Genealogical Abstracts from 18th-Century Virginia Newspapers

Genealogical Abstracts from
18th-Century
Virginia Newspapers

By Robert K. Headley, Jr.

Baltimore
GENEALOGICAL PUBLISHING CO., INC.
1987

Copyright © 1987 by
Genealogical Publishing Co., Inc.
Baltimore, Maryland
All Rights Reserved
Library of Congress Catalogue Card Number 87-80885
International Standard Book Number 0-8063-1199-1
Made in the United States of America

Dedicated to my father
ROBERT KIRK HEADLEY, SR
A Good Man and a True Virginian

ACKNOWLEDGMENTS

To produce a work of this kind I have had help from many people at many libraries. I take pleasure in acknowledging their help here: the Library of Congress (Periodical Reading Room staff); the Virginia State Library (inter-library loan, Reference Room, and manuscripts staffs); the Virginia Historical Society (library staff); the Prince George's County (Maryland) Library System (inter-library loan and Hyattsville Branch staffs); University of Maryland (McKeldin Library); Fredericksburg (Virginia) Public Library; College of William & Mary (Swem Library); Ms. Melanie Wisner (Houghton Library, Harvard University); Ms. Joyce Ann Tracy (American Antiquarian Society); my friend Robert W. Barnes; my family--Anne, Sarah, and Amy--for tolerating me during the long compiling of this work; and Dr. Michael Tepper of the Genealogical Publishing Company for his encouragement. Thank you all.

                                                      Robert K. Headley, Jr.
                                                      University Park, Maryland
                                                      December 1986

CONTENTS

1. ACKNOWLEDGMENTS — vii
2. INTRODUCTION — ix
3. SOURCES — xiii
4. ABBREVIATIONS — xix
5. ABSTRACTS — 1
6. INDEX OF PEOPLE — 383
7. INDEX OF PLACES, SHIPS, MILITARY UNITS, ETC. — 455

INTRODUCTION

The data abstracted herein have been collected from over 7,100 issues of eighty-one 18th-century Virginia newspapers. This has involved the scanning of original papers or microfilms of them in all of the major repositories of 18th-century Virginia newspapers. Only a few issues have not been utilized. To make up for some of the gaps in Virginia newspapers before 1736 and between 1740 and 1765, I have scanned papers from other states. These include the *Maryland Gazette*, the *American Weekly Mercury*, the *New York Post Boy*, the *Pennsylvania Chronicle*, and the [New Bern] *North Carolina Gazette*. I have abstracted all of the items on Virginians which I believe may be of some genealogical interest. In selecting items to abstract, I looked especially for those that gave at least two pieces of genealogical data. For example: age and place of residence; date of death and place of residence; date of death and names of executors/administrators; name of spouse and place of residence. The few items that do not meet this criterion have been included simply because they were interesting to me.

The following kinds of items have provided the basis of most of the abstracts: marriage notices, death notices, estate sales and settlements, advertisements for runaway servants/apprentices/slaves or military deserters, and court cases. Death notices may be full-fledged obituaries loaded with data, or they may be long flowery articles saying nothing except how wonderful the deceased was, or they may be simple statements that "so-and-so died." Advertisements of estate sales can provide data on next of kin or relatives, location of property, date of death, and relative worth. Advertisements for runaways or deserters can be the juiciest of all. They can provide minute descriptions down to manner of wearing the hair, tattoos, clothing, and personality. They sometimes give place of birth, age, date imported, name of the ship on which imported, occupation, and suspected destination. These records, indeed any record abstracted in this work, should be checked in the original source. There may be very interesting and useful data that was not abstracted.

I have tried to include all the names of runaways, whether black or white, where a surname was given. I regret not being able to include all the black and mulatto slaves who had only a single name; there is rich information there too. I have included all names of deserters when age, place of birth, or other data were provided. I have not included names of deserters when they were simply part of a list with no additional information. I have also omitted names of persons having letters at the various post offices. Many court cases, especially those of the High Court of Chancery (HCC) at Richmond, have been abstracted since they can provide so much information on relationships. Those of the HCC should prove especially valuable since the records of that court were destroyed during the Civil War. Usually the courts had information about a case printed when one or more of the parties, generally a defendant, could not be located "and appeared not to be an inhabitant of the Commonwealth." Advertisements for missing friends, relatives, or heirs have all been included, even when it was not known if the subject was living or had ever lived in Virginia.

Abstracts are given under the name of the deceased, the groom, the subject of the advertisement, the advertiser, or the main family in a court case. There are some exceptions, and I have had to be arbitrary in a few cases. Names of several deserters or runaways who ran away from the same location at the same time are filed by date under the heading "Deserters" or "Runaways." I have not usually corrected any spellings, and multiple spellings for some names abound. Any letters or words that were unclear as well as some clarifying data added by me are enclosed in square brackets. Names of persons appearing within an entry can be located by consulting the index.

Where I could be reasonably certain that two or more abstracts referred to the same person, I merged them into one entry.

Each entry includes a source reference, e.g., **VGGA 12 Dec 95**. This means that the entry was abstracted from the 12 December 1795 issue of the *Virginia Gazette and General Advertiser* . Occasionally there was more news than a printer could fit in his regular paper, so he would print a supplement, post script, or extraordinary; these are cited as **sup, ps,** and **ex** respectively. Thus, **VG 1 Apr 71 sup** refers to the supplement to the *Virginia Gazette* for 1 April 1771. The abbreviations for the newspapers can be found in the List of Abbreviations. No page numbers have been given since most 18th-century newspapers were only four pages long and it should be fairly easy to locate the source of the abstract. It may be helpful to note the general format of these newspapers:

> page 1 -- ads; major national or international news
> page 2 -- international and national news
> page 3 -- local news; ads
> page 4 -- ads; poems; anecdotes

Ads for settlements of estates often appeared on page 1 or 3 the first time, and then, in subsequent issues, were moved to page 4. Marriages and deaths were usually recorded under the local news heading.

Part 3 gives some information on the newspapers consulted for this work, including the dates of publication, changes of name, areas of coverage, and locations of major collections.

One of the most dangerous things about a publication like this is that readers will assume that everything useful has been gleaned from these newspapers. An abstractor is only human; I am certain that I have missed important data. I can only advise those who consult this work to be sure to check the originals. If you do not find a name in this publication, please do not assume that there is nothing on that person in the newspapers consulted. You should scan the newspapers for the appropriate area. Section 3 can help you locate these newspapers.

SOURCES

The listing below, based on Brigham (1947) and Parsons (1936), is arranged by place of publication. It provides, for each paper, a brief printing history, the major geographic area of coverage, and the locations of major collections.

ALEXANDRIA
The Columbian Mirror and Alexandria Gazette (CMAG), 1792-1800; covers the Alexandria area including Fairfax and Loudoun counties; major collections are at Harvard and LC; a mf covering the period 18 December 1793 to 6 December 1800 is available.
The Times. Alexandria Advertiser (TAA), 1797-1802; became *The Times; and District of Columbia Daily Advertiser* (TDCDA) in April 1799; covers the Alexandria area including Fairfax and Loudoun counties; major collections are at LC and Harvard.
The Virginia Gazette and Alexandria Advertiser (VGAxA), 1789-1793; covers the Alexandria area including Fredericksburg, Loudoun County, and Westmoreland County; major collection is at AAS; a mf is available.
The Virginia Journal, and Alexandria Advertiser (VJAA), 1784-1789; covers the Alexandria area including Berkeley, Fairfax, and Loudoun counties but may include information from Richmond, Powhatan, and Prince William counties; major collections are at AAS and the Missouri Historical Society; a mf covering the known issues is available.
DUMFRIES
Republican Journal: and Dumfries Advertiser (RJDA), 1795-1796; name changed to *Republican Journal and Dumfries Weekly Advertiser* (RJDWA); covers the Prince William area; the major collection is at Harvard; VHS has a mf of the Harvard copies.
The Virginia Gazette, and Agricultural Repository (VGAR), 1791-1793; covers the Prince William area; all of the known issues are at Harvard and AAS; copies are at LC.
FREDERICKSBURG
The Genius of Liberty; and Fredericksburg & Falmouth Advertiser (GLFFA), 1797-1798; became *The Genius of Liberty* (GL) in 1799; covers the Stafford and Orange County area; only seven issues are known: one at LC, three at AAS, and three at the Wisconsin Historical Society.
The Republican Citizen and Farmer and Planter's Chronicle (RCFPC), 1796-1797; covers the Stafford and Orange County area; the major collection is at Harvard; the VHS has a mf of the Harvard copies.
The Virginia Herald, and Fredericksburg Advertiser (VHFA), 1787-1820; became *The Virginia Herald, and Fredericksburg & Falmouth Advertiser* (VHFFA) 1795-1797, and the *Virginia Herald* in 1797; covers the Fredericksburg, Culpeper, Caroline, Essex, Fauquier, King George, Orange, Spotsylvania, Stafford, and Westmoreland areas; provides the best coverage of Northern Neck events until the late 19th century; major collections are at LC, AAS, and Harvard; mf copies are available at LC, VSL, and VHS; University Microfilms has a mf 1792-1809; Robert A. Hodge of Fredericksburg has prepared an extensive index.
LYNCHBURG
The Union Gazette (UG), 1793-1795; became the *Lynchburg and Farmer's Gazette* (LFG) in 1794; all the Lynchburg papers cover the same Amherst, Bedford, Appomattox, Campbell County area; the major collections are at Harvard and AAS; VHS has a mf of the Harvard copies.

Lynchburg Weekly Gazette (LWG), 1798-1801; only nine issues before 1800 are known, four of these are in the AAS.

Lynchburg Weekly Museum (LWM), 1797-1798; six issues are known, three are in AAS and two are at Harvard; VHS has a mf of the Harvard copies.

MARTINSBURG

The Berkeley Intelligencer (BI), 1799-1809; covers the Berkeley County area; the major collection is at the West Virginia Department of Archives; VSL has a mf of the 1799 issues.

The Potowmac Guardian and Berkeley Advertiser (PGBA), 1792-1800; a continuation of the paper of the same name published in Shepherdstown; became The Potomak Guardian (PG) in 1798; covers the Berkeley County area; the major collection is at Harvard; VSL has a mf.

NORFOLK

The American Gazette, and Norfolk and Portsmouth Weekly Advertiser (AGNPWA), 1792-1794; became *American Gazette, and Norfolk and Portsmouth Public Advertiser* (AGNPPA) 1794-1796; then in 1796, the name was shortened to *American Gazette* (AG) for a single issue; on 10 May 1796 the title was changed to *American Gazette & General Advertiser* (AGGA); the last issue was 7 November 1797; covers the Norfolk Borough and County, Nansemond County, and Portsmouth area in addition to some news of York, Prince George, Elizabeth City, and Gloucester counties; major collections are in AAS, LC, Harvard, the Philadelphia Library Company, and Norfolk Public Library; VSL has a mf of issues 1793 to 1797.

The Norfolk and Portsmouth Chronicle (NPC), 1789-1792; became the *Virginia Chronicle and Norfolk and Portsmouth General Advertiser* (VCNPGA) 1792-1793, the *Virginia Chronicle, & General Advertiser* (VCGA) in 1794, and the *Virginia Chronicle, &c* (VC) before it closed in late 1794 or early 1795; covers the Norfolk and Portsmouth area as well as Southampton and Princess Anne counties; major collections are at LC and the AAS; VSL has a mf of the LC collection.

The Norfolk and Portsmouth Gazette (NPG), 1789; covers the Norfolk and Portsmouth area; only three issues are known, all are at LC; VSL has a mf.

The Norfolk and Portsmouth Journal (NPJ), 1786-1789; covers the Norfolk and Portsmouth area as well as Princess Anne County and cities as distant as Alexandria, Petersburg, and Richmond; the major collection is at LC; VSL has a mf of the issues at LC.

Epitome of the Times (ET), 1798-1802; covers the Norfolk-Portsmouth area; major collections are at AAS and Harvard; a mf of the Harvard issues is at VSL.

Norfolk Herald (NH) began in 1794 as *The Herald, and Norfolk and Portsmouth Advertiser* (HNPA). In 1795 it became *The Herald* for about a month; then in December 1795 it became *The Norfolk Herald* (NH). A year later, in November 1796, it became *The Norfolk Herald & Public Advertiser* (NHPA). In February 1798 it again became *The Norfolk Herald*; covers the Norfolk, Portsmouth, and Princess Anne area as well as Elizabeth City, Nansemond, Warwick, and Isle of Wight counties; major collections are at LC, the University of Virginia, AAS, Harvard, and the Philadelphia Library Company; VSL has a mf of issues for 1794-95.

Virginia Gazette or, Norfolk Intelligencer (VGNI), 1774-1775; covers the Norfolk-Portsmouth area; major collections are at William and Mary and AAS; VSL has a mf and University Microfilms has one available.

Norfolk Weekly Journal and County Intelligencer (NMJCI), 1797-1798; covers the Norfolk-Portsmouth area; all known issues are in the collection of the Norfolk Public Library; VSL has a mf.

PETERSBURG

Independent Ledger and Petersburg and Blandford Public Advertiser (ILPB), 1793; the only issue located is in the LC; there is a mf at VSL.

The Virginia Gazette and Petersburg Intelligencer (VGPI), 1786-1800; covers the entire Petersburg area as well as nearby counties including Brunswick, Dinwiddie, Sussex, and Mecklenburg; major collections are at Harvard, AAS, and VHS; VSL has a mf of most issues.

The Virginia Star; and Petersburg Weekly Advertiser (VSPW); 1795; covers the Petersburg area; only six issues are known, five are at Harvard; VSL has a mf of these issues.

RICHMOND

The Richmond and Manchester Advertiser (RMA), 1795-1796, a continuation of *The Virginia Argus* (q.v.) in 1796; covers the Richmond area as well as Amelia, Goochland, Powhatan, and some more distant counties; major collections are at LC, Harvard, AAS, and the University of Chicago; VSL has a mf which includes many of these issues; there is also a mf available from University Microfilms.

Richmond Chronicle (RC), 1795-1796; a continuation of the *Virginia Gazette & Richmond Chronicle* (q.v.); covers the Richmond area; major collections are in the NYPL, Harvard, the Philadelphia Library Company, and LC; there is a mf at the VSL.

The Examiner (Ex), 1798-1804; covers the Richmond area as well as Caroline, Louisa, Goochland, Gloucester, and Prince William counties; major collections are at VSL, AAS, and Harvard; VSL also has a mf.

The Observatory; or, a View of the Times (OVT), 1797-1798; became *Dixon's Observatory* (DOB) in September 1798; covers the Richmond area; major collections are at AAS, Harvard, and VSL; a mf of these issues is at VSL.

Virginia Argus (Arg), 1796-1816; covers the Richmond area and adjoining counties especially Pittsylvania, Cumberland, and Goochland; major collections are at Harvard, LC, VSL, and AAS; VSL has a mf.

The Virginia Federalist (VF); 1799-1800; covers the Richmond and central Virginia area; the major collection is at Harvard.

The Virginia Gazette (VG), 1780-1781; a continuation of *The Virginia Gazette* published at Williamsburg; covers the Richmond-Williamsburg area and adjacent counties; major collections are at VSL, the Wisconsin Historical Society, and NYPL; the 1780 issues are included in the Virginia Gazette mf produced by the Massachusetts Historical Society and by the Institute of Early American History and Culture.

The Virginia Gazette, and General Advertiser (VGGA), 1790-1809; a continuation of *The Virginia Independent Chronicle, and General Advertiser* (q.v.); one of the best of the later 18th century Virginia newspapers for genealogical information, the VGGA covers the entire state with good coverage of Albemarle, Buckingham, Caroline, Chesterfield, Cumberland, Hanover, Henrico, King William, Louisa, Powhatan, and Prince Edward counties and the city of Richmond; major collections are at LC, VSL, William and Mary, AAS, and Harvard; VSL, VHS, and LC have a mf of issues at other institutions and a mf is available from University Microfilms.

The Virginia Gazette or(/and the) Independent Chronicle (VGIC), 1783-1789; became *The Virginia Gazette, and Public Advertiser* (q.v.) in 1789; covers the Richmond area; the major collection was reportedly at VHS but could not be located there in 1986; VSL has a mf of issues in the collections of VSL, William and Mary, Harvard, VHS, LC, NYPL, and the American Philosphical Society.

The Virginia Gazette, and Public Advertiser (VGPA), 1789-1793; covers the Richmond area; major collections are at Harvard and VSL.

The Virginia Gazette. And Richmond and Manchester Advertiser (VGRMA), 1793-1795; became *The Richmond and Manchester Advertiser* in 1795; covers the same area as the RMA; major collections are at LC, AAS, VSL, and the University of Chicago; VSL has a mf of most known issues.

Virginia Gazette & Richmond Chronicle (VGRC), 1793-1795; became the *Richmond Chronicle* (q.v.) in 1795; major collections are at LC, NYPL, and VSL; VSL has a mf of most known issues.

The Virginia Gazette: and Richmond Daily Advertiser (VGRDA), 1792-1793; became *The Virginia Gazette: and Richmond Advertiser* (VGRA) in late 1792; the major collection is at VSL which also has a mf.

The Virginia Gazette, or (and) Weekly Advertiser (VGWeA), 1781-1797; covers the entire state but especially New Kent, Princess Anne, James City, Henrico, Spotsylvania, and Chesterfield counties and the city of Richmond; the major collections are at William and Mary, LC, Harvard, VSL, AAS, and VHS; VHS has a mf of issues at LC, Harvard, AAS, and William and Mary; VSL has a mf covering issues 1781-1797; University Microfilms has a mf 1787-1789.

The Virginia Gazette, or, the American Advertiser (VGAA), 1781-1786; the major collections are at William and Mary, LC, NYPL, University of Michigan, VHS, and AAS; VSL has a mf of most known issues; University Microfilms has a mf 1782-1786.

The Virginia Independent Chronicle (VIC), 1786-1790; became *The Virginia Independent Chronicle, and General Advertiser* (VICGA) in 1790; covers the Richmond area but much data from throughout the state is also included; major collections are at VSL and LC; University Microfilms has a mf 1786-1789.

SHEPHERDSTOWN

The Impartial Observer (IO), 1797; the only issues known are at Harvard; a mf is available at the University of West Virginia, West Virginia Archives, and VSL.

The Potowmac Guardian, and Berkeley Advertiser (PGBA), 1790-[1798]; moved to Martinsburg in 1792 where it was published until 1798; the name was changed to *The Potomak Guardian* between 1798 and 1800; many issues are scattered about, but VSL has a mf of most of these issues from 1792 to 1798.

STAUNTON

The Staunton Gazette, or, the Weekly Western Star (SG), 1790; covers the Staunton area; the only issue known is at the University of Virginia; LC and AAS have photostats.

The Phenix (PH), 1798-1804; a continuation of the *Virginia Gazette, and Staunton Weekly Advertiser* (q.v.); covers the Staunton area; only three issues before 1800 are known.

The Staunton Spy (SS), 1793-1795; became *The Virginia Gazette* (q.v.) in early 1795; covers the Staunton area; three of the five known issues are in the AAS; a microprint is available at LC and other major libraries.

The Virginia Gazette (VGSWA), 1795-1798; became the *Staunton Gazette* in 1796 and the *Virginia Gazette, and Staunton Weekly Advertiser* in 1797; covers the Staunton area; the major collection is at Harvard; the University of Kentucky has a mf 1795-1796.

WILLIAMSBURG

The Virginia Gazette (VG), published by William Parks 1736-1750, then by Hunter, Royle, Purdie and Dixon, and Dixon and Hunter 1751-1778;

covers the entire state; major collections are at VHS, NYPL, LC, VSL, William and Mary, AAS, and the University of Michigan; an early mf was produced by the Massachussetts Historical Society; the Institute of Early American History and Culture, Williamsburg, produced a second mf in 1950 from originals at William and Mary, Colonial Williamsburg, Johns Hopkins, LC, Maryland Historical Society, VHS, VSL, and from photostats in other institutions; this latter mf contains 193 issues located after the earlier mf was made.

The Virginia Gazette (VGR), published by William Rind 1766-1773 and by John Pinkney (VGP) 1774-1776; covers the entire state; major collections are at LC, VHS, William and Mary, and AAS.

The Virginia Gazette (VGPu) and (VGCD), published by Alexander Purdie 1775-1779 and Clarkson and Davis until 1780; covers the entire state; major collections are at LC, the Maryland Historical Society, Colonial Williamsburg, and the University of Virginia.

The Virginia Gazette (VG), published by Dixon and Nicholson 1779-1780 when they moved to Richmond; covers the entire state; major collections are at VSL, Wisconsin Historical Society, and LC.

WINCHESTER

The Virginia Centinel; or, the Winchester Mercury (VCWM), 1788-1790; became *Bowen's Virginia Centinel & Gazette: or, the Winchester Political Repository* (BVCG) in 1790, and *Bowen's Virginia Gazette and the Winchester Centinel* (BVCG) in February 1796; in early 1798, it became the Winchester Gazette (WG); covers the Winchester area-- Frederick, Shenandoah, Berkeley, Hampshire, and Loudoun counties; the major collections are at the Handley Library in Winchester, LC, Harvard, and AAS; VSL has a mf of issues 1788-1800.

The Virginia Gazette, and Winchester Advertiser (VGWA), 1787-1791; covers the Winchester area; the major collection is at the Handley Library; VSL has a mf 1789-1791.

Willis's Virginia Gazette and Winchester Advertiser (WVGWA), 1790; covers the Winchester area; the few known issues are at the Handley Library; VSL has a mf.

KENTUCKY

LEXINGTON. *The Kentucky Gazette* (KG), 1787 + ; covers the entire state of Kentucky and parts of Ohio, Tennessee, and Virginia; major collections are at the Lexington Public Library, University of Chicago, LC, AAS, and Harvard.

MARYLAND

ANNAPOLIS. *The Maryland Gazette* (MG), 1727-1734; covers the entire state of Maryland and parts of Virginia and Pennsylvania; major collections at the Maryland Historical Society and New York Public Library; mf of all known issues prepared by John Carter Brown Library in 1925.

ANNAPOLIS. *The Maryland Gazette* (MG), 1745 + ; major collections are at the Maryland Historical Society, LC, AAS, and Harvard; a mf was prepared by Yale University in 1938.

BALTIMORE. *Maryland Journal and the Baltimore Advertiser* (MJ), 1773-1797; covers the Baltimore area, the state of Maryland and adjacent Virginia and Pennsylvania; major collections are at the Maryland Historical Society and LC.

NORTH CAROLINA

NEW BERN. *The No[rth] Carolina Gazette* (NG), 1751-1759; covers much of North Carolina and southern Virginia; major collection is at the North Carolina Department of Archives; LC has photostats.

The following published sources were also valuable:

Baber, Lucy H. M. et al. *Marriages and Deaths from Lynchburg, Virginia Newspapers 1794-1836*. Baltimore: GPC, 1980.

Barnes, Robert. *Gleanings from Maryland Newspapers, 1776-1785*. Typescript [Baltimore], 1971.

Barnes, Robert. *Marriages and Deaths from the Maryland Gazette, 1727-1839*. Baltimore: GPC, 1973.

Barnes, Robert. *Marriages and Deaths from Baltimore Newspapers, 1796-1816*. Baltimore: GPC, 1978.

Brigham, Clarence S. *History and Bibliography of American Newspapers, 1690-1820*. Worcester, Mass.: The American Antiquarian Society, 1947.

Cappon, Lester J. and Stella V. Duff. *Virginia Gazette Index*. Williamsburg: Institute of Early American Culture, 1950.

[Dorman, J. F.] "Extracts from the Virginia Gazette, 1755-1756," *Virginia Genealogist* 1, nos. 1-4 (1957), pp. 23-28, 80-85, 109-114, 169-178.

[Dorman, J. F.] "Marriages and Obituaries from Bowen's Virginia Centinel & Gazette Winchester, Virginia, 1792-1794," *Virginia Genealogist* 1, no.1 (1957), pp. 38-43.

[Dorman, J. F.] "Local Notices from the Virginia Gazette, 1780," *Virginia Genealogist* 3, no. 4 (1959), pp. 147-152; 4, nos. 1-4 (1960), pp. 33-37, 75-79, 132-138, 176-178; 5, nos. 1-4 (1961), pp. 37-39, 85-88, 117-124, 164-166; 6, no. 1 (1962), pp. 23-27.

[Dorman, J. F.] "Local Notices from the Virginia Gazette [,or, the American Advertiser]," *Virginia Genealogist* 25, nos. 3-4 (1981), pp. 163-170, 254-262.

Family Line Publications. *Western Maryland Newspaper Abstracts, 1786-1798*. Vol. 1. Silver Spring, Md., 1985.

Green, Karen Mauer. *The Kentucky Gazette 1787-1800*. Baltimore, 1983.

Hodge, Robert A. *An Index for the Virginia Herald and Fredericksburg Advertiser, 1788-1791*. Fredericksburg, 1969.

Hodge, Robert A. and Lois L. R. Hodge. *An Index to the Newspaper Death Notices, Fredericksburg, Virginia*. Fredericksburg, 1983.

Parsons, Henry S. *A Check List for American Eighteenth Century Newspapers in the Library of Congress*. Washington: GPO, 1936.

Scott, Kenneth. *Genealogical Data from the New York Post Boy, 1743-1773*. Washington, D.C.: National Genealogical Society, 1970.

Scott, Kenneth. *Genealogical Data from the Pennsylvania Chronicle, 1767-1774*. Washington, D.C.: National Genealogical Society, 1971.

Scott, Kenneth. *Abstracts from Ben Franklin's Pennsylvania Gazette, 1728-1748*. Baltimore: GPC, 1975.

Scott, Kenneth. *Genealogical Abstracts from the American Weekly Mercury,1719-1746*. Baltimore: GPC, 1974.

Scott, Kenneth. *Genealogical Data from Colonial New York Newspapers*. Baltimore: GPC, 1977 [Includes *New York Gazette*, *New York Weekly Journal*, and *New York Mercury*].

Virginia Genealogical Society. *Marriages and Deaths from Richmond, Virginia Newspapers, 1780-1820*. Richmond: Virginia Genealogical Society, 1983.

ABBREVIATIONS

AAS	American Antiquarian Society
abs.	absent
ac.	acre(s)
acc. to	according to
admr.	administrator(s)
admx.	administratrix
adv.	advertises
AG	American Gazette
AGGA	American Gazette and General Advertiser
AGNPPA	American Gazette and Norfolk and Portsmouth Public Advertiser
AGNPWA	American Gazette and Norfolk and Portsmouth Weekly Advertiser
aka	also known as
Alex	Alexandria
appr.	apprentice
Arg	Virginia Argus
att.	attorney
AWM	American Weekly Mercury
b.	born
bel.	belonging
BI	The Berkeley Intelligencer
BMG	[Baltimore] Maryland Gazette or the Baltimore General Advertiser
bn.	battalion
bur.	buried
BVCG	Bowen's Virginia Centinel & Gazette or the Winchester Political Repository; Bowen's Virginia Gazette and the Winchester Centinel
c.	circa, about
capt.	captain
chil.	children
CMAG	The Columbian Mirror and Alexandria Gazette
co.	county; company (military or commercial)
col.	colonel
compl.	complainant
cons.	consort
conv.	convict
cr.	creek
ct.	court
Ct. H.	Courthouse
d.	died
dau.	daughter
dec'd	deceased
def.	defendant
des.	deserted
disp.	dispatch
DOB	Dixon's Observatory
e.a.w.	estate accounts with
eld.	eldest
Eng.	England; English
enl.	enlisted
est.	estate
ET	Epitome of the Times (or Historical, Political and Commercial Miscellany)
ex.	executor(s); extraordinary (issue of a paper)

EX	The Examiner
exors.	executors
extx.	executrix
Fredsbrg.	Fredericksburg
GA	General Assembly
gdn.	guardian
GL	The Genius of Liberty
GLFFA	The Genius of Liberty and Fredericksburg and Falmouth Advertiser
Glouc.	Gloucester
H.E.	His Excellency
HCC	High Court of Chancery
HH & KF	household and kitchen furniture
HHF	household furniture
H.M's	His/Her Majesty's
HNPA	The Herald and Norfolk and Portsmouth Advertiser
husb.	husband
ILPB	The Independent Ledger and Petersburg and Blandford Public Advertiser
imp.	imported
in chanc.	in chancery
ind.	indentured
inst.	instant
IO	The Impartial Observer or Shepherd's-Town, Charles-Town and County Advertiser
K & Q	King and Queen
KG	King George
Kg. Geo.	King George
Kg. Wm.	King William
Ky.	Kentucky
LFG	Lynchburg and Farmer's Gazette
lt.	lieutenant
lt. col.	lieutenant colonel
LWG	Lynchburg Weekly Gazette
LWM	Lynchburg Weekly Museum
maj.	major
mar.	married
MC	[Frederick] Maryland Chronicle
MCent	Maryland Centinel
Md.	Maryland
merch.	merchant
mf	microfilm
MG	Maryland Gazette
MJ	[Baltimore] Maryland Journal and the Baltimore Advertiser
nfi	not further identified
NH	The Norfolk Herald
NHPA	The Norfolk Herald and Public Advertiser
NPC	The Norfolk and Portsmouth Chronicle
NPG	Norfolk and Portsmouth Gazette
NPJ	Norfolk and Portsmouth Journal
NWJCI	Norfolk Weekly Journal and County Intelligencer
NYG	New York Gazette
NYM	New York Mercury
NYPB	New York Post-Boy
NYPL	New York Public Library
NYWJ	New York Weekly Journal
OVT	The Observatory or a View of the Times

Pa.	Pennsylvania
par.	parish
PC	Pennsylvania Chronicle
PE	personal estate
pet.	petition
PG	The Potomak Guardian
PGBA	The Potowmac Guardian and Berkeley Advertiser
PH	The Phenix
plant.	plantation
pltf.	plaintiff
Pr. Anne	Princess Anne
Pr. Edw.	Prince Edward
Pr. Geo.	Prince George
Pr. Wm.	Prince William
pres.	presented
prop.	property
ps	post script
purs.	pursuant
Q.S.	quarterly session
RC	Richmond Chronicle
RCFPC	The Republican Citizen and Farmer and Planter's Chronicle
regt.	regiment
rem.	remainder
rep.	representative
Richm.	Richmond (City)
RJDA	Republican Journal and Dumfries Advertiser
RJDWA	Republican Journal and Dumfries Weekly Advertiser
RMA	The Richmond and Manchester Advertiser
run.	runaway
sd.	said
SG	The Staunton Gazette or the Weekly Western
sp.	spouse
SS	The Staunton Spy
Staff.	Stafford
sup.	supplement
surv.	surviving
SVG	The [Staunton] Virginia Gazette
svt.	servant
TAA	The Times. Alexandria Advertiser
TDCDA	The Times; and District of Columbia Daily Advertiser
UG	The Union Gazette
ult.	ultimo
Va.	Virginia
VC	The Virginia Chronicle &c
VCGA	The Virginia Chronicle and General Advertiser
VCNPGA	Virginia Chronicle and Norfolk and Portsmouth General Advertiser
VCWM	The Virginia Centinel; or, the Winchester Mercury
VF	Virginia Federalist
VG	The Virginia Gazette: Parks; Hunter, Royle, Purdie, Dixon; Dixon and Nicolson
VGAA	The Virginia Gazette, or, the American Advertiser
VGAR	The Virginia Gazette and Agricultural Repository
VGAxA	The Virginia Gazette and Alexandria Advertiser
VGCD	The Virginia Gazette: Clarkson and Davis
VGGA	The Virginia Gazette and General Advertiser

VGIC	The Virginia Gazette or the Independent Chronicle, The Virginia Gazette and the Independent Chronicle
VGNI	Virginia Gazette or Norfolk Intelligencer
VGP	The Virginia Gazette: Pinkney
VGPA	The Virginia Gazette and Public Advertiser
VGPI	The Virginia Gazette and Petersburg Intelligencer
VGPu	The Virginia Gazette: Purdie, Clarkson and Davis
VGR	The Virginia Gazette: Rind
VGRC	Virginia Gazette & Richmond Chronicle
VGRDA	The Virginia Gazette and Richmond (Daily) Advertiser
VGRMA	The Virginia Gazette and Richmond and Manchester Advertiser
VGSWA	The Virginia Gazette and Stanton Weekly Advertiser
VGWA	The Virginia Gazette, and Winchester Advertiser
VGWeA	The Virginia Gazette and Weekly Advertiser
VH	The Virginia Herald
VHFA	The Virginia Herald, and Fredericksburg Advertiser
VHFFA	The Virginia Herald and Fredericksburg and Falmouth Advertiser
VHS	Virginia Historical Society
VIC	The Virginia Independent Chronicle
VICGA	The Virginia Independent Chronicle and General Advertiser
VJAA	The Virginia Journal and Alexandria Advertiser
vs.	versus
VSL	Virginia State Library
VSPW	The Virginia Star; and Petersburg Weekly Advertiser
w.w.a.	with the will annexed
WG	Winchester Gazette
wid.	widow
Winch.	Winchester
Wmsbrg.	Williamsburg
WVGWA	Willis's Virginia Gazette and Winchester Advertiser
yrs.	years

Genealogical Abstracts from 18th-Century Virginia Newspapers

AARON, Tom, aka Tom, aka Aaron Negro, c. 40, ran away from John LUMKIN, Kg.Wm. Co. (VGGA 9 Nov 96)
ABBOT, Mrs. wife of Josiah ABBOT, hatter, of Richm., died. (RMA 6 Apr 96)
ABBOTT Family Accomack Co., Ct. of 1 Apr 96, in chanc: Richard ABBOTT, dec'd, by William STRAN his next friend (pltf) vs. Elizabeth, Jane, John, Sarah, and Margaret ABBOTT, infants, and remaining heirs of the said Richard ABBOTT, dec'd (defs). (VGGA 16 Nov 96)
ABBOTT, Mr. accidentally killed along with a Mr. SMITH by a Mr. MITCHUM in Middlesex Co. last Fri; ABBOTT is a distant relation of MITCHUM's. (VGPu 11 Aug 75)
ABBOTT, James, of Wm. and J. Abbott and admr. of Sam. ABBOTT dec'd, Fredsbrg. intends to leave for Europe in a few days. (VHFA 24 Nov 91)
ABBOTT, James, formerly a resp. merch. in this town [Fredsbrg], d. at Mr. Well's Tavern in this county on the 7th inst. on his way to Orange. (VHFA 9 Oct 95); e.a.w. Wm. GLASSELL of Fredsbrg. (VH 23 Apr 99)
ABBOTT, John, Irish svt, imp. in the *Justitia,* ran away from a vessel at Fredsbrg. (VGR 26 Jan 69)
ABBOTT, John, e.a.w. James ABBOTT (nfi). (AGNPPA 17 Mar 95)
ABBOTT, Samuel, merch. of Fredsbrg. d. on Monday. (VHFA 22 Jan 89); pet. to vest his real prop. in his children beyond the sea or in trustees for their use to be presented to next GA. (VHFA 1 Oct 89); est. to be sold. (VHFA 7 Jan 90)
ABBOTT, Wm., dec'd, his ex., Roger ABBOTT of Culp. Co., wishes to close his executorship. (VHFFA 3 Feb 97)
ABEL, Thomas, svt. ran away from Maj. Richard RANDOLPH, Henrico Co. (MG 1 Nov 34)
ABNEY, Lt. Wm., mar. Miss Eliza M'CLENECHAN on 23 Dec., both of Staunton. (VCG 29 Dec 94)
ABRAHAM, Capt. Mordecai, of Kg. Wm. Co., d. on Thurs. last. (VGGA 22 Feb 92); his ex. Christopher TOMPKINS and Wm. FLEET, will sell his slaves and other items. (VGGA 4 Apr 92); his ex. will sell all his lands in Caroline Co. (VGGA 26 Dec 92); his ex. will sell his land in Caroline Co. and stock in Kg. Wm. at his former plant. (VGGA 2 Jan 93) [Name also appears as ABRAMS]
ABSENCE, Billy, his relations are hereby notified that he made his exit last week in Gloucester. (VG 31 Oct 71)
ABYNON, George, dec'd, portions of his est. to be sold in Norfolk. (HNPA 31 Jan 95)
ACLAND, John, svt., tailor, ran away from John BLAND; supposed gone towards Carolina. (VG 20 Apr 69); ran away from Margaret HARPER, Petersburg. (VG 24 May 70)
ACOCK, John, tailor, from London, now of Loudoun Co. (VGR 13 Oct 68)
ACRILL, Capt. Wm., d. on Tues. night last at his house in Chas. City Co., of pleurisy (VG 24 Mar 38)
ADAM, Miss, dau. of the widow ADAM, d. after swallowing a small piece of money. (VJAA 18 May 86)
ADAM, Andrew, late of Loudoun Co., his 600 ac. est. between Goose Cr. and Leesburg adv. by Robert ADAM. (VJAA 26 Feb 84)
ADAM, James, dec'd, e.a.w. with Eliz. ADAM (nfi), Alexandria. (VJAA 13 Apr 86)
ADAM, Robert, of Alexandria, dec'd, e.a.w. Wm. HERBERT, Wm. WILSON, Roger WEST, and Wm. HUNTER Jr., admrs. w. w. a. (VGAxA 10 Sep 89)
ADAM, Wm., Scot, svt., c. 19, ran away from Wm. BARKLEY, Loudoun Co. (VGR 27 Sep 70)
ADAMS, Britain, appr., c. 13, ran away from Thos. LLEWELLIN. (VG 19 Mar 72)
ADAMS, James, sailor, ran away from the ship *Theodorick* at Broadway's in Appomattox, speaks broad inclining to the Yorkshire dialect. (VGR 8 Feb 70)
ADAMS, James, run. svt. from Jeremiah ALDERSON, Pr. Wm. Co.; b. in

Eng., c. 23, tailor, jailed in Augusta Co. (VGR 30 Sep 73)
ADAMS, Joseph, mar. Mrs. Jane DUKE of Scottsville in Powhatan Co., on Sat. 10th inst. (VGGA 14 Sep 91)
ADAMS, Josiah P., dec'd, his admr., Francis ADAMS, will sell all of his PE at the plant. near Centerville, Loudoun Co., where he lived. (CMAG 15 Apr 97)
ADAMS, Mary, has eloped from her husband, Henry ADAMS, Southampton. (VGPI 9 Sep 96)
ADAMS, Nathaniel, of Surry Co., dec'd, his admr., Wm. BOYCE, will sell the rem. of his est. in Surry Co. (VGGA 9 Dec 95)
ADAMS, Dr. Patrick, of Surry Co., d. a few days ago (VG 1 Dec 68); his ex., Richard BAKER and Alex. ADAMS, decline to admin. the will (VGR 17 Aug 69); his PE to be sold by his admr., James BELSCHES (VG 8 Mar 70)
ADAMS, Philip, [dec'd], his admr., Philip MALLORY, adv. that if James ADAMS, late of Kg. Wm. Co., son of Philip ADAMS, is living, he is desired to apply immediately for his legacy left him by the death of his grandmother DAVIS. (VG&N 7 Apr 81)
ADAMS, Mrs. Sally, spouse of Thos. B. ADAMS, Esq., d. in this city [Richm.] Tues. last. (VGRMA 15 May 94, VGGA 21 May 94)
ADAMS, Sylvester, dec'd, his admr. is George ADAMS. (VGGA 27 Nov 93)
ADAMS, Thos. Esq., d. 8 Jul. at the home of his friend, Dr. Corbin GRIFFIN of York (VIC 6 Aug 88)
ADAMS, Thos., dec'd, e.a.w. his ex. (nfi). (VGGA 9 May 92)
ADAMS, Thos., dec'd., e.a.w. his admr., Peter ELLIOTT, Norfolk. (AGNPWA 19 Mar 94)
ADAMS, Thos. B., Esq., of Richmond, mar. Miss Sally MORRISON of Chesterfield on Sat. (VICGA 3 Feb 90)
ADAMS, Thos. Bowler, Esq., d. on Fri. night last at Col. Richard ADAMS' in this city [Richm.] (VGRMA 1 Dec 94, VGGA 3 Dec 94); his ex., Richard ADAMS, Jr. of Richm., will sell his remaining PE (VGRMA 15 Jan 95); his ex. will sell his 393 ac. tract in Essex Co. and lots in Richmond (VGGA 8 Apr 95)
ADAMS, Wm., third son of Col. Rich. ADAMS, d. in Richm. on Tues. morn. last [2nd inst.] after a short illness; he was not more than 23 (VGWeA 7 Jun 87, VIC 13 Jun 87)
ADDISON, The Rev. Henry, d. on Mon. last [31 Aug.] at his seat in Pr. Geo. Co., Md. (VGAxA 3 Sep 89)
ADDISON, Col. John, wounded in a duel with Maj. Joseph MARBURY 12 Oct. near Alexandria. (VJAA 19 Oct 86)
ADKINS, Daniel, dec'd, e.a.w. his ex., Robert ADKINS, of Henrico. (VG 21 Apr 74)
ADKINS, Lucy, dec'd, the Commissioners in Sussex Co. will sell a tract of land bel. to the est. of Thos. ADKINS Sr. dec'd, lying on Nottoway River and Joseph Swamp in Sussex Co. on the premises where the late Mrs. Lucy ADKINS dec'd resided. (VGPI 21 Nov 97)
ADKINS, Wm., soldier, American born, went to visit his father in Berkeley Co., des. from Capt. Jos. BROCK's Co., 3rd U.S. [Regt.], Winchester. (BVCG 30 Jul 92)
ADKISSON, Solomon, e.a.w. his admr. and brother, Isaiah ADKISSON of Goochland Co. (VG 5 Feb 80)
AFFLAX, George, sent. to death Tues. last at Wmsbrg. for the murder of Col. PRESLEY (Wmsbrg. disp. of 15 Jun.) (NYPB 30 Jul 50)
AGEN, Mrs. M., wife of Thos. AGEN, d. on Thurs. eve (VGWA 25 Nov 89)
AGNEW, John, of Nansemond, intends for the West Indies soon and to return in the fall for his family when he proposes to dispose of his property in this country (VG 23 May 77)
AHL, Peter, Hessian [a long letter from G. S. Charles H. SWANGEL, Fred. Co., denouncing him and giving much biographic info.] (BVCG 14 Oct 93)
AIKEN, David, Scot, 35, sailor, ran away from the brigantine *Mally* in

18th-Century Virginia Newspapers

Hampton River on 2 Oct., supposed heading for Maryland (VG 6 Oct 52)
AINSWORTH, Geo., dec'd, e.a.w. his admr., John STEWART (TAA 20 Sep 97)
AITCHINSON (?), Wm. Esq., was mar. to Miss Polly ROBERTS on Thurs. eve. last [4 Jul.] by the Rev. James WHITEHEAD, both of Norfolk (VCNPGA 6 Jul 93)
AITCHISON, Wm. Esq., merch., formerly a rep. for the Borough of Norfolk in the Assembly, d. last week at Eastwood, his seat in Pr. Ann (VG & VGPu 8 Nov 76) [also given as ATCHESON]
AITKEN, Hugh, aka AIKEN, son of Wm. AITKEN of Learne, Co. Antrim, Ireland, who arrived in Pennsylvania about two or three yrs. ago, will hear something greatly to his advantage by applying to one of several persons (VG 20 Aug 72)
AITKIN, Robert, Jr., printer, mar. Miss Nancy PEARSON on Thurs. 13th inst. in Philadelphia (VGWeA 30 Aug 87)
AITON, Wm., Eng. svt., joiner, ran away from Gamaliel BUTLER, Annapolis, Md. (VG 16 Jan 56)
ALARD, Absalom, jailed for horse stealing, c. 25-30, escaped from jail in Martinsville (VGGA 3 Jun 95)
ALBERTI, Sr. Francisco, native of Italy and teacher of music for many years in this state, d. on Thurs. last in Richmond in an advanced age (VGIC & VGWeA 6 Aug 85)
ALDRED, Giles, conv. svt., c. 25, weaver, has much of the Welsh accent in his speech, ran away from John LEITCH, Pr. Edw. Co. (VG 18 Mar 73)
ALDRIDGE, Ann, wife of Richard ALDRIDGE, ran away (VJAA 2 Sep 84)
ALDRIDGE, W. Joseph, of Alexandria, mar. Mrs. Dorothy REYNOLDS of Norfolk on Sat. eve. last (NH 14 May 99)
ALEXANDER, Amos, mar. Miss Anne RICKETTS on Wed. eve. at Cameron, the seat of Jn. Thos. RICKETTS, Esq. by the Rev. Dr. MUIR (TAA 13 Oct 97)
ALEXANDER, Archibald, dec'd, his ex., John M'CLUNG and Wm. ALEXANDER of Lexington, will sell his plant. in Rockbridge Co. (BVCG 17 Sep 92)
ALEXANDER, Dr. Geo. D., dec'd, his est. to be sold at Fairfax Ct. H. 18 Jun; e.a.w. Robert ALEXANDER (nfi) (VJAA 24 May 87)
ALEXANDER, John, of Stafford Co., dec'd, his ex. are Seymour HOOE and Lucy ALEXANDER (VJAA 4 Nov 84)
ALEXANDER, John, dec'd, his ex. are Wm. ALEXANDER and Wm. Gibbons STUART, of Alexandria; they will sell 100 lots of ground contiguous to the town of Alexandria (VJAA 4 Aug 85, VGWeA 6 Aug 85)
ALEXANDER, Philip Esq., d. in Alexandria (VJAA 25 Jan 87); his stock and HHF will be sold by his ex., Wm. H. WASHINGTON (VGAxA 27 Jan 91); his ex. will rent for one year for the benefit of his heir all arable land bel. to sd. heir consisting of an island opposite the Federal City (TAA 15 Nov 97); his ex. will sell three Negroes to satisfy a debt due the est. by the est. of John LUKE, dec'd. (TAA 14 Dec 97)
ALEXANDER, Philip Thornton, of Kg. Geo. Co., allegedly shot and killed by Laurence WASHINGTON on 4 Mar. (VGAA 19 Apr 83)
ALEXANDER, Wm., Eng. svt., ran away from Robert PHILLIPS, Fredsbrg. (VGR 4 Feb 68)
ALEXANDER, Wm., lately arrived [in Alexandria] from Whitehaven, committed suicide on Tues. morn. last (VGAxA 17 Jun 90)
ALEXIS, David, ind. svt., silversmith, imp. last spring in the *Brilliant* from London to York R., ran away from Wm. RICHARDSON, Richm. (VGNI 22 Sep 74)
ALFRIEND, Abraham, dec'd, e.a.w. Wm. WILKINS Sr., security for Benj. ALFRIEND for the admin. of his father's est., Pr. Geo. Co. (VGR 5 Aug 73)
ALLAN, Mrs., cons. of Capt. James ALLAN, d. on Sat. morn. (VH 9 Apr 99)
ALLAN, Jacob, merch. of Wmsbrg., died (VG 4 Nov 73)
ALLANBY, Capt. Robert, of the *Peggy* of Liverpool lying up James River,

drowned last week (VG 20 Jun 66)
ALLAY, Barnaby, Irish svt., 50, ran away from John QUARLES, Jr., Kg. Wm. Ct. H. (VG 7 Nov 54)
ALLEGRE, Mrs. Jane, of Richm., d. on Sat. 22nd ult. at an advanced age (VGGA 2 Jan 93, VGWeA 4 Jan 93)
ALLEGRE, Wm., dec'd, his land in Fluvanna Co. near the land of Giles ALLEGRE (nfi) to be sold by Jane ALLEGRE, admx., Richmond (VGAA 2 Aug 83)
ALLEN Family, HCC, 19 Sep 93, Archibald MIDDLEMIST (pltf) and Phebe ALLEN (widow) and Nancy, otherwise called Anne ALLEN, Elizabeth ALLEN, Mary ALLEN, and Lucy ALLEN children and co-heirs of John ALLEN (defs); the defs. failed to answer the bill, and the court ordered the lot of land lately occupied by John ALLEN in Petersburg to be sold (VGPI 25 Oct 93)
ALLEN, Mrs., of Surry Co., wife of Col. Jn. ALLEN, d. last Sat. (VG 20 Oct 38)
ALLEN, Capt., of the British sloop of war *Rattler* on the West Indies Station, was executed at the Mole for an illicit commerce with one of his own sex (NHPA 19 Jun 97)
ALLEN, Beverly, jailed in Aug. Co. for the murder of Robert FORSYTH Esq., Federal Marshal for the state, escaped in late February (VGGA 23 Apr 94)
ALLEN, Henry, of Eliz. City dec'd, his ex., John ALLEN, Jr., will sell all of his HH & KF and a tract near Armistead's Mill Dam (VG 14 Nov 71, 14 May 72)
ALLEN, Capt. Hugh, of Norfolk, d. c. 24 Apr 90; e.a.w. his ex., Josiah HODGES of Norfolk (NPC 24 Apr 90, 7, 14 Aug 90, VCNPGA 23 Feb 93)
ALLEN, Jacob, merch., of Wmsbrg, d. on 4 Nov. in the prime of life (VGR 4 Nov 73)
ALLEN, James and Anne, dec'd, of Hanover Co., e.a.w. Capt. Wm. CRAIGHEAD of Hanover or the ex., James and Charles ALLEN, in Pr. Edw. (VG 4 Nov 75)
ALLEN, James, d. on the 20th ult. in Pr. Edw. Co. (VGGA 20 Nov 93)
ALLEN, Jesse aka Allen, Negro, c. 25, ran away from John JAMES, Staff. Co. (BVCG 29 Oct 92); c. 35, ran away from John JAMES, admr. of John JAMES dec'd, Staff. Co. about eight [sic] yrs. ago; he is supposed to be between Winchester and Martinsburg (BVCG 28 Dec 97)
ALLEN, John, mulatto, shoemaker, under articles of agreement for two yrs., ran away from John MUIRHEAD, Norf. 10 June last (VGR 30 Nov 69)
ALLEN, John and George, svts., lately imp. in the *Justitia* ; George is c. 25; ran away from the plant. of Thomas MONTGOMERIE, Dumfries (VG 12 May 74 ps)
ALLEN, John, Irish, c. 30, des. from Capt. Thos. LEWIS' Co. of riflemen now raising in Staunton, on the 9th inst. (BVCG 14 May 92)
ALLEN, Maj. John, dec'd, his land near Winchester will be sold by his extx., Ann ALLEN, and his ex., Joseph LUCKEY, Robert P. ALLEN, and Thos. ALLEN. (BVCG 26 Feb 96)
ALLEN, The Hon. John, member of the Exec. Council of this state, d. in this city [Richmond] on Mon. last (Ex 17 May 99)
ALLEN, John Jr., dec'd, his ex., Henry and Edward ALLEN, will sell all his PE and settle his est. accounts (VG 4 Apr 77, VGPu 7 Mar 77)
ALLEN, Maj. John, late of Henrico Co., dec'd, slaves to be sold by his admr., Julius ALLEN (Ex 24 Dec 98)
ALLEN, John H., appr. lad, ran away from Thos. NIXON, Norfolk, he was seen at Hampton about two months ago (NHPA 26 Aug 97)
ALLEN, Julius, dec'd, his ex., Julius ALLEN Jr., Samuel PRICE, and Myles SELDEN Jr. of Henrico Co., will sell his stock (VG 26 Dec 77, VGPu 13 Jun 77)
ALLEN, Matthew, appr. lad, well-known in Wmsbrg. and New Kent, ran away from Thos. PATE, Wmsbrg. (VG 10 Feb 76)
ALLEN, R. R., dec'd, his extx., Frances ALLEN, and ex., David ALLEN, will

sell his 300 ac. tract near Richmond (VGPu 27 Dec 76)

ALLEN, Richard Sr., of New Kent, dec'd, his ex., Richmond ALLEN, will sell his livestock, crops, HH and KF (VG 25 Nov 73); his ex. adv. that his legatees are to meet at his house in New Kent to divide the slaves of the dec'd. (VG 20 Jan 74); e.a.w. Richmond ALLEN (VGPu 14 Nov 77)

ALLEN, Richard, merch., in New Kent, drowned returning home from Cumberland Town last night (VGPu 21 Apr 75 sup)

ALLEN, Robert, dec'd, of Frederick Co., e.a.w. his ex., Martha ALLEN and Mont. ALLEN (BVCG 14 Jan 93)

ALLEN, Uriah, b. in Bucks Co., Pa., 27, shoemaker, des. from the 8th U. S. Regt., Culpeper Ct. H. (VH 13 Sep 99)

ALLEN, Ursula, Culpeper Co. Ct., 20 Nov 98, in chanc: John W. SMITH (comp.) against Isaac CAMPBELL, Francis BRANIN, and Thomas ALLEN, exors. of Ursula ALLEN, dec'd. (defs); it appears that CAMPBELL is not an inhabitant of this state (GLFFA 7 Dec 98)

ALLIAS, Thomas, appr., c. 16, ran away from Elias ADUDDELL (BVCG 7 Jan 92)

ALLINSON, John, mar. Miss Mary Ann EDWARDS of Norfolk Co., on Thurs. night [16 Aug.], by the Rev. Wm. BLAND (VCNPGA 18 Aug 92)

ALLISON, Mrs. Frances, cons. of Samuel ALLISON, died. (VGRC 30 Sep 94)

ALLISON, John Esq., att. at law, mar. Miss Frances Hill CURRIE, dau. of the Rev. Mr. David CURRIE dec'd, late of Lancaster Co; [incl. a poem] (VGGA 14 Dec 96)

ALLISON, Mary, of Alexandria, dec'd, e.a.w. Daniel ROBERDEAU (VJAA 22 Mar 87)

ALLMAND, Edward, dec'd, his ex., Maximilian HERBERT, Norfolk, will rent his dwelling house, garden and out houses on Ferry Point alias Washington and will sell three ferry boats and hire out some slaves (AGNPPA 15 Mar 96)

ALLMAND, Thomas, of Allmand & Powell; the firm was dissolved on 18 Aug. due to his death (HNPA 31 Aug 95)

ALLMOND, Eliz., has eloped from her husb., Wm. ALLMOND Sr., Isle of Wt. Co.(VG 15 Feb 70)

ALLORD, Absalom, suspected horse thief, c. 25, escaped from the Henry Co. District Jail at New London on 30 Oct. (LFG 1 Nov 94)

ALMOND, John, Eng. svt., ran away from the ship *Allerton* lying at Berkeley in James River, 30 Jul. (VG 21 Aug 52)

ALSOP, Frances, cons. of Maj. Benj. ALSOP, d. in this county on Sun. the 6th inst. (VH 22 Jan 99)

ALSOP, George, dec'd, his ex., Geo. ALSOP of Caroline Co., wishes to close his executorship (VHFFA 13 Dec 96)

ALSUP, Wm., of Hanover Co., d. Mon. 7th inst. in his 97th yr. [obit] (VIC 16 Jan 88)

ALTRITE, John, mar. Miss Syvella REILY on Sun. last, both of Winch. (WG 30 Jan 99)

ALVAS, Nancy, murdered by Wm. JOHNSON in Richm. on 20 Jul. (VGRMA 28 Jul 94)

ALVISE, Wm., Negro, 12, ran away from Robt. CRAWLEY, York Co., 28 Feb. last; said to live at Brunswick (VG 14 Nov 51)

AMBLER, Edw. Esq., rep. in Assembly for Jamestown, d. last Sun. morn. at the Treasurer's in Wmsbrg. (VG and VGR 3 Nov 68); e.a.w. his ex., Mary AMBLER, Jacquelin AMBLER, Ro. C. NICHOLAS, Jn. BLAIR Jr., and Wilson Miles CARY (VG 15 Dec 68); a watch was stolen from W. GOOSLEY with the inscription "Edward AMBLER Esq. obiit Oct 29, 1768, age 36" (VGPu 27 Sep 76 sup)

AMBLER, Edward Cary, of Wmsbrg. (or Jamestown) d. in his 16th (or 17th) year (VGP 23 Mar 75, VG 25 Mar 75)

AMBLER, Mrs. Fanny, sp. to John AMBLER, d. lately at Jamestown (VIC 26 May 88)

AMBLER, Jacquelin, Treasurer of Virginia, d. in Richm. on Wed. last [long obit. in VGGA] (VGGA 10 Jan 98, Arg 12 Jan 98, VGPI 16 Jan 98)

AMBLER, John, Esq., dec'd, two stallions and some house svts. of his to be sold in Wmsbrg. by his ex. and brother, Edw. AMBLER (VG 17 Oct, 20 Nov 66)

AMBLER, John, Esq., of Jamestown, mar. Miss Lucy MARSHALL of this city [Richm.] Sat. eve. last (VGGA 25 May 91)

AMBLER, John, Esq., of Jamestown, mar. Mrs. Catherine NORTON of [Winchester] Thurs. last (WG 27 Nov 99)

AMERICA, Geo., Virginia-born Negro, ran away from Thos WATKINS, Warwick Co. (VG 11 Apr 66)

American Prisoners; taken by Algerines and redeemed at Algiers, 12 Jul 96 [only Virginians given]: Geo. WELLS, mate, 26; Rich. HARRIS, seaman, 46; Sam. HENRY, seaman, 26; Chas. SMITH, seaman, 19; Thos. BURGESS, seaman, 20; Jn. LEMMAN, seaman, 40, Wm. WALLACE, capt., 48, of Norfolk. (AGGA 11 Nov 96)

AMMINETT, John, late of Chas. City Co., dec'd, his admr., James INNES and Wm. RADFORD, will sell eight Negroes (VGGA 17 Dec 94)

AMONS, Joseph [also given as EMONS], svt., ran away from Hannah [CRITENDON], New Kent Co., supposed he will be lurking around Wmsbrg. where are some of his shipmates who were imp. in the *Queensborough* last year (VG 18 Apr 51)

ANDERSON Family, HCC, 12 Mar 96; Benj. TOLER, surv. ex. of Jn. JONES, Cicely ANDERSON, admx. of Wm. ANDERSON, Nathaniel ANDERSON, admr. and Elkanah TALLEY and Mary his wife, admrs. of Jn. ANDERSON (pltfs.) and Eliz. JONES, widow and relict of Jn. JONES, Laney JONES, Rich. BANKS and Eliz. his wife, Chas. LAMBERT and Nancy his wife, Hardin BURNLEY and Geo. BRACKENRIDGE (defs.) (RMA 2 Jul 96)

ANDERSON Family, HCC, Archibald ANDERSON, Hen. GARRET and Martha his wife, David ANDERSON, Thos. MERIWETHER and Polly his wife, Francis ANDERSON, Eliz. ANDERSON, Lucy ANDERSON, Wm. ANDERSON, and Sarah ANDERSON, which sd. Archibald, Martha, David, Polly, Francis, Eliz., Lucy, Wm., and Sarah are chil. of David ANDERSON dec'd, the five last of whom are infants, Jasper ANDERSON, Waddy THOMPSON and Eliz. his wife, Nicholas ANDERSON, David ANDERSON, Sarah ANDERSON, Cicily ANDERSON, Nancy ANDERSON, and Edmund ANDERSON, which sd. Jasper, Eliz., Nicholas, David, Sarah, Cicily, Nancy, and Edmund are chil. of Richard ANDERSON dec'd, the last three of whom are infants, Ann MINOR, Matthew ANDERSON, Christopher HUDSON and Sarah his wife, Edmund ANDERSON, and Samuel ANDERSON (pltfs.) against Samuel GIST, Nathaniel ANDERSON, Thos. ANDERSON, and Samuel ANDERSON (Arg 18 Jan 99)

ANDERSON, Mrs., sp. of Geo. ANDERSON of Henrico, d. last Sat. (VGIC 22 May 84)

ANDERSON, Dr. Andrew, mar. Miss Betsey BURNET of New Kent Co. (VG 5 May 74)

ANDERSON, Dr. Andrew, of New Kent Co., died (VG and VGPu 15 Nov 76); his admr., Robt. ANDERSON, will sell all his PE (VGPu 31 Jan 77); e.a.w. his admr. (VGPu 3 Apr 78)

ANDERSON, Ann, of Hanover Co., dec'd, e.a.w. her admr., N. PATTESON, of Cumb. Co., who will sell her est. in Hanover (VGGA 11 Dec 93)

ANDERSON, Bartlot, dec'd, 500 ac. of his land in Pr. Edw. and Charlotte cos. and 125 ac. in Louisa Co. to be sold by his ex. at Hanover Ct. H. (VGR 12 Mar 67)

ANDERSON, Barttelot, magistrate, d. at his seat in Hanover Co. (VGGA 18 Oct 97)

ANDERSON, Benj., dec'd, of Hanover Town, e.a.w. his ex., Bartelot ANDERSON and Jn. ANDERSON, who will also sell a variety of HH and KF,

some livestock, surgeon's instruments, etc. (VG 24 Jul 79)
ANDERSON, Benj., late of Hanover Co., dec'd, e.a.w. his ex., Bartt. ANDERSON of Hanover Co. (VGGA 1 Aug 92)
ANDERSON, Mrs. Eliz., cons. of Ambrose ANDERSON, Esq., d. in Gloucester Town on Thurs. 26 Jul. (RC 27 Aug 96)
ANDERSON, Henry, dec'd, his admr. w. the will anxd., John PATERSON of Nottoway, will sell his 458 ac. tract there (VGPI 2 Aug 96)
ANDERSON, Jack, mulatto, c. 22, says he was b. in New York of free parents who live in Hanover Square near Mr. M'LEAN's printing office and that he was carried by water to Roanoke in North Carolina and sold to a Mr. Geo. MANNING who afterwards parted with him to a John TAYLOR in Grenville from whence he absconded; jailed in Alexandria as a runaway (CMAG 15 Nov 98)
ANDERSON, James, of Berkeley Co., imprisoned in Richm. for the murder of his wife; executed there on 18 Jul. (VGAA 5 Apr, 19 Jul 83)
ANDERSON, James, of Brookesbank, Essex Co., dec'd. (VHFA 31 Dec 89)
ANDERSON, James, of Richm., adv. that he will give up his blacksmith's shop below the capitol to his son, James ANDERSON, on 1 Jan. (VGRMA 9 Dec 93, VGGA 18 Dec 93 ex)
ANDERSON, James, d. 9 Jan. in Winchester in his 74th year (VCG 13 Jan 94)
ANDERSON, James, d. on Sat. the 8th inst. in Wmsbrg. (NH 13 Sep 98, DOB 17 Sep 98)
ANDERSON, Jeany, has eloped from her husband, Handsford ANDERSON of King and Queen Co. (VG 6 Oct 68)
ANDERSON, John, seaman, 20, ran away from the ship *Encouragement* of London lying at West Point, 8 Apr. (VG 10 Apr 52)
ANDERSON, Mrs. Mary, sp. of Daniel ANDERSON, d. in Petersburg (VGPI 13 Dec 96)
ANDERSON, Matthew, prob. of Hanover Co., dec'd, the case of Rich. DOBSON and Frances his wife against Wm. TAYLOR, Gent., General Court, Wmsbrg., 14 Apr 55, mentions Matthew ANDERSON, John GOODWIN and Mary his wife, John ANDERSON and Lucy ANDERSON, infants, and John SCOTT, Bartlett ANDERSON, and John ANDERSON, ex. of Matthew ANDERSON (VG 6, 13, 20, 27 Jun 55)
ANDERSON, Matthew, Virginian, 21, enl. by Capt. LEWIS, des. from the Va. Regt. at Ft. Cumberland (VG 26 Dec 55)
ANDERSON, Matthew, indicted for horse stealing at Dumfries, c. 35, escaped from jail (Ex 13 Dec 99)
ANDERSON, Michael, dec'd, his ex., Thos. ANDERSON of Louisa Co., will sell a 400 ac. tract in Louisa Co. on the fourth branch of Pamunkey (VGGA 11 Sep 98)
ANDERSON, N., of Louisa Co., mentions land of his late brother, David ANDERSON, in the same co. (DOB 8 Nov 98)
ANDERSON, Nathaniel, of Richm., has appointed his son, Wm. ANDERSON, to transact any of his business during his absence (VGGA 24 Dec 94)
ANDERSON, Capt. Nathaniel, of Caroline Co., d. on Sat. morn. last (Ex 20 Dec 98); his admr., Bathurst JONES and Wm. ANDERSON of Hanover Co., will sell all of his PE at the house of Mrs. ANDERSON near the White Chimneys in Caroline Co. and will also settle his est. (Ex 15 Mar 99)
ANDERSON, Col. Paulin, dec'd, of Amelia Co., his admr., Anderson SCOTT, will sell items of his est. (Arg 14 Nov 97)
ANDERSON, Pouncey, dec'd of Louisa Co., Michael ANDERSON, the ex. of his widow, Eliz. ANDERSON, dec'd, will sell 10 of her Negroes (VGGA 17 Aug 96)
ANDERSON, Richard, late of Louisa Co., dec'd, e.a.w. Joseph ANDERSON for the admx. (VGGA 7 Aug 93)
ANDERSON, Robert, of Norf., dec'd, his est. to be sold by his ex., Joshua PEED and extx., Eliz. BALENTINE (NPJ 28 May 88)

ANDERSON, Thos., late of Hanover, dec'd, 12 slaves which he lent to his wife, Fanny ANDERSON, to be sold by his ex. (Arg 20 Dec 99)

ANDERSON, Thos. Jr., of Hanover, mar. Miss Sally HOWARD, late of Buckingham (VG 28 Jan 75)

ANDERSON, Wm., late of Hanover Co., dec'd, e.a.w. his admr., Cicely ANDERSON (VGGA 26 Dec 92)

ANDERSON, Wm., dec'd, his act. ex., Samuel GIST of London, adv. that by the direction of his will, the house is to be continued under the management of proper persons in London until 1800 when his nephew, Francis ANDERSON, now in London and in the business will be of age to take charge of it himself (VGGA 19 Apr 97); Samuel GIST adv. that Francis ANDERSON (a native of Va.), nephew of the sd. Wm. ANDERSON, has lately withdrawn himself from his friends and business in London with the design, it is supposed, to return to Va.; he is not of age nor is he employed by his uncle's ex. to transact any business (VGGA 21 Feb 98)

ANDERSON, Wm., Esq., of London, dec'd, his tracts of land in Goochland, Hanover, Louisa, and Albemarle cos. to be sold (DOB 8 Nov 98, Arg 16 Apr 99)

ANDERSON, Wm. Jr., merch., mar. Miss Betsy MINOR, both of Richm., on Thurs. 26th Dec. (VGRC 31 Dec 93, VGWeA 3 Jan 94)

ANDRES, Eliz., wife of Martin ANDRES of Alexandria, has run away (VJAA 3 Jun 84)

ANDREWS Family, Cumb. Co. Ct. of QS, 3 May 94, in chanc: Robert SMITH (pltf) vs. Wm. and Garnet ANDREWS and Nancy ANDREWS who hath intermarried with Ambrose RANSONE, Jn. GRIFFIN and Mary his wife, and Nancy, Mary, and Jos. POLLARD infants and chil. of Isaac and Susannah POLLARD by Isaac POLLARD their guardian and next friend (VGGA 1 Jul 95)

ANDREWS, the Rev. Mr., of York, mar. Miss Betsy BALLARD of Princess Anne (VGP 5 Jan 75, VG 7 Jan 75)

ANDREWS, Mrs. Frances, wife of the Rev. Mr. ANDREWS of Nansemond, d. on Sat. 14th ult. in the flower of her age (VG 11 Nov 75)

ANDREWS, Robert, Esq., mar. Miss Molly BLAIR, dau. of John BLAIR Esq. of Wmsbrg., on Tues. 24th ult. in Wmsbrg. (VGWeA 28 Mar 95, VGRMA 30 Mar 95, VGGA 1 Apr 95)

ANDREWS, the Rev. Thomas, dec'd, e.a.w. his admr., James SMITH, Northumberland Co. (VGGA 1 Apr 95)

ANGE, Francis, of Somerset Co., Md., d. there about 2 mos. ago at a very advanced age; he was the son of John and Eleanor ANGE, b. in Stratford upon Avon, Warwickshire, Eng., came to Va. and served his time with Nicholas DEMAR on Rappahannock [long obit.] (VG 18 Jun 67)

ANSWINGER, George, des. from the barracks near Winchester; he came from near William's Port and has relations in Greenbrier (BVCG 30 Nov 95)

ANSWORTH, Michael, Eng. svt., silversmith, ran away from John FUNK, Fred. Co. (VG 12 Dec 55)

APPERSON, John, of Halifax Co., dec'd, three tracts of his tobacco land on Difficult Cr., Halifax Co., to be sold by his ex., Robert WOODING (VG 13 Oct 68)

APPERSON, Samuel, dec'd, his tract called "Poplar Spring" in Chas. City Co. to be sold by his ex., John APPERSON (VGR 18 Aug 68)

APPLEWHAITE, Benj., dec'd, e.a.w. his admr., Wm. ORR and John APPLEWHAITE (VGPu 7 Nov 77 sup)

ARBADO, Francis, black Frenchman, c. 30, des. from the *Manly* galley (VG 16 May 77)

ARCHDEACON, James, of Norf. Co., d. in an advanced age; his admx. is Parnel ARCHDEACON (NPC 19 Nov 91)

ARCHER, Mrs., sp. to Thomas ARCHER of Yorktown, died (VG 10 Jun 73)

ARCHER, Mrs., sp. of Edward ARCHER Esq. of Norfolk, died (NPC 8 May 90)
ARCHER, Mrs., cons. of Abraham ARCHER of York, died there (VGGA 31 Jan 98)
ARCHER, Chas., tailor and habit-maker from London, has commenced business in Martinsburg (PGBA 12 Jan 97)
ARCHER, Edw. Esq., mar. Mrs. WORMINGTON on Sat. last [12 Nov.] (NPC 19 Nov 91)
ARCHER, Mrs. Joanna, dec'd, of Wmsbrg. (VG 16 May 45)
ARCHER, John, dec'd, his ex., (nfi), will sell 20 of his slaves in Chest. Co. (VGGA 16 Jan 93)
ARCHER, Richard, of Amelia Co, d. on Tues. 16th ult. (RMA 10 Sep 96)
ARCHER, Thos. Sr., of Yorktown, died (VG 7 Apr 81)
ARCHER, Wm., inspector at Bollingbrook Warehouse, d. on Sun. last (VGPI 23 Jun 95, 16 Dec 96)
ARCHER, Wm., dec'd, of Dinwiddie Co., e.a.w. Wm. A, CRAWFORD agent for the admx., Mary ARCHER (VGPI 14 Mar 97)
ARCHIBALD, Bartholomew, svt., c. 18, ran away from Robert NORTH, Staunton (VG 23 Dec 75)
ARCHIBALD, Samuel, of Richm., adv. that Catherine ARCHIBALD, formerly his wife, eloped on the 4th inst. (VGWeA 30 Oct 88); dec'd, his admx., Kathreen ARCHIBALD of Richm., will sell has PE which includes the sloop *York* (RMA 9 Mar 96)
ARELL, David Esq., mar. Miss Phoebe CAVERLY [in Alexandria] (VJAA 12 May 85)
ARELL, Mrs. Eleanor, age 77, d. [in Alex.] on Thurs. morn. last (CMAG 30 Jul 96)
ARELL, Rich., dec'd, e.a.w. his admr., P[hilip]. G. MARSTELLER and Geo. JENKINS (CMAG 17 Sep 96)
ARELL, Samuel, dec'd, e.a.w. his ex., Elisha C. DICK and Philip G. MARSTELLER, who will also sell his PE (CMAG 5 Mar 96)
ARGYLE, Frederick, merch., of Richm., mar. Miss Rebecca WINSTON of Hanover Co. on Sat. eve. 9th inst. (VGGA 15 Nov 99, Arg 19 Nov 99)
ARMISTEAD, Bowles Esq., dec'd, his PE to be sold at the mansion house, Ely's Ford, Culpeper [Co.] (VHFA 6 Aug 89)
ARMISTEAD, Churchill, mar. Miss Betsey BOSWELL, both of Gloucester Co. (VGPu 7 Jul 75)
ARMISTEAD, Fanny, Negro, says she served her time with Wm. ROGERS of Spotsylvania, jailed as a runaway in K & Q Co. (VGPA [29] Dec 92)
ARMISTEAD, Col. Henry, of Caroline Co., dec'd, his est. in Caroline to be sold by his ex., Wm. ARMISTEAD in Gloucester Co. (VG 19 Jul 54, 29 Aug 55)
ARMISTEAD, Henry, d. at his house in Fredsbrg. on 20th inst. [Jul.] (VIC 8, 22 Aug 87)
ARMISTEAD, Henry, late of Fredsbrg., dec'd, his ex. is Wm. PEACHEY of Richmond Co. (VHFA 29 Apr 90)
ARMISTEAD, Mrs. Jane, of York Co., dec'd, her PE being sold by the sheriff; e.a.w. Frederick BRYAN (VG 19 Feb 67, 18 Feb 68)
ARMISTEAD, John, dec'd, 15 slaves of his est. to be sold at Hanover Ct. H. by his ex. (nfi) (VG 30 Jul 67)
ARMISTEAD, Col. John Esq., d. at his seat in New Kent Co. after a short illness; his admr., Wm. ARMISTEAD, of New Kent, will sell about 30 of his Virginia-born slaves (VG 8 May 79, 1 Jan 80)
ARMISTEAD, John Esq., late of Caroline Co., dec'd, his extx. is Lucy ARMISTEAD (VHFA 1 Jul 90); his admx. [sic] of Fredsbrg. will sell 40 of his slaves (VGAxA 11 Nov 90); portion of his est. bel. to his son, William, in Gloucester Co. to be sold for taxes (VGGA 24 Nov 90); his remaining PE to be sold in Caroline Co. and Fredsbrg by his admx. (VGGA 23 Feb 91)
ARMISTEAD, John, dec'd, Wm. ARMISTEAD (nfi) will sell a tract of his land on which Mary ARMISTEAD has lived for some years past near New Kent Ct. H. (VGGA 12 Sep 92)

ARMISTEAD, Martha, extx. of her late husband, Edward ARMISTEAD dec'd, adv. that he was security for Garden JEGGITT's gdnship of James HAY's orphan in York Co. (VG 7 Nov 71)
ARMISTEAD, Mary, has secretly taken a great part of furniture belonging to her husband, Wm. ARMISTEAD Sr. of Eliz. City Co. (NHPA 28 Aug 97)
ARMISTEAD, Moss, dec'd, e.a.w. his ex., Katharine ARMISTEAD and Wm. ARMISTEAD (VIC 9 Dec 89); e.a.w. his admr., Wm. ARMISTEAD, Eliz. City Co. (VGGA 22 Jun 91)
ARMISTEAD, Miss Nancy, eld. dau. of Thomas ARMISTEAD formerly of Petersburg, was killed in a carriage accident near Fleet's Mills on Sat. eve. last; her sister, Julia, and her mother were injured (NH 14 Jul 98)
ARMISTEAD, Westwood, Eliz. City Co., Ct. of 26 Aug. 86, in chanc: Robert WALKER (pltf.) against Alex. GRAHAM, Geo. GRAHAM, Jas. Bray ARMISTEAD, Robt. ARMISTEAD, exors. etc. of Westwood ARMISTEAD dec'd, Wm. BROUGH, Sarah DIXON, Rebecca DEWBREE exors. etc. of John DEWBREE dec'd, Thos. FENNY and Miles KING Gent. admrs. of Simon HALLIER dec'd, Wm. MOORE, Augustine MOORE Sr., Jos. NICHOLAS, John [PAUL], Warlich WESTWOOD Gent., Mary MALLERY exors. of Francis MALLERY dec'd and Samuel DEWBREE (defs.); it appears that Alex. GRAHAM and Geo. GRAHAM are not inhabitants of this country (VIC 13 Dec 86)
ARMISTEAD, Maj. William, dec'd, of New Kent Co., e.a.w. his admx., Mary ARMISTEAD, and admr., Wm. CLAYTON (VG 27 Nov 79)
ARMISTEAD, Capt. William, of New Kent Co., mar. Miss Betsy Stith ARMISTEAD of Eliz. City Co. on 23 Aug. (VGAA 13 Sep 83)
ARMISTEAD, Wm. Esq., of Gloucester Co., dec'd, his est. there to be sold by Maria ARMISTEAD, his extx., and Wm. NELSON, his ex. (VGAA 8 Oct 85); e.a.w. his extx. and ex. (VGAA 28 Jan 86); 50 of his slaves to be sold (VGAA 8 Feb 86)
ARMISTEAD, William, late of New Kent Co., e.a.w. his act. ex., J. DANDRIDGE (VGGA 2 Oct 93 ex)
ARMISTEAD. William, dec'd, e.a.w. his ex., R. ARMISTEAD of Eliz. City Co., who will also sell part of his PE (NH 28 Sep 99)
ARMSTRONG Family, Botetourt Co. Ct., Dec. 98, in chanc: Robt. ARMSTRONG, Alex. ARMSTRONG, Thos. ARMSTRONG, and Archibald ARMSTRONG devisees of Elinor ARMSTRONG dec'd (pltfs.) against Isabella ARMSTRONG, heiress of Andrew ARMSTRONG dec'd (def.); it appears that Isabella ARMSTRONG is not an inhabitant of the Commonwealth (Ex 24 Dec 98)
ARMSTRONG, Elizabeth, from Philadelphia, adv. that she has taken the public house for several years past occupied by Mr. Flo[rence] MAHONY in Martinsburg (PGBA 10 Mar 96, CMAG 26 May 96)
ARMSTRONG, Jacob, Negro, c. 30, says he belongs to Cornelius COLLICK in Lewis Town, Md., jailed in Surry Co. (VGR 18 Nov 73, 27 Jan 74)
ARMSTRONG, John, dec'd, his ex., Samuel PERRIN, Chas. BURTON, and David BOYD, will sell his valuable tract of land cont. 500 ac. on the south side of Dan River as well as the ferry known as Boyd's Ferry (VG 11 Sep 79)
ARMSTRONG, John, dec'd, e.a.w. his admr., Jas. TURNBULL (NH 28 May 99)
ARMSTRONG, John, dec'd, his ex., James KER, will sell his PE in Norf. (NH 28 Sep 99)
ARMSTRONG, Mary, of Louisa, will present a pet. at the ensuing GA for a divorcement from her husband, Wm. ARMSTRONG (VGGA 15 Nov 97)
ARMSTRONG, Mary, aka Mary RUSSEL, wife of John RUSSEL of Stafford, has left him; he will no longer pay her debts (VHFA 26 May 98)
ARMSTRONG, Robert, of or about Lynchburg, has applied to Geo. JUDE of Campbell Co. for a certificate of his freedom; JUDE certifies that the sd. ARMSTRONG served his time from his childhood to the age of 21 with trust and fidelity at which time he gave him his freedom (LWG 16 Feb 99)

18th-Century Virginia Newspapers   11

ARMSTRONG, Tom, mulatto, ran away from John JUDE, Cumb. Co. (VGR 13 Oct 68)

ARMSTRONG, William, conv. svt., Scot, blacksmith, 37, ran away from Jn. TURBERVILLE, Westmoreland Co. (VGNI 26 Jul 75)

ARMSTRONG, William, Eng., 40, ran off with two horses bel. to Matthew CROHON of Hampton (VJAA 13 Jul 86)

ARMSTRONG, William, from New Kent Co., exec. on Fri. last at the gallows near Richm. for breaking and robbing (VIC 11 Jun 88, VGWeA 12 Jun 88, NPJ 18 Jun 88)

ARMSTRONG, William, merch., of Winchester, mar. Miss Nancy BLAIR near Battletown on Tues. 8th inst. (BVCG 16 Mar 91)

ARNOLD, Mr. [ ], flatman, drowned last week (VJAA 17 Aug 86)

ARNOLD, Ann and her husband, William ARNOLD of Rockbridge Co. do not expect to live any longer together (BVCG 17 Sep 92)

ARNOLD, Daniel, mulatto slave, 17, ran away from Geo. RALLS, Loudoun Co., on 1 July (VJAA 12 Oct 86)

ARNOLD, James, of Halifax Co., c. 25, failed to appear to march with the 4th Co. of the 2nd Bn. for the State of Georgia (VGPu 9 May 77 sup)

ARNOLD, Mrs. Rebecca, d. on the 19th ult. at her seat near Lower Marlborough, Md. in her 77th year (VJAA 4 Dec 88)

ARNOTT, Mrs. Frances, of New Kent Co., dec'd, her ex. (nfi) will sell her plant. and land on Black Creek (VRG 24 Dec 72)

ARNOTT, Dr. Thomas, of New Kent Co., dec'd, his land to be sold by his ex., James LITTLEPAGE (Clerk of Louisa Court) and Julius King BURBIDGE (of New Kent) (VG 28 Aug 46)

ARTER, William, appr. carpenter, ran away from Francis SMITH Sr. and James GEDDY, Kg. Wm. Ct. H.; supposed gone to Bedford or North Carolina (VG 2 Apr 67)

ARTHUR, Charles R., d. on 20 Sep. 1796; his admr. with the will annexed, Wm. DU VAL, will sell the lease from Jn. HARVIE Esq. to Charles R. ARTHUR for about 30 ac. of land on the James River Company's canal near Richm. with a valuable mill, brewery, and distillery (VGGA 21 Sep 96, 10 May 97)

ARTHUR, Capt. Samuel, late commander of the ship *Flora* that arrived in Philadelphia on 12 Sep., d. on his passage from Liverpool (NPC 26 Sep 89)

ARUNDEL, Capt. Dohicky, killed in action in Gloucester Co. last Tues.-Wed. by the bursting of a mortar of his own invention (VG 13 Jul 76, VGPu 19 Jul 76)

ARUNDELL, John, aka Thomas LOCKE, appr., c. 16, ran away from Jos. COLEMAN (CMAG 8 Nov 96)

ASH, Jack, aka Johnny, Negro, ran away from Lewis BURWELL, King's Mill (VG 11 Feb 68)

ASH, James, intends to move from Winchester to Balto. (BVCG 15 Dec 94)

ASHBROOKE Family, Randolph Co. Ct., May 1798, in chanc: John CHENOWETH (compl.) against John JOINER and Rebecca his wife, Jacob LUNDER and Catharine his wife, Levi ASHBROOKE, Theodore BUTLER and Emma his wife, John ASHBROOKE, Edward P[ERRELL] and Rachel his wife, Thomas [TUCKER] and Phoebe his wife, Absolom ASHBROOKE, Eliz. ASHBROOKE, Aaron ASHBROOKE, Eli ASHBROOKE, Mary ASHBROOKE, Rhody ASHBROOKE, Amelia ASHBROOKE, Wm. ASHBROOKE, and Thos. ASHBROOKE, heirs of Levi ASHBROOKE dec'd (WG 27 Jun 98)

ASHBURN, Edward, b. in Whitehaven, bred a shipwright, worked some years in Jamaica then went to Georgia c. 1776-78; his brother, George ASHBURN, was bred a mariner and resided some years in Liverpool; about 1779-80 he sailed from New York to the Windward Islands and has not been heard of since; these two men would be about 60; George has a family in Liverpool; they may hear something to their advantage by applying to Geo. VENABLE, merch., Liverpool (VGGA 2 May 92)

ASHBURN, Capt. William, of the ship *Fly* at Bermuda Hundred, died (VG 28

Oct 73)
ASHBURN, William, cutler from London, has opened shop in Wmsbrg. (VG 14 Apr 74)
ASHBY, Catherine, has eloped from her husband, Robert ASHBY, of Fauquier Co. (VGWA 22 Feb 88)
ASHBY, Edward Esq., of Fauquier Co., mar. Miss Peggy PENTICOST of Mt. Sion [Frederick Co.], eld. dau. of Dorsey PENTICOST Esq. on Wed. last (VGWA 18 Jan 88)
ASHBY, Robin, of Fauquier Co., dec'd, e.a.w. his ex., John ASHBY (VCG 12 Mar 92)
ASHCROFT, Mary, widow of [?] ASHCROFT of New Kent Co. is lately dead; James, Robert, and Thomas MOORE, who reside on the southside of James River in Surry or Brunswick Co. are advised that she left behind some effects that may be of some service to her heir (VG 3 Oct 71)
ASHENHURST, Oliver and William, from Carlisle, [Pennsylvania?], have set up a tailor's business on Berk St. (PGBA 21 Apr 94)
ASHHILL, David, Irish svt., 35, ran away from Robt. VAULX and Jn. ELLIOTT, Westmoreland Co.; he may be headed for Norfolk (VG 2 May 51)
ASHLEY, Samuel, dec'd, his ex., Robt. C. WARREN, will sell his ordinary and the tract of land adjoining it six miles above Wmsbrg. on the road to Hanover (VGPu 17 Oct 77)
ASHTON, Richard W., merch. of Alex., mar. Miss Betsy CHAPIN (VJAA 16 Nov 86)
ATCHISON, Thomas, of Portsm., formerly a merch. in this county, died (VG 3 Oct 71)
ATHERTON, James, late of Wmsbrg., Va., now of Balto., dec'd, his ex. are Francis SMITH and John PROCTER (MJ 23 Feb 79)
ATHERTON, Lucy, her husband, James ATHERTON, adv. that she has behaved in a very unfriendly manner to him and he will not pay any of her debts (VG 4 Feb 75)
ATKERSON, James and Thomas, of Greensville Co., dec'd, e.a.w. their admr. Jn. ATKERSON (VGPI 25 May 98)
ATKINSON, Charles, of Fredsbrg, d. at Kingston, Jamaica on the 2nd ult. aged 22, of Yellow Fever (VHFA 23 Oct 94, VGRMA 27 Oct 94)
ATKINSON, David, of Henrico, aged 96, saith that about 62 yrs. ago, his brother-in-law, James PYRON, owned the land which now belongs to Thomas AUSTIN, and his brother, Henry ATKINSON, with whom he then lived, owned the land opposite thereto now the property of Nathaniel WILKINSON (deposition of 30 Mar. 84) (VGAA 3 Apr 84)
ATKINSON, Capt. John, dec'd, his ex., John ARCHER and James LADD, will sell his plant. cont. about 300 ac. and another cont. about 150 ac. in Chas. City Co. (VG 23 Oct 79)
ATKINSON, Mary, otherwise DAVIS, has eloped from her husband, James ATKINSON of Norfolk (VGR 1 Aug 71)
ATKINSON, Robert Esq., of Chesterfield Co., mar. Miss Polly MAYO at Powhatan, the seat of Col. Wm. MAYO, on Thurs. last (VGRMA 22 Dec 94)
ATKINSON, Roger Jr. Esq., mar. Miss Agnes POYTHRESS of Pr. Geo. Co., sixth dau. of the late Col. Peter POYTHRESS, on Sat. last (VIC 24 Sep 88)
ATTKINSON, William, dec'd, his land in Goochland and Hanover cos. to be sold by his ex., Joseph and Isaiah ATTKISSON [sic] (VGGA 30 Nov 91)
ATWOOD, Thomas, dec'd, e.a.w. his admr., Rich. WALSH, Norfolk (HNPA 29 Nov 94)
ATWOOD, William, appr., c. 16, ran away from Jas. DAMERON, Norfolk (NH 6 Jul 99)
AUBERY, Catherine, aka HAYNES, absconded from her husband, Wm. Arcutt AUBERY, with a young child, and is gone towards Fredsbrg. (VG 27 Jul 69)
AUBERY, Thomas aka SMITH, exec. at Wmsbrg. for horse stealing (Wmsbrg. disp. of 12 Jan.) (MG 1 Feb 53)
[AUFLER], Jeremiah, svt., 28, ran away from the ship *Duke of Cumberland* at

Bermuda Hundred in James River, 23 May (VG 25 May 39)
AUSTIN, Abner, d. in Hanover Co. on Sat. eve. the 1st inst. (RMA 4 Oct 96, VGGA 5 Oct 96)
AUSTIN, Henry, appr., 18-19, ran away from Jn. SMITH, bricklayer in Richm., expected to make towards Petersburg or Norfolk (VGAA 2 Aug 86)
AUSTIN, Israel, sailor, des. from the schooner *Sally* now lying at Burwell's Ferry; it is believed he is made towards Richm. where it is believed he intends to be married (VG 10 Jul 78)
AUSTIN, John, of Kg. Wm. Co., adv. that his wife, Susannah AUSTIN, has gone off with one of his Negroes and he will no longer be answerable for any bargain she makes (VGPu 28 Jun 76)
AUSTIN, Reubin, att. at law, of Manchester, d. on Sun. morn. after a short illness (Arg 12 Dec 96)
AUSTIN, Mrs. Sarah, wife of Capt. John AUSTIN Jr. of Hanover Co., d. on the 13th inst. (VGGA 22 Oct 99)
AVERY, Col. Edward, of Warwick Co., mar. Miss Mary WEST of Norfolk on Thurs. eve. (NHPA 6 May 97)
AVERY, Col. Isaac, of Norfolk, d. on Thurs. last (NH 19 Oct 99); e.a.w. his ex., John STRINGER (NH [30] Nov 99)
AVORIS, John, his admr., Thos. CHAPPELL and Jos. FOWLER of Dinwiddie will sell all of his est. consisting of 371 ac. (VG 13 Jul 76)
AXLEY, James, appr., carpenter, ran away from Francis SMITH Sr. and James GEDDY, Kg. Wm. Ct. H., supposed he is gone to Bedford on into North Carolina (VG 2 Apr 67)
AYLETT Family, P. AYLETT, gdn. of Wm. AYLETT, Kg. Wm. Co., mentions slaves in the possession of Maj. Gallohill MENNIS of Bedford Co. that are claimed by Mary AYLETT and that Wm. AYLETT, his ward, Anne AYLETT, and Rebecca AYLETT will bring a suit by their next friend for the recovery of the slaves (VGGA 6 Mar 93)
AYLETT, James, of Hanover, killed by Nathan PHILIPS (VG 5 Nov 72)
AYLETT, Capt. John, dec'd, his lands in Hanover and Louisa Cos. to be sold next April by Philip BUCKNER and Philip AYLETT (VG 9 Jan 46)
AYLETT, John, att. at law, mar. Miss Betsey DANDRIDGE of New Kent (VG 15 Apr 73)
AYLETT, John Esq., att. at law, of New Kent Co.(or, acc. to VG, of James City), d. of a pleurisy (VGPu 9 Feb 76, VG 10 Feb 76)
AYLETT, Philip, late of Kg. Wm. Co., dec'd, Thos. DANSIE, of the same co., is appointed gdn. to his children and will undertake admin. of the est. (VG 1 Aug 55)
AYLETT, Philip Esq., of Kg. Wm. Co., mar. Miss Betsy HENRY, dau. of H.E. the governor, on Thurs. (VIC and VGAA 18 Oct 86)
AYLETT, Col. William Esq., dec'd, several of his Negroes to be sold by Philip AYLETT, att. in fact for his ex., Wm. D. CLAIBORNE (VGGA 22 Jun 91); Philip AYLETT will sell several of his Negroes in Kg. Wm. Co. (VGGA 7 Aug 93)
AYRES, Rebecca, her husband (nfi), of Crooked Run, adv. that on the 6th of July, she absconded from him with a certain James CRAIG (who is about 25) and he suspects they are gone to North Carolina or Kentucky (WVGWA 10 Jul 90)
AYSCOUGH, Christopher and Anne, dec'd, e.a.w. the admr., Jacob BRUCE (VG 15 Oct 72)

BABER, Benjamin, dec'd, his ex., L. BERRY and Y. JOHNSON of Kg. Geo. Co., will sell his HH and KF (VH 19 Jul 99)
BABER, Thomas, son of Thos. BABER of Caroline Co., aged 17, has run away with Winifred BALEY, an "evil-disposed wench" whom he intends to marry (VG 31 Jul 46)

BACHELOR, Peter, Eng. conv. svt., c. 23, ran away from Jos. STROTHER, Culpeper Co. (VG 4 Jul 71)

BACKER, Frederick, Dutch svt., 20, ran away from Jn. TANKERSLEY and Jn. CATLETT, Port Royal [Caroline Co.] VHFA 23 Apr 89

BACKHOUSE, William, of Fredsbrg, mar. Miss Polly AVERY of Matthews Co. in Matthews Co. on the 16th inst. (RCFPC 22 Jun 96)

BACKHURST, Bolling, dec'd, e.a.w. his ex., J. BACKHURST of Chas. City Co. (VGWeA 12 Jul 87)

BACON, Langston, of Henrico Co., dec'd, his ex., Nathaniel BACON and John WILLIAMSON Jr., adv. his land and plant. on Chickahominy Swamp in Henrico for sale (VG 15 Aug 55)

BACON, Peter, of Norfolk, d. yesterday [23 Jul.] (VCGA 24 Jul 94)

BACON, Peter, mar. Miss Betsey SKINNER of Petersburg, Thurs. last (VGPI 29 Mar 96)

BACON, Samuel and Samuel D., dec'd, e.a.w. their admr., Wm. VAUGHAN, who will also sell 210 ac. of land belonging to the est. of Samuel BACON three miles by water from Norfolk (AGNPPA 5 Jan 96, NH 11 Dec 99)

BACON, the Rev. Mr. Thomas, rector of All Saints Par., Frederick, Md., d. Tues. 24th ult. [obit.] (VGR 23 Jun 68)

BADGETT, John, of Buckingham, warns that he will pay no debts of his wife, Milly BADGETT (VGWeA 6 Mar 84)

BADGETT, John, of Dinwiddie Co., forewarns all persons from harboring or entertaining his wife, Mary BADGETT (VGGA 13 Jan 96); he will no longer pay his wife's debts (VGPI 4 Oct 96)

BAGBY, John, dec'd, e.a.w. his ex., W. O. CALLIS of Louisa (Arg 3 Feb 97)

BAGGE, Robert, dec'd, a large tract of his land on the Rapidan River in Orange Co. to be sold in Fredsbrg. by his ex., Robt. SEAYRES and Jn. RENNOLDS (VG 18 Apr 55)

BAGNALL, John, conv. svt., c. 20, b. in London, was a tin plate worker, imported in Nov. last in the *Alexandria* and bought at Leedstown; ran away from Roger BECKWITH, Richmond Co. (VG 30 Jul 72)

BAGNALL, Richard, was mar. to Miss SELDEN on Wed. last at New Town by the Rev. Anthony WALKE, both of Norfolk (NHPA 4 Feb 97)

BAGWELL, John G., dec'd, late of Amherst Co., e.a.w. his admr., Wm. B. HARE of Warminster, Amherst Co. (Ex 12 Jul 99)

BAILES, John, Irish, carpenter, des. from Capt. James MACKILWEAN's Co. at Petersburg (VG 19 Jul 54)

BAILEY Family, Mecklenburg Co., Dec. Ct. 1795: Jonathan BAILEY, assignee of Samuel FARRAR (pltf.) against Warner MARTIN and Martha his wife, Henry BAILEY, Wm. FERRELL and Dolly his wife, Eliz. BAILEY, Jane BAILEY, Sarah BAILEY, and Gabriel BAILEY, children and co-heirs of Wm. BAILEY dec'd (defs.) (VGPI 9 Feb 96)

BAILEY, Mrs. Catharine, cons. of Chester BAILEY, d. in Fauquier Co. on 23 May (VHFA 2 Jun 98)

BAILEY, Charles, 23-24, b. in Va., enl. at Hanover Ct. H. 20 Sep. 94, des. from Ft. Nelson (HNPA 4 Mar 95)

BAILEY, Elizabeth, dec'd, e.a.w. her admr., Parke BAILEY, who notes that she was also the extx. of James SIMMS dec'd (Ex 7 May 99)

BAILEY, Francis, merch., d. on the 3rd inst. in Manchester; his funeral was attended by his brother masons of Manchester Lodge No. 14 (VGRMA 6 Jan 94)

BAILEY, James, dec'd, e.a.w. his ex., Daniel BAILEY of Westmoreland Co. (VGWeA 13 Aug 85)

BAILEY, John, appr. boy, ran away from Thos. ROBERTS, Nansemond Co., who suspects he is lurking about Hampton as he was born there (VGPu 24 Jun 77)

BAILEY, Joseph, and Wm. BULLINGTON, dec'd, e.a.w. their ex., Jos. BAILEY (VGWeA 20 Mar 84)

BAILEY, Josiah, Eng. svt., leather breeches maker, 25, ran away from Wm. BLYTH, Fredsbrg. (VGP 21 Sep 75)
BAILEY, Margery, conv. svt., ran away from Ann BECHAM, widow, Richmond Co. near Naylor's Hole on Rappahannock River (MG 2 Aug 34)
BAILEY, Robert, appr., 17, ran away from Robt. BROOKING, Culpeper on 16 Mar 89 (VHFA 8 Apr 90)
BAILEY, Samuel, conv. svt., c. 30, house joiner, has been in the country about two yrs., ran away from Wm. BUCKLAND (VG and VGR. 1 Aug 71)
BAILEY, Thomas, High Sheriff of Surry, d. on Sat. 30 Nov. (VG 12 Dec 71)
BAILEY, Thomas, Negro, blacksmith, c. 36, ran away from James GORDON Jr., Culpeper Co. (VHFA 31 Jul 94)
BAILEY, William, dec'd, his ex., Anne BAILEY, Roger TANDY, and Jn. BAILEY, will sell his ordinary in New Kent Co. (VG 13 Oct 74)
BAILEY, William, dec'd, e.a.w. Wm. EVANS, admr. for Yancey BAILEY, Buckingham Co. (RC 29 Dec 95)
BAILEY, William, orphan lad, bound as an appr. to James PATTON, ran away and may have gone to Warwick or Petersburg (NHPA 6 Nov 97)
BAILEY, William A., dec'd, those indebted to his est. are to pay Francis FOSTER and any claims are to be made to James BOYCE and Frede[r]ick WILLIAMS (VCNPGA 16 Mar 93, AGNPWA 27 Mar 93)
BAILIS, Rebecca, of Eliz. City Co., widow, dec'd, her land in sd. co. and the reversion of four Negro slaves...after the death of the sd. Mrs. BAILIS...being late the est. of James RICKITS dec'd (VG 14 Aug 46)
BAILLIE, Stephen, Eng. svt. boy, 15, ran away from Archibald MACCAUL, Essex Co. on 18 Nov. (VG 12 Dec 55)
BAILY, Thomas, svt., b. in Yorkshire, ran away from Jacob RICE, [Urbanna], Rappahannock (AWM 17 Mar 20)
BAIMBRIDGE, Dr. Absolam, mar. Miss TAYLOR, dau. of Jn. TAYLOR, merch., of Stephensburgh, last Thurs. [30 May] at Stephensburgh (BVCG 3 Jun 93)
BAIN, John, tailor, c. 24, ran away from Robt. NICOLSON, Wmsbrg. (VGR 19 Aug 73)
BAINE, Robert, merch., of this city [Richm.], d. last night [1 Apr.] (VGAA 2 Apr 85)
BAINE, Robert, dec'd, e.a.w. his ex., Jas. CRAWFORD and Jn. SCAMBLE, Norfolk (AGNPWA 25 Sep 93)
BAIRD, Mrs. Jane, wife of Jn. BAIRD Esq., of Greencroft, died (VG 3 Jul 79)
BAITY, David, redemptioner from Ireland, is at the house of James WRIGHT, Berkeley Co. (VJAA 8 Mar 87)
BAKER, Mrs., wife of Dr. BAKER of Alexandria, d. a few days ago in Charles Co., Md. (VJAA 30 Aug 87)
BAKER, Benjamin, dec'd, Jn. DORLON of South Quay is auth. to settle his est. per Wm. BAKER, ex. of Rich. BAKER who was ex. of Benjamin BAKER (VCNPGA 3 Aug 93)
BAKER, Blake Esq., dec'd, his est. in North Carolina to be sold by Mary BAKER extx. and Jn. BAKER and Jas. HOLDERNESS exors. (VG 2 Nov 69)
BAKER, Blake Esq., d. on Mon. 25th at 1:00 PM at his seat near South Quay in the flower of his age leaving a young family (VCNPGA 30 Mar 93)
BAKER, George, died (WVGWA 15 May 90)
BAKER, Isaac, Negro, c. 30, and his wife, Rachel, jailed in Berkeley Co. as runaways (PGBA 28 Dec 97)
BAKER, James, appr., 19-20, cabinet-maker, ran away from James WOODWARD, Norfolk (NH 27 Oct 98)
BAKER, Jerman Esq., att. at law near Petersburg, mar. Mrs. MURRAY, relict of the late James MURRAY of Pr. Geo. Co. (VG 7 Jan 73); d. at his seat at Archer's Hill, Chesterfield Co. on Fri. night last (disp. of 5 Sep.) (VGGA 5 Sep 92, VCNPGA 8 Sep 92, VHFA 13 Sep 92); his ex., Thos. G. PEACHY and Edmund HARRISON of Pr. Geo. will sell a large part of his PE and lease his

seat, Archer's Hill, for five years (VGGA 12 Sep 92, VGPI 27 Sep 92); his act. ex., Edmund HARRISON, will sell his PE upon the plant. near Petersburg (VGGA 10 Jul 93)

BAKER, Jerman, of Petersburg, mar. Miss M. B. EPPS, dau. of Col. Francis EPPS of Chesterfield (Arg 30 Nov 98)

BAKER, John, aka Gloucester, Negro, native of Jamaica, c. 40, formerly belonged to Dr. Jn. BAKER of Wmsbrg., ran away from Jn. FOX, Gloucester Co. (VGGA 1 Sep 90)

BAKER, John Frederick, late of Yorktown, dec'd, any claims against his est. to be made known immediately to the widow (nfi) (VG 25 Mar 80)

BAKER, Mary, svt., ran away from Thos. GREEN, Frederick Co., Md., along with svt. man Thos. DOWNRICHARDS (VGR 21 Sep 69)

BAKER, Col. Richard Esq., att. at law, clerk and rep. for Isle of Wight Co., d. on Sat last (VG and VGR 31 Oct 71)

BAKER, Richard, conv. svt., ran away from Jn. REED and Nicholas MILLER, Baltimore (VGR 6 Feb 72)

BAKER, Samuel, of Pr. Edw. Co., dec'd, e.a.w. his ex., Caleb BAKER and Andrew ELLIOTT (VGWeA 23 Nov 82)

BAKER, William, intends to move with his family from Alexandria to his plant. in Md. sometime in the next month (VJAA 18 Oct 87)

BAKER, William, appr. lad who ran away from Chudleigh SOUTHWICK in Jun. 1798, has been on board the *Constellation* frigate the last 12 mos. (NH 11 Jun 99)

BAKER, William H., dec'd, all of his PE will be sold at Littletown near South Quay (NH 22 May 98); his admx (nfi) will sell his nearly finished vessel in the town of Suffolk (NH 19 Jun 98)

BAKEWELL, Mrs. Mary, wife of T. BAKEWELL, merch., d. last Mon. (HNPA 8 Apr 95)

BALDING, William, Eng. ind. svt., carpenter and joiner, 22-23, ran away from the plant. of James PRIDE (VG 18 Aug 74)

BALDWIN, William, dec'd, his surv. ex., James CAMPBELL will sell his plant. of 360 ac. in Berkeley Co. 8 miles from Martinsburg (PGBA 23 Mar 97, BVCG 31 Mar 97)

BALDWIN, Dr. Zebulon, mar. Miss Susanna MILLER, both of Lynchburg, on Sun. eve. last (LFG 2 May 95); d. on Tues. eve. [long obit.] (LFG 18 Jul 95); his funeral sermon will be preached by the Rev. Chas. CRAWFORD on 22nd inst. at the Mason's Hall in Lynchburg (LFG 8 Aug 95)

BALEY, Abraham Jr., of Henrico Co., dec'd in 1771, e.a.w. his ex., Richard SHARP (VGIC 29 Jan 85)

BALFOUR, Colin, bar-keeper at Lindsy's Hotel, mar. Miss Hannah ROBERTS at the Eagle Tavern, Norfolk, on Sat. eve. (NHPA 29 May 97)

BALFOUR, James, of Hampton, died there (VGR 13 Apr 75, VG 15 Apr 75); his admr., Daniel BARRAUD, will sell the rem. part of his PE at Little England near Hampton (VGPu 14 Jul 75, 25 Aug 75); his ex., Thomas EATON and Augustine WILLIS, will sell 940 ac. of his land in Brunswick Co. near Fontaine's Cr. which he purchased of Gray BRIGGS (VG 26 Aug 75, VGP 31 Aug 75)

BALFOUR, William, appr., c. 20, ran away from Robert BORLAND, joiner and cabinet-maker, Portsmouth (NPJ 23 Apr 88, VIC 30 Apr 88)

BALL, Burges, wants to exch. his farm in Stafford Co., known as Travellers Rest for lands in any counties above the falls of the rivers, but would prefer Loudoun, Berkeley, or Frederick (VICGA 31 Mar 90)

BALL, Capt. George, d. at his house in Northumberland on Tues. 21st ult. (VGR 20 Sep 70)

BALL, John, dec'd, his widow and admx., Mary BALL of Fauquier, appoints Richard LEE and Henry LEE to settle his est. (VGR 20 May 73)

BALL, Mrs. Lettice, of Lancaster Co., mother of the late Dr. William BALL, died (VIC 5 Nov 88, VGWeA 6 Nov 88)

BALL, Lewis, dec'd, e.a.w. his extx., Rebecca TALBOT, at Westham (VGAA 18 Oct 83); two of his lots to be sold by his admr., James TAYLOR (VIC 1 Oct

BALL, Lewis, dec'd, Daniel L. HYLTON and Jesse SMITH will settle his est. (RMA 13 Aug 95)

BALL, Mrs. Mary, cons. of Burges BALL Esq., of Lanc. Co., died (VG 6 May 75)

BALL, Susanna, conv. svt., imported in the *Success's Increase* last Dec., ran away from Forceput near Fredsbrg. (VGR 7 Apr 74)

BALL, William, dec'd, his tract of land in Pr. Geo. Co. 6 miles below Blandford to be sold by Peyton HARVELL, Greensville Co. (ILPB 8 May 93)

BALL, William, from Amherst Co., des. from the camp of the 3rd Sub-Legion on Shockoe Hill (RC 23 Jun 95)

BALL, Capt. William, dec'd, his ex., Thomas PARKER and Laurence BUTLER, will sell his HH est. (BVCG 11 Nov 96)

BALLARD, Anne, has left her husband, Richard BALLARD, Bedford Co. (VG 23 Sep 75)

BALLARD, Col. Robert, mar. Miss PLOWMAN of Balto., Thurs. last (MJ 18 Jul 80)

BALLARD, William, Jr., pilot in Hampton, d. there of smallpox last Mon. (VG 27 Aug 72)

BALLENDINE, Abraham, free mulatto, hostler, d. on Thurs. 9th inst. (RMA 15 Jun 96)

BALLENDINE, John, dec'd, e.a.w. his ex., Thomas W. BALLENDINE of Richm. (VGAA 29 Jun 82); his ex. will sell all of his PE at the Falls of Potomac in Fairfax Co. (VGAA 19 Oct 82, 2 Nov 82)

BALLENDINE, John, [of Dumfries], dec'd (VGAR 14 Jun 92)

BALLENDINE, John, dec'd, e.a.w. T. BLACKBURN, Jesse EWELL, and James EWELL, all persons are desired to make known their demands against the est. of Thomas William BALLENDINE dec'd to Jesse EWELL, admr., Pr. Wm. Co. (VGGA 22 Nov 97)

BALLENDINE, Thomas William, dec'd, e.a.w. his admr., Jesse EWELL, Pr. Wm. Co. (TAA 2 Aug 97)

BALLENGE, Mr., murdered in Kentucky (PH 13 Feb 99)

BALLS, Lewis, dec'd, e.a.w. his admr., James TAYLOR (VGIC 22 May 84)

BALMAIN, the Rev. A[lexander], of Frederick Co. mar. Miss L. TAYLOR, dau. of E. TAYLOR of Orange Co. (VGAA 22 Nov 86)

BALMAIN, Andrew, merch., of New York and nephew of the Rev. Alexander BALMAIN, minister of the Protestant Episcopal Church in the parish of Frederick, d. on the 14th ult. at New York of Yellow Fever in his 31st year (WG 23 Oct 99)

BALMAIN, William, merch., d. last Fri. at Georgetown (VJAA 6 May 84)

BALOO, Thomas, his ex. is David PATTESON of Buckingham Co. (VGGA 28 Sep 96)

BALSAM, Elizabeth, dec'd, her admr., John Conrad GINTER, will sell her HH and KF at her house in Wmsbrg (VG 4 Mar 75)

BALTIMORE, Jemmy, Negro, 30-35, ran away from Alexander ROBERTSON of Blandford who believes he will make for Balto. where he formerly lived (VG 27 Nov 79)

BANGHAM, [Master], son of Humphrey BANGHAM, age 14, drowned on Sun. last (LFG 18 Jul 95)

BANISTER Family, HCC, 6 Oct 97, between Archibald M'CALL and Margaret M'CALL (pltfs.) and John BANISTER, grandson and heir at law of John BANISTER the elder, William RONALD and Alexander SHAW (defs.); this suit abates as to the defs. Jn. BANISTER and Wm. RONALD by their deaths and on the motion of the pltfs. by their counsel subpoenas to revive against Theodorick Blair BANISTER, John Monroe BANISTER, Frances Banister BOWDOIN, and Robert Banister WILSON, infants heirs of Jn. BANISTER dec'd, by Duncan ROSE now assigned their gdn. and against Betsy RONALD and Anne RONALD infants heirs of Wm. RONALD dec'd by William BENTLEY now assigned their gdn. and the def.

Alexander SHAW appears not to be an inhabitant of the country (VGGA 13 Dec 97)

BANISTER Family, HCC, 15 Sep 98, between David ROSS on behalf of himself and the other surv. partners of the late house of David Ross and Co. and Benjamin HARRISON and Co. (pltfs.) and Duncan ROSE surv. ex. of John BANISTER dec'd, Theodoric Blair BANISTER, John Monroe BANISTER, sons and devisees of John BANISTER the elder and infants by John BLAIR now assigned their gdn., Frances BOWDOIN an infant dau. of John BOWDOIN dec'd by Peter BOWDOIN now assigned her gdn., Robert Stewart Banister WIL[T]ON by Duncan ROSE now assigned his gdn., and Elizabeth Carter SHIPPEN the wife of Thomas Lee SHIPPEN the elder, and Thomas Lee SHIPPEN the younger and William SHIPPEN infants by the sd. ELIZABETH Carter SHIPPEN now assigned their gdn.; it appears that Elizabeth Carter SHIPPEN is not an inhabitant of Va. (VGGA 4 Dec 98)

BANISTER, Mrs. Elizabeth, spouse to Col. John BANISTER Esq. of Dinwiddie, died (VGPu and VG 11 Jul 77)

BANISTER, John Esq., of Dinwiddie, mar. Miss Nancy BLAIR, of Wmsbrg. (VG 26 Feb 79)

BANISTER, Col. John Esq., of Petersburg, formerly a del. in congress for this state, died [lately] at his seat near Petersburg (NPJ 8 Oct, 5 Nov 88, VGWeA 16 Oct 88); e.a.w. his ex. (nfi) in Petersburg (VIC 12 Nov 88);his ex., Neil BUCHANAN and Duncan ROSE, will sell his HHF and slaves at Battersea (VIC 11 Mar 89); e.a.w. his act. ex., Neil BUCHANAN and Duncan ROSE, Dinwiddie Co. (VICGA 14 Jul 90)

BANISTER, John Jr. Esq., dec'd, e.a.w. his admr., John DUNBAR, Chas. City Co. (VICGA 28 Apr 90)

BANKES, Capt. George, dec'd, his widow, Judith BANKES of Liverpool, has empowered Jacob ALLAN, Wmsbrg., to settle his est. in Va. (VG 22 Oct 72)

BANKS, Anne, conv. [svt.], ran away from James DAVIS living on the headwaters of Holston's River in Botetourt Co. (VGR 29 Oct 72)

BANKS, Gerrard Esq., d. on Fri. eve. last at his seat in Stafford by a stroke of apoplexy (VIC 20 Jun 87, VGWeA 21 Jun 87, VGIC 23 Jun 87)

BANKS, Henry Esq., of Richm., was mar. to Miss Patsy K. READ, dau. of Dr. J.K. READ of Norfolk Borough on Sat. eve. last at Norfolk by the Rev. Mr. EMMERSON of Portsmouth (NHPA 7 Nov 96, AGGA 8 Nov 96, VGGA 9 Nov 96 ex)

BANKS, John, mulatto, c. 20, ran away from Humphrey TAYLOR, Chesterfield Co. (VG 22 Mar 70)

BANKS, Thomas aka WILLIAMS, ostler, singing boy, pirate, fiddler, schoolmaster, clerk of Jefferson's Church in Chesterfield, [his epitaph] (VG 1 Jan 67)

BANNERMAN, Margaret, of Portsmouth, writes a letter accusing her husband, Benjamin BANNERMAN, of trying to possess himself of her fortune; she says that she mar. him in Oct. 1765 [Her husband has an ad in the same issue; additional details in later issues] (VG 21 Jan 68, 7 Jul 68, 20 Apr 69 sup, 25 May 69, 8 Mar 70)

BAPTIST, John T., French Negro, c. 25, lived lately with Mr. CRUER of Baltimore, a Frenchman, jailed in Norfolk Borough (NH 19 Sep 99)

BARBAFORE, William, died in prison (VG 23 Nov 39)

BARBER, Billy, Negro, c. 30-32, ran away from Bennett BROWNE, Urbanna; may have wives at Norfolk, Hampton, and Urbanna (VG 15 Jul 75)

BARBER, Daniel, Negro, owned by David COCKARNIN of Hanover Co., jailed in Norfolk (NPJ 2 Apr 88)

BARBER, James and Elizabeth, of York Co., dec'd, their admr. is Edward BOWCOCK (VG 24 Jan 51)

BARBER, John, of Harper's Wharf, Alexandria, his widow, Sarah BARBER, adv. a reward for info. where his body can be found and property restored; he was drowned on the 21st of Feb. between the Eastern Branch and

Greenleaf's Pt. (CMAG 7 Mar 97)
BARBER, Matthew, of Portsmouth, dec'd, e.a.w. his ex., William WHITEFIELD and Bernard MAGNIEN (VCNPGA 12 Jan 93)
BARBOUR, Lt., of the Virginia Line, d. lately in South Carolina (VGAA 14 Sep 82)
BARBOUR, Joseph, mulatto slave, 22, ran away from Ludwell GRYMES in Orange Co. (VGAA 4 Dec 84)
BARBOUR, Col. Philip, d. on Sat. 29th ult. [March] in this city [Richm.]; he was buried on Sun. in the churchyard of this city attended by the Grenadier and Light Infantry Companies (VGRMA 31 Mar 94, VGGA 2 Apr 94)
BARCHUS, George, pvt. in the Corps of Artillerists and Engineers, 21, tanner, b. in Queen Anne's Co. [Md.] but brought up in Kent Co., Md., [des. from Ft. Norfolk] (NH 21 Nov 99)
BARE, Billy, aka Billy, Negro, c. 25-26, ran away from Henry COWEN, Wmsbrg, about May 1798, has been seen in Richm. (VGGA 24 May 99)
BARKER, James, of Buckingham, upwards of 40, shoemaker, des. from Lt. Richard CRUMP's quota of state troops (VG 26 Dec 77)
BARKER, James, of or near Birmingham, Warwickshire, Eng., has been some time in North America and is supposed to be living in New York, asked to contact John RAWLINS, Baltimore, to hear of a handsome sum of money left him by relations in Eng. (VJAA 1 Sep 85)
BARKER, John, dec'd, his ex., Benjamin BRANCH, Manchester, will sell his HHF (VGRMA 1 Dec 94)
BARKSDALE Family, Spotsylvania Co. Ct., 2 Aug 96, in chanc: James ROBB, Edmund PENDLETON, and John HOOMES execs. of Robert GILCHRIST dec'd (compls.) against Francis COLEMAN, ex. of Daniel BARKSDALE dec'd, George BRONAUGH and Patty his wife, Joseph BARKSDALE, Edmund BARTLETT and Sarah his wife, George GAINES and Katey his wife, and Daniel BARKSDALE, which sd. Patty, Joseph, Sarah, Katey, and Daniel are the chil. of the sd. Daniel BARKSDALE dec'd (defs.); the defs. Joseph BARKSDALE, Edmund BARTLETT and Sarah his wife, and Daniel BARKSDALE appear not to be inhabitants of this state (VHFFA 1 Nov 96)
BARKSDALE, Daniel, dec'd, his ex. is Francis COLEMAN (VHFA 18 Mar 90)
BARKSDALE, Hickerson, formerly of Buckingham Co., but now a resident of South Carolina (VGGA 11 Apr 92)
BARKSDALE, William, late of Albemarle Co., dec'd, e.a.w. his ex., Samuel BARKSDALE of Charlottesville (VGGA 29 Mar 97)
BARLOW, John, aka Adam, Negro, 27, can read and write, ran away from Samuel SHREVE, Fairfax Co., he was seen in Alexandria and has been trying to procure a pass to go to Baltimore (TAA 31 Jan 98, CMAG 8 Feb 98)
BARMINGHAM, Capt. Christopher, d. this morn. about 8:00 (RC 15 Sep 95)
BARNARD, John, ind. svt., 24, ran away from the ship *Mary* from Ireland at Rich Neck, Warwick Co. (AGNPWA 19 Mar 94)
BARNER, Henry, soldier, c. 30, German-born, des. from Capt. Joseph BROCK's Co., 3rd U. S. R[egt.], Winchester (BVCG 28 May 92)
BARNES, Abraham, dec'd, e.a.w. his ex., Robert BOGGESS (VJAA 23 Jun 85)
BARNES, Henry, of Charlotte Co., dec'd, e.a.w. his ex., Henry BARNES and Gabriel BARNES (VGGA 4 Jan 97)
BARNES, Robert, Creole, appr., 18, ran away from William PATON, Alexandria (VJAA 23 Mar 86)
BARNES, Thomas, of Richmond Co., dec'd, 50 slaves and his HHF to be sold by his admr. William FLOOD (VG 19 May 68)
BARNES, Thomas, dec'd, e.a.w. his ex. (nfi) of New Kent Co. (VGGA 20 Jun 92)
BARNET, William, some years ago removed to Chatham Co., North Carolina; if he is living and will apply to James EARLY of Orange Co. who is ex. of James BARNET dec'd, he may receive the est. left his by his father (VGGA 16 Aug 99)
BARNET, William-Cole, Eng. svt., ran away from James BOYD, Spotsylvania Co. (VG 9 Mar 39)

BARNETT, John, appr., c. 19, his father lives in James City Co., ran away from Henry GARDNER, Chester-Hill, near Richmond (VGRMA 5 Feb 95)
BARNETT, Mary, her husband, John BARNETT, Trap Hill, Frederick Co., will no longer pay her debts (BVCG 2 Jul 92)
BARNETT, William, mar. Miss Fanny HIPKINS, dau. of John HIPKINS, at Port Royal (VHFA 16 Apr 89)
BARNS, Gerard, svt., c. 40, ran away from Ephraim FURR, Loudoun Co. (VGR 18 Oct 70)
BARNS, James, of Sussex Co., dec'd, his ex. (nfi) will sell the PE of Richard BARNS (VGPu 8 Mar 76)
BARON, James Esq., d. at Hampton the 16th [inst.]; he had been a commodore in the state navy (VIC 23 May 87)
BARR, John, aged 69, d. last week in Winchester (BVCG 1 Oct 92)
BARRADELL, Henry, att. at law, d. Wed. eve. [14th] at his brother's house in Wmsbrg (VG 16 Sep 37)
BARRES, Capt. Ralph, reportedly d. in London (VG 6 Jan 38)
BARRET, Anne, Eng. svt., 24, ran away from Willoughby NEWTON, Westmoreland Co. (VG 27 Feb 52)
BARRET, Capt. William, of Richmond, d. Fri. last at Airwell, Hanover Co. (VGGA 18 Jan 92); e.a.w. his admr., John BARRET also of Richmond (VGPA 14 Apr 92)
BARRETT, John, appr. shoemaker, ran away from Peter ELLIOTT (HNPA 12 Dec 95)
BARRETT, Martha, dec'd, her ex., Thomas BARRETT, will sell all her PE (VGPu 9 Feb 76, 4 Oct 76 sup)
BARRETT, Tabitha, dec'd, her tract of land in Lunenburg Co. to be sold by her ex., William NORVELL and William LIGHTFOOT (VGGA 10 Nov 90)
BARRETT, William, of Barrett's Ferry, d. at Wmsbrg. (VGAA 22 Mar 86)
BARRETT, William, dec'd, his ex., John PIERCE and John E. BAILEY, and extx., Tabitha BARRETT, will sell a tract of his land cont. 2740 ac. on Crooked Run in Lunenburg Co. (VGWeA 25 Oct 87, VGPI 1 Nov 87)
BARRETT, William, of Frederick Co., dec'd, his land near Winchester to be sold by his ex., Thomas BARRETT and Richard BARRETT (BVCG 18 Feb 93)
BARRINGTON, William, appr. shoemaker, c. 19, ran away from James DAMERON, Norfolk, it is believed he will make for New York (NH 28 Apr 96)
BARROM, Peter, of Charles City Co., dec'd, e.a.w. his ex., Laurence EGMON, who advises that his son, Fielding BARROM, a soldier in Col. HARRISON's Regt. of artillery, may receive a considerable legacy on application (VGAA 4 Dec 84)
BARRON, Capt. Richard, dec'd, his extx., Rebecca BARRON, and ex., Miles KING, will sell his plant. on James River within two miles of Hampton containing c. 100 ac. (VIC 14 May 88)
BARRON, Susanna, wife of Capt. Robert BARRON of this borough [Norfolk], d. on Tues. eve. last (NHPA 8 Jun 97)
BARRY, Capt., a French gentleman, drowned in Acquia [Cr.] between Dumfries and Fredsbrg on Sat. eve. last (VGGA 4 Feb 95)
BARRY, James, Irish ind. svt., c. 27, ran away from James PERRY, Montgomery Co., Md. (VCWM 19 Aug 89)
BARRY, James, Irish svt., 19-20, shoemaker, ran away from Thomas CORCORAN and John PRINGLE, Georgetown (VGWA 21 Oct 89)
BARRY, Mrs. Nancy, cons. of Thomas BARRY, merch., in this town [Staunton], d. on Tues. the 31st ult. leaving an only child, an infant nine days old [obit.] (SVG 8 Feb 97)
BARRY, Ned, svt., 50-60, has much of the brogue, ran away from James CROW near Staunton, Augusta Co. (VGPu 7 Jun 76)
BARTHOLOMEW, John, Eng. svt., 26, ran away from Robert HUTCHINGS in Petersburg (VG 7 Nov 51)
BARTLETT, Henry, merch., of Millwood, mar. Miss Eliza DAVIS in Jan. 1799

(WG 9 Jan 99)
BARTON, Amos, mate of the sloop *Neptune*, of and from Warren, R.I. now in this port [Norfolk ?], d. Thurs. eve. last (VCNPGA 21 Sep 93)
BARTON, John, Negro, c. 22, jailed in Norfolk Borough (HNPA 3 Dec 95)
BASCO, John, aka Basco, mulatto, ran away from Unity HOOPER near Cold Harbor, Hanover Co., he was purchased of Mr. FOSTER, Kg. Wm. Co. (Ex 17 Sep 99)
BASKERVILLE, George, of Mecklenburg Co., dec'd, his ex., John BASKERVILLE, will sell all lands belonging to his est. consisting of several very valuable plants. one on the Roanoke River (VGPu 16 Oct 78)
BASKERVILLE, George, son of John BASKERVILLE Sr. (VGAA 20 Dec 83)
BASS, Col. Joseph, of Chesterfield Co., dec'd, his est. accounts to be settled with the ex., Edward BASS and Peterfield TRENT, who will attend at Francis BASS's near the courthouse (VGAA 17 Aug 82, 12 Jul 83)
BASSETT, Mrs. Anna Maria, cons. of Burwell BASSETT Esq. of Eltham, New Kent Co., died (VGPu 19 Dec 77)
BASSETT, Miss Betsey, eld. dau. of Col. Burwell BASSETT Esq. of New Kent, d. suddenly, Sun. last in her 14th year (VG and VGR 25 Mar 73)
BASSETT, Col Burwell, dec'd, his ex., Burwell BASSETT, will sell his land and slaves in Hanover Co. and will also settle his est. (VGAA 22 May 93, VGRMA [18] Nov 93)
BASSETT, Miss Nancy, 2nd dau. of Burwell BASSETT Esq. of New Kent, d. in her 10th year (VG 29 Jul 73)
BASSETT, Master William, eld. son. of Burwell BASSETT Esq. of New Kent, d. on the 10th inst. at Studley the seat of Peter LYONS Esq. (VG and VGP 17 Nov 74)
BASSTONE, Edward, hosier, b. in Three Tun Alley, London, which he left about 50 years ago and was landed in Virginia and sold to one SHEPERD of Gloucester Co. for the payment of his passage; if he be living and will make application to O'Conner M'CRAMMUCK he will be informed of something greatly to his advantage (VGP 1 Jun 75)
BATEMAN, Peter, executed at Wmsbrg. on 10 Jan. for felony (VG 10 Jan 52)
BATES, Fleming, late of York Co., dec'd, e.a.w. his ex., Benjamin BATES (VGWeA 11 Sep 84)
BATES, Isaac, of York Co., dec'd, his ex., George CARRINGTON, adv. 487 ac. of land belonging to his est. about seven miles from Wmsbrg. near Fleming BATES's for sale (VG 24 Oct 55)
BATES, James, of York Co., dec'd, his slaves, livestock, and HHF to be sold by his admx., Elizabeth BATES (VGR 27 Jul 69)
BATES, James, dec'd, e.a.w. Samuel WINSTON, gdn., of Scimmino, York Co. (VG 26 Dec 77)
BATES, John, authorizes Fleming BATES to sell his 481 ac. tract on Skiminoe Cr. in York Co. next to the lands of James BATES dec'd (VGR 19 May 74)
BATES, John, of the 6th Virginia Continental Regt., under sentence of a General Court Martial to be shot for desertion, escaped from the public jail in Wmsbrg.; he is about 25 and will probably attempt to reach Georgia where he has lived for several years (VG 24 Apr 78)
BATES, Richard, svt., ran away from William LIGHTFOOT, Tedington (VG 24 Jan 52)
BATHGATE, Mrs., wife of William BATHGATE of Norfolk Borough, d. yesterday morn. [29 Nov.] (NWJCI 29 Nov 97, NHPA 30 Nov 97)
BATHGATE, William, of Norfolk, d. Sun. last; bur. with Masonic honors (NH 28 Aug 98, NWJCI 29 Aug 98); e.a.w. his admr., P. PROBY (NH 27 Sep 98, 12 Mar 99)
BATLE Family, HCC, 5 Mar 96, Charles DUNCAN (pltf.) and Lewis PARHAM and William BROWN son and ex. of Beverly BROWN who was surv. ex. of William BROWN and one of his residuary legatees, William BATLE son and heir at law of William BATLE dec'd, and John BROWN heir at law of William BROWN dec'd, Alexander Watson BATLE, Peyton HARWELL, and Sarah

PARHAM his wife, Mary BATLE, Francis Beverly BATLE, and Elizabeth Parham BATLE (defs.); it appears that John BROWN is not an inhabitant of the country (VGWeA 7 May 96)

BATON, John, c. 25, jailed on suspicion of murder in Wmsbrg, escaped (VGGA 27 Apr 96)

BATSON, George, Eng., enl. in Wmsbrg., but reportedly ran away from his master in North Carolina, des. from Capt. Thomas MASSIE's new recruits for the 6th Virginia Regt. (VGPu 21 Nov 77)

BATTAILE, Mrs., cons. of Hay BATTAILE, d. yesterday morn. in Caroline Co. (VHFA 6 Sep 92)

BATTE, Henry, dec'd, e.a.w. Richard BATTE (nfi) (VG 7 Mar 77)

BATTEAUX, Peter, appr., native of France, c. 17, ran away from Joseph PERKIN, New London, Va. (VGGA 10 Jun 95)

BATTERTON, Joseph, free Negro from the island of Nevis, his mother, Elizabeth, adv. for news of his whereabouts; he embarked on the sloop *Sally* for Md. on 30 Aug 1768 (VGR 29 Jun 69)

BAUGH, Robert, of Pr. Geo. Co., d. a few days ago (VGPI 27 Feb 95)

BAUGHAN, Austin, merch., mar. Miss Nelly HACKLEY in this town [Fredsbrg] on Thurs. last (VHFA 23 Apr 95)

BAXTER, Daniel, of Wmsbrg, bed-ridden with gout for upwards of 10 yrs., died (VGPu 16 Jun 75, VG 17 Jun 75 sup)

BAYLEY, Samuel, svt., c. 24, joiner, imported last Feb. in the *Justitia*, ran away from William BUCKLAND, Richmond Co. (VGR 26 Jul 70)

BAYLEY, Thomas, dec'd, his admr., John SHEPPARD and Thomas BAKER, will sell his plant. in Eliz. City Co. (VGGA 12 Dec 92)

BAYLEY, William Armistead, of Norfolk, dec'd, e.a.w. his ex., Frederick WILLIAMS and James BOYCE (NPC 2 Jun 92); his small plant. on Back River will be sold by his surv. ex., James BOYCE, Norfolk (NHPA 19 Jun 97)

BAYLIS, Hannah, wife of John BAYLIS, Stafford Co., who will no longer pay her debts (VG 12 Dec 45)

BAYLIS, Col. John, killed in a duel at Dumfries on 4 Sep. (MG 12 Sep 65, NYM 30 Sep 65, NYPB 3 Oct 65)

BAYLIS, Thomas, of Eliz. City Co., d. lately at Hampton in the 107th year of his age (NPJ 12 Mar 88)

BAYLOR, Mrs. Frances, relict of the late Col. John BAYLOR of New Market, Caroline Co., d. on 9 Jul. (VGAA 19 Jul 83)

BAYLOR, Col. George, of the 3rd Regt. of Lt. Dragoons, mar. Miss Lucy PAGE, dau. of Mann PAGE Esq. of Mansfield (VGPu 12 Jun 78)

BAYLOR, Col. John Esq., d. at his house in Caroline (VG 16 Apr 72, PC 4 May 72); his ex., John ARMISTEAD and Nathaniel BURWELL, have empowered Edmund PENDLETON Jr. to settle his est. (VG 23 Jul 72); his ex. will sell 50 choice blooded horses of his at Caroline Ct. H. (VG 24 Sep 72)

BAYLOR, John, of King and Queen, mar. Miss Sally PRITCHET of Middlesex (VGAA 13 Apr 82)

BAYLOR, Robert, of King and Queen (?), 1100 ac. of his land in the lower end of Spotsylvania Co. to be sold by his ex., Gregory BAYLOR and George BROOKE (VG 5 Sep 66 sup)

BAYNE, Mrs. Susanna, wife of Easworth BAYNE of Md., died (VJAA 30 Dec 84)

BAYNES, John, formerly of Whitehaven, d. suddenly at Piscataway last Tues. (VJAA 4 Aug 85)

BAYNHAM, Dr. John, dec'd, his ex., John BAYNHAM, will sell all his PE [in Caroline Co.] VGR 1 Sep 74)

BAYNHAM, Joseph, of Louisa, died (VGAA 23 Apr 85)

BAYNS, John, mechanic, of Norfolk, d. Sat. last [26 Sep.]; he was bur. on Sun. by his brethren of Lodge No. 1 (NPG 30 Sep 89)

BEACHAM, Susanna, of Cumberland Co., she and her mother, Sarah, jailed for the murder of her bastard son (VGAA 6 Aug 85)

BEALE, Charles, of Richmond Co., dec'd, his est. to be sold by Mary BEALE his

extx. (VGR 4 Dec 66)
BEALE, John, of Richmond, d. Thurs. last (VGGA 25 Apr 92); e.a.w. his act. ex., W. WISEHAM and W. RICHARDSON (VGGA 9 Jan 93)
BEALE, Thomas, aged 63, d. in Richmond Co. on Fri. 4th inst. (VH 22 Oct 99)
BEALL Family, York Co. Ct., 20 Nov 97, in chanc: James MADISON against Robert ANDREWS ex. of Samuel BEALL dec'd, Norbert BEALL, Matilda BEALL, and Harriet BEALL, devisees of the sd. Samuel BEALL dec'd; it appears that Matilda and Harriet BEALL are not inhabitants of this state (VGGA 27 Dec 91)
BEALL, Mrs. Anne, sp. of Samuel BEALL Esq., d. on Sun. 10th inst. in Wmsbrg (VIC 20 Sep 86, VGPI 21 Sep 86)
BEALL, George, late of Hampshire Co., dec'd, e.a.w. John THOMPSON (WG 23 Oct 99)
BEALL, Jeremiah, merch., murdered by Nicholas CURLETT in Winchester (VG 2 Jul 72)
BEALL, Samuel Esq., merch., of this city [Wmsbrg.], mar. Miss Nancy BOOTH of Frederick Co. (VG 12 Jun 79)
BEALL, Samuel, for many yrs. a resident in Wmsbrg., d. at New Town [Pennsylvania] of a cancer in his face (VGWeA 3 May 93, VGGA 8 May 93); his trustees, Nathaniel BURWELL, Robert ANDREWS, John PIERCE, and B. HOLMES will sell his HH and KF in Wmsbrg. (VGGA 19 Jun 93, 16 Apr 94)
BEARD, George, mar. Miss Elizabeth HUNTER, both of Fairfax Co. on Thurs. eve. (CMAG 22 Oct 96)
BEARD, Justice, dec'd, e.a.w. his admr., James RUSSELL of Traphill (PGBA 14 Jan 96)
BEARD, Robert, svt., abs. from Charles LEWIS' service in Wmsbrg. (VG 7 Sep 39)
BEASLEY, Martha, wife of William BEASLEY, Wmsbrg, who will no longer pay her debts (VG 24 Aug 51)
BEASLEY, Sarah, has eloped from her husb., Ambrose BEASLEY (VG 11 Dec 66)
BEAVER, Elizabeth, white svt. woman, c. 20, ran off from Joseph CALLAND, Cumberland Co., with a mulatto slave named Sancho c. 40 (VGR 17 Mar 74)
BEAVERS, John, Irish, c. 25, suspected of stealing money from James DOUGHERTY [Loudoun Co.] (VGAxA 17 Jun 90)
BEAZELY, John, of Caroline Co., dec'd, his admx. is Sarah BEAZELY (VH 30 Apr 99)
BECKLEY, John, has moved from Richmond to New York (VICGA 6 Jan 90)
BECKWITH, Sir Jonathan, d. in Richmond Co. on Tues. last at an advanced age (VHFFA 13 Dec 96)
BECKWITH, Richard M., mar. Miss Elisabeth S. BUCHANAN, dau. of Andrew BUCHANAN Esq. of Falmouth on Tues. last in Falmouth (VHFA 17 Feb 98)
BEDFORD, Jonas, who resided on Roanoke River about 40 miles from Salisbury, North Carolina and was in England in 1785 is asked to apply to Cumberland WILSON, merch., at Dumfries, or to the British Consul, Norfolk to hear something to his advantage (VCNPGA 23 Feb 93)
BEDGOOD, John, of Isle of Wight Co., c. 30, killed in a boating accident on Sat. 2nd inst.; he left a widow and three small children (VG 28 Mar 71)
BEDINGER, Daniel Esq., of Norfolk, mar. Miss Sally RUTHERFORD, dau. of Robert RUTHERFORD Esq. of Berkeley Co. on Tues. last (BVCG 30 Apr 91)
BEE, Isaac, mulatto, 18-19, his father was a freeman, ran away from Lewis BURWELL, Mecklenburg Co. (VG 8 Sep 74); mulatto slave, 30-40, can read and write, ran away from Richard LITTLEPAGE, Richm. (VGGA 13 Mar 93 ex)
BEELER Family, Fairfax Co., Sep. Ct. 1782 in chanc: Benjamin BEELER, admr. with the will annexed of Christopher BEELER dec'd. (compl.) against Joseph BEELER, son and heir of Christopher BEELER dec'd. (def.); the def. cannot be found (VGWeA 26 Apr 83 sup)
BEELER Family, HCC, [nd]: Christopher BEELER, Joseph BEELER, Catharine BEELER, Frederick BEELER, George KYZER, Benjamin KYZER, John

KYZER, Catharine KYZER, Molly KYZER, and Betsy KYZER, Benjamin BEELER Jr., Samuel BEELER, William BEELER, Benjamin BEELER, Michael BEELER, and Becky BEELER infants under 21 by their next friend (pltfs.) and Stephen HOLLINGSWORTH, Joseph BEELER, and Benjamin BEELER (defs.) (VGGA 26 Feb 99)

BEELER Family, HCC, 26 Sep. 99: Between Benjamin BEELER Jr. an infant son of Benjamin BEELER by Joseph CARY his next friend, George [KYZER], Benjamin [KYZER], John [KYZER], Catharine [KYZER], Jacob DUNCLE and Mary his wife, and Elizabeth [KYZER] by George [KYZER] her next friend children of George [KYZER] and Mary his wife, Samuel BEELER Jr., John HUCK and Mary his wife, Elizabeth BEELER and Benjamin BEELER, James BEELER, George BEELER, and Christopher BEELER infants by Samuel BEELER their next friend and children of Samuel BEELER, George BEELER, Charles BEELER, Joseph BEELER, and Frederick BEELER children of Frederick BEELER, Joseph BEELER, Christopher BEELER, Mary BEELER, an infant by Joseph BEELER her next friend, Dorsy PENTICOST and Catharine his wife and [?] BECQUITH and Mary his wife, and Samuel BEELER son of Christopher BEELER the elder (pltfs.) and Jesse HOLLINGSWORTH and Joseph BEELER and Benjamin BEELER admrs. of Christopher BEELER dec'd (defs.) (VGGA 29 Nov 99)

BEESON, Mrs. Julia, wife of Jesse BEESON, d. in Martinsburg (PGBA 28 Dec 97)

BEGG, John, mar. Miss Sally POOLE Thurs. eve. last, both of Norfolk (VCNPGA 13 Oct 92)

BEGG, Mrs. Phoebe, wife of John BEGG, merch., of Norfolk, a native of New York, d. Sat. eve. last in her 33rd year; she was buried in Elizabeth Churchyard (NPJ 17 Sep 88)

BEGG, Mrs. Rebecca, died yesterday (NHPA 11 Nov 97)

BELCHER, Thomas, Eng. svt., c. 28, imported into Patapsco River, Md. in Jul. 1765, ran away from Joseph WATKINS, New Kent Co. (VGR 16 Mar 69)

BELL, Adam, carpenter of a King's ship in the late war, supposed to have come to Va. in 1769 with his wife and two chil., has been left a legacy in England of £1500 by his old messmate, John MEARS, a gunner in the navy (VG 15 Oct 72)

BELL, David, father of Henry BELL of Buckingham Co., d. intestate on 28 Mar. 1770; his wife d. on 16 Apr. 1798 (Arg 25 Jan 99)

BELL, Hardy, Negro, took his wife, Nell c. 30, from the house of Robert FREEMAN in Warren Co. in Feb. 1796; Nell has passed for a free woman by the name of Becky JAMES or Betty BELL (NH 16 Nov 99)

BELL, Henry, of Buckingham Co., acting attorney for his brother, David BELL (VGGA 31 Apr. 93)

BELL, James, svt., painter, ran away from John CHAMPE, Loudoun Co. (VGR 11 May 69)

BELL, James, ind. svt., imported last Sep., miner, c. 40, ran away from Samuel HANSON, Charles Co., Md. (VG 24 Nov 74)

BELL, James, son of Joseph BELL, Esq., mar. Miss Sally ALLEN, dau. of James ALLEN, both of Augusta Co. on the 28th inst. (SVG 29 Apr 96)

BELL, James, mar. Miss Milly HANSBROUGH, dau. of Peter HANSBROUGH, all of Orange Co., on 23 May (VHFA 2 Jun 98)

BELL, John, blacksmith, intends to move from Wmsbrg. to Portsmouth (VG 14 Mar 66)

BELL, John, dec'd, his HH est. to be sold by his ex., Benjamin TATE and Henry BALL, Richmond (VGGA 14 Dec 91)

BELL, Capt. John, d. on Thurs. se'nnight at an advanced age near Karen's Town (BVCG 28 Jan 92)

BELL, John, of Petersburg, mar. Miss Mary Ann WALKER, dau. of Robert WALKER of Dinwiddie (VGPI 24 Mar 97)

BELL, John, Jr., of Orange Co., died (VHFA 6 May 90)

BELL, Mary, has left her husband, John BELL, Richm. (VGRMA 21 Jul 94)

BELL, Robert, Edward, and Samuel A., of Williamsburg, adv. that they are about

to remove to Md. (VGPu 14 Mar 77 sup)
BELL, Robert, printer (or bookseller, acc. to VGWeA) of Philadelphia, d. at Richmond on Thurs. last (VGAA and VGWeA 25 Sep 84, VJAA 30 Sep 84)
BELL, Sam, intends to move to Kentucky (VGRMA 20 Nov 94)
BELL, Mrs. Sarah, cons. of Thomas BELL, d. 2 Apr. in Orange (VHFA 14 Apr 98)
BELL, Thomas, d. at Orange Ct. H. on 11 Apr., age c. 23 (VHFA 18 Apr 98); e.a.w Alexander DAWNEY and Henry BELL, admrs. with the will annexed (VHFA 7 Jul 98); his admrs. will sell his land and tavern (VHFA 15 Jan 99)
BELL, William, of Orange Co., died (VGAA 15 Nov 83)
BELL, William, late of Orange Ct. H., dec'd, e.a.w. his ex. (nfi) (VHFA 4 Dec 94); his act. ex., Andrew SHEPHERD and Alexander DAWNEY, wish to settle his est. (VHFFA 4 Apr 97)
BELLAMAN, William, svt., ran away from Cornelius SALE of Essex Co. about 15 Dec 1736 (VG 20 Oct 38)
BELMAIN, the Rev. Alexander, of Frederick Co., mar. Miss Lucy TAYLOR, dau. of Erasmus TAYLOR, in Orange Co. (VJAA 23 Nov 86)
BELONG, Joseph, conv. [svt.], c. 35, b. in the west of Eng., joiner and painter, ran away from his owner in Annapolis, Md. (VGR 7 Jul 74)
BELSCHES, James Esq., b. in Perthshire, Scotland, d. a few days ago at Invermay near Cabin Point; he was an old and respected citizen who had resided in this state upwards of 50 years (NH 9 Jun 98)
BEMISH, Thomas, Eng. ind. svt., ran away from Daniel LIPSCOMB, Kg. Wm. Co. (VGPu 15 Sep 75)
BENFIELD, Sarah, Eng. svt., 30, speaks the Lancashire dialect, ran away from John STRETCH, Wmsbrg. (VG 29 Sep 52)
BENGER, Elliott, sole Deputy Postmaster-General of all H.M's Dominions in America, d. a few days ago in Virginia (MG 22 May 51)
BENGER, John, dec'd, his slaves and PE to be sold by his ex., William and Ben JOHNSON, Spotsylvania Co. (VG 4 Dec 66)
BENHAN, John, Eng. svt., 28, blacksmith, ran away from William Carr LANE, Loudoun Co. (VGR 12 May 68)
BENNET, Nathaniel, svt., c. 18, ran away from James DUNN, Berkeley Co. (VGWA 27 Oct 90, BVCG 10 Nov 90)
BENNET, Thomas, Negro, committed to jail in Wmsbrg. with his wife, Sarah JACKSON, who was born free and lived with the family of Thomas JEFFERSON Esq. near Charlottesville (VGGA 26 Sep 92)
BENNETT, Fisher, appr. tailor, 16-17, ran away from Lewis [WERCOR], Richmond (Arg 28 Feb 97)
BENNETT, George, Eng., 19, des. from the camp at Wmsbrg. last week (VG 31 Jul 46)
BENNETT, James, merch., mar. Miss M. WRIGHT, both of this town [Norfolk] on Thurs. eve. (HNPA 18 Jul 95)
BENNETT, William, dec'd, his admr. (nfi) will sell his plant. near Dumfries (VGR 6 Feb 72)
BENSHALL, Harrison, dec'd, e.a.w. his admr., Peter LUGG (VCGA 7 Jul 94)
BENSON, Mrs. Eleanor, cons. of John BENSON, d. in this town [Fredericksburg] on Wed. last (VH 24 May 99)
BENSON, Thomas, Irish svt., ran away from Nathaniel MORGAN, Fincastle Co. on Neck Cr. (VGPu 30 Jun 75 sup)
BENTHAL, John, appr., 18-19, ran away from John WARRINGTON, Norfolk (AGGA 16 Dec 96, 6 Jan 97, NHPA 17 Dec 96)
BENTLEY, George, appr. saddler, c. 19, ran away from Daniel MYTINGER, Stevensburg (BVCG 23 Sep 96)
BENTLEY, Mrs. Judith, cons. of Col. William BENTLEY, Powhatan Co., d. on the 25th ult. (VGGA 2 Jul 99)
BENTLEY, Thomas, Eng. svt., bound for four yrs., ran away from Philip Ludwell LEE, Westmoreland Co. (VG 16 Aug 70, VGR 30 Aug 70)
BENTLEY, Thomas, [of Richmond], dec'd, e.a.w. Joseph HOWARD his ex.

(VGAA 19 Nov 85)

BENTON, John, aka HOLLOWAY, executed Fri. last at Wmsbrg. for horse stealing (Wmsbrg. disp. of 2 Jul) (NYPB 3 Aug 47)

BERKELEY, Mrs. Mary, cons. of Nelson BERKELEY, merch., of this city [Richmond], d. on the 26th inst. (VGGA 29 May 93)

BERKELEY, Nelson Esq., of Hanover Co., dec'd, e.a.w. his ex., John MINOR Jr., Edmund BERKELEY, Nelson BERKELEY, and William BERKELEY (VGGA 9 Apr 94); his ex. will sell 30-40 of his slaves in Hanover Co. (VGGA 22 Oct 94)

BERKELEY, William, mar. Miss Betsey RANDOLPH, both of Richmond, on Thurs. last (Arg 10 Jan 97)

BERNARD, Sir Francis, lately died in England (VG 1 Apr 80)

BERNARD, Robert, b. in Glouc. Co., des. from the *Henry* galley (VGPu 6 Jun 77)

BERNELEY, Madam Elizabeth, Lewis RIVALAIN at the Insurance Office in Richmond seeks information on her (VGGA 27 Sep 99)

BERNITICUS, Henry, Dutch, hairdresser by trade, absconded from the employ of Joseph DELAHAYE (CMAG 12 Sep 99)

BERROW, Anne, has left her husband, John BERROW, Wmsbrg., and he will not pay her debts (VG 5 Dec 51)

BERRY, Elizabeth, Eng. svt., 35, b. in Lancashire, ran away from John M'DONALD, Frederick Co. (VGR 20 Jul 69)

BERRY, John, Irish svt., ran away from James TOONE, Rich. Co. (VG 22 Sep 38)

BERRY, John, Swedish, 30, ran away from the *Maryland Merchant* lying at Yorktown (VG 29 May 46)

BERRY, John, enl. in Fredericksburg., des. from Capt. Robert HODGSON's Independent Co. now raising for the service and defense of South Carolina (VG 3 Jul 46)

BERRY, Joseph, of Amelia, executed at the gallows on 9 Jul. [sic] for horse stealing (VG 8 Jul 73)

BERRY, Samuel, mulatto, shoemaker, ran away from Judith HARBERT, Hampton, supposed to be in Petersburg (VGR 18 Jul 71)

BERRYMAN, Isaac, late of Hanover Co., dec'd, e.a.w. his ex., Isaac BERRYMAN of Buckingham (VGGA 13 Sep 97)

BERRYMAN, Newton, merch., of Port Royal, mar. Miss A. HIPKINS, dau. of the late Leroy HIPKINS of Goldenvale, on Thurs. the 4th inst. (VH 9 Apr 99)

BETOUT, Peter, appr., 18, of French extraction, ran away from the Public Armory, New London, Va. (VGGA 13 Apr 96)

BETTIE, Christopher, aka BETTIS, executed at the gallows near Wmsbrg. last Fri. for horse stealing (Wmsbrg. disp. of 31 May) (MG 4 Jul 54)

BEVAN, Thomas, Eng. ind. svt., button maker, c. 25, came from London some time in May in the *Vulture*, ran away from James MILLER, Bladensburg, Md. (VGR 17 Jan 71)

BEVERADGE[S], Henry-Valentine, Eng. svt., came into the country last July on the *Dorsetshire*, ran away from Sam. HILLDRUP, Fredsbrg. (VG 24 Apr 46)

BEVERLE, Harry Esq., [of Caroline Co.], dec'd, his admr., John TENNANT and John WALSH, will sell his PE at his house near Port Royal (VG 10 Feb 74)

BEVERLEY, Harry S., merch., late of Fredsbrg., dec'd, e.a.w. his ex., Larkin STANARD (VHFA 3 Apr 94)

BEVERLEY, Robert Esq. the younger, of Essex Co., mar. Miss Jane TAYLOE, dau. of the late Hon. John TAYLOE, on the 27th ult. at Mt. Airy, Richmond Co. (VGGA 1 Jun 91)

BEVERLEY, Robert G., died in Kg. Geo. Co. (VHFFA 10 Mar 97)

BEVERS, John, appr., 18-19, ran away from Silas REES, Loudoun Co. (BVCG 5 Aug 93)

BEVILL, Edward, late of Mecklenburg Co., dec'd, e.a.w. his ex., William Wills GREEN and Francis Moore NEAL (VGPI 22 Dec 95)

BIBB, Thomas, dec'd, his legatees to meet at Amherst Ct. H. to receive their part of the money received at the sale of his est. (Ex 9 Aug 99)

BIBB, Capt. William, of Pr. Edw. Co., mar. Miss Sally WIATT of New Kent (VG 4

Dec 79)

BIBBIN, John, aka John, young mulatto, ran away from Samuel APPERSON, New Kent (VGPu 6 Sep 76, 6 Jun 77)

BICKARDIKE, Richard, dec'd, J. BRANAN, deputy sheriff, will sell all his est. for ready money (AGNPWA 10 Oct 92)

BICKERTON, Mrs. Anne, of Glouc. Co., d. lately in her 66th year (VGPu 7 Sep 75); her est. near York River to be sold by Samuel MAJOR, Richmond (VGAA 3 Jan 84)

BICKERTON, Maj. John Todd, of Hanover Co., died (VG 25 Feb 75); his ex. (nfi) will sell a 700 ac. tract in Albemarle Co. and a 1425 ac. tract in Louisa Co. subject to the dower of Mrs. Martha BICKERTON (VG 4 Nov 75); his surv. ex., Lewis WEBB, will sell the land and plant. whereon he formerly lived in Hanover Co. containing about 600 ac., Mrs. Martha IRWIN has dower in the land (VG 1 Jun 76)

BICKLEY, Sir. William, Bart., d. on Sat. last in Louisa Co. (disp. of 12 Mar) (VG 21 Mar 71)

BICKLEY, William Smith, native of Bristol, mar. Miss Judy Roy BUCKNER of Port Royal at Port Royal (VHFA 14 Mar 93)

BIDDLE, Charles, of the Virginia Company of Comedians, late from the Old American Co., d. on Sat. last (VGGA 1 Dec 90)

BIDDLE, John, of Pr. Anne Co., dec'd, his 255 ac. plant. there to be sold by his ex., Elizabeth BIDDLE, Robert WILLIAMSON, and Charles GASKING (VG & VGR 2 Feb 69)

BIGBEY, Elisha, of Pr. Wm. Co., dec'd, e.a.w. his admx., Susanna BIGBEY of Dumfries (TAA 27 Mar 98)

BIGELOW, William, dec'd, his heirs at law are John BATTE and Roderick BIGELOW [apparently of Dinwiddie Co.] (VGGA 15 May 93)

BIGGARS, James, from Bedford Co., executed for felony near Wmsbrg. Fri. last (VGR 1 Jun 69, NYPB 19 Jun 69)

BIGNALL, John, comedian, manager of the company, d. at Charleston [S. Carolina] (VGRMA 28 Aug 94, VHFA 4 Sep 94)

BIGNALL, Isaac, mar. Miss Harriot WEST, both of the Virginia Company of Comedians, on Thurs. last (NH 29 Mar 98)

BILLINGHAM, Edward, svt., b. in the north of Eng., 30, ran away from Sampson MATTHEWS, Staunton, Augusta Co. (VG 17 Oct 66)

BILLUPS, Capt. Robert, his schooner now upon the stocks, a sloop, and several other boats in addition to HH and KF will be sold by Mrs. BILLUPS and the admrs. (nfi) at his dwelling house in Gloucester Co. (VGPu 2 Feb 76)

BINGHAM, Roscow Cole, cadet in Capt. TIMPLE's Co. of Light Dragoons, d. at Gen. WASHINGTON's HQ after a short illness (VGPu 6 Jun 77)

BINGHAM, Stephen, of West Point, adv. that he will pet. the next assembly to invest him with the fee simple est. in a tract of land in Kg. Wm. Co. at present occupied by Col. Francis WEST; the land belonged to his brother (by the father's side), Roscow [given as Roscoe] BINGHAM, who d. under the age of 21; Mrs. WEST, wife to Col. Francis WEST and mother to his sd. brother had this tract given by her father for her life and after that to his brother Roscow [given as Roscoe] (VGWeA 23 Aug 87)

BINGLEY, Nathaniel, appr. lad, ran away from the ship *Hannah* when last at Gosport (NHPA 7 Oct 97)

BIRCH, Samuel, mulatto, c. 20, a Creole of Jamaica, ran away from the ship *Westmoreland* at Gosport (NHPA 23 Oct 97)

BIRCHETT, Robert, of Petersburg, mar. Miss Nancy TAYLOR, dau. of Richard TAYLOR of Pr. Geo. Co. in that county (VGPI 22 Mar 96)

BIRD, Col. George, of Middlesex Co., dec'd, his admr., Robert BIRD Jr., will sell all his PE (VGRMA 6 Nov 94)

BIRD, John, appr., 17, ran away from the brig. *Brenchley* of London (VGAxA 29 Apr 90)

BIRD, Richard, acc. to two depositions, a Capt. Samuel EDDINS, who was taken by an armed schooner commanded by Richard BIRD, had showed the sd. BIRD his commission, and BIRD said that he would set EDDINS ashore if he would go to Urbanna [Middlesex Co.] and inform BIRD's wife and mother-in-law that he was an officer of the King's on board the *St. Alban's* man-of-war and he likewise requested Capt. EDDINS to speak in favor of his brother-in-law who, sometime before, had been taken by Capt. BARRON, declaring that he was the sole cause of his sd. brother's going on board the *St. Alban's* (VGPu 1 May 78)

BIRK, John, Irish conv. svt., ran away from Richard GRAHAM, Dumfries (MG 26 Apr 59)

BISHOP, Richard, des. from the quota of state troops of Lt. John DUDLEY who believes he is lurking about Chas. City Co. where he has a family (VGPu 12 Sep 77)

BISSETT, Alexander, dec'd, his admx., Margaret BISSETT, will sell part of his est. including two likely 4-year old horses, a 2-year old bay colt, and a year old bay colt (VG 19 Mar 79)

BLACBURN, Jonathan, of Ky., mar. Miss Prudence BUFORD, dau. of Henry BUFORD Esq., on Thurs. last at the seat of Henry BUFORD in Bedford Co. (LWM 13 Nov 97)

BLACK, Dr. David, of Blandford, mar. Miss Nancy MACKENZIE, late of Wmsbrg. (VG 8 Oct 72)

BLACK, Dr. David, dec'd, e.a.w. John THWEATT of Pr. Geo. Co. who was authorized by the extx., Anne BLACK, and the ex., William M'KENZIE (VGWeA 20 Jul 82)

BLACK, David, dec'd, William HARRIS Jr., gdn. to Joanna M'KENZIE, heir at law to David BLACK, will lease BLACK's tenement in Petersburg (RMA 25 Jun 95)

BLACK, John, son of James BLACK dec'd late of Middletown Township, Chester Co., Pa., if he be living, by applying to James M'MINN or Robert MILLER, exors. to the dec'd, he may hear of a considerable est. left to him by his father; the sd. John BLACK left his father 14 years ago and it is said was a Capt. in Col. WASHINGTON's Legion of Light Horse (VGAA 12 Nov 85)

BLACK, Mary, claimed to be free born, c. 23, b. in Essex Co., dau. of a free yellow woman named Judy whose mother was Peggy BLACK and whose grandmother was an Indian (VIC 13 May 89)

BLACK, Robert, bricklayer, some time past left Philadelphia and is believed to reside at a place called Rock Bridge; if he will apply to the printer he will hear of something greatly to his advantage (VGGA 15 May 93)

BLACK, William Esq., of Chesterfield, died (VGWeA 2 Feb 82); his ex. (nfi) will sell all of his PE (VGAA 30 Mar 82); his PE to be sold (VGAA 4 May 82); purchasers at sales of his est. asked to discharge their bonds to Turner SOUTHALL Esq. of Richmond (VGAA 24 May 83); 16 of the slaves belonging to his est. to be sold at the Falls Plant. near Manchester (VGAA 29 Nov 83)

BLACK, William, of Chesterfield Co., d. on Fri. last in his 33rd year (VGWeA 16 Oct 84)

BLACKBURN, [?], eld. son of Col. BLACKBURN, drowned in the Potomac River (VG 24 Apr 52)

BLACKBURN, George, ind. svt., c. 22, pretty well learned, b. in Co. Durham, Eng., ran away from Thomas and Samuel PRETLOW, Surry (VG 29 Apr 75 sup)

BLACKBURN, Mrs. Mary, relict of the late Col. Richard BLACKBURN of Pr. Wm. Co., d. in an advanced age (VGPu 4 Aug 75 ps)

BLACKBURN, Maj. R. S., charged with the murder of Capt. George THOMAS, was found not guilty (Winchester disp. of 14 Oct.) (CMAG 18 Oct 96, VHFFA 21 Oct 96)

BLACKBURN, Capt. Richard Scott, of the U. S. Army, mar. Miss Ann BLAWS of Norfolk on Wed. last (NHPA 15 Jul 97)

BLACKBURN, Robert, soldier, 24, served his time with William WEBB, justice of the peace upon Little Land-Tatom, Md., des. from Lt. Col. BARTON's Co. in Col. DUNBAR's Regt. (VG 9 May 55)

BLACKBURN, Capt. William, of Middlesex Co., a Burgess in 1715, d. lately (VG 12 Jan 39)

BLACKBURN(E), William, of Great Brook St., Hanover Sq., London, came to Va. in 1754-55 and lived several yrs. with Maj. William TALIAFERO of K. and Q. Co., his friends have not heard from him for a long while and wish to know if he is alive (VG and VGR 20 Sep 70)

BLACKNALL, Charles, dec'd, his ex., Mary BLACKNALL and John DIXON, will sell his slaves (VG 11 Apr 71)

BLACKWELL, James, Negro, c. 22, claimed to be the property of Counsellor CARTER, Germantown Co., Pa., jailed in Alexandria (CMAG 18 Dec 93)

BLACKWELL, Robert, dec'd, e.a.w. his admr., James BLACKWELL of Halifax Co. (VGGA 22 Feb 99)

BLACKWELL, Samuel, of Northumberland Co., dec'd, a parcel of his slaves to be sold (VG 6 Nov 66)

BLADES, Caleb, appr., 18-19, ran away from Robert BORLAND, Portsmouth (HNPA 7 Feb 95)

BLAGDON, William, svt., from the west of England, ran away from Dr. Charles CARROLL, Patapsco River, Anne Arundel Co., Md. (VG 11 Jul 51)

BLAGROVE, Mrs., wife of the Rev. Mr. BLAGROVE, rector of Southwark Par., Surry Co., d. Mon. last in childbed (VG and VGR 23 Sep 73)

BLAGROVE, the Rev. Mr. Benjamin, rector of Southwark Par., Surry Co., mar. Miss Sally PELHAM of Wmsbrg. (VG and VGR 9 Dec 73); for many years chaplain to the House of Delegates, d. on Wed. in Richmond (VGRC and VGWeA 13 Sep 93)

BLAGROVE, John, asst. clerk of Norfolk Co. Ct., d. on Sun. eve. last (NH 24 Jul 98, NWCJI 25 Jul 98)

BLAIKLEY, Mrs. Catharine, of Wmsbrg., d. in her 76th year; she had been a midwife and had delivered over 3000 children (VG 24 Oct 71)

BLAIR Family, Rockbridge Co. Ct., 5 Nov 91, in chanc: James CARUTHERS (compl.) against William BLAIR and Mary his wife, William ANDERSON and Catharine his wife, and John BLAIR, heirs at law of William BLAIR dec'd, and [James] HAWTHORNE and Susannah his wife (VGGA 30 Nov 91)

BLAIR, Miss., 15-year old dau. of Jacob BLAIR of Augusta Co., was drowned in the Middle River on Thurs. the 13th inst. (WG 2 Oct 99)

BLAIR, Mrs. Anne, of Richmond, d. on Thurs. last in a very advanced age (VGRC 30 Sep 94)

BLAIR, Archibald Esq., of Richmond, mar. Miss Molly WHITING of Gloucester (VGAA and VIC 18 Oct 86)

BLAIR, Elizabeth, aka PLAYER, aka PRICE, sentenced to death for felony, 4 May (VG 5 May, 12 May 38)

BLAIR, Ely, Negro man, 35, ran away from William CHOWNING, Lancaster Co. (VHFA 31 Jul 98)

BLAIR, James, late of Pr. Geo. Co., dec'd, e.a.w. his ex., John BLAIR Jr. (VGR 15 Nov 70)

BLAIR, Dr. James, of this city [Wmsbrg.], mar. Miss Kitty EUSTACE from New York (VG 23 May 71); d. in his 32nd year on Sat. 26 Dec 1772 at Dr. GILMOUR's in Charlottesville, Albemarle Co. where he lately went upon a visit (VG 31 Dec 72, VGR 7 Jan 73); Catharine BLAIR will sell a moiety of his PE at his plant. in the forks of Hanover Co. and a moiety of his PE at Chickahominy in New Kent Co. (VG 23 Dec 73 sup)

BLAIR, James, merch., of Fredsbrg., mar. Miss Helen SHEPHERD, dau. of Andrew SHEPHERD Esq. of Orange Co. (VHFA 5 May 91)

BLAIR, [John or James], alderman of Wmsbrg., died (VG-Randolph 28 Sep 59)

BLAIR, the Hon. John, Gent., representative, Auditor, judge, Privy Councilor, and President of the Colony, d. on Tues. last in his 85th year (VG 7 Nov 71, PC

9 Dec 71);his sons, John and James BLAIR, will settle his est. (VG 21 Nov 71); all of his PE (as well as the PE of Dr. James BLAIR) to be sold by the ex., John BLAIR (the son and brother) (VG 2 Sep 73)

BLAIR, Miss Nelly, second dau. to the Auditor, John BLAIR Esq., of this city [Wmsbrg.], d. in her 14th year [elegy in VGR] (VG 4 Feb 73, VGR 11 Feb 73)

BLAIR, Robert, c. 16, ran away from Patrick WRIGHT, Richm. (VGWeA 16 Oct 84)

BLAKE, John, Irish svt., ran away from John CAWOOD on Piscataway Cr., Pr. Geo. Co., Md. (VJAA 25 Aug 85)

BLAKE, Moses, Negro, c. 30, was born free as his mother was emancipated by one HUNNICUT, came to the plant. of H. RANDOLPH, Chester Lodge (VGGA 8 Jan 99)

BLAKEY, Thomas, dec'd, his ex., Thomas BLAKEY and David PATTESON, will sell his PE (VG 28 Nov 77)

BLANCHARD, Thomas, was mar. to Miss Amy NEWTON, dau. of Col. Thomas NEWTON of Norfolk Borough, on Thurs. eve. last by the Rev. James WHITEHEAD (NPC 25 Feb 92); proposes to leave Norfolk at the beginning of Oct. to reside in Edenton, N.C. (VCNPGA 8 Sep 92)

BLAND, Mrs. Elizabeth, spouse of the Rev. William BLAND, rector of James City Parish, died (VG and VGR 17 Dec 72)

BLAND, Mrs. Elizabeth, spouse of Col. Richard BLAND of Jordan's in Pr. Geo. Co., died (VGPu 28 Apr 75, VG 29 Apr 75 sup)

BLAND, John, of Amelia Co., dec'd, his admx. (nfi) will sell all his PE (VG 18 Apr 77)

BLAND, Col. Richard Esq., of Pr. Geo. Co., more than 30 yrs. a rep. in GA for that co., d. in Wmsbrg. last Sat. eve. suddenly at Mr. TAZEWELL's in his 68th year; his son Richard BLAND of Pr. Geo. Co. intends to administer on his est. and sell all of his PE in that co. (VG and VGPu 1 Nov 76, VG 29 Nov 76, VGPu 6 Dec 76, VG 31 Jan 77)

BLAND, Col. Richard, of Jordan's, Pr. Geo. Co., d. last Wed. (VGAA 28 Jan 86)

BLAND, Richard, mar. Miss Susannah POYTHRESS, dau. of the late Col. Peter POYTHRESS of Pr. Geo. Co. in that co. on Mon. last (VGIC 29 Dec 87)

BLAND, Col. Theodore [also given as Theodoric], of Amelia Co., dec'd, e.a.w. his ex., Theodoric BLAND and William YATES (VGIC 27 Nov 84, VGAA 4 Dec 84)

BLAND, the Hon. Theodoric[k], rep. of Virginia in Congress, d. Tues. morn. (or Wed. morn. the 3rd inst.) at his lodgings in Broad St., New York [City] aged 49; he was buried in Trinity Churchyard (VGAxA 10 Jun 90, VICGA 16 Jun 90, VGWA 19 Jun 90)

BLAND, Thomas, merch., of Norfolk, d. yesterday; he will be buried this afternoon with Masonic honors (NH 7 Jan 96); of Thomas BLAND and Company, Norfolk, e.a.w. the surv. part., Robert BROUGH (AGGA 10 May 96)

BLAND, the Rev. Mr. William, of James City, mar. Mrs. WELLS of Warwick Co. on Sat. last (VGR 24 Jun 73)

BLAND, William, son of William BLAND of Norfolk, 19, absconded from the service of Hillary BUTT on 20 Nov. (VCGA 27 Nov 94)

BLANEY, Capt. David, mar. Miss Nelly MAXWELL, dau. of James MAXWELL Esq., last Wed. (HNPA 18 Apr 95); d. on Wed. last at his plant. at Ragged Island, Isle of Wight Co. (NH 8 Sep 98); his admx. and widow, Helen BLANEY, will sell his pers. prop. incl. slaves and a vessel on the stocks in Isle of Wight Co. and will lease his plant. called Chesterville on Back River in Elizabeth City Co. (NH 11 Dec 98)

BLANEY, Mrs. Helen, d. on Sun. eve. in her 25th year (NH 28 May 99)

BLANKINSHIP, Josiah, executed at the gallows near Wmsbrg. (VG 4 Dec 78)

BLASINGHAM, Benjamin Hope, appr. tailor, c. 17, ran away from Henry HALL Gloucester Co. (VG 7 Jan 73)

BLEDSOE, Col. Anthony, reportedly killed by Indians on Cumberland River (VIC 3 Sep 88)

BLETHYN, William, Welsh svt., ran away from William BYRD's at Westover, supposed to be gone towards Carolina (VG 27 Mar 52)

BLEWS, Samuel, from Birmingham [Eng.], adv. that he makes and sells all sorts of locks, hinges, screws, tongues, and cheaps for silversmiths (VGNI 14 Jul 74); of Norfolk Borough, dec'd, e.a.w. his ex., William GOODCHILD, and extx., Mary BLEWS, who will also sell a good assortment of gunsmith's, white and blacksmith's tools, and some guns, iron, and coal (VG 1 May 79)

BLUE, Stepney, Negro slave, went off with a free Negro woman named Easther ROBERTS who is reportedly his wife; he was the property of Mrs. Sarah MINGHAM who has mar. Nathan YANCEY, York Co. (VG 29 Sep 74)

BLUE, William, Negro, jailed in Norfolk Borough (NHPA 12 Jan 97)

BLUE, William, appr., c. 20, ran away from James WHITELOCK (PGBA 20 Apr 97)

BLUNDELL, Benjamin, tailor and habit-maker, late from London, has a shop on Church St. (NH 3 Apr 98)

BLUNT, Col. Richard, a rep. for Sussex Co., died (VG 14 Apr 74)

BLUNT, Capt. Thomas, of Southampton Co., dec'd, his land there to be sold (VGAA 15 Nov 83)

BLYTHE, William, appr., ran away from George BRITTON, Pr. Wm. Co. (TAA 6 Mar 98)

BOA, Cavan, of Alexandria, d. on Mon. last; he was a member of the Corps of Artillery and was buried in the Roman Catholic Burial Ground; e.a.w. his admr., Margaret BOA, corner Prince and Washington Streets (TAA 22 Aug 98, 6 Oct 98)

BOCKIUS, Jacob (or John acc. to OVT), mar. Miss Susannah "Sukey" PROSSER, both of Richmond, on Wed. eve. last [13 Jun.] (OVT 14 Jun 98, Arg 15 Jun 98, VGGA 19 Jun 98)

BOGGESS Family, Norfolk Borough Chancery case, 25 Aug 96, mentions Bennett BOGGESS, Robert BOGGESS, Ann BOGGESS, and Ruth MORRIS as heirs of their uncle John BOGGESS and aunt Mary (AGGA 15 Nov 96)

BOGGESS, John, dec'd, e.a.w. Hillary BUTT (NPC 18 Jun 91); a house belonging to his est. to be sold by Bennet[t] BOGGESS and Hillary BUTT, trustees for the heirs at law (VCNPGA 6 Oct 92)

BOGGESS, Robert, of Fairfax Co., dec'd, his admr., Robert BOGGESS, will sell items of his est. (VGR 1 Jul 73)

BOHANNAN, Capt. Ambrose, d. in Madison Co. on 30th ult. (VHFFA 9 Jun 97)

BOILE, Garet, adv. that Miss Polly EARVIN of Petersburg has breached her promise of marriage to him (VGGA 29 Aug 92)

BOLD, Thomas, appr. printer, c. 19, b. in Limerick, Ireland, ran away from John HAYES, Baltimore, [Md.] (VGAA 23 Aug 86)

BOLDERO, Mr., an eminent banker, died (VGWeA 16 Jul 89)

BOLLERE, John, who came into this country some years ago from Bordeaux, France and is "of the family of CLAUZEL," is advised to apply to the governor to be informed of some things much to his satisfaction (VG 11 May 39)

BOLLING, Col. Alexander, a rep. for Pr. Geo. Co., d. there last Thurs. (VG 18 Jun 67)

BOLLING, Archibald Esq., lately mar. Miss Jane RANDOLPH, second dau. of Richard RANDOLPH Esq. of Curle's (VG and VGR 17 Feb 74)

BOLLING, Archibald C., dec'd, e.a.w. his admr., Archibald BOLLING of Campbell [Co.] (LFG 2 May 95)

BOLLING, Mrs. Catharine, spouse of Robert BOLLING of Petersburg, d. on Sun 9th inst. (VGPI 11 Aug 95, RMA 20 Aug 95)

BOLLING, Edward, son of John and Elizabeth BOLLING, b. at Cobb's in Chesterfield [Co.], 9 Sep 1746 and d. at his plant. in Amherst [Co.] 18 Aug 1770 [elegy] (VGR 13 Sep 70)

BOLLING, Col. John, for many years a rep. for Chesterfield Co. in the GA, d. on Mon. the 5th at his seat at Cobb's in Chesterfield (VG-Randolph 16 Sep 57)

BOLLING, Col. Robert, the est. of Mrs. Anne BOLLING, lately dec'd, to be sold by

the ex., William STARK and Alexander BOLLING, at the late dwelling house of Col. Robert BOLLING on Appomattox River (VG 12 Dec 51)
BOLLING, Robert Esq., a rep. for Dinwiddie Co., died (VGPu 3 Mar 75 sup, VG 4 Mar 75)
BOLLING, Col. Robert, one of the delegates for Buckingham, d. suddenly last Fri. in Richmond (VGPu 28 Jul 75, VG 29 Jul 75); Thomas FLEMING adv. that claims are to be brought to Col. William FLEMING or Archibald BOLLING Esq. (VG 6 Apr 76)
BOLLING, Col. Robert Jr., late of Buckingham Co., dec'd, Powhatan BOLLING, (nfi) asks that persons who borrowed his books return them (VGRMA 10 Jul 94)
BOLLING, Robert, of Petersburg, mar. Miss Sally WASHINGTON, dau. of Lawrence WASHINGTON Sr., Esq., on Thurs. the 1st inst. at Mount Pleasant in Kg. Geo. Co. (VHFFA 13 Sep 96, RCFPC 14 Sep 96, RMA 17 Sep 96)
BOLLING, Sally, cons. of Robert BOLLING Esq. of Petersburg and dau. of Lawrence WASHINGTON of Kg. Geo. Co., d. in Richmond on Sat. eve. last, the 1st inst., after a short illness; she had mar. Robert BOLLING on the 1st ult. and was taken sick at Richmond on her way to Petersburg (RMA 4 Oct 96, VGPI 4 Oct 96, VGGA 5 Oct 96, VHFFA 7 Oct 96)
BOLLING, Capt. Samuel, of Fairfax Co., d. on Sun. night, 16 Dec, in his 33rd year [obit.] (TAA 20 Dec 98)
BOLLING, Mrs. Sarah, spouse to Archibald BOLLING Esq. of Goochland, died (VG 22 Apr 73)
BOLLS, William, Negro, shoemaker, jailed in Middlesex Co. (VGP 21 Sep 75)
BOLTON, William, appr., c. 19, ran away from James GARDNER, carpenter, Wmsbrg. (VG 19 Aug 73)
BOND, Benjamin, miller, c. 40, and Paul PRICE, a baker, 19-20, svts. belonging to John MITCHELSON of Virginia, broke out of jail in New Bern [N.C.]; they ran away some time ago from Virginia (NCG [7] Jul 53)
BOND, Richard, mar. Miss Polly GRAHAM, dau. of John GRAHAM, in Alexandria (VJAA 20 Sep 87)
BOND, Thomas, HCC, 20 Mar 97, between William Ward BURROWS and Polly his wife, David EASTON and Sarah his wife, which sd. Polly and Sarah are daus. of Thomas BOND dec'd, and Jane BOND widow and relict of the sd. Thomas BOND (pltfs.) and Alexander GIBBONY, James MORGAN, and Joseph KELSO; it appears that GIBBONY is not an inhabitant of this country (VGGA 3 May 97)
BOND, William, of Essex Co., dec'd, his ex., Alexander SAUNDERS, will sell his 125 ac. tract whereon he lived within a mile of the Lower Church in Essex Co. (VG 12 Dec 77, VGPu 12 Dec 77)
BONIS, William, of [Alexandria], d. on 13th inst. at Baltimore (CMAG 16 Jun 96)
[BONIZ], John, weaver and dyer, 45-50, escaped from jail in Frederick Town [Md.] (VGWA 1 May 90)
BONNA (also given as BONNAUND), new Negro form a place called Bonnaund in the I[g]bo country in Africa, ran away from Richard BOOKER, Chesterfield Co. (VG and VGR 24 Dec 72)
BOOKER Family, HCC, 15 May 92: Richard Marriott BOOKER surv. ex. of Richard BOOKER dec'd (pltf.) against William TAYLOR, Benjamin LANKFORD and Henrietta his wife who was the widow of [name missing], Josep[h] SCOTT and Elizabeth his wife, William DIX and Rebecca Marriott his wife, and Richard Edward BOOKER, the sd. Elizabeth, Rebecca, and Richard are chil. and devisees in the will named of Edward BOOKER dec'd, and John EISDALE admr. with the will annexed of the sd. Edward BOOKER dec'd, Frances BOOKER wid. of Parham BOOKER dec'd, and William PRICE and Susanna his wife, Richard BOOKER, and James BOOKER, the sd. Susanna, Richard, and James are chil. and devisees of the sd. Parham BOOKER, William Marshal BOOKER, and John BOOKER (VGGA 30 Jan 93)
BOOKER, Edward, [of Halifax Co.], his admr., John E[I]SDALE, will sell a tract

of his land in that co. on the south side of Staunton River near Booker's Ferry (VG 7 Nov 71)

BOOKER, Efford, late of Amelia Co., dec'd, e.a.w. his admx., Polly BOOKER, and admr., Jacob ROBERTS (VGPI 12 Oct 98)

BOOKER, George, of Amelia Co., dec'd, e.a.w. his ex., Richeson BOOKER and Efford BOOKER, who will also sell his land in Pr. Edw. Co. (VGGA 17 Oct 92)

BOOKER, John, conv. svt., c. 31, b. in Yorkshire, Eng., imported in the *Nassau* just arrived in Rappahannock from Liverpool, ran away from James DUNCANSON, Fredsbrg. (VG 21 Jun 70); [he apparently ran away again in 1772] (VG 23 Apr 72, 13 Aug 72)

BOOKER, John Esq., of Amelia Co., dec'd, his ex., John ARCHER and Joshua CHAFFIN, will sell his 835 ac. tract in Amelia Co. along with 40 Negroes and HH and KF, John BOOKER, Jr. will show the land; e.a.w. his ex. (VGPI 3 Nov 95, RMA 16 Mar 96)

BOOKER, Mrs. Mary, of Gloucester Co., d. in her 68th year (VG 28 Jul 74); her ex. (nfi) will sell her PE in Gloucester Co. (VGP 1 Dec 74)

BOOKER, Richard, merch. in Petersburg, an amiable young gent., d. on Wed. the 10th inst. (VG and VGR 18 Nov 73)

BOOKER, Lt. Richard, of the State Artillery, mar. Miss Betsy SWENLY of Hampton (VGPu 12 Jun 78)

BOOKER, Capt. Samuel, late of Amelia Co., dec'd, e.a.w. his ex., Marshall BOOKER and Richard BOOKER of Cumberland [Co.] (VIC 21 Jan 89)

BOOKER, Timson C., boy about 17, absconded from William DICK, Norfolk (NH 5 Mar 99)

BOON, Mrs. Elizabeth, the cons. of William BOON Jr. of Kg. Geo. Co., d. on the 20th inst. aged 16 [obit.] (VHFA 29 May 94)

BOON, William the Elder, lately dec'd, William BOON will sell the tract of land whereon he lately lived in Kg. Geo. Co. about 2 miles from Port Conway, containing about 370 ac. (VHFFA 9 Sep 96)

BOOTH, Charles, Eng. ind. svt., joiner, 20-21, ran away from William BRENT, Stafford Co. (VGNI 5 Jan 75, VG 7 Jan 75)

BOOTH, Elias, served his time to an eminent woolcomber in Norwich, went abroad, returned c. 1725-26, then returned to Va. where he married a dau. of one DEMISSY and had a son, William, who may be settled near Wmsbrg.; if any of them apply to Samuel METCALF, K and Q Co., they may hear something to their advantage (VG 23 May 66)

BOOTH, Mrs. Fanny, d. on Sun. the 1st in her 49th year (VGGA 2 Oct 93)

BOOTH, Mrs. Frances, relict of the late Dr. George BOOTH, d. in Gloucester Co. on the 21st ult. (VG 7 Jul 68)

BOOTH, George, dec'd, his admr., Robert BOOTH, will sell all his PE (VGPI 23 Aug 93)

BOOTH, George Jr., of Gloucester Co., dec'd, his ex., Thomas BOOTH and Philip TABB, will sell about 30 of his slaves at Gloucester Ct. H. (VGAA 7 and VGWeA 14 Dec 82); his slaves and PE to be sold at Gloucester Ct. H. by his surv. ex., Philip TABB (VIC 15 Oct 88)

BOOTH, John Cooke, dec'd, his ex., Gregory SMITH, will sell his land on Chickahominy River in James City Co. subject to the dower of Mrs. DRUMMOND (VGR 14 Oct 73)

BOOTH, Thomas, merch., died "about 3 weeks since" at his house in Gloucester Co. (VG 5 Nov 36)

BOOTH, William, conv. svt., sailor, has a wooden leg, ran away from Andrew LEITCH, Dumfries (VGP 10 Nov 74)

BOOTH, William, dec'd, his ex., Mordecai BOOTH, Battletown, will sell his plant. utensils (VGWA 22 May, 29 Sep 90)

BOSS, John, Scottish highlander, 15-16, ran away from John MITCHELL, Fredsbrg. (NYPB 13 Oct 46)

BOSTOCK, John, Eng., c. 21, committed to the borough prison as a runaway, supposed to have run away from John HOOD, Md. [See: Anthony JACKSON and William WARRICKER] (VGR 11 Oct 70)

BOSWELL, Edward, of Wmsbrg. intends to leave the colony immediately (VG 19 Jul 54)

BOSWELL, John, of Northumberland, dec'd, e.a.w. his ex., William GRESHAM (VG 2 Dec 73)

BOSWELL, Col. John, dec'd, e.a.w. his ex., Thomas JOHNSON, Minr. (VGIC 1 Nov 88)

BOSWELL, Richard, appr., c. 15, ran away from Peter TOFFLER (TAA 13 Jun 98

BOTETOURT, His Ex. the Rt. Hon. Norborne, Baron de, d. on Mon. 15th inst. Wmsbrg., aged 53 [obit] (VG and VGR 18 Oct 70)

BOTT, Col. John, d. at his house in Chesterfield Co. on Fri. the 8th inst. (VGPI 15 Apr 96); his admx., Ann BOTT of Chesterfield, will sell sundry articles of HH and KF (VGPI 17 Oct 97)

BOTTOM, William, of Amelia Co., dec'd, e.a.w. his ex., John BOTTOM (VGPI 28 Apr 97)

BOUCHER, John, aka CARROLL, appr., c. 19, ran away from John O'CONNOR, Alexandria and is now running at large in the town (TAA 20, 26 Sep, 3 Oct 97)

BOUGHAN, Francis, b. in Essex Co., 29, des. from Capt. Thomas WAGGONER's Co. (VG 28 Feb 55)

BOURK, William, Irish svt., ran away from Leroy GRIFFIN, Richmond Co. (VG 3 Jun 37)

BOUSH Family, HCC, John BOUSH and Robert BOUSH surv. partners of Samue BOUSH dec'd (pltfs.) and Charles S. BOUSH admr. with the will annexed of Goodrich BOUSH dec'd, Wilson BOUSH, James BOUSH, Solomon SHEPHERD and Anne his wife, Mary BOUSH, and Elizabeth BOUSH (defs.); the suit abates as to the def. Solomon SHEPHERD by his death (NH 5 Nov 99)

BOUSH, Capt. Goodrich, d. at Norfolk (VG 22 May 79)

BOUSH, John, eld. son of Samuel BOUSH of Norfolk mar. Miss Nancy WALLER 4th dau. of Benjamin WALLER Esq. of this city [Wmsbrg.] (VG and VGR 22 Apr 73)

BOUSH, John, mar. Miss Frances Moseley MUNFORD last Thurs. sennight at Norfolk (VGWeA 25 Jan 87); of Norfolk, dec'd, e.a.w. the extx., Frances M. BOUSH (VCNPGA 8 Sep 92)

BOUSH, Capt. Wilson, of Norfolk, mar. Miss Fanny LOYALL, dau. of Paul LOYALL Esq., of Norfolk, Thurs. last (VCGA 22 Sep 94)

BOUSH, Zachariah, appr. boy, ran away from John GRACIE, house carpenter, Norfolk (NH 24 Dec 99)

BOUSHELL, William Sr., dec'd, e.a.w. his ex., James BOUSHELL, Norfolk Co. (NH 23 Jun 96)

BOWCOCK, Henry, of York Co., dec'd, e.a.w. his ex., James SOUTHALL (VG 1 Apr 80)

BOWDEN, John, appr., c. 19, ran off from Philip COURTNEY (VGAA 9 Apr 85)

BOWDEN, Stephen, svt., ran away from William WRIGHT, Alexandria and may be heading for Baltimore or Philadelphia (VJAA 25 Aug 85)

BOWDOIN, [Mrs.], spouse of John BOWDOIN Esq., d. on Sat. the 11th inst. in childbed in Northampton Co. (VG 25 Sep 79)

BOWDOIN, Harry, aka Harry, mulatto, 23, ran away from Christopher M'CONNICO, Petersburg (VGPI 17 Oct 97, NHPA 23 Oct 97, VGGA 25 Oct 97)

BOWDOIN, John Esq., of Northampton, d. on the 11th inst. (VGP 19 Oct 75)

BOWDOIN, John Esq., of the Eastern Shore, mar. Miss Fanny BANISTER of Dinwiddie (VGPu 30 Oct 78); d. on the 5th inst. at Col. William PEACHEY's in Richmond Co. (VGAA 12 Apr 86)

BOWDOIN, Preeson, of Fredsbrg., intends to move to Norfolk in the fall of 1783 (VGAA 4 Oct 83)

BOWDOIN, Mrs. Rebecca, wife of Preston BOWDOIN Jr. Esq., d. yesterday at Jerusalem after a short illness (NH 18 May 99)

BOWEN Family, Botetourt Co. Ct., 9 Sep 94, in chanc: William BOWEN devisee o John BOWEN dec'd (pltf.) against Horatia Skillern BOWEN, William

BOWEN, and Christopher BOWEN sons and heirs at law of John BOWEN Jr. dec'd (defs.) (VGGA 15 Oct 94)

BOWEN, Daniel, aka JOHNSON, blacksmith, b. in Pa., c. 30, accused of stealing a horse from Jesse HOLLINGSWORTH in Baltimore (VGGA 12 Mar 94)

BOWEN, Evan Esq., d. yesterday of a tedious indisposition; his remains are to be removed from the house of Col. HAMILTON to the place of interment (NH 26 Jan 99); all persons having claims against him are requested to apply for satisfaction at the British Consul's Office (NH 29 Jan 99)

BOWER, Bartholomew, native of Haddington, Scotland, who has resided in Petersburg for several years, was found dead in a well at the seat of Richard HANSON near this town [Petersburg] on Sat. morn. (VGPI 2 May 97)

BOWIE, James Sr., of Caroline Co., dec'd, his est. being administered by J. TIMBERLAKE Jr. (VHFA 24 Sep 89)

BOWLER, Miss Catherine, of Richmond, d. on Wed. 19 Nov. (VGRMA 20 Nov 94, VGRC 21 Nov 94)

BOWLER, Dick, aka Dick, Negro, 35-40, handy house svt., ran away from William HETH, Henrico Co. (Arg 17 Oct 97, VGGA 18 Oct 97)

BOWLES, David, dec'd, William [K.] WAKELAND, his admr., will sell all his PE on Back Island Cr. in Buckingham Co. (VG 19 Dec 77)

BOWLES, John, of Hanover Co., dec'd, e.a.w. his ex., Benjamin BOWLES of Hanover (VGWeA 26 Dec 96)

BOWLES, John, a mulatto woman c. 28, named Ursula, and her dau., Rachel, c. 9, eloped or more probably were carried off from Benjamin D. WIL[L]IS by a black freeman, John BOWLES, who is husb. to the woman and has been a waterman; they are presumed to be in the neighborhood of Milton or Charlottesville as it is sd. BOWLES' mother lives near Charlottesville (VGGA 8 Nov 97)

BOWLES, N., mar. Miss Mary MINITREE at Petersburg (MCentinel 29 Feb 92)

BOWLES, Peter, of Hanover, intends to pet. the next GA for a divorce from his wife Sally BOWLES (Arg 14 Aug 98 sup)

BOWLES, Capt. Walter, of the 1st Virginia Regt., died (VG 11 Jul 77)

BOWMAN, Christian, a German, c. 60, formerly lived on the head of the north branch of the Potomac River in Va., farmer, 10 yrs. ago, the Mingos killed his wife and four chil. and took him captive, he lately escaped and has come to New York city intending to go to Holland to his brother, the principal swordmaker in Groningen (NYPB 31 Dec 67)

BOWNESS Family, HCC, 20 Sep 1798, William HODGSON (pltf.) and Mary BOWNESS the mother of Thomas BOWNESS, the brother, and Fanny BOWNESS, Mary BOWNESS, Elizabeth BOWNESS, and Margaret BOWNESS, the sisters, of William BOWNESS dec'd, and Edward ASHBY and Margaret his wife, Joseph Dorry PENTICOST, Catharine PENTICOST, Sarah PENTICOST, Lucy PENTICOST, Rebecca PENTICOST, George Washington PENTICOST, and Dorsey PENTICOST reps. of Dor[s]ey PENTICOST dec'd, and John BALL (defs.) (VGGA 4 Jan 99)

BOXLY, George, hatter, c. 19, ran away from William NICE, Richmond (VGRC 6 May 94)

BOYCE, Thomas, Eng. ind. svt., 30-40, ran away from William SETTLE, Fauquier Co. (VGR 4 Aug 74)

BOYD Family, any persons of the name of BOYD descended from the family of Trochbridge in Ayreshire, Scotland, on applying to Thomas MACUDIE, Fredsbrg., may hear something much to their advantage (VG 17 Jul 72)

BOYD, Mr., trader from Va., murdered in June on Broad River on the road from the Upper Cherokee Country to Va. about 30 miles from Loudon (Savannah, Georgia disp. of 23 Jul. citing S. C. Gazette of 7 Jul.) (NYM 18 Aug 66, NYPB 25 Sep 66)

BOYD, Betty, of Henrico, her late husb., James BOYD, d. seized in fee tail of the Penkil Est. in Scotland; she seeks to recover her dower right (VGGA 29 Sep 90)

BOYD, John, shoemaker, b. in New England, c. 30, des. from the College Camp of the 2nd Regt. (VGPu 6 Sep 76)

BOYD, Robert, merch., in Blandford, mar. Miss Susanna GILLIAM of Pr. Geo. Co. (VG 8 Apr 75)

BOYD, Samuel, of Black Cr., dec'd, his PE will be sold by his ex., Robert WHITE (VGWA 23 Jan 90, 23 Mar 91)

BOYD, Mrs. Susannah, of Dinwiddie, died (VG 2 May 77)

BOYDE, Dr. James, late of King and Queen Co. (VG 17 Feb 38)

BOYDE, John, ind. svt., says he belongs to John SMITH of Bucks Co., Pa., jailed in Winchester (VCWM 14 May 88)

BOYER, Elias, dec'd, e.a.w. his ex., Jacob SHUSTER, Norfolk (NH 15 Mar 98, 4 Oct 98)

BOYLE, John, merch., mar. Mrs. Mary Ann MACHI[N] on Tues. 1 Jul., both of Strasburg (BVCG 7 Jul 94)

BOYLE, Peter, Irish, shoemaker, enl. at Alexandria 15 Sep. 94, des. from Ft. Norfolk (AGNPPA 8 May 95)

BOZER, [Mrs.], and her four chil. were killed by Indians in Buchannon Settlement, Harrison Co., on Mon. the 12th ult. (Winchester disp. of 3 Aug.) (RC 11 Aug 95)

BRACKEN, the Rev. John (or William, acc. to VGPu), rector of Bruton Par., mar. Miss Sally BURWELL, dau. of the late Carter BURWELL Esq. of Carter's Grove (VGPu 13 Sep 76, VG 21 Sep 76)

BRADBY, Capt. James, of Surry Co., d. there last Tues. (VG 24 Feb 38)

BRADBY, Capt. James, of Surry Co., dec'd, his admx., Catharine Allen BRADBY, will sell his PE (VGR 27 Feb 72)

BRADFORD, Henry, d. last Tues. at Bladensburg, [Md.] (VJAA 10 Jun 84)

BRADISH, John, b. in Ireland, 52-53, enl. at Richmond 17 Aug. 94, des. from Ft. Nelson (HNPA 4 Mar 95)

BRADLEY, Miss Elizabeth, dau. of William BRADLEY of Petersburg, d. in her 15th year (VGPu 3 Jan 77 sup)

BRADLEY, Jane, has taken her dau., Lavinia, and eloped from her husband, John BRADLEY, in Surry Co. (VG 22 Feb 70)

BRADLEY, Walter, late of Chas. City Co., dec'd, e.a.w. his ex., James CLARK, who intends to give up the est. to the gdn. of the legatees (OVT 31 Aug 97)

BRADLEY, Capt. William, late of Culpeper Co., dec'd, his ex. is Absalom BRADLEY who will settle his est. (VHFFA 10 May 96)

BRADLY, Jesse, dec'd, e.a.w. Hales SHARP, Henrico Co. (VGGA 23 Jul 94)

BRAG, Allen, of Norfolk, d. on Sat. last (HNPA 1 Jul 95)

BRAGG, William, formerly an inhabitant of Culpeper living near Bradley's Ordinary, c. 40, des. from the camp near Gwyn's Island (VGPu 12 Jul 76)

BRAMBLE, Capt. John, mar. Mrs. Margaret WEST on Thurs., both of Norfolk (HNPA 16 May 95)

BRAMBLE, William, of Norfolk Borough, dec'd, e.a.w. his admr., John BRAMBLE, who will also rent a two-story house in Church St. (AGNPPA 15 May, 28 Aug 95)

BRANAN, Stephen, appr. tailor, c. 19, uncle to Richard STUART; it is supposed he and STUART are gone to Norfolk where the one has a sister and the other a mother (CMAG 14 Mar 96)

BRANCH, Archer, executed yesterday at the gallows near this city [Richmond] for horse stealing (VGWeA 29 Oct 96)

BRANCH, Benjamin, High Sheriff of Chesterfield Co., killed by a fall from his horse Sat. se'nnight (VGAA 10 May 86)

BRANCH, Christopher, dec'd, his ex., John ARCHER Jr. and Henry BRANCH, will sell his HH and KF (VG 15 Oct 72)

BRANCH, Olive, of Campbell Co.; he and his son, Anderson, were found guilty of murder by the General Court in Richmond, but were acquitted by the December court (VJAA 19 Oct 86, 4 Jan 87)

BRANCH, Samuel, late of Chesterfield Co., dec'd, all his stock will be sold by his ex., William BRANCH (VGRMA 5 Dec 93)

BRANCH, Thomas, dec'd, of Kingsland, Chesterfield Co. (?) (VG 24 Oct 66)
BRANDER, the Rev. John, late rector of Russell Parish, Bedford Co., d. on 2 Jan 1778 (VGPu 20 Mar 78)
BRANEY, Nancy, her husband, Patrick BRANEY of Richmond, adv. that she has been guilty of misdemeanors contrary to law (VGGA 30 Jan 93)
BRANHAM, Daniel, dec'd, his admr., Joseph BROCK, will sell his est. (VHFA 9 Jan 94)
BRANNAN, Timothy, Irish svt., jailed in Augusta Co. (VGR 17 Oct 71)
[BRANNEN], Daniel, James BLAKE was tried for his murder and found guilty of manslaughter (VHFA 8 May 95)
BRANSFORD, Robert M., printer of Lynchburg, mar. Miss Rachel COURTNEY of Richmond on Sat. last (VGRMA 18 Apr 93); formerly printer of *Lynchburg and Farmer's Gazette*, d. Sat. last in this city [Richmond] (OVT 30 Jul 98, VGGA 31 Jul 98)
BRANTON, John, aka Jack, Negro, c. 30, ran away from Charles COCKE, Charles City Co. (VGGA 28 Feb 98)
BRASENTON, William, appr., 18-19, ran away from George COLLINS, Portsmouth (VG 22 Oct 72)
BRASIER, Susannah, executed for murder on 13 Jan. [sic] (VGP 12 Jan 75)
BRAXTON, [?], son of Mr. BRAXTON, was killed in an accident in school in Kg. Wm. Co. a few days ago (Richm. disp. of 15 Apr) (VGPI 21 Apr 97)
BRAXTON, Carter Esq., a member of the Privy Council of the State, d. in Richmond (VGPI 17 Oct 97)
BRAXTON, George, dec'd, some of his est. to be sold at King and Queen Ct. H. (VG 18 Jun 67)
BRAXTON, Mrs. Mary, dau. of the late Col. CARTER and wife of George BRAXTON of K & Q Co., d. last Fri. [17 Sep.] after giving birth to a son who also died (VG 24 Sep 36) [The VG of 15 Oct 36 reported that the child was still living]
BRAY, Charles and Richard, appr. carpenter boys, both have fathers in K & Q Co. near the old church, ran away from John PRYOR of Norfolk (VIC 15, 22 Aug 87)
BRAY, Maj. James, Gent., dec'd, the ex., Carter BURWELL, desires debts for his goods bought by way of outcry to be paid to William PRENTIS, Wmsbrg. (VG 9 May, 6 Jun 45)
BRAY, Col. Thomas, of Nance's Neck, Chas. City Co., dec'd, his est. to be sold by Benjamin WALLER and William PRENTIS, the exors. (VG 29 Aug 51)
BREACH, Will, Negro, c. 30, says he was b. in Martinico and is free, a carpenter, jailed in Essex (VGR 27 Jan 74)
BREADNAX, Capt. William, late of Brunswick Co., e.a.w. his admr., James WALKER (VGR 20 Jun 71)
BREAKHILL, Capt., of the ship *John*, belonging to Liverpool, died (VG 12 Jun 72)
BREATHWAIT, Anne, late of Gloucester Co., dec'd, e.a.w. her ex., William ROBINS Jr. and Abraham ARCHER (VGWeA 25 Jun 85)
BREATON, Thomas, Irish ind. svt., c. 23, ran away from John CLIFFORD, Pr. Geo. Co., Md. (VGR 1 Sep 74)
BRECKINRIDGE, James Esq., of Botetourt Co., mar. Miss Nancy SELDEN of Richmond on Sat. eve. last (VGGA 5 Jan 91)
BR[E]CKENRIDGE, John, of Albemarle Co., will move to Kentucky next April where he will practice law (VGGA 5 Dec 92)
BREDIN, John, dec'd, e.a.w. his ex., William HERRING, John WAYTE, James CURRY, of Harrisonburg (BVCG 1 Oct 92)
BREILLAT, Thomas Ebenezer, child of Thomas BREILLAT, [died], his funeral will be on 21 Mar. at 4:00 (TAA 21 Mar 98)
BREND, Mrs. Elizabeth, consort of Thomas BREND of this city [Richmond], d. on Fri. last (VGGA 25 Jun 99)
BREND, Thomas, for many yrs. a respectable inhabitant of Richmond, bookbinder, d. on Sun. eve. last (Arg and VGGA 24 Dec 99)
BRENNON, James, aka John O'BRIAN, ind. svt., tailor, b. in Dublin, ran away

from William DAVIS, Yorktown (VGP 29 Jun 75)
BRENT, Henry, of Md., dec'd, his extx., Clare BRENT, will sell his 1200 ac. tract on Acquia Run in Stafford Co. (VGR 12 Mar 72)
BRENT, Richard, mar. Miss Rachel MOORE, Thurs. eve. (BVCG 7 Dec 95)
BRENT, Robert, son of George BRENT of Pr. Wm. Co. (VGR 16 Feb 69)
BRENT, William Esq., of Stafford Co., dec'd (VJAA 20 Jan 85)
BRENT, Col. William, of Stafford, mar. Miss Betsey AMBLER, eld. dau. of Jaquelin AMBLER Esq., Treasurer of this state, on Sat. 26th ult. (VGAA 9 Apr 85)
BRENT, Col. William Esq., Rep. of Stafford Co. and col. in the late army of this state, d. lately at his seat, Richland, in that county (VJAA 23 Jun 85, VGWeA and VGAA 25 Jun 85); e.a.w. his extx., Eleanor BRENT, and surv. acting ex., Daniel Carroll BRENT, who will sell several of his horses (VGAA 22, 29 Mar 86)
BRERETON, Thomas, original and ancient broker, etc., mar. Sally MARSHALL, the dau. of Maj. Thomas MARSHALL of Northampton Co., on Mon. eve. the 26th ult. (MJ 6 Mar 81)
BRERETON, Capt. Thomas, a native of Ireland and commander in the Virginia and Maryland trade from the port of Liverpool, d. in Baltimore yesterday [15 Nov.]; he had been a resident of Baltimore for a long time (VJAA 22 Nov 87)
BREWER, John, appr., shoemaker, c. 19, ran away from Thomas WATSON, Richmond (Arg 17 Mar 97)
BREWER, Richard, mar. Miss Nancy BLACKWELL of Md. (VGWeA 30 Oct 88)
BREWER, Sacville, dec'd, his ex. (nfi) will sell a 100 ac. tract of his land in Chas. City Co. (VG 26 Dec 77)
BREWSTER, John, svt., 25, blacksmith, ran away from Rock Creek, Frederick Co., Md., on 19 March (VG 10 Apr 52)
BRIANT, John, Irish svt., ran away from James LITTLEPAGE, Hanover Co. and is supposed to have gone to N. Carolina (VG 13 Jun 55)
BRICKEY Family, Botetourt Co., April Ct., 1798, in chanc: Daniel GOODWIN (pltf.) against John BRICKEY, Peter BRICKEY, Jared BRICKEY, John SLINKEY and Polley his wife, late Polley BRICKEY, John THOMPSON and Winney his wife, late Winney BRICKEY, William THOMPSON and Temperance his wife, late Temperance BRICKEY, Patsey BRICKEY, Christian BRICKEY, Nancy BRICKEY, and Milly BRICKEY, chil. and reps. of [M.] BRICKEY dec'd. (defs.); it appears that all the defs. except Peter BRICKEY are not inhabitants of the Commonwealth (LWM 19 May 98)
BRICKLES, George, appr. lad, ran away from John BEALE (CMAG 13 Oct 96)
BRIDEN, John, b. at Wainfrey within four miles of Moffat, Scotland; went to Virginia and mar. a planter's widow by whom he had a son, Robert BRIDEN; his parents d. and Robert also d. around 1745; he left the est. to his relations in Scotland: William, John, and Grizald BRIDEN; Mr. BELL of Dumfries has offered them £100 each for their shares of the est.; it is believed that Capt. James JOHNSON, b. near Moffat and in the employ of Mr. LUTWIDGE of Whitehaven, was left trustee to the sd. est. by Robert BRIDEN's will, but he also d. in Virginia; information on the est. believed to be on the James River is requested (VG 26 Sep 55)
BRIDGE, Daniel, b. in Ross, Herefordshire, Eng., supposed to be living in Md. or Va.; Thomas WHARTON Jr. in Philadelphia has a letter for him (PC 10 Oct 68)
BRIDGER Family, HCC, 6 Oct 96, William GOODRICH eld. son and heir at law of John GOODRICH (pltf.) and Esther BRIDGER, Lazarus LEVI and Sarah his wife, William HOGDEN, Joseph HOGDEN an infant by Dolphin DEW his gdn., Alexander GUTHRIE and Kesiah his wife, Robert PITT and Mary his wife, which sd. Esther, Sarah, William, Joseph, Kesiah, and Mary are heirs of Joseph BRIDGER dec'd, Mallory TODD ex. and formerly gdn. to the sd. Joseph BRIDGER dec'd (defs.); it appears that Robert PITT and Mary his wife are not inhabitants of the country (VGWeA 5 Nov 96)
BRIDGER, Miss, drowned at the beginning of March last when the schooner she

was on bound from Isle of Wight to Norfolk overturned (PC 6 Apr 72)
BRIGENDINE, Isaac, late of Charlotte Co., dec'd, e.a.w. his admr., William BRIGENDINE (VGPI 18 May 98)
BRIGGS, Miss, 10 year old dau. of Mr. [?] BRIGGS of Silver Springs, six miles from Harrisonburg, was killed in a fire (SVG 7 Dec 96)
BRIGGS, John, of New Kent Co., dec'd, his sloop and other items to be sold by his ex., Richard ALLEN and James BRIGGS (VG 29 Aug 66)
BRIGGS, John, of this city [Wmsbrg.], a native of Liverpool who had lived several yrs. with Mr. LAURANCE in Norfolk and had come here for his health about two months ago, died (VG 14 Aug 79)
BRIGGS, John, late of Nansemond Co., dec'd, e.a.w. his admr., George SPARLING (VGCD 19 May 80)
BRIGHTWELL, John, of Kg. Wm. Co., dec'd, his est. accounts and those of Elizabeth BRIGHTWELL, dec'd, with the Admr., John BRIGHTWELL (VGGA 10 Aug 91)
BRIGS, John, aka John DOYLE, appr., c. 19, tanner, ran away from John LINCOLN, Rockingham Co. (BVCG 23 Apr 92)
BRILL, Elizabeth, has left her husband, Harman BRILL (BVCG 13 Oct 94)
BRIMHEAD, William, Eng. svt. boy, ran away from Matthew WILLMAN, Hanover Co. and is supposed to have gone to Augusta Co. (VG 7 Nov 55)
BRINKER, Isaac, appr. to Frederick HAAS, tanner, of Winchester, drowned in Hollingsworth's Pond on 18 May (BVCG 20 May 93)
BRINKLEY, Peter, of Nansemond Co., 25, des. from Capt. David BELL's Co. of the Virginia Regt.; he may be going to N. Carolina (VG 5 Dec 55)
BRISCOE, Miss Elizabeth, of Woodville near Winchester, d. in Baltimore on 3 April in the bloom of life (BVCG 14 Apr 94)
BRISCOW, Peggy, dau. of Col. BRISCOW, d. near Winchester on the 6th inst. aged 10 (VCWM 12 Nov 88)
BRISTOR, William, dec'd, his admx., M. BRISTOR, and admr., John HOLT, will sell his dwelling house and all of his HH and KF at Blue Bottle, Gloucester Co. (VG 17 Aug 76)
BRITT, John, Irish, c. 26, served his time in Loudoun Co., des. from Alexandria (VGPu 27 Dec 76)
BRITTIN, Samuel, soldier, killed in Richmond Thurs. night [10 Jul] (VGAA 12 Jul 83)
BRITTON, Anderson, dec'd, e.a.w. his admr., Isaac SALLIE and William EDWARDS (RMA 10 Jan 96)
BRITTON, Joseph, of Frederick Co., dec'd, e.a.w. his admr., Jesse BRITTON (BVCG 26 Oct 95)
BRITTON, Nathan, appr., near 20, ran away from Jonathan WRIGHT (BVCG 18 Mar 96)
BROADBENT, Daniel, of Jones and Broadbent, merch., of Norfolk, d. in Sheffield, Eng., 19 Sep 1793 (VCNPGA 1 Feb, 1 Mar 94)
BROADDUS Family, Caroline Co. Ct., Nov. 1793, in chanc: Gray SAMUEL and Sally his wife, Warner Harwood BROADDUS, James ANDREWS and Molly his wife (pltfs.) against William BROADDUS, America BROADDUS, and Robert Loury BROADDUS infants by William SAUNDERS their gdn. (defs.) (VHFA 19 Dec 93)
BROADDUS, William, eld. son to Capt. John BROADDUS of Caroline Co., d. at his father's seat on Sat. the 19th ult. in his 22nd year (VGPu 13 Dec 76)
BROCAS, Richard, left Eng. 17 yrs. ago and resided at Wilmington in or about 1776; he was known to a family named QUINCE in Brunswick Co.; he is asked to apply to John BECKLEY, Richmond, to hear something to his advantage (VGAA 16 Oct 84)
BROCK, John Jr., was murdered near his house in Spotsylvania Co. on the eve. of 8 Aug. by four Negroes; he left a wife and several small chil. (VHFA 16 Aug 92, BVCG 3 Sep 92, SVG 15 Sep 92); two Negroes were executed at Mattepony on Mon. last for his murder (VHFA 20 Sep 92)
BROCK, Mrs. Sally, cons. of William BROCK merch. of this place [Fredsbrg.], d.

on Fri. morn. last (VHFA 5 Mar 95)

BROCK, William, dec'd, his admr., Joseph BROCK, will sell a slave and all of his PE in Fredsbrg. (VH 7 Oct 95)

BROCK, William, merch., of Fredsbrg., mar. Miss Betsey TOWLES, dau. of Col. Thomas TOWLES of Spotsylvania Co., on Mon. last (VHFFA 18 Dec 95)

BROCKENBROUGH, Thomas, d. on Tues. the 18th ult. in Richmond Co. (VHFA 4 Dec 94); his ex., John BROCKENBROUGH and Newman BROCKENBROUGH, will sell his slaves and items of his PE (VHFA 11 Dec 94, VGGA 31 Dec 94)

BRODIE, Dr. Ludowick, of Norfolk, dec'd, his PE to be sold by his admr., John PETERS (VCNPGA 23 Feb, 4 May 93)

BRODNAX, Mrs. Sarah, teacher, d. at Southam Glebe, Powhatan Co., aged 77 [obit.] (VICGA 17 Feb 90)

BROKENBERRY, Solomon, aka Solomon, mulatto, 20, ran away from Pritchard NEWBY, Alexandria, who presumes he is gone to the northward (CMAG 23 May 95); now near 22, ran away from NEWBY on 12 May 1793; he was seen in Baltimore and it is reported he took the stage for New York; he was seen in Boston in June 1795 (CMAG 2 Feb 97)

BROKER, Kitt, Negro, 48-49, ran away from Lewis MYERS, Richmond (Arg 9 May 97)

BROMLEY, Margaret, late FULKNER, will pet. the GA to dissolve her marriage with James BROMLEY (VGGA 21 Sep 91)

BROMLEY, Thomas, of Alexandria, died (VJAA 27 Jan 85)

BROOKE Family, HCC, 3 Jun 94: Thomas CONN (pltf.) and Robert CHRISTIE and Philip Jacob IRION, Lawrence BROOKE, Robert BROOKE, Fontaine MAURY and Betty his wife, John Taliaferro BROOKE, Francis Taliaferro BROOKE, and William BROOKE an infant (defs.); it appears that Robert CHRISTIE and Philip Jacob IRION are not inhabitants of this country (VGRC 29 Jul 94)

BROOKE, Mrs., spouse of H.E. Robert BROOKE Esq., governor of the Commonwealth, d. suddenly in Richmond on 5 July (RC 5 Jul 96, RMA and VGGA 6 Jul 96, NH and VGWeA 9 Jul 96)

BROOKE, Mrs. Franc[e]s, wife of Dr. Lawrence BROOKE, d. at Smithfield on 31 Oct., aged 32 (VHFFA 6 Nov 95)

BROOKE, Col. George Esq., of K & Q Co., late treasurer of the Commonwealth, d. in Richmond last Sun. morn. of an apoplectic fit; his ex., Robert PRICE, also of K & Q Co., will sell one moiety of a grist mill known as Brooke's Mill (VGAA 13 Apr, 26 Oct, 2 Nov 82, VGWeA 13 Apr 82)

BROOKE, Miss Hannah, 2nd dau. of Col. George BROOKE of K & Q Co., d. lately in the bloom of youth (VGR 27 Jan 74)

BROOKE, Humphrey, merch. of Kg. Wm. Co., d. last Sat. se'nnight (VG 27 Oct 38)

BROOKE, Richard Esq., d. on Sat. last at his seat in the neighborhood of this place [Fredsbrg.] in his 65th year (VHFA 13 Sep 92); e.a.w. his admr., Lawrence BROOKE, who will also sell his slaves and other items of his PE at his late residence, Smithfield (VHFA 10 Jan 93); his admr., Lawrence BROOKE of Smithfield, will hire out the Negroes belonging to his est. at William HERNDON's in Fredsbrg. (VHFFA 3 Feb 97)

BROOKE, Maj. Robert, of Culpeper Co., dec'd, his 1403 ac. tract in that county to be sold by his trustees, Robert BEVERLEY and John ROSE (VG 26 Mar 67)

BROOKE, Robert Esq., d. at his seat in Essex Co. (VHFA 28 Jan 90); his PE to be auctioned by his ex., Humphrey BROOKE and Edmund BROOKE (VHFA 11 Feb 90)

BROOKE, William., dec'd, a tract of his land in Orange Co. to be sold by his ex., John ROWZIE and Robert BROOKE (VG 2 May 66, 8 Oct 72)

BROOKE, William, dec'd, 30 of his slaves to be sold at Layton's Warehouses in Essex Co. by Richard HIPKINS (VG 18 Feb 68)

BROOKING, Charles, of Madison (formerly Culpeper) Co., dec'd, e.a.w. his ex., William BROOKING and Robert BROOKING (VHFA 1 Sep 95)

18th-Century Virginia Newspapers

BROOKING, Miss Fanny, eld. dau. of Mr. Vivian BROOKING of Amelia, d. of an accidental gunshot wound (VG 2 Dec 75)

BROOKING, Robert, of K & Q Co., d. in his 58th year (VG 28 Jan 73, PC 15 Feb 73

BROOKS, George, Negro, c. 30, lame, jailed under the name of Mingo, broke out of Norfolk Borough jail on the 23rd inst. (NH 26 Jan 99); jailed [again] in the borough jail; says he belongs to a Mr. HERT of Caroline Co. (NH 2 Feb 99)

BROOKS, John, aka Johnny, mulatto serving man, ran away from Benjamin HARRISON, Berkeley, and it is supposed he intends to Carolina (VGR 23 Jul 67)

BROOKS, John, appr., 18, ran away from Philip MICHAELS, Manchester (Arg 3 Feb 97)

BROOKS, Sarah, has eloped from her husband, Dudley BROOKE [sic], Chesterfield Co. (VG 2 Dec 73)

BROOKS, Thomas, killed by Mr. CRAWFORD in a fight in Manchester last Fri. (VGRMA 12 Aug 93)

BROOKS, William, dec'd, his ex., James LAREW, will sell a tract of his land adjoining the plant. of Mr. George WASHINGTON and John BRISCOE Esq. near Charlestown containing 50 ac. (BI 30 Oct 99)

BROUGHTON, James, late of Norfolk, dec'd, e.a.w. his admr., Charles STEUART (VG 24 Oct 51)

BROWDER, Isham, intends for S. Carolina soon (VG 9 May 66)

BROWN Family, Augusta Co. Ct., Aug. 1791, in chancery: various members of the GARDNER Family (q.v.) against John BROWN, Rebecca BROWN widow of Hugh BROWN dec'd, and Sally BROWN and Margaret BROWN infants, orphans of the sd. Hugh BROWN dec'd, by John BROWN their gdn. (defs.) (VGWA 17 Sep 91)

BROWN, Mrs., consort of Capt. John BROWN, merch., of this borough [Norfolk], d. on Sat. last (AGNPPA 17 May 96)

BROWN, Mrs., relict of the late Raleigh BROWN, d. in Stafford Co. yesterday morn. (VH 23 Apr 99)

BROWN, Abby, has left her husband, Thomas BROWN, Winchester, and gone off with another man (VCWM 20 Aug 88)

BROWN, Alexander, d. on the 16th ult. near the Red House, Pr. Wm. Co. [obit.] (VHFA 2 Jan 94)

BROWN, Mrs. Anne, wife of John BROWN Esq., Clerk of the General Court, d. on Sun. the 13th inst. (VGGA 16 Dec 95 ex, RMA 16 Dec 95, VGWeA 18 Dec 95, VGPI 22 Dec 95)

BROWN, Benjamin, aka William BROWN, accused of robbing Daniel FISHER near Bladensburg, Md.; described as having been b. in [Anne] Arundel Co., Md., living at or near Elk Ridge, 25-30, his wife is from some place on or near Rock Creek, a branch of the Potomac, and he has a sister living in the upper parts of Va. (VG 5 Sep, 17 Oct 55)

BROWN, Capt. Bristol, of Norfolk, d. in Port-au-Prince on 4 Jun. (NPJ 25 Jun 88); e.a.w. his admx., Sarah BROWN (NPJ 23 Jul 88)

BROWN, Catherine, ind. svt., c. 20, ran away from Henry GIRD and Co. (CMAG 13 Sep 96)

BROWN, Dr. Charles, d. on Sun. last was se'nnight in Wmsbrg. (VG 23 Jun 38)

BROWN, Daniel, from Va., c. 20, jailed Wed. last in New York City for shoplifting (NYPB 22 Sep 55)

BROWN, Daniel, late of Hampshire Co., dec'd, his ex. is Joseph NEVILLE (VJAA 21 Oct, 4 Nov 84)

BROWN, Dr. Daniel, dec'd, his ex., James CALLOWAY, adv. that his lot and improvements in Manchester are for sale (RMA 13 Jan 96)

BROWN, Francis, dec'd, "The Sergeant" adv. that persons having claims against his est. are to bring them to the next court (AGNPWA 10 Oct 92)

BROWN, Francis, dec'd, his admr., James BROWN of Petersburg, will sell the remaining goods belonging to his est. and also the lease of the shop formerly occupied by him (VGPI 13 Mar 95)

BROWN, Isaac, merch., lately from Eng., d. Sun. last at Newcastle (VGAA 27

Aug 85); his stock of goods [mostly cloth] and HHF to be sold; e.a.w. B. CRUMP of New Kent Co. or his admrs., William HAZLETT and Alexander MONTGOMERY of Richmond (VGAA 29 Oct 85)

BROWN, Jack, half Indian, c. 40, ran away from Augustine LONGAN (VGR 10 Mar 74)

BROWN, James, des. from Lt. John HALL, Suffolk (VG 3 Oct 55)

BROWN, James, c. 22, des. from the company of Capt. Francis TAYLOR, 2nd Va. Regt., who expects he is in N. Carolina (VGPu 12 Sep 77)

BROWN, James, Irish, c. 23, des. from the Virginia Artillery; he has reportedly been seen at Newbern, N. Carolina (VGPu 1 May 78)

BROWN, James Esq., lately from Ireland, d. on Thurs. last (NHPA 5 Nov 96)

BROWN, James, dec'd, e.a.w. his admr., John BROWN (SVG 21 Apr 97)

BROWN, James, dec'd, e.a.w. his admr., James KNOX of Petersburg, who will also sell all of his est. which includes coachmaker's and blacksmith's tools (VGPI 12 Oct 98)

BROWN, John, b. in Dublin, 25, des. from Capt. Robert HODGSON's Independent Company now raising for the service and defense of S. Carolina (VG 3 Jul 46)

BROWN, John, Scottish, 24, b. at Leith, ran away from the ship *Berry*, Sheppard's Warehouse on 8 Mar. (VG 27 Mar 52)

BROWN, John, Irish, 33, des. from Capt. David BELL's Company of the Va. Regt.; he may be going to N. Carolina (VG 5 Dec 55)

BROWN, John, of Norfolk, dec'd, portions of his est. to be sold by his ex., Robert NICOLSON and John BROWN (VG 27 Oct 68)

BROWN, John, of the Secretary's Office, mar. Miss Nancy GEDDY, dau. of James GEDDY of Wmsbrg. (VG 26 Mar 72)

BROWN, John, b. in Eng., but sometimes pretends to pass for a Virginian, des. from the *Hero* galley (VGPu 3 Jan 77 sup)

BROWN, John, late of Port Royal, dec'd, silversmith, his ex., James BROWN, will sell two of his lots in Port Royal and all of his HH and KF (VGPu 24 Oct 77)

BROWN, John, of Fredsbrg., dec'd, e.a.w. his ex., James BROWN (VGAA 16 Nov 82)

BROWN, John, murdered on his way from Petersburg to Bermuda Hundred on Fri. se'nnight (Richmond disp. of 22 Apr.) (VGAxA 29 Apr 90, WVGWA 8 May 90)

BROWN, John, fifer, b. in Pa., 35, des. from the camp of the 3rd Sub-Legion on Shockoe Hill (RC 1 Aug 95)

BROWN, John, Negro, c. 24, says he belongs to William KELTY near Dumfries, jailed in York, Pa. (Md. Gazette and Frederick-Town Weekly Advertiser 30 Mar 97)

BROWN, Capt. John Jr., late of Portsmouth, e.a.w. his admx., Frances BROWN (NHPA 27 Jul 97)

BROWN, Lewis, who lives on Deep Run in Henrico Co., des. from the State Troops (VGPu 11 Jul 77)

BROWN, Margaret, will present a pet. to the GA for a divorce from her husband, John BROWN, claiming that he had another lawful wife at the time of her marriage to him (VGSWA 20 Oct 97)

BROWN, Matty, Irish svt. woman, c. 29, has a sister who served part of her time with Jonathan SWIFT of Alexandria, ran away from James COLLINS, Fairfax Co. (VGAxA 3 Jun 90)

BROWN, Nancy, mulatto, 23-24, says she is free, was born in New York where she has parents, has been in Va. four or five years and spent her time between Petersburg and Norfolk, jailed in Norfolk Co. jail (AGNPPA 23 Oct 95)

BROWN, Peter, mulatto, printer (or painter), 35-40, raised near Petersburg, has a wife at Benjamin HUBBARD's, ran away from Peterfield TRENT, Osborne's (VG 16 Jun 74, VGR 30 Jun, 15 Sep 74)

BROWN, Polly, wife of James BROWN, Norfolk, has eloped from his bed and board (NPC 9 Jul 91)

BROWN, Richard, of Westmoreland Co., mar. Miss Nancy BLACKWELL of the same co. (or, acc. to the VIC, of Maryland) (VIC 29 Oct 88, VGIC 1 Nov 88)

BROWN, Dr. Robert, of Richmond, d. on Thurs. last after a short illness (VGIC 26 Mar 85); his ex., James LYLE and John M'KEAND, will sell part of his PE in Henrico Co. (VGAA and VGWeA 14 May 85); his ex., of Manchester, will rent his brick store in Richm. (VIC 7 May 88)

BROWN, Robert, Negro, jailed in Isle of Wight Co. as a runaway (VGGA 21 Mar 92)

BROWN, Stephen, of James City Co., dec'd, e.a.w. his admr., James WILLSON, Wmsbrg. (VG 22 May 52)

BROWN, Thomas, inn keeper, died, aged 61 (VHFA 14 Jan 90)

BROWN, Thomas, dec'd, his distillery below the Borough of Norfolk to be rented or sold by Samuel BROWN, Portsmouth (nfi) (VCNPGA 22 Dec 92)

BROWN, Thomas, of Portsmouth, dec'd, his wharf and warehouse to be rented or leased by his extx., Ann BROWN (VCNPGA 7 Sep 95)

BROWN, Thomas, of K & Q Co., dec'd, his ex., Lyne SHACKLEFORD, will sell 20 of his Negroes (VGGA 6 Jan 96)

BROWN, William, blacksmith, svt. to Richard ADAMS [of Richmond], ran away (VG 7 Mar 66)

BROWN, William, b. at Bently, Derbyshire, Eng., is supposed to have come into this colony with a son and family some time before 1716; he left several brothers and sisters in Eng.; he or his descendents may hear something to their advantage from Ben. WALLER, Wmsbrg. (VG 29 Nov 70)

BROWN, Dr. William, of Alexandria, mar. Miss [Kitty] SCOTT, dau. of the Rev. Mr. SCOTT of Pr. Wm. Co. (VGR 11 Mar 73)

BROWN, William, late Inspector in Blandford, dec'd, e.a.w. his ex., William BATTE and Beverly BROWN (VG 2 Mar 76)

BROWN, William, of James City, died (VGPu 20 Sep 76, VG 21 Sep 76); his ex. will sell his 318 ac. tract in James City Co. near Fox's Ordinary (VG and VGPu 25 Oct 76); e.a.w. his ex., John BROWN and John PIERCE (VGPu 6 Dec 76)

BROWN, William, of Winchester, desires to sell his house and lot in order to remove to Pennsylvania (VGWA 1 Oct 88)

BROWN, Dr. William, of Alexandria, dec'd, his extx., Catherine BROWN, will sell his medical equip. in Alexandria (VGAxA 1 Nov 92, BVCG 3 Dec 92); e.a.w. Mr. W. BROWN for settlement per the extx., Catherine BROWN of Chestnut Hill (CMAG 21 Jul 95)

BROWN, William, of Portsmouth, dec'd, e.a.w. the admx., Charlotte BROWN (VCGA 24 Jul 94)

BROWN, William, of James City Co., mar. Mrs. Maria PLEASANTS relict of Col. John PLEASANTS dec'd of Four Mile Cr., on Mon. 17th inst. (or on Mon. last acc. to the RMA and VGWA) (VGWA 15 Aug 95, RMA 15 Aug 95, RC 18 Aug 95, VGGA 26 Aug 95)

BROWN, William, Negro, c. 30, says he belongs to William KELTY near Dumfries, jailed in York, Pa. (Md. Gazette and Frederick-Town Weekly Advertiser 30 Mar 97)

BROWN, William, mar. Miss Susannah BUCHER on Thurs. eve. last, both of Winchester (WG 12 Jun 99)

BROWN, Maj. Windsor, d. in Alexandria (VJAA 9 Jun 85); his admr., John LOMAX of Alexandria, adv. for some Treasury Land Warrants belonging to the est. (VJAA 14 Sep 86)

BROWN, Winsor, dec'd, e.a.w. his admr., James LAWRASON of Alexandria (VGAxA 21 Jul 91)

BROWNE Family, HCC, 17 Mar 98, between William FLEET and Sarah his wife, Alexander LAWSON and Elizabeth his wife, Charles BROWNE, Basil BROWNE, Andrew Cochran BROWNE sons of Bennett BROWNE dec'd, infants by the sd. Wm. FLEET their gdn. and next friend, Mary BROWNE widow of the sd. Bennett BROWNE, and Priscilla Brooke BROWNE and Mary Hill BROWNE daus. of the sd. Bennett BROWNE, infants by the sd. Mary

BROWNE their gdn. and next friend, Charles BROWNE and Sarah BROWNE and Robert BROWNE infants by the sd. Charles BROWNE their next friend, which sd. Charles, Sarah, and Robert are chil. of Robert BROWNE dec'd (pltfs.) and the Rt. Hon. Patrick, Earl of Dumfries, William CUNNINGHAM, John M'DONALD, John ROBERTSON, Alexander M'CAUL, Robert FINLAY Jr., John BALLENTYNE, and William BROWNE formerly merchants in Glasgow, Robert CAMPBELL formerly of Queen Anne's Co. in Md. trustees and exors. of James BROWNE, William RICHMOND ex. of Basil BROWNE who was surv. ex. of Priscilla Brooke BROWNE and admr. with the will annexed of Robert BROWNE dec'd, James GOVAN, and Walter COLQUHOUN (defs); it appears that the defs. CUNNINGHAM, M'DONALD, ROBERTSON, M'CAUL, FINLAY, BALLENTYNE, Wm. BROWNE, CAMPBELL, and RICHMOND are not inhabitants of this country (VGGA 15 May 98)

BROWNE, Bennett Esq., merch. in Urbanna, mar. Miss Molly HILL of Essex (VGPu 9 Jun 75 sup); d. at his seat, Hill Park, Essex Co., on 19 Apr. (VHFA 30 Apr 89); his ex., James GOWAN of Kg. Wm. Co., will sell his livestock in Essex Co. (VGGA 24 Oct 92)

BROWNE, Betty, aka Amy, Negro woman, c. 30, ran away from Parker HARE, Petersburg (VGR 26 Oct 69)

BROWNE, Henry Gent., [of Surry Co.], dec'd, his PE to be sold at Richard WRINN's plant., Surry Co., by his ex., John EDMUNDS and William BROWNE (VG 15 Feb 70)

BROWNE, Henry, of Norfolk Co., d. on the 28th inst. (NH 31 Mar 98, NWJCI 4 Apr 98)

BROWNE, Col. Jesse, d. on Mon. the 3rd ult. at his seat in Southampton Co. aged 61; he was thoroughly versant in surgery (VG 3 Jan 71); e.a.w. his ex., Samuel BROWNE, John ATKINSON and Thomas JACK (VG 28 Feb 71, VGR 21 Mar 71); his son, Samuel BROWNE, proposes to continue the hospital and practice of surgery and physic as it was conducted by his father in Southampton Co. (VGR 21 Mar 71)

BROWNE, Dr. Samuel, of Southampton Co., dec'd, e.a.w. his admx., Mary BROWNE (VGPI 19 Jun 95)

BROWNE, William Burnel, of Kg. Wm. Co., dec'd, his admx., Judith BROWNE, will sell all his PE which includes a "fine toned harpsichord," plate, and china, and 30 slaves at his seat in Kg. Wm. Co. (VGWeA 30 Mar 86)

BROWNING, Christopher, Eng. svt., 24, ran away from William FREEMAN, Norfolk Borough (VG 24 Jan 52)

BROWNING, George, conv. svt., shoemaker, b. in Bristol, ran away from Christopher CURTIS, Pr. Edw. Co. (VG 24 Nov 74)

BRUCE, Alexander, dec'd, e.a.w. Philip CARBERY, Norfolk (VG 25 Jul 66)

BRUCE, Charles, of Orange Co., aged 59, d. in Fredsbrg. last Monday (VHFA 15 Dec 91)

BRUCE, Jacob, one of the Auditors of Public Accounts of Wmsbrg., died (VGPu 1 May 78); his admx., Rachel BRUCE, will sell all of his PE (VG 10 Jul 78, 15 May 79)

BRUCE, James, ind. shoemaker, c. 26, ran away from William Forsyth and Co., Portsmouth (VG 5 Mar 72)

BRUCE, James, ind. svt. from Scotland, seaman, 25, ran away from William BLACK, K & Q Co. (VG 23 Jul 72)

BRUCE, John, sailor, 24, ran away from the *Vernon* at Hampton (VG 14 Aug 46)

BRUCE, the Rev. Mr. John, d. Wed. night last (NPJ 29 Apr 89)

BRUCE, William, dec'd, his admr., Robert C. BRUCE of Caroline Co., will sell his slaves (VH 22 Jan 99)

BRUIT, Mr., of Caroline Co., killed himself (VG 21 Jul 38, NYWJ 28 Aug 38)

BRUMMIT, William, appr., 19, ran away from James CASSADY, Rockbridge Co. (BVCG 12 Mar 92)

BRUNET, Henry, mar. Mrs. BRUNET [sic], both of Norfolk, on Mon. last (NH 16 May 99)

18th-Century Virginia Newspapers 45

BRUNET, Peter, vendue-master of Norfolk Borough, d. on the 19th of June on his passage from Rhode Island to Norfolk (NHPA 1 Jul 97); e.a.w. his admrs., Gilbert ROBERTSON and William CUTHBERT, Norfolk (NHPA 16 Oct 97); his 68 ac. plant. on Elizabeth River will be sold by Henry BRUNET (nfi) (NH 10 Jul 98)

BRUNSKIL, the Rev. Mr., a native of Westmoreland in Eng. who about the year 1775 lived in a parish in Amelia Co., will hear of something to his advantage by applying to the printers (VGAxA 11 Nov 90)

BRUNTON, Richard, svt. from Yorkshire, miner, ran away from the plant. of the Hon. John CARTER (AWM 25 Jul 34)

BRUTON, John, svt., ran away from William WITHERS, Fauquier Co. (VGPu 10 Mar 75)

BRYAN, Benjamin, of Hampton, mar. the eld. dau. of Capt. Thomas DIXON and Sarah DIXON in 1769 (see: DIXON, John) (AGGA 23 Dec 96)

BRYAN, Benjamin, killed in a fight with John HILDRIP on Mon. eve. last in Fredsbrg. (VHFFA 9 Jun 97)

BRYAN, Edward, Irish svt., 30, weaver, ran away from John DALTON and Robert ADAM, Alexandria (VGR 23 Jul 67)

BRYAN, Frederick, for many yrs. deputy sheriff of York Co., d. Fri. 25 Jan at his house near Wmsbrg. (VG 24 Jan 71); e.a.w. his ex., William TREBELL, William MOODY and Frederick BRYAN Jr. (VG 4 Apr 71)

BRYAN, James, Irish svt., 35, ran away from the Potomac Co., Great Falls (VJAA 3 Aug 86)

BRYAN, John, of Richmond, d. on the 24th inst. in his 64th year (VGAA 29 Mar 86)

BRYAN, John, seaman, ran away from the ship *Hannibal* lying at the mouth of Quantico (VJAA 10 Aug 86)

BRYAN, John, Irish svt., 40, from Dublin, ran away from James WILEY, Newgate, Loudoun Co. along with Nancy MOORE (also from Dublin) (VJAA 19 Jul 87)

BRYAN, John, of Hardy Co., produces a statement from Agnes PARKER to whom he was formerly married that she renounces all attachment (WG 13 Mar 99)

BRYAN, Patrick, from Pa., des. from the 3rd U. S. Regt. near Alexandria (VGAR 12 Jul 92)

BRYAN, Simkin, dec'd, his PE to be sold at Mrs. Jane BRYAN's by his admr., Edward Champion TRAVIS and Joseph HORNSBY (VG 22 Aug 66)

BRYAN, Thomas, Irish, 28, des. from the 3rd U. S. Regt. near Alexandria (VGAR 12 Jul 92)

BRYAN, William, a youth of Northampton, d. on 4 Apr. (NPJ 23 Apr 88)

BRYAN, William, merch., mar. Miss Frances Booker WARBURTON, both of Wmsbrg., last week, by the Rev. Mr. BRACKEN (HNPA 27 Jun 95)

BRYANT Family, Rockingham Co., Ct. of Q.S., 25 Nov 93, in chanc: Casper MOYERS (pltf.) against Thomas BRYANT, Peter BRYANT, William BRYANT, Allen BRYANT, Rebecca BRYANT, John RUDDLE and Deborah his wife, John WARING and Alse his wife, William BRYANT and Mary his wife, and Sarah BRYANT heirs at law of Thomas BRYANT dec'd (defs.) (BVCG 13 Jan 94)

BRYANT, John, mariner and son to Mrs. Anne GOW dec'd, is asked to make application to Duncan M'DONALD and James KER, Norfolk, where he will find something very much to his interest (NHPA 6 Nov 97, AGGA 7 Nov 97)

BRYANT, Joseph, who lives in the upper end of Westmoreland Co., des. from Capt. John WILLIS' co. on their march northward (VGPu 11 Apr 77 sup)

BRYCE, John, d. recently (VJAA 13 Jul 86); of Alexandria, his est. accounts to be settled with Robert BRYCE and William WILSON the admrs. who are also selling several pieces of his property in Alexandria; his heir at law is Nicholas BRYCE (VJAA 10 Aug 86, 30 Aug 87)

BRYER, Robert, ind. svt., weaver, 31, ran away from the ship *Mary* from Ireland at Rich Neck, Warwick Co. (AGNPWA 19 Mar 94)

BUCHAN, John, late dec'd, e.a.w. his admr, John MUIR (CMAG 18 Apr 99)
BUCHANAN, Mrs., wife of Andrew BUCHANAN Esq., d. at Falmouth on Thurs. last (VHFA 27 Sep 92, VGRDA 1 Oct 92)
BUCHANAN, Archibald, of Kg. Wm. Co., d. in the bloom of youth (VG 4 Feb 73)
BUCHANAN, Ebenezer, appr., c. 19, ran away from James DAMERON, Norfolk (NH 6 Jul 99)
BUCHANAN, J., dec'd, e.a.w. his ex., James BELL and James GOLD, Rockbridge Co. (VGGA 10 Sep 99)
BUCHANAN, James, of the partnership of Buchanan and Simmons, dec'd, his admrs., Henry SIMMONS and Benjamin SIMMONS, will sell his PE at his late dwelling house at Cabin Point as well as some slaves bel. to the partnership of James BUCHANAN and Thomas SIMMONS dec'd (VG and VGR 7 Apr 74)
BUCHANAN, James, dec'd, his admr., Isaac HITE, will sell part of his est. in Falmouth (VG 24 Apr 78)
BUCHANAN, James, oldest merch. of this city [Richmond], d. early on Wed. morn., 10 Oct. (VGWeA 11 Oct 87, VIC 17 Oct 87)
BUCHANAN, Col. John, dec'd, e.a.w. his appointed ex., Andrew LEWIS, William PRESTON, and William CAMPBELL, Botetourt Co. (VGR 31 May 70)
BUCHANNON, Alexander Pitt Esq., of Baltimore, mar. Miss Sally HITE a few days ago at Woodville near Winchester (BVCG 3 Feb 94)
BOUCHER, Jacob, carpenter, of Winchester, d. Thurs. leaving a widow and children (WG 18 Sep 99)
BUCK, Billy, dark mulatto, c. 20, ran away from David COPELAND, Buckingham Co (VGGA 7 Oct 95)
BUCK, Charles Jr., of Shenandoah Co., mar. Miss Polly PRICE of Kentucky on Thurs. the 17th inst. (WG 6 Nov 99)
BUCK, Elizabeth, has threatened to involve her husband, Robert BUCK Jr., of Berkeley Co., in debt (PGBA 21 Apr 96)
BUCKLES, Robert Sr., dec'd, e.a.w. William BUCKLES his ex., who will sell 140 ac. of his land four miles from Shepherdstown (PGBA 12 Sep 91)
BUCKLESS, David, of Berkeley Co., mar. Miss Hanna CHIPLEY, dau. of Capt. William CHIPLEY of Frederick Co., on Wed. the 23rd inst. (WG 30 Jan 99)
BUCKLEY, John, Irish svt., hatter, 29-30, ran away from Henry BUDD, Alexandria (VJAA 2 Jun 85, VGAA 25 Jun 85)
BUCKNER, Dr. Horace, mar. Mrs. JONES, relict of the late Strother JONES Esq. of Culpeper Co. (VHFA 11 Aug 91)
BUCKNER, Jane, late of Albemarle Co., dec'd, her est. will be divided by 1 Dec. next by her ex., Philip BUCKNER (VGGA 31 Aug 91)
BUCKNER, John, of Gloucester Co., dec'd, e.a.w. his admr., Joseph CHAPMAN (VG 25 Mar 80)
BUCKNER, John Esq., of Gloucester, lately mar. Miss Dorothy SCROSBY of Middlesex (VGAA 3 Dec 85)
BUCKNER, Col. Mordecai, of the 6th Va. Regt., court-martialed on the 8th ult. fo shamefully misbehaving before the enemy in an action on the 23rd of Jan. last; he was cashiered (VGPu 7 Mar 77 sup); of Spotsylvania Co., dec'd, e.a.w. his admr., William STANARD (VGIC 28 Jun 88, VHFFA 24 Nov 95)
BUCKNER, Richard Jr., of Port Royal, declared to the world that Thomas MAGRUDER of Port Royal is a proven coward and a trifling puppy; they later fought a duel and wounded each other after which they settled their differences amicably (CMAG 12 Jan 97, 24 Jan 97)
BUDD, Mrs. Amy, d. on Wed. night the 11th inst. in her 38th year (CMAG 18 Dec 93)
BUFORD, Simeon, moving to Kentucky on 1 March next (VHFA 25 Sep 88); formerly of Northumberland Co. but now of Kentucky (VHFA 5 Aug 90)
BULGAR, Daniel, of Winchester, adv. that his wife, Elizabeth BULGAR, during his late absence, conducted herself in such an imprudent manner which a virtuous wife would shudder at the thought of and he will no longer pay any of her debts (WVGWA 18 Sep 90)

BULGER, John, svt., 17, ran away from Recovery Furnace, Spotsylvania Co.; he may have been carried off to Amherst Co. (VG 21 Jun 70)

BULL, Matthew, of Norfolk, intends going to New York for some time (NH 21 Mar 96)

BULLARD, Reuben, d. on Sun. the 19th inst. in this town [Fredsbrg.] in an advanced age (RCFPC 29 Mar 97)

BULLEN, Capt., friendly Catawba Indian, lately killed by enemy (nfi) as he was crossing the Potomac a few miles from Ft. Cumberland (Annapolis disp. of 14 Sep.) (NYPB 16 Oct 58)

BULLETT Family, HCC, 17 Sep 1799; James ROBINSON (pltf.) against Thomas BULLETT, and Thomas HARRISON exors. of Cuthbert BULLETT dec'd, who was heir at law of Thomas BULLETT dec'd, Helen BULLETT and the sd. Thomas BULLETT, Alexander Scott BULLETT devisees of the sd. Cuthbert BULLETT dec'd (defs.); it appears that Alexander Scott BULLETT is not an inhabitant of this country (Ex 22 Nov 99) (see also: BULLITT)

BULLEY, Dave, appr., c. 16, ran away from the schooner [*Ruby*] of S. BALLARD, Norfolk, who supposes that he went to Hampton as he came from there (AGNPPA 20 May 96)

BULLING, Richard, svt., an old man, ran away from John JOHNSTON and Joseph STANDFORD, Westmoreland Co. (VG 23 Feb 39)

BULLITT, Cuthbert Esq., dec'd, his ex., Thomas HARRISON, Pr. Wm. Co., and Thomas J. BULLITT, Talbot Co., Md., will sell 4728 ac. of his land in Bath Co. (VGGA 14 Nov 92)

BULLITT, John, executed near Staunton on 8 Nov. (SS 19 Oct, 9 Nov 93)

BULLOCK, Patterson, of Pr. Edw., adv. that he is about to remove to Kentucky and his wife, Rhoda BULLOCK, refuses to go with him (LWM 15 Jan 98)

BULLOCK, Thomas, Eng., 27, ran away from the snow *Industrious Bee* lying at Sandy Point (VG 5 Jun 52)

BULMAN, John, lived in the lower part of Pr. Geo. Co., Md., claimed his brother-in-law named John HESLEY 21-22, has not appeared for his service in Alexandria (VGPu 28 Feb 77)

BUNBURY, Mrs., wife of Capt. BUNBURY, d. on Wed. night at Portsmouth (NH 16 Feb 99)

BUNKLEY, John, svt., 30, ran away from Luke SUMNER, Chowan Co., N. Carolina (VGR 14 Apr 68)

BUNN, Arthur, svt., c. 30, ran away from Robert WALLACE, Augusta Co. (VGR 10 Jun 73 sup)

BUOYER, Mr., butcher, d. on Sat. last in Norfolk (NHPA 15 Feb 98)

BURBRIDGE, Thomas, dec'd, several of his tracts on Lewis's River to be sold (VHFA 1 Dec 91)

BURCH, William, mar. Miss Ann HOLLIDGE on 23rd ult. at Osborne's in Chesterfield Co. (Arg 2 Apr 99)

BURCHER, Mrs. Elizabeth, dec'd, e.a.w. John BURCHER and John HAY, Yorktown (VG 2 Jan 72)

BURDETT, John, of Wmsbrg., dec'd, a portion of his est. to be sold by his admx., Christiana BURDETT (VG 4 Sep 46)

BURE, Peter, dec'd, his ex., John COWAN and Peter BURE, will sell his stock and HH (PGBA 2 Mar 95)

BURFOOT, Lawson, dec'd, e.a.w. John FERGUSSON (VG 23 May 66)

BURGESS, Mrs. Anne, wife of the Rev. Mr. BURGESS of Isle of Wight Co., died (VG 25 Dec 71)

BURGESS, Hannah, dec'd, e.a.w. her ex., William PARRATT, Richmond (Arg 18 Apr 97)

BURGESS, the Rev. Henry John, dec'd, all his PE will be sold at his late dwelling house [in Southampton Co.] (NHPA 2 Nov 97)

BURGES[S], Mrs. Judith, wife of the Rev. Mr. BURGES[S] of Isle of Wight Co., d. on Wed. the 18th [ult.] (VG 11 Nov 75)

BURGESS, Offiah, dec'd, e.a.w. his admr., Joseph KINDER, Portsmouth (NH 18 Feb 96)

BURGESS, Thomas, late of Pittsylvania Co., dec'd, e.a.w. his admr., Thomas BURGESS and Anthony RUCKER, Amherst Co. (LWG 13 Oct 98)

BURK, Hannah, dau. of Patrick and Mary BURK, was taken prisoner by the Shawanese Indians but was relieved from them about three yrs. ago; she is now living at Ft. Pitt and is mar. to Robert ROSEBROCK; she has heard that her mother is living on Hogan's Cr., Orange Co., N. Carolina; she would like any info. on her mother's current whereabouts (VGP 22 Dec 74)

BURK, John, of Caroline Co., adv. that on 11 Sep. 1775, he agreed by virtue of a deed of trust from his brother, Thomas BURK, to sell a tract of 400 ac. in Bedford Co. (VGPu 17 May 76)

BURK, Patrick, svt., c. 30, b. in Va., saddler, ran away from James MITCHELL, Yorktown (AWM 12 May 37)

BURKE, [Master], eight year-old son of Dr. BURKE of Norfolk, was drowned on Sat. last (NH 25 Jun 98)

BURKE, Mrs., wife of Dr. BURKE, d. last Sat. (HNPA 1 Apr 95)

BURKE, Michael, of Petersburg, dec'd, his PE will be sold by C. C. De KLAUMAN, Sergeant (VGPI 9 Feb 96)

BURKE, Samuel, merch., of Norfolk, of [the firm of] Burke and Brunet, d. on 15 Feb. (HNPA 18 Feb 95); e.a.w. his ex., James HUNTER (HNPA 11 Mar 95)

BURKS, James, Irish svt., 19-20, ran away from John MASON, Lunenburg Co. (VG 1 Jun 69)

BURN, Francis, svt., 22, ran away from William KELLY, Orange Co. (VG 24 Apr 46)

BURN, James, Irish runaway svt., appears he was convicted to Md. in June 1758; jailed in Culpeper Co. (VGR 22 Mar 70)

BURN, Michael, svt., ran away from James [CRAP] Jr., Staff. Co. (VG 3 Nov 52)

BURN, Philip, Irish svt., 50, ran away from Henry GAINET and John FITZGERALD, Kg. Wm. Co., he is making towards the Potomac in Md. (VG 18 Jun 52)

BURNER, John Jr., son of John BURNER Sr., Shenandoah Co. (VGWA 15 Sep 90)

BURNET, Miss Martha, d. in the flower of her age (VG 11 Feb 73)

BURNET, Thomas, appr., 20, ran away from Simon SEXSMITH, Fredsbrg. (VH 14 Oct 97)

BURNETT, Richard, dec'd, e.a.w. his admr., Caston BURNETT, Dinwiddie Co. (VGPI 17 Feb 97)

BURNHAM, Solomon, svt., b. in Yorkshire, c. 26, farmer, ran away from Dorsey's Forge, Md. (VG 8 Dec 74, VGP 15 Dec 74)

BURNLEY Family, HCC, 5 Jun 1794: Edmund BROWN and Mary Bell his wife late Mary Bell BURNLEY (pltfs.) and Elizabeth Swan BOURNICHE admx. of Richard BURNLEY dec'd, Zachariah BURNLEY admr. with the will annexed of John BURNLEY dec'd, Hardin BURNLEY of Great Britain, Andrew MITCHELL, and Edmund LITTLEPAGE (defs.) (VGGA 25 Jun 94)

BURNLEY, John, dec'd, Zachariah BURNLEY (nfi) will sell all of the est. of the sd. dec'd in Kg. Wm. Co. consisting of 2000 ac. on the Pamunkey River (VGAA 13 Jul 82, VGWeA 20 Jul 82)

BURNLEY, Richard, dec'd, e.a.w. John WINGFIELD and Thomas LITTLEPAGE (VGAA 13 Jul 82)

BURNLY, Mrs., spouse of Hardin BURNLY, both of Richmond, d. on Tues. eve. last (VGWeA 3 May 93, VGGA 8 May 93)

BURNS, Anne, who came to Philadelphia from Bristol in the ship *Four Friends* in May last; if she will apply to Jesse and Robert WALN she will receive very agreeable and interesting info. (VGGA 11 Jan 97)

BURNS, Jeremiah, of Stafford Co., dec'd, his admx. is Ann JONES (VGAR 13 Dec 92)

BURNS, Capt. (or Maj.) Robert, d. on the 4th inst. at Staunton in Augusta Co. in his 38th year; e.a.w. his extx. Isabella BURNS also of Staunton (VGAA 12 Oct, 26 Oct 82, 1 Nov 83)

BURNS, Robert, d. here [Dumfries, Scotland] on the morn. of the 21st inst. [Jul]

(RCFPC 12 Oct 96)
BURNY, Edward, aka Barnaby BURNY, Eng. conv. svt., c. 25, has been a soldier, ran away from John CARLYLE, Alexandria, who had sent him towards Winchester along with one Martin WRIGHT an Irish conv. svt. c 40 (MG 16 Aug 59)
BURRAGE, John, Eng. svt., b. in the west of Eng., clock and watchmaker, ran away from Frances KNAPP (VGR 3 Aug 69)
BURRESS, Charles, of Kg. Geo. Co., intends to leave the state shortly (VGAA 20 Mar 84)
BURROUGH, Robert, carver, resident in the Par. of St. Mary's, Rotherithe, Surry, son of Richard BURROUGH (bookseller of London who d. c. 1728), who went to live at Cheynes, Bucks. in 1731 and from thence to Jamaica or some other part of America is asked to apply to one of various agents in Eng. and Va. to find out something to his advantage (VG 11 Apr 66)
BURROW, John Sr., of Dinwiddie Co., adv. that his son, John BURROW Jr., is under age and has left without his father's approbation (VGPI 7 Jun 87)
BURRUS, Jennings, dec'd, his plant. known as Goose Ponds in Caroline and Kg. Wm. cos. to be sold by his ex., Samuel BURRUS and Charles BURRUS; a portion of the plant. is subject to widow's dower (VGGA 21 May 94)
BURTON, Allen, mar. Miss Sally GOODIN, both of Amelia Co. (RMA 1 Aug 95)
BURTON, Billy, mulatto, 19-20, ran away from Robert DONALD, Warwick Co. (VG 25 Nov 75)
BURTON, Capt. Charles, dec'd, e.a.w. his admr., John BILLUPS of Gloucester (VGPu 7 Nov 77)
BURTON, Capt. Jesse, d. in an advanced age at his seat in Campbell Co. yesterday eve. (LFG 2 May 95); his ex., William HENDERSON and Alexander BURTON will sell a 514 ac. tract of his land in Campbell Co. about 5 miles from Lynchburg (LFG 8 Aug 95)
BURTON, John Jr., dec'd, e.a.w. his admr., Charles BURTON of Chesterfield (Arg 26 May 97)
BURTON, Martha, her husband, Joseph WARD, adv. that she has run him in debt and he will not pay any of her future debts (VGR 10 Jun 73 sup)
BURTON, Martin, of Henrico Co., d. a few days ago in his 69th year (VGGA 18 Apr 92)
BURTON, Mrs. Mary, relict of Martin BURTON dec'd, d. in this county on Sat. last (VGRMA 2 Apr 95)
BURTON, Peter Jr., late of Mecklenburg Co. dec'd, e.a.w. his ex., Joseph QUENICHETT of Nottoway (or Mecklenburg, acc. to VGPI of 26 Jul) or with his rep. Thomas BURTON (VGPI 26 Jul, 8 Nov 96)
BURTON, Thomas, mar. Miss Clementine PLEASANTS on Thurs. last, both of Henrico Co. ([VGRMA 3] Sep 93)
BURTON, William Allen, late of Cumberland Co., dec'd, e.a.w. his extx., Mary BURTON (VGPu 15 Sep 75)
BURWELL, [Mrs.], wife of the Hon. Lewis BURWELL Esq. of Gloucester Co., d. last Thurs. in her 28th year (VG 29 May 46)
BURWELL, Mrs. Anne, relict of the late James BURWELL Esq. of York Co. dec'd, died (VG 30 Oct 79); of York Co., e.a.w. her ex., Walter JONES, Nathaniel BURWELL, and John BRACKEN, who will also sell some of her livestock (VG 20 Nov 79)
BURWELL, Mrs. Ann, wife of Col. Lewis BURWELL of Mecklenburg Co., d. on Sat. the 14th ult. in her 43rd yr. leaving her husb. and 11 chil. (VIC 4 Mar 89)
BURWELL, Armistead, dec'd, his lands in Kg. Wm. Co. to be sold purs. to his will by his ex., Lewis BURWELL and Nathaniel BURWELL (VG 6 Jun 55)
BURWELL, Armistead, son of Lewis BURWELL Esq., of King's Mill, died (VG 28 Jan 75)
BURWELL, Carter, mar. Miss Lucy GRYMES dau. of the Hon. John GRYMES Esq., on 5 Jan. (VG 6 Jan 38)
BURWELL, Carter, dec'd, e.a.w. his sole ex., Nathaniel BURWELL (VG 17 Aug 76)

BURWELL, Edwin Esq., of Richmond, d. lately at Hampton in his 22nd year (VGGA 14 Mar 98, VHFA 24 Mar 98)

BURWELL, Mrs. Elizabeth, widow of Col. Lewis BURWELL naval officer of the Upper District of James River and one of the reps. in assembly, d. last Mon. se'nnight, aged 46 (VG 10 Oct 45)

BURWELL, Mrs. Elizabeth, lady of the Hon. Robert BURWELL Esq., d. Tues. last at York; she is to be bur. at Sandy Point (VG 8 Mar 70)

BURWELL, James Esq., of King's Cr. near Wmsbrg., died (VGPu 28 Apr 75, VG 29 Apr 75 sup); William RUSSELL (nfi) will settle his est. and sell his est.; his plant. near Winchester called Neville's, containing 1400 ac., will be rented by Anne BURWELL of King's Cr. (VGPu 13 Oct, 17 Nov 75)

BURWELL, John, mar. Miss Nancy POWELL, youngest dau. of Benjamin POWELL of Wmsbrg. (VG 5 Dec 71)

BURWELL, Mrs. Judith, of Carter's Cr., Gloucester Co., died (VGPu 12 Sep 77)

BURWELL, Lewis Esq., of Gloucester Co., mar. [Mrs.] Mary WILLIS dau. of Col. Francis WILLIS, during the week of 22 Oct. at Wmsbrg. (VG 29 Oct 36)

BURWELL, the Hon. Lewis Esq., President of H. M.'s Council of this Colony, d. yesterday morn. at his house in Gloucester Co. (Wmsbrg. disp. of 7 May) (MG 20 May 56)

BURWELL, Lewis Jr. Esq., of King's Mill, mar. Miss Lucy RANDOLPH of Wilton (VGPu 12 May 75 sup)

BURWELL, Lewis Esq., of Gloucester Co., died (VG 19 Mar 79)

BURWELL, Lewis Esq., of Gloucester Co., dec'd, his creditors to apply to Capt. Nathaniel BURWELL, Kg. Wm. Co.; his land there to be sold by his ex., Lewis BURWELL, Nathaniel BURWELL, and John PAGE (VGAA 12 Mar, 9 Jul 85)

BURWELL, Lewis Esq., of Gloucester Co., mar. Miss Judith CANNON of Richmond, on Sat. eve. last (VGWeA 4 Jun 89)

BURWELL, Mrs. Margaret, relict of Col. Nathaniel BURWELL, d. at her house in Kg. Wm. Co. (VG 3 Jul 79)

BURWELL, Nathaniel Esq., of Merchant's Hundred (Carter's Grove), mar. Miss Susannah "Sukey" GRYMES, dau. of the Hon. Philip GRYMES dec'd. of Brandon, on Sat. Last (VG and VGR 3 Dec 72)

BURWELL, Capt. Nathaniel, of the artillery, mar. Miss [Patsy] DIGGES, dau. of the Hon. Dudley DIGGES Esq. of Wmsbrg. (VG 11 Mar 80)

BURWELL, Col. Nathaniel, mar. Mrs. Lucy BAYLOR at Mansfield near Fredsbrg. (VGWeA 26 Feb 89)

BURWELL, Nathaniel Esq., of King's Cr., York River, d. last week (VHFA 10 Mar 91)

BURWELL, Nathaniel Bacon Gent., late of York Co., dec'd, his admrs. are the Hon. Philip LIGHTFOOT Esq. of York Co. and Col. Carter BURWELL and Col. Lewis BURWELL of James City Co. (VG 10 Apr 46)

BURWELL, the Hon. Robert Esq., mar. Mrs. BRAXTON of K & Q Co. (VGP 5 Jar 75, VG 7 Jan 75)

BURWELL, the Hon. Robert Esq., d. at his seat of Newington in Kg. Wm. Co. (VGPu 14 Feb 77)

BURWELL, Robert, dec'd, 3000 ac. of his land in Pr. Wm. and Loudoun Cos. known as Bull Run to be sold by Nathaniel BURWELL of Lancaster (VGAA 13 Sep 83)

BURWELL, Robert, dec'd, 40 of his slaves to be sold in Winchester (VJAA 13 Oct 85)

BURWELL, Mrs. Susannah, cons. of Nathaniel BURWELL Esq. of James City Co., d. last Thurs. eve. (VGWeA 31 Jul 88)

BURWELL, Mr. T., dec'd, his ex., Lewis BURWELL of Mecklenburg Co., will sell some of his livestock at his late dwelling near the forks of Roanoke River (VGGA 24 Dec 94)

BURWELL, Thacker Esq., of Kings Mill, mar. Miss Molly ARMISTEAD of New Kent (VG 24 Nov 74)

BUSH, Charles, svt. lad, b. 4 May 1749 and bound as a bastard to Richard QUINN, Culpeper Co., has run away from him (VGR 12 May 68)

BUSH, Henry, hat manufacturer, of Winchester, mar. Miss Betsey M'ALLESTER on Thurs. last in Berkeley Co. (VCWM 2 Sep 89, VGWA 2 Sep 89)

BUSH, Nicholas, of Sussex Co., dec'd, his est. in that co. on the north side of Nottoway River. to be sold by his ex., Joseph BUSH (VG 3 Sep 56)

BUSH, Solomon, heir at law of Matthias BUSH dec'd, summoned to Hardy Co. Ct. to answer a bill in chanc. exhibited against him by Daniel M'NEALE (VGIC 23 Jun 87)

BUSHUP, Elizabeth, Eng. ind. svt., c. 23, ran away from Gerrard ALEXANDER, Fairfax Co., who suspects she was carried away by Capt. TIPPLE's boatswain from Potomac River to Patuxent where the ship lies or that he has left her at the mouth of the river (MG 7 Nov 50)

BUTCHER, Lovy, Negro woman, c. 25, says she belongs to George M'CALL in Delaware, jailed in Pittsylvania Co. (VGGA 1 Nov 97)

BUTLER, Capt., of Philadelphia, d. on Wed. night of lockjaw as a result of a bullet wound received in a duel with one WATSON; he was bur. locally on Thurs. (NH 21 Apr, 12 May 98)

BUTLER, Mrs. Ann, whose maiden name was ROUTH and who about 10 yrs. ago lived at Risby, Brunswick Co., Va.; if she, or any of her chil., be living, they may hear of something to their advantage by applying to Mrs. Elizabeth ROUTH of Kirklington near Boroughbridge, Yorkshire; or, if either of the sons of Mr. David ROUTH, who is supposed to have d. at or near New Mill Cr. in Norfolk Co., Va. be living, he or they may also hear of something to their advantage by applying as above (VGAA 25 Oct 83)

BUTLER, Betsey, Negro, says she was raised on the Eastern Branch in Md. near the Federal City, was 16 last February, and was born free; jailed as a runaway in Dumfries (RJDA 12 Jun 95)

BUTLER, Charles, Eng. ind. svt., saddler and harness-maker, ran away from Miles TAYLOR, Richmond (VG 28 Apr 74)

BUTLER, Christopher, 35-40, an inhabitant of Hanover where his family still resides but who also has connections in Charlotte Co., failed to report for duty (VGPu 16 May 77 sup)

BUTLER, Edward, aka Robert DONALD, conv. svt., c. 27, tailor, ran away from Benjamin COLVARD and George DIVERS, Albemarle Co. (VG 16 Jun 74 sup, 21 Jul 74 sup)

BUTLER, Mansfield, of Hanover Co., d. on Tues. the 19th inst. in consequence of a stab which he received at the house of James HAZLEGROVE in an affray which took place on the Sat. night preceding the day of his death (VGGA 27 Sep 97)

BUTLER, Miss Nancy, of Pr. Geo. Co., died (VGPu 24 Jan 77)

BUTLER, Peggy, has left her husband, John BUTLER Jr. of Hanover Co. (VGGA 22 Apr 95)

BUTLER, Peter, Eng. svt., 24, brought over on the *Baltimore* to West Point, Kg. Wm. Co., on 14 Jun, ran away the same day. (VG 11 Jul 51)

BUTLER, Stephen, mulatto slave, 50, ran away from Leonard BOARMAN, Charles Co. [Md.] on 8 Dec 1784 (VJAA 9 Jun 85)

BUTLER, Thomas, aka Richard HOW, Eng. svt., 25, plasterer, ran away from Richard TALIAFERO on 19 Jun 1744; he may be in Norf. (VG 23 May 45)

BUTLER, Col. Thomas, late of Kg. Wm. Co., dec'd, his ex., Thomas BUTLER, will sell his land in Hanover Co. and his plant. called Tuckoman in Kg. Wm. (RMA 9 Jul, 12 Sep 95, VGGA 29 Jul, 9 Sep 95, 20 Jan 96)

BUTT, Hillary, mar. Miss Sally JAMES, Sat. night last [long poem] (VCNPGA 6 Apr 93)

BUTT, Peter, of Norfolk, dec'd, e.a.w. Richard BUTT (VCGA 5 Jun 94)

BUTTER, William, Irish conv. svt., ran away from Richard GRAHAM, Dumfries (MG 26 Apr 59)

BUTTS, Capt. Mark, mar. Miss Betsey WINTERBURY, both of Alexandria, last eve. (TAA 2 Mar 98)

BUXTON, Josiah, dec'd, e.a.w. James BUXTON of Nansemond (VG 19 Mar 79)

BUZELET, John, gardener from France, now in Alexandria (VGAxA 29 Apr 90)
BYARS, James, dec'd, his ex. (nfi) of Hanover, will sell his Negroes and PE (VGGA 17 Oct 92)
BYRD, Capt., eld. son of the Hon. William BYRD Esq., d. on 6 Jul. last in the south of France (VG 17 Oct 71)
BYRD, Miss Evelyn, eld. dau. of the Hon. William BYRD Esq., d. on Tues. last (VG 2 Dec 37)
BYRD, John Esq., died in Wmsbrg. (VGWeA 12 Dec 96, VGPI 13 Dec 96)
BYRD, Mrs. Maria, mother of the Hon. William BYRD Esq., d. yesterday morn. at Westover in an advanced age (VG 29 Aug 71)
BYRD, the Hon. William Esq., d. yesterday morn. at his seat of Westover, Charles City Co. (VG 3 Jan 77, VGPu 3 Jan 77 sup); his extx. is Mary BYRD (VG 22 Aug 77); his extx. will sell part of his est. (VG 19 Sep 77, VGAA 11 Jan 83)
BYRN, George, late surveyor of Pr. Wm. Co., dec'd, mention of his second son, Charles BYRN (VG 19 Mar 67)
BYRN, Joseph, adv. that sometime in 1769 or 1770, his brother, James BYRN of Frederick Co., borrowed some money from John ROUTY (VGPu 5 Apr 76)
BYRN, Samuel, dec'd, his ex., Peyton BYRN, will sell 275 ac. of woodland six-seven miles from Dumfries (RJDA 3 Jul 95)
BYRN, William, Irish svt., 23, wig-maker, ran away from W. BATTERSBY, Cumberland Co. (VG 10 Nov 52)
BYRNS, Garret, svt., ran away from service at Wood's Gap, Augusta Co. (VG 1 Aug 55)
BYWATER, Dr. Abraham, dec'd, e.a.w. his ex., William BLACK (VG 21 Jul 68)

CADMAN, Peter, lately arrived [in Norfolk] from Sheffield, Eng., died (NWJCI 4 O 97)
CAHILL, Richard, dec'd, e.a.w. his ex., James BYRNE of Petersburg (VGAA 29 No 83)
CAHOON, George, son of George CAHOON, 15-16, who was taken with three brothers and three sisters from Cumberland Co., Va. about 10 years ago by French and Iroquois Indians; he was later bought by a French officer; he arrived in New York from New Orleans on 19 Jul. in the brig *Africa* on his way to Trois Rivieres, Canada, attending on two sons of the surveyor General of New Orleans (NYM 27 Jul 67, PC 29 Jul 67, NYPB 30 Jul 67)
CALBOARD, Richard, house carpenter, ran away from Mary WHITE in Alexandria; he left town a great deal in debt and it is expected he is gone to Baltimore (CMAG 19 Aug 97)
CALDER, Thomas, dec'd, e.a.w. his admr., Didier COLIN (Arg 9 May 97)
CALDER, William, merch., d. on 26 Sep. at Cabin Point (VIC 15 Oct 88, VGWeA 1(Oct 88)
CALDWELL, Andrew, of Berkeley Co., dec'd, e.a.w. his ex., Charles M'DONALD and Sarah M'DONALD of Frederick Co. (PGBA 16 Nov 95)
CALDWELL, David, sailor, ran away from the ship *Prince William* on the Pamunkey (VG 18 Apr 51)
CALDWELL, David, dec'd, his 300 ac. tract in Charlotte Co. to be sold by his ex., Paul CARRINGTON and Robert CALDWELL (VGR 15 Jun 69)
CALDWELL, Henry, wishes to remove to Ky. and will sell his land in Pr. Edw. Co. (VIC 15 Oct 88 ex)
CALDWELL, the Rev. Joseph, of Winchester, was mar. to Mrs. Jane HOLLIDAY, also of Winchester, by the Rev. Alexander BALMAIN on last Thurs. (BVCG 24 Dec 92)
CALL, Capt. Daniel, late of Dinwiddie, dec'd, his est. to be sold (VGAA 28 Sep 82)
CALLAGHAM, Daniel, Irish conv. svt., ran away from Thomas LEE, Potomac, Va. (AWM 26 Jun 40)
CALLAGHAN, Robert, Irish svt., ran away from John CRANE and Leven POWEL Loudoun Co. (VJAA 21 Jul 85)
CALLAWAY, Robert, d. in Bedford Co. (VGGA 15 Oct, VGRMA 16 Oct 94)

CALLENDER, Capt. Eliezer Esq., d. on Fri. last, aged 51 (VHFA 15 Nov 92); late of Fredsbrg. of the firm of Callender and Henderson; his admr. is John CALLENDER Jr. (VHFA 7 Feb 93)
CALLENDER, Mrs. H., cons. of Capt. John CALLENDER of Fredsbrg., d. yesterday morn. (VHFA 21 Aug 94)
CALLENDER, Maj. John, an old and respectable officer in the American War, was bur. at the Episcopal Church on Tues. forenoon (CMAG 5 Oct 97)
CALLOUGHAN, John, appr. on the brig *Mercury*, c. 16, ran away (NH 4 Jul 96)
CALMES, Col. Marquis, d. a few days ago in Frederick Co. (BVCG 6 Jan 94); e.a.w. his ex., George CALMES and his extx., Betty CALMES (BVCG 28 Jul 94)
CALMES, William, Berkeley Co. Ct., 23 Nov 1795, in chanc: Thomas GRIGGS (compl.) vs. Robert THROCKMORTON and Marquis CALMES eld. son and heir at law of William CALMES dec'd (defs.) (PGBA 31 Mar 96)
CALVERT Family, Alexander COWAN of Norfolk has qualified to the will of John Savage CALVERT dec'd. and will administer the will of Jonathan CALVERT dec'd (NH 24 Mar 96)
CALVERT Family, Ct. for Norfolk Co., 21 Oct 1799, in chanc: Newton CALVERT and Rebecca CALVERT orphans of Jonathan CALVERT dec'd by Alexander COWAN their gdn. (pltfs.) against George MURPHY and Nancy his wife, John CRITCHIT, Sarah CRITCHIT, Richard CRITCHIT, and George CRITCHIT, Mary BRYANT, and Jonathan COOPER (defs.); it appears that John, Sarah, Richard, and George CRITCHIT are not inhabitants of Va. (NH 2 Nov 99)
CALVERT, Mrs. Elizabeth, wife of Dr. Jonathan CALVERT, Norfolk, d. Tues. last in her 30th year (NPC 24 Dec 91)
CALVERT, John, speaks in the North Country dialect, ran away from on board the *Scorpion* sloop (VGPu 4 Oct 76)
CALVERT, John Savage, capt. of one of the volunteer companies of Norfolk, d. last eve. [23 Dec] (HNPA 24 Dec 95, AGNPPA 29 Dec 95)
CALVERT, Dr. Jonathan, of Norfolk, d. Sat. last (VCNPGA 15 Dec 92); his HHF to be sold by his admr., John S. CALVERT (VCNPGA 29 Dec 92)
CALVERT, Maximilian, eld. son. to Maximilian CALVERT Esq., of Norfolk, a student at [William and Mary], age 17, d. suddenly on Mon. last [obit.] (VG 28 Jan 73, VGR 28 Jan, 11 Feb 73, PC 15 Feb 73)
CALVERT, Maximilian, of Norfolk, dec'd, e.a.w. John S. CALVERT, admr. with the will annexed (VCNPGA 26 Jan 93)
CALVERT, Samuel, appr., near 20, ran away from A. LAU[?]K, Winchester (BVCG 27 May 96)
CAMERON, Alexander, printer of the *Lucayan Herald*, d. lately at Nassau, New Providence (VGWeA 26 Nov 89)
CAMERON, Thomas, appr. tailor, 11, ran away from William JONES, Alexandria (VJAA 5 Apr 87)
CAMERON, the Rev. William, dec'd, at Chesterfield Co., Manchester Par., his est. will be settled with Eldridge HARRIS of Richmond (VGGA 31 May 97)
CAMM, Mrs. Elizabeth, relict of the late Rev. and Hon. John CAMM dec'd, died (VG 22 May 79); e.a.w. her admr., Samuel SHEILD and John BRACKEN, who will also sell all her HH and KF (VG 14 Aug 79)
CAMM, the Rev. Mr. John, Rector of York Hampton Par. and Prof. of Divinity at William and Mary College, mar. Miss Elizabeth HANSFORD eld. dau. of Charles HANSFORD, in York Co. on Sat. last (VG 13 Jul 69)
CAMMOCK, William Jr., dec'd, all his PE will be sold by his admx., Mary CAMMOCK, at the plant. of William CAMMOCK Sr. in Spotsylvania Co. (VGP 22 Dec 74)
CAMP, John, of Wmsbrg., d. on 30 Dec. in his 38th year (VG and VGR 30 Dec 73)
CAMP, Mary, dec'd, her PE will be sold by her exors. in Wmsbrg. (VGWeA 18 Dec 84)
CAMPBELL, Capt., of the ship *Devonshire* mar. Miss DUDLEY of Norfolk on Thurs. eve. last by the Rev. Mr. GLENDY (NH 30 Mar 99)
CAMPBELL, Mrs., wife of John CAMPBELL of Alexandria, d. very suddenly (VJAA 14 Jun 87)

CAMPBELL, Alexander Esq., attorney at law, mar. Miss Hetty HYLTON, eld. dau of William HYLTON Esq., lately from Jamaica, on Thurs. last (VGGA 18 Sep 93, VGWeA 20 Sep 93); late attorney of the U. S. for this district, d. suddenly at his house in Richmond on Mon. eve. last, 18 Jul. (RC 19 Jul 96, VGGA and RCFPC 20 Jul 96, NH 23 Jul 96, VGPI 26 Jul 96)

CAMPBELL, the Rev. Archibald, rector of Washington Par., Westmoreland Co., died (VG 4 Aug 74)

CAMPBELL, Archibald, late of Botetourt Co., dec'd, e.a.w. his admr., Israel CHRISTIAN (VGPu 30 Jun 75 sup)

CAMPBELL, Dr. Archibald, dec'd, e.a.w. his admr., Archibald CAMPBELL and Hamblin HARRIS of Cabin Point (VGAA 7 Jan 86)

CAMPBELL, Archibald Esq., attorney at law of Manchester, mar. Miss Lucy Cart STANARD dau. of William STANARD Esq. of this county [Spotsylvania ?] (VHFA 2 Jun 98)

CAMPBELL, Donald Esq., merch., of Norfolk, d. last Sat. and was bur. Mon. with Masonic honors (HNPA 11 Feb 95); his ex. (nfi) will sell his PE (HNPA 28 Feb 95) St. G. TUCKER, gdn. to Alexander CAMPBELL, will rent his large home for three yrs. (NH 30 Jan 96)

CAMPBELL, Duncan, [dec'd], e.a.w. his admr., Emily CAMPBELL, Norfolk (HNPA 15 Aug 95)

CAMPBELL, Dr. Ebenezer, dec'd, an assortment of his medicines, instruments, an books along with other items to be sold at Blandford on Appomattox River by his admr., Hugh MILLER, Richard [WEST], and Roger ATKINSON (VG 14 Aug 52)

CAMPBELL, Elizabeth, has left her husb., John CAMPBELL (PGBA 9 Sep 93)

CAMPBELL, Fanny, Irish svt., ran away from Hausimus ROSEBERRY, Berkeley Co. (VCWM 22 Apr 89)

CAMPBELL, Dr. Gustavus Brown, formerly of this town [Alexandria], d. on Wed. last at Dumfries (TDCDA 6 Dec 99)

CAMPBELL, Hugh, appr., 18, b. at sea, came from Albemarle Co., ran away from John RICHARDSON, Yorktown (VG 14 Aug 52)

CAMPBELL, Hugh Esq., merch., of Tappahannock; the contents of his store to be sold on 15 Aug. by his ex., William ROANE (VHFA 11 Aug 91)

CAMPBELL, James, Scottish svt., 26, ran away from Benjamin BERRYMAN, Kg. Geo. Co. (VG 30 Mar 39)

CAMPBELL, James, merch. in Essex Co., died (VG 7 Apr 74)

CAMPBELL, James, merch. of this town [Petersburg], mar. Miss LE PORTE, a French lady (VGPI 3 Nov 95)

CAMPBELL, John, Irish svt., ran away from John MITCHELL, Urbanna (VG 30 Mar 39)

CAMPBELL, John, with a party of 20 men from the Falls to Ft. Pitt, were all taken and killed by Simon GIRTY and his party acc. to a letter from Frederick (VGCD 27 Nov 79)

CAMPBELL, Lachlin, merch., d. last Mon. aged 43 (VHFA 5 Nov 89)

CAMPBELL, Mrs. Mary, d. at her seat in Spotsylvania Co. on Tues. last (VHFFA 1 Dec 95)

CAMPBELL, Robert, merch., mar. Miss Nancy ALLISON both of Richmond on Thurs. last (VGRMA 22 Dec 94)

CAMPBELL, William, saddler of Norfolk, dec'd, items of his est. to be sold by his admr., James REID of Norfolk; e.a.w. Francis FOSTER (nfi) (VCNPGA 6 Oct 92, 16 Mar 93, AGNPWA 10 Apr 93)

CAMPION, German, ind. svt., 30, b. in Derbyshire, farmer, ran away from John TURBERVILLE, Westmoreland (VGNI 26 Jul 75, VGPu 28 Jul 75)

CANDY, John, aka Edward WATKINS, from Caroline Co., executed on Fri. last at the gallows near Richmond for breaking into and robbing (VIC 11 Jun 88, VGWeA 12 Jun 88, NPJ 18 Jun 88)

CANE, Mary, Irish svt., c. 24, ran away from John SUITOR, Georgetown; she may have been carried off by John RILEY, Irish, c. 24 (VGWA 30 Sep 89)

CANE, Nicholas, of Albemarle Co. has died; his ex., John KEY, advises his chil. Daniel CANE, William SHAW, James CANE, John CANE, Cornelius CANE,

Edmund CANE, Jesse CANE, William FLIPPS, and David CANE that he has sold his PE and real est. (VIC 18 Mar 89)
CANN, James, dec'd, e.a.w. Thomas VEALE, Portsmouth; his extx. is Sarah CANN (AGGA 2 Sep 96)
CANN, John, of Pr. Anne Co., dec'd, his est. to be sold by the extx., Sarah CANN (VGR 12 Jan 69)
CANNADY, Jim, mulatto, c. 19, appr., ran away from William DICK, tin and copper smith, Norfolk (NH 15 Jan 99)
CANNON, Henry, appr. blacksmith, c. 18, ran away from John G. KEENOR, Little Cacapehon (WG 13 Mar 99)
CANNON, Mary, of Norfolk, dec'd, e.a.w. her admx., Mary CANNON (VCNPGA 22 Jun 93)
CANT, Capt. Constantine, d. on board ship [nd] (VG 7 Jan 37)
CANTRELL, William, Eng. svt., 19, from Warwickshire, imported last Whitsun from London, ran away from John MERCER, Stafford Co.; he may be making for Carolina (VG 13 Jun 66)
CAPPS, Cornelius, soldier, 2nd Regt. of Artillerists and Engineers, native of Va., 28, des. from the rendezvous at Kempsville; likely that he will go to P[u]ngo in Pr. Anne or to Currituck Co. N. Carolina (NH 29 Dec 98)
CAPUS, Jn. Anthony, citizen of France, d. in Va. 27 Oct 1791 (VCNPGA 8 Jun 93)
CARBERY, Philip, dec'd, his ex., William TREBELL, will sell his late dwelling house at the head of Mill Cr. in Norfolk Co. (VGWeA 13 Apr 82); his land in Botetourt Co. to be sold (VGAA 12 Apr 83)
CARDWELL, Thomas, dec'd, e.a.w. his ex., Henry THWEATT and extx., Obedience CARDWELL of Dinwiddie (VGPI 31 Jul 88)
CAREY, James, appr., c. 17, native of Ireland, ran away from Purdie and Dixon, Wmsbrg. (VG 31 Jan 71)
CAREY, Matthew, printer, mar. Miss Biddy FLAHAVAN, dau. of Roger FLAHAVAN of Philadelphia, in Philadelphia on Thurs. the 24th ult. (BVCG 16 Mar 91)
CARLILE, Anne, svt., c. 20, ran away from John BRITTAN, Chesterfield Co. (VG 24 Mar 68)
CARLILE, John, HCC, 12 May 1797; William BIRD and Catherine BIRD his wife (pltfs.) and William HERBERT and Charles LITTLE exors. of John CARLILE who was both a surv. partner and principal acting ex. of John DOLTON (defs.) (CMAG 28 Sep 97) [see also CARLYLE, Col. John]
CARLINE, James, adv. that he has commenced the business of p[a]inter and glazier formerly carried on by his father (NHPA 4 Jan 98)
CARLISLE, John Esq., of Calf Pasture in Augusta Co., mar. Mrs. WANLESS of the same (VGAA 22 Nov 83)
CARLYLE, Col. John, of Alexandria, dec'd, e.a.w. William HERBERT and Charles LITTLE, acting exors. (VGAA 2 Nov 82) [see also: CARLILE, John]
CARLYLE, Mrs. Sarah, wife of Col. John CARLYLE, merch. in Alexandria, and dau. to the late Hon. William FAIRFAX Esq. president of Virginia, d. in childbirth on 22 Jan. in her 33rd year (MG 12 Feb 61)
CARMACK, John, formerly of Md. but now of Holstein in Va., sold 250 ac. of land in Md. to Charles DORSEY in 1772; DORSEY has lately become insolvent (BVCG 13 Aug 92, VGPI 27 Sep 92)
CARMICHAEL, Dr. James, mar. Miss Betsey HACKLEY, both of Fredsbrg.; adv. that he has commenced the practice of medicine and will be found at Mr. Richard HACKLEY's, Fredsbrg. (VHFA 12 Jun 94)
CARMICHAEL, William Esq., late charge d'affaires, d. at Madrid on 9 Feb. (VHFA 8 May 95)
CARNEGGY, Wm., mar. Miss Betsy POWARS who reportedly received a bequest of £15,000 to £20,000 from the late Col. T. B. MARTIN, Jan. 1799 (WG 9 Jan 99)
CARNES, Arundale, svt., 17, imported last April in the *Tryall* from London; ran away from John TAYLOE's Neabsco Furnace (VG 29 Aug 66)
CARNES, Patrick Esq., officer in the late war, d. in S. Carolina (VJAA 3 Aug 86)
CARNEY, Bartholomew, Irish svt., c. 35, ran away from Mark KENTON and

Jeremiah OWEN, Fauquier Co. (VGR 11 Oct 70)

CARNYHAM, Mrs. Elizabeth, wife of Adam CARNYHAM, Loudoun Co., was delivered of a nine inch baby girl on last Sun. morn.[before 5 Jan.]; the mother is about 40 and has been mar. 20 yrs.; the child, her first born, was living and weighed about a pound on 12 Jan. (VGGA 25 Jan 92)

CARPENTER, Jonathan, dec'd, e.a.w. his admx., Elizabeth CARPENTER (VH 2 Oct 98)

CARPENTER, Joseph, Eng. svt., ran away from William LYNN, Fredsbrg. (VG 30 Jul 52)

CARPENTER, Nathaniel Esq., Collector of H.M's Customs, mar. Miss Nancy FANTLEROY last week (VG 17 Mar 68)

CARPENTER, Nicholas, killed by Indians in Harrison Co., 4 Oct. (VGGA 9 Nov 91 VGWA 19 Nov 91)

CARPENTER, Timothy, svt., ran away from the schooner *Billy* at Hobb's Hole; he was imported last winter in the *Hodgson* (VG 2 Sep 57)

CARPENTER, William, American, 21, brought up in Essex Co., Va., his father was a gent. of Devonshire in Eng.; he was killed in a duel by John PRIDE (a native of Amelia Co., Va., age 25) in Hyde Park, London, on Sun. morn. (London disp. of 23 Aug.) (VHFFA 21 Oct, RMA 22 Oct 96)

CARR, Archibald, stabbed a man (nfi) with a sword and killed him in Dumfries on Tues. eve. (CMAG 25 May 97)

CARR, Charles, seaman, reportedly from Va. with relations near Norfolk, killed in an accident on the schooner *Polly* at Charleston on 12 Nov. (HNPA 17 Dec 95)

CARR, Dabney Esq., attorney at law and a rep. for Louisa Co., d. at Charlottesville on Sun. 16 May in his 30th year (VG and VGR 27 May 73)

CARR, Elizabeth, wife of John Fendall CARR of Albemarle Co., ran away from him and he is no longer responsible for her debts (VGAA 22 Nov 83)

CARR, Maj. John, of Louisa Co., dec'd, his ex. (nfi) will sell his PE (RMA 21 Nov 95)

CARR, Capt. Samuel, of Albemarle Co., dec'd, e.a.w. his ex., Nathaniel ANDERSON, James MINOR, and Garland CARR of Albemarle (VG 16 Oct 78, VGWeA 10 May 83); his ex. will sell some of his slaves (VIC 16 Jan 88); his creditors are requested to meet with his ex. in Charlottesville on 1 Apr. (VGGA 30 Mar 96)

CARR, Thomas, conv. svt., c. 20, ran away from James MAGILL, Long Glade, Augusta Co. (PC 31 Aug 67)

CARR, Turner, commander of the sloop *Neptune* of and from Warren, R.I. now in this port, in a fit of religious frenzy jumped out of a window near 40 feet high and expired in a few moments (VCNPGA 21 Sep 93)

CARR, William, dec'd, e.a.w. his ex., Simon LUTTRELL and Thomas CHAPMAN of Dumfries who will also sell his merchandise, wheat, sloop, flat, and scow (VGGA 1 Feb 92, VGAxA 3 Mar 91); Pr. Wm. Co. Ct., 10 Aug 1799, in chanc: Thomas CHAPMAN surviving acting ex. etc. of William CARR dec'd (pltf.) against Robert CARTER and Benjamin DAWSON (defs.); it appears that CARTER is not an inhabitant of this country (TDCDA 26 Oct 99)

CARRELL, Benjamin, dec'd, his land and plant. containing 150 ac. in lower Surry Co. to be sold subject to the widow's dower by James SHELLY (nfi) (VG 25 Jul 66)

CARRICK, Patrick, Irish, seaman in the *Revenge* cruiser out of Capt. SLAUGHTER's Co. of the 8th Regt., ran away in marching up from Suffolk to Cumberland (VGPu 19 Jul 76)

CARRINGTON, Col. Edw., mar. Mrs. Elizabeth BRENT of Richmond on Sat. eve. last (VGGA 12 Dec 92)

CARRINGTON, Col. George, d. 7 Feb. at his seat in Cumberland Co. in his 74th year; his wife, Anne CARRINGTON, d. on 15 Feb. in her 73rd year [long obit.] (VGGA 5 Mar 85)

CARRINGTON, George Jr., late of Cumberland Co., dec'd, his ex. adv. that the division of his est. will take place immediately (VGIC 22 Dec 87)

CARRINGTON, George the Elder, late of Cumberland Co., dec'd, e.a.w. his admr. Joseph CARRINGTON and Mayo CARRINGTON (RMA 20 Apr 96)

CARRINGTON, the Hon. Paul Esq., a judge of the High Court of Appeals in his 6 year, mar. Miss SIMMS of Halifax, aged 15, on 6 Apr. (BVCG 9 Apr 92, MCent 25 Apr 92)

CARROL, Archibald, of Richmond, adv. that a report propagated in Yorktown by some Frenchman and others that he was married and had a family is an infamous falsity (VGWeA 10 Dec 85)

CARROLL, Archibald, of Norfolk, found guilty of murder Monday (VHFA 26 Jun 8, Irish, executed at Richmond on Fri. last for the "inhuman" murder of John M'GILL one of the seamen belonging to his vessel; he is supposed to be the person who carried the signals of the British fleet to the French whilst off the British Channel last war (NPJ 6 Aug 88, VGWeA 7 Aug 88)

CARROLL, Benjamin, dec'd, his admr. are William SEWARD Jr. and Jordan THOMAS (VG 30 Jan 52)

CARROLL, Daniel, waterman, of Alexandria, died (VJAA 22 Mar 87)

CARROLL, Patrick, Irish svt., b. c. 1717, ran away from John MARTIN, Kg. Wm. Co., seen near Hobb's Hole; he may be heading for Carolina or Sherando (VG 29 May, 6 Jun 45)

CARROLL, William, c. 30, jailed in Winchester on suspicion of being a runaway; says he is a freeman from Surry Co. (VGR 6 Sep 70)

CARTER Family, Henrico Co. Ct., 3 Jun 1799, in chanc: William SHACKLETON and Nancy his wife, Thomas OTEY and Frances his wife, which sd. Nancy and Frances are chil. and legatees of Benjamin CARTER dec'd. (pltfs.,) against James BERIFORD ex. of the late Benjamin CARTER dec'd and Theodoric CARTER, Elizabeth CARTER, Talitha P. CARTER, and Louisa CARTER also chil. and legatees of the sd. Benjamin CARTER dec'd; the sd. Talitha and Louisa being infants under 21 by the sd. Theodoric CARTER their gdn. (defs.); it appears that Elizabeth CARTER is not an inhabitant of this country (Ex 19 Jun 99)

CARTER, Mrs., wife of Col. Landon CARTER of Richmond Co. and dau. of the late Hon. William BYRD Esq., d. about a fortnight ago. (VG 12 Dec 45)

CARTER, Aaron, aka Aaron CASTEEL, aka Abraham SORTER, mulatto slave 26, raised on Addison MURDOCK's est. near Upper Marlboro, [Md.]; ran away from Joseph MOCKBEE, Upper Marlboro (CMAG 28 Oct 94, 23 May 95)

CARTER, Charity, Jacob CARTER (nfi) of Norfolk will not be answerable for any of her debts (AGNPPA 17 Jun 96)

CARTER, Charles, Virginian, 23, des. from Capt. Carter HARRISON's Co. (VG 5 Dec 55)

CARTER, Col. Charles, late of Kg. Geo. Co., dec'd, his ex., Landon CARTER and Charles CARTER, will sell his real estate (PC 8 Jun 67); 100 of his slaves will be sold at Rocky Ridge, Chesterfield Co. by his ex. (VG 25 Jun 67); 14,000 ac. of his land in Pr. Wm. and Fauquier cos. to be sold by his ex. (VG 6 Aug 67)

CARTER, Charles Esq., of Corotoman, mar. Miss Nancy MOORE second dau. of Col. Bernard MOORE (VG 29 Nov 70)

CARTER, Col. Charles, d. in Fredsbrg. on Fri. last in an advanced age. (VHFFA 3 May 96)

CARTER, [Mrs.] Charles, the lady of Charles CARTER Esq. of Corotoman, d. on the last of [January] (VGR 22 Feb 70)

CARTER, Edward Esq., d. on Sun. eve. in his 54th year (VHFA 26 Apr 92); e.a.w. his acting ex., Charles CARTER Jr. of Fredsbrg. (VHFA 5 Jul 92); his acting ex., of Culpeper [sic], will sell 100 of his slaves at Charlottesville (VGGA 16 Oct 93, VHFA 21 Nov 93)

CARTER, Elizabeth, her husb., Thomas CARTER Jr. of Northumberland Co., adv. that she has shamefully neglected the duties of a Christian and wife and he will not be bound by any contracts she may make (VG 26 Aug 75)

CARTER, Mrs. Elizabeth, spouse of Capt. Samuel CARTER of Pr. Edw. Co., d. on Mon. the 11th inst. in her 36th year (RMA 28 May 95)

CARTER, George Esq., dec'd, his estates in Pr. Wm., Fairfax, and Frederick cos. to be sold (VG 9 May 45)

CARTER, George Esq., of Corotoman, son of Charles CARTER Esq. of Shirley, died (VGWeA 6 Nov 88)

CARTER, James, of Pittsylvania Co., jailed for horse stealing, d. in the public jail in

Wmsbrg. last Wed. (VGP 30 Mar 75)

CARTER, Dr. James, of Wmsbrg., dec'd, his ex., John BRACKEN and Robert SAUNDERS, will sell all his slaves, furniture, and plate, cattle, corn, and plant. utensils (VGWeA 6 Dec 94, VGGA 10 Dec 94)

CARTER, James, late of Frederick Co., dec'd, e.a.w. Joseph CARTER, James CARTER, and A. W. CARTER, his exors. (WG 30 Jan 99)

CARTER, Jn. Esq., of Kg. Geo. Co., mar. Miss Philadelphia CLAIBORNE, youngest dau. of Philip Whitehead CLAIBORNE Esq. of Kg. Wm. Co. this eve. (VG 3 Oct 71); died (VGR 21 Oct 73); his ex., Philadelphia CARTER, Catesby WOODFORD, and Gawin CORBIN, will sell his est. (VG 23 Dec 73)

CARTER, Capt. John Gent., late of Spotsylvania Co., dec'd, e.a.w. the ex., William CARTER, John CARTER, and Joseph BROCK (VGAA 16 Oct 84); his ex. will sell six of his slaves at Spotsylvania Ct. H. (VHFA 11 Oct 92)

CARTER, John Esq., d. at his seat at Bull Run (VHFA 9 Apr 89); his admrs. in Loudoun Co. are Landon CARTER, Robert CARTER Jr., and Wormeley CARTER (VIC 16 Dec 89)

CARTER, John, late of Wmsbrg., dec'd, e.a.w. his ex., John CARTER (VGWeA 10 Aug 92)

CARTER, John, mar. Miss Matilda WRAY on Sat. (VGGA 18 Feb 95)

CARTER, Lemuel, capt. of the Norfolk Borough Artillery and member of the Common Council, d. on Mon. [2 Feb.] (HNPA 4, 21 Feb 95)

CARTER, Miss. Polly, dau. of Col. Charles CARTER of Ludlow, d. suddenly at Cleve [Kg. Geo. Co.] the seat of Landon Carter Esq. (VHFA 4 Oct 92)

CARTER, Mrs. Rebecca, spouse to Dr. William CARTER of Gloucester, died (VG 1 Apr 73)

CARTER, the Hon. Robert, President of the Council of Va., d. on 4 Aug. 1732 in his 69th year (AWM 7 Sep 32)

CARTER, Robert, of Westmoreland, was mar. by the Rev. Mr. MALCOLM to Miss Frances TASKER, youngest dau. of the Hon. Benjamin TASKER Esq. on Tues. last (MG 4 Apr 54)

CARTER, Capt. Robert, of Hanover Co., dec'd, e.a.w. his ex., John BLACKWELL and John CARTER Jr. (VG 14 May 72)

CARTER, Robert Sr., [died?] near the mouth of Willis' Cr., Cumberland Co. (VG-Randolph 7 May 52)

CARTER, Samuel, aka GASFORD, conv. svt., c. 23, ran away from the Rev. Mr. BOUCHER's in Pr. Geo. Co., Md.; he is the property of Clement BROOKE, Stafford Co., and was transported in the *Thornton* to Rappahannock River last Jun. (VGR 3 Dec 72)

CARTER, Lt. Thomas, a brave Va. youth, volunteer, killed 18 Apr. when a party of 15 soldiers under the command of Capt. John MERCER was attacked by Indians near Edward's Fort on Cape Capon about 20 miles above Winchester (Wmsbrg. disp. of 23 Apr.) (NYM 3 May, MG 6 May 56)

CARTER, Dr. Thomas, mar. Miss. BROADNAX of Petersburg on Sat. last (VGWeA 13 Aug 85)

CARTER, Walker R., mar. Miss Sarah C. C. STANARD, dau. of William STANARD of this county [Spotsylvania ?] (VHFA 4 Dec 94)

CARTER, William, third son of John CARTER, aged 23, mar. Mrs. Sarah ELLYSON relict of Gerard ELLYSON, aged 85, a sprightly old Tit with £3000 fortune, yesterday in Henrico (VG 14 Mar 71)

CARTER, Dr. William, mar. Miss Molly WRAY (VG 2 Dec 75)

CARTER, William, adv. that he intends to petition the next GA for the depreciation of pay due his dec'd brother, John CARTER, who served as a soldier in the 1st Va. Regt. (HNPA 16 Aug 94)

CARTER, Dr. William Sr., for many yrs. an inhabitant of Richmond but formerly Wmsbrg., d. on Wed. eve. last (VGGA 14 Jun 99); his ex., Joseph JACKSON and Charles SPENCER, will sell all his drugs, medicines, surgical instruments and shop furniture and all the necessary utensils for carrying on the druggist, apothecary, and chemical business at private sale and will also settle his est. (VGGA 9 Jul 99, Ex 30 Jul 99, VF 3 Aug 99, Arg 9 Aug 99)

CARTER, William C., of Richmond and Wmsbrg., adv. that his son, William, appears to be perfectly recovered from his late indisposition (VIC 15 Apr 89); adv. that he will not pay any debts of his son, William CARTER Jr. (VGGA 8 Sep 90)

CARTEY, John, Irish svt., blacksmith, ran away from William AYLETT, Westmoreland Co. (AWM 2 Aug 39)

CARTLIDGE, Charles, appr., 15-16, ran away from Martin HAGNER (TAA 18 Apr 98)

CARTMELL, Jacob, mar. Miss Rebecca CRI[S]T in Washington Co., Pa. (VGWA 29 Apr 89)

CARTMELL, Nathaniel, late of Frederick Co., dec'd, e.a.w. his ex., Thomas CARTMELL and Martin CARTMELL (BVCG 9 Nov 95)

CARTT, Thomas, svt., ran away from Benjamin CATTON, Yorktown; he is a tailor and has a mother in Charlestown, S. Carolina (VG 11 Aug 38)

CARTWRIGHT, John, gunner, upwards of 40, ran away from the *Norfolk's Revenge* galley in Chickahominy River (VGPu 14 Jun 76)

CARTWRIGHT, Thomas, Eng. svt., bricklayer, c. 22, ran away from William SHEDDEN, Essex Co. (VG 29 Jun 76)

CARTY, John, Irish svt., ran away from William AYLETT's Quarter in Essex Co. (VG 6 Apr 39)

CARVAN, Patrick, mariner, 26, ran away from the ship *Amelia* lying at Bermuda Hundred (VG 1 Jun 69)

CARVER, Alexander, of Kg. Wm. Co., dec'd, his 196 ac. tract of land there to be sold by his ex., Robert KING (VG 16 Sep 73)

CARVER, William, Scottish ind. svt., groom, c. 26, ran away from Daniel GRANT, Baltimore (VG 7 Apr 74)

CARWICK, John, appr., 18, ran away from Nicholas B. SEABROOK, Norfolk (VGN 5 Jan 75)

CARY, the Hon. Archibald Esq., speaker of the Senate, d. on Tues. last at his seat Chesterfield (VGWeA 1 Mar 87)

CARY, Claudius Peter, fencing master who was endeavoring to get out of the enemy's way, d. with fatigue in the Dismal Swamp (VG 22 May 79)

CARY, John, of Back River, Elizabeth City Co., mar. Miss Sukey ARMISTEAD of New Kent Co. (VG and VGPu 25 Jul 77)

CARY, Miles Esq., of Southampton Co., attorney at law and clerk of the Committee Claims to the Hon. the House of Burgesses, died (VG 19 Sep 66)

CARY, Miles, youngest son of Wilson Miles CARY Esq., of Hampton, died on the 16th inst.; he was bur. at Rich Neck, Warwick Co. (VG and VGR 21 Apr 74)

CARY, the Hon. Richard Esq., a judge of the General Court of this Commonwealth d. suddenly on Fri. night last at Mr. FORMICOLA's Tavern in Richmond (VIC 18 Nov 89, VGWeA 19 Nov 89)

CARY, Mrs. Sarah, cons. of Col. Wilson Miles CARY Esq. of Celeys, d. there on Thurs. 28 Feb., aged 62 (NH 2 Mar 99, Ex 5 Mar 99, VGGA 5, 8 Mar 99, Arg 5 Mar 99)

CARY, Thomas, dec'd, e.a.w. his admr., William REYNOLDS of York (VGWeA 6 Apr 82)

CARY, Col. Wilson, d. at his seat at Celeys near Hampton in an advanced age (VG 3 Dec 72)

CARY, Wilson Miles Esq., of Warwick Co., mar. Miss Sally BLAIR dau. of the Hon. John BLAIR Esq. Commander in Chief of this Colony, on 25 May (VG-Randolph 26 May 58)

CASEY, Francis, Irish svt., 19-20, ran away from the Potomac Co., Great Falls (VJAA 15 Jun 86)

CASEY, William, Eng. svt., 26, ran away from Edward VIELLER of Annapolis (VJAA 17 Feb 85)

CASH, Archdell, adv. that he was called a deserter under the name of Archibald CASH by Capt. Thomas EWELL; he denies being a deserter (VGPu 18 Jul 77)

CASHILL, Edmund, d. the eve. of the 2nd inst. at a tenement of Martin BAKER's near this city [Richmond]; he had arrived at Norfolk from Ireland about 18 months since; he came to the BEESON Fam. in which he died about seven weeks

before much emaciated with sickness and without money (VGRMA 11 Jun 93)
CASKIN, Lawrence, jailed in Frederick Co., says he came into Baltimore last May (VJAA 5 Jan 86)
CASON, Seth, late of Pr. Edw. Co., dec'd, his 425 ac. tract on Vaughan's Cr. in Pr. Edw. Co., will be sold by his ex. (nfi) (VGGA 15 Oct 99, Arg 5 Nov 99)
CASS, Anne, dau. of Daniel SHARP of Wakefield, Yorkshire, was, some yrs. ago, sold as a svt. to John PAGE of Wmsbrg. and by him again sold to Mr. PENMAN who sold her to a person whose name he does not remember, but believes she may live somewhere in N. Carolina; if the sd. Anne CASS will make known her place of residence or, being a svt., her master will notify his desire of disposing of her for the remaining time of service to the Hon. William FAIRFAX of Va., he will make the required satisfaction and give the sd. Anne an account of some proposals for her benefit (VG 6 Jun 55)
CASSANAVE, Peter, [dec'd.], his admrs. gave notice on 9 May 1797 that the divide of the assets would be made among his creditors on 16 Aug 1797, but they learne that by law they cannot make such dividend in less than 12 mos. after the deceas of the sd. CASSANAVE and that period has not yet elapsed; e.a.w. his admx., Anne CASSANAVE, and admr., Nicholas YOUNG of Georgetown (CMAG 28 Sep 97)
CASTLE, John, dec'd, e.a.w. his ex., John WHITE (VHFA 5 Feb 95)
CATLETT, George Esq., mar. Miss Fanny JOHNSON last Thurs. at Port Royal (VHFA 8 Dec 91)
CATLETT, George, mar. Miss Lucy BUCKNER dau of William BUCKNER, all of Port Royal in Caroline Co., on Fri. last (VHFA 16 May 98)
CATLETT, John, dec'd, e.a.w. his ex., John G. CATLETT, Port Royal (VHFA 15 Se 95)
CATLETT, John G., mar. Miss Nancy ROBB dau. of James ROBB Esq. in Port Roy on Mon. the 14th inst. (VHFFA 29 Dec 95)
CATLETT, Peter, dec'd, Ann CATLETT (nfi) will sell his livestock at his plant. in the fork of Shenandoah (VGWA 23 Mar 91)
CATTON, Dr. Benjamin, d. at York[town] this week (VGR 26 May 68); e.a.w. his e George RIDDELL, Yorktown; his PE to be sold at the dwelling house of Mrs. Mary CATTON, Yorktown (VG 20 Oct, VGR 27 Oct 68)
CATTON, William, from Kg. Wm. Co., 23-24, des. from the 15th Va. Regt. (VGPu 1 Apr 77)
CAUCO, George, Negro slave, ran away from George HOPE, Hampton (NPC 2 Jun 92)
CAUVY, John, dec'd, e.a.w. his admr., William HAXALL of Petersburg (VGPI 8 Jul 96)
CAVER, Alexander, late of Kg. Wm. Co., e.a.w his ex., Robert KING (VGPu 16 Oct 78)
CAY, Gabriel Esq., Comptroller of H.M's Customs for the Port of Hampton (or Low District of James River), d. on Mon. last in his 38th year (VG and VGR 10 Jan 71
CAYWOOD, William, Eng., 25, escaped from jail in Richmond (also given as Henrico) (VGAA 8 Nov 83, VGIC 15 Nov 83)
CEATON, John, Eng. svt., ran away from Adam REABURN, Augusta Co. (VGR 18 Oct 70)
CELLARS, John, Negro, 25, carpenter, cooper, reads and writes, ran away from Edward CARTER, Albemarle Co. (VGR 31 Oct 71)
CELSEY, Steycher, Eng. ind. svt., ships carpenter and caulker, c. 40, ran away fro Micajah JAMES, Baltimore, Md., about two yrs. ago and has made his escape from on board the boat *Molly* at New Point Comfort (VGPu 25 Oct 78)
CHA, John, 25, des. from the French frigate *Sybille* in Chesapeake Bay (VGAA 25 May 82)
CHALLIS, Hugh, Pittsylvania Co., Jan. Ct. 1799, in chanc: Elijah KING (pltf.) against John CHALLIS ex. of Hugh CHALLIS dec'd, who was ex. of John KING dec'd (def.); it appears the def. is not an inhabitant of this state (LWG 2 Mar 99)
CHAMBERLAIN, George, of Norfolk, d. suddenly on Tues. morn. last; his funeral on Wed. was attended by the master and brethren of the Norfolk Lodge (NPC 14

Jan 92)
CHAMBERLAINE, George, dec'd, e.a.w. Philip CARBERY, Norf. (VG 25 Jul 66)
CHAMBERLAYNE, Edward Pye, dec'd, his land in Buckingham Co. adjoining the land of Capt. Richard CHAMBERLAYNE to be sold by his ex., Rebecca CHAMBERLAYNE, Richard S. TAYLOR, and Philip W. [CLAIBORNE] (VGR 19 Oct 69 sup, VG 2, 8 Nov 70)
CHAMBERLAYNE, Richard Esq., d. at his seat in New Kent (VGPu 10 Jul 78); e.a.w. his ex., William CLAYTON and John ARMISTEAD (VG 4 Dec 78); his extx., Mary CHAMBERLAYNE and William CLAYTON of New Kent, will sell 400 ac. of unimproved land in Pittsylvania Co. (VG 19 Jun 79)
CHAMBERLAYNE, William, of New Kent Co., lately mar. Miss Peggy WILKINSON of Henrico (VGAA 7 Aug 84)
CHAMBERLYNE Elizabeth, dec'd, a slave of hers to be sold at Norfolk by her admr., Philip CARBERY (VG 7 Jan 68)
CHAMBERS, John, Eng. svt., c. 21, ran away from Henry JAMES and Mordecai GIST, Baltimore, Md., on the 10th inst. with Margaret GRANT, a mulatto, c. 20 (VG 22 Mar 70)
CHAMBERS, Joseph, d. in Martinsburg in an advanced age (PGBA 14 Apr 96)
CHAMBERS, Josiah, dec'd, e.a.w. his ex., John WATSON Jr. and Charles ALLEN Jr. (VGAA 14 Jan 86)
CHAMBLIS, John, 38, des. from James JOHNSON's Co. of the 6th Bn. of Continental Regulars (VGPu 26 Jul 76)
CHAMPAIGNE, Elizabeth, wife of Stephen CHAMPAIGNE, Norfolk, ran away from Philadelphia and eloped from his bed and board; her husb. believes she is living with John Baptist ARNO (or ARNAUD) [advertisement also appears in French in 28 Jul issue] (NH 25, 28 Jul 96)
CHAMPE, Col. John, d. on Sun. 25th ult. at Lamb's Cr., Kg. Geo. Co. (VGP 5 Jan, VG 7 Jan 75); his ex., William CHAMPE, will sell a large quantity of plate and elegant HHF belonging to his est. at Lamb's Cr. (VGP 15 Jun, VG 17 Jun 75 sup)
CHAMPE, William Esq., of Culpeper Co., dec'd, e.a.w. William CALDWELL of Kg. Geo. Co. or his extx., Mary CHAMPE in Spotsylvania (VGAA 28 Aug 84)
CHANDLER, George, of Norfolk, mar. Miss Polly LAWSON of Pr. Anne, Tues. last (VCNPGA 30 Mar 93)
CHANDLER, George, merch., of Norfolk, d. on Fri. last (NH 14 May 99); e.a.w. his admx., Mary CHANDLER, Norfolk (NH 6 Jun 99)
CHANDLER, Richard, dec'd, e.a.w. his ex., Sackville KING, at Oxford Iron Works in Campbell Co. or with Col. Tunstal QUARLES in Fluvanna Co. (VGAA 21 Jan 86)
CHAPIN, Mrs. Margaret, of Alexandria, died (VGAxA 3 Mar 91)
CHAPMAN, Carr, mar. Miss Sara THORNTON, younger dau. of the late Rev. Thomas THORNTON, in Dumfries on Sun. eve. last (VH 19 Jul 99)
CHAPMAN, Mrs. Eleanor, cons. of Maj. Henry Henley CHAPMAN, d. on the 20th ult. at Green Hill in Charles Co., Md., in her 29th yr. (CMAG 13 Aug 96)
CHAPMAN, John, of Spotsylvania Co., dec'd, his ex., Will. CHAPMAN and Ben. CHAPMAN, will sell his 1003 ac. tract in that co. and a 346 ac. tract in Orange Co. (VGPu 27 Sep 76)
CHAPMAN, John, aka TIMBERLAKE, executed on 25 Jan. near Richmond for robbery (or horse stealing acc. to VGAA) (VGWeA and VGAA 26 Jan 82)
CHAPMAN, Joseph B., appr., c. 15, ran away from John PHILPOTTS near Richmond (RC 5 Apr 96)
CHAPMAN, Richard, dec'd, the settlement and div. of his est. will take place at George GREEN's Tavern, Richmond on 1 Mar. (VGGA 6 Jan 96); Nathan. W. PRICE adv. that he is the only person legally auth. to settle the est. (VGGA 13 Apr 96)
CHAPMAN, Samuel, svt., b. in Eng., c. 28, ran away from Dorsey's Forge, Md. (VG 8 Dec, VGP 15 Dec 74)
CHAPMAN, Capt. William, of Brunswick Co., dec'd, his ex., Benjamin CHAPMAN, will sell his PE (VG 4 Apr 71)
CHAPPELL, Thomas, HCC, 19 May 1798, between Benjamin CHAPPELL, Agnes

CHAPPELL, and Aquila BINFORD and Mary his wife, Jane [ELLE] admx. of Thomas CHAPPELL dec'd, and Benjamin CHAPPELL ex. of John CHAPPELL dec'd (pltfs.) and John M. BINFORD, James BINFORD, Elizabeth BINFORD children and co-heirs of James BINFORD dec'd (defs); it appears that James and Elizabeth BINFORD are not inhabitants of this country (VGGA 10 Jul 98)

CHAPTER, Edward, dec'd, e.a.w. his admr., James TUCKER, Norfolk (NH 1 Feb 9⁴

CHARLTON, Francis Esq., merch. of Wmsbrg., d. there on Tues. (or Wed., acc. to VGGA) last; e.a.w. his admx., M. CHARLTON, and admr. William WISEHAM (NHPA 27 Jan 98, VGGA 31 Jan, 28 Feb 98); HCC, 20 May 1799, between John MOSS (pltf.) and Wallace & Muir, and Mary CHARLTON and William WISEHAM admrs. of Francis CHARLTON dec'd (defs.); it appears that Wallace & Muir are not inhabitants of this country (VF 13 Jul 99)

CHARLTON, Richard, of this city [Wmsbrg.], d. last Mon, at Richmond on his way from the springs (VG 2 Oct 79); his extx., Sarah CHARLTON, and ex., John M. GALT, will sell 3000 ac. of his land on the Ohio within two miles of the Falls (VG 19 Feb 80); a tract of his land at the Falls of the Ohio to be sold in Richmond on 2⁴ Nov. (VGAA 14 Sep 82)

CHASE, Capt. Lothrop, mar. Mrs. Elizabeth WARREN, both of Norfolk, on Sun. ev last (NH 11 Jun 99)

CHEATHAM, Thomas, dec'd, his ex. (nfi) of Chesterfield, will sell his large 3-story brick house [?in Manchester?] (VGPI 27 Sep 96)

CHEATUM, Josiah, c. 22, enl. in Amherst, des. from the 6th Va. Regt. at the College Camp (VGPu 5 Jul 76 ps)

CHEESEMAN, Samuel, formerly of Petersburg, late of Baltimore, dec'd, e.a.w. his admr., Samuel M'KEAN of Baltimore (VGGA 30 Nov 96)

CHELSON, Stephen, svt., 19, Virginian, ran away from James ROB, Lancaster Co (VG 3 Jul 46)

CHESHIRE, James, aka Chink, aka Jim, mulatto slave, c. 27, his father was an Indian named Cheshire; ran away from Paul MICHAUX, Cumberland (VG 26 Nov 72)

CHEVALLIE, John A. Esq., mar. Miss Sally MAGEE (VICGA 6 Jan 90); of Richmond, mar. Miss Kitty LYONS at Studley the seat of the Hon. Peter LYONS in Hanover on Thurs. last (VGRMA 19 May, VGGA 21 May 94)

CHEVIS, Capt. David, d. at his seat in Caroline Co. on Wed. the 21st ult. aged 66 (VHFA 5 Sep 93); of Spotsylvania Co. [sic], dec'd, his ex., John CHEVIS, will sell his stock and Negroes (VHFA 5 Feb 94)

CHEW, Henry, only child of Roger CHEW, d. on 4 Jan. in his 10th year in Alexandr (VJAA 5 Jan 86)

CHEW, Capt. John Sr., d. last Sat., aged 49, leaving a wife and numerous small children (VHFA 24 Sep 89)

CHEW, Larkin Gent., of Spotsylvania Co., dec'd, his livestock, etc. to be sold at his former ordinary by his ex., William BUCKNER and Oliver TOWLES (VGR 18 O 70)

CHEW, Larkin, d. in this county [Spotsylvania] on Wed. last in an advanced age (VHFFA 23 Sep 96)

CHEW, Mrs. Mary, d. at her seat in Spotsylvania Co. last Thurs. aged 57 (VHFA 2⁴ Sep 89)

CHEW, Robert, merch., d. on Fri. morn. last in his 36th year (VHFA 5 Jan 92)

CHEWNING, Samuel, mar. Mrs. Ann TAYLOR relict of the late Capt. John TAYLOR in this town [Fredsbrg.] (VH 14 May 99)

CHEWNING, Thomas, soldier, left Caroline Co. with his brother, John CHEWNII of Capt. Francis TAYLOR's Co., and des. from the co. of Capt. Samuel HAW Jr., 2nd Va. Regt. (VGPu 21 Mar 77 sup)

CHICHESTER, Richard Esq., dec'd, e.a.w. his extx., Sarah CHICHESTER (CMA 12 Aug 97)

CHILDRAY, Thomas, appr., ran away from William M'KIM; he is likely lurking about Four Mile Cr. where he is from (Arg 18 Jan 99)

CHILDRESS, John, c. 20, des. from the co. of Lt. John STOKES, 6th Va. Regt. (VC 1 Aug 77)

CHILDREY, William, of Pr. Edw. Co., executed at the gallows on 9 Jul. [sic] for robbery (VGPu 8 Jul 73)
CHILDS, Francis, ed. of the *Daily Advertiser* printed in the city of New York, mar. Miss Sarah BLANCHARD dau. of John BLANCHARD merch. of Elizabethtown, lately at Elizabethtown (VGWeA 23 Aug 87)
CHILES, James, of Louisa, adv. that he intends to remove his family and effects out of the colony some time next winter (VG 6 May 73)
CHILES, Micajah, of Albemarle Co., dec'd, his lots in Charlottesville to be sold by his ex., Chiles TERRELL and Thomas W. LEWIS (Ex 8 Nov 99)
CHILLINGSWORTH, Ralph, Eng. svt., plasterer, ran away from Richard ADAMS, Richmond (VGPu 29 Dec 75)
CHILTON, Col. Charles, late rep. of Fauquier Co., d. Fri. 25 Feb. 1791 [long obit.] (VGGA 28 Sep 91, VGWA 8 Oct 91)
CHISURE, John, of Norfolk, intends to leave Va. next spring and settle in the island of Nevis (VGR 30 Aug 70)
CHISM, John, Negro, c. 21, belongs to William GODARD on Lynch's Cr., Peedee River, S. Carolina, jailed in Norfolk (NHPA 3 Nov 96)
CHISMAN, Thomas, of York Co., d. Mon. after a short illness (VG 5 Apr 70); e.a.w. his ex., Diana CHISMAN, John CHISMAN, and John TOOMER of York Co. (VG 24 Jun 73)
CHISWELL, Charles, of Hanover Co., d. in Wmsbrg. on 4 Apr. of pleurisy and flux (VG 8 Apr 37)
CHISWELL, Col. John, who lately killed Robert ROUTLIDGE, d. last Wed., 15 Oct at his home in Wmsbrg. after a short illness (VG 17 Oct 66, NYM 3 Nov 66, NYPB 13 Nov 66)
CHOICE Family, Franklin Co. Ct. of Q.S, 7 May 1799, in chanc: James SMITH & Co. (compl.) against Tully CHOICE, John CHOICE, William CHOICE, Cyrus CHOICE, and Benjamin COOK (defs.); it appears that Tully, Wm., and Cyrus CHOICE are not inhabitants of the state (LWG 13 Jul 99)
CHOWNING, Josiah, of James City Co., dec'd, his admr., James JORDAN and Joseph ATKINSON, will sell all his PE (VGR 23 Apr 72)
CHRISTIAN, Mrs., relict of the late Col. CHRISTIAN and sister of Patrick HENRY Esq., d. at Norfolk on 4 May on her return form the West Indies where she had gone for her health (NPC 8 May 90, VICGA 12 May 90)
CHRISTIAN, Capt. Edward, mar. Miss Harriot RANSONE (PGBA 22 Dec 96)
CHRISTIAN, Israel, intends to move to Fincastle Co. on the Western Waters shortly (VG 4 Feb 73)
CHRISTIAN, Matthias, d. on Sat. last (VCNPGA 19 Oct 93); of Norfolk Co., his admx. is Ann ASHLEY (HNPA 31 Jan 95)
CHRISTIAN, Susannah, dec'd, her ex., Henry VAUGHAN, will sell her HH and KF (VGPu 23 May 77)
CHRISTIAN, Col. William, killed by Indians in Apr. in Ohio (VJAA 25 May 86)
CHRISTIE, Miss Charlotte, only dau. of James CHRISTIE, merch., of Norfolk, formerly of Norwich, Connecticut, d. on Wed. in her 14th yr. (NH 1 Oct 96)
CHRISTIE, Henry, who lately mar. Mr. CARTMELL's dau., of Frederick Co., reportedly killed by Indians on the Salt River (VGWA 25 Jun 88)
CHRISTIE, James, merch., of Norfolk, mar. Miss Esther MOSELEY of Dorchester, Mass. there on the 4th inst. (NH 30 Apr 99)
CHRISTIE, Thomas, appr., upwards of 18, ran away from David CARLILE, Frederick Co. (BVCG 17 Nov 94)
CHRISTMAN, Henry, dec'd, his admr. is John ROWT (BVCG 19 Aug 93)
CHRISTMAN, Isaac, mar. Miss Polly SUTER a few days ago, both of Frederick Co. (BVCG 23 Sep 96)
CHRISTOPHER, David, dec'd, e.a.w. his ex., Will. CHRISTOPHER and Edward FINCH of Mecklenburg (VGPI 28 Dec 86)
CHRISTOPHER, Hannah, from Mecklenburg Co.., d. in the public hospital for lunatics (VGPu 21 Aug 78)
CHURCHILL, Ann (or CHURCHWELL), has ill behaved and forsaken the bed and board of her husb., John CHURCHILL of Norfolk (NHPA 26 Jan 97); she

denies the allegations of her husband and claims that he has another wife, Sarah, living in England whom he mar. in Liverpool; Ann claims that she was mar. to him five yrs. ago by Mr. WHITEHEAD on Norfolk (NHPA 30 Jan 97)

CHURCHILL, Armistead, [dec'd], his ex. (nfi) to sell a tract of his land in Fauquier Co. (VG 22 Aug 66)

CHURCHILL, Mrs. Hannah, of Bushy Park, Middlesex Co., relict of Armistead CHURCHILL Esq., d. in her 70th year; her ex., Benjamin CHURCHILL, will sel all her HH and KF at her late dwelling house in that county (VGPu 13, 20 Sep 76 VG 21 Sep 76)

CHURCHILL, Col. William, dec'd, e.a.w. his admr. with the will annexed, Thomas E. CHURCHILL of Middlesex Co. (VH 21 Jun 99); his admr. will sell 30-50 of his Negroes at Urbanna, Middlesex Co. (VH [22] Nov 99, VGGA 3 Dec 99)

CLACK, Sterling, of Brunswick Co., dec'd, his property there and in Lunenburg Co to be sold pursuant to his will by his ex., James CLACK (VG 30 Jul 52)

CLAGETT, Thomas Esq., of Md., mar. Miss Julia DULANY, dau. of Benjamin DULANY Esq., of Alexandria, on Thurs. eve. last, by the Rev. Thomas DAVIS (CMAG and TAA 14 Apr 98)

CLAIBORNE, Col. Augustine, of Windsor, dec'd, e.a.w. his ex., John H. CLAIBORNE (VIC 20 Jun 87)

CLAIBORNE, Bathu[r]st Esq., of Windsor in Sussex Co., mar. Miss Polly CLAIBORNE [sic] of Manchester on Thurs. the 8th inst. (RMA 17 Sep 96)

CLAIBORNE, Herbert, of Sussex, mar. Miss Molly RUFFIN of Kg. Wm. Co. (VG 2 Nov 73)

CLAIBORNE, Herbert Esq., mar. Miss Polly BROWNE, both of Kg. Wm. Co. (VG Mar 81)

CLAIBORNE, Leigh, intends to set out for the Western Country in a few days and has appointed his father, William CLAIBORNE, living near Manchester, his attorney (VGRMA 9 Jan 94)

CLAIBORNE, Capt. Leonard, of Dinwiddie Co., d. on the 8th inst. in his 84th year (VGAA 27 May 85)

CLAIBORNE, Mrs. Mary, sp. of William CLAIBORNE of New Kent Co., died (VGWeA 20 Apr 82)

CLAIBORNE, Philip Whitehead, d. a few days after being elected a rep. for Kg. V Co. (VG 5 Dec 71); e.a.w. his ex., Carter BRAXTON, Peter LYONS, and George BROOKS (VG 2 Apr 72)

CLAIBORNE, Richard, of Lunenburg Co., dec'd, e.a.w. his ex., Edward DUDLEY Amelia Co. and William WARRICK, who will also sell all of his PE (VGPu 4 Oct 76, VG 24 Jul 79)

CLAIBORNE, Capt. Richard, of Lunenburg Co., [dec'd], e.a.w. his ex., Charles HAMBLIN Jr. (VG 16 Oct 78)

CLAIBORNE, Thomas, attorney at law, mar. Miss ROBINSON of Pr. Anne (VG 1 Jan 75)

CLAIBORNE, Thomas, dec'd, e.a.w. his ex., Arthur BOUSH and John WILSON o Norfolk (VG 19 Mar, 4 Sep 79)

CLAIBORNE, William Esq., of Hanover, mar. Mrs. BLACK of Chesterfield Co. on Sat. last (VGAA 3 May 83)

CLAIBORNE, William Charles Cole Esq., re-elected to represent Tennessee in Congress on the 1st inst., mar. Miss LEWIS of Nashville on 12 Aug. (VGGA 27 Aug 99)

CLAIBOURNE, Mrs. Elizabeth, cons. of Bathurst CLAIBOURNE of Dinwiddie C d. on Fri. the 12th inst. in Chesterfield Co.; she survived her marriage only sever days; [obit. in 23 Jun issue describes her as the dau. of Col. John BOTT of Chesterfield Co.][eulogy] (VGPI 16, 23 Jun 95)

CLAIBOURNE, William Presley, dec'd, his ex., Buller CLAIBOURNE, will sell p of his land in Sussex Co. (VGPI 25 Mar 96); his ex. will sell several of his Negroe in Dinwiddie Co. (VGPI 3 Jan 97)

CLARE, Edmund, dec'd, his ex., T. THROCKMORTON and James GIBBS, will se his furniture and livestock (BVCG 7 Dec 95)

CLARK, Mr., merch., of Norfolk, of the firm of Clark and Bixby, d. on Sun. (HNPA

Apr 95)
CLARK, Celia, mulatto girl, 14 yrs. old last Mar., ran away from her father, Gilly CLARK, in Richmond and is believed to be in Louisa Co. near Green Springs (DOB 17 Sep 98)
CLARK, David, Irish svt., wool comber and tobacco spinner, ran away from Alexander RAMSAY, York Co., Pa. (VGR 1 Aug 71)
CLARK, David Esq., senator for the district of Halifax, Charlotte, etc., d. on Sat the 17th ult. (VGGA 19 Jul 97)
CLARK, Edward, from St. Peter's of Hungate, Norwich, Co. Norfolk, Eng., says he has a brother, William CLARK, who came to Va. in 1724 and lived on Timber Neck Cr., James River; if William will apply to Mary ELLIS in Kg. Wm. Co. he may hear further particulars of the sd. Edward who is the only one of the family in England without heir (VGR 1 Jun 69)
CLARK, George, adv. that his wife, Mary CLARK, has betaken herself to drink and he will no longer pay any debts of her transacting (VGGA 12 Oct 91)
CLARK, George, of Richmond, intends to depart for Ky. about the last of next month (VGRC 30 Sep, 14 Oct 94)
CLARK, James, Irish svt., 28, ran away from James MOUNTGOMERY, Amherst Co. (VGR 22 Dec 68)
CLARK, John, Eng. svt., ran away from John MERCER, Marlborough, Stafford Co. (VG 2 May 55)
CLARK[E], Nancy, age about 15, murdered by David YOWELL in Culpeper Co. on Sun. eve. [30 Sep.] (VHFA 11 Oct 92, AGNPWA 17 Oct 92, BVCG 22 Oct 92)
CLARK, Robert, dec'd, e.a.w. his admr., Samuel INGLIS (VGNI 20 Apr 75)
CLARK, Samuel, svt., 33, cooper, imported from London on the *Lord Camden*, ran away from George LESLIE, Portsmouth (VG 26 Jan 69)
CLARK, Thomas, of Alexandria, mar. Miss Elizabeth JONES of Pr. Geo. Co., Md. on Thurs. eve. in Md., by the Rev. Mr. MESSENGER (CMAG 28 Sep 99)
CLARK, William, svt., joiner, c. 19, ran away from Stephen MITCHELL (VGP 7 Jul 75)
CLARK, William, of Norfolk, dec'd, his est. to be sold by his admr., Robert BAIN, baker (NPJ 26 Nov 88)
CLARK, Zachariah, appr. house carpenter, ran away from William M'KIM who supposes he has gone to Hanover Co. where he has relatives (RMA 13, 30 Jan 96); his brother, William CLARK of Kg. Wm. Co., adv. that he was illegally bound to M'KIM (RMA 27 Jan 96)
CLARKE, Arthur, svt., 26-27, ran away from Paul MENITREE, New Kent Co. (VG Jan 40)
CLARKE, Francis, dec'd, of Louisa Co., Wm. CLARKE ex. of Isaac CLARKE who was ex. of Francis CLARKE, dec'd, will sell his land there (VGGA 16 Nov 96)
CLARKE, Gedney, HCC, 9 May 85, Wm. VAUNS of Massachusetts (pltf.) against Gedney CLARKE ex., devisee, and heir at law of Gedney CLARKE dec'd, Mary CLARKE widow and relict of the sd. Gedney, and Bryan FAIRFAX late attorney in fact or agent for the sd. Gedney CLARKE dec'd and others (defs.); it appears that Gedney CLARKE and Mary CLARKE are not inhabitants of the country; notice to be published in Truro Par., Fairfax Co. (VGAA 16 Jun 85)
CLARKE, James Jr., dec'd (Arg 1 Oct 99)
CLARKE, John, late of Richmond, dec'd, his joiner's tools, HHF, and 1000 ac. of land in Ky. to be sold by his ex., Robert CRAIG and William McKECHNIE (Arg 2 Jul 99)
CLARKE, Stephen, ind. svt., tailor, c. 33, ran away from the *Lord Clive* at Norf. he may have gone to N. Carolina or to Sir Peyton SKIPWITH's plant. on the forks of Roanoke where his wife's brother, Robert READER (who came into the country on the same ship upwards of two yrs. ago) lives (VG 5 Dec 71, VGR 6 Feb 72)
CLARKE, Walter, Irish, c. 21, supposed to be a svt. of John CAMPBELL, merch. near New London in Bedford Co., jailed in Wmsbrg. (VGPu 16 Feb 76)
CLARKE, William, late of the house of Clarke and Bixby, dec'd, his [ex.] are Christ. FRY and John KEITH (NH 12 Mar 96)
CLARKE, Zachariah, HCC, 8 Mar 1797, between John SHORE surviving ex. of Jn.

SMITH (pltf.) and Lucy CLARKE extx. and Peter FOSTER ex. of Zachariah CLARKE dec'd (VGGA 7 Jun 97)

CLARY, Matthew, Irish svt., c. 25, ran away from William M'PHERSON, Berkeley Co. (VGWA 18 Mar 89)

CLASBY, Moses, aka Robert FOX, Negro, 24-25, says he belongs to John CORBII Kg. Wm. Co., jailed in Culpeper Co. (VGGA 12 Dec 92, 2 Jan 93)

CLAUSEL, John B., d. in Mecklenburg Co. on Sat. sennight (Arg 23 Jul 99)

CLAY Family, Pittsylvania Co., Ct. of Q.S, 20 Aug 1798, in chanc: William THORNTON and Lucy his wife (pltfs.) against Martha CLAY widow and relict of Charles CLAY dec'd, Eleazer CLAY, Charles CLAY, Thomas CLAY, Matthew CLAY, Green CLAY, Stephen LOCKETT and Mary his wife, [?] MURRAY and Betty his wife, Priscilla CLAY, and Martha CLAY (defs.) (VGGA 4 Jan 99)

CLAY, Agnes, has eloped from her husband, William CLAY of Cumberland Co. (VG 22 Sep 68)

CLAY,. Charles, of Powhatan Co., dec'd, his ex., Green CLAY, will sell his HHF and settle his est. then return to Ky. after the Oct. session of the GA (VIC 9 Sep 89); his ex. will; sell all his PE in Powhatan Co. (VICGA 10 Feb 90)' his ex. will; sell six of his slaves (VGGA 3 Sep 94)

CLAY, James, merch., of Richmond, lost at sea, 6 Jan. (VGAA 1 Feb 83)

CLAY, John, of Hanover Co., dec'd, items of his est. to be sold (VGAA 4 Jan 83)

CLAY, Sir. John, dec'd, his 460 ac. tract will be sold by his ex., Nathaniel WILKINSON and Richard CHAPMAN (VGIC 1 Nov 88)

CLAY, M., adv. that last Nov., he gave his bond to a certain John CALL then of Pittsylvania Co. but now of Mecklenburg Co. (RMA 4 Oct 96)

CLAY, Perciball, svt., blacksmith, ran away from Francis BROWN, Northumberland Co., (VG 31 Jul 46)

CLAYBORNE, William, and Frances his wife, will pet. the next GA to discontinue the ferry established from Rockets in Henrico Co. to the lands of William BLAC] on the opposite side in Chesterfield Co. (VGWeA 25 Sep 84)

CLAYPOOLE, Septimus, one of the proprietors of the *American Daily Advertiser*, Baltimore, mar. Miss Elizabeth POLK at the seat of Col. Nathaniel RAMSAY, Carpenter's Point, Cecil Co., [Md.] (VHFFA 23 Jun 97)

CLAYTON, Mrs., spouse of Jasper CLAYTON Esq. of Gloucester Co., died (VGPu : Mar 77 sup)

CLAYTON, Capt. Jasper Esq., of Gloucester Co., died; e.a.w. his ex., William CLAYTON, who will also sell all of his HH and KF (VG 22 May 79, 17 Jul 79)

CLAYTON, John Esq., H.M's Attorney General and Judge of the Court of Vice Admiralty of the Colony, First Justice of the Peace of James City Co., d. at his house on 18 Nov. (VG 18 Nov 37)

CLAYTON, John, clerk of Gloucester Co., died (VG 6 Jan 73); e.a.w. his ex., Willia CLAYTON of New Kent (VG 3 Feb 74, VGR 10 Feb 74)

CLAYTON, John Jr. Esq., son of Jasper CLAYTON Esq., of Gloucester Co., d. the lately [eulogy in VGP] (VG and VGP 13 Oct 74)

CLAYTON, Milly, her husband, William CLAYTON of Norfolk, will no longer pay her debts (VCGA 16 Jun 94); has absconded from her husband (NHPA 14 Dec 9

CLAYTON, Philip, mentioned in a Culpeper Co. chancery case as ex. and heir at law of Samuel CLAYTON dec'd (VH 25 Sep 98)

CLAYTON, Richard, mar. Mrs. Ann BRAGG relict of James BRAGG (of Richmon Co.) on the 10th inst. in that co. (VHFA 24 Oct 93)

CLAYTON, Thomas M.D., of Gloucester Co., son of the late Attorney General [Jo CLAYTON], d. lately (VG 26 Oct 39)

CLAYTON, Dr. Thomas, late of Gloucester Co., dec'd, e.a.w. his ex., Thomas WHITING (VGPu 16 Jun 75)

CLEALING, Andrew, Irish, carpenter and joiner, c. 25, jailed as a runaway in Elizabeth City jail (VGPu 20 Oct 75)

CLEAR, Richard, ind. svt., 30-40, joiner and house carpenter, calls himself Eng. believed to be Irish, ran away from John TURBERVILLE, Westmoreland Co. (VGNI 26 Jul 75)

CLELAND, Mrs. Margaret, spouse of Dr. W. C. CLELAND physician, d. at

Hamilton,. Scotland, on Mon. 5 Jun. last; she was the dau. of James ALLEN of Fredsbrg. (VIC 16 Aug 86)
CLEMENTS, Dr. Ewen, dec'd, his admrs., Pitman CLEMENTS and Meriwether SMITH, will settle his est. (VG 27 Oct 74)
CLEMENTS, Dr. John, dec'd, 40 of his slaves to be sold at Hobb's Hole by his ex., Pitman CLEMENTS (VG 22 Dec 68) [see above, Dr. Ewen CLEMENTS]
CLEMISON, George, of the house of Clemison and Johnson, merchants in Norfolk, d. in Charleston S. Carolina on 11 Aug. (AGGA 26 Aug 96)
CLENDENNING, Sarah, left her husband, Andrew CLENDENNING, on the night of the 13th inst. (BVCG 25 May 95)
CLERK, Alexander, Scottish svt., ran away from Francis WILLIS, Gloucester Co. (VG 10 Apr 52)
CLERK, James, svt., c. 27, speaks the Yorkshire intermixed with the brogue, ran away from Roger NORTH, Staunton, Augusta Co., who has learned that he worked in Louisa, Kg. Wm., and Hanover cos. and that he intended to work at ditching in Spotsylvania Co. (VGPu 16 Jun 75)
CLERK, Patrick, Irish svt., weaver, ran away from Lawrence WASHINGTON, Stafford Co., VGR 18 Jul 71)
CLERK, Philip, Irish svt., imported in the *Justitia*, ran away from a vessel at Fredsbrg. (VGR 26 Jan 69)
CLIFT, William Wombwell, of Hanover Co., d. of pleurisy some months ago at an advanced age; he was of a good family in Yorkshire (VG 10 Jun 37)
CLINCH, Christopher, dec'd, e.a.w. his admr., Samuel YEARGAN (VG 9 May 71)
CLOPTON, the Rev. Mr., d. at his seat in Cumberland Co. on 21 Dec. leaving a wife and five chil. (VGGA 30 Dec 95)
CLOPTON, Benjamin, dec'd, e.a.w. his admr., Waller CLOPTON and John BARNARD (VGGA 24 Aug 91)
CLOPTON, Mrs. Jenny, cons. of George CLOPTON, d. on 17 Dec. in Richmond in her 66th year leaving a husb. and six chil. (VGGA 30 Dec 95)
CLOUGH, Richard, late of Hanover Co., dec'd, part of his est. on Beaver Cr. in Louisa Co. to be sold by Mary CLOUGH, John CHISWELL, and Henry ROBINSON his exors. (VG 17 Oct 51)
CLOYD, David, living on waters of the James River not far from Looney's Ferry; his son reportedly killed on 20 Mar. by Indians (Philadelphia disp. of 3 May citing a letter from Staunton, Va.) (NYPB 10 May 64)
CLOYD, Michael, of Botetourt Co., adv. that his wife, Elizabeth CLOYD, eloped without any lawful reason and carried with her two of his chil. together with a considerable part of his property (VGAA 26 Feb 85)
CLUVERIUS, John, des. from the *Henry* galley (VGPu 6 Jun 77)
COAKER, Joseph, Virginian, des. from Capt. George MERCER's co. of Va. forces at Ft. Cumberland (VG 22 Aug 55)
COATES, Max., carpenter, d. on Fri. (NH 3 Oct 96)
COBBETT, Henry "Harry", dec'd, his widow and admx., Anne COBBETT of New Kent, desires to settle his est. (VG 13 Jun, VGPu 20 Jun 77 sup)
COBBS, Edmund, dec'd, e.a.w. his admr., Sarah COBBS and John L. COBBS of Bedford Co. (LWG 2 Mar 99)
COBIDGE, John, svt. from Essex Co., executed on 23 Nov. for the murder of a Negro (VG 23 Nov 39)
COBOGGEN, Peter Goffegon, c. 22, went away from Portsmouth and is supposed going to Beaufort, N. Carolina (VG 30 Jan 72)
COCHRAN, David, d. on the 27th ult. at New Castle in Hanover (VGGA 10 Oct 92)
COCHRAN, David, dec'd, his ex., Francis IRWIN (or IRVIN) and extx., Lucy COCHRAN, will sell 1940 ac. of his land in Fluvanna Co. (VGGA 16 Jul 94)
COCHRAN, James, merch. of Staunton, mar. Miss Magdalene MOFFETT dau of George MOFFETT Esq., of Augusta Co., on 6 Dec. (BVCG 24 Dec 92)
COCHRAN, Thomas, merch. of Fredsbrg., mar. Miss Betsey HANSBOROUGH dau. of Peter HANSBOROUGH of Kg. Geo. Co. (VHFA 16 Aug 92)
COCHRAN, William, dec'd, his ex., James COCHRAN, William COCHRAN, and Thomas [CURLET], will sell 450 ac. of his land in Frederick Co. (WG 20 Feb 99)

COCKE, Mrs., wife of John COCKE of Caroline Co., was delivered of a dead child which she had carried for upwards of 10 yrs. (VHFA 3 Feb 91)

COCKE, Col. Allen, of Surry Co., died (VGCD 9 Dec 80); his est. will be sold at his plant. in Fluvanna Co., in Goochland Co., and in Surry by his ex., Richard COCKE and Samuel KELLO (VGGA 23 Nov 91); his admrs. [sic], KELLO and COCKE, having been engaged in the admin. of his est. for several yrs., desire to close their transactions (VGGA 26 Feb 94)

COCKE, Mrs. Ann, d. at Swan's Point, Surry Co. on Fri. last, 22 May (VGPI 29 May, RMA 30 May 95)

COCKE, Capt. Benjamin, of Pr. Geo. Co., dec'd, his ex., James COCKE and Pleasant COCKE, will sell part of his PE (VG 17 Sep 72)

COCKE, Bowler Esq., d. at his seat at Shirley (VG 22 Aug 71)

COCKE, Col. Bowler Jr., dec'd, his ex., George WEBB, will sell a tract of his land in Hanover Co. (VG 19 Nov 72); his ex. will sell his livestock, HH and KF at his plant at Bremo (VG and VGP 1 Dec 74)

COCKE, Bowler, of Henrico, mar. Miss Molly WEBB of New Kent Co. (VG 14 Jan 7

COCKE, Charles, has determined to remove to a distant part of the state and will sell his farm in Charles City Co. (RMA 6 Jan 96)

COCKE, Edward, dec'd, his admx., Elizabeth COCKE, will sell his PE which includes material for a vessel calculated for Appomattox River with a 40-foot keel (VGR 23 Apr 72)

COCKE, Elizabeth, of Charles City Co., dec'd, her ex., John EDLOE, will sell all of her est. and rent her tract on the James River (VGPu 14 Nov 77)

COCKE, Col. Hartwell, Rep. for Surry Co., d. of a lingering illness (VG 23 Jul 72); his ex., John Hartwell COCKE, will sell his tract of tobacco land in Lunenburg Co. (VG 29 Oct 72)

COCKE, Henry, of Surry Co., dec'd, his ex., Lemuel COCKE, will sell all his PE at his plant. on the Otterdam Swamp in Surry Co. (VG 28 Nov 77)

COCKE, James Esq., of Wmsbrg., d. on Mon. (VGWeA [26] Jan 86)

COCKE, Col. John Hartwell, late of Surry Co., dec'd, e.a.w. his ex., William M'KENZIE and Richard COCKE Jr., who will also sell his plant. in Buckingham Co. (VGGA 16 Mar 91, 17 Oct 92); his ex., Richard COCKE of Surry Co., will leas a tract of his in Surry on which Robert COCKE now lives (VGGA 30 Sep 95 ps)

COCKE, Littlebury, dec'd, his extx., Rebecca Hubbard COCKE, will sell his PE at Westbury in Charles City Co. (VG and VGR 23 Sep 73); a tract of land in Charle City Co. which descended to him on the death of his mother, Mrs. Mary TYRIE, will be sold by Rebecca H. COCKE, James B. JOHNSON, and Rebecca JOHNSC (VG 15 Sep 74)

COCKE, Miss Lucy R., dau. of Richard COCKE Esq. of Greyland, Surry Co., d. on Thurs. the 11th inst. at Capt. William THOMPSON's in Halifax Co. (VGRMA 29 Sep 94)

COCKE, Richard, of Surry Co., mar. Miss Nancy CLAIBORNE, dau. of Col. Augustine CLAIBORNE, on the 19th ult. (VG 1 Dec 68)

COCKE, Col. Richard, d. on Thurs. last at his house in Surry Co. (VGR 12 Mar 72

COCKE, Richard, of Brunswick Co., dec'd, e.a.w. his ex., Lemuel COCKE (VGR 25 Nov 73)

COCKE, Robert, d. at his own house in Surry Co. on Tues. the 7th inst. in his 29th [obit. includes a poem /s/ "Maria" and a 2-line poem /s/ "Young." (VGPI 14 Jun 96); his admr., John NEWSUM of Cabin Point, will sell part of his PE at his pla in Southampton Co. (VGPI 29 Nov 96); e.a.w. his admr., John NEWSUM (Ex 2 Aug 99)

COCKE, Miss Susan, d. at Cabin Point on the 6th inst. in the bloom of youth (NH 13 Apr 97)

COCKE, Thomas, his ex., Thomas JOHNSON, will sell the plant. whereon he live on Black Water about 10 miles from Cabin Point containing about 800 ac. (VGWeA 28 Aug 84)

COCKE, Thomas W., of Thomas W. Cocke and Co., of Lynchburg, intends to remo to Ky. in a few weeks (LFG 14 Feb 95)

COCKE, William, late of Surry Co., dec'd, his ex. (nfi) will sell his 3000 ac. tract about three miles from Cabin Point (VG 11 Jul 77)

COCKE, William, dec'd, his surviving admr., Peter JEMM, will sell several Negroes at Cabin Point (VGPI 13 Jan 97)

COCKLE, John, (or COCKIL), Eng. conv. svt., barber, c. 25, has been four-five yrs. in the country, ran away from John ATKINSON, Fredsbrg. (VG 19 Mar 72); ran away from John ATKINSON and James NEWTON, Fredsbrg. (VGR 9 Dec 73)

COCKRAM, Charles, des. from the co. of Capt. Samuel HOPKINS, 6th Va. Regt., and is believed near the forks of the Roanoke (VGPu 11 Apr 77)

COCKRELL, Joseph, of Fairfax Co., dec'd, Susannah COCKRELL admx. of Christopher COCKRELL of Loudoun Co. who was ex. of Joseph COCKRELL dec'd, adv. that sometime in Feb. last, she made a power of attorney to E. ADAMS of Fairfax Co. to collect the money due on a certain number of bonds then in his hands due the est. of Joseph COCKRELL; she now revokes this power of attorney (CMAG 8 Mar 96, BVCG 15 Apr 96); e.a.w his admr., H. GUNNELL (CMAG 22 Sep 96)

CODY, Hannah, her husb., Redmond CODY of Petersburg, adv. that she has acted as a base, wicked, profligate wretch by having robbed him and his child and having absented herself from his house for some time and living in Petersburg and other places in the character of a loose, abandoned woman, that she has taken up with other men equally abandoned particularly with one Charles RICHARDSON at whose house she now resides in Chesterfield Co. and with one COURTNEY who resides in Richmond; he also notes that she consented to live separate from him before the Hustings Ct. of Petersburg on Tues. the 8th inst. (VGPI 15 Sep 95)

CODY, Simon, dec'd, e.a.w. his admr., N. WILKINSON, Norf. (AGNPPA 17 Mar 95)

COE, Joseph, passenger in the brig *Lydia* from Liverpool, d. last night in Norfolk (NHPA 2 Oct 97, NWJCI 4 Oct 97)

COFFEE, William, will pet. the Hon. Speaker and House of Assembly to sell a piece of land in Pr. Edw. Co. that his father (nfi) left his sister Betty who is lunatic and whom he supports (VGGA 17 Aug 96)

COGHLAN, James, carpenter lad, ran away from Pierce PURCELL in Washington; supposed to be lurking in Alexandria as he was seen attending a billiard table there a few days since (TAA 5 Feb 98)

COGO, Charles, mulatto, c. 35, ran away from Richard DENT, Pr. Geo. Co., Md.; he has a sister named Linda HUTTON in Alexandria (VGAxA 16 May 93)

COHAM, Robert, appr., c. 15, ran away from Charles PURCILL, Richmond (VIC 7 Jan 89)

COHAN, Jacob, of Cumberland Co., gives notice that he has been falsely charged with being a des. from Gen. PULASKI's Legion (VGWeA 20 Jul 82)

COHEN, Myer M., a worthy citizen, d. in this city [Richmond] (Ex 29 Jan 99); e.a.w. his admr., Samuel [MYER], who will also receive applications from those who placed watches in the hands of the dec'd (VGGA 26 Feb 99)

COHOON, Dr. Samuel, dec'd, his saw and grist mills on branches of Nansemond River near Suffolk to be sold by John C. COHOON (nfi) (VCNPGA 22 Sep 92)

COKE, John, of Wmsbrg., dec'd, his HH and KF to be sold by his extx., Sarah COKE, and ex., Samuel COKE (VG 12 Jan 69)

COKE, Prestly Thornton, appr., 17-18, ran away from the ship *Eliza* in this port [Alexandria] (CMAG 15 Dec 96)

COKE, Samuel, keeper of Col. BURWELL's Ferry, d. in his 36th yr. leaving a widow and numerous young family (VG 11 Feb 73); his admx., Judith COKE, will sell his PE and will rent his grist mill near Wmsbrg. (VG 18 Nov 73)

COLCLOUGH, Patrick, Irish svt., 24-25, schoolmaster, ran away from Joshua GIST, Frederick Co., Md. (VJAA 4 Nov 84)

COLDWELL, Andrew Jr., dec'd, e.a.w. his ex., Charles McDONALD (PGBA 14 Nov 91)

COLDWELL, Delphia, her husb., Thomas COLDWELL of Pr. Edw. Co., adv. that she has been a naughty and furious housewife for some yrs. and has threatened to ruin him; he will no longer pay any of her debts (VG 21 Jan 75)

COLE, Miss Ann, dau. of William COLE, d. on Sun. last at the hospital of Drs.

STRACHAN and HALL in Pr. Geo. Co. while under the smallpox (VGPI 26 Jul 96)

COLE, David, aka David, Negro, 28-30, ran away from Frankey SEAYRES, Henri Co. (VGGA 9 Jul 99)

COLE, James, svt., ran away from Richard LEE at the Naval Office in Charles Co., Md. on 6 Oct. (VG 24 Oct 51)

COLE, Josiah, dec'd, e.a.w. his ex., Heritage HOWERTON and Richard St.JOHN o Essex Co. (VG 6 Nov 79)

COLE, Mary, dec'd, her ex., George BARCLAY, will sell a tract of land apparently bel. to her est. in Goochland Co. (VG 29 Jul 73)

COLE, Dr. Walter K., d. on the 8th ult. at his seat in Jefferson Co. (VGRMA 3 Mar 94)

COLE, Col. William, any of his creditors to contact Capt. Miles CARY of Warwick Co. (VG 1 Sep 38)

COLE, William, svt., 24, ran away from the Patuxent Iron Works in Md. (VG 22 Jun 39)

COLE, William, of Warwick Co., dec'd, 1300 ac. bel. to his est. advertised for rent b Philip EDMONDSON gdn. to the heir at law (VG 21 Nov 55)

COLE, William the elder, by his will devised several specific and pecuniary legaci to his youngest chil. and all the rest to his eld. son, William COLE, on condition he satisfy the sd. pecuniary legacies; he has not done so and John MINGE, Philip EDMONDSON, and William ACRILL warn everyone not to purchase any of the slaves bel. to the elder COLE's est. (VG 27 Jun 66)

COLE, William, of James City Co., dec'd, e.a.w. his ex., Thomas MACHE[T] of Pr. Geo. Co. (VGIC 24 Apr 84)

COLEMAN, Francis, dec'd, his ex., Richard JOHNSTON, will sell his tract of land in Louisa Co. (VG 25 Mar 73)

COLEMAN, Henry, of Halifax Co., mar. Miss Ann GORDON of Petersburg, on Sa eve. the 13th inst. (VGPI 16 Jun 95)

COLEMAN, James, [dec'd], his admx., Betty COLEMAN, and admr., Thomas COLEMAN, will sell all his stock, HH and KF and settle his est. at his dwelling house at Orange [Ct. H.] (VHFFA 25 Nov 96)

COLEMAN, John, aka John NABB, Irish svt., ran away from John RALLS, Caroline Co. (VG 29 Sep 38)

COLEMAN, John, from Hampshire Co., executed near Wmsbrg. on Fri. for felony (VG 11 Dec 66, NYPB 1 Jan 67)

COLEMAN, Richard, dec'd, e.a.w. his ex., Richard COLEMAN and Robert COLEMAN (VHFA 14 Feb 93)

COLEMAN, Richard Jr., dec'd, e.a.w. his admr., Robert S. COLEMAN (VHFA 22 Sep 95)

COLEMAN, Robert, of Petersburg, mar. Miss Betsy HOLT of Wmsbrg. last eve. (VGWeA 24 Dec 85)

COLEMAN, Robert S., dec'd, e.a.w. his ex., Andrew CRAWFORD, Essex Co. (VG 14 Feb 71)

COLEMAN, Samuel, Deputy Collector of the Port of Norfolk, mar. Miss Sally MACLEAN, Sat. last [16 Nov.] at Norfolk (VCNPGA 23 Nov 93, MCent 11 Dec

COLEMAN, Thomas, Londoner, ind. svt., c. 25, committed to York [Co.] prison (VGPu 28 Jul 75)

COLEMAN, William, of Spotsylvania Co., adv. that his wife, Mary COLEMAN, absconded on the 28th of Dec. last and refuses to return home; he will not be answerable for any of her debts (VHFFA 4 Mar 96)

COLEMAN, Maj. Wyatt, late of Wmsbrg., d. on Sat, eve. last in [Richmond] after a very short illness (VGGA 13 Dec 97)

COLEMAN, Wyatt Sr., of this city [Richmond], d. this morn. (RMA 1 Aug 95)

COLEMAND, Bob, mulatto slave, 25, ran away from John HARDAWAY (VGR 2 May 71)

COLES, the Hon. Isaac Esq., Rep. from Va. to Congress, mar. Miss Catharine THOMPSON dau. of James THOMPSON of New York City, in that city on 2 J (VHFA 21 Jan 90)

COLES, Thomas, mariner, brother of William COLES, sailed from the Thames in a transport for Cork and from thence to Boston about the beginning of the late American War and is supposed to have settled in some part of the continent, is asked to send word to Mr. BRADFORD, printer, in Philadelphia, to hear something greatly to his advantage (VJAA 13 Jul 86)

COLES, Walter, Rep. in Assembly for Halifax Co., mar. Miss Mildred LIGHTFOOT dau. of the late William LIGHTFOOT of Charles City Co. (VG 19 Mar 67)

COLES, Walter Esq., of Albemarle Co., mar. Miss Eliza F. COCKE eld. dau. of Bowler COCKE Esq. of Turkey Island (VGGA 15 Nov 97)

COLES, Capt. William, late of Hanover Co., dec'd, his livestock to be sold by his admr., William DARRICOATT (VGAA 5 [Dec] 85)

COLFER, James, a young man of Pr. Anne Co., d. at Kempsville, Thurs. night last (VCNPGA 13 Oct 92); all his stock of dry goods to be sold by his ex., John KENNEDY and James LEAHY (VCNPGA 15 Dec 92)

COLL, Daniel, Negro, c. 30, ran away from Benjamin TALBOTT, Fairfax Co. (CMAG 20 Jun 97)

COLLAHAN, John, Irish, barber, des. from Capt. James MACKILWEAN's Co. at Petersburg (VG 19 Jul 54)

COLLARD, Samuel, of Alexandria, died (VJAA 22 Dec 85)

COLLET, Simon, svt., ran away from Col. SPOTSWOOD, Spotsylvania Co. (AWM 13 Apr 32)

COLLEY, Edward (or COLLY), late of Norfolk Co., dec'd, e.a.w. his ex., Baylor HILL of Norfolk (AGNPPA 17 Mar 95, HNPA 24 Aug 95)

COLLEY, Capt. William, mar. Miss Polly WILLOUGHBY, Thurs. eve. last (VCGA 2 Jun 94)

COLLIER Family, K & Q Co., Ct. of Q.S, 14 Aug 98, in chanc: John M'DOUALL and John JOHNSON surviving partners of John M'DOUALL (pltfs.) against Charles COLLIER survivor of Catherine COLLIER and Charles COLLIER extx. and ex. of John COLLIER dec'd, and Joseph COLLIER, Francis COLLIER, and Benjamin COLLIER (defs.); it appears that Charles COLLIER is not an inhabitant of this state (VGGA 2 Oct 98)

COLLIER, Edward, mar. Miss Elizabeth HUTCHESON, both of Richmond, on Sat. eve. last. (RC 16 Feb 96, RMA 17 Feb 96)

COLLIER, Lockey, of Elizabeth City Co., was murdered in his bed by his own Negroes in the night of the 29th ult. (VG 6 Nov 78)

COLLINS, Charles, d. in [Fredsbrg.] on Tues. last in an advanced age., he was a soldier in the Revolutionary War (VH 11 Oct 99)

COLLINS, Elijah, c. 22, his real name is Evan HARRY and he is the son of a gunsmith who formerly lived near the Brick Meetinghouse in Nottingham or Chester Co., Pa., des. from the Va. Regt. in Winchester (MG 8 Jul 62)

COLLINS, Jacob, Negro, c. 25, says he was once a slave, but was liberated by Joseph TURPIN, a Quaker, residing in Caroline Co., Md. (VIC 21 Jan 89); claims to be free and that he fought in the army of LAFAYETTE; jailed in Alexandria (VGAxA 5 Nov 89)

COLLINS, John, aka John BUTLER, Irish, allegedly robbed Matthew MAYES Jr. of Pr. Geo. Co. (VG 7 Dec 39)

COLLINS, John, carpenter of Richmond, d. yesterday eve. (VGRMA 4 Sep 94)

COLLINS, John, dec'd, e.a.w. his ex., William RICHARDSON of Richmond, who will sell all his PE (VGGA 12 Nov 94, 22 Apr 95)

COLLINS, John, aka Wiatt, mulatto, blacksmith, has a wife at Robert MORTON's in Culpeper Co. who is shortly to be removed to Ky., ran away from Gawin CORBIN, Caroline Co. (VHFA 6 Oct 95)

COLLINS, Owen, Negro, ran away from Henry COLLINS with his brother James; they have been seen lurking around Norfolk or on Broad Cr. (NH 2 Jun 98)

COLLINS, Thomas, of Hampshire Co., was found murdered on the night of Sat. the 18th inst. (VGWA 23 Apr 91)

COLLONEY, Richard, aka James O'DANIEL, Irish svt., ran away from Robert RENNOLDS, Caroline Co. (VG 29 Sep 74)

COLOUGNAC, John James, a French gentleman lately from New York, d. in

Richmond on Thurs. after a short illness (VGAA 4 Feb 86)
COLTON, William, ind. svt., ran away from John TURBERVILLE, Westmoreland Co. (VGNI 26 Jul 75)
COLVILLE Family, HCC, 4 Jun 96: George WASHINGTON, surv. ex. of Thomas COLVILLE (pltf.) and Thomas WEST ex., devisee, and heir at law of John WEST Jr. dec'd, who was one of the ex. of Thomas COLVILLE and the nearest relations of Catherine COLVILLE mother of the sd. Thomas COLVILLE of the names of STOT, WELLS (or WILLS), RICHARDSON, and SMITH or their descendants (defs.) (VGGA 6 Jul 96, CMAG 5 Dec 97)
COLVILLE, Col. Thomas Gent., formerly of Cecil Co., Md. where he was a rep., d. lately at Clish near Alexandria, aged 78 (MG 30 Oct 66); 600 ac. of his land in Fairfax Co. to be sold by his ex., Frances COLVILLE, George WASHINGTON, and John WEST Jr. (VGR 24 Dec 67)
COLVIN, John, dec'd, his admr., Roger STEWART, will sell his schooner in Portsmouth (VG 9 Dec 73)
COMBS, James, who left London about five yrs. ago to settle in Va., is hereby informed that his son, Richard COMBS, is now at Mr. [WOOTTON's] in Hampton and would be glad to know where he resides (VGPu 1 May 78)
COMPTON, John, dec'd, his extx., Catharine COMPTON of Richmond, will sell all of the goods and HHF (Arg 3 Jan 97)
COMPTON, William, aka William SMITH, late of Norborne Par., Berkeley Co., shoemaker, convicted of murder at the District Ct. of Winchester, escaped from jail in that town last Sep. and is now at large (VGGA 24 May 97)
COMRIE, Mrs. Margaret, wife of Dr. William COMRIE, d. at his house in Kg. Wm Co. on 9 Jun.; she was the niece to the late Thomas PARRATT (a Register in chancery) and sister to Josias BAINTONE (one of the present six clerks of sd. office) (VG 15 Jun 39)
CONDON, Patrick, aka William PETRE, Irish svt., 23, ran away from J. G. DOWDALL in Winchester in Nov. 1784; he had been imported into Alexandria in Jul. 1784 (VJAA 23 Dec 84); he was jailed in Dumfries then released and may now be in Falmouth (VJAA 24 Nov 85)
CONERLY, James, murdered by his svt., Day THOROUGHGOOD of Augusta Co. who was executed 10 Jan 1752 (VG 12 Dec 51, 10 Jan 52)
CONLEY, John, appr., 20, ran away from Esme SMOCK, Dumfries (VGAR 14 Jun 92)
CONLIFFE, John, mar. Miss Esther HUGHES, both of Richm. (VGWeA 15 Oct 85
CONNALY, Charles, dec'd, e.a.w. his ex., John W. CONNALLY of Nottoway (VGP 10 Nov 91)
CONNEL, Margaret, aka SULLIVANE, Irish svt., 40-50, ran away from Richard TAYLOR, Petersburg (VG 19 Sep 55)
CONNER, Mrs., aka Anne SLAUGHTER, persons are warned against trusting h or carrying her out of the state (VIC 24 Sep 88)
CONNER, Barney, Irish svt., 30, came from Cork in the summer of 1784 on the *Washington*, ran away with his wife and son, probably to Baltimore, from the es of Henry LYLES dec'd (VJAA 6 Jul 86)
CONNER, Bryan, executed for murder, 18 Nov. (VG 21 Oct, 18 Nov 37)
CONNER, Charles, son of Lewis CONNER, late of Norfolk, may hear something t his advantage by applying to William WISHART of Pr. Anne Co. (VGR 11 Mar 7
CONNER, James, dec'd, his admx., Frances CONNER, will sell 43 ac. of his land i Caroline Co. (VHFA 22 Aug 93)
CONNER, John, svt., sailmaker, ran away from Patrick CREAGH, Annapolis, [M (VG 15 Oct 36)
CONNER, Peter, Irish svt., ran away from Goochland Ct. H. (VGPu 14 Jun 76)
CONNER, Thomas, Irish svt., imported in the *Justitia*, ran away from a vessel at Fredsbrg. (VGR 26 Jan 69)
CONNOLLY, Dennis, conv. svt., c. 25, ran away from Michael COAGAR in the lower end of Rockingham Co. (VGPu 12 Jun 78)
CONOLLY, John, expert mechanic in the blacksmith business, Norfolk, d. on Sun [26 Oct.] leaving a wife and three chil. (NPJ 29 Oct 88, VGWeA 6 Nov 88)

CONOLY, William, Irish svt., 16-17, ran away from John DALTON and Robert ADAM, Alexandria (VGR 23 Jul 67)
CONOR, Nancy, svt., maid, ran away from John BOZLEY (PGBA 28 Dec 97)
CONRAD, Dr. Daniel, of Winchester, mar. Miss Rebecca HOLMES on Tues. last at Holmesgrove, Frederick Co., seat of the late Dr. Joseph HOLMES (BVCG 19 Feb 96)
CONRAD, Frederick, late of Frederick Co., dec'd, his stock of leather will be sold by his ex., John CONRAD and Frederick CONRAD (BVCG 27 Jan 94); Frederick CONRAD of Winchester will sell 500 ac. of his land in Hampshire Co. (BVCG 22 Jun 95)
CONRAD, Frederick Jr., of Winchester, mar. Miss Fanny THRUSTON on 25 Apr. at Mt. Sion the seat of Col. C. M. THRUSTON (BVCG 29 Apr 93)
CONRAD, John, of Winchester, merch., d. last night (BVCG 11 Aug 94); by his death, the partnership of George Hite & Co. is dissolved (PGBA 1 Sep 94); e.a.w. his admx., Elizabeth CONRAD, and his admr., John PEYTON (BVCG 15 Sep 94); Frederick CONRAD, surviving partner of John and Frederick CONRAD, will sell all their stock of leather (BVCG 13 Oct 94)
CONROY, Michael, Irish conv. svt., c. 25, shoemaker, ran away from Philip HALL and Isaac SHORT near Sno[w]den's Iron Works, Pr. Geo. Co., Md. (VGP 21 Sep 75)
CONWAY, James, adv. that his father, Cornelius CONWAY, has adv. that he obtained a deed to the father's lands near Charlestown in Berkeley Co. in a fraudulent manner (PGBA 19 May 94)
COODY, John, from Goochland Co., executed on Fri. last at the gallows near Richmond for the murder of his wife (VIC 11 Jun 88, VGWeA 12 Jun 88)
COOK, Mrs. Comfort, wife of Capt. John COOK of Norfolk and now abroad, d. suddenly on Fri. eve. last [23 Oct] (NPJ 29 Oct 88, VGWeA 6 Nov 88)
COOK, George, dark mulatto svt., bound to age 31, now c. 26, ran away from William KNOX, Culpeper Co. (VGPu 11 Apr 77)
COOK, Henry, dec'd, his est. was put into the hands of Robert YATES by the Gloucester Co. Ct. (VGGA 15 Jun 96)
COOK, Jacob, gunsmith, from Lancaster, Pa., has moved to Richmond to the house occupied by William COOK, coppersmith (Arg 22 Jan 99)
COOK, Roger, mulatto, 28, ran away from Francis EPPES, Pr. Geo. Co. (VGPI 3 Jul 98)
COOK, Thomas, late of Goochland Co., his 5000 ac. est. there to be sold (VG 11 Feb 3
COOKE, Henry, free Negro, b. in Gloucester Co., c. 24, indented to William FLOOD, Westmoreland Co., has run away (VG 19 Apr 70)
COOKE, Mordecai, d. on Tues. 13th inst. at his seat in Gloucester Co. (VGR 22 Feb 70)
COOKE, Thomas, ind. appr., ran away from the ship [*Delight*], Norfolk (HNPA 28 Dec 95, NH 2 Jan 96)
COOKUS Family, Cumberland and Berkeley Cos., Ct. of Q.S, 19 Mar 1790, in chanc: William DARK, Charles MORROW, and John LITTLEJOHN admrs. of Michael WELCH dec'd, (pltfs.) against Catherine COOKUS extx. and Henry BEDINGER ex., Henry COOKUS son and heir at law, Jacob COOKUS, Catherine COOKUS chil. and devisees of Henry COOKUS dec'd and Christian ORANDOEFF (defs.); it appears that ORANDOEFF is not an inhabitant of this county (WVGWA 17 Apr 90)
COOLEY, Elizabeth, wife of Peter COOLEY, Winchester, who will no longer pay her debts (VJAA 10 Aug 86)
[COOLEY], Mrs. Mary, of Wmsbrg., dec'd, John M. GALT, gdn. to the orphan, will settle the est. (VG 23 Jan 78)
COONEY, James, svt., 19-20, ran off in the company of Michael LINDSEY from Thomas HARPER, shoemaker, in Loudoun Co. (VJAA 9 Nov 86)
COONRED, George, murdered by John MOYERS from Greenbrier Co. who was imprisoned in Richmond (VGAA 13 Dec 83)
COONS, John and David, coppersmiths, of Berkeley Co., have opened a shop in Lexington, Ky. (KG 2 Jan 96)

COOPER, Betty, has eloped from her husband Francis COOPER (VGR 1 Aug 71)
COOPER, Charles, of Norfolk, dec'd, e.a.w. his admr., James GUY (VCGA 6 Oct 94
COOPER, Daniel Esq., d. at Longhill on the 15th of May last; he was 100 on the 7t May and was formerly one of the judges of Morrris Co. (nfi) (RJDA 19 Jun 95)
COOPER, Edmund, svt., 40, ran away from James LAIRD, Augusta Co. in Oct. 1768 (VG 14 Apr 68, VGR 7 Sep 69)
COOPER, Joel, of Alexandria, dec'd, e.a.w. his ex., Roger CHEW and William WARD (VJAA 21 Jun 87)
COOPER, John, planter, b. in Surry Co., 20, des. from Capt. Robert HODGSON's Independent Co. now raising for the service and defense of S. Carolina (VG 3 Jul 46)
COOPER, John, and his father, Charles COOPER, of Nansemond Co. will leave the U.S. in a short time (VGGA 12 Dec 92)
COOPER, Capt. Robert, d. yesterday eve. at Portsmouth (NHPA 7 Nov 96)
COOPER, Sal, Negro woman, c. 26, ran away from the est. of John BLAIR, Wmsbrg (VG 21 Nov 71, 27 Feb 72)
COOPER, Sam, Negro, c. 35, ran away from James GOVAN, Kg. Wm. Co., and may be headed for New England (VGGA 23 Mar 91)
COOPER, Will, Va. born Negro, 33, ran away from Peyton SKIPWITH, Pr. Geo. Co (VG 11 Apr 66)
COOPER, William Sr., dec'd, e.a.w. his admr., William COOPER Jr., who will also sell all of his PE (AGNPPA 25 Sep 95)
COOTE, Tom, aka Negro Tom, bel. to Luke CANNON, was found guilty of burgla and sentenced to death on 17 Jul. (RJDA 19 Jun 95)
COPLAND, Peter, of Charles City Co., dec'd, his plant. there to be sold by his ex., Charles COPLAND (VGAA 13 Dec 83)
COPLAND, Richard, apparently of Henry Co., mentioned in HCC case, 14 Mar 17 as the eld. son and heir to Peter COPLAND dec'd. (VGGA 24 Apr 93)
COPPER, Cyrus, vendue-master of Alexandria, died (VJAA 2 Jun 85); e.a.w. his admx., Elizabeth COPPER (VJAA 30 Jun 85)
CORBETT, Zachariah, appr., tailor, 18, ran away from William DUVALL, Alexandria (VJAA 10 May 87)
CORBIN, Francis Esq., of Edenton [N. Carolina], dec'd, his HH and KF to be sold his admx., Jean CORBIN (VGR 11 Aug 68)
CORBIN, Francis Esq., of the Reeds, Caroline Co., mar. Miss BEVERLEY of Esse Co. (VGGA 6 Jan 96)
CORBIN, Gawin Esq., of Caroline Co., mar. Miss Betsey JONES, eld. dau. of Col. Thomas JONES of Northumberland [Co.] (VGPu 10 May 76)
CORBIN, Mrs. Hannah, dec'd, e.a.w. her admr., George TURBERVILLE, who wil' also sell all her PE at Woodberry in Richmond Co. (VGAA 9 Nov 82, VGWeA 16 Nov 82); slaves bel. to her est. to be sold at Pickatone [sic] Mill, Westmoreland C (VGAA 4 Jan 83)
CORBIN, Col. John, all the PE of the late Mrs. Lettice CORBIN dec'd to be sold at Poplar Neck in Caroline Co., a quarter bel. to the est. of Col. John CORBIN dec'e by John TURBERVILLE the admr. (VG 7 Apr 68)
CORBIN, John Tayloe Esq., one of the reps. for K & Q Co., mar. Miss Molly WAL dau. of Benjamin WALLER of Wmsbrg., last Sat. eve. (VG and VGR 21 Feb 71)
CORBIN, Mrs. Martha, wife of Col. Gawin CORBIN, d. at his house in K & Q Co. 12 Jun. (VG 15 Jun 39)
CORBIN, Richard, eld. son. of Col. Gawin CORBIN, mar. Miss Betty TAYLOE da of the Hon. John TAYLOE Esq. (VG 29 Jul 37)
CORBIN, Richard Esq., of Laneville, K & Q Co., d. on Thurs. last in his 77th year [obit.] (VICGA 26 May 90)
CORBIN, Richard Esq., of Laneville, mar. Miss Rebecca Parks FARLEY of Wmsk on Sat. the 15th ult. (HNPA 6 Dec 94)
CORBIN, Richard, [of Middlesex Co.], dec'd, his admr., Thomas CHILTON and William C. BEALE, will sell all his HH and KF (VH 7 Sep 99)
CORBIN, Samuel, mulatto, 23, claims to be free, jailed in Norfolk (NH 10 Nov 98)
CORBIN, Thomas, late of Corbin Hall, Essex Co., dec'd, e.a.w. his ex., Francis

CORBIN and Carter BRAXTON (VH 7 Sep 99, VGGA 17 Sep 99)
CORCORY, Molly, has left her husb., James CORCORY, who adv. that she has behaved imprudently (WVGWA 15 May 90)
CORDILL, James, adv. that he never had anything to do with the est. of William and Sarah SMITH and that it was audited out of the hands of Dorothy CORDILL by Richard E. LEE and Donald CAMPBELL who was her security as an admx. (NH 2 Jan 96)
CORDON, Charles, dark mulatto, 38-41, ran away from John SMITH, Spotsylvania Co and may be heading north (VHFA 5 May 98)
CORGAN, James, Irish svt., 26-27, ran away from Anthony HADEN, Albemarle Co. (VG 21 Mar 71)
CORNHILL, James, Irish svt., 18, ran away from Samuel FOSTER, Pr. Wm. Co. (VHFA 7 May 89)
CORNICK, Amy, of Pr. Anne Co., adv. that she has administered on the est. of John CORNICK late of Pr. Anne, Gent., dec'd, and will also settle the accounts of the late John [SHORTZRAITZ] dec'd (HNPA 3 Dec 95)
CORNICK, Henry, of Norfolk, d. Thurs. [10 Jul.] (VCGA 14 Jul 94); his ex. is Smith BRICKHOUSE, Norfolk (HNPA 17 Jan 95)
CORNICK, John, dec'd, his admx., Amy CORNICK, will sell all of his HH and KF, livestock, and two tracts of land, one in the swamp and the other marsh (AGNPPA 9 Oct 95); e.a.w. his admx., Amy CORNICK of Pr. Anne Co. (NH 14 Jan 96); his admx., of Pr. Anne, Eastern Shore [sic], desires to settle his est. (NH 24 Aug 99)
CORNWALL, John, mar. Miss Kitty BARRAUD of this borough [Norfolk] on Thurs. eve. last (NH 6 Feb 96)
CORRAN, James, merch. of Petersburg, d. in Wilmington, N. Carolina (VGGA 8 Sep 90)
CORRAN, James, Lunenburg Co., Ct. of Q.S, 11 Nov 1796, in chanc: Henry CORRAN admr. of James CORRAN dec'd, which admr. is assignee of Lewis BURWELL surviving ex. of Edward R. YATES dec'd (compl.) against John BARRY, George CRAGHEAD attorney in fact for the sd. John BARRY, and Daniel ROBERTSON (defs.) (VGPI 23 Dec 96)
CORRIDAN, William, dec'd, e.a.w. James MITCHELL, Yorktown (VG 23 May 66)
CORRIE, Capt. John, late of Tappahannock, Essex Co., dec'd, his surviving ex., Beverly ROY of K & Q, will sell his houses and lots in Tappahannock (VGGA 19 Jun 93)
CORYTON, [Jonah], mar. Miss Kitty LYNN on Sun. the 12th inst. in Md. (CMAG 29 Oct 95)
COSBY, Ann, has eloped from her husb., James COSBY of York Co. (VG 24 Aug 76, VGPu 30 Aug 76)
COSBY, Fortunatus, of Louisa Co., intends to move to Ky. early in Oct. and practice law there (VGGA 17 Aug 96); of Fredsbrg., adv. that early in Sep. he intends to move to Ky. where he will settle and practice law (VHFFA 23 Aug 96)
COSBY, James, of Hanover Co., dec'd, e.a.w. his ex. (nfi) (VGGA 8 Feb 92)
COSGRAVE, John, svt., ran away from the ship *Becky* lying in James River; he has been seen in Roanoke (VG 12 Mar 52)
COSTE, Polly, her husb., Joseph COSTE of Norfolk, will not pay any debts she may contract (AGNPPA 5 Apr 96)
COTHMAN, Edward, mar. Miss P. THROGMORTON in Essex Co. on Tues. 3 Nov. (VHFA 29 Nov 92)
COTTON, Jack, Negro bel. to the heirs of Sam. M'CLANAHAN; he is believed to be the father of Theney (a girl) 15, Lucy 8, Primus 13, Jack 5, Jesse 2 by Marie 33, who all ran away from Ambrose KNOX, Nixonton, N. Carolina (VGGA 2 May 92)
COTTON, William Brook, master of the vessel *Dove* in Pasquotank River, has gone off with Polly GRIFFIN wife to John GRIFFIN, millwright, in Pasquotank Co., N. Carolina (VGNI 6 Oct 74)
COUCH, Samuel, of Goochland Co., d. Sun. morn. last (Arg 27 Dec 99)
COULTER, Hugh, intends to depart the colony for Great Britain immediately (VG 7 Nov 54)

COULTER, James, c. 25, jailed in Staunton as a runaway (VGR 10 Mar 74)
COUPLAND, David (or COPELAND), of Cumberland Co., mar. Miss Nancy HARRISON, second dau. of Benjamin HARRISON, at Berkeley, Charles City Co. on 9 Mar. (VGPu 10 Mar 75 sup, VGP 23 Mar 75)
COUPLAND, James, of Chesterfield, dec'd, his est. will be sold by his admr., David COUPLAND (VG 6 Aug 72)
COUPLAND, Joseph, shoemaker, 20, from Kg. Wm. Co., deserted, supposed to be gone to Pr. Edw. Co. (VG 28 Feb 55)
COURTNEY, John, Irish svt., 16-17, ran away from John CORDELL, Frederick C (VJAA 5 May 85)
COURTNEY, Peter, appr. house joiner, ran away from William M'KIM, Richmond (VGGA 22 Jun 91)
COURTNEY, Elder Thomas, Baptist minister of the Church of Christ, Black Cr., New Kent Co., d. in Richmond on the 25th inst. of smallpox (Arg 28 Apr 97)
COURTS, Mary, extx. of William COURTS dec'd, intends to move to Ky. with William COURTS of Culpeper about 20 Oct. next (VH 20 Sep 97)
COURTS, William, of Culpeper Co., dec'd, e.a.w. with his ex., Mary COURTS and Ben. GAINES (VGAA 4 Jan 83)
COURTS, William, dec'd, his admx., Betsey COURTS, will sell sundry articles of his est. in Charles Co., Md. (VGAxA 1 Aug 93)
COUSINS, Adam, of Fluvanna Co., adv. that he enl. with George THOMPSON, th of Albemarle Co. a lieutenant in Capt. BROWN's Co. for the colonial service, upon condition that if he were ever ordered out of Va. he should then be immediately discharged; THOMPSON has refused to honor the agreement (VGPu 28 Nov 77 sup)
COUSINS, John, dec'd, his est. to be sold at the plant. of Richard GRAVES, New Kent Co. by his admrs., William MARSTON and Freeman WALKER (VGR 19 Jan 69)
COUSINS, John, Negro, c. 27, says he bel. to Thomas FRANKLIN on Catawba River, S. Carolina, jailed in Charlotte Co. (VGGA 13 Dec 99)
COUTSMAN, Dr. Jacob, dec'd, the residue of his est. to be sold by Patrick CAVA Leesburg (VJAA 31 May 87)
COUTTS, Patrick, merch. of Richmond, died (VG and VGPu 27 Dec 76); his ex., William COUTTS, will sell all of his PE in Richm. (VG 14 Nov 77); his lots in Richm. to be sold (VGAA 6 Jul 91 sup)
COUTTS, the Rev. William, dec'd, his ex., Alexander M'ROBERT, Benjamin LEWIS, and John M'KEAND, will sell his lots in Richmond and land on Shocko Hill (VICGA 28 Jul 90)
COUZENS, Thomas, of Dinwiddie, adv. that his wife, Fanny COUZENS, has shamefully neglected and laid aside the duties of a Christian and a wife, and he will not be bound by any contracts she may make (VG 18 Sep 79)
Covenented Servants: Joseph HYNES, John BARTHOLEMUS, Nicholas WAL John BUTLER, Michael NOLEN, Timothy WARD, George CRAIG, Richard HARDEN, Francis BRETT aka Francis FITZGERALD, William BRADLEY, Frederick MARION, James M'MULLEN, Thomas GALLAGHER, Matthew WALSH, Michael DUNN, Peter CUNINGHAM, Thomas RUTLEDGE, Abraha KELLEY, Enoch ENNIS, Philip DIGNAN, Michael MERTON, Daniel LEWIS, Henry FRANKS, John WHITSTYENE, Samuel CHAMBERS, Lawrence DOOLAN, James M'GRAW, John KNOX, John MASON, Caleb ATHERTON, James M'INTYRE, James SHEELS, Daniel LANDEN, all ran away from the Potomac Co., Great Falls (VJAA 27 Apr 86)
COWAN, Alexander, of Norfolk, adv. that he qualified to the will of John Savage CALVERT dec'd and administered on the est. of Jonathan CALVERT dec'd and will settle their estates (NH 18 Feb 96)
COWAN, Ebenezer, merch., of Norfolk, d. on Sat. morn.; e.a.w. his ex., Alexander COWAN and James PAUL both of Norfolk (NH 29 Oct, 12 Nov 99)
COWAN, James, from Pa., reportedly killed by Indians on 8 Jul. 100 miles from the Ohio (VG 8 Sep 74)
COWGILL, John, ind. svt., c. 25, ran away from John HARRIS, Hanover Co. (VG

Jul 73)
COWICK, [?], from Albemarle Co, murdered recently; James ROACHE is suspected (VGWeA 2 Aug 87)
COWLES, Thomas, of Charles City Co., mar. Miss Elizabeth CRAWLEY of Wmsbrg. (VG 8 Sep 74); accidentally shot by his overseer on Wed, night last (VIC 22 Nov 86); e.a.w. his admr., Furnea SOUTHALL of Charles City Co. (VGIC 23 Jun 87)
COWLEY, Abraham, of Henrico Co., dec'd, his plant. there to be sold by his admr., John BROOKE (VGAA 3 May, 29 Nov 83)
COWLEY, Abraham, mar. Miss Peggy TANKARD last Sat. (VGIC and VGAA 9 Apr 85)
COWLEY, Mrs. Anne, of Henrico Co., died (VGWeA 16 Mar 82)
COWLING, Charles, appr., c. 17, ran away from the British brigantine *Europe* (NH 16 Oct 98)
COWLING, Josiah, d. after a short illness at his seat in Nansemond Co. in his 56th yr.; he left a wife and four chil.; he was upwards of 20 yrs. in the Methodist Episcopal Church (NH 28 Dec 99)
COWNE, William, mar. Miss Betsey QUARLES [of Kg. Wm. Co.] (VG 5 May 74)
COWPER, Philip, of Elizabeth City Co., dec'd, his ex., Edward COWPER and Roe COWPER, will sell his 160 ac. tract on Harris' Cr. (VG and VGR 17 Mar 74)
COWPER, Capt. Robert, d. Sat. eve. last at Portsmouth (AGGA 8 Nov 96)
COWPER, Wills, of Portsmouth, d. 2 Aug. at Cold Springs (AGGA 30 Aug 96); e.a.w. his son and Admr., John COWPER of Portsmouth (or Norfolk) (AGGA 20 Sep 96, 11 Apr 97, NH 22 Sep 96, NHPA 22 Apr 97); his heirs, John COWPER, Josiah COWPER, William COWPER, and Robert COWPER of Norfolk, will sell his tenements, warehouses, dwelling house, etc. in Suffolk Town (AGGA 7 Oct, 23 Dec 96, 6 Jan 97)
COX, Mrs., wife of Jacob COX, Alexandria, died (VJAA 13 Jan 85)
COX, Archildes, late of Amherst Co., dec'd, e.a.w. his ex., Volentine [sic] COX of Amherst (LFG 1 Nov 94)
COX, Edward, late of Henrico Co., dec'd, his HH and KF to be sold at Wilkinson's in Henrico Co. by his ex.; his est. to be settled with his ex., Joseph FRIEND and George COX (Arg 12 Apr, 26 Jul 99)
COX, Henry Jr., of Amelia, dec'd, his ex. is Francis Eppes HARRIS of Powhatan (VGGA 10 Aug 91)
COX, Howard, dec'd, his land on Mattaponi River in Kg. Wm. Co., where John MARTIN now lives, to be sold next Oct. (VG 31 Jul 46)
COX, John, late of Buckingham Co., dec'd, 1150 ac. of his land in Powhatan Co. to be sold by his ex., Benjamin MOSEBY (VGGA 17 Nov 90)
COX, John, a free mulatto boy, c. 12, native of Lancaster Co., by order of the sd. co. Ct., was bound by the Overseers of the Poor; he was carried off by a certain Jesse GARTON and William CORNELIUS of sd. co. a few weeks past and it is presumed they have sold him as a slave as they were seen in Fredsbrg.; CORNELIUS is c. 47 and GARTON is c. 25 (VHFFA 16 Aug 97)
COX, Mrs. Martha, spouse of Edward COX, d. in Chesterfield on Sat. last (VGRMA 22 Dec 94, VGGA 24 Dec 94)
COX, Mary, wife of John COX of Surry Co. who will no longer pay her debts (VG 20 Oct 52)
COX, Matthew, Virginian, 21, des. from Capt. Thomas WAGGENER's Co. of Va. forces (VG 22 Aug 55)
COX, Thomas, appr., c. 20, ran away from Thomas DAWSON, Yorktown (AGNPWA 19 Mar 94)
COX, Tom, aka Tom, mulatto, c. 40, ran away from the printer in Richmond (VGGA 2 Jul 94)
COX, William, svt., 17, ran away from Andrew CRAWFORD, Hobb's Hole (VG 16 May 71)
COX, William, of Charles Co., Md., mar. Joanna Catharine WEBSTER of Pr. Geo. Co., Md., by this event, Mary, the eld. sister of our informant became aunt, mother, and sister to the sd. William COX (VGAxA 1 Jul 90)
COX, William, of Madison Co., sentenced to death on 10 Jun. for passing counterfeit

money (VGRMA 26 May 94)

COX, William, mar. Miss Elizabeth WHITE on Thurs., both of Powhatan Co. (VGRMA 16 Feb 95, VGGA 18 Feb 95)

COXALL, William Cavalier, Eng. svt., carpenter, c. 20, says he was b. in the West Indies and brought up in London; imported this fall in the *Lord Camden* from London, ran away from George TURBERVILLE, Westmoreland Co. (VGR 29 Nov 70)

COYLE, Nicholas, of Capt. BEATTY's Lt. Inf. Co., Winchester, was badly wounded in an accident and his life is in despair (VHFA 15 May 94)

COYNE, James, sailed from Dublin, Ireland to New York in the ship *Draper* (or *Dragon*, acc. to VGGA) on 13 May 1797; if he will write a few lines to the Rev. James GRIFFIN in Alexandria, he can hear of something very interesting to him; it is certain that he intended settling either at Richmond, Petersburg, or Warrenton, N. Carolina (TDCDA 29 Oct 99, VGGA 10 Dec 99)

COZENS, [?], son of Mrs. COZENS of Gloucester Co., 14-15, murdered last week (VG 24 Nov 38)

CRABB, William, mar. Miss Polly TEMPLEMAN in Westmoreland Co. last Sat. (VHFA 21 Mar 98); letter from John M'CLANNAHAN denies the marriage as a malicious and notorious lie (VHFA 4 Apr 98)

CRAGDALLA, Miss Jenny, of Gosport, d. yesterday after a short illness (VCNPGA 7 Sep 93)

CRAICK, Dr. Robert, of Norfolk, dec'd, medicines and books bel. to his est. to be sol by his admr., Andrew SPROWLE (VG 21 Mar 55)

CRAIG, Adam, of Richmond, mar. Miss Polly MALLORY of Warwick Co. (VGWeA 12 Jul 87)

CRAIG, Alexander, member of the Common Council of Wmsbrg., d. in his 59th year; his ex., John M. GALT and Gabriel MAUPIN, will sell all of his stock in trade consisting of saddlery and harness furniture and will also settle his est. (VGP 10 Jan 76, VG 20 Jan, 24 Feb 76); his ex. will sell some of his lots in Manchester and on Shockoe Hill (VG 12 Feb 80); e.a.w. his ex. (VGAA 4 Oct 83)

CRAIG, David, late merch. of Alexandria, e.a.w. his admr., John CRAIG, who intends in a short time to leave this colony (MG 28 Feb 60)

CRAIG, George, Scottish ind. svt., gardener, 30-40, ran away from John TURBERVILLE, Westmoreland Co. (VGNI 26 Jul 75)

CRAIG, Jane, about a year ago, when she was living at Ft. Pitt, she intended marriage with William KELLY of Winchester and gave him a deed to 200 ac. of her land at Ft. Pitt; she later found out that he had a wife and two chil. (VGWA 19 Nov 88)

CRAIG, Robert, Scottish svt., weaver, ran away from William BRIGGS, Pr. Wm. Co. (VG 10 Dec 67)

CRAIG, Thomas, b. in Edinburgh, 27, des. from Capt. Robert HODGSON's Indep. Co. now raising for the service and defense of S. Carolina (VG 3 Jul 46)

CRAIGEN, John, HCC, 8 Mar 1797: John CRAIGEN and Phoebe COUCHMAN (pltfs.) and Michael THORN, John WILSON and Susanna his wife, George REID and Margaret his wife, Jonathan PARSONS, and Joseph OBANNON (defs.); it appears that the WILSONs and REIDs are not inhabitants of this country (VGGA 19 Apr 97)

CRAIGEN, Robert, late of Winchester, dec'd, his furniture, farming utensils, and land to be sold by John CRAIGEN of Hardy Co. his admr.w.w.a.(BVCG 19 Feb 9

CRAINE, William, skipper of a small vessel in Fredsbrg., killed in a scuffle with th sheriff on Mon. eve. last (VHFA 7 Mar 93); the sergeant, Mr. TOD, who was attempting to serve writs on him was tried for murder and acquitted (VHFA 2 May 93)

CRALLE, Mrs. Elizabeth, wife of John CRALLE Jr. of Cherry Point, d. Wed. last i her 19th year [obit.] (VGGA 26 Dec 92)

CRAMOND, John, intends to leave the colony soon (VG 2 May 66)

CRANFORD, Mr. and Mrs., living near Staunton, killed by Indians on 29 Sep. (Philadelphia disp. of 15 Nov.) (NYPB 22 Nov 64)

CRAP, James Sr., John CRAP and James CRAP Jr. of Stafford Co. forewarn the public not to deal with him as he is not possessed of his proper reason (VHFA 28 Mar 93)

CRAVEN, Josiah, appr., c. 19, ran away from John IREY near Leesburg, Loudoun Co. (CMAG 19 Apr 96)

CRAWFORD, Andrew; of Westmoreland Co., dec'd, his only and sole heirs are variously named as Anne CRAWFORD (VHFA 4 Sep 98); Margarett CRAWFORD, Ct. of Q.S, 25 Jul 98 (VH 19 Mar 99); Nelly CRAWFORD, chanc. case 24 Jun 99 (VH 30 Jul 99)

CRAWFORD, Joel, adv. that he intends to leave the state soon and desires the legatees of David CRAWFORD Sr. of Amherst Co., dec'd, to meet at his house to receive their legacies (VGPu 19 Sep 77)

CRAWFORD, John, appr. tailor, ran away from John M'CLELLAN, Lexington, Rockbridge Co. (BVCG 16 Dec 93)

CRAWFORD, John, for many yrs. an inhabitant of Richmond, d. on 2 Nov. in an advanced age. (RC 3 Nov, VGGA 4 Nov, RMA 5 Nov 95)

CRAWFORD, Mrs. Mary Ann, of Richmond, d. on Wed. eve. [8 Aug.] at an advanced age (OVT 9 Aug, Arg 10 Aug 98)

CRAWFORD, Col. William, killed by Indians near Pittsburgh in the spring of 1782 (VGAA 3 Aug 82)

CRAWFORD, William, late of Madison Co., dec'd, his ex., May BURTON Jr., will sell his land on Rapidan River (VH 30 Aug 99)

CRAWLEY, Benjamin, dec'd, his acting ex., Peter ROBINSON, will sell 20-30 of his slaves (VGPI 29 Dec 95)

CRAWLEY, David, dec'd, his ex., John CRAWLEY of Amelia, will sell 12 slaves, and a tract of his land containing 1070 ac. on Namozine Cr. in Amelia Co. which includes a mill (VGPI 10 Jan, 31 Jul 88)

CRAWLEY, John, of James City Co., dec'd, e.a.w. his extx., Elizabeth CRAWLEY; his legatees include Samuel TARRY[S], Thomas TARRY[S], Gracey TARRY[S], and Elizabeth TARRY[S] of Mecklenburg Co. (VGWeA 13 Nov 88)

CRAWLEY, John, of Amelia Co., dec'd, e.a.w. his ex., Alexander JONES (VGGA 16 Feb 91); his acting ex., Alexander JONES will sell 20-30 of his slaves (VGPI 3 Nov 95)

CRAWLEY, Nathaniel, of Wmsbrg., dec'd, his PE to be sold by his ex. (VG 7 Dec 69); e.a.w. his ex., Thomas COWLES and William GRAVES (VGR 8 Feb 70)

CRAWLEY, Robert, dec'd, his est. near Wmsbrg. to be leased by John FERGUSSON (nfi) (VG 14 Jan 75)

CRAWLEY, Rodham Kenner, appr., c. 18, has served about four yrs. to the business of house joiner; ran away from William GRESHAM, Northumberland Co. (VG 9 Dec 73)

CRAWLEY, Samuel, for many yrs. a resident of Wmsbrg., died (VGWeA 25 Jan 93)

CRAWLEY, Will, mulatto slave, c. 36, ran away from James SCOTT Jr., Fauquier Co., who suspects he has been seduced away by one Thomas MILES a weaver who ran from this county for hog stealing (VG 17 Jul 78)

CRAWSON, James, 18, des. from the U. S. Army, Winchester; says he was b. in Shenandoah Co. and has relations there and in Fauquier Co. (WG 22 May 99)

CREAGER, Peter, 19, des. from Capt. William CAMPBELL's Co., 7th U. S. Regt. (WG 18 Sep 99)

CREAMER, Patrick, ind. svt., c. 21, tailor, ran away from Andrew LEITCH, Dumfries (VGP 10 Nov 74)

CREIGHTON, Robert, [dec'd], e.a.w. his ex., William CREIGHTON Jr. and William RIDDLE, who will also sell his 600 ac. farm in Berkeley Co. (PGBA 9 Nov 97)

CRENSHAW, William Jr., dec'd, e.a.w. his ex., Rawleigh CARTER and William STOKES of Nottoway Co. (VGPI 15 Apr 96)

CRESSAP, Col. Daniel, of Allegheny Co., Md., d. a short time ago near Union Town, Pa. on his return from the expedition against the insurgents (BVCG 29 Dec 94)

CREW, James, of Hanover, dec'd, e.a.w. his ex., Malcolm HART of Louisa Co. (VGGA 2 Nov 96)

CREW, John, conv. svt., b. in Eng., c. 40, ran away from Robert ALEXANDER, Fairfax Co. (PC 7 Aug 67)

CREW, Josiah, c. 24, des. from Nicholas HOBSON's Co. of the 6th Regt. of Continental Regulars (VGPu 26 Jul 76)

CRINGAN, Mrs., sp. of Dr. John CRINGAN of Richmond, died (VGRMA 9 Dec 93, VGGA 11 Dec 93, VGWeA 13 Dec 93)

CRINGAN, Mrs. Jane, sp. of Dr. John CRINGAN of Richmond, d. on Sun. 26 Apr. at Eastwood, Pr. Anne Co. (NPJ 29 Apr 89, VGWeA 30 Apr 89)

CRINGAN, Dr. John, of Richmond, was mar. at Eastwood near Norfolk on Thurs. last [the 21st inst. acc. to VIC] to Miss Jane STEWART dau. of Charles STEWART Esq. of London, by the Rev. James SIMPSON of Pr. Anne Co. (NPJ 13 Feb 88, VIC 20 Feb 88); mar. Mrs. HYLTON of Sheffield, widow of Ralph HYLTON late attorney at law (VGGA 20 Mar 93)

CRINGHAN [sic], Dr. John, mar. Miss OGELSBY last week in Richmond (VGWeA 6 Feb 97)

CRISSOP, Michael, mentioned in a chanc. case, Ohio Co., 2 Aug 1796, as son of Michael CRISSOP (BVCG 16 Sep 96)

CRISTPONTNER, George, Dutch, des. from the U. S. service at Fredsbrg. (VHFA 12 May 95)

CRITCHER, Thomas, dec'd, his ex., Easther CRITCHER, Samuel MOORE, Nathaniel ROCHESTER, and Thomas CRITCHER, will sell about 1300 ac. of his land in Granville Co., N. Carolina (VG 9 Oct 79)

CRITMORE, Jesse, a draught from Norfolk Co., des. from the co. of State troops of Capt. John LEWIS in the 2nd Regt. (VG 7 Nov 77)

CROMPTON, Mrs., wife of Capt. CROMPTON, commander of H.M.S. *Seahorse*, gave birth to a dau. at his house in Gloucester (VG 4 Feb 37)

CROMWELL, Joseph, merch. of Martinsburg, mar. Miss Kitty DARRINGER of Lancaster (PGBA 9 Feb 97)

CROOKS, Robert, merch. of Norfolk, died [obit.] (VG 26 Sep 71)

CROSON, James, Eng. svt., ran away from Robert STOBO, Petersburg (VG 21 Aug 52)

CROSON, Robert, svt., tailor, b. in Va., c. 26, ran away from William WYATT, Wmsbrg.; sometime ago he was taken up in Charles City Co. and carried before Mr. HARDYMAN where he swore that he was no svt. and so was whipped and discharged (VG 15 Oct 36)

CROSS, James, merch. of Manchester, native of Glasgow, d. on Wed. the 10th inst. at Norfolk (VGWeA 25 Jan 87)

CROSS, Joseph, of Hanover Co., dec'd, his ex., John CROSS, will sell the remainder of his est. in that co. and also 400 ac. of land in Georgia to be sold by the patent (Arg 14 Nov 97)

CROSS, Nanny, Negro, served her time with Robert BURLEY on the Eastern Shor jailed in Suffolk Co. (NHPA 21 Sep 97)

CROSS, Richard, aka Richard BREEDING, svt, b. in Va., ran away from Samue EARLE, Pr. Wm. Co. (VG 13 Apr 39)

CROSS, Sarah, her husb., Joseph CROSS of Hanover, sent her to her father's for her health and she has not yet returned (VGGA 15 Aug 92)

CROUCH, Richard, conv. svt., c. 25, ran away from Anne MIDDLETON, Annapol: Md., who supposes he is gone towards N. Carolina as he is convicted for life (VGR 9 May 71)

CROUCH, Stephen, d. in this city yesterday morn. after a short and violent illness (Ex 29 Jan 99)

CROUCHER, Thomas, late skipper from Alexandria, dec'd, e.a.w. his admr., William COCKE of Dumfries (VGAxA 21 Jul 91)

CROUGHTON, Charles, mar. Miss Betsey HUDSON, Fredsbrg. (VHFA 29 Jul 90

CROW, David, killed on a salt boat at the mouth of Halfpone on the Cumberland, : Jan. (VGRMA 15 Apr 93)

CROWDER, William, of Dinwiddie Co., dec'd, e.a.w. his ex., Joshua SPAIN (VGPI 25 Mar 96)

CRULL, Catharine, of Monongalia, found guilty of murdering her husband (nfi) (VHFA 26 Jun 88)

CRUMLEY, William, of Berkeley Co., [dec'd], e.a.w. his ex., David FAULKNER ar

Sarah CRUMLEY (PGBA 1 Sep 94)
CRUMP, Goodrich, of Va., capt. in the 1st Va. Regt., found guilty of cowardice in the action of 4 Nov. at Germantown; cashiered at a general court martial held at Perkiomy, Pa. 7 [Nov.] 1777 (VG 28 Nov 77)
CRUMP, Jesse, appr., tailor, c. 19, ran away from Bennett WHITE, Newcastle (VGR 9 Sep 73, VG 23 Sep 73)
CRUMP, Lyddal, appr., [17 ?], [of New Kent Co.], ran away from George CLOPTON Jr., K & Q Co. (VGPu 4 Aug 75)
CRUMP, Richard, of New Kent Co., dec'd, his ex. is Benedict CRUMP (VGAA 21 Dec 82)
CRUMPLE, John, dec'd, Thomas CLAUGHTON will sell all his property which was left by will to his wife lying in Christ Church Town, Brighton Par., Chester Borough, Southampton, Eng. (TAA 13 Sep 97)
CRUMPTON, William, aka SMITH, convicted at the last district court of the murder of Nicholas YOUNG; he is to be executed at Winchester on Fri. 18 Nov. (PGBA 27 Oct 96)
CRUTCHER Family, Caroline Co., March Quarterly Term, 1797, in chanc: Henry CRUTCHER, Thomas CRUTCHER and Seabert CRUTCHER (the heirs of William CRUTCHER dec'd), Charles FOSHEE and Lucy his wife, John FOSHEE and Sarah his wife, Benjamin FICKLIN and Susanna his wife, Elizabeth SNEED, Coleman CRUTCHER, William CRUTCHER, and Robert CRUTCHER (heirs and reps. of Hugh CRUTCHER dec'd), Lunsford PITTS and Elizabeth his wife (pltfs.) against John SAUNDERS and Margaret his wife, Mary SNEED, Sarah CRUTCHER, and Thomas CRUTCHER (defs.); it appears that the defs. are not inhabitants of this commonwealth (RCFPC 26 Apr 97)
CRUTCHFIELD, Ralph, late of Hanover Co., dec'd, his ex. (nfi) will sell his land there (VGRMA 12 Jan 95)
CRUZ (or CRUG), Charles, late of Norfolk, dec'd, e.a.w. his admr., Frederick HEERMAN, Norfolk (NH 3 Nov 98)
CRYER, Edmund, aka Grievous, Eng. svt., b. at Leeds in Yorkshire, a very good shoemaker, has been in the country about four yrs., ran away from George LEE and Richard LEE in Westmoreland Co., he was seen crossing the river from Boyd's Hole to Md. (MG 20 Sep 49, 23 May 50)
CRYER, James, of Norfolk, intends to leave the state (NH 10 Apr 98)
CUBBIN, Andrew, of Petersburg, dec'd, e.a.w. his extx., Dorothy CUBBINS [sic] (VG 9 May 71)
CUBBIN, John, seaman, ran away from the ship *Hannibal* lying at the mouth of Quantico (VJAA 10 Aug 86)
CUDDY, William, Irish svt., 38, ran away from John SHORTWELL, Orange Co. and was last seen in Brunswick Co. (VG 26 Sep 45)
CUFFY, Moll, Negro woman, c. 35, claims to be free, jailed in Norfolk (VG 31 Mar 74)
CULBERTSON, William, late of Augusta Co., killed in the last Indian war (VGR 25 May 69)
CULLEN, John, Irish svt. bel. to Charles HAMMOND Jr., ran away from near Elk Ridge Church, Anne Arundel Co., Md. (VGR 26 Jul 70)
CULLY, John, aka John, mulatto, raised near Wmsbrg., ran away from George SHEPHERD, Orange Co. (VHFA 18 Sep 94)
CUNLIFF, John, merch., mar. Miss Esther HUGHES, both of Richmond (VIC 14 Oct 89)
CUNNINGHAM, [Edward], merch., of Cumberland Co., mar. Mrs. Ariana MACARTNEY of Richmond on Thurs. the 13th inst.[Aug.] [or 18th] (VGWeA 27 Aug 96, RMA 3 Sep 96)
CUNNINGHAM, James, dec'd, his land on Mill Cr. in Berkeley Co. to be sold by his ex., W. HENSHAW (VJAA 27 Oct 85)
CUNNINGHAM, James, dec'd, of Spotsylvania Co., his house to be sold by his admr., James LEWIS (VHFA 22 Oct 89); pursuant to a decree of Spotsylvania Co. Ct., the commissioners will sell four of his slaves at his late dwelling house in this county as well as some HHF of Ann CUNNINGHAM dec'd (VHFA 3 Dec 89)

CUNNINGHAM, James A., mar. Miss Mary MURPHY, both of Norfolk, on Sat. eve. by the Rev. Mr. WHITEHEAD (NH 23 Jul 99)

CUNNINGHAM, John, blacksmith, b. in Ireland, c. 23, resided on or near the Southwest Marsh, Frederick Co., wanted for counterfeiting (VGP 4 May 75)

CUNNINGHAM, John, of New York, tailor, has set up his business in Richmond (Arg 11 Oct 99)

CUNNINGHAM, Mrs. Margaret, sp. of Samuel CUNNINGHAM, d. on Mon. the 5th inst. at Somerton, Nansemond Co., age 33 (AGNPWA 14 Aug 93)

CUNNINGHAM, Mrs. Mary, wife of John CUNNINGHAM, merch., in Cumberland Co., d. on the 10th of last month; she was from Ireland (Arg 22 Mar 99)

CUNNINGHAM, William, dec'd, e.a.w. his admx., Elizabeth CUNNINGHAM, Norfolk (NHPA 5 Jan 97)

CUNNINGHAME, Loudon, killed in a hunting accident in Talbot Co., [Md.] in Nov. (VG 25 Dec 71)

CURD, James, dec'd, Jesse CURD and Samuel WOODSON (nfi) will settle his est. and sell a few of his Negroes, a wagon and team, HHF, and plant. utensils at his late dwelling house in the lower end of Goochland Co. (VGPA 5 Nov 91)

CURD, Richard and Sarah, of Goochland Co., dec'd, their ex., George UNDERWOOD, will settle their est. (VGGA 21 Sep 96)

CURETON, Thomas, of Pr. Geo. Co., dec'd, e.a.w. his ex., Nathan JONES of Surry Co., who will also sell all of his PE (VGPu 31 Oct 77, 21 Aug 78)

CURETON, William, dec'd, all persons indebted to his est. to make payments to Capt. Lemuel PEEBLES, acc. to an advertisement by Jeremiah CURETON for his ex., James CURETON (VGPI 24 Jan 97)

CURLE, Mrs., sp. to William Roscow Wilson CURLE Esq. of Hampton, died (VG 7 Apr 74)

CURLE, David W., dec'd, some of his Negroes to be sold by William Roscow CURLE his admr. (VG 10 Sep 67)

CURLE, John, des. from the *Hero* galley and is believed to be lurking somewhere in Amelia Co. (VGPu 21 Mar 77 sup)

CURLE, Col. William Roscow Wilson, delegate in convention for Norfolk Borough mar. Mrs. LYON relict of the late Walter LYON Esq. of Pr. Anne Co. (VGPu 6 Sep 76); dec'd, his admr., Moss ARMISTEAD, will sell a great variety of HH and KF at his plant. about a quarter of a mile from Hampton (VGAA 30 Mar 82--his name is given as CURTE); e.a.w. his admr., Moss ARMISTEAD of Hampton (VGAA 3 Dec 85)

CURLE, Wilson, dec'd, his ex., William LANGHORNE, will sell his land in Hampton (VGGA 23 Dec 95)

CUROTT, Lewis, dec'd, his admr., Nathaniel QUARLES of Manchester, will sell all of his est. and settle his est. (VGWeA 17 Dec 89, VICGA 10 Feb 90)

CURREL, William, appr., near 17, eloped from John HELM in Campbell Co. (VGAA 14 Jun 86)

CURRIE, Mrs. Anne, consort of Dr. James CURRIE of Richmond, d. on Sat. night last (VGWeA 15 Oct 96)

CURRIE, Eliza, late of Tappahannock [a eulogy] (VGWeA 24 Apr 84)

CURRIE, Dr. James, of Richmond, mar. Mrs. INGLES of Pr. Anne Co. (VIC 25 Nov 89, VGWeA 26 Nov 89)

CURRIE, John, of Fauquier Co., executed on 5 Dec. for horse stealing (VG 4 Nov, 9 Dec 73)

CURRIE, Peter, Virginian, 22, des. from Capt. David BELL's Co. of the Va. Regt.; supposed to be lurking in Albemarle Co. (VG 21 Nov 55)

CURRIN, Jane, has left her husb., Robert CURRIN of Essex Co. (VHFA 7 Jan 90)

CURRY, James, Negro, c. 25, says he belongs to William FITZHUGH near Fredsbr (Rights of Man 13 Jul 96)

CURRY, Nicholas, svt., sawyer, ray away from the snow *John* lying in Hampton Road (VGAA 17 Apr 84)

CURRY, Patrick, Irish ind. svt., joiner and cabinet-maker, 28, ran away from John ATKINSON near Battletown (VGWA 28 May 91)

CURRY, William, Scottish, des. from Capt. James MACKILWEAN's Co. at Petersburg (VG 19 Jul 54)
CURRY, William, Irish svt., 25, ran away from the Potomac Co., Great Falls (VJAA 17 Aug 86)
CURSEY, John, Negro, c. 22, broke out of jail in Norfolk Borough on 23 Jan. (NH 26 Jan 99)
CURTIN, Nancy and Chloe, Negro sisters, Nan is 20; Chloe is 19; ran away from Richard BRANDT, Pamunkey Neck, Charles Co. [Md.]; they are said to be in Alexandria (CMAG 1 Jul 97)
CURTIS, Christopher, dec'd, his land on Rappahannock River near Urbanna, Middlesex Co., to be sold; his wife is to have her thirds in the land during her life; mention is also made of his plant. in Caroline Co. (VG 10 Oct 66)
CURTIS, James, appr. boy, ran away from William ROW, Kg. Wm. Co., supposed going to Nansemond Co. (VG 1 Aug 71)
CURTIS, John, butcher in Wmsbrg., after gaming losses was found in bed with his throat cut on Sun. morn. last; he d. the following night (Wmsbrg. disp. of 23 Nov.) (MG 27 Dec 53)
CUSHING, Mr., of Salem, Mass., d. in [Alexandria] on Wed. morn. last (CMAG 10 Sep 96)
CUSSENS, John, aka Ben, Negro slave, 25-26, taken up last May in Petersburg but escaped; he was captured and escaped again in Powhatan Co. (VGGA 28 Mar 98)
CUSTIS, the Hon. John, one of H.M's Council of this Colony, d. last night at his house in this city [Wmsbrg.] aged 72 (VG-Randolph 23 Nov 49)
CUSTIS, John Parke Esq., lately mar. Miss Eleanor CALVERT of Md. (VG and VGR 17 Feb 74); stepson of His Excellency General WASHINGTON, d. a few days ago at Abingdon (Arlington) near Alexandria shortly after his return from the siege of York[town] and Gloucester (MJ 20 Nov 81); late of Fairfax Co., dec'd, e.a.w L. DANDRIDGE his admr. or Mr. Lund WASHINGTON of Fairfax Co. (VGAA 6 Apr 82); his admr. is named as David STUART (VGAA 9 Jul 85)
CUSTIS, Miss Martha, dau. of the late Daniel Parke CUSTIS, died (VG 1 Jul 73)
CUTE, Tom, aka Tom, Negro slave, 21-22, ran away from Bernard HOOE, Pr. Wm. Co., and is supposed heading for Philadelphia (BVCG 17 Jun 93)
CUTHBERT, Alexander, svt. from Perth, Scotland, 22, bricklayer, ran away from William BLACK, Pr. Geo. Co. and may be heading for Philadelphia (VG 25 Nov 67)
CUTHBERT, Maj. S. J., of Georgia, mar. Mrs. Catherine BLAIR of Wmsbrg. (VG 14 Feb 77)
CUYLER, Barend R., late of Norfolk, is now removed to New York (VG 14 Dec 69)

DABNEY, Col. Isaac, of Kg. Wm. Co., dec'd, his HHF to be sold on 12 Jul; e.a.w. his acting ex., Richard DABNEY (VGAA 3 Jul 84, 9 Jul 85)
DABNEY, John B., of [Alexandria], merch., mar. Miss Roxa LEWIS of Dedham, Mass. at Dedham (VGAxA 22 Nov 92)
DABNEY, William, of Richmond, merch., mar. Miss Hetty HYLTON, on Tues. last. (VGRMA 16 Feb 95, VGGA 18 Feb 95)
DABNEY, William, of Caroline Co., e.a.w. his admr., A. THORNTON (VHFA 4 Apr 98)
DADE, Francis, dec'd, e.a.w. William HUNTER per adv. by Townshend DADE the admr. of Fredsbrg. (VJAA 21 Apr 85)
DADE, Francis, age 14, d. of rabies last Mon. (VHFA 24 Jun 90)
DADE, Capt. Francis, late of Orange Co., his extx. was Sarah DADE (VHFA 27 Oct 91); his exors. (nfi) will sell his stock and plant. and grist mill on the Rapidan River (VHFA 20 Dec 92)
DADE, Franc[i]s, dec'd, Lawrence TALIAFERO gdn. to the chil., will hire out Negroes bel. to the est. at his blacksmith shop near the store at Rose-Hill (VHFFA 6 Dec 96)
DADE, Miss Kitty, of Alexandria, died (VJAA 13 Jul 86)
DADE, Rose, dec'd, formerly of Kg. Geo. Co., Va. but last of Charles Co., Md., e.a.w. her ex., Gerard B. CAUSIN (VGAA 15 Feb 86)

DAFFIN, Joseph, G. Esq., of Md., mar. Miss Betsy COOKE of Alexandria on Thurs. eve. (CMAG 9 Nov 99)

DAILYHUNT, James, dec'd, e.a.w. his admr., Robert BRYCE of Alexandria (VGWeA 28 Dec 82)

DAINGERFIELD, Robinson, of Kg. Geo. Co., merch., died (VG 4 Nov 73); his admrs., Thomas LOWRY and W. DAINGERFIELD, will sell all of his HH and KF (VGR 19 May 74); e.a.w. his admr., William DAINGERFIELD (VG 13 Nov 78)

DAINGERFIELD, Col. William, d. in an advanced age on the 29th ult. at his house in Essex Co. (VG 4 May 69)

DAINGERFIELD, Col. William, dec'd, e.a.w. his extx., Mary DAINGERFIELD, and ex., Thomas COLSON and Oliver TOWLES, who will also sell 20 of his slaves in Essex Co. (VGWeA 26 Oct 82); his ex., COLSON and TOWLES, will sell about 20 of his slaves at the house of Nathaniel GORDON in Orange Co. (VHFFA 7 Oct 96)

DAINGERFIELD, William Esq., of Belvidere, dec'd, e.a.w. his admr., Alexander SPOTTSWOOD (VGAA 26 Jul 83); his admr. will sell some of his HHF at his dwelling house on Rappahannock River (VGIC 5 Mar 85); his admr. will sell some of his PE at his late dwelling house (VHFA 4 Dec 94); William DAINGERFIELD (nfi) will sell part of his tract called Belvidere seven miles below Fredsbrg. (VHFFA 24 Nov 95)

DALBY, Mrs. Mary, consort of Philip DALBY Esq. of Winchester, d. Fri. morn. last, aged 25; she was bur. in the German Lutheran Burying Ground (VGWA 6 Jan 90)

DALGLEISH, Dr. Alexander, a young physician of Gloucester, d. on Mon. last, 24 Sep., [eulogy in VGR] (VG and VGR 27 Sep 70)

DALGLEISH, Dr. John, of Norfolk, died (VG 3 Oct 71)

DALGLEISH, Robert, merch., of Gloucester, died (VG 22 Mar 70); e.a.w. his admr., John DALGLEISH (VG 24 May 70); Archibald CAMPBELL of Norfolk, the admr., will settle his est. and that of Dr. Alexander DALGLEISH late of Gloucester Co. (VG 14 Nov 71)

DALLON, Michael, Irish svt., c. 19, tailor, ran away from Thomas CORCORAN and John PRINGLE, Georgetown (VGWA 21 Oct 89)

DALRYMPLE, John, merch., of Fredsbrg., mar. Miss Frances HESLOP of Dumfries, at Dumfries (VHFA 28 Apr 91); formerly a respected merch. of this town [Fredsbrg.], d. lately at Boyd's Hole (VHFA 11 Jan 99)

DALTON, James, son and heir of Timothy DALTON (see: David WOODSON) (VIC 10 Sep 88)

DAMERON, Oney S., dec'd, e.a.w. his extx., Martha DAMERON of Norfolk; those in N. Carolina who are indebted or have demands against his est. are to apply to William T. MUSE of Pasquotank Co. (NH 3 Oct 99)

DAMES, Charles, seaman, ran away from the ship *Brilliant*; he may have gone to his uncle, John DAMES, at Old Point Comfort (VG 7 Jul 74)

DAMMERY, Adam, appr., ran away from Patrick RYAN, Norf. (NH 23 Apr 96)

DANCE, Stephen, dec'd, HHF bel. to his est. to be sold by his ex., Matthew DANCE (VGAA 17 Jul 84)

DANCER, Capt. George, native of Eng., of the ship *Marlborough*, d. very suddenly on board his ship last Sun. from drinking brandy in which corrosive sublimate had been steeped by mistake (VGAA and VGWeA 25 Jun 85)

DANCER, John, mulatto svt., c. 25, ran away from John HIPKINS, K & Q Co. (VG 18 Feb 75)

DANCY, Francis, son of Edward DANCY; James HALL (nfi) will hire out Negroes bel. to his est. at Charles City Ct. H. (VGPu 22 Dec 75)

DANCY, John, Negro, ships carpenter, c. 45, says he was set free by Richard RATLIFF of N. Carolina, a Quaker, in Poquemon Co.; jailed in Hampton, Elizabeth City Co. (VGAA 21 Aug 84, VGIC 27 Nov 84)

DANCY, William, dec'd, his ex., William ACRILL, will sell his tract of land on Chickahominy River, Charles City Co. (VGR 9 Dec 73)

DANDRIDGE, the Hon. Bartholomew, of New Kent Co., judge of the General Ct

died (VGAA 23 Apr 85); 8000 ac. of his land on Elkhorn Cr. in Fayette Co. [Ky. ?] to be sold by his exors., John DANDRIDGE and William ARMISTEAD of New Kent Co. (VIC 18 Feb 89, VGAA 10 May 86)
DANDRIDGE, Miss Eliza Lewis, eld. dau. of Francis DANDRIDGE Esq. lately dec'd, d. on the 11th inst. at Turkey Island the seat of Bowler COCKE Esq. in her 16th yr. (RMA 14 May 95, VGGA [20] May 95)
DANDRIDGE, Francis, of Kg. Wm. Co., mar. Miss Lucy WEBB of New Kent Co. (VG 16 Apr 79); dec'd, his ex., Bowler COCKE, will rent his plant. called Huntington, in Kg. Wm. Co. and will sell all his HH and KF (VGGA 24 Sep 94, 9 Sep 95, VGRMA 2 Oct 94)
DANDRIDGE, Jane, widow of Nathaniel West DANDRIDGE, will sell her life est. in his plant. in Hanover Co. (VGAA 17 May 86)
DANDRIDGE, Capt. John, mar. Miss Betsy BOOTH of Westham, Henrico Co. on Sat. last (VGAA and VGWeA 2 Mar 82)
DANDRIDGE, John Esq., formerly of New Kent Co., d. on Wed. the 16th inst. at his residence in Pr. Geo. Co. (Ex 29 Jan 99)
DANDRIDGE, Mrs. Lucy, d. on Thurs. 15 Feb. at Richm. (VG 9 Mar 76)
DANDRIDGE, Nathaniel West, dec'd, his widow, Jane DANDRIDGE, informs the public that she never qualified or acted as extx. of the will of her late husb. and that Col. William DANDRIDGE was the only acting ex. (VGGA 11 Apr 92); e.a.w. his ex., William DANDRIDGE of Hanover Co. (VGGA 8 Jan 94)
DANDRIDGE, William Esq., of Kg. Wm. Co., mar. Mrs. CHAMBERLAYNE of New Kent (VGPu 17 Feb 75 sup)
DANGERFIELD, Henry Esq., mar. Miss Elizabeth THRUSTON dau. of Col. C. M. THRUSTON at Mount Sion last Sat. (BVCG 12 Aug 93)
DANGERFIELD, William, of Spotsylvania Co., mar. Miss Frances SOUTHALL dau. of Col. James SOUTHALL of Wmsbrg., on Fri. last (VGWeA 28 Jun 87)
DANIEL Family, HCC, 10 Sep. 1793, mention of John DANIEL, James DANIEL, Chestley DANIEL, and Overton DANIEL chil. of John DANIEL dec'd [apparently of Middlesex Co.] (VGGA 18 Dec 93)
DANIEL, Andrew, c. 20, des. from the French Co. in Wmsbrg. (VG 29 Aug 77)
DANIEL, Edward, aka James M'DONALD, Irish svt., blacksmith, 50, ran away from Benjamin GRYMES, Spotsylvania Co. (VGR 16 Feb 69)
DANIEL, George, dec'd, his admr., Thomas ROANE of Middlesex, will sell some of his slaves in Petersburg (VGGA 30 Sep 95)
DANIEL, Henry, dec'd, his ex., George DANIEL and Robert DANIEL, will sell his lots and houses in Urbanna (VGP 4 May, VGPu 5 May 75)
DANIEL, John, of Urbanna, Middlesex Co., dec'd, his ex. (nfi) will sell his lots and houses where he formerly kept an ordinary (VG 10 Jun 73)
DANIEL, Mrs. Marie, consort of Dr. John DANIEL of Dumfries, d. on 31 Oct. 1792 [eulogy] (VHFA 8 Nov 92)
DANIEL, Robert, dec'd, e.a.w. his ex., George DANIEL and Beverley DANIEL of Middlesex Co. (VGR 5 Sep 71)
DANIEL, Thomas, of Halifax Co.; Thomas TUCK is wanted for murdering him (VGGA 7 Jan 95)
DANIEL, Thomas, Caroline Co., March Ct., 1798, in chanc: Obadiah BOULWARE and Delphia BOULWARE his wife and Elizabeth RENNOLDS rep. of Thomas DANIEL dec'd (pltfs.) against Mary ISBELL, Gerard DONAPHIN and Nancy his wife and Henry PITTS (defs.); it appears that Mary ISBELL, Gerard and Nancy DONAPHIN [her name was also given as Mary DONAPHIN] are not inhabitants of this country (VHFA 18 Apr 98)
DANIEL, Walker, proposes going to practice as an attorney in the District of Kentucky this fall (VGAA 6 Jul 82)
DANIEL, William, Negro, b. in Wmsbrg., he and his wife, Sarah, who was born in Pa., claim to be free; jailed in New Kent Co. (VGGA 12 Jan 91)
DANIEL, William, dec'd, his admr., Henry DANIEL of Powhatan Co., will sell a tract of his land in Powhatan Co. on Appomattox River (VGRMA 16 Feb 95)
DANIELL, Miss Fanny, youngest dau. of Thomas DANIELL of this town [Fredsbrg.], d. lately in London in her 15th yr. (VH 21 May 99)

DANTIGNAC, Anne, will take depositions of Mrs. Anne DOWNMAN and Mrs. Elizabeth M'CREA in Pr. Wm. Co. in her suit against John DANTIGNAC (VICGA 26 May 90)

DANTIGNAC, John, summoned to General Ct. in Richmond to answer Anne DANTIGNAC of a plea for a divorce on the grounds of abuse, desertion, and adultery (VICGA 13 Jan 90)

D'ANVERS, John, Irish svt., 30, ran away from Robert LYON, Wmsbrg. (VG 4 Apr 55)

DARBY, Adam, of Fredsbrg., merch., mar. Miss Catherine SHEPHERD dau. of Andrew SHEPHERD of Orange Co. in that co. on Tues. last (VHFFA 18 Nov 96)

DARBY, John, of West Point, late of this borough [Norfolk], mar. Miss Lucy H. CHURCHILL dau. of Col. William CHURCHILL of Wilton, Middlesex Co. (VCNPGA 4 May 93)

DARBY, John, having declined business in this place [Alexandria] intends to remove to his farm in Richmond Co. (TAA 3 Nov 98)

DARCAS, James, aka Negro James, blacksmith, c. 28, has been in Pa., ran away from John GORDON, Northumberland Co. (VGGA 25 Jun 94)

DARCY, Thomas, tanner & currier, c. 28, jailed in Augusta Co. on suspicion of being a runaway svt. (VGR 10 Feb 74)

DARDEN, James, appr. tailor, ran away from Andrew SHULE, Lunenburg Co. (VGPI 22 Sep 97)

DARE, John, merch., mar. Miss Nancy CALLENDER dau. of Capt. John CALLENDER, both of Fredsbrg., last eve. (VHFA 25 Sep 95)

DARLING, George, mar. Mrs. Mazey ISLER, both of this town [Alexandria], on Thurs. last (CMAG 14 Mar 97)

DARNABY, William Sr., of Spotsylvania Co., dec'd, his admr., James OWEN, will sell his stock and 398 ac. tract there (VHFA 2 Oct 95)

DARNALL, Jeremiah, dec'd, e.a.w. his ex., James WRIGHT (RJDA 17 Jul 95)

DARRACOTT, Mrs. Catherine, of Hanover Co., d. in the flower of her age (VGP 2 Oct 75, VG 4 Nov 75)

DARRACOTT, Mrs. Cecilia, wife of Capt. John DARRACOTT of Hanover Co., d. the 19th ult.; she was bur. at the plant. of William MASSEY (late her father's) in New Kent Co. (VG 9 Dec 37)

DARRELL, Mary, dec'd, her acting ex., John HARPER, will sell all of her HHF (CMAG 12 Mar 95)

DAUGHRELY, John, Irish, 23-24, says he is a spinner by trade, des. from the new recruits of Cumberland Co. (VGWeA 5 Oct 82)

DAVENPORT Family, HCC, 1 Jun 1798; between Benjamin DAVENPORT, Willi [?] DAVENPORT, and Alix[u]s Madder DAVENPORT devisees of William DAVENPORT dec'd, and the sd. Thomas [Pasteur] DAVENPORT, William [Tersy] DAVENPORT, and William BARLOW exors. of the sd. William DAVENPORT (pltfs.) and Harrison JONES, Lucy JONES admx. of Elijah JONES, John JONES, Reuben JONES, Bedford DAVENPORT, and [Ishmas] HOBSON (defs.); it appears that John JONES is not an inhabitant of this count (Arg 10 Aug 98)

DAVENPORT, Mrs. Catharine, relict of George DAVENPORT of this city [Wmsbrg.], died (VG 18 Apr 71)

DAVENPORT, George Esq., attorney at law and clerk to several committees of th House of Burgesses, d. last Mon. (VG 9 May 66); e.a.w. his ex., Catharine DAVENPORT and Anthony HAYS, who will also sell his law books (VG 1 Aug 66)

DAVENPORT, James, clerk of Westmoreland Co., died (VGPu 23 Aug 76);his admr., Joseph PIERCE, will sell part of his est. at Mrs. Elizabeth RANSDELL's in Westmoreland Co. (VGPu 17 Oct 77); e.a.w. his admr. (VG 6 Nov 79)

DAVENPORT, Joseph, ind. appr., 19, tailor, ran away from James NOIX, Wmsbr (VGWeA 24 Apr 84)

DAVENPORT, the Rev. Joseph, rector of Charles Par., Poquoson, York Co., died (VIC 12 Mar 88, VGPI 13 Mar 88)

DAVENPORT, Joseph, printer, d. on Mon. last in Richmond (VGRMA [25] Nov 9!

VGWeA 29 Nov 93)
DAVENPORT, Mrs. Mary, relict of the Rev. Joseph DAVENPORT, d. lately in Poquoson, York Co. [obit.] (VIC 16 Apr 88)
DAVENPORT, Matthew, of Wmsbrg., d. on the 29th ult. at Mr. Haldenby DIXON's in Hanover Co. (VG 4 Jul 77)
DAVENPORT, Richard, of Albemarle Co., dec'd, e.a.w. his surviving ex., Samuel DYER (VGGA 13 Aug 94)
DAVENPORT, William, attorney at law of Warwick Co., d. lately in Wmsbrg. in the prime of life (VGGA 18 Mar 95, VGRMA 19 Mar 95)
DAVIDS, Walter, comedian, d. last Fri. (VHFA 22 Oct 89)
DAVIDSON, Robert, practitioner in physick and mayor of Wmsbrg., d. last week (VG 2 Feb 39)
DAVIES, David, d. of exposure near Winchester Sat. night; bur. at the Episcopal Burying Ground (VCWM 17 Feb 90)
DAVIES, Nicholas, of Bedford Co., d. on the 28th inst. [Sep.]; his heir, Henry DAVIES, requests all who have papers or other matters respecting the dec'd or his ext. will come forward with them (LFG 1 Nov 94)
DAVIS, Dr., of Charlestown, Berkeley Co., mar. Mrs. Elizabeth CONRAD, Winchester, in Jan. 1799 (WG 9 Jan 99)
DAVIS, Augustine, second son of Augustine DAVIS, printer of Richmond, drowned a short distance below Ross' Mill [obit. in VGRMA] (VGRMA 23 May 93, VHFA 30 May 93)
DAVIS, Miss C., of Petersburg, d. on Mon. eve. last (VSPW 11 Jun 95)
DAVIS, Charles, svt., 18-20, ran away from William PORTER, Thomas MILLER, and James LAVERTY Fredsbrg. (VGR 22 Sep 68)
DAVIS, David, appr. cabinet maker, c. 20, ran away from Benjamin BUCKTROUT, Wmsbrg. (VG 4 Apr 71)
DAVIS, Edward, Eng., 22, des. from Capt. Thomas WAGGENER's Co. of Va. forces (VG 22 Aug 55)
DAVIS, Edward, farrier, late of London, now resides in Richm. (VGGA 18 Jan 99)
DAVIS, Elizabeth, appr. girl near 14, ran away from Peter CHRISTMAN (BVCG 23 Dec 93)
DAVIS, George, dec'd, his ex., John JACKSON and Robert DANIEL, will sell three of his Negroes at Urbanna (VGR 3 Jun 73)
DAVIS, Gressit, dec'd, his admr., Abraham GREEN, will sell his stock of goods at his late store (VGPI 16 Jun 91)
DAVIS, Henry, seaman, ran away from the ship *Virginia* at Littlepage's Landing, New Kent Co.; he may be heading for Bristol Iron Mines (VG 18 Apr 45)
DAVIS, Henry, of Surry Co., dec'd, his land on Blackwater Swamp to be sold by his ex., Etheldred GRAY (VG 9 Nov 69)
DAVIS, James, claimed to be a native of Pa., b. on Brandywine Cr. about 12 miles above Chadsford where his father, Samuel DAVIS, owned a mill, absconded with money bel. to James WARDROP of Ampthill Mill on James River (VGGA 6 Oct 90)
DAVIS, John, sentenced to death for felony; repreived on 24 Nov. (VG 3, 24 Nov 38)
DAVIS, John, svt., West Country man lately imported from Bristol, ran away from Edward BARRADALL, Wmsbrg. (VG 11 May 39)
DAVIS, John Esq., merch. of Portsmouth, was mar. to Miss Elizabeth CHRISTIAN of Charles City on Sun. eve. last at Wmsbrg. by the Rev. Mr. J. BRACKEN (NHPA 20 Jul 97)
DAVIS, Lewis, dec'd, his ex., Nicholas MAGET, will sell 200 ac. of his land on the Nottoway River (VG 28 Nov 71)
DAVIS, Mary, middle-aged conv. svt., ran away from John CATLETT, Kg. Wm. Co. (VG 21 Jan 73); she may have changed her name to PHILIPS, she has been seen in Gloucester and Middlesex cos. (VG 25 Feb 73)
DAVIS, Nathan, country-born appr. lad, c. 17, ran away from John M'DOWGAL, Hanover Co. who believes he is now a soldier in Capt. NELSON's Co. of regulars at York (VGPu 9 Aug 76)
DAVIS, Philip, svt., 24, a Lancashire man, ran away from James POWELL, New

Town on the Eastern Branch of the Elizabeth River (VG 13 Oct 38)
DAVIS, Richard, Eng. svt., clock and watch mender, ran away from Edward HILL, Pr. Geo. Co., may have gone to Rappahannock (VG 4 Jul 66)
DAVIS, Richard, c. 21, jailed as a runaway in Richmond Co., says he came from Philadelphia (VGR 27 Sep 70)
DAVIS, Richard, late of Norfolk Borough, dec'd, e.a.w. his ex., Jonathan LYLE (VGR 26 Aug 73)
DAVIS, Capt. Richard, late of Nansemond Co., dec'd, e.a.w. his admr., Thomas DAVIS of Pr. Geo. Co. (VG 4 Sep 79)
DAVIS, Samuel, late of Pr. Edw. Co., dec'd, e.a.w. his admr., Ebenezer M. M'ROBERT (VGRMA 26 Mar 95)
DAVIS, Samuel Esq., of Portsmouth, d. yesterday [6 Mar.]; e.a.w. John DAVIS of Portsmouth; his admx., Mary DAVIS also of Portsmouth, will sell his PE (NH 7 Mar, 28 Apr 96, NHPA 3 Dec 96)
DAVIS, Capt. Samuel, a respectable merch. of Alexandria, d. on Thurs. eve. last; he was bur. yesterday afternoon in the Friends Burial Ground (TAA 17 Mar 98)
DAVIS, Thomas, Welsh svt., 40, ran away from the ship *Duke of Cumberland* at Bermuda Hundred in James River (VG 25 May 39)
DAVIS, William, dec'd, his admr., William PERKINSON, will sell his est. in Jamestown at the dwelling house of Thomas HARRIS dec'd (VG 2 Jul 71)
DAVIS, William, an editor of the *American Gazette*, was mar. to Miss Peggy HAYNES of Norfolk on Thurs. last by the Rev. James WHITEHEAD (VCNPGA 6 Apr 93)
DAVIS, William, of Isle of Wight Co., dec'd, his admr. with the will annexed, Josiah PARKER of Macclesfield, will sell all his PE (NH 20 Oct 96)
DAVISON Family, Harrison Co., Nov. 1798, in chanc: the heirs of Jacob REES (pltfs.) against David BRADFORD, David RALSTON, and Margaret DAVISON, Lucinda DAVISON, Ithmar DAVISON, Elizabeth DAVISON, and Ann DAVISON heirs of Hezekiah DAVISON (defs.) (WG 2 Jan 99)
DAVISON, Ithmar [given as Ithamar DAVISSON] infant son and devisee of Hezekiah DAVISON dec'd, Harrison Co. chancery case, 21 Nov 1799 (WG 25 Dec 99)
DAW, Milly, 19, ran off with her husband, Daniel a Negro aged c. 28, from Allen WILLIAMSON, Henrico Co. (VGAA 2 Apr 85)
DAWES, Caroline, appr. girl, c. 16, des. in a great hurry on the 23rd inst. from Philip WARNER in Alexandria; it is supposed that she has gone towards Annapolis [Md.] the residence of her brother (TAA 27 Dec 97)
DAWSON, Mrs. Elizabeth, relict of the late Rev. and Hon. William DAWSON, d. at Eltham in New Kent Co. in her 70th year (VG 16 Apr 79); late of Wmsbrg., e.a.w. John BECKLEY for the admr. (VGCD 11 Dec 79)
DAWSON, George, seaman, ran away from the ship *Virginia* at Littlepage's Landing, New Kent Co.; he may be heading for the Bristol Iron Mines (VG 18 Apr 45)
DAWSON, Henry, of Pr. Wm. Co., d. in the public hospital for lunatics (VGPu 8 No 76)
DAWSON, John, appr., c. 17, ran away from the British brigantine *Europe* (NH 16 Oct 98)
DAWSON, Mrs. Priscilla, of Wmsbrg., relict of the late Commissary DAWSON, d. at the house of William DAINGERFIELD near Fredsbrg. (VGP 23 Mar, VGPu 24 Mar, VG 25 Mar 75)
DAWSON, the Hon. and Rev. Thomas, one of H.M's Hon. Council, Commissary f the Lord Bishop of London, President of William and Mary College, and ministe of Bruton Par., d. Sat. last [3 Dec.] (Wmsbrg. disp. of 5 Dec 1760) (MG 8 Jan 61)
DAWSON, the Hon. Dr. and Rev. William, one of H.M's Council for the Colony of Virginia, President of William and Mary, and the Lord Bishop's Commissary for the Colony, d. Mon. last, 20 Jul., in Wmsbrg. (VG 24 Jul 52, MG 6 Aug 52); e.a.w, his admr., Thomas DAWSON (VG 28 Aug 52)
DAWSON, William, heir at law of John DAWSON dec'd, [of Bedford Co.] (VGAA 2 Apr 85)

DAWSON, William, eld. son of the late Hon. Commissary DAWSON, d. on Sat. eve. (VIC 18 Nov 89, VGWeA 19 Nov 89)

DAY, David, mulatto, ran away from Augustine SMITH, Middlesex Co. about three yrs. ago (VG 27 Jul 69)

DAY, John, dec'd, his ex., Thomas PEIRCE and William DAVIS, will sell all his PE and a valuable tract of his land containing 400 ac. and a grist mill and saw mill at his late dwelling house at Day's Neck, Isle of Wight Co. (VG 21 Sep 76)

DAY, John, appr. tailor, c. 16, ran away from Daniel DUNIVAN, Morefield (BVCG 17 Jun 96)

DAY, John, tailor, d. Tues. night in an advanced age (VH 8 Mar 99)

DAY, Samuel, enl. in Powhatan Co. but says he was b. in Albemarle Co. and has lived in Georgia or Carolina for some time, c. 30, des. from the 9th Va. Regt. (VG 26 Dec 77)

DAY, Thomas, of Isle of Wight Co., dec'd, his admr., John DAY, will sell his PE (VG 13 Aug 72)

DAY, William, middle-aged Eng. conv. svt., brought up to the farming "business," ran away from Gerard B. CAUSIN, Port Tobacco, Md. (VGR 6 Feb 72)

DAYLIES, William and Hannah, Irish svts., ran away from William TAITE, Northumberland Co. (VG 26 Mar 67)

DAYLY, Charles, Irish svt., c. 21, ran away from Thomas BLINCOE and Hardage LANE, Loudoun Co. (VG 18 Jan 70)

DEBAPTIST, John, of Fredsbrg., led to believe that his wife Frances "Franky" was guilty of breech of her connubial engagements, he acted a part very unbecoming; he now believes she is innocent (VHFA 13 May 90); on 11 Jun., Frances ran away leaving her husb. and four chil. (VHFA 24 Jun 90)

DEGRAFFENREID Family, HCC, 18 Mar 1796: Sarah DEGRAFFENREID and Vincent DEGRAFFENREID her eld. son and heir at law of Baker DEGRAFFENREID dec'd. (pltfs.) and Peter RUST ex. of Hannah RUST who was surviving extx. of Benjamin RUST, Anthony GARDNER admr. with the will annexed of Spencer BOYD dec'd, William HAWKINS, Spencer BOYD, Robert BOYD, John DI[D]LAKE, Betty BOYD wid. of James BOYD dec'd. and Vincent VASS and William BOYD an infant by William HAWKINS his gdn. (defs.) (VGGA 27 Apr 96)

DEGRAFFENREID, Ischarner, in 1764 he was a justice of the peace in this state [Va. ?] but what part is not known; George MEADE of Philadelphia desires to know if he is living or dead, if anyone can give information thereof and whether he left any children (Philadelphia 29 Oct 1785) (VGAA 3 Dec 85)

DEGRAFFENREID, Tes Charner [sic], late of Lunenburg Co., e.a.w. his admrs., Jonathan PATTESON and John BILLUPS (VGPI 20 May 96) [Torrence gives his name as Tscharner De GRAFFENREIDT]

DE LABORD, Capt. Peter, commander of a Spanish vessel which put into Norfolk in distress about four yrs. ago, a native of Spain and citizen of Cadiz, d. on Sun. last in Wmsbrg. (VGWeA 24 Jan 94)

DE LA COUR, Claude Simon, dec'd, e.a.w. his ex., P. DE RIEUX, Charlottesville (VGGA 16 Mar 91)

DE LA MARCH, the Hon. Baron, mar. Miss Mary MURRAY dau. of Patrick MURRAY of Alexandria (VJAA 12 Oct 86)

DE LA SOMET, John, of Fauquier Co., banished from France in 1684 for his religion and soon came to Va. to settle the Brenton Lands, d. in Fauquier Co. about a fortnight ago at the age of around 130 (Wmsbrg. disp. of 17 Oct.) (NYPB 13 Nov 66)

DE LA TURBEUFF, Monsieur, French settler on Clinch River, Russell Co., was murdered in his home by a set of about 12 conspirators about the last of April; three of them, including the noted Obadiah PAINE formerly of Bedford Co., were taken and condemned by the Russell Co. Ct. (Lynchburg disp. of 23 May) (RJDA 12 Jun 95, SVG 20 Jun 95, RMA 25 Jun 95, VSPW 16 Jul 95)

DE LA VILLE BRUNE, Chevalier, d. lately at St. Pierre, Martinique; after the taking of York[town] he was appointed to the command of the remaining division of the French fleet in York and Baltimore (VIC 20 Sep 86)

DE SEQUIRA, Dr. John, d. on the 30th ult. in Wmsbrg. in his 83rd year; he was b. in London, studied in Leyden, and had lived in Wmsbrg. for 50 yrs. (VGGA 18 Mar 95, VGRMA 19 Mar 95)

DE SIGENGUE, Julie, of K & Q Co., adv. that she has a power of attorney from her husband, Lewis DE SIGENGUE, dated in France 23 Apr. last (VGGA 11 Sep 93)

DEADFOOT, Peter, aka William SWANN, mulatto slave, 22, ran away from Thomas MASON, Loudoun Co., has relations in Pr. Wm. Co., Va. and Charles Co., Md. (VGR 22 Sep 68)

DEADRICK, Thomas, mar. Miss Nancy RAWORTH, both of Winchester, on Tues. the 18th inst. (VCWM 26 Aug 89)

DEAKINS, Col. William Jr., d. at Georgetown on Sat. last (TAA 6 Mar 98)

DEALE, Clement, conv. svt., ran away from Edmund TERRILL and Clement READE, Culpeper Co. (VG 4 Jun 72)

DEAN, Mr., nephew of Abel DEAN of Clifton near Bristol, supposed to be living near Wmsbrg., will hear something greatly to his advantage by applying to George BRAIKENRIDGE, Hanover Co. (VG 9 May 71)

DEAN, Hugh, svt., pretends to be German but is thought to be Irish, 35, ran away from Morgan GRAVEN, Hanover Co., on 10 Jun.; he was seen on Rappahannock River on 18 Jun. (VG 11 Jul 51)

DEAN, Jack, Negro, 25-26, says he was b. free in Washington, N. Carolina, has no pass, jailed in Norfolk Co. (AGNPPA 22 Jan 96)

DEAN, Joshua, London conv., c. 40, ran away from Alexander SPOTTSWOOD, Pos Master General, in Jun 1737 (NYG 17 Jul 38)

DEAN, Capt. William, dec'd, e.a.w. his ex., S. DEAN (VGWeA 20 Nov 84)

DEAN, Willis, of Nansemond, dec'd, e.a.w. his agent, James BUSTON (NHPA 18 Dec 87)

DEANE, Elizabeth, wid. of Elkanah DEANE, coachmaker of Wmsbrg., adv. that hi brother, William DEANE, feloniously carried off £240 which came from the public sale of his est. (VG 13 Dec 76)

DEANE, Elkanah, adv. that he served a regular apprenticeship to the noted Joseph CARNCROFT of Dublin, coachmaker, and for many yrs. past carried on the coachmaking trade in Ireland and New York; he has now removed with his family to Wmsbrg. (VG 25 Jun 72); dec'd, Elizabeth DEANE, the admx., will sell the houses and lots in Palace St. in [Wmsbrg.] and will also settle his est. (VGP 26 Oct, 16 Nov 75)

DEANE, John Allen, appr., c. 13, ran away from John SAUNDERS, Wmsbrg. (VG 21 Jun 70)

DEANE, Simeon, formerly a resident of Wether[s]field in Connecticut, d. on Fri. la in Wmsbrg. where he had resided for several yrs.; he was bur. on Sun. eve. at Bruton Par. churchyard; early in the war he was sent by Congress to negotiate some business of importance in Holland and at the French Court (VGWeA 3 Jul 88, VIC 9 Jul 88); e.a.w. his ex., B. WALLER and John CARTER of Wmsbrg. (VIC 27 May 89)

DEANS, James, late of Chesterfield Co., dec'd, e.a.w. the surviving ex., William FLEMING (VGAA 15 Feb 83)

DEBUTTS, John, dec'd, e.a.w. his ex., Samuel DEBUTTS of Trenthall (CMAG 30 Jun 96)

DEDMAN, Capt. [also given as Col.] Samuel, [of Mecklenburg Co.], dec'd, e.a.w. ex., William G. BAPTIST who will also sell 420 ac. of his land on Aaron's Cr. in Mecklenburg Co. (VGPA 13 Mar 90, VGRMA 18 Sep 94)

DEGEAU, Charles, French svt., 24-25, speaks French and German, ran away from Garland THOMPSON, Fredsbrg. [VGAA gives his name as DEGRAA] (VJAA 21 Apr 85, VGAA 23 Apr 85)

DEJARNATT, Anne, has withdrawn from the house of her husb., Munford DEJARNATT (VIC 2 Jul 88)

DELANEY, Michael, of Petersburg, d. a few days ago (VGPI 29 Dec 95)

DELANY, Sharp Esq., formerly a member of the state assembly and for many yrs. Collector of the Customs for the port of Philadelphia, died (NH 21 May 99)

DELANY, Dr. William, late of Culpeper Co., e.a.w. his admr., W. HENSLER

(VGCD 18 Dec 79)
DELBRIDGE, Nancy, has left her husband, Robert DELBRIDGE (VGGA 25 Nov 95)
DELK, Joseph, dec'd, Jacob BARNES of Southampton is legally empowered by David DELK, the admr. of Joseph, to settle the est. of the dec'd (VG 25 Oct 76)
DELKS, Dudley, mulatto, 24, b. in N. Carolina, des. from the camp at Wmsbrg. last week (VG 31 Jul 46)
DELLAMARE, Henry, svt., caulker, ran away from Patrick CREAGH, Annapolis, Md. (VG 16 Jan 56)
DELON, John, Irish svt., ran away from the Patuxent Iron Works, Md. (VJAA 28 Jul 85)
DELONY, Lewis Jr., of Lunenburg Co., dec'd, his plant. there to be sold by his ex., Henry DELONY (VG 9 May 51)
DEMOS, Catherine, a bound girl, ran away from Valentine KNOP (PGBA 5 Sep 95)
DEMOSS Family, HCC, 18 Mar 1796: Colbert ANDERSON (pltf.) and Sarah DEMOSS, Charles DEMOSS, William DEMOSS, Lewis DEMOSS, Katherine DEMOSS, and Throckmorton DEMOSS infants under 21 by Morgan MORGAN their gdn., Valentine UPP, James DUNLOP, and Joseph STEPHENSON and Anna his wife, and Thomas DEMOSS (VGGA 27 Apr 96) [NB. I suspect that Valentine UPP in this entry and Valentine KNOP in the previous entry are the same person.]
DENBOW, Bazzel, aka STEEL, appr., c. 20, ran away from David FAULKNER, Apple Pie Ridge (BVCG 7 Oct 96)
DENHAM, Mrs. Elizabeth, consort of Richard DENHAM of Richmond, d. on Thurs. eve. last (VGRMA 8 Dec 94)
DENNIS, Thomas Lodge, dec'd, his ex., William CRAGHEAD, will sell his livestock and other items at his plant. in Hanover Co. (VG 10 Nov 74)
DENNISTON, John, svt., shoemaker, 32-33, along with his wife, Hannah, c. 25., ran away from Daniel CAMPBELL, Falls of Rappahannock River about the end of last Feb.; it is supposed they are about Lancaster Town [Pa. ?] as they inquired the way thither (MG 7 Jun 53)
DENNY, George, dec'd, a slave bel. to his. est. to be sold in Pr. Anne Co. (VCNPGA 8 Sep 92); e.a.w. Dennis DAWLEY Sheriff of Pr. Anne Co. (NH 26 Jan 99)
DENNY, Henry, one of the oldest inhabitants of Winchester, d. on Fri.; he was believed to be between 90 and 100 (BVCG 7 Dec 95)
DENNY, Capt. Samuel, of the artillery, mar. Miss FALLEN of Northumberland Co. (VG 30 May 77) [Acc. to "Marriage License Records of Northumberland Co., Virginia 1735 to 1795" VHM 47: p. 47, Samuel DENNY mar. Elizabeth FALLIN, 6 May 1777.]
DENSY, John [see: John DANCY]
DENTON, John, dec'd, his ex. (nfi) will sell his land in Brunswick Co. (VGR 14 Jan 73)
DEPAK, Francis, French, des. from the quota of state troops of Lt. Edward DIGGES who believes he may have gone towards Petersburg as he came from there (VGPu 5 Sep 77)
DERBY, John, aka Derby FINN, from Westmoreland Co., executed near Wmsbrg. Fri. last for felony (VGR 1 Jun 69, NYPB 19 Jun 69)
DERRICK Family, Botetourt Co. Ct., 17 Sep 1797: John PITZER (pltf.) against Michael DERRICK, Adam FOX and Elizabeth his wife, Philip FRY and Mary his wife, and Barbara DERRICK, Jonathan DERRICK, Rosanna DERRICK, John DERRICK, and Eve DERRICK infants under 21 and heirs at law of John DERRICK dec'd by their gdns. (nfi), and Nicholas BOWMAN and Catharine his wife (defs.); it appears that Adam and Eliz. FOX, Philip and Mary FRY, and the DERRICKs are not inhabitants of the commonwealth (VGGA 1 Nov 97)
DERRICK, Thomas, late of Northumberland Co., dec'd, his admrs., John LELAND and William BELL report that John DERRICK and Joseph HAGUE took a pilot boat bel. to his est. (VGR 23 May 71)
Deserted from the Virginia Regt., Alexandria: John BILE of New England, c. 25; Jacob BILE of New England, c. 25; Thomas LOCKER b. in Md., 26; William TURNER, shoemaker, 30; John WILSON, shoemaker, 26; John M'INTOSH,

carpenter, 26; James GUIN, shoemaker, b. in Ireland, 45, seen in company with Elizabeth M'ABOY who lived in Stafford Co. (MG 18 Apr 54)

Deserted from the Virginia Regt., Winchester: Thomas LOCKER, b. in Md., 26, lived about the Eastern Branch of Potomac; Ignatius JONES, b. in Md., 23, enl. with Mr. POLSAN at Lower Marlborough; Peter BRILLINGER or PRELINGER, a Swiss or Dutchman, 28, late of Alexandria, butcher and formerly lived, as he said, about Monocacy, went away in company with his wife who is a slender woman; Patrick SMITH, enl. by Mr. POLSAN at Lower Marlborough (MG 23 May 54)

Deserted from Capt. David BELL's Co. of the Virginia Regt.: Peter CURRIE, fr Va., 22, lurking in Albemarle Co.; Nathaniel HALL, from Va., 23, formerly in Chesterfield Co. now supposed in Granville Co., N. Carolina; Robert MILTON, from Nansemond Co.; James HATTON, from England (VG 14 Nov 55)

Deserted from Capt. David BELL's Co. of the Virginia Regt.: Bryan RALEIGH Irish, 23; John BROWN, Irish, 33, tailor; Peter BRINKLEY, from Nansemond Co., 25; John PERITT, from Nansemond Co., 23, hatter; Dennis DOWLIN, Irish, 27; they may be going to N. Carolina (VG 12 Dec 55)

Deserted from Capt. Carter HARRISON's Co.: Richard WOOD, 20; Charles CARTER, 23; Francis ROBERTS, 23; Thomas HENSLEY, 20; James THOMSON, 23; all from Va. (VG 12 Dec 55)

Deserted from the Virginia Regt. at Ft. Cumberland: Matthew ANDERSON, Virginian, 21; William BUSHOP, 31; Francis HILL, 36; James TURNER, Virginian, 26; Charles LEWIS, Virginian, 25; James FERGUSON, Virginian, 44; James SMITH; William ROBINSON; Jacob LEWIS; Benjamin HEAD (VG 12 Dec 55)

Deserted from the detachment of the Va. Regt. at Maidstone, 10 Aug: Matthew FLOWER, from Md., 20; Thomas HAMMOND, from Md., 19; William STOCKSDILL, from Md., 17; Edward CONSTANTINE, from Md., 19; Cornelius CHAPMAN, from Md., 19; Abraham WHITTAKER, from Md., 19; [Robert] CRAIGHEAD, from Md.; Isaac WHITTAKER, from Md., 21; John DA[W]SON, from Md., 24; James LINCH, Irish, 26; Peter WILLIAMS, from Md., 20; Samuel SAUNDERS, from Md., 22; James BARNETT, from Md., 22; Francis BROTHERS, from Md., 21; P[?] CONSTANTINE, from Md., 18; George WILSON, from Md., 19; David GLENDENING, from Scotland, 35 (VG 27 Aug 56)

Deserters from the Virginia Regt.: Joseph COPELAND, Kg. Wm. Co., 26, planter Nathaniel SPENCER, Kg. Wm. Co., 22; William AVERY, Kg. Wm. Co., 22, carpenter; Andrew [HARRES], Pr. Wm. Co., 22, planter; [Ignatius] EDWARDS, Pr. Wm. Co., 30; Richard LEE, Pr. Wm. Co., 21; William [CONLEY], Pr. Wm. Co., 22; Joseph CHAPMAN, Pr. Wm. Co., 45; Thomas LEGG, Pr. Wm. Co., 20; John [BOLAND], Pr. Wm. Co., 25; William SMITH, Pr. Wm. Co., 20, saddler; [Osborn BARNS], Pr. Anne Co., 36, planter; Richard SMITH, Pr. Anne Co., 23; William BATTEN, Pr. Anne Co., 19; John [WHITBUST], Pr. Anne Co., 24; Thomas SHOR[T], Pr. Anne Co., 39; Charles EDWARDS, Pr. Anne Co., 21; [Hezekiah FENTRESS], Pr. Anne Co., 38; James JOHNSON, K & Q Co., 19, cooper; John [STEVENS], K & Q Co., shoemaker; [Isaac RAINES], Caroline Co., 19, planter; Nathaniel STEVENS, Caroline Co., 18; Samuel MARTIN, Amelia Co., 41; Richard SHORE, Amelia Co., 53; Thomas EDWARDS, Pr. Geo. Co., 42; Thomas [ROACH], Richmond Co., 40; George WILLIAMS, Richmond Co., 26, mulatto; James BUSH, Albemarle Co., 23; Thomas DOYLE, Albemarle Co., Irish; Thomas BURNET, Essex Co., 36, carpenter; James HAMILTON, Essex Co., 20; Joseph NOEL, Essex Co., 38, weaver; Hill SMITH, Chesterfield Co., 32; Francis [CHANDOIN], Chesterfield Co., 39, French, barber; John WOOTTEN, Chesterfield Co., 23, planter; William HOWERTON, Chesterfield Co., 26; John CARR, Chesterfield Co., 28, from Maryland; George SHORT, Chesterfield Co., 26; John HARP, Chesterfield Co.; Robert MATTERSON, Norf., 47, [from the Isle of Man], sailor; John DUNNABOW, Norf., 25, from Md., planter; Moses COOPER, Norf., 28, sawyer; William [PEYTEN], Norf., 24, planter; Joshua WILLIAMS, Norf., 32, ditcher; James COOPER, Norf., 24, shoemaker; Argel PEYTON, Norf., 26, carpenter; John CORBAN, Westmoreland Co., 27, English, [laborer]; William DEPRIEST, Goochland Co., 24, sawyer; Samuel PATE, Southampton Co., 21, carpenter; Thomas PATE, Southampton Co., 30, shoemaker; Henry SHARP, Southampton Co., 18, planter; Drury BASS, Southampton Co., 21; John BERRY, Culpeper Co., 20, carpenter; Thomas ROY, Culpeper Co., 25; John POWEL, Culpeper Co., 21, planter; Thomas MORGAN, Suffolk Co. 26, mulatto; Amos NEWSUM, Suffolk Co. 37; James RUTTER, Suffolk Co. 28, lawyer [sic]; John JOHNSON, Suffolk Co. 25, planter; Aaron [VELTS], Suffolk Co. 22, sawyer; James MITCHELL, Brunswick Co., 19, planter; Richard VAUGHAN, Brunswick Co., 29, shoemaker; Joseph SHEARL, Brunswick Co., 24, planter; William WALL, Brunswick Co., 30; Frederick COCK, Brunswick Co., 19; William RYLY, Brunswick Co., 18; Joseph CHAMBERS, Brunswick Co., 19, of Philadelphia; William BEATLY, Northumberland Co., 22, plasterer; Daniel WILKINS, Northumberland Co., 21, carpenter; Aaron DAMERON, Northumberland Co., 22, planter; William BATES, Northumberland Co., 23, wheelwright; Thomas SHORT, Northumberland Co., 21, planter; Spencer Morgan BETALY [sic], Northumberland Co., 21, wheelwright; William BEARCROFT, Northumberland Co., 22, planter; James RAY, Louisa Co., 25, Irish; Matthew JOHNSON, Louisa Co., 26, from Md., shoemaker; John DAVIS, Louisa Co., 31, planter; Morris ROBERTS, Louisa Co., 25; Thomas SHIFFLET, Louisa Co., 21; Peter FERGUSON, Louisa Co., 26; James TAYLOR, Orange Co., saddler; James RANDOLPH, Orange Co., 22, planter; Joseph HENSLEY, Orange Co., 21, plasterer; William NIXON, Orange Co., 24, carpenter; Benjamin COLLINS, Orange Co., 24; John JONES, Orange Co., 25; Joseph [FEWQUA], Charles City Co., 26, cooper; Benjamin SPENCER, New Kent Co., 19, planter; Matthew CHILDRES, Henrico Co., 23; James GARRET, Henrico Co., 27; David ELLEN, Henrico Co., 17; David ALLEY, Henrico Co., 19; William MASON, Henrico Co., 40, English, doctor; David HARRIS, Hanover Co., 23, planter; William HARDING, Hanover Co., 27; Gideon TUCKER, Hanover Co., 19; Thomas TUCKER, Hanover Co., 21; James ARCHER, Hanover Co., 30; Elisha BOWLS, Hanover Co., 22; John WOOLAMS, Hanover Co., 21; Philemon EDWARDS, Dinwiddie Co., 34; William GARDNER, Dinwiddie Co., 22; Isham PARHAM, Dinwiddie Co., 23; William BYRD, Dinwiddie Co., 20; William LYLES, Dinwiddie Co., 22; Richard WALL, Dinwiddie Co., 33, shoemaker; John SLAUGHTER, Dinwiddie Co., 27; William TYE, Dinwiddie Co., 27; all the above are soldiers lately drafted out of the militia of the colony to serve in the Va. Regt. (VG 2 Sep 57)

Deserted from John POSEY's [Co. of the Va. Regt. in Fredsbrg.] seven recruits including: John BARRY, from Alexandria, seen to cross over to Md. with his wife; James DEVINE, from Loudoun Co., b. in Dublin, mar. since he enl. to a freckled, red-headed girl; James FITZPATRICK, from Westmoreland Co., b. in Dublin, was a soldier in POSEY's Co. in 1758 and 1760, gardener and ditcher by trade (MG 24 Jun 62)

Deserted from the Halifax Regular Co. now in Wmsbrg.: Joseph Mitchell BLAIR 23; James TROOP, c. 23; William HILL, 19; all three enl. in Halifax Co. (VG 20 Apr 76)

Deserted from the Pittsylvania Regular Co. in Wmsbrg.: Philip ATKINSON, 30; Walter WALTERS, c. 35; William FREEMAN, c. 23; William DAVIS, a native of Great Britain (VGPu 10 May 76)

Deserted from the company of Charles FLEMING, 7th Regt. of Va. Forces at Gloucester Co.: Joseph HASKINS; Ephraim TURPIN, 17-18 (VG 25 May 76)

Deserted from the *American Congress* sloop of war, Yeocomico [River], Northumberland Co. on 10 May: Richard PEARL, b. in Va., 32; Randolph BIGGS, b. in Fairfax Co., 19; John MORGAN, b. in London, 21; James BARTLETT, b. in London, 24; William WOOD, b. in London, 22 (VGPu 21 Jun 76)

Deserted from on board the schooner *Liberty* lying in East River [New York]: Alexander DAWSON, b. in Britain, c. 30; John WILLIAMS, b. in N.Y. (VG 29 Jul 76)

Deserted from on board the *Scorpion* sloop of war, Yeocomico [River]: George PATTERSON, boatswain; James PARKS, John LOWERY, Thomas DAVIS, David REESE (VGPu 23 Aug 76)

Deserted from Capt. Arthur SMITH's Co. of Regulars, 4th Bn. of Va. Forces: J LANCASTER, b. in Isle of Wight Co., 25; Kenchen TURNER, b. in Isle of Wight Co. (VG 21 Sep 76)

Deserted from Thomas GASKIN Jr.'s Co. of the 5th Bn.: James SELF, corporal, 25; William SELF, brother of James, c. 23; Rodham Kenner CRALLE, c. 21; Francis WADDEY, c. 22; they were concerned in a mutiny the day before they des. (VGPu 27 Sep 76)

Deserted from the co. of Gross SCRUGGS of the 5th Bn.: Thomas HOLLAND, c Joseph PAYNE, c., 25, enl. in Bedford Co.; John FRANKLIN, enl. in Wmsbrg. but came from Hanover Co. (VGPu 27 Sep 76)

Deserted from the co. of Capt. Samuel Jordan CABELL, 6th Va. Regt.: Josiah JONES, c. 22; David BARNETT, 21; Joseph CANTERBURY, c. 28; they all enl. in Amherst Co. (VGPu 8 Nov 76)

Deserted from the sloop *Betsey and Polly* lying in York River: Zerubabel KELI mate, Va. born, c. 23; Abel WILLIS, seaman, c. 23; Francis MOORE, seaman, b. in New England, c. 21; Hugh HARRIS, seaman, c. 28 (VGPu 17 Jan 77)

Deserted from Capt. ALEXANDER's Co. of the 2nd Regt.: John LICHENS, Will OWENS, Thomas LOVE, William HARDY, Hugh NELSON; all enl. in Frederick Co. (VGPu 24 Jan 77)

Deserted from the 4th Troop of Horse, Fredsbrg.: Jeremiah BRADSHAW, of Amelia, c. 22; Charles IRBY, of Amelia, c. 19; Jesse HARPER, of Pr. Edw., c. 21 (VGPu 14 Feb 77)

Deserted from Capt. SMITH's Co., 2nd Georgia Bn.: William DORTON, Wmsbr William STRANGE, Brunswick Co.; John WILLIAMS; Robert WILKINS, Henrico; John LEE, Bedford; John STITH, Bedford; John VEST, Buckingham; Thomas KELLY (VG 28 Feb 77)

Deserted from the co. of Capt. William SMITH, 2nd Georgia Bn.: Patrick DUF' Irish, had been in the marine service; William HARDY, b. in or near Frederick Town, Md., c. 25; Owen CAWFIELD, Irish, weaver, has lived in Alexandria; Charles MELTON, b. in Loudoun Co. near Col. RUSSELL's; Charles PHILLIS, aka John FERR, lived near the Short Hills, Loudoun Co. (VGPu 7 Mar 77 sup)

Deserted from the 3rd Co., 2nd Continental Bn. recruited in Va. for the defer of Georgia: Robert TATE, 26-27; Andrew HARDY, recruited in Albemarle Co., 26-27; Bartlett ANDERSON, wagoner who marched as far as Pr. Edw. (VG 7 Mar 77)

Deserted from the 15th Continental Bn.: Nehemiah FENTRISS, Norfolk Co.; Richard PHILLIPS, Louisa Co.; Levi WHITEHURST, Pr. Anne Co.; Emanuel KELLY, enl. as E. KEMBLE (VG 21 Mar 77)

Deserted from the co. of Capt. John WEBB, 7th Va. Regt.: Reuben COX, 22, enl Essex Co.; Carter FLETCHER, c. 20, enl. in Essex Co.; Benjamin DEAN, c. 23, enl. in K & Q Co.; Curtis HARDY, c. 20, enl. in Middlesex Co. (VGPu 28 Mar 77 sup)

Deserted from the 15th Va. Regt.: William LYLE, country born, c. 28; William CATTON, 23-24; both are from Kg. Wm. Co. (VGPu 4 Apr 77)

Deserted from Capt. Charles FLEMING's Co., 7th Va. Regt., at Elk Ridge Landing, Md. on 5 Feb. last: Pleasant LOCKETT, Richard COX, Abraham LEAR, Joel JOHNSON (VGPu 4 Apr 77)

Deserted from the co. of Capt. John GREGORY, 15th Bn. of Continental troo Robert PEALE, c. 25, seen in N. Carolina; Samuel HOSCA, c. 35; Martin REDMAN, c. 22, shoemaker; George RATCLIFF, c. 30, native of Eng. (VGPu 11 Apr 77)

Deserted from headquarters at or near Princeton, the following soldiers be the co. of Capt. James LUCAS, 4th Va. Regt.: Aaron BROWN, sgt., c. 21; Joh EDMONDS, carpenter; James BLICK, c. 20; Robert JONES; from Brunswick Co. (VGPu 11 Apr 77 sup)

Deserted from Capt. Richard STEVEN's Co. of Caroline Co.: George HOLLOV

a young man; Thomas CHANDLER, lived in the lower end of Caroline Co.; John
MELONE, Henry WEBSTER, William STEVENS, James GRIGSBY, Joshua
DUNN, of Essex Co.; John TAYLOR (VGPu 18 Apr 77)
Deserted from the ship *Jane*: Anthony SAMATER, c. 23; Louis MORREL, and
one other (nfi); Spaniards, sailors (VGPu 18 Apr 77 sup)
Deserted from Wmsbrg.: Edward HAMMOND, c. 45; John ADAMS, whose proper
name is GRIGG, 30; James LINNEY, a young man (VGPu 25 Apr 77)
Deserted from the co, of Regulars of Capt. John NICHOLAS: John KERSEY, c.
supposed to have gone to Carolina as he mar. the dau. of one George BROWN of
Guilford Co.; William Harris TALIAFERRO, c. 21, cabinet maker, lived with his
uncle Peter TALIAFERRO in Culpeper Co. (VGPu 25 Apr 77)
Deserted from the 6th Va. Regt., Fredsbrg.: Peter BARHAM, c. 34; Jesse NEW, c.
20; Thomas ROACH, c. 24; all from Charles City Co. (VGPu 2 May 77 sup)
Deserted from the co. of Va. troops of Thomas HAMILTON, Alexandria: John
BULMAN, 21-22, lived in Pr. Geo. Co., Md.; Samuel WARNER, b. in Charles
Co., Md., 34-35; Edward WELLMAN, b. in Eng., 24-25, has lived some time in
Charles Co., Md.; James FRAZER, b. in Ireland, c. 25 (VGPu 2 May 77 sup)
Deserted from Capt. Wm. LANE's Co. of the 2nd Georgia Bn.: Stephen RICE,
Eng., 30; John MILLER, Eng., 32; Sylvester CARY, Irish, 25; all enl. in Loudoun
Co. (VGPu 9 May 77)
Deserted from the co. of Capt. James FOSTER, 15th Va. Regt.: John THOMAS,
in Amelia Co., but late from Pr. Wm., carpenter, 30-40; William PRATT, of
Charlotte Co., enl. in Amelia, 25; Joseph HOLLAND, of Amelia, c. 30; John
QUESENBURG, enl. in Amelia, 30-40; Benjamin JONES, of Amelia, 25;
Edmund MASSEY, of Amelia, 20; George LOVELL, enl. in Amelia but lately
came from N. Carolina, 25; Asa CAWLEY, of Cumberland Co., 18-19; John
QUINN, of Amelia, 21 (VGPu 16 May 77 sup)
Deserted from Capt. John WEBB's Co. of the 7th Va. Regt.: Reuben COX, c. 22;
Carter FLETCHER, c. 19; Rice GRAVES, c. 24; Vincent HUDSON, a lad;
William JONES, c. 21; all enl. in Essex; Benjamin DEANE, c. 21, enl. in K & Q
Co.; Curtis HARDY, c. 21, enl. in Middlesex Co. (VGPu 13 Jun 77)
Deserted from the 5th Va. Regt. at Wilmington in Pa. last Oct.: Job Martin, c.
25; Edmund FAIR, c. 22; William TALLER, c. 24; Joel DOSS, c. 25; John
SHEARMAN, c. 23; Zachariah KENNETT, c. 25 (VGPu 13 Jun 77)
Deserted from Wmsbrg. last Sep.: Thomas MARTIN, c. 25; Samuel SAUNDERS, c.
24 who des. from Bedford Co. in Feb. last (VGPu 13 Jun 77)
Deserted from the 10th Va. Regt.: [Lake] BROWN, of Cumberland Co.; Josiah
CLARK, Anderson GREEN, James HOPKINS of Buckingham (VGPu 13 Jun 77)
Deserted from the co. of Colonial Regulars now raising of John POPE: Wm.
CLARK, c. 20, carpenter; Charles SPROUSE, c. 30, planter; both of Louisa Co.
(VGPu 13 Jun 77)
Deserted from the co. of the 3rd Georgia Bn. of Isaac HICKS: Benj. SEAWARD,
24-25; Thomas WILLIAMS, 22-23 (VGPu 13 Jun 77)
Deserted from the co. of state troops of Thos. W. EWELL: Elijah BIGBY, saddler
living near Dumfries; Thomas COLE, mulatto, living in Pr. Wm. Co.; Archibald
CASE, living in Kg. Geo. Co.; John CHAPLE, living in Fairfax; William
JOHNSON, tailor, enl. in Colchester; John FARLEY, lived near Dumfries, but
has moved for fear of being apprehended; John HADEN, enl. at Dumfries, living
near Colchester (VGPu 20 Jun 77)
Deserted from the co. of Capt. Benjamin PORTER, 2nd Georgia Bn.: Gabriel
WILKINSON, lived on Back Cr., Frederick Co.; Timothy GERARD, enl. in
Frederick Co. c. 12 miles from Winchester; Aaron DILLEY, enl. on Mill Cr.;
William JENKINS, of Berkeley Co.; Randolph FUGATE, of Culpeper Co.;
Nathaniel BERRY, aka SMITH; Joseph PRICE, an Englishman; Jeremiah
BURLEY, of Kg. Wm. Co.; William DORTON, enl. in Wmsbrg.; William HOOD,
enl. in Wmsbrg.; Thomas ROBERTSON, of Frederick Co.; John PHILLIPS, of
Dunmore Co.; Benjamin JONES, of Spotsylvania Co. (VGPu 20 Jun 77 sup)
Deserted from on board the brig *Greyhound* lying at Minge's on James River:
William JOHNSON, 35; John STEPHENS, 23 (VGPu 4 Jul 77)

Deserted from Capt. Thomas BRESSIE's Co. of this state: John LEE, c. 25, from near Halifax in N. Carolina, his real name is apparently Daniel YOUNG; Ennall TOOLEY, 19-20, from Hertford Co., N. Carolina (VGPu 4 Jul 77)

Deserted from the co. of Continental Regulars raised in Washington Co., Va., Capt. Nathan REID: Thomas PRICE, b. in S. Carolina on Broad River; John CHAMBERS, b. in Eng.; Charles SINCLAIR, c. 20, b. in Va.; William WAKEFIELD, aka PRICE, b. in the west of Eng.; William KING, c. 20, b. in Va., he has a brother in Montgomery Co.; Prichard STONE, b. in Va., c. 35, has chil. living in Washington Co.; Robert HAMBLETON, 22-23; Robert GRAY, c. 20, believed to have gone to Amherst Co. (VGPu 4 Jul 77)

Deserted from Capt. Thomas THWEATT's Co. of Regulars: Benjamin TURNER 20; Roderick CARMICHAEL, c. 22; both enl. in Halifax Co. (VGPu 4 Jul 77)

Deserted from the co. of John WINSTON, 14th Va. Regt.: Richard O. WRIGHT, native, c. 19; Joseph CLARKE, native, c. 38; Williamson PLANT, c. 40; Philip M'DONALD, Irish, c. 25; believed in Fauquier or Culpeper Co.; John SORRELL, native, c. 25, believed in Amelia Co.; all enl. in Hanover Co. (VGPu 4 Jul 77)

Deserted from the ship *Tartar* lying at Frazer's Ferry on Mattaponi: Joseph MARTIN, c. 30; John BASS, near 50; both from Middlesex Co. (VGPu 8 Aug 77)

Deserted from Capt. John LEWIS' Co. of Colonial Troops: Henry FEAR, c. 40, tailor; Philip ATKINS, c. 30; James BOYD, c. 25; James JORDAN, aka William JOHNSTON, c. 20; all enl. in Bedford (VGPu 15 Aug 77)

Deserted from the co. of Capt. J. MOUNTJOY, 10th Va. Regt.: Jos. PHILIPS, 2 23, formerly lived in Augusta Co; James HAMILTON, c. 40, said to have gone to Carolina; Jeremiah CHRISTIE; John NELSON, 25, formerly followed the water business; William BETTESWORTH, 23; James JONES, 30, planter; all but the first came out of Stafford and King Geo. Cos. (VGPu 15 Aug 77)

Deserted from the co. of Capt. Jos. SPENCER, 7th Regt.: Daniel MUSICK, 25- enl. in Orange Co., but since has gone, it is understood, to Carolina; Thomas HILL, 23-24, enl. in Culpeper Co., but is supposed gone to the back inhabitants [sic]; James BERRY, mulatto, c. 30, enl. in Fredsbrg. but served his time with Thomas BELL of Orange Co. (VGPu 15 Aug 77 sup)

Deserted from the *Lewis* galley: Samuel WHARTON, c. 20; Henry OVERSTREE c. 25 (VGPu 22 Aug 77)

Deserted from the 2nd. Va. Regt. in New Jersey: Francis DRYSKILL, Irish, 35; STROTHER, lived near Wmsbrg.; Benjamin JONES, imagined lurking about Baltimore as his parents live near there; Joseph BRYANT, enl. in Kg. Geo. Co. where his parents live; William DENNY, Irish, c. 30; John SAUNDERS, Irish, c. 18; John STOKES, from Va., c. 30; Thomas CONNERAN, Irish, 20; Richard LEWIS, Eng., 35, formerly lived in Loudoun Co.; Thomas TAPP [or TRAP], sgt., 30, his pregnant wife went off with him; Philip RAGAN, corporal, 22, from Frederick Co.; Brice RAGAN, pvt., 20, from Frederick Co., brother of Philip; Henry MACE, pvt., from Frederick Co. (VG 5 Sep 77, VGPu 10 Oct 77)

Deserted from Col. William GRAYSON's Regt.: John RUSSELL, 21; George RUSSELL, 19; William HANNESS, 20; Reuben FARRINGTON, 20, believed to have made for some of the northern states; Joseph YOUNGER, c. 24; Abraham CHILDRESS, 30; James KYLE; the first four enl. in Pittsylvania Co.; the next two in Halifax Co., and the last in Charlotte Co., and it is noted that the three first mentioned have since enl. with Capt. John DOOLY and are gone with him to Georgia (VGPu 12 Sep 77)

Deserted from the brig *Northampton* at Frazer's Ferry on Mattaponi: John ANTHONY, Portuguese; Osmand SANDAL, Eng.; Thomas BROWN, Eng.; Thomas JEFFERY, a lad of c. 19 (VGPu 12 Sep 77)

Deserted from Capt. Thomas WEST's Co., 10th Va. Regt.: Jeremiah BROWN, carpenter, of Fairfax Co., 28; Hezekiah MATTENY, 22, shoemaker; James MADDOX, 27, planter; Henry JONES, 17, planter; Charles POTTER, 18, plante Davis RATCLIFF, 20, planter; Edward MEEKS, 30, planter; John HAYLY, 23, tailor; John SMITH, Eng., 30, wheelwright; John WILLIAMSON, 19, planter; William ROBERTS, Irish, 30, planter; William ANDERSON, Eng., 28, planter; George JOHNSON, Eng., 25, blacksmith; Joseph STOUTON, of Loudoun Co., 28

planter; James RUSH, 21, planter; Richard CROP, of Pr. Wm. Co., 18 (VGPu 19 Sep 77)
Deserted from the *Manly* galley: John HARFORD, sailor, c. 30; William WILKINS, marine sgt., c. 25 (VGPu 3 Oct 77)
Deserted from the 4th Georgia Bn.: James M'CORMICK, c. 27, shoemaker, b. in Ireland; James M'FARLAND, Scot, 23, tailor; John MITCHELL, 21, shoemaker, b. in Ireland; John HODGES, Scot, 30, sailor; Conor SULLIVAN, sgt., Irish, 25, weaver (VGPu 28 Nov 77)
Deserted from Capt. John LEWIS' Co. of State Troops in the 2nd Regt.: Philip ATKINS, reportedly gone towards Carolina; James JURDEN, aka William JONESTEN, tailor; both enl. in Bedford Co. (VGPu 28 Nov 77)
Deserted from the 2nd Georgia Bn. of Continental Troops: Jas. HARRIFIELD, c. 35, from Pr. Edw. Co.; Hawkins BRIANT, c. 21, from Bedford Co.; Thomas MOORE, c. 25, from Brunswick Co.; Charles BROOKS, c. 19, from Loudoun Co.; John COCK, c. 25, from Halifax Co, he reportedly is gone to an uncle's on Meherrin River; Joseph INGRAM, Scot, from Lunenburg Co.; Edward JAMES, c. 20, who reportedly is at one of his sister's in James City Co. near Cartright's Ordinary (VGPu 12 Dec 77)
Deserted from the *Manly* galley: James HODGES, c. 30; Isaac CARLTON, c. 20; both are marines (VG 19 Dec 77)
Deserted from the 3rd Georgia Bn. of Continental Troops: Caleb HUNTER, from Amelia Co., c. 23; Obadiah FERGUSON, c. 17; Isham DYKE, c. 18; John JOHNSON, c. 25; Ambrose LUCHAS, c. 21; David WOMACK, c. 16; William BARTLETT, c. 24; John Moore CLAY, c. 20; William WOODRUFF, c. 40; Alexa[n]der BARTLETT, c. 18; William JONES, c. 25; Andrew KING, c. 26, expected to be on Clinch River (VG 19 Dec 77)
Deserted from Capt. BRESSIE's Co. of State Troops: Joshua CAMPBELL, sgt., c. 22; Edmund LOVE; Charles SMITH; William GREGORY, enl. from N. Carolina, c. 27; James JOHNSTON, 35, formerly kept a school; John WAYLES, c. 30, enl. in Pr. Anne Co. (VG 26 Dec 77)
Deserted from Col. HARRISON's Bn. of Continental Artillery: Peter LAYLAND 30, obtained a furlough last Jul. to go to Northumberland Co. for 20 days; John FISHER, c. 20, obtained a furlough last Oct. for 25 days to go to Westmoreland Co. (VGPu 6 Mar 78)
Deserted from the State Artillery Co. of Capt. Hen. QUARLES: Thos. MOODY, from Lunenburg, c. 21; Richard [ASHLOCK], from Halifax, c. 16 (VGPu 27 Mar 78)
Deserted from Capt. DeLAPORTE: Patrick CARY, Irish, c. 26; Henry INGOT surnamed LA PUILLADE, French, c. 27, lately enl. at Edenton [N. Carolina]; Prittraud surnamed COEUR DE ROY, French (VGPu 1 May 78)
Deserted from the 2nd Georgia Regt. of Continental Troops: Thomas MARTIN, 22, resident of Chesterfield Co.; Thomas OWEN, [from] near Col. COLE's in Albemarle Co., c. 27; both are natives of Va. (VG 13 Nov 78)
Deserted from the Va. State Garrison Regt. of Infantry now stationed near Wmsbrg.: Thomas TISDALE, b. in Hanover Co., c. 23; Charles VALENTINE, mulatto, b. in Surry Co., 28; James COLLIER, b. in K & Q Co., 16; John BUNNS, b. in K & Q Co., 16 (VG 19 Mar 79)
Deserted from Wmsbrg.: Stephen HAWK, Eng.; William THOMPSON, Eng., nailer by trade, well known in Suffolk and Portsmouth (VG 9 Apr 79)
Deserted from the Wmsbrg. Garrison: James EGMON, from York Co., 19, supposed he enl. in the light horse and is stationed in Winchester; Charles VALENTINE, free Negro from Surry, it is thought he is with his wife in sd. co.; Philip MILLER, German, c. 20, a cooper by trade, supposed to work at Alexandria; John O'DEER, from K & Q Co., c. 16, cooper, supposed to be at his home; Thomas JOHNSON, Irish, sailmaker; Andrew WILSON, Scot, 28; Marshall DELASIE, fifer, b. in France, 21; Wilson JACKSON, from Nova Scotia, 33; William THOMPSON, Eng., 45; Thomas JAMES, Portuguese, 29, tailor; Samuel HAMOND, 25, was enl. in Hampton and des. from there; Harwell RANDOLPH, from Pr. Geo. Co., 30; Thomas TISDALE, from Hanover Co., 23,

used to drive a wagon for the Wmsbrg. Garrison, supposed to be with his wife in sd. co.; John ARMSTRONG, from Md., 29, has been a long time with the Indians; John LAWRENCE, from Richmond, 21 (VG 1 May 79)

Deserted from Wmsbrg., six recruits: Stephen HAWK, said he was on board the *Randolph* frigate when she was lost; William THOMPSON, sailor, well known in Suffolk and Portsmouth; John MITCHELL, said he came from Baltimore and had served three yrs. in the Continental Army as a sgt. in one of the Md. Bns.; William STONE, blacksmith, well known in James City and Dinwiddie Cos.; James WATERS, plasterer; Jean LAZERAT, French (VG 22 May 79)

Deserted, three recruits from the Pr. Wm. Co.: Andrew MURPHEY, Irish; James MILLER, Eng.; Robert WOODERFIELD, Eng. (VG 11 Sep 79)

Deserted from Richmond, two recruits: Robert TATE, from Va., c. 27, enl. as substitute for a division in Henrico Co.; John [WASH], who enl. as substitute for a division in Louisa, c. 25 (VGCD 27 Nov 79)

Deserted from the co. of State Artillery of Capt. Gideon JOHNSTON stationed York Garrison: John JOHNSTON, Irish; John LEWIS, Eng.; William BLACK, Irish; Peter LUTHIE, French; Christopher MAGEE, Eng.; George FITZPATRICK, Irish; Thomas NEWTON, Irish (VG 25 Mar 80)

Deserted from the ship *Hanover* at Richmond the following sailors: Thomas BOWMAN, c. 28; Thomas WEEKLY, c. 20; John BRIDE, c. 20; John MORRIS; Robert EDWARDS; Thomas PATTS; James WILLIAMS; all supposed to be English (VGAA 17 Dec 85)

Deserted from Capt. BROCK's Co. of new levies at Winchester: John POPE, otherwise John GARDINER, c. 23; Jacob SLY, c. 22 (VGWA 21 May 91)

Deserted from the Alexandria levies: Thomas M'KANN, 25; John SHUFFLETON 40 (VGWA 28 May 91)

Deserted from the Virginia Bn. of Levies: James GRAHAM, Irish; Andrew BENSON; Thomas HUGHS, Irish; John DOVE (VGWA 4 Jun 91)

Deserted from the 2nd Division of the Va. Bn. of levies: Absolom ELWOOD, en Alexandria; Michael JOHNSON, enl. in Alexandria; William TAYLOR, enl. in Alexandria; John REARDON, enl. in Leesburg; John NICHOLSON, enl. in Winchester; Sampson VIOLET; Edward TURNER; John MARRELL; John DWYER (VGWA 18 Jun 91)

Deserted from the rendezvous, 3rd U. S. Regt., Winchester: John COWDEN, country born, 18-20; Alexander DUKELAND, 17-18; Adam CHAMBERS, Irish, c. 33; John WOODFORD (BVCG 14 May 92)

Deserted from quarters, 1st U.S. Regt., Richmond: Joseph HINDS, Irish, 22; Patrick SCULLY, Irish, 26; Thomas CLARKE, Irish, 26; Charles WRIGHT, from Va., 22; William LUSTER, from Va., 20; Andrew PATTERSON, Irish, 30 (VGGA 27 Jun 92)

Deserted from Cap. Joseph BROCK's Co., 3rd U.S. Regt., Winchester: Henry MAHONY, William MURPHY, William YOUNGLOVE (BVCG 2 Jul 92)

Deserted from quarters, 1st U.S. Regt., Richmond: John O'NEIL, Irish, 27-28; Lovel CAIN, Irish, 40; John HINDS, Irish, 24; William ROBINSON whose real name is Arthur LAMB, Irish, 28, shoemaker; Reuben STATEN, from V., 22; William FAUSSET, Irish, 24; Benjamin FERGUSSON, from Va., 18 (VGGA 27 Jun, 25 Jul, 1 Aug 92)

Deserted from camp near Richmond: John CARNEY, b. in Alexandria, 19, shoemaker; John Lewis SIEBOLT, German, 42; George DICKERSON, aka CAMPBELL, from Va., 20, formerly lived in K & Q Co. (VGGA 26 Sep 92)

Deserted from the camp of the 3rd U.S. Regt. near Richmond: Richard JESS from Va., formerly of Essex Co., 22; John EDMUNDSON, from Va., kept school in Essex Co., 22; Edmund GREGS, from Va., lived in Essex Co., 19, carpenter (VGGA 26 Sep 92)

Deserted from the rendezvous of the 4th Sub-Legion, Staunton: Joseph STRATSMAN, German, 30, shoemaker; Edward MURPHEY, Irish, c. 40, shoemaker; William DIXON, says he was b. in Pa., his parents live in Amherst Co., 18-19 (VGGA 26 Sep 92)

Deserted from the camp of the Light Dragoons, Richmond: James AYDLE, c

Dutchess Co., NY, 18; Wyatt ATKINS, of Pittsylvania Co., 22 (VGGA 31 Oct 92)

Deserted from Fredsbrg.: James TAYLOR, Irish, plasterer; Charles McNIFF, Irish, plasterer; John ALLEN, young lad of Kg. Geo. Co.; Lewis JONES, young lad of Kg. Geo. Co.; Thomas NUTALL and William NUTALL both from Lancaster Co.; Lewis BICKERS, lad from Orange Co.; William LUTRELL, from Westmoreland Co.; William OMOHUNDRO, from Westmoreland Co.; James CLARK, from Westmoreland Co. (VHFA 15 Nov 92)

Deserted from Capt. Thomas LEWIS' Co. of Riflemen, [Greenbrier Ct. H.]: William and John RICHARDS, brothers, 25 and 22; Charles PEARCE, 20; William GREEN, c. 30; John SLOAN, c. 25; Larkin BAILINGE, c. 32; John ROBERTSON, c. 20 (BVCG 26 Nov 92)

Deserted from the 3rd U.S. Regt.: John HUFF, German; David JONES, from Va., along with his wife; William MULLINEAUX, Eng.; Henry WILLSTOCK, German; James WARNER, native (BVCG 3 Dec 92)

Deserted from Capt. Thomas LEWIS: William FOUGHT, Henry CAMPBELL, Samuel SWEARINGHAM, all three b. in Va. (KG 15 Dec 92)

Deserted from the 1st Troop, Light Dragoons, Ft. Washington: Mr. WELCH, c. 23, enl. in Botetourt Co.; Nat. BENNETT, c. 21, b. in Berkeley Co., enl. in Rockbridge Co. (KG 22 Dec 92)

Deserted from Ft. Hamilton: Samuel REMINE, c. 28; Isaac GRAY, c. 30; Mark DEMSEY, all natives of Botetourt Co. (KG 12 Jan 93)

Deserted from the 4th Sub-Legion, Winchester: Francis ONEAL, Irish, 28, has fathers-in-law [sic] in Loudoun Co.; Francis QUIN, Irish, 35, will probably head for Pa.; Stephen WAGGONER, Eng., upwards of 30; William M'GRATH, from Pa., 30, he and his wife were conveyed away by his brother-in-law, [?] LITTLE (BVCG 3 Jun 93)

Deserted from the camp of the 3rd Sub-Legion, Winchester: James M'REA aka James DOOGAN, Irish, 21; William CARLETON, Irish, 23, wounded in [Gen.] ST. CLAIR's defeat; David PETERSON, American, 20 (BVCG 24 Jun 93)

Deserted from the U.S. Infantry at Winchester or on the way to Ft. Pitt: Benj. ROBINSON, from Va., c. 24; James PLANT, from Va., c. 18; George SCHULTZ, Scot, c. 27; Thomas HARRISON, Irish, 26 (BVCG 1 Jul 93)

Deserted from the army at Winchester: Jeremiah HAMILTON, Irish, c. 20; Nicholas WATSON, Irish, above 40, his wife went with him (BVCG 11 Aug 94)

Deserted from the Ft. Pitt Expedition, 8th Brigade, in Richm.: Jn. NEWSUN, from Southampton; David POPE, from Southampton; Benjamin CREWS, from Sussex; Judkins JOHNSTON, from Sussex; William GLOVER, from Sussex (VGGA 8 Oct 94)

Deserted from Ft. Nelson: David POTTER, 32-33, b. in N. Jersey, cutler and nailer; Charles BAILEY, 23-24, b. in Va., enl. at Hanover Ct. H., butcher; William REESE, 25-26, b. in Pa., enl. at Fredsbrg., blacksmith; William WILSON, 24-25, Irish, enl. at Fredsbrg., stonemason; John BRADISH, 52-53, Irish, enl. at Richmond, shoemaker; John KELLY, 27-28, Irish, enl. at Richmond, upholsterer; Patrick KELLY, 22-23, Irish, enl. at Richmond, farmer and blacksmith (HNPA 4 Mar 95)

Deserted from the schooner *Endeavor* riding at anchor opposite the mouth of Acotink Cr.: John BOWEN, speaks Welsh and Eng.; James ROBERTS, a country born lad, c. 19 (CMAG 12 Mar 95)

Deserted from the camp of the 3rd Sub-Legion, Shockoe Hill, Richmond: Jn. CHILDERS, 22, b. in Albemarle Co., farmer; William SMITH, from Va.; George M'DONALD, b. in Philadelphia, Pa., 30, stonemason; John BYRD, from Va., supposed to be in Louisa Co. (RMA 5 Sep 95, 3 Dec 95, RC 8 Dec 95)

Deserted from the barracks in Winchester: George BURNS, 19-20, tanner, enl. at Libertytown, Md.; James M'CAULEY, Irish, 21, tailor (BVCG 12 Oct 95)

Deserted from Ft. Norfolk: Cornelius WILSON, 29, painter, Irish; Daniel DONOGHOE, Irish, c. 23, currier; John ALEXANDER, blacksmith, b. in Va. (NHPA 21 Jan 97)

Deserted from the Richmond rendezvous of the U.S. Army: Timothy MAHANE, laborer; William M'LELLAN, 24, laborer; John GORMAN, 26, seaman; all three are from Ireland (VGGA 14 Mar 98)

Deserted from Ft. Norfolk: Cuthbert SHELTON, from Va., 25; Benjamin WELLS b. in Southampton Co., c. 22, laborer; James LAMSON, native of Connecticut, c. 20 (NH 1 May 98, NWJCI 2 May 98)

Deserted from the Corps of Artillerists and Engineers: John BURROWS, c. 1 stonecutter, b. in Stafford Co.; William HOWELL, 21, farmer, b. in Westmoreland Co.; Richard SHERMAN, 28, ships carpenter, b. in Connecticut (NH 9 Feb 95)

Deserted from the co. of Capt. N. HENRY, 8th U.S. Regt., near Winchester: Ignatius ANDERSON, b. in Loudoun Co., 23; John DAVIS, b. in Hardy Co., 23; Samuel BONNER, b. in Hardy Co., 23; John GANBY, b. in Va., 20; William BONNER, b. in Hardy Co., 18 (WG 28 Aug 99, BI 18 Sep 99)

Deserted from the marine recruiting party at the Great Bridge: James DORMAN, b. in Accomack Co., bricklayer, 20; Samuel LOMAN, native of Camden Co., N. Carolina, 21 (NH 29 Aug 99)

Deserted from the U.S. frigate *Constitution*: Erastus BRUNSEN, sgt. of Marir. b. in Hartford Co., Connecticut, 21; Silas CUSHMAN, sgt., b. in Hampton Co., Mass. (NH 7 Sep 99)

Deserted from the armed schooner *Virginia*: William BAKER, c. 23; Davy LAMPERT, c. 24; Thomas DURHAM, c. 23 (NH 16 Nov 99)

Deserted from the U.S. Army: Peter CREAGER, 19, b. in Wythe Co.; James PHIPPS, 19, b. in Wythe Co.; Charles MORGAN, 19, b. in N. Carolina; John (aka Daniel) M'CLOUD, 22, b. in Guilford Co., N. Carolina; James KENNEDY, 29, b. in Kings Co., Ireland; Robert LYNCH, 35, b. in Lancashire, Eng.; James ROBERTS, 40, b. in Caroline Co.; George ELMORE, 27, b. in Frederick Co. (ARG 5 Nov 99)

DESHONCLE, John, French, des. from the quota of Lt. James W. BRADLEY of the state artillery; he was enl. at Portsmouth from a French vessel there (VGPu 14 Nov 77)

DESSIE, Aquilla, from Md., 26, des. from Capt. Thomas WAGGENER's Co. of Va. Forces (VG 22 Aug 55)

DEVERIX, James, Eng. svt., 20, ran away from William WYATT, Pr. Wm. Co. (VG 29 Jun 76)

DEVINE, John, appr., c. 11, ran away from M. GARBER Jr. in Staunton (SVG 4 Jan 97)

DEVOUX, Stephen, Eng. svt., 20, baker, ran away from Robert ADAM and Peter WISE, Alexandria (VG 6 Jun 66)

DIAL, Edward, dec'd, his admr. with the will annexed, William YOUNG, adv. a sale of his est. in Norfolk (VG 1 Aug 55)

DICK, Mrs., wife of William DICK of Norfolk, d. last Thurs. (HNPA 18 Apr 95)

DICK, Alexander, of Fredsbrg., died (VGWeA 4 Jan 83)

DICK, Maj. Alexander, dec'd, John MERCER is compelled to take upon himself the admin. of Maj. DICK's father, Charles DICK Esq., unadministered by the Major (VGAA 14 May 85)

DICK, George, sailor, ran away from the ship *Charming Peggy*, Georgetown (VJAA 17 Nov 85)

DICKENSON, Mrs. Ann, dec'd, Bernard WEBB claims that her land adv. for sale in New Kent Co. belongs to him [It is not clear whether her name is DICKENSON or BICKERTON, q.v.] (VGAA 20 Mar 84)

DICKENSON, Edward, dec'd, his extx. is Hannah DICKENSON, mentioned in Pr. Wm. Co. chancery case of 10 Aug 1799 (CMAG 26 Sep 99)

DICKERSON, David, of Gloucester Co. adv. that his son, William DICKERSON, will be but 16 on the 5th of Dec.; William was adv. as a deserter by Charles TOMPKIES (VGPu 8 Nov 76)

DICKERSON, William, a young fellow, b. in Gloucester Co., des. from Charles TOMKIES' Co. of Regulars at York (VGPu 25 Oct 76)

DICKERSON, William, dec'd, his land in Pr. Edw. Co. to be sold by Archelaus DICKERSON the admr. (VGAA 28 Jun 83)

DICKEY, John, dec'd, e.a.w. his ex., John DICKEY (VGWeA 12 Nov 85)

DICKIE, the Rev. Adam, of K & Q Co., dec'd, his schooner lying at Hobb's Hole to be sold by Anne DICKIE the admx. (VG 6 Jun 45, 12 Sep 45)

DICKINSON, Maj. Edmund B., dec'd, his admr., Robert NICOLSON, will sell 2'

ac. of his land a small distance from Petersburg (VG 24 Apr 79)
DICKINSON, Elisha, dec'd, e.a.w. his extx., Ann DICKINSON (VHFA 29 May 94)
DICKINSON, Francis, late of Norfolk, mar. Miss Catherine JOHNSTON dau. of Col. Richard JOHNSTON late of this county dec'd, in Caroline Co. on the 17th inst. (RCFPC 25 Jan 97)
DICKINSON, J., of Norfolk, intends to remove to Richmond in a few days (AGNPWA 27 Mar 93)
DICKSON, Capt. Henry, was mar. to Miss Virginia Averilla DOGGE at Pierceville the seat of Thomas PEARCE [sic] Esq. on Mon. eve. by the Rev. Mr. HUBBARD (NHPA 23 Mar 97)
DICKSON, Peter, of Norfolk, hairdresser, d. yesterday; e.a.w. his admr., George MITCHELL of Norfolk (HNPA 4 Oct 94, 15 Nov 94)
DICKSON, the Rev. Robert, rector of Lynhaven Par., Pr. Anne Co., died (VGPu 23 Aug 76)
DICKSON, Robert, of Norfolk, dec'd, his perfumery shop to be sold by his admr., George MITCHELL (NPJ 23 Jul 88)
DICKSON, Thomas, of Wmsbrg., died (VG 14 Nov 51)
DICKSON, William, was mar. to Miss Mary DAVIS, both of Portsmouth, on Thurs. last by the Rev. Mr. EMERSON (NH 13 Jun 99)
Died in an epidemic raging in Philadelphia: Samuel POWELL, John ROSS, Thomas WILLING, John MAYO (VGRMA [3] Oct 93)
DIGGES, Mrs. Anne, of York Co., d. in her 56th year (VGPu 22 Dec 75); e.a.w. her ex., Cole DIGGES, who will also sell all the HH and KF at Dr. Thomas POWELL's in Yorktown (VG 27 Jan 76)
DIGGES, Charles, eld. son of William DIGGES Esq., of Md., d. suddenly in the prime of life on Wed. 5 Apr. at Dumfries, Pr. Wm. Co. [obit.] (VGR 13 Apr 69)
DIGGES, Cole Esq., delegate for Warwick Co., d. in Wmsbrg.; e.a.w. his ex., Edward DIGGES and Thomas DIGGES, who will sell his HH and KF and livestock at his plant. in Warwick (VG 23 May 77, 20 Jun 77, VGPu 23 May 77, 6 Jun 77)
DIGGES, Cole, of Warwick Co., William DIGGES Sr. of Denbigh, Warwick Co., warns him not to sell certain slaves (VGGA 27 Nov 93)
DIGGES, Dudley, d. of smallpox at Wmsbrg. (VG 4 Feb 68)
DIGGES, Col. Dudley, old and respected inhabitant of Wmsbrg., d. at York on the 3rd inst. at an advanced period of life [obit.] (VICGA 12 May 90)
DIGGES, Dudley Jr. Esq., mar. Miss Polly DIGGES of Wmsbrg. last Thurs. sennight (VGAA 31 Dec 85)
DIGGES, Col. Edward, eld. son of the Hon. Cole DIGGES Esq. of H.M's Council, mar. Miss Anne HARRISON a dau. of the late Hon. Nathaniel HARRISON Esq. dec'd former Auditor of the Colony, on 9 Aug. (VG 10 Aug 39); d. Fri. last at his seat in York Co. in a very advanced age (VGR 30 Mar 69); e.a.w. the ex., William DIGGES Jr., William DIGGES, Dudley DIGGES Jr. (VG 2 Nov 69)
DIGGES, Mrs. Elizabeth, spouse of Dudley DIGGES Esq. of Wmsbrg., d. on Sat. last at Rosegill (VGWeA 31 Dec 85)
DIGIN, James, Bostonian, suspected of stealing a horse from Samuel DUVAL of Richmond (VGP 10 Jan 76)
DILLARD, James, of Amherst Co., dec'd, his admr., James DILLARD, will sell all his land, slaves, and stocks (LFG 13 Dec 94, LWM 21 Aug 97)
DILLARD, James Jr., d. in the flower of his age on 31 May (VGPu 7 Jun 76)
DILLING, John, appr., c. 17, ran away from Richard SIMPSON, Fairfax Co. (VGAxA 23 Jun 91)
DILLON, James, mar. Miss Phoebe BROWN (VHFA 24 Jan 93)
DILLON, Thomas, merch., of Cumberland Co., mar. Miss Betsy KEELING of the same co. on Wed. the 6th inst. (VGWeA 15 Mar 87)
DIRUPEARD, Joseph Valentine, French. tailor, des. from the camp. of the 3rd Sub-Legion, Shockoe Hill (RC 7 Jul 95)
DISMAKES, Reuben, 30, jailed in Richmond for murder, escaped on 17 Nov. (VGAA 13 Dec 83)
DISMAL, Jack, Negro, ran away from James HUNTER near Fredsbrg.

(VG 18 Feb 73)
DISMUKES, Benjamin, dec'd, e.a.w. John ELLIS, his ex., of Caroline Co. (VGGA 11 Apr 92)
DITTOND, Anthony Francis, of Spotsylvania Co., convicted of murdering a Mr. EVANS (q.v.) in Hanover Co., was executed by hanging near Wmsbrg. on 24 Nov. (VG 25 Aug, 20 Oct, 24 Nov 38, NYWJ 5 Feb 39)
DIXON, Beverly [also given as DICKSON], merch., of Wmsbrg., mar. Miss Polly SAUNDERS on Sun. last (VG and VGPu 1 Nov 76)
DIXON, Mrs. Charlotte, died in Wmsbrg. (VGWeA 12 Dec 96, VGPI 13 Dec 96)
DIXON, Capt. Edward, of Port Royal, died (VG 12 Jun 79); e.a.w. his ex., Harry DIXON and Turner DIXON (VG 31 Jul 79)
DIXON, Henry, of Halifax Co., adv. that his wife, Anne DIXON, has revolted from his bed and refuses copulation and has caused him to be put in prison (VG 26 May 68)
DIXON, John, of Newcastle, intends for Eng. in the spring with his family (VG 3 Oct 51)
DIXON, John, svt., 19-20, says he was b. in Eng., but is supposed to be Irish, ran away from John HOBDAY, Gloucester Co. (VG 10 Oct 55)
DIXON, John, of Hanover Co., dec'd, land and slaves of his to be sold by his ex., John DIXON (VG 17 Oct 66); his land in lower Louisa and upper Hanover Cos. to be sold by his ex. (VG 8 Oct 67)
DIXON, the Rev. John, dec'd, his ex., John PEYTON and John DIXON, will sell the public warehouses called Dixon's and Falmouth at the Falls of Rappahannock (VGPu 7 Nov 77 sup. VG 14 Nov 77); his ex. will sell about 40 of his Negroes at Gloucester Ct. H. (VGAA 12 Oct 82)
DIXON, John, public printer of this state, d. on Wed. last [27 Apr.] in his 51st year (VGGA 4 May 91, VHFA 5 May 91, S. Carolina Indep. Gazette and Georgetown Chronicle 4 Jun 91)
DIXON, John, admr., will settle the est. of his late father (nfi) (VGPA 17 Sep 91)
DIXON, John Esq., mar. Miss Peggy MOORE dau. of Cato MOORE Esq. (PGBA 1 May 96)
DIXON, John, Sarah DIXON of Portsmouth, adv. for runaway slaves that bel. to the est. of John DIXON and were lent to the wife of Benjamin BRYAN of Hampton during her lifetime and since her death, the sd. Benjamin has conveyed them to his son, William BRYAN, in Wmsbrg. (AGGA 9 Dec 96)
DIXON, John Jr., merch. in Gloucester Co., mar. Miss Elizabeth "Betsey" PEYTON second dau. of Sir John PEYTON Bart. of that county (VG and VGR 11 Feb 73)
DIXON, Mrs. Lucy, the admr., John DIXON, and the mortgagee, Thomas DIXON, will sell a 400 ac. tract in Culpeper Co. at her house in Fredsbrg. (VG 18 Nov 73)
DIXON, Roger, intends to move to Culpeper as soon as he can sell his est. near Fredsbrg. [long, detailed advertisement] (VG 21 Apr 68)
DIXON, Roger, d. at Fredsbrg. on Fri. the 22nd ult. [obit.] (VG 12 Jun 72); e.a.w. his brother in Wmsbrg., John DIXON, the admr. with the will annexed (VG 2, 9 Jul 72); John DIXON will sell his land in Culpeper, Spotsylvania, Albemarle, Orange, Louisa, and Hanover cos. (VG 30 Jul 72); additional lands to be sold pursuant to his will (VG 6 Aug 72)
DIXON, Roger, of Spotsylvania Co., dec'd, his wife, Lucy, and son, Roger, are mentioned in a court case of 7 Nov 1797 (VHFA 14 Feb 98)
DIXON, Mrs. Rosanna, wife of Col. John DIXON, printer, of Richmond, d. on Mon. morn. 5 Apr. (VICGA 7 Apr 90, VHFA 15 Apr 90, VGWA 24 Apr 90)
DIXON, Mrs. Sarah, d. on Wed. last about a mile from Portsmouth in her 69th year (NH 3 Nov 98)
DIXON, Capt. Thomas, dec'd, e.a.w. the admr., Carter BRAXTON (VGAA 22 Jun 82)
DOBBS, Christian, blacksmith, c. 40, lives about 17 miles below Charlottesville on the Three Chopt Road, believed to be of Dutch parents, jailed for breech of the peace, escaped from jail in Charlottesville (VGGA 15 Nov 97)
DOBBY, James, svt., 40, sailor, ran away from Charles GRIFFITH and Henry GRIFFITH Jr., Frederick Co., Md. (VGR 9 Jun 68)

DOBSON, Stephen, of Richmond, was found dead floating in Hampton Roads; he is supposed to have had a considerable sum of money as he sold a cargo of wheat in Baltimore; a liberal reward for any information is offered (NH 1 Jun 99)

DOBSON, Maj. William, late of Hampshire Co., dec'd, e.a.w. his ex., William DONALDSON and Jeremiah SULLIVAN (WG 23 Oct 99)

DOBY, John, a substantial planter in Surry Co., was returning home in his cart on 16 Dec. when his horses suddenly started off and he was thrown out and killed (VG 17 Dec 36)

Doctors who received the degree Doctor of Medicine at the Univ. of Pa. on the 21st inst. [only Virginians given below]: Thomas TRIPLET, of Alexandria; John CLAIBORNE, James T. HUBBARD, James STEWART, Isaac WEMSTON, William WELSH (CMAG 29 May 98)

DODD, Daniel, appr., ran away from James KELLY, Richmond Co., to whom he had bound himself to learn the carpenters and joiners trade in Feb. 1792 in Westmoreland Co. with the consent of his gdn.; he has a brother-in-law named CRAWLEY in Berkeley Co. and a brother named Griffin DODD in Mecklenburg Co. (VHFA 21 Feb 93)

DOEBER, Frederick Augustus Esq., mar. Mrs. GRANBERY of Suffolk (VG 4 Feb 75); dec'd, Christian DOEBER of Norfolk Co. adv. that some of the plate bel. to his est. all deciphered with the letters "I. C. G." is missing (VG 20 Dec 76)

DOGENS, Samuel [also given as DOGGINS or DOGERS], of Essex Co., dec'd, e.a.w. his admr., Richard HOLT (Arg 18 Jan 99)

DOHERTY, James, of Loudoun Co., 26, des. from the 3rd. U.S. Regt. near Alexandria (VGAR 12 Jun 92)

DOHONEY, Thomas, late of Orange Co., dec'd, e.a.w. May BURTON Jr. his ex. (VHFA 30 Jun 98)

DOIG, David, late Deputy Provost Marshal of West Florida; his friends in Scotland can inform him of something very much to his advantage (VG 2 Jul 72)

DOIL, Zachariah, 23, b. in Va. and raised in Powhatan Co., blacksmith, des. from the camp of the 3rd Sub-Legion, Shockoe Hill (RC 24 Oct 95)

DOLAN, Bridget, Irish svt., ran away from Joseph GILLIAM, Wmsbrg. (VG 31 Jul 45)

DOLD, Samuel, late ensign of Capt. GIBSON's Co. in the 4th Regt., U.S. Army, d. on Thurs. last in his 27th year (SVG 29 Mar 97)

DOLTON, Christopher, Irish conv. svt., c. 25, ran away from Andrew HAMILTON, Augusta Co. (VGR 15 Aug 71)

DONA[H]OW, Patrick, Irish svt., ran away from Jacob Andrew MINITREE, Charles Co., Md. (VG 7 Mar 51)

DONALD Family, Nottoway Co., Ct. of Q.S, 3 May 1798: Thomas PENNIX ex. of John PENNIX dec'd (compl.) in chanc. against Robert DONALD the elder, Andrew DONALD, Thomas DONALD the younger, Alexander DONALD the younger, and Robert DONALD the younger surviving partners of James and Robert Donald & Co., and Dicie BAGLEY admx. of James BAGLEY dec'd (defs.) (VGPI 25 May 98)

DONALD Family, U.S. Middle Circuit, District of Va., Nov. Term 1798, in chanc.: John LYNCH (pltf.) against Robert DONALD, Andrew DONALD, Thomas DONALD, and Alexander DONALD surviving partners of James and Robert DONALD & Co. (defs.); it appears that the defs. are not inhabitants of this country (LWG 16 Feb 99)

DONALD, Alexander, d. in Chesterfield Co. (VGRMA 5 Jan 95)

DONALD, George, of Richmond, an only child, aged 11, drowned on the 14th ult. [obit.] (VG 9 Jul 72)

DONALD, George, dec'd, e.a.w. his ex., Abraham COWLEY and James BUCHANAN, who will sell a 400 ac, tract of his land on Rockfish Cr. in Fluvanna Co. (VGPu 27 Mar 78)

DONALD, Robert, of Petersburg, mar. Miss Nancy OSBORNE of Chesterfield Co. (VG 27 Nov 79)

DONALD, Robert, dec'd, his ex., Alexander DONALD, Joseph WEISIGER, and James MURCHIE, will sell several tracts of his land in Henrico, Montgomery,

Botetourt, Bedford, Sussex, Campbell, Pr. Edw., and Amelia cos. (VGGA 18 Jul 92, VGPI 26 Jul 92)

DONALD, Robert, dec'd, Ann DONALD at Osborne's will rent his plant. on Appomattox River in Chesterfield Co. (VGPI 24 Jan 97)

DONALD, William, Bedford Co., March Ct. 1797, in chanc: Grizell GILES, James WEIR, and John KIPPEN extx. and exors. of William DONALD dec'd last surviving partner of William and James DONALD & Co. (compl.) against James PATTERSON and Francis REID (defs.); it appears that PATTERSON is not an inhabitant of the state (LWM 21 Aug 97); Patrick Co. Ct., Oct. 1797, in chanc: Grizel GILES, extx, and James WEIR and John KIPPEN , exors, of William DONALD surviving partner etc. (compl.) against James BUFORD Sr., James BUFORD Jr., and Christopher CLARK (defs.); it appears that the BUFORDS are not inhabitants of the state (LWM 15 Jan 98)

DONALDSON, Ebenezer, Scot. svt., ran away from on board the *Greenvale* at Ruffin's Ferry, Pamunkey River (VGR 26 Apr 70 sup)

DONALDSON, Elizabeth, has eloped from her husb., Alexander DONALDSON, Yorktown (VG 30 Sep 73)

DONALDSON, Col. John, killed by Indians on his way to Cumberland (VJAA 25 May 86)

DONALDSON, John, of Frederick Co., d. Mon. last (BVCG 27 Jan 97); his PE will be sold by his ex., Archibald MAGILL & James M'DONALD (BVCG 14 Apr 97)

DONALDSON, Mrs. Mary, consort of John DONALDSON, d. Thurs. morn. last, aged 23, [obit.] (VGWA 12 Aug 89)

DONALLY, Henry, Irish svt., c. 17, ran away from Mary BORDLAND, Hampton (VG 10 Dec 36)

DONIPHAN, Elizabeth, wife of William DONIPHAN who is no longer responsible for her debts (VHFA 7 Aug 88)

DONIPHAN, Gerrard, of Stafford Co., adv. that his wife has "derogated from the paths of virtue" and he will no longer pay her debts (VHFA 13 Aug 89)

DONNABY, Christy, of Orange Co., adv. that his wife, Abby COLEMAN, alias DONNABY, has appeared to him to be extravagant and he will not pay any of her debts (VGWeA 14 Sep 82)

DONNELLY, William, des. from the 3rd U.S. Regt. near Alexandria (VGAR 12 Jul 92)

DONOVON, Maj. Matthew Esq., of the 9th Regt., d. at Hesse in Gloucester Co. h was taken ill for pleurisy and d. in nine days (VGPu 9 Feb, VG 10, 24 Feb 76)

DONOHO, James, near 30, des. from the *Muskito* armed vessel; it is believed he is gone to Bedford Co. as his parents live near New London (VGPu 28 Jun 76)

DONVILLE, Ensign, French commanding officer of a group of Indians near Ft. Cumberland, killed and scalped in early Apr. (Wmsbrg. disp. of 16 Apr.) (MG 6 May 56)

DOODY, Joseph, dec'd, e.a.w. his ex., Ann DOODY and Henry HARRINGTON of Nansemond Co. (VGIC 9 Dec 86, NHPA 30 Nov 97)

DOOLITTLE, Jothan Ives, late of Yale College, Connecticut, is now assisting at the academy of Eldridge HARRIS, Richmond (Arg 19 Sep 97)

DOREN, John, Irish svt., c. 30, pretends to be a maltster and brewer, ran away from Daniel HORNBY, Richmond Co. (AWM 26 Sep 34)

DORISH, Balt[h]azar, killed fighting a fire in Richmond on Fri. morn. last (VGRMA 9 Jun 94, VGGA 11 Jun 94); his admx., Martha DORISH, and admr., Thomas WALKER, will sell items of his HHF in Richmond (VGRMA 24 Nov 94, VGWeA 28 Feb 95)

DORMAN, George, aka HOLDERNESS, Eng. conv. svt., c. 20, b. in London, ran away from Samuel LOVE Jr. in Loudoun Co. (VGPu 25 Jul 77)

D[O]RMAN, Thomas, b. in Somerset Co., Md., enl. at Norfolk 17 Aug. 17[94]; des from Ft. Norfolk (HNPA 13 May 95)

DORMER, the Rev. Mr. James, native of Eng., supposed to be in some part of N America, probably in S. Carolina; he has been away from his friends about 25 yrs. and any intelligence of this gentleman will be thankfully received by Jame

RIVINGTON, New York (VGAA 30 Aug 83)
DORSEY, Levin, mathematical instrument maker, mar. Miss Elizabeth TAYLOR, both of Norfolk, on Sat. eve. (NHPA 30 Jan 97)
DORTEVAL, Henry, of Richmond, dec'd, e.a.w. his admr., Francis GORLIER (VGGA 10 Jan 98)
DOUDING, John, adv. that his wife, Lucy DOUDING, has behaved in a very unfriendly manner to him and he will no longer pay any of her debts since he is going away as a listed soldier for three years (VGPu 10 Oct 77)
DOUGAL, Forrest, of Portsmouth, dec'd, his admr. is Barbara DOUGAL (HNPA 7 Mar 95)
DOUGHERTY, Constantine, d. on 4 Sep. at the home of James TAYLOR Jr. in Caroline; he was a person skilled in making saltpeter and had been recommended by gentlemen from the Jerseys, N.Y., Philadelphia, Md., etc. (VGPu 19 Sep 77)
DOUGHERTY, Enos, mar. Miss Jane CRAMPTON on Sun. eve. last, both of [Winchester] (WG 24 Apr 99)
DOGHETY, Patrick, mar. Mrs. Mary EDMONDSON on Mon. eve. last (WVGWA 24 Jul 90)
DOUGLAS Family, Frederick Co. Ct., Aug. 1788, in chanc: Robert SCOTT (compl.) against Archibald DOUGLAS eld. son and heir at law of James DOUGLAS dec'd, Margaret DOUGLAS and Catherine DOUGLAS daus. and devisees of the sd. James DOUGLAS dec'd, and Catherine DOUGLAS extx. and Alexander HENDERSON, William CARR, John RIDDLE, and George BRENT exors of the sd James DOUGLAS dec'd (VGIC 1 Nov 88)
DOUGLAS, the Rev. William, dec'd, e.a.w. his ex., Chiles TERREL of Louisa Co. (VGGA 7 Mar 98)
DOUGLA[S], William Esq., of Shelbourne Par., Loudoun Co., dec'd, his ex., Hugh DOUGLAS, will sell 150 ac. of his land there formerly purchased of Edward DULIN (VGIC 13 Dec 83, VJAA 4 Nov 84, VJAA 28 Jul 85)
DOUGLASS, James, brother to the present Dutchess of Douglass, d. at Dumfries, Pr. Wm. Co. on 17 (or 18) Nov. (VGR 27 Nov 66, 4 Dec 66)
DOUGLASS, John, dec'd, e.a.w. his admr., Charles CA[M]ABELL [sic] of Augusta Co. (VG 26 Dec 77)
DOUTHAT, Thomas Esq., of Staunton, mar. Miss Jane PRICE of Henrico Co. on Sun. 2 Jun. (BVCG 10 Jun 93, VGRMA 24 Jun 93)
DOUTHAT, William, d. about the 1st inst. at the Sweet Springs (SVG 29 Aug 95)
DOVE, James, late of Richmond, dec'd, e.a.w. his admx., Julia Lee DOVE (OVT 26 Jul 98)
DOWDLE, Hugh, executed on 6 Jul. for counterfeiting (VGAR 12 Jul 92)
DOWLAN, Michael, Irish svt., 24, ran away from the Potomac Co., Great Falls (VJAA 17 Aug 86)
DOWLIN, Dennis, Irish, 27, des. from Capt. David BELL's Co. of the Va. Regt.; he may be going to N. Carolina (VG 5 Dec 55)
DOWNER, John, dec'd, e.a.w. his admr., William DOWNER (VHFA 15 Sep 95)
DOWNING, James, c. 28, absconded from Lindsay's Mills near Port Royal where he was a miller; he is suspected of robbery; said to be from Downing's Town, Pa.; it is supposed he intends for Ky. or some of the southern states (VGRMA 5 Dec 93, VGGA 11 Dec 93, VGPI 3 Jan 94)
DOWNMAN, Joseph B. Esq., of Lancaster Co., d. in Culpeper Co. on Tues. last leaving a wife and nine children (VH 27 Sep 99)
DOWNMAN, Robert P., dec'd, e.a.w. his admr., William DOWNMAN [of Richmond Co.] (VGGA 27 Nov 93)
DOWNMAN, Travers, dec'd, his admr. (nfi) will sell all his est. at Cockpit Point (VG 11 Nov 73)
DOWNMAN, Travers, of Pr. Wm. Co., dec'd, e.a.w. his admrs., Thomas CHAPMAN and John COPPIDGE of Dumfries (VG 11 Dec 79)
DOWNMAN, William, of Richmond Co., dec'd, his PE to be sold at his late dwelling on the head of Morattico Cr. by his admr., James BALL (VG 17 Oct 66)
DOWNMAN, William, dec'd, his ex. are George ROBERTSON & Henry COUSINS

(VGPI 26 May 95)
DOWNS, Richard, from Petersburg, executed at the gallows on Fri. last for burglary (VIC 1 Aug 87, VGWeA 2 Aug 87)
DOYL, Thomas, svt., from Md., claimed to be a sailor from New York, committed to jail in Frederick Co. (VGR 8 Mar 70)
DOYLE, Alexander, dec'd, his admx. with the will annexed is Elizabeth DOYLE of Georgetown (CMAG 28 Feb 95)
DOYLE, John, 30, ran away from H.M.S. *Fewey* lying in Hampton on 23 Mar. (VG 10 Oct 45)
DOZIER, Richard, d. lately in Westmoreland Co., aged 89 (VGGA 1 Jun 91)
DRAGO, Benjamin, of Frederick Co., dec'd, e.a.w. his ex., John JOLLIFFE (WG 2 Jan 99)
DRENANE, Mrs. Mary, d. in Portsmouth in her 33rd year (HNPA 17 Dec 94)
DREW Family, Nansemond Co. Ct., 15 Aug. 1797, in chanc: Josiah COWLING admr. of John MACKIE dec'd. (compl.) against John DREW, Elizabeth ROBERTS, Julia HILL, Dolphin DREW, Josiah HOPKINS and Mary Cary HOPKINS his wife, and William DREW (defs.) (NHPA 23 Sep 97)
DREW, Capt. John, dec'd, John MACKIE will sell sundry Negroes bel. to his est. at Scotland Neck Quarter (VGPu 24 Jan 77)
DREW, William Esq., clerk of Berkeley [Co.], mar. Miss Hannah POWELL of Wmsbrg. (VGPu 15 Nov 76); late clerk to the senate, d. in Berkeley Co. (VGAA 29 Oct 85, VJAA 3 Nov 85); e.a.w. his acting ex., Benjamin POWELL Esq. of Wmsbrg. or Philip PENDLETON of Martinsburg, Berkeley Co. (VJAA 20 Apr 86, VGWA 7 Dec 87); his seat on Nullskin Run to be sold (VJAA 12 Oct 86)
DREWIDZ, [Master], son of Mr. DREWIDZ [sic] of West Point, was drowned above Yorktown on Mon. last (VGWeA 28 Aug 88)
DREWRY, Thomas, appr. tailor, c. 18, ran away from Archibald DIDDEP, Wmsb: who believes he will go to some of his relations in Kg. Wm. Co. (VG 19 Dec 77)
DREWRY, William, of Granville Co., N. Carolina, will hear of a considerable legacy having been left him by a deceased friend by applying to M. K. GODDARD, printer, in Baltimore (VG 2 Mar 79)
DRING, Elizabeth, dau. of Jonathan DRING of Watford, Herts., Eng.; who mar. Archibald WILSON; if she be living or has chil. living they will hear something considerably to their advantage by calling on the Rev. Dr. ROGERS in Philadelphia (VGGA 27 Apr 96)
DRISCOL, Thomas, dec'd, e.a.w. his admx., Catherine DRISCOL, Norfolk (NH 6 Oct 96)
DRISCOLL, Dr. Matthew, native of Baltimore, in Co. Cork, Ireland, is asked to apply to Messrs. Montgomery & Allen, merchants, Richmond, to hear something to his advantage [possibly concerning the est. of the late Cornelius DRISCOLL] (VGAA 18 Dec 84)
[DRISKELL], Michael, svt., 24, imported this year from Dublin in the *Burwell*; ran away from John TOWERS on board the *Carlisle* lying at City Point on James River (VG 3 Sep 56)
DRIVER, Miss, drowned at the beginning of Mar. last when the schooner she was in bound from Isle of Wight to Norfolk overturned (PC 6 Apr 72)
DRIVER, Charles, dec'd, e.a.w. his admr., Anne DRIVER and John DRIVER of Smithfield, Isle of Wight Co., who will also sell his PE which includes two sloops (VG & VGR 21 Feb 71)
DRIVER, John, svt., calls himself Eng. but has an Irish accent, tailor, ran away from John ATKINSON and James NEWTON, Fredsbrg. (VGR 9 Dec 73)
DRIVER, John, dec'd, e.a.w. his admr., Thomas SWEPSON and Edward ALLEN Suffolk (NHPA 16 Sep 97)
DRIVER, Capt. Samuel, master of the brig *Agness*, d. on his passage from the island of St. Vincent's (NH 7 Dec 99)
DROUGHT, Joseph, svt., ran away from Thomas INGALLS, joiner, in St. Mary' River, Md. (VG 31 Oct 45)
DRUM, Bryon, Irish svt., ran away from Philip CASSAY, Frederick Co., Md. (VG 18 Feb 75)

DRUMMOND, Mrs. Anne, of Wmsbrg., died (VGWeA 26 Jan 82)
DRUMMOND, George Esq., an eminent banker, died (VGWeA 16 Jul 89)
DRUMMOND, William, dec'd, his ex., John TYLER, and extx., Rachel DIXON, will sell his PE at his plant. Porto Bello (VG 1 Jul 73); his extx. will sell his plant. Porto Bello (VGR 16 Sep 73)
Drunken Frank, a woman in York Co., d. last Thurs. (VG 27 Oct 38)
DRURY, Michael, appr., 15-16 (in Oct. 1797) ran away from Samuel MARTIN near the Yellow Church, Stafford Co. who believes he may change his name to LEVAN; he ran away again in 1799 (VH 21 Oct 97, CMAG 16 Jul 99)
DRURY, Thomas, of Norfolk Co., dec'd, e.a.w. his ex., Mathias DRURY, Pr. Anne Co. (NHPA 2 Mar 97)
DRURY, Timothy, conv. svt., 16-17, ran away from William TRIPLET, Kg. Geo. Co. (VG 26 Sep 71)
DRYSDALE, Maj. [Hugh], [Lt.] Gov. of Virginia, [deputy to George Hamilton, Earl of Orkney], d. 17 Jul. (AWM 18 Aug 26, NYG 22 Aug 26)
DRYSDALE, Samuel, svt., 40, Virginian, ran away from Daniel Parke CUSTIS' plant. in Kg. Wm. Co. in Sep. (VG 28 Nov 55)
DUBERG, Edward, aka John UNDERWOOD, svt., brought up at Cambridge, ran away from Richard LEE and Thomas ATTWELL, Westmoreland Co. (VG 12 May 74)
DUCRECT, John Ecton, conv. svt. who came in on the *Justitia*, native of Berne, Switzerland, speaks good French and tolerable Eng. and Italian, ran away from Richard GRAHAM, Dumfries (VGPu 21 Jul 75)
DUDGEON, John, late of Halifax Co., dec'd, e.a.w. his admr., James M'CRAW (VGPu 23 Oct 78)
DUDLEY, George, of Gloucester Co., dec'd, his admx. (nfi) will sell sundry items of his HH and KF (VG 16 Mar 76)
DUDLEY, Capt. John, of Charles City Co., dec'd, his admr., James SOUTHALL Jr., Charles City Co., will sell all of his PE (VGAA 16 Nov 82)
DUDLEY, Marlow, dec'd, 900 ac. of his land near Clement's Mill, Amelia Co., to be sold by Joseph EGGLESTON and William MOULSON (nfi) (VG 29 Aug 66)
DUDLEY, Mrs. Mildred, wife of William DUDLEY of York Co., d. (VIC 15 Jul 89)
DUDLEY, Maj. Peter, mar. Mrs. RAWLINGS relict of the late Peter RAWLINGS in this county on 23 Jun. (VHFA 3 Jul 98)
DUDLEY, Robert, of K & Q Co., his brother William DUDLEY advertises a runaway slave (VGR 1 Jun 69)
DUDLEY, Capt. Thomas, late of K & Q Co., dec'd, e.a.w. his ex., Robert B. DUDLEY and Thomas DUDLEY (VG 9 Apr 79, 7 Sep 79)
DUFF, Arthur, svt., 30, ran away from Wm. KELLY, Orange Co. (VG 24 Apr 46)
DUFF, James, svt., ran away from John TRIMBLE, Augusta Co. (VGP 15 Jun 75)
DUFF, Nicholas, ind. svt., native of Wexford, Ireland, ran away from Henry GIRD, Alexandria (CMAG 31 Mar 96)
DUFFIELD, John, dec'd, e.a.w. his ex., Robert WELLS and James HOLLIDAY; his widow, Mary DUFFIELD, informs her friends and the public that she carries on the business as in her late husband's time (BVCG 23 Sep 96)
DUGAL, Elizabeth, c. 27, stole items from Lemuel ROBERTS, Norfolk Co., says she was b. in Pa. but may go to Carolina (VGR 27 Sep 70)
DUHAIL, Louis Etienne, Vice-consul of the French Republic at Norfolk and lately at Baltimore; [died], he was b. at Le Mans, France; buried at the Catholic Burying ground (NHPA 7 Oct 97)
DUKE Family, Louisa Co., Ct. of Q.S, 14 Mar 1797, in chanc: Frederick HARRIS, Garret MINON, and Zachariah LEWIS exors. of Richmond TERRELL dec'd (compls.) against George LUMSDEN and Ro[b]ert DABNEY acting ex. of Clevearss [sic] DUKE dec'd, Clevearse Duke (son of James) HARDEN and James DUKE, Samuel PETTUS and Amy his wife, Burnley DUKE, William SMITH and Ann his wife, Elizabeth DUKE, Mary DUKE, and Martha DUKE, Cleveasse SWIFT and Thomas SWIFT, Martin BAKER and Elizabeth his wife, Thomas SWIFT and Peggy his wife, Gabriel POINDEXTER and Molly his wife, Harriet SWIFT, Rebecca SWIFT, and Amy SWIFT, John DUKE, John HAWKINS and

Mary his wife, Joseph EGGLESTON and Mary his wife (who was the widow of Clevearse DUKE dec'd), Kaylen TAYLOR (who intermarried with Mary DUKE) Thomas SWIFT (who intermarried with Harriet SWIFT), William SWIFT (who intermarried with Rebecca SWIFT), Samuel BAKER (who intermarried with Amy SWIFT), Reuben SMITH (who intermarried with Elizabeth DUKE), Willia MILLS gdn. to Archibald SWIFT, Mary SWIFT, Charles SWIFT, Nancy SWIFT Sally SWIFT, Betsy SWIFT, Thomas SWIFT, William SWIFT, Maria SWIFT, and John SWIFT (orphans of Clevearse SWIFT dec'd and legatees of his est.) (defs.); it appears that Thomas and Peggy SWIFT, Gabriel and Molly POINDEXTER, and Thomas SWIFT are not inhabitants of the state (VGGA 3 May 97)

DUKE Family, HCC, 2 Jun 1798, Elizabeth DUKE widow of [?] DUKE dec'd and sister of the late John BURNLEY, Burnley DUKE (a son of the sd. Elizabeth), William SMITH and Ann his wife, Reuben SMITH and Elizabeth his wife, Richard K. TAYLOR and Mary his wife, and Patsy DUKE (pltfs.) and Zachariah BURNLEY admr. with the will annexed of John BURNLEY, and Hardin BURNLEY (defs.); it appears that Hardin BURNLEY is not an inhabitant of this country (VGGA 10 Jul 98)

DUKE, Cleavers, of Albemarle Co., will petition the next GA to pass an act for the sale of a tract of land in Louisa Co. which was willed to him by his grandfather, Cleavers DUKE dec'd (Ex 22 Oct 99)

DUKE, Cleviers, 22-23, des. from Chestertown (VGPu 6 Jun 77)

DUKE, Cosby, of Louisa Co. dec'd, e.a.w. with Betty DUKE the extx. and William PETTUS and George LUMSDEN (VGAA 12 Apr 83)

DUKE, Henry, of James City Co., [dec'd], e.a.w. William MOODY (nfi) of James City Co. (VG 13 Dec 76); e.a.w. William JONES (NFI) of Warwick Co. (VG & VGPu 18 Jul 77)

DUKE, John, of Hanover Co., dec'd, e.a.w. his ex., Richard KIMBROUGH and Henry DUKE of Hanover Co. (Ex 19 Apr 99)

DULANCY, Richard, Irish svt., c. 25, ran away from Marcus STEPHENSON, carver and gilder, Berkeley Co. (VG 23 Sep 75)

DULANY, Benjamin Esq., of Md., mar. Miss FRENCH of Fairfax Co. who has a fortune of £20,000 (VGR 11 Mar 73)

DULANY, Benjamin Jr. Esq., of this county [Fairfax], mar. Miss Eliza ROZER of Pr. Geo. Co., Md. (CMAG 20 Feb 96)

DULANY, Daniel Esq., barrister at law, d. on Sun. the 19th inst. in his 76th year (Balto. disp. of 20 March) (CMAG 30 Mar 96)

DULANY, Dr. Elkhany, of Woodstock, mar. Miss Peggy SNAPP dau. of Capt. Lawrence SNAPP of Shenandoah on Thurs. the 7th inst. (WG 13 Feb 99)

DULTON, Robert, of Surry in Eng., d. Wed. last in Richm. (VGAA 9 Jul 85)

DUNBAR, the Rev. Hancock, late minister of St. Stephen's Par., K & Q Co., die (VG 4 Dec 78)

DUNBAR, Ro[b]ert, of Falmouth, merch., mar. Miss Betsy THORNTON dau. of the late Francis THORNTON Sr. of the Fall-Hill on Sat. last near Fredsbrg. (VHFFA 11 Jun 97)

DUNBAR, William, arrived in Va. about two yrs. ago from the town of Portfoy, Banffshire, Scotland; if he will apply to William SMITH, Eden Academy, Somerset Co., Md., he will hear of something very interesting to him (VGAA 12 Jul 86)

DUNCAN, Charles, merch. of Blandford, mar. Miss Jeany GILLIAM of Dinwidd Co. (VG 15 Oct 72)

DUNCAN, Mrs. Elizabeth, wife of Thomas DUNCAN, d. last Thurs. in Martins burg (PGBA 9 Sep 93)

DUNCAN, Henny [sic], appr., 20, ran away from Aaron HEWES, Alexandria; h is believed heading for Ky. (BVCG 27 Aug 92)

DUNCAN, John, dec'd, his ex., Moses DUNCAN of Fauquier, will sell the tract c land whereon he lives bel. to the dec'd containing c. 165 ac. (VHFFA 11 Jul 97

DUNCAN, Lydia and Joseph, of Fauquier Co., dec'd, his ex., Howsen DUNCA and Joseph MAUZY and her ex., Howsen DUNCAN, will sell the rem. of both estates (VH 29 Nov 97)

DUNCAN, Matthew, late of Berkeley Co., dec'd, e.a.w. his ex., Thomas DUNCAN and Seth DUNCAN (PGBA 1 Jul 93)

DUNCAN, Rawleigh, HCC, 6 Jun 1797, between Simon COCKRELL (pltf.) and John DUNCAN heir at law of Rawleigh DUNCAN dec'd and Townshend DUNCAN (defs.); it appears that Townshend DUNCAN is not an inhabitant of this country (VGGA 28 Jun 97)

DUNCAN, Robert, appr. hatter, 17, ran away from Peter TOFFLER (CMAG 8 Oct 95)

DUNCAN, William, dec'd, those indebted to him are to settle with Charles COPELAND, attorney at law in Richmond, and anyone having any demands on him is to call on James DICKENSON in Norfolk (NH 26 May 96)

DUNCANSON, Lt. James, of the Va. Regt., killed 15 Oct. in an engagement with the French at Loyalhenning (NYM 30 Oct 58)

DUNCANSON, Col. James, of Fredsbrg., d. last Fri. aged [9]6; he was from Scotland and one of the oldest inhabitants in the town (VHFA 10 Mar 91); his ex. are Charles URQUHART and James BLAIR of Fredsbrg. (VHFA 12 May 91); his ex. announce a division of his est. on 1 May (VHFFA 11 Apr 97)

DUNCANSON, Mrs. Molly, wife of Col. James DUNCANSON, d. last Sun. in Culpeper in her 41st year (VHFA 14 Oct 90)

DUNCASTLE, Thomas, HCC, 15 Nov 1788, John DANDRIDGE and William ARMISTEAD exors. of Bartholomew DANDRIDGE dec'd who was the ex. of Thomas DUNCASTLE dec'd, and Henry Duke SHERMAN and Betsy his wife dau. and devisee and legatee of Thomas DUNCASTLE dec'd (pltfs.) against Thomas CARTWRIGHT and Adam BYRD (defs.); it appears that Thomas CARTWRIGHT is not an inhabitant of the country (VGWeA 12 Feb 89)

DUNDAS, John, merch., mar. Miss Nancy HEPBURN of Alexandria (VJAA 7 Apr 85)

DUNKERTON, Rebekah, aka MARTYR, has eloped from her husband, Tomkins MARTYR, Wmsbrg. (VG 2 Jun 74)

DUNLAP, Mrs. Deborah, consort of the Rev. William DUNLAP of K & Q Co.,. d. on Wed. the 15th inst. and was bur. in Stratton Major Church; she had been blind for nine yrs. (VG 4 Mar 75)

DUNLAP, Francis Franklin, son of the Rev. William DUNLAP of Stratton Major Par., K & Q Co. and chaplain to the 6th Regt., died (VGPu 10 May 76, VG 11 May 76)

DUNLAP, the Rev. William, rector of Stratton Major Par., K & Q Co., and chaplain to the 6th Regt. mar. Mrs. Johanna ROWE of Gloucester Co. (VGPu 26 Jul 76, VG 29 Jul 76); rector of St. Paul's Par., Hanover Co., died (VG 25 Sep 79); his ex., Ben. F. DUNLAP and Richard CHAPMAN, will sell all his HH and KF and a library of several hundred volumes (VG 9 Oct 79)

DUNLOP, Archibald, of Cabin Point, dec'd, his extx., Susanna DUNLOP, will sell his PE (VGGA 31 Jul 93)

DUNLOP, James, merch. of Port Royal, mar. Miss Betsey HILL of Essex Co. (VG 4 Aug 74); expects to leave the state this month (VHFA 14 May 89)

DUNLOP, William, merch., mar. Miss Jane BANKHEAD (VH 9 Aug 99)

DUNMORE, the Rt. Hon. the Countess of, gave birth to a dau. at the palace in Wmsbrg. on Sat. morn. last (VG 8 Dec 74 sup, VGP 8 Dec 74)

DUNN, Daniel, aka Daniel DIGGENS, conv. svt., c. 38, nailer, supposed to be in Norfolk, ran away from Samuel WILLITS, Harford Co., Md. (VG 10 Nov 74)

DUNN, Drury, of Dinwiddie Co., dec'd, his admr., William DUNN and Henrietta DUNN, will sell his slaves and other items of his est. (VG and VGR 31 Jan 71)

DUNN, Elizabeth, has eloped from her husband, Agrippa DUNN, of Essex Co. (VG 5 Aug 73)

DUNN, Henry, of Tappahannock, mar. Miss Lucy JULIAN dau. of the late Dr. JULIAN of this town [Fredsbrg.] on Sun. eve. (VH 29 Jan 99)

DUNN, Maj. Isaac B., of Lexington, [Ky.], committed suicide by shooting himself on Sun. last; he was bur. in the public burying ground in Lexington (Lexington disp. of 4 Jul.) (VGWeA 13 Aug 89)

DUNN, John, was mar. to Miss Mary BILLUPS, both of this borough, by the Rev.

Mr. WHITEHEAD on Tues. last (NHPA 12 Oct 97)
DUNORY, Daniel, of Southampton Co., his wife gave birth to triplets: Jemima, Kezia (who d. in two or three days), and Karenhappuch in Oct. (VG 3 Nov 68)
DUNSTAN, Joseph, of James City Co., adv. that his wife, Jane DUNSTAN, has eloped from his bed and board without any just cause (VG 1 Apr 80)
DURANT, Master Thomas, only son of Mr. L. E. DURANT of this borough, merch d. on Thurs. eve. (NH 26 Jan 99)
DURKHEIM, M., of Petersburg, adv. that he will move his family to Bridge Town in Northampton Co. (VGPA 23 Aug 93)
DURRETT, Henry, late of Caroline Co., dec'd, e.a.w. William DURRETT (nfi) (VH 19 Feb 99)
DUVAL, Mrs. Anne, wife of Maj. William DUVAL Esq., attorney at law, died on the 3rd inst. (VGRDA 4 Oct 92, VGGA 10 Oct 92)
DUVAL, Miss Anne P., dau. of Maj. William DUVAL of this city [Richmond], d. on Mon. the 25th (or acc. to RMA, Tues. the 26th), aged 16 (VGGA and RMA 27 Apr 96)
DUVAL, Benjamin, of Henrico Co., dec'd, his ex., Robert DUVAL, will sell his est. and land on Tuckahoe Cr. (VG 3 Jan 71, VGR 10 Jan 71)
DUVAL, Benjamin, mar. Miss Elizabeth WARWICK, both of Richmond, on Wed. (VGIC and VGAA 9 Apr 85)
DUVAL, Daniel, of Caroline Co., dec'd, his ex., Henry DUVAL and John DUVAL, will sell two tracts of his land in that co. (VG 3 Oct 77)
DUVAL, John, plans to move to Ky. next fall and will sell a tract of land in Caroline Co. (VHFA 14 Feb 98)
DUVAL, John P., senator for the District of Monongalia and Ohio, killed by Indians on 29 Jun. at the Great Kanawha (VGAA 23 Jul 85)
DUVAL, Robert, of Richmond, dec'd, his ex., Turner SOUTHALL, Zachariah ROWLAND, and William DUVAL, will sell his houses, lots, slaves, svts., and other items of his est. including a great variety of joiner's and carpenter's tools (VG 13 May 73)
DUVAL, Samuel, dec'd, a moiety of 100 ac. of land in Chesterfield Co. will be sold by his ex., Claiborne DUVAL; the other moiety to be sold by Philip DUVAL; William DUVAL, an attorney, is also mentioned (VGAA 14 May 85)
DUVAL, Samuel P., intends to move from Richmond to Ky. about the last of Oct. where he will settle in Lexington; he is currently at Maj. William DUVAL's on Shockoe Hill (VGRMA 15 Sep 94)
DUVAL, William, attorney at law, mar. Miss Nancy POPE eld. dau. of Capt. Nathaniel POPE of Louisa Co. on Thurs. last [in Richmond] (VG 25 Jun 72)
DWIGHT, Dr. M. W., d. at Kempsville on Sat. the 13th inst. (VHFFA 23 Aug 96)
DWYER, William, Irish svt., 21, ran away from the Potomac Co., Great Falls (VGAxA 21 Jul 91)
DYE, Reubin, Negro, c. 30, b. in Martinico, claims to be free; jailed in Pr. Wm. Co. (VGR 14 Oct 73)
DYER, William Clements, appr. hatter, 18-19, ran away from Nathan UPDEGRAFF, Winchester (VGWA 29 Sep 90)
DYKES, Mrs. Ann, wife of Mungo DYKES of Alexandria, died (VGAxA 11 Feb 90)
DYSON, Francis, dec'd, e.a.w. his admr., James DYSON, Norf. (AGGA 7 Oct 96)
DYSON, George, dec'd, his admr. and gdn. to his orphans, J. SLAUGHTER, will sell all his PE at Portsmouth (NH 21 Apr 96)
DYSON, Jonathan, dec'd, e.a.w. his admr., Paul LOYALL and Latimer HOLSTEAD, Norfolk (VGR 29 Oct 72)
DYSON, Lucy, wife of Robert DYSON of Dinwiddie who will pay none of her debts (VGPI 5 Jul 96)
DYSON, Manor, of Kg. Wm. Co., dec'd, his admr., James GOVAN of Kg. Wm., requests immediate payment from his debtors (VIC 12, 26 Dec 87)
DYSON, Mary, dec'd, a lot of hers in Newtown, Pr. Anne Co. to be sold by her ex., Nathaniel M'CLENEHAN (VGR 4 Dec 66)

EAGE, Edward, svt., ran away from William WITHERS, Fauquier Co. (VG 7

May 72)

EAKEN, Redmond, a pet. will be presented to the next GA to sell his lands; Jonathan MARTIN gdn. and Elenor MARTIN are the exors. (SS 9 Nov 93)

EALES, Thomas, left Henrico Co. in 1767; if he will come back and apply to Richard COTTRELL, he may hear of something to his advantage (VGR 23 Jun 68)

EARLY, Joel, of Culpeper,will settle in Georgia next spring (VHFA 25 Nov 90)

EARLY, Jubal, dec'd, e.a.w. his admr., John EARLY, Franklin Co. (LWG 13 Oct 98)

EARMAN, Henry, formerly a Hessian soldier, d. lately at Winchester; any creditor or relative is asked to apply to Peter Bryan BRUIN in Bath, Berkeley Co. (VGAA 21 Aug 84)

EARP, Caleb, formerly of this town [Alexandria], d. on Thurs. the 31st ult. at his house near the new Ct.H. (TDCDA 4 Nov 99); his admr., R. RATCLIFFE, will sell all the stock of goods bel. to the est. at the storehouse lately occupied by the dec'd near the new Ct. H. in Fairfax Co. (CMAG 26 Nov 99)

EASLY, Temperance, wife of Warren EASLY of Warwick in Henrico Co. who will no longer pay her debts (VG 11 Sep 46)

EASSON, James, merch., d. on the 30th ult. at his house in Smithfield (VG 9 Jul 67)

EAST, Capt. William, d. on the schooner *Swift* in James River on the 25th inst. (VGGA 31 Aug 96)

EASTIN, Thomas, late of Albemarle Co., dec'd, his est. will be divided on 1 Dec. next by his admr., William EASTIN (VGGA 31 Aug 91)

EASTON, David, having left this place [Alexandria] for Philadelphia, the business in the future will be carried on by James Miller & Co. (CMAG 21 Jun 96); merch., mar. Mrs. S. CRAIK on Tues. eve. (CMAG 22 Oct 96)

EASTWOOD, Elisha, dec'd, e.a.w. his ex., William PRITCHARD and Corns. EASTWOOD, Portsmouth (NH 23 Aug 98)

EATON, George, svt., 20, b. in London, imp. last Feb. in the *Neptune*, ran away from William PORTER, Thomas MILLER, and James LAVERTY, Fredsbrg. (VGR 22 Sep 68)

EATON, Capt. John, a rep. in assembly, d. at his house in James City Co. last Fri. (VG 5 Oct 39)

EATON, John, ship carpenter, c. 23, and Alice EATON, aka WALKER, c. 20 who probably travels as his wife, both Eng. conv. svts., ran away from Sampson MATTHEWS and George MATTHEWS, Richmond (VGR 27 May 73)

EATON, William, of York Co., d. suddenly last Sat. in Richm. (VIC 20 Jun 87, VGIC 23 Jun 87)

EATON, William Jr., dec'd, his ex., William EATON, will sell 1200 ac. of his land on the north side of Roanoke River near the sd. EATON's ferry commonly called Rawling's Ferry in the upper end of Northampton Co., N. Carolina and several valuable horses on the plant. where Mrs. Rebekah EATON now lives (VGPu 5 Apr, 7 Jun 76 sup)

ECHALDS Family, Halifax Co., Ct. of Q.S., 25 Mar 1794, in chanc: Rebecca ECHALDS and Sarah ECHALDS daus. of Joseph ECHALDS dec'd (compls.) against Abraham ECHALDS and Drucilla ECHALDS, Hawkins LANDRUM gdn. of David ECHALDS, Mary ECHALDS and Tabitha ECHALDS orphans of Joseph ECHALDS dec'd, Leonard BAKER gdn. of Moses ECHALDS, Obadiah ECHALDS, Rhoda ECHALDS, and Joel ECHALDS also orphans of Joseph ECHALDS dec'd, and John DILLON gdn. of John ECHALDS only child and heir at law of Jeremiah ECHALDS dec'd (VGRMA 28 Apr 94)

ECHOLS Family, Pittsylvania Co., Nov. Ct., 1799, in chanc: Theodorick B. M'ROBERT (pltf.) against William RAINEY admr. w.w.a. of Obadiah ECHOLS dec'd and gdn. of Philip I. ECHOLS, Samuel B. ECHOLS, Polly C. ECHOLS, Nancy ECHOLS, and Betsey ECHOLS, and Clement M'DANIEL gdn. of Obadiah ECHOLS and Elijah ECHOLS, Benjamin ECHOLS, and James ECHOLS (defs.); it appears that Benjamin and James ECHOLS are not inhabitants of this state (Arg 24 Dec 99)

ECKSTINE, Mary, her husb., Leonard ECKSTINE of Winchester, will no longer be responsible for her debts (VG 11 Oct 76)

EDINBURGH, John, svt., c. 30, ran away from William WAITE, Belhaven, Va. (MG 29 Aug 54)
EDLOE, John, late of Lunenburg Co., dec'd, a tract of his land in Charles City Co. to be sold (VGR 17 Nov 68)
EDLOE, John, mar. Miss BAILEY of Charles City Co. (VG 25 Feb 75)
EDMONDS, John, of Fauquier Co., dec'd, his PE to be sold by his admr., John EDMONDS (WG 16 Jan 99)
EDMONDSON, John Esq., dec'd, his admr., Lawrence ENNIS of Essex, will sell his slaves (VIC 4 Nov 89)
EDMONDSON, John, dec'd, e.a.w. his ex., Peter MANSON, Dinwiddie Co. (VGPI 27 Oct 91)
EDMONDSON, Eli, appr. chair maker, ran away from David RUSSELL, Winchester (BVCG 13 Aug 92)
EDMONDSON, James, dec'd, his admr., John BROCKENBROUGH, Tappahannock, will sell 28 of his Negroes (VHFA 18 Oct 92)
EDMONDTON, John Esq., dec'd, his plant. in Essex Co. to be sold by Lawrence LEWIS his ex. (VHFA 26 Nov 89)
EDMONSTONE, Andrew, of Richm., dec'd, his admr. is his brother, John EDMONSTONE, who intends to leave the colony soon (VG 17 Feb 74)
EDMUNDS, John Esq., att. at law, d. Thurs. last [8 Feb.] at his house in Sussex Co. (VG 15 Feb 70, VGR 22 Feb 70); his horses, law books, and HHF to be sold by his ex., William BLUNT and Sterling EDMUNDS (VG 13 Dec 70)
EDMUNDS, Col. Thomas, of Sussex Co., d. [recently]; he was an officer in the Revolutionary War [obit.] (VGGA 14 Sep 91)
EDWARD, Richard, of Surry Co., dec'd, e.a.w. his admr. w.w.a., Benjamin BLUNT, who will also sell his slaves, livestock, and crops (Ex 8, 25 Jan 99)
EDWARDS Family, HCC, 13 Sep 1794, between John ROBINSON (pltf.) and Alan JONES and Walter PETER acting ex. of William EDWARDS dec'd, who was the acting ex. of Nathaniel EDWARDS Jr. dec'd, and Benjamin EDWARDS who was devisee of the sd. William EDWARDS who was devisee of the sd. Nathaniel EDWARDS (defs.); it appears that Benjamin EDWARDS is not an inhabitant of this country (VGWeA 22 Nov 94)
EDWARDS, Col. Benjamin, dec'd, his plantations, Round Hill and Indian Town in Southampton Co. to be sold by his admr., Hen. BROWNE (VG 24 Jan, 19 Sep 51)
EDWARDS, David, appr., c. 17, ran away from John THOMAS, Hampshire Co. (BVCG 26 Oct 95)
EDWARDS, Isaac Esq., Auditor General of the Province of N. Carolina and a rep. in assembly for the town of New Bern [N. Carolina], d. in his 27th year (VGPu 17 Feb 75 sup)
EDWARDS, James, of Spotsylvania Co., dec'd, his ex. are Benjamin WALLER and John WALLER (VHFA 19 Nov 89)
EDWARDS, Margaret, has eloped from her husband, Mark EDWARDS of Chesterfield Co. (VG 24 Oct 66); she eloped (again ?) from Mark EDWARDS who expects that she is seduced by bad company (VGR 27 Apr 69)
EDWARDS, Nathaniel Jr., rep. for and clerk of Brunswick Co., d. of bilious fever on Wed. the 23rd inst. (VGR 31 Jan 71); e.a.w. his ex., William EDWARDS who will also sell his PE (VG & VGR 7 Mar 71)
EDWARDS, Thomas, of Northumberland Co., dec'd, his ex. (nfi) will sell his slaves, livestock, and HHF (VGR 19 Nov 72)
EDWARDS, William, dec'd, e.a.w. his ex., Nicholas FAULCON Jr. of Surry Co. (VGR 25 Nov 73)
EDWARDS, William, of Surry Co., mar. Miss Susan EDMUNDS of Sussex Co. (VG 9 Jun 74)
EDWERDS, Edith, dec'd, Humphrey EDWERDS of Louisa Co. will pet. the next GA to vest in fee simple to the heirs of Edith EDWERDS a tract of land in Powhatan Co. whereof Joseph B. LARK died possessed (VGRMA 30 Oct 94)
EGAN, Thomas, died (WVGWA 15 May 90)
EGBORN, Jacob, will pet. the GA for a divorce from his wife, Adelila EGBORN (VHFA 21 Aug 95)

EGE, Jacob, mar. Miss Betsy STUBBLEFIELD both of [Richmond] on Thurs. last (VGRMA 13 Mar 84); of Richmond, d. on Tues. morn. last [6 Oct] (VGGA 7 Oct 95, RMA 8 Oct 95); e.a.w. his admx., Elizabeth EGE of Richm. (RC 21 Mar 96)

EGER, Albert, baker of Winchester, d. of rabies on Sun. morn. last (Winchester disp. of 22 Jan.) (BVCG 22 Jan 96, RC 16 Feb 96)

EGGLESTON, Edmund, mar. Miss Jane S. LANGHORNE, both of Amelia Co. (RMA 21 Nov 95)

EGGLESTON, Mrs. Elizabeth, of James City Co., dec'd, her ex., Richard EGGLESTON and Richard TALIAFERRO, will sell a quantity of corn, HH and KF and other items [of her est.] (VGWeA 10 Dec 85)

EGGLESTON, John, son of Richard EGGLESTON of Powhatan Co., after having burned all his papers, cut his throat and expired in a short time last week (VGWeA 17 Jul 84)

EGGLESTON, Mrs. Judith, of Amelia Co., d. on Fri. the 3rd inst. in her 45th year (VGR 23 Dec 73)

EGGLESTON, Richard Esq., d. lately in Amelia Co. (RMA 2 Apr 96); e.a.w. his ex., Joseph EGGLESTON, William MERIWETHER, and Joshua CHAFFIN (VGGA 14 Sep 96)

EGGLESTON, Mrs. Sarah, cons. of Joseph EGGLESTON Esq. of Amelia Co., d. on the 10th inst. [obit. in VGRMA] (VGGA 17 Dec 94, VGRMA 18 Dec 94)

EGGLESTON, William, of Frederick Co., intends to settle over the mountains and will sell 800 ac. in Amelia Co. (100 ac. of which is subject to a widow's dower); mention is made of Joseph EGGLESTON in Amelia and Richard EGGLESTON in Cumberland Co. (VG 5 May 74)

EGLESTON, Richard Sr., adv. that John [ATHER] Jr. informed him that his son, William EGLESTON, just before he went to the northward (Sep. was twelvemonths) had lent upwards of £100 to a friend; he wishes to know if the debt was ever paid (VGPu 14 Nov 77)

EILS, Thomas, Virginian, jailed in Staunton as a runaway (VGR 10 Mar 74)

ELAM, Joseph, of Henrico Co., intends to inform the next GA to find out whether the RE of his dec'd nephew, Joshua STORRS, is subject to the payment of his debts (VGAA 28 Jan 86)

ELAM, Robert, intends to leave the colony soon (VG 23 May 66)

ELBUT, William, aka HUGHES, mulatto, c. 40, claims to be a Revolutionary [War] soldier, jailed in Wmsbrg. (VGAA 9 Jul 85)

ELDER, Dr. Thomas, of [Henrico Co.], dec'd, e.a.w. his admr., John POTTS of Richmond (VGRMA 1 Sep 94)

ELIN, Samuel, conv. svt., came from London last year in the *Forward Galley*; professes to be a carpenter and joiner, ran away from William WALKER, Westmoreland Co. (AWM 19 Jul 39)

ELIOT, John, of Middlesex Co., executed on 5 Dec. for burglary (VG 4 Nov, 9 Dec 73)

ELLASON, John, dec'd, if any of his offspring are living they may hear of something greatly to their advantage by applying to Samuel SWANN of Nansemond Co. or John SWANN of Cumberland Co. (VG 7 Jun 75)

ELLIOT, John, heir at law of Robert ELLIOT Gent., dec'd, summoned to Middlesex Co. Ct. to answer a bill in chancery (VGR 12 Jan 69)

ELLIOT, William, conv., from the north of Eng., farmer, ran away from the snow *Anne* at Port Royal (VG 9 Jul 72)

ELLIOT, William, dec'd, his admr., John HOOMES, will sell a tract of his land in Caroline Co. (VGGA 5 Dec 92)

ELLIOTT, Caleb, aka Caleb, Negro, ran away from Edmund BEEZLEY, Caroline Co. (VHFA 3 Jan 93)

ELLIOTT, Mrs. Elizabeth, late of Middlesex Co., her land there which was mortgaged by the late Mr. ELLIOTT to James MILLS dec'd, to be sold by her ex., Overton COSBY (VGAA 26 Jun 84)

ELLIOTT, George, of Petersburg, dec'd, e.a.w. Joseph HARDING in Petersburg or Richard ELLIOTT the ex. in Brunswick Co. (VGAA 28 Sep 82)

ELLIOT[T], the Rev. [James], mar. Miss [Elizabeth] BROCKENBROUGH [dau. c Arthur BROCKENBROUGH], both of Westmoreland Co. [bond 20 Nov 1792, Nottingham 1928: 22] (VGWeA 4 [Jan] 93)

ELLIOTT, John, of York Co., dec'd, e.a.w. his extx. and widow, Chivers ELLIOTT (VGWeA 4 Sep 84)

ELLIOTT, John, of the late house of Elliott and Purviance, merchants, of this borough, d. on Wed. (NHPA 10 Dec 96)

ELLIOTT, Mary, her husband, Thomas ELLIOTT of Fauquier Co., adv. that she "has conducted herself in such a manner as renders it necessary for me to caution any person from trusting her on my account, not that I accuse her of incontinency" (VG 15 Oct 72)

ELLIOTT, Richard Esq., late of Charlotte Co. [dec'd], e.a.w. his ex., Robert ELLIOTT (VGPI 1 Sep 97)

ELLIOTT, Robert, late of Middlesex Co., dec'd, e.a.w. his admr., Archibald RITCHIE of Tappahannock (VG 21 May 67, 5 Nov 67)

ELLIOTT, Robert, late of Portsmouth, dec'd, e.a.w. his admr., John ELLIOTT of Portsmouth (NHPA 7 Aug 97)

ELLIOTT, Solomon, trader to Carolina, was murdered in N. Carolina by one KELLY and his wife (VG 1 Oct 72)

ELLIOTT, Col. Thomas, late of Kg. Wm. Co., dec'd, the residue of his est. will be sold by his admr., Thomas ELLIOTT (VGGA 28 Oct 95)

ELLIS, Anne, conv. svt., imp. in the *Success's Increase* last Dec., ran away from Forceput near Fredsbrg. (VGR 7 Apr 74)

ELLIS, Francis, of Hanover, d. Sat. last (VGAA 30 Jul 85)

ELLIS, George, merch., of Richm., d. at Norfolk (VG 3 Oct 71)

ELLIS, Capt. John, late commander of the ship *Montague*, d. during his passage from Gibraltar to James River (MG 1 Sep 47)

ELLIS, John, son of William ELLIS on Tuckahoe Cr., Henrico Co. (VGAA 5 Apr 83)

ELLIS, John, merch. of Alexandria, died (VJAA 12 May 85)

ELLIS, John, of Henrico Co., son of William ELLIS, will rent a 600 ac. tract in Goochland Co. [may be the same as John ELLIS above] (VGGA 8 Oct 94)

ELLIS, John, of Henrico Co., dec'd, Susanna ELLIS and Jesse CURD, the gdns. to his orphans, will sell his est. (RMA 5 Nov 95)

ELLIS, John, d. on the 12th ult. in Caroline Co., aged 62 (RCFPC 5 Oct 96)

ELLIS, Mary, of Kg. Wm. Co., dec'd, John ELLIS of Hanover Co. (nfi) will settle her est. (VGPu 29 Dec 75)

ELLIS, Tempest, in the care of James SEAGROVE, Superintendent of Indian Affairs at St. Mary's; she is about 13, and was taken by the Indians near the Cedar Shoals on the Oconee from the house of a Mrs. SCARLET about seven yrs. ago; her friends are desired to send and take her away [It is not clear whether her name is ELLIS or ELLISON] (VGWeA 20 Aug 96)

ELLIS, Thomas, d. at his seat in Henrico Co. on the 15th inst. aged c. 50 (VGGA 2 Oct 95)

ELLIS, William, dec'd, his PE to be sold at Alexandria (VJAA 14 Sep 86)

ELLISON, Gerrard, of Chesterfield Co., dec'd, e.a.w. his ex., Abraham SALLE, Thomas BRANCH, and Daniel WEISIGER (VG 25 Apr 71)

ELLZEY, Capt. Lewis, d. at his seat on Popes Head, Fairfax Co. on 17 Oct. in his 85th year (VJAA 16 Nov 86)

ELLZEY, William, d. on the 24th ult. at his seat in Loudoun Co. in his 68th year; had been, for about 40 yrs., engaged in the profession of the law (CMAG 25 Feb 96); e.a.w. his ex., W. ELLZEY of Loudoun Co., who will also sell a large amount of his livestock, plant. utensils, and two slaves (CMAG 22 Sep 96)

ELSEY, William, heir at law and legatee of Edward WHITEHEAD dec'd of Frederick Co.; he will prefer a pet. to the present session of the GA to invest the real and PE of Edward WHITEHEAD in him and his heirs as his nearest relations in this country (VHFA 6 Sep 87, VGWA 26 Oct 87)

ELSIE, George, of Isle of Wight Co., 30, enl. by George MACKENZIE, has not reported to camp in Wmsbrg. (VG 31 Jul, 14 Aug 46)

ELTHERIDGE, Francis, svt., c. 30, a brass founder by trade but pretends to be skilled in the silversmith's business, ran away from Philip DELL, Northampton Ct.H. (MG 13 Dec 49)

ELTON, John, house carpenter, of Alexandria, dec'd, Isabella ELTON is his extx. and his exors. are Robert ALLISON and John SAUNDERS (VJAA 14 Oct 84, 6 Jan 85)

EMANUEL, John, Negro, claims to be free, jailed in Norfolk along with a little Negro boy named Jack CAWN (son of Fanny CAWN of Norfolk) (VG 18 Aug 74)

EMANUEL, Ralph, conv. svt., c. 22, just imp. in the *Justitia* from London, ran away from Andrew LEITCH near Leedstown (VG 22 Apr 75, 29 Apr 75 sup, VGP 28 Apr 75)

EMBLEY, Thomas, Berkeley Co. Ct., 19 Nov. 1794, in chanc: John HIGGINS (compl.) vs. John EMBLEY eld. son and heir at law of Thomas EMBLEY dec'd (def.); it appears that the def. is not an inhabitant of the commonwealth (PGBA 12 Jan 95)

EMMERSON, John, late from Eng., dec'd, e.a.w. his admr., James CATON, Norfolk (HNPA 28 Sep 95)

EMREY, Stephen, adv. that his wife, Catherine EMREY, has eloped from his bed and board (CMAG 24 Mar 96)

ENGLAND, Titus, dec'd, his property to be sold in Winchester by his admr. Daniel OVERACRE (VGWA 8 Oct 91)

ENOS, Robert, aged 20, d. yesterday (NH 4 Jul 96)

EPES, Miss Elizabeth, dau. of Col. Peter EPES of Pr. Geo. Co., d. a few days ago (VGPI 26 Jan 98)

EPES, Hamlin, of Dinwiddie Co., dec'd, e.a.w. his ex., Francis EPES of Amelia (VG 14 Oct 75)

EPPERSON, John, merch. of Buckingham Co., mar. Miss Betsy Ann WOODSON of Pr. Edw. Co. on the 17th ult. (Arg 22 Mar 99)

EPPES, Mrs. Amey, d. at her house in Dinwiddie Co. in her 76th year (VGPu 29 Aug 77)

EPPES, Edward, of Southampton Co., dec'd, a tract of his land on Meherrin River, formerly the property of George EPPES and subject to the dower of George EPPES' widow, to be sold by Francis EPPES, the ex. of Edward (VG 9 Mar 69)

EPPES, Francis, of Pr. Geo. Co., d. there lately (VG 4 Feb 37)

EPPES, Francis Esq., col. of the 2nd Regt. (or Lt. Col. of the 1st. Regt., acc. to VGPu) of the Va. Forces, d. in the prime of life at his own house in Dinwiddie Co. on 20 Dec. (VG & VGPu 27 Dec 76); e.a.w. his admr., Thomas SCOTT, who will also sell all of his PE including some valuable horses among which is the beautiful high bred horse *Mercury* (VGPU & VG 4 Jul 77)

EPPES, John W. Esq., of Chesterfield Co., mar. Miss Maria JEFFERSON dau. of Thomas JEFFERSON Esq. Vice-president of the U.S., on the 13th inst. (TAA 31 Oct 97)

EPPES, Peter, late of Charles City Co., dec'd, he was admr. to his late brother, Temple EPPES; e.a.w. his ex., William ROYAL[L] (VG 16 Jun 74); his ex. will sell about 20 of his slaves at Manchester (VGPu 11 Oct 76)

EPPES, Thomas, of Pr. Geo. Co., who hath devised the greatest part of a very considerable fortune to William POYTHRESS, an officer in the Continental Army, died (VG 25 Sep 79)

EPPES, Maj. William, dec'd, his admr. w.w.a. is Elizabeth EPPES of Dinwiddie Co. (VGPI 10 May 96)

EPPS, [?], son of Mrs. EPPS of Chesterfield Co., was murdered last Thurs. [12 Jun] by a Negro girl (Wmsbrg. disp. of 20 Jun) (NYM 21 Jul 66, NYPB 24 Jul 66)

[EPPS], Joel, dec'd, e.a.w. his admr., Banks MEACHUM of Sussex Co. (VGPI 7 Nov 97)

ERRINGTON, Mr., killed [in Essex Co.] by Miss Ann BROADRIC on the 15th ult. [long account] (HNPA 25 Jul 95)

Escaped Prisoners from the prison in Baltimore, 29 Dec 1776: William GOODRICH, from Va., partisan of Lord Dunmore, c. 34; Bridger GOODRICH, from Va., partisan of Lord Dunmore, c. 24; and three Scotch tories from N.

Carolina: Kenneth M'DONALD, c. 30, Alexander M'CLEOD, c. 30, Daniel
M'CLEOD, c. 30, Murdoch M'CASTLE, 28-30 (VG 7 Feb 77)
Escaped Prisoners from jail in Craven Co., N. Carolina: Michael KELLY, Irish
jailed for robbery; Matthias FARNAN, c. 28, jailed for robbery; James
RAWLINS, c. 40, jailed for high treason, has lived for two yrs. in Martin Co.
(VG 3 Oct 77)
Escaped Prisoners from jail in Richmond: Peter LYNCH, b. in Ireland, c. 30, ha
a wife and child in Philadelphia, formerly a soldier in Gen. WAYNE's Brigade;
William GALLEY, b. in Dublin, c. 24, formerly drove the Philadelphia stage
and is well known in Baltimore; both men jailed for highway robbery (VGWeA 7
Aug 84)
Escaped Prisoners from jail in Richmond: John MINNS, Eng., des. from
Tarlton's Legion, schoolmaster in Halifax, c. 23; John FOWLER, Irish, c. 22,
Albemarle Co.; John LANE, c. 18, Culpeper Co.; William DELAFIELD, c. 21,
Mecklenburg Co.; George MILES, Eng., c. 25, Henrico Co.; Charles EVANS,
free mulatto, c. 17, Buckingham Co.; Jesse TUCKER (son of William TUCKER)
of Powhatan, 19-20 (VGAA 30 Jul 85)
Escaped Prisoners from jail in Richmond, [8] Nov.: Alexander MOORE,
Nansemond Co., seaman, c. 30, b. in North Britain; Slaughter COWLING,
Nansemond Co., c. 20, b. in Va.; Ezekiel ABLE, Shenandoah Co., c. 30, a native;
Hugh JACKSON, from Culpeper, c. 23, a native; John BLACKWELL, from
Culpeper, c. 40, a native; John FOWLER, Nansemond Co., c. 22; William
PRESTON, Nansemond Co., c. 30, an Irishman bred to the sea; William
HAYES aka MAYES aka John KERSEY, from Amelia Co., c. 27, a Virginian;
James GOSS, from Pittsylvania, carpenter, c. 24, a native; John BAKER, from
Norfolk Co., c. 26, a sawyer; Andrew KELSEY, from Norfolk Co., c. 28, his
father lives in N. Carolina; John CHERRY, from Norfolk Co., c. 40, carpenter,
a native (VGAA 12 Nov 85)
Escaped Prisoners from Richmond Jail: John FOWLER, Irish, c. 22; James
CAMPBELL, Irish, c. 25; James GOSS, b. in Pittsylvania Co., c. 24; John
PRESTON, Irish, c. 28; Rowland GIBSON, [Virginian], c. 2[3]; Joseph MINOR,
Eng., c. 25; Thomas HICKLIN, Virginian, c. 22 (VGAA 30 Aug 86)
Escaped Prisoners from jail in Frederick Town, [Md.], 18 Mar.: Adam BONT:
weaver and dyer, 45-50; John SEEGFRIED, shoemaker, c. 35 (VGWA 3 Apr 90)
ESKRIGGE, George, of Eskrigge & Smith, Cartersville; formerly of Richmond, d.
on Fri. the 6th inst. at Cartersville (VGRMA 16 Jun, 11 Aug 94)
ESTEN, Capt. James, of the ship *Hanbury* from York River for London, d. on the
passage (VGP 5 Jan 75, VG 7 Jan 75)
ESTES, Abraham, of Spotsylvania Co., dec'd, his ex., Richard ESTES, will sell
about 400 ac. of his land adjoining Roger's Mill (VH 29 Nov 97)
ESTES, Robert, [of Lunenburg Co.], dec'd, his ex., Robert ESTES and Elisha ESTE
will sell the land and premises upon which the [Lunenburg] Ct. H. formerly
stood (VGP 9 Nov 75); his ex. will sell or rent 200 ac. of his land at Lunenburg
Ct. H. (VG 14 Sep 76); his ex. will sell 514 ac. of his land, the major part of a
tract whereon he lately lived and upon which Lunenburg Ct. H. stands (or
within a mile of the Ct. H.) (VGPu 1 Aug 77, 14 Nov 77); purs. to a decree of
Lunenburg Co. Ct., his ex. will sell the land and premises upon which the Ct.
H. formerly stood now occupied by Joseph SMITH and mortgaged to the exors.
for a debt due by the original purchaser to their testator's est. (VGPI 28 Dec 86)
ESTES, Triplett, merch., mar. Miss Sally LUCAS dau. of Zach. LUCAS in
[Fredsbrg.], on Thurs. eve. last (VH 26 Nov 99)
ESTHER, James, blockmaker, of Norfolk, died (VG 17 Oct 71)
ESTILL Family, Greenbrier Co..Ct., 29 Jan 1799, in chanc: Hugh CAPERTON an
Zachariah Fosterer ESTILL (compls.) against Bo[y]d ESTILL and Wallace
ESTILL (defs.); it appears that the defs. are not inhabitants of this state (PH 17
Jul 99)
ESTIS, Milly, dau. of Robert ESTIS Sr. of Lunenburg, mar. [Frederick] COX who
has moved to Pittsylvania Co. (VG 5 May 68)
ETHERIDGE, Mrs. Hanna, wife of Capt. P. ETHERIDGE, d. at Portsmouth on

Sun. last (NH 28 Aug 98, NWCJI 29 Aug 98)
EUBANK, James, dec'd, his ex. (nfi) will sell all his PE at his late dwelling in this country (VGGA 13 Dec 99)
EUSTACE, Nathaniel, [also given as EUSTIS], merch., formerly of Boston, d. this morn. (NHPA 14 Sep 97, VGPI 19 Sep 97)
EUSTIS, Abraham, of the partnership of Blodget & Eustis, Petersburg, d. on the 25th of Dec. 1788 (VIC 21 Jan, 18 Feb 89)
EVANS Family, Halifax Co., Ct. of Q.S., 22 Aug 1796, in chanc: Royall DANIEL attorney in fact for Samuel ROBERTS and Mary his wife (compl.) against George EVANS, [Berry] STRANGE and Frances his wife, Moses HENDROCK and Drucella his wife, Samuel BENTLEY attorney in fact for Samuel NORTHERN and Judith his wife, Sarah EVANS, Lucy EVANS, and Zachariah MEDLOCK and Eady his wife (defs.); it appears that George EVANS and the MEDLOCKs are not inhabitants of this state (VGPI 8 Nov 96)
EVANS Family, Montgomery Co. Ct., May 1799, in chanc: David PAINTER (compl.) against David EVANS and Peter EVANS heirs and reps. of Thomas EVANS dec'd (defs.); it appears that the defs. are out of this country (LWG 13 Jul 99)
EVANS, Miss, dau. of a Mr. EVANS and granddaughter of Mr. HOGG; she was kidnapped by Indians from the settlement of Clinch and ransomed by a British officer (VCWM 4 Feb 89)
EVANS, Mr., coachmaker, recently moved from Wmsbrg. to Rappahannock; murdered in Hanover Co. by Anthony Francis DITTOND (q.v.) (VG 11, 18 Aug 38, NYWJ 25 Sep 38)
EVANS, Mrs. Catherine, wife of Ephraim EVANS of Alexandria, died (VGAxA 6 May 90)
EVANS, Charles, mulatto, ran away from Benjamin JOHNSTON, Fredsbrg. (VGR 15 Mar 70)
EVANS, Elijah, appr., 20, millwright, ran away from Felix BEACHY, Shenandoah Co. (BVCG 30 Dec 96)
EVANS, Elizabeth, her husband, John EVANS Sr., will not pay her debts (PGBA 10 Mar 96); she adv. that Joseph EVANS Jr. has published a scandalous advertisement which he claims is in the handwriting of John EVANS Sr., her husband; the sd. John EVANS Sr. is aged, infirm, and disabled in body and mind, and acc. to her, John EVANS utterly denies that he had ordered or intended anything of the kind; she says that Joseph EVANS bears her a grudge (PGBA 17 Mar 96); John EVANS Sr. adv. that the advertisement of 25 Feb. so much complained of since by Mrs. Elizabeth EVANS, was done by his consent and at his request (PGBA 31 Mar 96)
EVANS, Evan, late of Delaware, now resides in Richmond where he deals in mill machinery (VGGA 4 Mar 95)
EVANS, George, aka George, mulatto, c. 25, plays well on the violin, ran away from Marsham WARING, Georgetown, who believes he has crossed over to Va. (VGGA 22 Oct 94, CMAG 28 Oct 94)
EVANS, John, Welsh, sailor, ran away from the brigantine *Mally* in Hampton River, 2 Oct., supposed heading for Md. (VG 6 Oct 52)
EVANS, John, who sometime in 1795 sailed in the *Polly* of Gloucester, New Eng., Capt. MAYO commander (a south sea man); if he will write to Mr. S. J. LILLEY, Peckham, near London, Eng., he will hear something to his advantage; Capt. Robert COWPER of Norfolk desires information on him (NH 13 Apr 99)
EVANS, Lucy, has eloped with all the HHF from her husband, Henry EVANS of Petersburg (VGPI 22 Jun 98)
EVANS, Martha, aka NASH, has absconded from her husband, Thomas EVANS, Norfolk (NH 29 Mar 98)
EVANS, Dr. Peter, of Pr. Anne Co., dec'd, his admr. w.w.a., Dennis DAWLEY, will sell his est. (HNPA 14 Dec 95)
EVANS, Philip, dec'd, his ex., William SMITH and George FRENCH, will sell his PE in Fredsbrg. (VHFA 30 May 93)

EVANS, Robert, appr. blacksmith boy, ran away from John HILL (TAA 9 Sep 97)
EVANS, Solomon, son of Nathaniel EVANS, dec'd, his friends may apply to Capt. BARTLET to see how they may obtain £50 sterling left by the dec'd (VCNPGA Sep 92)
EVANS, Thomas, svt., came in the country two yrs. ago, ran away from on board the *William and Anne* on the Eastern Branch of the Potomac (VG 31 Jul 46)
EVANS, Thomas, tailor, late from London, adv. that he has commenced business in Norfolk (NHPA 10 Apr 97)
EVANS, Thomas, mar. Mrs. BURKE wid. of Michael BURKE dec'd, both of Petersburg, on Thurs. last (VGPI 19 Sep 97)
EVANS, William, of Murfreesborough, N. Carolina, d. at Col. BROOKING's in Amelia Co. (VGRMA 5 Jan 95)
EVEREST, Richard, Eng., about 10 yrs. ago lived with a Mr. HOUGH, storekeep in Loudoun; he has been left a considerable legacy and is asked to contact Edward [VIDLER] in Annapolis, Md. (VJAA 25 Aug 85)
EVERITT, Willis, dec'd, Willis WILKINSON (nfi) will sell part of his est. at Everitt's Bridge (HNPA 21 Dec 95)
EVERSAGE, Michael, drummer, c. 30, enl. in Westmoreland Co., des. from the regt. in Wmsbrg. (VGPu 6 Jun 77)
EVRIE, John, Scot, svt., c. 29, weaver, ran away from N. W. DANDRIDGE, Hanover Co. (VG 18 Jan 70)
EWELL, Maj. James, formerly of Lancaster Co., d. a few days since in Pr. Wm. Co (RCFPC 26 Apr 97)
EWELL, Lt. Jesse, was mar. to Miss Mildred BEALE at Chestnut Hill, Richmond Ct. H., on Sun. the 17th inst. by the Rev. M. L. WEEMS (VH [22] Nov 99)
EWELL, Mrs. Sarah, spouse of Maj. James EWELL and eld. dau. of Col. Edwin CONWAY of Lancaster Co., d. on Sun. eve. 31 Oct. last in her 17th year (VGAA 15 Jan 85)
EWEN, John, [conv.] svt., joiner, c. 24 (in 1771), has been in the country since abo 1798, ran away from William BUCKLAND, Richmond Co. (VGR 15 Jun 69, 10 Jan 71)
EWING, Ebenezer, dec'd, e.a.w. Joseph FERGUSSON and David MILLER of Wmsbrg., his exors. (VGGA 20 Jan 96)
EWING, Esther, has eloped from her husband, John EWING (BVCG 2 Apr 92)
EYRE, John Esq., lately transported into this country for stealing paper, d. about three days after his arrival (VG 9 Apr 72, PC 27 Apr 72)
EYRE, Col. Littleton, d. at his house in Northampton Co. on Sun. the 26th ult. (V 7 Jul 68, VGR 14 Jul 68)
EYRE, Littleton Esq., of Northampton Co., d. on the 7th of May on the Eastern Shore [obit. in VIC] (VGWeA 21 May 89, VIC 10 Jun 89)
EYRE, Severn Esq., a rep. for Northampton, d. at Norfolk of a pleuritick disorder (VG & VGR 28 Jan 73); [a eulogy is printed in VG of 24 Jun 73]
EYRE, William, was mar. to Miss Gracy TAYLOR, youngest dau. of Robert TAYLOR Esq. of Norfolk by the Rev. James WHITEHEAD last eve. (AGGA 27 Sep 96)
EZELL, Jesse, of Ravenscroft Town, dec'd, his admx., Elizabeth EZELL, will sell his PE; she authorizes Timothy EZELL to receive all debts (VGPI 9 Feb 96)
EZELL, William, ran away from his father, Isham EZELL (VG 1 Apr 73)

FAIR, Henry, of Richmond, adv. that Sarah FAIR, by lawful marriage his wife, has withdrawn herself from him for no cause at all and he will not be accountable for any debts she may contract (VGWeA 23 Oct 88)
FAIRFAX Family, HCC, 12 Oct 1789: Ralph WORMELEY (pltf.) against George WASHINGTON, Wilson Miles CARY and George NICHOLAS exors. and Fer[di]nando FAIRFAX devisee of George William FAIRFAX dec'd, Sarah FAIRFAX and Bryan FAIRFAX heir at law and Elizabeth FAIRFAX devisee of the sd. George William FAIRFAX dec'd (defs.) (VIC 18 Nov 89)
FAIRFAX, Denny (late Denny MARTIN), HCC, 7 Jun 1797, between Henry BEDINGER (pltf.) and James STRADE, Denny FAIRFAX (late Denny

MARTIN), Robert STEPHENS, David HUNTER, Moses HUNTER, and Philip PENDLETON (defs.); it appears that Denny FAIRFAX is not an inhabitant of this country (VGGA 28 Jun 97)

FAIRFAX, Ferdinando Esq., of Berkeley Co., mar. Miss Elizabeth B. CARY youngest dau. of Wilson Miles CARY Esq., at Celeys near Hampton on Thurs. 18 [January] (NH 22 Feb 96, CMAG 3 Mar 96)

FAIRFAX, the Hon. George William, dec'd, tracts of his in Culpeper Co., Winchester, and Loudoun Co. will be sold by Wilson Miles CARY his ex. (VGGA 24 Nov 90)

FAIRFAX, the Rt. Hon. Thomas, Lord, Baron of Cameron and Proprietor of the Northern Neck, d. on 11 Dec. at his seat Greenway Court in Frederick Co. in his 98th year (VGWeA 5 Jan 82); e.a.w. his ex., Thomas Bryan MARTIN and Gabriel JONES, Greenway Ct. (VGWA 15 Feb 88, VIC 2 Apr 88)

FAIRFAX, Thomas, of Fairfax Co., mar. Miss Mary AYLETT dau. of Col. William AYLETT of Kg. Wm. Co. dec'd, on the 20th ult. at Evelington the seat of Alexander MOORE in Charles [City] Co. (VGGA 4 Nov 95, RMA 5 Nov 95, VHFFA 10 Nov 95)

FAIRFAX, the Hon. Col. William, President of H.M's Council of Va. and Collector of the Revenues for South Potomac, d. on the 2nd inst. (or Sat. the 3rd inst. acc. to Randolph) at his seat at Belvoir, Fairfax Co. (MG 15 Sep 57, VG-Randolph 16 Sep 57)

FAIRM, Peter, sailor of the ship *Juno*, broke out of Norfolk Co. jail (NH 5 Mar 99)

FAITHFUL, Jonathan, executed on 4 Jan. (VG 4 Jan 40)

FALCONER, Alexander, att. at law, mar. Mrs. Polly Harriet WYNNE of Franklin Co., N. Carolina (VGPI 17 Feb 97)

FALKNER, Usly, Patrick Co. Ct., 29 Nov 1798, in chanc: William FALKNER and Usly his wife who was Usly EDWARDS (pltfs.) against Isham SOLOMON (LWG 16 Feb 99)

FARGUSON, Robert, dec'd, 300 ac. of his land in Amelia Co. will be sold, pursuant to his will, by his ex., Benjamin BRIDGFORTH (VGAA 4 Jan 83)

FARGUSON, Sarah, who came ind. from Eng. about six yrs. ago and served her time with Charles LEWIS, dec'd, on Rappahannock, will hear of something much to her advantage if she will apply to the printer (VGR 14 Jul 74)

FARISH, John S., mar. Miss Jane WARD dau. of the late Capt. James WARD of this place [Fredsbrg.] on Thurs. last in this county (VH 25 Jun 99)

FARISH, Robert the Elder, Henry CHILES, the admr., adv. that he is about to settle his admin. of the est. of sd. FARISH and of Robert FARISH the Younger; any claims should be presented to him or to Hazlewood FARISH of Fredsbrg. (VHFA 22 Aug 93, VGGA 25 Sep 93)

FARLEY, James Parke Esq., mar. Miss Betsy BYRD eld. dau. of the Hon. William BYRD (VG 28 Mar 71); of N. Carolina, d. suddenly at the house of Mann PAGE Esq. in Gloucester (VG and VGPu 23 May 77)

FARLEY, James Parke, dec'd, his creditors who claim their debts. under the will of Francis FARLEY Esq. of the island of Antigua dec'd, are desired to state their demands to John DUNBAR the ex. (VIC 25 Nov 89)

FARLEY, Matthew, from Powhatan Co., executed on Fri. last at the gallows near Richmond for murder (VGWeA 5 , [19] Feb 89)

FARMER, Catherine, age 16, wife of William FARMER, Chesterfield Co., has eloped from his bed and board (VGAA 22 Feb 86)

FARMER, James, planter, b. in Va., 20, des. from Capt. Robert HODGSON's Independent Co. now raising for the service and defense of S. Carolina (VG 3 Jul 46)

FARMER, William, appr. tanner, c. 17, ran away from George [KING], Pr. Edw. Ct. H. (VGGA 6 Aug 99)

FARO, John, svt., 15, shoemaker, brought in last Jul. in the *Duke of Argyle*, ran away from [?] ARMISTEAD (VG 10 Apr 46)

FARQUHARSON, John, of Norfolk, dec'd, e.a.w. his admx., Margaret FARQUHARSON of Wmsbrg. (VGWeA 25 Sep 84)

FARQUHARSON, Mrs. [Margaret], spouse of John FARQUHARSON late of

Wmsbrg. [sic], dec'd, d. last week (VGWeA 6 Sep 87)
FARREL, Elizabeth, aka DEVINE, svt., ran away from the snow *John* lying in Hampton Road (VGAA 17 Apr 84)
FARREL, John, of Norfolk, d. last eve. (AGNPPA 16 Aug 96)
FARRELL, John, conv. svt., cooper, b. in Ireland, c. 35, ran away from M'Call & Shedden, Hobb's Hole (VG and VGR 26 Aug 73)
FARRELL, Martin, dec'd, e.a.w. his extx., Mary FARRELL Dinwiddie Co. (VGPI 7 Jun 87)
FARRER, William, d. on Sun. last in his 60th year (NH 6 Nov 98)
FARRILL, Thomas, Irish ind. svt., tanner, ran away from Miles TAYLOR, Richmond (VG 28 Apr 74)
FARRIS, Mitchell, of New Kent, dec'd, e.a.w. his admr., Littlebury ROYSTER of Henrico (VGGA 4 Mar 95)
FARRO, Joseph R., of Fayette Co., Ky., dec'd, his admx. (nfi) will sell his PE (disp. of 24 Aug) (VGGA 28 Sep 96)
FARTHING, Charles, Eng. conv. svt., ran away from Abraham LEWIS and Joseph LEWIS, Loudoun Co. (VGPu 31 Jan 77)
FASTON, Thomas, Scot, ind. svt., imp. in the *Betsy Richmond* last Feb., ran away from his owner (nfi) in Annapolis, Md. (VGR 7 Jul 74)
FAULCON, Nicholas, dec'd, his ex., Nicholas FAULCON and Edward FAULCON will sell his 340 ac. tract in Surry Co. (VGGA 27 Nov 93, 14 Jan 95)
FAULDER, Mrs., wife of Thomas FAULDER merch., d. on Sun. morn. (HNPA 7 Sep 95)
FAULDER, Thomas, late of Manchester, Eng., e.a.w. his admr., James TUCKER of Norfolk (NH 1 Feb 96, 13 Jun 96)
FAUNTLEROY, Mrs. Elizabeth, spouse to Samuel Griffin FAUNTLEROY Esq. c & Q Co., d. on Fri. the 21st inst. aged c. 32 (VGGA 3 Dec 94)
FAUNTLEROY, Dr. George, of Richmond Co., dec'd, his admr., Robert TOMLIN, will sell his medical supplies (VGR 20 Sep 70)
FAUNTLEROY, Capt. [Henry], [commander of the 10th Co., 5th Va. Regt. of Foo slain at the Battle of Monmouth (MJ 7 Jul [82])
FAUNTLEROY, Maj. Moore, of Crondall, d. 18 Jan.; he was bur. in the family burying ground on the 26th (VHFA 7 Feb 93)
FAUNTLEROY, Col. William, d. at his seat in Richmond Co. on Thurs. the 17th inst. aged 83 (VHFA 31 Oct 93)
FAUNTLEROY, William, of Richmond Co., dec'd, his ex., William HOOE of Kg. Geo. Co., will sell all of his PE (VH 11 Oct 97); his ex. will sell about 40 of his slaves at Westmoreland Ct. H. (VH [22] Nov 99)
FAUQUIER, the Hon. Francis Esq., Lt. Gov. and Commander in Chief of this Colony and member of the Royal Society, d. on 3 Mar. at the [Governor's] Palac in Wmsbrg. in his 65th year; he was buried in the north aisle of the church in Wmsbrg. (on Tues. last acc. to VG of 10 Mar.) (VG and VGR 3 Mar 68, VG 10 Mar 68, NYPB and PC 4 Apr 68)
FAY, Thomas, Irish svt., c. 18, ran away from Freer ARMSTON, Norfolk (VG 11 Jul 71)
FEARN, Meacham, of Middlesex Co., died (VG 21 Apr 74)
FEARSON, William, of New Kent Co., dancing master, d. suddenly at Tuckahoe i Goochland (VG and VGPu 23 May 77); e.a.w. his extx., Dorothy FEARSON of New Kent (VG 19 Sep 77)
FEATHERSTONE, Henry, soldier, 34 (but apparently near 40), b. in Ireland, ha: resided in Richmond for many yrs., has a wife--believed originally from Pr. Anne Co. near Norfolk--and a small child, a blacksmith by trade, des. from the 7th Regt. of Infantry (VGGA 24 Sep 99, NH 26 Sep 99, VF 5 Oct 99)
FEE, William, svt., 25-28, ran away from the Potomac Co., Great Falls (VJAA 18 May, 15 Jun 86)
FEELEY, Lt. Timothy, late of Winchester, dec'd, e.a.w. his ex., James WALKER (VGWA 20 Aug 88)
FEILD, James, of Petersburg, will go to Great Britain soon and will sell his medical utensils and chirurgical instruments (VG 7 Feb 71)

FEMSTER Family, Bath Co. Ct., 15 May 1799, in chanc: John FEMSTER and William FEMSTER (compls.) against Elizabeth FEMSTER relict of Thomas FEMSTER dec'd, John M'CREERY and Martha his wife, Robert SETLINGTON and Mary his wife, Adam BRAT[T]ON and Elizabeth his wife, Rachel CARLISLE (alias FEMSTER), Susannah FEMSTER, and Sarah BROWN dau. of Sarah FEMSTER dec'd who intermarried with Hugh BROWN dec'd (defs.); it appears that John and Martha M'CREERY are not inhabitants of the state (PH 17 Jul 99)

FENDALL, Philip Richard Esq., of Alexandria, mar. Miss Molly LEE of Pr. Wm. Co. (VGAxA 17 Nov 91)

FENNER, Thomas, of Swan's Point, adv. that a brother of his in London wrote to him in Jan., but he has not yet received the letter (VG 3 Jun 73)

FERGUS, Robert, of Amelia Co., 83, mar. Anne JONES, 14-15, as his third wife on 3 Mar. (VG 12 Mar 67, NYM 30 Mar 67)

FERGUSON, Abner, appr., c. 20, ran away from Thomas HUMPHREY Jr., Loudoun Co., suspected of being in Frederick or Berkeley Co. (BVCG 22 Jul 93)

FERGUSON, David, killed in a wagon accident between Winchester and Stephensburg on his way to Georgia on Sat.; he left a wife and five children (VCWM and VGWA 25 Nov 89)

FERGUSON, James, Virginian, 44, enl. by Capt. BELL, des. from the Va. Regt. at Fort Cumberland (VG 26 Dec 55)

FERGUSON, James, of K & Q Co., dec'd, his land there to be sold by his ex., Richard TUNSTALL (VG 6 Jul 69)

FERGUSON, the Rev. Robert, of Pr. Geo. Co., dec'd, his est. there to be sold on 11 Feb. (VG 19 Dec 51)

FERMEY, Thomas, Eng. svt., ran away from Robert STOBO, Petersburg (VG 21 Aug 52)

FERRALL, John, proprietor of the Norfolk Classical School, d. at Norf. on Mon. the 15th of Aug. (VHFFA 23 Aug 96, NH 26 Sep 96); late of Main St., e.a.w. his ex., Frederick HEERMANN, Norfolk (NHPA 4 Nov 97)

FERRALL, Will, aka Will BUTLER and Will CURTIS, yellow slave, house carpenter, ran away from Edward MATTINGLY, St. Mary's Co., Md., was seen in Va. (VGR 22 Sep 68)

FERREL, Anne, Irish svt., 25, ran away from John SUTTON and Michael GRETTER, Alexandria (NPJ 12 Dec 87)

FERRELL, William, Irish svt., ran away from Anthony STROTHER, Fredsbrg.; it is thought he is gone towards Mobjack Bay or York River (VG 17 Jul 52)

FERTE, [Dr.] J. G., adv. that he studied for 10 yrs. at the Univ. of Paris and has opened his practice in Norfolk (NH 28 Mar 96)

FESKIN, James, weaver, sailed from Port Glasgow the latter end of last year or the beginning of this year for Va.; if he will apply to Peter FESKIN, Wmsbrg., he will hear of something to his advantage (VG 4 Jul 71)

FEURY, Mrs. Fanny, cons. of Patrick FEURY and dau. of Theophilus SHANNAN, lately arrived from the West Indies, age 19, d. on Mon. the 20th inst. [June] [obit.] (VGGA 13 Jul 96)

FIDDES, Christopher, Irish svt., ran away from Francis HAGUE, Loudoun Co. (VGR 19 Oct 69 sup)

FIELD, Daniel Jr., of Culpeper Co., and Henry FIELD of Woodford Co. [Ky.], adv. land bel. to the est. of Henry FIELD Jr. dec'd in Bourbon Co. [Ky.] (KG 7 Nov 89)

FIELD, Elianor, late of Culpeper Co., dec'd, e.a.w. her ex., John McCOULL of Stephensburg (VHFFA 8 Jul 96)

FIELD, Henry, mar. Miss Frances HILL dau. of Col. Henry HILL, in Madison Co. on Tues. the 27th inst. (VHFFA 30 Sep 96)

FIELD, James, U.S. Middle Circuit, District of Virginia, Nov. Court, 1794 in chanc: Samuel GIST a subject of the King of Great Britain (pltf.) against Margaret FIELD extx. of James FIELD dec'd who was surviving partner of Theophilus FIELD; the aforesaid James FIELD and Daniel CALL late merch. and carrying on trade under the firm of Daniel Call & Co., and John Shaw FIELD (defs); it appears that Mary FIELD is not an inhabitant of this country

(VGWeA 14 Feb 95)
FIELD, John, ind. svt., from Hereford, 25-26, ran away from the snow *Carlisle* at Yorktown (VG 19 May 74)
FIELD, Col. John, his ex., Lawrence SLAUGHTER, will sell nine of his slaves in the upper end of Culpeper Co. (VGPu 7 Feb 77)
FIELD, Theophilus, merch. of Petersburg, d. a few days ago after being kicked by a horse (VGP 5 Jan 75, VG 7 Jan 75)
FIELD, Thomas, Irish svt., a very good joiner, ran away from William RAND a carpenter and joiner in Gloucester Co., supposed to be gone to Carolina and perhaps as far as Georgia (VG 17 Dec 36)
FIELDER, William Jackson, appr. baker, c. 16, ran away from George HUBER, Dumfries, he was seen at the Red House Races making for Winchester (CMAG 5 Oct 97)
FIELDS, William, appr. boy, ran away from Nathan ANDERSON (BVCG 9 Sep 96)
FIERER, Capt. (or Maj.) Charles, of Dumfries, dec'd, a capt. in the Va. State [Forces] during the late war; e.a.w. his ex., John WILLIAMS and Robert ALEXANDER also of Dumfries; they will sell his printing press and two land office military warrants for 2000 ac. each (VHFA 12 Feb 95, CMAG 28 Feb 95, RJDA 3 Jul 95)
FILLER, Joseph, appr., ran away from Michael BURNER, Shenandoah Co. (VGWA 10 Nov 90)
FILLIKINS, Abraham, Virginian, 22, des. from the camp at Wmsbrg. (VG 31 Jul 46)
FINCH, Agnes, dec'd, her ex., William FINCH, will sell her slaves, HHF and livestock at her dwelling house in Charles City Co. (VG 18 Jun 72)
FINCH, Edward, of Charles City Co., dec'd, e.a.w. his ex., Robert BENTFORD, Charles City Co., or William WRIGHT in Henrico (VGWeA 26 Mar 89)
FINCH, Richard, svt., ran away along with Comfort FINCH (nfi) from Dorothea BENGER, Spotsylvania Co. (VG 28 Feb 55)
FINDLEY, John, conv. svt., bricklayer, formerly bel. to Robert STOBO of Petersburg; ran away from Richard EPPES in Aug. 1753 from the house of Benjamin WARD in Amelia Co.; it is supposed he intends to go where one widow BUNDIE lives in N. Carolina or to Cape Fear to one NEIL, a Scotchman, who left Chesterfield Co. (MG 5 Sep 54)
FINLAY, David, dec'd, James PATTON, att. in fact for Amelia FINLAY heir at law of David FINLAY, will sell all of his real property in Alexandria (CMAG 9 Jun 95)
FINLEY, John, merch. of Alexandria, died (VJAA 13 Jan 95)
FINLEY, John, ind. svt., above 20, good fiddler, ran away from Samuel JOHN near Watkins' Ferry, Berkeley Co. (PGBA 28 Jan 96); returned of his own free will (PGBA 18 Feb 96)
FINNELING, Nicholas, Irish svt., tailor, c. 20, ran away from George LONG, Fredsbrg. (MG 25 Apr 54)
FINNIE, Mrs. the Younger, d. last Fri. at Portobello, she was from a very good an reputable family in Gloucester Co. (VGR 9 Feb 69)
FINNIE, Mrs., spouse of Col. William FINNIE of Richmond, d. on Fri. the 14th inst. (RMA and VGWeA 15 Aug 95, RC 18 Aug 95, VGGA 26 Aug 95)
FINNIE, Alexander, lately kept the Raleigh Tavern in Wmsbrg., intends to leave the Colony very shortly (VG 17 Nov 52)
FINNIE, Alexander, for many yrs. adj. to the Middle District of this Colony, d. yesterday at Porto Bello [York Co.] (VG 4 May 69); his land in York Co. to be sold; his widow has dower rights (VG 15 Jun 69)
FINNIE, Mrs. Elizabeth, spouse of Col. William FINNIE of Richmond, d. on Tues eve. last the 30th ult. (VGWeA 3 May 93, VGGA 8 May 93)
FINNIE, Miss Jane, dau. of Mrs. Joanna FINNIE of Pr. Geo. Co., d. last Thurs. morn. in her 13th year (VG 19 Feb 79)
FINNIE, John Austin, dec'd, Thomas TABB, att. in fact for Mrs. Joanna FINNIE and Miss Mary FINNIE, will sell a plant. or tract of land containing 500-600 ac on Ward's Cr. in Pr. Geo. Co., a tract of about 500 ac. on Pigeon Swamp in

Sussex Co., & many large tracts that appear to be in N. Carolina (VG 19 Jun 79)
FINNIE, Col. William Esq., Deputy Quartermaster-General, mar. Miss Betsy
CHAMBERLAYNE of James City Co. (VGPu 30 Aug 76, VG 31 Aug 76)
FIRMAN, Mr., att. at law, mar. Miss Nelly STEPHENS on Thurs. last at
Stephensburg (VCWM 22 Oct 88)
FISHER Family, Brunswick Co. Ct., Mar. 1799, in chanc: John FISHER, Daniel
FISHER, George FISHER, and Bolling FISHER heirs and residuary legatees of
Daniel FISHER dec'd (compls.) against George HICKS (def.) (VGPI 18 Jun 99)
FISHER, Eldred, of Norfolk, dec'd, his ex., James MARSDEN and Jonathan
EILBECK, will sell his est. which includes saddlery equipment (VG 10 Dec 72)
FISHER, George, svt., bookbinder, c. 26, broke jail at Wmsbrg.; he was assisted by
Andrew KELLY an Irish conv. svt., carpenter, c. 28 and John JONES aka
BAKER, an appr. carpenter, c. 18 (NYPB 19 Sep 65)
FISHER, James, merch. of Fredsbrg., aged about 54, d. on Thurs. (VHFA 31 Mar
98)
FISHER, John, has moved to Petersburg from Osborne's (VG 13 Jan 74)
FISHER, John, conv. svt., tailor, ran away from Andrew LEITCH, Dumfries (VGP
10 Nov 74)
FISHER, John, hatter, from Philadelphia, is in business in Petersburg (VGPI 31
Jan 93)
FISHER, Mrs. Mary, d. at Col. CLAIBORNE's in Sussex Co. in her 74th year
(VGPu 6 Mar 78)
FISK, Martin, merch., mar. Miss Elizabeth GILBERT dau. of Reyner GILBERT,
both of Norfolk, on Tues. eve. (NH 1 Aug 99)
FISKIN, Peter, Scot, svt., tailor, ran away from John ORR, Richm. (VG 23 Apr 72)
FITHER, John, svt. from Yorkshire, ran away from Zachariah HICKS, Pr. Geo.
Co. (VG 20 Apr 39)
FITZGERALD, Edward, merch. of Romney, Hampshire Co., d. on Wed. last
(VCWM 18 Nov 89)
FITZGERALD, John, Irish ind. svt., painter and glazier, c. 25, ran away from D.
TRUEHEART, Hanover Co., who expects he has gone down James River or to
Petersburg (VGIC 26 Mar 85, VGAA 9 Apr 85)
FITZGERALD, Col. John, of this place [Alexandria], d. on Mon. last; he was an
aide to Gen. WASHINGTON and since the war has filled an important office
under the Federal Govt.; his funeral was held on 4 Dec. [details of the funeral in
5 Dec. issue] (TDCDA 4, 5 Dec 99)
FITZGERALD, Maurice, Assistant Master of Languages at the Academy, mar.
Mrs. VALENTINE on Sun. eve. last (NPJ 9 Jan 88)
FITZGERRALD, Florence, Irish svt. man, c. 19, ran away, along with Florence
SWILAVAN, c. 50, from Edward SMITH of Richmond (VGR 14 Feb 71)
FITZHUGH, Daniel, of Westmoreland Co., mar. Mrs. DADE of Kg. Geo. Co.
(VGPu 18 Apr 77 sup); wishes to find out who inserted the marriage notice of
himself and Mrs. DADE so that he can have his man, George, give him a
genteel horsewhipping (VGPu 16 May 77)
FITZHUGH, Mrs. Eliza, wife of John FITZHUGH, Stafford Co., d. last Fri. in her
61st year; she was the mother of 13 children (VHFA 11 Mar 90)
FITZHUGH, Henry Esq., eld. son of Col. Henry FITZHUGH of Stafford Co., mar.
Miss Elizabeth STITH the dau. of Col. Drury STITH of Brunswick Co., on Fri.
the 26th ult. (VG 8 Nov 70); of Kg. Geo. Co., died (VGPu 27 Jun 77)
FITZHUGH, Henry Jr. Esq., mar. Miss Elizabeth C. CONWAY dau. of C.
CONWAY of Orange Co. (VHFA 17 May 92)
FITZHUGH, John, dec'd at Brandon in Pr. Geo. Co., his admr. (nfi) will sell the
stock late the property of Mrs. Elizabeth FITZHUGH dec'd (VGPI 17 Nov 91)
FITZHUGH, Lucy, will take depositions in the case of Dennis and William
FITZHUGH, infants, as plaintiffs in the HCC (Arg 8 Mar 99)
FITZHUGH, Miss Patsy, dau. of William FITZHUGH Esq. of Chatham, d. on Sun.
last (VHFA 3 Oct 93)
FITZHUGH, William Esq., of Va., mar. Mrs. ROUSBY, widow of John ROUSBY,
last week (MG 16 Jan 52)

FITZHUGH, William Esq., d. lately at Marmion his seat in Kg. Geo. Co. (VGGA 8 Sep 90)

FITZPATRICK, Daniel, Irish svt., ran away from William AYLETT and John BUSHROD[E], Westmoreland Co. on 8 Jul. (AWM 2 Aug 39, VG 17 Aug 39)

FITZPATRICK, Thomas, adv. that his wife, Mary FITZPATRICK, has ill-treated and absconded from him (CMAG 11 Aug 96)

FIVEATH, Capt. Peter, of Va., and Charlotte PARKS late of Waterford, Ireland, were mar. Wed. eve. the 12th inst. (BWG 14 May 84)

FLANNERY, Jeremiah, Irish ind. svt., c. 22, purchased from John MURRAY of Alexandria last fall, has run away from William ANDERSON, Augusta Co. (VGIC 26 Feb 85, VJAA 17 Mar 85)

FLEET, Edwin, of Hanover Co., dec'd, his extx., Frances FLEET, will sell his plant. near the Pamunkey River (VGGA 24 Dec. 94); his extx. will sell his plant. near Hanover Town (VGGA 4 Feb 95)

FLEET, William, of K & Q Co., intends to remove into the frontiers and wishes to sell his land on Mattaponi River (VG 4 Jul 71)

FLEMING, Adam Esq., of Wigto[w]n, Surry, d. on Tues. the 11th inst.; he was bur. at Cabin Point Chapel, on the 19th inst. (VG and VGPu 28 Feb 77); his ex., James WILLISON, will sell his plant. at the mouth of Chiapox Cr. on James River four miles from Cabin Point containing about 1100 ac. (VGPu 21 Mar 71)

FLEMING, Col. Charles, dec'd, e.a.w. William FLEMING (nfi) (VGRMA 11 Dec 94)

FLEMING, Charles, Negro, 30, ran away from Dover Estate, Goochland Co. (VGGA 25 Feb 95)

FLEMING, Henry, of the house of Fisher, Bragg, & Co., wholesale ironmongers and saddlers in Whitehaven, has opened a store in Norfolk (VG 29 Nov 70)

FLEMING, Col. John, lawyer, member of the Assembly for Cumberland Co., d. there on the 21st inst.; e.a.w. his ex., Thomas FLEMING and William FLEMING (VG 30 Apr 67, 4 Jun 67, 10 Nov 68); his ex. will sell 50 of his slaves (VGR 24 Dec 72)

FLEMING, John, Eng. ind. svt., c. 27, painter, drawer, and silversmith, ran away from Gavin HAMILTON, Wmsbrg. (or Norfolk) (VGPu 16 Jun 75, VG 24 Jun 75)

FLEMING, Capt. (or Maj.) John, of the 1st Va. Bn., killed in action near Trenton at the head of his company on 3 Jan.; acc. to VGPu of 14 Mar., he fell at the Battle of Princeton (VG 24 Jan 77, VGPu 7 Feb, 14 Mar 77)

FLEMING, Nathaniel, dec'd, collection of books from his est. to be sold by William URQUHART, Southampton (NPC 23 Jul 91)

FLEMING, Peter, of Norfolk, a native of Ireland, d. Wed. last in his 18th year; bur. in St. Elizabeth's Church yard (NPJ 16 Apr 88)

FLEMING, Peter, mulatto, 26, b. in Cumberland Co. near Sandy Ford Bridge of free parents and served his time with Richard GORDON to the carpenter's business near the aforesaid bridge, jailed in Alexandria (VJAA 21 May 89, CMAG 7 Mar 99)

FLEMING, Robert, dec'd, his admr., Benjamin HARRISON, Hanover Town, will sell his PE (VGGA 29 Apr 95)

FLEMING, Samuel, who mar. Margaret WETHERS of East Grinstead, Sussex, Eng.; if he or his lawful rep. will apply to Benjamin JOHNSTON of Spotsylvania Co. something to advantage may be heard of (VG 18 Jul 66)

FLEMING, Col. Tarlton, of Goochland Co., dec'd, his ex. (nfi) of Richmond, will sell slaves, livestock, and plant. utensils bel. to his est. (VIC 13 Dec 86)

FLEMING, Capt. Tarlton, of the U. S. Cavalry, d. lately at Ft. Washington (VGRMA 19 Jun 94); e.a.w. his admrs., William R. FLEMING and Thomas M. FLEMING (RMA 30 May 95); his admrs. will sell six of his slaves at Goochland Ct. H. (Arg 9 Dec 96)

FLEMING, Thomas, of Gloucester Co., age about 23, d. on Sun. the 12th inst. (VG 1 Jun 76)

FLEMING, Thomas, ship builder, d. in Alexandria, aged 63; he was one of the city's oldest inhabitants (VJAA 20 Apr 86); his est. to be settled with Betty

FLEMING, his extx., and George HUNTER his ex. (VJAA 14 Jun 87); his lot in [Alexandria] to be sold by his extx. and ex. (VGAxA 10 Jun 90)

FLEMING, William, of Goochland Co., will pet. the GA to vest in him the right to a tract of land which his brother Tarlton FLEMING d. possessed of (Ex 22 Oct 99)

FLEMMING, Capt. Robert, of Caroline Co., d. of consumption at his father's house in Hanover Co. last week (VG 10 Feb 38)

FLETCHER, John, Eng. svt., tanner, c. 25, ran away from William HOUSTON, Fredsbrg. (VG 1 Nov 70)

FLETCHER, Thomas, of Petersburg, d. on Wed. last (VGPI 13 May 96); his ex. is Thomas PETER of Cabin Point who will sell 12 of his slaves in Petersburg (VGPI 22 Jul 96)

FLET[C]HER, William, appr. boy, ran away from Charles BROWN, Fredsbrg. (VH 29 Jan 99)

FLIN, Timothy, Irish svt., with his young and lusty wife, Anne, ran away from Walter STEWART, Augusta Co. (VGR 23 Jun 68)

FLINN, Thomas, svt., c. 18, says he bel. to Thomas BADGET near Rocky Ridge; jailed in Bedford Co. (VG 21 Jul 74)

FLOOD, Dr. Nicholas, of Essex Co. [sic], for many yrs. an eminent practitioner in physic, died; his admx., Elizabeth FLOOD, and admrs., William PEACHEY and Leroy PEACHEY, will sell part of his PE at his late plant. in Richmond Co. (VGPu 19 Apr 76, 17 May 76); his admx. and admrs. adv. for a steward or manager for his plant. near Farnham Church, Richmond Co. (VG 14 Sep 76); e.a.w. his acting admr., William PEACHEY (VGAA 28 Jun 83)

FLOOD, Dr. William, dec'd, his ex. (nfi) will sell a variety of his plant. utensils, HH and KF, and livestock at Kinsale, Westmoreland Co. (VG 26 Aug 75)

FLORENCE, William, aka Windsor, Negro, c. 16, b. in the Indian town on the Pamunkey, son of Simon GILLET who lives in New Kent; jailed in York (VGR 26 Jul 70); ran away from William WATTS, Pr. Edw. Co. (VG 8 Nov 70)

FLOURNOY, Capt. Samuel, dec'd, e.a.w. his ex., Anthony MARTIN (VGGA 28 Dec 91)

FLOURNOY, Thomas, of Powhatan Co., dec'd, his ex., John HARRIS Jr. and Jordan FLOURNOY, will sell his land and plant. (VGRMA 27 Oct 94)

FOESE, John, of Chesterfield Co., dec'd, e.a.w. his admr., Francis GOODE (VGGA 28 Sep 91)

FOG, William, native of Great Britain, des. from the recruits bel. to Capt. James MASON's Co., 15th Va. Bn. (VGPu 11 Apr 77)

FOGG, John Jr., adv. that he mar. Ursula NOEL dau. of Taylor NOEL of Essex Co. on 20 Apr 1797 and found that she was pregnant at the time; she claimed that her father had had carnal knowledge of her body; FOGG will present a pet. for divorce to the next GA (VH 9 Aug 97, VHFFA 30 Sep 97); Taylor NOEL denies the charge and Ursula FOGG, of Caroline Co., also denied the charge saying that she had been deranged in her mind since her marriage to FOGG; James GARNETT and Agatha WOOLFOLK made depositions in support of NOEL (VHFFA 11 Oct 97); John FOGG Jr. renewed his accusations against NOEL and produced depositions by Reuben NOEL, Rachel KEESEE, Sally KEESEE, John FOGG Sr., Mrs. Anne SALE (wife of William B. SALE), Leonard SALE, and James UPSHAW Jr. to support his charge (VHFFA 11 Nov 97)

FOGG, William, ind. svt., c. 23, served his time in London under a blacksmith, ran away, along with Moses WILLIS a freeman and wagoner, from Edward TRAVIS, Brunswick Co.; they are believed headed for S. Carolina (VG 25 Aug 74)

FOLEY, Darby, Irish svt., ran away from John FITZGERALD, Kg. Wm. Co., seen near Hobb's Hole (VG 6 Jun 45)

FOLEY, Dennis, adv. that he will leave the continent in a short time; anyone indebted to him is requested to make payment to his wife, Elizabeth FOLEY (CMAG 14 Mar 97)

FOLGER, Barnard, late mariner, dec'd, e.a.w. Obed FOLGER of Fredsbrg. (nfi) (NHPA 27 Jul 97)

FOLK, John, 30, des. from the [army] barracks in Winchester; his relations live near Isaac's Cr. 18 miles from Winchester, but he is said to have a wife and family in Pa. (BVCG 25 May 95)

FONTAINE, Mrs. Alice, wife of the Rev. James Maury FONTAINE, d. on the 28th ult. at Ware Glebe, Gloucester Co. (VGPu 22 Dec, VG and VGP 23 Dec 75)

FONTAINE, Maj. James, with forces under Gen. HARMAR, killed by Indians in Kentucky (VHFA 2 Dec 90)

FONTAINE, the Rev. James Maury, Rector of Ware Par., Gloucester Co., mar. Miss Alice BURWELL (VG 25 Dec 71); dec'd, his admr. is Robert INNES who will sell some of his slaves in Gloucester Co. (VGGA 12 Oct 96)

FONTAINE, Col. Peter, dec'd, his extx., Eliza FONTAINE, will sell his tract in Halifax Co. (VGR 21 Oct 73)

FONTAINE, William, appr., 13 or 14, ran away from the rope walk of Joseph HARPER and Samuel HARPER in Alexandria; it is supposed that he has gone to Baltimore (TAA 9 Oct 97)

FORBES, James, of upper Isle of Wight Par., son of Alexander FORBES (who came into this colony many yrs. ago), is asked to apply to William MONTGOMERY, Yorktown, to hear of an est. left him in Britain (VG 10 Apr, 22 May 52)

FORBES, John, svt., c. 50, says he belongs to John HOOK in N. Carolina, jailed in Bedford Co. (VG 21 Jul 74)

FORBES, William, appr. silversmith, c. 20, ran away from James MURPHREE, Norfolk (VGNI 15 Jun 74, VG 16 Jun 74)

FORD, Daniel, d. on Fri. the 16th inst. near Dumfries in his 20th year of hydrophobia [long detailed article] (VH 3 Sep 99)

FORD, Robert, sailor, ran away from the brigantine *Mally* in Hampton River and supposed heading for Md. (VG 6 Oct 52)

FORD, Thomas, of Goochland, dec'd, e.a.w. John KEY of Albemarle Co. (VGGA 11 May 91)

FORDEM, James, Irish svt., 29, ran away from William HAYCOCK in Alexandria (VJAA 24 Aug 86)

FORDYCE, Capt., of the grenadiers of the 14th British Regt., killed in action on 9 Dec. at Great Bridge near Norfolk (VG 16 Dec 75)

FORLEAMS, Daniel, Virginian, 24, formerly lived in Powhatan Co., carpenter, des. from the 3rd Sub-Legion, Shockoe Hill (RC 24 Oct 95)

FORMAN, Gen. D., late of New Jersey, d. at sea on his return to Md. from the Natchez (NHPA 30 Oct 97, NWJCI 1 Nov 97)

FORMICOLA, Mrs., wife of Seraphino FORMICOLA of Richmond, d. on Mon. last (VIC 20 Jun 87, VGWeA 21 Jun 87, VGIC 23 Jun 87)

FORMICOLA, Serafino, informs the public that he has opened a tavern in the house opposite Mr. HOGG's Tavern in Richmond (VG 24 Feb 81); keeper of the Eagle Tavern in Richmond, d. Wed. last (VGGA 13 Oct 90); e.a.w. his ex., J. MARSHALL (VGGA 23 Feb 91)

FORRESTER, William, of Richmond Co., surgeon, murdered by Thomas GLASCOCK of the same co. planter aged c. 50; GLASCOCK's son, Gregory c. 22, is also mentioned (AWM 4 Feb 24)

FORSTER, Mr., mar. Mrs. KING of Petersburg on Sun. last (VGWeA 13 Aug 85)

FORSTER, Capt. John Collins, dec'd, his est. accounts and those of William FORSTER dec'd (nfi) to be settled with the ex., William GOODCHILD of Norfol (NPC 25 Feb 92)

FORSTER, William, of Norf., dec'd, e.a.w. Robert WILLS the ex. (VCGA 28 Jul 94

FORSYTH, Robert, of Fredsbrg., intends to move from the state in a few weeks (VGAA 12 Apr 83)

FORTUNE, John Jr., of Albemarle Co., dec'd, e.a.w. his admr., Peter DAVIE (VG 14 May 72)

FOSS, Thomas, supposed to be a deserter from the frigate *Constellation*, c. 25, escaped from jail in Fairfax Co. (TAA 5 Jun 98)

FOSTER, Capt. James, of the 15th Va. Regt., d. near Germantown, [Pa.] on the 15th ult. (VGPu 19 Dec 77)

FOSTER, Jonas, merch. of Birmingham, Eng., and brother to John FOSTER of th town [Alexandria], d. on Wed. morn. last; he had been a few months in this

country on a visit (CMAG 4 Mar 97)
FOSTER, Joseph, dec'd, his ex., John BLACKWELL, will rent his lands and houses on Pamunkey River and settle his est. (VGPu 28 Nov 77 sup)
FOSTER, Capt. Thomas, master of the ship *Lyon* lying in Norfolk harbor, died (NPC 3 Mar 92)
FOSTER, William, of Norfolk, dec'd, e.a.w. his ex., Robert WELLS (VCNPGA 23 Mar 93)
FOUNTAIN, James, Negro bel. to Elizabeth JENKINS of Alexandria, c. 25, jailed in Norfolk (NHPA 3 Nov 96)
FOUSHEE, Miss Ann, eld. dau. of Dr. William FOUSHEE of this city [Richmond], d. on Fri. the 10th inst. in the bloom of life [obit. in RMA] (VGGA and RMA 23 Mar 96)
FOUSHEE, Francis, of Northumberland Co., mar. Miss Fanny BEALE dau. of Thomas BEALE of Richmond Co. on the 21st inst. (VH 26 Oct 98)
FOUSHEE, Miss Nancy, dau. of Dr. William FOUSHEE of Richmond, d. on Sat. morn. last (RC 21 Mar 96)
FOUSHEE, Thomas, late of Stafford Co., d. in Alexandria on the 10th inst., a young man very much esteemed (RCFPC 25 Jan 97)
FOUSHEE, William, of Norfolk, mar. Miss Isabella HARMANSON of Northampton on 7 Mar (VGP 23 Mar 75)
FOWKE, Chandler Dinwiddie Esq., att. at law, d. in Charleston, S. Carolina on the 24th ult. (VHFFA 11 Dec 95)
FOWLER, James, appr., c. 15, ran away from Robert ANDERSON (CMAG 21 Jul 98)
FOWLER, John, conv. svt., c. 35, well acquainted with Va., Md., and Pa., plays on the fiddle and was brought up to the sea; transported in Capt. COOPER from Hull; ran away from Thomas DANSIE, Kg. Wm. Co. (MG 26 Jul 49)
FOWLER, John, son of John FOWLER late of Wapping St., London, sandman, went from Eng. as a svt. six or seven yrs. ago to some part of North America; if he will apply to Capt. David ROSS, commander of the ship *Betsey* at Norfolk, ROSS will inform him of matters greatly to his advantage (VGNI 23 Feb 75)
FOWLER, Matthew, sgt. in the 1st Regt., killed by accident last Sun. morn. at the camp near the college (VG 10 Aug 76)
FOWLER, Thomas, b. in Ireland, 21, enl. near Benedict Town, [Md.], des. from the Va. Regt. at Rock Cr. (MG 28 Jun 59)
FOWLER, Thomas, d. in Nov. last at the house of John TABB of Amelia Co.; he was a native of either Kerry or Cork in Ireland and came to the coast of Labrador some time in 1774; his legal rep. may hear something to his benefit by applying to E. MEADE, Amelia Co. (VGRMA 9 Mar 95)
FOX, James, murdered, John TROTMAN and John SPARKS were found guilty of the crime at Wmsbrg. (VG 12 Jun 52)
FOX, James M'Connell, of Washington Co., committed to jail in Richmond for the murder of a son of Mr. RUSSELL; FOX is a native of Pa., c. 22; he came into Greenbrier Co. about four yrs. ago where he mar. a young woman (VJAA 8 Nov 87); executed near Richmond on 25 Jan (VGWeA 31 Jan 88, VJAA 5 Feb 88, VGWA 8 Feb 88)
FOX, the Rev. Mr. John, minister of Ware Par. in Gloucester Co., mar. Mrs. RICHARDS relict of the Rev. Mr. RICHARDS late minister of the same par., yesterday was sennight (VG 17 Feb 38)
FOX, John, of Gloucester Co., adv. that he will meet at Pittsburgh on 10 May in order to have his land surveyed and if those persons undermentioned who were soldiers at the Battle of Little Meadows do not meet or some person for them, Mr. John MADISON will proceed to lay off his claims: David RICHERSON, Robert STOBO, Jacob VAN BRAM, John BAYNS a rep., James TOWERS, Andrew STEPHEN, Thomas NAPP, Arthur WATTS a rep., John FOX, Francis SELF, Robert STEWARD, Robert MURPHY, John SMITH, Alexander BONNY, William M'ANTHONY, and Mary HORN (VG 31 Mar 81)
FOX, John, mulatto, carpenter, ran away from John Taylo[e] CORBIN, Middlesex Co. (VGWeA 6 Dec 83)

FOX, John Esq., of Gloucester Co., e.a.w. his admr. Matthew ANDERSON and Anne FOX, who will also sell all of his livestock at his plant., Cheese Cake, in Gloucester Co. (VGAA 13, 27 Sep 86)

FOX, John, mar. Miss Nancy THRELKELD dau. of Col. Elijah THRELKELD of Stafford Co. (VHFA 27 Dec 92)

FOX, Robin, aka Robin, mulatto slave, c. 24, ran away from John W. DAVIS, Stafford Co. (VHFA 4 Dec 94)

FOX, Samuel, of Fauquier Co., will not pay debts of his wife Elisabeth and sons James and John since they "lately used me exceedingly ill" (VHFA 1 Dec 91)

FOX, Thomas, d. in an advanced [age] (VHFA 25 Oct 92); his ex., William Brown WALLACE, will sell two of his tracts in Kg. Wm. Co. (VGGA 17 Jul 93, 9 Oct 93); his ex. will sell his 150 ac. tract in Spotsylvania Co. (VHFA 11 Jul 93); his ex. of Stafford Co. will sell a tract of land pursuant to his will and by virtue of a power vested in him by Joseph FOX; the land is on the East-North-East River and contains 337 ac. (VHFFA 24 Mar 97)

FOX, William, indicted for the murder of his Negro svt., committed suicide last week (VHFA 17 Jul 95)

FOYLE, Robert, of Augusta Co., living at the head of Memonangehalla River--a branch of the Mississippi--together with his wife and five chil. the youngest about 10, were found murdered and scalped the 4th of last month supposed to have been done by the Indians about two mos. before (Wmsbrg. disp. of 8 Feb.) (MG 7 Mar 54, NYPB and NYM 18 Mar 54)

FRAME, Matthew, of Charlestown, merch., was mar. to Miss Massy GIBBS near Winchester by the Rev. Mr. HILL on Thurs. the 14th inst. (PGBA 18 Feb 93, BVCG 25 Feb 93)

FRANCIS, John, of New Kent Co., adv. that he intends to remove to Campbell C(shortly (VGWeA 15 Nov 83)

FRANCIS, Robert, committed for felony, c. 30, was in Pr. Edw. Co. jail some yrs. ago, escaped from jail in Charlottesville (VGGA 15 Nov 97)

FRANKLIN, Dr. Benjamin, d. on Sat. the 17th ult. in his 85th year (WVGWA 8 May 90); bur. on Wed. [an account of his funeral] (VICGA 5 May 90)

FRANKLIN, Jesse, appr., ran away from James BURKE who believes he is in Petersburg (Ex 7 Jun 99)

FRANKLIN, Thomas, his ex., Elisha WILLIAMS of Henrico, will divide the est. (10 Oct. next (VGWeA 30 Sep 91)

FRANKLIN, Thomas Sr., dec'd, e.a.w. his ex., Thomas WORSHAM and William SMITH of Chesterfield (VG 12 Feb 79)

FRANKS, Andrew, conv. svt., ropemaker, c. 26, ran away from William FEARSC Wmsbrg. (VG 15 Aug 71)

FRANKS, John, musician on H.M.S. *Flamsborough* drowned yesterday sennight (VG 1 Jun 39)

FRASER, Capt. Robert, d. last eve. after a few days illness; his funeral will be a house of Capt. DRIVER (NH 21 Mar 99); e.a.w. James THOMPSON who has t authorization of his admr. David FRASER (NH 15 Jun 99); his es., James THOMPSON of Norfolk, will sell one half of a brick house on Woodside's Whar adjoining Water St. (NH 22 Aug 99)

FRASER, Simon, dec'd, e.a.w. his brother and admr., Thomas FRASER of Petersburg (VGPI 30 Nov 94)

FRASER, William, Richard CHAPMAN of Hanover Co. adv. that FRASER who i his ward was accused of being a deserter by Capt. William LANE Jr. of Georgia; CHAPMAN says he has now got him in order to join his co. (VGPu 25 Apr 77) [see William FRAZER]

FRA[Z]ER, Mrs. Betsey, relict of the late John FRAZER, died (VHFA 8 May 95)

FRAZER, George, of Buckingham Co., intends to leave the colony soon (VG 5 Se sup)

FRAZER, James, d. in [Spotsylvania] Co. (VH 11 Jan 99); his ex., Anthony FRAZER and John FRAZER, will sell his furniture and stock (VH 23 Apr 99); his ex. will sell his tavern at Spotsylvania Ct. H. together with 143 ac. of land

adjoining (VGGA 25 Jun 99, CMAG 16 Jul 99, VH 19 Jul 99)
FRAZER, John, innkeeper, died (VHFA 28 Nov 93)
FRAZER, William, b. in Chesterfield Co. at or near Osborne's, c. 19, soldier in Capt. William LANE Jr.'s Co., enl. for the defense of Georgia, he has not reported for duty in Loudoun Co. (VGPu 6 Dec 76) [see William FRASER]
FRAZIER, Thomas, postrider, killed in a tavern brawl at Fredsbrg. on 15 Sep. by an officer of the Va. Regt. (NYM 10 Oct 57)
FRAZIER, Thomas, of Norfolk Borough, dec'd, e.a.w. his admr., William B. LAMB (NH 3 Mar 98)
FREELAND, Alexander, painter and glazier, lately from London, will carry on his business in Richmond (VGRMA 16 Jun 94)
FREELAND, Archibald, merch. of Manchester, mar. Mrs. Grace MACON of Powhatan Co. relict of John MACON, on Wed. the 17th inst. (RMA 31 Aug 96)
FREELOVE, John, svt., gardener, ran away from William AYLETT and John BUSHRODE, Westmoreland Co. (AWM 2 Aug 39, VG 17 Aug 39)
FREEMAN, Charles, Eng., c. 25, des. from the *Hero* galley (VGPu 26 Jul 76)
FREEMAN, I[s]ham, late of Henrico Co., dec'd, e.a.w. his admr., Isham GODDIN (VGGA 31 Aug 96)
FREEMAN, John, mar. Miss Nancy MOSSLEY on Thurs. eve. the 24th ult. at Pr. Anne (NH 2 Jan 96)
FREEMAN, William, of the 6th Va. Bn., des. from the sloop *Susannah* at Leedstown (VGPu 18 Oct 76)
French servants who ran away from M. THIEBAUD, Alexandria: Simon VADERCHAMP, 18, baker, speaks Eng. and Dutch; Peter Francis ANDRE, c. 26; Noel DE CLERY, c. 26; John Baptist BEAUCHE, c. 21, blacksmith; Joseph LE BLANC, c. 30, John GAILLIARD, 32 (VGAxA 3 Jun 90)
FRENCH, Capt. Hugh, d. on a ship bound from London to Potomac (VG 22 Jul 37)
FRENCH, Hugh, mar. Mrs. Ann DOUTHAT on Sun. the 15th inst. at the house of Col. William BOWYER (SVG 18 Jan 97)
FRENCH, James, dec'd, e.a.w. Messrs. Robert & Walter COLQUHOUN of Petersburg or James STRANGE of Manchester (VGPI 3 Nov 94, VGGA 28 Oct 95)
FRESON, Jacob, German, 20, baker, ran away from John SEYLE, Georgetown (VJAA 29 Jun 86)
FRIEND, William, of Osborne's, mar. Miss Kitty CRAIG dau. of James CRAIG of Wmsbrg. on Sun. the 26th ult. (VGGA 7 Mar 92)
FRIGHT, Matthew, Eng. ind. svt., 35-40, ran away from John HOLLADAY, Spotsylvania Co. (VGPu 25 Jul 77)
FRISKER, Tom, Negro, lately the property of Mr. FISHER in Pr. Anne Co., c. 30, broke jail in Norfolk (NH 29 Jan 99)
FRITH, George, dec'd, e.a.w. his ex., Samuel NELMS (VG 26 Feb 79)
FRY, Jacob, of Woodstock, Shenandoah Co., mar. Miss Elizabeth LYNN of Winchester in Jan 1799 (WG 9 Jan 99)
FRY, Col. Joshua, of Va., b. in Somersetshire, Eng., educated at Oxford, grammar master and then professor of mathematics at William and Mary College, commander of the forces gone to the Ohio, lately fell from his horse and died from the injuries at Wills Cr. (NYM 24 Jun, 15 Jul 55)
FRYE, William, svt., ran away with Mary SAVENAS the wife of Nicholas SAVENAS of Stafford Co. (VG 31 Oct 51)
FRYER, Capt. Richard, of Portsmouth, mar. Miss Nancy DAMERON of this borough on Sun. eve. last (NH 3 Sep 99)
FRYET, Bartholomew, svt., 22, ran away from Richland Farm bel. to Charles CARTER Esq. of Kg. Geo. Co. (VG 14 Dec 39)
FUDGE, John, dec'd, e.a.w. his admr., Patrick DWYER of Isle of Wight Co. (VG 22 Nov 76)
FULKS, Winney, of Richmond Co., d. in the public hospital for lunatics (VGPu 22 Nov 76)
FULLAM, Baker, a 31-year svt., c. 27, ran away from Thomas BLACKBURN near Dumfries, Pr. Wm. Co. (VGPu 17 Nov 75 sup)

FULLER, Thomas, famous African calculator, d. in Alexandria aged c. 80, he was owned by Mrs. Elizabeth COX and had been brought into this country at age 14 [for details of his arithmetical feats, see: VGWA 4 Mar 89] (VGAxA 9 Dec 90, VHFA 16 Dec 90)

FULLERTON, Alexander, Scot, svt., 20, ran away from Robert M'CLACHAN, Augusta Ct.H. (VG 18 Jul 51)

FULLIGAR, John, of Kg. Geo. Co., adv. that his wife has robbed his house and left her bed without any provocation for the third time and he will no longer pay any of her debts (VGPu 10 Oct 77)

FULMER, Mrs., wife of Joseph FULMER of Alexandria, died (VJAA 22 Mar 87)

FULTON, George, dec'd, e.a.w. his admr., John LAWSON, of Richmond (VGGA 1 Mar 97)

FULTON, Robert, dec'd, e.a.w. his ex., James FLETCHER, who will also sell his personal property consisting of furniture, a house frame, shingles and carpenter's tools (TAA 1 Dec 97)

FULTZ, Matthias, of Lower Merrion Township, Montgomery Co., [Pa.], aged 94, native of Germany, came to America in 1641, had six chil., three died without heirs, three daus. had 20 grandchildren and 67 great grandchildren (HNPA 25 Feb 95)

FUNK, Henry Sr., dec'd, his ex., Jacob FUNK of Storer's Town, will sell his seat of 1324 ac. in Shenandoah Co. (VGWA 3 Jul 90)

FURBUSH, William, appr., ran away from Bennett WHITE, Newcastle (VG 3 Nov 74)

FURGURSON, Benjamin, appr. hatter, c. 19, ran away from Jesse THORNTON, Richmond (VGRMA 16 Jan 94)

Furloughed from Wmsbrg. to go home last fall: George BURT, c. 23; Joseph STITH son of Richard STITH of Bedford Co., 18-19; George JONES, c. 26 (VGPu 13 Jun 77)

FURMAN, Augur Treadwell Esq., dec'd, his PE including law books will be sold by his admr., L. STEPHENS (VGWA 28 Oct 89)

FURMAN, Isaac, of Hampshire Co., 13-14, d. from rabies on 22 Sep. (VGWA 1 Oct 91)

FURRY, Daniel, of Shenandoah Co., jailed on suspicion of murdering his wife, Mary FURRY (WG 7 Aug 99); on 1 Oct., a Benjamin FURRY was found not guilty of murdering his wife (WG 2 Oct 99)

FURY, Patrick, of Norfolk, merch., was mar. to Miss Elizabeth NORTH dau. of William NORTH Esq., on Thurs. eve. at Cottage near Portsmouth by the Rev. Mr. EMMERSON (NH 8 Sep 98)

FYSON, Walter, formerly lived at Snailwell near Barnwell or New Market, farmer, is asked to contact Samuel BERRY, Bristol, to hear of an est. that has fallen to him (VG 2 Sep 57)

GABBET, Joseph Spires, appr., Irish, 16-17, ran away from the ship *Stanley* at Alexandria (VJAA 14 Oct 84)

GAFFNEY, Terrence, and his wife Jane GAFFNEY, Irish svts., aged c. 30 each, bought from James PORTER in Md., ran away from James EDMONDSON, Essex Co. \(VG 16 Aug 70)

GAINES Family, Halifax Co., Sep. Ct. in chanc: Dorothy GAINES mother of Francis GAINES dec'd, Thomas GAINES brother, and Mary GAINES and Dorothy GAINES sisters of the sd. decedent (petitioners) against Richard GAINES, John ROBERTS and Mary his wife, Absolom RUSSELL and Elizabeth his wife, and Edmund RUSSELL and Sanders RUSSELL chil. of Francis RUSSELL dec'd and Sarah GAINES, Thomas GAINES, Francis GAINES, Joseph GAINES, Solomon GAINES, Susanna GAINES, and Broddus GAINES chil. of Edward GAINES dec'd (defs.) (VGGA 4 Oct 99)

GAINES, Daniel, of Amherst Co., proposes to remove with his family in a few weeks to Wilkes Co., Georgia (VIC 18 Oct, VGAA 25 Oct, VGIC 28 Oct 86)

GAINES, Capt. Francis, of K & Q Co., died (VG 4 Aug 74)

GAINES, Maj. Harry, Rep. in Assembly for Kg. Wm. Co., d. lately (VG 16 Jul 67

GALASPIE, George, of Amherst Co., adv. that from the late behavior of his wife, Mary GALASPIE, he has reason to doubt her attachment to his interest and will not be answerable for any of her debts (VGPu 5 Jun 78)

GALBREATH, James, dec'd, his admr. is James CARFS, Norf. (NHPA 9 Nov 97)

GALDEN, Jesse, soldier in Capt. John POPE's Co. of Regulars, c. 25, des. from Wmsbrg. (VGPu 9 May 77)

GALE, John, Eng., sailor, well known in Hampton and Norfolk, suspected of robbing the ship *Fanny* on 17 Apr (NPJ 29 Apr 89)

GALES, Charles, appr., c. 22, ran away from James LANE and Joseph CROSS, Newgate, Loudoun Co. (VG 2 Dec 73)

GALLAWAY, Robert, d. in Bedford Co. (VGRC 17 Oct 94)

GALLEY, William, b. in Dublin, 24, formerly drove the Philadelphia stage and is well known in Baltimore; jailed in Richmond for highway robbery; he escaped along with Peter LYNCH on 3 Aug. (VGAA 7 Aug 84)

GALLOWAY, David, d. last Thurs. in Winchester (BVCG 11 Nov 93)

GALLOWAY, John, heir at law and admr. of his dec'd brother, Robert GALLOWAY late merch. at Fredsbrg., will pet. the next GA to suspend all process of escheat against the RE of his brother in Spotsylvania Co. (VGGA 22 Jul 95)

GALLOWAY, Robert, merch. of Fredsbrg., shot and killed by Benjamin GRYMES of Eagle's Nest, Kg. Geo. Co. (who is supposed to be insane) on Fri. morn. (VHFA 7 Aug 94, VGRMA 11 Aug 94); e.a.w. John GALLOWAY (VHFA 11 Dec 94); his admr., John GALLOWAY, will sell sundry dry goods and the HH and KF bel. to his est. at his store in Fredsbrg. (VHFA 1 Jan 95)

GALLUP, Ebenezer, of Richmond, intends to leave the state soon (VGGA [30] Apr 94)

GALT, Azel, a young man of this city [Richmond], d. in the island of Grenada (VGGA 21 May 94, VGRMA 22 May 94)

GALT, Charles Lee, child of James GALT of Wmsbrg., was christened sometime this week (VGP 16 Dec 75)

GALT, Miss Fanny, youngest dau. of Dr. John M. GALT of Wmsbrg., d. on the 15th [of Feb.] in her 11th year (VGGA 28 Feb 98)

GALT, Gabriel, d. at Richmond on Sat. 25 Oct. after a few weeks illness [obit. in VIC and VGWeA] (VIC 29 Oct 88, VGWeA 30 Oct 88, VGIC 1 Nov 88, NPJ 5 Nov 88, VHFA 6 Nov 88); his admrs., David LAMBERT and Jacob EGE of Richmond, will sell all of his PE (VIC 21 Jan 89)

GALT, James, clock and watchmaker, intends to leave Wmsbrg. for Shockoe near Richmond (VG 16 May 66)

GALT, Dr. John Minson, apothecary, surgeon, and man-midwife, just arrived in Wmsbrg. from London (VG 2 Feb 69); mar. Miss Judith CRAIG eld. dau. of Alexander CRAIG on 6 Apr (VGR 6 Apr 69)

GALT, William, son of Samuel GALT, watchmaker of Wmsbrg., has settled in Yorktown (VG 28 Mar 51)

GALT, William, eld. son. of Mrs. Elizabeth GALT of [Richmond], d. on the 17th ult. (VGGA 4 Oct 97)

GAMBILL, Mrs., wife of Matthew GAMBILL, d. on 23 Jan in Rockingham Co. (BVCG 3 Feb 94)

GAMBILL, H. J., mar. Mrs. Peggy BURNS, both of Harrisonburg, Rockingham Co., on Thurs. eve. last (WG 16 Oct 99)

GAMBILL, Matthew, of Staunton, mar. Miss Polly DEADERICK of Winchester on Mon. (BVCG 11 Feb 92)

GAMBLE, Archibald, merch. of New York, d. last week at New Market (VGWA 2 Nov 87)

GANNON, Henry, appr. blacksmith, c. 18, ran away from John G. KEENOR, Little Cacapehon (WG 20 Mar 99)

GARDEN, the Rev. James, dec'd, e.a.w. his admr. (nfi) in Pr. Edw. Co. (VG 4 Nov 73)

GARDENER, William, b. in Caroline Co., des. from Capt. Thomas WAGGONER's Co. (VG 28 Feb 55)

GARDINER, Miss, eld. dau. of Mr. James GARDINER at the Red House, Pr. Wm. Co., age about 17, drowned herself on Fri. the 8th inst. (TAA 16, 18 Jun 98)

GARDNER Family, Augusta Co. Ct., Aug. 1791, in chanc: Rebecca GARDNER relict and admx. of Thomas GARDNER dec'd, and Francis GARDNER and Thomas GARDNER dec'd (pltfs.) against various members of the BROWN Family (q.v.) (VGWA 17 Sep 91)

GARDNER, John, of Louisa Co., dec'd, slaves and 180 ac. bel. to his est. to be sold by his ex. (nfi) (RMA 23 Dec 95)

GARDNER, John, aka John, Negro, c. 25, blacksmith, ran away from William NASH, Caswell Co., N. Carolina (NHPA 27 Jul 97)

GARDNER, Matthew Jr., svt., 50-60, ran away from the ship *Duke of Cumberland* at Bermuda Hundred in James River (VG 25 May 39)

GARDNER, Mrs. Rachel, wife of Henry GARDNER, baker, d. in Alexandria (VJAA 4 Jan 87)

GARDNER, Tom, mulatto, c. 50, ran away from William BYRD, Buckland, Charles City Co. (VG 24 Nov 74)

GARLAND, Mrs. Frances Taylor, cons. of John GARLAND Esq. of Hanover Co., d. Wed. last in her 21st year; she was bur. in the family burying place at Aberdeen (VGAA 20 Dec 83)

GARLAND, J., of Hanover Co. will move to Lunenburg Co. (VIC 4 Nov 89, VICGA 6 Jan 90)

GARLAND, John Esq., of Hanover Co., mar. Miss BLACK of Chesterfield Co. on Sat. eve. last (VGAA 16 Nov 82)

GARLAND, John Esq., of Mayfield, Hanover Co., d. on Sat. the 7th inst. (RMA 14 Nov 95)

GARLAND, Thomas, d. in Hanover Co. (VGRC 11 Mar 94)

GARLAND, William, public surveyor, d. suddenly at Richmond [Co.] Ct. H. on 26 Aug. last (VGR 5 Sep 66); his son, Griffin GARLAND of Richmond Co., desires to settle his accounts and also those of his dec'd mother (VGP 4 May 75)

GARNER, Presley, c. 16, des. from the quota of state troops of Lt. William LAWSON who has been informed that he enl. with Lt. Thomas POLLARD on board Capt. CALVERT's galley (VGPu 21 Nov 77)

GARNETT, Thomas, dec'd, his land and plant. at Guineas Bridge to be sold by Thomas GARNETT his ex. (VHFA 13 Aug 89)

GARNETT, Thomas, of Travellers Rest, Stafford Co., former merch. in Fredsbrg d. in Fauquier Co. on Sat. last (VHFA 6 Jun 98); e.a.w. his ex., William ALEXANDER, Stafford Co. (VH 1 Feb 99)

GARNISH, Emmanuel, svt., 17-18, ran away from the snow *John* lying in Hampton Road (VGAA 17 Apr 84)

GARRARD Family, William GARRARD ex. and Mary GARRARD extx. of William GARRARD dec'd are mentioned in a chancery case in Stafford Co., 13 Jun 99 (VH 7 Sep 99)

GARRARD, Nathaniel, appr., 16-17, bound by his father to the saddling busines ran away from George WOLFF (PGBA 18 Aug 96)

GARRARD, William, desires to move to Ky. and will sell 606 ac. in Stafford Co. (VGAA 1 Mar 86)

GARRARD, William, dec'd, his land in Stafford Co. to be sold by his ex., William GARRARD (VIC 9 May 87)

GARRATT, Nicholas Potter, of Petersburg, d. on Fri. 18 Dec. (VGPI 29 Dec 95)

GARRETT, Mrs. Margaret, housekeeper at the college, died (VG and VGR 28 Jan 73); e.a.w. Emmanuel JONES (nfi) of Wmsbrg. (VG 14 Oct 73)

GARRISON, Dick, Negro, says he is free; he has a mulatto wife with him about 23 by the name of Fanny; jailed in Elizabeth City Co. (VGWeA 10 Dec 85)

GARTHRIGHT Family, William GARTHRIGHT ex. of John GARTHRIGHT dec'd, who was ex. of Samuel GARTHRIGHT and admr. of the estates of Benjamin GARTHRIGHT and Thomas GARTHRIGHT (Arg 24 May 99)

GARTS, Mrs. Peggy, wife of Peter GARTS merch. of Fredsbrg., d. last Thurs. (VHFA 12 Nov 89)

GARTS, Peter, merch. of Balto., mar. Miss Peggy LILLY dau. of Robert LILLY

merch. of this city [Fredsbrg.] on Tues. last (VHFA 27 Nov 88)
GASCO, David, aka David, Virginia born Negro, c. 35, ran away from Warren BEUFORD, Lunenburg Co. (VG 25 Dec 71)
GASKINS, John, took up a nine hogshead flat off the mouth of the Rappahannock River last Nov., dec'd (VG 30 Oct 66)
GASKINS, Melachiah and David CROW, killed by Indians on 24 Jan. in the Mero District; they were on a salt boat at the mouth of Half Pone on the Cumberland (Winchester disp. of 1 Apr.) (AGNPWA 10 Apr 93, VGRMA 15 Apr 93)
GATES, Mrs. Elizabeth, wife of the Hon. Maj. Gen. Horatio GATES, d. in Berkeley Co. on 2 Jun (MJ 11 Jul 83, VGAA 19 Jul 83)
GATES, John, killed in an accident in Staunton; on Sat. last a well caved in on John GATES, Anthony ENGLETON, and Christian GROVE, the former was crushed to death and the two latter very narrowly escaped unhurt; GATES left a wife and four small chil. (Staunton disp. of 16 Oct.) (TDCDA 4 Nov 99)
GATES, Robert, only son of His Excellency Gen. [Horatio] GATES of Berkeley Co., died (MJ 17 Oct 80)
GATEWOOD Family, HCC, John GOODWIN and Clara his wife (pltfs.) against Fleming GATEWOOD and Fullington GATEWOOD ex. or admr. of John GATEWOOD and Ca[ss]on BURNETT and Richard BURNETT ex. of Richard BURNETT dec'd who was admr. of Joseph BURNETT dec'd, Jeremiah BURNETT and Edmund PENDLETON Jr. Esq. (defs.) (VGGA 22 Jan 99)
GATEWOOD, Mrs., cons. of Henry GATEWOOD, d. in this county on Fri. night last (VHFFA 28 Feb 97)
GATEWOOD, Henry Sr., of Spotsylvania Co., dec'd, e.a.w. Henry GATEWOOD (nfi) (VH 2 Aug 99)
GATEWOOD, Philip, late of Shenandoah Co., dec'd, his livestock and HHF to be sold by his exors, John GATEWOOD, Charles CATLETT, and Isaac BOWMAN (BVCG 12 Aug. 93)
GATHRIGHT, Capt. Joseph, lately departed this life in Hanover Co. (RMA 4 Jun 95, RC 6 Jun 95)
GATLIFF Family, Greenbrier Co. Ct., 28 Nov 1797, in chanc.: William [P]ONEY and Leah his wife (late Leah GATLIFF) (pltfs.) against Charles GATLIFF and William LAFFERTY (defs.); it appears that Charles GATLIFF is not an inhabitant of this commonwealth (VGGA 10 Jan 98)
GAUF, Lewis, Negro, c. 20, says he is free and was bound to a certain widow NETHERLAND of Hanover Co., late of Halifax Co., jailed in Louisa Co. (VGPu 31 Oct 77)
GAULDING, Alexander, executed for highway robbery at Wmsbrg. (Wmsbrg. disp. of 12 Jan.) (MG 1 Feb 53)
GAUTIER, Nicholas, dec'd, his PE to be sold by William FOUSHEE admr. w.w.a. of Richmond (VIC 10 Dec 88)
GAY, Capt., mar. Miss E. WILLOUGHBY of this borough on Thurs. eve. (NHPA 31 Dec 96)
GAY, Daniel, of Chesterfield Co., dec'd, e.a.w. William SHORT for Polly GAY his extx. (Arg 7 Mar 97)
GAY, Capt. John, late of the ship *Fair Phebe*; if he be living in any part of this state, the printers hereof will inform him where he may hear of his brother Archibald (NH 9 Mar 99)
GAYLE, Robert, dec'd, his ex. is his brother Thomas GAYLE of Kingston Par., Gloucester Co. (VGAA 26 Jul 83)
GEADY, William W., mar. Miss Betsey PRENTIS in Petersburg on Thurs. last, both of that town (VGGA 23 Nov 96)
GEAL, Peter, sailor, ran away from the ship *Charming Peggy*, Georgetown (VJAA 17 Nov 85)
GEARY, John, svt., weaver, ran away from the snow *John* lying in Hampton Road (VGAA 17 Apr 84)
GEATTY, Jane, svt., ran away from the snow *John* lying in Hampton Road (VGAA 17 Apr 84)
GEDDES, Mrs., d. at Georgetown the 6th inst. (VGAxA 22 Nov 92)

GEDDY, James Jr., mar. Miss Euphan ARMISTEAD both of Petersburg (VGWeA 21 May 89)
GEE, Henry, of Pr. Geo. Co., enl. by George MACKENZIE has not rep. to camp in Wmsbrg. (VG 31 Jul 46)
GELDING, Isaac, ind. svt., house carpenter, c. 28, ran away from James SOUTHALL, Wmsbrg., who supposes that he has gone to Suffolk (VGP 2 Mar 75, VG 4 Mar 75)
GENNERY, Peter, aka Will, Negro, c. 28, plays the violin, has a brother named Charles in Alexandria, ran away from Rawleigh P. DOWNMAN, Pr. Wm. Co. (TAA 25 Oct 98)
GENTRY, John, killed by Indians on Tues. 31 Jan. on the waters of Harpeth, Mero District (Knoxville disp. of 13 Feb) (SVG 1 Mar 97)
GEOGHEGAN, Anthony, old and respected citizen of Richmond, d. in a very advanced age (VGRMA 9 Dec 93, VGGA 11 Dec 93, VGWeA 13 Dec 93)
GEORGE, Anne, late wife of William GEORGE of Norfolk who will no longer pay her debts (VG 14 May 72)
GEORGE, Catherine, dec'd, her est. in Orange Co. to be sold by her admr., Prettyman MERRY (VHFA 17 Mar 91)
GEORGE, John, of Caroline Co., adv. that his wife, Elsley GEORGE, has gone from his house and for some time past has not behaved as a wife to him; he will no longer pay any of her debts (VGPu 3 Oct 77)
GEORGE, John Jr., has moved from Urbanna to K & Q Ct. H. where he has opened a tavern (VICGA 31 Mar 90)
GEORGE, William, a doctor, b. on 20 Jul. 1746, possibly in Gloucester, Eng., ran away from his bail in Loudoun Co. (VGR 1 Nov 70)
GEORGE, William, Eng. svt., c. 34, carpenter and joiner, ran away from Dorsey's Forge in Md. (VG 8 Dec 74, VGP 15 Dec 74)
GERARD, Thomas, dec'd, his admr., T. WILLOCK of Norfolk, will pet. the next assembly to empower him to dispose of the landed property bel. to GERARD's est. in Va. (VGPI 30 Nov 94)
GHELSEMINO, Joseph, svt., 16, born in Ireland, ran away from John M'CLENACHAN, Alexandria (VJAA 27 Sep 87)
GIBBIN, Marcus, youngest son of the Rev. John GIBBIN of King's Co., Ireland, came to the back settlements in Philadelphia about 25 yrs. ago and was a schoolmaster; if he be living, he is requested to write to Mrs. Martha GIBBIN, Stephen St., Dublin; for further details, enquire of Marcus GIBBIN, Chesterfield Co. (VG 16 Jun 74)
GIBBONS, Mrs. Anne, d. last Sat. at York in her 97th yr. (VG 25 Aug 68)
GIBBONS, Lawrence, of York Co., mar. Miss Peggy NICOLSON of Wmsbrg. on Sat. eve. last (VGRMA 9 May 93)
GIBBORN, William, Irish svt., 22, ran away from Alexander STUART and Thomas MADDOX, Alexandria (VJAA 7 Oct 84)
GIBBS, Betsey, Negro, c. 16, jailed in Norfolk Borough (NH 26 May 96); escaped from jail on 29 May (NH 4 Jun 96)
GIBBS, John, if there be any such person now living in Va. as John GIBBS formerly of Hagedon, Essex, Eng., he may be benefitted perhaps by making himself known to Francis CORBIN, Caroline Co. (VGGA 29 Nov 97)
GIBBS, Stafford and Anne, dec'd, e.a.w. their ex., William GIBBS of Warwick Co. (VG and VGR 31 Mar 74)
GIBNEY, Hugh, bricklayer of Alexandria, dec'd (VJAA 12 May 85); e.a.w. his admr., Joseph FULLMER, of Alexandria (VJAA 23 Jun 85)
GIBSON, Mr., mar. Miss SAUNDERSON last week in Richm. (VGWeA 6 Feb 97)
GIBSON, Alexander, dec'd, e.a.w. his ex., Alexander GIBSON (SVG 15 Aug 95)
GIBSON, Henry, of Augusta Co., son of James GIBSON dec'd, late of Middlesex Co.; if he be living and will apply to William DEANE of Middlesex, he will hea of something greatly to his advantage (VG 18 Oct 76)
GIBSON, James, aka JOHNSON, svt., ran away from Shapleigh NEALE at Lit Wicomico River, Northumberland Co. (VG 31 Oct 45)
GIBSON, Dr. James, mar. Miss McCLANAHAN, both of Kempsville, there on

Mon. eve. (NH 29 Dec 98)
GIBSON, Capt. John, late of Kg. Wm. Co., dec'd, his ex. is Joseph GIBSON (VG 14 Feb 51)
GIBSON, Randall, executed at the gallows near Wmsbrg. last Fri. for felony (Wmsbrg. disp. of 31 May) (MG 4 Jul 54)
GIBSON, William, aka SHADBURN, appr., hatter, 20 (on the 27th of last May), ran away from James WALKER, Winchester (BVCG 30 Jun 94)
GIDDINS, Charles, svt., sawyer, c. 30, ran away from Samuel LONG, Warwick Co. (VGPu 2 Jun 75 sup)
GILBERT, George, dec'd, mentioned in a HCC case of 17 May 1794; his relict was Sarah GILBERT and his surviving admr. was David LAMBERT (VGRMA 24 Jul 94)
GILBERT, Robert, d. at Richmond (VGPI 14 Dec 86)
GILBERT, Robert, dec'd, a tract of his land four miles from Richmond to be sold (VGGA 20 Oct 90)
GILBERT, Sarah, for many yrs. a respectable resident of this city [Richmond], d. on Fri. eve. last (info. dated 20 Sep.) (VGGA 24 Sep 99)
GILBERT, Thomas, appr., 17, ran away from John BROWN near Wmsbrg. (VG 21 Mar 45)
GILBIRD, Thomas, appr., ran away from John BROWN living near the Capitol (VG 10 Oct 45) [Apparently the same person as Thomas GILBERT above]
GILCHRIST, Alexander, merch., mar. Miss Polly WISE both of Richmond on Thurs. eve. last (RC 31 May 96)
GILCHRIST, John, committed suicide in Norfolk on 21 Oct. leaving a wife and children (VGR 21 Oct 73); his ex., Archibald CAMPBELL, will rent out two plants. bel. to him lying in St. Bride's Par. (VGNI 5 Jan 75)
GILCHRIST, John Esq., dec'd, Tudor HINSON and John GILCHRIST will sell sundry tracts of his land in St. Bride's Par., Norfolk Co. (HNPA 18 Jul 95)
GILCHRIST, Robert Esq., d. Fri. last at Port Royal, Caroline Co., in his 69th year; he was a native of Scotland and came to Va. early in life [long obit.] (VICGA 21 Jul 90, VHFA 22 Jul 90); his 1500 ac. est. in Caroline Co. to be sold by his ex., Edmund PENDLETON Jr., John HOOMES, and James ROBB (VGGA 24 Nov 90, VHFA 2 Dec 90)
GILCHRIST, Thomas, of Norfolk, d. Wed. last (VCNPGA 31 Aug 93)
GILDART, Francis Esq., mar. Miss Ann MARTIN of Greenway Court, in Frederick Co. (VJAA 24 Nov 85)
GILDEA, Thomas, merch. late of Kempsville, dec'd, e.a.w. his ex., Samuel HARRISON of Norfolk (NHPA 13 Feb 97)
GILDING, Isaac, Eng. svt., house carpenter, ran away from James SOUTHALL, Wmsbrg. (VGNI 9 Mar 75)
GILES, Arthur, dec'd, his ex., Knowles GILES, John ROYSTER, and Judith GILES, will sell all his stock, etc. at the dwelling house of Nicholas GILES dec'd (VGGA 18 Dec 93)
GILES, Nicholas, dec'd, his admr., Knowles GILES, will sell his HHF in Manchester (VGRMA 18 Apr 95); his admr. adv. that Cannon GILES is authorized to settle and grant discharges (RMA 6 Jun 95)
GILES, Mrs. Rebecca Walker, cons. of Capt. William GILES of Richmond, d. on Sat. eve. last (Arg 12 Nov 99)
GILKISON, Maj. John, d. a few days ago in Frederick Co. (BVCG 1 Jul 93)
GILL, Peter, adv. that his wife, Frances GILL, has des. her bed and board (VG 22 May 79)
GILL, William, Irish ind. svt., c. 30, ran away from the Neabsco Furnace (VGPu 12 Jul 76)
GILLART, Felix, son of Felix GILLART, coachmaker and auctioneer of Long Acre, St. Martin's in the Fields, London; he went to sea and in 1789 or 1790 he was on a ship on the James River and was then called DELAP; if he will apply to Edmund PENDLETON Jr., of Caroline Co., he will hear of something much to his advantage (VGGA 6 Nov 93)
GILLIAM, Dr., educated at the Univ. of Edinburgh is now practicing in Petersburg

(VGPI 26 Oct 86)
GILLIAM, Isham, of Sussex Co., dec'd, e.a.w. his admr., John MASON, who will also sell all his est. (VGPI 27 Sep 92, 11 Aug 95)
GILLIAM, Robert, dec'd, consistent to a late adjudication, his ex., Reuben M. GILLIAM, will sell a few of his Negroes (VGPI 10 Jun 94)
GILLUM, Peter, dec'd, his ex., William GILLUM and John GILLUM, will sell his tract of 360 ac. in Hanover Co. (VG 5 Mar 72)
GILMER, Mrs., wife of Alderman George GILMER in Wmsbrg., d. last Tues. [week] (VG 10 Oct 45)
GILMORE, John, of Ker's Cr., Augusta Co., killed there with his wife and son on 17 Oct. by Indians (Philadelphia disp. of 1 Nov.) (NYPB 5 Nov 59)
GILMORE, Mrs. William, of Ker's Cr., Augusta Co., killed there on 17 Oct. by Indians (Philadelphia disp. of 1 Nov.) (NYPB 5 Nov 59)
GILPIN, Edward, b. in Pr. Geo. Co., Md., 22, des. from the 8th Regt. U.S. Army in Alexandria (CMAG 16 Jul 99)
GIST, Mordecai Esq., brig. gen. in the U.S. Army, d. in Charleston, S. Carolina (VGRDA 1 Oct 92)
GLASCOCK, Mrs. Elizabeth, wife of William GLASCOCK of Stephensburg, d. on 29 Nov. [obit.] (VGWA 2 Dec 89)
GLASS, Mrs., spouse of Thomas GLASS of Norfolk, d. on Thurs. last (VCNPGA 6 Oct 92)
GLASS, George, svt., 50, talks broad West Country, transported from Liverpool lately, ran away from Patrick MATTHEWS, York Town (VG 19 Dec 45)
GLASS, Robert, of Frederick Co., d. Tues. last (BVCG 30 Dec 96); his ex., Robert GLASS and James D. VANCE, will sell his PE (BVCG 10 Mar 97)
GLASSCOCK, George Esq., Rep. in the GA for Richmond Co., d. in Richmond on Sat. eve. last (VGGA 15 Jan 99)
GLASSELL, Andrew, of Culpeper, intends to leave the state in a few weeks (VHFA 29 Apr 90)
GLASSELL, John, aged 22, d. in Fredsbrg. on Sun. last (VHFFA 22 Nov 96)
GLENTWORTH, William, d. in this town [Winchester] very suddenly (WVGWA 26 Jun 90)
GLINN, Nicholas, Irish svt., 15, ran away from Jonathan SWIFT, Alexandria (VJAA 23 Mar 86)
GODDARD, Henry, aka MURPHY, appr., 18, ran away from John WILLIS, Hampshire Co. (BVCG 29 Apr 96)
GODDARD, William, printer of Baltimore, lately mar. Miss ANGEL of Providence Rhode Island [epigram] (VGAA 12 Jul 86)
GODFREY, Charles, dec'd, his PE to be sold by Nathaniel GODFREY the admr.; his house in Pr. Anne Co. burned (HNPA 18, 28 Feb 95); his admr, William WILLOUGHBY, will sell his PE (HNPA 22 Oct 95); e.a.w. his admr. (NH 23 Jun 96)
GODFREY, Nathaniel, d. on Tues. eve. last (NHPA 5 Jan 97, AGGA 6 Jan 97); e.a.w. his extx., Isabella GODFREY of Norfolk (NHPA 12 Jun 97)
GODWIN, Anthony, dec'd, e.a.w. his admr., Jeremiah GODWIN and Anthony GODWIN of Nansemond Co. (NH 22 Jun 99)
GODWIN, Col. Brewer, of Brewer's Neck, Isle of Wight Co., d. on the 6th inst. (NH 10 Oct 99)
GODWIN, Jonathan, dec'd, e.a.w. Anthony GODWIN who will transact the business for Mary KING (nfi) (VG 2 Oct 79)
GODWIN, Joseph, of Nansemond Co., mar. Miss Patty WILLIAMSON of the same Co. (VGPu 16 Oct 78)
GODWIN, Matthew, of Nansemond Co., dec'd, e.a.w. his ex., James GODWIN (VG and VGPu 14 Mar 77)
GODWIN, Robert, of York Co. was found dead on the road last Tues. morn; his mother, an old lady, died upon seeing his body (VG 10 Nov 74)
GODWIN, Mrs. Sarah, wife of Mr. GODWIN, comedian, d. at Richmond on 29 Mar (VHFA 7 Apr 91)
GODWIN, Thomas, of Nansemond Co., dec'd, e.a.w. his ex., Edwin GRAY and

Miles GODWIN (VG 18 Sep 79)
GOFF, Capt, master of a new ship from Liverpool, drowned Thurs. last when the ship went ashore on Cape Henry (Wmsbrg. disp. of 15 Jan.) (NYPB 19 Feb 67)
GOFF, Harry, Negro, claims to be free, c. 30, jailed in Fredsbrg. (VHFA 14 Jul 95)
GOGHERTY, Patrick, Irish svt., 27, ran away from Michael MADDEN, Alexandria, last seen going towards Leesburg (VJAA 4 Aug 85)
GOLD, Thomas, dec'd, e.a.w. his ex., William BROOKS (PGBA 18 Aug 96)
GOLDWELL, Nicholas, dec'd, his ex., John LACY, will sell a tract of his land cont. about 123 ac. in New Kent Co.; the sale will be held at Mrs. GOLDWELL's near Bottom's Bridge (VGPu 3 Oct 77)
GONNION, John, svt., 22, butcher, ran away from John STEUART, Middle River, Augusta Co. (VGR 14 Apr 68)
GOOCH, Lady, relict of the late Sir. William GOOCH, Governor of this Colony, d. at Bath in her 85th year (VGPu 5 May 75)
GOOCH, Sir William, Bart., late Governor of Va., d. recently in Eng. (VG 27 Feb 52, MG 12 Mar 52)
GOOCH, William Jr., dec'd; his son d. on 1 Jul. (Wmsbrg. disp. of 1 Jul.) (AWM 14 Jul 43)
GOOD, Thomas, svt., 35, b. in the north of Eng., ran away from Charles GRIFFITH and Henry GRIFFITH Jr., Frederick Co., Md. (VGR 9 Jun 68)
GOODALL, Charles, dec'd, two lots and PE of his to be sold in Hanover Town by Samuel OVERTON (nfi) (VG 1 Jan 67); e.a.w. Richard MORRIS and Samuel OVERTON (VG 27 Aug 67)
GOODCHILD, William, of Norfolk, dec'd, his PE to be sold by his ex. (VCNPGA 19 Jan 93); e.a.w. his ex., Robert WILLS (VCGA 28 Jul 94)
GOODE, Francis, of Chesterfield Co., mar. Miss Martha HUGHES of Powhatan on the 28th inst. (VGGA 11 Nov 95, RMA 12 Nov 95)
GOODE, Col. Francis, of Chesterfield Co., d. on Thurs. 23 Apr. on board the sloop *Fanny* on his way home from Philadelphia [obit. in RMA] (RMA 7 May 95, VGRC 9 May 95)
GOODE, John Esq., of Chesterfield Co., was mar. to Miss Lucy Herbert CLAIBOURNE at Grammarton on Sat. eve. the 11th inst. by the Rev. William HARRISON (VGPI 17 Nov 97)
GOODE, Richard B. Esq., att. at law, mar. Miss Sally H. WOODSON, both of Chesterfield Co., on Sat. eve. last (Arg. 12 Dec 96)
GOODE, Robert, of Henrico Co., mar. Miss Sally BLAND a dau. of Col. Richard BLAND, at Jordan's on Sat. last (VG 23 Jun 68)
GOODE, Thomas, Eng. ind. svt., c. 20, ran away from William SETTLE, Fauquier Co. (VGR 4 Aug 74)
GOODHUE, Hezekiah, American, des. from the co. of Capt. Thomas MERIWETHER (VGPu 7 Mar 77 sup)
GOODLET, Adam, of Orange Co., is going to Ky. in March 1791 (VHFA 8 Apr 90)
GOODMAN, John, of Pr. Wm. Co., dec'd (VGAR 14 Jun 92)
GOODRICH, Thomas, of Caroline Co., adv. that he intends to remove his family to Amherst Co. in Nov. (VGPu 11 Oct 76)
GOODRICK, Mr. [also given as Mr. GUTRIDGE], lately a resident of Alexandria, mar. a widow EDELEN at Fredsbrg.; he may hear of something to his advantage by applying to the printer (VGAxA 3 Sep 89)
GOODRIDGE, William, of Salisbury, Co. Wilts, left Eng. about 50 yrs. ago to reside in some part of this colony; if he or any of his descendents be living, they will be informed of something to their advantage by applying to John SMITH of Hanover Town (VG 2 Jun 68, VGR 9 Jun 68)
GOODSON, Mrs. Mary, of Wmsbrg., died, her ex., Humphrey HARWOOD and George REID, will sell all of her HH and KF (VGWeA 5 Jan, 2 Feb 82)
GOODSON, Thomas, Member of the GA for Isle of Wight Co., d. on Mon. last in Petersburg on his way home (VGRMA 11 Dec 94)
GOODWIN, Mrs. Elizabeth, cons. of Capt. William GOODWIN, d. at Rocket's on Sun. night the 3rd inst. leaving her husband and a young child (RC 5 Jul 96, VGWeA 9 Jul 96, VGGA 13 Jul 96)

GOODWIN, Harwood, intends to move to Georgia (VGAA 8 Oct 85)
GOODWIN, James, dec'd, Elizabeth GOODWIN (nfi) asks that all interest due his est. be payed (VG 3 Nov 63)
GOODWIN, John, dec'd, his 196 ac. tract in York Co. to be sold by Richard ANDERSON (VG 29 Apr 73)
GOODWIN, John, native of America, has resided sometime in Loudoun Co., des. from Col. GRAYSON's Regt. of Guards; it is expected he has made for the Western Frontiers (VGPu 6 Jun 77)
GOODWIN, John, late of Kg. Wm. Co., dec'd, e.a.w. his ex., Allen CHAPMAN (VG 10 Jul 78)
GOODWIN, Capt. John, late of York Co., dec'd, his admr., John MOSS of Yorktown, will sell all his PE (VGWeA 13 Nov 84, VGAA 3 Dec 85); e.a.w. his admr., John MOSS (VIC 3 Dec 88)
GOODWIN, Thomas, merch., mar. Miss Nancy SMITH dau. of William SMITH merch., both of this place [Fredsbrg.] (VHFA 11 Oct 92)
GOODY, John, from Goochland, executed near Richmond on Fri. night last for the murder of his wife which he denied to the last (NPJ 18 Jun 88)
[GOOSELEY], Cary, of Yorktown, killed in a riding accident last Sat. eve. (VG 2 Ju 72)
GOOSELY, John, son of Capt. George GOOSELY is suspected along with John REYNOLDS (son of William REYNOLDS), both of York Co., of mail robbery (RMA 10 Jan 96)
GOOSLEY, Ephraim, of York Co., dec'd, e.a.w. his admr., David JAMESON (VG 5 Jun 52)
GOOSLEY, William, of York Co., mar. Miss Ludwell HARRISON of Wakefield, in Surry Co. (VG 21 Jan 73)
GORDING, Abraham, appr. lad, ran away from James CROULY, Richmond (VGGA 13 Apr 91)
GORDON, Alexander, merch., mar. Miss Molly MURRAY of Pr. Geo. Co.; her sister, Peggy MURRAY, mar. Thomas GORDON (VG 13 Oct 74)
GORDON, Daniel, of Chesterfield Co. warns that he will not pay any debts of his wife, Charlotte GORDON (VGWeA 16 Nov 82)
GORDON, Daniel, of Manchester, adv. that he is going to remove to the Western Country (Arg 17 Feb 97)
GORDON, George, of Portsmouth, died (NPC 8 May 90)
GORDON, Hugh, of Petersburg, d. on Wed. eve. (VGPI 26 May 97)
GORDON, Col. James, of Lancaster Co., d. on the 2nd inst. in his 54th year [long obit.] (VG 14 Jan 68)
GORDON, James, dyer, he and his wife (nfi) were jailed as runaways from Md. in Isle of Wight Co.; they say they were b. in Scotland and came to Oxford, Md. six mos. ago in the *Molly* (VG 27 Oct 74)
GORDON, Col. James, of Lancaster Co., dec'd, his extx., Ann GORDON, will sell part of his PE (VHFA 30 Oct 94, VGGA 19 Nov 94)
GORDON, John, of Granville Co., N. Carolina, will sell 1000 ac. of land in Northumberland Co. between Point Lookout and Smith's Point (VG 30 Jul 72)
GORDON, John, from Pr. Edw., 24-25, jailed for horse stealing, escaped from jail in York Co. (VGR 4 Aug 74)
GORDON, John, of Pr. Geo. Co., mar. Miss Lucy POYTHRESS of the same co. (VGPu 21 Apr 75 sup, VGP 28 Apr 75)
GORDON, John, of Petersburg, died (VGWeA 20 Apr 82); his ex., Francis MUIR, Thomas GORDON, and William YATES, will sell his HH and KF at his late dwelling house four miles from Blandford (VGWeA 22 Jun 82); e.a.w. his admr., Francis MUIR (VGAA 14 Dec 82); slaves bel. to his est. will be sold at his plant. near Morton's Bridge, Charlotte Co. by his admr., Francis MUIR of Pr. Geo. Co. (VGGA 25 Aug 90)
GORDON, John, dec'd, his est. to be sold by his ex., William GORDON of Culpeper Co. (BVCG 14 Apr 94)
GORDON, Robert, merch., mar. Miss J. CURRIE, both of this city [Richmond], o. Sat. eve. last (VGGA 24 Dec 99, Arg 27 Dec 99)

GORDON, Samuel, merch., d. on the 14th inst. at Blandford on Appomattox in his 55th year (VG 25 Apr 71); he d. leaving a wife and heir at law, Alexander GORDON (VG 10 Oct 71)
GORDON, Samuel, [dec'd], any claims against his est. or the est. of Alexander GORDON are to be made to Neill BUCHANAN in Chesterfield Co. or Capt. William MURRAY in Pr. Geo. Co., per an advertisement by Mary GORDON the admx. of Alexander GORDON (VGCD 6 Nov 79)
GORDON, Thomas, served as a gardener with Col. BARNES of Md., c. 40, jailed in Northumberland Co. (VG 20 Oct 74)
GORDON, William, native of New Galoway, North Britain, came to Philadelphia from Belfast last fall and thence to Norfolk; he was lately seen in Philadelphia and Baltimore; a 20 guinea reward is offered (VCGA 14 Jul 94)
GORE, [Miss], dau. of John GORE of Culpeper, c. 20, killed by lightning on Sun. last (Fredsbrg. disp. of 7 Jul.) (NHPA 13 Jul 97)
GOSLING, John, of Charlotte Co., adv. that his wife, Susannah GOSLING, has sold sundry of his effects and made some considerable purchases without his knowledge; he will no longer pay any of her debts (VGPu 6 Jun 77)
GOSNEY, William, dec'd, his slaves to be sold by the Commissioners in Culpeper Co. (VH 2 Nov 98)
GO[SS]EGON, Peter, sentenced to death in April for Negro stealing was pardoned upon entering on board H.M.S. *Boston* bound for Eng. (VG 12 Jun 72)
GOTHARD, Joseph, ind. svt., cooper, ran away from John SYME and John CHRENSHAW of Hanover Co. (VG 21 Apr 74)
GOUGH, Capt. Joshua, drowned in the York River Thurs. last (VG 23 Sep 73)
GOULD, [?], son of Mr. GOULD, fell into the water and drowned at Harper's Wharf (TAA 25 May 98)
GOULD, Ignatius, young man who had lately arrived in Norfolk from Baltimore, d. on Sat. last (NHPA 4 Sep 97)
GOVAN, James, merch., mar. Miss Elizabeth GARLICK on 25 Nov. at Aylett's Warehouse (VIC 3 Dec 88, VGWeA 4 Dec 88)
GOW, Alexander, of Norfolk, dec'd, e.a.w. his ex., William DICK and James CRAWFORD (NPC 9 Jul 91)
GOW, Mrs. Ann, dec'd, e.a.w. her act. ex., James KER of Norf. (NHPA 16 Nov 97)
GOWDIE, John, executed last Fri. near Wmsbrg. for felony (Wmsbrg. disp. of 11 Jul.) (MG 8 Aug 54)
GOWEN, John, Negro, c. 33, said to be the property of Francis CORBIN of Caroline Co., jailed in Gloucester Co. (VGGA 11 Sep 98)
GOWEN, Johnson, mar. Miss Sarah RUSSEL, both of this county [Fairfax], last Tues. week (TAA 14 Mar 98)
GOWING, Rap, aka Anthony GILLIAT or Anthony, runaway from Alexander QUARRIER, Richmond; he may be on his way to Pa. (VGGA 6 Oct 90)
GOWNES, Daniel, dec'd, e.a.w. his admr., Dennis FOLEY, who will sell all of his PE at Samuel M'ATEE's near the Little Falls in Fairfax Co. (CMAG 8 Oct 95)
GRAFFENREAD, David, [also given as GRATENREAD in the 1767 account] mulatto, 37 (in 1767), ran away from Richard KING, Kg. Wm. Co. (VG 7 May 67, 17 Feb 74)
GRAHAM, Alexander, merch., late of Savannah-la-Mar, d. Sat. last (VCNPGA 3 Nov 92)
GRAHAM, Mrs. Catherine Macaully, d. at Binfield, Eng., on 23 Jun. (VHFA 8 Sep 91)
GRAHAM, Duncan the Elder, his admr. and also the admr. of Duncan GRAHAM the Younger is P[aul] WOOLFOLK of Hanover Co. (VGGA 14 Sep 91)
GRAHAM , Duncan Jr., his PE to be sold by the admr., Paul WOOLFOLK (VGGA 14 Dec 91); his admr. will sell his slaves in Caroline Co. (VGGA 13 Nov 93)
GRAHAM, Edward, merch. of Bedford Co., mar. Miss Peggy ALEXANDER of Lexington on 31 Dec 1792 (BVCG 7 Jan 93)
GRAHAM, Elizabeth, late of Pr. Wm. Co., dec'd, e.a.w. her ex., William GRAHAM (RJDA 12 Jun 95)
GRAHAM, George, of Richmond, d. yesterday morn. (VGRMA 11 Aug 94)

GRAHAM, James, from Westmoreland Co., was discharged from the public hospital for lunatics last week, he having [been] restored to his proper senses (VG 1 Apr 80)

GRAHAM, James, d. in Martinsburg on Sun. morn. last (PGBA 30 Mar 97)

GRAHAM, Jane, has left her husband, Thomas GRAHAM (WG 27 Jun 98)

GRAHAM, John, commonly called GRIMES, c. 23, a resident of Albemarle Co., des. from the recruits raised for the defense of Georgia; it is believed that he has gone to Pittsylvania Co. (VGPu 17 Jan 77)

GRAHAM, Col. Richard, of Dumfries, wishes to settle on the Western Waters (VI 18 Nov 89); d. at Philadelphia on Sat. 30 [Apr.] after a short illness; he was bur. there (CMAG 7 May 96, VHFFA 10 May 96)

GRAHAM, Tildsley, of Norfolk will pet. the ensuing GA for a divorce from his with, Catherine GRAHAM, and will no longer pay her debts (NH 24 Nov 98, 15 Aug 99)

GRAHAM, the Rev. William, Presbyterian minister from Kanawha Co., d. on Fri night last [acc. to VGGA] or Sat. last the 8th on Jun. [acc. to VF and Arg] in Richmond of a pleuritic complaint; he had worked to establish a seminary in Rockbridge Co.; he migrated to the Ohio River area two yrs. earlier (VGGA and Arg 11 Jun 99, VF 12 Jun, 28 Aug 99)

GRAMMAR, Robert, a young gentleman of this town [Petersburg], died (VGPI 1 Nov 87)

GRAMMER, Mrs., sp. of John GRAMMER of Petersburg, d. there on Mon. last (VGPI 21 Sep 86, VGAA 27 Sep 86)

GRANBERY, Josiah, merch. in Suffolk, died (VG 10 Dec 72, VGR 17 Dec 72)

GRANNEL, John, Irish svt., tailor, c. 25, ran away from Richard BURLAND, tailor, in Baltimore (VGAA 10 May 86)

GRANT, Bob, Negro, c. 22, claims he is free, says he formerly waited on one Capt. ROBINSON on board the brigantine *Peggy* at Port Royal, jailed in Elizabeth C: Co. (VGIC 13 Dec 83)

GRANT, Daniel, who lately kept tavern near Philadelphia, has opened an inn an tavern in Baltimore, Md. (VG 8 Jul 73)

GRANT, Mrs. Elizabeth Ruth, wife of Daniel GRANT master of the Fountain In Hotel, Baltimore, d. on 21 Sep., aged near 48 (NPG 30 Sep 89)

GRAPES, Jacob Sr., dec'd, his ex. is Jacob GRAPES (WG 6 Feb 99)

GRASTY, John, of Orange Co., 18, drowned in Pittsylvania Co. on 7 Jul. (VHFA : Jul 98)

GRATTAN, Capt. Richard, merch., of Staunton, mar. Miss Betsey GILMORE d. of Mr. Peachy GILMORE of Rockingham Co., Thurs. last (SS 19 Oct 93)

GRAVEN, Anderson, appr. shoemaker, c. 17, ran away from Job MILLS, Manchester; he is supposed to be in the neighborhood of John TODD's mill (or Kellie's Tavern) in Louisa Co as his father lives there (Ex 19 Jul, 9 Aug 99, Arg 9 Aug 99)

GRAVES Family, HCC, 19 Sep 1792: Sarah M'GEHEE, Lipscomb CRANK and Frankey, Nancy, Sally, John, Stephen, George and Betsey CRANK infants under 21 by their next friend William COOKE, Charles COSBY and Elizabeth his wife, Nancy, Frankey, Sally, Dabney, Sukey, Polly, and Babby SMITH infants under 21 by William COOKE their next friend (pltfs.) against John GRAVES, Samuel GRAVES, and James GRAVES chil. of John GRAVES and Mary his wife also under 21, William M'GEHEE, James M'GEHEE, George CRANK and Nancy his wife, William SMITH and Fanny his wife, James TRICE and William TRICE, William ARNATT and Susanna ARNATT and Bartholomew CHEWNING (defs.) [They are apparently of Spotsylvania Co.] (VGGA 13 Feb 93)

GRAVES, [?], d. from a fall last week in Alexandria (VJAA 16 Dec 84)

GRAVES, Mrs. Alice, dau. of John PIERCE of James City Co. and wife of John GRAVES of the same co., d. on Thurs. in her 21st year leaving a nursing infar (VGGA 25 May 91)

GRAVES, Elijah, late of Mecklenburg Co., dec'd, e.a.w. his ex., Howel GRAVES (VGPI 7 May 99)

GRAVES, Francis, d. on the 23rd ult. at his seat in Essex Co. aged 68 (VGGA 4 Apr 92)
GRAVES, Francis, d. yesterday eve. in this city [Richmond] (VGGA 20 Dec 97)
GRAVES, Frederick, appr. boy, c. 12, ran away from William DUNN, Norfolk (AGNPPA 12 Feb 96, NH 27 Jun 96)
GRAVES, Hannah, formerly Hannah STAFFORD, wife of John GRAVES Jr. has des. him (NPC 10 Mar 92)
GRAVES, John, mar. Miss Alice PIERCE dau. of John PIERCE Esq. of James City Co. on the 20th ult. (VIC 2 Dec 89, VGWeA 3 Dec 89)
GRAVES, John, appr. tailor, c. 18, ran away from Quentin CLARK, Norfolk (NH 25 May 99)
GRAVES, Joseph C., dec'd, his ex., William GRAVES, will sell all his PE and will rent his plant. called Windsor Shades on the Chickahominy River (VGGA 6 Aug 94)
GRAVES, Moses, mulatto, c. 26, escaped from jail in Newtown on Chester River, Md. (VG 17 Oct 71); jailed in Lancaster Co. (VGR 12 Mar 72)
GRAVES, Ralph, dec'd, his admr., John PIERCE, will sell all his slaves at the Raleigh Tavern, Wmsbrg. (VGGA 13 Jan 96)
GRAVES, Thomas, late of Spotsylvania Co., dec'd, his ex., Thomas GRAVES, William PETTUS, and Joseph GRAVES, desire his legatees to apply for the balance of their respective legacies any time after the 1st of next Jun. (VG 5 Mar 79); his ex. and the ex. of Mrs. Anne GRAVES dec'd, Rice GRAVES, will sell all the remaining part of both the sd. decedent's estates consisting of 399 ac. and other items (VGWeA 5 Oct 82)
GRAVES, William, of York Co., dec'd (VGAA 5 Oct 82)
GRAVES, William, Fielding FANT was acquitted of his murder in Fredsbrg. District Ct. (VHFA 9 May 93)
GRAVES, Maj. William, of Norfolk, mar. Miss Fanny ARMISTEAD of Elizabeth City Co. on Thurs. last in Hampton (AGNPPA 21 Apr 95, HNPA 22 Apr 95)
GRAY, Capt. David, of Berkeley Co., died (PGBA 5 May 96)
GRAY, Edward, native of Scotland, dyer, d. on Sat. eve. (RMA 1 Oct 95)
GRAY, Col. Edwin, dec'd, his 2000 ac. plant. near the town of Suffolk, on which Joseph GRAY (nfi) now lives, to be sold by his ex., Edwin GRAY (VGGA 16 Nov 91)
GRAY, French S., merch, aged 23, d. in Fredsbrg. (VHFA 16 Aug, VGGA 22 Aug 92); e.a.w. his ex., James DYKES (VHFA 25 Oct 92)
GRAY, George, dec'd, e.a.w. his admr., Peter Randolph BLAND (VG 10 Oct 66)
GRAY, George, of Stafford Co., dec'd, his PE to be sold by his admx., Mary GRAY (VGR 11 May 69)
GRAY, George, late of Stafford Co., dec'd, e.a.w. his admr., George WEEDON of Fredsbrg. (VG 31 Mar 74)
GRAY, George, of Richmond, intends to leave the state (VGGA 23 Aug 99)
GRAY, John, of Isle of Wight Co., c. 40, killed in a boating accident on Sat. the 2nd inst. (VG 28 Mar 71)
GRAY, John, aka Jack, mulatto, 21, ran away from Charles LOGAN, Powhatan Co. (VGAA 11 Dec 84)
GRAY, John, late merch. in Norfolk, dec'd, e.a.w. his admr., James COLQUHOUN and William GILLIES (VGIC 26 Mar 85)
GRAY, John, merch., mar. Miss Lucy ROBB dau. of James ROBB, at Port Royal on Fri. last (VHFA 20 Dec 92)
GRAY, John, a cripple, who for many years past has kept an Eng. school, d. at Wmsbrg. on Sun. last (VGWeA 24 Jan 94)
GRAY, Peter, Negro, c. 25, ran away from Isaac W. PLEASANTS, Goochland Co. (VGRMA 1 Sep 94)
GRAY, Mrs. Rebecca, cons. of Robert GRAY merch. of [Winchester], d. Sun. last; she will be bur. in the Presbyterian Burying Ground (WG 10 Jul 99)
GRAY, Richard, merch. of Winchester, d. on Tues. the 5th inst. [or, acc. to VGWA, last Sun. sennight] at the Sweet Springs, Augusta Co., in the prime of life (VGWA and VCWM 20 Aug 88); e.a.w. his admr., Joseph TIDBALL

(VCWM 10 Dec 88)
GRAY, Thomas, svt., 36, imp. from London on the ship *Rachel* in the summer, ran away from James ALLEN, Fredsbrg., on 27 Jul.; supposed to have gone towards N. Carolina (VG 20 Oct 52)
GRAY, William, of Surry Co., mar. Mrs. Elizabeth CHAMBERLAYNE widow of William CHAMBERLAYNE of New Kent Co., last Sun. (VG 14 Apr 38)
GRAY, William, conv. svt., 19, ran away from Patrick COUTTS, Richmond (VG 4 Feb 73)
GRAY, William, from Westmoreland Co., executed on 12 May for burglary (VGPu 12 May 75 sup)
GRAY, William, joiner, c. 22, suspected of stealing a horse from John FITZHUGH's pasture in Stafford Co.; it is believed that he was going to Bedfor Co. (VGPu 7 Jul 75)
GRAY, William, merch., d. at Port Royal (VHFA 11 Jan 99)
GRAY, William, merch. of Richmond, mar. Miss Jane GUERRANT of Goochland, Sat. eve. last (VGGA 15 Nov 99)
GRAY, William F., dec'd, Peggy GRAY and Thomas BURK (nfi) will rent his house in Port Royal (VHFA 18 Oct 92)
GRAY, Mrs. Zipporah, of Fredsbrg., d. on Wed. (VHFA 10 Jul 95)
GRAYSON Family, State of Md., 11 Aug 1796, in chanc: Robert FERGUSON and others vs. Robert CARTER and Hebe his wife, George GRAYSON, Robert GRAYSON, and Alfred GRAYSON and others heirs of William SMALLWOOD of Charles Co., [Md.], late dec'd; the CARTER's and GRAYSON's are residents of Va. (CMAG 27 Aug 96)
GRAYSON, Mr., native of Md. where he now lives is asked to acquaint the printer of the circumstances or situation of Mrs. Isabella WALLER of Plymouth, Eng. with whom he is well acquainted (VGR 7 Jul 74)
GRAYSON, Mrs., cons. of the Hon. William GRAYSON Esq. a senator of Va. in Congress, d. on Tues. the 22nd inst. in Frederick Co. (VCWM 30 Sep 89)
GRAYSON, the Hon. Col. William, U.S. senator, d. on 12 Mar. at Dumfries on h way to Congress; he was bur. in the family vault at the Rev. Spence GRAYSON's (VCWM 24 Mar 90, VICGA 24 Mar 90, VHFA 25 Mar 90); his admr., Joseph TIDBALL of Winchester, will sell his slaves and livestock (VGWA 19 Jan 91); his admr. will sell 2300 ac. of his land near Winchester (VGGA 2 Mar 91, VGWA 23 Mar 91)
GRAYTON, Robert, Irish, resident of Augusta Co., 34, des. from an escort conducting German prisoners of war from Winchester to Frederick, Md. (VGAA 22 Feb 83)
GREAVES, Mrs., spouse of Capt. William GREAVES of Norfolk, d. Sun. last (NP 17 Dec 91)
GREAVES, Col. William, of Norfolk, d. yesterday (NH 16 May 99)
GREEN Family, HCC, 18 Sep 1799: John MITCHELL surviving partner of Lenc Scott & Co. (pltf.) and Moses GREEN ex. of John GREEN who was ex. of William GREEN dec'd, Ann GREEN widow and relict of the sd. William GREEN, William GREEN, Francis Wyatt GREEN, Peter MARYE and Eleano: his wife, John POINDEXTER who mar. Ann one of the daus. of William GREEN, Henry CAMP and Elizabeth his wife, George THOMAS and Mary his wife, Daniel STRINGER and Milly his wife, Nathaniel PINHARD and Lucy Coleman his wife, and James SLAUGHTER admr. of Thomas SLAUGHTER dec'd (VGGA 22 Oct 99)
GREEN, Dr., of the House of Gardener & Green of Norfolk, d. on Sat. morn. (NH Oct 99)
GREEN, Abraham, of Amelia Co., mar. Miss Betsy BROWNE of Surry (VGPu 21 Nov 77)
GREEN, Mrs. Ann, [probably the wife of the late Col. William GREEN] whose ex John GREEN, will sell the reversion of her dower--two tracts of land in Culpeper Co. (VHFA 5 Sep 93)
GREEN, Dr. Baylie, dec'd, his medical equipment to be sold at the home of his

admr., John GIBBONS, York Co. (VG 31 Oct 55)
GREEN, Capt. Caleb, mar. Miss Hannah ROBINSON in [Alexandria] on Sun. eve. last (CMAG 1 Nov 96)
GREEN, Charles, light brown svt. or slave, c. 40 (in 1795), hostler and gardener, ran away from John TYLER, Greenway, Charles City Co., who believes he will go north (RMA 27 Jun 95, VGGA 15 Jul 95, Ex 28 May 99, Arg 4 Jun 99, VGGA 11 Jun 99)
GREEN, Francis Burwell, late of Pr. Geo. Co., dec'd, e.a.w. his admr., John GREEN (VGPI 28 Jun 96)
GREEN, George, Negro, c. 25, carpenter, says he is free, jailed in Botetourt Co. (VGWeA 5 Jan 82)
GREEN, George, of Nottoway Co., adv. that his wife, Elizabeth GREEN, has absconded from his bed and board (VGPI 30 Nov 94)
GREEN, John, of New Kent Co., dec'd, his est. there to be sold by his ex. (nfi) (VG 14 Sep 69)
GREEN, Col. John, d. on Mon. the 18th ult. in Culpeper Co., aged 60 [obit.] (VHFA 5 Dec 93); his acting ex., Moses GREEN of Culpeper Co., will sell his slaves and PE (VHFA 26 Dec 93, 2 Jan 94); his ex. will sell his 500-600 ac. tract and mill in Culpeper Co. (VHFA 5 Jun 94); Moses GREEN, ex. to Col. John GREEN and Col. William GREEN, will sell the reversion of Mrs. Ann GREEN's dower, c. 1000 ac. in Culpeper Co. (VHFA 12 Jun 94); his acting ex., Moses GREEN, will sell military lands in the district set apart for the officers and soldiers on the northwest side of the Ohio bel. to sd. est. (VHFFA 1 Apr 97); his acting ex. will sell his slaves (VH 14 Feb 98)
GREEN, Joseph, aka Joseph GALE, conv. svt., imp. last Nov. into Rappahannock River in the *Justitia*, c. 35, farmer, b. in Wiltshire, ran away from Nicholas FLOOD (PC 27 Apr 67)
GREEN, Joseph, Eng. svt., laborer, 35, ran away from Archibald M'CALL, Tappahannock (VG 11 Feb 68)
GREEN, Pleasant, Negro, c. 35, jailed in Norfolk Co., says he bel. to William BROWN at City Point (NH 29 Mar 98)
GREEN, Richard, appr., ran away from Samuel DUVAL, Henrico Co. (VG 14 Feb 51)
GREEN, Robert, Eng. svt., 24-25, ran away from the plant. of the Rev. Robert ROSS, Albemarle Co. (VG 5 Mar 52)
GREEN, Sarah, formerly the widow, Sarah PACKE; her husband, William GREEN of Wmsbrg., requests that any person indebted to her settle with him and not with George PITT (VG 28 Mar, 11, 18 Apr 55)
GREEN, Thomas, from Mecklenburg Co., executed for murder on the 9th inst. (VG 16 May 77)
GREEN, Thomas, forewarns all persons from employing or giving credit to William GREEN as he is underage (?) (RJDWA 7 Jul 96)
GREEN, Col. William, long a rep. for Culpeper Co., d. on Mon. the 6th inst. in his 43rd year (VGR 23 Aug 70)
GREEN, William, soldier, c. 28, b. in New Jersey but resided principally in Bucks Co., Pa., blacksmith, des. from the 7th U.S. Regt., Charlottesville Barracks (VGGA 26 Jun 98)
GREENE, Nathaniel, late of Rhode Island, is asked to apply to Messrs. Goddard and Langworthy, printers in Baltimore where he may hear of something to his advantage (VJAA 31 Mar 85)
GREENE, Samuel, of Culpeper Co., mar. Miss Elizabeth BLAIR of [Winchester], on Thurs. last (WG 29 May 99)
GREENFIELD, John, dec'd, several tracts of his land in Hampshire Co. to be sold by his ex., Angus M'DONALD and Alexander WHITE (VGR 15 Mar 70); his lots in Winchester to be sold by his ex. (VGR 21 Mar 71); his brother and heir at law is William GREENFIELD of Haddington, North Britain (VGR 30 May 71)
GREENHOW, John, of Wmsbrg., merch., age 64, mar. Miss HARMAN of James City Co. age 16 (VGAA 22 Mar 86)

GREENHOW, John, merch., d. in Wmsbrg. last week (VGWeA 6 Sep 87); his ex., Robert GREENHOW, will sell items of his est. in Richmond and Wmsbrg. (VGIC 6 Oct 87)

GREENHOW, John, mar. Miss Kitty VOSS, both of this city [Richmond] (VICGA 6 Jan 90)

GREENHOW, John, merch., of Richmond, mar. Miss Elizabeth DUVAL dau. of William DUVAL of Gloucester Co. (VGGA 18 Apr 92)

GREENHOW, John, merch. of Richmond, d. on Sun. eve. (VGGA 30 Sep 95, RMA 1 Oct 95); his admr., Samuel GREENHOW of Richmond, will sell all his PE (RMA 16 Dec 95)

GREENLEY, Elizabeth, conv., sentenced to death in Wmsbrg. for the murder of a fellow svt., executed on 26 Nov. near Wmsbrg. (VG 26 Nov 36, AWM 16 Dec 36, NYWJ 10 Jan 37)

GREENWAY, Mrs. Rebecca, widow of Capt. Joseph GREENWAY of this town [Alexandria], d. on the 9th inst. (CMAG 11 Mar 97)

GREENWICH, Thomas, an East India Indian, ran away from William COLSTON Richmond Co. (VGR 4 Aug 68)

GREGORIE, Mr. Sr., of the House of Gregorie & Barksdale, Petersburg, reportedly guillotined at Dunkirk last Aug. for having expressed sentiments inimical to the cause of France (VHFA 7 Nov 93)

GREGORY, Lt., of [Col. SCOTT's] 6th Va. Regt., was killed on or about 1 Feb. near Drake's Farm, N.J. (VG 7 Mar 77, VGPu 14 Mar 77)

GREGORY, Charles, of Pr. Geo. Co., dec'd, e.a.w. his extx., Margaret GREGORY, who will sell his est. (VGAA 29 Nov 83, VGWeA 10 Apr 84)

GREGORY, James, adv. that his wife, Elizabeth GREGORY, has left him without any provocation (VG 16 Aug 80)

GREGORY, John, of Charles City Co., dec'd, his surviving ex., Thomas HOLT and William GREGORY, will sell the remaining third of his est.; William GREGORY who is the admr. of Mildred GREGORY dec'd, will also sell all of her est. (VGPu 20 Oct 75)

GREGORY, Mrs. Mary, lady of Roger GREGORY Esq., d. on Sun. the 10th of Nov in Kg. Wm. Co. (VG 14 Nov 71)

GREGORY, Richard Fletcher, debtor, burned to death on 4 Dec. 1768 in a fire at the Amherst Co. jail (VG 15 Dec 68, PC 16 Jan 69, NYPB 23 Jan 69)

GREGORY, Richard, of Gloucester, died (VG and VGPu 31 Jan 77)

GREGORY, Richard Esq., of Petersburg, mar. Miss Elizabeth WILKINSON seco dau. of Col. Nathaniel WILKINSON of Henrico Co. on Mon. the 6th inst. (VIC 15 Jul 89, VGWeA 16 Jul 89)

GREGORY, Samuel, aka NAILING, appr., c. 18, ran away from Turner ANDERSON, Goochland Co., is believed to be in Loudoun Co. or vicinity (VGR 22 Sep 74)

GREGORY, Stith, dec'd, his ex., William GREGORY, will sell some of his PE (VGPu 15 Dec 75)

GREGORY, Capt. William, of Charles City Co., of the 6th Regt., died; e.a.w. his ex., John GREGORY and Francis IRBY (VGPu 7 Jun 76, 20 Sep 76, 29 May 78)

GREIG, Capt. Archibald, oldest commander in the Virginia and Maryland trade and a near relation to Admiral GREIG in the Russian service, d. from a fall from his horse Sat. last (VIC 29 Oct, VGIC 1 Nov, NPJ 5 Nov, VHFA 6 Nov 88)

GRESHAM, James, admr. of William GRESHAM dec'd, mentioned in a Northumberland Co. chancery case 19 May 1792 (VGGA 13 Jun 92)

GREVES, John, appr., c. 16, ran away from Quintin CLARK, Norfolk (NH 28 May 96)

GREY, John, slave, raised in Caroline Co., ran away from Thomas CARNEAL, Lexington, Ky. (KG 18 May 93)

GREY, Phillis, mulatto, c. 30, ran away from Isaac W. PLEASANTS, Goochland Co., who expects she will try to get the Robert PLEASANTS in Henrico Co. (VGGA 30 May 92)

GREY, Sally, aka Sall, mulatto slave, Virginia born, c. 25, has kin in Cumberland and Amelia Cos., ran away from Gabriel PENN, Amherst Co.

(VG 4 Aug 74)

GRIER, Susanna, absconded from the house of her husband, Robert GRIER, in Dumfries on 30 Oct last; he suspects she has run off with Anthony RICHARDS, c. 30, a former conv. svt. and may have gone to Norfolk (VGR 14 Dec 69)

GRIFFIN, Mrs. Elizabeth, dec'd [elegy dated 21 Sep.] (VGGA 2 Oct 98)

GRIFFIN, Sarah, from Augusta Co., d. in the hospital for lunatics in Wmsbrg. (VGGA 6 Oct 90)

GRIFFIN, Thomas B. Esq., d. at Belle Isle (VG 8 May 78); of Lancaster Co., his ex., William GRIFFIN, will sell a great variety of HH and KF and other items of his est. including a "pretty good library" (VGPu 29 May 78)

GRIFFIN, William, appr., 19, thought to be Irish but says he was b. in Caroline Co, ran away from John BROWN, Wmsbrg. (VG 30 Jan 52)

GRIFFIN, William Esq., mar. Mrs. ROBINSON widow of the late Speaker (VG 16 May 71)

GRIFFIN, Col. William, dec'd, his acting ex., Cyrus GRIFFIN and William MARSHALL, will sell his HHF and livestock at his late dwelling house in K & Q Co. (VGGA 8 May 93)

GRIFFIN, William, appr. lad, ran away from Chudleigh SOUTHWICK, sailmaker, at Norfolk who suspects he is secreted by his father (NH 11 Sep 98)

GRIFFITH, the Rev. David, late of Fairfax Co., d. at Philadelphia on Mon. 3 Aug. after a short illness; he was bur. in Christ Churchyard, Philadelphia (VHFA 13 Aug 89, VIC 19 Aug 89); a pet. will be pres. to the next GA to enable his admx., Hannah GRIFFITH, to sell some of his land in Ky. (VGAxA 1 Sep 91)

GRIFFITH, John, aka WELLS, a sailor aboard the *Virginia* frigate; he has a family on the Eastern Shore and is very well acquainted about Back River and Hampton, des. from Capt. PEARCE's Co. of Artillery (VGPu 15 Aug 77)

GRIFFITH, Owen, living with Landon CARTER, Richmond Co. "though in a little time free," has an account from his brother at the Duke of Montague's that some goods were sent him by his father who has since died; he will be going home to "really a very good estate." (VGR 6, 27 Sep 70)

GRIFFITH, William, Eng. svt., shoemaker, c. 30, ran away from Foushee TEBBS, Dumfries (VGR 7 Jun 70)

GRIFFITHS, Thomas, boatswain, middle aged, ran away from the ship *Amelia* lying at Bermuda Hundred (VG 1 Jun 69)

GRIFFITHS, Thomas, seaman, ran away from the ship *Hannibal* lying at the mouth of Quantico (VJAA 10 Aug 86)

GRIGSBY, Jem, aka James, slave, c. 22, ran away from Samuel LOVE's plant. near Leesburg (BVCG 16 Jul 92)

GRIMES, John, appr., 17, sailmaker, ran away from Joseph ROBERTSON, Alexandria (VJAA 7 Jul 85)

GRIMES, Mary, has des. her husband, John GRIMES, of Norfolk, without any provocation and he will no longer pay her debts (NH 1 Jun 99)

GRIMES, Philip, of Fairfax Co., adv. that his son, Philip GRIMES, has deserted his house because he will not consent that he should mar. a certain Bathsheba HOLLIS aka JACKSON who is a "melater" [mulatto ?]; his son is but 20 the 24th of Dec. next (VGPu 8 Aug 77)

GRIMES, Stephen, appr. carpenter, 20, ran away from George CORYELL, Alexandria (VJAA 4 Dec 88)

GRIMES, William, of Portsmouth, warns all persons that he will not pay any of the debts of his wife, Agatha GRIMES (VGWeA 7 Aug, VGAA 14 Aug 84)

GRINLY, David, native of Scotland who has been detained as a hostage in this state for several yrs., d. yesterday morn. (VGWeA 25 Oct 83)

GRISLEY, Jeffery, of Kg. Wm. Co. died (VG 14 Oct 73 sup); his admr. is John HOOK of Wmsbrg. (VG 9 Dec 79)

GROCOTT, John, Eng. svt., near 40, bricklayer and plasterer, ran away from John NEWTON, Westmoreland Co. (MG 12 Aug 62)

GROVE, Sally, left her husb., Henry GROVE of Martinsburg (PGBA 28 Dec 97)

GROVERMAN, William, merch., mar. Miss Kitty CONRAD on Fri. in Winchester (VGWA 22 Dec 90)

GRUME, Thomas, native of Va., with a family in Orange Co., des. from the state troops at Wmsbrg; he is believed lurking about Gloucester as chief of his relations live there (VG 3 Oct 77)

GRUMLEY, Michael, Irish svt., 25, ran away from Thomas WILLIAMS, Pr. Wm. Co. (VG 18 Jul 51)

GRYMES Family, General Ct., 7 May 1774, in chanc: Philip Ludwell GRYMES son and heir of the Hon. Philip GRYMES Esq. dec'd, and John GRYMES, Charles GRYMES, and Benjamin GRYMES the younger sons and devisees of the sd. Philip GRYMES (pltfs.) against Benjamin GRYMES Gent. one of the ex. of the will of the sd, Philip GRYMES dec'd (def.) (VGR 19 May 74)

GRYMES, Mrs. Anne, spouse to Charles GRYMES Esq., d. in Gloucester Co. (VGPu 18 Apr 77 sup)

GRYMES, B., intends to leave Va. for London in mid-August (VG 11 Jul 55)

GRYMES, Benjamin Esq., fourth son of the Hon. Philip GRYMES dec'd, mar. Miss Judy ROBINSON of Middlesex Co. (VG 14 Oct 73); intends to move to the Mississippi very shortly (VG 4, 18 Nov 73)

GRYMES, Benjamin, found not guilty by reason of insanity of the murder of R. GALLOWAY (VHFA 8 may 95)

GRYMES, Edward, Eng. ind. svt., bricklayer, c. 24, ran away from the plant. of James PRIDE (VG 18 Aug 74)

GRYMES, John, ind. svt. from Yorkshire, c. 25, cooper, says he belongs to Samuel COX, Blandford, committed to York prison (VGPu 28 Jul 75)

GRYMES, Mrs. Mary, relict of the Hon. Philip GRYMES dec'd, d. at her house in Wmsbrg. yesterday morn. (VG 21 Jan 68)

GRYMES, Philip Ludwell Esq., of Brandon in Middlesex Co., mar. Miss Judith WORMELEY dau. of Ralph WORMELEY Esq. of Middlesex, on Sun. last (VG and VGR 3 Jun 73)

GRYMES, Polly, Negro, c. 26, claimed to be free; served her time with Capt. George RICE near Winchester where she left her son John; jailed in Caroline (VHFA 19 Jun 94)

GUIER, Thomas, aka M'GUIER, Irish, 20, has been in the country about seven yrs., ran away from Robert WALLACE of Norfolk Borough (VG 10 Jan 52)

GUNN, James, dec'd, his ex., Turner SOUTHALL, James LYLE, James BUCHANAN, Patrick COUTTS, and John PENDLETON Jr., will sell his 400 ac tract near Richmond (VGPu 21 Apr 75, VG 22 Apr 75)

GUNTER, William, c. 40, des. from Capt. John WINSTON's Co. of the 14th Regt. (VGPu 12 Dec 77)

GUNTHER, John C., dec'd, e.a.w. his extx., Martha GUNTHER of Yorktown (VGGA 8 Jun 96, VGWeA 25 Jun 96)

GUNYON, Miss Anne, d. on Tues. eve. last in the bloom of life, at the house of Mr. GALVAN (RJDWA 18 Aug 96)

GURLEY, George, father of the Rev. George GURLEY, rector of St. Luke's Par. in this co., d. on 29 Dec. in Southampton Co. in his 73rd year (VG 10 Jan 71)

GUTHREY, Henry, [of Kg. Wm. Co.], dec'd, e.a.w. his admr., Alexander WHITE and Archibald GOVAN (VG 14 Jan 73)

GUTHREY, John, of Middlesex, sentenced to death for house breaking and robbery (VG 4 May 39)

GUTHRY, Simon, c. 40, jailed as a runaway in Richmond Co., says he came from Philadelphia (VGR 27 Sep 70)

GUY, Thomas T., of Caroline Co., d. on Sun. morn. last (RMA 21 Nov 95)

GWATHMEY, Owen, of Kg. Wm. Co., age 49, died (VG 21 Sep 76)

GWYN, Thomas, of Neath in the co. of Glamorgan, South Wales, d. on Sun. eve. last [27 Jan.] in his 27th year [long obit.] (NPJ 30 Jan 88); e.a.w. his ex., James CATON (NPJ 13 Feb 88)

HACKLEY, Mrs. Ann, aged 47, died (VHFFA 3 Nov 95)

HACKLEY, James, dec'd, his ex, Birkett DAVENPORT, adv. his lot in Fredsbrg for sale; for terms apply to Richard S. HACKLEY (nfi) (VHFFA 19 Apr 96); his ex. will sell the lots and houses bel. to his est. (VHFFA 11 Apr 97)

HACKLEY, Samuel, of Culpeper Co., d. lately at Hampton-Sydney Academy in his 22nd year (VGPu 30 Aug 76)

HADDON, Francis, dec'd, e.a.w. his admr., Allen HADDON, Petersburg (VGPI 22 Sep 97)

HAGART, the Rev. Mr., Baptist minister, killed by Indians in the Wilderness (VGRMA 21 Apr 94, VHFA 24 Apr 94)

HAGGETT, Edward, seaman, ran away from the ship *Virginia* at Littlepage's Landing, New Kent Co., may be heading for the Bristol Iron Mines (VG 18 Apr 45)

HAGGOT, James, 37, des. from H.M.S. *[Triton]*, alleged to be in Va. on board *Pamunkey Snow* up Pamunkey River (VG 9 May 51)

HAGINS, John, 26-27, committed to Elizabeth City Co. jail, supposed to be a runaway from Pennsylvania (VGR 29 Sep 68)

HAGLEY, George, dec'd, his son and admr., Peter HAGLEY of Berkeley Co.; adv. that his father passed a note to George HERGES [or HEIGES] for about £40 which he will not pay because it was unjustly obtained (PGBA 21 Apr 94)

HAGSET, John, Irish, des. from Capt. James MACKILWEAN's Co. at Petersburg (VG 19 Jul 54)

HAGUE, John, d. on Sun. night the 21st ult. in his 58th year (RMA 25 Jun 95, VGGA 1 Jul 95); e.a.w. his admx., Hannah HAGUE, and admr., John CRADDOCK of Rockett's (RMA 23 Jul 95)

HAILY, Thomas, Irish svt., 36 (acc. to VG, but c. 20 acc. to NYPB), ran away from Dr. William LYNN, Fredsbrg. on 31 Jul. (VG 14 Aug 46, NYPB 13 Oct 46)

HAINES, Robert, dec'd, his furniture, tools, and livestock will be sold by his ex., Thomas FAWCETT, Thomas SMITH, and Margaret HAINES of Frederick Co. (BVCG 26 Feb 96)

HAINES, Thomas, c. 20, jailed in Staunton on suspicion of horse stealing (WG 15 May 99)

HAIRSTON, Samuel Gent., of Campbell Co., dec'd, his est. to be sold by his ex., Robert ALEXANDER (VGAA 13 Jul 82)

HALDANE, James, coppersmith and brass founder from Philadelphia, now of Church St., Norfolk (VG 25 Dec 71)

HALE, Dr. William, d. at his house in the lower end of Goochland Co. the 3rd inst. (VGGA 20 Dec 97)

HALES, John, dec'd, e.a.w. his ex., Richard SHARP (VGWeA 30 Mar 86); e.a.w. Hales SHARP (nfi), Henrico Co. (VGGA 23 Jul 94)

HALFPENNY, John, Irish svt., 50-60, ran away from Thomas TURNER, Kg. Geo. Co. (VG 20 Apr 39)

HALKET, Jasper, store keeper with Neil CAMPBELL in Richmond, drowned on Mon. the 11th inst. [obit.] (VG 21 Mar 71)

HALL Family, Pr. Edw. Co., Quarterly Ct., 16 Aug. 1796: Samuel HALL and Thomas HALL against James HALL, Happy CHANDLER, Jemima HALL, George CHANDLER and Susanna his wife late Susanna HALL, and Polly MASSAY an infant under 21 by Elizabeth MASSAY her gdn. specially appointed to defend her interest, upon a petition that the interest of the several parties aforesaid in the lands in the sd. petition, should in place of a division to be preserved to them by an entire sale of the same.... It appearing to the court that William HALL late of this co., father of the sd. Samuel HALL, Thomas HALL, James HALL, Happy CHANDLER, Jemima HALL, Susanna CHANDLER wife of George CHANDLER, and Polly MASSAY, departed this life intestate [entitled] at the time of his death to 120 ac. of land lying in this co. subject to distribution among the parties aforesaid, that each distributor's share in sd. lands will not exceed $100, and it further appearing that the sd. James HALL and Happy CHANDLER are not inhabitants of this state (VGGA 1 Mar 97)

HALL, Almond, appr. printer, 19, ran away from F. X. MARTIN of New Bern

[N. Carolina], may be going to Petersburg (NPC 25 Feb 92)

HALL, Anne, svt., ran away from Charles OAKES, Kg. Wm. Co. (VG 4 Aug 38)

HALL, Armstead, dec'd, his ex., Thomas HILL and Robert WOODSIDE of Norfolk, will sell his cooper's tools (NHPA 13 Jul 97)

HALL, Mrs. Caroline, consort of Dr. Elisha HALL, d. in this town [Fredsbrg.] on Thurs. last (VH 28 Jun 99)

HALL, Claiborn, supposed to be in the upper end of Hanover Co., des. from the service of the Commonwealth (VGPu 2 May 77)

HALL, Durham, late of Norfolk Borough, dec'd, his ex. are Robert TUCKER and Christopher PERKINS (VG 7 Feb 51)

HALL, E., adv. that his son, B. H. HALL, has nearly finished his education in medicine (VH 31 May 99)

HALL, Master Elisha H., son of Col. Elihu HALL of Westmoreland Co., d. lately in Philadelphia (VHFFA 19 Aug 97)

HALL, Horatio Gates, aged 20, d. in Charleston [S. Carolina] on the 10th inst. on his way to Georgia; a native of Md. but lately of Philadelphia (VH 27 Sep 99)

HALL, Capt. James W., mar. the widow SWIFT lately at Hall's (NH 3 Mar 98)

HALL, Capt. James W., native of Whitehaven, Eng., d. suddenly at Hall's Mills near Portsmouth in the prime of his life on 14 Feb. (CMAG 7 Mar 99)

HALL, John, seaman, ran away from the ship *Hannibal* lying at the mouth of Quantico (VJAA 10 Aug 86)

HALL, John, merch., d. last Fri. in his 40th year; he was bur. in the Mason's Burying Ground (VHFA 23 Oct 88)

HALL, John H., d. on Sun. eve. (AGNPPA 21 Apr 95, HNPA 22 Apr 95); his creditors are requested to bring their claims to Polly Hopkins HALL or to the Norfolk Borough Court (HNPA 25 Apr, 20 May 95)

HALL, Mrs. Mary, relict of Capt. John H. HALL formerly of this borough, d. on Sun. eve. at Portsmouth (NH 11 Sep 98)

HALL, Nathaniel, Virginian, 23, des. from Capt. David BELL's Co. of the Va. Regt.; he was in Chesterfield Co. before he is supposed to have moved to Granville Co. near Col. EATON's in N. Carolina (VG 21 Nov 55)

HALL, Richard, att. at law in Md., mar. Miss Molly LEE of Va. (VG 28 Apr 74)

HALL, Dr. Robert, of N. Carolina, mar. Miss Wills NOBBS of Wmsbrg. (VGPu 7 Mar 77 sup)

HALL, Thomas, of Pr. Geo. Co., mar. Miss Molly POWER dau. of Maj. Henry POWER of James City Co., last Sun. (VG 30 Sep 37)

HALL, Thomas, Eng. conv. svt., c. 30, shoemaker, ran away from Murthy M'ABOY, Fauquier Co. (VGPu 11 Oct 76)

HALL, W. J., merch., of Alexandria, was mar. to Miss Gracie CRAIG at Capt. George HUNTER's in Baltimore on Wed. night last by the Rev. Dr. ALLISON (CMAG 28 Jan 97)

HALLAM, Mrs., spouse of Mr. HALLAM, comedian of Philadelphia, d. last week in Wmsbrg. (VGWeA 7 Dec 92, VHFA 13 Dec 92)

HALLEY, Nathaniel, dec'd, e.a.w. Mary HALLEY, his admx., and William HALLEY, his admr. (VGAxA 13 Jan 91)

HALLIDAY, George, of Somerset Co., Md., adv. that a certain Philip SULLIVAN (an Irishman who has been wounded in the shoulder and draws a pension of £18 a year from Mr. RANDOLPH at Annapolis) whom he had, for a long time supported in his family, went off with his wife and three small chil. and robbed him of all his property; he understands he went from Annapolis to Norfolk (HNPA 6 Dec 94)

HALLOM, Alexander, d. on Sat. the 27th ult. in Hanover Town, aged 22, after a short illness (VGGA 8 May 98)

HAMBLETON, John, Irish, ran away from Dr. Anthony STAFFORD, Nansemond Co. (VG 4 Aug 38)

HAMBLIN, Mrs. Christian, dau. of Lewis BURWELL Esq., of Mecklenburg Co, d. on Sun. the 23rd ult. in her 18th year (VGGA 16 Sep 95)

HAMILTON Family, HCC, 27 Sep 1797, between Jesse EWELL and James EWELL (pltfs.) and Alexander HAMILTON, Gavin HAMILTON, Elizabeth

HAMILTON, and Jacobina REID chil. of John HAMILTON dec'd, Robert LAWSON, Mary LAWSON, and Agnes LAWSON chil. of James LAWSON dec'd, John, Gavin, Francis, Thomas, Jacobina HAMILTON chil. and heirs of John HAMILTON dec'd and devisees in the will of the sd. John SEMPLE [sic], [missing] the widow, and [missing] the chil. of Henry LOCKHEAD dec'd, Francis KEYS and John KEYS heirs and devisees of Gresham KEYS dec'd, James LAWSON, Robert LAWSON, and Alexander HAMILTON the exors. named in the will of the sd. John SEMPLE dec'd; most of the defs. are not inhabitants of this country (VGGA 27 Dec 97)

HAMILTON, Andrew, dec'd, his ex., John M'CLOUD of Blandford, will sell all of his PE in that town (VGPI 30 Nov 94)

HAMILTON, Col. Andrew, d. lately in Greenbrier Co. due to a fall from his horse (VHFFA 19 Jul 96, RCFPC 20 Jul 96)

HAMILTON, Dennis Baptiste, accused of raping Polly BURDEN, is to be held for further trial at the District Ct. in Dumfries on 20 Oct. next (CMAG 27 Aug 96)

HAMILTON, George, Eng. svt., c. 26, joiner and carpenter, ran away from James TUFF of Va. (AWM 12 Aug 36)

HAMILTON, James, from Fredsbrg., reportedly killed by Indians on 8 Jul., 100 miles from the Ohio (VG 8 Sep 74)

HAMILTON, James, of Alexandria, mar. Miss DALTON of Killongford, Ireland, at Waterford in Ireland (CMAG 19 Jun 98)

HAMILTON, John, of Frederick Co., executed last Fri. near Wmsbrg. for murder (VGR 31 May 70)

HAMILTON, Robert, adv. that he has admitted his brother, James HAMILTON, into partnership (CMAG 22 Oct 96)

HAMILTON, Sukey, cook to the late governor, will be sold on 15 Dec. along with her seven year old dau. (VG 24 Nov 68)

HAMILTON, Capt. Thomas, of the State Legion, d. on 15 Sep. at Yorktown (VGAA 28 Sep 82)

HAMIL[T]ON, William, says he was born near Dumfries, Scotland, worked on the Western Branch of Elizabeth [River] and was last seen going for Edenton, N. Carolina; des. from Lt. FLEMING at Suffolk on 24 Sep. (VG 3 Oct 55)

HAMMACK, Riedy, of Frederick Co., dec'd, e.a.w. his extx., Elizabeth HAMMACK, and ex., John HAMMACK (VGWA 26 Mar 88)

HAMMOND Family, Hampshire Co., 18 Nov 1795, in chancery: Charles WELLS (compl.) against Richard CURSON and David M'MECHAN surviving trustees of William HAMMOND dec'd, and Margaret HAMMOND, Harriet HAMMOND, Camilla HAMMOND, Thomas K[?]O, Cumberland DUGAN and Margaret his wife, Nicholas R. MOORE and Sarah his wife, heirs of William HAMMOND dec'd (defs.) (BVCG 30 Nov 95)

HAMMOND, Isaac C., of Norfolk, intends to leave the state (NH 10 Apr 98)

HAMMOND, Joel, mar. Miss Rebecca DURELL of Petersburg on Thurs. last (VGPI 10 May 96)

HAMMOND, Mary Ann, wife of Stephen HAMMOND of Norfolk, who will no longer be responsible for her debts (VCGA 26 May 94)

HANAN, William, Eng. ind. svt., c. 25, shoemaker, ran away from Elias BARNABY and Archibald MIDLIMIST, Petersburg (VG 2 May 77)

HANBURY, John, merch. of this city [Wmsbrg.] d. at Coggeshall in Essex last Mon. (*London Chronicle* of 24 Jun 58) (VG-Randolph 24 Jun 58)

HANCOCK, George, of Chesterfield Co., dec'd, his ex., Arthur HANCOCK, will give his est. up to the legatees on 15 Apr. (VGGA 4 Jan 99)

HANCOCK, John, mar. Miss Ailcey NEWTON of Pr. Anne Co. (VCNPGA 19 Oct 93)

HANCOCK, Lt. John, mar. Miss Keziah READ of Pr. Anne Co. on Thurs. night (NH 25 May 99)

HANCOCK, Robert, of Norfolk, sentenced to death for the burglary of Samuel SMITH's storehouse (VG 16 Dec 37)

HANDLEY, Daniel, executed on 25 Nov. for robbery (VG 25 Nov 37)

HANEY, Thomas, appr. of Stephen MAHANY living on Cedar Cr., Shenandoah

Co., c. 18, was killed by lightning on Thurs. 2 Jul. (Rights of Man 29 Jul 95)

HANNA, George, drowned while attempting to cross the Roanoke River on Wed. the 30th ult.; it is understood he has left a wife and seven chil. (Winchester disp. of 13 Jun.) (VGGA 26 Jun 98)

HANNAH, Andrew, mar. Miss WILSON in Portsmouth on Thurs. eve. last (NH 6 Feb 96)

HANNAH, Capt. Nicholas, of the U.S. 3rd Sub-Legion, d. in Alexandria on Sat. 11 Oct. (BVCG 20 Oct 94)

HANNAM, Minty, left Eng. c. 1768 and was heard of at a Mr. Christopher CURDIFF's, Great Choptank River, Bollingbrook, Talbot Co., Md. in 1771; if he is alive he may hear of something to his advantage by writing to the Rev. Mr. Reader WAREHAM, Dorsetshire, Eng. (VIC 4 Mar 89)

HANNAY, Patrick, of the firm of Smith & Hannay, dec'd (VSPW 4 Jun 95); owing to his death, the business of Smith & Hannay was dissolved on the 11th inst. (VSPW 25 Jul 95)

HANOVER, William, Negro, 40, house carpenter, ran away from the plant. of William FITZHUGH Esq. in Kg. Geo. Co.; suspected of going to Lancaster Co. where his wife has been lately removed (VGR 5 Oct 69)

HANSBOROUGH, John, of Kg. Geo. Co., mar. Miss Nancy BANKS dau. of Adam BANKS of Madison, in Madison Co. on 9 Aug. (VHFA 28 Aug 98)

HANSFORD, Mrs. Ann, of the Borough of Norfolk, relict of the late Lewis HANSFORD Esq., d. Sun. morn. last [2 Nov.] in her 69th year; her PE will be sold at auction (NPJ 5 Nov, 3 Dec 88)

HANSFORD, Charles, of York Co., died (VG 8 May 78); e.a.w. his extx., Elizabeth HANSFORD (VG 5 Mar 79)

HANSON, Miss Nancy, dau. of Col. Samuel HANSON of Alexandria, d. last Tues. (BVCG 22 Jul 93)

HANSON, Richard, of Petersburg, intends for Great Britain soon (VG 20 Nov 66)

HANSON, William H., Deputy Collector at City Point, Richmond, d. on Wed. afternoon [Wed. last acc. to VH] in his 22nd year (VGGA 2 Oct, VH 12 Oct 98)

HAPPER, Samuel, his devisee is Thomas HAPPER; mentioned in a chancery case, Andrew MARTIN against Alexander GORDON et al., Norfolk Co. Ct. 20 Mar 1798 (NH 4 Apr 98)

HAPPER, William, of Charles City Co., dec'd, his extx., Mary HAPPER, and ex., William RITCHIE, will sell his est. (VGAA 21 Jan 86)

HARBEY, John, late of York Co., dec'd, e.a.w. his ex., Allen CHAPMAN (VG 10 Jul 78)

HARDAWAY Family, Brunswick Co. Ct., 29 May 1798, in chanc: William T. PENNINGTON and Mary his wife (formerly Mary HARDAWAY) gdn. of Hartwell HARDAWAY and Rebecca HARDAWAY (compls.) against John CLARKE ex. of Elisha CLARKE dec'd, John WILLIAMS, Jonas WILLIAMS, Lewelling WILLIAMS, William STAINBACK, and Richard PELKINGTON (VGPI 3 Jul 98)

HARDESEY, George, was mar. to Miss Polley CHIPLEY dau. of Capt. William CHIPLEY, last Thurs. by the Rev. Mr. MONTGOMERY (VGWA 20 Aug 88)

HARDESTY,, Mary, has left her husband, George HARDESTY, Loudoun Co. (PGBA 9 Sep 93)

HARDGRAVES, Charles, conv. svt., ran away from Edmund TERRILL and Clement READE, Culpeper Co. (VG 4 Jun 72)

HARDIE, John, conv. svt., 60 odd yrs. of age, pretends to be a miller by trade, speaks the West Country dialect, ran away from Spencer BALL and Richard HULL, Northumberland Co. (MG 11 Jul 54)

HARDIN, Erasmus, late of Dinwiddie Co., dec'd, his ex. (nfi) will sell his gristmill (VG 27 Aug 72 sup)

HARDIN, [Geor]ge, Irish, 35, des. from Capt. MERCER's Co. of Va. forces at Ft. Cumberland (VG 22 Aug 55)

HARDING, Charles, aka Dick, mulatto slave, c. 30, carpenter and joiner; he learned his trade from Lewis ALLMORN of Nansemond Co. who sold him to Edward VOSS, bricklayer; he ran away and lived in K & Q Co. then went to

Philadelphia and Hanover [Pa.] and later to Baltimore Co. [Md.] where he lived as a free man from about 1765 to 1772; a reward for his capture is offered by Samuel OWINGS Jr. and Alexander WELLS, Soldier's Delight, Baltimore Co., Md. (PC 20 Jul 72)

HARDING, George, late of Halifax Co., lately left to settle his affairs in Stafford Co. where he d. suddenly (VGR 11 Feb 68)

HARDING, Thomas, of Goochland Co., will leave the state on the last of Sep. (VGGA 9 Aug 99)

HARDING, William, b. in Va., enl. at Dumfries on 29 Jul 1794, des. from Ft. Norfolk (AGNPPA 8 May 95, HNPA 13 May 95)

HARDWICK, John, svt., 20, ran away from John AYLETT, Kg. Wm. Co. (VG 15 Jun 39)

HARDY, John, of Stafford Co., will not pay any debts which his wife, Hannah HARDY, contracts (VHFA 17 Jan 93)

HARDY, the Hon. Samuel Esq., delegate from Va. to the U.S. Congress, d. Mon. the 17th inst. at his home in Beekman St., New York [City]; [long obit. in VJAA] (VJAA 27 Oct, BMG 28 Oct, VGAA 29 Oct 85)

HARDY, William Esq., late a member of the GA from Isle of Wight Co., d. on 30 Dec. (VGGA 31 Dec 94, VGRMA 1 Jan 95, VGRC 3 Jan 95)

HARDYMAN, Capt. Littlebury, dec'd, his ex., William Green MUNFORD and Littlebury IRBY, will sell all his PE at Indiandale, Charles City Co. (VG 21 Nov 71)

HARDYMAN, William, of Charles City Co., mar. Miss Nancy BLACK dau. of William BLACK Esq. of Chesterfield Co. (VG 17 Jun 75)

HARE, Moses, dec'd, Moses HARE (nfi) will sell his plant. in Hertford Co., N. Carolina (VG 28 Jun 74 sup)

HARE, William, late of K & Q Co., dec'd, his ex. is William B. HARE of Amherst Co. (VGGA 12 Jun 98)

HARE, Dr. William B., of Amherst Co., mar. Miss Eliza CABELL dau. of Nicholas CABELL Esq. of the same co., on the 11th inst. (VGGA 24 Jul 93)

HARGRAVE, Samuel, of Caroline Co., dec'd, e.a.w. his acting ex., Jesse HARGRAVE (RMA 31 Aug 96 sup)

HARL, John, son of John HARL Sr., ran away from his father near the Falls of the Potomac, Loudoun Co.; his father adv. that he is under age and will not be of age til next Dec. 29 and his intention is to go to Abingdon, Washington Co., where his brother, Leander HARL, died and there forge his father's hand thinking to get what property Leander has left (CMAG 7 May 95)

HARLAN, Stephen, dec'd, his ex., Jesse HARLAN and Jehu HARLAN, will sell his PE (PGBA 26 Jan 97)

HARMAN, Anna, bound girl, ran away from Jacob BUCHER, Shepherdstown (WG 13 Mar 99)

HARMAN, James, aka Bob, Negro, ran away from Walter SMITH, Snow Hill, Worcester Co., Md. (CMAG 6 Apr 97)

HARMER, George Esq., native of Bristol, Eng., d. on Tues. last at Dr. GILMOUR's in Albemarle Co. (VIC 20 Sep 86, VGPI 21 Sep 86)

HARMER, William, c. 18, ran away from Tristram BUTLER, Alexandria (TAA 28 May 98); appr., 19-20, ran away from the schooner *Mercury* a Norfolk and Alexandria packet (CMAG 5 Nov 99)

HARMON, Ann, Eng. svt., c. 20, ran away from John CORRIES of Piscataway, Essex Co. (VG 1 Oct 36)

HARN, James, aka HARRINGHAM, Negro (or mulatto) ind. svt., ran away from William PEACHEY, Richmond Co. last Jul. (VG 4 Nov 63)

HARNESS, Michael, killed by Indians on 20 Aug. in Welton's Meadow on Loony's Cr. (Wmsbrg. disp. of 16 Sep.) (NYPB 6 Oct 63)

HARP Brothers, [two brothers, possibly from N. Carolina, who went on a killing spree in Ky. and Tennessee in 1798 and 1799]; Micajah HARP (c. 30-32) and his younger brother, Wiley, were believed involved in the following murders: Mr. STUMP, killed on Big Barren; Mr. LANGFORD, killed last winter in the Wilderness; the 12-14 year old son of Mr. TRABUE on Green River [Ky.]; [Mr.

DOOLEY]; Mr. HARDIN, killed about the middle of Jul. three miles below Knoxville; William BALLARD, killed on 24 or 25 Jul. near Knoxville; Isaac COFFEE, found dead on 25 Jul. on Beaver Cr. about eight miles from Knoxville; James BRAZEL (or BRASEL), brother of Robert found murdered on 29 Jul. on the road leading to Stockton's (or Stogden's) Valley in Cumberland Co., Ky.; John TULLY, killed in Stockton's Valley; the HARPs and their wives were arrested but escaped from jail in Danville, Ky. in late Aug.; on 22 Aug. they killed the wife and child of [Moses] STAGLE (or STIGALL) on Pond River, Muhlenberg Co., Ky. and two men [HUDGENS and GILMORE] near Robertson's Lick; they were pursued by a party of men [including Moses STAGLE] which captured Micajah HARP (or "Big Harp") and cut off his head; [Wiley HARP (or "Little Harp") was hanged several yrs. later in Miss.]. [For details, see: Lewis Collins' *History of Kentucky*, 1882, vol. II: 345-352] (KG 15 Aug, 5 Sep 99; WG 12 May, 21 Aug 99; VF 16 Oct 99)

HARPER, [Master], son of William HARPER, was drowned this morn. at Hartshorne's Wharf (TAA 22 Aug 97)

HARPER, Christopher, svt., bricklayer, with his wife, Ann HARPER c. 40, ran away from William WAITE, Belhaven (MG 29 Aug 54)

HARPER, Edward, merch., mar. Miss HIGGINSON at Alexandria (VJAA 15 Dec 85)

HARPER, Col. J. A., d. on Thurs. night last at his house in this borough [Norfolk] (NH 2 Mar 99)

HARPER, James, of Portsmouth, mar. Miss DUNN of the same place on 26 Nov (NPC 3 Dec 91)

HARPER, John, of Mecklenburg Co., dec'd, e.a.w. his ex., Wyatt HARPER (VGPI 25 May 98)

HARPER, Nathaniel, dec'd, e.a.w. his admr., Joseph Wells HARPER of Dinwiddie Co. (VGPI 20 May 96)

HARRINGTON, the Hon. Paul Esq., one of the judges of the High Court of Appeals, in his 65th year, mar. Miss SIMMS, aged 15, of Halifax Co. on Tues. the 6th inst. (VGGA 4 Apr 92)

HARRIS Family, HCC, 22 May 90: Thomas TREVILLIAN and William HARRIS, ex. of John HARRIS dec'd, and Robert HARRIS, and the sd. William HARRIS (pltfs.) against John THILMAN, John PITMAN, and Richard BOWLER (defs.) (VICGA 23 Jun 90)

HARRIS, Anne, svt., 30, big with child, ran away from Jacob Andrew MINITREE, Charles Co., Md. (VG 7 Mar 51)

HARRIS, Billy, black, executed at the gallows near [Richmond] yesterday (VGWA 20 Aug 96)

HARRIS, Charles, appr. barber, 18, ran away from William PEAK, York Co. (VG 18 Jul 51)

HARRIS, Edward, of Southampton Co., dec'd, e.a.w. his ex., Peyton HARRIS and James HARRIS of the same co. (VGGA 14 Mar 98)

HARRIS, Mrs. Elizabeth, of Jamestown, died (VG 25 Mar 80)

HARRIS, Jack, mulatto, c. 20, ran away from William HARDYMAN, Charles City Co. (VG 11 Jul 71)

HARRIS, James, appr., 18-19, ran away from Leven DORSEY, Norfolk (NHPA 27 Mar 97)

HARRIS, John, Welsh svt., ran away from Humphrey BROOKE, Kg. Wm. Co. (VG 4 Aug 38, AWM 21 Sep 38)

HARRIS, John, of Surry Co., dec'd, his lands there to be sold by his ex., Christopher MACRAE and Michael NICHOLSON (VG 7 Mar 71)

HARRIS, John, aka Johnny, mulatto slave who formerly waited upon the late Peyton RANDOLPH Esq., ran away from Edmond RANDOLPH, his nephew (VGPu 12 Dec 77)

HARRIS, John, of Caroline Co., dec'd, his ex. (nfi) will sell all his PE; George GUY, the admr., will sell the property of Mrs. Sarah HARRIS (nfi) dec'd (VG 30 Oct 78)

HARRIS, John, dec'd, commonly known as "Little Fighting Jack" of Hanover

Co., e.a.w. David CRENSHAW and John CHRISTIAN (nfi) (VGCD 30 Oct 79)

HARRIS, John, of Powhatan Co., desires to move to the Western Country and will sell his lands in Powhatan, Buckingham, and other cos. (VIC 22 Oct 88)

HARRIS, Capt. John, of Powhatan Co., mar. Miss Rebecca BRITTON of Chesterfield Co. on Sat. the 24th ult. (VGRMA 5 Jun 94)

HARRIS, John Skipp, late of Amelia Co., his admx., Sarah HARRIS of Cumberland Co., desires to settle all accounts (VG 25 Apr 77)

HARRIS, Jonathan Jr., of Fredsbrg., d. at Demerara [Guyana?] on the 21st ult. in his 20th year (VH 13 Aug 99)

HARRIS, Jordan, mar. Miss Betsy CANNON eld. dau. of Col. William CANNON of Buckingham Co. on Thurs. last (VIC 8 Apr 89)

HARRIS, Joseph, d. suddenly on Sun. night; he left a widow and four young chil. (PGBA 5 Sep 95); late of Martinsburg, e.a.w. his admx., Jane HARRIS (PGBA 28 Apr 96)

HARRIS, Lee, dec'd, e.a.w. his ex., William HARRIS and Joseph SHELTON (VGGA 19 Apr 97)

HARRIS, Mrs. Margaret, spouse of Hamlin HARRIS of Nottoway Co., d. there on the 31st ult. (VGPI 31 Jan 93)

HARRIS, Robert, aka Bob, slave, c. 28, raised in the HUBBARD Family in Gloucester Co., ran away from Robert BURTON, Granville Co., N. Carolina (VGGA 4 Apr 92)

HARRIS, Robin, aka Bob, mulatto, 28-30, ran away from Willis MILLS, Warminster, Amherst Co. (Arg 12 Mar 99)

HARRIS, William, svt., bricklayer, ran away from Dr. William FLOOD's where he was at work; he says his master's name is Joseph PEIRCE of Westmoreland Co.; jailed in Norfolk (VGR 12 Jul 70)

HARRIS, William, mulatto, enl. in the lower end of New Kent Co., but is expected to be lurking about Charles City Co.; des. from Capt. Thomas MASSIE's new recruits for the 6th Va. Regt. (VGPu 21 Nov 77)

HARRIS, William, late of Albemarle Co., dec'd, e.a.w. his ex., William HARRIS, John HARRIS, and Benjamin HARRIS (VGGA 19 Nov 94)

HARRISON Family, Fauquier Co., 25 May 1791, in chanc: Charles GARNER (compl.) against Benjamin HARRISON surviving ex. of Thomas HARRISON, Burr HARRISON, Jane HARRISON admx. of William HARRISON dec'd, Thomas GARNER son and heir of John GARNER dec'd, Vincent GARNER, Parish GARNER, and James GARNER (defs.) (VGWA 30 [Jul] 91)

HARRISON Family, Shenandoah Co. Ct., 14 Feb 1794, in chanc: Catherine HARRISON, Matthew HARRISON, Cuthbert HARRISON, Thomas HARRISON, and Mary-Ann HARRISON chil. and heirs at law of Burr HARRISON dec'd and the sd. Matthew HARRISON ex. of the sd, Burr HARRISON (compls.) (BVCG 21 Jul 94)

HARRISON, Mrs., the lady of Benjamin HARRISON Jr. Esq. of Brandon, d. last Mon. at Col. William ALLEN's in Surry Co. in the flower of her age (VG 26 Nov 67)

HARRISON, Mrs., spouse of Charles HARRISON Esq. of Huntington in Surry Co., d. on the 25th ult. (VGPu and VGP 10 Aug 75, VG 12 Aug 75)

HARRISON, Mrs. Anna, spouse of Benjamin HARRISON Jr. Esq. of Richmond, d. on Tues. morn. [28 Aug] (VIC 29 Aug 87, VGWeA 30 Aug 87)

HARRISON, Maj. Benjamin, son of the Hon. Nathaniel HARRISON Esq. former Auditor General of the Colony, mar. Miss Susanna DIGGES dau. of the Hon. Cole DIGGES Esq. one of H.M's Council, on 23 Aug. (VG 24 Aug 39)

HARRISON, Col. Benjamin, of Berkeley, Charles City Co., for many yrs. a rep. in the Assembly, was killed last Friday [12 Jul] with his two younger daus. when lightning struck his house (MG 16 Aug 45, AWM 22 Aug 45)

HARRISON, Benjamin Esq., dec'd, his PE will be sold at Berkeley in Charles City Co. by his admrs. [w.w.a] Benjamin HARRISON Jr. and Carter B. HARRISON (VGGA 28 Dec 91, 4 Jan 92)

HARRISON, Benjamin, late of Fauquier Co., dec'd, all his personal property to

be sold by his ex., Benjamin BOTTS of Dumfries (VHFA 14 Feb 98)
HARRISON, Benjamin Jr., of Berkeley, mar. Miss Sukey RANDOLPH eld. dau. of Col. Richard RANDOLPH of Curle's (VGPu 19 Apr 76 ps)
HARRISON, Carter Henry, late of Cumberland Co., dec'd, his ex., Robert C. HARRISON and Peyton HARRISON, adv. that the division of his est. will take place about the 1st of Jan. next [1797] (RMA 12 Sep 95, 28 May 96)
HARRISON, Gen. Charles, of Surry Co., d. at Osborne's on Thurs. the 12th inst. (VGWeA 13 Dec 93, VGGA 25 Dec 93); e.a.w. his admr., James BELSCHES, Cabin Point (VGGA 15 Jun 96)
HARRISON, Charles Sr., dec'd, e.a.w. his admr., Matt. M. CLAIBORNE (VGPI 29 Nov 96)
HARRISON, Capt. Cuthbert, of Pr. Wm. Co., dec'd, items of his est. to be sold by his ex., William ALEXANDER and Seth HARRISON (VGAA 18 Oct 83)
HARRISON, Cuthbert, att. at law of Harrisonburg, d. on the 26th ult. in Staunton (VHFA 8 May 95)
HARRISON, Capt. Henry, of Sussex Co., dec'd, his admr., Nathaniel HARRISON, will sell his PE (VG 2 Apr, 8 Oct 72, 1 Nov 76)
HARRISON, Jacob, mar. Miss Patsey PROSSER on Thurs. 31st ult., both of this city (VGGA 6 Jan 96)
HARRISON, James, [a eulogy to him by "A. M." of Caroline Co.; he d. in his 20th year] (VG 26 May 68)
HARRISON, James, late of Brunswick Co., dec'd, e.a.w. his ex., Robert HARRISON and Willie HARRISON (VGPI 13 May 96)
HARRISON, Matthew, appr. tailor, ran away from John S. SALUSBURY, Princess Anne Co. (VCGA 31 Jul 94)
HARRISON, Nathaniel, Virginian, of Pr. Geo. Co., 34, may have fled with his svt. Caesar (under sentence of death); a reward is offered (VG 12 Mar 52)
HARRISON, Nathaniel, dec'd, a tract of his land on Meherrin River in Brunswick Co. to be sold on 28 Apr. (VGAA 8 Feb 83); e.a.w. his ex., Edmund HARRISON, Robert GILLIAM, and William GILLIAM (VGAA 19 Jul 83)
HARRISON, Obadiah R., of Kg. Geo. Co., d. the 10th inst. (VHFA 21 Aug 94)
HARRISON, Peter E., late of Bute Co., N. Carolina, dec'd, e.a.w. his admr., Nath. HARRISON (VGPu 17 Oct 77)
HARRISON, Robert, late of Charles City Co., dec'd, Nathaniel HARRISON, the admr. of Henry HARRISON dec'd, will sell all of the PE of the sd. Robert HARRISON (VG 28 Oct 75)
HARRISON, the Hon. Robert Hanson, Chief Judge of the General Ct. of Md., d at his seat on Potomac, Charles Co., Md. on 2 Apr. in his 41st year (VHFA 15 Apr 90); e.a.w. his admr., Walter H. HARRISON (VGAxA 17 Jun 90)
HARRISON, Capt. Samuel, d. in [Alexandria] (CMAG 13 Feb 96); e.a.w. his admr., P. MARSTELLER, who requests that anyone indebted to the est. of his late wife, Barbara HARRISON, make immediate payments to him (CMAG 24 Jan 97)
HARRISON, Mrs. Susannah, dec'd, her admr., Nathaniel HARRISON, will sell 11 young Negroes and all of her PE at Wakefield in Surry Co. (VGPu 3 Oct 77)
HARRISON, Thomas, svt., c. 25, weaver, b. in the north of Eng., ran away from Alexander KNOX, Boyd's Hole (VG 3 Sep 72)
HARRISON, William, of Watt's Park, Dinwiddie Co., advises the public that his brother, Thomas HARRISON, who came into the country last fall has been imposing on his friends and William wishes the public to know that he is not responsible for his brother's actions (VG 3 Sep 67)
HARRISS, William, late of Surry Co., dec'd, e.a.w. James FLETCHER his admr. of Nottoway Co., who will also sell part of his est. on the plant. known as Broomfield and in Nottoway Co. at the plant. whereon Mr. [Hamlin] HARRISS now lives (VGPI 24 Nov 97)
HARROW, Mrs., consort of Gilbert HARROW of Fredsbrg, d. on Sun. last (RCFPC 25 Jan 97)
HARRY, James, killed on the north side of the Cumberland near the mouth of Red River in Mero District on 18 Feb. (VGRMA 15 Apr 93)

HARSHAW, Archibald, of Northampton Co., intends to leave the state for S. Carolina in a few weeks (VCNPGA 3 Nov 92)

HART Family, Augusta Co. Ct., 19 Aug. 1797, chancery case mentions Alexander ROBERTSON, David STEPHENSON, and John SMITH exors. of Silas HART dec'd, and Oliver HART, Silas HART, Josiah HART, Joseph HART, Edith HOUGH, John THOMAS, Betty THOMAS, Nelly THOMAS, and Joseph [COL]BERT heirs and heirs at law of Silas HART dec'd (VGSWA 20 Oct 97)

HART, Andrew, killed in an accident near Martinsburg on Thurs. eve. last (PGBA 19 May 94)

HART, Isaac, conv. svt. 16-17, calls himself a Jew, ran away from Richard BAYNE, Halifax Co. (VGNI 8 Sep 74)

HART, John, of the partnership of Allen & Hart, dec'd, e.a.w. his admr., James SEMPLE of New Kent Co. (VGPu 10 Jul 78)

HART, Silas, dec'd, his ex., David STEPHENSON, Alexander ROBERTSON, and John SMITH, will sell his 234 ac. tract in Rockingham Co. (BVCG 17 Mar 97)

HART, Thomas, Irish svt., tailor, c. 23, ran away from William BLYTH, Fredsbrg. (VGP 21 Sep 75)

HART, William, Irish svt., ran away from [?] in Chestertown, Md (VG 4 Sep 46)

HART, William, of Surry Co., d. a few days past (NPC 10 Oct 89)

HARTLEY, James, dec'd, e.a.w. his widow and admx., Letecia HARTLEY (CMAG 27 Aug 99)

HARTMANN, Sieur George Charles Frederick, formerly an NCO [or subaltern officer] in the Brunswick troops; in 1780 he resided in Loudoun Co.; he settled near Knowland's Ferry about three miles from the Potomac where he mar. a farmer's dau. who was a linen weaver and he took up the same profession; if he will apply to David ANDERSON Jr., Hanover Town, he will deliver into his hands proper credentials of his being heir to a very considerable inheritance in Brunswick; he must present himself there by the last of Feb. 1788 to claim it (VIC 15, 22 Aug 87, VJAA 6 Dec 87)

HARVEY, Mrs., relict of the late William HARVEY Esq., d. in Fredsbrg. Thurs. last (VHFA 2 Jun 98)

HARVEY, Dr. Mungo, native of North Britain, d. at his seat in Westmoreland Co. on his birthday, the 21st inst., aged 60 (VHFA 27 Mar 94)

HARVEY, William Esq., mar. Mrs. KERR of Norfolk (VG 4 Feb 75)

HARVEY, William, Irish, 22, absconded from the employ of Joseph DELAHAYE, hairdresser, of Alexandria (TAA 2 Mar 98)

HARVEY, William, Mayor of Fredsbrg., d. last Thurs. in his 50th year (VHFA 17 Mar 98); e.a.w. his admr., David C. KER and Jacob KUHN of Fredsbrg. (VHFA 2 May 98, GLFFA 3 Jul 98)

HARWOOD, Mrs., widow of Humphrey HARWOOD late of Wmsbrg., d. on San. last (VGWeA 19 Feb 89)

HARWOOD, Benjamin, mulatto son of a white man, c. 40, bel. to Sir Peyton SKIPWITH, ran off with a black boy, horse, and luggage bel. to Robert SKIPWITH between Petersburg and Hick's Ford (VG 10 Jul, VGP 21 Aug 78)

HARWOOD, Christopher, d. on Sat. last in K & Q Co. (VGRC 6 Apr 93); Margaret HARWOOD (nfi) will rent his tavern at K & Q Ct. H. (VGGA 21 Aug 93)

HARWOOD, Col. Humphrey, of Wmsbrg., d. on Sun. last (VGWeA 27 Nov 88, VIC 3 Dec 88); e.a.w. his ex., William HARWOOD Jr. of Wmsbrg. (VGWeA 30 Apr, 14 May 89, 26 Aug 90)

HARWOOD, Maj. Samuel, dec'd, e.a.w. his ex., John TYLER, of Charles City Co. (VGPu 29 May 78, VGAA 10 Jan 84)

HARWOOD, Thomas Sr., d. on Tues. eve. last at his seat near Richmond in his 53rd year (RMA 11 Jul 95); e.a.w. his admx., Frances HARWOOD of Henrico Co. (RC 3 Nov 95)

HARWOOD, Maj. William, of Warwick Co., d. after falling from his horse on Thurs. the 2nd inst. (VG 10 Jun 37)

HARWOOD, Capt. William, d. in K & Q Co. on the 16th inst. in his 39th year

(VGR and VG 30 Sep 73); his ex., Benjamin PENDLETON, will sell his slaves and other items at K & Q Ct. H. (VGR 27 Jan 74)

HARWOOD, William, d. at K & Q Ct. H. on the 16th of the present month in his 31st year leaving a wife and infant [obit.] (VIC 26 Aug 89); e.a.w. his ex., Benjamin PENDLETON and William COURTNEY (VGPA 13 Mar 90)

HARWOOD, William, dec'd, his ex., John ALLEN, will sell a tract of his land in Henrico Co. adjoining the lands of James HARWOOD, Elisha HARWOOD, and Maj. JONES (VICGA 14 Jul 90)

HARWOOD, William, arrived from Eng. about 1774 with his son aged 10-11 and is supposed to have settled near Fredsbrg. or Alexandria; he will learn something to his advantage by applying to T. GREEN, Printer, in Fredsbrg. (VHFA 24 Jun 90, VGAxA 1 Jul 90)

HASH, the Hon. Abner Esq., delegate for N. Carolina in the U.S. Congress, d. at New York on the 2nd inst. (VIC 27 Dec 86)

HASKINS Family, a pet. will be presented to the next Assembly for a law to empower the chil. of Edward HASKINS and Thomas HASKINS by their gdn. to make a title to the lands willed them by Creed HASKINS (VGGA 17 Sep 94)

HASKINS, Col. Creed, of Chesterfield Co., dec'd, his ex., Thomas HASKINS of the same co., will sell his tract near Bebil's Bridge (VGGA 17 Oct 92, 9 Oct 93)

HASLAM, James, Eng. svt., c. 25, ran away from William RENICK, Augusta Co. (VGR 8 Feb 70)

HASSET, Dennis, Irish ind. svt., 24, ran away from Peter CIRVILL, Alexandria (VJAA 21 Oct 84)

HASSET, Sarah, [Irish] svt., c. 20, b. in Co. Limerick, ran away from William JACKSON, Orange Co., N. Carolina last Nov. (VG 17 Feb 74)

HASWELL, John, from Westmoreland Co., recruit in the Va. Regt., des. from the camp in Fredsbrg. (MG 23 Sep 62)

HATCHER, Benjamin, of Manchester, mar. Miss Polly CRUMP of Powhatan Co. (VGGA 27 Jun 92)

HATFIELD, Richard, aka HATTER, Negro, born free but now indented; he has a brother at Col. CARY's and another at Mr. BALFOUR's; ran away from Samuel LAMBUTH, Smithfield (VG 18 May 69)

HATRIDGE, Robert, merch., late of Washington, N. Carolina, d. on Tues. eve. last (NPC 3 Dec 91)

HATTER, William, svt., 20, ran away from John AYLETT, Kg. Wm. Co. (VG 15 Jun 39)

HATTERSLAY, William, dec'd, his admr., Samuel HATTERSLAY of Alexandria, adv. that all those indebted to his are desired to make payment to Pomery & Isabel, merchants, in Alexandria (CMAG 29 Oct 95)

HATTON, George, b. in Nansemond Co., d. the latter end of Aug. at Amwell N. Jersey in his 103rd year; he had been a soldier under Bacon (Phil. disp. of 19 Sep.) (NYPB 23 Sep 51)

HATTON, James, Eng., des. from Capt. David BELL's Co. of the Va. Regt. (VG 21 Nov 55)

HATTON, Richard, conv. boy, 12-13, ran away from George GRAHAM [Dumfries] (VGR 23 Jul 67)

HATTON, Thomas, dec'd, e.a.w. his admr., Samuel HATTON, Indian Cr. (NHPA 14 Oct 97)

HATTON, William, aka JACKSON, svt., 28-30, ran away from Kingsbury Furnace Mine Bank near Baltimore, Md. (VGR 29 Sep 68)

HAUKS, John, ind. svt., 23, shoemaker, ran away from James Campbell & Co., Norfolk (VG 15 Feb 70)

HAW, Sally, free light mulatto woman, c. 19, reportedly ran away with a Negro man named Syphax from Lancaster Co. (VGGA 30 Sep 95)

HAWES, John, Dutch svt., 20, ran away from John TANKERSLEY and John CATLETT, Port Royal (VHFA 23 Apr 89)

HAWK, Richard, Eng. conv. svt., c. 55, ran away from Arthur EDWARDS and Thomas ASKREN, Loudoun Co. (VGPu 26 Jul 76)

HAWKINS, Benjamin, native of Eng., says he came into this country in 1767 an(

served his time with Mr. HARPIRON of Dunmore Co., jailed in Northumberland Co. (VGPu 2 Feb 76)

HAWKINS, Francis, of Norfolk, d. at Port-au-Prince the day after he arrived (NHPA 30 Jan 97)

HAWKINS, George Francis Esq., of Pr. Geo. Co., Md., dec'd, portions of his est. to be sold by his extx., Susanna T. HAWKINS (VJAA 3 Nov 85)

HAWKINS, James, appr., 18, ran away from the brig *Brenchley* of London (VGAxA 29 Apr 90)

HAWKINS, John, dec'd, his extx. is Mary HAWKINS who has moved to Ky. (VGGA 21 May 94, VGRMA 22 Dec 94)

HAWKINS, Joseph, of Spotsylvania Co., intends to move immediately to Ky. (VHFA 4 Nov 90)

HAWKINS, Mrs. Susanna, d. in Pr. Geo. Co., Md. (VGAxA 6 May 90)

HAWKINS, William, of Orange Co., dec'd, e.a.w. his admr., Reuben HAWKINS (VH 5 Nov 99)

HAY Family, HCC, 11 Mar 1797: Richard Henry [BRADFORD] and Peggy his wife (pltfs.) and William HAY in his own right and as ex. of John HAY and admr. of Peter HAY, and James BAIRD and John M'GEORGE surviving partners of John Hay & Co., Benjamin PARKER ex. of Dolly PARKER dec'd, John FORESTER and Elizabeth his wife, Jane WHITE and [?] exors. of Ninion MINZIES (defs.); it appears that James BAIRD, John M'GEORGE, John and Elizabeth FORESTER, and Jane WHITE and [?] are not inhabitants of this country (VGGA 19 Apr 97)

HAY, Mrs., cons. of William HAY Esq. of Richm., d. on Sat. last (Arg. 12 Dec 96)

HAY, Anthony, master of the Raleigh Tavern in Wmsbrg., d. of cancer on the 4th inst. leaving a large family (VG 13 Dec 70); e.a.w. his ex., William TREBELL and Robert NICOLSON, who will also sell his tavern and other items of his est. (VG 17 Jan 71)

HAY, Charles Esq., of Richmond, d. on Mon. 20 Jul (or the 21st acc. to VHFA and BVCG) at the seat of Sampson MATTHEWS Esq. [near] Staunton in Augusta Co. on his return from the Sweet Springs where he had been for the recovery of his health; he had been Clerk of the House of Delegates for several yrs. (VGGA 29 Jul 95 ps, RMA 30 Jul 95, VHFA 31 Jul 95, BVCG 10 Aug 95); e.a.w. his ex., George HAY of Richmond (RMA 12 Sep 95); his ex. will sell his house and lot in Richmond (VGGA 4 Nov 95)

HAY, Mrs. Elizabeth, relict of Anthony HAY of Wmsbrg., d. there on the 14th inst. (VIC 23 May 87)

HAY, Mrs. Grissel, of Wmsbrg., died (VG 8 May 78)

HAY, John, Scot, ind. svt., house joiner, ran away from Ry. RANDOLPH, Henrico Co. (VGR 13 Apr 69)

HAY, John, merch., at Cobham in Surry Co., mar. Miss JORDAN of Nansemond (VG 22 Mar 70)

HAY, John, of Yorktown, d. after a lingering illness (VGPu 5 Dec 77)

HAY, John, son of John HAY dec'd late a merch. of this city [Richmond], d. on Sun. the 1st inst. in his 2nd year (VGWeA 7 Sep 82)

HAY, John, of Richmond, mar. Miss Mary MAURY dau. of the late Rev. Walter MAURY of Orange Co., in Fredsbrg. on Fri. last (VHFFA 28 Feb 97)

HAY, Dr. Peter, physician, d. at his house in Wmsbrg. on [26 Nov.] at an advanced age; his library to be sold by his ex., Philip Whitehead CLAIBORNE (VG and VGR 27 Nov 66, VGR 29 Jan 67); his ex., Philip W. CLAIBORNE, widow Grissel HAY, and infant chil.: David, Robert, Lydia, Helen, and Mary, are summoned to Ct. of Hustings for Wmsbrg. to answer a bill in chancery (VG 8 Dec 68)

HAY, Peter, merch. of Richmond, died (VGWeA 16 Feb 82)

HAY, Miss Polly, sister of Charles HAY dec'd, d. on Sun. morn. last (RC 3 Nov 95, VGGA 4 Nov 95, RMA 5 Nov 95)

HAY, Thomas, one of the young gentlemen in the Secretary's Office, d. last Tues. eve. (VG and VGR 31 Mar 74)

HAY, William Esq., of Surry Co., att. at law, mar. Miss Betsey CARY of

Southampton (VG 22 Dec 74)

HAY, William, of Richmond, will travel to Philadelphia with part of his family; he has authorized his nephew, William FORRESTER, to manage his private affairs (VGGA 19 Oct 96)

HAYDON, Jarvis, dec'd, his ex., Jesse HAYDON, will sell a tract of his land containing 130 ac. in Spotsylvania Co. (VHFFA 19 Apr 96)

HAYES, James, of Richmond, mar. Mrs. HARDYMAN relict of the late William HARDYMAN Esq., on Sat. last (VGWeA 8 May 84)

HAYES, John, late of Lunenburg Co., d. in Petersburg (VGPI 17 Nov 91)

HAYES, Robert, merch. of Norfolk, d. yesterday [19 Oct.] (VCGA 21 Oct 94, VGRMA 27 Oct 94); his admx., Elizabeth HAYES [and admr.,] Thomas RITSON, will sell his ship the *Greenwood* in Norfolk (HNPA 5, 7, 31 Jan 95); his agent, John SAUNDERS, will settle the est. and sell the brig *Cary* (18 months old built at Norfolk) (AGNPPA 23 Jan 95, HNPA 11 Feb 95)

HAYES, Thomas, Irish ind. svt., coach and harness maker, 22-24, ran away from John GORDON, Baltimore (VICGA 30 Jun 90)

HAYMAKER, Mrs. Catherine, consort of Adam HAYMAKER of [Winchester], d. on Sun. last at an advanced age; she was bur. in the German Lutheran Burying Ground (WG 28 Aug 99)

HAYMAN, Charles Chasbar, mulatto, b. in Sweedland [sic], c. 20, ran away from Capt. Andrew MEED on Nansemond River (NYC 17 Nov 29)

HAYNES, Andrew, of Dinwiddie Co., dec'd, his land on White Oak Swamp to be sold by his ex., William EATON and [A.] HAYNES (VG 7 Nov 54)

HAYNES, Capt. George, mar. Miss Polly TALBOT Thurs. eve. (NHPA 15 Apr 97)

HAYNES, Col. Herbert, dec'd, his ex., Eaton HAYNES, William E. JOHNSTON, and Eaton P. PUGHE, will sell all his perishable est. and settle his est. (VGPI 25 Oct 93)

HAYNES, Solomon, mulatto, ran away from James SCROSBY (VG 3 Nov 68)

HAYNES, William, of Southampton Co., dec'd, his plant. there to be sold by his ex., Catherine HAYNES and Richard BAKER (VG 11 Dec 66)

HAYNES, William, d. on Mon. [23 Mar] in Princess Anne Co. (HNPA 25 Mar 95); his ex., James HAYNES, will sell all his PE (AGNPPA 6 Nov 95)

HAYS, Moses, dec'd, e.a.w. his admr., John TATE and Jacob KINNEY, Staunton (VGSWA 20 Oct 97)

HAYS, Capt. Samuel, killed by Indians 24 Feb. in Tennessee (BVCG 29 Apr 93)

HAYWARD, Mr., mar. Mrs. SPRINGER of this town [Norfolk] yesterday eve. [6 Dec.] (HNPA 7 Dec 95)

HAYWARD, Ezra, dec'd, his admx., Araminta HAYWARD of Norfolk, adv. that Capt. David WOODWORTH has cash bel. to his est. (NH 14 Apr, ET 4 Jul 98)

HAYWOOD, Catherine, has eloped from her husband, John HAYWOOD (NH 23 Jul 99)

HAYWOOD, Thomas, conv. svt., speaks good Eng., ran away from John PETTIT's in Westmoreland Co. (MG 21 Jul 57)

HAYWOOD, William, for several yrs. past has resided at Blackwell's Neck, Hanover Co., d. on Sun. the 6th inst. (VGWeA 17 Apr 88) [Probably the same as Willis HAYWOOD below]

HAYWOOD, William, dec'd, his admr., Robert JOHNSTON, will apply to the next GA to sell his mill and land in Hanover Co. (VGGA 31 Jul 93)

HAYWOOD, Willis, merch., d. on the 6th inst. at Pierson's Mills, Hanover Co. (VIC 16 Apr 88) [Probably the same as William HAYWOOD above]

HAZARD, Baker, mulatto, ran away from John SCOTT near the Pignut Ridge, Fauquier Co. (VGPu 25 Jul 77)

HAZLETON, George, of Norfolk, mar. in Richmond last week to Miss Amey DANIELL dau. of Thomas DANIELL of Richmond (VHFA 31 Mar 98); d. in Fredsbrg. Fri. last [5 Apr.[, aged 28 (VH 9 Apr 99, Arg 12 Apr 99)

HEAD Family, Orange Co. Ct., 29 May 1798, in chanc: George ARGENBRIGHT (compl.) against Elizabeth Jannett HEAD, Benjamin FORSON, and Sally FORSON, Betsy HEAD, Elizabeth HEAD, Lucy HEAD, Simon Benjamin

HEAD, James HEAD, and Sally RIDDLE (defs.); it appears that the defs. are
not inhabitants of the Commonwealth (VH 31 Aug 98)
HEAD, Benjamin, enl. by Capt. SPOTSWOOD, des. from the Va. Regt. at Ft.
Cumberland (VG 26 Dec 55)
HEAD, James, lately moved from Orange Co. to Georgia (VGGA 14 Dec 91)
HEAD, William, mulatto, c. 16, ran away from Henry MINSON, Charles City
Co. (VGR 9 Nov 69)
HEADEN, John, conv. svt., blacksmith, ran away from Charles M'CARTY and
Robert DOWNMAN, Richmond Co. (VG 5 Aug 73)
HEADFORD, John, Eng. svt., ran away from Benjamin FENDALL, Charles Co.,
Md. (VG 20 Jul 39)
HEANE, Joseph, of Loughborough, Co. Leicester, Gt. Britain, tailor, son of
Thomas HEANE of the same place, wheelwright; came to America about 10
yrs. ago and wrote to his father from Md. in 1775; he is asked to write to his
father or to Taylor & Rogers at New York to hear something greatly to his
advantage (VGAA 21 Feb 84)
HEART, Silas, late of Rockingham Co., dec'd, one of his ex. is John SMITH
(BVCG 8 Jul 96)
HEARY, Ann, has eloped from her husb., Matthew HEARY (NHPA 31 Aug 97)
HEATH, Maj. Henry, dec'd, his ex., Susannah HEATH, Jesse HEATH, and
Samuel LEE, will sell part of his PE at his late dwelling house in Pr. Geo. Co.
(VGPI 16 May 97)
HEATH, James, of Pr. Geo. Co., enl. by George MACKENZIE, has not reported
to camp in Wmsbrg. (VG 31 Jul 46)
HEATH, John, dec'd, e.a.w. his ex., Richard COCKE and Lemuel COCKE,
Cabin Point (VG 14 May 72)
HEATH, Thomas, of Kg. Geo. Co., was executed with his brother, Alexander
HEATH, near Wmsbrg. on Fri. last for housebreaking (VG 14 Jan 68)
HEATH, Thomas, son of John HEATH of Northumberland Co., d. last Sat. at
William & Mary College in his 15th year (VG 1 Apr 75)
HEATHCOTE, Michael, dec'd, his ex., James WALL, will sell his property in
Blandford (VGGA 24 Jul 93)
HEAVIN Family, Montgomery Co. Ct., 6 Jun. 1798, in chanc: William
HEAVIN and John HEAVIN devisees of Howard HEAVIN dec'd who was
devisee of John HEAVIN Sr. dec'd, and James HEAVIN and Richard
HEAVIN devisees of John HEAVIN Jr. dec'd who was devisee of the sd.
John HEAVIN Sr. dec'd (compls.) against [Reuben] RUTHERFORD (def.); it
appears that the def. is out of this country (Arg 10 Aug 98)
HEBBLETHWAITE, Robert, of Petersburg, d. a few days ago (VGPI 17 Oct 97)
HEDGES, Thomas, whereas Thomas HEDGES, late of Wmsbrg., carpenter,
went from thence about two yrs. ago intending, as he gave out, to go to S.
Carolina or Georgia; he is asked to adv. the printer where to write to him so
that he may be informed of an est. fallen to him in Oxfordshire; if he does not
make his right appear very soon, his uncle intends to enter upon it as heir
under pretense that the sd. Thomas is dead without issue (VG 19 May 38)
HEDGMAN, John, Virginia born Negro, c. 23, belongs to Mary WHARTON of
Hanover Co., jailed in Pr. Wm. Co. (VGR 17 Feb 74)
HEDGMAN, Peter, dec'd, a large tract of his land in Fauquier Co. on the North
Branch of the Rappahannock River to be sold by his ex. (VG 2 May 66
HELENFORD, Philip, aka ALLINFORD, svt., 26, b. in Suffolk, Eng., imp. in the
Justitia last fall, ran away from William TODD, K & Q Co. (VGR 14 Apr 68)
HELLIER, John, came to Va. many yrs. ago from Bristol and settled on the
freshes of the Rappahannock River; if any of his descendents apply to Roger
DIXON, Fredsbrg., they may be informed of a particular inquiry made after
them perhaps much to their advantage; DIXON has heard of a HILLIARD
Family that came from Bristol and settled near the late Col. TURNER on the
Rappahannock (VG 20 Jun 71)
HELLMAN, Thomas, Irish svt., 20, ran away from Anderson & Jamieson,
Alexandria, may be going to Baltimore (VHFA 5 Jun 88)

HELM Family, Loudoun Co. Ct., 12 Nov 1795, in chanc: Leven POWELL (compl.) against Achiles HELM commonly known by the name of Zachariah HELM eld. son and heir at law of Leonard HELM dec'd (def.); Achiles HELM appears not to be an inhabitant of the Commonwealth (CMAG 2 Jan 96)

HELM Family, Frederick Co., Nov. 1796, in chanc: Ambrose BARNET and Margaret his wife late Margaret HELM one of the legatees and daus. of Thomas HELM dec'd (pltfs.) against Meredith HELM and Joseph HELM exors. of Thomas HELM dec'd (defs.) (BVCG 25 Nov 96)

HELM, Martin, late of Berkeley Co., dec'd, e.a.w. his admx., Barbary HELM (PGBA 19 Jan 97)

HELM, Thomas, mar. Mrs. Elizabeth WALDING on Thurs. the 17th inst., both of Frederick Co. (BVCG 25 Mar 96)

HELM, Thomas, plans to move to Ky. next Oct. and will sell land near Elk Run Church in Fauquier Co. (VHFA 14 Feb 98)

HELPEN, Peter, Irish svt., 30, ran away from Joseph SIMPSON, Richmond Co. (VG 6 Oct 52)

HELPHINSTONE, Mrs. Catherine, relict of the late Peter HELPHINSTONE of Winchester, d. on Sat. last aged 61 years (BVCG 19 Feb 96)

HEMAN, John and Joseph, Eng., butchers, ran away from Amos DERROUGH, Alexandria (NHPA 10 Jun 97)

HEMMINGS, Moses, dragoon soldier, millwright, des. from the army near Philadelphia; his father lives near Winchester (BVCG 18 Mar 96)

HENCH, Elizabeth, her husband, Charles Frederick HENCH, will no longer pay her debts (WG 27 Jun 98)

HENDERSON, Mrs., wife of John HENDERSON formerly of Norfolk, d. on Tues. at the Great Bridge (HNPA 19 Nov 95)

HENDERSON, James, Negro, claimed to be free, born in Northumberland Co., may be the Negro adv. by Thomas GASKINS of that co., jailed in Nansemond Co. (VG 19 Nov 72)

HENDERSON, Dr. James, of Scottville, Powhatan Co., mar. Miss Polly OGILBY of Amelia Co. (VGGA 27 Jun 92)

HENDERSON, John, Scot., resident of Albemarle Co., 38, des. from an escort conducting German prisoners of war from Winchester to Frederick, Md. (VGAA 22 Feb 83)

HENDERSON, Thomas, appr., bound by order of Loudoun Co. Ct., c. 20, ran away from James RATEKIN (CMAG 7 May 95)

HENDERSON, William, aka William, Negro, c. 20, ran away from Edward CHAMBERLAIN, Kg. Wm. Co. (RMA 14 May 96)

HENDRICK, William, of Mecklenburg Co., dec'd, Judith HENDERSON, his admx. will sell a general assortment of European goods bel. to his est.; she has also empowered John HENDRICK of Manchester and Christopher HASKINS of Mecklenburg Co. to receive money due the est. (VGPI 22 Jun 98)

HENDRY, Deborah, dec'd, her admr. w.w.a., William HENDRY, will sell 140 ac. of her land on Burden's Marsh, Frederick Co. (WG 11 Sep 99)

HENERY, Dan, merch. of Baltimore, d. Wed. morn. (NHPA 14 Sep 97)

HENES, John, Eng. svt., 27, ran away from Robert ADAM and Peter WISE, Alexandria (VG 6 Jun 66)

HENING, David, dec'd, e.a.w. his admr., Samuel HENING of Culpeper Co. (GLFFA 19 Oct 98)

HENING, Samuel, of Culpeper Co., dec'd, his ex., David HENING, will sell his livestock and some HHF (VGP 6 Oct 74)

HENLEY, Turner, dec'd, his ex., Dudley RICHARDSON, will sell three of his Negroes at James City Ct. H. (VGPu 24 Jan 77)

HENNING, Mrs. Elizabeth, aged 74, died (BVCG 1 Oct 92)

HENNINGER, John Frederick, Jacob MICHAEL of Richmond adv. that he purchased of Mary Magdalena HENNINGER dau. of John Frederick HENNINGER late of Alexandria dec'd, all the right and interest which she had in equity or otherwise to any lands of which the sd. John Frederick HENNINGER died seized; the sd. Mary Magdalena HENNINGER having been born in Germany and not rendered a citizen of the U.S., he intends to pet. the next GA to confirm the right transferred to him by the sd. Mary Magdalena (CMAG 3 Sep 96); Ann SPADDEN adv. that she intends to apply to the next Assembly for an act to grant to her and her heirs that piece of ground in Alexandria with the improvements thereon which the sd. HENNINGER lately died seized (CMAG 17 Sep 96)

HENRY, Edward, att. at law, son of Patrick HENRY Esq., of Campbell Co., d. on Wed. morn. last at New Glasgow in Amherst Co. (LFG 1 Nov 94)

HENRY, Hugh Gent., late of the Jewel Office in the Tower of London, d. on 10 Sep. 1768, the chil. of his nephew, James HENRY, and his sisters Eleanor and Jane are to claim their shares of his est. from the HCC, London (VG 3 Nov 74)

HENRY, Joseph, merch. of Richmond, mar. Miss BREVOORT of New York (VGIC 26 Mar 85)

HENRY, Michael, who said he was a Frenchman, des. from the co. of Capt. James VAUGHAN, 7th Regt. of N. Carolina Continental troops (VGPu 2 May 77 sup)

HENRY, the Rev. Patrick, Rector of St. Paul's Par., Hanover Co., died (VG 11 Apr 77)

HENRY, Patrick Esq., of Charlotte Co., d. at his seat there on the 6th inst. [or 4th acc. to Ex.] (Ex. 14 Jun 99, VGGA 14 Jun 99, NH 15 Jun 99, VH 18 Jun 99, VGPI 18 Jun 99, WG 26 Jun 99)

HENRY, Robert, dec'd, items of his PE to be sold by his ex., George LAMON, Middletown, Berkeley Co. (WG 9 Jan 99)

HENRY, Samuel H., late of K & Q Co., dec'd, his ex., Robert POLLARD, will sell his 1900 ac. tract and grist mill on the Mattaponi River, K & Q Co. (VGGA 29 Jul 95, 6 Jul 96)

HENRY, William, aka Negro Billy, Negro, c. 28, ran away from Catesby JONES, Northumberland Co. (VHFA 8 Nov 92, VGGA 14 Nov 92)

HENSHAW, William, dec'd, his admx., Anne HENSHAW, will sell 10 slaves, 144-gal. still, farming equipment, and 120 ac. of grain in the ground bel. to his est. at his late mansion house (BI 30 Oct 99)

HENSLEY, John, adv. that he has been lately mar. to one Hannah WOOD in Spotsylvania Co; she has behaved herself so, he has quitted her and warns all persons from dealing with her on his account (VGPu 19 Jun 78)

HENSLEY, Thomas, Virginian, 20, des. from Capt. Carter HARRISON's Co. (VG 5 Dec 55)

HENSON, Bill, aka Negro Bill, c. 19-20, says he was b. in St. Mary's Co., Md. and that he bel. to a George NELSON who he says is gone to Ky., jailed in Alexandria (CMAG 7 Mar 99)

HENSON, Philip, [of Albemarle Co.], adv. that some yrs. ago, he mar. Mary SAUNDERS the dau. of Julius SAUNDERS and grandau. of William SAUNDERS; the sd. William SAUNDERS made a verbal gift to Mary of several slaves after the death of his wife, Mary SAUNDERS; upon the death of William, Julius SAUNDERS seized the slaves and claims them as his property (VG 8 Sep 68)

HENTON Family, Rockingham Co. Ct., 2[9] Mar. 1799, in chanc: William HENTON (comp.) against Peter HENTON, Thomas HENTON, Jacob GRIDER and Rebecca his wife late Rebecca HENTON, and Jugle BOWYER (defs.); it appears that Thomas HENTON, Jacob and Rebecca GRIDER, and Jugle BOWYER are not inhabitants of this Commonwealth (PH 17 Jul 99)

HENTON, Charles, mulatto, 19-20, ran away from Henry HOWARD, Elk Ridge, Md. (VGR 7 Dec 69)

HEPBURN, John, d. at Alexandria on Sat. last; his death was occasioned by a small bruise on his right leg which mortified so suddenly that he expired before any assistance could be given (VJAA 13 Dec 87)

HEPBURN, Thomas, of Baltimore, [dec'd], his admx. is Elizabeth HEPBURN (VCNPGA 28 Sep 93)

HERBERT, John, late merch. on James River, mar. Mrs. Frances ANDERSON and d. in 1704 or 1705; he left two sons Buttler HERBERT and Richard HERBERT, and a dau., Martha HERBERT, who mar. James POWELL about 1718; if any of his descendents apply to the printer they may hear something to their advantage (VG 7 Aug 52)

HERBERT, John, of Elizabeth City Co., dec'd, his plant. in Norf. Co. to be sold by Judith HERBERT (nfi) (VG 28 May 67)

HERBERT, Robert, native of Nevis, lately from Grenada; d. Thurs. last in his 24th year (NPJ 21 Nov 87)

HERBERT, Capt. Thomas, of Norfolk, d. Thurs. (VGRMA 11 Dec 94)

HERBERT, Capt. William, dec'd, his ex., Stephen TRIGG and James M'CORKLE, will settle his est. and sell all his stock, HH and KF at Poplar Camp, Montgomery Co. (VG and VGPu 30 May 77)

HERBERT, William, was mar. to Miss Nancy SNAIL by the Rev. James WHITEHEAD on [4 Apr.], both of Norfolk (VCNPGA 6 Apr 93)

HERDMAN, Thomas, commander of the ship *Harriet*, was lost on a voyage to Britain; his brother, James HERDMAN, is the admr. (VG 29 Jun 69)

HERN, John, aka Pooling HORNE, Eng. conv. svt., c. 24, imp. in the ship *Tayloe* last month, ran away from Alexander HENDERSON, Colchester (VG 10 Nov 74)

HERNDON, Edward, d. in this county on Mon. last in his 69th year (VH 3 May 99); his ex., John and Joseph HERNDON of Spotsylvania Co., will sell his land near Orange Springs; Edward HERNDON Jr. (nfi) is also mentioned (VH 11 Oct 99)

HERNDON, James, d. in this co. yesterday morn. in his 21st year (VHFFA 18 Apr 97, RCFPC 19 Apr 97)

HERNDON, Capt. John, dec'd, his land near Fredsbrg. to be sold (VHFA 12 May 91); his ex., Edward HERNDON and James LEWIS, will sell slaves, HH and KF bel. to his est. at Mrs. Mary HERNDON's in Spotsylvania Co. (VHFA 27 Sep 92); his ex. will sell two of his tracts on Massaponax; Mrs. HERNDON lives on one (VHFA 19 Sep 93); his ex. will sell his 277 ac. tract in Spotsylvania Co. (VHFA 9 Jan 94)

HERNDON, Reuben, dec'd, his admr., Thomas GARLAND and Harry GAINES, will sell a considerable part of his PE on his late plant. about five miles above K & Q Ct. H. (VG and VGPu 25 Jul 77)

HER[N]ERY, Arthur, d. at Gosport a few days ago (NWJCI 15 Aug 98)

HERRINGHAM Family, William, Mary, and Francis HERRINGHAM chil. of William HERRINGHAM late of Greenwich, Co. Kent, left Eng. about 25 years ago to go to the West Indies and then, it is believed, to Va.; if they or their survivors apply to Thomas HODGE near Leedstown, they will hear something greatly to their advantage (VGR 19 Feb 67)

HERRITER, Casper, was mar. to Miss Abbey M'KEEL, both of Norfolk, on Wed. eve. last by the Rev. Mr. BRUCE (NH 1 Oct 96)

HERRON, W., mar. Miss PLUME dau. of William PLUME Esq. of Norfolk on Thurs. eve. (NHPA 17 Feb 98)

HESS, [Balser], appr., ran away from William AINSWORTH, Shepherdstown (IO 11 Oct 97)

HESSCHIN, David, Irish svt., 23-24, has been in the country three years, ran away from Henry MILLER, Augusta Co. (BVCG 15 Dec 90)

HETH, Henry, mar. Miss Nancy HAIR, both of Richmond, on Sat. last (VGWeA 15 Nov 87)

HETH, Henry, dec'd, his acting ex., William HETH, Shillelah, will sell some tracts of his land in Hampshire Co. (VGGA 13 Jul 96)

HEWITT, Maj., d. on the 9th inst. at Falmouth (VHFFA 24 Nov 95, RC 28 Nov 9!

HEWITT, the Rev. Richard, rector of Hungar's Par. in Northampton Co., d. on Sat. 19 Mar. [long article in VGR] (VG 24 Mar 74, VGR 14 Apr 74); William HEWITT (nfi) of Wormeley's Cr. intends shortly to leave the colony and desires to settle the est. (VG 25 Nov 75); e.a.w. his admr., Edward HARWOOD, Warwick Co. (VG 30 Oct 78)

HEYDEN, Elizabeth, formerly Elizabeth BROWNING, wife of Lewis HEYDEN

Portsmouth, has des. him (NPC 2 Jun 92)

HIATT Family, Berkeley Co. Ct., 20 Aug. 1793, upon an injunction: Simeon HIATT (comp.) against Isaac HIATT and James HIATT (defs.); it appears that the defs. are not inhabitants of the Commonwealth (PGBA 16 Sep 93)

HICKEY, John, appr. carpenter, 13, bel. to Jacob SHUCK, and Edward HICKEY, 11, appr. hatter bel. to Peter HAUK, Alexandria, ran away and are supposed to have gone to their father's in Frederick Co. (BVCG 21 Oct 96)

HICKMAN, Col. John, late of Kg. Wm. Co., dec'd, e.a.w. his acting ex., Christopher TOMKINS (VIC 23 Apr 88)

HICKMAN, William, son of Thomas HICKMAN, mentioned in connection with a land transaction in Kg. Wm. Co. (VGR 8 Oct 72)

HICKS, Mrs. Ann H., consort of John HICKS merch. of this city [Richmond], d. yesterday morn. (VGGA 30 Dec 95)

HICKS, Mrs. Sarah, consort of John HICKS merch. of this city [Richmond], d. on the night of Sat. the 23rd inst. (VGRMA 27 Mar 94, VGGA 2 Apr 94)

HICLY, Edward, Eng. svt., 30, ran away from James LADERDALE, Augusta Co. (VGR 14 Jul 68)

HIGGINBOTHAM, Samuel, of Amherst Co., intends to remove to Georgia about 15 Nov. next (VGGA 24 Aug 91)

HIGGINS, John, b. at Alexandria, c. 30, convicted in New York City of counterfeiting and hanged on 12 Feb. (NYM 1, 22 Feb 62)

HIGGINSON, Joseph, conv. svt., native of London, 21-22, jobbing blacksmith, had been in the country four years as of last Sep., ran away from Samuel DANIEL near the Upper Church in Middlesex Co. (VGPu 7 Apr, VG 8 Apr 75)

HIGHAM, Sarah, of Richmond, intends to petition the GA for a divorce from her husband, Abraham HIGHAM (VGRC 30 Aug 93)

HIGTON, Paul, young Eng. conv. svt., talks broad, was a school master, ran away from John GORSUCH and Job GARRETSON of Baltimore (VGR 1 Aug 71)

HILDRIP, John, examined in ct. on Mon. last for the supposed murder of Benjamin BRYAN (RCFPC 14 Jun 97)

HILL, Mrs., consort of Baylor HILL Esq. one of the aldermen, d. on Tues. eve. (NHPA 2 Nov 97)

HILL, Amos, appr., shoemaker, c. 16, ran away from Thomas WATSON, Richmond (Arg 17 Mar 97)

HILL, Bayley, appr., 19, bricklayer and plasterer, ran away from Nicholas VOSS, Richmond, it is supposed he will make for Norfolk or Petersburg (VGRDA 27 Nov 92); bricklayer, served his time in Richmond under Edward VOSS [sic], des. from the camp of the 3rd Sub-Legion, Shockoe Hill (RC 7 Jul 95)

HILL, Caleb, mulatto, 32-33 [or 30-35 acc. to WVGWA], b. in K & Q Co., ran away from John DONOVAN, Winchester [or Hancocktown, Washington Co., Md., acc. to WVGWA] (VGWA 6 Jan 90, WVGWA 31 Jul 90)

HILL, David, dec'd, by virtue of a decree of the Ct. of Chancery of Pr. Edw. Co., his exors., John HILL and William HILL, will sell two thirds of the tract of land and also the reversion of the other third being the widow's dower lying on both sides of Sawney's Cr. containing about 300 ac. (VGWeA 6 Apr 93)

HILL, Elijah, conv. svt., ran away from Randolph SPICER, Fauquier Co. (VGR 15 Apr 73)

HILL, Francis, aged 36, enl. by Capt. BELL, des. from the Va. Regt. at Ft. Cumberland (VG 26 Dec 55)

HILL, Henry, only son of Joseph HILL of Annapolis, 25, d. the Wed. before 28 Aug. leaving a wife and young child (VG 26 Sep 51)

HILL, Col. Humphrey, of K & Q Co., died; he left a valuable donation to St. Stephen's Par. (VG 29 Apr 75 sup); e.a.w. his ex., John HILL, Edward HILL, and William HILL [or John EDWARDS and William HILL, acc. to VGPu] (VGPu 16 Jun 75, VG 17 Jun 75); his ex. will sell his 1400 ac. tract near Todd's Bridge in K & Q Co. (VGP 7 Sep 75, VG 9 Sep 75)

HILL, John, adv. that in a few weeks he will leave for the Western Country to survey, settle, and adjust some disputed land claims for Sir. Peyton SKIPWITH (VGPI 1 Jun 98)

HILL, Leonard Jr., d. in Stafford Co. the 22nd inst. in the bloom of youth (RCFPC 29 Mar 97)

HILL, Nathaniel, dec'd, e.a.w. the admr., Thomas WILLOCK (NPC 19 Mar 91)

HILL, Nathaniel, late of Antigua, killed in a duel with Edward PEYTON of Philadelphia in Norfolk Monday sennight [before 2 March] (BVCG 16 Mar 91) [But, see also: Edward PEYTON below]

HILL, Robert, mar. Miss Judith CHAPMAN dau. of Capt. William CHAPMAN in Madison Co. (VHFFA 30 Sep 96)

HILL, Samuel, dec'd, Negroes bel. to his est., will be sold by his ex., Charles HANSFORD, at the Halfway House between Wmsbrg. and York (VG 6 May 73)

HILL, Capt. Stephen, died at Boston (VJAA 3 Aug 86)

HILL, Thomas and James, twin mulatto boys, c. 13, chil. of Susanna HILL, a free woman who lived at Fredsbrg. with one Thomas MITCHELL a Scottish merch. and went away with him either to Scotland or Lord Dunmore, as they understand; came to the house of Joseph WOOLING, Albemarle Co. (VG 29 Jun 76)

HILL, William, of Halifax Co., intends to move in about two months with his family to the upper part of S. Carolina (VG 10 Nov 74)

HILL, William, dec'd, his chil. notified that they have a legacy left by the will of their grandfather, John HILL dec'd; Wm. HILL mar. in Kg. Wm. Co. about 1765, was a calico stamper, and d. leaving several chil. (VGAA 26 Mar 85)

HILL, William, mar. Miss Clarissa DAVIS, both of Essex Co., on Mon. 28 May (VHFA 9 Jun 98)

HILL, William C., of Cumberland Co., dec'd, the sheriff will sell his PE (VIC 18 Feb 89)

HILLENBRANT, Mr. J. G. Von, of Augsburg, Germany; his relations there are trying to contact him (VGGA 13 Oct 90)

HILLER, John, Eng. svt., 33, blacksmith, ran away from Robert STOBO, Petersburg (VG 12 Jun 52)

HILLEY, Francis, dec'd, his admr., David ROSS, will sell his 110 ac. tract at Goochland Ct. H. (VG 5 Sep 77)

HILLIAR, John, appr., c. 14, his parents live in or near Leesburg, ran away from John LLOYD (TAA 24 Aug 97)

HILTON, James, svt., 45-50, ran away from William HUGHES, Hanover Co. (VG 5 Mar 52)

HILYARD, Richard, late of Charles City Co., dec'd, e.a.w. his ex., Will LENNARD (VGPu 17 Oct 77)

HINDE, Dr. Thomas, Richard LITTLEPAGE adv. that he will sell 10 or 12 slave bel. to him at the doctor's plant. in the forks of Hanover (RMA 17 Aug 96)

HINDE, Thomas and John W., of Hanover Co., intend to remove to Ky. in a few months and authorize Richard LITTLEPAGE Esq. to represent them in Va. (RMA 20 Jul 96)

HINDHOUGH, Thomas, carpenter of the ship *Betsy*, murdered in Alexandria last Tues. (VJAA 4 Jan 87)

HINDS, David, Irish conv. svt., c. 35, ran away from Samuel LOVE Jr., Loudoun Co. (VGPu 25 Jul 77)

HINEKER, John Ludeavi, b. in Holland, enl. in Norfolk on 20 Dec. [1794], des. from Ft. Norfolk (HNPA 13 May 95)

HIPDITCH, William, Eng. conv. svt., ran away from Abraham and Joseph LEWIS, Loudoun Co. (VGPu 31 Jan 77)

HIPKINS, Lewis, dec'd, his PE will be sold at the dwelling of Mrs. HIPKINS about three miles from the Little Falls of the Potomac by his ex., Philip R. FENDALL, Robert YOUNG, and William WATERS, Alexandria (BVCG 8 Dec 94)

HIPKINS, Richard, of Westmoreland Co., dec'd, e.a.w. his admr., Joseph FOX

Jr. (VHFA 28 Aug 94)

HIPKINS, Samuel Gent., of Essex Co., dec'd, his 600 ac. tract there will be sold by his ex., Leroy HIPKINS and Samuel HIPKINS (VG 26 May 68)

HIRLEY, Patrick, Irish svt., ran away from Bush River Furnace, Md. (VGR 24 Dec 67)

HISELER, Michael, dec'd, his extx., Mary HISELER of Richmond, will sell his moveable est. including coppersmith's and tinman's tools (VGRMA 25 Jul 93)

HITCHCOCK, Edmund, dec'd, e.a.w. his admr., John HEAVENRIDGE of Petersburg (VGPI 27 Feb 95); John HEAVENRIDGE has authorized Dr. Cargill MASSENBURG to close his accounts and settle his admin. of the est. (VGPI 8 Nov 96)

HITE, Isaac, dec'd, e.a.w. his ex., Isaac HITE, of Frederick Co., who will also sell his PE (PGBA 18 Feb 96, BVCG 19 Feb 96)

HITE, Jacob, who lately removed from Berkeley Co. to the neighborhood of the Cherokee country with his family was reportedly murdered by the Indians (VGPu 30 Aug 76)

HITE, John, mar. Miss Delia REGAN in Winchester on 31 Jan. (BVCG 4 Feb 93)

HOBBS, James, ship carpenter, stole a boat from William RUFF, Newport News on 21 Sep; he may be going to Md. (VG 28 Sep 39)

HOBBS, Jesse, dec'd, his admr., Samuel LEE, adv. that he has part of the est. which would have descended to his dau., Elizabeth TOMLINSON, has she lived (VGPI 24 Oct 97)

HOBBS, Nathaniel, late of Dinwiddie Co., dec'd, e.a.w. his ex., Jordan REESE and Henry COUSINS (VGPI 22 Mar 96)

HOBBS, Robert, of Pr. Geo. Co., dec'd, e.a.w. his admr., Peter WILLIAMS (VGPu 20 Jun 77)

HOBDAY, Richard, appr., c. 17, ran away from Humphrey HARWOOD, Wmsbrg. (VG 5 Sep 71)

HOBDAY, Robert, aka DOBSON, appr., ran away from William TREBELL, Wmsbrg. (VG 3 Nov 63)

HOBDAY, William, mar. Mrs. Molly JAMEISON relict of the late George JAMEISON of [Pr. Anne Co.] on Sun. last (VCNPGA 30 Mar 93)

HOBDY, Edmund, appr. tailor, c. 19, ran away from Francis DURFEY, Charles City Co. (VG 21 Mar 71)

HOBZENBEELER, George, of Frederick Co., dec'd, e.a.w. his ex., Paul M'KEAVER and Joseph HOBZENBEELER (BVCG 29 Apr 96)

HOCKADAY, Mrs. Mary, consort of Col. John HOCKADAY, d. in New Kent Co. a few days ago (VGGA 20 Nov 93)

HOCKAD[A]Y, Col. John, of New Kent Co., d. a few days ago [long obit.] (Arg 12 Apr 99)

HODGE, John, appr., orphan [sic] bound to learn the trade of a cooper, c. 19, ran away from Daniel CURTIN, Alexandria (CMAG 17 Mar 95); CURTIN believes he has probably made for Baltimore where his father and mother live (CMAG 29 Sep 96); he is still a runaway (TAA 28 Sep 98)

HODGE, Thomas, merch., of Kg. Geo. Co., d. of an apoplectic fit (VGPu 15 Dec 75)

HODGES Family, Halifax Co., chancery case: William CARR (comp.) against William GLASS and Sarah his wife, Robert SHAW and Patsey his wife, Haily SHAW and Rebecca his wife, Jesse HODGES, Joseph HODGES, Chainey HODGES, and James HODGES heirs of James HODGES dec'd (Arg 18 Jan 99)

HODGES, James, mar. Mrs. Sarah DISON, Thurs. night (VCNPGA 18 Aug 92)

HODGES, Josiah Jr., of Norfolk, died yesterday (NH 11 May 99)

HODGES, Robert, executed at the gallows near this city [Wmsbrg.] (VG 4 Dec 78)

HODGSON, William, merch., was mar. to Miss Portia LEE eld. dau. of the late William LEE Esq. of Green Spring, James River, on Thurs. the 2nd inst. at the seat of Richard Bland LEE in this county [Fairfax] by the Rev. Mr. DAVIS (CMAG 14 May 99)

HOEMYER, Johannah, Dutch ind. svt., 18-20, ran away from Isaac M'PHERSON, Alexandria (VGAxA 11 Jul 93)

HOFFMAN, Jacob, from Baltimore, is now carrying on copper and tin manufacturing in Petersburg (VGPI 27 Sep 92)

HOFFMAN, Philip, from Hampshire Co. was executed near Wmsbrg. on Fri. for felony (VG 11 Dec 66, NYPB 1 Jan 67)

HOG, Joe, Negro, ran away from George CARSON, Norfolk; is believed going to Fredsbrg. where his mother is (NHPA 8 Jun 97)

HOGAN, James, served his time with Thomas RIGGS of Frederick Co., Md.; acc. to an advertisement by Peter PEARCE, HOGAN is said to have stolen property of Mary PEARCE of Fairfax Co. (VGP 19 Jan 75)

HOGAN, John, Irish svt., ran away from the Patuxent Iron Works, Md. (VJAA 28 Jul 85)

HOGAN, Mary, d. in Halifax Co. on 10 Jul., aged 91 (VG 22 Oct 67, NYPB 19 Nov 67)

HOGAN, Mary, left her four year old dau., Margaret, with a Frenchman, Nicholas WILLIAMS, living near Liberty Town, [Md.] last spring; the sd. WILLIAMS and his wife have taken her away (VGAxA 8 Nov 92)

HOGAN, Roger, appr. tailor, 19, ran away from William DUVALL, Alexandria (VJAA 10 May 87)

HOGE, Morgan, appr., 20, ran away from James MOORE and John COFFEE, Waterford, Loudoun Co. in Nov. 1786 (VJAA 15 Feb 87)

HOGG, Thomas, killed by Indians near the mouth of the Great Kanawha (VG 8 Sep 74)

HOGGAN, Patrick, executed last Fri. near Wmsbrg. for horse stealing (Wmsbrg. disp. of 11 Jul.) (MG 8 Aug 54)

HOGGARD, Nathaniel, of Pr. Anne Co., dec'd, his admx., Mary HOGGARD, will sell all his PE (NH 12 Dec 99)

HOGGARD, Thurmer, of Pr. Anne Co., died (VG 27 Nov 79)

HOGGART, Samuel, svt., 19, tailor, ran away from Thomas WILSON, Norfolk Borough (VG 31 Jan 51); supposed going towards Hanover or Fredsbrg. (VG 28 Feb 51)

HOLAMAN, Marhew, has eloped from her husband, John HOLAMAN of N. Carolina (VGPu 7 Apr 75)

HOLDEN, George, clerk of Accomack Co., died (VG 6 Jan 74)

HOLDEN, George Esq., of Gloucester Co., died (VGPu 18 Apr 77 sup)

HOLDEN, George, dec'd, his ex., John PERRIN, will sell about 25 of his Negroes at Gloucester Ct. H. (VGWeA 25 Oct 83)

HOLLADAY, Col. Anthony, of Nansemond Co., aged 70, died; e.a.w. his ex., Anthony GODWIN of Nansemond (VGPu 29 May 78, 10 Jul 78)

HOLLADAY, Joseph, of Stafford Co., dec'd, his ex. (nfi) will sell his 445 ac. tract in that co. (VHFFA 27 Nov 95)

HOLLAND, Elizabeth, dau. of William HOLLAND heretofore of James River in Va., shipwright and of Agnes his wife; she is believed to be living in or near New York [City] on or near James River or Yorktown in Va.; she may learn something greatly to her advantage by applying to Alexander COLDEN postmaster at New York or John DIXON postmaster at Wmsbrg. (VG 309 Aug 70)

HOLLAND, George Jr., of Goochland Co., dec'd, e.a.w. his court appointed admr., the sheriff, Thomas F. BATES (VGGA 27 Oct 90)

HOLLAND, John Esq., mar. Miss Elizabeth BROWN dau. of Clement BROWN both of Cumberland Co., on Sun. the 13th inst. (RMA 20 Aug 96)

HOLLAND, John Ellis, mulatto, c. 20, ran away from jail in Norfolk Borough (NHPA 23 Oct 97)

HOLLAND, Miss Susannah, of Amelia Co., age 15, killed by lightning on the 28th ult. (VG 14 Jul 74)

HOLLAND, William, formerly of Kg. Wm. Co. [in 1782 or 1783], has removed to Ky. (VGGA 17 Aug 96)

HOLLIDAY, Mrs. Ann, consort of James HOLLIDAY, merch., of Winchester,

d. on Mon. night in the bloom of life (VGWA 5 Jan 91)

HOLLIDAY, James, shoemaker of Alexandria, died (VJAA 30 Aug 87)

HOLLIDAY, James, merch. of Winchester, mar. Mrs. DARKE last week in Berkeley Co. (BVCG 18 Feb 93)

HOLLIDAY, Richard, of Winchester, merch., mar. Miss Anne M'DONALD a few days ago in Frederick Co. (BVCG 18 Feb 93)

HOLLIDAY, William Sr., merch. of Winchester, d. on 18 Jun. at an advanced age; he left a wife and chil.; he will be bur. in the Presbyterian Burying Ground [elegy in WVGWA 26 Jun.] (VGWA 19 Jun 90, WVGWA 19, 26 Jun 90); his extx., Jane HOLLIDAY, of Winchester, will sell part of his PE (VGWA 13 Oct 90)

HOLLIDAY, William, merch., of Winchester, mar. Mrs. BLAIR on Sun. eve. (VGWA 19 Jan 91)

HOLLIER, Col. Simon, dec'd, e.a.w. his admr., Miles KING (VGIC and VGWeA 22 Nov 83)

HOLLINGSHOW, Michael, aka HOLSHOO, Dutch svt., ran away from the Patapsco Iron Works in Md. on 1 Jul. and is supposed gone towards Va. (VG 30 Jul 52)

HOLLINS, John, merch., mar. Miss SMITH dau. of the Hon. John SMITH Esq., at Baltimore (VJAA 12 Jan 86)

HOLLINS, William, des. at Wmsbrg.; he is from the upper end of New Kent Co. (VGPu 2 May 77 sup)

HOLLIS, Henry, orphan boy, bound by the Overseers of the Poor to David FRY, Berkeley Co., has run away (PGBA 15 Dec 96)

HOLLOBACH, Mrs. Catherine, of Winchester, d. on Thurs. last, aged 77 (VGWA 24 Apr 90)

HOLLOWAY, David, mar. Mrs. Julia Lee DOVE on Thurs. eve. last, both of this city [Richmond] (Arg 19 Nov 99)

HOLLOWAY, Mrs. Elizabeth, dec'd, her dwelling house in Wmsbrg. to be sold (VG 6 Jun 55)

HOLLOWAY, James, of Pr. Geo. Co., dec'd, his ex., John POYTHRESS and Hamilton JONES, will sell his PE (VG 28 Nov 71)

HOLLOWAY, John, of Petersburg, dec'd, e.a.w. Christopher M'CONNICO his ex. or James YOUNG att. to Sarah HOLLOWAY the extx., who will also sell sundry articles bel. to his est. in Petersburg (VGAA 19, 26 Jan 82, 20 Mar 84)

HOLLOWAY, John, b. in Norwich, Eng.; he was 33 when Queen Anne came to the throne [1702]; he left Eng. in 1714 and was a soldier at the taking of Port Mahon, Gibraltar, and Vigo; he came to Va. in 1730, was overseer to Robin BIRD of K & Q Co. for 14 yrs., and mar. at age 67 to a woman aged 44--she d. in 1785 age 95--he has a son now 54; he d. on 19 Apr. at the age of 124 (VGGA 8 May 93, 28 May 94)

HOLLOWAY, Thomas S., mar. Miss MOORE dau. of Capt. Reuben MOORE in Culpeper Co. (VHFFA 30 Sep 96)

HOLLOWAY, William, executed last Fri. near Wmsbrg. for murder (VG 5 Dec 45)

HOLLYDAY, Mrs., wife of James HOLLYDAY, d. after a short illness (VJAA 6 Jul 86)

HOLMAN], Sarah, niece of Benjamin BROWN who is also her gdn.; she is under age and has eloped with one SNEAD (alias CRUTCHFIELD) (VG 27 Aug 56)

HOLMAN, Capt. William, d. at his seat in Goochland Co. on Sun. the 14th inst. aged 74 (VGGA 24 Aug 96)

HOLMAN, William Jr., of Goochland, ensign in the 9th Va. Bn., d. on Tues. 17 Sep. of a putrid fever (VG 8 Nov 76)

HOLMES, Mrs. Elizabeth, formerly DAVIS; Thomas DAVIS of Orange Co. notifies the heirs of John DAVIS late of Culpeper Co. dec'd, that because of her death, the Negroes bel. to the est. of J. DAVIS will be ready for delivery to them (VH 5 Oct 98); Ambrose and Robert JONES of Caroline Co. claim all the Negroes held by Elizabeth DAVIS under a bequest to her by the will of George

FLO[W]ER; after her death, the Negroes are given to Elizabeth DAVIS and her heirs; the last Elizabeth DAVIS mar. Charles Smith STERN and she d. without issue; Charles STERN remarried and had two daus. whom Ambrose and Robert JONES mar. (VH 30 Oct 98)

HOLMES, James Cunningham, accomptant, d. in Alexandria (VJAA 8 Sep 85)

HOLMES, Col. Joseph, d. at an advanced age at his seat in Frederick Co. last night (BVCG 24 Sep 92); some of his personal property will be sold at Holmesgrove near Winchester by his admx., Rebecca HOLMES and admr., Hugh HOLMES and David HOLMES (BVCG 29 Dec 94)

HOLMES, Samuel, aka John HARRIS, svt., tailor, ran away from William TAITE, Northumberland Co. (VG 21 Mar 66, 26 Mar 67)

HOLMES, William, mulatto, 45, from Kg. Wm. Co., deserted (VG 28 Feb 55)

HOLMS, John, aka COMMODORE, Irish svt., cooper, served as a soldier under Gen. BRADDOCK, ran away from Robert RUTHERFORD, Winchester (VG 14 Jun 70 sup)

HOLT Family, last sun. eve. the spouse of William HOLT near Wmsbrg. was safely delivered of two stout boys and a girl; all are well (VG 4 Nov 75)

HOLT, [Dantel], of Wmsbrg., d. in Petersburg (VGRMA 5 Jan 95)

HOLT, David, d. near Petersburg in an advanced age (VGIC 9 Dec 86, VGAA 13 Dec 86)

HOLT, David, dec'd, his extx., Betty HOLT of Chesterfield, has authorized Samuel DAVIS to settle his accounts (VGPI 30 Aug 87)

HOLT, Mrs. Elizabeth, relict of the late John HOLT, printer of the state of New York, and sister to the late William HUNTER Esq. of Wmsbrg., d. in Philadelphia in her 61st year on Thurs. last [before 27 Mar.] (NPJ 2 Apr 88)

HOLT, James Esq., senator for the district of Pr. Anne, Norfolk, and Nansemond cos., died (VG 12 Jun 79)

HOLT, John E., mar. Miss Sally LEE on Thurs. eve. last, both of Norfolk (NPC 1 Jan 92)

HOLT, John Hunter, of this city [Richmond], late an army officer, d. Fri. after a short indisposition (VIC 13 Jun 87)

HOLT, Randolph, dec'd, his admr., John HOLT, asks that books bel. to the est. be returned (VG 6 Sep 70); his admr. will sell his PE [mainly books] (VG 4 Apr 71)

HOLT, Richard, of Essex Co., dec'd, e.a.w. his admr., Richard HOLT (Arg 18 Jan 99)

HOLT, Stewart, dec'd, his co-heiresses, Nancy and Betsey HOLT, are sued by John HOLLAND in Northampton Co. (NHPA 4 Sep 97)

HOLT, Capt. Thomas, of Surry Co., dec'd, his admr., Henry COCKE, will sell his est. there and in Dinwiddie Co. (VG 3 Nov 74, VGP 10 Nov 74); his admr. will attend at Sammons's Tavern, Dinwiddie Co., to receive payment for the bonds due Capt. HOLT's est. for sundries sold at Namozeen Plant. (VGP 5 Oct 75)

HOLT, Capt. Thomas, dec'd, his admr., William HARRISS, will sell some of his slaves at Cabin Point (VGWeA 14 Dec 82, VGAA 21 Dec 82)

HOLTZCLAW, Henry, son of John HOLTZCLAW, of Fauquier Co. is summoned to appear in Fauquier Co. Ct. in a chancery case (VGR 26 Sep 71, VGAA 8 Oct 85)

HONEY, James, native of Perth in Scotland, but for many yrs. a resident of Wmsbrg., d. last Sun. sennight; his extx., Lucy HONEY, and ex., David MORTON, of Wmsbrg., will sell his HHF, wagon, set of cabinet maker's tools and carpenter's tools, and stock of timber on hand (including mahogany, black walnut, pine plank, etc.) (VGWeA 12 Apr, 17 May 87); e.a.w. William HARWOOD att. in fact for Lucy HONEY, surviving extx., who will also sell a 970 ac. tract in Jefferson Co. held by a patent of Jun. 1782 (VGWeA 23 Dec 91

HOOD, Benjamin, dec'd, e.a.w. his extx., Judith HOOD of Petersburg (VGPI 30 Nov 94)

HOOD, John, late of Flower de Hundred, Pr. Geo. Co., dec'd, his est. to be sold b William WILLIE (nfi) (VG 20 Jun 66)

HOOD, William, mulatto boy, claims to bel. to Henry MINSON, Charles City Co.; taken up in Halifax Co., N. Carolina (VG 21 Dec 69)

HOOE, Col. John, of Pr. Wm. Co., was drowned in the river near Colchester on the morn. of the 16th inst.; it is believed he committed suicide (CMAG 17 May 98); e.a.w. his ex., Bernard HOOE Sr. and Bernard HOOE Jr. of Pr. Wm. Co. (TAA 7 Jun 98)

HOOMES, Stephen Furnea, dec'd, e.a.w. William CLAYTON, New Kent Co. his ex. (VGR 16 Feb 69)

HOOPER, Richard, c. 20, has failed to return to the co. of Capt. James JOHNSON, 6th Va. Regt. and is still lurking about his father's in Lunenburg Co. (VGPu 11 Apr 77)

HOOPER, Thomas, of Hanover Co., dec'd, e.a.w. his extx., Unity HOOPER and ex., Edmund HOOPER (VGWeA 25 Sep 88)

HOPES, Thomas, Irish, des. from Capt. James MACKILWEAN's Co. at Petersburg (VG 19 Jul 54)

HOPEWELL, Rebecca, late Rebecca ADERTON, admx. of James ADERTON dec'd, now wife of George HOPEWELL, is a def. in a chancery case in Northumberland Co. Ct. brought by John CRAINE (VHFA 19 Mar 95)

HOPKINS, Arthur, dec'd, e.a.w. his ex., Samuel CALLAND, Pittsylvania Co. (VG 18 Oct 76)

HOPKINS, Dr. Arthur, of Albemarle Co., dec'd, e.a.w. his ex., William HOPKINS and James HOPKINS (VGWeA 14 Aug 84)

HOPKINS, John Esq., Receiver General of the Continental Loan Office for Va., mar. Miss Lucy LYONS second dau. of the Hon. Peter LYONS Esq. of Hanover (VIC 14 Oct 89, VGWeA 15 Oct 89, MC 7 Nov 89)

HOPKINS, Jonathan, dec'd, e.a.w. his ex., Matthias HOPKINS (NPC 18 Jun 91)

HOPKINS, Joseph, dec'd, his extx., Keziah HOPKINS of Pr. Anne Co., will sell 80 or 90 head of cattle bel. to his est. between Kemps and Great Bridge (NH 5 Oct 99)

HOPKINS, Samuel, of Mecklenburg Co., intends to remove to Ky. in Oct. next (VGPI 25 Jul 97)

HOPKINS, Samuel Jr., of Mecklenburg Co., intends to move to Ky. (VGGA 27 May 95)

HOPKINSON, the Hon. Francis Esq., District Judge of the U. S. for the State of Pennsylvania, d. suddenly on 9 May (VHFA 19 May 91)

HORBERT, Thomas, conv. svt., c. 30, silversmith, ran away from William ALEXANDER, Borton's Tract, Augusta Co. (VG 18 Feb 75, 4 Mar 75)

HORD, Maj. Thomas, of Stafford Co., dec'd, a pet. will be presented to the next GA to confirm the division of land and slaves, part of his est., left to his son Thomas HORD who d. under age (VHFA 10 Jul 94)

HORD, Thomas, late of Mecklenburg Co., dec'd, e.a.w. Thomas VAUGHN the admr. de bonis non (VGPI 7 May 99)

HORN, Richard, aka COLE, svt., 25, ran away from Robert VAULX and John ELLIOTT, Westmoreland Co. and may be headed for Norfolk (VG 2 May 51)

HO[R]NAGE, Richard, tallow-chandler, was inhumanly murdered in the house of Edward KING of Wmsbrg. last Tues. night; KING is now in jail together with two others who are supposed to be the murderers (VG 9 Oct 78)

HORNBLOWER, Dr. Joseph, of the *Roebuck* packet, died (Kingston, Jamaica disp. of 17 Sep.) (RC 7 Nov 95)

HORNBY, Maria, from Cork, Ireland, just arrived on the *Iris*, was drowned in Hampton Roads last Fri. night (NH 16 Oct 98, VH 23 Oct 98)

HORNE, John, aka Pooling HORNE, Eng. conv. svt., c. 24, imp. into Potomac River last month in the ship *Tayloe*, ran away from Alexander HENDERSON on Bull Run (VGP 10 Nov 74)

HORNER, Samuel, appr., 19, ran away from William PEARSON, Fredsbrg. (VHFA 30 Jun 98)

HORNSBY, Joseph, of Wmsbrg., mar. Miss Mildred WALKER dau. of Dr. Thomas WALKER of Albemarle Co. on the 8th inst. (VGR 26 Jan 69)

HORNSBY, Joseph, will sell his plants. in James City Co. and move to Ky.

(VGGA 17 Aug 96); left Wmsbrg. for Ky. in 1796; William HORNSBY (nfi) adv. that a Negro ran away from him just before he left (NH 21 Jun 98)

HORNSBY, Mrs. Margaret, spouse of Thomas HORNSBY merch. of this city [Wmsbrg.] d. last Sun. morn. [obit.] (VGR 1 Mar 70)

HORNSBY, Thomas, of Wmsbrg., d. in an advanced age (VG 28 May 72); e.a.w. Joseph HORNSBY (nfi); his ex. are Ben. WALLER, John PRENTIS, Joseph HORNSBY, and William HORNSBY of Wmsbrg. (VG 18 Jun 72, 2 Sep 73)

H[O]RRED, Hamilton, of Whitehaven, ran away from the *Delight* brig lying at Capt. DANIEL's (VG 7 Nov 54)

HORROCKS, Mrs. Frances, relict of the late Commissary, the Rev. Mr. James HORROCKS, d. last Sat. in her 26th year [obit. in VGR] (VG and VGR 16 Dec 73)

HORROCKS, the Rev. and Hon. James, Counselor of State to H.M. for Virginia, Commissary to the Bishop of London, President of William and Mary, and Rector of Bruton [Par.], d. on 20 Mar. at Oporto (VG 23 Jul 72, PC 25 Jul 72)

HORSLEY, William D., a young man lately from Eng., d. in Norfolk on Sat. night last (NWJCI 27 Sep 97)

HORTON, Tobias, capt. of a small schooner returning to Northumberland Co. from Norfolk, was murdered by two svts., Alexander JAMIESON, a Scot, and John SKERUM, Eng., on 4 Sep. (VG 26 Sep 45)

HOSPITAL, Andrew, Irish ind. svt., 19-20, ran away from A. BARNES [and] Thomas MASON [sic] near Leesburg (VCWM 15 Oct 88)

HOTZENBELLER, Stephen, dec'd, his ex. are Valentine SWISHER and Jacob HOTZENBELLER (BVCG 9 Sep 96)

HOUCK, Valentine, appr., ran away from John SMITH, Harrisonburg, Rockingham Co. (BVCG 10 Mar 97)

HOUGH, John, dec'd, his ex., William, Samuel, and Mahlon HOUGH, will sell his plant. containing 700 ac. in Loudoun Co. near Fairfax Meeting House 40 miles from Alexandria and also a house and lot in Leesburg, a 73 ac. tract in Shenandoah Co., and a 200 ac. tract in Hampshire Co. (CMAG 27 Apr 97)

HOUSE Family, Brunswick Co., Ct. of Q.S, 25 Mar 1795: John DRUMMOND compl. in chanc. against Joseph SEWARD, Nathaniel HARRIS, Joseph STACY, and Samuel HOUSE, John HOUSE, Henry HOUSE, Colley HOUSE, Patsy HOUSE, Mary HOUSE, Kesiah HOUSE, and Nancy HOUSE chil. of Lawrence HOUSE dec'd (defs.) [SEWARD appears to be the only inhabitant of Va. among the defs.; they all may have been originally from Brunswick Co.] (VGPI 26 May 95)

HOUSTON, Hugh, of Fredsbrg., dec'd, his admx. is Fanny HOUSTON (VGR 7 Jul 74)

HOUSTON, William, dec'd, e.a.w. with Hugh HOUSTON (nfi) who is carrying on the saddler's business in Fredsbrg. (VGR 17 Oct 71)

HOUSTON, William and Hugh, late of Spotsylvania Co., dec'd, e.a.w. John HOLLADAY Jr. (nfi) (VGPu 2 Feb 76)

HOWARD, Mrs., relict of the late Benjamin HOWARD of Buckingham Co., d. last Mon. in Hanover Co. (VG 1 Apr 75)

HOWARD, Maj. Benjamin, Clerk of Bedford Co. and one of the Burgesses for Buckingham Co., died; e.a.w. his admx., Sarah HOWARD (VG 9 Jan, 30 Jul 72)

HOWARD, George, appr. tanner, 18-19, ran away from Rudolph BLACK, Charlestown, Berkeley Co. (BVCG 6 Oct 94)

HOWARD, Jane, her husb., William HOWARD of Amherst Co., will not pay any of her debts (VGR 23 Apr 72)

HOWARD, John, aka JOHNSON, Irish svt., 30, formerly belonged to Thomas WHITING of Gloucester Co. dec'd, ran away from Joseph COCKE, Wmsbrg. (VG 15 May 46)

HOWARD, William, mar. Miss Nancy CHISMAN, both of York Co. (VG 12 Dec 77)

HOWE, James, Eng. svt., 4[0], ran away from Maj. Andrew CAMPBELL's in Frederick Co. last Nov. (VG 27 Mar 46)

HOWE, Robert Esq., late a general in the service of the U. S., d. lately at the house of Gen. CLARKE near Wilmington, N. Carolina (VGWeA 22 Feb 87)
HOWEL, Capt., of St. Martin's, drowned when the schooner *Virginia Packet* capsized on 31 May on its way to the West Indies (NHPA 10 Jun 97)
HOWEL[L], Sam, mulatto, 25, ran away from Wade NETHERLAND on James River in Cumberland Co. (VG 2 May 66)
HOWELL Brothers, Samuel, c. 28, and Simon, c. 25, mulatto svts., ran away from Wade NETHERLAND, Cumberland Co. (VG 16 Aug 70)
HOWELL, Charles, mulatto, 12-15, says he was b. free and that his parents live in Gloucester Co. from where he was stolen and taken to Warwick Co.; jailed in Chesterfield
HOWELL, Peggy, free mulatto, of Charlotte Co., reported that two of her chil., Peter TONEY and Edmund BOOKER, both c. 4-5, were kidnapped on 20 Jun. (VGGA 16 Jul 94)
HOWELL, Reuben, appr., ran away from James FAULKNER, Culpeper Co. (VH 3 Dec 99)
HOWERTON, Heritage, of Essex Co., dec'd, e.a.w. his admrs., Charles and Ambrose HOWERTON (VGGA 16 Dec 95 ex)
HOWLE, John, dec'd, his ex., Absolom HOWLE of New Kent Co., will sell his PE (VG 16 Sep 73)
HOWLE, Polly, absconded from her husband, Epaphroditus HOWLE of Henrico Co., with Charles PRICE on 26 Jan last (VGRMA 23 May 93)
HOWORTH, James, wishing to return to Europe, offers his land in Louisa Co. for sale (VHFA 17 Nov 91)
HOY, Richard, carpenter, came from Cork [Ireland] to Md. about 18 yrs. ago; his brother, John HOY, living on the Chickahominy River seeks information on him (VG 17 Feb 38)
HOY, Thomas, Irish svt., [3]1, ran away from [?] DEGRAFFENRIED, Pr. Geo. Co. (VG 26 Sep 45)
HUBARD, James, dec'd, e.a.w. his admr., Nathaniel BURWELL of Carter's Grove (VGWeA 26 Apr 83 sup)
HUBARD, James, dec'd, his est. was put into the hands of Robert YATES by the Gloucester Co. Ct. (VGGA 15 Jun 96)
HUBARD, James Jr., of Gloucester Co., mar. Miss Molly WHITING of K & Q Co. (VGPu 7 Jul 75)
HUBARD, James Sr., of Gloucester Co., d. on the 12th inst. (VG 22 Dec 74)
HUBARD, James B., dec'd, his est. was put into the hands of Robert YATES by the Gloucester Co. Ct. (VGGA 15 Jun 96)
HUBARD, John, dec'd, his est. was put into the hands of Robert YATES by the Gloucester Co. Ct. (VGGA 15 Jun 96)
HUBARD, Miss Peggy, of Gloucester Co., d. in the bloom of youth (VGPu 13 Dec 76)
HUBARD, William, formerly a merch. in Wmsbrg., d. last Tues. in his 49th year (VGR 26 Jan 69)
HUBARD, William, of Gloucester, mar. Miss Dolley COLE dau. of John COLE (VG 6 Feb 72)
HUBBARD, Benjamin, dec'd, his admr., James TAYLOR, will settle his est. and sell 11 of his Negroes at the Bowling Green in Caroline Co. (VGAA 19, 26 Jan 82)
HUBBARD, Capt. George, of London, dec'd, e.a.w. Peter LYONS (nfi) of Hanover Co. (VG 22 Aug 71)
HUBBARD, Nathaniel, mariner, dec'd, his heir (nfi) will receive 40 shillings being the balance due him till the 14th of Feb. at which time he was lost from the ship *John*, Bennet BOGGESS, master, on her passage to Liverpool (NPC 9 Jul 91)
HUBBARD, William, appr., who has about three and a half yrs. of his time to serve, ran away from Edmund JENNINGS of Chesterfield Co. who believes he is lurking about Charles City or Hanover Co. (Ex 26 Feb 99)
HUBBLE, William, Eng. svt., 26, ran away from Edward VIELLER of Annapolis

at Alexandria on 21 Jan. (VJAA 17 Feb 85)

HUDGINS, Capt. Westcomb, mar. Miss Nelly HARDY on Thurs. eve. last, both of this town [Fredsbrg.] (VH 5 Nov 99)

HUDLY, Thomas, svt., 40, ran away from A. CHURCHBILL (VG 11 Jul 55)

HUDNALL, Mrs. Jemima, consort of James HUDNALL, d. on Sat. the 17th inst. in Northumberland Co. (VHFA 29 Aug 93)

HUDNALL, William, the only son of James HUDNALL of Wicomico, d. of smallpox on the 7th inst. in his 22nd year (VHFFA 7 Apr 97)

HUDSON, Capt. Charles, of Hanover Co., dec'd, his est. to be sold by John DARRACOTT, John WINGFIELD, and Robert [?], his exors. (VG 28 Aug 46)

HUDSON, Christopher, late of Amelia Co., dec'd, e.a.w. his ex., Charles HUDSON of Amelia (VIC 11 Mar 89, VGRMA [13] Jan 94); his acting ex., Charles HUDSON of Amelia, will sell 10 or 12 of his slaves (VGWeA 4 [Jan] 93)

HUDSON, Elizabeth, of Amelia Co., dec'd, e.a.w. Francis HUDSON (RMA 11 Jul 95)

HUDSON, John, late of Albemarle Co., e.a.w. his ex., John SCOTT (VG 24 Jun 75)

HUDSON, John, b. in the north of Eng., c. 35, des. from on board the *Hero* galley; there is reason to suppose he will try to get to West Augusta as he has some land in the neighborhood of Pittsburgh (VGPu 20 Sep 76)

HUDSON, Col. John, of Portsmouth, died (NPC 24 Apr 90)

HUDSON, John, appr., 15, ran away from John RICHARDSON, Norfolk (AGNPPA 21 Apr 95)

HUDSON, Sarah, has eloped from her husband, John HUDSON of Chesterfield Co. (VG 20 Aug 72)

HUDSON, Thomas, Virginian, 28, has not returned to the camp at Wmsbrg. (VG 14 Aug 46)

HUDSON, William, appr. tailor, c. 19, ran away from Richard PHILLIPS of Essex Co.; he has been seen on his way to Lunenburg Ct. H. (VGR 31 Oct 71)

HUDSTON, George, dec'd, a tract of his land in Hanover Co. to be sold by his admr., Henry WATKINS, who expects to move to Ky. in the spring (VGGA 15 Jun 91)

HUGHES, Mrs., midwife, late from the West Indies, has moved to Norfolk with her dau. (VG 16 Dec 73)

HUGHES, Billy, aka Thomas [LESTER], Irish svt., ran away from Thomas DAN[SIE], Kg. Wm. Co. (VG 9 May 51)

HUGHES, David, alias LUELLIN, Welsh conv. svt., blacksmith, near 40, formerly bel. to Vincent ASKIN late of Charles Co., Md., dec'd, and ran away from his exors.; he worked a considerable time at the Eastern Shore as a free person and obtained a pass from some of the justices there which is signed by Capt. Robert VAULX and other justices of Westmoreland; ran away from Peter WAGENER Pr. Wm. Co., it is supposed that his wife is gone with him and that he will endeavor to escape out of Va. (MG 18 May 48)

HUGHES, John, of Amelia Co., dec'd, e.a.w. his ex., Richard BOOKER and Francis ANDERSON of Petersburg (VGPI 27 Sep 92)

HUGHES, John, appr., native of Va., his father at present keeps a tavern in Cartersville on James River, ran away from Thomas WHITE, blacksmith, at Alexandria who supposes he is gone towards Baltimore (TAA 6 Mar 98)

HUGHES, William, dec'd, his ex., John HUGHES and William HUGHES Jr., will sell several tracts of his land in Goochland Co., livestock, corn, fodder, HHF, and plant. tools at his late dwelling place on Allen's Cr. in the upper end of Hanover Co. (VGPA 5 Nov 91)

HUGHS, John, Irish svt., bel. to Dr. Ephraim HOWARD, ran away from near Elk Ridge Church, Anne Arundel Co., Md. (VGR 26 Jul 70)

HUIE, Capt [James] Jr., son to James HUIE Esq. of Glasgow, Scotland, mar. Miss Helen E. G. BULLITT dau. of the Hon. Cuthbert BULLITT Esq., near Dumfries on the 29th ult. (VHFA 23 Jun 91)

HULL, Col. Richard, of Northumberland Co., for many years a rep. in the

Assembly and magistrate for that co., d. in his 59th year (VGPu 7 Jun 76)
HULL, Robert, a man of color, d. on Thurs. the 8th ult., in his 53rd year; he was an honest man and a good citizen (CMAG 15 Dec 96)
HUMPHREYS, Mrs. Ann, [of Petersburg], died (NPJ 8 Oct 88)
HUMPHREYS, Daniel, Welsh ind. svt., c. 26, ran away from Samuel HARRIS, Wmsbrg. (VGPu 15 Nov 76)
HUMPHREYS, Ralph, of Hampshire Co., intends to move west out of Va. in Nov. (VCWM 3 Sep 88)
HUMPHREYS, William, Irish svt., ran away from John CAWOOD on Piscataway Cr., Pr. Geo. Co., Md. (VJAA 25 Aug 85)
HUMPHRY, David, seaman, ran away from the ship *Virginia* at Littlepage's Landing, New Kent Co., may be heading for Bristol Iron Mines (VG 18 Apr 45)
HUNDLEY, Ambrose, dec'd, his admr., Mack GOODE, will sell a colt bel. to his est. and also settle his est. (VGPu 20 Mar 78)
HUNDLEY, Charles, dec'd, his ex., Smith BLAKEY, will sell the tract of land whereon he lived near Hanover Town (Arg 27 Dec 96)
HUNDLEY, Wilkinson, dec'd, George HUNDLEY and John HUNDLEY in Amelia Co. will sell a tract of land containing 160 ac. in Kingston Par., Gloucester Co. whereon the dec'd formerly lived as well as the land adjoining on the head of Milford Haven containing 177 ac. whereon George HUNDLEY dec'd formerly lived (VGPu 18 Apr 77); his land in Gloucester Co. to be sold by John HUNDLEY (nfi) of Amelia Co. (VGAA 12 Mar 85)
HUNNICUT, Robert, dec'd, John HUNNICUT Jr. (nfi) will sell his 600 ac. tract in Pr. Geo. Co. (VG 26 Dec 77)
HUNT, Benjamin, dec'd, all his est. in Surry Co. to be sold by his admr., John WALKER (VG 8 Dec 68)
HUNT, Charles, merch. of Wmsbrg., d. there on Sat. last (VGGA 15 Oct 94, VGRMA 16 Oct 94, VGRC 17 Oct 94); his admx., Jane HUNT, will sell all of his PE (VGGA 4 Feb 95, HNPA 14 Feb 95); his admx. w.w.a., Jane HUNT, will settle his est. (HNPA 25 Jul 95, VGGA 29 Jul 95)
HUNT, Dick, c. 26, waiting man and shoemaker, mulatto, ran away from Thomas WILLIAMS, Nottoway Co. (VGPI 22 Dec 95)
HUNT, George, svt., ran away from William MEREDITH and is supposed to be gone towards the Northern Neck (VG 20 Oct 52)
HUNT, James, of Charlotte Co., dec'd, his ex. are David and Gilbert HUNT (Arg 10 Feb 97)
HUNT, John, merch. of Baltimore, d. Sat morn. last (VJAA 5 Jul 87)
HUNT, Mary, aka WILLIAMS, lusty, well-looking Eng. svt. woman, ran away from Anthony WALKE merch. in Petersburg, tis supposed she will change her name and put on man's apparel (VG 5 Jun 52)
HUNT, Nathaniel, late of Halifax Co., dec'd, e.a.w. his ex., David HUNT (Arg 10 Feb 97)
HUNT, Richard, aka Sip, Negro, c. 43, ran away from Salathiel VAUGHAN, Dinwiddie Co. (VG 15 Sep 74)
HUNT, Will, mulatto svt., ran away from John HARDYMAN, Charles City Co. (VG 24 May 51)
HUNT, William, tailor, of Wmsbrg., d. on 8 Apr. (VG 8 Apr 37)
HUNT, William, d. on Fri. 31 Mar. at his house in K & Q Co.; he was a vestryman of Stratton Major Par. (VGR 6 Apr 69)
HUNT, William, dec'd, e.a.w. his ex., William HUNT and George BRETT (VGPu 11 Apr 77)
HUNT, William, aka Will, mulatto, c. 40, ran away from Mr. DONALD's plant. in Pr. Edw. Co. (VGPu 13 Jun 77)
HUNTER, Mrs., wife of Miles HUNTER, printer, d. last week at Petersburg (VGAA 26 Jul 86, VIC 5 Nov 88)
HUNTER, Adam Esq., of Stafford Co., dec'd, e.a.w. Joseph ENNEVER, admr. w.w.a. (VHFA 19 May 68)
HUNTER, Archibald, of Rappahannock, reportedly guillotined at Dunkirk last

Aug. for having expressed sentiments inimical to the cause of France (VHFA 7 Nov 93)

HUNTER, David Sr., d. in Martinsburg (PGBA 13 Apr 97)

HUNTER, Capt. George, for many years a respectable merch. in Baltimore, d. on Sat. morn. last in his 67th year (Balto. disp. of 12 Jun.) (VHFFA 23 Jun 97)

HUNTER, George, merch., late of Alexandria, dec'd, e.a.w. his admr., George BEARD of Fairfax Co. (TAA 27 Mar 98); his admr. will sell all the goods, wares, and merchandise bel. to his est. in Fairfax Street, Alexandria (TAA 26 Apr 98)

HUNTER, Hugh, of Petersburg, d. on Fri. last; his only acting ex. is James BYRNE (VGPI 27 Sep 96, 23 Dec 96)

HUNTER, Ichabod, merch. of Richmond, d. at 10:00 on Mon. 3 Sep. (VGGA 4 Sep, OVT 6 Sep, VHFA 7 Sep 98)

HUNTER, James Esq., late of Stafford Co., dec'd, e.a.w. his ex., Adam HUNTER (surviving partner of James & Adam Hunter, Fredsbrg.) and Abner VERNON (VGAA 9 Jul 85, 16 Jul 85, VIC 16 Jan 88); about 100 slaves bel. to his est. to be sold in Fredsbrg. by his exors. (VJAA 11 Jan 87); his exors. will sell his 1100 ac. tract in Fauquier Co. (VHFA 19 Mar 89, VIC 16 Sep 89); e.a.w. his surviving ex., Adam HUNTER and Patrick HOME (VHFA 3 Jan 93); his exors. will sell his mansion house and plant. in Stafford Co. (VHFA 31 Jul 94, VGGA [20] May 95); his ex., Patrick HOME of Rappahannock Forge, desires to close his executorship and divide the est. (VHFFA 1 Nov 96); a large tract of his land in Fauquier Co. to be sold by his surviving ex., Patrick HOME (VHFA 28 Feb 98); his iron works and mills near Falmouth and Fredsbrg. to be sold by his ex. (VHFA 19 May 98, VH 31 Aug 98); HCC, 1! May 1798, between Adam HUNTER and Patrick HOME exors. of the testament and devisees of James HUNTER dec'd and James HUNTER also a devisee of the sd. James HUNTER dec'd (pltfs.) and Esther ROBINSON heretofore Esther FRAZER extx. of the testament of George FRAZER and one of his devisees, Henry VOWLES and Mary his wife, which Mary is dau. and devisee of the sd. George FRAZER, James WRIGHT clerk, and Peter WRIGHT, brothers of Alexander WRIGHT dec'd, and John GLASSELL (defs.); it appears that Peter WRIGHT, James WRIGHT, and John GLASSELL are not inhabitants of this country (VGGA 17 Jul 98)

HUNTER, James, aka James WOOD, appr. locksmith, c. 20, ran away from Christopher HIESKELL, Winchester (WVGWA 22 May 90)

HUNTER, James, late librarian, bookseller, and stationer in Norfolk, dec'd, his ex. are Samuel KERR and Thomas BROWN of Norfolk (HNPA 1 Oct 95, NH ! Jan 96)

HUNTER, Jane, has behaved in so imprudent a manner as to cause a separation from her husband, John HUNTER, Fairfax Co. (VGR 9 Feb 69)

HUNTER, John, late of Norfolk Borough dec'd, e.a.w. his admr., Joseph HARDING (VGR 4 Nov 73, VGNI 8 Sep 74)

HUNTER, John, ind. svt., native of London, ran away from Elkanah DEANE, Wmsbrg. (VGP 2 Feb 75)

HUNTER, John, Eng. svt., c. 25, ran away from Francis THOMAS, Frederick Co., Md. (VGPu 13 Oct 75)

HUNTER, Capt. John, d. in Apr. 1791; all of his sisters or their issue are to app to William W. PEPYS, Symonds Inn, Chancery Lane, [London] (VGRC 13 Jun 94)

HUNTER, John Jr., late of Hampton, dec'd, e.a.w. William HUNTER, his admr., of Norfolk (HNPA 20 Aug 95)

HUNTER, John Sr., late of Hampton, dec'd, e.a.w. his admx., S. HUNTER (RC 18 Aug 95)

HUNTER, Mrs. Margaret, d. in Wmsbrg. after a short indisposition (VIC 3 Oct 87, VGWeA 4 Oct 87, VGIC 6 Oct 87)

HUNTER, Miles, printer, of Richmond, mar. Miss Sally GARDINER of Hanover, on Sun. last (VGAA 17 May 86, VJAA 25 May 86); d. at Petersburg (?) on Fri. 12 Dec. (VIC 17 Dec 88, NPJ 24 Dec 88)

HUNTER, Moses, dec'd, his admr., Anne and David HUNTER, will sell some of his livestock, farming utensils, and a variety of HHF at Hazlefield (BI 2 Oct 99)
HUNTER, Mrs. Patsey, sp. of Miles HUNTER of Petersburg, died (NPJ 5 Nov 88)
HUNTER, Thomas T., of Petersburg, died (NPJ 8 Oct 88)
HUNTER, William, merch. of Hampton, d. lately (VG 26 Oct 39)
HUNTER, William Esq., one of H.M's Deputy Post Masters General of North America and printer of the GA of Va., d. Wed. sennight [5 Aug.] at his house in Wmsbrg. (MG 3 Sep 61, NYM 7 Sep 61, NYPB 10 Sep 61)
HUNTER, William, dec'd, e.a.w. Benjamin WALLER and Thomas EVERARD (VG 4 Jul 66)
HUNTER, William, printer, mar. Miss Betsey DAVENPORT dau. of the Rev. Joseph DAVENPORT Rector of Charles Par., York Co. (VGPu 10 Jan 77)
HUNTER, William, dec'd, e.a.w. his admx., Elizabeth TENANT of Pr. Anne (VGPu 10 Oct 77)
HUNTER, William, dec'd, e.a.w. Edward MOSELEY of Pr. Anne (VGPu 19 Jun 78)
[HUNTER], William, appr., cabinet maker, c. 20, ran away from John PRICE, Staunton (VGWA 15 Dec 90)
HUNTER, William, dec'd, a slave bel. to his est. to be sold in Pr. Anne Co. (VCNPGA 8 Sep 92)
HUNTER, William Jr. Esq., of [Alexandria], d. on Mon. eve. last [17 Nov.] [elegy in VGAxA reprinted in VHFA] (VGAxA 22 Nov 92, VHFA 6 Dec 92)
HUNTON, Thomas, adv. that his wife, Elizabeth, has behaved in a very uncommon manner to him of late and he will not be answerable for any of her debts (VGPu 8 Aug 77)
HUNTSBERGER, Henry, son of Jacob HUNTSBERGER (BVCG 8 Sep 94)
HURLY. Timothy, Irish, c. 40, suspected of stealing a horse from Robert RICHEY, Botetourt Town (VGGA 27 Jan 96)
HURST, Mr., lately became a resident of this borough [Norfolk] and one of the Norfolk Volunteer Co., d. yesterday (NH 16 Oct 98)
HURST, Henry, conv., ran away from Thomas ROBINS, Orange Co. (VGR 4 Aug 74)
HURST, Kemp, mar. Miss Sukey CALLENDER dau. of Capt. John CALLENDER, both of Fredsbrg. (VHFA 2 Oct 95); merch., d. at Norfolk yesterday sennight, formerly of Fredsbrg.; he left a widow and one child (VH 23 Oct 98)
HUSSLAR, George, dec'd, e.a.w. his admx., Nazy HUSSLAR (CMAG 25 Oct 96) [Also given as George ISLER, q.v.)
HUSTON, Peter, of Bladen Co., N. Carolina, d. suddenly at the house of William FARREL Jr. near Dumfries on 22 Feb. on his way to see his dau. in Baltimore (VGGA 11 Mar 95)
HUTCHINGS, Daniel, his extx., Elizabeth HUTCHINGS, will sell all his PE (VGWeA 26 Apr 83)
HUTCHINGS, Mrs. Elizabeth, of Norfolk, dec'd, e.a.w. her admr., Archibald WILLIAMSON (VCNPGA 18 Aug 92)
HUTCHINGS, Col. John, of Norfolk Borough, d. on Sun. morn. in his 77th year [long obit.] (VG 7 Apr 68)
HUTCHINGS, John Esq., of Norfolk, dec'd, e.a.w. his admrs. w.w.a., Thomas NEWTON Jr. [the sheriff] and John BOUSH, who will sell his tract "Holland" in Pr. Anne Co. (NPJ 4 Feb 89, VICGA 24 Feb 90, NPC 10 Jul 90, 28 Aug 90); e.a.w. Thomas NEWTON, surviving admr. w.w.a. (VCNPGA 23 Feb 93)
HUTCHINGS, Col. Joseph, formerly a rep. in Assembly for Norfolk Borough, d. in Richmond (VGPu 20 Sep 76, VG 21 Sep 76); his ex., John HUTCHINGS and Matthew PHRIPP, will sell his 300 ac. tract lying on Tanner's Cr., Norfolk Co., commonly called "Marley's" (VG and VGPu 4 Apr 77)
HUTCHINGS, Joseph, dec'd, his admr., J. BLAMIRE of Kempsville, will sell two of his Negroes (HNPA 10 Oct 95)

HUTCHINGS, Joshua Esq., dec'd, his lots in Norfolk Borough to be sold (VGAA 13 Sep 86)
HUTCHINGS, Mrs. Sarah, relict of Col. Joseph HUTCHINGS, d. Thurs. of smallpox (HNPA 16 May 95); e.a.w. Fred WILLIAMS of Norfolk, her ex. (HNPA 12 Aug 95)
HUTCHINGS, Capt. Thomas, Geographer of the U. S., d. on 28 Apr. in Pittsburgh (VHFA 21 May 89)
HUTCHINSON Family, Frederick Co. Ct., 4 Aug 1795, in chanc: Isaac BROWN (pltf.) against Jane HUTCHINSON widow and relict of James HUTCHINSON dec'd, John HUTCHINSON, Thomas HUTCHINSON, Alexander HUTCHINSON, Nancy HUTCHINSON, and James HUTCHINSON infants under 21, chil. and heirs of the sd. James HUTCHINSON dec'd (defs.) (BVCG 12 Oct 95)
HUTCHINSON, James, appr. shoemaker, ran away from Beaty CARSON, Winchester (WG 9 Jan 99)
HUTCHINSON, John, blacksmith, b. in Yorkshire, Eng., ran away from Thomas POLLARD, Lancaster Co. (VG 24 Sep 72)
HUTCHINSON, Joseph, appr. printer, 19, b. in Hartford, Conn., ran away from his master in Lansingburgh (NH 10 Sep 96)
HUTCHINSON, Robert, appr., c. 16, ran away from Robert LATHAN Pr. Wm. Co.; it is supposed he will try to get to Alexandria (TAA 9 Mar 98)
HUTCHINSON, Mrs. Sarah, dec'd, e.a.w. her admr., J. BLAMIRE of Portsmouth; he and J. CRAIG (nfi) will sell her house and lot (NH 26 Mar 96)
HUTT, John, mar. Miss Amelia P. HALL at Carville, Westmoreland Co. on Thurs. last (VHFFA 15 Dec 95)
HYBART, Mrs., late midwife to the Middlesex Lying-In Hospital, London, has fixed her residence in Richmond (VGGA 30 Nov 96)
HYDE, Mr., of Surry Co., murdered by one of his Negroes last Mon.; the Negro, who was later tried and hanged, also murdered HYDE's wife and three chil. (Wmsbrg. disp. of 18 and 25 Jan.) (MG 7 Feb 54, NYPB 25 Feb 54)
HYDE, Daniel, age 23, b. on the Eastern Shore of Va., sentenced to death in Rhode Island for piracy (AWM 24 Jul 23 [name also spelled HIDE])
HYLAND, Robert, for many yrs. past a door-keeper to the GA, d. last Wed. (VG 31 Jul 79)
HYLTON, Capt. John, Comptroller of the Customs in the Upper District of James River, d. at Bermuda Hundred (VG 18 Nov 73); his ex., Francis EPPES and John HYLTON, will sell his HH and KF at Bermuda Hundred (VG 4 Mar 75); his ex. will sell about 50 Virginia-born Negroes bel. to his est. at Manchester (VG 14 Sep 76); his ex. will sell 500 ac. of his land in Chesterfield Co. on James River (VGPu 27 Mar 78)
HYLTON, Ralph Esq., mar. Miss Polly WARD of Chesterfield Co. on Thurs. last (VICGA 3 Feb 90)
HYLTON, Ralph, att. at law, d. on Tues. the 28th ult. in Manchester (VGGA 7 Mar 92); his PE will be sold by Richard GOODE in Manchester (VGGA 4 Apr 92 ex)
HYORT, Charles Esq., att. at law, of Wmsbrg., mar. Miss Betsy WILLIS dau. of Francis WILLIS Esq. of Gloucester in that co. (VGRDA 31 Dec 92)
HYRIDS, Patrick, Irish, des. from Capt. James MACKILWEAN's Co. at Petersburg (VG 19 Jul 54)

IMRAY, John, dec'd, his surviving ex. are Robert BOLLING and Robert TURNBULL who will settle his est. (VGPI 16 Jun 91)
INGHAM, Joshua, mar. Miss Nancy WELCH both of Fredsbrg. on Sun last (VHFFA 25 Oct 96)
INGLES, Andrew, Scot, ind. svt., baker, ran away from James KIRK, Robert ADAM, and George PURVIS in Alexandria (VG 17 Jun 75)
INGLESTON, William, mar. Miss DAVIS dau. to the late Rev. Mr. Thomas DAVIS of Norfolk on Tues. last (VGNI 15 Jun 74)

INGLIS, Samuel Esq., merch., of Norfolk, mar. Miss Nancy AITCHISON dau. of William AITCHISON Esq. last Thurs. (VG and VGNI 7 Jul 74)
INGRAHAM, Mrs. Mary, wife of Nathaniel INGRAHAM of Alexandria, d. on the 14th ult. at Concord, Mass. while on a visit to her friends (VGWA 26 Mar 88)
INGRAM, John, of Norfolk Borough, d. suddenly on Sun. night last (NH 21 Mar 99); his admr., William G. INGRAM of Norfolk, will sell all of his HH and KF (NH 15 Oct 99)
INGRAM, Joseph, Irish conv. svt., c. 28 [in later issue given as Eng. conv. svt., 27], ran away from Henry COLEMAN, Spotsylvania Co.; he has reportedly changed his name to Joseph WAGPELS (VGP 3 Aug 75, 14 Sep 75)
INNES, Harry, intends to move to Lincoln Co., Ky. immediately where he will practice law (VGAA 4 Dec 84)
INNES, The Hon. Harry Esq., was mar. to Mrs. SHIELDS at Danville, Ky. on 9 Feb. by the Rev. John HURT, Chaplain to the Federal Army (VGGA 21 Mar 92)
INNES, James, Scot, [svt.], 24, ran away from Samuel DUVAL, Henrico Co. (VG 14 Feb 51)
INNES, Col. James, of Richmond, former Attorney General of Va., d. lately in Philadelphia; he was one of the commissioners from this state to settle British spoliations and was in the discharge of that duty when he died; e.a.w. his admx., Elizabeth INNES of Wmsbrg.; his admx. will sell his PE at Yarmouth, James City Co. (OVT 9 Aug 98, Arg 10 Aug 98, VGGA 6 Sep 99, 15 Nov 99)
INNES, the Rev. Robert, late of Caroline Co., dec'd, his land in Halifax Co. to be sold by his ex., Edmund PENDLETON, Alexander ROSE, John RICHARDS, and Hugh INNES (VG 8 Aug 66); his PE to be sold at the glebe house of Drysdale Par., Caroline Co. by his ex. (VG 29 Oct 67)
INNES, Dr. Robert, of Gloucester Co., died [long obit.] (Ex 19 Jun 99)
INNES, William, Irish svt., 20, blacksmith, ran away from Alexander BISSIT, Petersburg (VG 21 Jul 68)
INNIS Family, HCC, 9 Mar 1789, Patrick HENRY (pltf.) against [?] INNIS widow of Robert INNIS dec'd, Robert INNIS, James INNIS, and Harry INNIS chil. and devisees of the sd. Robert INNIS dec'd (defs.); it appears that Harry INNIS is not an inhabitant of this country (VGWeA 9 Apr 89)
INNIS, Hugh, one of the reps. for Pittsylvania Co., mar. Miss Hannah EGGLESTON of James City Co. (VG 9 Jan 72)
INSKEEP Family, Orange Co., Ct. of Q.S, 27 May 1795: James INSKEEP (compl.) against William PANNILL, Samuel INSKEEP, Abraham INSKEEP, George SPARK and Mary his wife, Samuel JAGGARD and Hope his wife, Samuel HAINS and Elizabeth his wife, Hannah INSKEEP, S[o]billa INSKEEP, and Priscilla INSKEEP (defs.) (VHFA 19 Jun 95)
IRBY, Charles, who was declared a deserter, adv. that he had gotten a replacement named Isaac CHAPMAN (VGPu 21 Mar 77)
IRBY, John, of Suffolk Co., dec'd, his PE to be sold by his ex., John EDMUNDS and Richard BLUNT (VG 14 Dec 69)
IREDALL, the Rev, John, of Culpeper Co., mar. Miss Hannah BAUGHAN of Fredsbrg. (VHFA 2 Apr 89)
IREDELL, the Hon. James Esq., one of the Associate Judges of the U. S. Supreme Ct., d. on the 20th ult. at Edenton, N. Carolina [obit. in Arg.] (VH 8 Nov 99, Arg 12 Nov 99)
Irish Svts.: Anthony M'GUIRE, shoemaker, 20; James HUGHES, 20; John CHAPMAN, blacksmith, 21; ran away from Samuel OWINGS and David SOUTHERLAND, Baltimore Co., [Md.] (VGAxA 8 Nov 92)
IRVINE, Dr. William, late of Lynchburg, dec'd, his ex., James GRAHAM and Samuel IRVINE, have authorized John DABNEY, att. at law, to settle his est. (LWM 15 Jan 98)
IRVING, Charles, dec'd, his extx. (nfi) of Buckingham Co., will sell 2200 ac. of

his land in Amherst Co. and 90 of his slaves (VGGA 17 Feb 96)
IRVING, Thomas, merch. of Petersburg, mar. Miss Betty MATTHEWS of the same, a few days ago (VGPI 19 Oct 75)
IRWIN, Edward Esq., quartermaster to Maj. BLAND's troop of horse, died (VGPu 18 Apr 77 sup)
IRWIN, Francis, Irish conv. svt., blacksmith, ran away from Samuel CANBY, Loudoun Co. (VGP 8 Jun 75)
IRWIN, Jones, late of Yorktown, dec'd, his brother and heir at law, John IRWIN of Dublin, shoemaker, gives power of attorney to sell his land in Kg. Geo., Warwick, and York cos. (VG 11 Apr 55, 13 Jun 55)
ISAACS, Isaiah, mar. Miss Hetty HAYES both of this city [Richmond] on Thurs. last (RMA and VGRC 9 May 95)
ISBEL, Peyton, escaped from public service at Point of Fork, 11 Oct. (VGAA 18 Oct 83)
ISBELL, Anne, her husb., William ISBELL of Goochland Co., adv. that she behaves in an ill-natured and indecent manner to him (VGGA 28 Dec 91)
ISLER, George, cooper, dec'd, e.a.w. his admx., Mary ISLER (CMAG 29 Oct 96) [see also George HUSSLER]
IVES, Joshua, dec'd, e.a.w. his ex., Edward MOORE (NHPA 31 Dec 96)
IVESON, George, of Gloucester Co., dec'd, 10 of his slaves to be sold by Richard GREGORY (VGR 24 Dec 67)

JACK, James, of Potomac in Berkeley Co., d. last Tues. sennight; he was among the first white children b. in this vale; he employed himself in cultivating the then wild woods and raised a respectable family; he desired to be bur. on the same plant. where he was born 61 yrs. ago (PGBA 14 Jan 96)
JACKSON, Anthony, Eng. svt., b. in Yorkshire, c. 20, ran away from John HOOD, Elk Ridge, Anne Arundel Co., Md. (VGR 27 Sep 70)
JACKSON, David, of Alexandria, dec'd, e.a.w. his admr., William LYLES (VJAA 11 May 86)
JACKSON, Fips, dec'd, his PE to be sold by his ex., Fleming BATES (VGR 22 Mar 70)
JACKSON, George, of Norfolk, will go to Eng. in a short time to recover his health; in his absence, Matthew JACKSON (nfi) and William JAQUES will carry on the business (VG 13 Feb 72)
JACKSON, Harry, mulatto, ran away from Thaddeus M'CARTY, Loudoun Co.; he has relations in the lower end of Fairfax Co. (VJAA 21 Apr 85)
JACKSON, Henry, dec'd, late of Brunswick Co., e.a.w. his admr. w.w.a., E. COOPER (VGPI 25 Apr 97)
JACKSON, James, blacksmith, c. 20, suspected along with John JACKSON (watchmaker, c. 20) of being connected with Lowe JACKSON in counterfeiting; both are sought by Va. authorities (MG 7 Nov 50)
JACKSON, Jane, of Richmond, will petition for a divorce from her husband, David JACKSON (Arg 23 Aug 99)
JACKSON, John, enl. in Fauquier Co., c. 22, deserted (VGPu 13 Jun 77)
JACKSON, Joseph O. B., d. on Tues. morn. last (VGGA 3 Jun 95, RMA 4 Jun 95, RC 6 Jun 95)
JACKSON, Low[e], sentenced to death at the Gen. Ct. in Apr. 1751 for counterfeiting the current coin and was reprieved til H.M's pleasure was known, is at length ordered for execution (Wmsbrg. disp. of 30 Mar. 1753); executed at the gallows near Wmsbrg. on 13 April; he is to be bur. in Nansemond Co. where he was born (VG 18 Apr 51, MG 12 Apr 53, 10 May 53)
JACKSON, Lucy, has eloped from her husband, Mingo JACKSON of Richmond (VGGA 9 Mar 99); Mingo JACKSON, hair dresser, adv. that Lucy JACKSON is not his wife but rather the wife of Mingo JACKSON the blacksmith (VGGA 12 Apr 99); she adv. that from the unjustifiable treatment she received at the hands of her husband, she feels at liberty to claim a separation from him until she can petition the next GA for a divorce (VGGA 16 Aug 99); her husband forbids all persons from harboring her (VGGA 27 Aug 99)

JACKSON, Major, aka Major, mulatto, ran away from M. ANDERSON who believes he may be hankering about in Richmond as he has an uncle near that place (known by the name of Tarlton) (VGGA 25 Mar 95)
JACKSON, Matthew, dec'd, his ex., Josiah JACKSON, will sell his 600 ac. tract in Pr. Edw. Co. (VGGA 7 Oct 95 ps)
JACKSON, Mrs. Milley, wife of William JACKSON of this place [Fredsbrg.], d. last Mon. (VHFA 27 Nov 88)
JACKSON, Miss Patience, of Chesterfield Co., d. in the bloom of life (VGPu 29 May 78)
JACKSON, Philip Whitehead, of Lunenburg Co., d. a few days ago (VGPI 21 Mar 97); his admr., Thomas GORDON, will sell his PE at Hungry Town, Lunenburg Co. (VGPI 28 Apr 97)
JACKSON, Richard, dec'd, his est. was sold in Nov. 1781 (VGAA 23 Aug 83)
JACKSON, Royal, Negro, c. 23, says he is free born and of the Par. of Kingston on the Eastern Shore of Va. and that he served his time to James DAVENPORT who moved from sd. place to Pittsylvania Co., came to the house of John DEPREIST Jr. in Campbell Co. who has doubts about his freedom (VGGA 13 Sep 97)
JACKSON, Thomas, ind. svt., coachman, c. 30, ran away from John SYME and John CHRENSHAW, Hanover Co. (VG 21 Apr 74)
JACKSON, Thomas, mar. Miss Nancy SMITH at Battletown (VGWA 29 Apr 89)
JACKSON, Thomas, appr., 19, ran away from Robert CREIGHTON, Martinsburg (PGBA 14 Nov 91)
JACKSON, William, from Va. where he was a freeholder in Augusta Co., apparently murdered at South Kingston, Rhode Island by Thomas CARTER also of Va. (NYPB 25 Mar, 8 Apr, 22 Apr 51)
JACKSON, William, eld. son and heir at law of Robert JACKSON dec'd, summoned to appear at Spotsylvania Co. Ct. to answer a bill of complaint (VGR 12 May 68)
JACKSON, William, svt., c. 27, ran away from William JENKINS, Frederick Co. (VG 24 May 70)
JACKSON, William, a young man of Norfolk, drowned in Norfolk River on Sun. the 6th inst. (VG and VGR 24 Jun 73)
JACKSON, William, d. suddenly last Sun. in Fredsbrg. in his 42nd year; his admr. is Richard S. HACKLEY (VHFA 7 Jul, 29 Sep 91); e.a.w . his admr. (VHFA 8 Nov 92)
JACKSON, William, shoemaker, c. 25, ran away from John HARRISON, Richmond (VGGA 8 Feb 92)
JACKSON, William, Negro, c. 40, jailed in Petersburg, says he bel. to William CARTER in Henrico Co. (VGPI 6 Aug 96)
JACKSON, William, Negro, 27-28, ran away from Thomas CRANDELL who believes he is gone towards Baltimore (CMAG 31 Dec 96)
JACOMI, Mary, has eloped from her husband, Emanuel JACOMI of Norfolk (AGNPWA 25 Sep 93, NHPA 8 May 97) [name also given as JACOME]
JACQUES, John, drowned in the Potomac two miles above Great Falls on the 13th inst.; his brothers living in Washington Co., Md., ask people to watch for his body (VJAA 26 Mar 89)
Jailed in Augusta Co.: Irish svts., William MORRIS (aka MORRISON) and Peter KINCHLER, and Eng. svt., Thomas HANSFIELD (VGR 31 Oct 71)
JAKINS, William, svt., 25, just imp. on the *Wilcox*, ran away from Peter RANDOLPH, Wmsbrg. (VG 16 May 55)
JAMES, Ann, has eloped from her husband, Elias JAMES of Loudoun Co. (VJAA 4 Dec 88)
JAMES, Edward, of Princess Anne Co., dec'd, his PE to be sold by his ex., John JAMES and Joshua JAMES (NPJ 4 Feb 89)
JAMES, Martha, of Loudoun Co., aged 90, d. last Sun. eve. [obit.] (VGWA 10 Sep 91)
JAMES, Richard, appr. lad with nearly three years to serve, ran away from George GAYLE, Mathews Co. (AGNPPA 28 Aug 95)

JAMES, Thomas, b. in Gloucester Co., blacksmith, 29, des. from the 7th U. S. Regt. of Infantry (NH 1 Oct 99)

JAMES, Maj. Thruston, of James City Co., d. on Wed. last after a short illness, in his 65th year (VG 5 Feb 80)

JAMES, William, of James City Co., mar. Miss Elizabeth PIERCE dau. of John PIERCE of the same co. on Sat. the 7th inst. (VGGA 25 May 91)

JAMESON, Mrs., relict of Thomas JAMESON lately dec'd, merch., of Yorktown (VG 14 Mar 71)

JAMESON, Dr. Alexander, of Blandford, Pr. Geo. Co., dec'd, his PE to be sold by his ex., Thomas YUILLE (VG 4 Jul 66)

JAMESON, Alexander, native of [New] Jersey, 29, des. from the Fredsbrg. rendezvous of the 4th U. S. Regt. of Infantry (VH 11 Jan 99)

JAMESON, David Esq., of Yorktown, d. on the 10th inst. (VGGA 24 Jul 93, VGRMA 25 Jul 93); his admrs. w.w.a., John, David, and David JAMESON Jr., will sell his lot and houses in Yorktown (VGGA 21 Aug 93); e.a.w. his admrs. w.w.a. of Wmsbrg. who will also sell his lot and houses in Yorktown (VGWeA 4 Oct 93)

JAMESON, Stanley, dec'd, e.a.w. his ex., Nathaniel PEED of Portsmouth (NH 6 Feb 96)

JAMESON, Thomas, merch. of Yorktown, died (VG 10 Jan 71); e.a.w his admr., Lewis TYLER (VG 9 May 71)

JAMIESON, John, tinsmith, came from Glasgow upwards of 10 years ago; his friends have not heard from him since 1775 when he desired them to address him to the care of Robert HAMILTON, Ferry Cr., Augusta Co. or Mr. Lamb LYLE, merch., Humber [sic] Co.; if the sd. JAMIESON is alive and will apply to Robert THOMSON, merch. Port Royal, Rappahannock, he will hear of something very much to his advantage (VGWeA 30 Oct 84)

JANES, Thomas, along with his wife, Ann JANES, both of Loudoun Co., declares that Miss Peggy PERRY is innocent of their charges against her character (VGAxA 10 Jun 90)

JANEY, Mrs. Margaret, d. Thurs. last at Raleigh near Four Mile Cr. (Arg 4 Jun 99)

JANNY, William, aka OLIPHANT, appr., c. 20, ran away from Abel JANNY, Frederick Co. (BVCG 20 Jul 95)

JAQUELIN, Edward, former justice of the peace, d. on 9 Nov. at his house at Jamestown in his 71st year (VG 16 Nov 39)

JAQUELIN, Mrs. Martha, d. on Wed. the 20th inst., aged 82, in Richmond (VGGA 26 Dec 92, BVCG 14 Jan 93)

JARDINE, John, conv. svt., from Cumberland [Eng.], ran away from John CARLYLE, Alexandria (VG 13 Aug 72)

JARVIS, Mrs., relict of the late John JARVIS of Fredsbrg., d. on Sat. night last (VHFFA 31 Jan 97, RCFPC 1 Feb 97)

JAVEN, Martha, has eloped from her husband, Daniel (SS 21 Sep 93)

JEEK, John, aka TEEK, of the Par. of South Brent, Somersetshire, left Eng. and came to this colony where he was reportedly employed as a bailiff or under sheriff to a Mr. JONES; he has not been heard of for eight yrs.; Humphrey HILL, K & Q Co., adv. for information on him (VG and VGR 20 Jan 74)

JEFFERS, Dominick, of Petersburg [poem on his death, signed "A. B."] (VGPI 3 Jan 94)

JEFFERS, Capt. John, killed in a duel in Petersburg on Sat. last (Petersburg disp. of 17 Nov.) by John W. JOHNSON [he is called John JEFFERSON Esq. in HNPA] (HNPA 19 Nov 95, RC 21 Nov 95, VHFFA 24 Nov 95)

JEFFERSON Family, Pittsylvania Co., Aug. Ct. 1798, in chanc: Samuel HOPKINS and John PUCKET (pltfs.) against Elizabeth JEFFERSON widow and relict of Peter F. JEFFERSON, Field JEFFERSON, William JEFFERSON, John JEFFERSON, Samuel JEFFERSON, George MURPHY and Frances his wife formerly Frances JEFFERSON, Judith JEFFERSON who are of lawful age, and Alexander JEFFERSON, Patsy JEFFERSON, and Elizabeth JEFFERSON infants under 21 by Elizabeth JEFFERSON their gdn

Thomas JEFFERSON, and Archer JEFFERSON (defs.); it appears that William and Samuel JEFFERSON and George and Frances MURPHY are not inhabitants of the state (LWG 13 Oct 98)
JEFFERSON, G., has removed for some yrs. into Lunenburg Co. and will sell a tract of land on Turkey Cr. in Pittsylvania Co. (VG 10 Sep 72); of Lunenburg Co. intends to remove into N. Carolina (VGPu 13 Sep 76 sup)
JEFFERSON, Luke, formerly a post rider, d. from a fall on Thurs. last (WG 2 Oct 99)
JEFFERSON, Thomas Esq., one of the reps. for Albemarle Co., mar. Mrs. Martha SKELTON the relict of Bathurst SKELTON (VG 2 Jan 72)
JEFFRIES, Mrs. Elizabeth, consort of John JEFFRIES, d. in Fauquier Co. on the 18th ult. (VH 2 Jul 99)
JEFF[S], Thomas, appr., 17-18, ran away from Lewis STEPHENS (BVCG 22 Apr 93)
JEGITTS, John, of Wmsbrg., dec'd, his houses and lots to be sold by Joseph JEGITTS (nfi) (VG 1 Nov 70)
JENIFER, Walter Hanson, doctor of physic, d. on 16 Dec after a short illness in Alexandria (VJAA 29 Dec 85)
JENKIN, William, d. at Winchester; he had attended Col. WASHINGTON upon his journey to Ft. Venango (VG 24 Mar 74)
JENKINGS, John, Eng. svt., 28, ran away from George TURBERVILLE, Westmoreland Co.; he had arrived in Va. in 1739 (VG 20 Jul 39)
JENKINS Family, Stafford Co., Ct. of Q.S, 11 Aug 1795, in chanc: William Griffin TURNER (pltf.) against Thomas JENKINS, George NICHOLS and Hester his wife, Thomas MILLS and Hannah his wife, William MILLS and Mary his wife, Sarah JENKINS, Anne JENKINS, William JENKINS, and Margaret JENKINS (defs.); the defs. Thomas JENKINS, Thomas and Hannah MILLS, William and Mary MILLS, Sarah, Anne, William, and Margaret JENKINS appear not to be inhabitants of the Commonwealth (VHFA 4 Sep 95)
JENKINS, Henry, appr., 18-19, ran away from Hugh GILKESON near Staunton, Augusta Co. (BVCG 9 Sup 93)
JENKINS, Mrs. Mary, of this town [Alexandria], d. yesterday morn. (CMAG 9 Jun 96)
JENKINS, Richard, aka Dick, Negro, c. 30, plays on the violin and is a good sawyer, ran away from Wood JONES, Amelia Co., in May 1759 (MG 10 Jul 60)
JENKINS, William, conv. svt., cabinet maker, c. 45, ran away from Thomas MILLER, Fredsbrg. (VG 2 Jul 72)
JENKINS, William, d. lately in Winchester, a worthy old man who had served with Brad[d]ock and Dunbar (VGR 24 Mar 74)
JENKINS, William, d. on Sun. last in Fredsbrg.; he was bur. with Masonic honors (VHFA 1 Jan 95, VGRMA 5 Jan 95)
JENNINGS, Moody, late of Hanover Co., dec'd, e.a.w. his surviving ex., Charles COLLEY (VIC 26 Mar 88)
JERDONE Family, HCC, 9 Mar 1797, William JERDONE surviving ex. of Charles JERDONE (pltf.) and Benjamin JOHNSON and John MILLER acting ex. of Michael JOHNSON, Reuben JERDONE son of Matthew JERDONE, Charles SCOTT, John HARRIS son of John HARRIS, William CABELL and Peggy his wife, John WYATT and Jemima his wife, Matilda ROSE relict of Hugh ROSE, and Mary WINSTON relict of Geddes WINSTON (Arg 9 May 97)
JEREMIAH, Thomas, from Wales, c. 40, came from Philadelphia to the Head of Elk two yrs. ago and to Alexandria last May with his wife, who is from Ireland; he is suspected of aiding svts. to run away (NPJ 12 Dec 87)
JESSIE, William, Virginian, 23, des. from Capt. Thomas WAGGENER's Co. of Va. forces (VG 22 Aug 55)
JETER, Winnifred, of Nottoway Co., dec'd, widow of Thomas JETER dec'd of Amelia Co., e.a.w. her admr., Henry JETER (VGGA 11 Sep 98)

JETT, Mrs. Catharine, d. on 15 Nov. in Westmoreland Co; she was bur. in the family burial ground near Leedstown; she had become a widow in the early part of her life; she had four daus. (VJAA 30 Nov 86)
JETT, Francis, dec'd, slaves bel. to his est. to be sold at Mattox Bridge by his exors. of Westmoreland Co. (VJAA 8 Feb 87)
JETT, Francis, dec'd, e.a.w. his admx., Bersheba JETT, of Stafford Co. (VHFFA 30 Oct 95)
JOBSON, Philip Yeates, dec'd, his admrs. (nfi) adv. for the heir (nfi) who will receive about £15 (VG 19 Dec 71)
JOHN, [?], on the 22nd ult. a son of Gregory JOHN of Petersburg was baptized by the Rev. William HARRISON; he also mar. the father and mother, grandfather and grandmother, the grandmother twice, and the great grandfather and great grandmother (VGPI 4 Jul 97)
JOHNS, Daniel, sailor, 18-19, ran away from the ship *Boyne* at Gosport (VG 24 Jan 71)
JOHNS, Jesse, c. 19, resided in Amherst Co. for three yrs. past, des. from the co. of James FRANKLIN (VGPu 7 Mar 77)
JOHNSON Family, Louisa Co., Ct., 17 May 1792, in chanc: James JOHNSON and Keziah his wife (pltfs.) against Christopher JOHNSON and Thomas JOHNSON exors. of David JOHNSON dec'd (defs.); it appears that Christopher JOHNSON is not an inhabitant of this state (VGGA 25 Jul 92)
JOHNSON, Mr., traveling man from New York, murdered in Orange Co. on 17 Aug. (VHFA 28 Aug 88)
JOHNSON, Mrs., wife of John JOHNSON [also occurs as JOHNSTON, q.v.] hatter, d. on Thurs. last (HNPA 22 Aug 95)
JOHNSON, Agnes, her husband, Henry JOHNSON of Spotsylvania Co., accuses her of having taken up with another man and of conspiring to take his est. away and commit him to the local mad house (VHFA 26 Jun 94)
JOHNSON, Andrew, merch., d. last week at Petersburg (VGWeA 14 May 85)
JOHNSON, Andrew, late of Manchester dec'd, his ex., William LAPRADE, will sell his lands on the west side of the Blue Ridge and in Culpeper Co. (VGGA 24 Apr 93)
JOHNSON, Ben, aka Ben, mulatto, c. 32, ran away from William HOSKINS, K & Q Co.; he had run away 18 months previously and was caught in New Castle, Delaware about a month ago, but he [escaped by] passing as a free man in Philadelphia; he is probably headed for Philadelphia or New York (VGGA 26 Jul 99, VH 2 Aug 99)
JOHNSON, Benjamin, dec'd, his ex., Nathan BELL, will sell his 416 ac. tract in Hanover Co. (VGGA 9 Sep 95, RMA 26 Sep 95)
JOHNSON, Billy, Negro, c. 20, jailed as a runaway in Richmond; says he was b. in Accomack Co. and that his mother, Katy JOHNSON, his brother, Harry, and other relations live there; his father, Billy JOHNSON, is dead and was well known to Mr. Ezekiel YOUNG Clerk of that co.; his brother, Harry, has Col. CROPPER's slave, Sukey, for his wife (VGGA 13 Nov 98)
JOHNSON, David, late of Louisa Co., dec'd, e.a.w. his ex., Christopher JOHNSON (VIC 20 Feb 88)
JOHNSON, Dorothy, has behaved unseemly towards her husband, B. JOHNSON of Fredsbrg. (VGR 26 Jul 70)
JOHNSON, Edward, late of Chesterfield Co., dec'd, e.a.w. his ex., William and Andrew RONALD (VGWeA 27 Apr 82, VGAA 11 May 82)
JOHNSON, George Esq., eminent practitioner of law, one of the reps. in assembly for Fairfax Co., d. on [31 Aug.] in Alexandria (MG 4 Sep 66, VG 19 Sep 66)
JOHNSON, George, appr. shoemaker, 18-19, ran away from James MOORE near Leesburg (VGWA 8 Oct 91)
JOHNSON, Henry, Eng. svt., ran away from Robert PHILLIPS, Fredsbrg. (VGR 4 Feb 68)
JOHNSON, Henry, of Surry Co., to be hanged for horse stealing (VHFA 26 Jun 88)

JOHNSON, James, late of Charles City Co., dec'd, a tract of his land to be sold by his ex., Richard COCKE and Benjamin COCKE (VG 7 Nov 31)
JOHNSON, James, Thomas BRIGHTWELL found not guilty of being an accessory to his murder in Orange Co. (VHFA 19 Mar 89)
JOHNSON, James Bray Esq., mar. Miss Rebekah COCKE of [Chesterfield Co.] (VG 15 Jul 73); d. at Westbury in Charles City Co. (VG and VGCD 27 Nov 79); of Richmond, dec'd, his ex., John TYLER and William JOHNSON of Richmond, will sell 20 of his slaves (VGAA 1 Nov 83, 10 Jan 84, VGIC 15 Nov 83)
JOHNSON, Jean, is not contented to live with her husband, John JOHNSON Sr. of Stafford Co. (VG 16 Jul 72)
JOHNSON, John, b. in Dublin, 27, des. from Capt. Robert HODGSON's Independent Co. now raising for the service and defense of S. Carolina (VG 3 Jul 46)
JOHNSON, John, seaman, Scot, 23, ran away from the ship *Encouragement* of London lying at West Point (VG 10 Apr 52)
JOHNSON, John, svt., ran away from Armistead CHURCHILL, Middlesex Co. (VG 12 Jun 52)
JOHNSON, John, recruit, carpenter, des. from the 1st Va. Regt.; he was an inhabitant of Amelia Co. (VGPu 25 Apr 77)
JOHNSON, John, bricklayer of Alexandria, drowned last Fri. (VJAA 26 Mar 89)
JOHNSON, John, dec'd, his ex., William WEBBER Jr. and John GUERRANT Jr., will sell his est. in Goochland Co. (VIC 18 Nov 89)
JOHNSON, the Rev. Mr. Josiah, one of the masters of the college, mar. Miss Mildred MOODY last Thurs. (VG 26 May 68); Rector of Bruton Par., Master of the Grammar School in William and Mary College, and Professor of Humanity, d. on Sun. last (VG and VGR 8 Apr 73); his ex., John CAMM and James CARTER, will sell all his PE (VG 10 Jun 73)
JOHNSON, Moses, Negro, c. 24, property of Samuel [TROSS] of the Eastern Shore of Md., jailed in Norfolk Borough (NH 3 Aug 99)
JOHNSON, Pamela, has quitted the bed and board of her husband, Frederick JOHNSON, who will no longer pay her debts (AGNPPA 15 Sep 95)
JOHNSON, Col. Philip, [dec'd], claims against his trust est. to be settled with John WATKINS Esq. of New Kent Co. per the ex. of James B. JOHNSON who are John TYLER and William JOHNSON (VGAA 11 May 82)
JOHNSON, Col. Richard, of Newcastle, died (VG 10 Oct 71)
JOHNSON, Col. Richard, dec'd, four college lots formerly his property to be sold (VGAA 20 Dec 83)
JOHNSON, Robert, of Orange Co., dec'd, e.a.w. his admr., Grace JOHNSON and Andrew SHEPHERD (VGPu 10 Feb 75)
JOHNSON, Samuel, Eng. svt., baker, acquainted with the City of London and says he was in the East Indies, ran away from John DRAPER, Wmsbrg. (VG and VGR 11 Nov 73)
JOHNSON, William, svt., 25, ran away from John GRATTAN, York Co., Pa. (VGR 4 Feb 68)
JOHNSON, William, Eng. svt., c. 16, arrived in Va. in 1768 on the *Justitia* from London; John JOHNSON (nfi) wishes information on him (VG 16 Apr 72)
JOHNSON, Sir William, d. at Johnson Hall the 11th inst. (VGNI 4 Aug 74)
JOHNSON, William, appr., 17-18, b. in or near Wmsbrg., bound to a staymaker in Surry Co. by the James City Ct., ran away from the brig *Innermay* at Brandon on James River (VG 21 Jan 75, VGNI 16 Feb 75)
JOHNSON, William Esq., of Frederick Co., mar. Miss REYNOLDS of Richmond Co. on Sun. last (VGWA 1 Jul 89)
JOHNSON, William, by trade a cooper, murdered a woman named Nancy ALVAS on Sun. 20 Jul. and has since fled the city of Richmond; he is about 28 (VGRMA 28 Jul 94, VGWeA 2 Aug 94)
JOHNSON, William, c. 28, des. from the rendezvous at Wmsbrg. (BVCG 8 Jun 95)
JOHNSON, William, of the late firm of Clemison & Johnson, merch., mar. Miss

Sally HAYNES on Thurs. last at the seat of Col. DAWLEY in Pr. Anne Co. (NHPA 19 Nov 96)

JOHNSON, William, dec'd, e.a.w. his ex., Stephen JOHNSON, of Goochland Co. (VGGA 28 Dec 96)

JOHNSON, William, appr., son of Jeremiah JOHNSON of Richmond, painter, 18, ran away from Morgan WINGMORE (VGGA 11 Jan 99)

JOHNSTON Family, Caroline Co. Ct., 13 Mar 1789, in chanc: Joshua ARNOLD and Priscilla his wife, Cary BULLARD, Daniel JOHNSTON and Clary JOHNSTON (pltfs.) against Jebediah JOHNSTON ex. of Daniel JOHNSTON dec'd, and John SAUNDERS and Betsy SAUNDERS his wife (defs.); it appears that John and Betsy SAUNDERS are not inhabitants of this country (VGIC 6 Jun 89 sup)

JOHNSTON Family, HCC, 9 Mar 1791: Jennings BURRUS and Elizabeth his wife and Mary JOHNSTON and John JOHNSTON infants by the sd. Jennings BURRUS their next friend (pltfs.) and Benjamin WINN admr. w.w.a. of Aquilla JOHNSTON dec'd, William DUERSON and Elizabeth his wife, Richard JOHNSTON, Sarah JOHNSTON, Molly JOHNSTON, Nancy JOHNSTON, James JOHNSTON, and Aquilla JOHNSTON infants under 21 which sd. Elizabeth, Richard, Sarah, Molly, Nancy, James, and Aquilla are the chil. of Aquilla JOHNSTON dec'd, George GOODLOE, James STEVENS and Mary Byrd his wife, John GOODLOE, Joseph RAWLINGS and Elizabeth his wife, Robert GOODLOE, Aquilla GOODLOE, Henry GOODLOE, and George GOODLOE infants under 21 which sd. Mary Byrd, John, Elizabeth, Robert, Aquilla, Henry, and George are the chil. of Priscilla late the wife of George GOODLOE the elder and one of the daus. of Aquilla JOHNSTON the elder dec'd (defs.); the families are apparently of Spotsylvania Co. (VGRMA 25 Apr 93)

JOHNSTON Family, Charlotte Co. Ct., 6 Mar 1799, in chanc: Caleb JOHNSTON, David BAILEY and Jeane his wife, James JOHNSTON, and Patsey JOHNSTON which sd. Caleb, Jeane, James, and Patsey are the chil. of Samuel JOHNSTON dec'd (pltfs.) against William JOHNSTON, Samuel JOHNSTON, and Holcombe ROBERTSON and Ruth his wife (defs.); it appears that the defs. are not inhabitants of this state (Arg 19 Apr 99)

JOHNSTON, Mrs., consort of Richard JOHNSTON merch., of this town [Fredsbrg.], d. on Tues. eve. last (VH 15 Feb 99)

JOHNSTON, Andrew, of Petersburg, his ex., James CROSS, will sell all of his HH and KF (VGWeA 30 Jul 85)

JOHNSTON, Mrs. Ann, widow of Richard JOHNSTON, dec'd; pursuant to an order of Caroline Co. Ct., the tract of land formerly assigned her as her dower will be sold (VHFA 25 Sep 94)

JOHNSTON, Elisha, aka George WILKES, now in Winchester jail under sentence of death for horse stealing, was pardoned (CMAG 15 Oct, 9 Nov 99)

JOHNSTON, George Esq., aide-de-camp of Gen. WASHINGTON, died (VGPu 13 Jun 77); his ex., Archibald JOHNSTON and Leven POWALL, will sell five half-acre tracts bel. to his est. in Leesburg, Loudoun Co. (VGPu 29 Aug 77)

JOHNSTON, Jane, has left her husband, William JOHNSTON (SVG 8 Apr 96)

JOHNSTON, John, tailor, of Fredsbrg., died (VHFA 8 May 95)

JOHNSTON, John, hatter, mar. Mrs. WALLER, both of this borough, last Thurs. eve. [name also given as JOHNSON; see: Mrs. JOHNSON] (NH 24 Aug 99)

JOHNSTON, John, shot and killed by James BROWNING who was found guilty of justifiable homicide by a Culpeper Co. Ct., 24 Dec 1791 (VHFA 12 Jan 92)

JOHNSTON, John W., mar. Mrs. KAY of Halifax, N. Carolina on Sun. last in Petersburg (VGPI 30 Jun 95)

JOHNSTON, Philip, of James City Co., d. on the 15th inst. (VGWeA 19 Mar 89)

JOHNSTON, Rachael, has eloped from her husband, James JOHNSTON of Augusta Co. (BVCG 10 Dec 92)

JOHNSTON, Richard, merch., mar. Miss Nancy WALKER dau. of the late Thomas WALKER, in Fredsbrg. on Thurs. last (VH 2 Jul 99)

JOHNSTON, Robert, dec'd, his ex., Robert B. CHEW of Fredsbrg., will sell his remaining est. at Port Royal (VHFA 9 Apr 89, 23 Jun 91, 7 Jul 91) [Name also given as JOHNSTONE and JOHNSON]

JOHNSTON, Dr. Robert, native of Dumfries, Scotland, d. at his seat in Isle of Wight Co. on the 20th ult. after a short illness in his 68th year (NH 5 Sep 99)

JOHNSTON, Thomas, aka Samuel WILLIAMS, 22, private in the Corps of Artillerists and Engineers, cordwainer, b. in Carlisle, Pa., des. from Ft. Norfolk (NH 21 Nov 99)

JOHNSTON, Capt. William, late of Caroline Co., dec'd, his lot and houses in Port Royal and tract of land in Orange Co. to be sold by his ex. (VGR 10 Aug 69); his acting ex. are Robert and Benjamin JOHNSTON (VGR 28 Dec 69); some of his property in Port Royal and Orange Co. to be sold by the acting ex. (VGR 8 Feb 70, 14 Feb 71)

JOHNSTON, William, merch. of Norfolk, was mar. last eve. to Miss Sally HAYNES of Pr. Anne Co. by the Rev. Anthony WALKE (AGGA 18 Nov 96)

JOHNSTONE, Mr., killed in Berkeley Co. near Robert RUTHERFORD's Mill by John CONOWAY and [James] M'CABE on Mon. eve. last; he left a wife and seven chil. (Winchester disp. of 6 May) (VHFA 16 May 93)

JOHNSTOUN, Capt. John, of the *Lord Camden* was lost on his passage to London in 1770; any of his debtors are requested to inform Joseph LANE of Westmoreland or William CARR of Dumfries (VG 21 Jan 73)

JOLES, Dick, mulatto slave, 24, ran away from Anthony WINSTON, Bosworth, Hanover Co. (VG 12 Jun 52)

JOLLEY, Joseph, des. from John PLEASANTS' Co. of the 5th Bn., he has a family in the lower end of Henrico Co. (VGPu 20 Sep 76)

JOLLIFFE, Amos, mar. Miss Margery PERRY dau. of Ignatius PERRY of Frederick Co., a few days ago (BVCG 3 Nov 94); of Frederick Co., d. Sun. last (WG 6 Mar 99); his PE to be sold by his ex., Archibald MAGILL (WG 9 Oct 99)

JOLLIFFE, William and Elizabeth, of Frederick Co., dec'd, their legatees are James BRUCE for himself and Lydia his wife, Archibald MAGILL for Mary and Elizabeth JOLLIFFE, and Amos JOLLIFFE (BVCG 18 Nov 96)

JONES Family, HCC, 12 Mar 1796: Benjamin TOLER surviving ex. of John JONES, Cicely ANDERSON admx. of William ANDERSON, Nathaniel ANDERSON admr. and Elkanah TALLEY and Mary his wife admrs. of John ANDERSON (pltfs.) and Elizabeth JONES widow and relict of John JONES, Laney JONES, Richard BANKS and Elizabeth his wife, Charles LAMBERT and Nancy his wife, Hardin BURNLEY, and George BRACKENRIDGE (defs.) (RMA 14 May 96)

JONES, Mr., overseer in Accomack Co., reportedly murdered two or three weeks ago by two Negro men (MG 6 Dec 53, NYPB 31 Dec 53)

JONES, Abraham, dec'd, his est. in Pr. Geo. Co. to be auctioned in Jul. by his ex., Peter JONES, Abraham COCK, and Frederick JONES (VG 20 Jun 45); Peter JONES, an infant, is his son and heir (VG 4 Jul 45)

JONES, Allen, dec'd, his ex., W. GOOSLEY, will sell several tracts of his land in Warwick and York cos. (VIC 20 May 89)

JONES, Miss Ann, younger dau. of the late John JONES Esq., d. at Hampton on Sun. the 14th (NH 22 Feb 96)

JONES, Miss Anne, dau. of Mrs. Mary JONES of Hanover Co., d. on Thurs. 30 Jun. (RMA 2 Jul 96, VGGA 6 Jul 96)

JONES, Archer, murdered, Thomas MERIMAN, 22-23, is wanted by Cumberland Co. authorities to stand trial for the murder (Ex 15 Nov 99)

JONES, Caleb, of Richmond, merch., mar. Miss Polly SOUTHALL of Hanover, on Thurs. the 28th ult. (VGRMA 15 Apr 93)

JONES, Charles B., of Brunswick Co., mar. Miss Sarah NORFLEET of Southampton Co. on Tues. the 28th ult. (VGPI 21 Mar 97)

JONES, Charles B., Clerk of Brunswick Co. Ct., died (VGPI 10 Oct 97)

JONES, Daniel, of Amelia Co., dec'd, his ex., Francis FITZGERALD of Nottoway Co., will sell some of his horses and other property on his late est. adjoining the plant. whereon Amelia Old Ct. H. stands (RMA 12 Dec 95, 30 Dec 95,

VGPI 22 Dec 95); his acting ex., Francis FITZGERALD, will sell a tract of his land on Butcher's Cr. in Mecklenburg Co. (VGPI 18 Nov 96)

JONES, Edward, Eng. svt., in Frederick Co. prison says he ran away from Capt. Nathaniel CHEW, commander of the ship *Hannah* in Patuxent River, Md. (VG 17 Oct 51)

JONES, Edward, of Pr. Wm. Co., forewarns all persons from harboring or maintaining his wife, Jane JONES, as she has eloped from him and he will no longer pay any of her debts (RJDWA 18 Aug 96)

JONES, Elizabeth, has left her husband, Vinkler JONES, Granville [Co.], N. Carolina (VG 1 Apr, 13 May 73)

JONES, Emmanuel, Preceptor of Brafferton, mar. Miss Molly MACON [or MEKIN, acc. to VGR] of Gloucester Co. (VG and VGR 7 Apr 74)

JONES, Frederick, dec'd, John WITHERS gdn. to Elizabeth and Augustine JONES will sell a plant. bel. to the heirs of Frederick JONES dec'd on Nottoway River in Dinwiddie Co. (VGPI 5 Jul 96)

JONES, Gabriel Esq., Capt. in the 1st Va. Regt., d. at his seat in Culpeper Co. (VGPu 18 Apr 77 sup)

JONES, Henry, of Caroline Co., d. on Fri. the 5th inst. by a fall from a horse (VGRMA 15 Apr 93)

JONES, the Rev. Mr. Immanuel, Minister of Petworth Par., Gloucester Co., d. at an advanced age this week (VG 1 Feb 40)

JONES, Capt. James, dec'd, his ex., Robert and Hambleton JONES, will sell his ordinary known as Burges's near Petersburg in Dinwiddie Co. and 400-500 ac. of land pursuant to his will (VG 9 Jul 72)

JONES, James, Welsh conv. svt., ran away from Daniel and Menoah SINGLETON, Orange Co. (VGR 22 Jul 73 sup)

JONES, Capt. James, dec'd, his plant. known as High Hills, in Sussex, to be rented out by James BERRYMAN (nfi) (VG 17 Feb 76)

JONES, James, adv., that his son, Lunsford JONES, who was declared a deserter by Lt. James MERIWETHER, is only 17 and denies that he is a deserter (VGPu 8 Aug 77)

JONES, James, late of Caroline Co., dec'd, e.a.w. his ex., Thomas JONES (VG 5 Feb 80)

JONES, John, Welsh svt., 40, ran away from John DANBY, Nansemond Co. (VG 20 Apr 39)

JONES, John, Eng., suspected of stealing a horse in Chowan Co., N. Carolina, supposed to be gone towards Suffolk Co. (VG 22 Jan 67)

JONES, John, Eng. svt., 35, ran away from Andrew BURD, Augusta Co., may have altered his name in Fredsbrg. (VG 5 Mar 67)

JONES, John, of Gloucester Co., dec'd, his 300 ac. tract there to be sold by John JONES and others (VGR 8 Nov 70)

JONES, John, seriously wounded by William GOODCHILD during a fray in Wmsbrg.; he now lies at the point of death (VG 5 Dec 71)

JONES, John, conv. svt., shoemaker, c. 36, b. in Liverpool, may speak Welsh, ran away along with Elizabeth LEWELLIN, also Welsh, c. 25, from Patrick LOCKHART, Botetourt Co. (VG 26 May 74)

JONES, John, of Henrico Co., c. 29, failed to join the co. of B. C. SPILLER, Capt of State Troops at Wmsbrg. (VG 19 Dec 77)

JONES, Maj. John, of Warwick Co., dec'd, his extx., Constance JONES, will sel' all of his HH and KF and other items of his est. including a tract of 110 ac. adjoining his plant. and another tract of land on Saltford Cr., Elizabeth City Co. containing 150 ac. (VG 30 Oct 78); any claims are to be made known to Francis JONES Esq. of Warwick Co. (VG 12 Feb 79)

JONES, John, of Buckingham Co., adv. that his wife, Tabitha JONES, eloped from his bed and board (VG 2 Oct 79)

JONES, Capt. John, late of Hanover Co., dec'd, e.a.w. his ex., William ANDERSON, John ANDERSON, and Benjamin TOLER (VGAA 6 Aug 85)

JONES, John, dec'd, e.a.w. his admx., Phebe JONES, Fredsbrg. (VHFA 10 Jul 95)

JONES, John, of Bedford Co., dec'd, e.a.w. his admr., Lewellen JONES and Jesse ANDERSON (VGGA 14 Jun 97)
JONES, Joseph, of James City Co., dec'd, his admr., George HUGHES (also of James City Co.) will settle his est. and sell all of his PE (VG 17 Aug 76, 4 Jul 77)
JONES, Ludowick, of Middlesex Co., d. in his 27th year (VGPu 13 Dec 76)
JONES, Martha, formerly lived with Peter ELLIOTT as his wife; he now banishes her irrevocably and will not pay any debts contracted by her (NPC 10 Jul 90)
JONES, Mrs. Mary and William POTTER, of York Co., dec'd, e.a.w. the surviving admr., Baker PERKINS (VG 4 Nov 75)
JONES, Mrs. Mary, wife of Joseph JONES Esq. of Kg. Geo. Co., died (VGPu 18 Jul 77)
JONES, Mrs. Mary, lady of Maj. Cadwallador JONES, d. in Northampton Co., N. Carolina on the 27th ult. (VGPI 11 Jul 97)
JONES, Meriwether Esq., of Spring Garden, Hanover Co., mar. Miss Lucy Franklin READ eld. dau. of Dr. READ of Hanover Town (VIC 11 Feb 89, VGWeA 12 Feb 89)
JONES, Peter, of Brunswick Co., dec'd, e.a.w. his ex., Buckner STITH (VGPI 17 Jul 95, 13 Dec 96)
JONES, Philip, [svt.], 22, ran away from Emery HUGHES, James City Co., supposed gone towards Brunswick Co. (VG 24 Jan 51)
JONES, Reuben, of Fauquier Co., executed near Richmond on 29 Jul. for Murder (VGAA 30 Jul 85, VJAA 4 Aug 85)
JONES, Richard, dec'd, his ex., Samuel CLAY of Halifax Co., will sell all of his HH and KF and livestock (VGGA 18 Oct 97)
JONES, Robert Jr., dec'd, 1800 ac. of his land in Mecklenburg Co. to be sold by Allen JONES and Willie JONES (nfi) (VG 17 Oct 66)
JONES, Robert, dec'd, his ex., John SCOTT, will sell his land in Pittsylvania and Charlotte Cos. (VGR 10 Jan 71)
JONES, Robert, of Amelia Co., dec'd, items of his est. to be sold by his ex., Samuel JONES (VGAA 14 Sep 82)
JONES, Robert, dec'd, his ex., Richard JONES, will sell his tract in Mecklenburg Co. (VGGA 24 Jul 93)
JONES, Mrs. Sally, dec'd, her admr. w.w.a., M. JONES, will sell her land called Spring Garden on Pamunkey River 18 miles from Richmond (VGAA 16 Jul 94)
JONES, Samuel, late of Halifax Co., dec'd (VG 7 May 67)
JONES, Samuel, appr. to Matthew LANGSTONE in Cumberland Co., obtained leave to go down to Warwick Co. to see his mother and has not returned (VGPu 29 Nov 76)
JONES, Samuel, of Pr. Wm. Co., dec'd, his ex., William ALEXANDER and James GWATKIN, will sell his 400 ac. tract in Pr. Wm. about 14 miles from Dumfries and his 200 ac. tract near Reno's Ordinary about 9 miles from Dumfries (VGPu 20 Dec 76 sup)
JONES, Samuel, native of Wales, late in the employ of Messrs. Randall & Atkinson, dec'd, e.a.w. his ex., Peter LUGG (ET 12 Nov 98)
JONES, Capt. Servant, Magistrate and Inspector of Tobacco of Warwick Co., died; his ex. (nfi) will sell his PE (VG and VGR 4 Feb 73)
JONES, Stephen, aka Stephen, mulatto, 15-16, his mother belongs or did belong to Samuel HIGH on Neuse River, N. Carolina, ran away from Didier COLIN in Richmond (OVT 31 Aug, 4 Sep 97)
JONES, Strother, dec'd, Gabriel JONES advises his "legal (not gambling) creditors" to send their demands to Col. Isaac ZANE (VGWA 29 May 90); Gabriel JONES advises that he is att. in fact for the extx., Frances JONES (VGWA 27 Oct 90); by Nov. 1791, Frances JONES has remarried and is Frances BUCKNER (VGWA 19 Nov 91)
JONES, Thomas, seaman, ran away from the ship *Virginia* at Littlepage's Landing, New Kent Co., and may be heading for the Bristol Iron Mines (VG

18 Apr 45)
JONES. Thomas, Eng. svt., shoemaker, brought into Rappahannock by Capt. GRACE, ran away from Matthew WELLMAN, Hanover Co. (VG 18 Sep 46)
JONES, Thomas, Welsh svt., speaks several languages, ran away from James PATTIE near Port Royal, Caroline Co. (VG 7 Jan 68)
JONES, Thomas, svt., 20, ran away from Charles GRIFFITH and Henry GRIFFITH Jr., Frederick Co., Md. (VGR 9 Jun 68)
JONES, Thomas Esq., att. at law, dec'd, of Edenton, N. Carolina, his ex., Daniel EARL and Walter FERGUSON and Charles BONFIELD, will sell all his PE as well as tracts, houses and lots near Edenton and in Edgecombe Co. (VG 28 Feb 77)
JONES, Thomas, of Orange Co., adv. that he intends to remove to Ky. with his family some time next fall (VG 31 Jul 79)
JONES, Thomas, dec'd, e.a.w. his admr., Thomas CLAY of Dinwiddie Co. (VGWeA 24 Apr 84)
JONES, Col. Thomas, of Kg. Wm. Co., dec'd, his admr., Thomas JONES, will sell 20 of his Negroes and other items of his est. and will also settle his est. (VGAA 18 Oct, 1 Nov 86); his admr., of Hanover Co., will settle his est. and sell several likely Virginia born slaves (VGWeA 24 Jul 88)
JONES, Thomas, late of Norfolk Borough, dec'd, his ex. are James CATON and Benjamin POLLARD (HNPA 11 Mar 95)
JONES, Thomas, of Stafford Co., mar. Mrs. Sarah BROWN relict of T. BROWN of Fredsbrg., in Fredsbrg. on Fri. last (VHFFA 29 Dec 95)
JONES, Thomas Esq., mar. Miss Sally NEEDHAM on Thurs. last at Hampton (NH 16 Mar 99)
JONES, Dr. Walter, of Richmond Co., mar. Miss Alice FLOOD of Westmoreland (VG 21 Jan 73)
JONES, William, c. 30, carpenter, b. in Pr. Wm. Co., des. from the Md. Forces in Conococheague (MG 21 Jul 57)
JONES, William, aka Richard CHAPMAN, from Southampton Co., executed near Wmsbrg. Fri. last for felony (VGR 1 Jun 69, NYPB 19 Jun 69)
JONES, William, of the 6th Va. Bn., des. from the sloop *Susannah* at Leedstown (VGPu 18 Oct 76)
JONES, William, dec'd, his ex., Elisha MERIDETH, will sell two tracts of his land in Blackwell's Neck in the lower end of Hanover Co. (VGIC 22 Dec 87)
JONES, William, Negro, c. 30, claimed to be free; jailed in Alexandria (VGAxA 13 Jan 91)
JONES, William, of Mecklenburg Co., dec'd, e.a.w. his ex., Wood JONES (VGPI 13 Dec 96)
JONES, William, merch., mar. Miss Sally SIMONS dau. of David SIMONS, all of this place, in Fredsbrg. on Tues. eve. last, by the Rev. Mr. STEPHENSON (RCFPC 28 Dec 96, VHFFA 30 Dec 96)
JOPLING, Thomas the elder, of Amherst Co., d. on Mon. the 24th ult. in a very advanced age (VIC 9 Sep 89); e.a.w. his ex., James and Josiah JOPLING (VIC 9 Dec 89)
JORDAN, Henry, mar. Miss Mary Amena EVAN last eve. (RJDWA [2 Oct 95])
JORDAN, James, Scot, svt., tailor, 35, ran away from Andrew CUBBIN, Petersburg (VG 20 Apr 69)
JORDAN, Col. Samuel, late of Buckingham Co., dec'd, e.a.w. his admr., William CABELL (VGGA 20 Jul 91)
JORDAN, William, of Richmond Co., dec'd, his slaves and land in Richmond and Culpeper cos. to be sold by his son, John M. JORDAN, who intends to leave the colony soon (VG 22 Apr 57)
JOUETT, Mr., dec'd, his land in Hanover and Louisa Cos. to be sold (VG 28 Mar 45)
JOUETT, Robert Esq., of Charlottesville, mar. Miss Alice LEWIS of Henrico C on Sat. eve. (VGGA 28 Jan 95, VGRMA 29 Jan 95)
JOUETT, Col. Robert, of Charlottesville, d. on Sun. 5 Jun. [obit.] (VGGA 22 Ju 96)

JOURDAN, Francis Esq., of Louisa Co., mar. Miss Polly BYERS of Hanover Co. last week (VH 28 Jun 99)

JOYCE, Anthony, dec'd, his admr. is Benjamin JACOB of Bowling Green [Caroline Co.] (VHFA 22 Oct 89)

JOYNER, Jesse, Negro, c. 40, emancipated for the life of one Molly JOINER who is lately dead and has since been purchased by Henry ADAMS, Southampton Co., from whom he has run away (NH 8 Dec 98)

JOYNER, John, Eng. svt., c. 30, calls himself a ship carpenter, ran away from Alexander SPOTSWOOD's Iron Works (AWM 12 Aug 36)

JOYNER, Nehemiah, planter, b. in Va., 22, has relations in Toss Knot, Edgecombe Co., N. Carolina, des. from Capt. Robert HODGSON's Independent Co. now raising for the service and defense of S. Carolina (VG 3 Jul 46)

JUDAH, Mr. B. H., merch., mar. Mrs. MOSES, dau. of Mr. DELYON of [Richmond] (Arg 2 Dec 96)

JUDE, John, late of Powhatan Co., dec'd, e.a.w. his ex., Samuel Hyde SAUNDERS (VGAA 26 Jan 82)

JUHAN, Mr., musical instrument maker, d. yesterday in Petersburg (VGPI 24 Mar 97)

JULIAN, Dr. John, of Fredsbrg., dec'd, e.a.w. his admx., Margaret JULIAN (VGAA 12 Mar, 24 Sep 85)

JULIAN, Mrs. Phebe, d. at her house in Spotsylvania Co. in her 67th year; Charles JULIAN will sell the tract of land in Spotsylvania Co. which she formerly occupied (VHFA 3 Apr 94)

JUSTIS, Peter, of Norfolk Borough, d. after being accidentally shot near Newport [N. Carolina] on Sat. last (NPJ 9 Apr 88)

KA[F]KADENUS, [?], a German redemptioner, 35, ran away from John BROWNLOW and Richard SIMCOCK (VHFA 13 Nov 88)

KATING, Arthur, ind. svt., 35-40, bricklayer, ran away from Humphrey HARWOOD, Wmsbrg. (VG 21 Dec 69)

KAVANAGH, Matthew, carpenter. lately of New Port in the Province of Nova Scotia, removed from thence in 1789 to some part of the U. S. supposed to be Ky.; his brother, Patrick KAVANAGH of Halifax, Nova Scotia, asks him to write to him as it would be much to his advantage (Ex 26 Mar 99)

KAY, Mr. and Mrs., from the Richmond area, d. of poisoning by a Negro man (VGGA 12 Dec 92)

KAY, John, appr., 18, ran away from William MERCHANT, Dumfries (VGAR 17 Nov 91)

KAY, John, c. 13, wandered away from his home near Port Royal on 16 Mar. (VHFA 30 Apr 95)

KAY, Joseph, dec'd, his admr., Samuel PAINE and Alexander KAY of Richmond, will sell his PE (VGGA 27 Feb 93)

KEAN, Henry, merch. of Norfolk, mar. Mrs. HICKS of Norfolk (NPC 24 Apr 90)

KEAN, John, late cashier of the Bank of the U. S., d. at Philadelphia on the 2nd inst. (VHFA 12 May 95)

KEAN, John, c. 40, jailed for passing counterfeit money and possible counterfeiting, escaped from Staunton jail on 7 Aug. (SVG 15 Aug, VGGA 19 Aug 95)

KEARFOOT, Elizabeth, has left her husband, Samuel KEARFOOT (BVCG 14 Dec 95)

KEARNES, John, dec'd, e.a.w. his extx., Margaret KEARNES of Portsmouth (NH 20 Jul 99); his extx. will sell the remainder of his PE at The Mills on Deep Cr. (NH 3 Oct 99)

KEATING, Andrew, 30, committed to jail as a rioter and at the suit of a certain Mary FRAWD; broke out of Fairfax Co. jail (VJAA 27 Jul 86)

KEATING, Patrick, Irish ind. svt., 22, ran away from Henry HUDALE, Shenandoah Co. (BVCG 9 Apr 91)

KEATING, William, appr., 17, ran away from John PETERS, Norfolk (NPJ 17

Sep 88)

KEATING, William, formerly resided in London as an att. and is now supposed to be near Winchester; if he will apply to Samuel PLEASANTS, printer of Richmond, he will hear of something interesting to him (RMA 26 Nov 95, BVCG 14 Dec 95)

KEATTING, John, Eng. svt., an old soldier formerly under the command of Col. STEPHEN, ran away from Robert STEVENSON, Augusta Co. (VGR 11 Aug 68)

KEAY, Philip, of Va., was sent a letter from a relative in Whitechurch, Shropshire, Eng. (VG 29 Nov 70)

KEDEY, Mrs. Catherine, formerly of Mr. WEST's Company of Comedians, d. on Mon. last (NHPA 17 Nov 96)

KEEFE, William, Irish svt., ran away from the Patuxent Iron Works, Md. (VJAA 28 Jul 85)

KEELING, Andrew, aka Morris FITZJARREL, Irish conv. svt., joiner, ran away from Charles M'CARTY and Robert DOWNMAN, Richmond Co. (VG 5 Aug 73)

KEELING, Leonard, of James City Co., dec'd, his land there to be sold by Benjamin WILSON his ex. (VGR 4 Dec 66, 22 Sep 68)

KEELING, Thomas, of Pr. Anne Co., dec'd, e.a.w. his admr., Adam KEELING (NH 14 Jul 98, 10 Nov 98)

KEELING, Thorowgood, dec'd, a house bel. to his est. in Portsmouth to be sold by Paul PROBY (nfi) (VCNPGA 6 Oct 92)

KEELING, William, was mar. to Miss Mary WHITE in Pr. Anne Co. on Tues. last by the Rev. Anthony WALKE (VCNPGA 27 Oct 92)

KEENAN, Lawrence, b. in Ireland, c. 23, des. from Col. GRAYSON's Regt. (VGPu 16 May 77 sup)

KEENE, Capt. Newton, a magistrate for many years, d. on the 2nd inst. at his house in Northumberland Co. (VGR 17 Dec 70); his ex., Richard LEE and David BOYD, will sell his 1400 ac. tract in Loudoun Co. (VG and VGP 20 Oct 74); his ex. will sell his 250 ac. tract in Fairfax Co. (VGP 9 Feb 75); e.a.w. his surviving ex., Richard LEE (VGIC 22 Dec 87)

KEENE, William, of James City, d. on the 14th inst. in an advanced age (VGGA 28 Feb 98)

KEILLY, John, Irish svt., ran away from John CRAINE and Leven POWELL, Loudoun Co. (VJAA 21 Jul 85)

KEITH, Watts, mar. Miss Polly BLAMER on 5 May (PGBA 5 May 96)

KELL, Mr., native of Gt. Britain, tailor, living in Wmsbrg., d. suddenly last week (VGWeA 28 Feb 84)

KELLAM, Capt. Henry, of Kempsville, dec'd, his plant. near that town to be sold by his ex., William WHITE (NPC 26 Sep 89)

KELLER Family, HCC, 7 Mar 1796, between Adam SHERMAN Jr. surviving ex. of George KELLER dec'd, Jacob KELLER, Elizabeth SNAPP late Elizabeth KELLER, Adam SNAPP Jr. and Mary his wife, John SNAPP and Madelina his wife, Jacob SNAPP and Barbara his wife chil. and devisees of the sd. George KELLER (pltfs.) and Thomas BRYAN, Martin and Gabriel JONES exors. and devisees of Denny FAIRFAX devisee of Thomas Lord FAIRFAX (RC 5 Apr 96)

KELLER, Capt., killed by Indians in Ohio in Apr. (VJAA 25 May 86)

KELLEY, Capt. Thadey, native of Ireland, d. at the house of James PRICE, Henrico Co., in 1788; he left a son who has since died (VGGA 29 Apr 95)

KELLO, Richard Esq., d. lately in Southampton Co. (VIC 3 Jun, VGWeA 4 Jun 89)

KELLOCH, Mary, svt., b. in Eng., c. 17, ran away from Jane NEILE in Fredsbrg who has since heard that she went with one JARVIS, a drummer in the Va. Regt. (MG 3 Feb 63)

KELLY, Abraham, of Gates Co., N. Carolina, c. 21, jailed in Norfolk Borough as a man of bad fame (NHPA 5 Jun 97)

KELLY, Corporal Alexander, b. in Armagh, Ireland, weaver, 28, des. from

Capt. William PRESTON's Co. of Riflemen, 4th Sub-Legion, Montgomery Ct. House (SVG 16 Sep 96)

KELLY, Andrew, Irish svt. man, brick maker, ran away from James PARSONS, Alexandria (VGPu 20 Sep 76)

KELLY, Edmund, adjutant [also given as Lt.] of the 5th Va. Regt., reportedly killed on or about 1 Feb. in a skirmish near Drake's Farm, N. Jersey (VG 21 Feb, 7 Mar 77, VGPu 21 Feb 77, 14 Mar 77)

KELLY, Maj. George, of Norfolk Borough, d. on Tues. last [obit. in AGGA] (NH 27 Oct 96, AGGA 28 Oct 96, RMA 5 Nov 96)

KELLY, George, dec'd, of Newton & Kelly, e.a.w. his admx., Katy KELLY of Norfolk (NHPA 22 Apr 97, ET 25 Jul 99)

KELLY, Henry, mulatto, c. 17, ran away from someone (nfi) in Hanover Co. (VGWeA 22 Mar 87)

KELLY, John, b. in Ireland, 27-28, enl. in Richmond on 12 Sep. 1794, des. from Ft. Nelson (HNPA 4 Mar 95)

KELLY, Michael, Irish svt., along with his wife, Margaret, both of whom speak Irish, ran away from William HAYTH, Bedford Co. (VG 16 May 71)

KELLY, Patrick, b. in Ireland, 22-23, enl. in Richmond on 12 Sep. 1794, des. from Ft. Nelson (HNPA 4 Mar 95)

KELLY, Sarah, woman prisoner of the Indians, taken near Winchester, was retaken from them at the Kittanning in Sep. (MG 30 Sep 56)

KELLY, Thomas, Irish conv. svt., c. 26, ran away from James PERRY, Montgomery Co., Md. (VGPu 18 Apr 77)

KELLY, Walter, killed by Indians below the falls of the Great Kanawha (VG 8 Sep 74)

KELLY, William, killed by Indians on Muddy Cr., a branch of Green Brier (VG 8 Sep 74)

KELLY, William, svt., ran away from John STEED of Bath in Berkeley Co.; he took his bagpipes with him (VJAA 29 Sep 85)

KELLY, William, bricklayer, drowned near Fredsbrg. on Sun. last (VHFA 1 Aug 93)

KELSEY, Stephen, des. from Capt. Nat. BURWELL's Co. of artillery last Feb. and is supposed to be gone to N. Carolina (VGPu 3 Oct 77)

KELSICK, Mrs. Elizabeth, relict of Capt. KELSICK, d. on Sat. morn. last in her 61st year (NPJ 24 Dec 88)

KELSICK, Elizabeth, late of Norfolk, e.a.w. her ex., Ben. E. JOHNSON, Norfolk Co. (NH 23 May 96)

KELSICK, Richard, of Norfolk Borough, dec'd, e.a.w. his ex., Joseph HUTCHINGS (VGR 12 May 74)

KELSICK, Samuel B., of Richmond Co., warns persons not to rent or lease lands of the late Capt. Samuel KELSICK dec'd, because he means to have a division (VH 20 Aug 99)

KELSO, Nathan, late of Manchester dec'd, e.a.w. his admr., Robert KELSO of Pr. Edw. Co. (VGGA 12 Oct 91)

KEMON, James, appr., 18-19, ran away from William NORRIS, Centerville, Loudoun Co. (TAA 22 Jan 98)

KEMP, George, saddler of Norfolk Borough, d. on Thurs. morn. last (NHPA 13 Feb 97, AGGA 14 Feb 97); e.a.w. his admr., William ANDERSON of Norfolk (NHPA 21 Aug 97)

KEMP, James, for many yrs. a resident of Richmond, d. there on 15 Dec. with a stroke of the paralytic (apoplectic) (VGGA 16 Dec 95 ex, VGWeA 18 Dec 95, RMA 19 Dec 95)

KEMP, Matthew, Clerk of the Secretary's Office of James City Court, d. last Sun. in Wmsbrg., aged 44 (VG 14 Dec 39)

KEMP, Peter, late of Gloucester Co., dec'd, e.a.w. his ex., John and Peter KEMP (VGPu 19 Apr 76)

KEMP, Sarah, dau. of Thomas and Ann KEMP late of Gloucester Co. dec'd; she d. intestate according to a motion of her admr., James SINGLETON, in Frederick Co. Dec. Ct., 1799 (WG 11 Dec 99)

KEMPTON, Ephraim, dec'd, e.a.w. his admr., Christopher FRY of Norfolk (NH 1 Aug 99)

KENDAL, William, son and heir of Col. Custis KENDAL of Northampton Co., mar. Miss Nancy PARSONS on Thurs. the 17th inst. (VG 7 Nov 71)

KENDAL, Capt. WOFFENDAL, d. on the 5th inst. at his seat in Kg. Geo. Co. (VHFA 11 Sep 95)

KENDALL, Mr., of Kg. Geo. Co., famous for curing the dropsy, d. the beginning of Feb., aged 84 (VGPA 13 Mar 90)

KENDALL, Col. Custis, mar. Miss Susannah GORE, both of Northampton Co., on the 16th ult. (VGWeA 17 Apr 84)

KENDRICK Family, Shenandoah Co. Ct., 13 May 1794, in chanc: John SMITH and Elizabeth his wife late Elizabeth KENDRICK o of the daus. of Abraham KENDRICK dec'd (compls.) against Alexander HITE and Philip HOFFMAN exors. of the sd. Abraham KENDRICK dec'd, Jacob KENDRICK, Abraham KENDRICK, Benjamin KENDRICK, Jacob FUNK admr. of Christian KENDRICK dec'd, Catherine KENDRICK, and Christian STOVER and Barbara his wife late Barbara KENDRICK widow and relict of the sd. Abraham KENDRICK dec'd (defs.) (BVCG 11 Aug 94)

KENDRICK, Hannah, has left her husband, Abraham KENDRICK (WG 6 Jun 98)

KENDRICK, William, appr. bricklayer, ran away from Francis SMITH Sr. and James GEDDY, Kg. Wm. Ct. H.; it is supposed he has gone to Bedford Co. or into N. Carolina (VG 2 Apr 67)

KENNA, Mr. J., comedian, d. on Tues. eve. (RMA 24 Sep 95)

KENNAN, John, Irish svt., 16-18, ran away from Sampson MATTHEWS, Augusta Co. (VGAA 31 Jul 84)

KENNEDY, Capt. Alexander, a native of Scotland, d. Sun. last, aged about 60 (VHFA 15 Oct 89)

KENNEDY, Archibald Esq., d. in Lexington, Ky. on 8 Jan. 1797 (RCFPC 22 Feb 97)

KENNEDY, Mrs. Isabella, wife of John KENNEDY of Charlestown merch., d. on Thurs.. last in the bloom of life (WG 28 Aug 99)

KENNEDY, John, Irish svt., c. 26, had been discharged from some Regt. in Eng., ran away from the ship *Catherine* at Norfolk (VGNI 23 Feb 75)

KENNEDY, John, d. on Wed. night last (HNPA 4 Oct 94); merch., d. at the Great Bridge in Norfolk Co. on the 2nd inst. (VGGA 15 Oct 94); his est. to be sold on 26 Jan. by his admr., J[ames] HUNTER (HNPA 17 Jan 95); e.a.w. his admr., James HUNTER of Norfolk (NHPA 6 Jul 97); several tracts of his land near Great Bridge to be sold for his heirs (NHPA 14 Sep 97)

KENNEDY, John, cabinet maker of Baltimore, mar. Miss Isabella GRAY dau. of Robert GRAY merch. of this town [Winchester], on Sun. eve. last (BVCG 7 Apr 97)

KENNEDY, John, dec'd, Robert OTWAY, att. for the heirs, will sell two tracts of land and his remaining real est. at the Great Bridge (NH 22 Feb 98)

KENNEDY, Dr. Nathan, from Jamaica, practitioner of physic, surgery, and midwifery, offers his services to the inhabitants of Martinsburg (PGBA 28 Dec 97)

KENNEDY, Sam, mulatto slave, c. 21, absconded on 9 Jun. from Norfolk where he was sent to embark for Jamaica with several other slaves brought from thence to attend on William HYLTON's family (VGGA 19 Jun 93)

KENNER, Mrs. Eleanor, consort of Rodham KENNER of Frederick Co., d. on Mon. the 21st ult., aged 30 (WG 6 Nov 99)

KENNER, Rodham Esq., a rep. in the GA, d. in the prime of life at his seat in Northumberland Co. (VGPu 7 Mar 77 sup)

KENNON, Col. Richard, dec'd, e.a.w. his ex., Edward OSBORNE of Chesterfield Co. (VGR 14 Jun 70)

KENNON, Col. William, dec'd, his plant. in Amelia Co. to be sold (VG 26 Sep 51)

KENNON, William Esq., dec'd, Francis WILLIS (nfi) will sell four valuable tenements bel. to his est. in Charles City Co. (VG 19 Dec 77)

KENNON, William, dec'd, his land in Charles City Co. to be sold (VGAA 22 Feb 83)
KENNY, Andrew, of Stafford Co., c. 25, has a wife and child in Culpeper Co., des. from the barracks at Fredsbrg. (VHFA 6 Oct 95)
KENT, Mr., who reportedly lived in Lancaster Co. and who enl. under Capt. Wright WESTCOT to serve on board the *Norfolk Revenge* galley; his heirs are desired to apply to Joseph SCOTT Jr. in Suffolk Co. or John EVANS in Nansemond Co. for a sum of money left at his decease (VG 17 Jul 78)
KENT, Jack, Negro [or mulatto acc. to HNPA] man-slave, 30-40, plays the fiddle well, ran away from Cornelius CALVERT Sr., Norfolk (HNPA 8 Oct 95, NH 2 Jan 96)
KENT, James, mulatto, c. 40, ran away from John SNYDER and John THOMPSON, Hampshire Co. (WG 27 Nov 77)
KENYON, Ellen, of Freeman Ford, Fauquier Co., dec'd, her est. to be sold or rented (VHFA 11 Aug 91)
KENYON, James, dec'd, his land in Stafford Co., six miles below Fredsbrg., to be sold by James WE[S]T his ex. (VHFA 23 Jul 89)
KEPHART Family, Rockingham Co. Ct., 28 Mar. 1799, in chanc: Andrew BAZEL and Elizabeth his wife late Elizabeth KEPHART (comps.) against Christopher KEPHART, Henry KEPHART, Nancy KEPHART, Henry ARMENTROUT, and Charles SP[R]EKER (defs.); it appears that Christopher KEPHART is not an inhabitant of this Commonwealth (PH 17 Jul 99)
KEPPELL, Catherine, widow, only dau. and heiress of Michael GROSS dec'd and sole extx. of Henry KEPPELL of Frederick Co. (BVCG 11 Aug 94)
KER, Mrs., wife of James KER of Norfolk, d. on Tues. last (NH 22 Sep 96)
KER, David, att. at law and Clerk of Middlesex Co., died (VG 13 Aug 72); his ex., James GREGORIE, will sell all his PE at Urbanna, Middlesex Co. (VG 19 Nov 72); HCC, 9 Mar. 1799, between David C. KER and James GREGORY ex. of David KER dec'd and gdn. to the pltf. and Overton COSBY, Edmund BERKELEY, and Edmund SPRATT; it appears that James GREGORY is not an inhabitant of this country (Ex 19 Apr 99)
KER, Dr. David Corbin, was mar. to Miss Margaret BENSON dau. of John BENSON, all of Fredsbrg., on Wed. last by the Rev. Mr. STEPHENSON (VHFFA 16 Sep 96, RCFPC 21 Sep 96)
KER, Edmond, hatter, reportedly killed by Archibald CARR in a fight in Dumfries on 22 [May] (NHPA 5 Jun 97)
KER, James, vendue master, mar. Miss GOLDIN [also given as COLDIN] both of Norfolk Borough, on Sat. eve. last (NHPA 6 Feb 97, AGGA 7 Feb 97)
KER, Mrs. Ruth, wife of James KER formerly of this city [Richmond], d. on the 19th ult. in Norfolk (VGGA 12 Oct 96 ex)
KERBY, John, of Charles Par., dec'd, his ex., Thomas KERBY, will sell the remainder of his HH and KF (VG 24 Nov 74); his ex. will settle his est. (VG 13 Jun 77)
KERBY, Robert, late of York Co., e.a.w. Merritt MOORE (VIC 30 Apr 88)
KERCHEVAL, John, dec'd, his ex. (nfi) will sell his Negroes and stock (VGWA 29 Oct 88)
KERCHEVAL, Mary, wife of William KERCHEVAL and dau. of Mr. BEALL, desires to sell a tract of her father's land in Berkeley Co. (BVCG 27 Aug 92)
KERR Family, HCC, mention of Ann KERR widow and relict of Edward KERR dec'd and their chil. George KERR and Ann KERR who are infants (Arg 11 Jun 99)
KERR, Alexander, silversmith of Wmsbrg., d. Sun. last (VG 20 Oct 38)
KERR, David, appr., ran away from William BALL, Cumberland (VGWA 30 [Jul] 91)
KERR, George, executed last Fri. for murder (VG 27 Dec 51)
KERR, George Sr., of Westover, dec'd, e.a.w. John KERR (nfi) (VG 9 Nov 69)
KERR, George, appr., ran away from the ship *Mary Ann* at City Point (VGPI 16 Jun 91)

KERR, James, young gentleman of Richmond, d. of bilious fever (VGIC 25 Oct 88, NPJ 5 Nov 88)
KERR, James Jr., late of Richmond, dec'd, e.a.w. his admr., James KERR of Albemarle Co. (VGIC 6 Jun 89 sup)
KERR, John, of Charles City Co., adv. that some time ago he was unfortunate enough to marry a woman by the name of Mary Maria Milmount PARRIS but has since found her right name was Elizabeth BEVER and finding himself thus imposed upon and her conduct different from that of a good woman, he has separated from her and will no longer pay any of her debts (VG 6 Apr 76)
KERR, John, of Henrico Co., dec'd, e.a.w. his ex., John CLARK (VG 9 May 71)
KERR, Thomas, svt., ran away from John BOTKIN, Augusta Co. (VG 22 Dec 68)
KERWELL, Charles, Eng. svt., ran away from William FICKLIN, Kg. Geo. Co. (VG 18 Sep 46)
KERYS, James, aka MURPHY, Irish svt., ran away from Charles NELSON [also given as NEILSON], Pr. Geo. Co. in Apr. 1751; he was apprehended in Carolina and ran away again in July (VG 4 Apr 51, 8 Aug 51)
KEY, James, appr., ran away from Michael STIEBER, baker, Alexandria (VGAxA 19 Sep 93)
KEY, James, appr. tailor, c. 14 last fall, ran away from John KEY, Petersburg (VGPI 30 May 97)
KEY, Jesse, of Albemarle Co., but for sometime past a resident of this city [Richmond], d. on Sun. last in the bloom of youth (VGWeA 23 Aug 87)
KEY, Martin, late of Albemarle Co., dec'd, e.a.w. John, Tandy, and Joshua KEY his exors. (VGGA 11 May 91)
KEYON, Joseph, Irish svt., ran away from John CANADAY, Fairfax Co. (VG 31 Jul 46)
KEYS, David, appr. hatter, 17, ran away from William BALL (BVCG 24 Sep 92)
KEYS, Thornton, mar. Miss Christiana RAZER in Fredsbrg. on Wed. eve. (VH 12 Jul 99)
KEYSER, Mrs., aka Mrs. MORRISS, French, short and very lusty, c. 36, speaks very good Eng. and several other languages; suspected of stealing items from the store of Joseph CLERICO at Manchester (VGIC 28 Oct 86)
KIBLE, Richard, conv. svt., came from London this year in the *Forward Galley*, professes to be a carpenter and joiner, ran away from William WALKER, Westmoreland Co. (VG 6 Jul 39, AWM 19 Jul 39) [name also given as KIBBLE]
KIBBLE, Robert, of Richmond, d. on Fri. eve. last (VGRMA 1 Dec 94, VGGA 3 Dec 94); e.a.w. his ex., Richard DENNY and Alexander GILCHRIST, who will also sell his PE consisting of unfinished saddles, harness, leather, etc. (VGRMA and VGRC 25 Apr 95)
KIBBY, John, appr., c. 18, ran away from John DUNCAN, Loudoun Co. (CMAG 22 Feb 98)
KID, David, appr. miller, 16, ran away from M. DONALD and A. SIMRALL, Frederick Co. (BVCG 1 Apr 96)
KIDD, John, of Philadelphia, merch., d. at Norfolk (VG 3 Oct 71); e.a.w. his admrs., Alexander KIDD and Amos WICKERSHAM of Portsmouth (VG 7 Nov 71)
Killed by Indians at the mouth of the Great Kanawha, 10 Oct. 1774: Col. Charles LEWIS, Col. John FIELD, Capt. John MURRAY, Capt. Robert M'CLENACHAN, Capt. Samuel WILLSON, Capt. James WARD, Lt. H. ALLEN, Ensign BRACKEN, Ensign CUNDIFF (VGP 10 Nov 74)
Killed by Indians: Capt. Joseph FAIN, Caleb JONES, Joseph ALEXANDER, Van PIERCEFIELD, William LANG, Jonathan DEAN, John BRANNON, William ENGLISH, John MEDLOCK, Robert HESTON, George MATTHEWS, Isaac ANDERSON, Charles PAYNE, Luthor JOHNSTON, Hermon GREGG, George BUL[L]Y; they were members of a party commanded by Capt. FAIN that left Houston Station on Nine Mile Cr., crossed the Tennessee River, and was ambushed by Cherokees on 8 Aug.

(VCWM 10 Sep 88, NPJ 1 Oct 88)
Killed by Indians on the headwaters of Dunkard Cr., Washington Co. [Pa. ?], on 25 Apr.: Joseph CUMBRIDGE and his wife, William THOMAS and two children (VGWA 3 Jun 89)
Killed by Indians in Harrison Co.: four members of William JOHNSON's family on 19 Sep. and Mr. [MUICK's] wife and two chil. on 22 Sep. (VCWM 18 Nov 89)
Killed by Indians during the expedition under Brig. Gen. HARMAR against the Miami towns: Maj. WYLLYS and Lt. FROTHINGHAM of the Federal troops; Maj. FOUNTAIN, Capt. THARP, Capt. SCOTT, Capt. M'MUTREY, Lt. CLARK, Lt. ROGERS, Ensign SWEET, Ensign BRIDGES, Ensign HIGGENS, and Ensign THRELKELD of the militia (VGAxA 23 Dec 90)
Killed by Indians in Ky. on 4 Nov 1791: Gen. BUTLER, Col. OLDHAM, Majors BROWN, HART, CLARK, FERGUSON, Capts. BRADFORD, TIPTON, SMITH, PURDIE, NEWMAN, PHELAN [also given as PHILON], KIRKWOOD, PEATE [also given as PRATT], PRICE, SWEARENGEN, CUBBS [also given as CRIBBS], GUTHRIE [also given as GUTHERIE], Lts. WARREN, SPIER [also given as SPEER], LICKINS [also given as LUKINS], M'NICKLE, M'MATH, HOPPER, RIED [also given as REED], KELSO, BOYD, Ensigns BEALLY [also given as BEATTY], COBBS, BROOKS, BALSH [also given as BALCH], CHASE [also given as CHAFE], TURNER, PURDIE, Quartermasters WARD, REYNOLDS [also given as REYNOLD], SAMPLE, Adjutants ANDERSON, BURGESS, Dr. GRAYSON; all were members of a force under Gen. ST. CLAIR which was attacked by Indians 15 miles from the Maume Village (KG 12 Nov 91, VGGA 7 Dec 91, NPC 10 Dec 91)
Killed by Indians in Mero District: Col. Isaac BLEDSOE (9 Apr.), John HARMAN, [?] DOWDEY (on 11 Apr. near the mouth of Sycamore, Tennessee Co.), Henry HOWDESHELL and Samuel PHARR (on 14 Apr. near Gen. RUTHERFORD's), John BENTON (on 18 Apr. on the road between Capt. REEFE's and Col. WINCHESTER's Mill), Richard SHAFFER and [?] GAMBRELL (26 Apr.), John JERVIS (on 27 Apr. at Greenfield), Francis RAMER (on 28 Apr. near Dripping Springs) (VGRMA 6 Jun 93)
Killed by Indians near Ft. Recovery, Ky. on 30 Jun.: Maj. M'MAHAN, Capt. HARTSHORN, Lt. CRAIG, Cornet TORRAY (PGBA 28 Jul 94, VCGA and VGRMA 4 Aug 94)
Killed by Indians on the Cumberland Path [in Tennessee] near the Crab Orchard on 13 Aug.: Paul CUNNINGHAM, Daniel HITCHCOCK, William FLENNIKIN, Stephen RENFRO[E] (VGGA 10 Sep 94, VGRMA 22 Sep 94)
Killed by Indians and Canadian Militia near Ft. Defiance, Ky. on 20 Aug. 1794: Capt. Robert CAMPBELL (of the dragoons), Lt. Henry B. TOWLES (of the 4th Sub-Legion) and the following Ky. Volunteers: John JACKSON, Alexander INNES, William MITCHELL, Thomas MOORE, William STEELE, Benjamin BELL, and James WILEY (BVCG 29 Sep 94, VCGA 6 Oct 94, VGRMA 6, 13 Oct 94, VGRC 3 Oct 94, HNPA 4, 7 Oct 94)
Killed by Indians in Tennessee, Nov. 1794: John LAWRENCE, William HAINES, Michael HAMPTON [Acc. to HNPA they were killed in Summer Co.] (VGRMA 26 Jan 95, HNPA 31 Jan 95)
Killed by Indians in Tennessee, [Dec. 1794]: Col. John MONTGOMERY (HNPA 31 Jan 95)
Killed in a naval action against a privateer or pirate ship on 10 Jul. [acc. to VGGA] or 19 Jul. [acc. to VH] on board the U. S. *Planter* **out of Hampton Roads**: John LEETCH, Samuel HUFFMAN, William JOHNSON, William CHESTER (NH 10 Sep 99, VGGA 13 Sep 99, VH 17 Sep 99)
KIMBELL, Catherine, and her husband, John KIMBELL, of Frederick Co. intend to separate (BVCG 2 Jun 94)
KIMBERLIN, Jacob, killed by Indians near New River in [Oct.] 1763 (VG 4 Nov 63)
KIMBROUGH, John, dec'd, his ex., John BUMPASS and Fortunatus GREEN,

will sell the tract of land in Hanover Co. where he lived, seven miles from the Ct. H. containing 275 ac. (RMA 20 Aug. 96)

KINCAID, Adjutant, of the 12th Regt., mar. Miss Agatha CHINN of Winchester (VGPu 21 Feb 77)

KINCAID, Mr., of Manchester, mar. Miss Betsy CARY dau. of the late Archibald CARY Esq. Speaker of the Senate (VGWeA 12 Jul 87)

KINDALL, John, of Orange Co., dec'd, e.a.w. his admr., May BURTON Jr. (VHFA 18 Sep 94)

KINDLE, Ransom, 17-18, des. from the barracks in Winchester; lived with his father on the Blue Ridge Mountain seven miles from Barry's Ferry (BVCG 7 Sep 95)

KINDRECK, Christopher, of Frederick Co., killed in a wagon accident last week leaving a wife and five chil. (VGWA 25 Jun 88)

KING Family, est. accounts of Dr. John KING, Michael KING, and Mary KING to be handled by James KING of Nansemond Co., the ex. (NHPA 20 Jan 98)

KING, Alexander, merch. of Frankfort, mar. Miss Sarah M'ALISTER dau. of James M'ALISTER Esq. of Springfield, in Hampshire Co. on 11 Dec. (BVCG 17 Dec 92)

KING, Miss Catharine, of Henrico Co., d. of smallpox on Sun. night last (VGRMA 3 Apr 94)

KING, George, Eng. svt., c. 40, ran away from Patrick MURRAY, Winchester (VGPu 6 Jun 77)

KING, Col. Henry, of Hampton, died (VG 12 Dec 77); his ex., Miles KING, will sell a valuable water lot in the town of Hampton whereon the dec'd lived (VGIC 22 Nov 83)

KING, James Jr., HCC, Cyrus GRIFFIN (pltf.) and Robert TURNBULL surviving partner of James KING Jr. dec'd, James KING Sr. ex. or admr. of sd. James KING Jr. and the sd. James KING Sr., Charles DUNCAN, William COLE, and Robert TURNBULL surviving partners of the firm of Duncan & Turnbull (defs.); it appears that James KING [Sr.] is not an inhabitant of this country (VGWeA 7 May 96)

KING, John, [svt.], 25, ran away from Thomas WILLIS, Isle of Wight Co. (VG 28 Feb 51)

KING, John, merch. of Hampton, mar. Miss Nancy STARKE (VG 24 Nov 74)

KING, John, of Norfolk, dec'd, his lots and houses to be rented out by William NEWSUM (nfi) (NPJ 18 Feb 89)

KING, John, late of Liverpool, mariner, son of Esther KING late of Kg. Wm. Co., Va. but at the time of her death of Liverpool; he is entitled to a considerable portion of the est. of Mrs. Anne CLOWES of Liverpool, widow, dec'd; he has not been heard of or seen in Liverpool for the past six yrs. (VICGA 26 May 90)

KING, Thomas, ind. svt., c. 30, b. in Eng., bricklayer, ran away from his owner in Annapolis, Md. (VGR 7 Jul 74)

KING, Thomas, dec'd, his admr. and acting legatee, Sackville KING, will sell his est. in Louisa Co. (VGGA 11 Dec 98)

KING, William, comedian, who lately arrived here [Norfolk] from New York, d. on Thurs. morn. last (NH 3 Oct 96)

KINGAN, John, merch. of Ft. Cumberland, mar. Miss Fanny WALKER dau. of James WALKER hat manufacturer of Winchester, on Thurs. last (BVCG 14 Oct 93)

KINNEY Family, nine slaves, several of whom are mulattoes, to be sold in Louisa Co. (VGGA 17 Feb 96)

KINSBURY, Damilian, age 57, mar. Miss Anne HARDING, age "53 years rising 54 this spring" both of Fairfax Co., on Sun. morn. last in [Alexandria] (CMAG 22 Mar 96)

KINSEY, Noka, free African, d. on 8 Aug. in his 70th year; he lived about 30 yrs. in the family of John PEMBERTON as a coachman [from the *Philadelphia Gazette* of 14 Aug.] (WG 28 Aug 99)

KINSMAN, Janet, of Port Tobacco [Md.], admx. of John KINSMAN, adv. that she is going to remove shortly to Va. and wishes to settle the est. of John

KINSMAN dec'd; she still keeps tavern at the sign of the ship in Port Tobacco (MG 7 Jan 62)

KIRBY, Mr. P., formerly of Limerick, Ireland, d. yesterday [Wed.] morn. at the house of Dr. O'GRADY (NH 27 Oct 96, AGGA 28 Oct 96)

KIRBY, William and Thomas, of Dinwiddie Co., dec'd, e.a.w. their admr., Samuel T. KIRBEY (VGPI 9 Feb 96)

KIRK, Miss, eld. dau., c. 10, of Mrs. KIRK, killed by a galloping horse on Sat. last (VGAxA 15 Jul 90)

KIRK, Mrs. Bridget, d. on Sat. morn. last (CMAG 7 Mar 97); e.a.w. her admr., Archibald M'LEAN, who will also sell all of her pers. property (CMAG 1 Jun 97); e.a.w. her admr. (TAA 28 Apr 98)

KIRK, Edward, appr. hatter, c. 19, ran away from Henry BUSH, Winchester (BVCG 18 Aug 94)

KIRK, James Esq., late mayor of Alexandria, died (VJAA 6 Apr 86); portions of his est. in Alexandria to be rented by his admx., Bridget KIRK (VJAA 6 Jul 86)

KIRK, Patrick, late of Winchester, dec'd, e.a.w. his admr., Edward DYER (BVCG 26 Oct 95)

KIRK, Thomas, transported from London around 1765; around 1771 he informed relations that he was an usher to a Mr. HART, a schoolmaster, in Baltimore or some place in Md.; he reportedly left Md. and resided in Berkeley Co., Va. near Winchester where he kept a school; he reportedly d. in 1783, however, a Mr. KIRK was in Winchester last year and is now in Baltimore; if Thomas KIRK or any of his issue are alive they have a legacy in Eng. (VCWM 14 May 88)

KIRK, William, of Kittcuton, Loudoun Co., acts as agent for John KIRK of Lancaster Co., Lampeter Township, Pa. in securing stolen horses (VG 4 Nov 63)

KIRKPATRICK, Thomas, merch. of Alexandria, dec'd, e.a.w. his ex., Robert ADAM, Robert McCREA, John GIBSON, and William HUNTER Jr. (VJAA 20 Jan, 3 Mar, 26 May, 11 Aug 85)

KIRTLEY, Elijah, intends to move to Ky. next spring (VHFA 13 Jan 91)

KIRTLEY, Francis, dec'd, e.a.w. his ex., Francis KIRTLEY (VG 30 Dec 75)

KIRTLEY, Capt. William, dec'd, his former plant. and tracts in Madison Co. will be sold by his ex., Isaac DAVIS Jr. and Adam BANKS (VHFFA 6 Nov 95)

KISSADY, John, appr., 16-17, ran away from William THOMPSON, Washington, D.C., who suspects he might have returned to Richmond where Robert THOMPSON (William's brother) lives (RMA 25 Jun 95)

KITCHINGMAN, William, Eng. svt., ran away from Col. Henry WILLIS in Spotsylvania Co. (VG 9 Mar 39)

KITTEN, John, means to leave this state in the course of one month for Baltimore (CMAG 9 Aug 96)

KITTLER, John Charles, Dutch svt., breeches-maker, c. 23, speaks good French and several other languages but bad Eng., ran away from Casper HERRITER, Suffolk Co. (VG 8 Jun 76)

KLEINHOFF, Mrs., wife of John KLEINHOFF merch. of Alexandria, died (VJAA 2 Sep 84)

KLEINHOFF, George, of Chesterfield Co., d. on Mon. last (VGWeA 8 Nov 93); his ex., Arthur GRAVES and John Jocelyn KLEINHOFF of Chesterfield, will sell his plant. near Falling Rock [also given as Falling Creek] Church (VGRMA 16 Dec 93, VGGA 18 Dec 93)

KLEINHOFF, John, late of Alexandria, his assignees are James HENDRICKS and Daniel GRAY (VJAA 11 Aug 85)

KNAPHAUSEN, Baron, [former] Hessian general in America, d. in Berlin on 2 Jun. aged 59 (VHFA 29 Oct 89)

KNIGHT, Cecilia, has left her husband, John KNIGHT of Stafford Co. (VHFFA 18 Dec 95)

KNIGHT, Richard, merch., d. last week in Norfolk [disp. of 6 Mar.] leaving a widow (VG 21 Mar 71); his admr., John LAWRENCE and John

GREENWOOD, will sell all his PE (VG 13 Jun 71)
KNIGHT, Richard, ran away from the schooner *Jerushia* (CMAG 19 Jan 96)
KNIGHT, Vincent, aka Joshua, aka John PRICE, executed in Fredsbrg. on Thurs. last for horse stealing (VHFA 23 Nov 92)
KNOWLES, Corben, mar. Miss Lucy BELL a few days past (VGPI 4 Apr 97)
KNOWLES, John, aka HURLEY, Irish svt., blacksmith, ran away from Samuel STEVENS, Talbot Co., Md. (VG 3 Sep 67)
KNOX, James, mar. Miss Sally TURNER, both of this town [Petersburg] on Sat. last (VGPI 7 Mar 97)
KNOX, John, murdered near his home in Stafford Co.; his brothers, Robert and William KNOX, offer £105 reward for his suspected murderers (VG 15 Jun 69); two slaves suspected of his murder were caught, tried, found guilty, and hanged at Stafford Ct. H. (VGR 20 Jul 69)
KNOX, John Brumley, des. from the 3rd U.S. Regt. near Alexandria (VGAR 12 Jul 92)
KNOX, Robert, of Fauquier Co., dec'd, his extx. petitions the GA to sell a tract of land to pay off his debts (VHFA 6 Oct 91)
KNOX, Sarah, aka HOWARD, aka WILSON, conv. svt., says she was b. in Yorkshire, had been in the army for several yrs. in Flanders and at the battle of Culloden where she lost her husband; may pretend to be a dancing mistress; ran away from David CURRIE, Lancaster Co.; she was imp. from Whitehaven in the *Duke of Cumberland* with other conv. among whom was one William FORRESTER (VG 3 Jul 52, MG 25 Jan 53)
KNOX, Mrs. Sarah, spouse of James KNOX of Petersburg, d. Wed. last (VGPI 1(Jan 98)
KNOX, Thomas, of Wmsbrg., intends to leave the colony soon (VG 1 Jan 67)
KNOX, William, merch. of Philadelphia, mar. Miss Peggy GORDON of Petersburg on Wed. last (VGPI 10 Feb 97)
KOONTZ, Michael, [appr.] shoemaker, c. 20, ran away from Joseph CARSON, Winchester (BVCG 29 Oct 92)
KREAGAR, Peter, appr. tailor, c. 20, ran away from Richard WEIGHTMAN (TAA 3 Aug 97)
KUO, Thomas, Eng., c. 35, committed to the borough prison as a runaway, supposed to have run away from John HOOD in Md. [see: Anthony JACKSON and William WARRICKER] (VGR 11 Oct 70)

LABILLE, Louis, upholsterer from Paris, lately arrived from Philadelphia, adv. that he has taken a house in Fairfax St. [Alexandria] where he will carry on the above business (CMAG 18 Aug 96)
LACEY, James, appr., ran away from William WARDEN, Alexandria (VJAA 14 Jul 85)
LACY, Hugh, Irish svt. bel. to Dr. Ephraim HOWARD, ran away from near Elk Ridge Church, Anne Arundel Co., Md. (VGR 26 Jul 70)
LADD, James, of Charles City Co., adv. that he has been called on by the acting ex. of Amos LADD dec'd for a settlement of the partnership of Amos & James Ladd which dissolved in 1790 by the death of Amos LADD (RMA 27 Jul 96)
LADD, Dr. Joseph Brown, the celebrated and highly esteemed author of those productions of genius which lately appeared under the signature of Arouet, d. at Charleston, S. Carolina of wounds he received in a duel (VGIC 9 Dec 86
LADD, Thomas, merch., mar. Ann BELL dau. of Nathan BELL of Hanover Co. at the Friend's Meeting House in this city [Richmond] on Wed. last (Arg 9 Aug 99)
LAGRIZE, Eliza, whose maiden name was JONES, escaped upwards of two years since from the horrid massacre at Cape François and [has been] wandering about without the means of restoring herself to her friends, having been long in quest of her uncle, James JOHNSTONE, has reason to believe he has established himself somewhere in America; she asks that anyone with knowledge to contact her through the Rev. John MURRAY, Boston, Mass. (RJDWA 23 Jun 96)

LAING, Ketty, her husband, William LAING, adv. that, using a fictitious name, she mar. another husband named MULHOLLAND when she was on tour to the Western Country (BVCG 28 Jan 93)
LAMAN, Joseph, e.a.w. his ex., George and Rachel LAMAN who will also sell his stock and PE at his dwelling house at Buckle's Town (PGBA 6 Apr 97)
LAMB, John, svt., 25, ran away from John GRATTAN, York Co., Pa. (VGR 4 Feb 68)
LAMB, John, c. 22, des. from Capt. Joseph SPENCER's Co. of Regulars before they left Orange Co.; he was bred in Orange near Col. BURNLEY's (VGPu 12 Jul 76)
LAMB, Richard, dec'd, his admr., Walter LAMB, will sell his PE in Mecklenburg Co. (VGPI 28 Sep 86)
LAMB, Thomas, b. in Sussex Co. where his father now lives, speaks some French, des. from the York rendezvous of the 7th U.S. Regt. (VGGA 11 Oct 99)
LAMB, William B., of Norfolk, mar. Miss Margaret KERR dau. of Samuel KERR merch., on Mon. eve. last (VCGA 11 Apr 94)
LAMBERT, Charles Sr., d. on Mon. the 1st inst. at his place in Bedford Co. in the 100th year of his age (DOB 15 Nov 98)
LAMBERT, David, mar. Miss Sally EGE on Sun. last, both of Richmond (VGWeA 5 Oct 82)
LAMBERTON, Capt., reported killed by Indians near Point Pleasant on the other side of the Ohio around 1 Aug. (VGAA 13 Aug 85)
LAMBETH, Mary, dec'd, her est. to be sold at West Point by William MEREDITH and John MARTIN (nfi) (VG 27 Feb 52)
LAMELY, William, lately from Eng., skinner, d. in Alexandria (VJAA 8 Sep 85)
LAMMOND, Thomas G., adv. that his wife, Peggy LAMMOND, has absented herself from his bed and board and conducted herself otherwise in an improper manner (CMAG 21 Jul 95)
LANCASTER, John, and Amelia his wife of Portsmouth having this day separated by mutual consent, he adv. that he will not be answerable for any debts his wife may contract after this date (NH 8 Aug 99)
LAND, Barton, murdered by William STONE near Hickory Bridge, Pr. Anne Co. on the 27th ult. (VHFA 11 Aug 95, SVG 15 Aug 95)
LAND, Richard, of Orange Co., murdered by a slave (VG 10 Jun 37)
LANE, James Sr., dec'd, his land in Loudoun Co. will be sold by his ex., Aaron LANE, William LANE, and H. LANE (CMAG 18 Dec 93)
LANE, James Hardage, dec'd, e.a.w. his ex., George LANE, who will also sell all of his real and personal est., except the Kentucky land, at the plant. near Centerville commonly called Newgate in Loudoun Co. whereon he formerly lived (CMAG 28 Jan 97)
LANE, John, Serjeant of Wmsbrg., dec'd, his ex. is James HOLDCROFT (VG 23 Jul 72)
LANE, Joseph, of Westmoreland Co., died (VGAA 5 Apr 86)
LANE, Mrs. Martha, d. on 9 Feb. at the house of Capt. Benedict MIDDLETON in Westmoreland Co., aged 78 (VGR 10 Mar 74)
LANE, Michael, Irish conv. svt., ran away from Samuel CANBY, Loudoun Co. (VGP 8 Jun 75)
LANE, Nathaniel, c. 21, des. from Thomas MASSIE's Co. of Continental Regulars, Wmsbrg. (VGPu 17 May 76)
LANE, Rachel, of Winchester, adv. that she was mar. to Larkin LANE (VCWM 18 Jun 88)
LANG, Thomas, printer, d. on Fri. the 25th inst. in his 30th year; he was bur. in the Free Quaker's Burial Ground [in Philadelphia] (VHFA 7 Feb 93)
LANGE, William, seaman, middle-aged, b. in North Britain, ran away from the ship *Encouragement* of London lying at West Point (VG 10 Apr 52)
LANGFORD, John, a noted and skilled musician, d. on Christmas Eve in Hanover Co. leaving a widow and six or seven small chil. (VG 7 Jan 37)
LANGFORD, Thomas, of Pittsylvania Co. suspected of being murdered on his

way to Ky. last Dec. 12 by two men and three women supposed to be of the name of ROBERTS (KG 2 Jan 99, VGGA 22 Jan 99, Arg 22 [Jan] 99) [name also given as LANKFORD]

LANGHORN, David B., appr., ran away from Samuel SWANN, Richmond (VGGA 26 Aug 95)

LANGHORN, William, d. lately at his house in Warwick; he had been a magistrate for almost 40 yrs. (NHPA 30 Sep 97, NWJCI 4 Oct 97)

LANGHORNE, John, of Cumberland Co., dec'd, his ex., Cary and Sarah HARRISON will sell his tract of land there (VGGA 16 Nov 96)

LANGHORNE, Mary, dec'd, e.a.w. her admr., John HOBSON of Cumberland Co. (RMA 18 Oct 96)

LANGHORNE, Maurice, dec'd, his Negroes to be sold in Cumberland Co. by the sheriff (VGGA 16 Mar 91)

LANGLEY, Mrs., relict of Robert LANGLEY dec'd, dep. this life at her house near Petersburg on Fri. last (VGPI 3 Jan 97)

LANGLEY, Elizabeth, dec'd, all her PE will be sold by Thomas LEWIS (nfi) in Dinwiddie Co. (VGPI 4 Jul 97)

LANGLEY, Lemuel, dec'd, e.a.w. his admr., Lemuel LANGLEY (AGNPPA 15 Mar 96, AGGA 6 May 96)

LANGLEY, Robert, late of Dinwiddie Co., his admr., Thomas ATKINSON, will sell his HH and KF (VGPI 17 Jun 96)

LAN[G]STON, Thomas, mar. Miss Chloe LAWSON at Norfolk on Thurs. 11 Mar. (VG 1 Apr 73)

LANGSTON, Thomas, d. at Suffolk on Tues. morn. 21 Apr. (VG 8 May 78); e.a.w. his admx. (nfi) of Suffolk (VGPu 16 Oct 78)

LANIER Family, Greensville Co., Ct. of Q.S, Mar. 1798 in chanc: Mary LANIER widow of Thomas LANIER dec'd, William LANIER and others (compls.) against Colin LANIER and others (defs.) (VGPI 27 Jul 98)

LANKFORD, Elizabeth, her husband, William LANKFORD of Chesterfield Co. will not pay her debts (VGGA 13 Nov 93)

LAORENCE, Bartholomew, dec'd, e.a.w. his admr., John BROOKES of Portsmouth (ET 12 Nov 98)

LAPORTE, Bajieux, dec'd, e.a.w. his admrs., Lacoste and A. BAGNERS of Fredsbrg. (VGAA 4 Jan 83)

LAPORTE, Victor, of Petersburg, d. on Sat. last (VGPI 2 Aug 96)

LAPPIN, Isaac, svt. boy, bound by order of ct. to William JOHN, Berkeley Co., ran away (PGBA 3 Sep 92)

LAPSLEY, Thomas, son and heir at law to William LAPSLEY dec'd, summoned to Rockbridge Co. Ct. to answer a bill in chanc. exhibited against him by Alexander STUART (VGAA 25 Dec 84)

LARBY, Eliphalet [or Lifelet], of Great Cape Capon Cr., Orange Co., hunter, murdered on 30 Apr. (or sometime in May) by runaway svts.; Peter HECKIE was convicted of the murder and executed at Wmsbrg. on 18 Nov. (VG 10 Jun, 21 Oct, 18 Nov 37, AWM 21 Jul, 15 Dec 37)

LARI, Capt., of the ship *Hudibras* lately from Guernsey, d. on Mon. last (NH 8 Sep 96)

LARK Family, Mecklenburg Co., June Ct. 1795, in chanc: Frederick COLLIER and Ann his wife (pltfs.) against Mary LARK, Samuel LARK, Jacob FOX and Elizabeth his wife, Augustine WRIGHT and Sarah his wife, John HOLMES, Walter LEIGH, and Joshua SMITH (VGPI 4 Sep 95)

LARKIN, Patrick, of Northumberland Co., adv. that his wife, Betty LARKIN, has taken up with a certain Daniel FENAUGHTY (VHFA 24 Jul 94)

LARSH, Charles, acc. to his motion in Montgomery Co. Ct., Sep. 1794, his father, Paul LARSH, d. intestate leaving two chil., the sd. Charles and Hannah an infant living outside the Commonwealth of Va. (BVCG 20 Oct 94)

LARUE, Alexander, dec'd, e.a.w. his admr., James RIND, Richmond (RMA 28 May 95)

LARUE, Isaac Sr., of Frederick Co., dec'd, his admr., James LARUE and Jabez LARUE, will sell his slaves and livestock (BVCG 7 Sep 95)

LASSETTER, Elisha, brought to jail in Richmond for murdering his uncle by roasting (VJAA 3 Aug 86); executed at the gallows near Richmond on Fri. last (VGWeA 1 Feb 87)

LATIL, Mrs. Lucy, cons. of Joseph LATIL Esq. of this city [Richmond], d. on Sat. last (VICGA 20 Jan 90, VHFA 28 Jan 90)

LATIMER, Edward, dec'd, his admr., William LATIMER and Thomas ALLEN, will sell the land whereon he lived three miles from Hampton in Elizabeth City Co. (VGWeA 9 Feb [82]

LATIMER, Roe, dec'd, e.a.w. his admr., James LATIMER in Chesterfield (VG 15 May 79)

LAUDERBACK Family, Shenandoah Co. Ct., 13 May 1794, in chanc: Matthias LAUDERBACK, and Joseph LAUDERBACK (compls.) against David LAUDERBACK, John LAUDERBACK, Abraham LAUDERBACK, Adam BOYER and Christina his wife, Godlove HOVEMASTER and Sarah his wife, Ernest Frederick MATHONEY and Susanna his wife, John BEVERAGE and Elizabeth his wife, Eve LAUDERBACK, Peter HENAY and Barbary his wife heirs at law and reps. of David LAUDERBACK dec'd (BVCG 23 Feb 95)

LAUGH, John, ind. svt. from Holland, barber, c. 27, ran away from John WHITE, Alexandria (CMAG 24 May 94, BVCG 26 May 94)

LAUGHLIN, Richard, merch., d. in Caroline Co. on the 23rd ult. (VH 7 May 99)

LAUGHLIN, Thomas, of Henrico Co., dec'd, his est. accounts being discharged by James LAUGHLIN at Cold Harbor (Arg 25 Jan 99)

LAUGHTON, Henry, of Wmsbrg., died (VG 12 Dec 77)

LAVERSTON, Henry, appr. gunsmith, c. 19, ran away from John SHOUGH, Martinsburg (PGBA 13 Apr 97)

LAVINDER, William, late of Baltimore Co., Md., dec'd, e.a.w. his admr., Robert LAVINDER of Stafford Co. (VHFA 26 May 95)

LAWLESS, John, hostler, b. in Amherst Co., des. from Capt. Henry BOWYER's troop of light dragoons, Ft. Washington (KG 22 Jun 93)

LAWLOR, John, of Culpeper Co., adv. that his wife, Susannah LAWLOR, has eloped from his bed and board for sometime past and he will not pay any of her debts (VIC 29 Nov 86)

LAWRANCE, Fed, mulatto lad, ran away from Edward HARRISON, Pr. Geo. Co. (VCNPGA 18 Aug 92)

LAWRENCE, Capt. John, of Hanover Co., dec'd, e.a.w. his ex., William and James LAWRENCE (VGGA 15 Jun 91)

LAWRENCE, John, tailor, missing and supposed drowned (VHFA 5 Mar 95); his body was found recently (VHFA 9 Apr 95); e.a.w. his admr., William SMITH and William PEARSON (VHFA 10 Jul 95)

LAWRENCE, William, formerly of Richmond, died (VGGA 28 Jan 95)

LAWSON, David, was mar. to Miss Susan DENBY, both of Norfolk, on Sat. eve. by the Rev. Mr. WHITEHEAD (NH 12 Nov 99)

LAWSON, John Esq., of S. Carolina, mar. Miss Betsey BILLUPS of Gloucester Co. (VGPu 27 Jun 77)

LAWSON, Robert Esq., dec'd, his admr. is George JENKINS of Charles Co., Md. who requests those indebted to his est. to make immediate payment to William TRIPLETT Jr. near Colchester (CMAG 22 Aug 99)

LAWSON, Thomas, of Norfolk, dec'd, e.a.w. his ex., Daniel McPHERSON (NPC 12 Jun 90)

LAYPOLD, John, of Rocket's, d. on Sat. last (VGGA 18 Feb 95)

LAYTON, Isaac, of Philip Lane near London Wall, London, jeweller, went to N. America in 1766 and resided in Philadelphia and Va. under the assumed name of Charles FREEMAN, in Jul. 1774, he resided at Alexandria in Potomac in Va.; Nicholas TOKE late of Lenton in Kent Gent., who d. on 7 Apr. [1783], left the sd. LAYTON £500 and a share of the clear residue of his est.; he is asked to contact John OFD Esq. at Lincoln's Inn, London (VGWeA 20 Aug 85, VGGA 5 Nov 85)

LEADAM, William, came to America some yrs. ago from the town of Beverly in Eng. and lived somewhere about Ocracoke, N. Carolina; he may hear something to his advantage if he apply to the postmaster in Wmsbrg. (VG 4 Aug 74)

LEAK[E], John Jr., of Licking-Hole, Goochland Co., intends to move to S. Carolina on 30 May to practice law there (VGRMA 15 May 94) [A Josiah LEAK Jr. of Goochland announced that he would not move to S. Carolina on 1 Jun.; it is not clear if one or two persons are involved (VGRMA 29 May 94)]

LEAKE, Josiah, att. at law, mar. Miss Elizabeth HATCHER on the 23rd inst., both of Goochland Co. (Arg 29 Mar 99)

LEAKER, James, Eng. svt., b. in Powlet, Somersetshire, yeoman, 23, ran away from Samuel GARLICK, Kg. Wm. Co. (VG 12 Mar 67)

LEAR, Mrs. Frances, wife of Tobias LEAR Esq. of Washington, died (RMA 6 Apr 96)

LEAR, Tobias Esq., of Georgetown, mar. Mrs. Fanny WASHINGTON of Mt. Vernon (CMAG 6 Aug 95)

LEATH, Barbara, of Manchester, adv. that she has lately returned to the tavern in the south end of Manchester formerly kept by Peter LEATH dec'd and last year by Zachariah BROOKS (VGGA 20 Aug 94)

LECAT, James, appr., c. 16, ran away from James CRAWFORD, Norfolk (NHPA 14 Nov 96)

LECKIE, Andrew, aged 33, d. on 14 Nov. (VHFA 27 Nov 88)

LECKIE, Andrew, merch., mar. Miss BROKENBROUGH on Thurs. eve., both of this town [Norfolk] (NHPA 6 May 97)

LEE Family, Middlesex Co. Ct., 26 May 1796, in chanc: Isaac KIDD (compl.) against Thomas CRITTENDEN, James TRICE and Frances his wife who was Frances LEE widow of James LEE dec'd, and James LEE and Robert LEE chil. of the sd, James LEE dec'd (defs.) (VGGA 15 Jun 96)

LEE, Gov. [Henry], mar. Miss Anne CARTER dau. of Charles CARTER Esq. at Shirley [Charles City Co.] on Tues. 18 Jun. (VGRMA 20 Jun 93, VGGA 26 Jun 93, BVCG 1 Jul 93)

LEE, Mrs., relict of the late R. LEE of Norfolk, died (NPC 24 Apr 90)

LEE, Algernon Sydney, youngest son of Gov. Henry LEE, d. on the 9th inst. at t' seat of Richard Bland LEE Esq. in Loudoun Co. (CMAG 13 Aug 96)

LEE, Mrs. Anne, widow of the late Col. R. H. LEE, d. on Sun. 10 Jan. after an illness of seven days at Chantilly in Westmoreland Co. (CMAG 2 Feb 96)

LEE, Arthur Esq., former diplomat, d. at Urbanna, Middlesex Co. (VGRDA 21 Dec 92); d. on 12 Dec. (VHFA 3 Jan 93); or on 15 Dec. (VHFA 10 Jan 93),; or on 18 Dec. (VGGA 19 Dec 92), or last Wed. (BVCG 31 Dec 92) aged 51; a letter about his life is in VHFA of 10 Jan 93

LEE, Barret, Negro, 30, claimed to have served Benjamin ELK, Pr. Geo. Co., Md. until 21; committed to Fairfax Co. jail (VJAA 19 Jul 87)

LEE, Cassius, son of the late Richard Henry LEE Esq., d. on 8 Jul. at Princeton, N. Jersey (VHFA 20 Jul 98)

LEE, Edmund J., of this town [Alexandria], mar Miss Sarah LEE dau. of the late Col. Richard Henry LEE of Chantilly on Mon the 23rd inst. (CMAG 26 May 96)

LEE, Edward, Irish, 27-28, served his time in Loudoun Co., des. from Alexandria (VGPu 27 Dec 76)

LEE, Edward, laborer, d. on Sunday (VJAA 1 Jul 84)

LEE, Francis, late of Amherst Co., dec'd, e.a.w. his ex., Richard HARRISON (LWM 13 Nov 97)

LEE, Francis Lightfoot Esq., mar. Miss Rebecca TAYLOE a dau. of the Hon. John TAYLOE, Thurs. last (VG 16 Mar 69); d. at his seat in Richmond Co. on Wed. the 11th (VHFFA & RCFPC) or Wed. the 18th ult. (VGGA) in his 63rd year (VGGA 8 Feb., NHPA 13 Feb, VHFFA 14 Feb, RCFPC 15 Feb 97)

LEE, George Esq., of Loudoun Co., mar. Miss Eveline Byrd BEVERLEY dau. of Robert BEVERLEY Esq. of Blandfield, in Essex Co. on the 13th inst. (VH 26 Oct 98)

LEE, Green, younger son of Col. Henry LEE, d. at Stratford, Westmoreland Co. on the 28th ult. (VGAxA 5 Aug 90)

LEE, the Hon. Henry, Senator for Fairfax and Pr. Wm. Cos., d. at the seat of Richard Bland LEE, Leesburg, on the 5th inst. [or on the 15th acc. to VIC], in his 58th year (VJAA 23, 30 Aug, VIC 29 Aug, 5 Sep 87)
LEE, James, of Norfolk, sentenced to death for robbery (VG 4 May 39)
LEE, James, svt., b. near Manchester, Lancashire, 35, ran away from Jonathan BOUCHER, Fredsbrg. (VG 1 Jun 69)
LEE, Col. John, dec'd, e.a.w. Richard LEE (nfi) (VGR 11 Dec 66); John LEE of Essex Co. will settle with his debtors and creditors; Mary LEE of Westmoreland Co. is acting extx. (VGR 14 Apr 68)
LEE, John, c. 25, from near Halifax, N. Carolina, his right name is supposed to be Daniel YOUNG, des. from Capt. Thomas BRESSIE's Co. (VGPu 18 Jul 77)
LEE, John Esq., dec'd, e.a.w. his ex., Muscoe GARNETT and William YOUNG of Essex Co. (VGPu 22 Aug 77)
LEE, Capt. John, d. last Sep. in Orange Co., he was 82 and grandson to Col. Richard LEE who settled in Va. during the reign of Charles I (VGPA 13 Mar 90)
LEE, Kendall Esq., of Northumberland Co., dec'd, his exors., W. and G. LEE, will sell a tract of his land on Matchipongo Inlet in Northampton Co. containing about 1000 ac.; e.a.w. his ex., William LEE (VG 24 Mar 81, VGAA 20 Sep 83)
LEE, Ludwell Esq., of this co. [Fairfax], mar. Miss Betsy ARMISTEAD of Fredsbrg., in Hanover Co. on the 30th ult. (CMAG 8 Jun 97)
LEE, Mrs. Matilda, wife of Col. Henry LEE, d. on 16 Aug. in Westmoreland Co. (VGAxA 19 Aug 90)
LEE, Mrs. Mildred, consort of Thomas LEE Esq., d. on Wed. night last at Park-Gate (RJDWA 16 Sep 96)
LEE, Master Philip, eld. son of Henry LEE, Gov. of Va., d. on Tues. the 17th inst. in Rich. (VGGA 25 Jul 92)
LEE, the Hon. Philip Ludwell Esq., one of H.M's Hon. Council of this Colony, d. the 28th ult. at his seat of Stratford in Westmoreland Co.; the following day his wife gave birth to a son (VGPu 3 Mar 75 sup, VG 11 Mar 75)
LEE, Mrs. Rebecca, wife of Francis Lightfoot LEE Esq. of Manokin, d. on Sat. last (VHFFA 10 Jan 97, RCFPC 11 Jan 97)
LEE, Richard, only son of Richard LEE Esq. of Westmoreland, d. on Sat. the 21st ult. at Lee Hall (VGRMA 1 Aug 93)
LEE, Richard Esq., of Lee Hall, Westmoreland Co., d. on Fri. the 10th inst. in his 71st year (VGRMA 16 Oct, VGRC 17 Oct, VHFA 23 Oct 94); e.a.w. his admr., Richard Bland LEE, of Sully, Loudoun Co.) (CMAG 21 Nov 95); his admr. w.w.a., Richard Bland LEE, will sell a tract of his land at the head of Dry Run in Berkeley Co. containing 245 ac. as well as tracts in Hampshire Co. and other real est., slaves, and livestock (CMAG 5 May 96, WG 6 Jun 98, VH 14 Sep 98)
LEE, Richard Bland, member of Congress, mar. Miss COLLINS dau. of Stephen COLLINS merch. of Philadelphia, at Germantown on the 19th ult. (VHFA 3 Jul 94, BVCG 7 Jul 94)
LEE, Richard Henry, d. on the 19th ult. in his 64th year [obit.] (VHFA 17 Jul 94); e.a.w. his ex., William Augustine WASHINGTON and Corbin WASHINGTON, Westmoreland Co., who will also sell his HHF at Chantilly in the same co. (VHFA 4 Sep 94)
LEE, Theodoric Esq., mar. Miss Kitty HITE a few days ago at Woodville near Winchester (BVCG 29 Apr 93)
LEE, the Hon. Thomas, President of the Colony of Va., d. on 13 Nov. (MG 21 Nov 50, NYPB 24 Dec 50)
LEE, Thomas, of Johnston Co., N. Carolina, being about to remove to Ky. will barter for Negroes the plant. whereon he lives containing 750 ac. on both sides of Mill Cr. a branch of Ne[u]se River (VG 11 Mar 80)
LEE, Thomas Esq., of the Senate, eld. son of Richard Henry LEE Esq., mar. Miss Mildred WASHINGTON youngest dau. of the late John Augustine WASHINGTON and niece to Gen. WASHINGTON (VIC 29 Oct 88, VGWeA

30 Oct 88, VGIC 1 Nov 88, NPJ 5 Nov 88)
LEE, William, of Westmoreland Co., mar. Miss Hannah LUDWELL eld. dau. of the Hon. Philip LUDWELL, on Tues. 7 Mar. in London (VGR 25 May 69)
LEE, William, [conv.], cooper, ran away from James KIRK, Robert ADAM, and George PURVIS, Alexandria (VG 17 Jun 75)
LEE, William, of Cumberland Co., d. in Manchester on Fri. last (VGRMA 23 Jun 94)
LEE, Willis, of Fauquier Co., was mar. to Miss Polly RICHARDS dau. of John RICHARDS of Fredsbrg., last eve. by the Rev. Mr. STEVENSON (VH 6 Dec 99)
LEEDS, Polly, second dau. of Jedediah LEEDS merch. of [Richmond], d. on Fri. eve. last (VGGA 10 Jan 98)
LEES, Mary, has withdrawn herself from the bed and board of her husband, John, of Winchester, and on the 22nd [of Jul.] she gave him a violent blow which he thought very indecent of her (BVCG 28 Jul 94)
LEFAVOUR, John, Virginia born, des. from the co. of Capt.. George Lee TURBERVILLE, 15th Va. Regt.; he enl. in Westmoreland Co. (VGPu 11 Apr 77)
LEFEVRE, John, highwayman, b. in the Jerseys, broke jail in Carlisle Pa. and Frederick Co., Va. (VGR 31 May 70)
LEFTWICH, Augustine, dec'd, his ex., Thomas LEFTWICH and David SAUNDERS of Bedford, will settle his est. and sell his HHF, plant. utensils, and livestock and two tracts of land on the road between New London and Liberty (LFG 1 Aug 95)
LEFUEUR, David, of Cumberland Co. and his chil., David Jr., James, and Catherine (the wife of Robert THOMPSON) are entitled to sums of money under the will of David LEFEUER of London dec'd whose ex. cannot locate him (VG 21 Jun 70)
LEGG, Amos, mulatto, c. 21, bred as a sailor, ran away from William MEREDITH K & Q Co.; sometime past he was taken up by Capt. DAWSON of Norfolk in Jamaica and brought home; it is believed he will try to get on a ship and leave the country (VG 22 Aug 66); [He may have run away a second time (VGR 23 Jul 67)]
LEGG, Capt. John, vendue master of this town [Fredsbrg.], d. on Tues. morn. (VH 12 Apr 99); his ex., William LOVELL and William DRUMMOND, will sell his stock of goods; Thomas LEGG (nfi) is authorized to receive his debts and grant discharges (VH 7 Jun 99)
LEGON, William, of Amelia Co., dec'd, e.a.w. his ex., James M'GLAHON (Ex 8 Mar 99)
LEGRAND, the Rev. Nash, mar. Miss Peggy HOLMES dau. of the late Col. Joseph HOLMES dec'd, last Thurs. at Holmes Grove near Winchester (BVCG 11 Mar 93)
LEIGH, Ferdinando, d. near Petersburg in his 64th year (VG 30 Oct 79); e.a.w. William CLAIBORNE Sr. of Petersburg (VG 19 Feb 80); his heir at law is his son, William LEIGH of Chesterfield Co. (VGAA 12 Jul 83)
LEIGH, Richard, intends to move from Mecklenburg Co. to James City Co. abot Christmas next (VG 10 Nov 74 ps)
LEIGH, Roscow, of Va., merch., d. on the 3rd ult. on board the brig *Nancy* on her passage from Martinico (VGWeA 8 Nov 93)
LEIGHTON, James, Eng. conv. svt., b. in Cambridgeshire, c. 20, imp. last summer, ran away from Isaac ZANE, Frederick Co., Va. (VGP 16 Nov 75)
LEIPER, Dr. Andrew, was mar. to Miss Fanny TRENT, both of this city [Richmond], by the Rev. Mr. BUCHANAN on 27 Apr. (VGRMA 28 Apr 94, VGGA [30] Apr 94); of this city [Richmond], d. yesterday morn. after a short illness (DOB 18 Oct 98); his HH and KF, medical books, and instruments to k sold by his admr., Joseph GALLEGO (Arg 7 Jun 99 ex)
LEITCH, Maj., died (acc. to a Philadelphia letter of 8 Oct.) (VGPu 18 Oct 76)
LEITCH, Capt. Alexander, of the ship *Eliza* lately arrived from London, died; had been mar. only a fortnight earlier (VG 10 Nov 74)

LEITCH, James, of Norfolk, dec'd, e.a.w. David LEITCH and James BOUSHELL (NPJ 18 Jul 87)
LELAND, the Rev. Mr. John, Churchwardens, John EUSTIS and William NUTT, adv. that there is a vacancy in Wicomico Par. [Northumberland Co.] due to his death (VGPu 3 Apr 78); e.a.w. his ex., William NUTT of Northumberland Co. (VGPu 21 Aug 78)
LEMOINE, Dr. Ferol, formerly of the Hotel Dieu, Paris and Surgeon Major of the military hospitals of France, adv. that his residence is in the upper end of Lancaster Co. where he offers his services to the public (VHFA 10 Jul 94)
LEMOUNT, Cornelius, dec'd, e.a.w. his admr. w.w.a., Joseph WHITE, Pr. Anne Co., who will also sell several of his Negro slaves (AGNPPA 12 Jul 96, AGGA 19 Jul 96)
LENNARD, John, of Westham, Henrico Co., dec'd, e.a.w. Mary LENNARD his admx. (VGAA 16 Aug 83)
LENNIS, Capt. Francis, dec'd, e.a.w. his admr., William BALLARD of Hampton (VGCD 30 Oct 79, VG 13 Nov 79)
LENNO, Peter, aka Philip LENNO, aka Peter JERRO, and Elizabeth his wife, sometimes called Elizabeth WILKERSON, and Mary SULLIVAN are summoned before the justices of Spotsylvania Co. in chanc. to answer a certain bill exhibited against them by James HUNTER Esq. (VGWeA 26 Oct 82)
LENNON, Andrew, appr., c. 19, ran away from the snow *St. Bees,* Norfolk (VGNI 15 Jun 75)
LENOX, Joseph, of Petersburg, d. on Tues. last (VGPI 7 Apr 97)
LEONARD, Charles, native of Cologne, Germany, has long resided in this colony and was famous for his excellent but capricious performance on the violin; he played his last solo in the house of Mr. Blovet PASTEUR of Wmsbrg.; he d. in his 76th year at Wmsbrg. (VGPu 20 Sep, VG 21 Sep 76)
LEONARD, Nicholas, dec'd, e.a.w. his ex., Anna LEONARD and Jonathan JONES (PGBA 9 Nov. 97)
LEONARD, Price, young man of this county, d. on Thurs. eve. [or Fri. morn. acc. to VGRMA] last of smallpox (VGRMA 10 Feb 94, VGRC 11 Feb 94)
LESHER, Susanna, has eloped from her husband, John LESHER, Shenandoah Co. (BVCG 18 Jun 92)
LESHLEY, Sarah, dec'd, e.a.w. her admr., Joseph WILLSON, Augusta Co. (SS 1 Feb 94)
LESTER, John, appr., 16-17, ran away from John SHEPPARD (CMAG 17 Dec 96)
LETRUITE, Anthony, appr., c. 17, ran away from John JOHNSTON who suspects he will try to go on board some vessel from Baltimore (CMAG 31 May 96)
LETUZ, G. H. M. P., [sells and repairs musical instruments], mar. Miss Mary MALLORY on Thurs. eve. (NHPA 6 May 97)
LEVI, John, professes to be a Jew and says he was b. in Eng. and bred to the buckle making business, suspected of stealing some jewelry out of Jacob EGE's shop in Richmond (VGIC 29 Jan 85)
LEVI, Lazarus, late of Isle of Wight Co., dec'd, e.a.w. his admr., William MALLORY and Jno. MURRY (NHPA 4 Nov 97)
LEVINGSTON, Capt. John, mar. Miss Tabitha HERBERT, Sat. last, both of Norfolk (VCNPGA 15 Dec 92)
LEVINGSTON, Sukey, Negro woman, 22, says she was b. in Scotchtown, Isle of Wight Co., taken up by Stephen HOPKINS, Norfolk, before May 1792 (VCGA 26 May 94)
LEVINGTON, Dr. Justice, surgeon of the privateer brig *Northampton,* mar. Miss Angelica LAFONG of Wmsbrg. (VG 1 Aug 77)
[LEVSEY], Thomas, escaped from the guard in Botetourt Co. after being tried there for counterfeiting; he is about 30 and it is supposed he will make for Henry Co. where he formerly lived (VG 4 Sep 79)
LEWEL[L]IN, Christopher, aka Charles LANE, svt., 21-22, b. in London, bred a blacksmith, imp. in the *Rachel* in 1750; ran away from William

TALIAFERRO, K & Q Co. on 10 Jul 1752 (VG 21 Aug 52); ran away from John HOBDAY, coachmaker, Gloucester Co. who imagines he has gone towards Philadelphia or followed a woman whom he has kept company with to Md. (MG 2 Aug 53)

LEWELLING, Samuel, appr., bound an orphan to Daniel M'PHERSON, tailor, Norfolk, from whom he has run away (HNPA 7 Sep 95)

LEWIS Family, U. S. Middle Circuit, District of Va., Nov. 1794, chancery case mentions John PETIT, John LEWIS and David ALLEN, ex. of John LEWIS dec'd, David ALLEN and Aphia his wife, Peter TAYLOR and Sarah his wife, chil. and devisees of the sd. John LEWIS dec'd (VGGA 11 Mar 95)

LEWIS Family, Albemarle Co. Ct., 6 Aug. 1795, in chanc: Francis BROWNING (pltf.) against Henry GRAVES and Rachel his wife, Rebecca LEWIS, Priddy LEWIS, James LEWIS, Polly LEWIS, James POOL and Rebecca his wife, George JOHNSON and Susanna his wife, John STOVALL, and Mary STOVALL, heirs of David LEWIS dec'd (defs.) (VGGA 23 Sep 95)

LEWIS, Mrs., spouse of Warner LEWIS Jr. Esq. of Gloucester, died (VGPu 8 Nov 76)

LEWIS, Capt. Addison, of the Light Horse, mar. Miss Sukey FLEMING (VG 16 Apr 79)

LEWIS, Addison, of Gloucester Co., dec'd, e.a.w. his ex., Thomas LEWIS (VGGA 6 Jan 96)

LEWIS, Mrs. Betty, relict of the late Col. Fielding LEWIS of Fredsbrg., d. at her seat in this co. (VHFFA 11 Apr 97)

LEWIS, Charles, Virginian, 25, enl. by Capt. BELL, des. from the Va. Regt. at Ft. Cumberland (VG 26 Dec 55)

LEWIS, Charles Esq., slain [in the battle] at Point Pleasant [now West Va.] on 10 Oct. 1774, [long eulogy by a schoolmaster in Fincastle Co. appeared in VGPu in Mar. and a revised, authorized version was later published in VGP] (VGPu 17 Mar 75, VGP 25 May 75)

LEWIS, Col. Charles, of Albemarle Co., dec'd, e.a.w. his ex., Nicholas LEWIS, Charles L. LEWIS, and Charles HUDSON (VGWeA 28 Aug 84)

LEWIS, Charles, d. yesterday at his seat near Richmond (VGRMA 22 Aug 93)

LEWIS, David, late of Va., but now in S. Carolina in the District of 96, all debts to be paid to his att., William Terrell LEWIS of Albemarle Co. (VG 8 Apr 75)

LEWIS, Evans, Welsh, 35, imp. last summer, ran away from Robert WALLACE of Norfolk Borough (VG 10 Jan 52)

LEWIS, Fielding Esq., of Berkeley Co., mar. Miss Betsy DADE of Alexandria (VJAA 26 Mar 89)

LEWIS, Fielding, dec'd, his ex., John and George LEWIS, will sell 50 of his slaves and, at the dwelling house of Mrs. Betty LEWIS dec'd adjoining Spotsylvania Ct. H., all of his HH and KF (VH 7 Oct 95)

LEWIS, Fielding J., eld. son. of John LEWIS, aged 24, d. in Fredsbrg. Mon. last (VHFA 21 Mar 98)

LEWIS, George, aka George, Negro, ran away from Robert RAWLINGS, Richmond (VIC 3 Sep 88, VGWA 11 Sep 88)

LEWIS, Henry, mar. Miss Eliza HUFF dau. of Lawrence HUFF of [Alexandria] on Tues. eve. (TAA 26 Jan 98)

LEWIS, Howel, mar. Miss Nancy BOLLING, both of Goochland Co., on the 16th inst. (VGIC 24 Apr 84)

LEWIS, Howell, of Fredsbrg., mar. Miss Nelly POLLARD of Richmond on Sat. eve. (VGGA 30 Sep 95, RMA 1 Oct 95)

LEWIS, Isaac, wagonmaker, says he is a native of Pa., jailed in Essex Co. as a runaway (VGPu 1 Dec 75)

LEWIS, Isham, dec'd, e.a.w. his exors., John THOMAS and Edward MOORE of Albemarle Co. (VICGA 9 Jun 90)

LEWIS, Jacob, enl. by Lt. WILLIAMS, des. from the Va. Regt. at Ft. Cumberland (VG 26 Dec 55)

LEWIS, James, svt., ran away from John JAMESON, tailor, in Hampton (VG 20 Jun 55)

LEWIS, James, att. at law, mar. Miss Jane WALKER dau. of the late Thomas WALKER of Fredsbrg. in Fredsbrg. on Thurs. last (VH 13 Sep 97)
LEWIS, John, svt., 18, ran away from John CARTER, Wmsbrg. (VG 6 Jun 45)
LEWIS, John, 25, ran away from the snow *Industrious Bee* lying at Sandy Point (VG 5 Jun 52)
LEWIS, the Hon. John Esq., for many yrs. a member of H.M's Council for this Colony, d. on Thurs. the 17th inst. of the gout in his stomach at his house in Gloucester Co. (Wmsbrg. disp. of 25 Jan.) (MG 7 Feb 54)
LEWIS, John, of New Kent Co., his poor health makes it necessary for him to leave the colony (VG 10 Sep 67)
LEWIS, John, att., of Spotsylvania Co., dec'd, his ex., John Z. LEWIS, Robert LEWIS, and Nicholas LEWIS, will sell a tract of his land in Culpeper Co. containing about 1500 ac. (VGAA 26 Oct 82); and his son, John Zachary LEWIS, both dec'd; their est. accounts to be settled with the ex., Joseph BROOK [also given as BROCK] of Spotsylvania Co. (VGAA 9 Oct 84, 26 Nov 85)
LEWIS, John Sr., late of Pittsylvania Co., dec'd, e.a.w. his ex., John LEWIS Jr. and Robert LEWIS (VGGA 10 Sep 94)
LEWIS, John W., son of Col. Robert LEWIS of Goochland Co., d. on the 8th inst. in his 17th year (VGAA 17 Dec 85)
LEWIS, Mrs. Mary Anne, consort of John LEWIS, d. suddenly on Fri. last [5 Apr.] in Fredsbrg. (VH 9 Apr 99, Arg 12 Apr 99)
LEWIS, Nicholas, of Spotsylvania Co., dec'd, e.a.w. Thomas TOWLES his acting ex. (VGAA 25 Oct 83)
LEWIS, Peter, mulatto, 25-30, ran away from Edward MARKS, Pr. Geo. Co., who suspects that he may attempt to go to Baltimore or Philadelphia (AGGA 10 Feb 97)
LEWIS, Richard, of Stafford Co., dec'd, e.a.w. his admr., Thomas SOWELL, who will sell a valuable sawmill and grist mill with lands and timbers belonging to the sd. mills in Fauquier Co. and a piece of land in the sd. co. containing 450 ac. (VG 8 May 79); his PE to be sold by Thomas SOWELL for Ann LEWIS the admx. (VGAA 27 Jul 82)
LEWIS, Robert, late of Spotsylvania Co., dec'd, his only son and heir is Robert LEWIS under 21 whose gdn. is John Zachary LEWIS Gent.; the siblings of Robert LEWIS Sr. are: John Zachary LEWIS, Nicholas LEWIS, Zachary MEREWETHER and Jane his wife, and David Wood MEREWETHER and Mary his wife (VGAA 16 Aug 83)
LEWIS, Robert, nephew and aide de camp of the President of the U.S., mar. Miss Judith Walker BROWN dau. of William Burnet BROWN Esq. on the 15th inst. at Elsing Green, Kg. Wm. Co. (VGGA 30 Mar 91)
LEWIS, Miss Sally, dau. of Charles LEWIS, d. yesterday at Marrin's Hill near this city [Richmond] (VGRMA 25 Jul 93)
LEWIS, Col. Thomas, reportedly killed by Indians about 12 miles from Point Pleasant on the other side of the Ohio around 1 Aug. (VGAA 13 Aug 85); later reported rescued by Shawnees (VGAA 10 Sep 85) [See also: VJAA 25 Aug, 1 Sep 85, VGWeA 20 Aug 85]
LEWIS, Thomas, of Rockingham Co., d. on Sat. last (SG 5 Feb 90)
LEWIS, Waller, mar. Miss Sally WINN in Spotsylvania Co. on the 16th inst. (VHFFA 22 Dec 95)
LEWIS, Warner Esq., son of Col. Warner LEWIS, dec'd, his ex., Philip L. GRYMES, William NELSON, Burwell STARKE, Mann PAGE Jr., and Matthew ANDERSON, will sell a tract of his land in Powhatan Co. (VGGA 7 Mar 92)
LEWIS, Warner, mar. Miss Courtney NORTON at Philadelphia on 12 Apr., both of Va. (BVCG 7 May 92)
LEWIS, Warner Esq., member of the Hon. Senate of this Commonwealth, d. on Sat. the 22nd. of Dec. at the family seat, Warner Hall, in Gloucester Co. (Ex 1 Jan 99)
LEWIS, Warner Jr. Esq., of Gloucester Co., mar. Miss Molly FLEMING of

Cumberland Co. (VGPu 12 Sep 77)
LEWIS, Capt. William, d. lately at Norfolk; he had been appointed superintendent of the light house at Cape Henry (VHFA 29 Nov 92); e.a.w. James LEWIS (nfi) (VHFA 4 Apr 93)
LEWIS, Col. William, d. yesterday [27 Nov.] at his seat in Henrico (VGRMA [28] Nov 93, VGWeA 29 Nov 93)
LEWIS, William, of Wmsbrg., dec'd, e.a.w. Charles LEWIS, his admr., of York Co. (VGGA 5 Mar 94)
LEWIS, Capt. William, dec'd, his admr., James LEWIS Sr. of Fredsbrg., will sell three slaves and his HH and KF at his late dwelling house in Fredsbrg. (VHFA 8 May 94); his remaining est. will be sold on 1 Aug. by his admr. (VHFA 10 Jul 98)
LEWIS, William, late of Henrico Co., dec'd, e.a.w. his admx., Judith A. LEWIS (VGGA 25 Nov 95); his admr., Francis LEWIS, will sell his livestock, HH and KF, etc. at the late dwelling house of Mrs. Judith A. LEWIS dec'd (VGGA 14 Feb 98)
LEWIS, William, Negro, c. 26, bel. to William HICKMAN of Wilton on James River, jailed in Norfolk Borough (NH 17 Oct 96)
LIBITER, John, aka LEADBEATER, Eng., c. 35, imp. in the *Nassau* just arrived in Rappahannock from Liverpool, ran away from James DUNCANSON, Fredsbrg. (VG 21 Jun 70)
LIBSCOMB, Moses, lad of c. 18, excellent hair dresser and shaver, ran away from John DARROUS, Richmond, and may be going north to Philadelphia or New York (VGRMA 16 Feb 95)
LIBSCOMB, Mrs. Peggy, wife of Nathaniel C. LIBSCOMB Esq., d. in Hanover Co. on Fri. morn. last (RMA 4 Jun 95, RC 6 Jun 95)
LIDDERDALE, John, merch. of Wmsbrg., mar. Miss Elizabeth ROBERTSON dau. of William ROBERTSON Esq., last Fri. eve. (VG 3 Mar 39)
LIDDLE, Adam, b. in Scotland, 18-20, ran away from on board the *Scorpion* sloop (VGPu 4 Oct 76)
LIETCH, Alexander, of Pr. Geo. Co., dec'd, his admx., Margaret LIETCH, will sell all his PE (VG 8 Jul 75)
LIGHTBURN, Joseph, executed on 23 Nov. for robbery in Pr. Wm. Co. (VG 23 Nov 39)
LIGHTFOOT, Mrs., relict of the late William LIGHTFOOT Esq., d. a few days ago in an advanced age at Teddington (VGIC 22 Nov 83)
LIGHTFOOT, Armistead, ward of William NELSON of York Co., land in New Kent and Hanover Co. was given to him by his father (nfi) (VG 1 Aug 55)
LIGHTFOOT, Armistead, of Yorktown, mar. Nancy BURWELL dau. of the late Lewis BURWELL (VG-Randolph 28 Sep 59)
LIGHTFOOT, Armistead Esq., d. at his house in Yorktown (VG 19 Sep 71); of Goochland Co. [sic], his PE will be sold by William MITCHELL deputy sheriff of York Co. (VGR 12 Mar 72)
LIGHTFOOT, Col. Goodrich, of Orange Co., d. there lately (VG 14 Jul 38)
LIGHTFOOT, John, of Brunswick Co., dec'd, e.a.w. the admr., Robert RUFFIN of Surry Co. (VG 6 Feb 52)
LIGHTFOOT, Mrs. Mary, relict of the late Hon. Philip LIGHTFOOT Esq. one of H. M's [Council] of this colony, d. at York[town] in her 79th year; she is to be bur. in the family vault at Sandy Point; William ALLEN of York Co. (nfi) will sell her PE (VGPu 30 Jun 75 sup, 10 Nov 75, VG 1 Jul 75)
LIGHTFOOT, Miss Nancy, fourth dau. of the late William LIGHTFOOT Esq. of Sandy Point dec'd, d. on Tues. 29 Jun. (VG 1 Jul 73, VGR 8 Jul 73)
LIGHTFOOT, William Esq., dec'd (VGR 23 Jun 68)
LIGON, Anne, has eloped from her husband, William LIGON of Amelia Co. (VGR 1 Nov 70)
LILLE, John, dec'd, e.a.w. his admr., Richard BLAKE (VG 24 Jul 79)
LILLY, Mrs. Ann, wife of Robert LILLY of Fredsbrg., d. Mon. night last (VHFA 24 Jul 94)
LILLY, Robert, dec'd, his admr., Edmund WINDER of Fredsbrg., will sell his PE (VH 10 May 99)

LILLY, Robert, appr. to the printing business, c. 18, ran away from Yundt & Brown, Baltimore (NH and VH 13 Aug 99)
LINDER, Jacob, of Berkeley Co., d. between 2 Aug. 1787 and 22 Sep 1789 (VCWM 30 Sep 89)
LINDSAY, James, of Caroline Co., dec'd, his ex., Daniel and Reuben LINDSAY, will sell some of his slaves and HH and KF; they request the attendance of Mr. John LINDSAY of N. Carolina and the heir of Jacob LINDSAY dec'd of Pittsylvania Co. (VGAA 12 Oct 82)
LINDSAY, John, aka John, Negro, c. 23, ran away from Ezekiel MOUNT. Loudoun Co. (VHFFA 30 Sep 96)
LINDSAY, Maj. William, Collector of the Customs for this district, d. in Rhode Island at Newport, on the 3rd inst. (NHPA 9 Sep 97, VH 13 Sep 97)
LINDSEY, Benjamin, was mar. to Miss Amelia ROBINSON, both of Alexandria on Wed. eve., by the Rev. Mr. MUIR (TAA 9 Feb 98)
LINES, Dickson, c. 15, lived sometimes in Fredsbrg. with a barber, ran away from William NICE, hatter, in Richmond; it is supposed he is either gone to Fredsbrg. or got on board some vessel as he has been used to follow the sea (VGPA 25 Jun 91)
LINGOE, Thomas, mar. Jane IFERLOW at Norfolk on 16 May 1784; her former husband later returned to claim her; LINGOE claims to be wholly exonerated from the bands of matrimony (VGAA 14 Aug 84)
LINLEY, John, svt., from Yorkshire, 27, ran away from Francis TOMKIES, Gloucester Co.; he is believed heading for the Eastern Shore and Philadelphia (VG 11 Apr 55)
LINN, Jacob, son of George LINN of [Winchester] aged 10, d. on Mon. last (WG 16 Oct 99)
LINNY, John, svt., ran away from William WILLCOCK and James TAYLOR, Wmsbrg.; he may be headed north (VG 8 Aug 51)
LINSEY, William, native of James City Co., which he left some yrs. ago, the admr. of his mother, Elizabeth LINSEY dec'd, who is Edmund LINSEY, adv. that William or his heirs may receive their legacies (VICGA 6 Jan 90)
LIPSCOMB, Ambrose, dec'd, his ex., John P. LIPSCOMB, will sell five Negroes, his stock of cattle, HH and KF, and other items of his est. in Kg. Wm. Co. (VGPu 27 Oct 75)
LIPSCOMB, William, of Richmond, dec'd, some of his HH to be sold by his admx., Sarah LIPSCOMB (Ex 6 Dec 98)
LIPSCOMBE, Ambrose, of Hanover Co., d. on 21 Oct. (VGGA 29 Oct 94); his admrs. (nfi) will sell his PE (VGGA 26 Nov 94)
LIPSCOMBE, Mrs. Elizabeth, wife of Ambrose LIPSCOMBE, d. lately at Hanover (VGAA 14 May 85)
LITERALL, John, c. 22, was a wagoner for William RICHARDS, Culpeper Co., des. from the barracks at Fredsbrg. (VHFA 6 Oct 95)
LITHGOW, Hector, served in H.M's 77th Regt. in Halifax, Nova Scotia about 1764, d. in the East Indies in 1784 possessed of a considerable fortune which he left to his sons, John and Hugh LITHGOW, who were b. in Halifax and lately resided there and also to Frances SWEETING their mother; the sons or their mother may receive information on the est. by applying to Messrs. Brymer & Belcher at New York, Thomas Pope Esq. at Philadelphia, or Archibald Gay, Laetitia Court (VHFA 3 Jul 88, NPJ 23 Jul 88)
LITTLE, James, of the firm of Little & Thompson of Winchester, mar. Miss Elizabeth SOWERS dau. of John SOWERS of Frederick Co. on Thurs. last (WG 26 Jun 99)
LITTLE, William, master and commander of an American vessel from Norfolk; on Thurs. morn., Michael BLANCH a Spaniard, James COLLEY an American, and Francis COLE a black, were found guilty of his murder and executed (London disp. of 29 Jan.) (AGNPPA 1 Apr 96)
LITTLE, William and Olive REESE, dec'd, e.a.w. their admr., Robert MABRY, of Southampton (VGPI 3 Jul 98)
LITTLEPAGE, Edmund, of Newcastle, d. on Mon. the 8th inst. in the bloom of

youth, due to the bite of a mad dog (VGGA 24 Nov 90)
LITTLEPAGE, Col. James, of Hanover Co., dec'd, his land in Hanover Co., Orange Co., and Louisa Co. to be sold (VG 27 Nov 66); e.a.w. Peter RANDOLPH, William BYRD, and Geddis WINSTON (VG 11 Dec 66)
LITTLEPAGE, William, mar. Miss Sukey SMITH of Hanover Co. (VGWeA 17 Aug 82)
LITTLETON, Col. Esq., d. at his home in Northampton Co. on Sun. the 26th ult.; he was many yrs. a judge of the court and rep. of the co. (VG 7 Jul 68)
LIVELY, John, of Hanover, adv. that his wife, Constant, made an elopement from him about 12 months ago and went up and down the neighborhood to make him appear as ridiculous as she could; he will no longer pay any of her debts (VGWeA 11 Oct 83)
LIVELY, William, ind. mulatto, c. 23, ran away from Lewis BOATEN, Culpeper Co. (VGR 15 Jul 73)
LIVINGSTON, Mr., son of the late governor of New York, d. last Fri. in Richmond (VGAA 27 Sep 86) [see: Peter V. B. LIVINGSTON below]
LIVINGSTON, John, merch., mar. Miss Pleasant WALTERS a few days ago in Frederick Co. (BVCG 4 Feb 93)
LIVINGSTON, Muscoe, of St. Anne's Par., Essex Co., dec'd, his land and plant. there to be sold by Andrew RONALD and James BROWN (nfi) (Arg 26 Mar 99, 10 May 99)
LIVINGSTON, Peter V. B. Jr., of New York, d. on Sat. the 23rd inst. in Richmond at the house of William CLAIBORNE Esq.; he was bur. locally (VIC 27 Sep 8) [see: Mr. LIVINGSTON above]
LIVINGSTON, Capt. Samuel, d. near Gosport last Fri. (VCGA 21 Oct 94)
LIVINGSTON, Sarah, under pretense of visiting her parents in Worcester Co., Md., she has eloped with her chil. from her husband, George LIVINGSTON of Gloucester Co. (VGR 6 Apr 69)
LIVINGSTONE, George, late of Gloucester Co., dec'd, e.a.w. his admr., Cornelius LIVINGSTONE (VGR 11 Mar 73)
LIVINGSTONE, John, appr., ran away from James BENTLEY in Gloucester Co. who suspects he is harbored at his mother's, Mary GUTTERY, of K & Q Co. (VGPu 18 Apr 77)
LLOYD, Edward, of Md., mar. Elizabeth TAYLOE eld. dau. of the Hon. John TAYLOE Esq. of Va. on 12 Nov. (VG 26 Nov 67, MG 10 Dec 67)
LLOYD, Enoch, dec'd, his ex., Jacob and Sarah WATKINS, will sell a tract of his land in Loudoun Co. (VG 13 Nov 78)
LLOYD, Joseph, Eng. conv. svt., house carpenter and joiner, c. 21, ran away from Rawleigh DOWNMAN, Lancaster Co. (VG 30 Dec 73)
LLOYD, Joseph, late of Orange Co., d. at the home of Ambrose ANDERSON of Gloucester Town on the 6th inst. (VGGA 15 Oct 94)
LLOYD, Robert Esq., of Queen Anne's Co., Md., d. on Mon. the 16th inst. [obit.] (VGR 2 Aug 70)
LOAFMAN, Abraham, appr. to Francis LOCKETT who adv. that he is under 14 and has reportedly enl. into the artillery service (VG 19 Sep 77)
LOCKHART, Capt., reportedly killed by Indians near Point Pleasant on the other side of the Ohio around 1 Aug. (VGAA 13 Aug 85)
LOCKHART, Daniel, dec'd, e.a.w. Hugh M'PHERSON (nfi) (HNPA 19 Nov 95)
LOCKLEY, John, native of England, for many yrs. a worthy citizen of this state, d. on Mon. eve. last at Rocket's (VGAA 4 Feb 86)
LOFFLAND, Charles, mar. Miss Mary PROATZMAN, both of Harrisonburg, Rockingham Co., on Thurs. last (WG 13 Nov 99)
LOFTEN, Benjamin, late of Norfolk Borough, dec'd, e.a.w. his admr., Thomas REED (HNPA 10 Oct 95)
LOGAN, Charles, d. Thurs. eve. last at his seat in Powhatan Co. (VGRMA 10 Jul 94); e.a.w. his admx., Mary LOGAN, and admr., Goodrich CRUMP, who will also sell his PE (VGRMA 26 Jan, 12 Mar 95); e.a.w. his admx., Mary PLEASANTS, and his admr., Robert C. PLEASANTS (RMA 11 Jun 96)
LOGGINS, William, aka Will, Negro, c. 30, ran away from Robert S.

COLEMAN, Spotsylvania Co. (VH 3 Dec 99)
LOGWOOD, Archibald, dec'd, a tract of his land in Chesterfield Co. to be sold by his ex., Edmund LOGWOOD, Edward MOSELEY, Robert HASKINS, William LOGWOOD, and Edward FRIEND (VGAA 13 Nov 84)
LOGWOOD, Edmund, late of Powhatan Co., dec'd, his ex., Edmund LOCKETT of Chesterfield Co., will sell his lands in Bedford Co., Richmond, Manchester, Charles City Co. and Ky.; Maj. Thomas LOGWOOD of Bedford Co. is mentioned (VGGA 16 Jul 99)
LOGWOOD, Thomas, of Powhatan Co., mar. Miss Polly PATTERSON on 10 Nov. at the home of Capt. Henry FLOOD in Buckingham Co. (LFG and LWM 13 Nov 97)
LOGWOOD, William, of Chesterfield Co., mar. Miss Jenny WALKER of Baltimore (VGWeA 31 Dec 85)
LOKY, Thomas M'Collester, mar. Mrs. Kitty GESS, both of this town [Alexandria] (CMAG 12 Mar 96)
LOMAN, Dennis, svt., c. 22, ran away from Robert ALLISON (VCWM 22 Apr 89)
LOMAX, John, for many yrs. a noted tavern keeper in Alexandria, d. recently (VJAA 25 Jan 87, VGWeA 1 Feb 87); e.a.w. his admx., Rachel LOMAX (VJAA 18 Oct 87); his admx. and Joseph THOMAS will pet. the GA to sell two of his unimproved lots in Alexandria (VGAA 21 Sep 91); the several persons to whom he by his nunc. will devised his lands and tenements in Alexandria give notice that they intend to present a pet. to the next GA to pass an act to confirm to them the estates given them by that will (CMAG 8 Sep 96)
LOMAX, Lunsford Esq., died (VG 9 Jul 72, PC 20 Jul 72)
LOMAX, Lunsford Jr., of Caroline Co., d. on Sun. the 10th ult. after a short illness [obit. (VGR 7 Mar 71)
LONDON, John, Negro svt., 26, ran away from Benjamin DAY, Fredsbrg. (VH 17 May 99)
Long Daniel the Fiddler, runaway Negro, suspected of being in Petersburg; he was at Suffolk and Broadway where he passed for a freeman by the name of Sam; he is remarkable for using his bow with the left hand (VGPI 7 Jun 87)
LONG, Armistead, [mar.] Miss Betsey BALL dau. of Col. Burges BALL in Fredsbrg. on Sat. last (VHFA 27 Jun 93)
LONG, Bromfield, his acting ex., Bromfield LONG Jr. of Culpeper will sell all of his est. consisting of a 150 ac. tract on Rapidan River in Culpeper Co. five miles above Germanna and a tract in Orange Co. (VHFFA 14 Oct 96)
LONG, Ellis, has des. his wife, Elizabeth, and six chil. in Stephensburg (BVCG 28 May 92)
LONG, James, of Blandford, dec'd, e.a.w. his extx., Elizabeth LONG, who will also sell some of his HHF and a complete set of wigmaking utensils (VG 6 Jun 71)
LONG, John, appr., 17, ran away from Robert WHITACRE, Alexandria (VJAA 8 Feb 87)
LONG, Peter, dec'd, his ex., Conrad CREBS and admx., Elizabeth LONG, will sell his livestock and furniture (WG 11 Dec 99)
LONG, Reuben, late of Culpeper Co., dec'd, e.a.w. his admr., Nimrod LONG (VHFA 7 Mar 93)
LONG, Thomas, a Scotch rebel, ran away from Jacob Andrew MINITREE, Charles Co., Md. (VG 7 Mar 51)
LONGACRE, Joseph Jr., of Frederick Co., mar. Miss Sally HITE of Hardy Co., on 12 Mar. (BVCG 25 Mar 93)
LONGDEN, Mrs. Lucy, relict of Thomas LONGDEN, died (VJAA 9 Mar 84)
LONGDEN, Robert, of Alexandria, d. last week at Darby, Pa. (TAA 28 Oct 97)
LOOKUP, John, dec'd, his admr. is Alexander PURDIE (VG 17 Nov 74)
LOPDELL, Henry, kept a school for some yrs. on York River; he has not been heard of for some time; if he applies to Col. George BRAXTON on York River, he will receive information of something much to his advantage (VG 8 Jun 39)

LORDAN, John, native of Ireland, d. in Alexandria on 24 Aug. (VJAA 25 Aug 85)

LORDE, John, of Kg. Wm. Co., adv. that his wife. Jane LORDE, has eloped from his bed and board without any provocation (VGAA 5 Jun 84)

LORIMER, George, merch. in Urbanna, mar. Miss Hannah Thacker TIMBERLAKE of Middlesex Co. (VG 20 Oct 74); of Middlesex Co., dec'd, e.a.w. his admr., Samuel KLUG; Hannah Thacker LORIMER adv. for a governess (VGAA 10 Jan 84, 13 Nov 84)

LORTON, Robert, dec'd, his admr., Thomas LORTON, will sell all his PE at Lester's Ferry, Charles City Co. (VG 15 Dec 74)

LOTHIAN, Elizabeth, dau. of Baillie John LOTHIAN of Bruntisland, in N. Britain; she has been in this country about nine yrs.; if she will send to the post office, she will receive a letter from a relation of hers, "...she must acquaint the printer...what was her grandmother's name by the mother's side but for what reason, he disna ken" (VG 31 Mar 74)

LOUGHEREY, Philip, Irish svt., 18, ran away from David KENNEDY, Berkeley Co. (VJAA 12 May 85)

LOVE, Alexander, of Osborne's, proposes going to Sweden early in the summer and requests all his debtors to pay their debts; he will sell his property at Osborne's along with his distillery and brewery (VGWeA 19 Jan 82)

LOVE, [Allan], Superior Ct. held in Petersburg, 23 Apr. 1797, in debt, mentions John GREEN for the benefit of Fanny LOVE admx. w.w.a. of [Allan] LOVE dec'd (pltf.) against Benjamin TUCKER Sr. (VGPI 1 Aug 97)

LOVE, Mrs. Jane, d. on 5 Jan. at Salisbury, Loudoun Co. in her 45th year leaving a husband and 12 chil. (VHFA 13 Jan 91)

LOVE, John Esq., mar. Miss Betsey WATSON dau. of Josiah WATSON [of Alexandria] (VCWM 4 Jun 88)

LOVE, Dr. William, dec'd, his admr., Alexander MORSON of Falmouth, will sell a small assortment of drugs and medicines (VH 6 Sep 97)

LOVEDAY, Joseph, conv., c. 23, ran away from the ship *Justitia* at Leedstown (VG 9 Apr 72)

LOVELL, William, eld. son and heir at law of George LOVELL dec'd; the sheriff of Halifax . is commanded to summon him to appear before the justices of that co. to answer a bill in chancery exhibited against him by William HAWKINS Jr. (VGPu 21 Aug 78)

LOVET, Reuben, appr., c. 19, ran away from John HAMILTON, tailor, Norfolk (NH 16 Jun 96)

LOVETT, Daniel, Pr. Geo. Co., Ct. of Q.S, 15 Aug. 1798, in chanc: James WOODEND and Jane his wife (compl.) against Daniel LOVETT and Rebecca his wife and Thomas GALT and Vandevan LEONARD (defs); it appears that the LOVETTs are not inhabitants of the Commonwealth (VGPI 12 Oct 98)

LOVETT, Joshua, appr. boy, ran away from James ABBOTT (ET 28 Jun 98)

LOVITT, John, dec'd, e.a.w. his admr., Thomas STONE of Pr. Anne Co. (NHPA 3 Jul 97)

LOW, James, Eng., 30, des. from Capt. Thomas WAGGENER's Co. of Va. forces (VG 22 Aug 55)

LOWE, Thomas, appr., native of Bermuda, 16-17, ran away from Andrew JAMIESON, Alexandria (CMAG 31 May 96, NH 9 Jun 96 sup)

LOWERY, John, appr., 15-16, ran away from Lewis JOHNSON, Albemarle Co. (VGGA 7 Sep 91)

LOWNDES, Christopher, of Bladensburg [Md.], dec'd, his ex. are Benjamin and Francis LOWNDES (VJAA 7 Apr 85)

LOWRY, Edward, appr., c. 17, ran away from Joseph TULEY, Frederick Co. (BVCG 13 Oct 94)

LOYAL, Mrs. Frances, spouse of Paul LOYAL Esq. of Norfolk, d. Thurs. last (VCNPGA 12 Jan 93)

LUCAS, Fielding, of Fredsbrg., mar. Miss Eliza WITHERS dau. of James WITHERS of Fauquier Co., in Fauquier Co. on Thurs. last (VHFA 2 May 98)

LUCAS, Miss Sally, of Norf., d. Wed. last in the prime of life (VCNPGA 6 Oct 92)

LUCAS, Mrs. Sally, consort of Fielding LUCAS of this town [Fredsbrg.], d. on Sat. last (VHFA 5 Mar 95)

LUCAS, William, son of Thomas LUCAS and Passibella his wife, who was b. in Accomack Co., is requested to apply to William BEAVANS in that co. to be informed of something greatly to his advantage (VG 25 Apr 55)

LUCAS, William, of Norfolk, cautions masters of vessels and others not to carry his son, Daniel LUCAS, out of the borough without his consent since he is under age (AGNPPA 25 Mar 96)

LUCK, Samuel Sr., of Spotsylvania Co., dec'd, his ex. is Samuel LUCK (VHFA 10 Dec 89)

LUDEMAN, Maj. William, dec'd, e.a.w. his ex. (nfi) who requests that his debts be paid (VIC 16 Apr 88, 23 Apr 88 ex)

LUDIMAN, Maj. John, native of Germany, a brave officer, d. in Richmond last Thurs. [9 Mar.] (VGAA 15 Mar 86, VJAA 23 Mar 86)

LUDWELL, Philip Esq., only son of the Hon. Philip LUDWELL Esq., dec'd, mar. Miss Fanny GRYMES eld. dau. of Col. Charles GRYMES (VG 29 Jul 37)

LUDWELL, the Hon. Philip Esq., member of H.M's Council in this Colony, d. in England (VG 4 Jun 67); his HHF to be sold at his seat, Green Spring, by his ex. (nfi) (VG 12 Nov 67)

LUMKIN, John, of Kg. Wm. Co., 22-23, guilty of killing a slave bel. to Sarah LUMKIN of the same co., has absconded (VGGA 4 May 96)

LUNEY, Peter, b. in Philadelphia, but now of Va., c. 23, arrived in Philadelphia after having been a prisoner of the Indians (NYM 25 Jul 57, 1 Aug 57) [name also spelled LEWNEY]

LUPTON, Joseph, mar. Miss Elizabeth CARTMELL dau. of Thomas CARTMELL on Thurs. (WVGWA 24 Jul 90)

LUPTON, Joseph, dec'd, e.a.w. his ex., David and Jonathan LUPTON (BVCG 28 Jan 92)

LUSCOMBE, William, svt., 17-18, ran away from Roger NORTH, Staunton (VGPu 26 May 75 sup)

LUSK, Capt. James, of the ship *Speirs* just arrived from Glasgow, fell overboard off the Western Islands and was lost (VG 29 Dec 68)

LUTZ, Michael, dec'd, e.a.w. his admx., Catherine LUTZ of Alexandria, who adv. that the tanning business will be carried on as usual (CMAG 4 Feb 96)

LYALL, William, from Kg. Wm. Co., c. 28, des. from the 15th Va. Regt.; claims that he was regularly enl. with Drury RAGSDALE in Col. Charles HARRISON's Regt. of Artillery and may be found in York Garrison (VGPu 11 Apr 77, 18 Apr 77 sup)

LYAN, David, Irish svt., 27, ran away from the Potomac Co., Great Falls (VJAA 3 Aug 86)

LYDE, Maj. Cornelius, of Kg. Wm. Co., son of Mr. [?] LYDE merch. of Bristol, d. last week (VG 27 Jan 38)

LYELL, Richard Davis, c. 28-30, escaped from Gloucester Co. jail (VIC 21 Oct 89)

LYLE Family, HCC, 12 Mar 1791; Robinson, Sanderson, & Rumney (pltfs.) against William HUNTER Jr., Andrew WALES, Thomas HEWETT, and Robert LYLE ex. of Robert LYLE dec'd and Martha LYLE widow and relict of William LYLE, Jane LYLE and Robert LYLE chil. of the sd. Robert LYLE and his devisees (VGAxA 19 May 91)

LYLE, Farrell, came from Ireland about five yrs. ago and landed at Hobbs' Hole; if he will apply to James MULLAGHAN, Kingston Par., Gloucester Co. he may hear of something to his advantage (VGPu 11 Oct 76)

LYLE, James, Clerk of the District Ct., d. in Staunton on 13 Apr. (BVCG 29 Apr 93)

LYLE, James Jr., of Manchester, mar. Miss Sally GOODE dau. of Col. Robert GOODE of Chesterfield Co., last Sat. eve. (VGGA and RMA 22 Jun 96)

LYLE, Robert, merch. of Alexandria, mar. Miss Martha HEWITT of Bladensburg [Md.] (VJAA 24 Nov 85)

LYLES, Capt. Henry, d. on Thurs. morn. and bur. at the Presbyterian Meeting House; the brethren of Lodge No. 39 attended (VJAA 6 Apr 86); e.a.w. his admrs., William LYLES and James HENDRICKS of Alexandria (VJAA 27 Apr 86); lived in the tavern in Alexandria called the Alexandria Inn and Coffee House, which is to rented (VJAA 11 May 86)

LYMEBURNE, Capt., formerly of the ship *Roba and Betsey*, d. a few days ago in Wmsbrg. (HNPA 29 Oct 95)

LYNAR, Mary, of Richmond, adv. that her husband, John LYNAR, has behaved in a cruel and unbecoming manner to her, has turned her out of doors, destitute of support, and is about to sell certain freehold property (VGWeA 30 Aug 87, 6 Sep 87)

LYNCH, Francis, of Norfolk Borough, mar. Miss Polly DRYNANE of Gosport (NH 3 Oct 99)

LYNCH, Head Esq., Postmaster General of America, d. Mon. last at his house in Caroline Co. (Wmsbrg. disp. of 10 Jun.) (AWM 14 Jul 43); tracts of his land in Caroline and Orange Cos. to be sold pursuant to his will by William DUDLEY (nfi) (VG 30 Apr 52)

LYNCH, Peter, b. in Ireland, 30, has a wife and child in Philadelphia, formerly a soldier in Gen. WAYNE's Brigade; jailed in Richmond for highway robbery; escaped with William GALLEY (VGAA 7 Aug 84)

LYNCH, Robert, who is underage, has run away from his father, George LYNCH (SVG 14 Feb 95)

LYNE, Col. George, of K & Q Co., d. lately after a short illness [long obit.] (VGAA 31 Jan 84)

LYNE, John, of Richmond, dec'd, dwelling house, lot, PE, and two ships bel. to his est. to be sold by his ex., W. LYNE (Arg 8 Mar 99, VGGA 19 Mar 99 sup)

LYNN, Adam, of Alexandria, died (VJAA 15 Jun 86); a lot bel. to his est. to be sold by Katherine LYNN, his extx., and his exors., Peter WISE and Philip WEBSTER (VJAA 17 Aug 86)

LYNN, Robert, b. in Londonderry [Ireland], 26, soldier, resided at Conicogce [sic], Md., des. from Col. DUNBAR's Regt. (VG 9 May 55)

LYNN, Dr. William, dec'd, his ex. (nfi) will sell a lot of his land in Fredsbrg. (VGR 5 Sep 71)

LYON, Mr., of Alexandria, d. last night (NHPA 14 Sep 97)

LYON, Daniel, dec'd, his ex., William MOSS, will rent his plant. two miles from St. Peter's Church in New Kent Co. and settle his est. accounts (VGPu 15 Mar 76, VGAA 19 Apr 83)

LYON, John, of P[erson] Co., N. Carolina, dec'd, e.a.w. his ex., John WORNACK and John FARRIER (VGGA 13 Jan 96)

LYON, Dr. John, late of Pr. Anne Co., dec'd, e.a.w. his ex., J. BLAMIRE, Portsmouth (NH 23 May 96)

LYON, Walter, att. at law, of Pr. Anne Co., died (VG 14 Jan 75)

LYONS, John, white svt., ran away from Dennis RYAN, Petersburg (VGIC 22 May 84)

LYONS, John Esq., of Hanover Co., mar. Miss Anne (of Cleve) CARTER of Kg. Wm. Co. on Fri. the 24th ult. (VIC 12 Aug 89)

LYONS, Mrs. Mary, spouse of Peter LYONS Esq., att. at law, died (VG 4 Mar 73)

LYONS, Peter Esq., of Hanover Co., mar. Miss Judith BASSETT of Wmsbrg. (VG 30 Dec 73)

LYONS, Peter Jr. Esq., d. in Richmond, yesterday morn. [Fri. 21 Dec.] (VGRMA 22 Dec 94, VGGA 24 Dec 94, VGWeA 27 Dec 94)

M'ADAM, Dr. Joseph Jr., late surgeon's mate in the 5th Va. Regt., died (VGPu 16 May 77)

M'ADOOE, John, of Botetourt Co., adv. that his wife, Anne, has eloped from his house and bed after the most tender treatment for upwards of 20 yrs. (VG 21 Jun 70)

M'ALESTER, Daniel, adv. that his wife, Emma M'ALESTER, eloped without any just cause on 12 May last and he will not be accountable for any of her contracts (TAA 6 Sep 97)

M'ALESTER, James Jr., merch., formerly of Winchester, d. lately in N.

Carolina (BVCG 12 Oct 95)
M'ALISTER, Mrs. Elizabeth, consort of John M'ALISTER, d. Wed. last at Buffalo Marsh (BVCG 28 Oct 96)
M'ANDREE, Sarah, dec'd, e.a.w. her ex., Jacob BRUCE, Wmsbrg. (VG 10 Dec 72)
M'AN[N]ULTY, [?], found dead in a field near Winchester early of Sat. morn. 20 Oct.; the jury's verdict was that he was intoxicated and perished with the cold (BVCG 21 Oct 92, VGRDA 27 Oct 92)
M'AULAY, Thomas, executed at the gallows near this city [Richmond] on Fri. last, for a rape (Richmond disp. of 10 Aug.) (*Pittsburgh Gazette* 2 Sep 86) [see: M'CAULEY, Thomas]
McAUSLAND, Humphrey, dec'd, e.a.w. his admrs. w.w.a., William DRUMMOND and Adam DARBY, Fredsbrg. (VHFA 8 Nov 92, 12 Jun 94, VGGA 5 Dec 92)
M'BRIDE, Francis, an aged man, resident of Pendleton Co. near the South Branch of Potomac, d. on the 30th ult. [Dec.] at the home of George RALLS, Loudoun Co. (VGAxA 14 Jan 90)
M'BRIDE, James, ind. svt., 17-18, ran away from Adam HART, Hog Cr., Frederick Co. (BVCG 10 Feb 97)
M'CAA, William, dec'd, his widow, Sarah M'CAA, will continue to keep his tavern, the King's Arms Tavern at Hampton (VGPu 7 Jul 75, VG 29 Jul 75)
M'CABE, Laughlin, dec'd, e.a.w. Cornelius CALVERT [Jr.] the surviving ex., of Pr. Anne Co. (VCNPGA 13 Oct 92, HNPA 31 Aug 95)
M'CABE, William, appr. hatter, c. 17, ran away from Howson SEATON (BVCG 15 Sep 94)
M'CALL, Miss Katherine Flood, heir of the late Dr. Nicholas FLOOD, of Richmond Co., is now of age (VGGA 25 Aug 90)
M'CALLASTER, Elizabeth, has eloped from her husband, Matthew, of Augusta Co. (VGR 2 May 71)
M'CALLION, James, b. in New Castle, Pa., 24, des. from Richard CALL's troop of Light Horse, Fredsbrg. (VGPu 21 Feb 77)
M'CALLUM, Daniel, late merch. at Osborne's, e.a.w. his ex., George MARKHAM and Joseph FRIEND (Arg 26 Jul 99)
M'CAMY, William, dec'd, his extx., Isabella M'CAMY, and ex., John [M'CAMY], will sell his land below Jennings' Gap in Augusta Co. (PH 12 Dec 98)
M'CANN, Peter, jailed in Isle of Wight Co. as a vagrant, but is suspected of being the svt. who ran away from Robert RUTHERFORD (VG 19 Jul 70) [see: HOLMS, John]
M'CARTNEY, the Rev. James, Rector of St. Patrick's in Pr. Edw. Co., died (VGPu 21 Jul 75 sup, VG 22 Jul 75) [name also given as MACARTNEY]
M'CARTNEY, Nicholas, Irish svt., c. 27, ran away from Zachariah HENDRICK, Cumberland Co. (VGR 17 Feb 74)
M'CARTY, Cornelius, svt., of the Potomac Company, jailed for attempted murder of Michael BURNET near the Falls Church (VJAA 9 Nov 86)
M'CARTY, Daniel, appr., c. 19, wheelwright, ran away from William COSBY, Wmsbrg. (VG 9 Jan 72)
M'CARTY, John, Irish ind. svt., weaver, ran away from Thomson MASON, Loudoun Co. (VGPu 12 Sep 77)
M'CARTY, John, journeyman printer, d. near Norfolk (VICGA 28 Apr 90)
M'CARTY, Michael, svt., laborer, ran away from the snow *John* lying in Hampton Road (VGAA 17 Apr 84)
M'CARTY, Col. Thaddeus, dec'd, his ex., James BALL Jr., James GORDON, and Will. SYDNOR, will sell his late dwelling plant. in Lancaster Co. on the Western Branch of Corotoman River containing 280 ac. (VGWeA 22 Nov 87, VIC 5 Dec 87)
M'CARTY, William, Irish svt., 30, ran away from the Potomac Co., Great Falls, supposedly with Daniel CRONEAN, 25, and his wife (VJAA 13 Jul 86); ran away again, on 10 Nov., with William JOHNSON an Irish freeman (VJAA

16 Nov 86)
M'CARTY, Mrs. Winifred, wife of Daniel M'CARTY Esq., of Westmoreland Co., d. on 23 Feb. (VHFA 10 Mar 91)
M'CAUGHEY, Joseph, blacksmith, d. in Richmond on Sat. morn. last [4 July] (RMA 4 Jul 95, RC 7 Jul 95)
M'CAULEY, Thomas, executed near Richmond last Fri. [4 Aug.] for rape (VJAA 10 Aug 86) [see: M'AULAY, Thomas]
M'CAULY, Alexander, merch. of Norfolk, d. on Tues. at Yorktown, leaving a wife and a young and beautiful offspring (VH 19 Jul 98, OVT 23 Jul 98, VGGA 24 Jul 98, NWJCI 25 Jul 98)
M'CAUSLAND, Thomas, denies that he has been intimate with Polly TEARE and has made her pregnant, as she has been propagating a number of false and malicious tales about him (PGBA 4 Jan 96)
McCAW, Dr. James Drue, mar. Miss Sally HARRIS, Tues. eve. last in Hampton (VCNPGA 5 Jan 93)
M'CLANACHAN, John, of Augusta Co., dec'd, e.a.w. his ex., Alexander St. CLAIR (VG 22 Apr 75)
M'CLANAHAN, John, hatter, c. 21, enl. in Greenbrier Co., des. from Corporal SILLS' Co. (KG 12 Jan 93)
M'CLANEN, Henry, executed at the gallows near this city [Wmsbrg.] (VG 4 Dec 78)
M'CLANNAHAN, John, mar. Miss Fanny PIERCE in Westmoreland Co. last Fri. (VHFA 21 Mar 98); his letter of denial stating that the marriage notice was a malicious and notorious lie (VHFA 4 Apr 98)
M'CLA[R]Y, David, b. in Franklin Co., Pa., 24, des. from the camp of the 8th U. S. Regt. near Harper's Ferry (WG 18 Dec 99)
M'CLATCHY, James, dec'd, his surviving partners in James McClatchy & Co. are: John CUNNINGHAM, Edward CUNNINGHAM, and Edward DILLON, of Cartersville (VGGA 19 Mar 94)
M'CLEAN, Archibald, principal of an academy in Alexandria, was mar. to Miss Mary JONES dau. of the Rev. Mr. David JONES of Chester[field] Co., on Tues. morn. last by the Rev. Dr. ROGERS (TAA 29 Aug 97)
M'CLEAN, Matthew, age 24, ran away from H.M.S. *Fewey* lying in Hampton, on 23 Mar. (VG 10 Oct 45)
M'CLELLAN, James, dec'd, his admr., William MAITLAND, will sell all of his PE at Charlotte Ct. H. (VGPI 26 May 97)
M'CLENACHAN, Col. Alexander, for many yrs. a citizen of this place [Staunton], d. on Tues. 28 Mar. (SVG 5 Apr 97, BVCG 14 Apr 97); e.a.w. his admr., W. ABNEY (SVG 21 Apr 97)
M'CLENEHAN, Capt. William, of Pr. Anne Co., dec'd, e.a.w. his ex., John PAYNTER and Cornelius CALVERT Jr. (NPC 26 Mar 91); e.a.w. Cornelius CALVERT Jr., the surviving ex. (VCNPGA 26 Jan 93, HNPA 31 Aug 95); the sheriff of Pr. Anne will sell 12 of his Negroes to satisfy two executions (HNPA 12 Nov 95)
M'CLOUD, [?], native of the north of Scotland, killed himself by cutting his throat on Sat. eve. last in Richmond (VGWeA 14 Jun 87)
McCLOUD, Alexander, adv. that his wife, Nancy McCLOUD, has eloped withou' any just provocation (VH 2 Sep 97)
M'CLOUD, Joseph, dec'd, e.a.w. his admr., Levi REUBIN (VGWeA 16 Dec 91)
M'CLURG, Dr. James, of this city [Wmsbrg.], mar. Miss SELDEN of Hampton (VG 22 May 79)
M'CLURG, Dr. Walter, of Hampton, dec'd, e.a.w. his ex., James M'CLURG, who will also sell surgical instruments, apothecary apparatus, and medicines (VGWeA 10 Apr 84)
M'CLUSE Family, Frederick Co. Ct., 5 Aug. 1790, in chanc: John M'CLUSE admr. of David M'CLUSE dec'd, Thomas JONES and Elizabeth his wife, late Elizabeth M'CLUSE, admx. of the sd. David M'CLUSE dec'd (compls.) against James G. DOWDALL and Edward M'GUIRE surviving exors. of Robert RUSSELL dec'd, James RUSSELL, Francis RUSSELL, Margaret

RUSSELL, and Amelia RUSSELL devisees of the sd. Robert RUSSELL dec'd (defs.); it appears that James, Francis, Margaret, and Amelia RUSSELL are not inhabitants of this country (WVGWA 21 Aug 91)

M'CONNICO, Mrs. Anne, spouse of Christopher M'CONNICO Esq., mayor of Petersburg, d. on Fri. last; she was only 27 (VGAA 15 Feb 86)

M'CONNICO, Christopher Esq., of Petersburg, mar. Miss Nancy BOLLING of Pr. Geo. Co. on Sat. last (NPJ 19 Nov 88)

M'CORD, David, appr., 13, ran away from John SENSENEY (BVCG 25 Nov 96)

M'CORKLE, William, c. 19, b. in Augusta Co., des. from the 4th Regt., U. S. Army (VGSWA 20 Oct 97)

M'CORMACK, James, appr., 18, ran away from John BOGUE, supposed to be gone towards Water Branch, Bull Run near the house in Pr. Wm. Co. where his relations live; he has been heard to express himself that he wished to go with them to Ky. (TAA 19 Dec 98)

M'CO[R]MICK, Hugh, continental soldier in the 16th Regt. of Guards, had a wife in Buckingham Co., des. from Leesburg (VG 23 Jan 78)

McCOULL, Neil, merch. of Fredsbrg., native of Scotland, d. on 27 Apr. in the 52nd year of his age; his extx. is apparently Ann McCOULL; John McCOULL (nfi) is also mentioned (VHFA 5 May, 29 Dec 91); e.a.w. John McCOULL and Ann McCOULL who will also sell his 1200 ac. tract in Spotsylvania Co. (VHFA 5 Jan 92)

M'COY, George, aka John, mulatto slave, c. 28, can speak English and Dutch, ran away from Jacob BARRIER [also given as BERRIER], Augusta Co. (VGGA 31 Apr 93, BVCG 27 May 93)

M'CRAW, Daniel, Scottish highlander, belonged to Charles DICK in Fredsbrg., ran away (VG 14 Aug 46)

M'CREADY, Robert, intends to leave the state in a few weeks and desires to sell his property (NPC 2 Jun 92)

M'CREADY, John, passenger in the sloop *Venus* from Baltimore who arrived in Norfolk on Sun. last may obtain his property at Christopher COFFIN's (NHPA 5 Nov 96)

M'CROSK[E]Y, Mrs. Charlotte, wife of the Rev. Samuel Smith M'CROSK[E]Y of Northampton, d. suddenly at Mr. PINCKARD's in Lancaster Co. while on a visit to her friends (VG and VGPu 30 Oct 78)

M'CULLOCH, Anthony, Fairfax Co., August Ct. 1791, in chancery: James M'CULLOCH admr. and Margaret M'CULLOCH admx. w.w.a. of Anthony M'CULLOCH dec'd (compls.) against the Rt. Hon. Charles BENNETT Earl of Tankerville admr. w.w.a. of the Rt. Hon. Charles BENNETT Earl of Tankerville dec'd, Henry Astley BENNETT, Robert Townshend HOOE, Charles LITTLE, Anthony STEWART, and Robert LAWSON (defs.); it appears that Charles BENNETT and Henry Astley BENNETT are not inhabitants of this country (VGPA 5 Nov 91) [see also: VICGA 7 Apr 90]

M'DANIEL, Michael, Irish svt., 14-15, ran away from Jonathan SWIFT, Alexandria (VJAA 12 Apr 87)

M'DONALD Family, HCC, 1 Jun. 1793, Isaac HITE Jr. and Archibald M'DONALD exors. of Mary M'DONALD dec'd who was devisee of John M'DONALD dec'd (pltfs.) and Jane CAMERON and Angus M'DONALD heirs at law of John M'DONALD dec'd and Charles LEWIS Registrar of the Land Office (defs.); it appears that Jane CAMERON and Angus M'DONALD are not inhabitants of this country (VGRC 12 Jul 93)

M'DONALD, Angus, late of Frederick Co., dec'd, e.a.w. Anna M'DONALD (VGWA 10 Sep 91)

M'DONALD, Charles, appr., c. 19, ran away from John WARRINGTON, Norfolk (HNPA 1 Jul 95)

M'DONALD, Daniel, appr., 17, ran away from Jacob WEAVER, Shenandoah Co. (BVCG 25 Nov 96)

M'DONALD, Dennis, ind. svt., ran away from George NORVELL, Hanover Co. (VG 16 Jun 74)

M'DONALD, Elizabeth, has absconded from her husband, Patrick M'DONALD

(VHFA 7 Mar 93)
M'DONALD, Dr. J., d. near Winchester (VGPI 14 Dec 86)
M'DONALD, James, merch., of Frederick Co., mar. Miss Polly RICE also of Frederick Co., last Thurs. (BVCG 7 Jan 93)
M'DONALD, James, appr., c. 20, ran away from John DAY, Falmouth (VHFA 4 Jul 93)
M'DONALD, Dr. John, d. at his house near Winchester on 27 Oct. (VJAA 9 Nov 86, VGAA 13 Dec 86)
M'DONALD, John, appr. saddler, 20 in June next, ran away from George HESSLER, Winchester (WG 20 Feb 99)
M'DONALD, Mrs. Mary, widow of Dr. John M'DONALD, d. on Fri. the 2nd inst. at the house of her father, Isaac HITE (VCWM 7 Jan 89); her PE will be sold by Isaac HITE Jr. on her plant. near Hopewell Quaker Meeting House (VGWA 4 Feb 89); pursuant to her will, the land whereon the late Dr. John M'DONALD lived will be sold by her ex., Isaac HITE Jr. (VGWA 12 Aug 89)her ex., Isaac HITE Jr. and Archibald M'DONALD, will sell her 35 ac. tract of land in Hampshire Co. on Potomac River (PGBA 28 Jul 94) [name also given as MACDONALD]
M'DONALD, William, svt., cooper, from the north of Scotland, has been in the country about a year, ran away from Gardner FLEMING, Suffolk Co. (VG 1 Oct 67)
M'DOUGLE, Dougle, of Hanover Co., dec'd, e.a.w. his admr., John M'DOUGLE (VGAA 27 Dec 83)
M'DOUGAL, Peter, dec'd, his admr. with the nunc. will annexed is Angus M'DONALD, Hampshire Co. (BVCG 31 Mar 97)
M'DOWEL, Samuel, Scot, 32, b. at Newport, Glasgow, ran away from the *Berry*, Sheppard's Warehouse (VG 27 Mar 52)
M'DOWELL, Mr., of Augusta Co., killed in Dec. 1742 by Shawan Indians (NYPB 4 Apr 43)
M'DOWELL, Mary, adv. that her father, James M'DOWELL, devised her 336 ac. in James City Co. which she has been kept out of (VGGA 25 May 96)
M'DOWELL, Robert, of Norfolk, of [William] Johnson & M'Dowell, tobacco manufacturers, d. on 6 Sep (NWJCI 6 Sep 97)
M'DUEL, Sam, aka John, aka HENSON, mulatto, c. 30, ran away from Edward COX, Goochland Co., suspected that he is going to Pa. (VGGA 1 Jul 95)
M'FADDEN Family, Berkeley Co. Ct., 27 May 1796, in chanc: Thomas VIOLET (compl.) vs. Richardton STEWART and James ARMSTRONG exors. of Alexander M'FADDEN dec'd, James CAMPBELL and James M'FADDEN the Elder dec'd who was heir at law of Alexander M'FADDEN dec'd (PGBA 23 Jun 96)
M'FARLAN, Robert, Scottish svt., ran away from the plant. of the Rev. Mr. Robert ROSS, Albemarle Co. (VG 5 Mar 52)
M'FARLANE, Alexander, dec'd, e.a.w. his admx. and widow, Mary M'FARLANE of Portsmouth [or Norfolk acc. to NHPA] (NHPA 25 May 97, NH 6 Mar 98, 27 Jun 99) [name also given as M'FARLINE]
M'FARLANE, Frederick, mulatto svt., 23 - 28, ran away from John STUART, Stafford Co. (VG 8 Nov 70)
M'FARLINE, John, ran away from the ship *Mary Ann* at City Point (VGPI 16 Jun 91)
M'FARQUHAR, John, dec'd, his admr., John BURNS of Petersburg, will sell all of his PE including carpenter's tools, HH and KF (VGPI 13 Jun 94)
M'FEARSON, John, appr., 16, ran away from the brig *Brenchley* of London (VGAxA 29 Apr 90)
M'FEELLY, James, appr., 15-16, ran away from John DARLINGTON (VGWA 25 Jun 91)
M'FEELY, Isaac, appr., 17, ran away from Joseph LONGACRE Jr. near Marlboro's Iron Works (WG 25 Sep 99)
M'FEETERS, James, dec'd, his admx., Elenor WILSON, is a compl. in a chancery case, Rockbridge Co. Ct., May 1797 (VGSWA 20 Oct 97)

M'GEHEE, Carr., dec'd, 527 ac. of his land in Caroline Co. to be sold by his ex., Henry CHILES; his legatees are: Gideon GOOCH and Benjamin HUTCHINS of N. Carolina, Samuel M'GEHEE of Amherst Co., and John M'GEHEE of Bedford Co. (VGGA 24 Nov 90)

M'GIBBON, John, Irish ind. svt., 46, jailed in Winchester, says he bel. to William BARTON, Montgomery Co., Md. (VCWM 28 May 88)

M'GILL, Andrew, Scot, svt., blacksmith, ran away from John SHIPHARD, Wmsbrg., who has heard that he was seen going towards N. Carolina (VGP 20 Jul 75, VG 29 Jul 75, 7 Oct 75)

M'GILL, Mrs. Elisabeth, wife of Col. Charles M'GILL of Winchester, d. in this co. [Spotsylvania?] on Thurs. sennight (VHFA 10 Feb 91)

M'GILLIVRAY, Col. Alexander, celebrated chief of the Creek Nation, died (VGGA 30 May 92, NPC 2 Jun 92)

McGOWN, Archibald, of Norfolk, dec'd, e.a.w. his exors., Daniel McPHERSON and John HAMILTON (VCNPGA 6 Oct 92)

M'GRATH, Mrs. Eleanor, wife of Chris. C. M'GRATH Comedian, d. on Sat. eve. last at Port Tobacco, Md. during the company's performing there (CMAG and RJDWA 3 Nov 96)

M'GRATH, Terrence, svt., laborer, ran away from the snow *John* lying in Hampton Road (VGAA 17 Apr 84)

M'GRAUGH, Robert, 21, ran away from the ship *Allerton* on 28 Aug. (VG 31 Oct 51)

M'GUIRE, Edward, ind. svt., c. 19, ran away from David LUPTON near Winchester (BVCG 8 Oct 92)

M'GUIRE, Edward, HCC, 21 Mar. 1797, between John M'ALISTER (pltf.) and Richard QUINCE and Sarah Elizabeth M'ALISTER admr. and admx. of James M'ALISTER and Edward M'GUIRE (defs.); it appears that QUINCE and Sarah Eliz. M'ALISTER are not inhabitants of this country (VGGA 10 May 97)

M'GUIRE, Edward Jr., of Winchester, merch., mar. Miss Elizabeth HOLMES of Holmesgrove, Frederick Co., on Thurs. the 10th inst. (BVCG 18 Mar 96)

M'GUIRE, James, executed last Fri. in Wmsbrg. for murder (VG 24 Jan 51)

M'GUIRE, James, soldier, 25, b. in Boston, but his dialect is that of the north of Ireland, des. from the rendezvous at Kempsville (NH 7 Mar 99)

M'GUIRE, Richard, Irish svt., 18, from Dublin, ran away from John SUTTON, Alexandria (VJAA 22 Nov 87)

M'GUIRE, Thomas A., of Richmond, schoolmaster, killed himself on Fri. night last (VIC 9 Dec 89, VGWeA 10 Dec 89)

M'GUIRE, William Esq., att. at law of Winchester, mar. Miss Polly LITTLE of Berkeley Co. last Wed. (BVCG 16 Apr 92)

M'HENRY, Ann, of Alexandria, dec'd, e.a.w. her admr., Jesse TAYLOR and Patrick BURNS who will also settle the est. of the late James M'HENRY (CMAG 17 May 98)

M'HENRY, James, has left his wife, Ann M'HENRY, of Alexandria, and is expected to leave the country (VGAxA 3 Jun 90); late of Alexandria, dec'd, e.a.w. his admx., Ann M'HENRY (CMAG 9 Mar 97)

M'INTIRE, Samuel, ind. svt., c. 16, ran away from John LARICK of Frederick Co. (BVCG 7 Apr 97)

M'INTOSH, Lachlin, 52, d. on Mon. eve. last in this town [Fredsbrg.] (VH 8 Mar 99)

M'INTYRE, Alexander, of Leesburg, dec'd, his extx. is Jane M'INTYRE (VGAxA 10 Sep 89)

M'IVER, John, merch., mar. Miss Peggy COUPER, both of this town [Alexandria] (VGAxA 9 Dec 90)

M'KAY, George, Eng. svt., ran away from Robert PHILLIPS, Fredsbrg. (VGR 4 Feb 68)

M'KEAND, Mrs., consort of John M'KEAND merch., d. on Mon. last (VGWeA 12 Nov 89)

M'KEAND, John, of Richmond, d. on Sun. last (VGGA 2 May 92); his ex.,

Alexander M'ROBERT, will sell his HH and KF (VGGA 27 Jun 92)

M'KECHNIE, George, adv. that he is an upholsterer and paperhanger from North Britain and last from London, and has set up shop in Richmond (RMA 13 Jan 96)

M'KEDDIE, Daniel, Scot., svt., c. 18, ran away from Benjamin DUVALL, Caroline Co. (MG 15 Jun 48)

M'KEE, Sam, mulatto, ran away from Thomas CRANDELL (CMAG 21 Aug 94)

M'KENDRICK, Archibald, of Richmond, will leave the colony soon (VG 22 Apr 75)

M'KENNY, Francis, brother to Anne M'KENNY (since DE LA HOYDE) late of S. Carolina; if he be living, he may hear of something to his advantage by applying to George SIKES of Charleston, S. Carolina (VG 30 Oct 78)

M'KENNY, John, appr., 16-17, ran away from James WALKER (VGWA 7 Oct 89)

M'KENNY, Luke, appr., c. 9, ran away from Ambrose BARNETT, Battletown, Frederick Co. (BVCG 29 Apr 96)

M'KENZIE, Mrs. Joanna, of Wmsbrg., dec'd, e.a.w. her ex., James CARTER (VG 19 Feb 67)

M'KENZIE, Dr. William, d. on Fri. last in Manchester (VGRMA 3 Jun 93); sundry moveable property of his to be sold by his ex., [William] FOUSHEE, William HARRIS, John MURCHIE (VGRMA 25 Jul 93)

M'KIM, William, mar. Miss Betsy ELLIOTT, both of Richmond, on Thurs. 26 Dec. (VGRC 31 Dec 93, VGWeA 3 Jan 94)

M'KINLAY, William, Irish svt., c. 23, ran away from Francis THOMAS, Frederick Co., Md. (VGPu 13 Oct 75)

M'KINZIE, Capt., of H.M's 43rd Regt., a native of Va. is reportedly slain at the Battle of Charlestown (VG 12 Aug 75)

M'KINZIE, Daniel, of Fluvanna Co., dec'd, his heir at law was Alexander M'KINZIE and his widow is Sarah (VGGA 27 Oct 90)

M'KINZIE, Donald, of Petersburg, merch., mar. Miss Sally HARRISON of Richmond on Thurs. eve. (VGGA 28 Jan 95, VGRMA 29 Jan 95)

M'KNIGHT, Capt. John, was mar. to Miss Kitty PIERCY, both of this town [Alexandria], on Tues. eve. [or Wed. acc. to TDCDA] by the Rev. Mr. SWANN (TDCDA 1 Nov 99, CMAG 2 Nov 99)

M'KOY, Jacob, mar. Miss Mary HAINES, both of Frederick Co., on Wed. last (WG 16 Jan 99)

M'KUE, John, Irish svt., blacksmith, ran away from William AYLETT and John BUSHROD, Westmoreland Co. (AWM 2 Aug 39)

M'LAUGHLIN, James, of Berkeley Co., adv. that sometime since, he exchanged his property in Berkeley Co. for land in Ky. and is now on the point of removing, but his wife, Elizabeth M'LAUGHLIN, refuses to sign the deed of conveyance and also refuses to go with him; he will no longer be answerable for any of her proceedings or pay any of her debts (PGBA 19 May 94)

M'LAURIN, The Rev. Mr., Rector of Southampton [Par.] in Cumberland Co., d. suddenly at the house of John BASKERVILLE (VGR 22 Jul 73)

M'LAURINE, Joseph, of Chesterfield Co., mar. Miss Sukey ELLIS of Hanover Co. yesterday (VGRC 12 Jul 93)

M'LEAN, James, Scot., svt., c. 28, ran away from Samuel WOOD, Richmond (VG 27 Oct 74)

M'LEAN, John, printer, native of Glasgow, d. at Norfolk on Mon, the 18th inst. in his 32nd year [obit. in VIC] (VIC 27 May 89, VGWeA 28 May 89)

M'LEAN, Samuel, dec'd, his ex., Andrew WALES, will pet. the next GA to authorize him to sell the real est. of M'LEAN to pay his debts (CMAG 16 Aug 96); his acting ex., Andrew WALES, will sell a lot of ground on Queen St. [Alexandria] (CMAG 24 Oct 99)

M'LEOD, Capt. George, formerly of the ship *New York*, d. on Sat. last (NH 30 Apr 99)

M'LEOD, John, native of Scotland, appr., c. 15, ran away from John EWING, Portsmouth; he is supposed to have gone to Carolina (VGNI 13 Oct 74)

M'MACHAN, Robert, of Augusta Co., convicted of murder, was executed Fri. last near Wmsbrg. (VGR 1 Jun 69, NYPB 19 Jun 69)

M'MAHAN, Michael, barber, of Alexandria, died (VJAA 30 Mar 86)

M'MECHAN, William, merch., mar. Miss Nancy WILKINSON, on Thurs. last (CMAG 5 Nov 96)

M'MECHEN, William, intends to remove to Norfolk in a few days (TDCDA 20 Nov 99)

[McMEHON], Cornelius, Irish conv. svt., 30-40, ran away from Richard BOATMAN, Lancaster Co. (VG 22 Oct 36)

M'MIKEN, Hugh, merch., of Norfolk, d. at Wmsbrg. after a short and violent illness on the 22nd inst. in his 32nd year (VG 23 Jun 74, VGNI 30 Jun 74, VGP 27 Oct 74) [name also given as M'MEKIN]

McMUNN, George, mar. Miss Elizabeth SITTLER dau. of Isaac SITTLER coppersmith, in Winchester a few days ago (BVCG 23 Dec 93)

M'MURDO, G., intends to leave the colony in six-eight months and will let his plant. in Pr. Geo. Co. (VG 7 Nov 51)

McMURTY, Capt., of the militia, killed by Indians in Ky. (VHFA 9, 16 Dec 90)

McNEELY, Hugh, merch., mar. Miss Polly KIGER dau. of George KIGER saddler of Winchester, on Thurs. eve. last (VGWA and WVGWA 3 Apr 90) [name also given as M'NEALLY]

M'NUTTE, Robert, appr. bound by his father to the saddling business, c. 16, ran away from John RICHARDSON who was removing out of the state (PGBA 12 Jan 95)

M'PHERSON, Mrs., of Caroline Co., dec'd, the land whereon she lived to be sold; Archibald M'PHERSON (nfi) is also mentioned (VG 7 Jan 73)

M'PHERSON, Daniel, dec'd, his admr., Simon FRAZER, will sell three of his slaves in Richmond (VGWeA 20 Mar 84)

M'PHERSON, Daniel, of Daniel & Isaac M'Pherson, dec'd, of Alexandria (VGAxA 2 Dec 90)

M'PHERSON, John, appr., c. 17, ran away from David OSBORN (BVCG 19 Aug 96)

McQUEEN, Daniel, svt., b. in London, 21, transported in the *Caesar* in 1736, ran away from Benjamin PORTER, Orange Co. (VG 3 Nov 38)

M'QUILKEN, Samuel, appr. shoemaker, ran away from Joseph PASSMORE, Winchester (WG 9 Jan 99)

M'QUILKING, Thomas, bound boy, ran away from James CHAMBERLIN now dec'd acc. to an adv. by Elijah CHAMBERLIN his admr. (PGBA 9 Mar 97)

M'QUIRE, Patrick, Scot, svt., c. 45, smith and farrier, ran away from Samuel WOOD, Richmond (VG 27 Oct 74)

M'RAE, John, mulatto, c. 30, b. in [Yorkshire], Eng., committed to jail in Surry Co. (VG 24 May 70)

M'RAE, John, d. in Richmond (VGGA 15 Oct 94)

M'RAE, Nancy, eloped from her husband, John M'RAE (VGGA 14 Aug 93)

M'RAE, Philip, d. at Richmond at a very advanced stage of life (VGRMA 16 Oct 94, VGRC 17 Oct 94); his ex., Christopher and John M'RAE, will sell his lots in Richmond (RMA 12 Dec 95)

M'REDIE, Thomas, merch., of Fredsbrg., dec'd, son of Thomas M'REDIE; his brother and heir at law is William M'REDIE (VG 14 Mar 55)

M'ROBERT, Alexander, dec'd, his ex., James WATT of Buckingham Co. requests those indebted to settle their accounts with John BROOKE of Henrico Co. (DOB 11 Oct 98)

M'SHERRY, Bernard, dec'd, e.a.w. his admr., Richard M'SHERRY, who will also sell some of his PE (PGBA 5 Jan 97)

M'SHERRY, Richard, and STARKEY, their firm plans to remove from Martinsburg to Baltimore about 1 Oct. next (PGBA 5 Sep 95)

M'WILLIAMS, John, is advised that he has a letter from his wife, Anne M'WILLIAMS, at the Wmsbrg. Post Office (VG 19 Aug 73)

MABON, James, capt. in the late army of the U. S., d. Thurs. last (VGAA and

VGWeA 28 Aug 84)
MACARTNEY, Robert, merch. of Richmond, d. on Sat. night (VGGA 15 Apr 95 post)
MACAULAY, Patrick, d. in Norfolk on the 3rd inst. (VICGA 13 Jan 90)
MACCOY, Susanna, has taken up with another man and left her husband, Robert MACCOY of Pr. Anne Co. (VCNPGA 15 Jun 93)
MACEE, John, sentenced to death for stealing a horse (VG 5 May 38)
MACEY, John, aka John MURPHEY, svt., 24, ran away from William WYATT, Wmsbrg., he was seen in N. Carolina using the name John MURPHEY (VG 1 Sep 38, 15 Dec 38)
MACGEHEE, Jacob, dec'd, e.a.w. his acting ex., William MACGEHEE of Cumberland Co. (RMA 13 Jan 96)
MACGILL, Mrs. Catherine, wife of N[athan] MACGILL merch. of Norfolk, d. on Mon. night last (NHPA 5 Jan 97, AGGA 6 Jan 97)
MACGILL, John, d. on Wed. last (HNPA 25 Jul 95)
MACGILL, Nathan, merch., mar. Miss Kitty TAYLOR last eve. (AGNPPA 29 May 95)
MACHARG, Elizabeth, dec'd, any claims against her est. or the est. of Alexander MACHARG dec'd, will be settled by her ex., M. ALEXANDER (VGPI 27 Feb 95)
MACHENRY, John, of Washington Co., forewarns all persons from having any dealings with his wife, Hannah MACHENRY, as he will not be liable for any of her contracts (VGGA 14 Dec 96)
MACHIR, Alexander, of Strasburg (commonly called Stover's Town) dec'd, e.a.w. his ex., John CROWDSON, W. O. WILLIAMS, and James MACHIR (VGWA 3 Jul 90)
MACKAY, James Esq., a native of Scotland, now of Georgia, d. in Alexandria on his way to Mt. Vernon (VJAA 1 Dec 85)
MACKAY, Miss Katherine, d. at Kirnam the seat of Mrs. CAMPBELL of Westmoreland (VGPu 24 Jan 77)
MACKAY, the Rev. William, dec'd, William MISKELL of Richmond Co., trustee for the admx. (nfi), requests creditors to acquaint him with the nature and amount of their claims (VG 8 Nov 76)
MACKAY, William, of Portsmouth, dec'd, e.a.w. his ex., Bernard MAGNIEN (NPC 10 Sep 91)
MACKENSIE, Dr., of Charles City Co., mar. Miss Johanna TYLER eld. dau. of John TYLER of James City Co. on 16 Feb. (VG 17 Feb 38)
MACKENZIE, Dr. Kenneth, of Wmsbrg., dec'd, his shop, books, and medicines to be sold by his ex., James CARTER and George RIDDELL (VG 21 Mar 55)
MACKEY, John, ind. svt., tailor, 20, ran away from Thomas CROSS, Norfolk (AGNPWA 19 Mar 94)
MACKEY, Michael, Irish svt., 27, ran away from the Potomac Co., Great Falls on 25 Dec. along with Patrick ROWELEN a freeman (VJAA 4 Jan 87)
MACKIE, Andrew, his widow, Martha, of Smithfield, adv. that she is revoking the power of att. she gave to Dr. William COCKE of Cabin Point to settle her husband's est. (NH 28 Aug 98)
MACKIR Family, HCC, 7 Mar 1795, between the reps. of Joist HILE, Robert GREEN, William DUFF, and Robert M'COY dec'd (pltfs.) and Scot MACKIR, William WORTHINGTON and Betsy his wife, Peggy MACKIR, Sarah MACKIR, and John MACKIR chil. and devisees of Alexander MACKIR dec'd and heirs at law of Angus MACKIR dec'd another of the chil. and devisee of the sd. Alexander MACKIR dec'd (defs.); it appears that William and Betsy WORTHINGTON, and Peggy MACKIR are not inhabitants of this country (RC 23 May 95)
MACKNELL, William, ind. svt., from Whitehaven, c. 19, ran away from the snow *Carlisle* at Yorktown (VG 19 May 74)
MACKOY, the Rev. Mr., Rector of Hanover Par., Kg. Geo. Co., mar. Miss Barbara FITZHUGH dau. to Maj. John FITZHUGH of Stafford Co. dec'd, on the 6th ult. (VG 2 Mar 39)

MACKS, Lewis, a volunteer in Capt. HICKS' Co. now on duty at Hampton, d. last Fri. (VGPu 20 Oct 75 sup)

MACKUE, John, Irish svt., ran away from William AYLETT and John BUSHRODE, Westmoreland Co. (VG 17 Aug 39)

MACLAURIN, the Rev. Robert, Rector of Southam [Par.] in Cumberland Co., d. on the 5th inst. (VG 22 Jul 73)

MACLEAN, John, an old and respectable inhabitant of this borough, d. Sun. last (NWJCI 6 Dec 97)

MACLEOD, James, late of Yorktown, dec'd, e.a.w. Thomas NEWMAN; his admx. is Mary MACLEOD (VGGA 4 Apr 92)

MACOMB, Eleazer, son of James MACOMB merch. of Richmond, d. on Tues. in his 16th year [obit.] (VGAA 24 Sep 85)

MACON, John Esq., of Cumberland Co., a rep. for that co. in the GA, d. lately (VGGA 27 Nov 93, VGWeA 29 Nov 93)

MACON, Mrs. Sarah, spouse to William H. MACON Esq. of New Kent Co., d. on Sat. 21 Sep. (VGWeA 26 Oct 82)

MACON, Col. William, of New Kent Co., dec'd, his ex., William and Henry MACON, will sell his livestock, crops, and HH & KF (VG 18 Nov 73, 17 Mar 74)

MACON, William, late of Cumberland Co., dec'd, e.a.w. his ex., John DODSON and Warren WALKER, and extx., Sally MACON (VGGA 22 Nov 97)

MACON, William Sr., of New Kent Co., adv. that his son, Hartwell MACON, has gotten into debt and that he will receive nothing more from his father (VG 17 Oct 71)

MACOUN, Thomas, Irish svt., ran away from Robert CHESLEY, St. Mary's Co., Md. (VG 17 Aug 39)

MACPHERSON, Archibald, late of Fredsbrg., dec'd, his lot and houses there to be sold by his ex., Charles DICK (VG 28 Feb 55)

MACPHERSON, Daniel, dec'd, his admrs. (nfi) will sell his est., which includes a schooner, at Warwick (VG 1 Oct 72)

MACRAE, Allan, late merch. in Dumfries, e.a.w. his ex., Thomas LAWSON and John LEE (VG 11 Dec 66)

MACREDIE, Thomas, dec'd, his land on Shenando River in Augusta Co. to be sold by Alexander CUNINGHAME att. for the heir (VG 8 Aug 66)

MADDEN, Hannah, dec'd, her ex., Robert ALLISON and Dennis RAMSAY, will sell the plant. whereon the late Michael MADDEN lived containing about 80 ac. (CMAG 13 Apr 99)

MADDEN, John, tailor, 28, ran away from the ship *Amelia* lying at Bermuda Hundred (VG 1 Jun 69)

MADDEN, Michael, mar. Miss Hannah RAMSAY dau. of William RAMSAY, both on Alexandria (VJAA 29 Jul 84)

MADDIN, Cornelius, Irish svt., ran away from Capt. Robert DUDLEY of K & Q Co. (VG 9 Feb 39)

MADISON, A[mbrose], dec'd, his admx., Mary W. MADISON, will sell 300 ac. of land, the property of Tavernor BEAL, in Orange Co. (VHFA 7 Aug 94)

MADISON, the Rev. James, President of William and Mary College, mar. Miss Sally TAITE of this city [Wmsbrg.] last Wed. (VG 1 May 79)

MADISON, James Esq., member of Congress from this state, mar. Mrs. D. TOD of Philadelphia, in Frederick Co. [Va.] (VGRMA 6 Oct 94, VGRC 7 Oct 94)

MADISON, John, late of Kg. Wm. Co., dec'd, e.a.w. his admr., Edward HILL of K & Q Co. (VGIC 12 Jun 84)

MADISON, John, dec'd, his son and admr., Henry MADISON of Hanover Co., will settle his est. (VGGA 22 May 98)

MADISON, Mrs. Mary Willis, relict of the late Maj. Ambrose MADISON, d. at her seat, Woodley Vale, in Orange Co. on 14 Mar. (VHFA 28 Mar 98)

MAGEHE, Childs, b. in Va., 22, des. from the U. S. Army at Staunton (SVG 21 Oct 96)

MAGILL, Archibald, merch. of Winchester, mar. Miss Nancy LISLE on Thurs. last (VCWM 21 Jan 89)

[M]AGILL, Col. Charles, of Winchester, mar. Miss Polly T[HRUST]ON of Frederick Co. last Thurs. (BVCG 28 May 92)
MAGILL, John, of the Corporation of Winchester, dec'd, e.a.w. his ex., Charles MAGILL (BVCG 30 Jul 92)
MAGRUDER, Brooke, d. in Montgomery Co., Md. in his 27th year (VGAR 13 Oct 91)
MAGUIRE, Margaret, her husband, Patrick MAGUIRE of Georgetown, will no longer pay her debts (VJAA 26 May 85)
MAGUIRE, Richard, Irish svt., b. in Dublin, 18, ran away from John SUTTON and Michael GRETTER, Alexandria (NPJ 12 Dec 87)
MAHANY, John, c. 25, says he was imp. from Cork [Ireland] about five yrs. ago and sold at Quantico to William STEWARD of Pittsylvania Co., jailed as a runaway in Essex Co. (VGPu 5 Jan 76)
MAHON, William, svt., shoemaker, ran away from the snow *John* lying in Hampton Road (VGAA 17 Apr 84)
MAHONEY, Timothy, Irish svt., 18-19, ran away from Henry M'CABE and Alexander M'INTYRE, Alexandria (VJAA 27 Apr 86)
MAHONY, Florence, forewarns any person from taking an assignment on two notes passed by him to Anne FITZGERALD now Anne M'ELWAINE sometime in Apr. 1790 (PGBA 30 Sep 93); adv. that he has removed from Martinsburg to Winchester and opened a tavern at the sign of the Harp and Crown (PGBA 31 Mar 96)
MAIBEN, James, from Ireland, settled in this country about 1770; his friends in [Co.] Sligo are anxious to be informed if he is still alive; information to be sent to James DUNLOP, Port Royal (VHFA 24 Jul 88) [name also given as MAVEN]
MAITLAND, Mrs. spouse of William MAITLAND, d. in Petersburg (VGPI 21 Jul 97)
MAJOR Family, HCC, 18 Mar. 1796, between John PERKINS admr. of his late wife, Betty PERKINS (pltf.) and Francis MORELAND and George BRASFIELD ex. of William MAJOR dec'd, Thomas TRICE admr. of Mary his wife, Solomon PATILLO and Sarah his wife, and the sd. Francis MORELAND and Nancy his wife, and Bernard MAJOR ex. of Christian MAJOR who was extx. of Bernard MAJOR (defs.) (RMA 27 Apr 96)
MAJOR, Edmond, planter in Va. or Md., d. about 40 yrs. ago leaving two daus.; if they or their descendents apply to Cary MICHELL in Hampton, they may hear something to their advantage (VG 27 Oct 68)
MAJOR, Samuel, printer, d. on Tues. last near Wmsbrg. (VGAA 5 Feb 85)
MAJOR, Samuel Jr., dec'd, e.a.w. his admr., William MAJOR (VHFA 14 Feb 98)
MAJOR, Thomas, his trustees, John MAJOR and Thomas PORTER, adv. that he has made a deed of trust of his whole est. to them which is recorded in Culpeper Co. in Va. and they thought proper to give the notice as they are determined to answer no contract made by sd. [sic] Francis MAJOR (KG 26 Nov 91)
MALBURNE, Evan, appr., c. 19, ran away from John GRACIE house joiner and undertaker (NH 12 May 98)
MALLORY, Francis, appr. lad from Elizabeth City Co. and par., son of Edward MALLORY dec'd, ran away from George BILLUPS, Norfolk (VCNPGA 9 Mar 93)
MALLORY, Johnson, of Hampton, mar. Miss Nancy BOUSH of Norfolk on Thurs. eve. (NHPA 15 Jul 97)
MALLORY, Mrs. Mary, dec'd, e.a.w. her ex., Miles KING of Hampton; he notes that after her debts are fully paid, Mr. G. H. LETUZ will be entitled to one third of the est. (NH 7 Apr 98)
MALLORY, Thomas, age 91, d. in Hanover Co. on the 25th ult. (VGGA 17 Jan 98)
MALONE, Elizabeth, her husband, John MALONE, of Sussex Co. will not be responsible for her debts as she has absconded from his bed; he forewarns al

persons except her father, Daniel RANEY, from harboring or entertaining her (VGPI 3, 17 Feb 97)

MALONE, Mary, all of her PE of which she d. possessed, the est. of William MALONE dec'd as also 150 ac. of land late the property of Drury MALONE dec'd, will be sold by the commissioners in Dinwiddie Co. (VGPI 27 Jun 97)

MALONE, Patrick, Irish ind. svt., c. 20, ran away from James FRANKLIN near Baltimore. Md. (VG 25 Mar 73)

MAN Family, Patrick Co. Ct. of Q.S, 28 Apr. 1798, in chanc: Isaac PENINTON (compl.) against Jonathan HANBY, Joseph FRANCIS, John MANKIN, George LENT, Washington MAN, John MAN, Constant Harden MAN, William Miller MAN, Sally MAN, Peter Nicholas MAN, and Anna alias Agnes MAN chil. and heirs of John MAN dec'd (defs.); it appears that Joseph FRANCIS is not an inhabitant of the state (LWM 19 May 98)

MAN, Francis, Eng. svt. from Huntingdonshire, blacksmith, ran away from William AYLETT and John BUSHRODE, Westmoreland Co. (AWM 2 Aug 39, VG 17 Aug 39)

MAN, George, of Flat Cr. [Tennessee] found killed by Indians on 28 [Jan.] (VGRMA 9 Mar 95)

MANBY, John Esq., Collector of H.M's Customs on the Eastern Shore of Va., c. 50, says he was b. in Yorkshire, but has a wife in London where he had been some time an officer in the customs, says he has a son, an officer in some of the foot regiments now in Eng., ran away from his bail on 24 Jun. last from Accomack Co.; it is thought he will try to reach New York or some other port where he may get a ready passage to Gt. Britain or towards Canada by the way of Albany as he pretends an acquaintance with Gen. GAGE; a reward is offered by Abraham MITCHELL of Philadelphia, merch. (MG 9 Jul 61)

MANGUM, William, des. from the co. of Capt. Samuel HOPKINS, 6th Va. Regt.; he has relations in Sussex (VGPu 11 Apr 77)

MANLY, Devereux Jarret, of Petersburg, d. on Mon. last, e.a.w. his acting ex., Joseph BADGER, who will also sell a variety of articles in the coachmaking business bel. to his est. (VGPI 17 Mar 97)

MANLY, Mrs. Sarah, relict of John MANLY Esq., d. in Alexandria (VJAA 13 Oct 85)

MANN, Mrs., spouse of Henry MANN cabinetmaker [of Richmond], d. on Mon. the 18th inst. (VGGA 20 Mar 93)

MANN, Elizabeth, her husband, John MANN Sr. of Nottoway Co., will no longer be responsible for her debts (VGPI 7 May 99)

MANN, Rachael, eloped from her husband, Michael MANN of Norfolk, on the 7th inst. (NH 10 Jul 98)

MANN, Robert, d. on Sun. the 19th ult. at his seat in Essex Co.; he was 73 last June (VGGA 6 Dec 97)

MANNING, John, young man c. 23, b. in Va., ran away from John SMITH, carpenter, in Annapolis (MG 31 Dec 28)

MANSFIELD, Thomas, dec'd, George MAGEE of Alexandria adv. that his decease makes it necessary that every account wherein he had an interest should be closed (TAA 1 Sep 98)

Manslaughter: four Irishmen convicted of manslaughter in Pittsylvania Co. now in jail in Wmsbrg.: James M'DONALD (aka M'DANIEL), laborer, 20; Edward SWENY, butcher, 32; Edward LUPTON, shoemaker, 25; Patrick RYAN, 25 (VG 27 Oct 74)

MANSON, William, merch. of Hanover Town, dec'd, e.a.w. his admr., Thomas FOX, of Kg. Wm. Co. (VGGA 5 Apr 99)

MARABLE, Matthew, d. in Mecklenburg Co. (VGAA 12 Apr 86)

MARBURY, Col. Leonard, [his quarrel with Col. John ADDISON is described in a long article which contains much information on MARBURY] (VJAA 14 Sep 86)

MARCHAND, Mr., d. on Sun. morn. (Arg 14 Feb 97)

MARECHAL, Matthew, French, c. 16, appr., ran away from Michael

RABORG, Fredsbrg. (VHFA 24 May 92)
MARIE, Peter, 30, des. from the French frigate *Sybille* in Chesapeake Bay (VGAA 25 May 82)
MARINER, Dr., came to Va. from Bristol about 1758 with his son, James; they may hear something to their advantage by applying to the post office in Wmsbrg. (VG 17 Dec 72)
MARINER, George, 30, b. in New England, ran away from the snow *Industrious Bee* lying at Sandy Point (VG 5 Jun 52)
MARKEL, Barney, escaped robber, aged 35 (VHFA 10 Feb 91)
MARKER, Jacob, wagon maker of Stephensburg, d. on 1 Dec (VCWM 2 Dec 89)
MARKHAM, James, appr., 20, ran away from George KEMPER, Fauquier Ct. H. (BVCG 20 Jan 97)
MARKHAM, John, of Chesterfield Co., dec'd, his ex., Benjamin WATKINS, Vincent MARKHAM, and George MARKHAM, will sell his plant. about four miles from Warwick (VG 25 Jul 71)
MARKHAM, John, son of William MARKHAM, he was granted a power of att. in Campbell Co. by John and Rebecca H. FARRAR of Chesterfield Co. (VGGA 3 Jan 98)
MARKHAM, John, Campbell Co. Ct., 9 Oct. 1798, in chanc: Samuel BRANCH for the benefit of Absolom MELTON (pltf.) against John MARKHAM heir at law of John MARKHAM dec'd (def.); it appears that the def. is not an inhabitant of the state (LWG 13 Oct 98)
MARKHAM, Ned, aka Ned, Negro, ran away from Francis McGUIRE in Ohio Co. (VHFA 5 Sep 93)
MARKLAND, John, appr., 16-17, ran away from Hugh GAINE, New York; he may have sailed to Jamaica (VG 3 Sep 72)
MARKS, Peter, dec'd, e.a.w. his ex., Jo. Jo. [sic] MONROE, Charlottesville (RMA 19 Mar 96)
MARLATT, Abraham [Sr.], his chil., Abraham MARLATT Jr. and Richard MARLATT, and Richard BARDINE (nfi), call in question his mental faculties and caution all persons from purchasing any kind of prop. of, selling to, or in any manner dealing with him (PGBA 18 Feb 96); he denies that he is incapable of transacting business; he is determined to leave this part of the country and wishes to sell his home place of 300 ac. about three miles from Martinsburg (PGBA 10 Mar 96)
MARLEY, Mrs., spouse of William MARLEY of Norfolk, d. after a short illness (NPC 3 Dec 91)
MARNIX, John and Jemima, of Norfolk, dec'd, e.a.w. their ex., William WILLOUGHBY (VCNPGA 29 Dec 92)
MARQUART, John, appr., c. 18 yrs. and 6 mos. old, bound by his father to learn the hatter's trade, ran away from John HERMAN, Martinsburg (PGBA 16 Nov 95)
MARQUES, William, plans to move to the Western Country (WG 2 Jan 99)
MARQUET, Charles Louis, a soldier of the Duke of Lauzun's Legion, b. in Alsace, 25, des. from the *Romulous* (VGAA 22 Mar 83)
MARR Family, Patrick Co. Ct., 29 Nov. 1798, Sherod HARRIS (pltf.) against Susannah HARDAMAN heretofore Susannah MARR admx. of John MARR dec'd, George Lent Washington MARR, John MARR, William Miller MARR, Sally MARR, Constant Harden MARR, Peter Nicholas MARR, and Anna alias Agnes MARR, chil. and heirs of the sd. John MARR dec'd (defs.); it appears that George Lent Washington MARR is not an inhabitant of this state (LWG 16 Feb 99) [the name also appears as MAN, see: MAN Family, above]
MARRABLE, Benjamin, of Charles City Co., dec'd, his admr., Edward MARRABLE, will sell his rem. PE (VG 2 Dec 73)
MARRABLE, George, of Charles City Co., dec'd, his land to be sold by his admr., Benjamin MARRABLE (VGGA 9 Dec 95)
Married by the Rev. William BLAND in the Borough of Norfolk within a

18th-Century Virginia Newspapers 227

few days: James LAMBERT and Miss Mary WILSON; Thomas LAMBERT and Miss Agnis WILSON; Joshua MARTIN and Frances COLLINS; Lewis DRIBON and Elizabeth COOPER; John POOL and Molly WRAY; James ARLINGTON and Catherine NUTT; Err BARCLIFT and Miss Ann SEYMOUR, Malachi DEMBY and Ann TIGNER; Isaac LEVY and Judah HILL; Dormand TOWNSEND and Ann MATHIAS; William ETHEREDGE and Anne M'COY; and on Sat. last Hillary BUTT and Miss Sally JAMES (VCNPGA 6 Apr 93)

MARRIOTT, Mrs., wife of Mr. MARRIOTT, comedian in the Va. Company, d. on Tues. morn. (AGNPPA 11 Sep 95)

MARRIOTT, Mathias, dec'd, his extx., Elizabeth MARRIOTT, and John WATKINS (nfi), will sell his running mare at Surry Ct. H. (VG 1 Dec 74); Jacob FOULCON, gdn. to the orphans, will lease his late plant. in Surry Co. one mile from the Ct. H. on the head of Gray's Cr. (VG 23 Oct 79)

MARSDEN Family, HCC, 7 Mar. 1795; Preeson BOWDOIN surviving partner of Phripp & Bowdoin (pltf.) and Mary MARSDEN admx. of James MARSDEN dec'd, and John Greenhow MARSDEN son and heir of the sd. James MARSDEN (defs.) (NH 26 Oct 99)

MARSDEN, James, dec'd, his admx., Mary MARSDEN, will sell sundry articles bel. to his ext. at the plant. of Daniel TRUEHART near the Meadow Bridges in Hanover Co.; she has reason to believe that a marriage contract entered into by Mr. MARSDEN and herself may have been lent to some person in order to copy another from it and requests its return; she has authorized Samuel COLEMAN of Richmond to settle her husband's est. (VGAA 16 Feb 82)

MARSDEN, James, dec'd, partner of Francis SMYTH of Richmond (VGAA 8 Jun 82); e.a.w. William DUVAL (nfi) (VGAA 19 Apr 83)

MARSH, Hollan, enl. at Northumberland Ct. H., des. from the 7th U. S. Regt., Yorktown (VGGA 29 Nov 99)

MARSHAL, Edward, soldier in the 8th Regt., des. from the College Camp (VGPu 16 Aug 76)

MARSHALL Family, Hampshire Co. Ct., 15 Mar. 1788, in chanc: Christopher MARSHALL, Charles MARSHALL, and Daniel WILLIAMS and Sarah MARSHALL admx. and Christopher MARSHALL Jr. and Charles MARSHALL admrs. of Benjamin MARSHALL dec'd (compls.) against John SPORE, Bryan BRUIN, Andrew GRAFF, and Benjamin MESHIE (defs.) (VGIC 21 Jun 88 sup)

MARSHALL, Francis, dec'd, his ex., Alexander MARSHALL, will sell all of his livestock and HH & KF, and settle his est. as well as the est. of Mrs. Mary MARSHALL dec'd (VGWeA 21 Nov 95)

MARSHALL, George, late of Kg. Geo. Co., dec'd (VHFA 17 Jul 98)

MARSHALL, James, murdered in Westmoreland Co. on 26 Jan. allegedly by Jonathan PIPER; a reward is offered for PIPER's capture (VG 2 May 51)

MARSHALL, James, d. lately at the Hon. Mr. CARTER's in Westmoreland Co.; he was formerly an usher at William and Mary (VGR 15 Apr 73); he is reported alive and well at this date (VGR 22 Apr 73)

MARSHALL, John, of Louisa Co., dec'd, his surviving partner and admr., Robert HART of Spotsylvania Co., will sell a great variety of HH & KF and plant. and store utensils (VG 27 Nov 79)

MARSHALL, John Esq., member of the Hon. Privy Council, mar. at Richmond Miss Polly AMBLER of that city on Sun. last (VGAA 11 Jan 83)

MARSHALL, Lucy, has eloped from her husband, William MARSHALL (VG 10 Oct 66)

MARSHALL, Scotter, conv. [svt.], c. 26, ran away from James DAVIS living on the headwaters of Holston's River in Botetourt Co. (VGR 29 Oct 72)

MARSHALL, William, mar. Miss Alice ADAMS youngest dau. of Richard ADAMS Esq. of Richmond, on the 20th ult. (VIC 9 Jul, VGWeA 10 Jul 88)

MARSHALL, Dr. William, of Gloucester Co., d. on the 16th inst. at the house of

John ANDERSON Esq. in Kg. Wm. Co. (RMA 21 May 96); his acting ex., Thomas FOX of Kg. Wm. Co., will sell his books, manuscripts, HH & KF (VGGA 13 Jul 96); his acting ex. will sell 700 ac. of his land (VGGA 12 Oct 96)

MARSTELLER, Lewis, bur. yesterday afternoon; he had been an officer of the Alexandria Dragoons (TAA 21 Aug 98)

MARSTON, William, of New Kent Co., dec'd, his ex., John ARMISTEAD and Joseph VAIDEN, will sell stock of various kinds and HH & KF (VGPu 28 Mar 77 sup)

MARSTON, William and William VAIDEN, late of New Kent Co., dec'd, e.a.w. their ex., Joseph VAIDEN of Charles City Co. (VGIC 29 Jan 85)

MARTIN, Archibald, native of Ireland, a young man of good character, d. on Mon. the 15th inst. (NH 18 Jul 99)

MARTIN, Christopher, Irish svt., in Frederick Co. jail, says he bel. to Matthias BODELEY of Cecil Co., Md. (VG 17 Oct 51)

MARTIN, Christopher, of Chesterfield Co., dec'd, his PE to be sold by his admr., John MARTIN (VG 5 Sep 66 sup)

MARTIN, Jacob, Negro, says he bel. to James GREENWOOD of Mecklenburg Co., jailed in Hanover Co. (Ex 19 Apr 99)

MARTIN, James, of Wmsbrg., dec'd, e.a.w. Benjamin BUCKTROUT who will also sell his HH & KF (VGR 21 Apr 68, 11 May 69)

MARTIN, James, Irish, c. 25, des. from the *Hero* galley (VGPu 26 Jul 76)

MARTIN, James, of Caroline Co., dec'd, his admr., J. MARTIN, has money for his legatees (VGGA 24 Oct 92)

MARTIN, Col. John, the houses and land whereon he lately lived in Caroline Co. to be sold by Col. Lewis BURWELL of Wmsbrg. and John MARTIN (nfi) att. at law of Kg. Wm. Co. (VG 12 Jun 52); a tract of his land in Halifax Co. to be sold by his ex. (VG 27 Aug 56)

MARTIN, John, Welsh svt., ran away from James ARMSTRONG in Augusta Co. (VG 7 Nov 54)

MARTIN, Col. John, dec'd, his extx., Elizabeth MARTIN, will sell all the rem. slaves bel. to his est. at Kg. Wm. Ct. H. (VGPu 19 Jan 76)

MARTIN, Mary, has left her husband, James MARTIN of Deep Cr., Norfolk Co. (NHPA 8 Jul 97)

MARTIN, Ned, aka Ned, Negro, 25-26, ran away from Francis M'GUIRE, near Buffalo Cr., Ohio Co. (BVCG 9 Sep 93)

MARTIN, Thomas, of the city of Bristol, dec'd, tracts of his land in Louisa and [Kg. Wm.] cos. to be sold by John ROBINSON and Humphrey HILL (VG 27 Jun 51)

MARTIN, Thomas, Irish, 26, ran away from the snow *Industrious Bee* lying at Sandy Point (VG 5 Jun 52)

MARTIN, the Rev. Thomas, Rector of St. Thomas Par., Orange Co., d. some short time past (VGR 20 Sep 70)

MARTIN, Thomas, late of Frederick Co., dec'd, e.a.w. his ex., George RUBLE and Underhill BARTON (BVCG 11 Jun 92)

MARTIN, Thomas, of Albemarle Co., dec'd, e.a.w. his ex., Samuel MURRIL, George MARTIN, and Tandy KEY (VGRC 29 Jul 94); e.a.w. his ex., George MARTIN and Tandy KEY (VGGA 28 Aug 98)

MARTIN, William, planter, b. in Pasquotank, N. Carolina, 19, des. from Capt. Robert HODGSON's Independent Co. now raising for the service and defense of S. Carolina (VG 3 Jul 46)

MARTIN, William, merch., late of St. Lucia, passenger in the sloop *Martha*, d. on the 16th ult. (VHFFA 13 Jan 97)

MARVAULT, Simon, of Norfolk, dec'd, e.a.w. his admr., William SMITH also of Norfolk (NPC 7 Aug 90, 19 Mar 91)

MARYE, James, of Spotsylvania Co., dec'd, e.a.w. his ex., John CHEW (VGWeA 26 Oct 82)

MARYE, Mrs. Mary, wife of the Rev. James MARYE of Spotsylvania Co., d. on Sun. 7 Oct. (VGR 1 Nov 70)

MASK, Thomas, late of Hanover Co., dec'd, his ex., William MASK, adv. 224 ac. of land bel. to his est. in Goochland Co. for sale (VG 28 Nov 55)
MASKALL, Thomas, Eng. svt., 26, ran away from George TURBERVILLE, Westmoreland Co. (VG 20 Jul 39)
MASON, Mrs. Anne, widow and relict of Col. George MASON, d. on 13 Nov. at her house in Stafford Co. in her 63rd year (MG 23 Dec 62)
MASON, Benjamin, appr. tanner and cutter, he was 20 the 3rd. of last month, ran away from Jabez LARUE (BVCG 9 Sep 96)
MASON, George Esq., of Va., mar. Ann EILBECK dau. of William EILBECK, merch. of Charles Co., Md. on 3 Apr. (MG 2 May 50)
MASON, George, acc. to news from Lexington, [Ky. ?] of 7 Sep., he was killed by Indians on Wed. last near Licking Cr. salt works (VIC 24 Oct 87)
MASON, the Hon. George Esq., d. on the 14th ult. at Gunston Hall (VGAxA 8 Nov 92)
MASON, George, mar. Miss Mildred SANDERS dau. of the Rev. Mr. Nathaniel SANDERS, both of Orange Co., on the 13th inst. (VHFFA 19 Aug 97)
MASON, Col. James, of Greensville Co., dec'd, his plants. in Southampton and Brunswick cos. to be sold (VGAA 9 Oct 84)
MASON, James, aka James, mulatto, has a mother and some relations in Hampton, ran away from James INNES near Richmond (VGGA 21 Sep 96)
MASON, John, svt., ran away from David REYNOLDS, Norf. (VGR 12 May 74)
MASON, John, svt., 22-23, barber, ran away from Walter LENOX, Wmsbrg. (VGP 13 Jul 75)
MASON, John, mar. Miss Polly PARSONS, Alexandria (VJAA 11 Aug 85)
MASON, John, writes from Frederick Co. jail on 13 Feb. 1788 that he grew up in Cumberland Co., Pa. then moved to Frederick Co., Md., Frederick Co., Va. and then to Washington Co., Md.; he is a mason and plasterer (VGWA 15 Feb 88)
MASON, Maj. John, dec'd, the ex. of J. and W. MASON dec'd, for William MASON is William MASSENBURG who will handle their est. accounts and sell land bel. to Maj. John MASON in Sussex Co. (VGPI 29 Dec 95)
MASON, Mrs. Mary, wife of Thomas [also given as Thomson] MASON Esq. of Loudoun Co., d. on Mon. 21 Oct. at Westwood the seat of the Rev. Mr. SCOTT in Pr. Wm. Co. on her return home from a visit to her father (VGR 31 Oct 71, MG 14 Nov 71)
MASON, Miss Sally, third dau. of Maj. John MASON of Sussex Co., d. on the 11th inst. in her 17th year [or 19th year acc. to VG] (VG and VGR 23 Sep 73)
MASON, Stephen Thomas, member of the GA, mar. Miss Polly ARMISTEAD of Louisa Co., in Richmond (VGAA 17 May 83)
MASON, Thomas Esq., of Loudoun Co., mar. Mrs. Elizabeth WALLACE of Elizabeth City Co. on Sun. 23 Nov. (VGPu 5 Dec 77)
MASSENESEG, Col. Nicholas, died in Va. (PC 25 May 72)
MASSEY, Miss Nelly, d. at the seat of Thomas COLSON Esq. in Spotsylvania Co. on Wed the 7th inst. aged 13 (VHFA 22 Aug 93)
MASSIE, William, dec'd, his dwelling house to be sold (VG 25 Jul 51)
MASSIE, William, of New Kent Co., dec'd, his ex. (nfi) will sell his stock, HH & KF (VGGA 19 Jun 93 ex)
MASTIN, Isabella, has left her husband, Elijah MASTIN of Spotsylvania Co. (VHFA 12 Jul 92)
MATHEWS, Betsey, aka Peggy, mulatto woman, c. 20, escaped from persons bringing her back to Sterling EDMUNDS, Brunswick Co. (VGGA 24 May 99) [see: Betsy MATTHEWS below]
MATHEWS, Beverly, appr., tailor, 15, ran away from Curtes HAYNES, Pr. Edw. Co. (Arg 26 Apr 99)
MATHEWS, Drury, dec'd, his admr., Joseph PAUP, will sell part of his PE on the premises in Brunswick Co. (VGPI 11 Aug 95)
MATHEWS, the Hon. Sampson, mar. Mrs. Catherine PARK, Richmond, last week (VGAA 14 Jun 83)
MATHEWS, William, of Stafford Co., dec'd, in his will he left his son, William MATHEWS, a legacy; if the son will apply to the ex. (nfi) he may receive it

(VGWeA 8 Nov 83)
MATHISON, David, Scot, ind. svt., c. 25, gardener, ran away from William BRENT, Stafford Co. (VGNI 5 Jan 75, VG 7 Jan 75) [name also given, in VGNI, as David MATHESONS]

MATTHEWS, Mrs., wife of Joseph MATTHEWS, d. in Staunton (BVCG 3 Feb 94)

MATTHEWS, Mrs., relict of the Rev. John MATTHEWS late of Essex Co., d. last Sun. (VHFA 7 Apr 98)

MATTHEWS, Mrs. Anne, late of Yorktown, dec'd, e.a.w. her admr., James MOIR of Wmsbrg. (VG 21 Aug 79)

MATTHEWS, Capt. Baldwin, of York Co., found dead in his house on 31 Mar, in his 68th year (VG 1 Apr 37)

MATTHEWS, Betsey, mulatto girl, c. 21, from Petersburg, says she is free but has no papers, jailed in Norfolk Borough (NH 2 Feb 99) [see: Betsey MATHEWS above]

MATTHEWS, Constantine, executed on 23 Nov. for a robbery in Caroline Co. (VG 23 Nov 39)

MATTHEWS, Francis, Irish conv. svt., 19-20, ran away from Philip HALL and Isaac SHORT near Sno[w]den's Iron Works, Pr. Geo. Co., Md. (VGP 21 Sep 75)

MATTHEWS, James, conv., sentenced to death in Wmsbrg. for horse stealing, executed on 26 Nov. (VG 26 Nov 36, AWM 16 Dec 36, NYWJ 10 Jan 37)

MATTHEWS, John, Jr., merch., at Laytons, mar. Miss Maria C. McCARTY of Lancaster Co., on Tues. last at Brooke's Bank, Essex Co. (VHFFA 13 Dec 96)

MATTHEWS, Jude, Irish conv. svt., c. 25, ran away from Coleman READ, head of Nomini River, Westmoreland Co. (AWM 2 Aug 39, VG 17 Aug 39)

MATTHEWS, Dr. Philip S., of Essex Co., d. on Wed. night the 27th ult. (VHFA 11 Sep 94)

MATTHEWS, Richard, of Louisa Co., d. on Mon. the 8th inst. (VGRMA 15 Apr 93)

MATTHEWS, Sol, of Norfolk, proposes to pet. the ensuing assembly to be emancipated in consequence of his services during the late war; he means to apply for the country to purchase him from his present master (VCNPGA 15 Sep 92)

MATTHEWS, Thomas, warns all persons that he will not be answerable for any debts of his wife, Sarah MATTHEWS (VG 8 Aug 77)

MATTHEWS, William, of Pr. Edw. Co., dec'd, e.a.w. his ex., William T. WALKER, and extx., Sarah MATTHEWS (Arg 2 Jul 99)

MATTHIAS, Henry, appr., 18-19, ran away from William CONSOLVO, tailor, Norfolk NHPA 14 Jul 97, NH 29 May 98)

MATTHIAS, Matt., dec'd, e.a.w. his admr., Joshua MATTHIAS (NH 23 Apr 96)

MATTHIAS, Peter, dec'd, his ex., Charles LATTIMORE, will sell all his PE and real est. on the main road from Norfolk to Princess Anne (NH 23 Jan 96, 7 Mar 96)

MATTOX, William, ind. svt., along with his wife, Mary, ran away from William TINSLEY near Hanover (VG 18 Aug 74)

MAUND, John James Esq., att. at law, of Westmoreland Co., mar. Miss Fanny CARTER dau. of Robert CARTER Esq. of Nomini (VHFA 13 Aug 89, VGWA 19 Aug 89)

MAUND, Nicholas, ind. svt., c. 45, b. in Yorkshire, wheelwright and wagon maker, ran away from James LANE and Joseph CROSS, Newgate, Loudoun Co. (VG 2 Dec 73)

MAUPIN, Daniel, d. on 20 Sep. at his seat in Albemarle Co.; he was b. on 25 Mar. 1700; he leaves a wife and upwards of 200 descendents (VIC 22 Oct 88)

MAUPIN, George Washington, son of Gabriel MAUPIN of Wmsbrg. was baptized last Sun. (VG 7 Oct 75)

MAURY Family, Orange Co. Ct. of Q.S, 25 Nov. 1795, in chanc: John GLASSELL (compl.) against John D. GRYMES, William MOORE and Elizabeth his wife, Robert SANDFORD and Hannah Philippa his wife, Mary

MAURY, James WALKER, Ludwell MAURY, Leonard Hill MAURY,
William Grymes MAURY, Penelope MAURY, Ann MAURY, and Mary
MAURY chil of the above sd. MAURY [sic] (defs.) (VHFFA 4 Dec 95)
MAURY, Mrs., consort of James MAURY merch. of Liverpool, d. there
sometime in July (VHFA 2 Oct 94)
MAURY, the Rev. Mr. James, Rector of Fredericksville, d. lately in Albemarle
Co. [long obit.] (VG and VGR 24 Aug 69)
MAURY, James B., late of Fredsbrg., d. in Paris on the 19th of Oct. last
(VHFFA 3 Feb 97)
MAURY, Matthew, dec'd, the whereabouts of a bale of goods bel. to his est. is
requested by his ex., Daniel CLAIBORNE (VG 20 Mar 52)
MAURY, the Rev. Walker, Minister of Elizabeth River Church and Master of
the Norfolk Academy, d. Sat. eve. last [11 Oct.] in his 36th year leaving a wife
and child (NPJ 15 Oct 88, VHFA 23 Oct 88, VGIC 25 Oct 88)
MAURY, Walker, dec'd, his admx., Mary MAURY, will sell all his PE at
Berlington, Orange Co. (VHFFA 27 Nov 95)
MAXEY, William, adv. that his wife, Elizabeth, absconded from him on Thurs.
the 10th inst. and he does not mean she shall waste any more of his property
(VGGA 7 Dec 96)
MAXWELL, John, svt., laborer, ran away from the snow *John* lying in
Hampton Road (VGAA 17 Apr 84)
MAY, Anne, intends to open a school in the house of her father, Edward MAY,
in Prince St. [Alexandria] (TAA 16 Aug 97)
MAY, John, of Botetourt Co., reportedly killed by Indians on his passage down
the Ohio near the mouth of Scioto about the 20th of Mar. [1790] (WVGWA 22
May 90, RMA 13 Oct 95); dec'd, e.a.w. his admr., David ROSS, Richmond
(VGGA 14 Oct 95)
MAY, John, dec'd, his widow is Anne MAY of Chesterfield Co. (VGGA 5 Sep
92)
MAY, John, of Fredsbrg., intends to leave in a few weeks (VHFA 28 Jul 91)
MAY, John, late of Chesterfield Co., dec'd, his est. there will be administered
by the sheriff (VGGA 9 May 92)
MAY, Thomas, a likely young fellow, b. in the upper end of K & Q Co., des. from
Gregory SMITH's Co. of Regulars at York (VGPu 22 Nov 76)
MAYER, Frederick, Dutch, d. in Savannah, Georgia on 1 Jan. last; he came
there early in 1782 and on his death devised a large est. to Thomas ADAM
with whom he had served in Capt. Alexander KIRKPATRICK's Co. of the
Continental Army; ADAMS des. at Old Cumberland Co. Ct. H. in Va.;
ADAMS' father lived in Nansemond Co. (WVGWA 17 Apr 90)
MAYLE, Dr. Charles, dec'd, his admr. (nfi) will sell his imported horse *Carver*
at the dwelling house of Mrs. Lydia MAYLE, Great Bridge, Norfolk Co. (VG
4 Oct 76); a pet. to be presented to the next assembly for payment of damages
suffered at the Great Bridge by our troops to his est. in 1776 by Samuel
HATTON of Norfolk, gdn. to MAYLE's orphans (VCNPGA 18 Aug 92)
MAYNARD, Nathaniel, dec'd, his 640 ac. tract on Sturgeon Run, Brunswick
Co., to be sold by Mary MAYNARD his extx. and John ROYSTER and
William Green MUNFORD, his ex. (VG 12 Mar 67, 6 Sep 70)
MAYO Family, HCC, 1 Jun 1793: Joseph PRENTIS, John PIERCE, and
William RUSSELL admrs. w.w.a. of Benjamin POWELL dec'd (pltfs.)
against John POWELL, William MAYO, John MAYO, William SMITH,
and John BECKLEY ex. of John MAYO dec'd, and George MAYO devisee of
the sd, John MAYO (defs. [They are apparently of Henrico Co.] (VGGA 26
Jun 93 ex)
MAYO, Mrs. Anne, relict of Col. William MAYO, d. on the 28th ult. in her 73rd
year (VGR 30 Dec 73)
MAYO, George Esq., late a rep. from Chesterfield Co. in the state legislature, d.
on Sun. the 2nd. inst. at Richmond in his 28th year after a short illness [obit.
in OVT] (VGGA 4 Sep 98, OVT 6 Sep 98, VHFA 7 Sep 98, NH 8 Sep 98)
MAYO, John, of Richmond, adv. that in 1782 or 1783, he gave a bond to a certain

William HOLLAND then of Powhatan Co. but who has since removed to Ky. (RMA 3 Sep 96)

MAYO, Dr. John, son of Joseph MAYO of Powhatan Co., d. on Mon. the 18th ult. during his attendance on the medical lectures at Philadelphia (VGGA 2, 5 Apr 99, Arg 5 Apr 99)

MAYO, Joseph, dec'd, e.a.w. his admr. w.w.a., Paul CARRINGTON, Joseph CARRINGTON, and Miles SELDEN; he had plants. on Tuckahoe Cr. in Goochland Co., in Henrico Co., in Manakin Town in Chesterfield Co., near the fork of the James in Cumberland Co., and in Mecklenburg Co. (VGWeA 12, 19 Nov 85)

MAYO, Joseph Jr. Esq., of Powhatan, Henrico Co. [sic], d. on his passage from Lisbon to Boston on 24 May in his 29th year (VGAA 23 Jul 85, VJAA 28 Jul 85); the GA determined that his slaves should be emancipated in accordance to his will (VJAA 4 Jan 87)

MAYO, Joseph, dec'd, e.a.w. his exors., James EDMUNDS Jr., Charles WATTS, and John DILLARD of Amherst Co. (VGGA 29 Mar 99)

MAZE, Elizabeth, executed on 23 Nov. for the murder of her bastard child in Lancaster Co. (VG 23 Nov 39)

MAZZEI, Philip, warns all persons from trusting Mrs. Petronilla MAZZEI, his wife, as he was induced from her behavior to allow her a certain annual sum for her separate maintenance from the 1st of Nov. 1781 which she has demanded since her return to this country (VGAA 17 Jul 84, VGWeA 24 Jul 84)

MEAD, David Esq., of Nansemond Co., mar. Miss Sally WATERS of Wmsbrg. on Thurs. last (VG 19 May 68)

MEADE, Mrs., wife of Maj. MEADE of Nansemond Co., d. lately (VG 26 Oct 39)

MEADE, Col. Andrew, of Nansemond Co., a former justice of the peace and rep. in assembly, d. on Sat. sennight (VG 28 Mar 45)

MEADE, Andrew, of Brunswick Co., dec'd, e.a.w. his ex., Buckner STITH (VGPI 9 Jun 95, 16 Dec 96)

MEADE, Mrs. Elizabeth, spouse of Richard Kidder MEADE Esq. of Pr. Geo. Co. died (VG 20 Jan 74)

MEAGHAN, John, Irish svt., 22, ran away from Richard Bland LEE, Loudoun Co. (VJAA 25 Jan 87)

MEAGHAN, Robert, Irish svt., 24, of the Potomac Company, broke out of Fairfax Co. jail (VJAA 27 Jul 86)

MEANLY, John, dec'd, his house and lot at Shed Town and his PE will be sold by his ex., John NEW of Richmond (VGRMA 12 Jun 94)

MEASE. Mrs. Betty, consort of Robert MEASE of Alexandria, d. on Sun. morn. last; she was bur. in the Presbyterian Burying Ground (TAA 27 Mar 98)

MEAUX, John, of Mercer Co., Ky., appoints his son, John G. MEAUX, his att. to recover all sums of money which are due to him in Va. [The document is dated 24 Jan 1797 and witnessed by Samuel M'DONALD, Richard MEAUX, and N. B. MEAUX (VGGA 15 Mar 97)

MECHUM, Robert, Irish svt., 20, ran away from the Potomac Co., Great Falls (VJAA 15 Jun 86)

MECOM, John, from Southampton Co., executed last Sat. for murder (VGPu 14 Feb 77)

MEDLICOT, Dr. James, executed near Winchester on 26 Nov. for the murder of John HEFFERSON, a journeyman ropemaker (VGWA 1 Dec 90)

MEEKS, Jesse, 28-29, des. from Chestertown [Md. ?] (VGPu 6 Jun 77)

MEEKUM, Lewis, of Isle of Wight Co., killed in a fall about three weeks since (VG 9 Dec 37)

MEI[R]K, Mr., of New Kent Co., mar. Miss OLIVER of Hanover Co. (VGWeA 21 May 89)

MEIVIN, James, svt., Scot, 35, ran away from the Potomac Company, Great Falls (VJAA 15 Jun 86)

MERCER, Col. George, dec'd, a lot in Alexandria formerly bel. to him, to be sol by his brother, J. MERCER of Fredsbrg. (VJAA 3 May 87)

MERCER, Gen. Hugh, dec'd, e.a.w. John TENNENT and George WEEDON his ex., Fredsbrg. (VGAA 7 Dec 82, 4 Jan 83, VGWeA 14 Dec 82); land bel. to his est. on the Yohogany River to be sold by his ex. (VGAA 25 Sep 84)

MERCER, John Esq., eminent lawyer, d. on the 14th inst. after a short illness at his seat at Marlborough, Stafford Co., aged 64 (VG and VGR 27 Oct 68); his extx. is Anne MERCER; his library will be sold by James MERCER (nfi) (VGR 15 Dec 68)

MERCER, Mrs. Isabella, relict of the late Gen. Hugh MERCER, d. on 17 Sep. in Fredsbrg. (VHFA 22 Sep 91, VGAR 29 Sep 91)

MERCER, the Hon. James Esq., for many yrs. one of the judges of the General Ct., d. in Richmond on 30 Oct. (VGGA 6 Nov 93, VHFA 7 Nov 93, SS 9 Nov 93, BVCG 11 Nov 93); e.a.w. his admr., John T. BROOKE and James M. GARNETT, who will also sell some HH & KF and about 380 books (VHFA 12 Feb 95); his admrs. will sell some valuable Cape Sheep and other livestock at the Retreat Farm (VHFA 26 Mar 95); 3000 ac. of his land near Middleburg in Loudoun Co. to be sold by his admrs. (VHFA 27 Jun 98)

MERCER, Capt. John, Virginia volunteer, killed [on 18 Apr.] when he and 15 soldiers under his command were attacked by Indians near Edward's Fort on Cape Capon about 20 miles above Winchester (Wmsbrg. disp. of 23 Apr) (NYM 3 May 56, MG 6 May 56)

MERCER, the Hon. John F. Esq., Va. delegate in the U. S. Congress, mar. Miss SPRIGGS eld. dau. of Richard SPRIGGS Esq. of Annapolis, in that city on Thurs. the 2nd inst. [or 3 Feb. acc. to VJAA] (VJAA 24 Feb 85, VGIC 26 Feb 85)

MERCER, the Rev. Silas, d. in early Jul. in Georgia (RCFPC 7 Sep 96)

MEREDITH, John, intends to move up the country next fall and wishes to sell his plant. in K & Q Co. (VG 11 Jul 71)

MEREDITH, Ralph G., of K & Q Co., the distribution of his est. is ordered to be made in April next (Arg 22 Jan 99)

MEREDITH, Samuel, of K & Q Co., dec'd, e.a.w. his admr., Ralph G. MEREDITH and William MEREDITH (VGAA 28 Jun 83)

MEREDITH, Samuel Sr., of K & Q Co., adv. for a horse that was given to his son by his cousin, William MEREDITH (VGR 24 Dec 67)

MEREDITH, William, of K & Q Co., dec'd, his HH items to be sold by William MEREDITH (nfi) (VG 2 May 66) [name given as MERIDETH]

MEREDITH, William, of K & Q Co., dec'd, his moveable est. to be sold by his admx., Ann B. MEREDITH (VGAA 31 Jan 84)

MEREDITH, William, dec'd, his seat on Mattaponi River in K & Q Co., containing 537 ac., to be sold by William MEREDITH Jr. (nfi) of K & Q Co. (VGPI 3 May 87)

MERIMEN, Thomas, of Cumberland Co., 22-23, jailed for the murder of Archer JONES on 19 Oct., has escaped (Ex 8 Nov 99)

MERIWETHER, Ann, of Richmond, is the wife of the late John MERIWETHER (VGGA 12 Oct 91)

MERRIT, Rowsey, formerly of Essex Co., the printer is seeking information on his current residence (VGGA 29 Sep 90)

MERRY, Prettyman, of Orange Co., intends to move to Ky. in the spring (VH 25 Jan 99)

MERRYMAN, Thomas, an inhabitant of Caroline Co., des. from the *Muskito* cruiser lying at Warwick (VGPu 13 Sep 76)

MESSER, John, Dutch, svt., ran away along with his wife from James MERONEY (VGR 13 Apr 69)

MESSHIE Family, Hampshire Co. Ct., in chanc: John MESSHIE (compl.) against Christopher MESSHIE, Jacob MESSHIE, Barbara MESSHIE, Elizabeth MESSHIE, and Mary MESSHIE (defs.) (BVCG 7 Jan 93)

MESSMORE, George, son of Nicholas MESSMORE of [Winchester], d. on Sat. last in the prime of life (WG 27 Nov 99)

MESTON, Capt. William, of Philadelphia, d. on Wed. last in Richmond after a lingering illness (VGAA 5 Feb 85)

METTAUER, Joseph, of Pr. Edw. Co. will pet. the next legislature for permission to institute a suit in the HCC for the dissolution of his marriage with Jemima METTAUER (VGGA 19 Oct 96)

MEUX, Richard, dec'd, e.a.w. his ex., Thomas and William MEUX (VGPu 3 Jan 77)

MEUX, Thomas, late of New Kent Co., dec'd, his widow and admx., Agnes MEUX, desires to settle his est. soon (VGGA 31 Dec 94)

MEYERS, John, adv. that on Tues. eve. his wife, Anna, absconded from his house; she is the mother of a young child (TAA 14 Sep 97)

MICHELL, Reuben, of Richmond, dec'd, e.a.w. William MICHELL of Goochland Co. (VGAA 13 Sep 83)

MICKELL, Capt. George, dec'd, e.a.w. his admx., Susannah MICKELL of Norfolk (NH 28 Jan 96)

MICKLEBERROUGH, Capt. Robert, dec'd, e.a.w. his ex., Thomas HACKETT of Caroline Co. (VGGA 17 Nov 90)

MIDDLEMIST, Archibald, boot and shoemaker, one of the oldest inhabitants of Petersburg, d. on Sun. last (VGPI 7 Nov 97)

MIDDLETON, Capt., of the ship *York* of Liverpool, d. in Gloucester Co. a few days ago (VG 11 Dec 66)

MIDDLETON, Horatio, late of Charles Co., [Md.], dec'd, e.a.w. his surviving ex., George WARD and Joanna his wife (CMAG 12 Apr 96)

MIDDLETON, Robert, of Westmoreland Co., long a vestryman of Cople Par., d. in his 71st year (VG 30 Dec 73)

MIDDLETON, Thomas, of Fredsbrg., is about to leave the state (VHFA 17 Mar 91)

MIDDLETON, Capt. William, of Liverpool, dec'd, e.a.w. Peter LYON of Hanover Co., att. for the exors. (VG 12 Nov 69)

MIDDLETON, William, adv. that his wife, Lucinder [later corrected to Lucinda], left him without any just cause and he will not pay any of her debts (TAA 4 Dec 97)

MIERS, Sarah, a Dutch woman, svt., ran away from Patrick CREAGH, Annapolis [Md.] (VG 15 Oct 36)

MILBORN, John, svt. c. 30, forge carpenter, indented himself to the Hon. John TAYLOE and Presley THORNTON Esqs. as a svt. for the term of three yrs. in order to discharge a debt of about £35 due by bond, ran away from the Occoquan Iron Works (MG 16 Sep 62)

MILBURN, Samuel, svt. from the west of England, 27, ran away from Dr. Charles CARROLL, Patapsco River, Anne Arundel Co., Md. (VG 11 Jul 51)

MILBY, Adiel Esq., Rep. for Northampton, killed in a shooting accident (VGP 23 Mar, VGPu 24 Mar, VG 25 Mar 75)

MILES, James, appr., c. 19, went off with his mother, Mary MILES, a widow, from Michael STIEBER, baker, Alexandria (VGAxA 24 Nov 91)

MILHADO, Aaron, dec'd, e.a.w. his admx., Mary MILHADO of Portsmouth (NH 28 Sep 99)

MILLER Family, Rockingham Co. Ct., 28 Mar 1799, in chanc: John DAVIS (compl.) against Samuel MILLER, John LEWIS and Rachel his wife late Rachel MILLER, James MILLER, James MOFFETT and Hannah his wife late Hannah MILLER, William MILLER, Henry MILLER, and Patsey MILLER infants, heirs, and devisees of Henry MILLER dec'd (defs.); it appears that James and Hannah MOFFETT are not inhabitants of this commonwealth (PH 17 Jul 99)

MILLER, Mr., from Va., murdered in Jun. on Broad River about 30 miles from Loudon (Savanna, Georgia disp. of 23 Jul. citing *South Carolina Gazette* of 7 Jul.) (NYPB 25 Sep 66)

MILLER, Mrs. Ann, in her 60th year, relict of Capt. Matthias MILLER, d. on Wed. morn. last (NPJ 20 Feb 88)

MILLER, Catherine, has refused to live with her husband, Henry, of Rockingham Co. (BVCG 7 Apr 97)

MILLER, David, d. on Tues. eve. last in Wmsbrg. [or Thurs. eve. last acc. to

OVT] (OVT 23 Jul 98, VGGA 24 Jul 98)
MILLER, David, native of Scotland, and for many yrs. an inhabitant of this borough, d. on Sun. morn. (NH 16 Oct 98)
MILLER, Hans, Prussian, former sergeant, 50-55, suspected of having kidnapped a 2-3 year old girl named Catharine from the house of her father, Henry WOLFORD, in Renssel[n]erville [sic] [NY] (VGGA 20 Mar 93)
MILLER, Henry, of Augusta Co., c. on the 10th instant in an advanced age (BVCG 18 Mar 96)
MILLER, Henry, dec'd, e.a.w. his ex. (nfi) at the Mossy Creek Iron Works (SVG 3 Jun 96)
MILLER, Hugh, of Appomattox, intends to leave the country for Britain by the 1st of Aug. (VG 29 May 52)
MILLER, James, mulatto slave, c. 38, ran away from Richard C. WEBB the ex. of George GRASTY dec'd, Fauquier Co., on 12 Jun 1784 (VIC 21 Jan 89)
MILLER, James, merch., mar. Miss Betsey ROBB dau. of James ROBB Esq., lately in Port Royal (VH 9 Aug 99)
MILLER, John, Eng. svt., 28, blacksmith, ran away from William Carr LANE, Loudoun Co. (VGR 12 May 68)
MILLER, John, son of Francis and Susanna MILLER of London, left Great Britain on the *Litchfield* for Md. or Va. in 1752; he or his heirs are requested to apply to Aeneas M'LEAN, New York, to hear of something greatly to their advantage (VGR 9 Feb 69)
MILLER, John, late of Berkeley Co., dec'd, e.a.w. his extx., Hannah MILLER, and ex., Alexander MILLER and Thomas SHARP (PGBA 18 Feb 96)
MILLER, Margaret, aka GRAVES, Eng. svt., 36, ran away from Moses PHILLIPS, Stafford Co. (VGPu 15 Aug 77)
MILLER, Mason, dec'd, e.a.w. his admr., Thomas MATTHEWS, Norfolk (VGNI 23 Aug 75)
MILLER, Michael, d. on Fri. [8 Nov.] (BVCG 11 Nov 93)
MILLER, William, a Scotchman, formerly bel. to Capt. STEVENSON's Co. of the 8th Regt., enl. at Ft. Pitt, des. from the *Hero* galley (VGPu 19 Sep 77)
MILLER, William, late of Henrico Co., dec'd, his land to be sold by his admr., John MILLER (VGRMA 12 Aug 93)
MILLE[R]SON, Fanny, wife of Ward MILLESON, Pr. Anne Co., has left her husband (NHPA 6 May 97)
MILLES, Philip, joiner and cabinetmaker, came to Va. in 1773; if he will apply to Capt. William ANDERSON of Hanover, he will find letters giving him an account of something much to his advantage, acc. to an advertisement by James MILLER, Yorktown (VG 29 Jul 75)
MILLOW, Thomas, appr., 19, baker, has served eight of 10 yrs., ran away from John SMITH, Wmsbrg. (NH 5 Feb 99)
MILLS, James, merch., of Urbanna, mar. Mrs. BOYD relict of Walter BOYD of Blandford (VG 14 Nov 71)
MILLS, John, dec'd (VJAA 2 Nov 86)
MILLS, John Esq., merch., of Alexandria and Fairfax Co., d. of an epileptic fit on 24 Dec. [1783] at Shooter's Hill; e.a.w. his admr., Robert T. HOOE, Charles SIMMS, and William BROWN, who will pet. the GA to empower them to sell his RE to pay his debts (VJAA 5 Feb 84, 16 Dec 84, 14 Jul 85, VGAA 21 Aug 84)
MILLS, Philip, ind. svt., may have run away from Henry MANN in Yorktown (VGNI 22 Sep 74)
MILLS, Robert, Irish ind. svt., imp. last Sep., gardener, c. 22, ran away from Samuel HANSON, Charles Co., Md. (VG 24 Nov 74)
MILNER, James, att. at law in Halifax, N. Carolina, killed in a riding accident (VG 31 Dec 72); e.a.w. his acting ex., Joseph MONTFORT and Andrew MILLER (VG 4 Feb, 11 Mar 73)
MILNER, Samuel, of Nansemond Co., killed by George KIER [also given as KERR] a lunatic (VG 24 Jan, 18 Apr 51)
MILSON, Charles, svt., bel. to Robert ANNER, Westmoreland Co., Pa., jailed in

Botetourt Co. (VGPu 23 Jun 75)
MILTON, Robert, b. in Nansemond Co., pretends to be a doctor, des. from Capt. David BELL's Co. of the Va. Regt. (VG 21 Nov 55)
MILVEN, Robert, seaman, Scot, ran away from the ship *Encouragement* of London lying at West Point (VG 10 Apr 52)
MILVIN, Peter, aka Isaac MALVIR, Negro, c. 24, from Boston, printer, jailed in Middlesex Co. (VGAA 9 Jul 85)
MILWOOD, Benjamin, of Richmond Co., sentenced to death for robbing a house; executed on 1 Jul. (VG 17 Jun, 1 Jul 37)
MIMM, Gilbert, mar. Miss Fanny SIMRALL on Thurs. (BVCG 5 Aug 93)
MINER, William, mar. Miss Mildred LEWIS dau. of John LEWIS, Fredsbrg. (VHFA 28 Jan 90)
MINGE, Capt. David, late of Charles City Co., dec'd, e.a.w., his extx., Christina MINGE of Waynoake (VGAA 8 Mar 83, 10 Jan 84)
MINNIS, Charles, of York Co., dec'd, e.a.w. his ex., Augustine MOORE (VG 28 Oct 73)
MINOR, Col. Garritt, d. on the 25th ult. in Louisa Co. (Ex and VGGA 12 Jul 99)
MINOR, Henry, appr., 16, ran away from Richard HOLT Jr. in Essex Co. (VGR 15 Mar 70 sup)
MINOR, Spence, ex. of Nicholas MINOR, dec'd, e.a.w. his admx., Mary MINOR (TAA 25 Jun 98)
MINOR, William, a young man, d. in Richmond on Wed. eve. last (VGRC 17 Oct 94)
MINOR, William, late of Richmond, dec'd, e.a.w. his admr., Dabney MINOR (VGGA 10 Dec 94, 20 Apr 96)
MINSER, Jacob, late of Frederick Co., dec'd, e.a.w. his admx., Rebecca MINSER (WG 22 May 99)
MINSON, Elizabeth, of Charles City Co., adv. that her husband, Henry MINSON, who for a number of yrs. has been capt. of several vessels on the James River, has left her with his five chil. without any reason and a few days ago she learned that he was brought to Wmsbrg. as a tory and has never since heard of him; she requests information on his current whereabouts; she has reason to believe he is in Hampton or Norfolk (VGPu 21 Jun 76)
MISKELL, William, late of [North] Farnham Par., Richmond Co., his admr., Thomas GARNETT, adv. that a pet. will be presented to the next GA for a power to sell his RE (VGPA 18 Jun 91); his admr. will sell his lands in Richmond Co. (VHFA 12 Sep 93)
MISKELL, William, dec'd, David OLIVIER of Fredsbrg. (nfi) will pet. the next GA for permission to sell that part of William MISKELL's RE which descended to OLIVIER's late wife and "none belongs to her children" (VGGA 13 Aug 94)
MIS-QUA-C[P]O-NA-CAW or Red Pole, of the Shawanoese Nation, d. on the morn. of the 28th [Jan.] at Ft. Fayette (Pittsburgh) (CMAG 16 Feb 97)
MITCHELL, Capt., of Va., mar. Miss DAFFIN (MJ 21 May 82)
MITCHELL, Alexander Esq., age 101 and much afflicted with the palsy, was mar. to Miss Jane HAMMOND age 16, both of Buckingham Co., on the 13th ult. by the Rev. Mr. CHASTAIN; the parties applied previously to a circuit preacher, the Rev. Mr. SAUNDERS, who refused to perform the ceremony alleging that the intended union was contrary to nature (VGGA 20 Dec 97)
MITCHELL, Andrew, of New Castle, d. on Thurs. the 4th inst. (VGRMA 15 Dec 94, VGGA 17 Dec 94); e.a.w. his admr., Thomas CHRISTIE of New Castle and James BROWN of Richmond (VGGA 18 Mar 95, 3 Aug 96)
MITCHELL, Archelous, late of Charles City Co., dec'd, e.a.w. his ex., James BRADLEY and Henry VAUGHAN (VGGA 28 Sep 91)
MITCHELL, Cary, late of Frederick Co., dec'd, e.a.w. his ex., Archibald BROUNLEY and Frances MITCHELL (WG 6 Mar 99)
MITCHELL, Henry, dec'd, e.a.w. Daniel GRINNAN Jr.; his surviving ex. is James BLAIR of Fredsbrg. (VHFA 19 May, 31 Aug 98)

MITCHELL, James, of Yorktown, d. in his 68th year (VG 30 Jan 72); his extx., Jane [also given as Janet] MITCHELL of Yorktown will sell his PE (VG 28 May, 4 Jun, 23 Jul 72, 11 Feb 73)

MITCHELL, James, formerly an eminent merch. at Glasgow, d. at Alexandria last Tues. on his way to New York (VJAA 21 Jun 87)

MITCHELL, Dr. John, of Urbanna, intends to sell his house and move to England (VG 28 Nov 45)

MITCHELL, Mary, dau. of James and Ann MITCHELL, d. in Dumfries on Fri. eve. last, aged 2 (RJDWA 2 Sep 96)

MITCHELL, Randle, Negro, jailed in Winchester, claimed to be free, from Powhatan otherwise Port-Ann Co. [sic] (VGWA 17 Sep 91); escaped from jail on 23 Sep. (VGWA 24 Sep 91)

MITCHELL, Samuel, late of Richmond Town, dec'd, e.a.w. his ex., Thomas PROSSER and Turner SOUTHALL (VGR 15 Nov 70, VGAA and VGWeA 24 Jan 84)

MITCHELL, Thomas, of Amherst Co., intends for Scotland in a few weeks (VG 14 Nov 71)

MITCHELL, William, dec'd, his houses and lot in Hampton to be sold by his admr., Cary SELDEN (VGR 20 Apr 69)

MITCHELL, William, of Mecklenburg Co., forewarns all persons from purchasing any part of the est. of Richard RAGSDALE which he received by his wife, Judith M'KNIGHT, from William MITCHELL (VGPu 21 Nov 77)

MOBBS, Martha, svt., 24, ran away from William ROANE, Essex Co. (VG 5 Oct 39)

MOFFAT, John, merch., late from Ireland, d. in Richmond last Mon. (VGIC 15 Nov 83)

MOFFET, John, dec'd, e.a.w. Francis ASH who was security for Sandford BREEDWELL and wife, MOFFET's exors. (WG 6 Mar 99)

MOFFIT, Thomas, of [Baltimore], dec'd, e.a.w. his admr., George LINDINBERGER Jr. of Baltimore (NH 25 Feb 96)

MOHUN, Elizabeth, extx. of Joel MOHUN dec'd, is a pltf. in a HCC case, 29 May 1788 (VIC 24 Sep 88, VICGA 5 May 90))

MOHUN, Joel, of Norfolk, dec'd, a tract of land he purchased from Charles RUDDER to be sold by his extx., Elizabeth MOHUN and his ex., James TAYLOR (NPJ 12 Dec 87)

MOIR, the Rev. Mr. James, dec'd, his plant. to be sold by his ex. (nfi) at Tarborough Town, N. Carolina (VG 17 Dec 67)

MOLAN, Dr., of Philadelphia, drowned off the coast of N. Carolina, 17 Oct., he was a passenger on the ship *George and Patty Washington* (TAA 14 Nov 98)

MOLLOY, John, Irish sailor, ran away from the ship *Fairfield* now at Norfolk (VG 3 Jan 71)

MOLLOY, Patrick, Irish svt., 20, ran away from David BOYD, Northumberland Co. on 19 Aug. (VG 29 Oct 67)

MOLLOY, Thomas Esq., of Pr. Edw. Co., dec'd, e.a.w. Sarah MOLLOY, his extx., and Grief GREEN and Owen HASKINS, his exors. (RMA 31 Oct 95)

MONCRIEF, Henry, Scot, svt., c. 30, ran away from Isaac ZANE, Frederick Co. (VG 12 Sep 77)

MONELLY, James, 23, tanner and currier, jailed as a runaway in Winchester (VCWM 17 Jun 89)

MONKS, John, of Hardy Co., dec'd, his admr. is John SMITH (BVCG 16 Jun 94)

MONROE, Andrew, of Kinsale, Westmoreland Co., dec'd, his admr. w.w.a. is John MONROE; who will sell tracts of his in Westmoreland Co. (VHFA 4 Apr 98)

MONROE, John, svt., apothecary, 27, ran away from Patrick COUTURE, Richmond (VG 16 May 66)

MONROE, John, dec'd, all his est. to be sold at the plant. of Mrs. Sarah MONROE, Fairfax Co., by Edward BLACKBURN, his ex., and Sarah MONROE, his extx. (VJAA 12 Jan 86)

MONROE, Joseph Jones Esq., mar. Miss Elizabeth KERR dau. of James KERR Esq. of Albemarle Co., on 19 Mar. in Albemarle Co. (VGGA 30 Mar 91)
MONTAGUE, Clement, aged 70, mar. Mrs. Hannah LEWIS aged 25, widow of James LEWIS dec'd, in this county [Spotsylvania] (VHFA 22 Sep 91)
MONTFORT, Capt., killed by Indians near Ft. Jefferson (BVCG 25 Jun 92)
MONTFORT, John, dec'd, e.a.w. his ex., Henry MONTFORT of Halifax, N. Carolina, who will sell several tracts of his land in Tryon Co. (6000 ac. commonly called "The Great Cove", another 2000 ac. tract), in Orange Co., in Bute Co., a 4000 ac. tract in Halifax Co., and sundry other tracts (VG 27 Apr 76, 16 May 76)
MONTFORT, Joseph, dec'd, his ex., Henry MONTFORT of Halifax Town, N. Carolina, will settle his est. and sell large tracts of his land in Tryon, Orange, Bute and Halifax Cos. in N. Carolina (VG 23 Jan 78) [It is not clear if this person is the same as John MONTFORT above.]
MONTGOMERIE, Thomas, of Dumfries, dec'd, his ex., James DUNLOP and John RYBURN, will sell part of his PE and his lots in Dumfries and on Quantico Cr. (VHFA 6 Sep 92)
MONTGOMERY, James, of Amherst Co., dec'd, e.a.w. his admr., Robert WRIGHT (VGPu 29 May 78)
MONTGOMERY, Col. John, killed by Indians on 27 [Nov. 1784] on the northwestern frontier of Sumner Co., Tenn. (VGRMA 26 Jan 95)
MOODY Family, HCC, [nd]: William CALL (pltf.) and John MARSHALL, Elizabeth MOODY widow and relict of Henry MOODY dec'd, William MOODY eld. son and heir at law of the sd. Henry MOODY, Francis MOODY, Henry MOODY, Jesse TAYLOR and Phoebe his wife, and Mary MOODY, which sd. Henry, Francis, Phoebe, and Mary are chil. and heirs of the sd. Henry MOODY dec'd, and Charles [BARTON] and Richard BA[S]KERVILLE (defs.) (VGGA 20 Apr 96)
MOODY Family, Mecklenburg Co., Quarterly Ct., 17 Oct. 1796, in chanc: John MARSHALL (pltf.) against Richard BASKERVILLE, Henry MOODY, and Francis MOODY, which sd. Henry and Francis are sons of Henry MOODY dec'd, Charles CAMPBELL and Phoebe his wife, Abraham BEUFORT and Mary his wife, which sd. Phoebe and Mary are daus. of the sd. Henry MOODY dec'd, Elizabeth Beufort MOODY and P. MOODY (infants) are chil. of William MOODY dec'd who was also a son of Henry MOODY dec'd (defs.) (VGPI 9 Dec 96)
MOODY, Benjamin, of Fairfax Co., dec'd, slaves, etc. of his est. to be sold at auction by his ex., Thomas MOODY (VJAA 23 Mar 86, 8 Mar 87)
MOODY, Ishmael, dec'd, e.a.w. his extx., Ann ORRELL (VG 14 Nov 77)
MOODY, Jesse, Negro, c. 35, says he is free, formerly the property of David CLEMENTS of Pr. Geo. Co.; he was raised by a certain Richard CLARK; jailed in Pr. Wm. Co. (Ex 12 Jul 99)
MOODY, John, smith and farrier from Philadelphia, but late from Norfolk, adv. that he has opened a shop in Wmsbrg. (VGPu 28 Jun 76)
MOODY, John, late of [Wmsbrg.], dec'd, e.a.w. his admx., Margaret MOODY (VG 2 Mar 79)
MOODY, John, merch, of Richmond, mar. Miss Elizabeth P. PRICE of Fluvanna Co. on Sat. eve. (Arg 30 Dec 96)
MOODY, Matthew Sr., d. in a very advanced age at the Capitol Landing (VGP 8 Jun 75, VGPu 9 Jun 75 sup); William RUSSELL of Wmsbrg. will settle his est. (VG 29 Jul 75)
MOODY, Philip Jr., of James City Co., mar. Miss Kitty MOODY eld. dau. of Matthew MOODY of Richmond on Thurs. last [acc. to VGRMA] or Sat. last [acc. to VGGA] (VGGA 1 Apr 95, VGRMA 2 Apr 95)
MOODY, Samuel, drowned in Moorcock Cr. by Chickahominy Ferry on 15 Dec. (VG 23 Dec 37)
MOODY, Samuel, dec'd, his admr., John BOGUE of Alexandria, will sell his est. (CMAG 2 Jan 96)
MOONE, Capt., drowned some time ago; his body was recovered last Sun. and

bur. in the Episcopal Burial Ground (VJAA 19 Apr 87)

MOORE Family, Pr. Edw. Co. Ct., 20 May 1799, in chanc: William MORTON (pltf.) against Thomas MOORE and John WATKINS, Jesse HAMLET and Molly MOORE extx. and exors. of George MOORE dec'd (defs.) (VGGA 9 Jul 99)

MOORE, Mr., a journeyman tailor, drowned in the Potomac last Thurs. (VJAA 7 Jul 85)

MOORE, Mr., killed by Indians around 20 Jan. about 10 miles from Lincoln Ct. House, Ky. (VJAA 5 Apr 87)

MOORE, Mrs., of Pr. Anne Co., died (VGWeA 30 Nov 82)

MOORE, Anne, lately a prisoner in Chesterfield Co. jail, 25-30, escaped therefrom (VGR 14 Jul 68)

MOORE, Col. Bernard, of Kg. Wm. Co., died (VG 15 Apr 75)

MOORE, Bernard Esq., of Kg. Wm. Co., mar. Miss Lucy LEIPER niece of Dr. Andrew LEIPER of Richmond, on Sat. last (VGWeA 8 May 88)

MOORE, Elizabeth, has eloped from her husband, Filmer MOORE of York Co. (VG 2 May 71); she is staying with her father [Charles MILES] since her husband said his mother would rather live in a hollow tree than with her (VG 9 May 71)

MOORE, Francis, of Orange Co., adv. that all contracts he makes must have the consent of his son, Reuben MOORE (VHFA 22 May 94)

MOORE, Col. Francis, d. in Orange Co., aged 85 (RCFPC 10 Aug 96); his land in Orange Co. will be sold by his ex., Alexander DAWNEY (VH 23 Jul 99)

MOORE, George, Pr. Edw. Co. Ct., 15 Jul. 1799, in chanc: Jeremiah ALDERSON (pltf.) against Molly MOORE extx. and John WATKINS and Jesse HAMILTON exors. of George MOORE dec'd, and Thomas MOORE (defs.); it appears that Thomas MOORE is not an inhabitant of the state (Ex 16 Aug 99)

MOORE, Harbin, aged 75, mar. Mrs. TUTT aged 72, in Culpeper (VHFA 24 Jan 93)

MOORE, Henry, of Colchester, d. on 12 Mar. (VGR 15 Apr 73)

MOORE, James, Irish svt., ran away from John SCHOOLAR, Caroline Co. on 27 Dec.; he may be headed for N. Carolina (VG 1 Feb 40)

MOORE, James, of Pr. Anne Co., dec'd, his land in that co. to be sold by his admx., Mary MOORE (NPJ 5 Mar 88)

MOORE, Jemmy, Negro, c. 40, says he formerly bel. to Len BROOKS of Essex Co. but is now free, jailed in Surry Co. (VG 9 Sep 73)

MOORE, John, c. 24, a soldier in the troop of Light Dragoons of Cadwallader JONES at Fredsbrg., des., he was b. in Md. and is now a resident in Halifax Co. (VGPu 4 Jul 77)

MOORE, John, dec'd, e.a.w. his ex., George BILLUPS (AGNPWA 25 Sep 93)

MOORE, Joseph, dec'd, his extx., Sarah MOORE, and ex., John WATKINS, will sell ten of his Negroes in Pr. Edw. Co. (VGPA 5 Jan 93)

MOORE, Lewis, formerly of Berkeley Co., now of Mason Co., Ky. has opened a tavern at Limestone (PGBA 15 Dec 96)

MOORE, Mrs. Mary, relict of the late Daniel MOORE, [died lately] (VIC 16 Apr 88)

MOORE, Maurice, of Clifton Mills, adv. that his wife, Catherine, has eloped from his bed and board (CMAG 22 Sep 96)

MOORE, Michael, svt. boy, 17-18, ran away from the snow *John* lying in Hampton Road (VGAA 17 Apr 84)

MOORE, Robert, of Powhatan Co., dec'd, his admr., M. MONTAGUE also of Powhatan, will sell his plant. containing c. 520 ac. all of his HH and KF and will also settle his est. (VGGA 29 Mar 97)

MOORE, Capt. Stephen, was mar. to Mrs. Phoebe ARELL, both of this town, by the Rev. Mr. DAVIS, last eve. (CMAG 1 Mar 96)

MOORE, William, late of Freeman's Bridge, Sussex Co., dec'd, his PE to be sold by his admr., John VERELL (VG 27 Aug 67)

MOORE, William, from Charlotte Co., c. 22, jailed for robbery; escaped from jail

in York Co. (VGR 4 Aug 74)
MOORE, William, aka John KENNOR, executed on 13 Jan. for burglary (VGP 12 Jan 75)
MOORE, William, comedian, d. in Fredsbrg. on Wed. sennight (VHFA 17 Jul 94)
MOORELAND, Young, dec'd, e.a.w. the ex. of his extx., Samuel THOMAS of Warwick Co. (VG 1 Dec 74)
MORAN, Mrs., consort of Thomas MORAN of Norfolk, d. on Thurs. eve. (NH 26 Jan 99)
MORAS, Citizen, of Bordeaux [France], resident in Port Royal, Martinique, arrived in the continent since sd. island fell into the power of the English; his brother-in-law wishes to know his residence and asks that he write to him in care of Citizen MYERS, Norfolk, who will forward letters to the French ship *L'Eclatant* on board which Citizen FAGE, Officer of Health and son-in-law of the widow MORAS resides (AGNPPA 21 Apr 95)
MORE, Michael, Irish svt., 20, ran away from John SEARS, Bushtown, Harford Co. [Md.] (VJAA 23 Nov 86)
MORECOCK, Thomas, dec'd, his ex., Henry SOUTHALL, will sell his plant., Tomahun, in Charles City Co. (VGGA 27 Nov 93)
MORGAN, Abel, of Ashby's Gap, Fauquier Co., adv. that his wife, Jean, hath at sundry times eloped from him and he will no longer pay any of her debts (VGPu 3 Jan 77 sup)
MORGAN, Abel, dec'd, his admx., Diana MORGAN, will handle his est. and will sell material for carrying on the burr-making business (Arg 23 Mar 98)
MORGAN, Charles, son of William MORGAN of Fauquier Co., wants to purchase land in Fayette Co. [Ky.] (KG 24 May 88)
MORGAN, George, dec'd, his admr., Rauleigh [sic] MORGAN, and admx., Drusella MORGAN, will sell his stock, HHF, and farming utensils (PGBA 18 Feb 96)
MORGAN, Jacob, dec'd, e.a.w. his admr., William FITZGERALD, Amelia Co. (VG 12 May 74)
MORGAN, James, svt., c. 21, ran away from Robert SMITH, Baltimore (VGWA 14 Jan 89)
MORGAN, John, of Middlesex Co., dec'd, 400 ac. of his land there--subject to the widow's dower--to be sold by the trustees, Robert DANIEL, Will CHURCHILL, Augustine SMITH, and George DANIEL (VG 12 Jan 69)
MORGAN, Dr. John, medical professor at the College of Philadelphia, d. a few days ago at Philadelphia (VHFA 29 Oct 89)
MORGAN, Nathaniel, executed on 23 Nov. for horse stealing in Pr. Geo. Co. (VG 23 Nov 39)
MORGAN, [Wathing], dec'd, e.a.w. his ex., William BROWN, of City Point (VG 7 Dec 69)
MORGAN, William, Eng. svt., silversmith and watch mender, ran away from Edward HILL, Pr. Geo. Co. (VG 25 Jul 66)
MORGAN, William, late of Berkeley Co., dec'd, e.a.w. his ex., John MORROW and William MORGAN (PGBA 4 Jan 96)
MORGAN, Zachariah, dec'd, his ex., Abraham MORGAN and Thomas SWEARINGEN, will sell his stock and farming equipment (PGBA 8 Mar 98)
MORLAND, Francis, of Cabin Point, dec'd, his admr., Archibald DUNLOP, will sell all of his HH and KF (VGWeA 10 Apr 84)
MORRIS, Capt., of the Eng. brig *Charlotte*, drowned about six miles below Craney Island on Nansemond River on Wed. last (NH 4 May, VH 10 May 99)
MORRIS, Anne, has eloped from her husband, Edward of Amelia Co. (VGR 17 Oct 71)
MORRIS, Benjamin, dec'd, two Negro boys bel. to his est. will be sold by his admr., John MORRIS in Richmond (VGRMA 7 Apr 94)
MORRIS, Charles, of Westmoreland Co., dec'd, his ex., Euell MORRIS and John BUTLER, will sell all of his est. including the 600 ac. tract whereon he lived (VH 21 Oct 97)

MORRIS, Charlotte, wife of Philip MORRIS of Portsmouth, has left him "without any provocation" (NH 21 Apr 96)

MORRIS, Daniel, sailor, b. in Rhode Island, 22, suspected of robbing his ship, the *Fanny*, on 17 Apr. (NPJ 29 Apr 89)

MORRIS, Edmund, Irish ind. svt., c. 28, ran away from James PERRY, Montgomery Co., Md. (VCWM 19 Aug 89)

MORRIS, Henry, adv. that he has bought a tract of land in Pr. Edw. Co. from his father, John MORRIS (VG 14 Dec 69)

MORRIS, Isaac, dec'd, his admr. w.w.a., John BEADEL of Amelia Co., adv. that he is ready to pay all demands against the est. and notes that he is accused by Moses MORRIS (nfi) of refusing to settle regularly with him (VGPu 5 Dec 77)

MORRIS, Isaac, dec'd, e.a.w. his ex., John CLARK and William WOOTTEN of Pr. Edw. Co. (VGPI 11 Aug 95)

MORRIS, James, Welsh svt., ran away from William BYRD's at Westover; he is supposed to be gone towards Carolina (VG 27 Mar 52)

MORRIS, Moses Sr. Esq., mar. Miss Masey DICKINS, both of Amelia Co., on Tues. the 2nd. inst. (RMA 20 Aug 96)

MORRIS, Patrick, Irish svt., 20, ran away from the Potomac Co., Great Falls (VJAA 17 Aug 86)

MORRIS, Sylvanus, of Hanover Co., dec'd (VG 3 Jul 46)

MORRIS, Thomas, of [Norfolk], dec'd, e.a.w. Mr. Hillary BUTT; his admr. is Ruth MORRIS (NPC 24 Apr 90)

MORRIS, Will, Negro, c. 40, ran away from the schooner *Amelia* lying at Portsmouth (VG 4 Oct 70)

MORRIS, William, late of Henrico Co., dec'd, e.a.w. his ex., Joseph SHEPHERD (VGPu 6 Jun 77); e.a.w. Benjamin SHEPPARD [sic] of Henrico Co., acting ex. of Joseph SHEPPARD dec'd, who was MORRIS' ex. (VGRMA 19 Jan 95)

MORRIS, William, dec'd, e.a.w. his admr., Henry MORRIS Jr. of Brunswick Co. (VGPu 10 Jul 78)

MORRISON, Alexander, appr. saddler, 17-18, ran away from Henry FRIDLEY, Winchester (BVCG 19 Feb 96)

MORRISON, Andrew, Berkeley Co. Ct., 26 Mar. 1795, in chanc: James WINNING (compl.) vs. Nathaniel MORRISON, devisee of Andrew MORRISON dec'd, and Thomas JONES (defs.) (PGBA 9 May 95)

MORRISON, Clowd, Scot, ind. svt., shoemaker, ran away from Elias BARNABY and Archibald MIDLEMIST, Petersburg (VG 2 May 77)

MORRISON, Henry, Irish svt., ran away from William WILLCOCK and James TAYLOR, Wmsbrg.; he may be headed north (VG 8 Aug 51)

MORRISON, John, Clerk of the Ct. of Pr. Geo. Co., d. last week (VGPI 18 Mar 90)

MORSE, James, of this town [Fredsbrg.], d.last Tues. eve. (RCFPC 23 Nov 96)

MORSON, Arthur Esq., d.Wed. last at his seat in Stafford Co. (VHFA 2 Jun 98)

MORTIMER, Charles, intends to leave Norfolk (HNPA 24 Jan 95)

MORTIMER, Capt. John, came from Rathmilton in the north of Ireland a few months ago to buy some land; he d. on the 14th inst. [later corrected to 4 Nov.] at the seat of Landon CARTER Esq. in Pr. Wm. Co. (VG 17 Nov 74, 8 Dec 74)

MORTON, Henry, of Petersburg, d. on Wed. night (VGPI 5 Aug 96)

MORTON, Jane, of Fairfax Co., dec'd, e.a.w. her admr., Arch. MORTON (CMAG 11 Mar 97)

MORTON, Jeremiah, merch., mar. Miss Mildred JACKSON dau. of the late William JACKSON Esq. dec'd. (VHFA 12 Jan 92)

MORTON, John, of Kg. Geo. Co., murdered about three weeks ago by one of his slaves (VGRMA 9 Mar 95, VGPI 13 Mar 95, VHFA 19 Mar 95); his admrs., George, Robert, and Joseph MORTON, will sell eight of his slaves in Kg. Geo. Co. (VHFA 14 Aug 95)

MORTON, Joseph Gent., of James City Co., dec'd, his slaves to be sold by his ex.

(nfi) (VG 9 Nov 69, VGR 30 Nov 69); his manor plant. in James City Co. on the Chickahominy River as well as several other nearby tracts to be sold by his ex., Jonathan BECKWITH (VG 19 Apr 70)
MORTON, Robert B. and Robert B. [sic], as acting exors. for Joseph MORTON of Mason Co., Ky., adv. that on 15 Oct. 1794, Robert B. MORTON, Joseph MORTON, George MORTON, and John MORTON passed four bonds to Christopher McCONNICO; they forewarn all persons from taking an assignment of the bonds as they are determined not to pay them as McCONNICO has no right to the land sold them (VHFFA 26 May 97)
MOSBY, Benjamin, mar. Miss Polly CROUCH on Mon. eve. (VGGA 29 Mar 97, Arg 31 Mar 97)
MOSBY, Benjamin Jr., son of Littlebury MOSBY, aged 19, drowned in the James River in Cumberland Co. [long obit.] (VG 18 May 69)
MOSBY, Mrs. Hannah, consort of Col. Littlebury MOSBY of Powhatan Co., d. on Sat. the 9th inst. [obit.] (VGRMA 21 Aug 94)
MOSBY, Capt. Littlebury Jr., mar. Miss Mary P. HASKINS, both of Powhatan Co., on Thurs. the 3rd. inst. (VIC 9 Dec 89)
MOSBY, Samuel, mar. Miss Polly ANDERSON, both of Richmond, on Thurs. eve. last (VGRMA 2 Jun 94)
MOSBY, Wade, of Powhatan Co., mar. Miss Sukey TRUE[HEA]RT of Hanover Co. (VGAA 23 Apr 85)
MOSELEY Family, Norfolk Borough, Ct. of Q.S., 27 Aug. 1798, in chanc: Anthony WALKE, John LAWRENCE, and Alexander MOSELEY exors. of Anthony WALKE dec'd (pltfs.) against William Francis BICKERTON ex. of William BOWDOIN dec'd and Edward Hack MOSELEY ex. of Edward Hack MOSELEY dec'd (defs.) (NH 13 Sep 98)
MOSELEY, Capt. Andrew, of Henrico Co., d. when thrown from his horse (VG 15 Oct 36)
MOSELEY, Basset, of Norfolk, dec'd, e.a.w. his admr., Alexander MOSELEY (VCNPGA 5 Apr 94)
MOSELEY, Col. Edward H., of Pr. Anne Co., for many yrs. a magistrate and rep. of his co. and an officer of the customs in the Lower District of James River, d. on the 27th ult. (VGWeA 16 Nov 82)
MOSELEY, Col. Edward Hack Jr. Esq., one of the reps. for Pr. Anne Co., mar. Miss Patsy WESTWOOD of Elizabeth City Co., on Thurs. the 24th ult. (VG and VGR 3 Mar 74)
MOSELEY, Elizabeth the Elder and the Younger, e.a.w. the ex., William WHITE, Norfolk Co. (AGNPPA 21 Apr 95)
MOSELEY, Mrs. Frances, d. last Sat. (HNPA 1 Apr 95)
MOSELEY, Joseph, late of Buckingham Co., dec'd, e.a.w. his ex., Robert and Daniel MOSELEY (VGGA 21 Mar 98)
MOSELEY, Matthew, son of Anthony MOSELEY, came over from Eng. in 1734; if he or his chil. are alive and apply to Bassett and Alexander MOSELEY, Norfolk, they may hear something to their advantage (VGR 12 May 68)
MOSLEY, Francis, late of Buckingham Co., e.a.w. his ex., Edward MOSLEY and Thomas SANDERS (VGIC 13 Dec 83)
MOSS, Henry, free Negro, 42, b. a free Negro in one of the lower counties of this state, arrived in Winchester last Fri. eve. on his way to Philadelphia; his father was black and his mother a mulatto but he has turned white; he was in the Virginia Line in the late war (BVCG 1 Jul 96)
MOSS, James, dec'd, e.a.w. his admr., William BETHELL Jr. of Henrico Co. (VGRMA 1 Sep 94); his admr. will sell his land in New Kent and Goochland Cos. (VGGA 8 Apr 95, RMA 30 May 95)
MOSS, John, svt., ran away from William FOSTER, Botetourt Co. (VG 7 Oct 73)
MOSS, John, dark mulatto, 22, shoemaker and cooper, absconded from Powhatan Co. with Maryann SCOTT the wife of Henry MOSS, who suspects he may be lurking about Wmsbrg., York, or Queen's Cr. and will probably make for the Eastern Shore (VGWeA 26 Apr 83)
MOSS, Robert, of Yorktown, dec'd, tailor, e.a.w. his widow and admx., Julia, who intends for Eng. as soon as she can settle her affairs (VG 27 Dec 51)

MOSS, Thomas, Negro, ind. to Lawrence EGMOND, 25-26, ran away from the plant. of William LIGHTFOOT in Charles City Co. and it is supposed he is gone towards Newcastle as he has a wife there (VG 19 Jul 54)
MOSSOM, the Rev. David, dec'd, his 240 ac. plant. on Pamunkey River in New Kent Co. to be sold by his ex., George WEBB, William CLAYTON, and Lewis WEBB (VG 20 Aug 67)
MOULSON, Mrs. Mary, of Amelia Co., dec'd, her admr., Richard EGGLESTON, will sell her livestock etc. (VGRMA 8 Dec 94)
MOULSON, William, of Amelia Co., died (VG 4 Mar 75); e.a.w. William GILES and Richard EGGLESTON Sr. (VGPu 28 Nov 77)
MOUNSEY, Miss, milliner, lately from England, has a large assortment of millinery for sale at the house of John WISE, Alexandria (CMAG 27 Feb 96)
MOUNTAIN, Robert, married with one child, adv. that he is an Eng. farmer who has been in America upwards of eight yrs.; he worked in East Jersey for four yrs. and served Lewis BURWELL Esq. of Gloucester Co.; he desires employment (VG 2 Dec 73)
MOUTER, Mr., of N. Carolina, mar. Miss SOUTHALL younger daughter of Col. James SOUTHALL in Wmsbrg., on Sat. last (VGGA 13 Jun 92)
MOWAT, Commodore H., d. on the 14th inst. of an apoplectic fit as he was giving orders on the quarterdeck of H.M.S. *Assistance* (under his command); he was bur. at Hampton on Tues. last (NH 19 Apr 98)
MOXLEY, [?], a child of William MOXLEY of this co. [Spotsylvania], died Mon. last (VHFA 18 Sep, 25 Sep 88)
MOXLEY, Elijah, appr., c. 11, ran away from the sloop *Saucy Fox*, Norfolk (AGGA 16 Sep 96)
MOXLEY, Daniel, appr., ran away from Joseph FULLMER, Alexandria on 4 Sep. 1789 (VGAxA 7 Jan 90)
MOXLEY, John, dec'd, sold a tract of land in Hampshire Co. to Conrad MYRE (VJAA 5 Oct 86)
MOXLEY, Thomas, of Alexandria, dec'd, two of his houses in Alexandria to be rented out by his admx., Hester MOXLEY (VJAA 26 Jul 87)
MOXLY, William, adv. that he and Anne MOXLY have separated by mutual consent and that she is not deemed by him as his wife (TAA 18 May 98)
MUIR, Mr., his body was found bur. near the house of William JONES of Pr. Geo. Co.; it was believed that he was murdered by JONES and one ABBETT (VGPI 26 Oct 86)
MUIR, Gilbert, traveling merch., left Wmsbrg. on 3 Mar. 1785 for Baltimore, but being then in a bad state of health and never hearing from him since, it is supposed he is dead (VGAA 14 Jun 86)
MUIR, John, dec'd, est. accounts for him and for Robert MUIR dec'd, to be settled with Eliz. MUIR of Alexandria the extx. of John (VGAxA 12 May 91)
MUIR, Robert, of Alexandria, d. suddenly (VJAA 21 Dec 86)
MULHALL, Thomas, svt., laborer, ran away from the snow *John* lying in Hampton Road (VGAA 17 Apr 84)
MULLEN, Arthur, aka Hobble DAVIS, Irish svt., 22, ran away from the Potomac Co., Great Falls (VJAA 15 Jun 86)
MULLEN, John, Eng., soldier in the 12th Co. of Infantry, 3rd Sub-Legion, committed suicide on 10 Jun. (VGRMA 22 Jul 93)
MULLIN, William, of Stafford Co., d. on 28 Aug. in Middlesex Co., aged 57 (VHFA 8 Sep 91)
MULLINS, Henry, dec'd, his ex., John MULLINS and Conoly MULLINS of Goochland Co., will sell all of his Negroes and rent his plant. about three miles from Cartersville (VGGA 9 Oct 98)
MULLOY, Capt. John, of Liverpool, dec'd, e.a.w. Peter LYON of Hanover Co., the att. for the exors. (VG 12 Nov 67)
MULRAIN, Thomas, svt., c. 25, b. in St. Kitts in the West Indies but chiefly bred in Scotland, ran away from Batholomew [sic] FRYATT, Frederick Co. (VGR 12 Jul 70)
MULRAIN, Thomas, cabinetmaker, c. 45, reportedly obtained a horse from the 10-11 year old son of Edward FLOOD living near Bruce's Mill, in a

clandestine manner (BVCG 27 May 93)

MUMFORD, Robert, late of Amelia Co., dec'd, e.a.w. his ex., Vivion BROOKING (VGPI 26 Oct 86)

MUMFORD, Thomas, of Amelia Co., dec'd, e.a.w. his ex., Samuel BOOKER and Thomas MUMFORD (VGAA 25 Jun 85)

MUNFORD, Edward, of Dinwiddie Co., dec'd, 12 of his slaves to be sold by Joshua POYTHRESS and George TURNBULL his admrs. (VG 30 Nov 59)

MUNFORD, John, late a merch. of Fredsbrg., d. last Sat. in Alexandria (VHFA 3 Aug 98)

MUNFORD, Capt. Theodorick, d. at Col. John BANISTER's in Dinwiddie (VG 8 Oct 72); e.a.w. his ex., Robert MUNFORD, Theodorick BLAND, and John BANISTER (VG 19 Nov 72); Robert MUNFORD of Mecklenburg Co. adv. that all persons having demands against the est. should apply to him (VGPu 4 Jul 77 sup)

MUNFORD, William G. Esq., of Charles City Co., died (VGAA 5 Apr 86)

MUNRO, Hugh, merch., of the house of Gilbert Robinson & Munro of Norfolk, d. on 23 Mar. last at Port-au-Prince (NH 11 Apr 96)

MUNROE, George, appr. house carpenter, ran away from Joseph FULLMER (VJAA 27 Apr 86)

MURCHIE, Matthew, of Manchester, d. on Sun. eve. last (RMA 17 Aug 96)

MURDOCK, Capt. John, dec'd, slaves bel. to his est. to be sold in Fauquier Co. by his admr., William BRONAUGH (VGR 28 Jul 68)

MURDOCK, Joseph, mar. Miss Elizabeth SPAIN in Petersburg, on Thurs. last (VGPI 21 Mar 97)

MURDY, George, Irish svt., weaver, c. 20, ran away from George SELL, Frederick Co., Md. (VGPu 8 Mar 76)

MURPHEY, Mrs., spouse of Martin MURPHEY, Norfolk, died (NPC 9 Apr 91)

MURPHEY, Anne, wife of James MURPHEY, left his plant. in Lunenburg Co. in a clandestine manner the morn. of 5 Jun. (VG 12 Jun 52)

MURPHEY, James, svt., laborer, ran away from the snow *John* lying in Hampton Road (VGAA 17 Apr 84)

MURPHEY, John, Eng. conv. svt., ran away from John MAY, Botetourt Co. (VG 11 Nov 75)

MURPHREE, James, late of Southampton Co., dec'd, but formerly of Norfolk Borough, e.a.w. his extx., Susannah MURPHREE (VGAA 12 Oct 82)

MURPHY, Bartholomew, Irish svt., 20, ran away from Daniel ROBERDEAU of Alexandria (VJAA 13 Jan 85)

MURPHY, Daniel, Irish, soldier in Col. HARRISON's Regt. of Artillery, des. from Gosport (VGPu 14 Nov 77)

MURPHY, George, native of Pa., tanner, his relations are supposed to live near the Sweet Springs, d. on his passage from Cape François to Norfolk on 7 Oct.; for 18 months past he worked at Mr. CLEMENT's tanyard in Portsmouth (NH 5 Nov 99)

MURPHY, James, Irish svt., tailor, c. 30, ran away from George LONG, Fredsbrg. (MG 25 Apr 54)

MURPHY, James, butcher, dec'd, e.a.w. his admr., Francis HYLAND, Richmond (VGRMA 19 May 94)

MURPHY, Jeremiah, svt., 25, imp. in Baltimore last May, ran away from Hugh STEUART (VJAA 11 Nov 94)

MURPHY, John, Irish conv. svt., joiner, speaks proper Eng., has been upon the stage and appears to be the complete gentleman, ran away from John PATTERSON, Alexandria (MG 14 Aug 60)

MURPHY, John, native of Armagh, Ireland, 26, des. from a co. of recruits of the 2nd Regt. of Art. and Eng. (VGGA 22 Mar 99)

MURRAY Family, HCC, 1 Jun. 1796: James ROSE and Co. (pltfs.) against William MURRAY ex. of John MURRAY, and William MURRAY, James MURRAY, and John MURRAY devisees of the sd. John MURRAY (VGGA 3 Aug 96)

MURRAY Family, HCC, 6 Oct. 1796, between William ALLEN (pltf.) and William MURRAY the Elder surviving ex. of John MURRAY dec'd, James

MURRAY, William MURRAY the Younger, and John MURRAY infants by William MURRAY the Elder their gdn., Jesse BROWN, and Margaret MURRAY another infant by the sd. William MURRAY the Elder her gdn. (defs.); it appears that the def. William MURRAY is not an inhabitant of this country (VGGA 1 Feb 97)

MURRAY, Francis, Irish svt., 25, ran away from the Potomac Co., Great Falls, supposedly with Daniel CRONEAN, 25, and his wife (VJAA 13 Jul 86)

MURRAY, George, mar. Miss Olivia LOWRY, both of [Alexandria] (VGAxA 12 Jan 92)

MURRAY, Maj. George, d. a few days ago in Frederick Co. (BVCG 16 Jun 94)

MURRAY, George, dec'd, his admx. (nfi) will sell his HH & KF at his plant. near Greenway Court (BVCG 1 Dec 94)

MURRAY, Hanson, an ind. appr., 16, ran away from Henry NICHOLSON (CMAG 28 Feb 99)

MURRAY, James, dec'd, his 2500 ac. tract near Genitoe Bridge, Amelia Co., to be sold by his ex., James MURRAY of Pr. Geo. Co. and John MURRAY (VG 2 Apr, 20 Aug 67)

MURRAY, James Esq., Capt. of His Britannic Majesty's Corps of Queen's Rangers, d. on Mon. last in his 31st year (Norfolk disp. of 1 Apr.) (VGWeA 9 Apr 89)

MURRAY, John, dec'd, e.a.w. his admr., William ROAN and Rachel MURRAY (VGR 26 Oct 69)

MURRAY, John, Irish svt., 21-23, stocking weaver, ran away from Marcus STEPHENSON, Berkeley Co. (VG 23 Sep 75)

MURRAY, John, of Mecklenburg Co., dec'd, his ex., William MURRAY and William YATES, will sell several of his Negroes and other items bel. to his est. (VGAA 26 Oct 82, 8 Nov 83)

MURRAY, John, merch., of Alexandria, mar. Miss Patty M'CLENACHAN (VJAA 11 Jan 87)

MURRAY, Mary, aka CLARK, aka ATKINS, executed near Wmsbrg. on 23 May (VG 23 May 55)

MURRAY, Michael, Irish conv., 21, ran away from Edward STEVENSON, Little Pipe Cr., Frederick Co., Md. (VG 11 Jun 67)

MURRAY, Nancy, Irish svt., 33-34, ran away from James COLLINS living near the Old Courthouse (VJAA 29 Jun 86)

MURRAY, Peter, a young gentleman, d. on Tues. last (TDCDA 28 Nov 99)

MURRAY, Robert, merch., d. on Sun. morn. last; he had been a resident of Manchester for several yrs. (VIC 5 Mar, VGWeA 6 Mar, NPJ 12 Mar 88)

MURRAY, Capt. William, of Pr. Geo. Co., mar. Miss BOLLING of Chesterfield Co. (VG 27 Nov 79)

MURRAY, William, tailor, of Fredsbrg., d. on 26 Jan. (VHFA 27 Jan 91)

MURRAY, William, dec'd, his admr., Jas. MURRAY of Caroline Co., will sell two tracts of his land in Caroline Co. near Port Royal (VHFFA 27 Jun 97)

MURRAY, William Yates, printer, of Fredsbrg. (?), a young man, d. on Sat. last (VGPI 11 Oct 96, VHFFA 14 Oct 96)

MURRELL, John, brother of Sarah MURRELL late of Gloucester Co., will receive a legacy from her est. (VGR 27 Jan 74)

MURROE, John, Irish svt., ran away from Matthew KENNER Jr., Northumberland Co. (VG 10 Nov 38)

MURRY, George, Irish svt., 27, tinman and coppersmith, ran away from Thomas WILKINSON, Alexandria (VJAA 29 Mar 87)

MURRY, James, svt., 32-35, ran away from the Potomac Co., Great Falls (VJAA 18 May 86, 15 Jun 86)

MUSE Family, HCC, 8 Mar. 1799: William FOUSHEE (pltf.) and Lawrence MUSE and Jane his wife, Thomas ROANE and Mary Elizabeth Mills his wife, and Hudson MUSE and James GREGORIE (defs.); it appears that James GREGORIE is not an inhabitant of the country (Ex 19 Apr 99)

MUSE, Mrs. Ann, formerly THOMPSON, a tavern in Westmoreland Co. to be rented or leased for and during her life by Wm. NELSON (VHFFA 22 Dec 95)

MUSE, Hudson Esq., Collector for the Port of Tappahannock, mar. Miss Agnes

NEILSON at Urbanna on Thurs. eve. 30 Dec. 1790 (VGGA 19 Jan 91, VHFA 27 Jan 91); d. lately in Middlesex Co. (VH 5 Jul 99); his admrs. w.w.a., Thomas and Elliott MUSE, will sell all his PE at his seat, Hampstead (VH 8 Nov 99, Ex. 15 Nov, 6 Dec 99)

MUSE, Capt. James, dec'd, his admrs. w.w.a., Richard and James MUSE, will sell his tract of 137 ac. in Westmoreland Co. (VHFA 4 Jul 93)

MUSE, Lawrence, of Tappahannock, mar. Mrs. Jane SOUTHALL at Urbanna on the 1st inst. (VGGA 19 Jun 93, VGRMA 24 Jun 93, VHFA 27 Jun 93)

MUSGROVE, Eliphalet(h), of James City Co., was executed near Wmsbrg. on 6 May for murder (VGR 6 May 73, VG 3 Jun 73)

MYERS Family, the co-partnership of Samuel MYERS and brothers will be dissolved by mutual consent on 6 Aug. next; /signed/ Samuel MYERS, M. M. MYERS, and Samson MYERS (VGGA 21 Jun 97)

MYERS, Christopher, [dec'd], e.a.w. W. W. Williams and Co., his admrs., of Matildaville (CMAG 27 Feb 98)

MYERS, Isaac, appr., 18, ran away from Anthony CRUM, Frederick Co. (BVCG 11 Jun 92)

MYERS, Jacob Esq., of Baltimore, was mar. to Miss Liza ROSS eld. dau. of David ROSS Esq. of Cobham, on the eve of the first inst., by the Rev. Dr. HOPKINS (VGGA 10 May 97)

MYERS, Mrs. Jane, widow of the late Capt. Christopher MYERS formerly Engineer to the Potomac Co., has been encouraged by the directors and a number of her husband's friends to open a tavern in the house occupied by him at the Great Falls; she intends to open it in the second week of Sep. (CMAG 27 Aug 99)

MYERS, John, mar. Mrs. Margaret BOWYER relict of Henry BOWYER dec'd, both of this town, on Thurs. eve. (CMAG 16 Nov 99)

MYERS, Peter, dec'd, e.a.w. his ex., Matthew MYERS of Wmsbrg. (VGWeA 16 Dec 91)

MYERS, Mrs. Sarah, consort of Samuel MYERS of Petersburg, d. on Mon. last (RMA 15 Oct 95)

MYERS, Solomon M., merchant, died (VGPI 17 Nov 91)

MYLES, George, Berkeley Co. Ct., 23 Aug. 1793, in chanc: George MYLES eld. son and heir at law of George MYLES dec'd (compl.) against David WATKINS, Jane LOGAN widow, extx., and devisee of James LOGAN dec'd, Bryan BRUIN, and James WILSON (defs.); it appears that BRUIN and WATKINS are not inhabitants of the commonwealth (PGBA 9 Sep 93)

MYNER, John, appr., tailor, 16, ran away from Adam YOUNG (VGWA 19 Nov 91)

NAILOR, Barton, appr. to James REED of Loudoun Co., ran away on 20 Jun. (VCWM 19 Nov 88)

NAIRNE, Alexander, dec'd, his ex., George MURRAY of Fredsbrg., will settle his est. (VHFA 12 Oct 98)

NALLE, Martin, dec'd, his land in Culpeper Co. to be sold by William NALLE (nfi) (VHFA 23 Jul 89)

NANCE, Mrs. Mary Ann, dau. of Adam LINDSEY of Norfolk, d. in her 19th year (VCGA 14 Aug 94)

NAPIER, Thomas, of Fluvanna Co., intends moving to Georgia soon (VGAA 1 Nov 83)

NASH Family, Pr. Edw. Co. Ct., 17 Nov 1794, in chanc: Thomas READ and Mary READ ex. and extx. of Clement READ the Younger dec'd (pltfs) against Alfred MOORE ex. etc. of Francis NASH and John NASH Sr. ex. etc. of John NASH dec'd (defs.) (VGGA 31 Dec 94)

NASH, Abner Esq., of Pr. Edw. Co., mar. Miss Matilda PENN dau. of Col. Gabriel PENN of Amherst Co., on Thurs. the 12th ult. (VGGA 1 Aug 92)

NASH, John, dec'd, e.a.w. his admr., Samuel HATTON of Indian Cr. (NH 5 May 96); his admr. will sell 240 ac. of his land in Norf. Co. (NHPA 15 Jul 97)

NASH, Thomas Sr., dec'd, e.a.w. his ex., Thos. and Wm. NASH (NH 13 Jun 96)

NASH, William, Eng. svt., bricklayer, ran away from John WILLIS,

Brunswick Co. last March (VG 9 May 45)

NASH, William, appr., 17, ran away from Thomas WILKINSON, Alexandria (VJAA 15 Jul 84)

NATTALL, Thomas, brother of Matthias NATTALL of Gloucester Co. (VG 16 May 71)

NEAL, John, of Lunenburg Co., dec'd, e.a.w. David ABBERNATHA and P. POINTDEXTER of Mecklenburg Co.,the acting exors. (VGPI 9 Feb 96)

NEAL, Lewis, appr., c. 19, ran away from Nathaniel SHEPARD, Richmond (RC 4 Jun 96)

NEALE, Mrs. Anne (or LADBROOK), from Daventry in Northamptonshire, left London on 3 Feb. 1713; about three yrs. ago she was known to live with a lady on Bristol or Rappahannock River in Va.; if she will apply herself to the printer she will meet with a letter from her brother, John NEALE, which contains something to her advantage (MG 9 Jun 30)

NEALE, Edward, Irish svt., barber, ran away from John STEVENSON, Baltimore, Md. and is believed gone to Va. (VG 6 Jul 69)

NEALE, Mrs. Elizabeth, of Warwick Co., d. in her 22nd year after a short illness (VGP 9 Mar 75)

NEALE, Thomas, dec'd, his widow and extx., Anne NEALE, adv. that he d. intestate (VIC 26 Aug 89)

NEALE, William, Irish svt., ran away from William FICKLIN, Kg. Geo. Co. (VG 18 Sep 46)

NEALE, William, dec'd, 1800 ac. of his land in Orange and Spotsylvania Cos. to be sold by his ex., Thomas ROSE (VGR 1 Jun 69 sup)

NEAVERS, John, Eng. svt., ran away from Thomas BLINCOE and Hardage LANE, Loudoun Co. (VG 18 Jan 70)

NEAVES, Christian, extx. of William NEAVES dec'd of Goochland Co. (VGR 16 Jun 68)

NEBAKER, George, d. on Sun. last in Petersburg (VGPI 11 Jul 97); the co-partnership of Clarke & Nebaker was dissolved on 10 Aug. due to his death, acc. to an advertisement by William CLARKE the surviving partner (VGPI 1 Sep 97)

NECKS, Capt. Robert, commander in the Va. trade for many yrs., lately arrived from London, d. at Norfolk (VG and VGP 29 Sep 74)

Negro Tom, to have been executed this day, is reprieved (RJDA 17 Jul 95)

Negroes Released by the French Legion: Negroes delivered up by Gen. CHOISY, Commander of the French Legion, to Col. Thomas READ of Charlotte Co. and sent to Richmond: David COLE, 34, of New York, says he is free; John COLE, 26, of New York, says he is free; Charles SCOTT, 23, says he bel. to Chastaine COCKE of Amelia Co.; John JACK, 20, says he is free (VGWeA 30 Mar 82)

NEIL, Abraham, mar. Miss Rachel WOODROW, on Thurs. eve. (WVGWA 24 Jul 90, VGWA 28 Jul 90)

NEILL, Joseph, of Frederick Co., dec'd, e.a.w. his ex., Lewis NEILL and John M'PHERSON (BVCG 8 Apr 96)

NEILSON, Charles Esq., of Middlesex Co., dec'd, his admr., W. FOUSHEE of Richmond, will sell a number of his Negroes in Richmond and in Urbanna and will also settle his est. (VGAA 7 Jan 86)

NEILSON, Mrs. Charlotte, of Middlesex Co., dec'd, her est. will be sold by her admr. w.w.a., W. FOUSHEE (VGGA 10 Aug 91)

NEILSON, John, d. on Fri. the 5th inst. at Mount Hermon, Kg. Geo. Co. in his 40th year; he was bur. at Falmouth where he had resided as a merch. above 20 yrs. (VG 11 Jul 71)

NEILSON, John, merch. in Dumfries, died (VG 22 Oct 72)

NELMES, David, infant, orphan of David NELMES; his gdn. is Archibald NELMES who was a pltf. in a Nansemond Co. chancery case against James BEST and Susanna his wife (who are apparently not residents of Va.), James HAMMON and Eleanor his wife, Demsey MURPHEY and Rachel his wife, and Sarah and Mary NELMES (VCGA 31 Jul 94)

NELMES, Thomas, appr., 20, ran away from Robert BORLAND joiner and

cabinetmaker, Portsmouth (NPJ 23 Apr 88, VIC 30 Apr 88)
NELSON, Hugh Esq., second son of His Hon. the President, mar. Miss Judy PAGE eld. dau. of the Hon. John PAGE Esq. (VG 16 May 71)
NELSON, Col. John, late of Louisa Co., dec'd, e.a.w. his admx., Rebecca NELSON (VGGA 20 Jul 91)
NELSON, Mrs. Lucy, lady of the Hon. Thomas NELSON Esq. of York Co., died (VG 17 Feb 81)
NELSON, Nathaniel Esq., mar. Miss Jeanie PAGE third dau. of the late Hon. John PAGE of North River (VGPu 12 Jun 78)
NELSON, Nathaniel Esq., of Yorktown, d. at Bermuda (VGGA 26 Jul 86)
NELSON, Nelly, wife of John of Pr. Wm. Co., who will no longer pay her debts (VG 26 Jan 52)
NELSON, Robert, of Yorktown, mar. Miss Molly GRYMES third dau. of the Hon. Philip GRYMES Esq. dec'd (VG 27 Oct 74)
NELSON, Thomas, merch., d. last Mon. at his house in Yorktown in a good old age; he had lived there 40 yrs. (VG 10 Oct 45)
NELSON, Thomas, late of Kg. Wm. Co., dec'd, his exors., William NELSON, Thomas NELSON, and J. NELSON, will sell several pieces of his land in Yorktown (VIC 2 Apr, 30 Apr 88)
NELSON, Gen. Thomas, of York Co., former governor of Va., d. at his seat in Hanover Co. on Sun. the 4th inst. [or 14 Jan. acc. to VCWM] (VIC 14 Jan 89, VGWeA and VHFA 15 Jan 89, NPJ 21 Jan 89, VCWM 28 Jan 89); his heirs and devisees, William NELSON Jr., Thomas NELSON Jr., Philip NELSON, Francis NELSON, and Hugh NELSON Jr., will sell 8000 ac. of his land in Hanover Co. (VGGA 26 Feb 94, VHFA 27 Mar 94)
NELSON, Thomas Jr. Esq., capt. in the 1st Va. Regt., mar. Miss Sally CARY eld. dau. of Wilson Miles CARY Esq. of Fluvanna Co. (VGPu 25 Sep 77)
NELSON, William, eld. son of Thomas NELSON merch. in York Co., mar. Miss Elizabeth BURWELL at Mrs. PAGE's in Gloucester Co. yesterday sennight (VG 10 Feb 38)
NELSON, the Hon. William Esq., President of H.M's Council of Va., d. on 19 Nov. at his house in York Co. in his 61st year (VG and VGR 19 Nov 72); e.a.w. Thomas NELSON, Thomas NELSON Jr., Hugh NELSON, and Ro. C. NICHOLAS (VG 15 Jul 73)
NELSON, William, of Gildersom near Leeds in Great Britain, d. in Pr. Geo. Co. on 30 Oct. 1775; Peter WILLIAMS (nfi) has his books, papers, and effects (VG 25 Nov 75, VGP 30 Nov 75)
NELSON, William Jr. Esq., Clerk of Caroline Co., mar. Miss Lucy CHISWELL (VG 29 Nov 70); he and his new married lady appeared in Stratton Major Church, K & Q Co., for the first time since their marriage on 25 Nov. (VG 17 Jan 71)
NESBIT, Mary, Rockbridge Co., May Ct. 1797: John ROBINSON (compl.) against Samuel NESBIT and Mary his wife late Mary BERRY (defs.); it appears that the defs. are not inhabitants of this commonwealth (VGGA 7 Jun 97)
NESBITT, Hugh, late of Richmond, dec'd, e.a.w. Samuel MOSBY, sergeant (Arg 22 Nov 96)
NESTOR, Richard, of Portsmouth, died (NPC 24 Apr 90)
NETHERLAND, John, of Powhatan Co., adv. that his son, Littleberry NETHERLAND who is under 21, has a nervous complaint that impairs his faculties (VGGA 21 Nov 92)
NETHERLAND, Mrs. Mary, B. NETHERLAND of Fayette Co., Ky., agent for John NETHERLAND, adv. for several runaway slaves whom he believes are being detained at the instigation of Mrs. Mary formerly the wife of John NETHERLAND of Va. from whom she is separated (KG 8 Apr 97)
NETHERLAND, Wade, late of Cumberland Co., dec'd, e.a.w. Anne NETHERLAND (nfi) (VG 13 Jan 74)
NEVISON, the Rev. Mr. John, Rector of Meherrin Par., Brunswick Par., died (VG 13 Apr 69)
NEW, William, late of Henrico Co., dec'd, e.a.w. his admx., Mary NEW (VGAA

9 Jul 85); [his admx. named as Edith NEW in the VGAA issue of 23 Jul 85]

NEWBY, Edward, of Lancaster Co., d. Wed. last near Stephensburg, aged 23 (VGWA 15 Oct 91); Ozwald NEWBY will meet those indebted to his est. in Winchester on the first day of Jan. court (BVCG 19 Nov 92)

NEWBY, James, mar. Miss Betsy WALKER, Fredsbrg. (VHFA 15 Jan 89)

NEWCOMB, Jesse, of Petersburg, mar. Miss Margaret WILLOUGHBY of Norfolk (NH 24 Oct 99)

NEWEL, William, a soldier that marched out to S. Carolina, d. in camp and left about $100 with Capt. William FITZGERRALD, Amelia Co. (VG 16 Oct 79)

NEWHOUSE, Lewis, d. on Tues. eve. last at the seat of William ALEXANDER Esq. near this city [Richmond] on his return from Baltimore to Charleston, S. Carolina where he carried on an extensive mercantile trade; he was a native of Sweden and had held a commission in the Swiss Guards in the service of Louis XVI (VGRMA 10 Feb 94)

NEWLANDS, James, went from Glasgow five or six yrs. ago, c. 35, to one of H.M's plantations as an ind. svt.; he has lately succeeded to a considerable fortune; Alexander NEWLANDS, skinner, in Edinburgh seeks information on him (VG 21 Apr 38)

NEWMAN, Mr., fell off a ship at Blandford Wharf and was drowned on Tues. last (VSPW 4 Jun 95, VGPI 5 Jun 95)

NEWMAN, Michael, of Henrico Co., executed in Richmond on 5 Dec. for robbery (VGAA and VGWeA 6 Dec 83)

NEWMAN, Richard, Negro, 40-50, ran away from James LEWIS, Hanover Co. (VGGA 6 Jun 92)

NEWMAN, Susannah, of Richmond Co., d. lately at the Public Hospital for Lunatics (VG 1 Apr 80)

NEWMAN, Thomas, merch. of Yorktown, d. lately at Northampton Ferry on his way home from New York (VGGA 28 Feb 98); e.a.w. his admx., Martha NEWMAN, and admrs., Corbin GRIFFIN and Charles YOUNG, who will sell all his PE including a sloop, slaves, wet and dry goods at York[town] and all the wet and dry goods in his store at Gloucester Ct. H. (VGGA 24 Apr 98, NH 3 May 98)

NEWSAM, George and Edward SLATER, architects and builders from London and Dublin, have commenced business in Winchester (VGWA 7 Sep 87)

NEWSOM, Sally, has left her husband, Benjamin NEWSOM of Pr. Geo. Co. (VGPI 9 Feb 96)

NEWSUM, Mrs. Lucy, of Petersburg, d. a few days ago (VGPI 10 May 96)

NEWSUM, Robert, dec'd, his ex., Thomas BARRETT and Francis RUFFIN, will sell the rem. part. of his est. (VGPu 16 May 77 sup); e.a.w. his ex., Francis RUFFIN (VGPI 26 Jul 92)

NEWTON, Mrs., spouse to Andrew NEWTON merch. of Accomack Co., d. on Tues. the 22nd inst.; she was the dau. of Thomas GOLDIE of Mains dec'd, Keeper of and Writer to His Majesty's Signet in Edinburgh [obit.] (VGR 31 May 70)

NEWTON, Andrew Esq., Comptroller of the Customs for the Port of Accomack, died (VG 14 Apr 74)

NEWTON, George, conv. svt., farmer, b. in Yorkshire, imp. in the *Justitia* this spring; he has been in some office about the Custom House in London; ran off with a Negro man from James TUTT, Spotsylvania Co. (VGNI 15 Jun 75)

NEWTON, Henry, of Caroline Co., dec'd, e.a.w. his ex., Henry NEWTON (VHFA 12 Feb 95)

NEWTON, John, svt., c. 20, an Asiatic Indian by birth [or mulatto acc. to VGPu], has been in Va. about 12 mos. but claims to have lived in England 10 yrs. in the service of Sir Charles WHITWORTH; ran away from William BROWN, Pr. Wm. Co. (VG 13 Jul 76, VGPu 19 Jul 76)

NEWTON, Lemuel, d. at Kemp's Landing in Pr. Anne Co. (VG 22 May 79)

NEWTON, Mrs. Rebecca, of Pr. Anne Co., and formerly of Norfolk, died (VG 12 Feb 79)

NEWTON, Thomas, merch., late of Norfolk, dec'd, e.a.w. his admr., Thomas WRIGHT (HNPA 29 Oct 95, AGNPPA 30 Oct 95, NH 2 Jan 96, AGGA 17

May, 16 Sep 96)
NEWTON, Capt. Thomas Sr. Esq., d. at Norfolk on Sat. the 13th inst. in his 82nd year (HNPA 17 Dec 94, VGRMA 22 Dec 94, VGGA 24 Dec 94)
NEWTON, Capt. Willoughby, d. at his seat in Westmoreland Co. on the 11th inst.; had been a judge of the co. ct. for many yrs. (VGR 19 Feb 67); e.a.w. his ex., Richard LEE (VGR 23 Jul 67)
NICE, William, of Richmond, mar. Miss Nancy COLEMAN of Henrico on Thurs. last (VGRMA 11 Aug 94)
NICHOLAS, Maj. Abraham, former Adjutant General of the colony, d. last Sun. morn. (VG 8 Sep 38)
NICHOLAS, Mrs. Anne, relict of the late Hon. Robert Carter NICHOLAS Esq., d. yesterday [5 Dec.] at Wmsbrg. (VIC 6 Dec 86, VGIC 9 Dec 86, VGAA 13 Dec 86, VGPI 14 Dec 86)
NICHOLAS, Charles, svt., joiner, ran away from Lewis DEBNY, Wmsbrg. (AWM 18 May 21)
NICHOLAS, George Esq., Clerk of Dinwiddie Co., d. on Sat. 9 Mar. [obit. in VGR] (VG 14 Mar 71, VGR 21 Mar 71)
NICHOLAS, Col. George, of Va., mar. Polly SMITH dau. of John SMITH of Baltimore (MJ 5 Jan 79)
NICHOLAS, George, of Charlottesville, intends to remove to the district of Ky. next Feb.; persons having accounts to settle with him of with the est. of Robert C. NICHOLAS dec'd are desired to make application prior to that time (VIC 17 Sep 88, VGIC 25 Oct 88)
NICHOLAS, Col. George, Professor of Law and Politics at Transylvania Univ., d. in Lexington Ky. on the 25th ult. (VF 17 Aug 99, VH and VGGA 27 Aug 99, WG 28 Aug 99)
NICHOLAS, John, executed at the gallows near Wmsbrg. on 21 Nov. for murder (VG 21 Nov 55)
NICHOLAS, John Esq., Clerk of Dinwiddie, mar. Miss Dolly Pleasants BRIGGS eld. dau. of Gray BRIGGS (VGPu 18 Apr 77 sup)
NICHOLAS, John Esq., of Albemarle Co., mar. Miss Louisa CARTER of Wmsbrg. there on Thurs. last (VGWeA 7 Aug 88)
NICHOLAS, John the Elder, d. on Wed. 4 Nov. in his 75th year at his seat on James River in Buckingham Co. [obit. in RMA] (VGGA 11 Nov 95, RMA 12 Nov 95)
NICHOLAS, Philip Norborne Esq., of Richmond, mar. Miss Mary SPEAR of Baltimore, at Baltimore on the 11th inst. (Arg 26 Feb 99)
NICHOLLS, William, locksmith who served his time with John GOLAT, Fairfax Co., is suspected of stealing a horse from Stephen WEST, Pr. Geo. Co., Md.; NICHOLLS left a wife in the neighborhood; he was b. in England from which he was imp. (VG 29 Nov 76)
NICHOLS Family, Frederick Co. Ct., 5 Jun. 1799, in chanc: Joseph HARDEN and Daniel MAGRUDER (pltfs.) against Levi SMITH, William TALBOT, Hezekiah MAGRUDER and Susannah his wife late Susannah TALBOT, Isaiah NICHOLS, Benjamin NICHOLS, Edward NICHOLS, Nathan HARDEN and Rebecca his wife late Rebecca NICHOLS, Perry BELL and Elizabeth his wife late Elizabeth NICHOLS etc., Casandra NICHOLS, the sd. Casandra, Elizabeth, Rebecca, Benjamin, Isaiah, Samuel, and Daniel being the heirs or legal reps. of Susannah NICHOLS late Susannah TALBOT who together with the sd. Susannah and William are the heirs or other legal reps of Edward TALBOT dec'd (defs.) (WG 3 Jul 99)
NICHOLS, Nicholas, age 17, drowned in the Potomac at Georgetown last Thurs. (VJAA 14 Jun 87)
NICHOLSON, Daniel, dec'd, all his PE including blacksmith's tools to be sold at Rockett's by his admr., John NICHOLSON (OVT 7 Sep 97)
NICHOLSON, James, for many yrs. a steward and gardener at William and Mary College, died; his est. goes to his relations in Scotland (VG and VGR 28 Jan 73); e.a.w. his ex., Robert NICOLSON [sic], Wmsbrg. (VG 18 Feb 73)
NICHOLSON, John, merch., of Baltimore, mar. Miss Susanna PEACHEY dau. of Col. William PEACHEY of Milden Hall, Richmond Co., on 26 Apr.

(VHFA 14 May 89)
NICHOLSON, Joshua, dec'd, his snow to be sold in Norfolk by his ex., James NICHOLSON, William NICHOLSON, Matthew GODFREY and Daniel HUTCHINGS (VGR 24 Mar 68)
NICHOLSON, Robert, of Brunswick Co., d. on Sun. 6 Jun. in the flower of his age leaving a widow (VGR 1 Jul 73)
NICHOLSON, Robert, mar. Miss Betsey DYSON last Wed. (HNPA 21 Feb 95)
NICHOLSON, Robert, d. on Mon. eve. (HNPA 17 Dec 95); his ex., James DYSON Sr. of Norfolk, will sell all his PE (AGNPPA 22 Dec 95)
NICHOLSON, William, his heir at law is Thomas NICHOLSON; mentioned in the chanc. case of Andrew MARTIN against Alexander GORDON et al., Norfolk Co. Ct., 20 Mar. 1798 (NH 4 Apr 98)
NICOLSON, Henry, of Wmsbrg., d. on the 17th [inst.] (VGGA 28 Feb 98)
NICOLSON, Mrs. Martha, consort of William NICOLSON of this city, d. on Mon. last (VGGA 25 Jun 99)
NICOLSON, Robert, an old and highly respectable inhabitant of Wmsbrg., d. on Fri. last in [Richmond] (VGGA 19 Jul 97)
NICOLSON, William, dec'd, his admr., Max. HERBERT, will sell all of his HH & KF (NH 2 Nov 99)
NIGHSWONGER, John, of Frederick Co., dec'd, his plant. between Stephensburg and Strasburg will be sold by Peter NIGHSWONGER (nfi) (BVCG 12 Aug 96)
NIMMO, James, mar. Miss Elizabeth THOROWGOOD on Sun. the 4th inst.; she was from Pr. Anne Co. [also a poem commemorating the event] (VGNI 15 Jun 75)
NIMMO, William Esq., for many yrs. a rep. in the legislature of the state for Pr. Anne Co., d. on Wed. last at Kempsville (NH 26 Jan 99)
NISEWANGER, John, proposes moving to the Western Country in a short time (VCWM 7 Oct 89)
NIVES, William, svt., c. 20, ran away from William WITHERS, Fauquier Co. (VG 7 May 72)
NIVISON, William, dec'd, e.a.w. his admr., John NIVISON (NH 2 Mar 99)
NOBLE, Robert, aka Bob, Negro, c. 22, ran away from David ALLEN, Richmond (VGGA 7 May 99)
NOBLE, Thomas, late of Berkeley Co., dec'd, e.a.w. Joseph LAMAN of Darkville (PGBA 12 Jan 95)
NODEN, Charles, dec'd, his ex. (nfi) of Northampton, N. Carolina will sell 325 ac. of his land on the north side of the Roanoke River within three miles of Halifax Town (VG 4 Nov 75)
NOELL, Reuben, dec'd, e.a.w. his admr., Reuben GARNETT, Essex Co. (VGPu 22 Aug 77)
NOLAND, Philip Jr., dec'd, his land on Potomac River to be sold by Thomas NOLAND his ex.; his widow, Mary NOLAND, settles her right of dower (VJAA 22 Sep 85)
NOLAND, Thomas, Irish svt., 24-25, ran away from Richard ARELL, Alexandria (VG 23 May 71)
NOLLE, John, of Culpeper, dec'd, his PE to be sold by his ex., John and Francis NOLLE (VHFA 26 Mar 89)
NOONAN, William, native of Ireland, ran away from John BAIRD, Appomattox (VGNI 23 Feb 75)
NORMAN, Mrs. Frances, wife of Dr. Samuel NORMAN lately from Eng., d. in Alexandria (VJAA 30 Sep 84)
NORMAN, Ross, free Negro, condemned to death for a rape, to be executed on Fri. 6 Jun. (Winchester disp. of 6 May) (VGPI 9 Jun 97)
NORRIS, Alexander, Scot, svt., house carpenter, ran away from Reginald GRAHAM, Dumfries, who supposes he went to James River or Norfolk (VGPu 31 Mar 75)
NORRIS, Mrs. Sarah, relict of the late Joseph NORRIS dec'd, d. in Lancaster Co. on 30 Aug. in her 64th year (VH 9 Sep 97)
NORRIS, Septimus, mar. Miss Peggy BROWN on Thurs. last in Fauquier Co.,

both of that co. (VHFFA 10 Nov 95)
NORRIS, Septimus, d. at Fauquier Ct. House on Wed. morn. the 3rd. inst. [obit.] (VH 12 Apr 99)
NORRIS, Thomas, svt., tailor, ran away from Philip GRYMES, Brandon, was seen on the James River and may be headed for Carolina (VG 20 Feb 52)
NORRIS, William, mar. Miss Sally EVANS, Alexandria, on Tues. eve. last (VJAA 21 May 89)
NORTH, Joseph, merch. in Portsmouth, mar. Miss Polly PEART of Norfolk Co. (VGPu 12 Jun 78)
NORTH, Roger, of Staunton, merch., dec'd, e.a.w. his admx., Catherine NORTH (VG 14 Feb 77); his admx. will let his house and store on the main street in Staunton for a term of yrs. (VGPu 2 May 77, VG 8 Aug 77)
NORTHCOTT, Thomas, appr., 19-20, b. on the Western Branch, Norfolk Co., ran away from James WALKER, Norfolk (VGNI 28 Jul 74)
NORTHUP, Joseph, silk-dyer, late from Boston, has set up shop in Norfolk (VGR 12 Mar 72)
NORTON, Daniel Esq., merch., of Winchester, was mar. to Miss Caroline Henrietta TUCKER of Norfolk, by the Rev. Anthony WALKE, on Sat. eve. the 3rd. inst. at Norfolk (NPJ 7 Jan 89, VHFA 15 Jan 89, VCWM 21 Jan 89); plans to move from Winchester to Norfolk (BVCG 6 Aug 92); formerly of Winchester but late of Norfolk, merch., aged 31, d. on Sun. last [obit.] (HNPA 9 Nov 95)
NORTON, David, aka David, Negro, c. 20, ran away from Thomas HARDAWAY, Dinwiddie Co. (VGGA 23 Dec 95)
NORTON, John Hatley Esq., mar. Miss Sally NICHOLAS eld. dau. of Robert Carter NICHOLAS Esq., Treasurer of this colony (VG 30 Jan 72); mar. Miss Kitty BUSH (WVGWA 3 Apr 90); d. on Mon. last; the funeral sermon was preached by the Rev. [Alexander] BALMAIN (BVCG 14 Apr 97)
NORTON, Mrs. Sarah, dau. of the late Robert Carter NICHOLAS of Wmsbrg. and consort of John Harley NORTON of [Winchester], d. on Fri. the 5th inst., aged 35 yrs. and six months; her 10-year old dau., Sarah NORTON, d. 11 hours later (VGWA 12 Oct 87)
NORVELL, George, of Hanover Co., d. in his [93rd] year (VGAA 5 Apr 86)
NORVELL, William, dec'd, his admr., Reuben NORVELL, will sell all his PE at the late dwelling house of Martha NORVELL dec'd in Hanover Co. (VGGA 28 Feb 98)
NOUCHET, Peter, a handsome-faced French West Indian, not more than 20, is wanted for counterfeiting a check on the Baltimore Office of Discount and Deposit (PGBA 15 Dec 96, VGPI 16 Dec 96); acc. to a Baltimore disp. of 11 Sep., his trial took place on Fri. last and he was found guilty and sentenced to a year's imprisonment and a fine of £200 (TAA 13 Sep 97) [his name was also given as Peter NOTCHET and Peter NOUCHEL]
NOUGHTIE, James, Scot, svt., tailor, 22, ran away from Andrew CUBBIN, Petersburg (VG 20 Apr 69)
NOUGHTON, Thomas, Irish svt., ran away from John THOMPSON Jr., Pr. Edw. Co. (VGP 17 Nov 74)
NOURSE, James Esq., dec'd, bonds given at the sale of his personal effects come due in Nov. and may be paid to William NOURSE at Charlestown, Berkeley Co. (VJAA 6 Oct 85); his ex., Joseph NOURSE, James NOURSE, and William NOURSE, advise that they will apply to the GA for an act to enable them to sell a certain tract of land bel. to the est. of the dec'd in Berkeley Co. (VJAA 8 Dec 85)
NOWLING, Thomas, appr., c. 20, ran away from Francis BUTT, Norfolk; it is believed he has gone to his uncle's on the Eastern Shore (NHPA 31 Aug 97)
NOX, Sukey, her husband, Edward NOX, warns persons from entertaining or harboring her (VHFA 11 Sep 94)
NUCCLES, William, appr., c. 16, ran away from Joseph M'ADOMS, Amherst Co. (WG 11 Sep 99)
NUGENT, Andrew, Irish, house joiner, ind. svt., ran away from Stephen JOHNSTON, Fredsbrg. (VG 24 Oct 71)

NUGENT, James, aka James M'MULLEN, of Capt. ROGER's Troop of Horse, hanged in Pittsburgh on Sun. last for desertion and stealing a horse (Pitts. disp. of 6 Oct.) (AGNPWA 24 Oct 92)

NUNALLY, Daniel, of Chesterfield Co., died, aged 103 (VGPI 13 Mar 88)

NUNNELLEE, Bartlett, dec'd, his admr., Edward NUNNELLEE, will sell his real and PE (LWM 13 Nov 97)

NUTTLE, John, 21-22, was bred to the sea, des. from the co. of Capt. N. BURWELL of Continental Artillery who supposes he has gone to Philadelphia (VGPu 3 Oct 77)

O'BANNON, John, of Fauquier Co., dec'd, e.a.w. his ex., William O'BANNON (VGCD 18 Dec 79)

O'BRIAN, John, aka James BRENON, Irish ind. svt., b. in Dublin, c. 21, tailor, ran away from William DAVIS, Yorktown (VG 24 Jun 75, 24 Jan 77, VGPu 7 Feb 77)

O'BRYAN, Matthew, jailed in Halifax Co. on 14 Apr.; he is suspected of being Matthew THARP (q.v.) (VGR 6 May 73)

O'BRYAN, Patrick, of Pr. Wm. Co., executed near Wmsbrg. on 4 Jul. for felony (VG 4 Jul 66)

OCINHYSER, John, Dutch svt., baker, ran away from Peter BOWERS in Kg. Geo. Co. (VGPu 24 Feb 75)

O'CONNOR, Timothy, appr., c. 12, ran away from Solomon MARKS in Richmond who has information that he now sails in a vessel from Petersburg and Norfolk to Philadelphia and claims that he values himself much on being of the ancient and noble family of the O'Connors of Henrico Co. (RC 25 Mar 96)

O'FARRELL, John, merch., mar. Miss Polly SYLING of Martinsburg on Wed. last (VGWA 6 Jan 90)

OGILBY, Richard, of Amelia, dec'd, e.a.w. James HENDERSON his present acting ex., Powhatan (RMA 17 Sep 95)

OGLE, Benjamin Esq., of Berkeley Co., dec'd, e.a.w. William HARDAGE of Shenandoah Co. (VJAA 31 Mar 85)

OGLE, James, 20-25, jailed for horse stealing, escaped from Staunton jail on the 7th inst. (SVG 15 Aug 95, VGGA 19 Aug 95)

OGLE, Samuel Esq., bur. in the church in this city [Annapolis] on [5 May] (MG 3, 7 May 52, VG 29 May 52)

OGLE, Thomas, svt., shoemaker, claims to be English but appears to be Irish, ran away from Benjamin JOHNSON, Fredsbrg. (VGP 20 Oct 74)

OGLEVIE, Mrs., spouse of the Rev. Mr. OGLEVIE, d. Wed. last in this city (Richmond) (VGAA 2 Apr 85)

O'GRADY, Dr. William, of Norfolk, mar. Miss Polly CALVERT dau. of John CALVERT Esq. of Norfolk, at Kempsville in Pr. Anne Co. on Mon. last [23 Nov.] (AGNPPA 24 Nov 95, HNPA 30 Nov 95)

O'HARA, Patrick, Irish, 35, des. from the camp of the 8th U.S. Regt. near Winchester (WG 16 Oct 99)

O'HARROW, John, appr., 15, his father is Thomas O'HARROW who lives in Middlesex Co., ran away from John HAMILTON, Norfolk on 15 Jun. 1793 (HNPA 8 Apr 95)

O'LAUGHLIN, Cornelius, merch. of Winchester, mar. Miss Catherine "Kitty" HOOE [or HOWE acc. to BVCG] dau. of Col. John HOOE of Pr. Wm. Co. on 2 May at Swan Point (BVCG 13 May 93, VGAxA 16 May 93)

OLDERAGE, Godlip, svt., 28, ran away from Robert HUTCHINGS, Petersburg on 11 Aug. (VG 22 Sep 52)

OLDHAM, Capt. Samuel, of Kg. Wm. Co., d. on 25 Feb. aged 91; he was a judge and magistrate for many yrs. in Westmoreland and Kg. Geo. Cos. (VGPA 13 Mar 90)

OLFORD, Elizabeth, has left her husband, George OLFORD, of Shenandoah Co. (BVCG 16 Sep 96)

OLIVER, James, kept the Sign of the United States Arms in Winchester, was killed in a wagon accident while delivering goods to a merch. across the

Allegheny; his wife was ill after childbirth and her life is despaired of (BVCG 2 Mar 95, VHFA 12 Mar 95)

OLIVER, James, of Caroline Co., dec'd, his exors. (nfi) of Hanover Town will sell his PE (VGGA 16 Apr 99)

OLIVER, Joseph and John, sons of Joseph OLIVER and Mary KNAP of the Island of Guernsey, may hear of something to their advantage by applying to William FOSTER, surgeon, in Guernsey (VGGA 7 Dec 91)

OLIVER, Sarah, of Augusta Co., has eloped from her husband, John OLIVER (VIC 17 Dec 88)

OLIVER, Thomas, dec'd, his admx., Rachel OLIVER, will settle his accounts and will carry on as formerly both in the wet and dry good[s] line (RJDWA 26 May 96)

OLIVER, William, of Sussex Co., dec'd, his admr. is Edward ANDERSON (VGPI 9 Feb 96)

O'NEAL, Owen, Irish svt., 31, ran away from Henry M'CABE and Alexander M'INTYRE, Alexandria (VJAA 27 Apr 86)

O'NEAL, Thomas, dec'd, e.a.w. his ex., Henry PITTS (VH 12 Apr 99)

O'NEAL, Timothy, Irish svt., 22, ran away from James KENNERLY, Augusta Co. (VGR 5 Sep 71)

O'NEIL, T. H., of Baltimore, mar. Miss Eliza SAUNDERS of Wmsbrg. on Tues. last in Norfolk (NHPA 29 Dec 96)

O'NEILL, Thomas, mentioned as the heir at law of John O'NEILL in a Frederick Co. chancery case, Mar. 1797 (BVCG 31 Mar 97)

ONG, Isaac, dec'd, his carpentry tools will be sold by his admr., John FLIEGER, at auction in Staunton (SVG 26 Sep 95)

ORAM, Benjamin, svt., b. in London, 16, ran away from John James HULETT, James City Co. (VG 15 Aug 55)

ORANGE, James, Eng., lately a grenadier of the 17th British Regt. from which he des. six or eight weeks ago, des. from the company of Capt. Thomas MERIWETHER (VGPu 6 Jun 77)

ORENDORFF, Elizabeth, has eloped from her husband, C. ORENDORFF Jr. of Shepherdstown (VGWA 18 Aug 90)

ORENDORFF, John, late of Frederick Co., dec'd, e.a.w. his ex., Elias KACKLEY and Jacob WHITE (WG 6 Mar 99)

ORIXBRIGS, Richard, was mar. to Mrs. BROWN, widow of Francis BROWN, in the bloom of her life, on the 5th inst. at Gloucester by the Rev. Josiah BELLAMY (AGGA 11 Nov 96)

ORMESTON, John, merch. of Wmsbrg., intends for Wilmington, N. Carolina (VG 18 Apr 66)

ORR, Mrs., widow of Capt. Hugh ORR, d. lately in Wmsbrg. in her 79th year (VGWeA 4 Dec 88)

ORR, Capt. Hugh, of Norfolk, d. at Islington near London on 10 Feb. last (NHPA 20 Apr 97); late of Portsmouth [sic], e.a.w. his admr. Thomas ALLEN of Norfolk (NHPA 23 Oct 97)

ORTON, Reginald, of Yorktown, intends to return home to England shortly (VG 5 Jun 52)

ORTON, Thomas, son of Reginald ORTON and a minor, is attempting to get a license to marry Margaret McQUEEN against his father's wishes (VG 10 Nov 52)

ORTON, Thomas, Eng. conv. svt., c. 30, ran away from the Mossy Cr. Iron Works, Augusta Co. (VG 13 Nov 78); c. 30, des. fro, the York Garrison (VG 9 Apr 79)

OSBORN, Isaac, mulatto, slave, c. 36, a handy jack-of-all-trades, ran away from James SMITH, Dumfries; his former master was William TEBBS (TAA 17 May 98)

OSBORN, John, conv. imp. in the *Brickdale*, ran away from John GLASSELL, Fredsbrg. (VG 1 Oct 72)

OSBORNE, Charles, of Wmsbrg., intends to leave the colony soon (VG 25 Feb 5:

OSBORNE, John, Eng. svt., 25, ran away from Willoughby NEWTON, Westmoreland Co., 19 Feb. (VG 27 Feb 52)

OSBORNE, John, dec'd, e.a.w. his admr., Robert DONALD and Daniel M'CALLUM (VIC 12 Nov 88)
OSBORNE, John, of Blandford, merch., mar. Miss Jane HARRISON of Pr. Geo. Co., on Thurs. last (ILPB 8 May 93)
OSBORNE, Miss Nancy, d. on Mon. the 13th at Chestnut Hill, Chesterfield Co. (VGGA 22 Feb 92)
OSBORNE, Capt. Thomas, Justice of the Peace of Pr. Wm. Co., d. on 10 Apr. (VG 29 Apr 37)
OSBORNE, Thomas, who arrived at Charlestown, S. Carolina in a vessel from England three or four months ago, b. in Sheffield, Yorkshire, c. 38, set out from Charlestown for this province about 10 weeks ago; if he will call upon or write to the publisher of this paper he will hear of something greatly to his advantage (VG 11 Jun 67)
OSBORNE, Thomas, dec'd, his ex. (nfi) will sell his PE near Osborne's, Chesterfield Co. (VGGA 22 Feb 92)
OSBORNE, Thomas Jr., late of Chesterfield Co., dec'd, e.a.w. his ex., George MARKHAM and Joseph FRIEND (Arg 26 Jul 99)
OSWALD, Col. Eleazer, printer, of [Philadelphia], died (CMAG 22 Oct 95)
OSWALD, Thomas, of Kg. Geo. Co., intends for Britain next spring and will sell his land in that co. (VG 8 Oct 72)
OTTY, Elizabeth, has eloped from her husband, Thomas OTTY, Rockbridge Co. (BVCG 18 Nov 96)
OUNSTED, John, ind. svt., farmer, ran away from William DANGER, James City Co. (VGPu 27 Sep 76 sup)
OUTLAND, John Sr., of Isle of Wight Co., dec'd, e.a.w. his ex., Robert N. COOKE (NH 7 Feb 99)
OVERALL, Capt. William, killed by Indians in the Mero District on 22 Jan on the trace from Ky. to the Dripping Spring along with one BURNELL (Winchester disp. of 1 Apr.) (AGNPWA 10 Apr 93, VGRMA 15 Apr 93)
OVERBY, Jeremiah, late of Dinwiddie Co., e.a.w. his admr., Armistead DAVES (VGPI 4 Sep 95, 17 Jan 97)
OVERTON, James [Jr.], att. at law, d. on 20 Feb. in the District of Ky. (VICGA 19 May 90, VGWeA 20 May 90); e.a.w. his admr., John OVERTON, Louisa Co. (VICGA 5 May 90); his brother, John OVERTON Jr. [given as James OVERTON Jr. in the 19 May issue but corrected to John on 9 Jun.] att. at law of Ky. will finish his law business (VICGA 19 May 90, 9 Jun 90)
OVERTON, Col. Samuel, of Hanover Co., d. at Winchester (VGPu 30 May 77)
OVERTON, Thomas P., dec'd, his admr., Samuel FORD, Amelia Co., will sell his slaves, livestock, etc. (RMA 15 Oct 95)
OWEN, Hobson, of Henrico Co., for many yrs. the principal Inspector of tobacco at Shockoe Warehouse, d. on Thurs. after an illness of only three days leaving a widow and chil. (RC 6 Aug. 96, VGGA 10 Aug 96); e.a.w. his admx., Judith OWEN, of Henrico (VGGA 25 Jan 97); his admx. of Henrico, will sell all of his stock, HH & KF, and plant. utensils (VGGA 8 Nov 97)
OWEN, Jesse, son of David OWEN of Powhatan Co., d. the 22nd ult. in his 15th year [obit] (VIC 8 Apr 89)
OWEN, Thomas, dec'd, his ex., William BURTON of Henrico, will sell his land on Chickahominy Swamp, Henrico Co. (VGRMA 26 Jan 95)
OWENS, Edward, merch., d. on Wed. last (HNPA 25 Jul 95); e.a.w. Rose OWENS (nfi) of Norfolk (HNPA 8 Aug. 95, NH 2 Jan 96)
O'WILLIAMS, Mrs., the lady of Dr. Edward O'WILLIAMS, d. at Shepherdstown the 2nd ult. (VGWA 1 Jul 89)
OWL, John, aka William LAYNE, svt., 35, ran away from James FINDLY, Albemarle Co. on 14 Feb. (VG 18 Apr 45)
OWRAM. Mrs., wife of Thomas OWRAM, died (WVGWA 15 May 90)
OXEN, William, aka Anthony PURSELL, Irish svt., claims to bel. to Robert WALKER of Essex Co., jailed in Wmsbrg. (VG 4 Sep 46)

PACE, Robert C., dec'd, his HHF to be sold at auction in Fredsbrg. (VGAA 15 Mar 83)

Co., died lately (VG and VGR 11 Aug 74)
PAGE, the Hon. John Esq., of North River, Gloucester Co., d. on Sat. morn. last at Mansfield the seat of Mann PAGE Esq. near Fredsbrg. (VG and VGP 6 Oct 74); his ex. are Mann PAGE, Mann PAGE Jr., and John PAGE Jr. (VG 10 Nov 74)
PAGE, John Esq., of Hanover Co., mar. Miss Maria BYRD dau. of Col. William BYRD dec'd of Charles City Co. (VGWeA 29 May 84)
PAGE, John Esq., of Caroline Co., d. last Thurs. (VIC 6 May 89); e.a.w. his admx. w.w.a., Elizabeth PAGE (VIC 12 Aug 89); HCC, 12 Aug. 1790: Lucy PAGE, William NELSON and Elizabeth NELSON infants by Hugh NELSON their gdn. and next friend and the sd. Hugh NELSON and William NELSON exors. of Nathaniel NELSON dec'd (pltfs.) vs. Elizabeth PAGE admx. of John PAGE dec'd (VGGA 8 Sep 90)
PAGE, the Hon. John Esq., of Va., mar. at New York, Miss LOWTHER dau. of William LOWTHER Esq. of New York, on 27 Mar. (VHFA 15 Apr 90, WVGWA 24 Apr 90)
PAGE, John, mar. Miss Betsey MALLORY, both of Hampton, on Thurs. last (AGNPPA 21 Apr 95)
PAGE, John Jr. Esq., mar. Miss Betsey BURWELL only dau. of Lewis BURWELL Esq. of King's Mill (VG 11 Jul 71)
PAGE, Mann, dec'd, lots bel. to his est. in Hanover Town to be sold (VGAA 2 Nov 82, 22 Mar 83); of Mansfield, Spotsylvania Co., a chanc. suit against his est. was initiated; his surviving exors. are John PAGE, Mann PAGE, and Benjamin HARRISON (VGAA 3 Jul 84); 20 of his slaves to be sold by his ex., John PAGE of Gloucester Co. (VGAA 8 Feb 86)
PAGE, Mann Jr. Esq., of Mansfield, mar. Miss Molly TAYLOE 5th dau. of the Hon. John TAYLOE Esq. of Mount Airy in Richmond [Co.] (VGPu 10 May 76)
PAGE, Mrs. Mary, dec'd, her PE to be sold by her admrs., Gabriel MAUPIN and James SHIELDS (VG 16 Jul 67)
PAGE, Mrs. Mary, consort of Robert PAGE, died leaving her husband and a numerous family of chil. (VGRC 11 Mar 94)
PAGE, Matthew Jr., att. at law of Hanover Co., d. in Fauquier Co. on 1 May (VHFA 9 May 98); e.a.w. Samuel RICHARDSON att. at law, Hanover Town, or Gwyn PAGE, the admr., in Pr. Wm. Co. (VHFA 24 Aug 98, VGGA 28 Aug 98); his admr. will sell 20-30 Virginia-born slaves at Leesburg on 14 Jan next (TAA 18 Nov 98); GWYN PAGE will sell a tract of his land in Pr. Wm. Co. (VGGA 10 Sep 99, Ex 22 Oct 99)
PAGE, Robert, d. lately in Hanover of gout and dead palsy (VG 21 Jan 68)
PAGE, Robert, of Hanover, mar. Miss Molly BRAXTON eld. dau. of Col. Carter BRAXTON of Kg. Wm. Co. (VG 14 Oct 73)
PAGE, Robert Esq., of Mansfield, mar. Miss Elizabeth CARTER of Kg. Geo. Co. by publication of the banns in church (VG 7 Oct 75)
PAGE, Robert Esq., att. at law, mar. Miss Sally PAGE of Hanover Co. (VGWeA 24 Jan 88)
PAGE, Robert Esq., d. on Sat. last in Hanover Co. (VGRC 21 Nov 94); late of Hanover Co., his ex. (nfi) will sell some of his livestock (VGGA 31 Dec 94)
PAGE, Robert, late of Hanover Co., dec'd, e.a.w. his ex., William Fleming GAINES (VGGA 8 Mar 99)
PAGE, Thomas, Eng. svt., lived most of the time in London, ran away from William TAITE in Wmsbrg. (VG 21 Nov 45)
PAGE, William, of Alexandria, d. [lately] (VGAxA 5 Aug 90)
PAGE, William B. Esq., of Loudoun Co., mar. Miss Nancy LEE of this town [Alexandria] on Thurs. eve. last (CMAG 12 Aug 97)
PAINE, Thomas, d. in Paris in 1795 (RMA 16 Jan 96)
PAINTER, Rees, appr., c. 16, ran away from Henry SPRINKLE, Harrisonburg, Rockingham Co. (BVCG 22 Jun 95)
PALFREMAN, [Ae]ron, tutor, d. on 22 Oct. in his 46th year (VGGA 23 Nov 91)

PALMER Family, HCC, [nd]: Ann PALMER an infant dau. of John PALMER by John ECHOLS her next friend, and Alice PALMER, Thomas PALMER, and Robert PALMER infant chil. of Isaac PALMER by the sd. James ECHOLS their next friend (pltfs.) and William PALMER, Robert PALMER, Rawleigh PALMER, and Joseph PALMER (defs.) (VGGA 13 Sep 97)

PALMER, Jeffrey, of Kg. Wm. Co., dec'd, his 400 ac. tract on the Mattaponi River to be sold by his ex., Thomas CLAIBORNE, William DANDRIDGE, and William FRAZIER Jr. (VG 11 May 69, 14 Dec 69)

PANCAS, Miss, late from Philadelphia, d. in Alexandria (VJAA 15 Sep 85)

PANCOAST, David, late of Alexandria, dec'd, e.a.w. Philip WANTON (nfi) (TDCDA 26 Oct 99)

PANKEY, John, of Chesterfield Co., adv. that he made an assignment to his brother, Stephen PANKEY Jr. of Chesterfield Co., of all debts due him on his private account (VGPu 29 Aug 77)

PANKEY, Stephen Jr., his ex., Bernard MARKHAM and Smith BLAKEY, will sell all of his stock, HH & KF, at his late dwelling house about six miles from Manchester (VGWeA 12 Dec 96)

PANNILL, David, late of Kg. Wm. Co., dec'd, e.a.w. his admr., John PANNILL (Arg 21 Mar 97)

PANNILL, Joseph, of Wilkes Co., Georgia, adv. that previous to the commencement of the war, he contracted several debts in Va.; he now asks his creditors to send their claims to Thomas FARISH of Orange Co. or transmit all accounts to him in Ga. (VGIC 9 Dec 86)

PARBERRY, James, of Franklin Co., reportedly killed by Indians on his way from Ky. (VHFA 23 Nov 92)

PARHAM, William, of Sussex Co., dec'd, his ex., W. MASON and Thomas PARHAM, will sell about 3000 weight of fine pork and sundry other items of his est. (VGPu 5 Dec 77)

PARISH, Charles, of Lunenburg Co., dec'd, e.a.w. his admr., Thomas BLACKWELL (VGPI 6 Feb 98)

PARISH, Joel, late of Spotsylvania Co., dec'd, e.a.w. John PARISH (VH 23 Sep 97) [name also given as PARRISH]

PARK, Edward, late of Richmond, dec'd, e.a.w. his extx., Catharine PARK (VGAA 26 Jan 82); his extx. intends to leave the state and rent his tanyard in Richmond and a dwelling house in Staunton (VGAA 26 Apr 83)

PARK, James, dec'd, e.a.w. his admrs., Thomas McCOY and Jane PARK (PGBA 10 Sep 92)

PARK, Stephen, Eng. svt., 45, ran away from Thomas WILLIAMSON, Southampton Co. (VG 18 Apr 51)

PARKE, Benjamin, merch. of Fredsbrg., mar. Miss TALIAFERRO dau. of Col. John TALIAFERRO of Kg. Geo. Co. on Thurs. last (VHFA 6 Dec 92)

PARKER, Alexander, appr. carpenter, 18, ran away from W. QUARLES Jr., Point of Fork (VHFA 11 Aug 91); The reply of his father, A. PARKER, as to why he withdrew his son from QUARLES' service (VHFA 25 Aug 91)

PARKER, Mrs. Elizabeth, consort of Richard PARKER Esq., Judge of the Ct. of Appeals, d. on the 20th ult. in her 66th year (VGGA 31 Jan 98)

PARKER, George, aka George, Negro, bel. to Alexander VOSS, Falmouth, has a brother bel. to Maj. BUTLER across the "Ridge," ran away on 21 Oct. (VH 26 Oct 98)

PARKER, James, of Suffolk in Nansemond Co., intends to leave the colony (VG 20 Oct 52)

PARKER, John, Irish appr., blacksmith, 19, ran away from James YOUNG, Alexandria, supposed he is gone to Frederick Town [Md.] or Baltimore (CMAG 19 Jun 94)

PARKER, Joseph, merch. in Smithfield, mar. Mrs. Mary BRIDGER relict of Col. Joseph BRIDGER of Isle of Wight Co. (VG 17 Jun 73)

PARKER, Patrick, dec'd, his ex., J[ames] HUNTER, will sell that part of Holland bel. to his est. at Kempsville (NHPA 18 May 97); HCC, James CURRIE (pltf.) and James HUNTER ex. of Patrick PARKER and Mary

PARKER his widow who has renounced all benefits under his will and
Solomon Wilson & Co. and Elizabeth HAYES admx. of Robert HAYES and
creditors of the sd. Patrick PARKER (defs.) and between Solomon WILSON
and Robert TAYLOR late merch. and partners under the firm of Solomon
Wilson & Co. (pltfs.) and James HUNTER ex. of Patrick PARKER dec'd and
Mary PARKER his wife and devisee (defs.) (NH 6 Nov 98)

PARKER, Richard, joiner and house carpenter, who came lately from England,
if he will inquire at the post office he may hear of something to his
advantage (VG 26 May 68)

PARKER, Richard, Irish, 35-40, des. at Wmsbrg. (VG 24 Jan 77)

PARKER, Maj. Richard, of the 5th Va. Regt., reportedly killed on or about 1 Feb.
in a skirmish near Drake's Farm, N. Jersey (VG 21 Feb, 7 Mar 77, VGPu 21
Feb 77)

PARKER, Robert, dec'd, his plant. near the New Bridges, Hanover Co., will be
sold (VGAA 18 Jan 83)

PARKER, Sacker, a rep. of Accomack Co., d. there lately (VG 14 Jul 38)

PARKER, Thomas, svt., b. in Philadelphia, ran away from Matthew KENNER
Jr., Northumberland Co. (VG 10 Nov 38)

PARKER, [William], his ex., William PARKER and Thomas PETERS, publish
his will which mentions a son, William PARKER, a dau., Mary MINTON,
and other chil., Lucy PETERS, Martha PARKER, Susanna PARKER, and
Judith PARKER (VGR 23 Jun 68); of Sussex Co., 10 of his slaves to be sold by
his ex., William PARKER and James PETERS (VG 1 Dec 68) [It is not clear
if his ex. is Thomas or James PETERS]

PARKER, William, Eng. ind. svt., 21, blacksmith, ran away from Archibald
M'KENDRICK, Richmond Town, who suspects he will attempt to return to
Britain (VGPu 3 Mar 75)

PARKER, William, dec'd, his ex., John PARKER, will sell his dwelling house
in Port Royal (VGPu 30 May 77)

PARKER, Capt. William, of Spotsylvania Co., dec'd, his ex., Benjamin
ROBINSON and James POWELL, will sell the tract of land whereon he lived
as well as his PE (VH 11 Oct [97]); his ex. will sell his slaves (VH 1 Feb 99)

PARKHURST, Dr. Samuel, late of Connecticut, d. in Culpeper Co. on the 13th
inst. (VHFFA 23 Aug 96)

PARKS, Andrew, merch., of Fredsbrg., mar. Miss Harriott WASHINGTON
dau. of the late Samuel WASHINGTON and niece of the President, in this
co. [Spotsylvania], on Fri. last (VHFFA 19 Jul 96, RCFPC 20 Jul 96)

PARKS, William, late printer of [the *Virginia Gazette*], died; he took passage in
Capt. WATSON, and went on board the 22nd of Mar. in good health but was
soon seized with a pleurisy of which he d. the 1st of Apr. and was bur. at
Gosport [Wmsbrg. disp. of 24 May] (MG 13 Jun 50); e.a.w. his ex., John
SHELTON, Wmsbrg. (VG 12 Mar 52)

PARMER, John, appr., tailor, 13-14, ran away from Edward MAXEY,
Cumberland Co. (VGR 9 Feb 69)

PARRISH, John Simog, American, 30-38, suspected along with one Joel
PARRISH, of forgery (VGGA 30 Sep 95 ps)

PARROT, Benjamin, ind. svt. from London, 32, house carpenter, came in on
the *Elizabeth* two months ago, ran away from Joshua POYTHRESS Jr., Pr.
Geo. Co. (VG 16 Jun 74)

PARROT, Capt. Robert, mar. Miss Sally READ in this town on Sun. eve. (VH
Apr 99)

PARROT, William, Negro, says he is free and was b. about a mile from
Wmsbrg., jailed in Norfolk Co. (VGPu 27 Oct 75)

PARRY, Thomas, John MULLINS of Middlesex Co. requests that he apply for
his part of the est. of William MULLINS dec'd (VGPu 31 Oct 77)

PARSONS, David, mar. Miss Katy MILLER, both of Hampshire Co., on Tues.
last (BVCG 8 Apr 96)

PARSONS, Capt. James, of Alexandria, died (VJAA 3 Feb 85)

PARSONS, James, of Back River, d. lately on board the schooner *Sally* on her

passage to Jamaica (AGNPPA 16 Oct 95)
PARSONS, John, dec'd, e.a.w. his ex., William Ap Thomas PARSONS, Elizabeth City Co. (VICGA 14 Jun 90)
PARSONS, John, late of Pr. Anne Co., dec'd, e.a.w. his ex., Josiah SLACK, Norfolk (NHPA 6 Apr 97, 21 Aug 97)
PARSONS, the Hon. Samuel H., one of the judges of the Western Territory, drowned in Big Beaver Cr. (VGWA 9 Dec 89)
PARSONS, Thomas, his ex., J. WISE and Dr. Tully R. WISE, Kg. Wm. Co., will sell his houses and lots in Wmsbrg. (AGNPPA 9 Feb 96)
PARSONS, William, late of Henrico Co., dec'd, e.a.w. his ex., Samuel PARSONS, of Goochland Co. (VGWeA 9 Aug 87)
PARTIN, William, Virginian, 35, des. from Petersburg (VG 28 Feb 55)
PARTLOW, John, dec'd, his extx. is Sarah PARTLOW and his exors. are Benjamin WALLER, Thomas MINOR, and Lewis PARTLOW (VHFA 1 Dec 91)
PASLAY, William, dec'd, e.a.w. his admr. William AKERS Jr. of Buckingham Co. (VGPu 14 Nov 77)
PASTEUR, the Rev. James, Rector of St. Bride's Par., Norfolk, was taken ill at the altar on Sun. the 16th inst. and d. the following Tues. (VG and VGR 27 Jan 74)
PASTEUR, John, dec'd, his ex., Solomon WILSON, Isle of Wight Co., will sell all his PE (NHPA 12 Oct 97)
PASTEUR, Dr. William, appr., has run away from Alexander GORDON, Norfolk (VG 2 Jul 72); of Halifax Co., denies that he is still apprenticed to GORDON (VG 30 Jul 72); d. on Sat. last in Wmsbrg. (VGGA 22 Jun 91, VGWeA 24 Jun 91)
PATE, Matthew, of Hanover Co., dec'd, his admr. is Jeremiah PATE (VICGA 17 Mar 90)
PATERSON, Robert, dec'd, e.a.w. his admr., Ninian MENZIES (VG 19 Nov 72)
PATERSON, Robert, of Hanover Co., dec'd, e.a.w. his admr., Robert DONALD, Warwick Co. (VG 2 Sep 73)
PATTEHUSER, John, aka John PATTERSON, appr., native of Germany, 25, ran away from Frederick CONRAD, Winchester (VJAA 26 Aug 84)
PATTERSON, Mrs., spouse of John PATTERSON, Portsmouth, died (NPC 24 Apr 90)
PATTERSON, James, svt., 25, shoemaker, ran away from William TREBELL, Wmsbrg. (VG 4 Nov 63)
PATTERSON, James, dec'd, late manager of the est. of the Hon. William BYRD Esq. at the Falls, e.a.w. his ex., Mary PATTERSON, Thomas PROSSER and Charles PATTERSON (VG 16 Apr 67)
PATTERSON, James, ind. svt. lad, ran away from Alexander GORDON, Charles City Co. (VG 7 Jan 73) [see also: James PATTESON}
PATTERSON, James, of Richmond, dec'd, Miles TAYLOR will settle his est. (VG 22 Jul 73)
PATTERSON, Capt. James, late of Portsmouth, dec'd, his PE is in the hands of Marsden Maxwell and Co. [Norfolk] (VG 11 Mar 73); e.a.w. his Admrs., James MARSDEN and James MAXWEL[L] (VGNI 6 Oct 74)
PATTERSON, James, Virginian, 20, des. from the co. of Capt. Thomas MASSIE, 6th Va. Regt., he was decoyed off by his father and carried to Louisa or Albemarle Co. (VG 11 Jul 77)
PATTERSON, Leonard, of Fredsbrg., dec'd, his ex. is Juda[h] PATTERSON (VHFA 15 Apr 90)
PATTERSON, Lewis, Negro, speaks broken Eng. and French, says he bel. to John JONES of S. Carolina, jailed in K & Q Co. (VG 1 Sep 74)
PATTERSON, Paul, Negro, 35, claimed to bel. to Samuel KELSEY [should be KELSICK] of Richmond Co., committed to jail in Georgetown, Montgomery Co., Md. (VJAA 8 Nov 87)
PATTERSON, Samuel, att., d. lately in Mecklenburg Co. (VGWeA 25 Sep 84)
PATTESON Family, HCC, 12 May 1790: David PATTESON (pltf.) against David

LEITCH [also given as LEITH] att. in fact for Elizabeth PATTESON the extx. of Leonard PATTESON dec'd, and Sarah FISH (defs.) [The defs. are probably of Buckingham Co.] (VICGA 19 May 90, VGGA 29 Sep 90))

PATTESON, James, ind. svt. lad, ran away from Alexander GORDON at Rocky Ridge (VG 30 Apr 72) [see also: James PATTERSON]

PATTON, Hugh, merch., of Richmond, d. on Fri. morn. last (VICGA 27 Jan 90, VHFA 28 Jan 90); e.a.w. his ex., James BROWN, who will sell his stock of dry goods, wines, and HHF (VICGA 9 Jun 90)

PATTON, Col. James, murdered by Indians on the last day of July on the head branches of the Roanoke (VG 8 Aug 55, NYPB 25 Aug 55)

PATTON, Robert, merch., mar. Miss Nancy MERCER dau. of the late Gen. Hugh MERCER, on Tues. eve. last (VHFA 18 Oct 92)

PATTON, William, native of Ireland, d. in New Kent Co. lately (VGGA 22 May 98)

PAUL, Cornet Hugh, mar. Miss Eleanor FACKLER on 22 Dec., both of Staunton (BVCG 29 Dec 94)

PAUL, James, of Richmond, will not pay any debts of his wife, Ann PAUL (VGRMA 11 Apr 95); warns all persons from giving credit to his wife, Anne PAUL (Ex 12 Feb 99)

PAUL, William, of Fredsbrg., adv. that his wife left him some time ago and before she ran him into debt (VG 20 Sep. 70); his wife, Fanny, presents her side (VG 25 Oct 70)

PAULY, Lewis Abraham, mar. Miss Jane ALLEGRE of this city [Richmond] on Thurs. last (VGAA 12 Mar 85)

PAYNE, Benjamin, intends to leave the state (NH 7 Jun 98)

PAYNE, George, of Goochland Co., dec'd, e.a.w. the court appointed admr., the sheriff Thomas F. BATES (VGGA 27 Oct 90)

PAYNE, George, of Westmoreland Co., dec'd, e.a.w. his ex., William and John PAYNE (VHFA 21 Jul 95)

PAYNE, John, svt., b. in Md., c. 25, ran away from Richard BOWES, Yeocomico River, Northumberland Co.; it is believed he will make for Pa. or N. Carolina (MG 7 Jul 63)

PAYNE, John Elliot, dec'd, his ex., William PAYNE of Caroline Co., will sell 12 of his slaves (VGGA 13 Nov 93)

PAYNE, Capt. Merryman, of Lancaster Co., dec'd, his ex., Merryman PAYNE and Henry TOWLES, will sell some of his slaves, a yoke of oxen, and other items of his est. (VG 25 Nov 73)

PAYNE, Mrs. Susanna, consort of William PAYNE of Leeds, d. in Falmouth on Mon. last (VHFA 17 Jul 95)

PAYNE, Col. William, mar. Miss Elizabeth DORREL, both of this county [Fairfax], on Thurs. last (CMAG 20 Feb 96)

PAYNTAR, John, dec'd, e.a.w. the extx., Susanna PAYNTAR (VCNPGA 15 Jun 93)

PAYRAS, Dr. John, late of Yorktown, dec'd, his est. and dwelling there to be sold pursuant to his will by Samuel PRICE, his ex. (VG 5 Jun 52)

PEACHEY, Leroy, only son of Leroy PEACHEY Esq. of Richmond Co., d. on Tues. night last in his 17th year; he was a student in the Winchester Academy [obit.] (VGWA 11 Jan 88)

PEACHEY, Thomas Griffin, eld. son. of Col. William PEACHEY, d. on Sun. the 29th ult. at his father's house in Richmond Co., aged 22; he took his degree as bachelor of arts at Dickenson College, Carlisle, [Pa.] on 28 Sep. 1790 (VGWeA 10 Aug 92) [his name is given as Francis G. PEACHEY in VHFA of 9 Aug 92]

PEACHEY, Miss Winifred, dau. of Col. Leroy PEACHEY of Richmond Co., d. in Frederick Co. on Tues. 6 Aug. (BVCG 29 Aug 93) [or on Tues. the 15th inst. acc. to VHFA 29 Aug 93]

PEAK, Humphrey, d. at his plant. near Alexandria (VJAA 13 Jan 85)

PEARCE, Benjamin, who enl. in K & Q Co., is desired to repair to Wmsbrg. immediately to join the 1st Bn., 1st Va. Regt. (VGPu 4 Jul 77 sup)

18th-Century Virginia Newspapers   261

PEARCE, Elizabeth, has absconded from her husband, Jeremiah PEARCE of Caroline Co. (VG 9 Jul 72)

PEARCE, Francis, dec'd, pursuant to his will, his acting ex., George WILLIAMSON of Henrico, will sell his land near Richmond (VGRMA 4 Sep, 17 Nov 94) [also given as PEIRCE]

PEARCE, Gilbert, executed at the gallows near this city [Wmsbrg.] for murder (VG 1 May 79)

PEARCE, Jeremiah, late of Cumberland Co., dec'd, e.a.w. his ex., Miller WOODSON (RMA 13 Feb 96)

PEARCE, Robert, svt., 30, ship carpenter, ran away from Patrick CREAGH, Annapolis, Md. (VG 16 Jan 56)

PEARCE, Maj. Valentine, of Pr. Wm. Co., mar. Miss Eleanor "Nelly" ORR of Loudoun Co. (VGAR 17 Nov 91, VGAxA 24 Nov 91) [also given as PEERS]

PEARCE, William, conv. svt., c. 25, just imp. from London in the *Justitia*, ran away from Andrew LEITCH near Leedstown (VG 22 Apr 75, 29 Apr 75 sup, VGP 28 Apr 75)

PEARSE, Samuel, appr., c. 18, ran away from Andrew and Robert M'KIM, Richmond (VGGA 17 Apr 98)

PEARSE, William, svt., c. 25, carpenter, ran away from Man[n] PAGE, Gloucester Co. (AWM 8 Jul 25)

PEARSEY, Charles, late of Orange Co., dec'd, e.a.w. his ex., May BURTON Jr. (VHFA 18 Sep 94)

PEARSON, George, c. 40, ran away from the brig *Neptune,* may try to get to Alexandria (VHFA 14 Aug 95)

PEARSON, W., dec'd, M. PEARSON of Wmsbrg. requests that any demands against the est. be brought in (VG 8 May 78) [probably the same person as William PEARSON below]

PEARSON, William, of Wmsbrg., tanner, d. after a few days illness leaving a widow and chil. (VG and VGPu 17 Jan 77); Mary M. PEARSON (nfi) of Wmsbrg. will lease his tan works and dwelling house near Wmsbrg. (VGPu 7 Mar 77)

PEARSON, William, mar. Miss Nelly ATKINSON in Fredsbrg. on the 20th inst. (VHFFA 22 Dec 95)

PEART, George, ind. svt., c. 22, shoemaker, b. in Co. Durham, England, ran away from Thomas and Samuel PRETLOW, Surry Co. (VG 29 Apr 75 sup)

PEAY, Henry, of Kg. Wm. Co., enl. with Lt. RAINES, and has since enl. in the Georgia Service (VGPu 11 Apr 77)

PEBWORTH, Robert, svt., 23, ran away from Francis SEARLON, Pr. Wm. Co. (VG 10 Aug 39)

PECK, Miss Priscilla, dau. of Simeon PECK of Manchester, d. on Thurs. last by the fall of a piece of timber on her head (VGWeA 7 Aug 88)

PEEBLES, Capt. Lemuel, dec'd, e.a.w. his ex., Heartwell PEEBLES, Pr. Geo. Co. (VGPI 14 Jul 97)

PEELING, Sarah, has left her husband, John PEELING of Winchester (BVCG 27 May 93)

PEERS, Charles, late of New Kent Co., dec'd, e.a.w. Anderson PEERS (nfi) (VGAA 1 Oct 85)

PEETE, Samuel, is selling his plant.; his son, Richard, will attend courts to settle his accounts (VG 24 Mar 68)

PEGEL, John Jacob, Dutch svt., baker, 44-45, ran away from John SEYLE, Georgetown (VJAA 22 Jun, 29 Jun 86)

PEIRS, Anderson, dec'd, his ex., John LAPRADE, will rent his mill in Goochland Co. (VGGA 10 Sep 94) [also given as PEERS]

PELHAM, Peter Jr., Clerk of Brunswick Co., mar. Miss [Bethina] BROWN of Southampton Co. (VG 22 Oct 72)

PENDERGAST, Edward, Irish svt., c. 18, ran away from Richard JONES, Bladensburg [Md.] (VGAxA 10 Feb 91)

PENDERGAST, Capt. James, of the ship *America,* bel. to Joseph ANTHONY & Co., was scaling some guns at Kensington yesterday at 1:00 when one of

them burst and killed him instantly (CMAG 12 Jun 98)
PENDLETON, James, dec'd, his ex., John PENDLETON and William C. BROWN of Culpeper Co., will sell his lands in that co. (VHFA 19 Dec 93)
PENDLETON, John, of Caroline Co., mar. Miss Nancy LEWIS in Wmsbrg. on Sun. last (VGWeA 24 Sep 89)
PENDLETON, Mrs. Mary, spouse of John PENDLETON of Richmond, d. lately at Clifton in Hanover Co. (VGWeA 6 Nov 84)
PENDLETON, Miss Sally, of K & Q Co. [a poem on her death] (VGR 31 Mar 74)
PENISTON, Anthony Colin, dec'd, e.a.w. his admr., Thomas PENISTON, Pr. Geo. Co. (VGPu 2 Jun 75)
PENN, Col. Gabriel, d. on Mon. the 8th inst., aged 57, at his seat in Amherst Co. (VGGA 24 Jan 98)
PENN, John Esq., of Caroline Co., intends to remove to N. Carolina soon (VG 5 May 74); of N. Carolina, d. [lately]; he was a delegate to Congress for many yrs. (VIC 24 Sep, VGWeA 25 Sep, NPJ 8 Oct 88)
PENN, Solomon, Irish svt., ran away from on board the *Greenvale* at Ruffin's Ferry, Pamunkey River (VGR 26 Apr 70 sup)
PENN, William Esq., a lt. in Capt. JAMESON's Troop, died (VGPu 18 Apr 77 sup)
PENN, William, if any relation to William PENN late practitioner of physic in the British settlement at the Bay of Honduras, dec'd, are living, they are requested to apply to Alexander MACAULEY at York or to the printers where they may hear of something to their advantage (AGNPPA 21 May 94)
PENNEROY, Daniel, who left Philadelphia about 12 yrs. ago, probably to settle in Md. or Va., will hear something to his advantage if he will apply to Edward EVANS, Philadelphia (AWM 17 May 39)
PENNINGTON, Joshua, dec'd, his est. in Sussex Co., to be sold by his ex., Marcus PENNINGTON and Waddel JOHNSON; they will also sell some of the est. of John PENNINGTON (nfi) dec'd (VG 2 Jun 68)
PENNY, John, of the ship *Saratoga*, mar. Miss Betsy HILL of this town [Alexandria], on Sat. eve. last (TAA 18 Oct 97)
PENTICOST, James, svt., ran away from Richard JOHNSON, Culpeper Co. (VGR 21 Sep 69)
PEOPLES, the Rev. Jacob, supposed name of a dissenting clergyman whose body was found five miles above the mouth of Tye River in Amherst Co. on Sat. 21 May; he was apparently from "the back parts of Pennsylvania" (VGR 16 Jun 74)
PEPPERS, Catharine, from Bedford, executed for murder on 3 [sic] June (VG and VGR 2 Jun 74)
PERFECT, Christopher, Eng. svt., 19, ran away from George TURBERVILLE, Westmoreland Co.; he had arrived in Va. in 1739 (VG 20 Jul 39)
PERFUME, Harry, Negro, c. 30, jailed in Gloucester (VG 17 Feb 74)
PERINE, Matthew, appr., 16-17, ran away from David PARKINS (BVCG 24 Mar 94)
PERITT, John, of Nansemond Co., 23, des. from Capt. David BELL's Co. of the Va. Regt.; he may be going to N. Carolina (VG 5 Dec 55)
PERKINS, Capt. Hardin, of Buckingham Co., d. on the 11th inst., aged 60 (VGGA 24 Sep 94)
PERKINS, Joshua, mulatto, 24-25, des. from the Va. troops at Wmsbrg. (VGPu 6 Jun 77)
PERKINS, Mary, dec'd, her ex., John, David, and Isaac PERKINS, will sell her plant. containing 300 ac. about seven miles above the New Kent Ct. H., the land may be viewed by applying to Nathaniel PERKINS (nfi) on the premises (VGPu 24 Oct 77)
PERKINS, William Sr., of Dinwiddie Co., d. on the 23rd inst., aged 75 (VGPI 29 Mar 93)
PERKINSON, William, adv. that his wife, Anne PERKINSON, has eloped from his bed and board (VGCD 6 Nov 79)
PERKINSON, William, of Amelia Co., dec'd, e.a.w. his admr., Dabney

MORRIS of Nottoway Co. (VGPI 25 Oct 96)
PERRIN, Capt. John, d. in Gloucester Co. (VG 22 Feb 70)
PERRIN, John, of Gloucester Co., dec'd, e.a.w. his admr., Francis WILLIS and Thomas LEWIS (VGGA 21 Mar 92)
PERROW, Charles, dec'd, e.a.w. his extx., Frances PERROW, and ex., Isaac BRYANT and Charles PERROW of Buckingham Co. (VGGA 13 Dec 97)
PERRY, Dr., d. on Tues. last (NH 18 Oct 98)
PERRY, Capt. David, of Staunton, mar. Miss Rosetta MAY of Winchester on Thurs. eve. (BVCG 29 Dec 94)
PERRY, Mrs. Jane, spouse of Dr. PERRY of Norfolk, d. on Thurs. last leaving her husband and four chil. (VCNPGA 3 Nov 92)
PERSON, John, late of Southampton Co., dec'd, his land in Surry Co. to be sold by his ex., John and Henry PERSON (VG 17 Nov 52)
PERSON, John, late of Southampton Co., dec'd, e.a.w. his extx., Dorcas PERSON, and his ex., William and Benjamin PERSON (VG 24 Sep 67); e.a.w. his ex., Benjamin PERSON and Richard CLIFTON (VG 9 May 71)
PERSON, Thomas, dec'd, his PE to be sold by his admr., Jesse WILLIAMSON, Brunswick Co. (VGR 26 Jul 70)
PESCUD, Thomas, dec'd, e.a.w. Hawkins READE of York Co. (VGGA 21 Mar 92)
PETER, John, of Surry Co., dec'd, items of his est. to be sold by his ex. (nfi) (VG 3 Nov 63)
PETER, Mrs. Margaret, spouse of Thomas PETER, merch. at Cabin Point, d. on Sun. the 25th inst. (VGGA 28 Nov 92)
PETERS, Joh[n], sailmaker, of Norfolk, d. on Fri. last leaving a widow and chil. [obit.] (AGGA 11 Oct 96)
PETERS, John, dec'd, e.a.w. his admx., Ann PETERS, Norfolk (NHPA 6 Mar 97)
PETERS, John, adv. that his wife, Polly, has absconded without any just cause and he will no longer pay any of her debts (TAA 10 Jan 98)
PETERSON, John Jr., of Dinwiddie, died (VGR 25 Feb 73)
PETES, John, reportedly killed by Indians on Crooked Cr., near Knoxville, Tenn., on the 22nd inst. [Jan.] (BVCG 18 Feb 93)
[PETHERAM], James Butler, Eng., svt., 26, has been in the country about a year, ran away from Lemuel REDDICK, Suffolk Town (VG 6 Oct 52)
PETTIGREW, James, merch., mar. Miss Polly TAYLOR (VHFA 4 Mar 90)
PETTUS, Dick, Negro, cooper, raised in New Kent Co., ran away from John MILLER, Botetourt Co. (VGGA 1 Jul 95)
PETTUS, Thomas, of Mecklenburg Co., dec'd, e.a.w. his admrs., William and John PETTUS (VGPI 15 Aug 97)
PETTUS, Col. William, late of Spotsylvania Co., dec'd, his land there on the north fork of the Pamunkey River to be sold by his acting ex., William PETTUS of Louisa Co. (VH 19 Oct 98)
PETTWAY, John, dec'd, his ex., Sterling HARWELL and William PETTWAY, will sell his land on Smith's Cr., Warren Co., N. Carolina (VGPI 8 Nov 96)
PETWAY, Thomas, of Surry Co., dec'd, his est. in Cobham Town to be sold by Thomas HOLT (nfi) (VG 13 Jun 55)
PEYTON, [?], of Gloucester Co., d. about a fortnight ago in a riding accident (VG 27 Oct 38)
PEYTON, [?], lady of Sir. John PEYTON of Gloucester, Bart., died (VGPu 5 Jun 78)
PEYTON, Mrs. Anne, wife of Thomas PEYTON Esq. of Gloucester Co., eld. son of Sir John PEYTON Bart., died in the prime of her age a few months after their marriage, on Fri. the 10th inst. (VG 17 Jan 77, VGPu 7 Feb 77)
PEYTON, Edward, of Philadelphia, was killed by Nathaniel HILL in a duel in Norfolk, on Mon. sennight (VHFA 10 Mar 91) [But, acc. to BVCG of 16 Mar., HILL, q.v., was killed by PEYTON.]
PEYTON, Col. Henry, of Pr. Wm. Co., dec'd, his est. on Broad Run, Pr. Wm. Co. to be sold by his ex. (VJAA 6 Dec 87); his grist mill and plant. about 18

miles above Dumfries in Pr. Wm. Co. to be sold by his ex., Cuthbert
BULLITT, James EWELL, and John PEYTON (VIC 10 Dec 88); Cuthbert
BULLITT, trustee and ex., and James EWELL and John PEYTON, his ex.,
will sell his remaining slaves (VIC 18 Feb 89); slaves involved in litigation
brought by Mrs. VALIN to be sold by his ex. (VGAxA 11 Feb 90)

PEYTON, Sir John Bart., d. suddenly in Gloucester Co. on Wed. eve. the 27th
ult.; it is said that his death was occasioned by eating a hearty supper of
roasted oysters and afterwards milk (WVGWA 17 Apr 90); his admx., Mary
PEYTON of Mathews Co., adv. that Negroes bel. to his est. will be sold at
Petersburg (RMA 30 Jan 96)

PEYTON, Dr. John, dec'd, his admx., Mary, of Richmond, will sell 20-30 of his
slaves at Gloucester Co. (VGGA 17 Feb 96)

PEYTON, John R. Esq., d. on Tues. 5 Feb. at Stoney Hill his seat in Stafford Co.
(VH 12 Sep 99); e.a.w. his ex., John HOOE of Fauquier Co. (VH 10 Sep 99)

PEYTON, Thomas Esq., of Gloucester Co., mar. Miss Nancy WASHINGTON of
the same co. last Sat. [Gloucester disp. of 13 May] (VG 25 May 76)

PEYTON, Capt. Thomas, of the 1st Co., Stafford Light Infantry, d. on Mon. the
5th inst. at his house in Stafford Co. [obit.] (VHFA 15 Jan 95); dec'd, his ex.,
Samuel H. PEYTON and Henry PEYTON, will sell his dwelling house and
plant. containing 400 ac. on Acquia Run in Stafford Co. (RJDA 17 Jul 95);
e.a.w. with Cuthbert BULLITT (VICGA 18 Aug 90, VGGA 25 Aug 90)

PHELPS, Mr., mar. Mrs. Elizabeth HEWES at Col. HITE's (VGWA 29 Apr 89)

PHILE, Miss Harriet, d. in Petersburg (VGPI 21 Jul 97)

PHILIPS, Alexander, des. from the new levies, Winchester, says he was mar.
about three weeks ago to a widow HOWARD living eight miles from
Winchester (BVCG 18 Jun 91)

PHILIPS, Charles, svt., smith and farrier, ran away from the plant. of the
Hon. John CARTER (AWM 25 Jul 34)

PHILIPS, John, Irish, des. from Capt. DICKENSON's Co., 1st Va. Regt., at
headquarters in the Jerseys; supposed to be lurking about Hampton (VGPu
25 Apr 77)

PHILIPS, Thomas, aka HAMILTON, conv. svt., c. 25, b. in Hertfordshire; ran
away from William THOMSON, Stafford Co. (VG 11 Mar 73)

PHILIPS, William, Welsh svt., ran away from Robert LORTON, Capitol
Landing near Wmsbrg. (VG 4 Jan 40)

PHILIPS, William, ind. svt., c. 20, ran away from Rebekah SMITH near
Winchester (VGPu 4 Jul 77 sup)

PHILIPS, Young, appr., wheelwright, c. 18, ran away from Thomas PHILIPS,
Martinsburg (VGWA 15 Aug 87)

PHILIPSON, Dr. Robert, dec'd, his ex. is Thomas CARY Jr. of Warwick Co.
(VG 15 May 46)

PHILLIPPIE, Frederick, of Richmond, adv. that his wife, Sally PHILLIPPIE,
has eloped from his bed and board (DOB 29 Nov 98)

PHILLIPS, Mrs. Ann, wife of Capt. Richard PHILLIPS of Louisa Co. and eld.
dau. of Col. William JOHNSON, d. lately (VGAA 13 Nov 84)

PHILLIPS, James, late of Charles City Co., executed on Fri. last for a burglary
and robbery committed in Pr. Geo. Co. (VGWeA 6 Dec 87)

PHILLIPS, John, a likely young man, des. from Nicholas HOBSON's Co. of the
6th Regt. of Continental Regulars (VGPu 26 Jul 76)

PHILLIPS, Josiah, executed at the gallows near this city [Wmsbrg.] (VG 4 Dec
78)

PHILLIPS, Col. Richard Jr., dec'd, e.a.w. his admr., John WADDY of Louisa
Co. (VGGA 19 Jun 93)

PHILPOTTS, Francis, mar. Miss Elizabeth CASEY, both of this city
[Richmond], on Sat. night last (DOB [19] Nov 98)

PHIPPS, James, age 19 and seven months, des. from Capt. William
CAMPBELL's Co., 7th U. S. Regt. (WG 18 Sep 99)

PHOSET, Thomas, svt., weaver, ran away from Sampson DORELL, Fairfax Co.
(VGR 17 Nov 68)

18th-Century Virginia Newspapers 265

PHRIPP, John, of Norfolk, dec'd, e.a.w. Matthew PHRIPP (nfi) (VGR 22 Dec 68)
PHRIPP, Capt. John, late of Norfolk, d. in his 93rd year (VGPu 8 Nov 76)
PHRIPP, John, mar. Miss Sally KEELING in Pr. Anne Co. (VCNPGA 19 Oct 93)
PHRIPP, John Esq., d. at his seat in Pr. Anne Co. on Tues. (NH 6 Oct 96, AGGA 7 Oct 96); his admr, James RAMSAY of Norfolk, will sell his personal property (NHPA 12 Dec 96)
PHRIPP, Matthew Esq., of Norfolk Borough, d. after a lingering illness (VG 26 Feb 80); late of Norfolk Co., e.a.w. his ex., Alexander MOSELEY (VGCD 19 May 80); of Phripp & Bowdoin, Fredsbrg., the surviving partner is Presson BOWDOIN; PHRIPP was living in Norfolk Borough (VGAA 26 Jan 82, 6 Jul 82, 26 Jul 83, VGWeA 2 Mar 82, 26 Apr 83 sup)
PICKETT, Mr., drowned along with his wife and sister (nfi) in the Potomac (VG 24 Apr 52)
PICKETT, George, of Richmond, mar. Mrs. Margaret FLINT late of Baltimore (VIC 21 Oct 89, VGWeA 22 Oct 89)
PICKFORD, Charles, Eng. svt., 25, ran away from the Hon. John CARTER Esq., Charles City Co. (VG 30 Nov 39)
PIED, [?], 16 year old son of Joshua PIED, d. on Sat. last (NPJ 16 Apr 88)
PIERCE, Isaac, lately dec'd, e.a.w. Francis ROBINS of Alexandria, who will also sell his blocks, mast hoops, handspikes, and stock of lignum vitae (VGR 20 Jun 71)
PIERCE, Isabella, Eng. svt., ran away from Thomas LEWIS on the mouth of Doeg Cr., Fairfax Co. (VG 9 May 45)
PIERCE, Jeremiah, dec'd, e.a.w. his ex., Miller WOODSON, Cumberland Co. (VGGA 18 May 96)
PIERCE, John, Irish, resident of Augusta Co., 35, des. from an escort conducting German prisoners of war from Winchester to Frederick, Md. (VGAA 22 Feb 83)
PIERCE, Mrs. Sarah, of Hanover Co., died in an advanced age (VG 4 Mar 79)
PIG, William, Negro, says he bel. to Dr. William CLARKE of Charlotte Co, jailed in Essex Co. (VGPu 24 Nov 75)
Pilots Drowned at Norfolk: the pilot boat, *Idle Times*, bel. to Mr. LATTIMER of Hampton, was driven ashore in Lynhaven Bay on Thursday night, 22 Jan., and before any assistance was given, the following had perished: John PRICE, John HOUSE, Edward BULLY, Rox CUNNINGHAM, and a lad named RUDD, all pilots from Hampton (VGWeA 7 Feb 95)
PINCKARD, the widow, late of Wmsbrg., d. on Tues. morn. in Norfolk Borough at the house of Col. BIRD where she was on a visit (NH 31 May 98)
PINDALL, Thomas, of Fairfax Co., adv. that his wife, Ann PINDALL formerly Ann RHODES, absconded from his bed and board on 30 Oct. with an Irishman named James CAIN, c. 26, and their eld. dau., Ann, c. 12; his wife is c. 48 and was pregnant when she left (VGAxA 10 Nov 91, VGGA 14 Dec 91)
PINKARD, Jonathan, Eng. ind. svt., watchmaker, c. 23, ran away from Samuel JEFFERYS, Philadelphia (VG 29 Apr 73)
PINKERTON, Wilson, executed at the gallows near this city for murder (VG 1 May 79)
PINKNEY, Charles, mar. Miss Clara MOODY, both of Richmond, on Tues. eve. last (RC 5 Feb 96)
PINKNEY, John, of Wmsbrg., is obliged in a short time to quit the state and reside in N. Carolina (VG 27 Jun 77); formerly of Wmsbrg., printer, d. in N. Carolina (VG 5 Sep 77); e.a.w his admr., Jacob BRUCE, of Wmsbrg. (VG 17 Oct 77)
PIPEMAN Family, Court of Hustings, Fredsbrg., 26 Mar. 1790: Charles YATES (pltf.) against Elenor PIPEMAN and Kitty PIPEMAN daus. and coheirs of Benjamin PIPEMAN dec'd (defs.); it appears that Elenor is not an inhabitant of this country (VHFA 20 May 90); by virtue of a decree of the Ct. of Hustings founded on a deed of mortgage executed by Benjamin PIPEMAN

and Rebecca his wife to Charles YATES Gent. to secure the payment of a debt due from PIPEMAN to YATES, one half lot of ground in Fredsbrg. will be sold (VHFA 30 Dec 90)

PISTOW, John Christopher, German redemptioner, came in the brig *Rappahannock*, ran away from Isabella ROSS, Caroline Co. (VHFA 19 Feb 89)

PITCHER, Billy, aka Billy, Negro [slave], c. 18, ran away from Joseph CABELL on James River near Warminster, Buckingham Co. (LWG 13 Jul 99)

PITCHER, Lucy, her husband, John PITCHER of Shenandoah Co., warns that he will no longer pay any of her debts (VHFA 1 Jan 95)

PITCHER, Richard, d. on 10 Mar. 1784 [his epitaph is published] (RCFPC 28 Dec 96

PITMAN, John, of Falmouth, will pet. the GA to vest legal right to him for a tract of land in Kg. Geo. Co. formerly the property of William PITMAN dec'd (VGAA 12 Oct 91)

PITMAN, William, of Kg. Geo. Co., executed on 12 May for the murder of his Negro lad (VGPu 12 May 75 sup)

PITSBARGER, John, Dutch, 19, enl. in Pendleton Co., des. from the 4th Regt., U. S. Army (VGSWA 20 Oct 97)

PITT, Mrs. Eleanor, relict of the late William PITT merch., d. in Wmsbrg. on Tues. eve the 10th inst. in her 42nd year (RC 21 Nov 95)

PITT, George, svt., imp. in the *Justitia* in the fall of 1766, served in the 11th Regt. of Foot under Maj. MARKHAM, ran away from Samuel HIPKINS and Griffin GARLAND, Richmond Co. (VGR 25 Aug 68)

PITT, Robert, att. at law, of New Kent Co., d. on Wed. the 13th inst., (VGR 21 Jan 73); his ex. (nfi) will sell his plant. in New Kent Co. two miles above the Long Bridge (VG 23 Sep 73)

PITT, Mrs. Sarah, spouse of Dr. George PITT of Wmsbrg., d. last Mon. morn. in her 47th year [obit. in VGR] (VG and VGR 12 Nov 72)

PITT, William, died lately at Lilliput near Wmsbrg. (VGWeA 26 Jan 86)

PIT[T]S, John, of Caroline Co., nearly 80 years old, committed to the Fredsbrg. jail for horse stealing (VHFA 21 Aug 98)

PLANTIFF, Jack, aka Jack JACKSON, Negro, c. 30, speaks like a West India Negro, says he came from Ky., jailed in [Alexandria] (CMAG 16 Jul 99)

PLATER, His Ex. George Esq., Governor of Md., d. in Annapolis, Md. on Fri. the 10th inst. (VGGA 29 Feb 92)

PLEASANTS Family, HCC, [nd], between Robert POLLARD (pltf.) and Thomas PLEASANTS (admr. of John PLEASANTS), Thomas Mifflin PLEASANTS, and Richard PLEASANTS infants under 21 by Thomas PLEASANTS their gdn., Austin MORRIS and Polly his wife, Philip SHEPPARD, Edmund JAMES and Susanna his wife, and Moseby SHEPPARD, John SHEPPARD, Elizabeth SHEPPARD, and Ann SHEPPARD infants under 21 by the sd. Philip SHEPPARD their gdn. (defs.) (VGGA 10 Jan 98)

PLEASANTS, Miss, of Goochland Co., d. in a riding accident on Fri. last (VGAR 13 Oct 91)

PLEASANTS, James Jr., att. at law, has moved from Goochland Co. to Manchester (VGRMA 12 Mar 95)

PLEASANTS, John, d. on the 13th ult. at his house at Curle's in Henrico Co., aged 75 (VG 12 Sep 71)

PLEASANTS, John, dec'd, his son and ex., Robert PLEASANTS, will sell his mill on Fine Cr., Cumberland Co. (VGR 30 Sep 73)

PLEASANTS, John, of Henrico Co., mar. Miss Peggy JORDAN of Isle of Wight Co. (VG 2 Jun 74)

PLEASANTS, Col. John, of Four Mile Cr., died (VGWeA 13 Dec 93); late of Henrico Co., his admr., Thomas PLEASANTS Jr., will rent his land on Four Mile Cr. (VGRMA 22 Sep 94)

PLEASANTS, John Scott, of Richmond, mar. Miss Sally LOWNDES of Alexandria (VGAxA 6 May 90)

PLEASANTS, John, Jonathan, and Thomas, dec'd, e.a.w. Robert PLEASANT

18th-Century Virginia Newspapers 267

(nfi) who will also sell a tract of land in Charlotte Co. containing 1700 ac. and a tract in Cumberland Co. containing 345 ac. bel. to the est. of Jonathan PLEASANTS (VG 11 Apr 77)

PLEASANTS, John and Jonathan, late of Henrico Co., dec'd, a pet. will be pres. to the next GA to confirm the freeing of their slaves (VGGA 8 Sep 90)

PLEASANTS, Joseph, late of Nansemond Co., dec'd, three tracts of his land to be sold by Lemuel REDDICK and Exum SCOTT, both of Nansemond Co., or John PLEASANTS Jr. in Henrico (VG 20 Mar 52)

PLEASANTS, Mrs. Mary, consort of Robert C. V, d. at Bell Meade, Powhatan Co., on the 13th inst. (Arg 26 Feb 99)

PLEASANTS, Robert, Jr., dec'd, any demands against his est. or that of his widow, Eliza PLEASANTS, to be made known to his admr., Robert PLEASANTS (RMA 4 Jun 96)

PLEASANTS, Robert Cary, mar. Mrs. Mary LOGAN widow of Charles LOGAN, on Thurs. last, the 10th inst., at Bell Meade, Powhatan Co. (RMA 16 Dec 95)

PLEASANTS, Samuel, printer, mar. Miss Deborah LOWNES, both of Richmond, on Sat. eve. 18 July (RC 21 Jul, VGGA 22 Jul, VHFA 28 Jul 95)

PLEASANTS, Thomas Jr., of Four Mile Cr., d. on Sun. the 10th inst. at the house of Dr. Cringan in this city [Richmond]; he left a widow (VGGA and RMA 13 Jan 96); his acting ex., Samuel PLEASANTS, will sell all his PE (RMA 4 May 96)

PLEDGE, William Sr., dec'd, the Commissioners in Goochland Co. will sell several of his slaves to pay off a debt to David ROSS (VGRMA 12 May 94)

PLEDGER, Thomas, living near Baker's Ordinary, Isle of Wight Co., 40, enl. by George MACKENZIE, has not reported to camp at Wmsbrg. (VG 31 Jul, 14 Aug 46)

PLUM, Lewis W., potter, mar. Miss Susannah [DOXAY], both of Alexandria, on Thurs. eve. (CMAG 9 Nov 99)

PLUNKET, Anne, executed at Wmsbrg. on 26 Nov. for the murder of her bastard child (NYWJ 21 Feb 43)

POE, John, escaped from jail in Winchester on 17 Jul; his brother-in-law is Jesse BROWN (BVCG 3 Aug 95)

POLLARD, Anne, from Hampshire Co., d. in the hospital for lunatics (VGP{u 24 Jan 77)

POLLARD, Benjamin Esq., was mar. to the widow NORTON, both of Norfolk, on Thurs. eve. at the seat of Col. NEWTON by the Rev. James WHITEHEAD (NHPA 9 Nov 97)

POLLARD, Jonathan, svt., from the west of England, ran away from Gerard ELLYSON, Chesterfield Co. (VGR 19 Feb 67)

POLLARD, Joseph, d. lately in Goochland Co. in his 91st year leaving a widow aged 87 and seven chil. [obit.] (VGGA 11 Jan 92)

POLLARD, Sarah, dec'd, her ex. is Francis COLEMAN (VHFA 18 Mar 80)

POLLARD, William, of Hanover Co., dec'd, e.a.w. his admr., Robert POLLARD of K & Q Co. or William POLLARD of Hanover Co. (VGGA 19 Sep 92)

POMPEY, Billy, aka Billy, Negro, c. 23, good ship carpenter, can read and write, ran away from John GILLIAM Sr., Pr. Geo. Co. (VGPI 22 Mar 96, RMA 13 Apr 96)

PONSONBY, John, 22, absconded with a horse bel. to Thomas REED, Alexandria, in Oct. 1786 (VJAA 10 May 87)

POOL, George, appr., c. 16, tailor, ran away from John WOODSIDE, Norfolk, whom he had served about two years (VGR 8 Aug 71)

POOL, Howard, of Norfolk, d. on Sun. last (NHPA 10 Aug 97); e.a.w. Samuel and Robert POOL, Norfolk (NHPA 1 Feb 98, NH 22 Feb 98); Robert POOL will rent a two-story frame house in the commons (NH 29 Mar 98) [name also given as POOLE and POULE]

POOL, Mrs. Mary, consort of Howard POOL, Norfolk, d. on Sun. morn. in her 55th year (NPJ 26 Nov 88)

POOL, Capt. Samuel, of Norfolk Borough, d. on Thurs. last (NH 24 Feb 98)

POOR, Thomas, dec'd, his ex., James SCRUGS, will sell some of his slaves in Goochland Co. (VIC 12 Nov 88)
POORE, James, c. 18, des. from Samuel HOPKINS' Co. of regulars in the 6th Va. Regt.; he was b. in some of the northern provinces (VGPu 16 Aug 76)
POPE, Mrs. Lucy, consort of Nathaniel POPE Esq. of Louisa Co., d. on Thurs. the 23rd ult. (VIC 5 Aug 89)
POPE, Mrs. Mary, consort of Dr. Matthew POPE of Henrico Co., formerly a resident of Yorktown, d. lately near Richmond (VGWeA and VGAA 12 Jan 82)
POPE, Matthew, of Yorktown, intends to return to England as soon as he settles his affairs (VG 17 Jun 73)
POPE, Capt. Piercy Smith, of the U. S. Artillery, d. at Natchez last July [obit.] (VGGA 10 Dec 99, Ex 17 Dec 99, TDCDA 20 Dec 99)
POPE, William Esq., of Goochland Co., mar. Miss Ann WOODSON of Powhatan (VGGA 6 Jun 92)
POPE, William, att. at law, has moved from Goochland Co. into Powhatan Co. (VGGA and RMA 3 Feb 96)
POPJEE, William, conv. svt., hatter, arrived in the *Justitia* in Apr., ran away from Sampson and George MATTHEWS, Staunton (VGR 6 May 73 sup)
PORROCK, William, from Amherst Co., d. on the 17th ult. at the Lunatic Hospital in Wmsbrg. (VGWeA 26 Aug 90)
POR[T]EOUS, Mr. Ivey, late of Philadelphia, d. of consumption in Norfolk on Sun. eve. (NPJ 12 Dec 87)
PORTEOUS, Capt. William, of Pr. Geo. Co., dec'd, e.a.w. J. and J. J. THWEATT, his admrs. (VGPI 17 Dec 99)
PORTER, Mr., merch., from New England in Port-au-Prince, d. there on 24 [Dec. 1790] (VGGA 16 Mar 91)
PORTER, Charles, of Orange Co., dec'd, e.a.w. his ex., Camp PORTER, John WHARTON, and Thomas FARISH (VHFA 17 May 92); his ex. will sell all his PE (VHFA 30 Oct 94)
PORTER, Capt. David, dec'd, his admr. (nfi) intends to pet. the next Assembly for a payment to Capt. PORTER's est. for the destruction of his property on the South Branch (NPJ 1 Oct 88)
PORTER, Edward, executed on 13 Jan. for horse stealing (VGP 12 Jan 75)
PORTER, Sarah, appr., c. 15, ran away from James LARUE, Long Marsh (BVCG 25 Mar 96)
PORTER, William, merch., of Fredsbrg., mar. Miss Polly DUNCANSON dau. of the late James DUNCANSON Esq. of this place [Fredsbrg.], on Thurs. last at the seat of James DUNCANSON in Culpeper Co. (VHFFA 6 Sep 96, RCFPC 7 Sep 96)
PORTERFIELD, Alexander, dec'd, his extx., Elizabeth PORTERFIELD, and ex., Matthew PORTERFIELD and George HARLAN of Berkeley Co., will sell some of his slaves, livestock, and farming equipment (BI 18 Sep 99)
PORTERFIELD, Mrs. Rebecca, consort of Gen. Robert PORTERFIELD of Augusta Co., d. on Tues. the 3rd inst. (OVT 23 Jul 98, VGGA 24 Jul 98)
PORTLOCK, Nathaniel, of Norfolk Borough, dec'd, e.a.w. his extx., Rebecca PORTLOCK (VG 29 May 52)
PORTLOCK, Nathaniel, dec'd, a pet. by his legatees to have their legacies paid (VCNPGA 8 Sep 92)
PORTLOCK, Samuel, of Norfolk, dec'd, e.a.w. his ex., Samuel and John PORTLOCK (NPJ 28 May 88); two chests of his carpenter's tools to be sold by his ex., John SMALLWOOD (NPC 10 Jul 90)
POSEY, John Price, executed on Fri last [25 Jan.] near Richmond (VGWeA 31 Jan 88, VJAA 5 Feb 88, VGWA 8 Feb 88)
POTTER, David, 32-33, b. in New Jersey, enl. at Norfolk on 11 Nov. 1794, des. from Ft. Nelson (HNPA 4 Mar 95)
POTTER, Dr. Henry, late of Spotsylvania Co., dec'd, his est. to be sold by his admr., John GRYMES (VG 24 Apr 46)
POTTER, Sarah, appr., 13, ran away from Robert STOREY, Round Hill (WG 2

Jan 99)

POTTIE, Christopher, of Winchester, his wife Mary has absented herself from his bed and board (BVCG 21 Jul 94)

POTTIE, George, dec'd, e.a.w. his acting ex., Archibald DICK of Louisa Co. (VIC 2 Apr 88); a chancery case mentions his extx. Mary POTTIE (VGGA 28 Sep 91 ex); Archibald DICK Jr. of Caroline adv. that he has settled the est. and delivered the residue to George POTTIE Esq., the heir and devisee (VGGA 19 Oct 96)

POTTINGER, James, late innkeeper in Fredsbrg., d. yesterday, aged 34 (VHFA 20 Jun 93); his admr., George FRENCH, will sell all his PE (VHFA 4 Jul 93)

POTTINGER, Mrs. Margaret, wife of James POTTINGER of Fredsbrg., died (VHFA 11 Aug 91)

POTTLE, William, svt., c. 30, ran away from Thomas TURNER, Kg. Geo. Co. (VG 11 Aug 38)

POTTS Family, Berkeley Co. Ct., 22 Nov. 1792, in chanc: John POTTS eld. son and heir at law and Elizabeth POTTS dau. and legatee of Jonas POTTS dec'd (compls.) against George BEELER admr. etc. of William VESTALL dec'd who was admr. of John VESTALL dec'd who was ex. of Jonas POTTS dec'd, and William VESTALL eld. son and heir at law of the sd. William VESTALL dec'd who was the eld. son and heir at law of the sd, John VESTALL dec'd (defs); it appears that BEELER is not an inhabitant of this country (PGBA 18 Feb 93)

POTTS, John, [in a long advertisement] accuses his wife, Johannah, of trying to secure his property and run him into debt (PGBA 22 Sep 96)

POTTS, John Jr., merch., of Alexandria, mar. Miss Eliza RAMSAY (VJAA 29 Jun 86)

POTTS, Martha, has absented herself from her husband, Thomas POTTS of Pr. Geo. Co. (VGPu 7 Feb 77)

POTTS, Nathan, des. from the barracks in Winchester; he formerly lived within five miles of the Vinyard Tavern (BVCG 30 Nov 95)

POULTNEY, Thomas, merch., of Alexandria, mar. Miss Nancy THOMAS dau. of Evan THOMAS of Md. (VGAxA 29 Apr 90)

POULTON, Mrs., spouse of Capt. Jesse POULTON of Norfolk, died (NPC 24 Apr 90)

POUND, John, son and heir of Morris POUND dec'd of Fairfax Co., summoned to answer a bill in chanc. in that co. exhibited against him by William SAVAGE and Margaret his wife extx. of the will of Charles GREEN dec'd and Spence GRAYSON admr. of Benjamin GRAYSON dec'd (VGR 1 Aug 71)

POUND, Lot, appr. saddler, reportedly working in Bath or Greenbrier Co., ran away from William SMOCK, Fredsbrg. (VHFA 17 Jul 94)

POUND, Morise, a native of Shafousen, Switzerland, who started a vinyard in Va., d. on 18 Nov.; his sons, John and Jacob, will carry on the business (PC 27 Nov 69)

POVALL, Peter, commonly called POVEY, of Oswestry, Shropshire, England, sailed from Liverpool on the *Hope* in Mar. 1759; he left the ship in Philadelphia that same year; information on his whereabouts is desired (VG 18 Jan 70)

POVALL, Robin, late of Henrico Co., dec'd, his ex., William ROYALL of Charles City Co., invites the several claimants against the est. to bring in their accounts (VGWeA 21 May 85)

POWELL, Mrs., spouse of Benjamin POWELL Esq. of Wmsbrg., died (VGWeA 12 Jan 82)

POWELL, Benjamin, d. at his farm near Wmsbrg. on Sat. the 20th inst. in his 63rd year (VGGA 1 Dec 90)

POWELL, Burr, of Loudoun Co., adv. that on 15 Oct. 1792, Aaron OWINS, now of Mason Co., Ky., sold him a small tract of land in Fauquier Co. and caused a deed to be executed for it by his father, William OWINS, in whom the legal title was and received in part consideration for sd. land a bond drawn in the name of his father, Levan POWELL, to convey him 100 ac. on the north fork of Licking; it appears that the land in Fauquier Co. had been mortgaged before its sale (KG 1 Apr 97)

POWELL, David, svt., brickmaker, 40, ran away from John JOHNSTON and Joseph STANDFORD, Westmoreland Co. (VG 23 Feb 39)

POWELL, Edward and Robert, of Greensville Co., dec'd, e.a.w. their ex., Matthew DAVIS (VGPI 21 Apr 97)

POWELL, Elizabeth, mulatto woman, ran away from John ALMAND, Goochland Co. (VGR 22 Dec 68)

POWELL, James, Collector of the King's Duties in the District of Pocomoke, Accomack Co., died (VG 12 Jan 39)

POWELL, Jannatt, of Orange Co., advises James HEAD and Elizabeth Jannatt HEAD, his wife, and Sally RIDDLE all of Georgia of his intention to take depositions to prove his right to certain Negroes (VHFA 16 Jun 95)

POWELL, Leven Jr., of this town [Alexandria], mar. Miss Eliza ORR of Loudoun Co. on the 26th ult. (CMAG 3 Oct 97)

POWELL, Matthew, svt., b. near Bristol, England, ran away from Joseph SIMPSON, Richmond Co. (VG 6 Oct 52)

POWELL, Seymour, late of Yorktown, dec'd, e.a.w. his extx., Jane POWELL (VGWeA 5 Oct 82, 11 Jan 87)

POWELL, Thomas, c. 25, des. from the ship *Tartar* lying at Frazer's Ferry, Mattaponi River; he enl. under the name Thomas NEWTON and is expected to go to Georgetown, Md. as that was his place of residence (VGPu 17 Oct 77)

POWELL, Thomas, late of Southampton Co., dec'd, e.a.w. his admr., Thomas HOLLIDAY (NH 21 May 99)

POWELL, William, svt., over 40, b. in an inland county of England, ran away from Richard GRAHAM, Dumfries (VGR 26 Oct 69)

POWELL, William, of Warwick Co., [dec'd], e.a.w. his ex., Benjamin POWELL of York Co. and Thomas C. AMORY of Warwick Co. (VGWeA 30 Mar 86)

POWER, Maj. Henry, former justice of the peace and rep. in the assembly, d. on 20 Dec. at his house in James City Co. (VG 21 Dec 39)

POWER, Major, dec'd, e.a.w. his ex., Robert H. SAUNDERS and Daniel WADE (VGGA 14 Oct 95)

POWERS, Edward Jr., d. on Tues. the 23rd inst. in James City Co. in the bloom of youth (VGRC 30 Sep 94)

POWERS, John, dec'd, his plant. in Kg. Wm. Co. to be sold by his ex., William POWERS and Daniel LIPSCOMB (VG 1 Jan 67)

[P]OWIS, Samuel, tailor and shoemaker, c. 40, b. in the west of England, ran away from Abraham JARRETT (VGR 4 Aug 74)

POYTHRESS, Joshua, dec'd, e.a.w. his admx., Elizabeth POYTHRESS and admr., Archibald ROBERTSON (VGPI 20 Sep 87); his surviving admr. and gdn. of Susanna POYTHRESS, Archibald ROBERTSON, will sell his HH & KF and other items of his est. at Flower de Hundred his late residence (VGPI 1 Nov 87); ROBERTSON will sell 35 of his Negroes at Flower de Hundred (VGPI 29 Nov 96)

POYTHRESS, Col. Peter, of Pr. Geo. Co., dec'd, e.a.w. his ex., William MAYO Jr. (VGAA 8 Feb 86, VIC 1 Aug 87)

POYTHRESS, Maj. William, dec'd, his ex. will sell all his PE at his plant. on Little Roanoke in Charlotte Co. (VG 30 Dec 75)

POYTHRESS, William, late of Pr. Geo. Co., dec'd, e.a.w. his ex., Peter POYTHRESS of Branchester (VG 18 Jul 77)

POYTHRESS, William, will sell part of the Flower de Hundred tract of land on the James River which was devised to him by his father (nfi) (VGPI 18 Mar 90)

POYTHRESS, Maj. William, his admx. is Mary POYTHRESS of Pr. Geo. Co. (VGPI 29 Dec 95)

PRATT, Dr. Shubael, formerly of Connecticut, d. in Alexandria (VJAA 18 Aug. 85)

PRATT, Thomas, conv. svt., 36, millwright and pump maker, ran away from

Sampson and George MATTHEWS, Staunton; he had arrived in the *Justitia* in April (VGR 6 May 73 sup)

PR[E]BY, Thomas, Eng. svt., 40, biscuit maker, ran away from Richard TALIAFERRO on 19 June 1744; he may be in Norfolk (VG 23 May 45)

PRENTICE, Ebenezer, dec'd, e.a.w. his admr., Jedidiah LEED, Richmond, who will also sell his effects (VGRMA 8 May 94)

PRENTIS, Daniel, of Wmsbrg., mar. Miss Betsey GODWIN of Warwick Co. (VG 10 Sep 72)

PRENTIS, Miss Elizabeth, dau. of the late William PRENTIS merch. of Wmsbrg., d. on Fri. the 5th inst., at the house of David MEADE Esq. in Nansemond in her 18th year (VGR 11 Oct 70)

PRENTIS, Col. John, merch., of Wmsbrg., died (VGP 2 Nov, VGPu 3 Nov, VG 4 Nov 75); his ex. (nfi) will sell all of his HH & KF at his plant. in James City Co. (VG 23 Dec 75)

PRENTIS, Mrs. Mary, relict of the late William PRENTIS, d. last Sat. morn. in her [6]8th year (VG 14 Apr 68)

PRENTIS, William, of Wmsbrg., dec'd, his PE and tracts of land in York Co. to be auctioned off for the benefit of his chil. (VG 28 Jul 68); a tract of his land in James City Co. to be sold (VG 13 Oct 68)

PRENTIS, Capt. William, of this city [Wmsbrg.], d. in his 33rd year (VG and VGR 18 Feb 73)

PRENTIS, William, printer, mar. Miss Polly GEDDY, both of Petersburg (VIC 11 Mar, VGWeA 12 Mar, VGWA 25 Mar 89)

PRESLEY, Col. [Peter], murdered by his own servants (VG-Randolph 10 May 49)

PRESSON, Samuel, late of York Co., dec'd, e.a.w. his ex., Nicholas PRESSON also of York Co. (VG and VGPu 28 Nov 77)

PRESTON, Francis Esq., att. at law of Montgomery Co., mar. Miss Sally B. CAMPBELL only dau. of the late Gen. William CAMPBELL dec'd of Washington Co., on 10 Jan. (VGGA 30 Jan 93)

PRESTON, Col. John Esq., of Montgomery Co. [or Botetourt acc. to OVT], mar. Miss Polly RADFORD eld. dau. of William RADFORD Esq. of Richmond, on Mon. eve. last the 11th inst. (OVT 14 Jun 98, Arg. 15 Jun 98, AGGA 19 Jun 98)

PRESTON, Col. William, dec'd, e.a.w. his acting ex., John BROWN, John PRESTON, and Francis PRESTON of Montgomery Co. (VGIC 15 Nov 83)

PREWET, James, appr. lad, bound to John CROPPER Jr. to learn the occupation of a farmer, has about 18 months to serve (NH 11 May 99)

PRICE, Mrs., consort of Nathaniel PRICE merch. of Richmond, d. on Sat. last (RC 29 Mar 96)

PRICE, the Rev. Dr., d. on Tues. morn. 18 [month not given] at his house on Newington Green near London (VHFA 23 Jun 91)

PRICE, Mrs. Ann, spouse of John PRICE of Henrico Co., d. last Wed. (VIC 13 Jun 87)

PRICE, Capt. Barrett, of Henrico Co., d. on Thurs. last leaving a wife and numerous offspring (VGRMA 8 Sep 94); his ex., William PRICE, will settle his est. and sell 50 ac. of his land about four miles from Richmond (RMA 20 Jun 95)

PRICE, Ellis J., printer, mar. Miss Sally FLEMMING (PGBA 5 May 96)

PRICE, James, dec'd, his ex., Randolph PRICE, will sell his PE which includes house joiner's and cabinet maker's tools (VG 17 Dec 72)

PRICE, Mrs. Jane, consort of Nathaniel W. PRICE merch. of this city [Richmond], d. on Sat. eve. last (VGGA and RMA 30 Mar 96)

PRICE, John, formerly lived with George T...[remainder of name unclear] and John CHAMBER, Queen Anne's Co., Md. is earnestly entreated by his brother (nfi) to return to England (VG 25 Oct 95)

PRICE, John, dec'd, his extx., Anne PRICE, and ex., John LEE, will sell 300 ac. of his land near Rappahannock River (VG 4 Jun 72)

PRICE, John, mar. Miss Nancy KENNON, both of this city [Richmond], on Fri.

eve. (VGAA 19 Apr 86)
PRICE, John, dec'd, his ex. (nfi) of Hanover Co., will sell his crops and HH & KF (VGGA 17 Oct 92)
PRICE, John W., of Henrico Co., d. on Mon. eve. the 11th inst. and was bur. on Sun. last at his seat about five miles from this city [Richmond] attended by upwards of 100 of his bother masons (VGGA 20 Jul 91); his ex., Peter and Lewis PRICE, will settle his est. and sell items of his est. (VGGA 26 Oct 91, 9 Jan 93)
PRICE, Capt. Joseph, mar. Miss Lucy BURTON, both of this co., on Thurs. last (VGRMA 11 Dec 94)
PRICE, Capt. Leonard, of Goochland, dec'd, his ex. (nfi) will sell items of his est. (VG 8 Oct 72)
PRICE, Peter, adv. that he will pay no debts contracted by his wife, Jane PRICE, from this date, she having abused his confidence and otherwise ill treated him (CMAG 31 May 96)
PRICE, Randolph, dec'd, his ex., John WESSON, will sell part of his est. at his late dwelling house in Surry Co. (VG 19 Mar 79)
PRICE, Mrs. Rebecca, of Surry Co., spouse of Randolph PRICE, died (VGPu 21 Mar 77 sup)
PRICE, Samuel, c. 30, lately master and owner of a coasting schooner in Georgia, wanted there for robbery and piracy (VG 23 Dec 75)
PRICE, Samuel, of Henrico Co., dec'd, e.a.w. James PRICE and John W. PRICE, his exors. (VGAA 27 Jul 82, 14 Sep 82)
PRICE, Capt. William, of Fluvanna Co., mar. Miss Sally LEWIS dau. of Col. Robert LEWIS of Goochland Co., on Thurs. the 29th inst. (VIC 12 Dec 87, VGWeA 13 Dec 87)
PRICE, William, mulatto, jailed [in Fredsbrg.] (VHFA 1 Aug 93)
PRICE, William, mar. Miss Lucy DUVAL, both of Richmond, on Thurs. (VGRMA 16 Feb 95, VGGA 18 Feb 95)
PRIDE, Halcott, dec'd, his ex. (nfi) will sell sundry articles of HH & KF in Petersburg (VGP 12 Oct 75)
PRIDE, William, of Dinwiddie Co., near Petersburg, dec'd, some of his livestock and HHF to be sold by his ex., William EATON and Henry BATTE (VG 29 Dec 52)
PRIMUS, Charles, young Negro, has a relation at Mr. H. SKIPWITH's in Cumberland Co., ran away from Benjamin PARKER (VGGA 17 Sep 94)
PRINGLE, John, late bar keeper to Mrs. CAMPBELL of this city [Wmsbrg.], dec'd, e.a.w. his admr., John LOCKLEY (VG 1 Dec 74)
PRINGLE, Richard, of Kg. Geo. Co., dec'd, e.a.w. his ex., Theodorick FITZHUGH (VGGA 30 Mar 84)
PRINGLE, Sarah, has left her husband, Richard PRINGLE of Gloucester Co. (VG 10 Sep 72); she has exhibited a bill against her husband at the General Ct. of Chancery in Wmsbrg. (VG 22 Oct 72)
PRINTZ, Michael, of Winchester, mar. the widow PRICE of Frederick Co. on Thurs. last (WG 6 Mar 99)
PRIOR, Mrs., spouse of John PRIOR of Norfolk, died (NPC 24 Apr 90)
PRIOR, John, dec'd, e.a.w. Dr. Frederick WILLIAMS of Norfolk or Samuel PRIOR of Charles City Co. (VCNPGA 2 Mar 93)
PRITCHARD, Mrs. Margaret, consort of Stephen PRITCHARD, d. on Tues. the 3rd inst. in her 46th year (BVCG 13 Jan 97)
PRITCHETT, Peter, c. 24, des. from the 14th Regt. and is supposed to be lurking in the upper end of Dinwiddie Co. (VGPu 5 Sep 77)
PROBY, Mrs., consort of Paul PROBY an alderman of the borough, d. on Tues. 9 [Dec.] (NPJ 17 Dec 88)
PROCTOR, Jonathan, of Md., but late of Va., dec'd, e.a.w. his admr., Tully ROBINSON of Norfolk Co. (HNPA 7 Feb 95)
PROSSER, Mrs., consort of Maj. Thomas PROSSER, d. on the Brook in this co. on Sun. last (RMA 4 Oct 96)
PROSSER, John, of this city [Richmond], mar. Miss Polly POOLE of Henrico, o

Sat. eve. last (VGGA 9 Oct 98, DOB 11 Oct 98)

PROSSER, Jonathan, tailor, with many yrs. experience in London, continues his business in Wmsbrg. (VG 7 Jan 73)

PROSSER, Maj. Thomas, d. on Sun. last at his seat in Henrico Co. (VGGA 9 Oct 98, DOB 11 Oct 98

PROTHERO, Mary, came to Va. from Bristol about six or seven yrs. ago with Sarah SYFERS (when both were about 20) and lived with one COLEMAN, a biscuit baker on York River; if she will apply to Capt. John CAWSEY of the ship *Brothers* now lying in Pamunkey, she may hear something to her advantage (VG 18 Feb 68); her husband, Robert TAYLOR of Bedford Co., adv. that she ran off with a silversmith named CUTTINGS and that they will go to Eng. to get some money she is heir to by the death of Thomas PROTHERO of Bristol (VG 6 Jul 69)

PRUCE, Thomas, Eng. conv. svt., ran away from Daniel and Menoah SINGLETON, Orange Co. (VGR 22 Jul 73 sup)

PRUDDEN, Mrs., killed by a slave in Nansemond Co. (VG 4 Feb 37)

PRY, Richard, appr. wheelwright and chairmaker, 19-20, ran away from John JAMISON, Martinsburg (PGBA 27 Oct 96)

PRYOR, Arthur, dec'd. a tract of land he purchased of Charles STUNKS in Lunenburg Co. to be sold by his ex., John WALLER and Christopher PRYOR of K & Q Co. (VG 27 Mar 52)

PRYOR, John, of this city [Richmond], mar. Miss Nancy WHITING of Gloucester on Thurs. last (VGGA 19 Oct 96)

PUGH, Daniel, dec'd. lands claimed by him in Harrison, Hardy, and Randolph cos. to be sold by his ex., John PRUNTY (BVCG 9 Nov 95)

PUGH, Joseph, late of Shenandoah Co., dec'd, e.a.w. his admr., William RICHARDSON (WG 9 Oct 99)

PUGH, Col. Theophilus, of Nansemond Co., d. last Fri. (VG 21 Nov 45)

PULLAM, James, b. in Goochland Co., 26, pvt. in the 2nd Regt. of Artillerists and Engineers, des. at Federal Spring (VGGA 2 Jul 99)

PULLETT, Joseph, of York Co., dec'd, e.a.w. Frederick BRYAN (nfi) (VG 25 Jun 67)

PUNTER, Henry, dec'd, his PE to be sold by his admr., W. GRAVES of Charles City Co. (VGGA 11 Apr 92); his houses and plant. in Charles City Co. to be leased by his admr. William GRAVES (VGGA 28 Jan 95)

PURCEL, Thomas, merch., of the House of Blight, Brothers, & Co., Norfolk, d. on 4 Oct. (VCNPGA 6 Oct 92)

PURCELL, Henry, dec'd, demands against his est. to be made known to Henry PURCELL of Gloucester Co.; his admr. is Peter PURCELL of the same co. (VGCD 19 May 80)

PURCELL, John, Irish, 30-32, wanted for escaping from Henrico Co. jail (VGAA 8 Nov 83, VGIC 15 Nov 83)

PURCELL, William, of Gloucester Co., dec'd, e.a.w. his ex. (nfi) (VGPu 29 Nov 76)

PURDIE, Alexander, printer, of Wmsbrg., mar. Miss Peachy DAVENPORT on 31 Dec. (VGR 31 Dec 72); printer to the Commonwealth, died (VG 16 Apr 79); his ex., Ro. ANDERSON and J. M. GALT, will settle his est. and sell all of his PE (VG 8 May 79)

PURDIE, Alexander, son of Alexander PURDIE printer dec'd, late of Wmsbrg., who served as a soldier in the last campaign under General WAYNE, d. on Sat. night last (VGWeA 15 Oct 96)

PURNAL, John, appr. cooper, near 18, ran away from Jacob HAINES, West Nottingham, Cecil Co., Md., who expects he intends going near Winchester in Va. (PGBA 5 May 96)

PURNER, James, appr., shoemaker, ran away from Abner WELLS (BVCG 17 Feb 97)

PURTLE Family, Frederick Co. Ct., 3 Dec 1799, in chanc: John HODGSON and Martha his wife late Martha PURTLE, James TODD and Jane his wife late Jane PURTLE (the sd. Martha and Jane being the heirs and legal reps. of

Nicholas PURTLE dec'd) (pltfs.) against Meshach SEXTON et al. (defs.) [see also: USHER Family] (WG 18 Dec 99)

PURVIANCE Family, HCC, 7 Mar. 1795, between John HAZLEHURST (pltf.) and Robert PURVIANCE, John HENRY, Henry, [Letitia,] Elizabeth, Susanna, and Isabella PURVIANCE chil. and co-heirs of Samuel PURVIANCE (defs.); the defs. are not inhabitants of this country (RC 23 May 95)

PURVIANCE, John, for many yrs. an eminent merch. in Philadelphia, d. in Nelson Co., Ky. at the beginning of Jan. last (WVGWA 17 Apr 90)

PURVIS, Francis, planter of this county [Spotsylvania], murdered returning home from his son's house about a mile from his own (VHFA 4 Dec 88, VGWA 24 Dec 88)

PURVIS, James, of Spotsylvania Co., dec'd, his PE will be sold by James DUDLEY and Burrell LEAVIL (nfi) (VH 18 Sep 98)

PURYEAR, Hezekiah, dec'd, e.a.w. his ex., Ellis PURYEAR and Hezekiah PURYEAR (Arg 30 Nov 98)

PURYEAR, John, dec'd, e.a.w. his ex., Samuel PURYEAR, William PURYEAR, and Edward FINCH of Mecklenburg Co. (VGPI 28 Dec 86)

PURYEAR, Obediah, journeyman chairmaker, ran away from Elkanah DEANE, Wmsbrg. (VGP 23 Mar 75)

PUTTERILL, Thomas, ind. svt., butcher, a Lincolnshire man, came in the *Liberty* last Apr., ran away from Richard LEE, Westmoreland Co. (VG 8 Jul 73, VGR 22 Jul 73 sup); escaped from custody in Essex Co. (VG 19 Aug 73); reportedly came from Old Nansemond Town, ran away from Richard LEE and Thomas ATTWELL, Westmoreland Co. (VG 12 May 74) [name also given as PUTRELL and PUTTRELL]

PYLAND, Richard, of Surry Co., dec'd, Robert PYLAND (nfi) will sell his tract of land there (VG 3 Feb 74)

PYNES, Nathaniel, of Kg. Wm. Co., dec'd, his admr., Drury RAGSDALE, will pet. the next GA for the emancipation of Nat, a Negro man bel. to the est. (VIC 22 Oct 88)

QUACCA, George, Negro, c. 24, ran away from George HOPE, Hampton (VGWeA 20 Aug 85)

QUARLES, Isaac, of Kg. Wm. Co., mar. Miss SOUTHERLAND of the same co. (VG 5 May 74)

QUARLES, Col. James, of Kg. Wm. Co., dec'd, his ex., William AYLETT and John QUARLES Jr., will sell all of his PE (VG 24 Oct 71); some of his est. is in the hands of Col. John QUARLES and other legatees acc. to his ex., William AYLETT (VGR 18 Nov 73)

QUARLES, Roger, of Caroline Co., dec'd, e.a.w. his ex., Francis TOMPKINS and John QUARLES (VGGA 6 Aug 94)

QUARLES, Tunstall, late sheriff and coroner of Fluvanna Co., intends to move to the Western Country (VGGA 4 Oct 92); intends to move to Ky. on or about 1 April (VGGA 6 Mar 93)

QUARRIER, Alexander, coachmaker from Philadelphia has decided to settle in Richmond (VGAA 26 Apr 86)

QUARRIER, Mrs. Elizabeth, consort of Maj. Alexander QUARRIER of [Richmond], d. on Thurs. morn. last (VGGA 27 Sep 97)

QUASH, John, aka Quash, Negro, c. 30, ran away from Bourne PRICE, Bedford Co. (VG 8 Nov 76)

QUASH, Will, aka Will DAMAR, Negro, c. 35, ran away from the est. of John MAYO dec'd. (VGAA 24 May 86)

QUICK, George, 21-22, of Dutch extraction, b. in Loudoun Co., his father lived at Beazentown [in Carolina?]; convicted of horse stealing at a court held in Dumfries, escaped from jail (VGIC 4 Jul 89 sup)

QUIGLEY, John, his body was found hanging by the neck in a cabin near Bucklestown on Mon. morn. last; on examination of his children, who are very young, it appeared that on Thurs. morn. previous, QUIGLEY differed with his wife upon a trivial circumstance having at that time a pair of sharp-pointed shears in his hand, thrust them into her body which put an end to her life, after which he bur. the body in the garden (Martinsburg disp. of 6 Jul.) (VGGA 26 Jul 97)

QUIGLEY, Robert, ind. svt., 23, out of the ship *Mary* from Ireland, weaver, ran away from Rich Neck, Warwick Co. (AGNPWA 19 Mar, AGNPPA 21 May 94) [also given as TWIGLEY]

QUIN, Charles, executed on 23 Nov. for the murder of a Negro in Essex Co. (VG 23 Nov 39)

QUINN, James, desires to move to the Western Country and will sell his land in Rockingham (WG 6 Jun 98)

QUINN, Richard, dec'd, his son, James QUINN of Rockingham Co., has been informed that his father's debts were not paid off (VH 7 Oct 95)

QUINN, Richard, dec'd, his ex., Belfield CAVE and James WOOD, will sell two of his tracts in Madison Co. (VHFFA 1 Dec 95)

QUISENBERRY, Aaron Sr., of Orange Co., dec'd, e.a.w. his admrs., Aaron and Moses QUISENBERRY (VHFA 1 Sep 95)

RABORG, Michael, boot and shoemaker from Baltimore has opened his shop in Fredsbrg. (VHFA 2 Aug 92)

RACKETT, Thomas, his son, Ludwell RACKETT of Amelia Co., will pet. the next GA for leave to dispose of the est. his father left him as he thinks proper (VGGA 13 Aug 94)

RAGLAND, Edmond, of New Kent Co., appr., [18], ran away from George CLOPTON Jr., K & Q Co. (VGPu 4 Aug 75)

RAGLAND, Evan, dec'd, e.a.w. John and Evan RAGLAND (nfi) (VGGA 15 Jun 96)

RAGLAND, George, dec'd, his ex., William RAGLAND and John VEAL, will sell his land in Northampton Co., N. Carolina (VG 17 Sep 71)

RAGLAND, Maj. Samuel, late of Louisa Co., dec'd, e.a.w. his admr. w.w.a., Samuel OVERTON Jr. (VGGA 22 Jan 99)

RAILEY, Daniel, Irish, c. 30, jailed as a runaway svt. in Orange Co. along with Conner CORNEE (also Irish and c. 30); they say that they came to S. Carolina on a ship commanded from Capt. WILSON (VG 13 May 73)

RAINBERD, Jessath, Eng. svt., ran away from Richard LEE at the Naval Office in Charles Co., Md. (VG 24 Oct 51)

RAINES, Hartwell, of Brunswick Co., dec'd, his admr. is Nathaniel RAINES (VGPI 7 May 99)

RAINES, John, of Southampton Co., executed in Richmond on 5 Dec. for horse stealing (VGAA and VGWeA 6 Dec 83)

RAINES, William, saddler, appr., c. 17, his parents live in Caroline Co., ran away from John M'ENERY, Richmond (VGWeA 25 Jan 93)

RAINEY, David, d. in Petersburg (VGPI 21 Jul 97)

RAKESTRAW Family, Charlotte Co. Ct., 3 May 1796, in chanc: William BARKESDALE (compl.) against John RAKESTRAW heir of Robert RAKESTRAW and Mary RAKESTRAW widow of Robert RAKESTRAW (defs.) (RMA 7 May 96)

RAKESTRAW, John, brother of Robert RAKESTRAW of Charlotte Co. is mentioned (VGAA 12 Apr 83)

RALEIGH, Bryan, Irish, 23, des. from Capt. David BELL's Co. of the Va. Regt.; he may be going to N. Carolina (VG 5 Dec 55)

RALF, John, aka RELFE, HCC, 16 Sep. 1794: John HIGGENS (pltf.) and Tench FRANCIS and Richard NEAVE, Peter HODGSON, and Samuel GARDNER assignees of the est. of John RALF otherwise called John RELFE and John LEGAN (or LAGAN) (defs.); it appears that the defs. are not inhabitants of this county (VGWeA 22 Nov 94)

RAMSAY, Allen, late of Edenton, [N. Carolina], merch., e.a.w. his ex., William T. MUSE and Alexander MILLEN of Edenton, who will also sell his store of European and India goods (NH 19 Sep 99)

RAMSAY, Miss Amelia, of Alexandria, died (VGAxA 24 Nov 91)
RAMSAY, Mrs. Ann, of Alexandria, relict of the late William RAMSAY, d. on Sat. last in her 55th year; she was bur. next to her husband (VJAA 7 Apr 85)
RAMSAY, Col. Dennis, merch., mar. Miss Jenny TAYLOR dau. of Capt. Jesse TAYLOR merch. of Alexandria (VJAA 24 Nov 85)
RAMSAY, Dr. James, of Norfolk, mar. Mrs. Margaret BOUSH (VGWeA 12 Jul 87)
RAMSAY, Dr. James, of Norfolk, dec'd, his est. is unadministered by Dr. John RAMSAY; the new admr. is James RAMSAY (NPJ 12 Dec 87)
RAMSAY, Dr. James, a colonel of the 54th Regt. of Militia, d. [recently] (NHPA 18 Dec 97); e.a.w. his admr., John HUTCHINGS (NHPA 30 Dec 97)
RAMSAY, John and James, formerly of Lancaster Co., sons of John and Jane RAMSAY dec'd; Dale CARTER and Samuel YAP adv. that they may hear something to their advantage if they return to Lancaster Co. before 10 May 1769 (VGR 28 Apr 68)
RAMSAY, Mrs. Margaret, wife of Dr. James RAMSAY and dau. of James TAYLOR Esq. of Norfolk Borough, d. on Mon. eve. [27 Oct.] in her 23rd year (NPJ 29 Oct 88, VGWeA 6 Nov 88)
RAMSAY, Patrick, dec'd, his acting extx., Elizabeth RAMSAY, will sell his 900 ac. tract in Brunswick Co. and a 402 ac. tract two miles from Petersburg (VGPI 29 Mar 93); Elizabeth RAMSAY of Petersburg will sell 400 ac. of his land on Tomaheaton Cr. in Dinwiddie Co. (VGPI 12 Apr 96)
RAMSAY, Miss Sally Douglas, d. last Fri. night after a short illness (VJAA 24 Nov 85)
RAMSAY, Samuel, native of Scotland, d. on Mon. the 3rd. inst. in the bloom of life after an illness of a few days; he left behind him here no particular or near connection (OVT 6 Sep 98, VGGA 11 Sep 98)
RAMSAY, Thomas, mulatto, c. 22, a miller by trade, ran away from the mill of Stump, Ricketts & Co. on Cameron near Alexandria; he has a number of relations in and about Baltimore (CMAG 19 Apr 94)
RAMSAY, William Esq., of Alexandria, d. on 10 Feb. in the 69th year of his age; "first inhabitant of Alexandria;" he was bur. in the Episcopal churchyard on 12 Feb. (VJAA 17 Feb 85); persons having books belonging to him are asked to return them to William RAMSAY (nfi) (VJAA 23 Jun 85)
RAMSAY, William, native of Delaware, Assistant in the Continental Commissioner's Office for the accounts of S. Carolina and Georgia, d. lately in Charleston (VJAA 22 Nov 87)
RAMSEY, Patrick, HCC, 7 Jun. 1793: Elizabeth RAMSEY extx. of Patrick RAMSEY dec'd who was surviving partner of Gordon & Ramsey, merchants and partners (pltfs.) and John PERKS of Bristol, Peter LYONS, George WEBB, Joseph THORPE, James DREW, William DIGHTON, and ex. of George THOMAS dec'd (defs.) (VGWeA 16 Aug 93)
RANCOME, Thomas, conv. svt., c. 30, ditcher and well digger by trade, ran away, along with conv. svt. Elizabeth WILLIAMS alias WILLOUGHBY c. 25, from Richard BARNES, Richmond Co.; it is supposed that they will go towards Philadelphia (MG 24 Mar 47)
RAND, William, dec'd, pursuant to his will, his HHF and several tracts of land in Isle of Wight and Southampton cos. will be sold by his extx., Sophia RAND, and ex., Lewis ALLMAND; also mentioned are John RAND in Smithfield and William RAND in Southampton Co. (VG 9 Jan 72)
RAND, William, of Smithfield, dec'd, his admrs., Walter RAND and James PITT, will sell his houses and lots there (VIC 22 Apr 89)
RANDAL, Mrs., wife of John RANDAL merch., d. on Tues. last (NHPA 4 Feb 97)
RANDALL, Capt. George, was considered insane in 1789; in Feb. 1794 he left home and said he was going to Frederick Co.; he was in Madison Co. but has not been heard of lately; Griffin GARLAND of Richmond Co. will pay for information and for anyone to care for him until he can send for him (BVCG 6 May 96)

RANDALL, Richard and Joseph, sons of Christopher and Hannah RANDALL of the Parish of St. Magdalen, Burmondsey; if they apply to Capt. George DOBBIE at Hobb's Hole they may hear of a considerable legacy left to them; Joseph RANDALL is believed to be in Md. (VG 26 May 68)

RANDALL, Samuel, conv. svt., c. 28, bricklayer, ran away from John HAZLEGROVE, Fredsbrg. (VGR 9 Dec 73)

RANDOLPH Family, U. S. Middle Circuit, District of Virginia, Nov. term, 1794, in chanc: William JONES surviving partner of Farell & Jones (pltf.) against Benjamin HARRISON of Brandon, Benjamin HARRISON the Younger of Berkeley ex. of the will of Peyton RANDOLPH dec'd, William RANDOLPH, Richard Kidder RANDOLPH, and Peyton RANDOLPH sons and devisees of the sd. Peyton RANDOLPH dec'd (VGGA 26 Aug 95)

RANDOLPH, Mrs., wife of William RANDOLPH of Tuckahoe, Goochland Co., gave birth to a dau. on 1 Jan.; this was the first child after about four yrs. of marriage (VG 10 Feb 38)

RANDOLPH, Mrs., relict of [?] RANDOLPH Esq. of Va., d. lately in England (VG 1 Apr 80)

RANDOLPH, Mrs., of Chatsworth, died (VGWeA 27 Apr 82)

RANDOLPH, Mrs., wife of Harrison RANDOLPH, d. in [Richmond] (VGAA 8 Nov 86)

RANDOLPH, Adam, appr., 18-19, ran away from Thomas ALLEN, tailor, Norfolk; it is supposed he has gone to N. Carolina where he has some relations (NPJ 6 Aug 88)

RANDOLPH, Mrs. Anne, spouse of Thomas M. RANDOLPH Esq. of Tuckahoe, died (VIC 11 Mar 89, VGWeA 12 Mar 89)

RANDOLPH, Anne, a pet. will be presented to the next GA praying for a divorce between Anne RANDOLPH and John RANDOLPH her husband (RMA 12 Nov 96)

RANDOLPH, Mrs. Betty, relict of the Hon. Peyton RANDOLPH dec'd, d. on the 21st ult. in Wmsbrg. (Pennsylvania Gazette 12 Feb 83); late of Wmsbrg., her house there to be sold (VGAA 1 Feb 83); her admr. is Benjamin HARRISON Jr. of Richmond (VGGA 26 Oct 91)

RANDOLPH, Beverly, eld. son of the Hon. William RANDOLPH Esq., mar. Miss Betty LIGHTFOOT niece of the Hon. Philip LIGHTFOOT Esq., yesterday sennight (VG 30 Dec 37)

RANDOLPH, Beverly Esq., of Chatsworth, mar. Miss Martha COCKE eld. dau. of James COCKE Esq. of Wmsbrg., on Sat. last (VG 21 Jan 75)

RANDOLPH, Col. Beverly, d. on Tues., 7 Feb., at his residence on Green Cr. in Cumberland Co. in his 43rd year; though debilitated by an hereditary gout at a very early part of his life, he never shrunk from his portion of military duty; he was in arms at different periods from 1775 to the end of our late Revolutionary War; in 1781, at the head of a regt. of the yeomanry of his country, he gained honor in the action at Guilford Ct. H. under the orders of Gen. GREEN; in the same year, he served in the combined American and French armies before Yorktown (VGGA 15 Feb, Arg 17 Feb, VHFFA 21 Feb, RCFPC 22 Feb, VGPI 24 Feb 97); his ex., William RANDOLPH and Creed TAYLOR, will sell his HHF and 20 of his Negroes at his plant. in Cumberland Co. (Arg 28 Mar, VGWeA 1 Apr 97)

RANDOLPH, Edmund Esq., Att. Gen. of Va., mar. Miss Betsy NICHOLAS second dau. of the Treasurer (VGPu 30 Aug 76, VG 31 Aug 76)

RANDOLPH, Mrs. Elizabeth, consort of Ryland RANDOLPH, d. a few days ago in Petersburg (VGPI 16 Mar 98)

RANDOLPH, Harrison Esq., mar. Miss Betsy STARKE, both of Wmsbrg. (VG 19 Mar 79)

RANDOLPH, Henry Esq., mar. Miss Lucy WARD on Sat. last in Chesterfield Co. (VGWeA 7 Dec 82)

RANDOLPH, Isham, aka Isham ALLEN, Negro, 21-22, ran away from Landon CARTER, Fauquier Co.; he is believed to be in Stafford or Kg. Geo. Co. (VG 25 Feb 75)

RANDOLPH, Mrs. Jane, spouse of Thomas Isham RANDOLPH Esq. of Chesterfield Co., d. a few days ago (VG and VGR 17 Feb 74)

RANDOLPH, Sir John, d. on Wed., 2 Mar. at his house in Wmsbrg. after a long indisposition, aged 44; he was bur. in the Chapel of William and Mary; he was a brother of Col. Richard RANDOLPH and was related to the ISHAM's of Northamptonshire on his mother's side (VG 4, 11 Mar, AWM 31 Mar 37)

RANDOLPH, John Esq., H.M's Att. Gen., dec'd, Peyton RANDOLPH, John BLAIR, and James COCKE, by virtue of a deed of trust to them will sell his est. in Wmsbrg. (VGP 19 Oct 75)

RANDOLPH, John Esq., of Chesterfield Co., mar. Miss Nancy POYTHRESS dau. of Col. Peter POYTHRESS of Pr. Geo. Co. (VGPu 2 May 77 sup)

RANDOLPH, John Esq., his creditors are asked to meet with his son, Edmund, in Richmond in March (VGGA 1 Feb 83)

RANDOLPH, Nancy Kennon, dau. of William RANDOLPH Esq. of Charles City Co., d. in the bloom of life on Wed. last at Capt. Joseph WEISIGER's in Pr. Geo. Co. (VGRMA 11 Apr 95)

RANDOLPH, Paul, appr., tailor, ran away from Robert BENSON, Portsmouth (VCGA 24 Apr 94)

RANDOLPH, Peter, son of the Hon. William RANDOLPH Esq., mar. Miss Lucy BOLLING dau. of Col. Robert BOLLING of Pr. Geo. Co. on 20 Jul. (VG 21 Jul 38)

RANDOLPH, the Hon. Peter Esq., Surveyor Gen. of H.M's Customs and a member of the council of this colony, d. on 8 Jul. at his seat at Chatsworth in Henrico Co. (VG 16 Jul, PC 3 Aug 67); a dwelling house part of which was his property will be sold in Wmsbrg. by Carter BRAXTON and William RANDOLPH (nfi) (VG 8 Oct 67); e.a.w. his ex., Archibald CARY, Richard RANDOLPH, John WAYLES, and Seth WARD (VG 18 May 69); his PE to be sold at Chatsworth, Henrico Co. by his ex. (VG 13 Jul 69); his PE in Halifax, Charlotte, Chesterfield, and Cumberland cos. to be sold (VG and VGR 7 Sep 69); slaves bel. to his est. to be sold at Manchester on 15 Apr. by Archibald CARY and Richard RANDOLPH (VGAA 22 Mar 83)

RANDOLPH, Peter Esq., of Wilton, Henrico Co., d. after a short illness (VG 13 Oct 74)

RANDOLPH, Peter Esq., mar. Miss Sally [GREENHILL] of Amelia Co. (VGPu 16 Oct 78)

RANDOLPH, Peter Esq., of Chatsworth, mar. Miss Elizabeth SOUTHALL second dau. of Col. James SOUTHALL of Wmsbrg., on Sat. last in Wmsbrg. (VGWeA 5 Feb 89)

RANDOLPH, Col. Peter, dec'd, e.a.w. Creed TAYLOR (nfi) (Arg 18 Jan 99)

RANDOLPH, Peter S., of Richmond, d. on Sat. eve. last (Arg 19 Nov 99)

RANDOLPH, the Hon. Peyton Esq., d. on Sun. 23 Oct. in Philadelphia of an apoplectic stroke in his 54th year [or 53rd acc. to VGP]; he was late President of the Continental Congress and Speaker of the House of Burgesses (VGPu 3 Nov, VGP 9 Nov, VG 11 Nov 75); e.a.w. his ex., Betty RANDOLPH and James COCKE (VGPu 12 Jan 76); his remains were brought from Philadelphia to Wmsbrg. and interred in the family vault in the College Chapel (VG 29 Nov 76)

RANDOLPH, Peyton Esq., d. on Sat. the 15th inst. at his seat near Richmond (VGIC 22 May, VJAA 27 May 84); of Wilton, e.a.w. his acting ex., Ben. HARRISON Jr. (VGWeA 17 Jul 84)

RANDOLPH, Peyton Jr. Esq., of Wilton, mar. Miss Lucy HARRISON dau. of Col. Benjamin HARRISON of Berkeley (VGPu 5 May 75)

RANDOLPH, Col. Richard Esq., d. at his seat at Curles (VJAA 15 Jun 86); e.a.w. David Meade RANDOLPH of Curles (VGAA 16 Aug 86); e.a.w. his ex., Richard and D. M. RANDOLPH of Curles (VGWeA 22 Mar 87); his ex., Richard RANDOLPH, David Meade RANDOLPH, Brett RANDOLPH, and Ryland RANDOLPH are pltfs. in a HCC suit, 10 Mar 1789 (VIC 1 Apr 89)

RANDOLPH, Richard, eld. son of Richard RANDOLPH dec'd of Curles, Henrico Co., d. on Mon. last (disp. of 20 Mar.) in his 42nd year in Wmsbrg.

where he was bur. (eulogy) (VGGA 26 Mar, NH 30 Mar 99)
RANDOLPH, Richard [Jr.], of Cumberland Co., d. on the 16th inst. (VGPI 17 Jun, RMA 22 Jun 96)
RANDOLPH, Ryland, of Turkey Island dec'd; his admr. w.w.a., Richard RANDOLPH, will sell his PE (VGAA 12 Mar 85); his brother, Richard RANDOLPH of Curles, Henrico Co., has obtained letters of admin. w.w.a. on the whole est.; he will be ready to bring the question on his claim before the HCC at the next session in Nov. (VGAA 25 Jun 85); his late residence, Turkey Island, 17 miles below Richmond on the James River, to be sold by Thomas M. RANDOLPH, David M. RANDOLPH, and Benjamin HARRISON (VGGA 15 Sep 90)
RANDOLPH, Ryland, of Pr. Edw. Co., mar. Miss Betsy FRASER of Petersburg (RMA 11 Jul 95)
RANDOLPH, Thomas Jr. Esq., mar. Miss Patsey JEFFERSON eld. dau. of His Ex. Thomas JEFFERSON Esq. at Monticello in Albemarle Co. on Mon. the 22nd ult. (VICGA 3 Mar 90)
RANDOLPH, Col. Thomas Mann Esq., native of Va., d. on Wed. 20 Nov. in Richmond (VGRMA 25 Nov, VGGA 27 Nov, VGWeA 29 Nov 93); of Tuckahoe, his ex. (nfi) will sell more than 100 of his slaves at Scottville in Powhatan Co. (VGRMA 23 Oct 94); HCC, 7 Jun. 1796, between Thomas M. RANDOLPH and William RANDOLPH acting ex. of Thomas Mann RANDOLPH (pltfs.) and Elizabeth RANDOLPH, John MURCHIE, William MEWBURN, Thomas THOMPSON, Carter PAGE ex. of Archibald CARY, James WARDROP, Thomas MASON, Richard POTTS and Ann EVANS admrs. w.w.a. of Thomas ELDER, John BLAIR surviving partner of Prentis & Co., Benjamin HARRIS, and Samuel FLOURNOY exors. of James HARRIS and Daniel ASTIN (defs.) (VGGA 31 May 97)
RANDOLPH, William Esq., mar. Miss Mary SKIPWITH dau. of the late Sir. William SKIPWITH Bart. (VG 26 Nov 67)
RANDOLPH, William, of Chesterfield Co., mar. Miss Polly KENNON dau. of the late Col. Richard KENNON of Charles City Co. (VG 7 Jan 73)
RANDOLPH, William Esq., dec'd, his admrs. (nfi) will sell all his PE at Mr. GUNN's in Richmond Town (VG 11 Mar 75)
RANDOLPH, William, of Charles City Co., is about to remove to Ky. (VGGA 30 Nov 91)
RANDOLPH, William, of Petersburg, d. yesterday (VGPI 24 Nov 97)
RANKIN, Capt. Benjamin, of Berkeley Co., dec'd, e.a.w. Judith RANKIN, his extx., and James CRANE, his ex. (VJAA 1 Mar 87)
RANKIN, Thomas, conv. svt., c. 30, b. in Cheshire, Old England, and served part of his time with Richard BARNES of Richmond Co. and is an old runaway; ran away from Thomas RUTHERFORD, Frederick Co., living near the mouth of the Shenando River (MG 15 Sep 47)
RANNELLS, William, of Hampshire Co., aged 76, d. a few days ago (BVCG 22 Sep 94)
RANSDELL, Edward Jr., only son of Edward RANSDELL of Westmoreland Co., d. on 24 Feb. (VGR 4 Mar 73)
RANSOME, James, of Gloucester Co., demised 50 ac. of land to Abraham SAVEY and his wife Sarah on 23 Nov. 1670 for 99 yrs.; G. WYTHE now possesses the land and is adv. for the person entitled to the reversion (VG 8 Mar 70)
RANSONE, James, dec'd, his eld. son and heir at law, Richard RANSONE, was a def. in a HCC case brought by Charles JONES and his wife, Letitia, 1 Aug. 1789 (VICGA 31 Mar 90)
RARIDEN, Michael, Irish svt., 26-27, cooper, ran away from Joshua GIST, Frederick Co., Md. (VJAA 4 Nov 84)
RATHER, James, Negro boy, 13-14, says he bel. to Linton TAZEWELL, Wmsbrg., jailed in Norfolk Borough (NH 18 Feb 96)
RAVENS, William, of Kg. Wm. Co., dec'd, his slaves and livestock to be sold by his admrs. (nfi) (VG 10 Dec 67)

RAVENSCROFT, Col. Thomas, formerly a rep. from Pr. Geo. Co., d. lately (VG 28 Jan 37)
RAWLEIGH, Mrs. Patsey, consort of William RAWLEIGH of [Richmond], d. on the 25th inst. (VGGA 2 Aug 97)
RAWLINGS, Robert, of Richmond, died (VGWeA 24 Sep 89); e.a.w. his admr., William MARSHALL (VGGA 20 Apr 91)
RAWORTH, Francis, native of England, d. on Thurs. (BVCG 5 Aug 93)
RAY, Jonathan, HCC, 5 Mar. 1793: Roger ATKINSON (pltf.) and Anne RAY admx. etc. of Jonathan RAY dec'd [apparently of Chesterfield Co.] (def); it appears that the def. is not an inhabitant of this country (VGGA 17 Apr 93)
RAY, William, dec'd, e.a.w. his admr., Daniel GAY [sic] of Henrico Co. (VGWeA 22 Nov 94)
REA, Ashton, late of Hampton. d. on Mon. last (NHPA 14 Sep 97)
REA, Sampson, merch., of Norfolk, d. in St. Bartholomew's on 23 May (VCGA 24 Jul 94); his dry goods to be sold on 28 Aug.; e.a.w. his admrs., Phinehas DANA and William REA (VCGA 21 Aug 94, NHPA 31 Jul 97)
READ, Col., of Va., d. at Philadelphia (MJ 2 Sep 77)
READ, Mrs. Frances, wife of Dr. READ of Hanover Town, d. on the 7th inst. (VIC 17 Dec 88)
READ, Mrs. Huldah, wife of Dr. John K. READ of Hanover Co., d. in her 21st year (VG 24 Oct 71)
READ, Col. Isaac, late of Charlotte Co., dec'd, his ex. are John COLEMAN and Thomas READ (VG 9 Oct 78)
READ, Dr. J[ohn] K., has removed to Norfolk from Richmond where he will practice the profession of physic (HNPA 8 Aug 95); mar. Mrs. MAXWELL relict of Capt. James MAXWELL late of Norfolk on Sat. eve. last (NH 27 Jun 96, AGNPPA 28 Jun 96, RC and RMA 2 Jul 96)
READ, James, b. in Grantham, Lincolnshire; was a tailor, came to N. Carolina where his uncle was governor and later moved to Va. where he d. on 30 Dec. 1769 in St. Stephen's Par., K & Q Co. (VG 18 Jan 70)
READ, John, Irish svt., c. 35, ran away from Jacob PECK in Staunton, Augusta Co. (VGPu 4 Jul 77 sup)
READ, John, svt., 20, ran away from James COCHRAN near Elk Run Church, Fauquier Co. (VJAA 7 Sep 86)
READ, Minor, d. on Sun. last, age 20 (VGWeA 5 Nov 88)
READ, Thomas, soldier in Capt. TERRELL's Co., 5th Regt., aged 18, died (VG 21 Sep 76)
READ, Thomas, late master of the ship *Alliance* and during the late war a capt. in the American Navy, d. on 26 Oct. [in Philadelphia ?] (NPJ 12 Nov 88)
READ, William, ind. svt., speaks West Country dialect, ran away from John WEST, Kg. Wm. Co. (VG 7 Feb 71)
READ, William, chief surgeon of the U. S. frigate *Constitution*, d. yesterday in his 25th year [or 28th acc. to TAA]; [he was apparently bur. in Norfolk] (NH 27 Sep 98, TAA 3 Oct 98)
READE Family, Hawkins READE of York Co., adv. that the est. of John READE dec'd is settled and requests that Mrs. Ann HAYNES, Robert READE, and John READE of Halifax Co. come to get the bonds (VGGA 29 Jul 95)
READE, the Rev. Mr., Minister of Stratton Major Par. in K & Q Co., mar. Miss Frances YATES dau. of the Rev. Mr. Bartholomew YATES late minister of Christ Church in Middlesex Co., the week before last (VG 17 Feb 39)
READE, Benjamin, of Portsmouth, dec'd, e.a.w. Robert SHEDDEN, his admr. (VG 2 Feb 69)
READE, Capt. Gwyn, of Gloucester Co., dec'd, his tract of land there to be sold by his extx., Dorothy ARMISTEAD, and ex., Robert READE (VG 15 Sep 68)
READE, Isaac, executed for murder at the gallows near Richmond on Fri. last (VGWeA 1 Feb 87)
READE, John, dec'd, e.a.w. Hawkins READE of York Co. (VGR 10 Feb 74, VGGA 21 Mar 92)
READE, Mrs. Mary, of York Co., relict of Samuel READE dec'd, d. in her 59th

year (VG 18 Feb 73); her livestock, HH & KF, etc. will be sold by her admr., Anthony ROBINSON (VG 1 Apr 73)

READY, Patrick, Irish svt., 32, ran away from the Potomac Co., Great Falls (VJAA 3 Aug 86)

REAGAN, Michael, his ex., Nicholas REAGAN, will sell his 700 ac. plant. in Fairfax Co. on Hunting Cr. Run (VGP 25 May 75)

REARDON, Patrick, attempted suicide near Baltimore on 17 June; claims to have a wife and family in Alexandria; it is doubted that he will survive (VSPW (2 Jul 95)

REASOR, John, executed at the gallows near this city [Wmsbrg.] (VG 4 Dec 78)

REAT, Mrs., wife of William REAT of Fredsbrg., d. on Tues. last (VHFA 10 Jul 95)

RECTOR, Christopher, sailmaker of H.M.S. *Triton*, 31, absent from duty at Norfolk (VG 12 Oct 52)

REDD, George, anxious to remove to the Western Country and will sell about 1800 ac. in Pr. Edw. Co. (VGGA 2 Jul 99)

REDD, Capt. Samuel, of Caroline Co., dec'd, e.a.w. his ex., William REDD and S. TEMPLE (VGGA 5 Sep 92)

REDDITH, James, mar. Miss Nancy DAVIS in Caroline Co. on the 4th inst. (RCFPC 10 Aug 96)

REDFORD, Milner, dec'd, his ex., John and Milner RADFORD, will sell all his PE (VGWeA 6 Aug 85)

REDMAN, Francis, Irish svt., ran away from Sam. THORNBERY, John SHIPPEY, and William BEAVARS, Lancaster Co. (VGR 7 Sep 69)

REDMON Family, Charlotte Co. Ct., 7 Nov. 1792, in chanc: Thomas REDMON, James LOGGINS and Anne his wife, Mary MALONE, Mildred REDMON, John CREWS and Sarah his wife (pltfs.) against Mahaney REDMON, dau., and Benjamin REDMON, son, of William REDMON dec'd (defs.); it appears that the defs. are not inhabitants of this state (VGWeA 4 [Jan] 93)

REDWOOD, John, dec'd, e.a.w. his admr., W. REDWOOD, James City Co. (VGWeA 26 Apr 87)

REED, Henry, ind. svt., c. 22, coachmaker, ran away from Isaac SIMMONS, Anne Arundel Co., [Md.]; he was reportedly seen in Berkeley Co. with another ind. svt. named John WHITE (VGR 18 Aug 74)

REED, Hugh, dec'd, e.a.w. his admr., Robert LYLE (CMAG 21 Apr 96)

REED, John, 16-17, ran away from Mary DRAKE living near Shepherdstown (PGBA 18 Feb 93)

REED, Robert, Eng. svt., 40, ran away from Robert GILKISON and David HOGSHEAD near Jenning's Gap (VGR 27 Oct 68)

REED, Sarah, bound svt., 17, ran away in a white bed gown and linsey petticoat from William BUCKLES Jr. (PGBA 10 Mar 96)

REEDER, Thomas, of [Alexandria], died (VGAxA 13 Dec 92)

REES, David, merch., of Baltimore, mar. Mrs. Mary ROTHERY at Portsmouth on Thurs. last (NPJ 12 Nov 88)

REES, John, says he comes from Va. and was b. in North Wales, c. 21, jailed in Charles Co., [Md.] on suspicion of being a runaway; it is thought he des. from some regt. [along with John THOMAS, q.v.] (MG 30 Apr 61)

REES, Thomas, a Welshman, svt., ran away from Matthew SATCHELL, Portsmouth (VGNI 13 Sep 75)

REESE, William, b. in Pennsylvania, 25-26, enl. at Fredsbrg. on 27 Sep. 1794; des. from Ft. Nelson (HNPA 4 Mar 95)

REEVES, James, svt., bricklayer, b. in London, ran away from Hugh HICKLEN, Augusta Co. (VGPu 7 Jun 76)

REID, Dick, Negro, 19-20, says he bel. to Thomas MATHEWS of Granville Co., N. Carolina who has lately removed from Charles City Co., Va.; jailed in Isle of Wight Co. (NH 12 May 98); escaped from Isle of Wight jail (ET 28 Jun 98)

REID, Fanny, of Norfolk, adv. that she had administered on the est. of John REID dec'd and has qualified as extx. to the will of her late husband, James

REID dec'd (HNPA 26 Oct 95, NH 2 Jan 96)
REID, James, mar. Miss Fanny WESTCOTE, both of Norf. (VCNPGA 8 Sep 92)
REID, James, merch. of Norfolk, d. on Thurs. eve. last (HNPA 15 Aug 95, RMA 20 Aug 95)
REID, Dr. John, dec'd; a slave bel. to his est. will be sold in Pr. Anne Co. (VCNPGA 8 Sep 92)
REID, John and James; of Norfolk, dec'd, Fanny REID, wife of James REID, will sell all the rem. stock of dry goods at their store and also their brigantine *Janet* (AGNPPA 30 Oct 95); e.a.w. Fanny REID, extx. and admx. (AGGA 6 May 96)
REID, Katherine, wife of Andrew HARPER and dau. of the late Rev. Mr. Alexander REID [sic], minister of the Gospel at Kemney in Aberdeenshire, North Britain, d. on Sun. morn. last at Portsmouth, aged 33 (NPJ 22 Oct 88)
[REILEY], Martin, of Winchester, tailor, d. on Wed. last in his [64th] year (VGWA 5 Nov 91)
REILLY, Molly, Irish, c. 30, with a child, Polly, about 8; she is suspected of stealing items from Ann GRAVES, Richmond (Arg 6 Jan 97)
REMNANT, John, dec'd, e.a.w. his ex., William ANDERSON (VJAA 30 Aug 87)
RENAUD, John, merch., of Petersburg, d. on Sat. last; e.a.w. his admx., Areanea RENAUD of Petersburg (VGPI 4 Jul, 18 Aug 97)
RENN, Anne, has eloped from her husband, Joseph RENN of N. Carolina (VG 24 Nov 68)
RENNOLDS, Thomas, conv. svt., shoemaker, ran away from the plant. of Ann SMITH, Middlesex Co. (VG 24 Sep 36)
REVEL, James, of Essex, executed at the gallows on 9 Jul. [sic] for burglary (VG 8 Jul 73)
REVELL, Mrs. Ann, consort of Edward REVELL and third dau. of Edward KER Esq. of Accomack Co., d. on 10 Apr. [long obit.] (NPJ 23 Apr 88)
REVIS, William, of Sussex Co., dec'd, e.a.w. his admr., Timothy REVIS (VGPI 19 May 97)
REYNOLDS, Henry, appr. blacksmith, 18, ran away from Washer BLUNT, Alexandria (VJAA 6 Dec 87)
REYNOLDS, James M., baker, dec'd, his admr., Gilbert ROBERTSON of Norf., will sell his PE and settle his est. (NHPA 11, 25 Nov 97, NH 3 Apr 98)
REYNOLDS, John, merch., mar. Miss Hannah FOULDER on Sun. (AGGA 7 Feb 97)
REYNOLDS, Samuel, dec'd, e.a.w. his extx., Dorothy REYNOLDS of Norfolk (NH 9 Oct 98); Dorothy ALDRIDGE, late Dorothy REYNOLDS, adv. that those indebted to his est. or to his widow since his decease are requested to make immediate payment to John REYNOLDS (nfi) (NH 16 May 99)
REYNOLDS, Capt. Thomas, late of York Co., his HHF to be sold by his ex. who note that the death of Mrs. REYNOLDS makes it necessary to call on those who borrowed money from Capt. REYNOLDS' est. immediately to discharge their bonds (VG 7 Apr 68)
REYNOLDS, Thomas, late of Kg. Wm. Co., dec'd, e.a.w. Nathaniel REYNOLDS his ex. (VGGA 22 Jun 91)
REYNOLDS, Capt. Thomas, killed by Indians on 20 Mar. last on his way from Slate Cr. Iron Works to Morgan's Station in Ky. (VGGA 29 Jun 91, PGBA 11 Jul 91)
REYNOLDS, William, merch. in York Co., mar. Miss Nancy PERRIN of Gloucester (VG 14 Apr 74)
REYNOLDS, Capt. William, of Henrico Co., mar. Miss Betsey WHITLOCK of the same co. on the 2nd inst. (VGGA 13 Oct 90)
REYNOLDS, Capt. William, d. at his seat in Henrico on Wed. eve. the 3rd inst. (DOB 15 Nov 98)
REYNOLDS, William, of Henrico Co, dec'd, his trustee, William SAVAGE, will sell his land in Henrico and Hanover Cos. (Arg 18 Jan 99, Ex 29 Mar 99)
RHODES, Benjamin, aged 20, mar. Miss Elizabeth ADAMS a maiden lady in

her 62nd year on Tues. last (disp. of 10 Apr.) in Surry Co. (VG 15 Apr 73)
RHODES, Nancy, has separated from her husband, John RHODES (VGR 18 Oct 70)
RICAUD, Mrs., wife of Francis RICAUD, both of this city [Richmond], d. on Wed. eve. (VGRMA 20 Nov 94, VGRC 21 Nov 94)
RICE Family, Frederick Co., Ct., 9 Nov. 1798: Micajah ROACH and James M'DONALD exors. of George RICE dec'd, Micajah ROACH and Ruth his wife, Joshua WILSON and Mary his wife, George RICE an infant under 21 and over 14 by Elizabeth RICE their [sic] mother and next friend, William M'CORMICK and Elizabeth his wife heirs and devisees of George RICE dec'd (pltfs.) against Andrew WAGGENER, Jacob LARUE, and Edmund RICE exors. of John RICE dec'd, and George RICE, Edmund RICE, John RICE an infant under 21, and James RICE an infant under 21, children and devisees of the sd. John RICE dec'd (defs.) (WG 2 Jan 99)
RICE, Edward, of Hackwood near Kemps, d. a few days ago at the Bay Side (NH 19 Jul 98, NWJCI 25 Jul 98)
RICE, Elizabeth, her husband, Richard of Norfolk, will pay none of her debts (NH 13 Oct 96)
RICE, Capt. George, of Frederick Co., dec'd, his ex., James M'DONALD and Micajah RO[A]CH, will sell his stock, HH and KF at his late dwelling house at Long Marin, Frederick Co. (BVCG 8 Jul 96, PGBA 14 Jul 96)
RICE, John, Irish, 35-40, formerly an innkeeper in Woodstock, apprehended near Frankfort for suspected horse stealing (BVCG 2 Dec 93)
RICE, John, dec'd, a pet. will be presented to the GA to convey the right and title of John RICE and that of his reps. to certain lands in Frederick Co. to George RICE's devisees (WG 9 Oct 99)
RICE, Mary, svt., ran away from Edward BAKER, Gloucester Town (VG 10 Nov 52)
RICE, William, conv. svt., b. in Shropshire, Great Britain, c. 27, ran away from Francis TALIAFERRO, Spotsylvania Co. (VGPu 5 Sep 77)
RICHARDS, Clement, of New Castle, intends to leave the state in about two months to go south (VGGA 11 Sep 93 ex); intends to leave for S. Carolina in a few weeks (VGGA 24 Sep 94)
RICHARDS, George, printer and one of the editors of the *Virginia Journal*, d. in Alexandria on Fri. last (acc. to VHFA) or last Sat. morn. (acc. to VIC) in the prime of life (VHFA 9 Jul, VIC 15 Jul, VGWeA 16 Jul 89); e.a.w. Philip MARSTELLER; his admr. is William HUNTER Jr. (VGAxA 3 Sep 89)
RICHARDS, James, drum-major to the 2nd Regt., adv. that his wife, Eleanor RICHARDS, has behaved in such a manner that he can no longer trust her and will not be answerable for any transaction of hers (VGPu 7 Jun 76)
RICHARDS, John, dec'd, e.a.w. his ex., Daniel TRIPLETT, Falmouth (VGAA 21 May 85)
RICHARDS, John, mar. Miss Polly DIXON dau. of the late Col. John DIXON of Richmond at the seat of Holenby DIXON Esq. in Hanover on Sat. the 12th inst. (VGRMA 17 Jul 94, VGGA 23 Jul 94)
RICHARDS, John, studied physick, surgery, and midwifery at the College of Edinburgh and Glasgow and practiced for a considerable number of years in Ireland, is now practicing medicine in Alexandria (CMAG 31 Oct 99)
RICHARDS, Miss Kitty, d. in the bloom of youth and beauty at Daniel TRIPLETT's in Culpeper (RCFPC 3 Aug 96)
RICHARDS, Kitty, appr. girl, c. 16, ran away from Joseph FULLMER (CMAG 8 Feb 98)
RICHARDS, Richard, of Alexandria, merch., mar. Miss Nancy GARNETT dau. of Thomas GARNETT of Traveller's Rest, on Thurs. night (VHFFA 11 Jul 97)
RICHARDS, Capt. William, dec'd, a tract of his land in K & Q Co. to be sold by his ex. (VGGA 5 Jan 91); his slaves to be sold on 23 Dec. at Fredsbrg. by his ex., Thomas RICHARDS of K & Q Co. (VHFA 24 Nov 91); Martha RICHARDS and Thomas RICHARDS will sell the land in K & Q Co.

whereon he lived (VGGA 13 Mar 93)

RICHARDSON, Mrs. Abigail, d. yesterday morn. after a short illness, in an advanced age (VGRC 5 May 95)

RICHARDSON, Charles, svt., ran away from George MURRILL, Albemarle Co. (VGR 19 Apr 70)

RICHARDSON, David, of Hanover Co., appoints his grandson, Samuel RICHARDSON att. at law, to be his agent (VICGA 14 Apr 90)

RICHARDSON, David Sr., dec'd, e.a.w. his admrs., John and Samuel RICHARDSON of Hanover Co. (VGGA 16 Jul 94)

RICHARDSON, Hales, merch., of Norfolk, d. on Monday (HNPA 1 Apr 95); John BURCHER of Norfolk is authorized to settle his est. (HNPA 20 May 95); William ROYSTER (nfi) will be in Norfolk in Nov. to settle his est. (NH 13 Oct 96)

RICHARDSON, John, of New Kent Co., dec'd, his widow is Sarah RICHARDSON (VGAA 16 Aug 83)

RICHARDSON, Jordin, mar. Miss Betsy MASON eld. dau. of Col. David MASON of Sussex Co. (VG 4 Feb 75)

RICHARDSON, Laurana, admx. to George RICHARDSON dec'd, will pet. Congress next July for a duplicate of a Loan Office certificate which was granted him on 26 Feb. 1779; the original was destroyed by the British (VICGA 14 Apr 90)

RICHARDSON, Mary, svt., c. 26, jailed in Pr. Wm. Co. (VGR 14 Oct 73)

RICHARDSON, Thomas, appr., Virginia born, 20, ran away from John BALL, New Kent Co.; it is supposed he has made for Shenando (VG 24 Oct 51)

RICHARDSON, Thomas, merch., of Annapolis, Md., killed by lightning in Baltimore on Fri. last (VGR 7 Jul 68)

RICHARDSON, William, son of John RICHARDSON of Stafford, England, came to Md. and was a svt. in 1754 to Samuel TIPTON on the Patapsco; he will hear something to his advantage by applying to the printer (VG 1 Jan 67)

RICHARDSON, William, blacksmith, dec'd, e.a.w. his admr., Burwell ROBERTS of Caroline Co. (VGGA 8 Apr 95)

RICHARDSON, William, watchmaker, mar. Miss Elizabeth THENABELL, both of Norfolk, on Sat. eve. last (NHPA 28 Nov 96, AGGA 29 Nov 96)

RICHARDSON, William, b. in Ireland, possesses a knowledge of herald painting, des. from the 7th U.S. Regt. (WG 25 Dec 99)

RICHESON, Mrs., spouse to James RICHESON of Kg. Wm. Co., died (VG 3 Jan 77, VGPu 3 Jan 77 sup)

RICHESON, James, of Kg. Wm. Co., dec'd, e.a.w. Holt RICHESON, Peter RICHESON, and David PANNILL also of Kg. Wm. Co. who will also sell all of his PE (VGPu 17 Jan 77); e.a.w. his ex., David PANNILL (VGPu 18 Jul 77)

RICHESON, Mrs. Sukey, spouse of Col. Holt RICHESON of Kg. Wm. Co., died (VGCD 9 Dec 80)

RICHESON, Thomas Sr., dec'd, his ex. (nfi) will sell a Negro bel. to his est. in Caroline Co. (VGGA 4 Feb 95)

RICHMOND, John, late of Louisa Co., dec'd, a pet. will be presented to the GA to vest his est. in the heirs of James DIXON dec'd late of Goochland Co. (VGRMA 1 Sep 94)

RICHMOND, Skipwith, of Edgecombe Co., N. Carolina, d. there on 28 [Jul.] in his 23rd year (VG 1 Sep 74)

RICHTER, Charles, adv. that the public are hereby forewarned from crediting Mary JACKSON better known by the name of Mary RICHTER, the latter name having no foundation as he was never lawfully married to her; he is resolved for the future to pay no debts of her contracting (CMAG 24 Mar 96)

RICKARD, James, appr., c. 18, cooper, ran away from Robert M'MIN, Cumberland, [Md. ?] (PGBA 9 May 95)

RICKMAN, Dr. William, of Charles City Co., mar. Mrs. Betsy HARRISON dau. of Col. Benjamin HARRISON of Berkeley (VGPu 5 May 75); dec'd, his ex., Elizabeth RICKMAN of Charles City Co., will sell his HHF and surgical instruments (VGWeA 20 Sep 83)

RIDDELL, Dr. George, of Yorktown, dec'd, e.a.w. Susanna RIDDELL (VGAA 10 Jan 84, VGWeA 17 Jan 84) [Name also given as RIDDLE]

RIDDELL, Mrs. Susanna, d. lately in Wmsbrg.; her ex., Jacquelin AMBLER and Robert ANDREWS, will sell a variety [of her] HH and KF at her house in Wmsbrg. (VGWeA 10 Dec, 24 Dec 85, VGAA 24 Dec 85); dec'd, [of Richmond] (VIC 31 Oct 87)

RIDDELL, William, of Orange Co., [dec'd], e.a.w. his ex., James and Lewis RIDDELL (VG 14 Nov 77)

RIDDICK, Esther, HCC, [nd], Robert Moore RIDDICK (pltf.) and Amey CARY widow and extx. of Henry STEPHENS and Edward WOODCOCK exors of Robert CARY heretofore of...Great Britain dec'd and Samuel RIDDICK eld. son and heir at law of Esther RIDDICK dec'd (defs.); it appears that Amey CARY, Henry STEPHENS, and Edward WOODCOCK are not inhabitants of this country (RMA 4 Jun 95)

RIDDICK, Capt. Jason, of Nansemond Co., formerly an officer in the Continental Army, died (VGWeA 30 Nov 82)

RIDDICK, Josiah, of Nansemond Co., dec'd, his ex., Wills COWPER and Josiah GRANBERY, will sell his crops and livestock as well as land in Suffolk Co. (VG 19 Nov 72)

RIDDICK, Col. Lemuel, Rep. for Nansemond Co., died (VGPu 15 Dec 75); e.a.w. his ex., Edward RIDDICK of Nansemond (VGPu 2 May 77 sup)

RIDDLE Family, Caroline Co., August Ct., 1797, in chanc: Richard RIDDLE, Thomas RIDDLE, John RIDDLE, Thomas INSKO and Mary his wife, William VAUGHAN and Gennett his wife, John [FAMER] and Liddy his wife, Edmund McDANIEL and Anne his wife, William PICKETT and Mary his wife, Sally NORMAN (widow), Joseph MARTIN and Milley his wife, James LAUGHLIN and Martha his wife, and Enoch RUSSELL and Ruth his wife (pltfs.) against William RIDDLE, Reuben CHAPMAN and Christopher BLACKBURN (defs.); it appears that William RIDDLE is not an inhabitant of this country (VHFA 14 Mar 98)

RIDDLE, Joseph, merch., of Martinsburg, mar. Miss Sally KEARSLEY dau. of John KEARSLEY Esq. of Shepherdstown, a few days ago (VCWM 30 Sep 89)

RIDDLE, Thomas, of Orange Co., murdered by his slave, who also murdered Richard LAND (VG 10 Jun 37, AWM 21 Jul 37, NYG 25 Jul 37)

RIDDLE, William, ind. svt., 18, from Aberdeen, Scotland, ran away from William AUSTIN, Bedford Co.; it is believed he is headed for Caroline Co. (VG 14 Sep 69)

RIDER, Ralph Edward, Eng. svt., ran away from John HOOD, Pr. Geo. Co., last Dec.; he has been seen in New Kent Co. (VG 28 Mar, 25 Apr 51)

RIDGELY, Capt. Francis, of [?] Landing, N. Carolina, dec'd, his admr. is Joshua RIDGELY (VGAA 23 Apr 85)

RIDLEHURST, John, of Hampton, dec'd, his PE to be sold by his admr., Francis RIDLEHURST (VGR 15 Mar 70 sup)

RIDLEY, James, of Fredsbrg., denies a report that he had used his wife and daus. in such a cruel manner as to have forced them from his house and obliged them to seek aid to carry them to Baltimore (VHFA 7 Mar 98)

RIDLEY, William, provides more data on the family of James RIDLEY; he alleges that James left Baltimore with Ann CROSSLEY alias SHUFFLETON and went to Winchester; Jane RIDLEY and daus. thank the people of Fredsbrg. for helping them "seek shelter where the envenomed darts of an old man and Ann SHUFFLETON cannot reach to their disadvantage" (VHFA 10 Mar 98)

RIFFITTS, Mr. J., comedian, d. yesterday (HNPA 1 Jul 95)

RIGAUDEN, Francis, des. from the French frigate *Sybille* in Chesapeake Bay (VGAA 25 May 82)

RIGG, Rachel, aka DALF, ran away from Peregrine FREELAND, Lower Marlborough, Calvert Co., Md. (VJAA 6 Jul 86)

RIGG, Richard, dec'd, his books etc. to be sold in Frederick Co. by his ex., John M'COOLE (VJAA 11 Aug 85)

RIGGEN, Moses, Virginian, 24, des. from Capt. Carter HARRISON's Co. at Petersburg (VG 24 Oct 55)

RIGNEY, William, appr., 18, ran away from James MOORE and John COFFEE, Waterford, Loudoun Co. in Nov. 1786 (VJAA 25 Jan 87)

RILEY, Edward, Irish, des. from Alexander DICK's Co. of marines at Hobb's Hole (VGPu 30 Aug 76)

RILEY, James, Irish, 30, resident of Augusta Co., des. from an escort conducting German prisoners of war from Winchester to Frederick, Md. (VGAA 22 Feb 83)

RILEY, John, Irish svt., c. 19, ran away from Thomas PARROT, Mecklenburg Co. (VG 1 Apr 73)

RILEY, Patrick, Irish svt., bel. to Charles HAMMOND Jr., ran away from near Elk Ridge Church, Anne Arundel Co., Md. (VGR 26 Jul 70)

RILEY, Patrick, Irish svt., ran away from Patuxent Iron Works, Md. (VJAA 28 Jul 85)

RIND, Mrs. Clementina, of Wmsbrg., relict of William RIND printer, d. on Sun. last [a poem on her death is in VGP of 20 Oct 74]; her admr. is John PINKNEY (VG and VGP 29 Sep 74, VGP 23 Feb 75)

RIND, James, mar. Miss Sally SEABROOK on Thurs. eve. last at the seat of Mrs. SEABROOK in Hanover Co. (VGRMA 17 Nov 94, VGRC 18 Nov 94)

RIND, William, dec'd, his ex., Sophia RIND and Lewis ALMAND, will sell his land in Isle of Wight Co. near Smithfield (VGR 12 Mar 72)

RIND, William, Printer to the Colony, d. on 19 Aug. at Wmsbrg. (VG 19 Aug 73, PC 30 Aug 73), [obit] (VG 26 Aug 73); e.a.w. his admr., William RUSSELL (VGR 18 Nov 73)

RINNEY, David, dec'd, e.a.w. his admr., David M'RONALD of Petersburg, who will also sell his PE (VGPI 19 Sep 97)

RION, John, dec'd, e.a.w. his ex., William BOUNTIN (VGWA 14 Jan 89)

RITCHIE, Archibald, dec'd, e.a.w. his acting ex., William RITCHIE (VGWeA and VGGA 12 Jun 84); e.a.w. John REYNOLDS Jr. of Tappahannock (VGAA 10 Sep 85); due to the death of William RITCHIE of Tappahannock who was his acting ex., William RUFFIN of Brunswick will be his acting ex. (VGGA 17 Dec 94)

RITCHIE, Daniel, dec'd, William WINGO Jr. (nfi) will sell all his PE at the plant. of Mary RITCHIE in Kg. Wm. Co. (VG 26 Dec 77)

RITCHIE, William, d. at Tappahannock on Sun. last (VHFA 4 Dec 94); he was the acting ex. of Archibald RITCHIE (VGGA 17 Dec 94, VHFA 1 Jan 95)

RITENOUR, Elizabeth, has eloped from her husband, John RITENOUR (BVCC 18 Nov 96)

RITTENHOUSE, Dr. David, d. on Sun. the 26th ult. at Philadelphia (CMAG 2 Jul 96)

RIVERS, Robert, conv. svt., shoemaker, ran away from James HOLLOWAY, Stafford Co. (VGR 28 Jul 74)

RIVERS, Robert, dec'd, e.a.w. his ex., Thomas RIVERS, who will also sell his stock of horses, cattle, hogs, plant. utensils, etc.; the Commissioners will sell his 700-800 ac. plant. in Greensville Co. pursuant to a court decree (VGPI 15 Nov 96)

RIVERS, Thomas, of Brunswick Co., dec'd, e.a.w. Thomas SAUNDERS, the acting ex. (VGPI 22 Sep 97)

RIVES, Benjamin, dec'd, a tract of land in Pr. Geo. Co. to be sold by his admr., Glaister HUNNICUTT (VG 3 Mar 74)

RIVES, Christopher, killed by lightning in Sussex on Thurs. the 16th inst.; he left a wife and six small chil. (VG 30 Jul 72)

RIVES, Joseph, of Brunswick Co., enl. by George MACKENZIE, has not reported to camp in Wmsbrg. (VG 31 Jul 46)

ROACH, David, b. in Orange Co. and resided in Rockingham Co., 24, des. from an escort conducting German prisoners of war from Winchester to

Frederick, Md. (VGAA 22 Feb 83)
ROACH, Jett, native of Va., c. 25, well acquainted in N. and S. Carolina convicted of horse stealing at a ct. held in Dumfries; he escaped from jail (VGIC 4 Jul 89 sup)
ROACH, Thomas, native of Limrick, Ireland, 43, ran away from the Powder Magazine in Baltimore of which he had the charge; he is suspected of carrying off the powder (RMA 2 May 95, VSPW 11 Jun 95)
ROAN, Tom, Negro, blacksmith, c. 30, ran away from D. BLANEY, Isle of Wight Co. (NH 5 Jun 98)
ROANE, Alexander, merch., of Fredsbrg., mar. Miss Betsy ALCOCK of Caroline Co. (VHFA 8 Dec 91)
ROANE, Mrs. Ann, consort of the Hon. Spencer ROANE, d. on Wed. the 2nd inst. at the house of Mr. P. AYLETT in Kg. Wm. Co. after a short illness (Ex 28 May 99)
ROANE, Christopher, dec'd, his admr., James ROANE, will settle his est. (VGPI 5 Jul 96)
ROANE, the Hon. Spencer Esq., member of the Hon. the Council of State, mar. Miss Anne HENRY eld. dau. of His Ex. Gov. Patrick HENRY Esq. last Thurs., at his seat at Salisbury in Chesterfield Co. (VGAA and VIC 13 Sep 86, VGPI 14 Sep 86)
ROANE, Thomas, merch., mar. at Tappahannock, Miss Mary Eliza NELSON both of that place, on the 13th inst. (VHFA 21 Aug 95)
ROANE, Col. William, dec'd, land in Essex Co. to be rented (VHFA 5 Nov 89)
ROANE, William, of K & Q Co., magistrate, committed suicide with a musket [included is a copy of his suicide note] (RMA 4 Jun 95, RC 6 Jun 95, VGPI 9 Jun 95)
ROARK, Eleanor, svt., 30, ran away from William KELLY, Orange Co. (VG 24 Apr 46)
ROBB, Peter, conv. svt., baker, b. in Scotland, rather turned of 30, ran away from M'Call & Shedden, Hobb's Hole (VG and VGR 26 Aug 73)
ROBB, Robert Gilchrist, mar. Miss Nelly BANKHEAD on Thurs. the 8th inst. at Port Royal (VHFFA 13 Sep 96, RCFPC 14 Sep 96)
ROBERDEAU, Gen. [Daniel], of Winchester, dec'd, his ex., Alexander SMITH, will sell all his PE (CMAG 29 Oct 95)
ROBERDEAU, Isaac, of [Alexandria], mar. Miss Susan BLAIR of Philadelphia at Germantown, Pa. on the 7th inst. (VGAxA 22 Nov 92)
ROBERTS Family, Washington Co. chancery case mentions Sarah FOREST, wife of Philip FOREST, and Mary ROBERTS, both daus. of David ROBERTS dec'd (Arg 4 Jun 99)
ROBERTS, Capt. Benjamin, of Culpeper Co., dec'd, e.a.w. his ex., Daniel FIELD (VHFA 14 Aug 95)
ROBERTS, Charles, d. on the 10th inst. at the dwelling house of James M'CARMACK in Bullskin, aged 116 (PGBA 28 Apr 96)
ROBERTS, Christopher, dec'd, e.a.w. his ex., William ROBERTS of Nansemond Co. (VG 8 May 78)
ROBERTS, Esther, lately from Philadelphia, if she be in Norfolk or its vicinities, she will hear of something to her advantage by calling at the house of Mr. WINROW, Norfolk (NH 10 Nov 98)
ROBERTS, Francis, Virginian, 23, des. from Capt. Carter HARRISON's Co. (VG 5 Dec 55)
ROBERTS, George, free born Negro, b. in Accomack Co., c. 30, indented for two yrs., ran away from George CAPRON, Dismal Swamp Canal, Norfolk (NHPA 6 Apr, 16 Sep 97, NH 15 Mar 98)
ROBERTS, Humphrey, dec'd, e.a.w. his ex., Edward ROBERTS of Norfolk, who intends for Europe in three weeks (AGNPWA 25 Sep 93); e.a.w. John TAYLOR (VCNPGA 28 Sep 93)
ROBERTS, Isaac, conv. svt., speaks Yorkshire dialect, ran away from John REED and Nicholas MILLER (VGR 6 Feb 72)
ROBERTS, John, Campbell Co., Aug. Ct., 1790, in chanc: Richard ELAM

(compl.) against Olive ROBERTS heir at law of John ROBERTS dec'd (def.); it appears that the def. is not an inhabitant of this state (VGPA 18 Jun 91)
ROBERTS, John, dec'd, his admr., John GORDON of Northumberland Co., will sell several of his Negroes (VGGA 19 Jun 93)
ROBERTS, Joseph, aka Daniel, Negro, c. 30, ran away from Elijah TROMAN, James City Co.; he has reportedly been harbored by the Baptist Negroes in New Kent Co.; he had a free pass signed by Mat. and Lucy ROBERTS (VGGA 27 Jan 96)
ROBERTS, Margery, shot and killed on the night of 30 Nov. 1784 in Chesterfield Co. (VGAA 24 Sep 85)
ROBERTS, Richard, conv. svt., 17-18, ran away from Benjamin COLVARD and George DIVERS, Albemarle Co. (VG 16 Jun 74 sup, 21 Jul 74 sup)
ROBERTS, Thomas, of Halifax Co., adv. that he intends to remove to Ky. next Mar. (Arg 17 Feb 97)
ROBERTS, William, aka William SIMMONS, Eng. svt., shoemaker, 23, ran away from Peter PRESLEY, Northumberland Co. (VG 17 Nov 38)
ROBERTS, William, Eng. conv. svt., 44-45, blacksmith, ran away from John GORSUCH and Job GARRETSON of Baltimore (VGR 1 Aug 71)
ROBERTSON, Mrs., consort of Mr. [?] ROBERTSON of Baltimore, d. Thurs. last (WVGWA 10 Jul 90)
ROBERTSON, Archibald, dec'd, his PE and land in Dinwiddie Co. to be sold by his admx., Elizabeth ROBERTSON in Pr. Geo. Co. (VG 15 Jun 69)
ROBERTSON, Daniel, d. on Wed. the 14th inst. in Camden Co., N. Carolina (NH 22 Sep 96)
ROBERTSON, Mrs. Fanny, of Norfolk Co., d. of smallpox on Wed. eve. (AGGA 20 May 96)
ROBERTSON, Col. George, of Chesterfield Co., d. on Wed. last; his acting admr., James ROBERTSON and John BRANDER, will settle his est. (VGPI 15 Sep 97, 7 Nov 97)
ROBERTSON, Capt. John, mar. Miss Betsy MOXLEY, Alexandria (VJAA 7 Apr 85)
ROBERTSON, John, merch. of the firm of Robertson & Gibson (Portsmouth) and Gibson & Robertson (Norfolk), d. on Mon. morn. at Portsmouth (HNPA 1 Oct 94); his admr. is William GILLIES (HNPA 4 Feb 95)
ROBERTSON, John, Negro, c. 25, jailed in Kg. Geo. Co. (VGGA 24 Sep 99)
ROBERTSON, John A., of Amelia Co., mar. Miss Elizabeth ROYALL of Nottoway dau. of John ROYALL, on Thurs. 19 Nov. (RMA 12 Dec 95)
ROBERTSON, Joseph, sailmaker, Alexandria, died (VJAA 18 May 86); his sail loft to be let by Daniel ROBERDEAU (VJAA 8 Jun 86)
ROBERTSON, Miss Martha, of Halifax Co., d. on 20 Sep. 1785 in her 23rd year [poem] (VGAA 4 Feb 86)
ROBERTSON, Capt. Robert, mar. Miss Susanna DEADMAN on Thurs. last (VGR 16 Mar 69)
ROBERTSON, Capt. Robert, late of Yorktown, dec'd, e.a.w. his extx., Sarah ROBERTSON (VGWeA 26 Apr 83 sup)
ROBERTSON, Seymour, dec'd, William MASSENBURG, ex. of William MASON dec'd, will sell a tract of ROBERTSON's land in Sussex Co. (VGPI 25 May 98)
ROBERTSON, Sidney, age 16, left H.M.S. *Nautilus* in Virginia some time ago; he was recently seen in Norfolk (VG 4 Nov 63)
ROBERTSON, Susannah, wife of Moses ROBERTSON of Northumberland Co., who will no longer pay her debts (VG 31 Jul 46)
ROBERTSON, Thomas, Eng., des. from the company of state artillery of Capt. Henry QUARLES (VG 9 Apr 79)
ROBERTSON, William, Eng. svt., shoemaker, ran away from Jacob PECK in Staunton (VGPu 8 Aug 77)
ROBIN, William, an alien, now and for many yrs. back a Greenwich pensioner; a pet. will be presented to the next GA for an act conveying the right that may, on office found, appear to be in the Commonwealth to his

est....to John ROBINS [sic], Richmond Co. (VHFFA 27 Oct 95)
ROBINET, Peter, a French citizen, d. in Va. on 24 Feb. 1792 (VCNPGA 8 Jun 93)
ROBINSON, Mrs., of Essex Co., wife of the Hon. John ROBINSON Esq. one of H.M's Council of the Colony, d. on Sat. sennight (VG 11 Aug 38)
ROBINSON, Anthony, of York Co., dec'd, his ex., Merritt MOORE, will sell all of his HH and KF at his late dwelling house in the lower end of York Co. (VG 11 May 76)
ROBINSON, Benjamin, dec'd, e.a.w. his admr., Charles Carter ROBINSON (VHFFA 30 Oct 95); his ex. will sell all his crop of corn and fodder with equipment and stock at his former plant. in Spotsylvania Co. (VHFFA 25 Dec 95)
ROBINSON, Christopher Esq., of Middlesex Co., d. on the 8th inst. [or acc. to VGR, on Mon. the 18th inst.] (VG and VGR 28 Jul 68); his PE to be sold by his ex., Richard CORBIN and Ralph WORMELEY (VG 15 Dec 68)
ROBINSON, Christopher, son of the late Charles ROBINSON Esq. of Middlesex Co., d. on 23 Oct. last (VG 2 Dec 75)
ROBINSON, Christopher Esq., dec'd, his ex., William CURTIS, will sell 750 ac. of his land in Gloucester Co. (VGAA 6 Jul 91 sup); his ex. will sell 600 ac. of his land in Gloucester Co. (VGGA 12 Sep 92, 7 Aug 93)
ROBINSON, Francis, of Lunenburg Co., dec'd, e.a.w. his admr., Lucretia ROBINSON and Everard DOWSING (VGPu 16 Oct 78)
ROBINSON, Harry, of Kg. Wm. Co., att. at law, died (VG 3 Oct 71)
ROBINSON, Harry, att. at law, late of Kg. Wm. Co., dec'd, e.a.w. his ex., Bartlet ANDERSON of Hanover Co. (VGGA 1 Aug 92); his ex. will sell 400 ac of his land on Mattaponi River in Kg. Wm. Co. (VGWeA 10 Aug 92, VGAA 7 Nov 92, 6 Mar 93)
ROBINSON, James, of Louisa Co., c. 20, des. from Ben. POLLARD's Co. of marines (VGPu 30 Aug 76)
ROBINSON, James, from Pr. Wm. Co., executed near Richmond for burglary (VGWeA and VGAA 26 Jan 82)
ROBINSON, the Hon. John, President of H.M's Council, d. on Thurs. night at the house of the Hon. William NELSON at York (MG 30 Aug 49, VG-Randolph 31 Aug 49)
ROBINSON, John, Speaker [to the Hon. House of Burgesses] m. Miss Sukey CHISWELL dau. of Col. CHISWELL of this city [Wmsbrg.] (VG-Randolph 21 Dec 59); Speaker to the House of Burgesses and Treasurer of the Colony, d. on Sat. night last [obit. and poem] (VGR 1 May 66) [or, acc. to VG, member of the GA for the county of K & Q, d. last Sun.] (VG 16 May 66); e.a.w. his admrs., Peter RANDOLPH, Edmund PENDLETON, and Peter LYONS (VG 13 Jun 66); his HH and KF to be sold by his admrs., Edmund PENDLETON and Peter LYONS (VG 4 Aug 68); e.a.w. Edmund PENDLETON and Peter LYONS, the surviving exors. (VGAA 26 Apr 83)
ROBINSON, John, about 50 of his slaves to be sold by his admr., Richard CORBIN (VG 3 Nov 68)
ROBINSON, John, svt., ran away from John G. FRAZER, Kg. Wm. Co.; he probably intends for Baltimore (VG 7 Dec 69)
ROBINSON, Master John, only son of the late Speaker, d. at the house of William NELSON Esq. in Caroline Co.; his body was brought to K & Q Co. where it was bur. on a high point near Mattaponi River [elegy] (VG 27 Jan 74)
ROBINSON, John and Thomas, brothers from the lower end of Henrico Co., des. from John PLEASANT's Co. of the 5th Bn. (VGPu 20 Sep 76)
ROBINSON, John Esq., dec'd, his ex., Will. O. WINSTON and John WARDEN, will sell sundry Va. born slaves and other items at his late dwelling house in the forks of Hanover (VGAA 15 Jan 85, VGIC 29 Jan 85)
ROBINSON, John, of Fredsbrg., d. there on Tues. last (VHFFA 8 Dec 95); e.a.w. his ex., William ROBINSON (VHFFA 23 Sep 96)
ROBINSON, John, Negro, 25, jailed in Kg. Geo. Co., claimed to be free (VH 23

Jul 99)
ROBINSON, John Cotton, committed suicide by hanging himself in Alexandria on Mon. 31 May (VJAA 3 Jun 84, VGIC and VGWeA 12 Jun 84)
ROBINSON, Joseph, of Caroline Co., dec'd, tract of land known as "The Mount" to be sold (VHFA 4 Dec 88)
ROBINSON, Joseph, jailed in Norfolk for passing counterfeit bank notes; escaped on 29 Nov.; his residence is in Wilmington, N. Carolina, but he was b. in New Hampshire Co., Mass. (NHPA 9 Dec 97)
ROBINSON, Matthew, merch., was mar. to Mrs. Margaret BOA on Tues. by the Rev. Mr. GRIFFIN of the Roman Catholic Church (CMAG 18 Apr 99)
ROBINSON, Capt. Maximilian, of Kg. Geo. Co., dec'd, his ex. (nfi) will sell 40 valuable slaves at his plant. near Leedstown (VGPu 21 Mar 77 sup)
ROBINSON, Michael, late of Fredsbrg., dec'd, e.a.w. his ex., William and John ROBINSON of Spotsylvania Co. (VGAA 20 Mar 84, 21 Jan 86)
ROBINSON, Robert, joiner and carpenter, c. 28, b. in the south of Scotland, worked in Edinburgh and Kelso-upon-Tweed; purchased three weeks ago at Mundy Point on Potomac from on board the *Friendship*, ran away from Mungo HARVEY, Lancaster Co. (VGPu 23 Jun 75)
ROBINSON, Thomas, age 31, b. in Pr. Geo. Co., Md., committed to jail in Frederick Co. on suspicion of being a runaway svt. (VG 30 Oct 66)
ROBINSON, Tully, dec'd, e.a.w. his ex., Ben. E. JOHNSON, Norfolk Co. (NH 23 May 96)
ROBINSON, William, enl. by Capt. PEACHEY, des. from the Va. Regt. at Ft. Cumberland (VG 26 Dec 55)
ROBINSON, the Rev. Mr. William, the Lord Bishop of London's Commissary for this colony and Rector of Stratton Major Par., d. Tues. eve. last at his house in K & Q Co. (VG 7 Jan 68); his PE to be sold by his admrs., Richard CORBIN and Christopher ROBINSON (VG 31 Mar 68)
ROBINSON, William, aka Thomas, from York Co., executed near Wmsbrg. on 27 Jun. (VG 27 Jun 71)
ROBINSON, William Esq., late of Westmoreland Co., dec'd, e.a.w. his ex., Beckwith BUTLER (VGAA 2 Oct 85)
ROBINSON, Col. William, of Pr. Anne Co., dec'd, his admr. w.w.a., James SIMPSON, will sell his PE (NPJ 25 Feb 89)
ROBINSON, Maj. William Esq., of Spotsylvania Co., d. on Sun. the 13th inst. aged 83 (VHFA 24 May 92); [listed as ROBERTSON but corrected on 21 Jul.] e.a.w. his ex., Benjamin ROBINSON (VHFA 8 May, 21 Jul 95)
ROBISON, James, seaman, 24-25, escaped from Fairfax Co. jail in Alexandria (CMAG 22 Aug 99)
ROBISON, John, svt., 28, ran away from Andrew M'CLU[R], Augusta Co. (VG 23 Jun 68)
ROCK, Mrs. Nancy, consort of Capt. Charles ROCK, d. on the 24th inst. at Rockett's after a short illness (DOB 27 Sep 98)
ROCKET, Baldwin, of Henrico Co., died (VGWeA 16 Mar 82)
ROCKETT, Francis Ware, appr., 14-15, tailor, ran away from John SUMPTER, Manchester (VG 13 May 75)
RODDY, Rachel, widow and admx. of Charles RODDY dec'd, Shenandoah Co. (VGWA 21 May 91)
RODELPHUS, Nanny, has eloped from her husband, George DAVEY [or DEWEY] (VG 8 Apr 75)
RODGERS, David, dec'd, e.a.w. his admrs., William Kook WACKLAND and Mary WACKLAND, Buckingham Co. (VG 16 Nov 69)
RODGERS, Mary, heir at law of Adam RODGERS dec'd (VGWeA 28 Aug 84)
ROE, William, dec'd, his land on Summer Duck Run, Fauquier Co. to be sold by Richard BAKER, his ex. (VHFA 13 Jun 98)
ROGERS, Charles, appr., 18, absconded from this printing office (AGNPPA 18 Mar 96)
ROGERS, Elizabeth, wife of Thomas ROGERS, has eloped from her husband with Henry ORENDORFF (who reportedly changed his name to DOFF)

about a year ago (BVCG 9 Jul 92)

ROGERS, Giles, of Albemarle Co., dec'd, e.a.w. his ex., Robert DAVIS, Achilles ROGERS, and Parmenas ROGERS (RMA 17 Sep 95)

ROGERS, Hugh, ind. svt., c. 21, carpenter and sawyer, ran away from Thomas RIGDON, Georgetown; he came to Alexandria near 12 months ago from Dublin (VG 7 Oct 73)

ROGERS, Maj. John, of Caroline Co., d. on Wed. last, the 16th inst., at the Eagle Tavern in Richmond (VGRMA 21 Apr 94, VGGA 23 Apr 94, VHFA 24 Apr 94); his admr. w.w.a. is Thomas ROGERS of Hanover Co. (VGGA 10 Dec 94)

ROGERS, Miriam, wife of Joseph ROGERS late of Chowan Co., N. Carolina, dau. of Capt. Joseph TODD of Southampton Par., Bermuda; any of her descendants are asked to apply to John MALLORY and Mallory TODD, Isle of Wight Co. (VGAA 17 Jul 84)

ROGERS, Richard, came to America from England in about 1750; he was keeping school in Lunenburg Co. in 1754 when he was last heard of; information is sought on him by persons in London (VG 20 May 73)

ROGERS, Capt. Samuel, of Norfolk Borough, dec'd, e.a.w. his ex., John TUCKER and Nicholas WONYCOTT (VG 24 Aug 51)

ROGERS, Sarah, of Cumberland Co., was last week discharged from the Public Hospital in this city; she having recovered her right senses (VG 20 Nov 79)

ROGERS, Thomas, watchmaker, d. a few days ago in Church St. (NHPA 10 Dec 96)

ROGERS, William, of Yorktown, dec'd, his est. to be auctioned (VG 4 Jan 40)

ROGERS, William, of Norfolk, dec'd, e.a.w. his extx., Priscilla ROGERS (NPJ 23 Jul 88)

ROLLEY, James, ind. Irish svt., 24-25, ran away from James WOOD, Northampton Co., N. Carolina (VG 23 Sep 73)

ROLLINS, William, white svt., c. 21, ran away from Francis SMITH Jr., Chesterfield Co. (VG 9 Sep 73); came down as a wagoner with the Chesterfield Volunteers and was placed near the [Governor's] Palace; ran away from Francis SMITH, of Chesterfield, who suspects he is on board the man of war (VGP 13 Jul 75)

ROMJEU, Betsey, her husband, John ROMJEU of Front Royal, adv. that he will not pay her debts since she has not conducted herself in a proper manner (WG 4 Sep 99)

RONALD Family, agreeable to a decree of the HCC between James LYLE (pltf.) and Peter STONER and William BENTLEY admr. of William RONALD dec'd, B[et]sey RONALD and Nancey RONALD infant chil. of William RONALD by the sd. William BENTLEY their gdn., a 1214 ac. tract in Powhatan will be sold (VGGA 19 Jul 99)

RONALD, Andrew Esq., att. at law, d. on Sat. eve. [or last Sun.] in Richmond (Arg and VGGA 4 Jun 99, EX 7 Jun 99); e.a.w. his ex., William WISEHAM, of Richmond (VGGA 12 Jul 99)

RONALD, Mrs. Sarah, spouse of Andrew RONALD Esq. of Richmond, d. last Wed. night in the flower of her age (VIC 28 May, VGWeA 29 May 88, NPJ 4 Jun 88)

RONALD, William Esq., of Powhatan Co., d. on Sun. last at the seat of David ROSS in Cumberland Co. of a sudden stroke of the palsy on the road about five minutes after leaving Mr. ROSS' house to return to his own (VGPA 9 Feb 93); his admr., William BENTLEY of Powhatan Co., will sell his moveable est. (VGGA 24 Jul 93); his orphans' gdns. are William BENTLEY, John SWANN, and Samuel PLEASANTS; Andrew RONALD (nfi) is mentioned (VGGA 2 Oct 93); his orphans' gdns. adv. that his est. is now in a situation to enable them to pay all legal demands (VGRMA 9 Jan 94)

RONALDSON, James, of Smithfield, intends to leave the Colony soon for Great Britain (VG 9 May 66)

RONEY, Capt. John, late of Richmond, dec'd, e.a.w. his admr., Martin MIMS (VGGA 8 May 98)

ROOKINGS, James, of Pr. Geo. Co., dec'd, ship carpenter, e.a.w. his ex., Elizabeth ROOKINGS, Robert JONES Jr., and John NICHOLSON (VG 21 Feb 51); tract of land and plant. on James River between the mouths of Ward's and Flower de Hundred Creek to be sold pursuant to his last will for payment of his debts (VG 27 Mar 52)

ROOTES, Elizabeth, consort of the late George ROOTES Esq., d. on Tues. eve. last in this place [Martinsburg] (VGRMA 23 May 93)

ROOTES, George Esq., att. at law, late of Richmond, d. on Tues. the 7th inst. at Martinsburg, Berkeley Co. (BVCG 20 May 93, VGRMA 23 May 93)

ROOTES, Thomas Reed, dec'd, 100 ac. of his land in Kg. Wm. Co. will be sold at his late dwelling house in K & Q Co. by his ex. (nfi) (VG 20 Jun 66); mention of the will of the late Maj. Philip ROOTES (VG 1 Aug 66)

ROPER, Mrs., spouse of Jesse ROPER of Richmond, d. last Tues. (VGWeA 22 Mar 87)

ROPER, John, d. on Mon. last at Rockett's (VGGA 18 Sep 93); his admr., John HAGUE of Rockett's, will sell his HH and KF and tavern (VGRMA 10 Oct 93)

ROPER, John, dec'd, e.a.w. his admr., Jesse ROPER of Richmond (VGGA 29 Jul 95)

ROSE, Mrs., spouse of William ROSE [of Richmond], d. on the 12th ult. (VGGA 20 Mar 93)

ROSE, Alexander Esq., of Kg. Geo. Co., dec'd, his seat at Grantswood to be sold by his ex., Gavin LAWSON and Thomas FITZHUGH of Falmouth, who will also settle his est. (VGAA 11 Oct, 15 Nov 86)

ROSE, Duncan, dec'd, his ex., J[ohn] BANNISTER, Neil BUCHANAN, and Duncan ROSE, will sell all his real and personal est. including 1300-1400 ac. within six miles of Petersburg, as well as tracts in Surry, Pr. Geo., and Mecklenburg Cos. (VGWeA 7 Jan 86, VGAA 22 Mar 86); his ex. will sell several tracts of his land in Dinwiddie, Pr. Geo., Surry, and Mecklenburg Cos. (VGPI 13 Mar 88)

ROSE, Fanny, free Negro, drowned last Wed. (VJAA 5 Oct 86)

ROSE, Col. Hugh, d. at his seat in Amherst Co. on 18 Oct., aged 52 (VGRMA 6 Nov 94); e.a.w. his ex., Patrick ROSE and William CABELL Jr. (LFG 14 Feb 95, VGAA 25 Feb 95); his ex. will sell 2300 ac. of his land in Henry Co. (VGGA 25 Nov 95, PGBA 18 Feb 96)

ROSE, Mary, has left her husband, Ezekial ROSE, of Hampshire Co. (PGBA 14 Apr 94)

ROSE, Peyton Randolph, son of William ROSE of Wmsbrg., to be baptized on 1 [Nov.] (VGP 16 Nov 75)

ROSE, Roderick Esq., of Grenada, d. yesterday (NH 17 Oct 99)

ROSS, John, Scots highlander, 16, ran away from John MITCHELL, Fredsbrg. (VG 14 Aug 46)

ROSS, John, ind. svt., from the Highlands of Scotland, c. 18, ran away from the sloop *Lark* landed at Hardy's Ferry (VG 30 Sep 73)

ROSS Miss Peggy, d. a few days ago in Wmsbrg. (VGWeA 16 Dec 91)

ROSS, the Rev. Mr. Robert, of Albemarle Co., dec'd (VG 5 Mar 52)

ROSS, Sarah, of Petersburg, adv. that whereas her husband, Francis EDWARDS, formerly of Wmsbrg. but late of this town has illegally possessed himself of a mulatto boy named Jack bel. to her orphan son and is now trying to dispose of him in Richmond; the boy is the property of the est. of John ROSS dec'd of York Co. (VGWeA 20 Sep 87)

ROSS, Thomas, post rider, killed by Indians about three weeks ago [Winchester disp.] (South Carolina Gazette 21 May 93)

ROSS, Thomas, Negro, formerly the property of James FORSTER on York River, jailed in Norfolk Borough (NH 9 May 96); escaped from jail on 29 May (NH 4 Jun 96)

ROSS, William, son of William ROSS, shoemaker on the South Branch of Potowmack, is a prisoner of the French and Indians at or near Ft. Detroit (NYPB 2 Jan 58)

ROSSEAU, Henry, dec'd, his admr., Alexander HENDERSON of Dumfries, will sell all of his PE on Popeshead Run in Fairfax Co. and settle his est. (RJDA 14 Aug 95, CMAG 27 Aug 95) [Also given as ROUSSAU]

ROSSON, Jerome, of Culpeper Co., dec'd, his acting admr., Joseph ROSSON, will sell all of his livestock, plant. utensils, and HHF and settle his est. (VHFFA 1 Nov 96)

ROTHERY, Charles, printer, d. on Tues. the 10th inst. in Richmond (VGGA 18 Mar 95, VGRMA 19 Mar 95)

ROTHERY, Daniel, of Norfolk, d. yesterday after a short illness (HNPA 27 Sep 94); a portion of his est. to be sold on 24 Feb. (HNPA 21 Feb 95)

ROTHERY, Capt. Henry, dec'd, e.a.w. George ABYVON of Norfolk (VGR 21 Apr 69 sup)

ROTHERY, Mary, intends to leave the state shortly and requests anyone indebted to her or to Maj. William ORANGE, late of the Borough of Norfolk, to make immediate payment (NPJ 8 Oct 88)

ROTHERY, Matthew, of Norfolk, dec'd, his wife and extx., Mary ROTHERY, will sell his ship, tracts of land, water grist mill, and a large tract on New Mill Cr., Norfolk Co. (VG 2 Apr, 1 Oct 72)

ROTHROCK, Mrs., wife of George ROTHROCK of Fredsbrg., d. in Orange Co. on Fri. last (VHFA 28 Aug 94)

ROUGHSEDGE, William, late of Prescot, Lancaster, imp. as a transport in the *Swaile* in 1763 and bound to Mr. BURCH of Wicomico, Charles Co., Md., may hear of something to his advantage by applying to Jacob ALLAN, Wmsbrg. (VG 25 Apr 71)

ROULETT, John Sr., of Pr. Edw. Co., dec'd, his ex., John and Mackness ROULETT, will sell four of his Negroes and his livestock (VGPu 10 Jan 77)

ROURK, Patrick, of Richmond, intends for Ireland next summer (VGAA 24 Jan 84)

ROUTLIDGE, Robert, of Pr. Edw. Co., killed on 3 Jun. last by Col. John CHISWELL at the tavern of Benjamin MOSBY at Cumberland Ct. H. [long detailed articles] (VG 18 Jul, 15 Aug, 12, 19 Sep, 10 Oct 66)

ROW, William, Eng. conv. svt., 18-19, ran away from Archer MATHEWS on the levels of Greenbrier (VGPu 16 Aug 76 sup)

ROWAND, Thomas, dec'd, portion of his est. to be sold by John ROWAND his admr. at Macho[t]ick Neck, Westmoreland Co. (VJAA 15 Dec 85)

ROWE, Lyne, dec'd, his admr., Overton COSBY, will sell all his est. in Gloucester Co. (VG 12 Nov 72)

ROWE, Mrs. Rebekah, late of Gloucester Co., dec'd, e.a.w. Zachariah and Jasper ROWE (nfi) (VGPu 1 Aug 77)

ROWLEY, Col. William, of Kg. Geo. Co., aged 62, mar. Miss Nancy GRIGSBY of the same co. in her 63rd year, a maiden lady, and who, it is said, is in a likely way of increasing the colonel's family (VG 6 May 73); late of Kg. Geo. Co., dec'd, e.a.w. his ex., Richard TAYLOR of Caroline Co. (VGPu 4 Aug 75)

ROWLS, Francis, conv. svt., shoemaker, speaks the West Country dialect, ran away from Spencer BALL and Richard HULL, Northumberland Co. (MG 11 Jul 54)

ROWSAY, William, of this city [Wmsbrg.], mar. Miss Fanny TABB of Yorktown (VG 13 Nov 79)

ROWSAY, William, dec'd, a tract of his land in York Co. on King's Cr. to be sold by his admrs., Samuel BEALL and Benjamin POWELL (VIC 28 Nov 87)

ROWZAY, Mrs. Barbara, died in childbed (VGPu 13 Dec 76)

ROWZEE, John, dec'd, his ex., Richard ROWZEE, will sell all of his stock and plant. utensils, etc. at the Neck Plant. in Essex Co. (VGPu 16 Oct 78)

ROWZEE, William Esq., d. on Fri. the 12th inst. in his 50th year at his seat in Essex Co. [obit.] (VH 19 Apr 99)

ROY, James, dec'd (VHFFA 13 Dec 96)

ROY, John Beverly, his widow and extx. is Anne ROY apparently of Caroline Co. (VGWeA 17 Apr 84)

ROY, Mungo, mar. Miss Nancy POPE, both of this city [Richmond] on Wed. eve. (VGGA 6 Dec 99)

ROYLE, Joseph, printer of the *Virginia Gazette* and member of the partnership of Joseph Royle & Co., dec'd (VG 7 Mar, 4 Jul 66)

ROYSTER, George, of Mecklenburg Co., dec'd, claims against his est. to Thomas VAUGHAN, Deputy Sheriff of Mecklenburg Co. (VGPI 2 May 97)

ROYSTER, John, dec'd, e.a.w. his ex., John HALES (VGR 13 Apr 69)

ROYSTER, John, dec'd, four Negroes bel. to his est. to be sold in Henrico Co. by the admrs. (nfi) of Elizabeth GILES dec'd who was his extx. (VGGA 1 Jan 94)

ROYSTON, John, [appr.], son of Richard Wiatt ROYSTON of Gloucester Co., 19 last Sep., ran away from Samuel DANIEL, Middlesex Co.; suspected of being with his acquaintances in Bedford or Pr. Wm. Co. (VG 8 Mar 70)

ROYSTON, John, dec'd, e.a.w. his admr., Nelson ANDERSON Jr. (VGCD 18 Dec 79)

ROYSTON, William, age 52, mar. Miss Mary ROLLINS, age 16, in Caroline Co. on Thurs. last (VHFA 4 Apr 93)

ROZEY, Conrad, an aged, honest man, d. yesterday in Martinsburg from the kick of a stud horse during the election of Mon. last (PGBA 28 Apr 96)

RUARK, Daniel, Irish svt., c. 22, tailor, ran away from Richard CADDEEN, Westmoreland Co. (VGR 23 Aug 70)

RUBEL, Arrabella, has eloped from her husband, John RUBEL (BVCG 15 Oct 92)

RUBSAM[E]N Family, HCC, 14 Sep. 1799, between John WIDEWILT (pltf.) and Thomas BANKS surviving ex. of Jacob RUBSAM[E]N, Daniel RUBSAM[E]N, Balthasar RUBSAM[E]N, and Maria Catharine RUBSAM[E]N legatees of the sd. Jacob RUBSAM[E]N dec'd, Reuben COUTTS and William Archer COCKE, James COCKE, John ROYALL Jr., Elizabeth ROYALL, Mary COCKE, Joseph COCKE, Richard COCKE, and John COCKE heirs of Charles COCKE dec'd (defs.); it appears that Thomas BANKS and Daniel, John, Balthasar, and Maria Catharine RUBSAM[E]N are not inhabitants of this country (VF 26 Oct 99)

RUBSAMEN, Jacob Esq., of Manchester, Va., d. lately in Philadelphia (VGGA 2 May 92); his ex., W. M'KENZIE and Thomas BANKS will sell his HHF (VGGA 23 May 92); his lands to be sold by his surviving ex., Thomas BANKS of Manchester (Arg 27 Dec 99)

RUD, William, son of John and Avis RUD, late of Henrico Co., but last of Chesterfield Co., he left Va. about 16 yrs. ago designing as he said for Annapolis in Md.; if he be living and will apply to his brother, Thomas RUD in Chesterfield Co. or to the printer of this paper, he may hear of something to his advantage (MG 27 Dec 49)

RUDD, Elizabeth, some yrs. ago she came out of the co. of Warwick, Eng. and is supposed to be living in some part of America; she is asked to contact her father, Samuel RUDD of Charles City Co. (VG 26 Sep 45)

RUFFIN, Col. John, d. on Sat. the 21st inst. [or on Sun. last acc. to VGPu] after a very short illness (VG and VGPu 27 Jun 77)

RUFFIN, John and Thomas, dec'd, their brother, Francis RUFFIN of Mecklenburg Co., is their ex. and will settle their estates (VGPu 1 May 78)

RUFFIN, Robert, plans to move to Kg. Wm. Co. from Dinwiddie Co. (VG 24 Nov 68)

RUFFIN, Robert, son of Col. RUFFIN of Kg. Wm. Co. and one of the young gentlemen in the Secretary's Office, d. in Wmsbrg. on Tues. last in his 19th year (VG and VGR 15 Jul 73)

RUFFIN, Robert Esq., late of Kg. Wm. Co., dec'd, e.a.w. his ex., Herbert CLAIBORNE (VGPu 23 May 77)

RUFFIN, Capt. Thomas, of the 7th Regt. of Va. Forces on Continental establishment, stationed in Wmsbrg., died (VG 13 Apr 76)

RUFFIN, William, of Surry Co., dec'd, his brother, John RUFFIN Jr., desires to give satisfaction to his creditors (VG 12 Aug 73); his ex., John RUFFIN

and John H. COCKE, will sell all of his HH and KF (VG 30 Mar 76); his ex., John H. COCKE, will sell, rent, or lease two plants. in the lower end of Surry Co. and sell all of his livestock (VG 15 Aug, 19 Dec 77)
RUFFNER, Peter, dec'd, e.a.w. his admx., Mary RUFFNER of Shenando Co. (VG 12 Jun 79)
RUMNEY, Edward, c. 40, charged with aiding and assisting Lowe JACKSON in counterfeiting double dubloons, has escaped from Fairfax Co. jail (MG 7 Nov 50)
RUMNEY, Dr. William, of Alexandria, dec'd, his ex. is Robert ADAM (VJAA 3 Mar 85)
Runaway Svts: Edmund THOMAS, carter and husbandman, Eng., c. 25; Henry REDWOOD, sawyer, speaks West Country dialect, c. 30; George MACDONALD, tailor, c. 22; Solomon GARR, miller, West Countryman, c. 30; John COLE, wheelwright, speaks West Country dialect, c. 30; ran away from Col. SPOTTSWOOD, Germanna (AWM 31 May 22)
Runaways from Thomas NEVETT and Thomas WATKINS, Cambridge, Md: Thomas ABLEWHITE, Jane SHEPHERD, Eng., Francis O'CONNER, Irish, Mary BARNES, Jane HARLETT, Scottish (VG 22 Oct 36)
Runaway svts. from John LEWIS, Gloucester Co.: John TOMLINS, c. 26; John MAYNARD, plasterer, c. 26; Thomas LEE, joiner, c. 50; George BARRY, barber, 16-17; William WATERS (a svt. bel. to the Rev. Mr. Thomas HUGHES), joiner or chairmaker, 20-22, also went away with them; LEE, BARRY, and WATERS are convicts imp. in the ship *York* into York River last Mar.; LEE reportedly has a relation in Philadelphia or New York; TOMLIN and MAYNARD are indented for four yrs. and were imp. in the brigantine *Priscilla* in Jun. last (VG 19 May 38)
Runaways from the ship *Spencer* now lying at Port Miccou, Rappahannock River: William WALLACE, c. 22; Charles SPINKS, c. 27; Edward DICK, c. 23; John WALKER, 26; all seamen (MG 16 Jun 47)
Runaway Eng. svts: William ALEXANDER, Edward WILLIAMS, Henry JOHNSON, George M'KEY; ran away from Robert PHILLIPS, Fredsbrg. (VG 28 Jan 68)
Runaways from the ship *Fortune* wrecked in the Chesapeake Bay: Joseph DURRANT (shipwright), Thomas GILES (carpenter), Mary GILES, Thomas RUFF (carpenter), Edward LAWRENCE (plasterer), William CLARK (surgeon), James HITCHINGS (sailor), John THOMAS (farmer), George ELLAR (carver), William SAUNDERS (farmer), Thomas RATCHFORD (drawer), Thomas NEAL (stocking weaver), Ambrose WILLMOTT (drawer), Robert WIGGENTON (turner), Margaret WIGGENTON, James FOSTER (weaver), Richard CRAP (tailor), John DAVIES (wheelwright), Elizabeth HAYES, Mary WEBB (mantua maker) (VG 28 Sep 69, VGR 5 Oct 69)
Runaway conv. svts.: James BARBER, Eng., c. 25; John BATE, Eng., c. 23; John BATES, Eng., 27-28; John TOMLINSON, Eng., c. 35; ran away from Benjamin HOWARD, Elk Ridge Landing, [Md.] (VGR 18 Jul 71)
Runaway svts: Edward RYLOT, c. 27; John POLLARD, c. 25; John BISSEY, c. 20; William NORRIS; Henry WITMORE; ran away from Edward STEVENSON, Frederick Co., Md. (VG 12 Mar 72)
Runaway convicts: William NICHOLSON, c. 21; William SMITH, c. 27; Peter KNIGHT, Patrick BURN; Joseph WADE, c. 40; Alexander CLUBB; all are seamen except CLUBB who is a shoemaker; ran away from the ship *Thornton* lying at Leedstown (VG 23 Jul 72)
Runaway convicts: Daniel SUTHERLAND, Lauchlane WILL, William M'WILLIAM, William ELDER, Donald ELDER, Alexander M'DONALD; all are Highlanders; SOUTHERLAND is the only one among them who can speak Eng. distinctly; ran away from the ship *Donald* near Richmond (VG 15 Apr 73)
Runaways from Neabsco Furnace: Joseph LOVEDAY, conv. svt. from the West of Eng., c. 23; Tynie ROACH, conv. svt., c. 20; James M'LANE, Scot, ind. svt. (VG 8 Jul 73)

Runaway Eng. conv. svts.: John RICHARDSON, house carpenter and joiner, c. 28; Joseph REEVES, bricklayer and plasterer, c. 21; Richard BENNETT, jobbing blacksmith, c. 18; John EATON, ship carpenter, c. 25; William STEEL, cabinetmaker, c. 17; Alice WALKER who passes for EATON's wife; imp. in Mar. into Rappahannock in the *Justitia* from London (VG 12 Aug 73)
Runaways from the ship *Chance* [at Norfolk]: Thomas GLASS, ind. svt., ship carpenter, 45; John WHATMORE, ind. svt., house joiner, c. 21; James EARLY, young ind. svt., barber (VG 19 Aug 73)
Runaway conv. svts: Oliver MARTIN, Irish, 22, house carpenter and joiner; Jonathan BOOTHMAN, Eng., 23; Paul PRESTON, b. in Pa., 30; John THOMPSON, b. in New Eng., 35; John GAGAHAGEN, Irish, 43, grocer; ran away from on board the *Taylor* at Four Mile Cr. (VG and VGR 11 Nov 73)
Runaway conv. svts: David JONES, Welsh, c. 40; Elizabeth COWAN, Scottish, c. 50; William GRAY, Eng. c. 21; ran away from Caleb WORLEY and Hugh ALLEN, Botetourt Co. (VG 2 Dec 73)
Runaway svts: Robert WALKER, b. in Surry, 26; Ralph LAWSON, b. in London, 23; Francis GRANGER, b. in the north of Eng., 30; James WATSON, b. in Scotland, 20; Robert WOOD, b. in the north of Eng., 30; Lydia HEATHCOTE, b. in London, 25; ran away from the *Justitia* at Leedstown (VG 24 Mar 74)
Runaways from Samuel KEMPTON and Hercules MULLIGAN, New York: James DOUGLAS, ind. svt., b. in Scotland, c. 32, brass founder, has an uncle living between Norfolk and Wmsbrg.; James WARDOPE, ind. svt., b. in Scotland, c. 40, tailor; Archibald SCOT, ind. svt., b. in Scotland, c. 22, tailor, supposed gone toward Philadelphia (VGNI 5 Jan 75)
Runaway Eng. svts.: John BROWN, c. 35; Abraham PETERS, c. 28, says he is a Jew and talks very good Dutch; John COOLEY, c. 22, plasterer; William CHILDS, c. 21, carver and gilder; Thomas ABLE, c. 25; William BLANCHLET, c. 27; Thomas SHARP, c. 15; ran away from their masters near Bush River, Harford Co., Md. (VGPu 21 Apr 75)
Runaways from the Continental brig *Morris* lying in Rappahannock River at Port Micou: Edward Arthur BIRMINGHAM, Irish, c. 22; John RAWORTH, American, 21-22 (VG 17 Jul 78)
Runaway Irish svts. from the Potomac Co.: Cornelius M'CARTY, 26; Hugh TAYLOR, 23; William CURRY, 26; James COLLINS, 22; William BOHANNAN, 25; James M'CORMACK, 20; Arthur LAMB, 20; Daniel DUNLEAVY, 25; James KEGGAN, 22; Edward RYAN, 28; Michael DOREN, 21; Daniel HENNESSY, 25; William NUNAN, 24 (VJAA 14 Jun 87)
Runaway Irish svts. from the Potomac Co.: Philip BLAKE, 26; Hugh TAYL 23 (VJAA 30 Aug 87)
Runaway Irish svts. from the Potomac Co.: Edward MOORE, 26; Daniel HOULTON, 23; Tobias CAVENAGH, 20; James SHERRIDAN, 25; Samuel KINGSTON, 40 (VJAA 4 Dec 88)
Runaway Irish svts. from the Potomac Co.: Cornelius COLEMAN, 25; John RIELY, 31; Patrick CARNEY, 25 (VJAA 4 Oct 87)
Runaway ind. svts. engaged in France: Peter SPURK, from Treves, German watchmaker, c. 25, speaks French and German; Mark RAVEL, French, baker, c. 26, speaks French and a little Latin; Anthony RAVEL, his brother, c. 21; Charles BETIN, c. 22, speaks only French; Joseph FOUTLAIE, stocking weaver, c. 23, speaks only French; Joseph PETIT, gardener, 25, speaks only French; Joseph PRADEL, gardener, 26, speaks only French; Joachim ROCEAU, gardener, 20, speaks only French; Anthony HARVIN, stonemason, 25, speaks only French; John HARVIN, his brother, 19, speaks only French; ran away from DE BARTZ, Winchester; they were seen on the road to Philadelphia (WVGWA 24 Jul 90)
Runaway French ind. svts: Louis Joseph MATEY, laborer, c. 24; James PENNE, laborer, c. 24; Louis PONTIFFE, blacksmith, c. 21; ran away from

MALARTIE, Winchester (VGWA 1 Sep 90)
Runaway sailors: James ROBB, b. in the north of Eng., William TATE, Charles THOMPSON; John FIELD; William WILLIAMS aka Alick an ind. svt., c. 23, speaks much in the Scotch accent; ran away from the ship *Elizabeth* lying at Alexandria, seen at Nanjemay (VGPu 24 Feb 75)
Runaway sailors: William WHARM, 20; John TOLKIN, native of Bremen; Charles VINCENT; ran away from the brig *Commodore Hood* (VGAxA 22 Apr 90)
Runaway sailors: James HAWKINS, 18; John BIRD, 17; John M'FEARSON, 16; ran away from the brig *Brenchley* of London (VGAxA 22 Apr 90)
Runaway slaves: Jesse MOODY, Negro man, shoemaker, c. 35; Hannah SMITH, Negro, claims to be free, b. in Northumberland Co., c. 30; Sarah STARK, Negro, claims to be free, b. in Northumberland Co., c. 35; jailed in Pr. Wm. Co. (Ex 9 Aug 99)
Runaway slaves: William STUART, Negro, c. 45; Judah HOWARD aka Jenny, c. 18; jailed in Pr. Wm. Co. (Ex 1 Nov 99)
RUSSEL, **Christopher**, dec'd, e.a.w. his admr., George LANE of Dumfries (RJDA 19 Jun 95)
RUSSEL, **Joseph**, dec'd, e.a.w. his admr., Frederick HERMANN, Norfolk (HNPA 3 Dec 95)
RUSSEL, **William**, age 15, a pupil at the Winchester Grammar School, d. on 20 Jan. in Shenandoah Co. (BVCG 10 Feb 94)
RUSSELL **Family**, James G. DOWDALL and Edward M'GUIRE surviving exors. of Robert RUSSELL dec'd, James RUSSELL, Francis RUSSELL, Margaret RUSSELL, and Amelia RUSSELL devisees of Robert RUSSELL dec'd were defs. in a Frederick Co. chancery case, 5 Aug. 1790 [see also: M'CLUSE Family] (WVGWA 21 Aug 90)
RUSSELL, [?], son of Capt. William RUSSELL of Va., supposed killed on the frontiers of Fincastle in Sep. last [or on 20 Oct. by Cherokee Indians along with Daniel BOONE of Va. and a son of John DRAKE of Va. acc. to PC citing a Baltimore disp. of 27 Nov. (PC 6 Dec 73, VGR 23 Dec 73)
RUSSELL, **Armistead** Esq., of New Kent Co., mar. Elvy CLAYTON of the same co. (VG 12 Jun 79)
RUSSELL, **Charles**, dec'd, his admx., Susannah RUSSELL, will sell part of his est. in Pr. Geo. Co. (VGPI 18 Mar 96)
RUSSELL, **Mrs. Elizabeth**, wife of William RUSSELL of Wmsbrg., d. on 16 Feb. in the bloom of her life (VGAA 5 Mar 85)
RUSSELL, **James**, svt., ran away from George WOOLSEY of Norfolk while in Currituck Co., N. Carolina (VGR 8 Feb 70)
RUSSELL, **Capt. James**, mar. Mrs. SCOTT (PGBA 14 Jan 96)
RUSSELL, **John**, of Kg. Wm. Co., dec'd, his admr., William AYLETT and James RUSSELL, will sell his slaves and furniture (VG 17 Oct 71)
RUSSELL, **Dr. Joseph**, dec'd, his admr. is Fred. HEERMANN (RMA 4 Oct 96)
RUSSELL, **Katherine**, Irish svt., 18, ran away from John SMITH Jr., Orange Co. on 20 June (VG 31 Oct 45)
RUSSELL, **Mary**, has behaved very indecent to her husband, Thomas RUSSELL Sr. of Warwick Co., and will not live with him (VG 6 Nov 66)
RUSSELL, **Mary**, des. her husband, William, Orange Co. (VHFA 25 Nov 90)
RUSSELL, **Nehemiah**, late of Orange Co., dec'd, several of his slaves to be sold by his ex., William RUSSELL (VG 28 Nov 51)
RUSSELL, **Samuel**, merch., [of Wmsbrg.], mar. Mrs. LANIER last week (VGR 31 Dec 72)
RUSSELL, **William**, mar. Miss Betsy FARROW of this city [Wmsbrg.] (VGP 5 Jan 75, VG 7 Jan 75)
RUSSELL, **William**, of Wmsbrg., mar. Miss Molly CAMPBELL also of Wmsbrg., on Sat. last (VGWeA 24 Dec 85)
RUSSELL, **Gen. William**, of Washington Co., dec'd, his admx. Elizabeth RUSSELL, and admr., William RUSSELL, will sell some of his stocks in Richmond (VGGA [20] May 95, VGPI 26 May 95)

RUSSELL, William, grocer, late of Richmond, dec'd, e.a.w. his extx., Sarah RUSSELL, and ex., Samuel COUCH (Arg 27 Nov 98)

RUSSWORM, Francis, of Nansemond Co., who played such a sweet fiddle, drowned on 15 Jun. (VG 24 Jun, 9 Sep 73) [also given as RUSSWURM]

RUTHERFORD, Archibald, appr. house joiner, 18-19, ran away from John SLOTE, Winchester (BVCG 7 Oct 93)

RUTHERFORD, John, Scot, c. 28, suspected of carrying a Negro woman named Suckey away from Isaac HITE, Frederick Co. (VGWA 21 Oct 89)

RUTHERFORD, Miss Peggy, of Norfolk, d. on Mon. last in her 20th year (NPC 18 Jun 91); [eulogy to her by a student of William and Mary] (NPC 23 Jul 91)

RUTHERFORD, Miss Susannah, dau. of Benjamin RUTHERFORD of Winchester, aged 24, d. last Tues. (BVCG 16 Jun 94)

RUTHERFORD, Thomas, son of Robert RUTHERFORD Esq., d. a few days ago in Berkeley [Co.] (VGWA 23 Nov 87)

RUTHERFORD, Thomas, merch., of Richmond, mar. Miss Sally WINSTON of Hanover Co. on Sat. last (VGWeA 26 Aug 90)

RUTHERFORD, Van, of Charlestown, adv. that the death of Thomas RUTHERFORD Jr. dissolved the partnership of Thomas & Van Rutherford (PGBA 28 Jul 96)

RUTTER, Adam, of Berkeley Co., executed on 5 Dec. for horse stealing (VG 4 Nov, 9 Dec 73)

RYAN, Charles, svt., 25, ran away from Thomas CARVAN, Alexandria (VJAA 9 Nov 86)

RYAN, James, conv. svt., cabinet maker, ran away from Stephen MITCHELL, Yorktown (VG 3 Jun 73)

RYAN, Col. Michael, mar. Miss Frances DUDLEY at Richmond (VJAA 9 Jun 85)

RYAN, Patrick, saddler, mar. Miss LEE, both of this borough [Norfolk], on Sun. eve. (NHPA 19 Jan 97)

RYAN, Thomas, Irish svt., ran away from Henry GAINET and John FITZGERALD, Kg. Wm. Co.; he was making toward Potomac in Md. (VG 18 Jun 52)

RYAN, Thomas, breeches maker, of Winchester, d. on Sun. morn. (VGWA 1 Oct 91)

RYANS, Edward, Irish svt., c. 25, ran away from Bazil WATERS, Montgomery Co., Md.; he is suspected of running off with an Irish free woman named Bell MAGUIRE (VGWA 24 Jun 89)

RYLEY, Thomas, appr., 15-16, ran away from John BOGAN, Millwood (BVCG 28 Apr 94)

RYLY, James, Irish, 24-25, cooper, jailed as a suspected runaway in Leesburg (VGAxA 23 Sep 90)

SACHEWADE, John, appr., ran away from Daniel TROUT, Strasburg (BVCG 26 Oct 95)

SACK, Thomas, Eng., c. 47, weaver, and his son, John SACK, c. 20, also a weaver, des. from the 4th Co. of the 2nd Bn. for the State of Georgia; they were enl. in Henry Co. (VGPu 9 May 77 sup)

SADLER, Richard, svt., ran away from John CHAMPE, Kg. Geo. Co. (VG 11 Apr 55)

SADLER, William, of Fluvanna Co., lately dec'd, e.a.w. his admr., John SADLER (VGGA 18 Nov 95)

ST. MOYER, Barney, deserter, 22, from Berkeley Co. (Washington Spy 23 Nov 92)

SALEM, James, runaway, c. 25, says he bel. to Ralph PICKETT of Portsmouth jailed in Hanover Co. (VGGA 1 Nov 97)

SALKRIG, James, Scot, svt., tailor, 36, ran away from John HALPIN, Wmsbrg.; he is supposed to be gone towards the Northern Neck (VG 30 Mar 39)

SALLARD, John, of Richmond Co., dec'd, e.a.w. his ex., Walker TOMLIN,

George SISSO[N], and Ben. BRANHAM (VGWeA 4 Jan 83)
SALLY, Josiah, aka Joe, mulatto, sailor, ran away from Charles STEUART, Norfolk (VG 24 Jan 52)
SALTER, Tom, aka Tom, Negro slave, c. 38, ran away from Henry LEE's plant. in Loudoun Co.; he is suspected of being near a plant. of Charles CARTER in Hanover Co. where he has a wife named Sebra (VGR 9 Mar 69)
SALTER, William, of Surry Co., died (VG 12 Mar 79)
SAMPSON, Charles and Mary, of Goochland Co., dec'd, e.a.w. their ex., John GUERRANT, Thomas HATCHER, and Stephen SAMPSON (VGAA 26 Jun 84)
SAMUEL, Peter, French Negro boy, ran away from John CLAMEN, Washington, N. Carolina (NH 16 Feb 99)
SAMUEL, Reuben, called R. S. HURT, son of James SAMUEL of Culpeper Co. dec'd and grandson of Thomas SAMUEL of Caroline Co. dec'd; James SAMUEL d. intestate last Nov.; Reuben has an uncle named Reuben SAMUEL in Caroline Co. [an exchange of letters] (VHFA 26 Mar 95, 16 Apr 95)
SAMUEL, Capt. Reuben, d. in Caroline Co. on the 8th inst. (VHFA 17 Jul 95)
SANDEFUR, Abraham, dec'd, e.a.w. with his ex., Stephen COOKE of Cumberland Co. (VGGA 15 Feb 92)
SANDERS, William, Eng. conv. svt., c. 22, ran away from Josias CLAPHAM, Fairfax Co. (MG 30 Jun 47)
SANDERSON, Jesse, formerly of New York, d. in Richmond on the 23rd inst. (VGGA 29 Mar 97, Arg 31 Mar 97)
SANDS, Thomas, svt., 26, ran away from Patuxent Iron Works in Md. on 11 Jun. (VG 22 Jun 39)
SANFORD, Daniel Esq., dec'd, e.a.w. his ex., George CALLIS, Great Bridge (VCGA 12 Jun 94)
SANFORD, Robert, of Orange Co., intends to remove to Ky. in a few days (VHFFA 21 Oct 96)
SAUNDERS, Mrs., spouse of Robert SAUNDERS, d. in Wmsbrg. (VGWeA 12 Dec 96, VGPI 13 Dec 96)
SAUNDERS, John, said to be living on James River, is asked to apply to the Governor to get a letter from Eng. of consequence to him (VG 13 Jul 39)
SAUNDERS, Capt. John, late of Norfolk Borough, dec'd, e.a.w. his admr., Alexander ROSS (VG 24 Oct 51)
SAUNDERS, John, mulatto, 23, ran away from William PICKETT, Pr. Wm. Co. on 27 Mar. last (VG 2 Sep 57)
SAUNDERS, John, ind. svt., 41, native of Wales, barber, ran away from Anthony GEOGHEGAN, Richmond Town (VGP 2 Mar 75)
SAUNDERS, John, of Alexandria, d. on the 18th inst. [obit.] (VGAxA 20 May 90)
SAUNDERS, John, of Norfolk, late of Fredsbrg., was mar. to Miss Elizabeth PROBY of Norfolk on Sat. eve. last by the Rev. William WHITEHEAD (NPC 3 Dec 91)
SAUNDERS, John, merch., of Wmsbrg., d. on Mon. the 14th inst. in his 59th year; his admr., Robert SAUNDERS, will sell all of his slaves (VGWeA 25 Jan 93, 13 Dec 93)
SAUNDERS, John, appr., 19, ran away from David GRAHAM, Baltimore (VGRC 30 Aug 93)
SAUNDERS, John, merch., of Norfolk, mar. Miss GALT of Wmsbrg., at Wmsbrg. on Thurs. last (NH 2 Jun 96)
SAUNDERS, Mrs. Mary, wife of John Hyde SAUNDERS of Cumberland Co., d. on 23 Sep. after having been mar. 18 months and nine days; she left behind an infant dau. (VG 19 Dec 71)
SAUNDERS, Matthew, of Petersburg, d. on Thurs. 21 Nov. at Norfolk in the prime of life (VCNPGA 23 Nov 93, VGWeA 29 Nov 93)
SAUNDERS, Richard, dec'd, his ex., Samuel BROWN, will sell a tract of his land situated in Spotsylvania and Orange Cos. on the branches of Arseforemost containing 200 ac. (VG 8 Mar 79)

SAUNDERS, Robert, resident of Louisa Co., 35-40, failed to report for duty (VGPu 16 May 77 sup)

SAUNDERS, Samuel, a youth, son of Jesse SAUNDERS of Lunenburg Co., d. on the 12th inst. at the house of Lipscomb WASH in Powhatan Co. (VGGA 18 Oct 99)

SAUNDERS, Mrs. Sarah, wife of John SAUNDERS of Wmsbrg., d. there on the 28th ult. (VGPI 17 Nov 91)

SANDERSON, Mrs., wife of Capt. SANDERSON of Alexandria, died (VJAA 30 Aug 87)

SAVAGE, George, lately of the Secretary's Office, has mar. Miss KENDALL a young lady possessed of an independent fortune of at least £6000 (VGR 16 Feb 69)

SAVAGE, George, mar. Miss Elizabeth HARMANSON of this county, on Thurs. the 13th inst. (VGR 17 Feb 74)

SAVAGE, George, printer, mar. Miss Elizabeth M. GARTHRIGHT of Henrico Co., last evening (VGGA 22 Nov 99)

SAVAGE, John, of Warminster, mar. Miss Aggy DOBBINS eld. dau. of George DOBBINS Esq. of Amherst Co., on Sat. the 12th inst. (OVT 31 Aug 97)

SAVAGE, Mrs. Margaret, wife of Col. Lyttleton SAVAGE of Northampton Co., died (VG 17 Dec 72)

SAVAGE, Matthew, Va. born ind. svt., has relations near Wmsbrg., indented himself in Ireland, c. 45, ran away from William DEAKINS Jr., Georgetown, Frederick Co., Md. (VGR 24 Dec 72)

SAVAGE, Nathaniel L., dec'd, e.a.w. his ex., Thomas L. SAVAGE and Nathaniel L. SAVAGE of New Kent Co. (VGWeA 15 Jul 91)

SAVAGE, Richard, svt., tailor, ran away from Reginald ORTON, Yorktown (AWM 12 May 37)

SAVAGE, Thomas Littleton Esq., of New Kent Co., mar. Miss Mary Burton SAVAGE dau. of Col. Littleton SAVAGE of Northampton Co. (VIC 17 Jun 89, VGWeA 18 Jun 89)

SAVAGE, Dr. William, age 49, d. at his seat near Bass Town on the 27th ult. (New Bern disp. of 8 Apr.) (VGIC 24 Apr 84); of Edenton, N. Carolina, dec'd, e.a.w. his ex., Edward RICE and John COWPER also of Edenton [later exors. were named as: S. DICKINSON, Walter JONES, and William P. FLOOD] (VGAA 29 May, 5 Jun, 25 Dec 84)

SAVAGE, William, dec'd, late partner of Arthur MAXWELL, Alexandria (VJAA 31 May 87)

SAVANO, Capt. Lewis, master of the schooner *Betsey* from N. Carolina, d. last Fri. morn. at the counting house of Luman BISHOP in Manchester (Arg 24 May 99)

SAWS, Sally, claims to be a free-born Negro from New York, dau. of Thomas SAWS, 25, came to the house of Allen JONES, Yorktown, after the siege (VGAA 18 May 82); pregnant, ran away from Allen JONES of Bourbon (VGWeA 8 May 84)

SAWYER, Charles, conv. svt., c. 20, Londoner, ran away from Thomas PRICE and Thomas MICHUM, Annapolis, Md. (VGR 2 Jun 74)

SAYERS Family, HCC, 6 Apr. 1781, upon an appeal from a decree of the co. ct. of Chesterfield, James MARTIN and Hannah his wife and John REYNOLD ex. etc. of Robert SAYERS dec'd (appellants) against Robert SAYERS, Edward SAYERS, William Hardyman SAYERS, Isham SAYERS, and Elizabeth SAYERS infants under 21 by Edward SAYERS their father and next friend (appellees); it appears that the appellees are not inhabitants of the country; publication of this order will be made in the *Virginia Gazette* and also published in the several churches or chapels of the par. of St. Anne in Essex Co. (VG 14 Apr 81)

SAYERS, Robert, svt., 26, ran away from Accokeek Iron Works, Stafford Co. (VG 3 Nov 52)

SCARBOROUGH, James, conv. svt., 25, from the North of Eng., ran away from Thomas PRICE and Thomas MICHUM, Annapolis Md. (VGR 2 Jun 74)

SCARBURGH, [?], eld. son. of Col. Edmund SCARBURGH, drowned in York River on his way to Accomack Co. on 17 Sep. (VG 21 Sep 39)
SCASBROOKE, Col. Henry, of Warwick Co., d. in his 73rd year (VG and VGR 8 Apr 73)
SCASBROOK[E], Mrs. Martha, relict of the late Col. Henry SCASBROOKE of Warwick Co., d. in her 58th year; her ex., Miles WILLS, will sell all of her HH and KF (VGPu 21 Jun 76, 28 Feb 77)
SCHERER, Samuel, mar. Miss Hannah TANKARD, both of Richmond (VGWeA 20 Apr 82)
SCLATER, Sacharell, dec'd, e.a.w. his ex., William GRAVES and John DICKESON of York Co. (VG 13 Nov 79)
SCLATER, William Sheldon, of York Co., died (VG 5 Dec 77)
SCOT, John, aka Joe, Va. born slave, c. 21, ran away from Richard BROWDER (VGR 24 Dec 72)
SCOT, Ned, aka Joe, mulatto slave, c. 17, ran away from John COBBS, Chesterfield Co. (VGR 9 Nov 69)
SCOTT Family, HCC, William CALL (pltf.) and Mary Slowman SCOTT extx. of Thomas SCOTT, Thomas SCOTT, Francis SCOTT, James SCOTT, and Frederick SCOTT sons and devisees of Thomas SCOTT dec'd by the sd, Mary Slowman SCOTT assigned their gdn., John BOISSEAU, Martha LANIER ex. and extx. of Lewis LANIER the Eld., and Lewis LANIER the Younger (defs.) (VGPI 9 Dec 96)
SCOTT, Mrs., cons. of Thomas SCOTT of Richmond, d. on Thurs. morn. last (Arg 26 Nov 96)
SCOTT, Charles, of Powhatan Co., intends to move to the Western Country (VGAA 1 Oct 85)
SCOTT, Charles R., merch., of Alexandria, mar. Miss Lucinda STANTON dau. of Col. STANTON of Fauquier Co., at Fauquier Ct. H., on Thurs. the 8th inst. (CMAG and TAA 15 Nov 98)
SCOTT, Daniel, resident of Cumberland Co., and eld. son of Gen. Charles SCOTT of Ky., d. on Fri. last at the seat of George MAYO in Chesterfield Co. (VGRMA 28 Oct 93)
SCOTT, Edward, a rep. of Goochland Co., d. there lately (VG 24 Mar 38)
SCOTT, Capt. Francis, master of a schooner from N. Carolina, drowned near Hampton on Sun. last (VG 21 Apr 38)
SCOTT, Col. George, d. last week in Berkeley Co. (VCWM 17 Sep 88); e.a.w. his ex., Philip PENDLETON, Moses HUNTER, James CAMPBELL, and David GRAY (VGWA 6 May 89)
SCOTT, Israel, mulatto, appr. forgeman, c. 20, ran away from Robert GOGGIN, Elk Ridge, Franklin Co. (LFG 24 Oct 95)
SCOTT, Jack, Negro, Va. born, says he bel. to Peter HUNTER, Warwick Town, jailed in Surry (VG 9 Sep 73)
SCOTT, Jack, aka Davie, Negro, c. 27, ran away from John ARUNDELL, Richmond (VGGA 6 Sep 99)
SCOTT, Jacob, free-born mulatto, c. 17, appr., ran away from Peter JENKINS, cooper, Norfolk (NHPA 11 May 97)
SCOTT, James, merch., of Alexandria, mar. Miss Phebe MUIR dau. of the late George MUIR, in Fredsbrg. on Thurs. eve. (VHFA 23 Jun 98)
SCOTT, the Rev. James, dec'd, land held in common with the late Rev. John MONCURE in Pr. Wm. Co., to be sold by his admr., T. BLACKBURN (VJAA 22 Sep 85)
SCOTT, James Jr. Esq., dec'd, his ex. are Elizabeth SCOTT and Cuth. BULLITT (VGAA 16 Oct 84)
SCOTT, Jesse, Negro, c. 40, says he bel. to Col. Joseph BASS, Chesterfield Co., jailed in Pr. Wm. Co. (VGGA 30 Jul 94)
SCOTT, John, Negro, jailed in Chesterfield Co., claimed to be free; came from Cape Fear River, N. Carolina (VG 1 Oct 72)
SCOTT, the Rev. Mr. John, d. on his way home from Berkeley Co. to Fauquier Co.; formerly of Somerset Co., Md.; to be bur. at the Episcopal Church in

Winchester (VJAA 5 Aug 84); his PE to be sold at Westwood, Pr. Wm. Co. (VJAA 21 Oct 84); his extx., Eliza SCOTT sells his tracts in Fauquier and Fairfax Cos. (VJAA 24 Feb 85); 600 ac. of his land in Fauquier Co. on Elk Run to be sold by his extx. (VJAA 19 Jul 87)

SCOTT, John, was mar to Miss Fanny PAINE dau. of William PAINE, on Sun. eve., by the Rev. James STEVENSON, all of this town [Fredsbrg.] (VH 16 Oct 98)

SCOTT, John, Negro, c. 25, says he was freed by William LADD of Charles City Co.; jailed in Northumberland Co. (VGGA 13 Nov 98 ex)

SCOTT, John, mulatto, waterman, c. 25, ran away from Windsor Mills near Petersburg (NH 3 Aug 99)

SCOTT, Joseph, of Nansemond, dec'd, partner of William SCOTT dec'd; e.a.w. his ex., Jacob RANDOLPH and Joseph PRITLOW (VCNPGA 24 Aug 93, AGNPWA 25 Sep 93)

SCOTT, Joseph, HCC, 31 May 1799, between Ann SCOTT admx. w.w.a. of Joseph SCOTT (pltf.) and David MEADE, Lewis BURWELL, and [unknown] (defs.); it appears that MEADE is not an inhabitant of this country (VF 13 Jul 99)

SCOTT, Miss Maria, d. on Sat. last in Church St. [Norfolk?] in her 18th year (RMA 24 Sep 95)

SCOTT, Mary, formerly of Pa., d. in Winchester on Tues. the 15th inst. in her 83rd year (WG 23 Jan 99)

SCOTT, Nancy, Negro, with two chil., says she is free, but is believed to bel. to Harden BURNLEY in Hanover; jailed in Wmsbrg. (VGWeA 28 May 85)

SCOTT, Peter, for 40 yrs. a common councilman of this corporation, d. in his 81st year (VG 2 Dec 75); his ex., Alex. CRAIG and Robert NICOLSON, will sell cabinet makers tools, mahogany, walnut, and pine plank, and new items of furniture bel. to his est. (VG 13 Jan 76); his old house in this city [Wmsbrg.] which he had rented and lived in for 43 yrs. was burned down last Sun. night by accident (VGPu 26 Jan 76)

SCOTT, Poll, aka Sall SCOTT, "as an abandoned strumpet as the co. of Berkele can produce has lately had a mulatto child," ran away from John VAN METER (PGBA 18 Aug 96)

SCOTT, Richard, vendue-master, Norfolk, dec'd (VG 2 May 66); e.a.w. Philip CARBERY (VG 25 Jul 66); his widow and relict is Mary SCOTT (VGR 12 Mar 67)

SCOTT, Robert, dec'd, his admr., James BUCHANAN of Petersburg, will sell the remaining part of the lease on the garden on New St. lately occupied by the dec'd (VGPI 17 Feb 97)

SCOTT, Samuel, Negro, c. 30, says he was free born in Charles Co., Md., escaped from jail in Alexandria (TAA 22 Jan 98)

SCOTT, Thomas, Scot, conv. svt., tailor, ran away from Richard CADDEEN, Westmoreland Co. (VG 28 Jul, 6 Oct 74)

SCOTT, Thomas, of Culpeper Co., adv. that Thomas CLAYTON of Orange Co. intermarried with his dau., Frankie, and has in his possession some slaves which he did not intend to give to him the sd. CLAYTON (VGWeA 24 Apr 88)

SCOTT, Thomas, an old and respectable inhabitant, d. in Madison Co. on Sun. last (VHFFA 29 Jul 96)

SCOTT, Thomas, apothecary, mar. Mrs. FOWLER of Richmond on Tues. eve. last (LWG 16 Mar 99)

SCOTT, Thomas, Scotchman by birth, seaman, 24-25, escaped from jail in Alexandria (CMAG 22 Aug 99)

SCOTT, William, Scot, 28, des. from Capt. Thomas WAGGENER's Co. of Va. Forces (VG 22 Aug 55)

SCOTT, William, merch. of Fredsbrg., d. there on the 6th inst. (VG 30 Apr 67)

SCOTT, William, d. on the 18th inst. at his seat, Strawberry Vale (VJAA 25 Oct 87)

SCOTT, William, of Pr. Wm. Co., dec'd, the ex., Charles R. SCOTT, asks that all persons having claims against his est. or the est. of Robert SCOTT dec'd of Loudoun Co. bring them forward (CMAG 7 May 95)

SCOTT, William, of Orange Co., dec'd, his admr. is May BURTON Jr. (VHFA 13 May 90); his legatees are the chil. of his brothers, Thomas and John SCOTT, and his sister, Barbara MORTON (VGGA 21 May 94)

SCOTT, William, of Nansemond Co., dec'd, he was a partner of Joseph SCOTT dec'd; e.a.w. his admrs., Peggy SCOTT and Jacob RANDOLPH (VCNPGA 24 Aug 93, AGNPWA 25 Sep 93)

SCOTT, William, mar. Mrs. OLIVER, both of Dumfries, on Sun. eve. last by the Rev. Mr. GRAYSON (RJDWA 16 Sep 96)

SCOTT, William, dec'd, his ex., J. W. HARPER and W. MASON of Dinwiddie Co., will sell a tract of his in the lower end of Brunswick Co. (VGPI 16 Jan 98)

SCREECH, William, elderly seaman, ran away from the ship *Thomas* now at Bermuda Hundred (VG 12 Jun 72)

SCRIVNER, Joseph, merch., of Wmsbrg., died (VG 20 Aug 72); his ex., William TREBELL and Robert NICOLSON, will sell portions of his est. (VG 20 Aug 72)

[SCROSBY], Elizabeth, wife of James [SCROSBY] who will no longer pay her debts (VG 27 Mar 46)

SCRUGGS, Henry, of Cumberland Co., dec'd, his ex., Littleberry SCRUGGS, adv. that a division of his est. will take place on 1 Jan. next (Arg 25 Sep 98)

SCULLY, Edward, Irish ind. svt., c. 26, says he was a soldier in the American Army for sometime but was taken to Britain a prisoner and came out indented; ran away from Patrick WRIGHT, Richmond (VGWeA 16 Oct 84)

SEABORN, James, dec'd, e.a.w. his admr., George SEABORN (BVCG 29 Oct 92)

SEABROOK, Capt. Charles, dec'd, several ships and other items of his est. to be sold at Yorktown by his ex., Thomas REYNOLDS (VG 24 Jan 52)

SEABROOK[E], Capt. Nicholas B., d. in this city [Richmond] on Mon. last (VICGA 30 Jun 90); e.a.w. his ex., John SEABROOK[E] of Hanover Co. (VGGA 27 Mar 93)

SEARS, Albin, dec'd, e.a.w. his admr., Elliott RICHESON of Caroline Co. (VGGA 25 Dec 98)

SEARS, Miss Mary, d. on Mon. the 9th inst. at the house of Capt. George GUY in Caroline Co., aged about 16 (RMA 16 May 95)

SEARS, Willard, went to Petersburg or Richmond the latter end of March from Norfolk; information on him is sought (VGGA 27 May 95)

SEARS, William, appr. house carpenter, c. 20, ran away from John GARY near Sussex Ct. H. (VG 31 Mar 74)

SEATON, Capt. Charles, of Bristol, for many yrs. commander of a ship in the Va. trade, d. of a dropsy on Sat. last at Roger GREGORY's in Kg. Wm. Co. (VG and VGR 14 Feb 71) [also given as SETON]

SEATON, Richard, of Gloucester Co., dec'd, his land there to be sold by the sheriff (VGAA 21 Aug 84)

SEAWELL, Benjamin, died (VGR 11 Feb 73)

SEBOR, Henry, mar. Miss Hannah GRAPES, on Thurs. last, both of Frederick Co. (VGWA 22 Dec 90)

SEEGFRIED, John, shoemaker, c. [3]5, escaped from jail in Fredericktown, [Md.] (VGWA 1 May 90)

SEGAR, Miss Elizabeth, her uncle is named as Richard SEGAR (VIC 21 Oct 89)

SEGAR, John, of K & Q Co., mar. Miss Lucy ANDERSON of Petersburg a few days ago (VGPI 11 Jul 97)

SEGGA[T]T, John (see: SUGGITT, John)

SEHON, J. S., of Hardy Co., mar. Miss Polly WAGGONER dau. of Maj. Andrew WAGGONER (PGBA 16 Nov 95)

SEITZ, Frederick William, of Manheim, Germany; left London on a transport sailing for America in Aug. 1777 when he was 17; his aged father and unhappy family are trying to get in touch with him; any information is to be sent to the publisher of the *Philadelphia Gazette* or to Mr. Unich HENCKE, Secretary to the Amsterdam and American Post Offices in Hamburg (VHFFA 11 Jul 97)

SELDEN, Miss Ann, of Norfolk, d. on Wed. last [or Thurs. last acc. to the NHPA] in Petersburg in the bloom of youth (VGPI 25 Aug 97, NHPA 31 Aug 97) [also given as SELDON]

SELDEN, Maj. James, of Lancaster Co., dec'd, his ex., John SELDEN, will sell 20 of his slaves (VGPu 3 Jan 77)

SELDEN, John, dec'd, Elizabeth SELDEN (nfi) will sell part of his PE at his late dwelling house near Blandford, Pr. Geo. Co. (VGPu 12 Dec 77)

SELDEN, Miles, mar. Miss Betsey ARMISTEAD of Wmsbrg. (VG 31 Mar 74)

SELDEN, the Rev. Miles, Rector of Henrico Par. near Richmond, d. last Thurs. (VGAA 2 Apr 85, VJAA 7 Apr 85)

SELDEN, Samuel Esq., d. at his seat in Stafford Co. in his 64th year (VHFA 18 Nov 90)

SELDEN, the Rev. William, of Elizabeth City Par., died (VGAA 25 Oct 83)

SELDON, John, late of Blandford, dec'd, e.a.w. his ex., Robert ARMISTEAD (VGIC 12 Jun 84)

SELMAN, Isaac, appr., c. 16, bound by order of the Ct. of H[u]stings for the town of Alexandria, ran away from William MILLNER and John M'CALLMONT (CMAG 28 May 95)

SEMPLE Family, HCC, 19 Mar. 1796: John Walker SEMPLE and Robert Baylor SEMPLE ex. of Elizabeth SEMPLE dec'd who was surviving extx. of John SEMPLE dec'd (pltfs.) and Robert NELSON and Susannah his wife, Polly ROBINSON, William WEST and Lucy his wife, and Elizabeth COOK, Fanny COOK, and John THROCKMORTON infants by Robert THROCKMORTON the Elder their gdn., Edmund PENDLETON and Peter LYONS admrs. of John ROBINSON dec'd, and Susannah GRIFFIN wid. of the sd. John ROBINSON, John COOK and John TAYLOR, and Robert THROCKMORTON the Eld. (defs.) (VGGA 27 Apr 96)

SEMPLE, John Esq., att. at law, d. in K & Q Co. (VG 22 Feb 70); his est. containing 1200 ac. and subject to the dower of Elizabeth SEMPLE, his wid., in the whole, to the dower of Joanna PRINCE wid. of Francis PRINCE, in 100 ac. part thereof, and for the life of Sarah ROBERTS, wid., in 50 ac. another part thereof, to be sold by the sheriff (VG 27 Sep 70)

SEMPLE, John, of Pr. Wm. Co., died, he had carried on extensive iron works there for many years (VG 23 Sep 73)

SENEY, the Hon. Joshua Esq., member elect to represent the 7th District in Me in the U.S. House of Reps., d. on Sat. the 20th inst. at his seat in Queen Anne Co., Md [obit.] (TAA 31 Oct 98)

SENNET, John, aka James, son of John SENNET and Sarah ABBOT formerly residents of New York who removed from thence to Madeira when John parted with Sarah; if he will apply to the printer he will hear something to his advantage (VGGA 7 Nov 92)

SETTLE, Fielding, of Culpeper Co., adv. that his wife, Mary SETTLE, has eloped from his bed and board without any just cause (CMAG 28 Feb 97)

SEWARD, Benjamin, Virginian, des. from the recruits bel. to Capt. James MASON's Co., 15th Va. Bn. (VGPu 11 Apr 77)

SEWARD, Capt. William Coffield, dec'd, his ex., Nicholas and Jacob FAULCON, will sell his plant. known as Scotland Neck, containing 1180 ac. adjacent to the town of Cobham in Surry Co. (VGWeA 8 Nov 83)

SEWILL, Henry, dec'd, his admr. (nfi) will sell all his est. at the Great Bridge (HNPA 29 Oct 95)

SEXTON, Andrew, Negro slave, cooper or carpenter, formerly slave of James COOTS, Charles Co., Md., ran away from Col. Alexander SPOTSWOOD (AWM 20 Mar 33)

SEXTON, Hagai, aka Hankey, mulatto woman, 22-23, b. in Caroline Co., ran away from Wm. SMITH, Fredsbrg. (VG 31 Oct 71)

SEXTON, Isaac, dec'd, his admr., Rich. BUTT, will sell his est. in Norfolk (NH 23 Jul 96, 13 Oct 96)
SEYMOUR, John, of Norfolk, died (NPC 19 Nov 91)
SEYMOUR, John B., appr., ran away from Rich. BAILEY, cabinet maker, Norfolk (NH 27 Feb 96)
SEYMOUR, Thomas B. and John B., appr., ran away from Rich. BAILEY, cabinet maker, Norfolk (HNPA 19 Dec 95)
SEYMOUR, Robert, of Warwick Co., d. in his 66th year; he was nearly related to the noble family of Somerset and it was thought he had no bad title to the dukedom (VG 14 Jan 73)
SHACKLEFORD, James, dec'd, his extx., Judith SHACKLEFORD of Hanover Co., will sell a tract of his land containing 143 ac. about one mile from Hanover Ct. H. (VG 15 May 78)
SHACKLEFORD, John Esq., att. at law, of K & Q Co., d. on Thurs. 22 Jan. (VIC 18 Feb 89, VGWeA 19 Feb 89, NPJ 25 Feb 89)
SHACKLEFORD, Zachariah, dec'd, e.a.w. his admx., Lettice SHACKLEFORD of Blandford (VGPI 23 Feb 96)
SHADRICK, Job, of Orange Co., dec'd, e.a.w. his ex., Arculus HAWKINS (VHFA 7 Aug 95)
SHANKLIN, Davy, aka Davy, Negro, c. 22, his father lives with Mr. Lund WASHINGTON of Hayfield and he has numerous relations and acquaintances in the neighborhood of the Gum Spring, ran away from Francis ADAMS, Centerville, Loudoun Co. (CMAG 28 Jun 96)
SHANNAHEN, William, native of Ireland, svt., 25, ran away from Andrew DANIELL, Berkeley Co. (PC 20 Dec 73)
SHANNON, Hugh, of Hampshire Co., dec'd, e.a.w. his ex., Jeremiah REID and Paul M'IVER (BVCG 22 Jun 95)
SHAPTER, Edward, late of Backfastlief, dec'd, e.a.w. his admr., J. TUCKER of Norfolk (NH 13 Jun 96)
SHARKEY Family, Botetourt Co. Ct., 13 Oct. 1795, in chanc: The Rev. Edward CRAWFORD, Nicholas CARPER, James DALSELL, Wm. SNODGRASS, David LITTLE and Sam. WALKER for and in behalf of the Sinking Springs Congregation of Presbyterians (pltfs.) against Nicholas SHARKEY, James SHARKEY, Patrick SHARKEY, John SHARKEY, Peter WILEY and Mary his wife, Adam WOODS and Anne his wife and Adam PECK and Elizabeth his wife reps. of Patrick SHARKEY dec'd, and James MONTGOMERY, Wm. MONTGOMERY, Sam. MONTGOMERY, Joseph MONTGOMERY, Robert MONTGOMERY, and John SIMPSON and Mary his wife reps. of Robert MONTGOMERY dec'd (VGGA 25 Nov 95)
SHARKEY, Michael, merch., from Ireland, d. on Sun. eve. last (VGAA 28 Aug 84)
SHARP, Alexander, of Norfolk, dec'd, e.a.w. his admr., Robert BAIN (NPC 12 Jun 90)
SHARP, Martha, of Chesterfield, executed Fri. last for the murder of her child (VG 11 Jun 67, PC 22 Jun 67, NYPB 2 Jul 67)
SHARP, Richard, dec'd, e.a.w. Hales SHARP of Henrico Co. (VGGA 23 Jul 94); his admrs., William ROYSTER and Hales SHARP, will sell all of his PE (VGGA 16 Dec 95); e.a.w. Hales SHARP one of the admrs. (VGGA 25 Oct 97)
SHARP, Richard, dec'd, e.a.w. Thomas BINFORD for the admr. (nfi) (VGGA 15 Jun 96)
SHARP, Robert, of Henrico Co., is 83 and has 156 descendents all now alive (VG 30 Mar 69)
SHAVERS, Jacob, aka Ben WILLIAMS, mulatto slave, 45-50, property of Henry STEPHENS, Johnston Co., N. Carolina, jailed in Surry Co. (VGGA 2 Sep 95)
SHAW, John, Eng. conv. svt., 18-19, ran away from Wm. MARMADUKE near Westmoreland Ct. H. (VGPu 6 Oct 75)
SHAW, John, Irish, former soldier in the Md. Line, wounded in the Battle of Germantown, may have aided a mulatto svt. to escape from James PERRY, Montgomery Co., Md. (VJAA 29 Jun 86)

SHAW, Robert, Scot, ind. svt., baker, ran away from James KIRK, Robt. ADAM, and Geo. PURVIS of Alexandria (VG 17 Jun 75)

SHEDDEN, Mrs. Mary, widow of John SHEDDEN merch. of Norfolk, d. on Thurs. last (VGNI 25 Aug 74)

SHEERMAN, Capt. Arnold, capt. of the galliot *Fraw Tabitha* from Bremen, Germany, bound for Baltimore stranded on the eastern end of Wreck Island [Northampton Co.] on 24 Feb. last, was drowned (VGWeA 14 May 85)

SHEETS, Jacob, Dutch, ran away from John WIMMER, Berkeley Co. (VJAA 27 Oct 85)

SHEHAN, David, svt., 24, ran away from the brigantine *Greyhound* lying in Baltimore harbor; he was seen on the road below Bladensburg and is supposed now near Alexandria (VJAA 7 Sep 86)

SHEILD, Mrs. Rebecca, relict of Maj. Robert SHEILD late of York Co., d. on Sun. last (VG 18 Mar 75)

SHEILD, the Rev. Samuel, Rector of Drysdale Par., Caroline Co., mar. Miss Molly HANSFORD of York Co. (VGPu 7 Jul 75)

SHELBY, Maj. Evan, killed by Indians in the Mero District near the mouth of Red River on the north side of Cumberland on 18 Jan.; James HARRY was also killed there (Winchester disp. of 1 Apr.) (AGNPWA 10 Apr 93, VGRMA 15 Apr 93)

SHELDREAKE, Mary, her husband, George, of Norfolk, will not pay any of her debts (NH 12 May 98)

SHELL[E]MAN, John, merch., of Norfolk, d. suddenly on Sun. last (AGGA 21 Jun 96, NH 23 Jun 96); e.a.w. his [joint] admrs. James LEAHY and Andrew BYRNE of Norfolk (NH 28 Jul 96, NHPA 15 Feb 98)

SHELTON Family, Patrick Co. Ct. of Q. S., 14 May 1793, in chanc: Samuel STAPLES (compl.) against Eliphaz SHELTON as gdn. for [Elop] SHELTON, Abigal SHELTON, Liberty SHELTON, and Mary SHELTON, Abraham PENN, att. in fact for Ralph SHELTON Jr., Patrick SHELTON, Jeremiah SHELTON, Wm. M. GEH[C]E, and Julius ROBERTSON, also against Dudley RUTHERFORD, Wm. ARNOLD, Wm. JONES, Roger SHELTON, Aziriah SHELTON, Ezakiah SHELTON, and James SHELTON heirs of Ralph SHELTON dec'd. (defs.); it appears that RUTHERFORD, ARNOLD, and JONES are not inhabitants of this country (LFG 5 Apr 94)

SHELTON, the Rev. Mr., Baptist minister, killed by Indians in the Wilderness (VGRMA 21 Apr 94, VHFA 24 Apr 94)

SHEPARD, Samuel Esq., Auditor of this state, mar. Miss Polly MOSS dau. of Capt. John MOSS, both of Richmond, on Sat. 25 Mar. (VGGA 29 Mar 97, Arg 31 Mar 97, VGWeA 1 Apr 97)

SHEPHARD, Alexander, of Orange Co., mar. Miss Eliza MADISON eld. dau. of Francis MADISON of Madison Co., on 23 Feb. (VHFA 3 Mar 98)

SHEPHERD, Dr. John, of Norfolk, member of the Queen's Independent Co., d. on Tues. last in the bloom of youth [obit.] (VGR 26 Aug 73); his admrs., John LAWRENCE and John GREENWOOD, will sell his PE at Norfolk (VG and VGR 9 Sep 73)

SHEPHERD, Joseph, mar. Miss Judith BROWN eld. dau. of John BROWN Esq. of Richmond, on Sat. eve. last (VGGA 26 Dec 92, VGPA [29] Dec 92, VGRDA 31 Dec 92) [also given as SHEPPARD and SHEPARD]

SHEPHERD, Mrs. Mary, consort of Alexander SHEPHERD of Orange Co., d. at Orange Ct. H. on the 3rd inst. (VHFFA 7 Apr 97)

SHEPHERD, Smith, dec'd, his ex., Smith SHEPHERD of Pr. Anne Co., will sell his PE (NH 26 Jan 99)

SHEPHERD, Solomon, late of Nansemond Co., dec'd, his admx. w.w.a., Anne SHEPHERD, has authorized Robert BROUGH Esq. of Norfolk to settle his est. (HNPA 24 Dec 94, 5 Jan 95, AGNPPA 23 Jan 95); his admx. will sell several of his slaves in Norfolk (NH 19 Jun 98)

SHEPHERD, Thomas, mar. Miss Peggy MURDAUGH at the seat of Josiah MURDAUGH Esq. in Nansemond Co. on Thurs. eve. last (NHPA 1 Jul 97)

SHEPPARD, Mrs. Anne, spouse of Nathaniel SHEPPARD of Richmond, and dau. of John BROWN of Richmond, d. on Mon. [acc. to VGPI], Tues. [acc. to VGWeA], or Wed. [acc. to Arg.] in the bloom of youth

SHEPPARD, Benjamin, of Henrico, dec'd, e.a.w. his ex., Austin MORRIS and Edmund JAMES (VGGA 19 Jul 97)

SHEPPARD, Joseph, of Richmond, d. on Fri. last of the smallpox in the natural way [sic] (VGRMA 20 Jan 94) [given as SHEPPEARD]

SHEPPARD, Joseph, dec'd, e.a.w. his acting ex., Philip SHEPPARD, who will sell his PE in Richmond (VGGA 1 Oct 94, 23 Sep 95)

SHEPPARD, Joseph the Elder, dec'd, persons having claims against the est. are to make them known to John M. SHEPPARD in Richmond acc. to an advertisement by the ex. (nfi) of Benjamin SHEPPARD dec'd who was the ex. of the sd. Joseph SHEPPARD dec'd (Arg 14 Nov 97)

SHEPPARD, Nathaniel, mar. Miss Nancy BROWN dau. of John BROWN of Richmond in that city, both of Richmond, on Thurs. eve. last (RMA 19 Mar 96, RC 21 Mar 96, VGPI 22 Mar 96, VGGA 23 Mar 96)

SHEPPARD, Nathaniel, mar. Miss Polly PENDLETON on Thurs. eve. last, both of Richmond (VGGA 26 Nov 99) [given as SHEPHARD]

SHERGOLD, William Berrow, came some yrs. ago from Eng. and is supposed to live now in Pasquotank, Perquimans, or Currituck Cos., N. Carolina; he is asked to apply to the printer of this paper to hear something considerable to his advantage (VG 12 Sep 45)

SHERMAN, Thomas, of New Kent Co., dec'd, his admx., Frances SHERMAN, and his admr., James OTEY, will sell all of his PE (VG 22 Nov 76)

SHERMER, Mrs. Anne, relict of the late John SHERMER of James City Co., died (VG 21 Jan 75)

SHERMER, John, of James City Co., died (VG 14 Jan 75); his ex. (nfi) will sell his land in James City and Kg. Wm. Cos. (VG 25 Feb 75); e.a.w. Thruston JAMES, Dudley RICHARDSON, and George BOOTH (VG 18 May 76); one of his ex., Dudley RICHARDSON, adv. that the bonds due his est. are divided: one part payed to the heirs of Mrs. Anne SHERMER dec'd and the other part with the open accounts left in RICHARDSON's hands to collect for Richard SHERMER of England [contains a long list of names] (VG 3 Aug 76); Dudley RICHARDSON, trustee, of James City Co., adv. that all persons indebted to the est. devised to Richard SHERMER of Gt. Britain by the late John SHERMER are desired to make speedy payment (VG 4 Mar 79); e.a.w. his ex., Th[r]uston JAMES, Dudley RICHARDSON, and George BOOTH, who ask his legatees to meet at Wm. KEENE's in York Co. (VGCD 30 Oct 79)

SHERMIDINE, Polly, formerly MILLISON, has left her husband, John SHERMIDINE of Norfolk (NHPA 9 Nov 97)

SHERRARD, Mrs., wife of Robert SHERRARD, d. in Winchester (WVGWA 10 Jul 90)

SHERRY, Charles, conv. svt., cabinet maker, ran away from Wm. SCOTT, Dumfries (VGPu 28 Feb 77)

SHIELD, James, dec'd, his ex., John P. SHIELD, will sell about 40 of his slaves at Piney Point, James City Co., where he lived (RC 21 Nov 95)

SHIELD, James Jr., of James City Co., mar. Miss Patsy VAUGHN of Goochland Co. (VGWeA 12 Jan 82)

SHIELD, Maj. Robert, of York Co., died (VG 20 May 73); e.a.w. his ex., Samuel SHIELD, Thos. NELSON Jr., Hinde RUSSELL, and Thos. PESCUD of York Co. (VG 4 Nov 73)

SHIELD, Sarah, svt., ran away from the snow *John* lying in Hampton Road (VGAA 17 Apr 84)

SHIELDS, Mrs., spouse of Maj. James SHIELDS of York Co., d. near Wmsbrg. leaving a number of children (VGWeA 24 Jan 88) [see Mrs. Susanna SHIELDS below]

SHIELDS, Dennis, Irish svt., 16, ran away from John CARLYLE, Alexandria (VG 17 Sep 67)

SHIELDS, James, dec'd, Henry WETHERBURN of Wmsbrg. has empowered Thomas CARTER, also of Wmsbrg., to collect all debts due to the est. (VG 27 Mar

52)
SHIELDS, Matthew, member of the Bruton Par. vestry, d. of hemiplegia on Mon. morn. last (VG 4 Apr 66); his tract in York Co. was to be sold by Wm. PEARSON dec'd (VG 3 Sep 67)
SHIELDS, Mrs. Susanna, spouse of Maj. William SHIELDS, d. near Wmsbrg. leaving numerous offspring (VIC 30 Jan 88) [see: Mrs. SHIELDS above]
SHIELDS, Thomas, reportedly killed on the 4th inst. on Pigeon River [Knoxville letter dated 24 Mar.] (Arg 18 Apr 97)
SHIELDS, William, dec'd, his admrs., Daniel BOYCE and Josiah SMITH, will sell his PE in Powhatan Co. (RMA 25 May 96)
SHIELDS, William, mar. Miss Polly THOMPSON, both of this county [Augusta], on Thurs. last (VGSWA 20 Oct 97)
SHIELS, Robert, Eng. svt., 26, ran away from Peter PRESLEY, Northumberland Co. (VG 17 Nov 38)
SHILLING, Michael, of Baltimore, 14, comb maker, killed by lightning on 10 Aug. (VCNPGA 18 Aug 92)
SHINN, George, dec'd, a tract of his in Stafford Co. to be sold (VHFA 24 Jul 88)
SHIP, Daniel, svt., c. 20, b. at Marmion, Kg. Geo. Co., ran away from Wm. Beverly FITZHUGH, Caroline Co. (VGAxA 1 Sep 91)
SHIRKEY, Michael, merch., of Richmond, died (VGWeA 28 Aug 84)
SHIRLEY, John, appr., orphan of Philamon SHIRLEY of K & Q Co., ran away from Edwards MILLER, Kg. Wm. Co. (VGGA 10 Sep 94)
SHIVELY, Catherine, has eloped from her husband, Jacob SHIVELY, and gone off with Jacob WISE (VGWA 28 Jul 90, BVCG 4 Aug 90)
SHORE, Henry S., merch., mar. Miss Patsey WINSTON, both of Richmond, in Richmond on Sat. eve. last (VGRMA 26 Jan 95, VGGA 28 Jan 95)
SHORE, Dr. John S., of Newcastle; John SHORE Jr., Henry S. SHORE, and Samuel SHORE adv. that they will sell a 542 ac. tract of his land in the upper end of Hanover Co. (RMA 31 Aug 96)
SHORE, Samuel Esq., Superintendent of the U.S. Navy Yard at Gosport, mar. Miss E. MALE on Sat last (HNPA 28 Sep 95)
SHORES, Mr., schoolmaster, of Alexandria, died (VJAA 30 Aug 87)
SHORT, John, mulatto, c. 50, ran away along with his son, Tom, c. 19, from John M'CLENACHAN, Pr. Wm. Co. (VGAxA 27 Jan 91)
SHORT, Thomas, Scot, seaman, middle-aged, ran away from the ship *Encouragement* of London lying at West Point (VG 10 Apr 52)
SHORT, Thomas, native of Va., [lived] with a family in Chesterfield Co., des. from the state troops at Portsmouth (VGPu 12 Sep 77)
SHREVE, Mrs. Hannah, wife of Benjamin SHREVE merch. of Alexandria, died (VJAA 30 Dec 84)
SHREVE, Miss Mary, d. in [Alexandria] on the 2nd inst. (VGAxA 11 Jul 93)
SHREVE, Miss Rebecca, d. in [Alexandria] on the [3rd inst.] (VGAxA 11 Jul 93)
SHROCK, Jacob, of Hagerstown, [Md.], mar. Miss Amelia HEISKELL dau. of Frederick HEISKELL merch in Woodstock, Shenandoah [Co.] (BVCG 1 Jul 93)
SHROPSHIRE, James, appr., c. 18, ran away from John JOHNSTON in company with a lad named Samuel BAYLY; they were seen about 12 miles from Leesburg inquiring the road to Charlestown (CMAG 4 Aug 96)
SHRUM, George, appr., c. 20, ran away from Anthony SOURBEER (BVCG 15 Sep 94)
SHUGARS, Martin, tavern keeper in Alexandria, died (VJAA 22 Dec 85)
SHU[L]ER, Jacob, saddler, of Blandford, dec'd, e.a.w. his ex., Wm. CHAPPELL of Petersburg, who will also sell all his property (VGPI 19 Nov 93)
SHULS, John, aka John MONGOLD, appr., blacksmith, 17-18, ran away from Bernard VANDEREN, Loudoun Co. (VJAA 27 Jul 86)
SHUM, Adam, dec'd, e.a.w. his extx., Prudence SHUM of Alexandria (CMAG 2 Jan 96)
SHUTER, Mary, wife of William SHUTER, Frederick Co., who will not pay her debts after 9 Dec. (VJAA 16 Dec 84)

SIBBALD, George, brother of Capt. SIBBALD of Philadelphia, c. 50, drowned on 27 Mar. a little above the mouth of the Rappahannock near Fleet's Bay (VG 18 Apr 45, AWM 9 May 45, MG 10 May 45)

SICK-QUO-IN-NE-YOU-HEE, aka John WALKER, one of the chiefs of the Cherokee Nation, was mar. to Miss Ann Jane DURANT of Philadelphia, in Philadelphia on Thurs. the 5th inst. by Hilary BAKER Esq. (CMAG 14 Jan 97)

SIDEBOTTOM, Peter, from Stafford Co., was executed near Wmsbrg. on 6 May for horse stealing (VGR 6 May 73)

SIDES, Benjamin, late of Stephensburg, dec'd (BVCG 11 Mar 93)

SIFORD, Mrs. Catharine, consort of Michael SIFORD of [Staunton], d. on Thurs. the 11th inst. (Phenix 17 Jul 99)

SILING, Andrew, adv. that his books were formerly kept by his wife who is now dec'd (PGBA 13 Feb 95); [series of depositions mentions Andrew SILING and his wife and their dau., Polly OFERRALL the wife of John OFERRALL; it is noted that the SILING's speak German] (PGBA 16 Nov 95); [in a ct. case of 26 Sep 95, he is the pltf. and the defs. were Barbary FURNEY and Erasmus UHLER, admx. and admr. of Hans Adam FURNEY; it was noted that the defs. were not inhabitants of this country] (RC 29 Dec 95); he requests all persons indebted to him in the old book formerly kept by his wife, Catharine, dec'd, to make immediate payment (PGBA 2 Feb 97) [also given as SYLING]

SIM, Robert, mar. Miss Elizabeth KING of Upper Marlborough, [Md.] (VJAA 19 Jan 86)

SIMMONS, Charles, mulatto, c. 21, son of a white man named SIMMONS, ran away from Thos. L. LEE, Stafford Co. (VGAxA 13 Sep 92)

SIMMONS, Philip, appr., hatter, c. 16, ran away from Wm. STANHOPE (ET 12 Nov 98)

SIMMONS, Thomas, of Brunswick Co., dec'd, his ex. (nfi) will sell his land there (VG 8 Dec 74)

SIMMONS, William, executed in Wmsbrg. for robbery and being supposed accomplice in the murder of Col. PRESLEY (VG 24 Jan 51)

SIMMONS, William, of Southampton Co., dec'd, e.a.w. his ex., Peter BUTTS, Ben. RUFFIN Jr., and Edwin GRAY (VGPu 21 Aug 78)

SIMMONS, Maj. William, of Surry Co., dec'd, his extx. (nfi) will sell two likely looking breeding wenches that are good spinners and other items of his est.; she will also settle his est. (VG 13 Nov 78)

SIMMONS, William, late of Surry Co., dec'd, his admr., Wm. SIMMONS Jr., will sell his slaves (VGGA 21 Nov 92)

SIMMS, James, tailor, d. on Wed. last in Richmond (VGRC 6 Dec 93); e.a.w. his extx., Elizabeth SIMMS, and ex., David HOLLOWAY and Wm. BURNS (VGGA 26 Feb 94); his ex., David HOLLOWAY, Wm. BURNS, and Parke BAILEY, will sell some of his PE in Richmond (Ex 26 Feb 99, VGGA 1 Mar 99)

SIMMS, Mrs. Margaret, consort of Thomas SIMMS of Alexandria, died in childbed on the morn. of the 28th inst.; she will be bur. at the burial ground of the Presbyterian Church (TAA 29 Dec 97)

SIMONDS, Mrs., consort of David SIMONS [sic] in this town [Fredsbrg.], died (VHFA 15 May 94)

SIMONS, Mrs., wife of Abraham SIMONS formerly a resident of this co. [Spotsylvania], d. in Wilkes Co., Georgia, on Sat. the 16th ult. (VH 7 Oct 97)

SIMPSON Family, Fairfax Co., Aug. Ct., 1789, in chanc: the Rev. William STUART (pltf.) against Glassford & Henderson, Alexander HENDERSON, Robert BOGGESS, Gilbert SIMPSON, Moses SIMPSON, and Richard SIMPSON ex. of George SIMPSON dec'd, Thomas [KIRLEY], Gerrard BARNETT, and Jarvis HAMMON (defs.) (VGIC 6 Oct 87)

SIMPSON, Abraham, dec'd, e.a.w. his admr., Joseph BROCK of Spotsylvania Co. (VGR 17 Oct 71); his admr. adv. that his est. will not be sufficient to pay all his debts (VGR 3 Dec 72)

SIMPSON, Alexander, aka Alexander SMITH, runaway svt., c. [20], jailed in Spotsylvania Co. along with one Anne BAILEY (VGR 20 Jun 71)

SIMPSON, John, svt. boy, ran away from the ship *Industry* at Four Mile Cr., James River (VG 18 Jan 70)

SIMPSON, Moses, of Fairfax Co., dec'd, 30 slaves and items of his est. to be sold at his home near Wolf Run by his ex., Rich. SIMPSON and Wm. SIMPSON (VJAA 25 Jan 87)

SIMPSON, Robert, age 50, ran away from the ship *Allerton* on 28 Aug. (VG 31 Oct 51)

SIMPSON, Southy, of Accomack Co., senator from that district, died (VG 26 Mar 79)

SIMPSON, Thomas, svt., a Yorkshire man, farmer, pretends to shoemaking, ran away from John WORMLEY, York Co. (MG 26 Jul 49)

SIMPSON, Thomas, mar. Miss Anne WALKER (VHFA 5 Nov 89)

SIMPSON, Thomas, tailor, d. yesterday from a stroke on the head with a stone; the blow was given on Fri. eve. by John HURLEY who had worked as a journeyman with the dec'd (CMAG 12 Apr 96); Wm. SUMMERS of Alexandria adv. that he will pay any claims against his est. if legally authenticated (CMAG 30 Apr 96)

SIMPSON, William, Eng. svt., ran away from Thomas BRANSON, Stafford Co. (VG 21 Jul 68)

SIMS, Ignatius, appr. tailor, c. 19, ran away from Timothy SULIVAN (CMAG 6 Sep 96)

SIMS, James, late of York Co., dec'd, e.a.w. John HAWKINS (nfi) of Hanover Co. (VGP 24 Nov 74)

SIMS, Thomas, mar. Miss FRISTER, both of this place [Alexandria] on Sun. eve. last (TAA 20 Nov 98)

SIMS, William, of Albemarle Co., dec'd, his admr., Achilles DOUGLASS and Nimrod BRAMHAM of Albemarle Co., will sell sundry goods and chattels of the dec'd and settle his est. (VH 6 Sep 97)

SINGER, Isaac, Eng. svt., c. 25, ran away from Archer MATHEWS on the levels of Greenbrier (VGPu 16 Aug 76 sup)

SINGLETON, Capt. Anthony, of Richmond, mar. Mrs. RANDOLPH widow of the late Peyton RANDOLPH Esq., of Wilton, on Thurs. last the 9th inst. (VGWeA 16 Oct 88, VIC 22 Oct 88); d. lately at Newport, Rhode Island where he had gone for his health (VGGA 21 Oct 95)

SINGLETON, Isaac, late of Gloucester Co., dec'd, a tract of his land in Ware Par. to be sold, subject to the widow's dower, by his ex. (VGR 9 Feb 69)

SINGLETON, Margaret, dec'd, her PE as well as several slaves bel. to the est. of Peter SINGLETON dec'd to be sold by Thos. WISHART Jr. and Thos. LAWSON admrs. (NPC 9 Jul 91)

SINGLETON, Richard Hunt, dec'd, e.a.w. Mary SINGLETON (nfi) of Wmsbrg. (VGR 24 Mar 74)

SINGLETON, Robert, d. at Dunkirk, K & Q Co., on Thurs. eve. the 12th inst. after a severe illness of 15 days (VGGA 24 Jul 98)

SISRATH, Francis, German ind. svt., lately from Rotterdam, c. 35, can speak little or no Eng., says he followed the distilling business in his own country; ran away from Samuel KERCHEVAL, Frederick Co.; his indenture, dated 5 Oct. 1789, is signed "Francis X SISRALL" and was made in Baltimore Co., [Md.] (WVGWA 15 May 90)

SISTARE, Gabriel, John SISTARE (nfi) of New London, adv. that Gabriel SISTARE, about 15, left Belville on the Ohio near Marietta, with an intent, it is supposed, of going to Alexandria and from thence to sea, on 27 June last; he has not since been heard of (TAA 30 Oct 97, CMAG 2 Nov 97)

SITTLE, William, of Louisa Co., dec'd, his ex., Wm. THOMSON and Robert WASLEY, will sell his livestock, HHF, and slaves (VIC 9 Dec 89)

SITTLER, Miss Fanny, dau. to Isaac SITTLER, coppersmith of Winchester, d. on Mon. last (BVCG 16 Mar 91)

SKAIFE, the Rev. Mr. John, Rector of Stratton Major Par., K & Q Co., educate

18th-Century Virginia Newspapers 311

at St. John's College in Cambridge, d. on 4 Nov.
SKAIFE, Mrs. Susanna, widow of the Rev. Mr. John SKAIFE, died at the home of Geo. GILMER [apothecary], Wmsbrg., on 1 Nov. (VG 5 Nov 36)
SKELTON, Bathurst, d. Fri. last in his 25th year (VG 6 Oct 68)
SKELTON, John, from Beckermount near Whitehaven, tailor, left Eng. about 14 yrs. ago; his brother (nfi), aboard the *Waters* lying in James River, requests information on him (VG 27 Oct 68)
SKIDMORE, Benjamin, mentioned in a chanc. ct. case in Randolph Co., 24 May 1796, as heir at law of Edward SKIDMORE dec'd (BVCG 16 Sep 96)
SKIDONORE [sic], Jeremiah, murdered in Bedford Co. last Dec. by his svts.; has a small est. in the hands of his admr., Robert ALEXANDER (VG and VGR 14 Apr 74)
SKINKER, Col. John, late of Kg. Geo. Co., dec'd, his admr. w.w.a., John and Wm. SKINKER, will settle his est. and sell all of his HH and KF (VHFA 17 Aug 98, VH 31 Aug 98)
SKINNER, Dr. Alexander, of Richmond, d. there on Fri. last after a few hours illness in his 45th year (VIC 19 Nov, VHFA and VGWeA 20 Nov 88, NPJ 3 Dec 88, VGWA 10 Dec 88)
SKINNER, Burdit, of Kg. Geo. Co., d. intestate seized in fee simple of a tract in that co.; the inheritance of the land falls on several reps., some of whom are resident in Ky. (VH 23 Oct 98)
SKINNER, Ned, aka Ned, Negro, ran away from John BAIRD, Pr. Geo. Co. (VGPI 26 May 95, RMA 9 Jul 95)
SKINNER, William, dec'd, his admx., Elizabeth SKINNER, will sell all his HH and KF (VG 2 May 77)
SKINNER, William, late of Petersburg, dec'd, e.a.w. Andrew HAMILTON (VGAA 5 Oct 82)
SKIPWITH, [Anne], the lady of Sir. Peyton SKIPWITH Bart., d. on Tues. last in childbed at Hog Island in Surry Co. (VG 18 Sep 79)
SKIPWITH, Fulwar, intends to leave the country and settle in Martinique (VICGA 14 Jul 90)
SKIPWITH, Henry, mar. Miss Tabitha WAYLES of Charles City Co. (VG 15 Jul 73)
SKIPWITH, Col. Henry Esq., of Cumberland Co., mar. Mrs. Elizabeth Hill DUNBAR of Wmsbrg. on Sat. eve. last (VGGA 17 Dec 99, Arg 20 Dec 99)
SKIPWITH, Sir Peyton, of Mill Farm, Mecklenburg Co., mar. Miss MILLER lately arrived from Gt. Britain (VIC 15 Oct 88, VGWeA 16 Oct 88)
SKIPWITH, Robert Esq., mar. Miss Betsy NICHOLAS of Dinwiddie Co. (VGP 5 Jan 75, VG 7 Jan 75)
SKIPWITH, Sir Thomas George Bart., of Newtola Hall, Eng., dec'd, has left to Gray SKIPWITH eld. son of Sir. Peyton SKIPWITH Bart. of Priestwold in Va., a landed est. of £4900 sterling (VGGA 2 Mar 91, VHFA 10 Mar 91)
SKYRIN, the Rev. Henry, Rector of Elizabeth City Par., d. near Hampton on Sat. last (HNPA 11 Mar 95)
SLANEY, Capt. Charles Plowden, of H.M's 21st Regt. of Lt. Dragoons and brother to William SLANEY Esq. of Park Place, Shropshire, d. this morn. at the house of the British Consul in Norfolk (NH 19 Sep 96)
SLATE, James, tailor from London, opened shop in Wmsbrg. (VG 21 Jul 74)
SLATER, Edward, of Winchester, mar. Miss Elizabeth KEAN dau. of John KEAN of the Sweet Springs (VGWA 5 Nov 88)
SLATER, Edwin W., of New Kent Co., dec'd, e.a.w. his admx., Mary SLATER (Arg 22 Oct 99)
SLAUGHTER, Anne, of Fairfax Co., mentions her husband, Thomas SLAUGHTER, her father, Wm. CLIFTON of Fairfax Co., and her dec'd mother, Elizabeth CLIFTON (VG 9 Dec 73)
SLAUGHTER, Mrs. Ann, dec'd, e.a.w. James PATTON (CMAG 19 Feb 99)
SLAUGHTER, George, of Culpeper Co., proposes moving to Ky. sometime this winter; Robert SLAUGHTER Jr. has full and ample powers to settle all of his concerns (VG 13 Nov 79)

SLAUGHTER, James, of Culpeper Co. intends to remove to Ky. in about four weeks (VHFA 9 Oct 95)

SLAUGHTER, Robert S., c. 25, jailed in Fredsbrg. by the Spotsylvania Co. Ct. for horse stealing, escaped on Wed. (VH 28 Sep 98, GLFFA 19 Oct 98)

SLAUGHTER, Capt. Shelden, d. on Wed. 26 Nov. (VGPu 5 Dec 77)

SLOAN, Dunbar, of the house of Sloan & Pagan, mar the widow M'HUCHIN on Sat. night (NH 27 Nov 98)

SLUSHER, Frederick, of Stephensburg, denies that his dau., Catharine, was "in an indiscreet manner" before her marriage (VCWM 14 May 88)

SMALLWOOD, Bayn, soldier in the 2nd Regt. of Artillerists and Engineers, 45, b. in Charles Co., Md., des. from the rendezvous at Kempsville (NH 26 Jan 99)

SMALLWOOD, John, dec'd, his admx. (nfi) will sell the residue of his PE (VCGA 31 Jul 94)

SMALLWOOD, John, dec'd, his admx., Mary B. SMALLWOOD, has revoked the power of Robert SHELTON of Portsmouth, to settle her dec'd husband's est. (NHPA 14 Dec 97)

SMALLWOOD, Gen. William, former governor of Md., d. lately at Woodward, Pr. Geo. Co., Md. (VGGA 29 Feb 92)

SMALLWOOD, William Esq., dec'd, his extx. (nfi) will sell 30 Negroes at his plant. at Pasbytansy and 12 Negroes at his plant. in Culpeper Co. (VHFA 29 Nov 92)

SMARR, John, dec'd, e.a.w. his ex., Robert SMARR, and extx., Sarah SMARR (CMAG 9 Feb 96)

SMEDDLE, Richard, Eng. svt., 23, ran away from H. U. ST. GEORGE, Surry Co.; it is suspected that he went to Hampton or Norfolk (VG 14 May, 2 Jul 67)

SMELT Family, HCC, 2 Jun. 1789: Wm. POLLARD Jr. and Elizabeth his wife, Reuben BUTLER and Anne his wife, Dennis SMELT, John HALL and Lucy his wife, Anne SMELT and Lucy SMELT children of Wm. SMELT dec'd by Anne SMELT their gdn. and next friend (pltfs.) against Robert Payne WARING, ex. of Wm. TODD dec'd, who was ex. of the Rev. John SMELT and of Anne SMELT dec'd, Samuel GRIFFIN, Fauntleroy and John MACON (defs.) (VIC 24 Jun 89)

SMELT, Mrs. Anne, dec'd, William TODD will sell her tract of land in K & Q Co. (VG 16 Dec 73)

SMILEY, John, b. in Pa., cooper, enl. in Dumfries on 31 Jul. 1794, des. from Ft. Norfolk (AGNPPA 8 May 95, HNPA 13 May 95)

SMITH Family, Rockingham Co., Ct. of Q.S., 27 Mar. 1793: Isaiah SHIPMAN (comp.) against Wm. SMITH and John DAVIS ex. of Abraham SMITH dec'd, and Henry SMITH devisee of the sd. Abraham SMITH (defs.) (BVCG 6 May 93)

SMITH, Mrs., spouse of William SMITH of Norfolk, d. last Sat. (HNPA 25 Mar 95)

SMITH, the Rev. Mr., Rector of Portsmouth for upwards of 30 yrs., d. on the 6th inst. (VGR 14 Jan 73)

SMITH, Aaron, Negro, c. 23, son of Rose SMITH a free mulatto who lives at the Piney Woods in Perquima[n]s Co., N. Carolina; he was bound out to Benj. SMITH, a Quaker, in the same co. at the age of 12; jailed in Richmond (VICGA 7 Jul 90)

SMITH, Abraham, native of Philadelphia, c. 25, escaped from jail in Suffolk Co. (NH 4 Jan 96)

SMITH, Alexander, aka Duffy, appr., 16-17, ran away from Andrew JAMIESON, Alexandria (CMAG 31 May 96, NH 9 Jun 96 sup)

SMITH, Capt. Alexander H., of the ship *Ardent* of Baltimore, d. on 2 June in Alge[c]iras, [Spain] in consequence of a wound he received in an engagement with five French privateers (NH 20 Aug 99)

SMITH, Anne, has eloped from her husband, Samuel, and is "being entertained" by her father, John WILKINSON, of New Kent Co. (VG 15 Oct 67)

SMITH, Anne, has eloped from her husband, Robert SMITH of Richmond Co. (VGR 12 Jan 69)

SMITH, Arthur, of Surry Co., dec'd, his HH goods to be sold on 19 Jun. by his admx., Elizabeth SMITH (VG 13 Jun 55)

SMITH, Augustine, late of Middlesex Co., dec'd, e.a.w. his ex., John SMITH (VG 24 Nov 74)

SMITH, Dr. Augustine J., mar. Miss Susannah TAYLOR on Wed. eve. last, in [Alexandria] (CMAG 26 Mar 96)

SMITH, Baldwin Matthews, of Lancaster Co., dec'd, some of his slaves to be sold at Lancaster Ct. H. by his admr., John SMITH (VG 4 Nov 63)

SMITH, Col. Burgess, of Lancaster Co., died (VGP 9 Feb 75, VG 11 Feb 75); his admrs., Philip SMITH, Burgess BALL, and Thomas B. GRIFFIN, will sell 25 of his slaves, HH and KF, etc. (VGP 23 Mar 75, VG 25 Mar 75)

SMITH, the Rev. Charles Jeffery, dec'd, e.a.w. his ex., Julius King BURBEDGE and Bartholomew DANDRIDGE, who will also sell his land on the Chickahominy River in New Kent and Charles City Cos. (VG 24 Jan 71, VGR 31 Jan 71)

SMITH, the Rev. Charles, Rector of Portsmouth Par., Norfolk Co., died (VG 14 Jan 73)

SMITH, Christopher, svt., 16-17, ran away from the snow *John* lying in Hampton Road (VGAA 17 Apr 84)

SMITH, Christopher, mar. Miss Elizabeth YOUNG, both of this town [Winchester], on Fri. last (WG 20 Feb 99)

SMITH, David, adv. that his wife, Frances, has eloped from him and he will no longer be answerable for her debts (VG 10 Jul 78)

SMITH, Edward, late of York Co., dec'd, his land near Fredsbrg. to be sold; his extx. is Agnes SMITH (VG 27 Dec 51)

SMITH, Elizabeth, svt., 25, ran away from Alexander M'INTYRE, Leesburg; she was formerly indented to Capt. GRAY from Boston (VGR 15 Oct 72)

SMITH, Elizabeth, of Henrico Co., dec'd, e.a.w. her ex., Drury WOOD (VGGA 20 Jul 91)

SMITH, Elizabeth, has absconded from her husband, John SMITH, for over two yrs. and calls him "Old Devil" and tells him she had rather have a copper snake there [in her bed] than him (PGBA 28 Dec 97)

SMITH, Mrs. Elizabeth, of Hanover Co., d. on the 16th inst., aged 85 (Arg 25 Oct 99)

SMITH, Mrs. Elizabeth Garland, consort of Jesse SMITH of Henrico, d. on Wed. the 17th inst. in her 50th year (RMA 20 Aug 96)

SMITH, Francis, of Hanover Co., dec'd, e.a.w. his ex., Thomas SMITH, who will also sell a large tract of land in Louisa Co. (VGPu 12 Jan 76, VG 13 Jan 76); Granville SMITH and Geo. WILLIAMSON, exors. of Thomas SMITH, who was ex. of Francis SMITH, will sell 18 slaves, HH and KF bel. to Francis SMITH at the late dwelling house of Elizabeth SMITH near Hanover Ct. H. (Ex 15 Nov 99, 6 Dec 99)

SMITH, Francis, merch., mar. Miss Anne MARSDEN, both of Norfolk, on Wed. eve. last (NH 12 Dec 99)

SMITH, George, a waterman, found dead on a small flat just above the mouth of Carter's Cr., Gloucester Co., last Mon. (VGR 15 Aug 71)

SMITH, George, dec'd, his ex., Anne SMITH, Samuel WHITE, and James MORTON, will sell 800 ac. of his land in Charlotte Co. (VIC 26 Aug 89)

SMITH, George, of Little Cacapehon, dec'd, e.a.w. his admr., John M'BRIDE, and admx., Elizabeth SMITH (WG 16 Oct 99)

SMITH, Hannah, Negro woman, c. 30, says she is free, was b. in Northumberland Co., and lived with James ALLEN until she was 18 then with Thos. HARRISON in Petersburg and with James STRANGE in Manchester; jailed in Pr. Wm. Co. (Ex 12 Jul 99)

SMITH, Henry Middleton Esq., mar. Miss SULLY, late of the theatre, lately, in Charleston, S. Carolina (Norfolk disp.) (RMA 7 May 95)

SMITH, Howard, dec'd, e.a.w. his admr., Daramis SMITH of Goochland

(VGWeA 12 Nov 85)
SMITH, Dr. J. B., d. in Alexandria last Mon., on his way to Connecticut from Charleston, S. Carolina (VJAA 28 Dec 86)
SMITH, James, of Isle of Wight Co., age 40, des. from H.M.S. *Hector* in Elizabeth River, on 17 Oct. (VG 2 Nov 39)
SMITH, James, enl. by Capt. PEACHEY, des. from the Va. Regt. at Ft. Cumberland (VG 26 Dec 55)
SMITH, James, supposed to be a runaway svt. from Md., c. 20, jailed in Middlesex Co. (VG 29 Oct 72)
SMITH, James, Scot, conv. svt., ran away from John M'DONALD in Goochland Co. (VG 19 Nov 72)
SMITH, James, mulatto, came to the plant. of James HUBARD in Gloucester Co., claimed to be a Pamunkey Indian (VGAA 15 Nov 83)
SMITH, Jean, widow and admx. of Wm. SMITH, has sold a tract of land in Augusta Co. (VGGA 13 Jun 92)
SMITH, John, of Gloucester Co., mar. Miss Molly JAQUELIN, youngest dau. of Edward JAQUELIN of Jamestown on 17 Nov. (VG 18 Nov 37)
SMITH, John, Eng. svt., 27, came in Capt. JOHNSON in Potomac River and was bought for a schoolmaster, ran away from Thos. CHILTON, Westmoreland Co. (VG 31 Oct 45)
SMITH, John, b. in Gloucester Co., des. from Capt. Thomas WAGGONER's Co. (VG 28 Feb 55)
SMITH, John, svt. from Md., blacksmith, belonged to Dr. Geo. STEWART in Annapolis, jailed in Frederick Co. (VGR 8 Mar 70)
SMITH, John, of Northumberland Co., dec'd, his tract in that co., known as Fleet's Bay, containing 1611 ac. to be sold pursuant to a decree of the General Ct. (VG 12 Jun 72)
SMITH, John Esq., merch. and a rep. for Hanover Co., d. at his seat in Hanover Co. in the flower of his age; he left no chil. (VG and VGR 28 Jan 73, PC 15 Feb 73); his lands in Hanover and Goochland Cos. to be sold by his ex., Wm. ANDERSON (VG 15 Apr 73); his livestock, land in Goochland and Henrico Cos. to be sold at his late plant. in Kg. Wm. Co. by his ex., Wm. ANDERSON who is also the admr. of Joseph SMITH (VG and VGR 14 Oct 73); his ex., Wm. ANDERSON, will sell his 2000 ac. tract opposite Elk Island in Goochland Co. and other land; the est. of Joseph SMITH (nfi) dec'd is also mentioned (VG 21 Apr 74); e.a.w. Wm. ANDERSON (VG 16 Apr 79); his ex. was Wm. ANDERSON who removed to Gt. Britain and was replaced by John SHORE (of Clifton) whose son, Thos. SHORE (of Petersburg) has the [est.] books and papers (VGIC 6 Aug 85)
SMITH, John, recruited in Chesterfield Co., des. from the recruits of the 1st Va. Regt. (VGPu 25 Apr 77)
SMITH, John, one of the orderly men at the State Hospital, was found dead at the lower end of Wmsbrg. last Mon. morn.; he is supposed to have been murdered in the night (VG 6 Nov 78)
SMITH, John, mar. Miss Sally WALLER youngest dau. of Benj. WALLER Esq., late of Wmsbrg. (VGWeA 24 Jan 88)
SMITH, John, appr. painter, native of Va., c. 20, ran away from (nfi) (VCWM 4 Jun 88)
SMITH, John, native of Delaware, 19, des. on his way from Staunton to the rendezvous at Greenbrier Ct. H. (BVCG 25 Jun 92)
SMITH, John, of the Great Bridge, mar. Miss Elizabeth BOUSH of Pr. Anne Co. (VCNPGA 7 Sep 93)
SMITH, John, Irish, 22, des. from the camp of the 3rd Sub-Legion, Shockoe Hill (RC 24 Oct 95)
SMITH, John, aka James TAYLOR, b. in London, c. 35, plasterer; he was in Capt. BROWN's Co. of Baltimore bel. to the 1st Regt. of Artillery, des. from Samuel EDDIN's Co. of Artillery and Engineers at Richm. (VGGA 9 Jul 99)
SMITH, John, dec'd, e.a.w. his extx., Mary-Anna HUNTER of Portsmouth (NH 28 Sep 99)

SMITH, Joseph [sic], [of Hanover Co.], dec'd, his admr., Wm. ANDERSON, will sell his livestock and HH and KF (VG 5 Aug 73) [probably an error for John SMITH who d. in Jan. 1773, see above]

SMITH, Joseph, Scot, painter, c. 33, ran away from Fredsbrg. (VGPu 25 Aug 75)

SMITH, Jury, b. in Kg. Wm. Co., des. from the service of the Commonwealth (VGPu 2 May 77)

SMITH, Col. Lawrence, d. at his house in Yorktown on Tues. morn. last (VG 2 Mar 39)

SMITH, Lawrence, of York Co., dec'd, his land there to be sold by his admr., Wm. MITCHELL (VGAA 1 Nov 83)

SMITH, Lawrence, dec'd, his ex., Thomas SMITH, will sell a 400-500 ac. tract of his joining the town of York (VIC 24 Dec 88, VGWeA 1 Jan 89)

SMITH, Louis, b. in Brunswick Co., c. 20, enl. out of Capt. PELHAM's Minute Co. at York, des. from Capt. CRUMP's Co., 1st Va. Regt. (VGPu 13 Sep 76)

SMITH, Mrs. Margaret, dec'd, her ex., David BOYD of Northumberland Co., will sell her PE at Shooter's Hill in Middlesex Co. which was the seat of the late Augustine SMITH Esq. (VGPu 16 May 77 sup)

SMITH, Marshall, appr., c. 19, tanner, ran away from Daniel GARWOOD, Culpeper Co. (BVCG 22 Dec 94)

SMITH, Martha, of Pittsylvania Co., has eloped from her husband, Edward SMITH (VGPu 13 Jun 77)

SMITH, Mrs. Mary, wife of Jonathan SMITH, tailor, of Winchester, aged about 40, d. on Thurs.; she was bur. on Fri. at Stephensburg (BVCG 17 Sep 92)

SMITH, Mrs. Mary, wife of Hugh SMITH of this town [Alexandria], d. on Sat. last (CMAG 7 Feb 97)

SMITH, Mrs. Mary E., consort of Col. Larkin SMITH of K & Q Co., d. on Fri. the 10th ult. after a long illness (VHFFA 21 Feb 97, RCFPC 22 Feb 97, VGGA 1 Mar 97)

SMITH, Meredith, Tappahannock, Essex Co., 25 Aug. 1797, in chanc: Wharton QUARLES (compl.) against George Wm. SMITH admr. of Meredith SMITH dec'd and Lettice Lee RUTT, Francis West QUARLES and Lucy Daingerfield his wife and Edwin Bathurst SMITH an infant under 21 (defs.) (VGGA 20 Dec 97)

SMITH, Meriwether, of Essex Co., mar. Miss Betsey DANGERFIELD of K & Q Co. on Thurs. the 3rd inst. (VGR 24 Aug 69)

SMITH, Meriwether, [of Essex Co.], dec'd, his admr., George W. SMITH, will sell part of his PE at the plant. of Paradise in Essex (VGRMA 8 May 94, VHFA 15 May 94); his admr., of High Meadow, will sell five of his slaves (VGRMA 29 Jan 95)

SMITH, Milly, her husband, John SMITH of Petersburg, adv. that she has eloped from her residence (VGPI 13 Jun 94)

SMITH, Ned, Negro, b. in the West Indies, bel. to Wm. CHAMP on Rappahannock River, jailed in Halifax N. Carolina (VG 5 Mar 67)

SMITH, Obadiah, of Chesterfield Co., died (VGPu 21 Mar 77 sup)

SMITH, Robert Esq., dec'd, his ex., Josiah COLLINS and James [INADELL], will sell the remaining part of his est. at Edenton, [N. Carolina] (VGWeA 20 Apr 82)

SMITH, Robert, of Powhatan Co., dec'd, est. accounts of Wm. SMITH dec'd (who was admr. of Robert SMITH) with Josiah SMITH the ex. of Wm. SMITH (VGGA 20 Apr 91)

SMITH, Robert Esq., mar. Miss BORUM dau. of John BORUM Esq., at Horn Harbor, Mathews Co., on Thurs. last (HNPA 29 Oct 95)

SMITH, Sam, of Norfolk, intends to depart the colony in June (VG 24 Apr 46)

SMITH, Samuel, of Bedford Co., dec'd, e.a.w. his admr., James TAYLOR of Henry Co. (VGAA 19 Apr 86)

SMITH, Samuel, dec'd, e.a.w. his admr., John SALLIE of Chesterfield Co. (Ex 14 Jun 99)

SMITH, Sarah, has left her husband, James SMITH (NH 16 Jun 96)

SMITH, Thomas, seaman, ran away from the ship *Virginia* at Littlepage's Landing, New Kent Co., and may be headed for Bristol Iron Mines (VG 18 Apr 45)
SMITH, Capt. Thomas, of Gloucester Co., mar. Miss Nancy PLATER of the same co. (VG 16 Jan 72)
SMITH, Thomas, merch., of Richmond, mar. Miss Betsey WARREN of New Kent Co. (VG 5 Nov 72)
SMITH, Thomas, of Kg. Wm. Co., dec'd, his admrs., Wm. and Harry SMITH, will sell his slaves (VG 19 Nov 72)
SMITH, Thomas, Eng. ind. svt., house carpenter, ran away from J. ARMISTEAD in New Kent Co. (VG 29 Jul 76)
SMITH, Thomas, of Sussex Co., who called himself a native of Eng., dec'd, e.a.w. his admr., Marcus PENNINGTON (VG 2 Oct 79)
SMITH, Thomas, of Louisa Co., will settle his executorship of his late dec'd father, Francis SMITH (VIC 9 May 87)
SMITH, Thomas, printer, of Richmond, d. yesterday morn. (VGRMA 20 Jan 94)
SMITH, Capt. Thomas, d. a few days ago at Oak Hill, Fauquier Co. (BVCG 15 Jul 96, RCFPC 20 Jul 96)
SMITH, Thomas, dec'd, his ex., James JOHNSON of Isle of Wight Co., will sell part of his PE including 100 head of cattle at his dwelling house, one half mile from Smithfield (NH 5 Sep 99)
SMITH, William, of Brunswick Co., intends to sell his 625 ac. of land there and move into Pittsylvania Co. next fall (VGR 18 Jul 71)
SMITH, William, conv. svt., c. 22, ran away from Jonathan NIXON, Frederick Co., near Bladensburg, Md. (VG 3 Jun 73)
SMITH, William, Scot, c. 23, ran away from John COCKBURN, Newcastle; he is believed to be making for Wilmington, N. Carolina as he has a brother's widow living there who moved from Va. some time since (VGP 29 Dec 74)
SMITH, William, Irish svt., 45, ran away from Sampson MATHEWS, Richmond (VGAA 14 Aug 84)
SMITH, William, aka Billy, free Negro from Bermuda, 25, in the possession of James BRANCH, Chesterfield Co. (VGAA 18 Dec 84)
SMITH, William, Irish svt., carpenter, ran away from John EVANS, Alexandria (VJAA 8 Dec 85)
SMITH, William, grocer, d. in Alexandria (VJAA 20 Apr 86)
SMITH, William, of Alexandria, dec'd, e.a.w. his admr., Colin MACIVER (VJAA 15 Jun 86)
SMITH, William, of Fairfax Co. [?], dec'd, a lot bel. to his est. in Alexandria to be sold pursuant to a decree of Fairfax Co. Ct. (VJAA 31 Aug 86)
SMITH, Col. Wm., of Essex Co., dec'd, his land five miles from Tappahannock to be sold (VHFA 22 Apr 90)
SMITH, William, appr., c. 19, b. in Ireland, ran away from George CORYELL, Alexandria (VGAxA 13 Jan 91)
SMITH, William, late of New Mill Cr., Norfolk Co., [dec'd], e.a.w. John NEVISON; his admx. is Bethia[h] SMITH of New Mill Cr. (VCNPGA 3 Aug 93, AGNPWA 19 Mar 94)
SMITH, William, dec'd, e.a.w. his ex., John SMITH, Spotsylvania Co. (VHFA 15 May 94)
SMITH, William, mar. Mrs. MOORE on Sun. eve. (NH 4 Jul, AGGA 5 Jul 96)
SMITH, William, soldier, 18 yrs. and eight months, native of Gloucester Co., des. from the main barracks at Norfolk (NH 1 Dec 98)
SMITH, William Sr. Esq., of Powhatan, d. on the 16th inst. at an advanced age (VICGA 27 Jan 90)
SMITH, William H., mar. Miss Elizabeth CROUCH of Richmond on Sat. last (VIC 7 Jan 89)
SMITHE, William, appr., 16, ran away from John BOGAN, Winchester, and is believed to be going to his mother's near Muse's Mill (VGWA 20 Aug 91)
SMITHE[R], James, mar. Miss Kitty KIGER dau. of Geo. KIGER saddler, all of

Winchester, on Sun. 19 Oct. (BVCG 27 Oct 94)
SMITHER, John, indent. appr., c. 17, ran away from John HUBER, Dumfries (CMAG 7 Sep 99)
SMITHER, John B., dec'd, his ex. is Thomas FRAYSER of New Kent Co. (VGGA 2 Oct 98)
SMITHERS, Godfrey, mulatto, c. 21, ran away from Abraham NICHOLAS, James City Co. (AWM 26 Sep 34)
SMITHSON, William, dec'd, a quantity of leather bel. to his est. to be sold by his admr., Rich. HANSON of Petersburg (VG 22 Sep 68)
SMOOT, Alexander, merch., mar. Miss Eliza HIPKINS at Golden Vale, Caroline Co., on Thurs. the 15th inst. (VHFA 22 Aug 93)
SMOOT, Alexander, of Tappahannock, will sell his distillery on Piscataway Cr.; he desires to settle in Baltimore (VHFFA 6 Nov 95)
SMOOT, Solomon, appr. blacksmith, ran away from Daniel SMITH, Frederick Co. (WG 16 Oct 99)
SNALE, Will, runaway Negro bel. to the Par. of Elizabeth River (AGNPPA 22 Jan 96)
SNEAD, Sarah, has absconded from her husband, William (VGR 18 Jul 71)
SNEED, Zachariah, of Pittsylvania Co., dec'd, e.a.w. his admr., Wm. SNEED (VGGA 29 Nov 97)
SNICKERS, Edward, d. at Battletown (WVGWA 26 Jun 90)
SNIDER, Selagh, has left her husband, Henry SNIDER (PGBA 28 Jul 94)
SNOOCK, Joseph, Eng. ind. svt., laborer, ran away from Robert MOORE, Georgetown (VGP 16 Nov 75)
SNOW, Hyman, from Norfolk Borough, d. in the Hospital for Lunatics in Wmsbrg. (VGGA 6 Oct 90)
SNYDER, Jacob, jailed for the murder of Joshua STRIKLER by stabbing him in the belly with a knife in Hardy Co. (Winchester dateline of 29 July) (VHFFA 5 Aug 96)
SNYDER, Mary, ind. svt., 17-18, ran away from Thomas LEWIS, near Winchester (WG 27 Nov 99)
SOLACUTTA, commonly called "Hanging Maw," a great and beloved chief of the Cherokees, aged 65, d. at his house near Tellico Blockhouse, Tennessee (CMAG 26 May 96)
SOLE, John, Eng. ind. svt., c. 19, shoemaker, ran away from John APPERSON, New Kent Co. (VG 24 Feb 76)
SOMERVILLE, Alexander, son of Geo. SOMERVILLE, age 2 yrs., d. on Fri. last (VGWA 5 Nov 88)
SOMERVILLE, James, old inhabitant and for many yrs. a merch. in Fredsbrg., d. at Port Royal, where he had gone for his health, on Tues. last, aged 57 (VHFA 28 Apr 98); e.a.w. Walter COLQUHOUN, James BLAIR, Daniel GRINNAN, and James SOMERVILLE Jr., his exors. (VHFA 16 May 98); his exors. will rent his wharves and warehouses (VH 2 Nov 98)
SOMMERVILLE, Joseph, d. at Bath on the 24th ult. (PGBA 9 Mar 97)
SOREL, John, des. from Capt. WINSTIN's Co. of Continental Infantry; it is expected he will try to get to N. Carolina (VGPu 18 Apr 77)
SOUDER, James, aka John, shoemaker, 18, from "the Jerseys" escaped from jail in Winchester (VGWA 24 Sep 91); a John SOUDER, an ind. svt., c. 18, ran away from John IRWIN, Westmoreland Co., Pa. near Ft. Pitt (VGWA 27 Aug 91)
SOUTHALL, Philip Esq., of Richmond, mar. Miss Jenny NEILSON of Urbanna on Sun. sennight (VIC 24 Sep 88, VGWeA 25 Sep 88)
SOUTHALL, Pleasant, a young man much lamented, d. in Richmond on Tues. eve. last [6 Mar.] (VGGA 7 Mar 98, Arg 9 Mar 98)
SOUTHALL, Maj. Stephen, of Richmond, d. on Sat. eve. last (Arg 5 Mar 99)
SOUTHALL, Col. Turner, of Southall and Hay, Richmond, dec'd, the surviving partner is Wm. HAY (VGGA 10 Aug, 12 Oct 91)
SOUTHALL, William, merch., of Richmond, d. at Bermuda on 22 Jan. (NH 6 Feb 96, VGGA 10 Feb 96)

SOUTHARD, William, late of Loudoun Co., dec'd, e.a.w. his acting ex., Hardadge LANE (VJAA 28 Jul 85); his acting ex. requests that Anne PEYTON dau. of John SMITH and Margaret his wife, niece of the sd. Wm. SOUTHARD, apply for a £20 legacy left her in his will (VGWeA 6 Aug 85)

SOUTHGATE, John, merch., mar. Miss Fanny STARK, both of Norfolk, on Thurs. eve. last (NH 23 Apr 96)

SOWERBUTTS, Richard, of Chesterfield Co., executed near Wmsbrg. on 27 June (VG 27 Jun 71)

SOWERS, James, mar. Miss Eliza KERFOOT, both of Frederick Co., in Jan. 1799 (WG 9 Jan 99)

SPAIN, Isaac, appr., 18, ran away from John GARY near Sussex Ct. H. (VG 31 Mar 74)

SPANGENBERG, Dr. Frederick, dec'd, e.a.w. his admr., John STEWART, of Alexandria (VGAxA 12 May 91)

SPANGLER, Mary, extx. to David SPANGLER dec'd of Franklin Co. (VGGA 18 Dec 93)

SPARENBURG, John, ind. Dutch svt., c. 23, purchased at Philadelphia last April off a ship from Amsterdam, ran away from Samuel COUCH, Richmond, who believes he will make towards Philadelphia (VGWeA 24 Dec 85)

SPARKS, John, executed on 3 July in Wmsbrg. for the murder of James FOX (VG 3 Jul 52, NYPB 27 Jul 52)

SPARKS, John Whitlif, appr., 18, ran away from Johnzd [sic] TONGUD, Warrenton, Fauquier Co. (VHFA 3 Jul 98)

SPARROW, Betsey, has eloped from her husband, John SPARROW, of Norfolk (NH 7 Jun 98)

SPEARS, Thomas, joiner, b. in Bristol, c. 20, ran away from George WASHINGTON, Fairfax Co., (VGP 28 Apr 75 sup, VGPu 5 May 75)

SPEARS, William Sr., late of Cumberland Co., dec'd, e.a.w. his admrs., Wm. and Robert SPEARS (RMA 20 Jul 96, Arg 7 Feb 97) [also given as SPEAIRS]

SPECHT, George, boot and shoe maker from Philadelphia, adv. that he has moved to Richmond (VGGA 26 Dec 92)

SPENCE, Catherine, called the "Old Post Woman" who lived many yrs. in this colony; any of her children are asked to apply to John MARTIN, Kg. Wm. Co., to be informed of something to their advantage (VG 4 Sep 46)

SPENCER, Charles, merch., mar. Miss Elizabeth CARTER, both of this city [Richmond], on Sat. eve. (VGGA 30 Sep 95, RMA 1 Oct 95)

SPENCER, Daniel, Irish svt., c. 45, ran away from Mark KENTON and Jeremiah OWEN, Fauquier Co. (VGP 11 Oct 70)

SPENCER, Mrs. Elizabeth, of Petersburg, d. yesterday (VGPI 13 Jul 98)

SPENCER, Harry, Negro, 50, ran away from Charles BRUCE, Spotsylvania Co. may have gone to Carolina (VG 21 May 67)

SPENCER, Richard, who kept a store or tavern at Pittsburgh about 10 or 12 yr ago and was afterwards an officer in the American Army; if he is alive and will apply to David ANDERSON Jr., Hanover Co., he will hear of something to his advantage (VGIC 28 Oct 86)

SPENCER, Thomas Sharp, reportedly killed by Indians near Crab Orchard, Tennessee on [1 May] (VGRMA 12 May 94)

SPENNY, William, dec'd, e.a.w. his ex., D. M'PHERSON and D. M'DONALD (HNPA 18 Feb 95, AGNPPA 7 Apr 95)

SPICER, Absolom, appr. ship carpenter, his parents live in Caroline Co., ran away from Samuel LEMBERD, Isle of Wight Co. (VG 16 Apr 67)

SPIERS, Harris and Joshua BUTTS, of Columbia Co., Georgia, purchased about 15 Negroes a few days ago from Benj. DREW of this co. [Southampton]; on the 15th, they set out on their way home; about three miles from Southampton Ct. H. (near Jerusalem) the Negroes mutinied and cut their throats from ear to ear (NH 22 Oct, VH and TDCDA 29 Oct 99) [SPIERS first name also given as Horace]

SPIKE, Sarah, Negro woman, c. 35, says she is free, b. in Northumberland Co. near the Isle of Wight [sic] and raised by John DAWLIN, then lived with a certain James WARREN in Norfolk Co.; jailed in Pr. Wm. Co. (Ex 12 Jul 99)

SPITTEN, George, Negro, 28 jailed as a runaway in Norfolk Borough (NH 5 Sep 99)

SPOONER, the Rev. Mr., of Elizabeth City Co., has died and his par. there is vacant (VGGA 1 Oct 99)

SPOONER, George W. B., merch., mar. Miss Betsey WALLACE dau. of Col. G. B. WALLACE, both of this place [Fredsbrg.] (VHFA 4 Oct 92)

SPOTSWOOD, Col., of Orange Co., intends to leave Va. with his family next year (VG 26 Oct 39)

SPOTSWOOD, Alexander Esq., of Spotsylvania Co., dec'd, his lands in Culpeper and Orange Cos. to be sold by John SPOTSWOOD (nfi) (VG 18 Apr 51, 30 Jul 52, 10 Nov 52)

SPOTS[WOOD], Alexander, mar. Miss Betsy LEWIS, Fredsbrg. (VHFA 26 Mar 89)

SPOTSWOOD, Hugh, of Gloucester Co., dec'd, e.a.w. his ex., Hugh WALKER (VGR 17 Nov 68)

SPOTSWOOD, John, eld. son of the late Hon. Alexander SPOTSWOOD Esq. former Governor of this Colony, mar. Miss Mary DANDRIDGE dau. of the late Hon. William DANDRIDGE Esq. who was commander of one of H.M's ships of war and one of the Honorable Council of this Colony, on 24 Oct. in Kg. Wm. Co. (VG 7 Nov 45)

SPOTSWOOD, John Esq., of Spotsylvania Co., mar. Miss Sally ROWZEE, youngest dau. of John ROWZEE of Essex Co., on 19 Sep. (VG 3 Oct 71)

SPOTSWOOD, John Jr., of Fredsbrg., mar. Miss Polly GOODE eld. dau. of the Hon. Col. Robert GOODE, on Thurs. night the 29th ult. at Richmond (VGGA 4 Nov 95, RMA 5 Nov 95, VHFFA 10 Nov 95)

SPRATT, Dr., d. yesterday sennight at Urbanna (VHFA 27 Dec 92)

SPRING, Nicholas, mar. Miss Elizabeth HICKS, both of this co. [Augusta] on the 25th inst. (SVG 26 Aug 96)

SPRINGATE, William, conv. svt., b. in Wales and bred in Bristol, ran away from Daniel CHAMIER, Baltimore (VGR 1 Aug 71)

SPRUCE, Absolom, svt., 25-30, ran away from Jonathan BOUCHER, Caroline Co. (VG 16 Aug 70)

SPURLOCK, Jack, Va. born Negro, ran away from Thomas DANSIE, Kg. Wm. Co. (MG 15 Mar 49)

STABLER, Edward, dec'd, several of his lots in Petersburg to be sold by Wm. STABLER (VIC 7 May 88); e.a.w. his ex., Samuel HOUGH, Mahlon HOUGH, and Wm. STABLER (VGIC 4 Jul 89 sup)

STABLER, Edward, dec'd, those indebted are to settle accounts with Daniel DODSON (VGPI 9 Sep 96)

STACEY, Anne, wife of John STACEY of York Co., has left him and he will no longer pay her debts (VG 27 Feb 52)

STAINBACK, Littlebury, dec'd, e.a.w. his ex., Francis STAINBACK (VG 27 Jun 77)

STANARD, Mrs. Jane W., consort of Beverly STANARD, Orange Co., and second dau. of Judge FLEMING, d. Tues. last at her father's seat, Summerville, Chesterfield Co. [long obit.] (Arg 19 Mar 99)

STANDLEY, Moses, appr., c. 19, ran away from John TOMPKINS, Fluvanna Co.; he visited his parents in Caroline Co. at Christmas and never returned (VHFA 19 Mar 95)

STANHOPE, Price, of James City Co., dec'd, e.a.w. his admr., Joseph HORNSBY, who will also sell his HH and KF at his late plant. in James City Co. (VG 23 Sep 75, 13 Jan 76) [name also given as STANUP]

STANHOPE, William, of Norfolk Borough, mar. Miss Sally JOHNSTON of Pr. Anne Co., on Sun. eve. (NH 1 Oct 99)

STANLEY, Agatha, of Caroline Co., was this day discharged from the Public Hospital in this city, she having perfectly recovered her senses (VG 3 Jul 79)

STANLEY, Eleanor, dec'd, e.a.w. her ex., John STANLEY of Hanover Co. (VG 1 May 79)
STANTON, Capt., of the Va. Militia, killed on 9 Aug. by Indians at a fort above Pearsall's on the South Branch near Fort Cumberland (NYM 29 Aug 63)
STANWORTH, Henry, executed last Fri. for murder (VG 27 Dec 51)
STAPLES, John, dec'd, his ex., Nathaniel STAPLES, will sell a tract of land on which he formerly lived about 10 miles above Richmond containing about 100 ac. (VIC 24 Dec 88)
STAPLES, Richard, svt., ran away from the ship *Becky* lying in James River; he was seen in Gloucester Co. (VG 12 Mar 52)
STARK, the Hon. Bolling Esq., mar. Mrs. ORR of [Richmond] on Sat. last (VGAA 15 Jan 85); d. early Fri. morn. at his house in Richmond [obit.] (VIC 30 Jan 88); e.a.w. his ex. Wm. STARK, Belfield STARK, and Daniel FISHER (VIC 2 Apr 88)
STARK, William Jr., dec'd, his admr., William STARK, will sell all his PE (AGNPPA 1 Jan 96)
STARKE, John, dec'd, e.a.w. his admr., Moses AUSTIN and Elisha PRICE of Westham (VIC 25 Feb 89); his admrs. will petition the GA for permission to sell his lands (VGGA 14 Sep 91)
STARKE, Col. John, d. lately at his seat in Hanover Co. (Ex 22 Nov 99)
STARKE, Richard, att. at law and clerk of two committees of the House of Burgesses, died (VG 30 Jul 72)
STARKE, William Esq., aide de camp to Lord Sterling, d. of smallpox at John ARMISTEAD's, Caroline Co. (VGPu 21 Feb 77)
STARKE, William, of Dinwiddie Co., mar. Mrs. Sukey EDWARDS of Brunswick Co. (VG 6 Nov 79)
STARKE, William A. Esq., son of the late Richard STARKE Esq., of Wmsbrg., d. of smallpox on the 13th ult., aged 17 (VG 14 Mar 77)
STAUNTON, John, aka WILSON, Eng. svt., wheelwright, ran away from John SHIPHARD, Wmsbrg., who has heard that he was seen going towards N. Carolina (VGP 20 Jul 75, VG 7 Oct, 29 Oct 75) [name also given as STANTON]
STEAD, Solomon, mar. Miss Nancy CORNICK dau. of the late John CORNICK dec'd, in Pr. Anne Co. on Tues. last (NH 2 Jan 96)
STEEL, Capt., of the *Brunswick*, killed on the voyage from Glasgow to Va. (VGR 23 Jun 68)
STEEL, Ann, has eloped from her husband, John STEEL (WG 6 Mar 99)
STEEL, John, Eng. conv. svt., cabinet maker, c. 18, ran away from Sampson and Geo. MATTHEWS, Richmond (VGR 27 May 73)
STEEL, Joseph, conv. svt., hatter, c. 30, ran away from Jonathan NIXON, Frederick Co., near Bladensburg, Md. [sic] (VG 3 Jun 73)
STEEL, Robert, late of Norfolk, dec'd, e.a.w. his admr., Daniel BARRAUD (VGNI 9 Mar 75)
STEELY, Jacob, merch., of Wythe Co., on his way northward he was murdered on 15 Nov. within half a mile of Greenville in Augusta Co.; the murderer is supposed to be from Surry Co., N. Carolina and passed by the name of Hall LEE (Staunton disp. of 18 Nov.) (BVCG 25 Nov, Arg 26 Nov, RCFPC 14 Dec 96)
STEPHEN, Gen. Adam, d. on Sat. the 16th ult. at Martin[s]burg, Berkeley Co., in an advanced age; he was a native of Scotland and an officer under BRADDOCK [obit.] (VGGA 10 Aug 91); his land and mill near Martinsburg to be sold by his ex., Robert STEPHEN, Ephraim GAITHER, Moses HUNTER, and David HUNTER (BVCG 16 Apr 92)
STEPHEN, Capt. Alexander, late an officer in H.M's Royal American Regt., d. on 8 May in Frederick Co. (Philadelphia disp. of 19 May) (NYPB and PC 23 May 68)
STEPHENS Family, Mecklenburg Co., Quarterly Ct., Aug. 1797, in chanc: John STEPHENS, John CARTER and Polly his wife (pltfs.) against Joshua STEPHENS, Debbie STEPHENS, Joseph STEPHENS and Hailey STEPHEN

infants under 21 by Debbie STEPHENS their gdn., and the sd. Debbie STEPHENS widow of Thomas STEPHENS dec'd (defs.) (VGPI 20 Oct 97)

STEPHENS, Mrs., consort of Samuel STEPHENS, d. early yesterday morn. in the vicinity of this place [Fredsbrg.] (VH 21 May 99)

STEPHENS, Ann, wife of Joseph STEPHENS, Frederick Co. (VJAA 21 Oct 84)

STEPHENS, James, now in the public jail, Wmsbrg., in justice to Elizabeth his wife's character; he denies being the author of an advertisement lately published in this gazette charging her with having defil[ed] his bed, etc.; he believes her to be a virtuous woman (VGPu 1 May 78)

STEPHENS, Thomas, tailor, 28-30, des. from the barracks at Winchester (BVCG 26 Oct 95)

STEPHENSON, Capt. James, mar. Miss CUNNINGHAM in Berkeley Co. (BVCG 28 May 92)

STEPHENSON, John, millwright in Cumberland Co., intends to leave the colony around 1 Aug. with John KERR (VG 20 Jun 51)

STEPHENSON, John, merch., of Berkeley Co., mar. Miss Eleanor MACLIN, at Winchester on Sun. last (WG 6 Mar 99)

STEPHENSON, Richard, late of Berkeley Co., dec'd, e.a.w. his ex., Daniel KENNEDY (PGBA 28 Jan 96)

STEPTOE, Mrs. Elizabeth, d. at her house in Westmoreland Co. on Mon. the [27th] ult. (VGR 6 Sep, 20 Sep 70)

STERNE, David, of Caroline Co., d. on Mon. eve. the 6th inst. in an advanced age (RCFPC 22 Feb 97)

STERRETT Family, Shenandoah Co., Ct. of Q.S., 16 Aug. 1793, in chanc: Joseph STERRETT, John STERRETT, John LOWRY and Joseph WILSON exors. and John, James F., Sarah, and Joseph STERRETT chil. and heirs at law of James STERRETT dec'd, which sd. John, James F., and Joseph are under 21 by John STERRETT their gdn. and next friend (pltfs.) against Joseph PUGH, Wm. RICHARDSON and Rebecca his wife, heir at law, devisee, etc. of Benjamin PRICE (defs.) (BVCG 9 Sep 93)

STERRETT, David, killed in a duel with Thomas HADFIELD (PGBA 27 Jun 91)

STERRETT, James, eld. son and heir at law of Joseph STERRETT dec'd (compl.) against Joseph PUGH eld. son and heir at law of Joseph PUGH dec'd, Wm. RICHARDSON and Rebecca his wife and the heir at law and other legal rep. of Benj. PRICE (defs.), Shenandoah Co., chancery case, 31 Aug. 1792 (BVCG 19 Nov 92)

STETSON, Capt. George, d. yesterday in Water St. (NH 2 Jun 96)

STEUBEN, Baron Frederick William Augustus de, late Maj. Gen. in the army of the United States, d. on the 27th (acc. to VGGA and HNPA) or 28th (acc. to VHFA) of Nov. of a paralytic shock at his seat in Steubenville, NY (VGGA and HNPA 31 Dec 94, VHFA 8 Jan 95)

STEVENS, Edward Jr., d. in Culpeper Co. on Fri. the 13th inst. aged 23 (VHFA 26 Mar 95)

STEVENS, Joseph, dec'd, eight of his lots in Tappahannock, his slaves at his dwelling house in Caroline Co. and 1000 ac. in Goochland Co. to be sold by his ex., Robert FARISH (VG 1 Aug 66)

STEVENS, William, elderly seaman, ran away from the ship *Thomas* now at Bermuda Hundred (VG 12 Jun 72)

STEVENSON, Mr., reportedly killed by Indians along with his family not far from Madison Ct. H., Ky, about five weeks ago (Winchester disp. of 1 Oct.) (AGNPWA 10 Oct 92)

STEVENSON, Miss Fanny, of York Co., fetched away in the very prime of life [eulogy by a young lady] (VG 30 Dec 75)

STEVENSON, the Rev. James, Rector of Berkeley Par., Spotsylvania Co., mar. Miss Fanny LITTLEPAGE of Hanover Co. (VG 16 Jan 72)

STEVENSON, Mrs. Janet, of Petersburg, died (VG 16 Oct 79)

STEVENSON, William, late of Yorktown, dec'd, e.a.w. Allen JONES; his ex. is Frances STEVENSON (VGAA 18 Oct 83); his son and admr., John STEVENSON of Lunenburg, authorizes Allen JONES of York Co. to settle his est. (VGWeA 1 May 84, VGAA 8 Oct 85)

STEWARD, Mr., of N. Carolina, murdered at the home of Robert M'CREDIE, Norfolk; M'CREDIE and his wife were arrested on suspicion of murder (NPC 10 Mar 92)

STEWART, Alexander, native of Scotland, suspected of stealing a horse from John COCKBURN, Newcastle (VG 6 Jul 76)

STEWART, Andrew Jr., dec'd, 350 ac. of his land in the Northwest Wood to be sold by his ex., Geo. D. WISE (NPC 10 Sep 91)

STEWART, Arthur, merch., of Richmond, died (VICGA 13 Jan 90)

STEWART, Charles, late of Brunswick Co., dec'd, his land in Sussex and Greensville Cos. to be sold by his ex., John RIVES (VGAA 25 Oct 83)

STEWART, Charles, of Richmond, d. after a short illness (VGWeA 25 Sep 88)

STEWART, George, dec'd, his ex., Hugh STEWART and John GRAY, request those indebted to his est. to settle quickly and those having demands against his est. to bring them to the house where Joseph LEMEN lives in Middletown (PGBA 18 Feb 93)

STEWART, Dr. Gibbon, age 40, d. at his seat in Kg. Geo. Co. (RCFPC 20 Jul 96)

STEWART, James, Scot, svt., 25, ran away from John MITCHELL, Urbanna (VG 30 Mar 39)

STEWART, James, appr., wheelwright, 19, ran away from Daniel HOYE who believes he will make for Md. (VG 30 May 66) [name also given as STUART]

STEWART, James, late of Brunswick Co., dec'd, two of his ordinaries, one on Meherrin River and the other in Sussex Co., to be let or leased by his ex., John and Rich. STEWART (VG 24 Nov 68)

STEWART, Jane, has eloped from her husband, Walter STEWART of Staunton (VGR 20 Jul 69)

STEWART, John, merch., of Richmond, mar. Miss Katey [or Kitty] HAIR[E] of Richmond on Thurs. last (VGAA and VGWeA 28 Feb 84)

STEWART, John, native of Lancaster Co., Pa., 33, des. from the 4th U.S. Regt. of Infantry between Winchester and Cumberland (WG 17 Jul 99)

STEWART, Richard, appr., tailor, c. 19, ran away from James CALDER and James MELAN [also given as MELVIN], Georgetown, Potomac, with his uncle Stephen BRANHAM, [also given as BRENAN] c. 19, also an appr. tailor ; they are believed going to Norfolk as the one has a sister and the other a mother there (CMAG 14 Mar 97, NHPA 27 Mar 97, BVCG 7 Apr 97) [name also given as STUART]

STEWART, Richard, HCC, 5 Jun. 1799, between Robert STEWART (pltf.) and John BELL admr. of Richard STEWART, John HEWET and Charles LINGARD (defs.); it appears that HEWET and LINGARD are not inhabitants of this country (VF 13 Jul 99)

STEWART, Thomas and Joseph MOULDER, adv. that they have lately arriv from Philadelphia to carry on the sailmaking business in Norfolk (VGNI 22 Sep 74)

STIFF, Frances, has behaved in a very uncommon manner to her husband, John, of late and he will not be answerable for any of her debts (VGPu 26 May 75 sup)

STIP, Martin, late of Berkeley Co., dec'd, e.a.w. his ex., John and Frederick STIP (PGBA 19 Jan 97)

STIR, Gerrard, a free mulatto sailor bel. to the schooner *Duly-Ann* lying at Fredsbrg. killed by accident on Tues. night last (VHFFA 27 May 96)

STITH, Anderson, dec'd, his lands in Pr. Geo., Halifax, and Kg. Wm. Cos. to be sold by his extx., Joanna STITH, at Pr. Geo. Ct. H. (VG 6 Nov 66, 10 Sep 67)

STITH, Bassett Esq., merch., of Richmond, mar. Miss Polly LONG of N. Carolina (VICGA 14 Jul 90)

STITH, Drury, of Brunswick Co., dec'd, e.a.w. his admr., Thomas STITH (VG 14 Mar 71)

STITH, Drury, of Brunswick Co., dec'd, his admx., Mary STITH, will rent his grist mill in that co. (VGPI 18 Mar 90); his admr., Christopher M'CONNICO, will sell all his HH and KF (VGPI 16 Jun 91)

STITH, Mrs. Elizabeth, d. at her house in Surry Co. in an advanced age (VG 24 Feb 74)
STITH, Griffith Esq., of Northampton Co., d. on 18 Jan. (VCGA 30 Jun 94); his trustees, James LYON, N. GOFFIGAN, John EYRE, will sell his plant. (VCGA 13 Nov 94)
STITH, Joanna, widow of Anderson STITH Esq. of Hampstead, Kg. Wm. Co., d. on Sun. last (acc. to the Halifax, N. Carolina, newspaper of the 9th inst. [Sep.]) in her 64th year (VGRMA [3] Oct 93)
STITH, Joseph, who was advertised as a deserter from the 5th Va. Regt., claims that he had enl. at the age of 15 with the approval of his father and after some time serving as a minute soldier, enl. with Capt. TERRELL; he became ill and applied for a furlough and late procured for $40 one James WEAVER of Bedford. to enter the service in his room; WEAVER is now a soldier in Capt. TERRELL's Co. (VGPu 20 Jun 77)
STITH, Miss Judith, of Wmsbrg., dau. of the late president STITH of the college, d. on Mon. eve. last (VG and VGR 17 Jun 73)
STITH, Mrs. Rebecca, spouse of Maj. John STITH of Westbury in Charles City Co., d. on Sat. last (VGWeA 5 Apr 87)
STITH, Col. Robert, of Kg. Geo. Co., d. on 21 Nov. [obit.] (VGAxA 23 Dec 90)
STITH, the Rev. Mr. William, of Henrico Co., mar. Miss Judith RANDOLPH, sister of William RANDOLPH of Tuckahoe, on 13 Jul. (VG 28 Jul 38)
STITH, the Rev. William A. M., President of William and Mary, d. on Fri. sennight (VG 3 Oct 55)
STITH, William, dec'd, pursuant to his will, about 1500 ac. of his land on Herring Cr., Charles City Co. will be sold by his ex., Robert WALKER (VG 2 Jan 72)
STOARIE, William, Virginian, 20, des. from Capt. Thomas WAGGENER's Co. of Va. Forces (VG 22 Aug 55)
STOCKDELL, Mr. J., d. on the 13th inst. in Henrico Co. (OVT 23 Jul 98, VGGA 24 Jul 98)
STOFFENBURG, John Charles, Polander, 27, ran away from the *Berry*, Sheppard's Warehouse (VG 27 Mar 52)
STOKES Family, Lunenburg Co., Ct. of Q. S., 15 May 1795, in chanc: Wm. HERRING admr. w.w.a. of Martha STOKES dec'd (compl.) against Arthur HERRING and Mary his wife, John TUCKER and Prescilla his wife, Joel TUCKER and Polly his wife, lately Polly EVANS, which sd. Prescilla and Polly are the chil. of Wilmouth EVANS dec'd, Batte STOKES and Wiley STOKES son and dau. of Shadrack STOKES and Feraby STOKES dau. of Rich. STOKES dec'd (defs.) (VGPI 9 Jun 95)
STOKES, Col. David, att. at law of Mecklenburg Co., dec'd, his admrs. are Mary M. STOKES and David STREET (VGPI 18 May 98)
STOKES, Margaret, her husband, John STOKES of Alexandria, will not be responsible for her contracts (VGAxA 17 Jun 90)
STONE Family, Cumberland Co. ct., 27 Sep. 1785, Anderson STONE infant son of Thomas STONE dec'd by William Cortito HILL his next friend, Isaac BEACHAM and Prudence his wife and Wm. C. HILL (pltfs) against Wm. STONE infant son and heir of Thomas STONE and Wm. FARIS ex. of Thomas STONE and Marble [sic] STONE gdn. of Wm. STONE (defs.) (VGAA 15 Oct 85)
STONE, Daniel, merch., mar. Miss Jenny VAUGHAN, both of Norfolk Borough, last eve. (NH 17 Aug 99)
STONE, Thomas, svt., ran away from James MILLS, Yorktown (VG 10 Jan 51)
STONE, the Hon. Thomas Esq., member of the Senate of Md., d. on the morn. of the 5th inst. in this place [Alexandria] (VJAA 11 Oct 87)
STONE, William, of Henrico Co., dec'd, his plant. there to be sold by Stith BLAKEY his ex. (VGAA 20 Jul 82)
STORRS, Gervas, of Henrico Co., mar. Miss Patsy TRUEHEART dau. of Daniel TRUEHEART of Hanover Co. on Sat. eve. last (RMA and VGGA 22 Jun 96)
STORRS, Joshua, of Henrico Co., a much respected merch., died (VG 11 Dec 79)

STORRS, Joshua, dec'd, e.a.w. his admr., Gervas STORRS of Henrico Co. (VGRMA 9 Mar 95)

STORRS, Mrs. Susanna R., consort of Gervas STORRS of this co., d. in the bloom of life on Thurs. last at The Contention, the seat of James PLEASANTS Sr. in Goochland Co. (VGRMA 16 Dec 93)

STOTT, Ebenezer, merch., of Petersburg, mar. Miss Eliza PHILE dau. of Frederick PHILE Esq. naval officer for the Port of Philadelphia, in Philadelphia on the 15th ult. (VGWeA 3 Sep 89)

STOURS, James, from Albemarle Co., executed in Richmond on 18 Jul. for horse stealing (VGAA 19 Jul 83)

STOVAL Family, HCC, 23 May 1789, Wm. GALT (pltf.) against Wm. CUNNINGHAM and Co., Thos. STOVAL and Mary STOVAL exors. of Geo. STOVAL Jr. dec'd and Geo. M'DANIEL Sr. (defs.) (VGIC 4 Jul 89 sup)

STOVALL Family, Bedford Co. Ct., Nov. 1793, in chanc: Henry JETER (compl.) against John SHARP, Augustine LEFTWICH Sr. and Elizabeth his wife, late Elizabeth STOVALL, exors. of John STOVALL dec'd, and Bartholomew STOVALL, Ralph STOVALL, Barnes STOVALL, Risden ROBERTSON and Mary his wife, John STONE and Elizabeth his wife, Jabez LEFTWICH and Delilah his wife, Ann STOVALL and Hezekiah STOVALL chil. and legatees of John STOVALL dec'd (defs.); it appears that Bartholomew, Ralph, and Barnes STOVALL, Risden ROBERTSON and Mary his wife, John STONE and Elizabeth his wife, Ann STOVALL, and Hezekiah STOVALL are not inhabitants of this country (UG 25 Jan 94)

STOVALL, Bartholomew, of Powhatan Co., dec'd, his acting ex., Littleberry and Jesse STOVALL, will sell his 400 ac. tract which includes a grist mill and other items of his PE (RMA 29 Oct 96, Arg 2 Dec 96)

STOVALL, Jim, mulatto, 45, ran away from Rich. JAMES in Cumberland Co., who supposes he is in the Richmond Area (Arg 12 Oct 98, NH 23 Oct 98)

STOVER, Peter, native of Germany, founder of Stovertown, Shenandoah Co., d. on Tues. the 13th inst. aged 83 (WG 21 Aug 99)

STRACHAN, Alexander Glass, has declined his practice as a physician in Kg. Wm. Co. and intends to settle in the town of Blandford (VG 28 Feb 71)

STRACHAN, Dr. Alexander, of Richmond, d. on Thurs. last in an advanced age (VGWeA 26 Feb 89)

STRACHEY, Henry, of K & Q Co., dec'd, his HH goods and plant. to be sold by his admr. (nfi) (VGR 16 Nov 69)

STRANGE, John, Negro, c. 20, ran away from Mann PAGE near Hanover Town (NH 26 Nov 99)

STRAS, Mrs., consort of Geo. F. STRAS of this city [Richmond], d. on Tues. last (VGGA 14 Jun 99)

STRAS, George F., mar. Mrs. SOUTHALL on Fri. eve. (VGGA 26 Nov 99)

STRATON, John Jr. Esq., of Northampton Co., mar. Miss Lucy DIGGS of York Co. on Thurs. last (VCNPGA 23 Feb 93)

STREATER, Willis, dec'd, e.a.w. Stephen C. GRAHAM of Suffolk Co. (VCGA 12 May 94)

STREET, Benjamin, Capt. of the Artillery Co. of the Borough and proprietor of the Eagle Tavern, d. on Thurs. morn., 18 Feb., leaving a widow and four chil. (AGNPPA 19 Feb 96, NH 20 Feb 96); e.a.w. his admx., Martha STREET (AGGA 27 May 96, NH 21 Apr 98)

STRIBBLING, John, mar. Miss Sally DRUMMOND on Mon. last near Battletown (BVCG 28 Jan 92)

STRIBBLING, William, late of Battletown, e.a.w. Bu[s]hrod TAYLOR; his admr. is Wm. HODGSON of Alexandria (BVCG 15 Apr 93)

STRIBLING, Thomas, mar. Miss Betsy SNIGGERS at Battletown (VGWA 10 Dec 88)

STRIBLING, William, mar. Mrs. HUMPHREYS at Battletown (VGWA 29 Apr 89)

STRICKLAND, George, Jacob SNYDER was charged with his murder and found guilty of manslaughter for which he was branded (Winchester disp.

of 14 Oct.) (CMAG 18 Oct 96) [see: Joshua STRICKLER]
STRICKLAND, Henry, dec'd, e.a.w. his admr., Rich. CHEW (BVCG 25 Jun 92)
STRICKLAND, Joseph, appr. tailor, 16-17, ran away from James EDMONDSON, Winchester (VGWA 29 Sep 90)
STRICKLER, Benjamin, dec'd, his admr. is Isaac STRICKLER (BVCG 9 Sep 96)
STRICKLER, Joshua, murdered in Hardy Co., Jacob SNYDER was charged with his murder but found guilty of manslaughter (BVCG 29 Jul, 14 Oct 96) [In the 14 Oct. issue, the name of the victim was given as STRICKLAND; see George STRICKLAND]
STRIEBEL, William, German, ind. svt., c. 30, miller, ran away from Wm. STRAIN, Franklin Co., Pa. (VGWA 23 Nov 87)
STRINGER, Mrs. Elizabeth, spouse of John STRINGER of James City Co., died (VG 2 Dec 75)
STRINGER, Thomas, svt., 25, ran away from Kingsbury Furnace Mine Bank near Baltimore. Md. (VGR 29 Sep 68)
STRINGER, William, Eng. svt., 28, ran away from Rich. BANKS, Kg. Wm. Co., (VGR 12 May 68, 7 Sep 69)
STRITE, Mrs., consort of the Rev. Mr. STRITE, Lutheran minister in [Winchester], d. on Sun. night last a few days after her delivery in child birth, in her 24th year [obit.] (VGWA 11 Jan 88)
STRITE, the Rev. Christian, mar. Miss Sukey BARR on Thurs. eve. (VGWA 21 Oct 89)
STROBIA, Mrs. Mary, consort of John STROBIA of Richmond, d. on Sun. last (RC 26 May, VGGA 27 May, RMA 28 May 95)
STRODE, James, dec'd, his ex., Henry BEDINGER and Abrah. SHEPHERD, will sell about 9000 joint shingles and a quantity of building timber bel. to his est. in Martinsburg (PGBA 20 Jun 95)
STROLE, Adolph, late of Winchester, dec'd, the elders of the Lutheran Church in Winchester propose to prefer a petition to the next session of the Assembly to invest his est. in the petitioners for the use of sd. church (VGWA 15 Aug 87)
STRONG, Capt. Edward, dec'd, e.a.w. his admr., George CALLIS of Norfolk Co. (VG 25 Sep 79)
STROTHER, James, reportedly killed by Indians in Ky. (VG 15 Sep 74)
STROTHER, John, dec'd, his admr., John STROTHER of Culpeper Co., will sell 3500 ac. of his land there and 500 ac. between Chester's and Thornton's Gaps in Culpeper Co. and settle his est. (VHFA 14 Jul, BVCG 20 Jul CMAG 8 Aug 95)
STROTHER, William, late of Kg. Geo. Co., dec'd, several tracts of his land to be sold by Anthony STROTHER living near the Falls of the Rappahannock (VG 4 Aug 38)
STROUD, Elizabeth, her husband, Wm. STROUD of Mecklenburg Co., will not pay any of her debts (VGGA 9 Oct 93)
STUARD, Thompton, her husband, Francis STUARD of Petersburg, will not pay any of her debts (VGPI 13 Jul 98)
STUART, Dr., of Alexandria, mar. Mrs. CUSTIS relict of the late John Parke CUSTIS Esq., on Thurs. the 20th ult. (VGWeA 6 Dec 83)
STUART, Alexander, late of Cumberland Co., dec'd, e.a.w. his ex., Alexander TRENT and Wm. POWELL (VGGA 7 Jan 95)
STUART, Charles, [of Petersburg], died (NPJ 8 Oct 88)
STUART, John, ind. svt., tailor, 30-35, ran away from on board the *Jenny* lying at Broadway (VG 2 Jun 74)
STUART, William, Negro, c. 45, traveling with a black woman named Betty who says she was b. free in Annapolis, [Md.]; they ran off with a slave from the plant. of James WALKER in Buckingham Co. (VGGA 11 Jun 99); jailed in Pr. Wm. Co. (Ex 12 Nov 99)
STUART, William Gibbons, mar. Miss Molly FITZHUGH dau. of Col. Henry FITZHUGH of Stafford Co. (VGPu 3 Jan 77 sup)

STUBBLEFIELD, Robert B., appr. cabinet maker, 17-18, ran away from Edward SLATER, Winchester (BVCG 7 Oct 93)

STUBBLEFIELD, Thomas, of Fairfax Co., dec'd, portions of his est. to be sold by his admx., Joanna STUBBLEFIELD (VJAA 28 Apr 85)

STUDSON, Capt. George, mar. Miss Eliza MACHIE (HNPA 21 Feb 95)

STURDEY, William, adv. that his wife, Phillis, late of Stafford Co., has eloped from her bed and board for no reason known to him unless occasioned by a certain John WITHERS Jr. who lately moved to a place called Sinking Cr. in Botetourt Co. to which place he expects the sd, Phillis is gone (VGPu 20 Jun 77)

STURDIVANT, Ann, dau. of John STURDIVANT of Pr. Geo. Co., d. on the 11th inst. (VGPI 20 Sep 87)

STURDIVANT, Capt. Joel, dec'd, his ex., John STURDIVANT, will sell all his PE on Ward's Cr., Pr. Geo. Co. (VG 17 Oct 77)

STURDIVANT, John Sr., dec'd, e.a.w. his ex., Joel STURDIVANT (VGPI 25 Oct 93)

STURDIVANT, William, of Dinwiddie Co., dec'd, items of his PE to be sold by his ex., John and Joel STURDIVANT (VGR 19 Jan 69)

STYERS, Mrs. Sarah, wife of Jacob STYERS baker, d. in Fredsbrg. on Wed. last (Fredsbrg. disp. of 17 May) (VGPI 23 May [97])

[SUGGITT], John, of Richmond Co., a student at the [Winchester] Academy, d. on Sat. eve. at age 16 (VGWA 16 Apr 88) [name given as SEGGA[T]T]

SUGGS, Mrs., wife of Capt. George SUGGS tailor, of Norfolk, d. on Mon. [acc. to AGNPPA] or Tues. [acc. to NH] last (NH 5 May 96, AGNPPA 6 May 96)

SUGGS, George, mar. Mrs. S. MICKLE on Sat. eve. (NH 4 Jul, AGGA 5 Jul 96)

SUICKERS, Edward, d. at Battletown (WVGWA 26 Jun 90)

SULIVANT, Joseph, dec'd, e.a.w. his admr., Vincent BRENT (VGAA 28 Aug 84)

SULLENGER, Thomas, dec'd, e.a.w. his ex., Thomas SULLENGER who intends to go to Ky. next spring (VIC 17 Dec 88)

SULLIVAN, David, from Essex Co., d. at the hospital for lunatics (VGPu 24 Jan 77)

SULLIVAN, Dennis, Irish svt., ran away from Alexander STUART and Thomas MADDOX, Alexandria (VJAA 7 Oct 84)

SULLIVAN, Humphrey, says he is a native of Cork and was in Pulaski's Horse in S. Carolina, suspected of stealing a horse from James ROURKE, Upper Marlboro, Pr. Geo. Co., Md. (CMAG 19 Jan 96)

SULLIVAN, Owen, Irish svt., ran away from Alexander STUART and Thomas MADDOX, Alexandria (VJAA 7 Oct 84)

SULLIVAN, Timothy, dec'd, e.a.w. his extx., Elizabeth SULLIVAN (TAA 4 Jan 98)

SULLIVANT, John, of Lancaster Co., brought to General Ct. for the murder of Col. TAYLOR; he was discharged by proclamation (VGWeA 10 Apr 84)

SULLIVANT, John, late of Charlotte Co., dec'd, e.a.w. his admrs., John PETTY and Robert GILLIAM (VGPI 7 Nov 97)

SULLY, Del., mar. Miss Salley INNIS, both of Richmond, on Mon. last (VGWeA 3 Jan 94)

SUMMER, David, appr. tailor, ran away from Martin RILEY (VGWA 15 Dec 90)

SUMMERS, George, of Loudoun Co., adv. that his dau. Betty SUMMERS has charged goods to him without his knowledge and his wife Susannah SUMMERS has left him (VGAxA 15 Sep 91)

SUMMERS, John, d. in his 103rd year, he was b. in Md. within 30 miles of [Alexandria] and settled in [Alexandria] in 1715; he leaves nearly 400 descendents (VGAxA 9 Dec 90, VHFA 16 Dec 90)

SUMMERS, William, mar. [Mrs.] Isabel ELTON, Alexandria (VJAA 1 Nov 87); of Alexandria, d. yesterday (TAA 28 Oct 97); e.a.w. his extx., Isabel SUMMERS, and ex., George SUMMERS (CMAG 5 Dec 97)

SUMNER, Thomas, dec'd, his ex., Samuel COHOON, will sell his PE which

includes a sloop and some lots in Suffolk Town (VG 27 Aug, 10 Sep 72)
SUMNEY, Je[ss]e, appr., 17, ran away from Edmund GRAVES, Chesterfield Co. (VG 5 Jun 52)
SUMRALL, Jesse, c. 18, des. from the rendezvous of the 4th U.S. Regt. at Winchester; he has relations on Back Cr. in [Frederick] Co. (WG 5 Jun 99)
SUNDAY, Jack, [Negro] slave, 35, ran away from Richard RANDOLPH, Cumberland Co., VGR 31 Jan 71)
SUNDERLAND, John, native of Lancashire, Eng., merch., d. in Fredsbrg. last Fri. in the flower of his youth (VHFA 6 Jan 91)
SUTHERLAND, John, late physician in Fredsbrg., dec'd, e.a.w. Col. Fielding LEWIS of that town (VG 26 Aug 73)
SUTOR, Ruth, has eloped from her husband, James SUTOR of Frederick Co. (BVCG 30 Dec 96)
SUTTLE, James, aka Nathan ALLEN, escaped from jail in Loudoun Co. where he had been committed on suspicion of having counterfeited notes of the Bank of Baltimore, but he was acquitted; he was tried and fined on another count by a petit jury (CMAG 20 Jun 95, 23 Jun 95)
SUTTON, Mrs., wife of John SUTTON, merch, of Alexandria, died (VJAA 2 Sep 84)
SUTTON, Edward, svt., ran away from Robert JACKSON, Fredsbrg. (VG 1 Aug 51)
SUTTON, John, b. in Va., 26, des. from the New York Regt. in New York City (NYPB 17 Jul 58)
SWAINE, James, of Charles City Co., d. on Thurs. the 28th ult. after a short illness (VGWeA 11 Jun 89)
SWANN Family, HCC, 17 Oct. 1789: Thomas HUBBARD and Mary Blaikley his wife one of the daus. of Thompson SWANN and Jennett Carson his wife both dec'd (pltfs.) against Griffin STITH and Wm. STITH admrs. de bonis non of Griffin STITH dec'd, John SWANN Sr. surviving ex. of Thompson SWANN dec'd, and Thomas Thompson SWANN (VICGA 17 Mar 90)
SWANN, John Esq., of Pasquotank Co., [N. Carolina], dec'd, a runaway from his est. is adv. by Abraham KIRBY (NPC 25 Feb 92)
SWANN, John, merch., mar. Miss Anna WILSON dau. of Wm. WILSON, all of this town [Fredsbrg.], on Sun. eve. (VH 7 May 99)
SWANN, Samuel, late of Nansemond Co., dec'd, his ex., John SWANN, adv. that the bonds taken on the sale of his est. will become due on 24 May (VG 20 Apr 76)
SWANN, Samuel, of Powhatan Co., dec'd, his ex., John SWANN and Geo. TAYLOR, will sell his PE at his plant. (VGGA 11 Oct, Arg 18 Oct 99, Ex 19 Nov 99)
SWANN, Thomas T., of Cumberland Co., dec'd, items of his est. to be sold by his admr., Wm. MAYO, at the home of Mrs. Judith SWANN near Cumberland Old Ct. H. in Powhatan Co. (Arg 13 Aug 99)
SWANSON, John, appr. seaman, c. 18, speaks very broad Yorkshire, ran away from the ship *Brilliant* (VG 7 Jul 74)
SWANWICK, John, a rep. from Philadelphia in the Federal Councils, d. on 31 Jul., [long obit.] (OVT 9 Aug 98)
SWEARINGEN, Capt. Josiah, dec'd, his admrs., Henry BEDINGER and Josiah SWEARINGEN of Shepherdstown, will sell his stock, HHF, and farming utensils, and settle his est. (PGBA 16 Nov 95, IO 13 Sep 97)
Swedish Seamen Runaways: Swen HOLMSTROM, Jonas GIERTBERG, and Erland FALKENQUIST; ran away from the brig *Thetis* lying at Norfolk (NH 8 Sep 98)
SWENEY, Ann, of Norfolk Borough, dec'd, her house and lot to be sold by her ex. (nfi) (NPC 10 Jul 90)
SWIFT, Godwin Esq., for many yrs. a magistrate for this co., d. in a very advanced age (PGBA 8 Mar 98)
SWIFT, Jacob, late of Philadelphia, d. at his seat at Hall's Mill on 10 Jul. (VCGA 14 Jul 94)

SWIFT, Jonathan, merch., of Alexandria, mar. Miss Nancy ROBERDEAU eld. dau. to Gen. ROBERDEAU of Alexandria (VJAA 29 Sep 85)

SWINGLE, Peter, late of Berkeley Co., dec'd, e.a.w. his admr., Elijah HAWKE (PGBA 12 Jan 97)

SWINTON, Anne, of Caroline Co., will petition the next GA for a right to the whole of the tract of land she lives on which escheated to the Commonwealth by the death of George SWINTON (GLFFA 19 Oct 98)

SYDEBOTHAM, William, dec'd, his admrs. are D. ROSS and R. CRAMPHIN of Alexandria (VGAxA 1 Aug 93)

SYDERS, Martin Christian, pvt. in the U.S. infantry, b. in Ireland, des. from the rendezvous at Port Tobacco, [Md. ?] (TAA 12 Apr 98)

SYDNOR, Fortunatus, dec'd, e.a.w. Fortunatus SYDNOR of Richmond; his ex. is Thos. HOWLITT (VICGA 21 Jul 90)

SYDNOR, Robert, of Hanover Co., dec'd, e.a.w. his acting ex., Robert SYDNOR (VGGA 17 Aug 91)

SYKES, Samuel J., native of Eng., left there some time last summer, d. in Richmond on Fri. last (RC 19 Jul 96, VGGA 20 Jul 96)

SYME, Col., of Virginia, mar. Miss Sally HOOPS dau. of Adam HOOPS Esq., in Philadelphia on Thurs. night [10 Mar. ?] (PC 21 Mar 68, VG 14 Apr 68)

SYMMER, Dr. John, dec'd, his land in Gloucester and Middlesex Cos. to be sold by his ex., Robert and Alexander DALGLEISH (VG 29 Oct 67)

SYPHRET, Lawrence, of Frederick Co., dec'd, e.a.w. his ex., Andrew SYPHRET (BVCG 29 Jul 96)

TABB, John Esq., of Amelia Co., mar. Miss Frances PAYTON eld. dau. of Sir John PEYTON of Gloucester Co. (VG 22 Mar 70); late of Amelia, dec'd, e.a.w. his admx., Frances TABB, and admr., Wm. B. GILES of Amelia (VGPI 12 Oct 98)

TABB, John, Clerk of Mecklenburg Co., died; he was succeeded by John BROWN in the Secretary's Office (VGPu 7 Jul 75); e.a.w. his admr., Mary TABB and Noah DORTEL (VG 24 Feb 76)

TABB, John, of Amelia Co., intends to leave the country early next year with his family (VGAA 15 May 84)

TABB, John, son and heir at law of Thomas TABB is mentioned in a Charlotte Co. chancery case of Nov. 1791 against Larkin WELLS son and heir at law of Elijah WELLS; it appears that Larkin WELLS is not an inhabitant of this state (VGGA 28 Dec 91)

TABB, John Esq., dec'd, (Arg 18 Oct 99)

TABB, Col. Thomas, long a member for Amelia Co., d. on Mon. the 27th ult. [obit.] (VGR 7 Dec 69, PC 25 Dec 69)

TABB, William, of Bute Co., N. Carolina, will sell his land there as he intends to move to Va. (VG 1 Jul 73)

TAFF Family, HCC, 13 May 1790: Geo. YERBY and the sd. Geo. YERBY ex. of John YERBY dec'd, and Thomas YERBY eld. son and heir at law of the sd. John YERBY dec'd (pltfs.) against Peter TAFF and William TAFF ex. and devisees of Thomas TAFF, Ellen TAFF widow of the sd. Thomas TAFF, Priscilla TAFF, Mildred DEANE, Woodbridge TAFF, Francis TAFF, Travis TAFF, Betty TAFF, Anne TAFF, and Nancy Walker ALLISON devisees of the sd. Thomas TAFF, and Alice PALMER, Thomas PALMER, Robert PALMER, Betsey ISLES and Absolom ISLES the sd. Alice, Thos., Robt., and Betty [sic] chil. of Betty TAFF one of the daus. of Thomas TAFF dec'd, and Thomas BROOKE who mar. Anne TAFF another dau. of the sd. Thomas (defs.); it appears that Thomas PALMER is an inhabitant of Thilchappel Par., Co. Lancaster, Eng. (VICGA 18 Aug 90, VGGA 25 Aug 90)

TAGGART, Francis, late of Romney [Hampshire Co.], dec'd, e.a.w. his admx., Lucy TAGGART, and his admr., Edward DYER (BVCG 12 Aug 96)

TAIT, John, sold a tract of land in Louisa Co. to Rich. SWIFT without making a proper conveyance and has since moved to Caroline Co. (VG 19 Dec 77)

TAITE, Maj. William, of Northumberland Co., dec'd, 25 of his slaves to be sold

by his ex., Presley THORNTON, Thos. JONES, Rodham KENNER, and Newton KEENE (VGR 27 Oct 68)
TALBOT, Henry Esq., d. on Thurs. eve. at Tanner's Cr. (NHPA 2 Jan 97, AGGA 3 Jan 97)
TALBOT, Henry George, taken on suspicion of being a svt. (VGNI 9 Mar 75)
TALBOT, Robert, age 63, b. in London, committed to Frederick Co. jail on suspicion of being a runaway svt. (VG 30 Oct 66)
TALBOT, S. B., dec'd, his admr., Mary TALBOT, will sell his PE (NH 23 Jul 99)
TALBOT, Solomon B., of Norfolk Co., mar. Miss POLLY [TABB] of Bute Co., N. Carolina (VG 24 Apr 78)
TALBOTT, Edward, late of Frederick Co., dec'd, e.a.w. his admrs., Daniel MAGRUDER and Edward TALBOTT (BVCG 8 Apr 93)
TALBOTT, John, late of the Western Branch, Norfolk Co., dec'd, e.a.w. John R. MOORE, acting for the admx., Tamer TALBOTT (NH 1 Aug 99)
TALBOTT, William, of Chesterfield Co., dec'd, his slaves and livestock to be sold by Wm. WEST and Haly TALBOTT (VG 24 Nov 68)
TALBUT, John, dec'd, his extx., Ann TALBUT, and ex., Benj. TALBUT, will sell a tract of his land containing 134 ac. in Pr. Geo. Co., Md. about four miles from the Eastern Branch (CMAG 18 Feb 97)
TALBUTT, Benjamin, dec'd, his PE will be sold by Sarah TALBUTT, his extx., and Elisha PHELPS, his ex. (BVCG 9 Apr 91)
TALIAFERRO, Baldwin, of Orange Co., mar. Miss Anne Washington Burwell SPOTSWOOD dau. of Gen. Alexander SPOTSWOOD of Spotsylvania Co., on Mon. last [Mon. the 13th inst. acc. to RCFPC] (VHFFA 17 Mar 97, RCFPC 22 Mar 97)
TALIAFERRO, Charles, late of Amherst Co., dec'd. e.a.w. his admrs. w.w.a., Wm. and Roderick TALIAFERRO (VGGA 9 Oct 98)
TALIAFERRO, Hay, mar. Miss Lucy THURSTON in Orange Co. on 15 Apr. (VHFA 21 Apr 91)
TALIAFERRO, Hay, mar. Miss Susannah Fitzhugh CONWAY dau. of Catlett CONWAY, all of Orange Co., on the 15th inst. (RCFPC 22 Mar 97)
TALIAFERRO, John Esq., of Hayes, d. on 8 Apr. in Fredsbrg., aged 44 (VHFA 9 Apr 89); part of his est. to be sold at his plant. on Rappahannock River by his ex., John TALIAFERRO [Jr.] of Kg. Geo. Co., who will also sell his stock and slaves (VHFA 15 Sep 91, 5 Jan 92)
TALIAFERRO, John, mar. Miss Alice LECKIE, both of Culpeper Co., on the 12th inst. (VHFA 19 Mar 95)
TALIAFERRO, John, mar. Miss Betsey GEDDY, both of Petersburg, yesterday eve. (VGPI 31 Mar 97)
TALIAFERRO, Lawrence Esq., d. in Orange Co., last Mon. (VHFA 14 Apr 98)
TALIAFERRO, Miss Mary Thornton, dau. of Col. John TALIAFERRO of Dissington, Kg. Geo. Co., d. on Wed. the 7th inst., aged 18 (VHFA 15 Jan 95)
TALIAFERRO, Richard Gent., of Port Royal, dec'd, e.a.w. his admr., Edmund PENDLETON; his heir at law is Zachary TALIAFERRO (VG 17 Oct 51); his land in Halifax Co. to be sold by his admr. (VG 6 Jun 53)
TALIAFERRO, Maj. Richard Esq., of James City, d. in his 74th year with the gout in his head (VG 3 Jul 79, VGCD 3 Jul 79)
TALIAFERRO, Richard, late of Gloucester Co., dec'd, some of his slaves to be sold by his ex., Philip TALIAFERRO, and his extx., Elizabeth TALIAFERRO (VGGA 26 Oct 91 ex)
TALIAFERRO, Robert, of Blenheim, dec'd, his ex. is Wm. TALIAFERRO (VHFA 17 Nov 91); his ex., Wm. and Robt. TALIAFERRO, will sell all his stock, HH and KF (VHFA 6 Dec 92)
TALIAFERRO, Zacharias, dec'd, any claims against his est. to be brought to Richard TALIAFERRO who intends to leave the state in Nov. (LWG 13 Jul 99)
TALLY, the Rev. Elkana, mar. Mrs. ANDERSON, relict of Col. Jn. ANDERSON of Hanover Co. (VIC 11 Feb 89, VGWeA 12 Feb 89)
TALLEY, Nathaniel, of Hanover Co., dec'd, e.a.w. his admr., Nathaniel

TALLEY (VG 23 Oct 79)
TALLY, Zebulon, of Hanover Co., his father, Nathaniel, warns all ministers not to marry him and Mourning ABBOT, as he is under age (VG 12 Jan 69)
TAMAR, Edward, aka Bob, Negro slave bel. to Wm. TREBELL of Wmsbrg., lately brought home from H[e]rtford Co., N. Carolina where he was harbored for three yrs. by one VAN PELT on Chinkopin Cr.; he passed for a freeman and has a wife there; he spent some time in Charleston S. Carolina; ran away in Apr. 1767 (VG 16 Apr 67) [First name also given as Edmund]
TANKERSLEY, John, d. at Port Royal, aged about 42 (VHFA 17 Feb 91); Reuben TURNER (nfi) will sell his est. including his lease of a tavern [in Port Royal] (VHFA 13 Dec 92)
TANNER, Branch Sr., dec'd, his ex., Branch TANNER, will sell his slaves near Amelia Ct. H. (VGGA 13 Nov 93)
TANNER, Edward, mar. Miss Nancy CRESTMAST, both of Warren Co., N. Carolina, on Thurs. last (VGPI 28 Mar 97)
TANSELL, John Frederick Spooner Corbin, aka Corbin TANSELL, John SPOONER, appr., ran away from Wm. PEARSON, Fredsbrg. (VHFA 29 Aug 93)
TAPLEN, John, svt., ran away from Charles NEILSON, Hampton (VG 8 Aug 55)
TARPLEY, Adam, planter, b. in Goochland Co., 18, des. from Capt. Robert HODGSON's Independent Co. now raising for the service and defense of S. Carolina (VG 3 Jul 46)
TARPLEY, Charles, of Brunswick Co., dec'd, e.a.w. Benj. BLICK, sheriff of Brunswick Co. (VGPI 9 Dec 96)
TARPLEY, Mrs. Elizabeth, of Wmsbrg., died, aged 61 (VG 12 Jun 72); her ex., John BLAIR and James COCKE, will sell her dwelling house and lots in Wmsbrg. (VG 13 Aug 72)
TARPLEY, John, of Morattico Hall, intends to leave the colony towards the latter end of next summer and is selling six small plantations in Richmond Co. and 1000 ac. in Pr. Wm. Co. (VG 30 Apr 67)
TARPLEY, Maj. Travers, late of Richmond Co., dec'd, e.a.w. [his ex.], John BELFIELD and Rich. MITCHELL (VG 28 Jan 73)
TARRY, Samuel, of Amelia Co., dec'd, a chancery suit was brought by his admrs., Peter JOHNSTON and Thomas YUILLE and Peter TARRY an infant by Peter [JOHNSTON] his next friend against John PINNOCK, Edw. BOOKER, and James CLARKE (VG 5 Sep 66 sup)
TASKER, Benjamin Esq., President of the Council in the Province of Md., d. on the 19th inst. [long obit.] (VG and VGR 30 Jun 68)
TATE, Benjamin, of Richmond, mar. Miss Anna POE of Henrico Co., on Tues. eve. last (VGRMA 24 Jul 94)
TATE, Joseph, dec'd, 490 ac. of his land in Guilford and Surry Cos., N. Carolina to be sold by his ex., Adam TATE, John TATE, and Joseph TATE (VG 19 May 74)
TATE, Capt. Joseph, of the 2nd Bn. of the N. Carolina Continental troops, d. at Alexandria on the 2nd. inst. of a malignant fever; he was bur. in the churchyard at Alexandria (VG 20 Jun 77, VGPu 27 Jun 77)
TATE, Robert, dec'd, his admr., Francis TATE of Newcastle, will sell all of his HH and KF (VG 3 Oct 77)
TATHAM, John, cabinet maker, served part of his time in London and part in Carolina, has a wife and four chil., had sent a letter to his brother, Thomas TATHAM, Pontefract, Yorkshire, from Va.; he is asked to send [another] letter to his brother No. 20, Queen St., Bloomsbury, London, to learn something greatly to his advantage (NPJ 21 Nov 87)
TAYLER, John, late of Berkeley Co., dec'd, e.a.w. his ex., William and John TAYLER (PGBA 21 Apr 94)
TAYLOE, John Jr. Esq., only son of the Hon. John TAYLOE Esq. on of H.M's Council of this Colony was mar. at the house of Ralph WORMELEY Esq. in

18th-Century Virginia Newspapers 331

Middlesex Co. to Miss Rebecca PLATER dau. of the Hon. George PLATER Esq. one of His Lordship's Council of the Province of Md., on the 11th inst. (Wmsbrg. disp. of 23 July) (MG 11 Aug 47)

TAYLOE, John Esq., d. at Mt. Airy, [Richmond Co.], a few days ago (MJ 11 May 79)

TAYLOE, the Hon. John Esq., dec'd, debtors to his est. for dealings at [Neabsco] and Occoquan Furnaces to settle with Robert HAMILTON (VJAA 17 Nov 85)

TAYLOE, Col. William, of Lancaster Co., d. on 8 [Jan.] in his 72nd year, [obit.] (VGR 22 Feb 70)

TAYLOR, Mr., lately of Liverpool, d. in Alexandria (VJAA 7 Oct 84)

TAYLOR, Mrs., spouse of Col. John TAYLOR of Richmond Co., died (VGWeA 1 Feb 87) [NB. The surname is probably an error for TAYLOE.]

TAYLOR, Mrs., d. on Tues. the 14th inst. at the house of James HERRON (VGGA 22 Feb 92)

TAYLOR, Abraham, hatter, c. 21, escaped from Rockingham Co. jail where he was awaiting trial for murder (BVCG 16 Dec 93)

TAYLOR, Alexander, Irish svt., joiner, ran away from Col. LUDWELL, Green Spring (AWM 14 Jul 20)

TAYLOR, Mrs. Anne, spouse of Wm. TAYLOR merch. of New Kent Co., died; she was bur. in the family graveyard at Winterham in Amelia Co. (VG 21 Jan 75)

TAYLOR, Anne, HCC, 6 Aug. 1790: Richard Merriot BOOKER surviving ex. of Richard BOOKER (pltf.) against Wm. TAYLOR and Anne his wife (defs.); the cause abates as to the def. Anne, by her death on 6 Aug. 1790 (VGGA 27 Oct 90)

TAYLOR, Charles, att. at law of Southampton Co., d. on Thurs. the 18th inst.; he was bur. in the churchyard of this city [Richmond] (VGWeA 27 Dec 94); [an elegy on his death submitted by a friend] (VGGA 11 Feb 95)

TAYLOR, Drury, age 22, des. along with his brother, Wm. TAYLOR age 15, from the Frontier Bn. under Lt. Col. Wm. PEACHEY at Staunton, Augusta Co.; they were enl. in Albemarle Co. (VG 30 Nov 59)

TAYLOR, Eleazer, appr. tailor, 18-19, ran away from Adam KIGER, Winchester (BVCG 24 Sep 92)

TAYLOR, Mrs. Esther, wife of George TAYLOR of Alexandria, died (VGAxA 22 Apr 90)

TAYLOR, Mrs. Fanny, consort of William TAYLOR of Fredsbrg, d. on Fri. eve. in Caroline Co. (VHFA 21 Aug 95)

TAYLOR, Col. Francis, dec'd, a tract of his land in lower Caroline Co. to be sold by his ex., James TAYLOR and Edmund PENDLETON (VG 1 Dec 68)

TAYLOR, Francis Stubbs Esq., was mar. to Miss Ann Fox LINDSAY, both of this borough [Norfolk], on Thurs. eve. last by the Rev. John IRELAND, at the seat of Wm. BUCKLEY near Baltimore, Md. (NWJCI 11 Oct 97, NHPA 12 Oct 97)

TAYLOR, George, age 19, ran away from his father Edward TAYLOR living on Back Cr., Frederick Co. (VGWA 18 Jul 87)

TAYLOR, George, dec'd, his land near Newcastle, Hanover Co., to be sold by his ex., Edmund TAYLOR (VGGA 20 Jul 91)

TAYLOR, Col. George, of Orange Co., dec'd, his ex., Francis TAYLOR and Benj. TAYLOR, will sell many items of his est. and 280 ac. of his land three miles below Orange Ct. H. (VHFA 23 Nov 92, 11 Apr 93)

TAYLOR, George, merch., mar. Miss Love HOOKER, on Thurs. eve. (CMAG 19 Mar 96)

TAYLOR, George Keith Esq., Rep. from Pr. Geo. Co. in the GA, mar. Miss Jane MARSHALL of [Richmond] on Sat. eve. last (VGGA 24 Dec 99, Arg 27 Dec 99)

TAYLOR, Hancock, reportedly killed by Indians in Ky. (VG 15 Sep 74)

TAYLOR, Hugh, Irish svt., 22, ran away from the Potomac Co. at Great Falls (VJAA 15 Jun 86)

TAYLOR, Humphrey, Scot. svt, 16, ran away from John CATLETT, Kg. Wm. Co. (VGR 9 Feb 69)

TAYLOR, Jacob, appr., 20, ran away from Lund WASHINGTON at Norfolk; it is conjectured he went to sea in the brigantine *Nancy* (CMAG 30 Jul 96)

TAYLOR, James, dec'd, his ex., James GALT, will sell his dwelling house with 32 ac. of land one mile from Wmsbrg. (VGWeA 25 Sep 84)

TAYLOR, James, appr., c. 18, carpenter and house joiner, ran away from Reuben ARNOLD, Spotsylvania Co. (VGRMA 29 Jul 93)

TAYLOR, James, a bound boy, 20, ran away from John BERKELEY (PGBA 22 Sep 96)

TAYLOR, James, coppersmith from Liverpool, is now conducting business in Richmond (VGGA 28 Sep 96)

TAYLOR, James, b. in Eng., 35, des. from the 8th Regt., U.S. Army, in Alexandria (CMAG 16 Jul 99)

TAYLOR, Jesse Jr., merch., of Alexandria, mar. Miss Mary SMITH dau. of the late Austin SMITH Esq., on 31 Jan at Hackwood the seat of Col. John SMITH near Winchester (BVCG 4 Feb 93); died last Mon. (BVCG 2 Dec 93)

TAYLOR, John, merch., of Norfolk, dec'd, e.a.w. the ex., Margaret TAYLOR and John WILLOUGHBY (VG 27 Oct 52)

TAYLOR, John, merch., of Norfolk Borough, died [elegy in VGR] (VG 17 Sep 72, VGR 10 Dec 72)

TAYLOR, John, who enl. under Lt. Henry QUARLES of the 15th Bn., des. from Kg. Wm. Co.; he is an inhabitant of Gloucester Co. (VGPu 11 Apr 77 sup)

TAYLOR, Capt. John, mar. Miss Sally GARNER in Fredsbrg., on 7 Jan. (VHFA 21 Jan 90)

TAYLOR, John, appr. boy, ran away from Geo. PAYNE, Berkeley Co. (BVCG 15 Dec 94)

TAYLOR, John, appr. boy, ran away from John ROE in Fredsbrg. (RCFPC 3 Aug 96)

TAYLOR, John, coppersmith from Liverpool, is working in Richmond where he makes stills (VGGA 7 Jun 97, OVT 31 Aug 97) [see also: James TAYLOR]

TAYLOR, Joseph, from Albemarle Co., executed at the gallows on Fri. last for horse stealing (VIC 1 Aug 87, VGWeA 2 Aug 87)

TAYLOR, Lowdell Blackey, of New Kent Co., died (VGPu 20 Sep, VG 21 Sep 76)

TAYLOR, Miss Patsey, d. in Wmsbrg. (VGGA 31 Jan 98)

TAYLOR, Ralph, conv. svt., a North Country man, ran away from Patrick CREAGH, Annapolis, [Md.] (VG 15 Oct 36)

TAYLOR, Richard, of the house of Gilliat & Taylor, merch., mar. Miss Eliza CALVERT dau. of John CALVERT Esq., on Sat. eve. in Market St. (NHPA 2 Jan 97, AGGA 3 Jan 97)

TAYLOR, Robert, of Norfolk, mar. Miss Sally BARRAUD eld. dau. of Daniel BARRAUD merch., in that place, last Thurs. (VG 3 Oct 71)

TAYLOR, Robert Jr., mar. Miss Nancy RITSON on 28 Jul. (AGGA 29 Jul 96)

TAYLOR, Simon, late of Hampshire Co., dec'd, e.a.w. his ex., Robert PARKER and John TAYLOR (VCWM 9 Sep 89)

TAYLOR, Thomas, Eng. svt., b. in Somersetshire, ran away from John WORMELEY, Lancaster Co. (VG 11 Feb 73)

TAYLOR, Thomas, mar. Mrs. J. SHEPPARD, both of [Richmond], on Thurs. eve. last (VGGA 14 Jun 97)

TAYLOR, Thomas Sr., late of Loudoun Co., dec'd, e.a.w. his ex., Thomas TAYLOR Jr. in Frederick Town [Md. ?] or Benj. H. CANBY in Leesburg; his ex. will sell his plant. in Frederick Co., Md. containing 448 ac. plus other tracts in Frederick Co., [Md. ?] and in Loudoun Co. (CMAG 28 Sep 97, 3 Oct 97, 29 May 98)

TAYLOR, Maj. William, dec'd, a tract of his land on Little River, Hanover Co., to be sold by his ex. (nfi) (VG 21 Mar 66, 12 Nov 67)

TAYLOR, William, rep. in Assembly for Lunenburg Co., mar. Miss Patty WALLER eld. dau. of Benj. WALLER of Wmsbrg. (VG 19 Mar 67)

TAYLOR, William, of Southampton Co., dec'd, his ex., Henry TAYLOR, will sell his slaves and stock (VGPu 20 Dec 76 sup)

TAZEWELL, Mrs. Dorothy Elizabeth, spouse to Henry TAZEWELL Esq. of Brunswick Co., died (VGPu and VG 23 May 77)

TAZEWELL, Henry, of Brunswick Co., mar. Miss Dorothy Elizabeth "Dolly" WALLER third dau. of Benj. WALLER Esq. of Wmsbrg. (VG and VGR 13 Jan 74)

TAZEWELL, Henry Esq., senator from Va., in the U.S. Congress, d. in Philadelphia on the 24 of Feb. (VGGA 29 Jan 99, Ex 1 Feb 99, WG 6 Feb 99, PH 13 Feb 99)

TAZEWELL, John Esq., of Wmsbrg., d. after a lingering illness (VG 7 Apr 81); his ex. (nfi) will sell the houses and 100 ac. of his land on which they stand in Wmsbrg. formerly the property of Jn. RANDOLPH Esq. but now bel. to the est. of the dec'd (VGWeA 15 Feb 83)

TEARE, Robert, of Suffolk, intends to leave this part of the country as soon as the settlement of his affairs will permit (NH 6 Sep 98)

TEASE, William, of Augusta Co., dec'd, his ex., Robert LOVE, and extx., Mary TEASE, will sell his slaves (VIC 21 Oct 89)

TEBBS, Foushee, dec'd, his est. near Dumfries, near Winchester, and in Hampshire Co. to be sold by his ex., Willoughby TEBBS (VJAA 12 May 85); his lands in Frederick and Hardy Cos. and houses and lots in Dumfries to be sold by his ex. (VGAxA 12 Aug 90); his ex., Willoughby TEBBS and Samuel TEBBS, will sell 520 ac. of his land in Frederick Co. (BVCG 11 Feb 93) [name also given as TIBBS]

TEBBS, Foushee Esq., of Richmond Co., mar. Miss Ann QUARLES dau. of Capt. Henry QUARLES of Essex Co. on Thurs. the 17th inst. (VH 25 Jan 99)

TEBBS, Capt. Thomas, of the 2nd Regt., died (VG and VGPu 17 Jan 77)

TEBBS, Willoughby Esq., lately mar. at Dumfries, Miss Betsy CARR dau. of Wm. CARR Esq., merch. (VJAA 14 Sep 86)

TEDD, [Mr.], a butcher, d. suddenly in Wmsbrg. last Tues. (VG 18 Apr 51)

TEDFORD, Lt. James, of the U.S. troops, reportedly killed by Indians near Henry's Station south of the Ohio on 28 Aug. (VGRMA [7] Oct 93, VGGA 16 Oct 93)

TEDMAN, Luke, lately arrived in Norfolk from Sheffield, Eng., d. this morn. (NHPA 30 Sep 97)

TEMPLE, Mrs., consort of Liston TEMPLE of Richmond, d. on Sun. eve. (OVT 9 Aug 98)

TEMPLE, Col. Samuel, d. on Tues. the 23rd inst. at his seat in Caroline Co. (OVT 30 Jul 98)

TEMPLEMAN, William, merch., at Fredsbrg., d. lately (VG 19 Nov 72, PC 5 Dec 72); his ex. is Richard TEMPLEMAN of Norfolk (VG 28 Jan 73)

TENANT, Miss Kiziah, of Pr. Anne Co., d. on the 7th of last month in her 19th year after a short illness (VGWeA 14 Dec 82)

TENNENT, Dr. John, d. on Sat. the 29th ult. at his seat in Caroline Co., aged 63 (VHFA 17 Jul 94); his admr., John TENNENT, will sell his est. at his dwelling house near the Bowling Green (VHFA 28 Jul 95) [name also given as TENNANT]

TENNENT, John H., of Caroline Co., son of Dr. John TENNENT of Port Royal (VHFA 22 Jul 90) [also given as TENNANT]

TENNISON, Joseph, appr. boy, ran away from Geo. HILL (TAA 7 Sep 97)

TERELAGH, Daniel Connor, svt., plays the bagpipes, ran away from Miles BARROTT, Bedford Co., last year (VG 25 Mar 75)

TERREL, John, Irish svt., ran away from Thomas INGALLS, joiner, in St. Mary's Co., Md., he had been a svt. in Md. before (VG 31 Oct 45)

TERRELL, Edmund, dec'd, e.a.w. his ex., Wm. WILLIS of Culpeper (VHFFA 14 Oct 96)

TERRELL, James, svt., 21-22, leather breeches maker, ran away from Geo. COUSINS, Chesterfield Co. (VG 28 Mar 66)

TERRELL, Jonathan, adv. that he is not a deserter but obtained a discharge due to ill health (VGPu 23 May 77)

TERRELL, Richard, will undertake business in Ky. where he will reside in Lexington (VGGA 4 Oct 92); has opened a commission office in Lexington (BVCG 31 Mar 94)

TERRELL, Richmond, dec'd, his ex., Wm. CLAYTON, Richmond ALLEN, and Richard ALLEN, will sell his PE at his plantation in New Kent Co. (VGR 15 Aug 71, VG 7 Nov 71, 12 May 74) [In the VG and VGR of 21 Nov 71, his ex. were named as Frederick HARRIS, Zachariah LEWIS, and Garret MINOR; they were to sell his land]

TERRELL, William, dec'd, six of his slaves to be sold at Charles City Ct.H. by his admr., Marston WILLIAMS (VG 15 Jan 67)

TERRETT, Miss Peggy Hunter, d. in Fairfax Co. on Sat. the 8th inst. (TAA 12 Dec 98)

TERRY, William, a legatee of Stephen TERRY dec'd late of Hanover Co.; he left Caroline Co. around 1764 and may have been in the 96 District of S. Carolina in 1786 (VIC 29 Jul 89)

TEUWELL, Matthew, dec'd, his extx., Mary TEUWELL, will sell his houses and lots in Wmsbrg. (VG and VGP 22 Dec 74) [also given as TEWELL]

THACKER, Mrs. Elizabeth, dec'd, her est. in Middlesex and K & Q Cos. to be sold by Henry WASHINGTON, her admr. (VG 7 Nov 51)

THACKER, Capt. Henry, dec'd, his land in Kg. Wm. Co. being sold by his ex., Mrs. Mary Elizabeth THACKER of Middlesex Co., and Col. Wm. ALLEN of Surry Co. (VG 1 Jan 67)

THACKER, [Henry], son of the late Rev. Chichley THACKER, d. on Fri. last at the Glebe in Blissland Par., New Kent Co. in his [?] year (VG 12 Dec 71)

THACKSTON, Sarah, her husband, James THACKSTON of Pr. Edw. Co., will pay no more of her debts (VGR 29 Oct 72)

THARP, Matthew, Irish conv. svt., gardener, ran away from Joseph PEIRCE, Westmoreland Co. (VG 20 Aug 72, VGR 29 Oct 72)

THAXTON, Saras, mulatto, c. 18, ran away from Hugh FRAZER, Charlotte Co. (VGGA 2 Jan 93)

THEEDS, Coleman, and his wife, Elizabeth, parted by mutual consent on 12 Jun. 1773 (VG 10 Feb 74)

THELABALL, Lewis, late of the Borough of Norfolk, dec'd, his house and lot there to be sold by his ex., Matthew GODFREY (NPJ 29 Apr 89)

THENABELL, George, dec'd, e.a.w. his acting ex., Wm. WHITE of Norfolk Co. (NH 12 Mar 96)

THILMAN, P. Jr., dec'd, his admrs., John THORNTON, Edmund TAYLOR, John DAY, and Samuel DAY, will sell a Negro in Hanover to discharge a debt due to P. WOOLFOLK the ex. of Capt. P. THILMAN dec'd (VGGA 1 Apr 95)

THILMAN, Paul Esq., mar. Miss Barbara O. WINSTON, both of Hanover Co., on Mon. the 22nd inst. (Arg 26 May 97)

THILMAN, Richard, a pet. will be pres. to the House of Delegates to enable some of his lands to be sold in order to [make] a more equal division thereof between his brothers and sisters, some of whom are under 21 (VGGA 25 Aug 90)

THOMAS Family, HCC, 9 Mar. 1797, between Bogle, Somerville & Co. (pltfs.) and Richard THOMAS, James THOMAS, George THOMAS, Joel DOGGETT, Geo. DOGGETT, and John PIPER and [?] his wife (defs.); it appears that the PIPER's are not inhabitants of this country (VGGA 19 Apr 97)

THOMAS, Benjamin, late of Pr. Wm. Co., dec'd, e.a.w. his ex., Benj. THOMAS (RJDWA 3 Nov 96)

THOMAS, Charles, of Warwick Co., intends to leave the colony in late Sep. (VG 4 Sep 46)

THOMAS, Charles Esq., dec'd, e.a.w. his ex., Alex. MOSELEY of Norfolk (VGAA 24 Apr 84, VGWeA 12 Jun 84)

THOMAS, Elizabeth, Welsh, ind. svt., c. 25, ran away from [?], Loudoun Co. (VGR 3 Aug 69)
THOMAS, Capt. George, late of Berkeley Co., killed at Bath on Mon. eve. last by Maj. [or Capt.] R. BLACKBURN who was charged and imprisoned at Martinsburg (Martinsburg disp. of 1 Sep., Winchester disp. of 2 Sep.); BLACKBURN was later found not guilty; e.a.w. his admr., John KERNEY (CMAG 6 Sep 96, VGPI 15 Sep 96, BVCG 16 Sep, 14 Oct 96, PGBA 27 Oct 96)
THOMAS, John, says he comes from Va., and was b. in London, c. 40, jailed in Charles Co., [Md.] on suspicion of being a runaway; it is thought he des. from some regiment, along with John REES, q.v. (MG 30 Apr 61)
THOMAS, Capt. John, late of [Portsmouth], dec'd, e.a.w. his ex., John M'EVOY (NHPA 6 Apr 97)
THOMAS, Joseph, of Orange Co., dec'd, he d. in May 1773; his ex., Thomas BARBOUR, will settle his est. as well as the est. of his relict, Sarah THOMAS, who d. in May 1795 (VHFFA 9 Jun 97)
THOMAS, Rees, dec'd, e.a.w. his admr., Evan THOMAS (BVCG 10 Jun 93)
THOMAS, Richard, seaman, 30, ran away from the ship *Amelia* lying at Bermuda Hundred (VG 1 Jun 69)
THOMAS, Rowland, of Orange Co., desires to remove from the colony and will sell his lands in that co. (VG 1 Apr 75)
THOMAS, Mrs. Ruth, of Loudoun Co., d. of asthma on 30 Mar. (BVCG 14 Apr 94)
THOMAS, Sarah, dec'd, her admr., Henry FINCH, requests that her legatees come and receive their proportionable parts of her est. (VGPu 20 Jun 77)
THOMAS, William, svt., ran away from Joseph BARKER living on Charles' Beaver Dam, Kg. Geo. Co., on 29 Apr.; he may be headed for Hampton (VG 20 Jun 51)
THOMAS, William, dec'd, e.a.w. his ex., William THOMAS and Thomas FAVER of Essex Co. (VGR 21 Nov 71)
THOMAS, William, of Northumberland Co., d. in Jan. last, aged 78 (VGPA 13 Mar 90)
THOMAS, William, dec'd, e.a.w. his ex., Daniel THOMAS and Eleanor THOMAS of Fauquier Co. (WG 23 Oct 99)
THOMASSON Family, Louisa Co., Ct. of Q. S., 11 Nov. 1798, in chanc: Temperance Dumas THOMASSON, Unity Smith THOMASSON, Patsey THOMASSON, and David Hix THOMASSON infants of tender years by Unity THOMASSON their next friend (pltfs.) against Lewis THOMASSON and Nancy his wife, Nelson FOSTER and Betsey his wife, Fanny, Polley, John, Winney, and Wright THOMASSON (defs.) (VGGA 22 Jan 99)
THOMPSON Family, Montgomery Co., April Ct., 1799, in chanc: Patrick M'MANES and Sarah his wife (compls.) against James THOMPSON, Henry THOMPSON, John THOMPSON, Patton THOMPSON, and Samuel HICKMAN and Peggy his wife, late Peggy THOMPSON, Hanson GARDNER and Nancy his wife, late Nancy THOMPSON, Wm. GLOVER and Isabella his wife, late Isabella THOMPSON, Wm. FARLEY and Elizabeth his wife, late Elizabeth THOMPSON, Violet CARTY and Clay FARLEY and Letty his wife, late Letty CARTY daus. of Mary CARTY dec'd, late Mary THOMPSON, chil. and co-heirs of Wm. THOMPSON dec'd (defs.); it appears that the GARDNER's, GLOVER's, M'MANESes, and Violet CARTY are not inhabitants of the Commonwealth [There was a second case with Gordon CLOYD as compl. against Patrick M'MANES and all the above defs.] (Arg 14 May 99)
THOMPSON, Mr., from Madeira, mar. Miss Nancy PLEASANTS dau. of Robert PLEASANTS of Henrico Co. (VGIC 22 May 84)
THOMPSON, Alexander, grocer, of Richmond, dec'd, e.a.w. Hunt & Adams his admrs. (VIC 31 Oct 87)
THOMPSON, Amos, indented boy, c. 14, ran away from Persons MEANLY, Petersburg, and is supposed to be gone towards Carolina (VGR 29 Oct 72)
THOMPSON, Andrew, of Westmoreland Co., sentenced to death for the

burglary of Benedict MIDDLETON's house; executed on 13 Jan. (VG 16 Dec 37, 13 Jan 38)

THOMPSON, Anne, svt., "tolerable lusty," ran away from Geo. WOOLSEY, Norfolk (VGR 8 Feb 70)

THOMPSON, Bartholomew, formerly an inhabitant of Norfolk, taken by the enemy on board the *Franklin* and carried to New York; he was confined on board the prison ship where he caught jail fever; soon after his discharge he had a relapse of that cruel disorder at Philadelphia on his way to Va. which carried him off in the flower of his age (VG 17 Jul 79)

THOMPSON, Charles, of York Co., murdered on 5 Jul. by his deranged wife; he left a number of chil. (VG 6 Jul 69, NYPB 31 Jul 69)

THOMPSON, Charles R., adv. that he has removed his store to Richmond Co. and requests all those to whom he is indebted to call on Mr. W. S. THOMPSON for settlement (CMAG 22 Nov 96)

THOMPSON, Cornelius, blacksmith, des. from the *Page* galley and is believed lurking around the lower end of Fauquier Co. as his family lives there (VGPu 24 Oct 77)

THOMPSON, Cornelius, mar. Miss Polly COUCHMAN in Berkeley Co. (BVCG 28 May 92)

THOMPSON, Dekar, of Falmouth, d. on 30 Dec. last (VG and VGR 12 Jan 69); his surviving partner, Charles YATES, desires all debtors to Dekar Thompson & Co. to pay their debts (VG 2 Feb 69); a lot of his in Falmouth to be sold by his ex., Arthur MORSON and Edw. MOORE (VGR 7 Sep 69)

THOMPSON, Israel, dec'd, his ex., Jonah THOMPSON, Samuel THOMPSON, and Wm. HOUGH of Loudoun Co., will sell all of his PE (CMAG 12 Mar 95)

THOMPSON, James, Virginian, 23, des. from Capt. Carter HARRISON's Co. (VG 5 Dec 55)

THOMPSON, James, dec'd, e.a.w. his ex., Thomas BALLARD and James BULLIFANT, Charles City Co. (VG 12 Dec 77)

THOMPSON, John, svt., 18, b. in Blissland Par., New Kent Co., has relations in Goochland Co., ran away from Wm. WYATT in Wmsbrg. (VG 1 Sep 38)

THOMPSON, the Rev. John, Rector of St. Mark's [Par.] in Culpeper Co., died (VG 22 Oct 72)

THOMPSON, John, of Pr. Geo. Co., son of John THOMPSON of Sussex Co. (VG 24 Dec 72)

THOMPSON, John, black lad, says he bel. to Wm. HACK of Accomack Co., jailed in York Co. (VGPu 7 Jul 75 sup)

THOMPSON, Capt. John, of Sussex Co., dec'd, e.a.w. his ex., Geo. RIVES (VG 27 Nov 79)

THOMPSON, John, late of Halifax Co., dec'd, e.a.w. his ex., W. and James THOMPSON (RMA 25 May 96)

THOMPSON, John, late of Culpeper Co., dec'd, e.a.w. his admr., Garland THOMPSON (VHFFA 20 Sep 96 ex)

THOMPSON, John, a young man, d. in this city [Richmond] on Thurs. morn. last after a short illness (DOB 29 Oct 98)

THOMPSON, John Esq., att. at law and author of "Curtains" and several other political essays, d. on Thurs. last [acc. to VGGA] or Fri. last [acc. to Ex] in Petersburg, aged 23; he was a member of the Petersburg Troop of Light Horse (VGGA and Ex 29 Jan 99)

THOMPSON, Littleberry, executed on 31 May at Wmsbrg. for murder (Wmsbr disp. of 31 May) (NYPB 28 Jun 64)

THOMPSON, Mary, has eloped from her husband, John THOMPSON (VGWA 27 Feb 90) [Her name was given as Hannah THOMPSON in the VGWA issue of 6 Mar 90]

THOMPSON, Mary, eloped from her husband, Richard THOMPSON, on 10 Fel (VGGA 13 Mar 93 ex); her letter of explanation notes that Richard is her second husband (VGGA 20 Mar 93)

THOMPSON, Mary, her husband, Jacob THOMPSON, accuses her of embezzling his property and refusing to cohabit with him (BVCG 18 Nov 96)

THOMPSON, Mrs. Prudence, one of the oldest inhabitants of Portsmouth, d. on Sat. last in her 58th year (VCGA 12 May 94)
THOMPSON, Robert, dec'd, William THOMPSON (nfi) will sell a 200 ac. tract of his land in Amelia Co. (VGPu 29 Aug 77)
THOMPSON, Roger and G., of Fluvanna Co., intend to move to Ky. within a month (VGGA 21 Mar 92)
THOMPSON, Samuel Esq., commander of H.M.S. *Rippon*, mar. Miss Betsey BLAIR youngest dau. of the Hon. John BLAIR Esq. one of H.M's Council, last [Tues.] (VG 23 Mar 69)
THOMPSON, Samuel, dec'd, e.a.w. his admr., Samuel THOMPSON, in Orange Co. (VHFA 1 May 94)
THOMPSON, Thomas, merch., of Norfolk, died (VG 26 Sep 71); e.a.w. his ex., Matthew PHRIPP and John LAWRENCE (VG 9 Jan 72); his ex. will sell his tanyard, houses, land, etc. near Norfolk (VG 17 Sep 72)
THOMPSON, Thomas Esq., of Richmond, mar. Miss Jane Isabella SYME dau. of Col. John SYME, at Rocky Mills in Hanover Co. on Sat. eve. last (VGRC 5 May 95, RMA 7 May 95, VGGA 13 May 95)
THOMPSON, Thomas, native of Ireland and formerly a wine merch. in the island of Madeira, d. on the 5th inst. at the Rocky Mills (VGGA 15 Nov 99)
THOMPSON, William, of Portsmouth, dec'd, e.a.w. his admr., John THOMPSON (VG 29 Jul 73)
THOMPSON, William, merch., mar. Miss Polly CHANDLEE, both of [Winchester], on Tues. last (BVCG 22 Jan 96)
THOMSON, Dr. John, of Petersburg, dec'd, his apothecary's shop will be run by Robert MASSENBURG (VGAA 9 Jul 85)
THOMSON, John, dec'd [obit. and poem] (Arg 5 Feb 99)
THOMSON, Robert, of Louisa Co., dec'd, e.a.w. his ex., Samuel BROCKMAN (VGPA 13 Mar 90)
THOMSON, William, Eng. svt., bookbinder, c 35, ran away from James ALCORN, Botetourt Co. (VG 24 Nov 74)
THORNBURG, Benjamin, late of Berkeley Co., dec'd, e.a.w. his admr., Robert EACHUS (PGBA 13 Feb 95)
THORHNILL Family, Bedford Co. Ct., Mar. 1795, in chanc: John FOLDEN (compl.) against Edw. HANCOCK and Sarah, late Sarah WORMAX, his wife, John THORHNILL, Wm. THORHNILL, Ezekial THORHNILL, Leonard THORHNILL, Amstead THORHNILL, Reuben THORHNILL, Sarah THORHNILL, James THORHNILL, Barnett THORHNILL, Edna THORHNILL, Bryant THORHNILL chil. and heirs of Wm. THORHNILL dec'd; the sd. Sarah, James, Barnett, Edna, and Bryant are infants under 21 by Wm. THORHNILL their gdn. (defs.); it appears that John THORHNILL, Ezekial THORHNILL, and Leonard THORHNILL are not inhabitants of this country (LFG 1 Aug 95)
THORNTON, Charles, dec'd, his ex., Robert WARREN, will sell 320 ac. of his land convenient to Thornton's Ordinary in Pr. Wm. Co. (VGPu 12 Jun 78)
THORNTON, Mrs. Frances, relict of Wm. THORNTON of Gloucester Co., died (VG 9 Sep 73)
THORNTON, Col. Francis, of Kg. Geo. Co., lately dec'd, e.a.w. his ex., Wm. THORNTON, of Richmond (VGIC and VGWeA 27 Nov 84)
THORNTON, Francis Esq., of Spotsylvania Co., mar. Miss Sally INNIS dau. of the Hon. Harry INNIS of the District of Ky., on Sat. the 2nd inst. at Mount Comfort the seat of James INNIS Esq. (VGGA 20 Jun 92)
THORNTON, George, dec'd, his extx., Mary THORNTON, and ex., Francis THORNTON of Fredsbrg., will sell 13 blooded horses bel. to his est. (VGWeA and VGAA 21 Sep 82)
THORNTON, Maj. George, of Spotsylvania Co., dec'd, Thomas POSEY is acting for the extx. (nfi) (VGIC 12 Jun 84)
THORNTON, James, of Orange Co., dec'd, e.a.w. his ex., Daniel THORNTON and Thomas BRYANT (VHFA 31 Jul 94)
THORNTON, Jesse, hatter, of Richmond, stabbed himself to death on Sat. eve.

last (VGPI 23 Aug, RMA 24 Aug, 20 Sep, RC 27 Aug 96); his extx., Sarah
THORNTON of Richmond, adv. that the hatting business in the future will
be carried on under the name of S. THORNTON and E. COMPTON (Arg 23
Dec 96)

THORNTON, John Esq., of Stafford Co., mar. Miss Catherine "Kitty" YATES of
Gloucester Co. fourth dau. of the Rev. Robert YATES (VG and VGPu 5 Sep
77)

THORNTON, John, late of Caroline Co., dec'd, his admrs. are Wm.
WOODFORD and John TALIAFERRO; any debts to his est. to be paid to Maj.
Benj. DAY of Fredsbrg. (VGPu 19 Jun 78)

THORNTON, John Esq., att. at law, late of Loudoun Co., dec'd, his est. acc.
with Samuel LOVE Jr. his ex. (VJAA 20 Jan 85, VGAA 16 Apr, 23 Apr 85,
VGGA 1 Dec 90)

THORNTON, John Tayloe Esq., d. on Sat. last at his seat in Northumberland
Co. (VHFFA 16 Sep 96); his admr., Presl[e]y THORNTON, will sell all of his
stock, HHF, plant. utensils, a 20-ton schooner, and a valuable mill, and 15-
20 Negroes at his seat (VHFFA 1 Nov 96)

THORNTON, Luke, mar. Miss Lucy SLEET in Orange Co. on [Thurs. last] (VH
2 Jul 99)

THORNTON, Mrs. Mary, spouse of Sterling THORNTON Esq. of Gloucester
Co., d. in the flower of her age (VGPu 22 Nov 76)

THORNTON, Peter Esq., of Northumberland Co., mar. Miss Sally
THROCKMORTON of Gloucester Co. (VG 23 May 71)

THORNTON, Presley, Lt. of Northumberland Co., mar. Charlotte NELSON
(VG-Randolph [?] Jun 58)

THORNTON, the Hon., Presley Esq., member of H.M's Council of this colony, d.
on Fri. last at his house in Northumberland Co. [obit. in VGR] (VG and
VGR 14 Dec 69)

THORNTON, Presley Esq., mar. Miss Sally INNES dau. of Harry INNES Esq.
at the seat of Col. James INNES near this city [Richmond], on Sat. eve. last
(VGGA 13 Jun 92) [VGGA of 20 Jun. corrects this, stating that it was
Francis THORNTON Esq., q.v., who mar. Sally INNES.]

THORNTON, Presley Esq., of Northumberland House, mar. Miss Susan STITH
dau. of Col. Robert STITH of Kg. Geo. Co., on Thurs. the 8th inst. (VHFA 13
Oct 95)

THORNTON, Reuben, dec'd, his tract of 1346 ac. in Caroline Co. to be sold by his
ex., James TAYLOR and Geo. THORNTON (VGR 16 Jun 68)

THORNTON, Reuben, of Amherst Co., dec'd, his admr., Anthony THORNTON
of Caroline Co., will sell three of his slaves (VH 29 Jan 99)

THORNTON, Mrs. Sarah, wife to Peter Presley THORNTON Esq. of
Northumberland Co., died (VGPu 27 Jun 77)

THORNTON, Seth, of Caroline Co., dec'd, his est. being administered by John
THORNTON of Kg. Geo. Co. (VHFA 4 Aug 91); e.a.w. his ex., F.
THORNTON of Caroline Co. (VHFA 4 Sep 95)

THORNTON, Sterling, late of Henrico Co., dec'd, e.a.w. his ex., John
PLEASANTS (VIC 28 Mar 87)

THOROUGHGOOD, Col. John, of Pr. Anne Co., d. lately (VIC 24 Oct 87, VGPI 1
Nov 87)

THOROWGOOD, John, mar. Miss Patty WHITE on Thurs. eve. last on the
Western Shore in Pr. Anne Co. (VCNPGA 3 Nov 92)

THOROWGOOD, Nicholas, intends to move from Norfolk to Philadelphia in a
short time (VCGA 21 Jul 94)

THORP, Christopher, of Surry Co., dec'd, his ex., Wm. BROWNE and Nicholas
FAULCON Jr., will sell all his est. (VG 26 Dec 77)

THORP[E], Matthew, Irish conv. svt., c. 27, ran away from Gilbert
CAMPBELL, Westmoreland Co. (VGR 10 Jan 71); jailed as a runaway in
Augusta Co. (VGR 23 May 71)

THORPE, Peterson, dec'd, his admr., Timothy THORPE, will sell part of his
est. and rent a plant. bel. to the est. on Meherrin River about four miles

18th-Century Virginia Newspapers 339

below Hick's Ford (VGPu 21 Nov 77)
THORPE, Thomas, of K & Q Co., dec'd, his HH goods to be sold by his ex., Graham FRANK (VG 30 Nov 59)
THRIFT, George, late of Fairfax Co., dec'd, e.a.w. his ex., John OVERALL, John ADAMS, C. W. LANE, and Luke FRIZZLE (TAA 8 Nov 98)
THRIFT, John, conv. svt., ran away from Robert M'KITTRICK, Augusta Co. (VGPu 26 May 75 sup)
THROCKMORTON, Gabriel, of Gloucester Co., d. about a fortnight since in his 77th year (VG 20 Jan 38)
THROCKMORTON, John, late of Gloucester Co., dec'd, his ex., Robert THROCKMORTON, will sell his tract of land on Ware River in that co. in which the widow has her dower (VGPu 13 Sep 76)
THROCKMORTON, Capt. Mordecai, of [Hanover Co. ?], dec'd (VG 19 Nov 67)
THROCKMORTON, Col. Robert, of Gloucester Co., d. on Mon, the [25th] ult. in his 63rd year (VGR 6 Sep 70)
THROCKMORTON, Robert Esq., of Berkeley Co., d. last Mon. (BVCG 23 Sep 96); his admr., John DAVENPORT, will sell his HHF and livestock (PGBA 5 Jan 97, BVCG 20 Jan 97)
THROCKMORTON, William, printer, lately publisher of a paper at Staunton, he had lived in Winchester, Richmond, and Alexandria, d. on 3 Aug. at 2:00 (Charleston disp. of 4 Aug.) (VGGA 17 Aug, VHFFA 19 Aug, RMA 20 Aug 96)
THRUSTON, Miss Ann, of Orange Co., dec'd, e.a.w. her admr., John NETHERLAND Jr. in Powhatan Co. (VICGA 17 Mar 90)
THRUSTON, Miss Nancy, formerly of Orange Co., d. on the island of Barbados on 22 Dec. [1789] (VHFA 28 Jan 90)
THUILLIER, Mr. F. R., of Norfolk, d. on Mon. last [or Tues. last acc. to TDCDA] after a short illness (NH 17 Oct 99, TDCDA 28 Oct 99)
TH[U]RMAN, [Mary], has eloped from her husband, Andrew THURMAN of Hanover Co. (VGRMA 25 Jul 93)
THURSTON, William Plummer, dec'd, e.a.w. Nicholas TALIAFERRO, Culpeper Co. (VHFA 8 Oct 89)
THWAITES, Mary, wife of John THWAITES of Norfolk, who will not pay any of her debts (NHPA 1 Apr 97)
THWEAT, Miles, sometime before his death, he obtained a bond from Francis EPES on condition of the reversion of the time of a mulatto girl named Fanny HARRIS (VGR 12 Mar 67)
TICKELL, the Rev. Mr. Joseph, Rector of Trinity Par., Louisa Co., d. a few days ago (VG 1 Dec 68)
TIDBALL, Capt. James, merch., of Winchester, mar. Miss Eleanor M'DONALD on Thurs. the 7th inst. (WG 13 Feb 99)
TIEFFIER, [?], stocking weaver, native of Duzes, Languedoc; Pierre SEGUIN a grenadier in Burgoyne's Infantry that arrived from France on 11 Sep. is seeking information on him (VCNPGA 22 Sep 92)
TIGNOR, Anne, has left her husband, Thomas TIGNOR, and carried with her three of his chil. and one Negro man (VGGA 19 Apr 99)
TILEY, James, dec'd, e.a.w. his admr., Ben. PAYNE (AGNPWA 10 Oct 92)
TILLETT, Samuel, dec'd, his ex., Giles TILLETT and Samuel TILLETT, will sell his 184 ac. plant. on Sandy Run in Fairfax Co. six miles from Occoquan Mills which is now in the possession of Caleb STONE (CMAG 16 Jul 99)
TILLEY, George, dec'd, e.a.w. his admx., Ann TILLEY, Martinsburg, who will sell his HHF and store goods and who cautions persons against taking off rails and stakes from the field bel. to his est. (PGBA 12 Jan, 2 Mar 95)
TIMBERLAKE, Miss Ann, of Kg. Wm. Co., d. on the 31st ult. in her 34th year [a letter she wrote mentions her sister, Betsey, and brothers, Richard, William, Henry, and John] (VGGA 20 Feb 93)
TIMBERLAKE, Francis, dec'd, e.a.w. Furnew SOUTHALL (VG 19 Feb 80)
TIMBERLAKE, Joseph, merch., d. lately at Port Royal (VHFFA 10 Mar 97)
TIMMINGS, Daniel, mar. Miss Elizabeth RAILEY, both of Richmond, d. on

Sun. morn. last (VGRMA 4 Dec 94)

TINKER, Jeremiah Esq., grandson of the late Gov. GIBBS; his mother was dau. and heiress of GIBBS; a tract of land bel. to him in Pr. Anne Co. to be sold (VGR 16 Jun 74)

TINSLEY, Charles, of Newcastle, d. lately in Fredsbrg. (disp. of 8 Feb.) of smallpox (VG and VGR 17 Feb 74); late of Hanover Co., his admr., Wm. TINSLEY, will sell his stock, HH and KF, and other items at his late dwelling house in Newcastle (VG 17 Mar 74)

TINSLEY, John, of Chesterfield Co., adv. that his wife, Anne MAJOR, eloped about three months ago and he will not be answerable for her debts (VG 23 May 77)

TINSLEY, Thomas, of Hanover Town, dec'd, his admx., Agnes TINSLEY, will sell his slaves and PE; his tavern in that town will be let by Leighton WOOD Jr. (VGR 4, 18 Aug 74, VG 11 Aug 74, VGPu 17 Nov 75 sup)

TINSLEY, William, of Newcastle, dec'd, his admx., Mary TINSLEY, will sell all his PE (VGWeA 21 Sep 82)

TIPPER, James, butcher, came to this place [Annapolis ?] about 13 or 14 yrs. ago and served his time here with Daniel WELLS; if he be living and will apply to the printing office he will hear of something worth inquiring about; after he left Annapolis, he lived sometime in Upper Marlboro from whence he removed over to Va. and is supposed to live now not far from Alexandria (MG 21 Jan 62)

TIPPETT, John, svt., ran away from Joseph MORTON formerly of Richmond Co., but now of Orange Co. (VG 15 May 39)

TIPPIN, Charles, aka TIPPINS, svt., gardener, ran away from Wm. REYNOLDS, Annapolis, Md. (VGP 16 Nov 75)

TITSWORTH Family, Isaac TITSWORTH adv. that on 5 Oct. 1794, his family and that of John TITSWORTH were attacked by Indians on the Red River, his wife, John TITSWORTH and his wife, one of his children and one of Isaac's children were killed; three chil. of Isaac's and one of John's were captured; one of his chil. was killed and a dau., Peggy c. 13, was captured (VGRMA 5 Feb 95)

TOBIAS, Christopher, of Pr. Anne Co., dec'd, e.a.w. his admr., Bargey KEITH of Port Norfolk (NH 10 Sep 99)

TOD, Dr. George, d. in Caroline Co., aged 80 (VHFA 11 Mar 90)

TOD, [George], merch., mar. Miss Polly SMITH dau. of Wm. SMITH last eve., all of this place [Fredsbrg.] (VHFA 7 Mar 98)

TODD, Col. [John], killed in an engagement with an Indian force near Lexington, Ky. [on 19 Aug.] [He was the brother of Col. Levi TODD and Capt. Robert TODD; for additional details, see *Calendar of Virginia State Papers* 3: 333-334] (VGAA 5 Oct 82)

TODD, Betty, late of Manchester, dec'd, e.a.w. her ex., Wm. MACKENZIE of that town and Wm. DANDRIDGE (VG 24 Apr 78, 28 Aug 79)

TODD, the Rev. Mr. Christopher, of Brunswick Par., Stafford Co., dec'd, his ex., Thos. LOWRY and Bernard TODD, adv. that eight head of his cattle strayed from Brunswick Glebe; his ex. will sell all of his HH and KF (VG 28 Nov, 5 Dec 77, VGPu 5, 12 Dec 77)

TODD, Richard, late of Baltimore Co., Md., dec'd, e.a.w. his admr., Thomas TENANT, Baltimore (NH 23 Jun 98)

TODD, Robert, late of Norfolk, merch., dec'd, his windmill and other houses built upon the Glebe to be sold by his admr., John WATSON of Suffolk (VG 28 Mar 55)

TOFFLER, Peter, hatter, of Alexandria, drowned while attempting to cross the river on the ice (TAA 23 Dec 97)

TOLER, Henry, merch., of Richmond, mar. Miss Cyntha [sic] SOUTHALL, on Thurs. the 28th ult. (VGRMA 15 Apr 93)

TOLER, William, of Hanover Town, dec'd, e.a.w. his admr., Benjamin TOLER (VGGA 10 Nov 90)

TOLLS, Reuben, Va. born Negro, ind. svt., 23, ran away from Nicholas Brown

SEABROOK, Norfolk (VG 16 Jan 72)
Tom (famous African calculator), see: Thomas FULLER
TOMKIES, Charles, of Gloucester, practitioner of physick and surgery, d. on Sun. sennight (VG 20 May 37)
TOMLINSON, Samuel, conv. svt., ran away from Thomas Wm. IRWIN, Yorktown; he was seen in New Kent Co. (VG 19 Nov 36)
TOMPKINS, William, dec'd, his ex., John MINOR, Ben. TOMPKINS, and Francis TOMPKINS, will sell his tract of land in Hanover Co. on Stag Cr. (VGPu 19 Sep 77); his ex. will sell a tract of his land in Hanover Co. containing near 600 ac. (VG 31 Oct 77)
TONEY, Davey, Negro, c. 22, ran away from the Appomattox Canal (VGPI 18 May 98)
TOOLEY, Ennell, from Hertford Co., N. Carolina, 19-20, des. from Capt. Thomas BRESSIE's Co. (VGPu 18 Jul 77)
TOOMER, John, late of York Co., dec'd, e.a.w. his ex., John MOSS and William GARROW (VIC 3 Dec 88)
TOOMEY, Daniel, Irish svt., ran away from Thomas CLARKE, Fredsbrg.; he is supposed to be headed for Winchester (VJAA 22 Jun 86)
TOPIN, John, Eng. conv. svt., c. 55, has been in this country about nine months, ran away from Arthur EDWARDS and Thomas ASKREN, Loudoun Co. (VGPu 26 Jul 76)
TOPPING, William, c. 30, from Chowan Co., N. Carolina, disappeared on his way to Philadelphia in Jan. to solicit the recovery of an est. (VG 12 Aug 74)
TORBORN, Dr. William, of Charles City Co., dec'd, his ex., Peter DUN, will sell all his PE (VG 15 Jul 73)
TOURET, Nicholas, French, appr., saddler, 18-19, ran away from John LAMOINE, Alexandria; he is believed to have absconded on the schooner *Amazon* bound for Norfolk and France (VCGA 9 Jun 94)
TOWELL, John, aka TOOL, Irish, ran away from the *Delight* brig lying at Capt. DANSIE's (VG 7 Nov 54)
TOWLES, Miss Eliza M., dau. of Col. Henry TOWLES of Lancaster Co., d. on the 14th ult. aged 27 (VHFA 7 Aug 95)
TOWLES, Col. Henry, d. suddenly at his seat in Lancaster Co. on the 13th [acc. to VGGA] or 18th [acc. to VH] ult. aged 53 (VH 3 Dec 99, VGGA 6 Dec 99)
TOWNES, Richard, operated stage-carriages between Richmond and Norfolk, dec'd; his brother, William TOWNES, has taken his business over (VCNPGA 22 Jun 93) [also given as TOWNS]
TOWNES, William, proprietor of the stages between Petersburg and Norfolk, d. on Tues. last (VGPI 31 Mar 97)
TOWNSEND, Henry Esq., mar. Miss Rebecca CHESLEY the third dau. of John CHESLEY Esq. of St. Mary's Co., Md., at Hayes', Montgomery Co., Md., on 11 Dec. (VJAA 29 Dec 85)
TOWNSEND, Capt. James, of the brig *Eliza*, d. at sea on 13 [Feb.] on his passage from Madeira to New York (VGPA 13 Mar 90)
TRABUE, William, dec'd, his ex., Robert HASKINS, will sell his land in Chesterfield Co. (VICGA 20 Jan 90)
TRACEY, Daniel, mar. Miss Fanny BUTT, both of Norfolk, on Thurs. night (NH 25 May 99)
TRACEY, James, captured by Shawnee Indians in 1763 on Stinking Cr., New River; he escaped [in the spring of 1773] and went to his former home to learn that his father and family had removed "to what they called Virginia;" he is now in Fredsbrg. seeking information on his family (VGR 16 Dec 73)
TRACEY, Michael, Irish svt., c. 25, ran away from Andrew WALES, Alexandria (VGR 2 Aug 70)
TRAMMELL, Gerrard, d. in his 86th year (VJAA 6 Jul 86)
TRAUTWINE, Mrs. Jane, formerly of Winchester, d. in Hardy Co., on Sat. the 5th inst. in her 53rd year (WG 23 Jan 99)
TRAVIS, Champion Esq., Rep. for Jamestown, mar. Miss Betsey BOUSH of

Norfolk dau. of Samuel BOUSH Clerk of that co. and borough (VG and VGR 3 Dec 72)

TRAVIS, Edward, of Jamestown, mar. Miss Betsey TAITE (VG 2 Apr 72)

TRAVIS, Capt. Edward, of the Navy, mar. Miss Clarissa WALLER of Wmsbrg. (VG 26 Feb 79)

TRAVIS, Edward Champion Esq., d. a few days ago at his plant. near this city, of a dropsy in his 59th year (VG 21 Aug 79)

TRAVIS, Mrs. Elizabeth, spouse of Edward TRAVIS Jr., of James City, died [elegy in VGR] (VG and VGR 28 Jan 73)

TREBELL, Mrs. Sarah, consort of William TREBELL of James City, d. at his seat in Martin's Hundred on James River on Mon. the 9th inst. [obit. in VIC] (VGWeA 12 Feb 89, VIC 18 Feb 89, NPJ 25 Feb 89)

TREBELL, William, d. on Sun. the 11th inst. at his seat near James City Co. near Wmsbrg. where he was the owner and master of the Rawleigh Tavern, aged 68; e.a.w. his ex., John M. GALT of Wmsbrg. (VIC 14 Oct 89, VGWeA 15 Oct, 3 Dec 89)

TRECHET, Pored de, b. in France, 25, sometimes calls himself the Count de Bueil, des. from the *Romulous* (VGAA 22 Mar 83)

TRENT, Mrs., spouse of Alexander TRENT Esq., of Cumberland Co., d. on Tues. the 16th inst. (VGGA 24 Dec 94)

TRENT, Alexander, eld. son of Peterfield TRENT Esq. of Chesterfield Co., d. on 13 Jul. in his 13th year (VGAA 7 Aug 84)

TRENT, Alexander, late of Powhatan Co., dec'd, his trustees, Alex. TRENT Jr. and Peterfield TRENT Jr., will sell some slaves and livestock at Cumberland Ct. H. (VGRMA 2 Jun 94); his exors. (nfi) of Cumberland Co., will sell one moiety of his part of sundry lots in Manchester (Arg 22 Nov 96)

TRENT, Mrs. Angelica, spouse of Peterfield TRENT of Richmond, d. yesterday morn. in her 46th year (VGPA 9 Feb 93)

TRENT, Peterfield, merch., of Richmond, mar. Miss WILKINSON of Chesterfield Co. on Sun. the 3rd inst. (VGR 21 Mar 71)

TRENT, Peterfield, eld. son of Peterfield TRENT of this city [Richmond], d. on 1ᶠ Dec. last in his 18th year (VGGA 15 Jan 73)

TRENT, Peterfield Esq., of Richmond, d. yesterday [19 Nov.] in an advanced age (VGRMA 20 Nov 94, VGRC 21 Nov 94)

TRETON, William, svt., 20, baker, ran away from John SEYLE, Georgetown (VJAA 22 Jun 86)

TRICKETT, Jasper, filesmith, left Sheffield, Eng., unknown to his parents and went to Va. where they have heard he is overseer to some gentleman; if he will write to his relations he may hear something to his advantage by applying to John WARRINGTON, Wmsbrg. (VGR 30 May 66)

TRIGG, Col. [Stephen], killed in an engagement with an Indian force near Lexington, Ky. [on 19 Aug.] [For additional details, see *Calendar of Virginia State Papers* 3: 333-334] (VGAA 5 Oct 82)

TRIMBLE, Donald, drowned last eve. [14 Jun.] when a longboat bel. to the brig *Ann* from Glasgow going from Norfolk to Hampton Road was upset by a squall (extract from Lindsay's Norfolk Hotel diary) (Pennsylvania Gazette 1 Jul 89)

TRIPLETT, Daniel, dec'd, lots bel. to his est. in Port Royal to be sold (VG 14 Aug 52)

TRIPLETT, Thomas, dec'd, his admx., Sarah TRIPLETT, will sell his slaves and HHF (VGAxA 13 Jan 91)

TRIPLETT, Dr. Thomas, having finished a regular study of medicine, purposes practicing in its various branches in the city of Alexandria and its vicinity (CMAG 19 Jun 98)

TRIPLETT, Titus, Deputy Clerk of this place [Alexandria ?], d. in the bloom of youth after a short illness, accounts against his est. to be presented to G. DENEALE, of Alexandria (CMAG 30 Jul 96, 13 Aug 96)

TRIPLETT, William, dec'd, e.a.w. his admr., Daniel TRIPLETT, Madison Co., who will also sell his stock and his mill on Mattox Cr. (VHFA 27 Mar 94

sup, VH 21 May 99)
TRISCOE, Tom, Negro, c. 28, broke out of jail in Norfolk Borough on the 23rd inst. (NH 26 Jan 99)
TROUNSER, Samuel, 32, des. from H.M.S. [*Triton*]; he is alleged to be in Va. on board *Pamunkey Snow* up Pamunkey River (VG 9 May 51)
TROUT, Geor[g]e, appr., 18-19, ran away from Wm. BEVERIDGE, Fauquier Co. (CMAG 7 May 96)
TRUAN, Francis, a native of France, came to America and served in the army under the Count d'Estaing in Georgia or some of the Southern States; he is to apply to Mons. de GAMBLE, New Orleans, to be informed of a considerable sum of money he may command; when last heard of he was a merch. in Richmond (VHFA 8 Jul 90)
TRUEHEART, Aaron Bartholomew, d. last Sat. in Long's Court, St. Martin's Street, Leicester Fields, [London]; he had care of the Cherokee Indians now in town (Pennsylvania Gazette 24 Jan 67)
TRUEHEART, Bartholomew, mar. Miss Polly SEABROOK on Thurs. eve. last at the seat of Mrs. SEABROOK in Hanover Co. (VGRMA 17 Nov 94, VGRC 18 Nov 94)
TRUEHEART, Bartholomew, of Hanover Co., mar. Miss Betsey MOSBY dau. of Littlebury MOSBY Esq. of Powhatan Co., on Tues. the 23rd inst. (DOB 1 Nov 98)
TRUEHEART, Mrs. Elizabeth, consort of Maj. Wm. TRUEHEART of Hanover Co., d. on the 22nd inst. [acc. to Ex] or the 24th inst. [acc. to Arg] (Arg and Ex 29 Jan 99)
TRUEHEART, Mrs. Polly, consort of Bartholomew TRUEHEART, d. on Wed. night last in the bloom of youth [obit.] (RMA 18 May 96)
TRUGEN, Mrs., in consequence of the late decease of her husband, she judges it advisable to decline the business of storekeeping; she has taken an apartment in the house occupied by Mr. STEEL, boot and shoemaker, where she will immediately open the business of mantua maker (CMAG 26 Jan 96)
TRUGEN, Edward, dec'd, e.a.w. his admr., J. T. RICKETTS and R. YOUNG of Alexandria, who will also sell a variety of items from his est. at the dwelling house of Mrs. TRUGEN, his widow (CMAG 2 Jan 96)
TRUMP, James, Eng. svt., 26, baker, ran away from Robert ADAM and Peter WISE, Alexandria (VG 6 Jun 66)
TUCKER Family, HCC, 27 Sep. 1792: Thomas NEWTON Jr. and Martha his wife, Elizabeth TUCKER otherwise Elizabeth FAULKNER, which Thomas, Martha and Elizabeth are joint devisees of John TUCKER dec'd (pltfs.) against Alex. GRAY and Mary his wife, Wm. HARVEY and Frances his wife, Wm. PENNOCK and Anne his wife, Daniel NORTON and Caroline his wife, James TAYLOR Jr., Geo. Lee TURBE[R]VILLE and Betty Taylor his wife, Orrick CHILTON and Felicia his wife, Wm. Curry BEALE and Anne his wife, John BOWDOIN and Courtney BOWDOIN infants under 21 by Preeson BOWDOIN their gdn., and Rich. Henry CORBIN and Jane CORBIN infants under 21 by Francis CORBIN their gdn., Wm. PENNOCK and Joanna TUCKER and Thomas APPLETHWAITE and others ex. etc. of John TUCKER late of the island of Barbados dec'd (defs.) (VGGA 2 Jan 93)
TUCKER, Mrs., consort of the Hon. St. George TUCKER Esq. of Chesterfield Co., died (VIC 30 Jan 88)
TUCKER, Gawin Corbin, [dec'd], e.a.w. his admr., Wm. PENNOCK of Norfolk (NH 4 Sep 98)
TUCKER, Henry, late of Halifax Co., dec'd, e.a.w. his admr., Neil JAMIESON of Norfolk (VG 16 May 71, VGR 5 Sep 71)
TUCKER, Capt. James, mar. Miss Ann MACAULEY in Pr. Anne Co., on Sat. last (VCNPGA 6 Oct 92)
TUCKER, Capt. John, late of Norfolk, dec'd, e.a.w. his ex., Jn. HUTCHINGS, Edw. C. TRAVIS, and Henry TUCKER (VG 21 Jun 70)
TUCKER, John, late of Hampshire Co., c. 25, who had been removed to the district jail in Moorfield to be tried for horse stealing, has escaped (VGGA 26

Jun 98)

TUCKER, John, Chief Assistant in the Land Office, d. suddenly on Wed. morn. last in Richmond; he was bur. with Masonic honors (VGGA 1 Mar 99, NH 7 Mar 99); his admr. w.w.a., Henry YOUNG, will sell his HHF (VGGA 21 Jun 99)

TUCKER, Mrs. Mary, wife of George TUCKER and third dau. of the late James Parke FARLEY Esq., d. at Wmsbrg., aged 22 [poem in NH] (NH 6 Jun 99, Ex 28 Jun 99)

TUCKER, Raines, appr. carpenter, 17, ran away from Robert JONES, Southampton (VG 20 Jun 66)

TUCKER, Robert, merch., of Norfolk, mar. Miss Hannah CORBIN dau. of Col. Gawin CORBIN of K & Q Co. on 17 May (VG 18 May 39)

TUCKER, Col. Robert, d. on Wed. the 1st inst. at Norfolk (VG 9 Jul 67, NYPB 30 Jul 67); e.a.w. his ex., Thomas NEWTON Sr. and John [or James] TAYLOR (VG 24 Sep 67); 50 of his slaves to be sold at Norfolk by his ex. (VG 18 Aug 68); tracts of his land in Norfolk Co. to be sold (VG 13 Oct 68)

TUCKER, Robert, of Norfolk Co., died (VG 25 Sep 79)

TUCKER, Robert, dec'd, his admrs. are Stith PARHAM and Wm. EPPES (VGPI 4 Sep 95)

TUCKER, Col. Robert, dec'd, his admrs., James TAYLOR and Thomas NEWTON of Norfolk, have empowered James TAYLOR Jr. to settle his est. (NHPA 5 Jun 97, AGGA 7 Nov 97)

TUCKER, Robert Jr., of Norfolk, dec'd, his land on Wind Mill Point adjoining Portsmouth to be sold by his exors., Thomas NEWTON Jr. and Preeson BOWDOIN (VGAA 5 Apr 83, 21 Feb 84)

TUCKER, William, son of John TUCKER, of [Amelia Co.] (VG 7 Apr 74)

TUCKER, Capt. William, dec'd, his ex., Paul LOYALL and Henry BRESSIE, will sell six of his slaves at Norfolk Ct. H. (VGNI 28 Jul 74)

TUDOR, Samuel, Eng. conv., c. 19, ran away from the sloop *Betsy* out of Corotoman River, Lancaster Co. along with Alex. RICHARDSON a Virginia born Negro c. 21 (VGR 7 Mar 71, VG 28 Jan 73)

TUELLS, Mrs., wife of Enoch TUELLS of Norfolk, was delivered this week of her fourth pair of twins; she is 29, has been mar. 11 years, and has 15 chil.; Mr. TUELLS is 34 (AGGA 2 Aug 96)

TUMBLING, George, appr., 16, suspected of robbing his master, Peter DIXON of Norfolk (NPC 25 Feb 92)

TUMMINS Family, Botetourt Co. Ct. of Q. S., 12 Nov. 1793: Elizabeth VANDINE heiress at law of Jacob VANDINE dec'd (pltf.) against Samuel TUMMINS, Mary TUMMINS, and Winefred TUMMINS, heirs to Edward TUMMINS dec'd (defs.) (VGGA 18 Dec 93)

TUNSTALL, Richard, Clerk of K & Q Co., his daus. (nfi) aged 11 and 12 drowned last Sun. sennight (Wmsbrg. disp. of 8 Jul.) (Pennsylvania Gazette 4 Aug 43)

TUNSTALL, Col. Richard, of K & Q Co., dec'd, his ex., Rich. TUNSTALL and Geo. BROOKE, will sell a tract of his land containing 700-800 ac. in Amelia Co. (VG 16 Oct 78)

TUNSTALL, Col. Richard, late of K & Q Co., dec'd, his legatees (nfi) will sell the tract of land whereon he resided containing 574 ac. on Mattaponi River in K & Q Co. (VHFA 17 Aug 98, VH 31 Aug 98)

TUPMAN, Capt. Francis, of Fredsbrg., d. at Leedstown on his return from the West Indies, aged about 36 (VHFA 28 Aug 98)

TURBERVILLE, George, of Peckatone, Westmoreland Co., died (VGWeA 4 Feb 93); his extx., Martha TURBERVILLE, will sell all his slaves and personal property (VH 2 Apr 99)

TURBERVILLE, John, of Hickory Hill, mar. Mrs. Anne BALLENDINE, both of Westmoreland Co. (VGWeA 4 Feb 93)

TURBERVILLE, Mrs. Martha, the consort of John TURBERVILLE Esq., d. at Hickory Hill, Westmoreland Co. on the night of the 8th inst. in her 53rd year (VHFA 19 Jan 92)

TURKEL, Thomas, Eng. ind. svt. lad, ran away from on board the sloop *Washington* lying at Broadway's on Appomattox (VGPu 20 Dec 76)

TURNBULL, Charles, merch., of Petersburg, mar. [Mrs.] COLE of Charles P[arish], York Co. (VG-Randolph [?] 59)

TURNBULL, George, of Dinwiddie Co., dec'd, his land there and two lots in Petersburg to be sold by Charles TURNBULL (nfi) (VG 4 Nov 63)

TURNBULL, James, ind. svt., tailor, ran away from Andrew HAMILTON, Blandford (VG 13 Oct 74)

TURNBULL, Robert, a petition will be pres. to the next GA for the dissolution of his marriage to Sarah BUCHANAN formerly Sarah LEE, Petersburg (VGGA 20 Jul 91)

TURNBULL, Thomas, appr., c. 17, ran away from the British brigantine *Europe* (NH 16 Oct 98)

TURNER, Arthur, late of Brunswick Co., dec'd, his ex., Thomas TURNER and Philip and Colin PEARSON, will sell his real and personal est. consisting of 400 ac. joining Meherrin River in Southampton Co. which he purchased of Maj. John RUFFIN and livestock including two covering horses (VGPu 13 Jun 77)

TURNER, Brian, native of Eng., kept school in Petersburg, drowned Thurs. last (NPJ 2 Apr 88)

TURNER, Charles, native of Scotland near Tweed, clock and watch cleaner, lived in Alexandria upwards of 16 yrs., d. last Jan. intestate; any heirs should apply to his admr., Robert MUIR (VGPu 8 Nov 76)

TURNER, Dorrel, of Caroline Co., dec'd, his admr., James TAYLOR, will sell his stock and furniture (VH 15 Jan 99)

TURNER, George, dec'd, Reuben TURNER (nfi) will sell his land in Kg. Wm. Co. (VG 17 Dec 72)

TURNER, George Esq., d. lately in Caroline Co. (VH 25 Jun 99)

TURNER, James, Virginian, 26, enl. by Capt. BELL, des. from the Va. Regt. at Fort Cumberland (VG 26 Dec 55)

TURNER, Capt. John, late of Nansemond Co., dec'd, his land in Brunswick Co. to be sold by his ex., Simon TURNER and James HOLT (VG 14 Aug 52)

TURNER, John, executed on 23 May near Wmsbrg. for murder (VG 23 May 55)

TURNER, John, Eng. svt., shoemaker, ran away from George DONALD, Richmond (VG 7 Mar 66); aged 30-40, ran away from George DONALD [again ?] (VG 5 Feb 67)

TURNER, John aka Johnny, Negro, 40, ran away from the est. of Col. Carter BURWELL (VGR 4 Aug 68)

TURNER, John, merch., of Wmsbrg., died (VGPu 16 Jun 75, VG 17 Jun 75 sup); his ex., Wm. PEARSON and Wm. TURNER, have discharged Geo. REID from the management of his business and settling the est. of Allan & Turner, merchants (VGP 13 Jul 75, VG 22 Jul 75)

TURNER, John, of Richmond, adv. that his wife, Sarah, eloped without any provocation (VGAA 14 Jan 86)

TURNER, Joseph, uncle to a certain Washington TURNER a young lad who formerly lived in Alexandria; if he will call on Joseph RIDDLE he will hear something that is of consequence to a particular friend of his (CMAG 16 Jun 98)

TURNER, Peter, Negro, c. 30, broke jail in Norfolk Borough (NH 1 May 98)

TURNER, Mrs. Sinah, d. in this town [Alexandria] on Fri. last (CMAG 21 Jun 96)

TURNER, Col. Thomas, dec'd, 60 of his slaves and a 500-600 ac. tract of land in Kg. Geo. Co. to be sold at Nanzatico by his ex., Wm. A. WASHINGTON and John FAUNTLEROY (VHFA 8 Nov 87, VIC 5 Dec 87)

TURNER, William, enl. in Amelia Co., des. from Capt. Wm. SANFORD's Co. of the 2nd Regt., Wmsbrg. (VGPu 17 Jan 77)

TURNER, William, late of this city [Wmsbrg.], merch., died (VG 18 Dec 79)

TURPIN, Mrs. Caroline M., consort of Dr. Philip TURPIN of Salisbury in Chesterfield Co., d. there on Wed. the 20th inst. (VGRMA 25 Nov 93, VGGA

27 Nov 93, VGWeA 29 Nov 93)
TURPIN, Dr. Philip, mar. Mrs. M'CALLUM relict of Daniel M'CALLUM of Osborne's, on Sat. eve. last (Arg 12 Dec 96)
TURPIN, Col. Thomas, d. on the 20th inst. at his house in Powhatan Co., aged 83 (VICGA 30 Jun 90)
TURPIN, Col. Thomas and Peterfield, of Powhatan Co., dec'd, e.a.w. their ex., Thomas, Wm., and Horatia TURPIN (VGGA 10 Nov 90)
TURPIN, Thomas Sr., merch., d. at his seat in Powhatan Co. (VGGA 29 Mar 97, Arg 31 Mar 97); late of Powhatan Co., his acting ex., Horatia TURPIN, will sell the 990 ac. tract where he resided (Arg 14 Nov 97) [NB. It is not clear if the name in the above two entries is Horatio or Horatia]
TUTE, Capt. John, d. at his house near Jamestown on Wed. last (VG 18 Nov 37)
TUXENT, Curry, Negro, 50, carpenter and cooper, ran away from Capt. John WILLIAMS, Northumberland Co.; he is thought to be gone towards James River (VGR 4 Aug 68)
TWENTYMAN, Benjamin, of Orange Co., 70, mar. Mrs. Betty NUTTY, 50, on 26 Jan (VHFA 4 Feb 90)
TWOPENCE, Elizabeth, of Essex Co., sentenced to death for murdering her bastard child (VG 4 May 39)
TWOPENCE, John, Negro, 40, ran away from Robert BEVERLY, Blandfield, Essex Co. (VG 11 Apr 77, VGPu 11 Apr 77 sup)
TWYMAN, George, mentions his son, Abraham, who is under age (VGGA 13 Apr 91)
TYE, John Sr., reportedly killed by Indians on the frontiers of Hawkins Co., [Tennessee] on 5 Jan. (VGGA 25 Feb 95)
TYLER, Ben, aka Ben, Negro, c. 25, brought from Talbot Co., Md., ran away from R. WORSHAM at Broadway near Petersburg (NH 29 Jan 99)
TYLER, Charles, of Amherst Co., adv. that his wife, Mary, has eloped and he will pay no debts of her contracting (VGPu 23 Oct 78)
TYLER, George C., of this co. [Pr. Wm.], mar. Miss Cecilia CAMPBELL of the same on 3 Nov. (VGAR 17 Nov 81)
TYLER, Henry, d. on the 2nd. inst. in Sussex Co. in his 73rd year (VGR 27 Jan 74)
TYLER, John, of James City Co., magistrate, vestryman in James City Par., and marshal of the court of Vice Admiralty of Wmsbrg., d. last Thurs., aged 55 (VG 26 Aug 73, VGR 2 Sep 73); e.a.w. John TYLER (nfi) (VGR 23 Sep 73)
TYLER, John, of Charles City Co., mar. Miss Polly ARMISTEAD of the same (VGPu 29 Dec 75 sup)
TYLER, John, of Essex Co., dec'd, his land on Piscataway Cr. to be sold by Archibald McCALL, whom his chil., if they be alive, are asked to contact (VGAA 21 Feb 84)
TYLER, John, was executed yesterday for shooting his uncle (VGAA 29 Jan 85)
TYLER, Lewis, att. at law, dec'd, his admr. w.w.a., Geo. CALDWELL, will sell a valuable tract of land on Turnip Cr. in Charlotte Co. whereon the sd. TYLER lived containing upwards of 900 ac. subject to the dower of the sd. TYLER's widow (VGPu 28 Nov 77)
TYLER, Lyttleton, ship carpenter, formerly of Alexandria, killed in an accident while working on the bridge over Colchester River (TAA 15 Sep 97)
TYLER, Mrs. Mary, spouse of Judge TYLER, d. on the 22nd inst. (VGGA 29 Mar 97, Arg 31 Mar 97)
TYLER, William, dec'd, his admr., Rodman BLANCETT, will sell two of his lots in Dumfries (RJDWA 11 Feb 96, 5 May 96)
TYLER, William and Peggy, son and dau. of Francis TYLER, may hear of something to their advantage by applying to John MASSENBURG, Sussex Co. (VGGA 22 Aug 92)
TYREE, Tarlton [or Dalton], appr., son of Wm. TYREE of New Kent Co., 19, ra away from Job MILLS in Manchester along with his brother, John TYREE, 21 (DOB 20, 24 Sep 98)

ULERIDGE, Thomas, Eng. svt., ran away from Thomas BRANSON, Stafford Co. (VG 21 Jul 68)
UNDERJUE, William, Indian-born mulatto boy, b. c. 1779, bound as a shoemaker to Lemuel BAILEY, Norfolk; he ran away from his master in May 1794 and Sep. 1797 (VCGA 19 May 94, NHPA 21 Sep 97, NH 11 Oct 98); well-known notorious lad, ran away [again] from Lemuel BAILEY (NH 25 May 99)
UNDERWOOD, James, dec'd, his ex., Rich. ADAMS and Geo. PARKE, will sell his HH and KF at Cumberland Town as well as a tract of his land adjoining the land of Thomas UNDERWOOD in Goochland Co. (VG 18 Nov 73)
UNDERWOOD, Col. Thomas, of Goochland Co., mar. Mrs. Jane DANDRIDGE of Hanover Co., on Thurs. the 15th inst. (VGRMA 26 Jan 95)
UNDERWOOD, William, att. at law, dec'd, e.a.w. his ex., Andrew BUCHANAN, Falmouth (VG 16 Jan 72)
UNDERWOOD, William, a young man of Goochland Co., d. on Thurs. last in Richmond (RC 6 Aug 96)
UPCOTT, Capt., master of a vessel in the service of Capt. PERRIN of Gloucester Co.; his body was found floating in the river near Gloucester Town last Sun. sennight (VG 21 Oct 37)
UPSHUR, Thomas S. Esq., att. at law, d. lately in Northampton Co. [elegy dated 29 Nov. 1792] (VCNPGA 26 Jan 93)
URIE, William, dec'd, his admr., Geo. LORIMER, will sell all his est. including a pilot boat at Urbanna, Middlesex Co. (VG 10 Jan 71)
USHER Family, Frederick Co. ct., 3 Dec. 1799, in chanc: John HODGSON et al (see: PURTLE Family) (pltfs.) against Meshach SEXTON, Thomas USHER, Josiah USHER, James USHER, Ann USHER, Robert USHER, Elizabeth USHER, Sarah USHER, and Samuel USHER heirs and devisees of Thomas USHER dec'd, Joseph USHER, Thomas USHER, Samuel JOHNSON and Joseph DONALDSON exors of the will of Thomas USHER dec'd (defs.) (WG 18 Dec 99)
USHER, John, conv., from the north of Eng., weaver, ran away from the snow *Anne* at Port Royal (VG 9 Jul 72)
USTUS, Thomas, Irish svt., 20, ran away from Greenberry GAITHER, Montgomery Co., Md., may have run off with Cornelius and Elizabeth ROGERS, also natives of Ireland (VJAA 15 Mar 87)

VADRILL, Mr., French, kept a store in K & Q Co., committed suicide at the house of Geo. TODD, Richmond, an inquest was held on 16 Aug. (WVGWA 28 Aug 90)
VAIDEN, William, of New Kent Co., dec'd, e.a.w. his ex., Joseph and Jacob VAIDEN (VGPu 29 Aug 77)
VALENTINE, Caesar, free Negro, executed near Wmsbrg. (VG 30 Nov 59)
VALENTINE, Edward, mar. Miss Elizabeth SINGLETON of Pr. Anne Co. on Sun. eve. last (NPC 23 Jul 91)
VALENTINE, Edward, dec'd, e.a.w. his admr., Joseph VALENTINE, Caroline Co. (VGGA 25 Nov 95)
VALENTINE, Harry, svt., 18, b. in Leicestershire, has been in the country about three yrs. and is the property of Samuel HIPKINS of Totuskey Bridge, Richmond Co.; he ran away from Samuel HIPKINS and Griffin GARLAND, Richmond Co. (VGR 25 Aug 68)
VALENTINE, Jacob, of Kg. Wm. Co., dec'd, his ex., Batchelder VALENTINE and Jacob VALENTINE, will sell his 383 ac. tract in Henrico Co. in which his widow has her dower (VG 1 Dec 74)
VALENTINE, Jenny, mulatto girl, ran away from Thomas BROWN in Fredsbrg. and is now lurking about Richmond at the house of one Hannah MACKLAND; she has a mother in Wmsbrg. (VGWeA 12 Jun 88)
VALENTINE, John, of Richmond, mar. Miss Anne MOORE (VG 27 Jun 77)
VALENTINE, John, of Norfolk, dec'd, his admx. is Ann FITZGERALD (NPJ 5 Mar 88)

VALENTINE, Joseph, late of York Co., dec'd, e.a.w. Rich. C. GRAVES and Stanhope VAUGHAN (VG 13 Jun 77)
VALENTINE, Thomas, mulatto, broke jail in St. Mary's Co., Md. on 4 Aug.; he may be in Alexandria (VJAA 15 Sep 85)
VALLENICAR, Mr., d. on Tues. the 3rd inst. at Manchester (VG 13 Dec 76)
VANASTAN, John, mulatto boy, c. 16, ran away from on board the brig *Jane* at Norfolk (NH 28 Dec 99)
VANCE, Mrs. Mary, consort of William VANCE of Frederick Co., d. a few days since in her 32nd year (VGWA and BVCG 23 Mar 91)
VANCE, William, d. on 12 Sep. in Frederick Co. (BVCG 17 Sep 92); e.a.w. his ex., John GILKISON and James D. VANCE (BVCG 22 Oct 92); his PE will be sold at his plant. near Newtown (BVCG 29 Oct 92)
VANCOUVER, Charles Esq., killed by Indians at the forks of Sandy [in Ky.] about seven weeks ago (VGGA 25 May 91)
VANDEWALL, Col. Markes, vendue master of [Richmond], mar. Miss Susannah "Sukey" LEWIS dau. of Charles LEWIS of Henrico Co. [or Hanover Co. acc. to VIC] (VIC 21 Oct 89, VGWeA 22 Oct 89)
VANDEWALL, Mrs. Susannah, consort of Col. Markes VANDEWALL of Richmond, d. yesterday morn. (VGRMA 26 Jun 94)
VANHORNE, Abraham, killed in a fight with John CRANE a few miles from Shepherdstown on Tues. last (PGBA 11 Jul 91); e.a.w. John VANHORNE (nfi) (BVCG 20 Aug 92)
VANHULT, Joseph, of Norfolk Borough, mar. Miss Elizabeth WHITEHOUSE, on Tues. eve. at the seat of Col. DAWLEY in Pr. Anne Co. (NH 1 Mar 98)
VAN METTER, Mr., killed with his son at Sovern's Valley, Ky. by Indians about 20 Jan. (VJAA 5 Apr 87)
VASS, James, merch., of Falmouth, mar. Miss Susanna BROOKE of Pr. Wm. Co. on the 12th ult. in that co. (VH 8 Oct 99)
VAUGHAN Family, Goochland Co. ct., 16 Apr. 1799, in chanc: John H. PURRINGTON and Clarissa his wife and Daniel THOMAS and Mary his wife which sd. Clarissa and Mary are daus. of Matthew VAUGHAN dec'd (pltfs.) against Mary VAUGHAN widow and relict of Matthew VAUGHAN dec'd, James VAUGHAN, and Hudson VAUGHAN, Jack VAUGHAN, Washington VAUGHAN, and Matilda VAUGHAN by the sd. James VAUGHAN their gdn. assigned to defend them in this suit, Elis S. PEERS, John BASS and Nancy his wife, Philip RICE and Patsey his wife, Ambrose KNIGHT and Arpasia his wife, which sd. James, Hudson, Jack, Washington, Matilda, Elizabeth, Nancy, Patsey, and Arpasia are chil. and with the pltfs. Clarissa and Mary, co-heirs of the sd. Matthew VAUGHAN dec'd (defs); it appears that Philip and Patsey RICE are not inhabitants of this country (Arg 14 May 99)
VAUGHAN, Abraham, dec'd, his est. committed to the care of the sheriff of Charlotte Co. (VGPI 16 May 97)
VAUGHAN, James, c. 23, des. from the College Camp, enl. in Amherst in the 6th Va. Regt. (VGPu 5 Jul 76 ps)
VAUGHAN, James Jr., formerly of Richmond, d. by a fall from a horse at Amelia Ct. H. on Sat. eve. last (RMA 4 Jun 95, RC 6 Jun 95)
VAUGHAN, Philip, svt., 27, claims to have a brother in Va., ran away from the Baltimore Iron Works, Md. (VGR 1 Jun 69)
VAUGHAN, Salathial, dec'd, e.a.w. his ex., Peter VAUGHAN of Dinwiddie Co. (VGAA 14 Sep 82)
VAUGHAN, William, of New Kent Co., the slaves now in his possession are entailed on his eld. son, James VAUGHAN (VG 27 Mar 46)
VAULX, Robert, of Westmoreland Co., dec'd, his ex., John BUSHRODE and Augustine WASHINGTON, adv. his slaves for sale (VG 22 Aug 55)
VAUTERS, David, formerly a deputy commissary to Col. BARBER, is absent without leave from the co. of Capt. John CAMP (VGPu 4 Apr 77)
VAUX, Mr., killed along with members of his family by Indians at a fort on Holston's River in Augusta Co. (Wmsbrg. disp. of 9 Jul.) (MG 29 Jul 56)

VEALE, Samuel Esq., dec'd, e.a.w. James HARPER of Portsmouth (HNPA 29 Oct 95, NH 2 Jan 96); the gdn. to his orphan is A. SLAUGHTER who will lease his plant. near Portsmouth (HNPA 2 Nov 95); his children's gdns. are pressing his ex., James HARPER of Norfolk, for money (NHPA 2 Nov 97)
VEALE, Thomas, dec'd, part of his est. on the Southern Branch about five miles from Portsmouth to be sold by his ex., Samuel VEALE, James CANN, Wm. C. VEALE, and Thomas VEALE (VCNPGA 21 Dec 93)
VEALE, Thomas Esq., mar. Miss Polly PICKETT dau. of Capt. PICKETT of Portsmouth, in that city, last week (NH 1 Jan 99)
VEALL Family, HCC, 13 May 1793: Rich. Evers LEE and Paul PROBEY acting ex. of Rich. TAYLOR dec'd, and Rich. BAILY and [?] admr. of Mary his late wife which sd. Richard and Mary are legatees in the will named of the sd. Rich. TAYLOR (pltfs.) and Samuel VEALL, Demse VEALL, Wm. VEALL, Nancy VEALL, and Paul Dale LUKE and Sally his wife, which sd. Samuel, Demse, Wm., Nancy, and Sally are co-heirs and the sd. Paul Dale LUKE is admr. de bonis non of Demse VEALL dec'd by Elizabeth his late wife (defs.) (VGWeA 16 Aug 93)
VENABLE, Miss Fanny, of Pr. Edw. Co., d. at the Rising Sun Tavern on Sat. last on her return from a tour of the lower parts of this state for the recovery of her health (VGGA 14 Jun 99)
VENTUS, Joshua, dec'd, e.a.w. his admx., Mary VENTUS of Portsmouth (NHPA 1 Feb 98)
VERMONNET, Maj., of Washington City, mar. Mrs. Jane BRADFORD relict of the late Maj. BRADFORD of this co. [Spotsylvania], lately in Albemarle Co. (VHFFA 7 Oct 96)
VERNON, Abner, of Stafford Co., drowned on Wed. eve. last while attempting to ford the Rappahannock (VHFA 13 Dec 92, VGGA 19 Dec 92); drowned on 5 Dec.; his body was not found until 13 Feb. (VHFA 21 Feb 93); e.a.w. his admr., John STRODE of Culpeper Co. (VHFA 5 Dec 93)
VERNON, John, aka John, mulatto, 28, ran away from Byrd CHAMBERLAYNE, Kg. Wm. Co. (VGGA 8 Jun 96, NH 18 Jun 96)
VEST, James, son and heir of John VEST dec'd, of Buckingham Co., summoned to ct. (VG 5 Nov 72 sup)
VEST, John, appr., c. 14, ran away from Luman BISHOP, Manchester; he is supposed to be in Buckingham Co. with a relation, Rainy CHASTEEN (RMA 20 Aug 95)
VICKERY, Mrs., wife of Capt. Eli VICKERY, d. on Tues. last (NH 13 Dec 98)
VIGNON, Louis, of Louis Vignon & Co., tin and coppersmiths from Paris who have opened a manufactory in Norfolk (HNPA 8 Aug 95)
VINCENT, William, only surviving son of Abraham VINCENT of Dublin, woolen draper; he left Eng. as steward of a man of war and is now supposed to reside in Va.; news of him is sought (NYM 21 Jun 62)
VINTJOLE, Mingo, Irish, speaks bad Eng., bad French, and bad Spanish, des. from Capt, De CLOVAY's Co. in the French Regt. at Wmsbrg. (VG 6 Jun 77)
VIOLET, Thomas, appr. saddler, has run away from Wm. SHOPE, Charlestown (PGBA 28 Dec 97)
VIOLET, William, of Berkeley Co., reportedly killed his [son]-in-law on 2 Sep. (SS 12 Oct 93)
Virginia Troops killed in action on the banks of Monongahela on 9 Jul. unde Gen. BRADDOCK: Capt. POLSON, Capt. PERONIE, Lt. HAMILTON, Lt. WRIGHT, Lt. SPLITDORFF, Mr. McNEAL (a wagoner) (NYPB [11 Aug 55])
VLIN, Samuel, svt., ran away from Wm. WALKER, Westmoreland Co. (VG 6 Jul 39)
VOBE, Mrs. Jane, dec'd, her acting ex., David MILLER, Osborne's, will sell her PE (VIC 5 Aug 89)
VOSS, Lt. Edward, one of the officers of the co. of artillery stationed at Norfolk, d. on Tues. last in Petersburg (HNPA 31 Aug 95, VHFA 4 Sep 95)
VOWLES, Mrs., cons. of Capt. H. VOWLES, d. lately in Staff. Co. (VH 9 Oct 98)

VOWLES, Capt. Walter, of the 1st Regt. of Va. Troops, died (VGPu 11 Jul 77); e.a.w. his admr., Thomas VOWLES of Falmouth (VGPu 28 Nov 77)

WADDELL, Elizabeth, has eloped from her husband, John WADDELL of Fauquier Co., and run off with Geo. LINTON (VGR 12 May 68)

WADDELL, James G., of Louisa Co., mar. Miss Lucy G. GORDON dau. of James GORDON, on Thurs. last at Germanna (VHFFA 11 Jul 97)

WADDILL, William, goldsmith, mar. Miss A. EVANS of this city [Richmond] (VGAA 6 Dec 86, VGIC 9 Dec 86)

WADDRINGTON, Dr., of Georgetown, Md., was mar. to Miss Betsy BOOTH in Wmsbrg. on Thurs. last by the Rev. John BRACKEN (VGWeA 21 Feb 88)

WADE Family, HCC, 1 Jun. 1789: Benj. WADE, Joseph WADE, Elizabeth WADE widow, relict and extx. of Henry WADE dec'd, Andrew WADE and Martha WADE widow, relict, and extx. of William WADE dec'd, which sd. Benj., Joseph, Henry, Andrew, and William were sons of Andrew WADE dec'd (pltfs.) against William ROBERTSON ex. of Andrew WADE dec'd (def.) (VGGA 27 Oct 90)

WADE, Edmund, late of Hanover Co., dec'd, e.a.w. his ex., Charles TALLEY of Buckingham Co. (VGGA 26 Sep 92)

WADE, Capt. Edward, of Halifax Co., dec'd, late lt. to Capt. COCKE's Co. of the 6th Bn. of Va. forces, e.a.w. his ex., Samuel PERRIN (VG and VGPu 11 Oct 76); his ex. will sell his PE at his late plant. near Bond's Ferry on Staunton River in Halifax Co. (VGPu 25 Sep 77)

WADE, Edward, mar. Elizabeth THURMON originally of Hanover Co.; they recollect when Hanover was the frontier of Va.; they began their courtship about 50 or 60 yrs. ago and were not mar. until the 27th ult. (VGWeA 10 Sep 89)

WADE, Hampton, of Halifax Co., dec'd, kept stores in Amelia, Lunenburg, and Halifax Cos., accounts to be paid to Edward WADE (nfi); his admrs. are John BAIRD and Wm. STOKES (VG 5 Feb 67); his plant. on the Dan River to be sold by his admr. (VG 2 Nov 69)

WADE, Jacob, of Bedford Co., adv. that his wife, Anney WADE, absconded with a certain Edmund DOWDY on 16 Oct.; they were seen in Pittsylvania Co. on the 18th; she has forfeited his confidence in her as a wife (LFG 1 Nov 94)

WADE, Robert Jr., dec'd, several large tracts of his land in Pittsylvania and Halifax Cos. to be sold by his ex., Wm. STOKES (VG 5 May 68)

WAGENER, Peter, att. and only son of the Rev. and Worshipful Peter WAGENER Esq. of the co. of Essex in Eng. mar. Miss Katy ROBINSON only dau. of the Hon. John ROBINSON Esq. one of H.M's Council, at Piscataqua, Essex Co. [Va.?], on 5 Jul. (VG 20 Jul 39)

WAGENER, Col. Peter, Clerk of the Fairfax Co. Ct., d. in Colchester on Sat. morn. last in his 58th year [obit.] (TAA 30 Apr 98); e.a.w. his ex., G. DENEALE, who will also rent for 10 yrs. the noted stand in Colchester called "The Stone Ordinary" and several lots adjoining (TAA 23 Oct 98, CMAG 27 Oct 98)

WAGER, William, of Elizabeth City Co., dec'd, e.a.w. his admr., Geo. BOOKER (VGAA 23 Apr 85)

WAGGONER Family, Berkeley Co. Ct., 28 Aug. 1795, in chanc: Wm. WILSON admr. of John WILSON dec'd (compl.) versus Mary Barbara WAGGONER widow, Abraham WAGGONER, Elizabeth WAGGONER, Jacob WAGGONER, John WAGGONER, Joseph WAGGONER, Catharine WAGGONER, Mary WAGGONER, and F[....] WAGGONER children and heirs of Christopher WAGGONER dec'd (defs.) (PGBA 16 Nov 95)

WAGSTAFF, John, c. 20, enl. near York[town], des. from Capt. Thomas NELSON's Co. of regulars of the 1st Va. Regt., Trenton, N.J., on 4 Dec. 1776 (VGPu 17 Jan 77)

WAIDE, William, dec'd, a tract of land bel. to his est. near Hanover Town to be sold at Kg. Wm. Ct. H. by his ex., John HICKMAN (VGAA 10 May 86)

WAIN, Joseph, Eng. svt., imp. last Whitsun from London, b. in Bucknell, Oxfordshire, 22, ran away from John MERCER, Stafford Co.; may be making for Carolina (VG 13 Jun 66)

WAITE, Mrs. Jane, dec'd, e.a.w. Richard E. BEALE, Fauquier Co. (VHFA 26 Feb 95)

WAITE, Obed, of Winchester, mar. Miss Mary Anne HARRISON dau. of Matthew HARRISON of Loudoun Co., last Thurs. (BVCG 3 Mar 94)

WAKER, Randolph, native of Va., des. from the state troops at Wmsbrg.; it is supposed he will go to Buckingham Co. to his father (VG 3 Oct 77)

WALDEN, Charles, of Caroline Co., dec'd, his ex., John and Charles WALDEN, will sell tracts of his land on the Mattaponi River; his widow is to have part of the tract in Kg. Wm. Co. for life (VG and VGR 31 Jan 71)

WALDEN, Charles, dec'd, his ex., John WALDEN, will sell a lease of 300 ac. of land about three miles from Falmouth in Stafford Co. for 23 yrs. and also settle his est. (VG 6 Nov 78)

WALDEN, John, late of Caroline Co., dec'd, his ex., John TAYLOR, will sell his 500 ac. tract (VGGA 26 Nov 94)

WALDEN, Lewis, dec'd, e.a.w. his admr., John WALDEN of Caroline Co. (Ex 29 Mar 99)

WALKE, Anthony, son of Anthony WALKE late of Appomattox, absconded from Balfour & Barraud, Norfolk (VG 10 Nov 68)

WALKE, Anthony, dec'd, e.a.w. his ex., Anthony WALKE, John LAWRENCE, and Alexander MOSELEY of Pr. Anne Co. (VGWeA 22 Jun 82)

WALKE, Anthony Sr. Esq., d. on the 18th ult. in his 76th year [long letter about him] (VG 29 Dec 68)

WALKE, Anthony Sr. Esq., of Pr. Anne Co., died (VG 13 Nov 79)

WALKE, John, second son of Anthony WALKE Esq., of Pr. Anne Co., died (VGNI 16 Aug 75)

WALKE, Mary, dec'd, e.a.w. her admr., Wm. BOUSH of Pr. Anne (NH 16 Jun 96)

WALKE, Mrs. Mary, relict of the late William WALKE Esq. of Pr. Anne Co., d. on Wed. eve.; e.a.w. her admr., Cornelius CALVERT Sr., Norfolk (NH 22 Sep 98, 6 Oct 98)

WALKE, Col. Thomas, commandant of Pr. Anne Co., d. on Tues. last (NHPA 6 Apr 97); his admr. w.w.a., James ROBINSON of Pr. Anne Co., will sell the remainder of his personal property (NH 17 Mar 98)

WALKE, William, dec'd, his widow, Mary WALKE Jr. [sic] of Pr. Anne Co., has appointed her father, Cornelius CALVERT Sr., her agent to settle her late husband's est. (HNPA 15 Aug 95); his extx., Mary WALKE, will rent or lease his plant. on a branch of Lynnhaven River in Pr. Anne Co. (NH 2 Jan 96); e.a.w. his admr., Cornelius CALVERT Sr. of Norfolk (NH 6 Oct 98)

WALKER Family, HCC, 4 Jun. 1791: Mary WALKER admx. de bonis non of John WALKER dec'd and John WALKER, Francis WALKER, and Edmund WALKER children of the sd. John WALKER dec'd (pltfs.) against Thomas SIMPSON admr. of John WALKER dec'd, Archibald GOVAN, Geo. LUMSDEN, and James GOVAN (defs.); it appears that Archibald GOVAN and Thos. SIMPSON are not inhabitants of this country (VGPA 5 Nov 91)

WALKER, [?], Eng. conv. svt., carpenter and joiner, 35-36, often uses the words "in regard to that," ran away from John WORMELEY at Mr. GRIFFIN's in Lancaster Co. (VG 12 Aug 75)

WALKER, Mrs., wife of Hugh WALKER of Culpeper Co., was struck by lightning but is recovering (VHFA 18 Sep 88)

WALKER, Adam, ind. shoemaker, c. 21, ran away from Wm. Forsyth & Co., Portsmouth (VG 5 Mar 72)

WALKER, Benjamin, attorney, of Caroline Co., d. last Mon. sennight (VG 8 Sep 38); his est. to be auctioned on 19 Nov. (VG 9 Nov 39)

WALKER, Mrs. Dorothy, relict of the late Robert WALKER of Fredsbrg., d. there (VHFFA 11 Apr 97)

WALKER, Elijah, member of the mounted infantry for the Mero District

[Tennessee] was reportedly killed by Indians on 5 Jan. (VGGA 25 Feb 95)
WALKER, G., of Elizabeth City Co., intends to move to Brunswick Co. (VGR 12 May 68)
WALKER, George, of Brunswick Co., dec'd, e.a.w. his ex. David MEADE, Wm. WITHERS, and Andrew MEADE (VGGA 7 Dec 82, VGPI 9 Feb 96)
WALKER, George, intends for Scotland immediately; he will sell the house and lots of Wm. WALKER in Port Royal (VGGA 25 Apr 92)
WALKER, Col. James, late of Pittsylvania Co., dec'd, his admr., Thomas GORDON, will sell all his PE except the Negroes (VG 7 Nov 77)
WALKER, James, watch and clockmaker, has opened shop in the house formerly occupied by his father, Thomas WALKER, in Fredsbrg. (VHFA 19 May 91)
WALKER, James, hatter, native of Ireland, resident of Winchester for 25 years, d. on Fri. last (WG 26 Jun 99); his PE to be sold by his admrs., Joseph GAMBLE and John BRADY, and his admx., Rachael WALKER (WG 17 Jul 99)
WALKER, Jean, dau. of William WALKER in the old town of Aberdeen, Scotland; she came to Va. about 50 yrs. ago; John DAVIDSON, cooper at Falmouth, and James DAVIDSON, cooper at Milner's in Nansemond Co., came to Va. three yrs. ago to seek her; they have been unsuccessful (VG 5 May 68)
WALKER, John, of Urbanna, dec'd, his est. to be auctioned (VG 18 Apr 45)
WALKER, Dr. John, of Hanover Co., d. suddenly while from home (VG 10 Mar 74); e.a.w. his admr., Thomas SIMPSON (VG and VGR 14 Apr 74); 15 of his slaves will be sold at Hanover Ct. H. by his admr. (VG 14 Jul 74); his admr. will sell a complete set of shop utensils, surgeon, and midwifery instruments at Hanover Town (VGPu 12 May 75, VGP 1 Jun 75); his land in Hanover Co. to be sold by Mary WALKER (nfi) (VGAA 20 Apr 83)
WALKER, John, dec'd, his house in Urbanna to be sold by his ex., Christopher ROBINSON, Alex. FRAZIER, and Wm. TALIAFERRO (VG 9 May 45)
WALKER, John, of Fauquier Co., adv. that his [son], Wm. WALKER, eloped from him since 14 Dec. last (VGPu 23 May 77)
WALKER, John, late of Washington Par., Westmoreland Co., teacher (VGAA 21 May 85)
WALKER, John, appr., 15-16, ran away from the brig *Frances* [at Norfolk] (NHPA 27 Mar 97)
WALKER, Lucy, dau. of the late Thomas WALKER, d. in this town [Fredsbrg.] on Sat. last, aged 19 (VH 23 Apr 99)
WALKER, Ned, aka Walker, Negro, bred in Westmoreland Co., purchased three yrs. ago from Mr. HUTT of Charlestown, ran away from Wm. RIDDLE living in Martinsburg (BI 11 Dec 99)
WALKER, Capt. Robert, of Charles City, late in the London trade, mar. Miss Susan HARRISON of Wakefield, Surry Co. (VG 2 Jun 74)
WALKER, Robert, native of Scotland who resided in T[oe]ks in the Par. of Dunotter in that country until his departure for this colony which was about 44 or 45 yrs. ago and the only accounts his friends received concerning him, lives on Rappahannock River; if he se still living, he may by applying to the printer hear of something greatly to his advantage (VGP 13 Jul 75)
WALKER, Capt. Robert, of Charles City Co., dec'd, e.a.w. Stith HARDYMAN who is authorized by the extx., Susannah WALKER (VGAA 16 Mar 82, 17 May 83)
WALKER, Robert, of K & Q Co., mar. Miss Nancy F. POWELL of Amherst Co., on Tues. the 1st inst. (VGGA 23 May 92)
WALKER, Robert, dec'd, his admr., David BRIGGS, will sell his PE (VHFFA 9 Aug 96)
WALKER, Robert, of Kingston, Dinwiddie Co., d. on Thurs. night 19 Oct. in his 69th year [long obit.]; he left a widow and 10 chil. (VGPI 27 Oct 97)
WALKER, Robert, Surveyor of the Port at City Point and principal clerk in the Collector's Office for six years, d. on Thurs. eve. last in his 24th year (VGGA

18th-Century Virginia Newspapers 353

2 Oct 98, VH 12 Oct 98, LWG 13 Oct 98)
WALKER, Robert Sr., d. yesterday in an advanced age (VHFA 16 Oct 95)
WALKER, Dr. Thomas, d. at Castle Hill on 7 Nov. in his 81st year (VGGA 12 Nov 94)
WALKER, Thomas Esq., late agent for the Royal Co., died (VGGA 15 Apr 95)
WALKER, Thomas, of Richmond, tailor, d. last night after an illness of only two days (RC and RMA 25 Jun 96)
WALKER, Maj. William, late of Stafford Co., dec'd, e.a.w. Col. Nathaniel HARRISON of Stafford (VG 17 Oct 51)
WALKER, William, aka SMITH, svt., gardener, came in the *Scarsdale* in 1771, ran away from Rich. LEE, Westmoreland Co. (VG 8 Jul 73, VGR 22 Jul 73 sup); escaped from custody in Essex Co. (VG 19 Aug 73)
WALKER, William, of Brunswick Co., dec'd, e.a.w. his ex., Benj. JONES (VGPI 22 Sep 97)
WALKINSHAW, James, of Nansemond Co., intends to leave the colony soon (VG 4 Nov 63)
WALL, Benjamin, of Southampton Co., des. from Capt. Nathaniel FOX's Co. of the 6th Va. Regt. (VGPu 2 May 77)
WALL, James, svt., b. in London, 19, ran away from John James HULETT, James City Co. (VG 15 Aug 55)
WALL, Capt. James Sr., dec'd, his ex., James WALL, Seymour POWELL and James MASON, will lease his plant. and houses in Brunswick Co. near Hick's Ford (VG 26 Dec 77)
WALL, John, planter, b. in Northampton, N. Carolina, 22, des. from Capt. Robert HODGSON's Independent Co. now raising for the service and defense of S. Carolina (VG 3 Jul 46)
WALL, Robert, b. in Brunswick Co., Va., c. 21, on 25 Jul. he stole about 1400 pistoles and £150 from Edward LANGFORD at the house of Mrs. Mary BRADOCK [or BRADDICK acc. to NYM] in New London, Connecticut (NYPB and NYM 30 Jul 53)
WALL, Susanna, her husband, William WALL of Portsmouth, will not pay any of her debts (NH 1 Aug 99)
WALLACE, Mr., drowned in the river while crossing from Gosport on Tues. (HNPA 21 Mar 95)
WALLACE, Capt. Antonio, of this borough [Norfolk], d. on Thurs. last (NHPA 21 Aug 97); e.a.w. his admx., Elizabeth WALLACE of Norfolk (NH 3 Mar 98); F. S. HARRISON of Norfolk is appointed agent to settle his est. (NH 23 Oct 98)
WALLACE, Dr. James, late surgeon of Col. BAYLOR's Regt. of Cavalry of Va., d. in Jacksonborough, S. Carolina on 12 Dec. 1790 in his 35th year (VHFA 27 Jan 91)
WALLACE, Joseph Dunstan, of James City Co., adv. that his wife, Jeane Dunstan WALLACE, has eloped from him and endeavors to involve him in debt and he will no longer pay any of her debts but if she will return to him she shall be cordially received and all former animosities shall be forgot (VGWeA 12 May 91)
WALLACE, William, from Berkeley Co., executed for murder on the 9th inst. (VG 16 May 77)
WALLER, Hardress, of Norfolk Co., dec'd, e.a.w. Ann WALLER (nfi) (VGAA 15 Jun 82)
WALLER, John, appr., c. 15, ran away from Thomas LLEWELLIN (VG 19 Mar 72)
WALLER, John Esq., Clerk of Spotsylvania Co., mar. Miss Judith PAGE of Hanover Co. (VG 24 Nov 74)
WALLER, John, Eng., 26, des. from the 1st U.S. Regt. (WG 23 Jan 99)
WALLER, Joseph, Eng., 26, printer, des. from the 1st U.S. Regt., Charlottesville (VH 29 Jan 99) [NB. the above John and Joseph may be the same person.]
WALLER, Robert Esq., of Wmsbrg., mar. Miss Nancy CAMM dau. of the late

John CAMM of York Co. President of William and Mary College, lately in Poquoson, York Co. (VIC 18 Mar 89, VGWeA 19 Mar 89)
WALLER, Robert Esq., dec'd, A. SLAUGHTER gdn. of Robert and Edward HICKS grandchildren of the sd. WALLER will sell a valuable plant. at Great Bridge (NH 3 Dec 99)
WALLER, Thomas, carpenter from Yorkshire, ran away from Col. A[lexander] SPOTSWOOD's works (AWM 25 Oct 33)
WALLER, William, merch., mar. Miss Sally MACON of Hanover Co., last Tues. (VIC 6 Dec 86, VGIC 9 Dec 86)
WALLER, William, dec'd, his admx., Elizabeth WALLER of Bellefield near Yorktown, will sell a considerable part of his PE; e.a.w. Col. William Hartwell MACON of New Kent Co. or Robert H. WALLER of Wmsbrg. (Ex 12 Apr 99)
WALROND, Benjamin, Thomas MULLIN adv. that he is informed that WALROND has removed to Halifax Co. in Va. and that if he does not apply to MULLIN in New Kent Co. in a short time...for the money due him on account of his wife, that he shall think himself under no obligation to pay any interest on the sd. money (VGPu 3 Apr 78)
WALROND, William, dec'd, a large tract bel. to him in Louisa Co. and a smaller tract in Kg. Wm. Co. to be sold pursuant to his will by his ex., John QUARLES, at Kg. Wm. court in May (VG 24 Apr 52)
WALSH, Richard, Irish svt., c. 22, ran away from Wm. FLEM[M]ING, Cumberland Co., he may have run away with a Scottish svt. named Mary TANKER (VG 19 Jul 70)
WALSOM, Thomas, conv. barber, c. 27, ran away from James KIRK, Robert ADAM, and Geo. PURVIS, Alexandria (VG 17 Jun 75)
WALSTON, Samuel, appr., 18, ran away from Leven DORSEY, mathematical instrument maker, Norfolk (NH 17 Oct 96)
WALTER, Jacob, German ind. svt., baker, c. 22, ran away from Diederick SHECKEL, baker, Alexandria (VGAxA 13 Jan 91)
WALTERS, Sarah, has eloped from her husband, Rich. C. WALTERS, Yorktown (VGGA 31 Oct 92)
WALTHAL, Branch, adv. that his wife, Mary Patterson WALTHAL [also given as Mary Peterson], eloped from him on the 19th [of Jun. ?] (VGPI 23 Jun 95, VSPW 2 Jul 95)
WALTHOE, Nathaniel Esq., of Wmsbrg., d. on 23 Aug.; he was educated at Oxford and was for many yrs. clerk to H.M's Privy Council of this colony (VGR 23 Aug 70); e.a.w. his ex., Henry WALLER (VG 1 Nov 70); his ex., Benjamin WALLER [sic], will sell his wearing apparel in Wmsbrg. (VG 16 Mar 71)
WALTON, Col., of Isle of Wight Co., d. suddenly (VG 26 Oct 39)
WALTON, Capt. George, of the 1st Bn. of Georgia troops, d. in his 20th year at Col. HARRIS' near Savannah (VGPu 31 Oct 77)
WALTON, John B., mar. Mrs. Nancy BAGNOIS both of Richmond, on Tues. last (RMA 8 Oct 96)
WALTON, Robert, late of Cumberland Co., dec'd, e.a.w. his ex., Geo. WALTON (VG 26 Mar 72)
WALTON, Thomas, Eng. conv., from Yorkshire, 28, ran away from Edw. STEVENSON, Little Pipe Cr., Frederick Co., Md. (VG 11 Jun 67)
WALTON, William, lately arrived from Va., d. on Sat. last at Kensington Gore, Eng. (London disp. of 15 Nov.) (PC 17 Jan 74)
WAMOCK, Pleasant, appr. tailor, 16-17, ran away from John KEY, Petersburg (VGPI 30 May 97)
WANING, Henry, mar. Miss Nancy EDWARDS last eve., both of this town (VGPI 28 Dec 86)
WANNUNBURG, Frederick, Dutch ind. svt., 24-25, ran away from Isaac M'PHERSON, Alexandria (VGAxA 11 Jul 93)
WAR, Peter, Negro, bel. to Garnet BURLEY, Orange Co., jailed in Frederick Co. (VGAA 30 Jul 85)

18th-Century Virginia Newspapers 355

WARBURTON, Maj. John, lately mar. Miss Betsey HARRIS, both of James City Co. (VGAA 26 Jun 84)

WARD, Benjamin, late of Chesterfield Co., dec'd, e.a.w. his ex., Joseph EGGLESTON, Stephen COCKE, and Daniel HARDAWAY of Amelia (VGIC 15 Nov 83)

WARD, Betsey, five year old dau. of Abigail WARD widow of Samuel WARD of Guilford, was burned to death on Tues. eve. last while her mother was on a visit to Massachusetts (WG 6 Nov 99)

WARD, Christopher, svt., from Yorkshire, shoemaker, ran away from Maj. Rich. RANDOLPH, Henrico Co. (AWM 31 Oct 34, MG 1 Nov 34)

WARD, Capt. Edward, of Halifax Co., dec'd, his ex. (nfi) will sell his PE (VG 19 Sep 77)

WARD, George, Eng. svt., 22, ran away from Anderson & Jamieson, Alexandria last Sun; may be going to Baltimore (VHFA 5 Jun 88)

WARD, Capt. James, of Fredsbrg., dec'd, e.a.w. his admx., Jane WARD (VGAA 31 Jul 84); his admx. will sell several of his Negroes at Fredsbrg. (VHFA 6 Sep 87)

WARD, James, 25, des. from the 3rd U.S. Regt. near Alexandria (VGAR 12 Jul 92)

WARD, Leonard, dec'd, his ex., Rich. EG[G]LESTON[E] [Sr.] and Wm. WALKER, will sell his est. in Chesterfield Co. (VG 27 Oct 74); his ex. will sell sundry Negroes and stock (VGPu 18 Oct 76)

WARD, Littleton Dunmore, appr., ran away from Alex. McFARLANE, Portsmouth (VCGA 28 Jul 94)

WARD, Seth, of Chesterfield Co., dec'd, his PE to be sold by his ex. (nfi) (VGAA 11 Dec 84)

WARD, Seth, of Chesterfield Co., mar. Miss Patsey NORVELL of Hanover Co. on Thurs. eve. last (RMA 6 Feb 96)

WARD, William, seaman, b. in Dublin, des. from the ship *Neptune* of Boston (AGNPWA 27 Mar 93)

WARD, William, dec'd, e.a.w. his extx., Cicely WARD of Alexandria, who will sell all of his PE (CMAG 21 Aug 94)

WARDEN, Amos, mulatto son of Abraham WARDEN of Pr. Wm. Co., was carried of by Henry GRYMES (VHFA 10 Sep 89)

WARDEN, George, appr. boy, ran away from Geo. BILLUPS, Norfolk (NH 4 Jul 99)

WARDEN, Jesse, des. from on board the *Muskito* cruiser at Warwick; it is believed he is harbored by his relations in Henrico or Hanover Co. as he has been an inhabitant of those cos. (VGPu 13 Sep 76)

WARDEN, Timothy, appr., c. 16, ran away from Geo. KIGER, Winchester (BVCG 8 Jul 93)

WARDROP, Mrs., native of Scotland, now of Ampthill near Richmond, d. on Tues. the 10th inst. (VGRC 13 Sep 93)

WARDROP, Daniel, merch., of Manchester, d. on Thurs. last in his 26th year; he was bur. at Ampthill the seat of his brother, James WARDROP Esq. (VGGA 23 Feb 91)

WARE, John, of K & Q Co., d. in his 52nd year (VG 2 Apr 79)

WARE, John, of K & Q Co., d. in March last (VGGA 19 Jun 93)

WARE, Spencer, orphan, his gdn. is Robert WARE of K & Q Co. (NPC 19 Mar 91)

WARING, Master Lawson, son of Wm. WARING of Essex Co., d. on Sun. last in Fredsbrg. (RCFPC 25 Jan 97)

[WARLMAN], Daniel, svt., 46, ran away from Wm. FITZPATRICK in the forks of [Hardware] River, Albemarle Co. (VG 12 Mar 52)

WARNER, Thomas, schoolmaster who served his time in the lower parts of Va., pretends to be a watchmaker; he came to Darby, Pa. in June 1733 where he kept school; he got a woman with child and had to marry her about 29 May; he has run away abandoning his wife and child (Pennsylvania Gazette 13 Jun 34)

WARREN Family, Norfolk Borough, Ct. of Q. S., 25 Au. 1796, in chanc: Wilson WARREN, Toulson WARREN, Susannah WARREN, and Polly WARREN by James WARREN their father and next friend (compls.) against Bennett BOGGESS, Robert BOGGESS, Ann BOGGESS, and Ruth MORRIS (defs.) (AGGA 22 Nov 96)

WARREN Family, Brunswick Co. Ct., Mar 1799, in chanc: Frederick LANIER and Tempy his wife (formerly Tempy WARREN) widow and relict of Benj. WARREN dec'd (compl.) against James and Hartwell BASS exors of Benj. WARREN Jr. and Martha JACKSON (formerly Martha WARREN), Wm. OGBORNE and Hannah his wife (formerly Hannah WARREN), Henry HYDE and Rebecca his wife (formerly Rebecca WARREN), Ferrel HARPER and Ritter his wife (formerly Ritter WARREN), Elizabeth LASHLEY (formerly Elizabeth WARREN), Marriott WARREN, Wm. MITCHELL Jr. and Elizabeth his wife, John WARREN, Wm. WARREN, and Thomas WARREN (defs.) (VGPI 18 Jun 99)

WARREN, Christopher, Irish svt., weaver, 35, ran away from Geo. SELL, Frederick Co., Md. (VGPu 8 Mar 76)

WARREN, Mrs. Frances, wife of John WARREN, d. in Norfolk Borough on Sat. morn. last (NH 15 Jun 99)

WARREN, John, formerly of Snow Hill, Md., d. in Fredsbrg. on Tues. last (VHFA 19 Jun 95); his admr., John BROWNLOW, will sell his personal property (VHFA 28 Jul 95)

WARREN, Miss Nancy, of New Kent Co., [dec'd], an elegy on her death (VGP 21 Sep 75)

WARREN, Thomas, of Richmond, dec'd, his admr. (nfi) will sell his entire est. (VGGA 16 Jan 93) and will hire out his slaves in Richmond (VGGA 1 Jan 94)

WARRICKER, William, Eng. svt., c. 25, ran away from John HOOD, Elk Ridge, Anne Arundel Co., Md. (VGR 27 Sep 70)

WARRINGTON, Mrs., wife of the Rev. Mr. Thomas WARRINGTON, was found dead by one of her daus. (VG 13 Apr 69)

WARROCK, W., jeweller, mar. Miss Mary CROANE of this borough [Norfolk], on Sat. last (HNPA 9 Nov 95)

WARTON, Thomas, conv. svt., b. at Hackney near London, 18, ran away from A. HAMILTON, Gloucester Co. (VG 9 Apr 72)

WARWICK, Jacob, of Surry Co., mulatto, 25, enl. by Geo. MACKENZIE, has not reported to camp in Wmsbrg. (VG 31 Jul, 14 Aug 46)

WARWICK, Joseph, formerly skipper of a vessel and is commonly about Hobb's Hole, is absent without leave from the co. of Capt. John CAMP (VGPu 4 Apr 77)

WASHERS, Betty, ran away from Thomas WHITE (TAA 7 Jun 98)

WASHINGTON Family, HCC, 18 May 1793: John TINSLEY and Anne his wife which sd. Anne was the widow of Henry WASHINGTON dec'd and is now extx. of his will and James QUARLES ex. (pltfs.) and Nathaniel WASHINGTON and Frances Maria WASHINGTON and Anne Catharine WASHINGTON infants under 21 by Robert QUARLES their gdn. (defs.); it appears that Nathaniel WASHINGTON is not an inhabitant of this country (VGRC 30 Aug 93)

WASHINGTON, Mrs., wife of Col. Samuel WASHINGTON, d. lately in Berkeley Co. of smallpox by inoculation (MJ 14 Apr 77)

WASHINGTON, Mrs. Anne, dec'd, her ex., Burditt ASHTON, will sell her PE at her plant. on Pope's Cr. (VGR 2 Jun 74)

WASHINGTON, Miss Betty, of Gloucester Co., dau. of Maj. John WASHINGTON, d. there lately (VG 25 Feb 37)

WASHINGTON, Corbin Esq., of Fairfax Co., only surviving brother of Judge WASHINGTON and a nephew of the late Gen. George WASHINGTON, d. on the 10th inst. at Bushfield, Westmoreland Co. (TDCDA 20 Dec 99)

WASHINGTON, Gen. George, d. in Alexandria on Sat. eve., the 14th, about 11 o'clock (TDCDA 16, 20 Dec 99, VF 18 Dec 99, NH 19 Dec 99, Arg 20 Dec 99, V

21 Dec 99, Ex 20, 24 Dec 99, CMAG 24 Dec 99, BI 25 Dec 99)
WASHINGTON, Maj. George Augustine, of Mount Vernon, d. at the seat of the late Col. BASSET in New Kent Co. (VHFA 28 Feb 93)
WASHINGTON, John Esq., of Liberty, died (VGAA 5 Apr 86)
WASHINGTON, Mrs. Lucy, dau. of the late Nathan CHAPMAN and wife of Samuel WASHINGTON, d. in Alexandria last night [6 Aug.] (MG 19 Aug 62)
WASHINGTON, Mrs. Mary, mother of President George WASHINGTON, d. at her home in Fredsbrg. on the 25th ult., aged 82 [obit.] (VGWA 2 Sep 89, VGWeA 3 Sep 89); her livestock to be sold at the plant. four miles below Fredsbrg. (VHFA 22 Oct 89)
WASHINGTON, Mrs. Mary, consort of William A. WASHINGTON and eld. dau. of Richard Henry LEE Esq. dec'd, d. at Harwood [also given as Haywood] on the 2nd inst., aged 30 (VHFFA 24 Nov 95, RC 28 Nov 95)
WASHINGTON, Samuel Esq., of Berkeley Co., dec'd, items of his est. to be sold by his ex., John A. WASHINGTON, Charles WASHINGTON, and James NOURSE (VGAA 14 Sep 82)
WASHINGTON, Thacker, dec'd, his ex., Wm. P. FLOOD, will sell 40-50 Negroes, hogs, 60-70 head of sheep, other livestock, and plant. utensils and will rent out the rock and herring fisheries bel. to his est. in Kg. Geo. Co. (VH 2 Nov 98, CMAG 6 Nov 98)
WASHINGTON, Thomas, Brunswick Co. Ct., 29 Mar 1796, in chanc: Sarah WASHINGTON admx. of Thomas WASHINGTON dec'd (compl.) against Geo. WALTON and Joseph BENNITT (defs.); it appears that BENNITT is not an inhabitant of the commonwealth (VGPI 8 Nov 96)
WASHINGTON, Warner, of Frederick Co., mar. Miss Mary WHITING dau. of Francis WHITING of Gloucester Co. on Thurs. the 18th [ult.] (VGR 1 Nov 70)
WASHINGTON, Capt. William, of Westmoreland Co., dec'd, his ex., John WASHINGTON of Caroline Co., will sell 20 of his slaves (VHFA 31 Jan 93)
WASHINGTON, Col. William Augustine, of Westmoreland Co., mar. Miss Sally TAYLOE dau. of the late John TAYLOE Esq. of Mount Airy, at Mansfield the seat of Mann PAGE Esq. in this co. [Spotsylvania] (VH 14 May 99)
WASSELL, George, Eng. ind. svt., c. 17, shoemaker, ran away from Gavin HAMILTON, Wmsbrg. [also given as Norfolk] (VGPu 16 Jun 75, VG 24 Jun 75) [name also given as WASSILL]
WATERMAN, Solomon, dec'd, his admr., Willis WILSON, will sell his est., which includes a small schooner at the Great Bridge (VGNI 23 Aug 75)
WATERS, James, appr., b. in Scotland, c. 19, Edward KER of Accomack Co., adv. that he was carried off on the sloop *Sally* by Lynde VALENTINE and may be bound for Antigua (VG 16 Apr 72, VGR 23 Apr 72)
WATERS, John, b. in Leesburg, Loudoun Co., blacksmith, 24, des. from Capt. Wm. PRESTON's Co. of riflemen, 4th Sub-Legion, Montgomery Ct. H. (SVG 16 Sep 96)
WATERS, William, d. last Sat. eve. at his house in Wmsbrg. (VG 4 Jun 67); his slaves and livestock to be sold at his plant. in Halifax Co where Benj. BOXLEY now lives, by John TAZEWELL his ex. (VG 24 Dec 67); his lots and houses in Wmsbrg. to be sold by his ex. who notes that his widow is entitled to her dower in the above (VG 13 Oct 68)
WATKINS Family, Pittsylvania Co., Quarterly Ct., 21 Nov. 1797: Jonas HOLLAND (pltf.) against Matthew RAULY and Judith his wife, Geo. HARSTON and Elizabeth his wife, Stephen LYO[N] and Elinor his wife, James SNEED and Parthena his wife, Hodge ROBERTSON and Elizabeth his wife, and Willis WATKINS, Ledwell WATKINS, Benj. WATKINS, Isaiah WATKINS, Ichabod WATKINS, Conny WATKINS, Elly WATKINS, Elizabeth Anne WATKINS, Peter PERKINS, Nicholas WATKINS, Hardin PERKINS, Parthina BOSTUCK, Susanna MARR, Anne HARDIN, Mary HARDIMAN, Nicholas Tate PERKINS, Charles PERKINS, Anne

WALKER, Meekey MARLES, Mary PERKINS and all the husbands of the respective female defs., John WIMBISH, Wm. WIMBISH, Samuel WIMBISH, Nancy PANNELL, Polly LAMPKIN, Sharp LAMKIN, heirs at law of John WIMBISH, and Benj. ADAMS, Nicholas SCALES, Joseph SCALES, Robert SCALES, Peter SCALES, Polly JACKSON, and Parthina SCALES (defs.); it appears that Willis, Ledwell, Benj., Isaiah, Conny, Elly, Elizabeth, and Anne WATKINS are not inhabitants of this state (VGGA 10, 31 Jan 98)

WATKINS, Benjamin, of Chesterfield Co., dec'd, his livestock and other items to be sold (VGAA 25 Jan 83)

WATKINS, Henry, formerly of Hanover Co., but now of Ky., gave power of att. to Richard LITTLEPAGE to sell his land in Hanover Co. (VHFA 10, 31 Mar 91)

WATKINS, James, Negro, says he is free, that he was b. in New Jersey and left that state some yrs. before the war, c. 55, jailed in Albemarle Co. (VGGA 14 Feb 98)

WATKINS, John, from Henrico Co., executed on 12 May for rape (VGPu 12 May 75 sup)

WATKINS, John, of Surry Co., d. in his 45th year (VGPu 23 May 77)

WATKINS, John, dec'd, his admr., Wm. HILL, will sell several of his slaves at the next Kg. Wm. Ct. (VGIC 15 Nov 83, VGWeA 15 Nov 83, VGAA 22 Nov 83, 20 Dec 83)

WATKINS, John, of New Kent Co., dec'd, goods lately imported from London to be sold by his ex., Wm. CLAYTON (VGAA 14 May 85)

WATKINS, John Jr., d. on Sat. last in Surry Co. (VGPI 6 Oct 97)

WATKINS, Joseph, of Chesterfield Co., dec'd, e.a.w. his admr., James RAILEY and James PERY (VGGA 20 Nov 93)

WATKINS, Nicolson, of Surry, d. on Tues. the 8th inst. at the Great Bridge in Norfolk Co. (VGPI 31 Jan 93)

WATKINS, Robert, of Swan Bay, Surry Co., dec'd, his est. to be sold by his admr., Thomas BAILEY (VG 26 Feb 67); his admr. w.w.a. is Thomas BAILEY Gent. and his sisters and coheirs are Rebekah (wife of Rich. FIGURES) and Charity (wife of Nathaniel HICKS); they are involved in a chancery suit (VG 28 Jan 68)

WATKINS, Robert, Rich. YARBROUGH of Dinwiddie Co. reports that WATKINS, who is from Va., is now settled in St. Eustatia and desired him to inform the public should any vessel or tobacco addressed to him fall into St. Croix or St. Thomas's, his connection in them [sic] islands will remove the difficulties that would otherwise attend (VG 16 Aug 80)

WATKINS, Samuel, of Nottoway Co., dec'd, his admx., Betsey WATKINS, will sell most of his PE (VGPI 22 Dec 95)

WATKINS, Thomas Sr., dec'd, his will was presented in Henrico Co. Ct., 5 Feb. 1781, and proved by the oath of Jesse WILLIAMS one of the witnesses; it was ordered to be certified for further proof and, on the motion of Wm. CURD who intermarried with Mary a dau. of the sd. Thomas WATKINS dec'd, that letters of administration w.w.a. be granted him on the est. of the sd. dec'd; it appearing to the ct. that Elizabeth SMITH widow of Wm. SMITH dec'd another dau. of the sd. Thomas WATKINS is co-heiress with the sd. Mary (VG 24 Feb 81)

WATKINSON, William, Eng. svt., ran away from John TURBERVILLE, Westmoreland Co. (VG 3 Nov 68)

WATLINGTON, Paul, of Abington Par., Gloucester Co., d. on the 12th inst. aged 77 (VG 21 Mar 77)

WATSON, Capt., master of a brig bel. to Va., killed by slaves when the ship was in the River Gambia (Philadelphia disp. of 14 Aug.) (NYM 18 Aug 66, NYPB 21 Aug 66)

WATSON, Capt. Andrew, of Norfolk, d. on Sat. last (NH 24 Apr 98)

WATSON, Mrs. Anne, wife of Capt. Edward WATSON, d. on Mon. night (HNPA 3 Sep 94)

WATSON, Elizabeth, aka Elizabeth STEWART, svt., 40, b. in Ireland, ran aw from Charles JENKINS, Fredsbrg. (VG 10 Jul 52)

WATSON, James, Irish, c. 20, came to the home of James GORDON sometime in Aug. and said that he was a svt. to John WAYMAN in Md. (VGP 26 Oct 75)

WATSON, John, dec'd, Julius ALLEN Sr. will rent the plant bel. to his orphan, Joseph WATSON, on the south side of Pamunkey River in Hanover Co. (VGPu 27 Sep 76)

WATSON, Joseph, a rep. for Dunmore Co., died (VG 23 Sep 73)

WATSON, Nathaniel, ind. svt., supposed to bel. to Robert RUNDELL of Baltimore Co., Md., jailed in Winchester (BVCG 14 May 92)

WATSON, Maj. Philip, dec'd, e.a.w. his admrs., John HYLTON and James BALFOUR, who will also sell his slaves and livestock (VG 5 Feb 67, VGR 19 Feb 67)

WATSON, Mrs. Rebecca, of Charles City Co., dec'd, her HH effects to be sold by her exors. (nfi) (VGAA 17 Apr 84)

WATSON, Solomon, executed near Winchester on 11 Jun. for horse stealing; he was b. in Delaware in 1749 [an account of his life is given] (WVGWA 12 Jun 90)

WATSON, William, appears from his dialect to be a Yorkshire man, 30-35, jailed as a runaway in Westmoreland Co. (VGR 8 Oct 72)

WATSON, William, late of Albemarle Co., dec'd, e.a.w. his ex., John KEY and David WOOD (VIC 2 Sep 89)

WATTLES, Capt. Nathaniel, mar. Miss Betsy TAYLOR, on Thurs. eve. (CMAG 28 May 96)

WATTS Family, HCC, 20 Mar. 1792: Thomas MERIWETHER (pltf.) against Thomas PRICE acting ex. of Shadrach WATTS dec'd and Ann WATTS widow of the sd. Shadrach (VGGA 20 Jun 92)

WATTS, Edward, a young man, d. on Tues. last in Baltimore; he was bur. in St. Paul's burying ground on the 13th (CMAG 19 Feb 99)

WATTS, James, mulatto, c. 19, b. in Richmond, has a mother who is a white mulatto bel. to the est. of the Rev. Mr. COUTTS dec'd; believed to be attached to a girl bel. to Col. SYMS; a reward is offered for apprehending him (VGIC 28 Jun 88)

WATTS, John, Eng. conv. svt., shoemaker, c. 26, ran away from John GARDNER, K & Q Co. (VGR 14 Feb 71)

WATTS, William, sheriff of Dinwiddie Co., died (VGRMA 5 Jan 95)

WAUGH, Alexander, late of Orange Co., dec'd, his ex., [Alex. WAUGH], will sell his Negroes and two tracts of land containing 200 and 250 ac. respectively (VHFA 24 Jan 93); e.a.w. his ex. (VHFA 2 May 93)

WAUGH, Billey, aka Billey, Negro [slave], c. 38, ran away from Joseph CABELL on James River above Warminster in Buckingham Co. with his wife Judah c. 36 (LWG 13 Jul 99)

WAX, Henry, appr., c. 16, ran away from Jonathan LONG, Stephensburg (BVCG 30 Sep 93); [in the BVCG of 16 Dec 93, WAX explains his actions and accuses LONG of many crimes]

WAYLAND Family, Culpeper Co. [ct.], 20 Nov. 1798: David JONES and Hannah his wife (late Hannah WAYLAND) and Adam WAYLAND by the sd. David JONES his next friend (compl.) against John WAYLAND and Godfrey YAGER exors. of Adam WAYLAND dec'd and the sd. John WAYLAND, Godfrey YAGER and Mary his wife, Morton CHRISTOPHER and Elizabeth his wife, Joshua WAYLAND, Lewis WAYLAND, and Daniel [ULTZ] and Mary his wife (defs.) (VHFA 15 Jan 99)

WAYLES, John Esq., att. at law, d. on Fri. last at his house in Charles City Co. (VG and VGR 3 Jun 73)

WAYNE, His Ex. Anthony, Commander in chief of the Federal Army, d. on Wed. night the 14th inst. at Presqu'isle [there is a long biographical sketch from the *Philadelphia Gazette* in the Arg. of 24 Jan.] (Arg 6, 24 Jan 97, VGPI 10 Jan 97, SVG 11 Jan 97)

WEAKLY, Susanna, svt., says she was b. in Lincolnshire, her speech is north

of Eng., ran away from John SILBEY, Stafford Co. (VG 4 Jul 45)
WEAKS, Zachariah, ind. svt., 18, ran away from Geo. HUNTER, Fairfax Co. (VGAxA 17 Feb 91)
WEATHERED, Anthony, svt., ran away from John LANE, K.P.G., Wmsbrg. (VG 8 Aug 51)
WEAVER, Richard, Negro, c. 19, ind. svt., ran away from Robert DUDLEY, K & Q Co. (VGR 21 Mar 71)
WEBB Family, Essex Co., 15 May 1791, in chanc: Francis WEBB (pltf.) against James WEBB ex. of Mary WEBB Jr. who was extx. of James WEBB dec'd and Mary WEBB (defs.) (VGGA 1 Jan 92)
WEBB Family, HCC, 12 May 1796: Francis WEBB, James GRAY and Lucy his wife, James WEBB, Albion THROCKMORTON and Mary his wife, William WEBB, Geo. WEBB, and Wm. F. TUNSTALL and Jane his wife, which Francis WEBB, James WEBB, Wm. WEBB, and Geo. WEBB are sons of James WEBB (who was brother of Thomas WEBB dec'd and legatee of the sd. Thomas) and which Lucy, Mary, and Jane are daus. of the sd. James WEBB last mentioned and legatees of the sd. Thomas, Wm. WEBB and John WEBB brothers and legatees of the sd. Thomas, Samuel [SAMITH] and Mary his wife and Philip [VASS] and Eliz. his wife, which Mary and Eliz. are sisters and legatees of the sd. Thomas, and Overton COSBY a legatee of the sd. Thomas (pltfs.) and Rawleigh COLSTON admr. with the testament annexed of Thomas WEBB and surviving partner of Webb & Colston (def.) (WG 25 Sep 99)
WEBB, Miss Elizabeth, [an elegy to her] (VGGA 5 Nov 99)
WEBB, Foster, of New Kent Co., d. on 5 Apr., aged 59, he left a wife and eight chil. (VGGA 22 Apr 95)
WEBB, Foster Jr. Esq., mar. Miss Theodosia COCKE, both of Richmond (VGA/ 24 Sep 85)
WEBB, Mrs. Frances, dec'd, e.a.w. her admr., Wm. WATERS, Wmsbrg. (VG 29 Aug 66)
WEBB, George Sr., d. at the seat of George WEBB in Goochland Co., on Wed 26 Sep, in his 65th year (VGGA 4 Oct 92)
WEBB, James Sr. Esq., of the Great Bridge, died (VGPI 1 Nov 87)
WEBB, Richard, aka Dick WEBB, mulatto svt., 25-30, ran away from Hunter' Forge near Falmouth (VG 13 Nov 78)
WEBB, Rodman, enl. at Northumberland Ct. H., des. from the 7th U.S. Regt., Yorktown (VGGA 29 Nov 99)
WEBB, William, appr. tailor, ran away from Charles COPPEDGE, Dinwiddie Co. (VG 10 Nov 68)
WEBBER, William, dec'd, e.a.w. his ex., Daniel GUERRENT and John LAPRADE of Goochland Co. (RMA 3, 23 Dec 95)
WEBSTER, John, of Pr. Wm. Co. [also given as Pr. Edw. Co.], c. 22, des. from the co. of Capt. Abner CRUMP (VGPu 14 Mar, 13 Jun 77)
WEBSTER, William, brickmaker, b. in Scotland, rather turned of 30, ran away from Geo. WASHINGTON, Fairfax Co. (VGP 28 Apr 75 sup, VGPu 5 May 75)
WEBSTER, William, Eng. svt., hatter, 23, ran away from Wm. REYNOLDS, Annapolis, Md. (VGP 16 Nov 75)
WEEDON, Mrs. Catherine, relict of the late Gen. George WEEDON of Fredsbrg., d. on Thurs. last (VHFFA 28 Mar 97, RCFPC 29 Mar 97)
WEEDON, George Esq., late major general in the U.S. Army, d. on Mon. eve. last in Fredsbrg. (VGGA 25 Dec 93)
WEEKS, Billy, aka Billy, Negro, c. 30, purchased from Rich. H. CORBIN Esq. Middlesex Co., where he has a wife; he was permitted to visit her before Christmas and never returned to John HOPKINS in Richmond (VGGA 11 Jan 99)
WEEKS, Peter, mulatto lad, says he bel. to John PARKER of Accomack Co., jailed in York Co. (VGPu 7 Jul 75 sup)
WEELER, William, appr., 13-14, ran off with his mother, Rachel

CALLAGHAN, from Laurence TRIMPER, Staunton (SVG 26 Sep 95)
WEIGHTMAN, Richard, mar. Miss Betsy CHEW, Alexandria (VJAA 14 Apr 85)
WEIR, Richard, of Richmond, plans to leave the colony (VG 6 Oct 52)
WEISIGER, Joseph, dec'd, his admrs., Anna and Daniel WEISIGER, will sell his personal property at his late dwelling house (VGPI 16 May 97)
WELLMAN, John, Negro, upwards of 40, says he was b. in France and is a freeman and lived in the town of York before coming to this country, jailed in Henrico (VG 7 Apr 74)
WELLMAN, Matthew, dec'd, his surviving ex., Peter LYONS and Bart. ANDERSON, will sell two of his tracts of land and some Negroes at the late dwelling of Mrs. Anne WELLMAN in Hanover Co. (VGGA 29 Apr 95)
WELLS, George, appr., c. 20, ran away from John DUFFIELD, Winchester (VGWA 29 Sep 90)
WELLS, Jeremiah, Eng. conv. svt., b. in Sussex, ran away from R. JONES, Northumberland Co. (MG 28 Sep 48)
WELLS, Larkin, son and heir at law of Elijah WELLS, Charlotte Co., was mentioned in a chancery case (VGGA 28 Dec 91)
WELLS, Richard, Eng. ind. svt., ran away from John NORTON, Loudoun Co. (VG 9 Jan 72)
WELLS, Samuel, b. in Rhode Island, c. 25, wanted for robbery and piracy in Georgia (VG 23 Dec 75)
WELLS, William, conv. svt., imp. this spring in the *Justitia*, ran away from Francis CHRISTIAN, [North] Farnham Par., Richmond Co. (VG 10 Jun 75)
WELSH, George, mar. Miss Eliza EGE on Sun. eve. last, both of this city [Richmond] (VGGA 1 Mar 99)
WELSH, James, ind. svt. c. 25, shoemaker, bel. to Thomas CARTER of Lancaster Co., ran away (VGNI 28 Jul 74)
WELSH, James, Irish svt., shoemaker, ran away from W. FORSYTH, Norfolk (VGNI 5 Jul 75)
WELSH, Miss Peggy, dau. of John WELSH, aged about 16, d. in Fredsbrg. (VHFA 6 Jun 93)
WELSH, Thomas, Irish svt., c. 21, ran away from Samuel INGRAM and Joseph MEARS within nine miles of English Ferry on New River, Fincastle Co. (VGPu 30 Jun 75 sup)
WELSH, William, appr., c. 14, ran away from Jacob KIGER, Winchester (VGWA 13 Mar 90)
WEMMER, Jacob, of Franklin Co., adv. that his wife, Elizabeth, has conducted herself so vile as to threaten his [life] and swears that she will have revenge at the risk of life and reported that she will destroy his living as fast as possible; he will no longer be answerable for any of her contracts (LWM 6 Nov 97)
WENTWORTH, Capt. Samuel, d. lately at his house in Smithfield (VG 23 Jul 67); his PE including two schooners to be sold at Smithfield, Isle of Wight Co., by his admx., Mary WENTWORTH (VG 20 Aug 67)
WERCY, Louis, adv. that he is a French tailor (RMA 13 Oct 95)
WERNECK, Col. Frederick, dec'd, e.a.w. his admr., R. MAR[E]CK of Petersburg (VGPI 5 Sep 97, VGGA 22 Nov 97)
WESLEY, John, d. in London on 2 Mar. [long obit.] (VHFA 28 Apr 91)
WEST Family, Berkeley Co. Ct., 21 May 1790, in chanc: Philip PENDLETON (compl.) against Hannah WEST, Stephen WEST, Sophia WEST, Margaret WEST, Robert WEST, and Harriot WEST (defs.) (BVCG 16 Jun 90)
WEST Family, HCC, 30 Jun. 1794: Philip PENDLETON (pltf.) and Hanna WEST widow and extx. of Stephen WEST, Sophia WEST, Margaret WEST, Richard WEST, and Harriot WEST chil. and devisees of the sd. Stephen WEST, and Rich. PARRIS (defs.); it appears that PARRIS is not an inhabitant of this country (VGRC 29 Jul 94)
WEST Family, Campbell Co., Ct. of Q. S., 15 Nov. 1797, in Chanc: Charles

HALL (compl.) against Walter WEST, John WEST, Elizabeth WEST, Alley WEST, Rachel WEST, Nancy WEST, and Katy WEST chil. and heirs at law of Walter WEST dec'd (defs.); it appears that the defs. are not inhabitants of the state (LWM 15 Jan 98)

WEST, Mrs., wife of Geo. WEST Esq., died (VJAA 4 Aug 85)

WEST, Francis Esq., of Kg. Wm. Co., d. on [2]8 June last aged 94 (VGGA 6 Jul 96)

WEST, George, b. in Hanover Co., 18, des. from Rich. CALL's troop of light horse, Fredsbrg. (VGPu 21 Feb 77)

WEST, Col. George, d. at Cameron, the funeral sermon was by the Rev. Dr. GRIFFIN (VJAA 20 Apr 86)

WEST, George, late of Loudoun Co., dec'd, e.a.w. the ex., Charles LITTLE and Wm. WEST (VJAA 14 Sep 86)

WEST, J., mar. Mrs. BIGNALL, both of the Virginia Company of Comedians, at Norfolk on the 22nd inst. (RMA 30 May 95, VSPW 4 Jun 95)

WEST, John Jr., late of Fairfax Co., dec'd, e.a.w. his ex., Geo. and Wm. WEST (VGPu 12 Jun 78)

WEST, Mrs. Nancy, wife of Roger WEST, d. at Dumfries (VJAA 13 Oct 85)

WEST, Mrs. Susanna, consort of the Rev. Dr. Wm. WEST, d. at Baltimore on the 13th inst. (VJAA 26 Jul 87)

WEST, Mrs. Sybil, d. in her 83rd year; she was bur. in the family vault near Alexandria (VJAA 7 Jun 87)

WEST, Thomas, overseer, c. 25, had lived at the plant. of John GAILLARD, St. Stephen's Par., S. Carolina from which he was believed to have carried off three Negroes (VG 14 Jan 73)

WEST, Thomas, of Norfolk Borough, merch., mar. Miss Peggy WILLOUGHBY on Sun. eve. last [26 Oct.] (NPJ 29 Oct 88, VGWeA 6 Nov 88)

WEST, Thomas Wade, manager of the Virginia Company of Comedians and of the Alexandria Theater, d. on 28 July at Alexandria, in his 53rd year (VH 30 Jul 99, 6 Aug 99)

WEST, Capt. William, d. last Mon. sennight in Loudoun Co. (VGR 19 Oct 69 sup)

WESTBROOK, Thomas, c. 20, b. at Wraton, Southampton Co., des. from a recruiting party of H.M's 56th Regt., Annapolis, Md. (MG 9 Jun 63)

WESTCOTE, Miss Margaret, of Norfolk, d. Thurs. last in the bloom of life (VCNPGA 8 Sep 92)

WESTON, James, of Brunswick Co., failed to report back from furlough to the 1st Va. Regt.; he served in the campaign at Norfolk in Capt. MEADE's Co. of the 2nd Va. Regt. (VGPu 14 Nov 77)

WESTON, Nicholas, svt., b. in Yorkshire, 23, ran away from Taverner BEAL, Orange Co. (VG 11 Apr 55)

WESTWOOD, James, dec'd, his extx., Elizabeth WESTWOOD, will sell several of his slaves in Hampton (VG 10 Dec 72)

WESTWOOD, William, of Elizabeth City Co., d. on the 2nd inst., aged 73 (VG and VGR 14 Jun 70); e.a.w. his ex., James WALLACE and Hen. KING, who will also sell several tracts of his land in York Co. and Elizabeth City Co. (VG 19 Jul 70)

WESTWOOD, Maj. William, d. on Mon. night at Hampton (NH 1 Aug 99)

WESTWOOD, William, of Norfolk Borough, dec'd, e.a.w. his admr., John S. WESTWOOD in Hampton (NH 17 Sep 99)

WHALAND, Peter, Irish ind. svt., women's shoemaker, 18-20, ran away from A. Barnes Thomson MASON [sic] near Leesburg (VCWM 15 Oct 88)

WHALEY, James, dec'd, mention of land formerly bel. to him in Goochland Co. (VG 3 Apr 52)

WHALON, Stephen, aka STACKHOUSE, appr., near 19, ran away from John CAPPER (BVCG 8 Apr 93)

WHARTON, Henry Penn, of Philadelphia, mar. Mrs. Mary CURLE relict of the late Col. CURLE at Hampton on Thurs. last (NH 6 Sep 98)

WHARTON, Thomas, of Wmsbrg., dec'd, e.a.w. his ex., Thomas DAWSON

(VG 30 Jul 52)
WHEALON, Daniel, Irish svt., 30, ran away from Daniel PARKS, Wmsbrg. (VG 12 Dec 45)
WHEATLEY, Joseph, dec'd, e.a.w. his admx., Mary WHEATLEY (VHFFA 8 Jul 96)
WHEELAN, Dennis, Irish svt., engraver, ran away from Hamilton COOPER, Winchester (VGWA 16 Nov 87)
WHEELER, Maurice, from Lancaster Co., executed near Richmond pursuant to his sentence for murder (VGAA 30 Nov 82)
WHEELER, Tom, mulatto, 40, committed to jail in Pr. Anne Co. (VG 20 Oct 68)
WHEELIN, Richard, of Richmond, d. on Wed. last (RMA 10 Sep 96)
WHERDON, Mary, formerly Mary SMITH, wife of Nathaniel WHERDON, Frederick Co. (VGWA 23 Mar 91)
WHICHCOTTON, Lt., of the S. Carolina Regt., reportedly killed about 25 miles from Ft. Moore in Western Va., acc. to a letter from Augusta Co. dated 14 Nov. [1758] (MG 12 Jan 59)
WHIDDON, John, of Norfolk Co., dec'd, his extx., Mary WHIDDON, will sell two tracts of his land, one in Norfolk Co. and one in Pr. Anne Co. (AGNPPA and AGGA 2 Aug 96, AGGA 16 Sep 96)
WHIL[E]S, John, mar. Miss Prudence MAY, all of Warren Co., N. Carolina (VGPI 4 Apr 97)
WHITAKER, Simon, dec'd, his HHF to be sold by his ex., Humphrey HARWOOD (VG 22 Jan 67)
WHITAKER, William, ran away from William FITZHUGH, Kg. Geo. Co. (VJAA 27 Apr 86)
WHITE, Capt., of Col. VOSE's Bn. of infantry, was killed at Yorktown (VGAA 22 Dec 81)
WHITE, Master, son of Robert WHITE merch., d. on Sun. morn aged 7; Robert WHITE lost his 4-year-old dau. on 6 Sep.; he has lost four of his chil. in about as many weeks (HNPA 7 Sep 95)
WHITE, the Hon. Alexander Esq., state senator, mar. Mrs. Sarah HITE in Berkeley Co. lately (VJAA 10 Jun 84)
WHITE, the Rev. Archibald, Rector of St. David's [Par.] in Kg. Wm. Co., died (VGPu 18 Oct 76)
WHITE, Maj. Armistead, d. in Culpeper Co. aged about 40 (VHFA 7 Oct 90)
WHITE, Bennett, dec'd, his ex., Ben. OLIVER and Joseph BRAND, will sell all of his est. in the town of Newcastle, Hanover Co. (VGPu 4 Apr 77)
WHITE, C. A., a ring was found in Wmsbrg. with the inscription: "C. A. White, Nat. 2 Sep. 1762, Ob. 6 Jul. 1774" (VGP 2 Nov 75)
WHITE, Charles, Eng. conv. svt., stocking weaver, b. in Rutlandshire, c. 28, imp. last summer, ran away from Isaac ZANE at the Marlborough Iron Works, Frederick Co. (VGP 16 Nov 75, 29 Jun 76); has been apprehended twice, once in Fredsbrg. under the name of JOHNSON, and then in Manchester in Chesterfield Co. (VG 22 Nov 76)
WHITE, Daniel, Scot, sailor, ran away from the ship *Fairfield* now at Norfolk (VG 3 Jan 71)
WHITE, David, executed on 23 Nov. for the murder of a Negro in Essex Co. (VG 23 Nov 39)
WHITE, Mrs. Elizabeth, wife of the Hon. Alex. WHITE Esq. a delegate in the Assembly for Frederick Co., d. near Winchester on 24 Oct. (VGAA 9 Nov 82, MJ 26 Nov, 3 Dec 82)
WHITE, George Christopher, d. in Amelia Co. on 19 June last, bequeathed his whole est. to Maria and Gutlieb DILDEY, of Roppin, Marquisate of Brandenburg, who are his nieces (daus. of his sister Catharine by her first husband Peter DILDEY) (VG 6 Aug 72); his ex., Benj. WARD and Thomas JONES, will sell items of his est. (VG 29 Oct 72)
WHITE, Henry, mar. Miss Sally ALLAN dau. of James ALLAN in Fredsbrg. on Thurs. eve. last (VHFA 23 Jun 91)
WHITE, James, age 26, ran away from H.M.S. *Fewey* lying at Hampton, on 23

Mar. (VG 10 Oct 45)
WHITE, Jeremiah, late of Orange Co., dec'd, e.a.w. his admr., William WHITE (VHFFA 4 Nov 96)
WHITE, John, ind. svt., from Berwick, north of Eng., ran away from John KILTY, Anne Arundel Co., Md. (VGR 7 Jul 74)
WHITE, John Esq., Postmaster of Baltimore, d. there on 20 May, aged 36, leaving a widow and five small chil. (VICGA 2 Jun 90)
WHITE, John, Irish svt., c. 22, ran away from Jacob KELSEY, Shenandoah Co. (BVCG 2 Jul 92); believed to have been jailed in Winchester using the name Dennis M'CANN (BVCG 30 Jul 92)
WHITE, Capt. John, of Norwich, Connecticut, d. on Sat. last at Rockett's (VGWeA 13 Sep 93)
WHITE, John Esq., dec'd, his admr. (nfi) of Kg. Wm. Co., will sell 30-40 of his Negroes at Westwood near Hanover Town (VGGA 4 Feb 95)
WHITE, Jonathan, Negro, 22-23, ran away from David MAITLAND, Petersburg (NH 7 Jul 96)
WHITE, Lucy G., consort of John WHITE, d. in Staunton, on Sun. last (VGSWA 20 Oct 97)
WHITE, Rhoda, of Richmond, adv. that her husband, Samuel WHITE, petitioned the GA for a bill of divorcement, but it was not granted because he could bring no lawful cause against her; she warns the public that she is his wife and forewarns any person from marrying him as she is determined to have the law instituted against them; she adds that she means following him out of the state (RC 16 Feb 96)
WHITE, Samuel, of Hanover, age about 100, d. of throat cancer (VGWeA 4 Jan 83)
WHITE, Samuel, of Richmond, adv. that his wife, Rhoda, has behaved in a very unbecoming manner and he will no longer pay her debts (VGRC 15 Aug 94); adv. that he will petition the next GA to pass an act of divorce between his wife, Rhoda, and himself (RC 3 Oct 95)
WHITE, Thomas Esq., dec'd, all his lands in Chowan Co., N. Carolina, to be sold (NPJ 9 Apr 88)
WHITE, William, of Richmond, merch., mar. M[r]s. THILMAN of Hanover (VGAA 23 Apr 85)
WHITE, Col. William, of Louisa Co., mar. Mrs. Elizabeth WHITE of Hanover Co., on Wed. the 18th inst. (VGWeA 26 Jul 87)
WHITE, Col. William, dec'd, e.a.w. his admr., John WHITE Jr. (VICGA 21 Apr 90); his admr. will sell his PE in Hanover Co. (VICGA 2 Jun 90); his land in Louisa Co. to be sold by his ex., John WHITE Jr. (VGGA 20 Oct 90); his ex. will sell [his] 270 ac. tract on Pamunkey River (VGRMA 5 Dec 93)
WHITE, Capt. William, of Hanover Co., mar. Mrs. Mildred ELLIS of the same co., on Thurs. eve. the 5th inst. (VGGA 6 Sep 99)
WHITECOTTON, George, appr., hatter, 20-21, ran away from Wm. PEARSON, Fredsbrg. (VHFA 5 Jul 92)
WHITEHEAD, Mrs., wife of the Rev. James WHITEHEAD of Norfolk, d. this morn. (VCGA 4 Sep 94)
WHITEHEAD, Dr. Alexander, was mar. to Miss Nancy MOSELY dau. of Capt. H. MOSELY of Norfolk, on Wed. eve. by the Rev. James WHITEHEAD (NH 23 Nov 99)
WHITEHEAD, Ben, of the Indian breed and almost white, 18-19, carpenter, ran away from S. KELLO, Southampton (VICGA 13 Jan 90)
WHITEHEAD, James, appr., 16-17, ran away from Jacob POE, Winchester (BVCG 21 Jul 94)
WHITEHEAD, the Rev. James, mar. Mrs. Clara ROTHERY, both of this town [Norfolk], on Thurs. last (HNPA 23 May 95)
WHITEHEAD, Josiah, Virginian, from Pr. Anne Co., des. from the Corps of Artillerists and Engineers at Ft. Norfolk (NH 6 Oct 96)
WHITEMAN, Magdalena, has eloped from her husband, Henry, of Frankfort, Pendleton Co. (SVG 20 Jun 95)

WHITFIELD, George, of Portsmouth, cautions all persons not to trust his wife, Elizabeth WHITFIELD, as he will no longer pay any of her debts (NH 26 Sep 99)

WHITING, Francis, late of Berkeley Co., dec'd, demands against his est. are to be made to John WHITING Jr. of Gloucester (VGPu 13 Sep 76)

WHITING, Francis, dec'd, his admr., Henry WHITING, will sell 30 of his Negroes in Berkeley Co. (VGWeA 14 Dec 82)

WHITING, Henry, late of Pr. Wm. Co., dec'd, e.a.w. his ex. Humphrey F. WHITING or John PEYTON of Gloucester Co. (VGPu 1 Mar 76)

WHITING, Dr. John R., of Stephensburg, Frederick Co., mar. Miss Nancy LANE of Culpeper, Thurs. last (WG 27 Nov 99)

WHITING, Mrs. Mary, relict of Beverley WHITING of Gloucester Co., d. on Mon. the 24th inst. (VGR 27 Sep 70)

WHITING, Peter Esq., of Gloucester Co., mar. Hannah WASHINGTON dau. of Col. Warner WASHINGTON, of Fred[erick] Co., on Tues. the 10th inst. (VCWM 18 Jun 88)

WHITING, Peter Beverly Esq., of Gloucester Co., killed in a riding accident on 28 Nov. [long obit.] (VGAA 21 Dec 82, 4 Jan 83); his extx., Elizabeth WHITING, will sell all his remaining est. (VIC 30 Sep 89)

WHITING, Capt. Thomas, one of the reps. for Gloucester Co., mar. Miss Elizabeth SEAWELL, on Tues. the 16th ult. (VGR 1 Nov 70); [as Col. Thomas WHITING] of Gloucester Co., dec'd (VGAA 13 Dec 83)

WHITING, Thomas, mar. Mrs. PERRIN widow of John PERRIN, in Gloucester Co. (VGGA 20 Mar 93)

WHITING, Thomas, appr., ran away from Geo. REED, coppersmith, Winchester (BVCG 17 Jun 96)

WHITING, Thomas, d. on the 26th ult. at his seat on York River in Gloucester Co, aged 35 (NH 21 Mar 99)

WHITLEY, Jacob, of Fredsbrg., innholder, d. last Thurs., aged 61 (VHFA 10 Sep 89)

WHITLOCK, Josiah Sr., late of Pr. Edw. Co., dec'd, e.a.w. his ex., Geo. MOORE and Thos. FLOURNOY (VGR 30 Aug 70)

WHITLOCK, William, of Caroline Co., dec'd, pursuant to his will, a tract of his land on Polecat Swamp containing by estimation 200 ac., two dwelling houses, and a good apple and peach orchard will be sold by Wm. WHITLOCK (nfi) (VG 4 Dec 78)

WHITLOCK, William, Clerk of Petersburg District Ct., died (VGPI 10 Oct 97)

WHITNEY, Francis, dec'd, e.a.w. his admx., Elizabeth WHITNEY, of Norfolk (NHPA 30 Oct 97)

WHITNEY, Jeremiah, dec'd, all his est. to be sold by his admx., Susannah WHITNEY (VGAA 13 Jul 82)

WHITNEY, John, aka MERRYMAN, conv. svt., was executed on 21 Jan. at Fredsbrg.; he was part, with Michael KENNEDY, of a gang of thieves that was active there and in Falmouth (VG 3 Feb 74)

WHITTER, James, appr., c. 10, ran away from Geo. TROUTWINE, Hardy Co. (WG 27 Jun 98)

WHITTLE, Conway, was mar. to Mrs. Frances M. BOUSH relict of the late John BOUSH Esq. dec'd of Norfolk, by the Rev. James WHITEHEAD, on Wed. eve. last (VCNPGA 20 Apr 93)

WHITWELL, Mrs., wife of Capt. WHITWELL, d. recently at Chatham, Eng. of smallpox (VG 23 Jan 56)

WHYTE, Francis, who lived with Anne GOW, Patrick BURKE, and Mrs. BROWN, is a thief, liar, and drunkard acc. to Anne GOW; WHYTE is suing her for his character (NHPA 21 Aug 97)

WHYTE, Richard, merch., late of Dublin, dec'd, his ex., Mary WHITE and Thomas DAWSON, adv. that they had empowered Thomas SMITH to collect debts in America and try to locate Alexander WHYTE his son and heir; they have since revoked his power of attorney; Alexander WHYTE is believed to be in Va. since he wrote to a friend in Bristol and the letter was dated

"Virginia"; he is asked to bind himself in £700 to the ex. for the use of the est. and his sister Euphemia; his bond should be conveyed to Wm. ALLEN Esq. of Philadelphia (VG 2 Sep 57); an adv. in Nov. 1759 stated that sundry advertisements had been inserted in the *Virginia Gazette* in 1757 enquiring after Alexander WHITE son and heir of Richard WHITE which ads. were directed to be charged to Robert JACKSON of Fredsbrg.; JACKSON says that he knows nothing of the ads. or matter (VG 30 Nov 59)
WICKETT, Billy, Negro boy, jailed in Isle of Wight Co. (VG 8 Jul 73)
WICKHAM, Jesse, appr. tailor, 15, ran away from James EDMONDSON, Winchester (VGWA 18 Jun 91)
WICKHAM, Mrs. [Maria], [an elegy] (VGGA 5 Feb 99)
WICKLIFF, Charles, son of David WICKLIFF of Fauquier Co., to mar. Miss NELSON of Westmoreland Co. (VGAR 11 Apr 93)
WIGGENTOR, James, of Culpeper Co., mar. Miss Sally PENDLETON dau. of Wm. PENDLETON of Berkeley Co. (PGBA 19 May 96)
WIGHT, John, of Connecticut, d. in Richmond on Sat. last after a short illness (VGRC 13 Sep 93)
WIGLAY, John, svt., a West Country man, imp. in the *Litchfield* about a year ago, ran away from Geo. and Rich. LEE, Westmoreland Co. (MG 20 Sep 49)
WILBAR, H., late master of the Steinhouse Academy, Brighthelmstone, Eng., is opening an academy in Richmond (Ex 29 Mar 99); he has fitted up an apartment in his academy for the reception of young ladies (Ex 19 Jun 99); has opened his academy at the house, late Miller's Tavern, opposite the Swan (Ex 12 Jul 99)
WILBOURNE, Thomas, of Cumberland Co., dec'd, e.a.w. his ex., Joseph CARRINGTON (VGGA 12 Jan 91)
WILCOCKS, Isaac, dec'd, his est. in lower Middlesex Co. will be sold by Rich. JONES (VG 13 Sep 70)
WILD, Thomas, of York Co., adv. that he intends to go to Charleston, S. Carolina as soon as he can (VIC 6 Dec 86)
WILIE, the Rev. Mr., Rector of Albemarle Par., Sussex Co., d. on Good Friday [obit. in VGPu 19 Apr. 76 ps] (VGPu 19 Apr 76, VG 20 Apr 76) [also given as WILLIE]
WILKES, John, Negro, 28-30, has a fondness for the sea, ran away from J. B. NICKOLLS (CMAG 17 Sep 96)
WILKINS, James, late of New Mill Cr., Norfolk Co., dec'd, all his moveable property will be sold by Willis WILKINS (nfi) (HNPA 12 Aug 95)
WILKINS, John, merch., d. on Sat. last (VGNI 15 Sep 74)
WILKINS, John Sr., of Pr. Anne Co., died (VCNPGA 30 Mar 93)
WILKINS, Joseph, of Flower de Hundred, dec'd, his land and ferry there to be sold by his admr., Geo. NOBLE and Joshua POYTHRESS (VG 24 Sep 67, VGPu 30 Aug 76)
WILKINS, William, late of Northumberland Co., d. as a result of "severe correction and cruel treatment" from Rawleigh BRYANT who has since fled (VGR 16 Nov 69)
WILKINSON, Miss Betsey, of Nansemond Co., d. suddenly in the flower of her age (VG and VGR 8 Apr 73)
WILKINSON, Edward, of Chesterfield Co., dec'd, his ex., Benj. BRANCH, will sell his corn and fodder at his plant. in Amelia and Chesterfield Cos. (VG 12 Dec 71)
WILKINSON, Mrs. Elizabeth, relict of John WILKINSON late of Philadelphia, died, aged 72 (VJAA 26 Jan 86)
WILKINSON, Capt. George, Commander of the ship *Madeira Packet* of London, d. last Fri. of an apoplectic fit at Warren's Ordinary, New Kent Co. (VG 10 Sep 67)
WILKINSON, Jesse, of Pr. Geo. Co., dec'd, his admx., Mary WILKINSON, will sell all of his est. there (VGPI 28 Feb 97)
WILKINSON, John, svt., ran away from Wm. LIGHTFOOT, Tedington (VG 24 Jan 52)

WILKINSON, John, aka Jack, mulatto, ran away from Mann PAGE, Spotsylvania Co. (VGR 27 Sep 70)
WILKINSON, John, late of New Kent Co., dec'd, e.a.w. his ex., Jesse HEARD (VGAA 8 Jun 82)
WILKINSON, Col. Lyddall, dec'd, his extx. (nfi) will sell his tract of land in New Kent Co. (VGGA 8 Jun 96)
WILKINSON, the Rev. Thomas, of Amelia Co., dec'd, e.a.w. his ex., Thomas Griffin PEACHEY, James HENDERSON, and Wm. FITZGERALD (VGAA 23 Apr 85)
WILKINSON, Thomas, dec'd, e.a.w. his admr., Jane WILKINSON of Alexandria (VGAxA 2 Dec 90)
WILKINSON, William, of Nansemond Co., dec'd, Willis WILKINSON (nfi) adv. for claims against his est. (HNPA 14 Feb 95)
WILLCOCKS, Edward, d. of smallpox at the hospital on Mon. eve. (VGPI 1 Jul 96)
WILLCOCKS, John, Eng. conv., 21, ran away from Edw. STEVENSON, Little Pipe Cr., Frederick Co., Md. (VG 11 Jun 67)
WILLER, Marshall, Negro, jailed as a runaway in Pr. Edw. Co. (VGAA 15 Feb 92)
WILLESS, William, gunsmith and brass founder from Birmingham, late of Wmsbrg., has removed to Norfolk (VGR 2 Aug 70)
WILLETT, Charles, one of the editors of the *Norfolk Herald,* was mar. to Miss Charlotte WATSON, both of Norfolk, last eve. by the Rev. James WHITEHEAD (AGNPPA 20 May 96)
WILLEY, Francis, infant under 21, son and heir of James WILLEY dec'd, of Fincastle Co., summoned to appear there in court to answer a bill in chancery (VGR 12 May 74)
WILLIAMS, Capt., mar. Miss Jane [or Jenny, acc. to VGAA] CHARLTON of Richmond (VIC and VGAA 18 Oct 86)
WILLIAMS, Mr., lived at the plant. of the Hon. Robert CARTER Esq. near Wmsbrg., was thrown from his horse and killed last week (VGR 6 Jul 69)
WILLIAMS, Andrew, 27-28, speaks West of Eng. dialect, escaped from the sheriff in Baltimore, Md. (VGR 1 Aug 71)
WILLIAMS, Anthony, ind. svt., from Monmouthshire, 25-26, ran away from the snow *Carlisle* at Yorktown (VG 19 May 74)
WILLIAMS, Bartlett Esq., att. at law, mar. Miss Sally CLOUGH of New Kent Co., on Fri. sennight (VGAA 29 Dec 81)
WILLIAMS, Brazure, of Charles City Co., dec'd, e.a.w. his ex., Samuel PRYOR (VGGA 7 May 94)
WILLIAMS, Chaplain, son and heir of Capt. WILLIAMS dec'd of Southampton Co., summoned to appear in court to answer a bill in chancery exhibited against him and Stephen WILLIAMSON by Thomas WILLIAMSON and John HYNDMAN merch. (VG 11 Apr 71)
WILLIAMS, Christopher, Irish svt., c. 25, ran away from John MOUNTJOY, Stafford Co. (VGR 23 Apr 72)
WILLIAMS, Edward, Eng. svt., ran away from Robert PHILLIPS, Fredsbrg. (VGR 4 Feb 68)
WILLIAMS, Edward, b. in Wales, c. 30, ran away from Abraham JARRETT (VGR 4 Aug 74)
WILLIAMS, Dr. Frederick, mar. at Chestnut in Surry Co. on 10 Apr. by the Rev. Mr. BURGHES to Miss Mary HUTCHINGS dau. of John HUTCHINGS Esq. late of this place (NPJ 23 Apr 88); Capt. of the militia of this town [Norfolk], d. yesterday morn. (HNPA 22 Aug 95); e.a.w. his admx., Frances WILLIAMS (AGNPPA 15 Mar 96, AGGA 6 May 96)
WILLIAMS, Frederick, appr. tailor, 20, ran away from Geo. SUGGS (VCGA 11 Apr 94)
WILLIAMS, George, of Frederick Co., dec'd, his est. to be sold by his ex., John S. WOODCOCK (BVCG 12 Mar 92, 12 Aug 93)
WILLIAMS, George, late of Fairfax Co., dec'd, his ex., Jeremiah MOORE and

Geo. WILLIAMS, will sell a tract of his land in Fauquier Co. near Rector Town containing about 200 ac. (CMAG 16 Jul 95)

WILLIAMS, Hezekiah, overseer, killed by Negro Moses who was acquitted because of extenuating circumstances in Alexandria (VGAxA 27 Jan 91)

WILLIAMS, Jacob [Jr.], dec'd, items of his est. to be sold by his admrs., John SMITH and Joseph WILLIAMS, at the house of Wm. SMITH in Caroline Co. (VGGA 25 Feb 95); his admrs. will attend John ELLIS' Tavern in Caroline Co. to settle his est. (VGGA 18 May 96)

WILLIAMS, James, of Dinwiddie Co., native of this country, blacksmith, 87, recently came to Wmsbrg. as an evidence in the General Ct. (Wmsbrg. disp. of 2 Nov.) (NYPB 20 Nov 69)

WILLIAMS, James, carpenter, killed in a fight with Thomas ROSS in Fredsbrg.; ROSS was acquitted of his murder in Fredsbrg. District Ct. (VHFA 23 Nov, 29 Nov 92, 9 May 93)

WILLIAMS, Mrs. Jane, consort of Capt. Thomas WILLIAMS of Richmond, d. on Mon. morn. after a long illness (VIC 3 Oct 87, VGWeA 4 Oct 87, VGIC 6 Oct 87)

WILLIAMS, Jane, has sworn the peace against her husband, John S. WILLIAMS (BVCG 26 Aug 93)

WILLIAMS, John, svt., West Country man, ran away from Wm. RICHARDS, Drysdale Par., K & Q Co. (VG 15 Jun 39)

WILLIAMS, John, dec'd, his land in Henrico Co. to be sold by his ex., Robert PLEASANTS (VGR 21 Jul 68)

WILLIAMS, John, Eng. conv. svt., ran away from Henry WILLIAMS, Pittsylvania Co. (VGPu 4 Aug 75)

WILLIAMS, John, seaman in the *Revenge* cruiser out of Capt. STINSON's Co., from West Augusta Co., of the 8th Regt., ran away in marching up from Suffolk to Cumberland (VGPu 19 Jul 76)

WILLIAMS, Capt. John, dec'd, e.a.w. his admr., Wm. NUTT [of Northumberland Co.] (VGPu 21 Aug 78)

WILLIAMS, John, seaman, ran away from the ship *Hannibal* lying at the mouth of Quantico (VJAA 10 Aug 86)

WILLIAMS, John, Eng., c. 36, mason, des. from the rendezvous in Staunton (RMA 24 Sep 95, SVG 26 Sep 95, RC 3 Oct 95 ex)

WILLIAMS, Col. John, of Halifax Co., dec'd, his admrs., Wm. WILLIAMS and John B. SCOTT, will sell his stock and other items of his est. (VGPI 5 Aug 96, Arg 19 Nov 96)

WILLIAMS, John Sr., d. lately in Culpeper Co. (VH 5 Mar 99)

WILLIAMS, Lesenberry, dec'd, e.a.w. his ex., R. WILLIAMS, Daniel HAIR, and extx., Sarah WILLIAMS of Pr. Geo. Co. (VGPI 23 Jun 91)

WILLIAMS, Mrs. Mary, relict of the late Jacob WILLIAMS, d. on Thurs. eve. last (NPJ 13 Feb 88)

WILLIAMS, Mary, has left her husband, Edward WILLIAMS of Norfolk, and frequents houses of bad fame (NHPA 3 Aug 97); she replies that her husband had sold all her clothes and furniture and taken up with a most abandoned prostitute and that she hopes "that a dissipate life and virulent disorder will soon free me and the world of such an abominable nuisance to society" (NHPA 17 Aug 97)

WILLIAMS, Gen. Otho H., d. on the 15th inst. on his way from Baltimore to the springs (VHFA 24 Jul 94)

WILLIAMS, Richard, Welsh svt., ran away from Samuel WASHINGTON, Kg. Geo. Co. (VG 11 Apr 55)

WILLIAMS, Richard, dec'd, his property will be sold at Frankfurt by his ex., Ezekiel WHITMAN (VGWA 25 Jun 88)

WILLIAMS, Robert, of Pittsylvania Co., dec'd, his admx., Sarah WILLIAMS, will sell his stock, HH, and KF (VGGA 7 Aug 93)

WILLIAMS, Robert, dec'd, Mace FREELAND and Spice PENDLETON will present a petition to exclude Elizabeth JONES from the act entitled "An act to vest the est. of Robert WILLIAMS equally among Mace FREELAND, Spice

PENDLETON, Elizabeth JONES and their heirs" (VGRMA 15 May 94)
WILLIAMS, Samuel, late of Richmond Co., dec'd, his extx., Betty Ann
WILLIAMS, and ex., W, PEACHEY, will sell his 400 ac. tract in Halifax Co.
on Bandy Cr.' Luke WILLIAMS who lives in that co. will show the land (VG
24 Oct 77, VGPu 31 Oct 77, VGAA 14 Aug 84)
WILLIAMS, Thomas, of Dinwiddie Co., dec'd, his plant. and land there to be
sold by his ex., Francis EPES and Thomas WILLIAMS; they will also sell
his land near Petersburg (VG 24 Sep 67, 16 May 71)
WILLIAMS, Col. Thomas, d. in Pr. Geo. Co., Md. on 22 Feb. (VJAA 25 Mar 84)
WILLIAMS, Thomas, merch. of this town, mar. Mrs. Jane BOND formerly of
Philadelphia on Sun. eve. last [it is not clear whether this was an
Alexandria or Boston marriage] (CMAG 7 May 95)
WILLIAMS, William, of Wmsbrg., lost his wife lately and intends to sell
household goods and women's clothing and leave for Eng. (VG 2 Jan 52)
WILLIAMS, William, of Norfolk, drowned at Petersburg on 7 Jul. (VCGA 14
Jul 94)
WILLIAMS, William, light complexion, 32, says he is free, b. in Henrico Co.,
jailed in Norfolk Borough (NH 10 Nov 98)
WILLIAMS, William C. Esq., of Culpeper, mar. Miss Alice BURWELL of
Richmond on Fri. eve. last (VGGA 19 Mar 94)
WILLIAMSON, Archibald, native of North Britain, who had resided in
Wmsbrg. a few yrs., was bur. on Sun. last in the churchyard of this city (VG
16 Apr 79)
WILLIAMSON, Dabney, mar. Miss Lucy BURTON, both of this city
[Richmond], on Thurs. last (RMA 18 May 96)
WILLIAMSON, Mrs. Eleanor, died (BVCG 6 Jan 94)
WILLIAMSON, the Hon. Hugh, delegate in Congress from N. Carolina, mar.
Miss Maria APTHORP dau. of Charles Ward APTHORP at Bloomingdale
near New York [City] on 3 [Jan.] (NPJ 4 Feb 89)
WILLIAM[S]ON, James, d. in Falmouth in an advanced age (VH 24 May 99)
WILLIAMSON, John, dec'd, his trustees (nfi) will sell a tract of his land in
Louisa Co. (VG 1 Oct 72)
WILLIAMSON, John, of Amelia Co., mar. Miss Molly ANDERSON of
Richmond (VGWeA 27 Apr 82)
WILLIAMSON, John the Younger, dec'd, 400 ac. of his land near the
courthouse in Lunenburg Co. to be sold by Robert and Samuel
WILLIAMSON agreeable to his will and pursuant to an order of Henrico
Co. Ct. (VG 26 Sep 66)
WILLIAMSON, Samuel, of Henrico Co., d. on the 28th ult. (VGGA 9 Jul 99)
WILLIAMSON, Thomas, of Thos. Williamson & Co., late of Norfolk, dec'd,
e.a.w. Robert TUCKER, the surviving partner, and Lewis HANSFORD, the
ex. (VG 17 Apr 52, 8 Dec 52)
WILLIAMSON, Thomas, from Henrico Co., executed of Fri. last at the gallows
near Richmond for murder (VGWeA 5 Feb 89)
WILLIAMSON, Willoughby, dec'd, e.a.w. his ex., Joshua WHITEHURST of Pr.
Anne Co. (HNPA 8 Aug 95, NH 5 May 96)
WILLIARDS, [D]aniel, 26, des. from Capt. Geo. MERCER's Co. of Va. forces at
Ft. Cumberland (VG 22 Aug 55)
WILLIE, William, nephew to the Rev. William WILLIE (VG 30 Jul 72)
WILLIS Family, Halifax Co., Ct. of Q. S., 21 Aug. 1794: Joseph HUGHES
(compl.) against Mary WILLIS admx. of Wm. WILLIS dec'd, Rich.
WILLIS, John WILLIS, Edward WILLIS, Sterling WILLIS, Drury WILLIS,
Thomas WILLIS, Sherwood WILLIS, Wm. HOPWOOD and Anne his wife,
John ALLGOOD and Sarah his wife, and Elizabeth DANIEL infant and
orphan of Thomas DANIEL and Elizabeth his wife also dec'd (defs.)
(VGRMA 1 Dec 94)
WILLIS, Mrs. Ann, consort of Maj. John WILLIS, d. in this county
[Spotsylvania] (VH 8 Mar 99)
WILLIS, Edward, late of Henrico Co., dec'd, e.a.w. his admr., Thomas SMITH

of Charlotte Co. (VGWeA 7 Feb 95)
WILLIS, Mrs. Elizabeth, d. on the 9th inst. in Gloucester [Co.] [long obit.] (VG 11 May 69 sup, VGR 11 May 69)
WILLIS, Francis, dec'd, his ex., John WILLIS, will sell his plant. White Hall [in Gloucester Co.] containing 800 ac. (VGGA 25 Jun 99)
WILLIS, George, late of Winchester, dec'd, hatter, e.a.w. his admr., James WALKER (BVCG 7 Jul 94)
WILLIS, George, native of Britain, des. from a British man-of-war two or three yrs. past, worked as a shoemaker in Georgetown, Fredsbrg., Falmouth, and Dumfries; he is suspected of fraud (Arg 4 Jun 99)
WILLIS, Col. John, of Brunswick Co., dec'd (VG 13 Nov 66); e.a.w. John or Francis WILLIS (nfi); some of his horses to be sold at Gloucester Ct. by his extx., Mildred WILLIS (VG 27 Nov 66); Mildred WILLIS of Brunswick Co. adv. that his horse, Janus, is to be available to service mares at Richard JAMES' in Cumberland Co. (VG 9 Apr 67)
WILLIS, Mrs. Mildred, of Brunswick Co., dec'd, 50 of her slaves to be sold by her ex., John WILLIS, Francis WILLIS, and Augustine WILLIS (VG 9 Mar 69)
WILLIS, Robert Carter, dec'd, slaves bel. to his est. to be sold at Martinsburg, Berkeley Co., by his extx., Martha WILLIS (VJAA 7 Dec 86)
WILLIS, Walter, dec'd, e.a.w. his admr., Andrew KIDD of Portsmouth (NH 2 Feb 99)
WILLIS, William, gunsmith from Birmingham has opened shop near the playhouse, Wmsbrg. (VG 22 Sep 68)
WILLIS, Capt. William, late of Warwick Co., dec'd, e.a.w. his ex., Willis WILLS and Thomas HAYNES (VGR 24 Mar 74)
WILLISON, James, dec'd, his ex., Carter B. HARRISON and Thomas J. ANSON of Cabin Point, will sell his PE at his late dwelling house in Surry Co. (VGPI 1 Nov 87, VGWeA 15 Nov 87)
WILLMAN, Mr., mar. Mrs. YOUNG widow of the late T. YOUNG, in Norfolk Borough on Tues. eve. (NH 1 Mar 98)
WILLMAN, Matthew, late of Hanover Co., dec'd, e.a.w. his ex., Bartt. ANDERSON of Hanover Co. (VGGA 1 Aug 92)
WILLMORE, Sarah, aka WILLMOTT, svt., 23, ran away from Robert VAULX and John ELLIOTT, Westmoreland Co., and may be headed for Norfolk (VG 2 May 51)
WILLOUGHBY, Col. John, of Willoughby Point, d. last Tues. (NPC 19 Mar 91); e.a.w. his admr., Thomas RITSON (NPC 18 Jun 91); portion of his Willoughby Point est. to be sold by his acting ex., Thomas RITSON of Norfolk (NPC 2 Jun 92)
WILLOUGHBY, Thomas, dec'd, his ex., Philip RITTER, will sell a tract of his land on Tanner's Cr. in Norfolk Co. (VGIC 27 Nov 84)
WILLOUGHBY, Thomas, ward of Thomas WALKE, has been devised a part of the plant. of the late Col. John WILLOUGHBY (HNPA 19 Nov 95)
WILLOUGHLY [sic] Family, Amherst Co., March Ct., 1798, in chanc: Joshua WILLOUGHLY and Joshua WILLOUGHLY for Alexander WILLOUGHLY, Richard HENDERSON, Jeremiah PICKETT, and Charity WILLOUGHLY (compl.) against Philip SMITH and Wm. WILLOUGHLY (defs.); it appears that Wm. WILLOUGHLY is not an inhabitant of the state (LWG 13 Jul 99)
WILLS, Benjamin, of Warwick Co., dec'd, his ex. (nfi) will sell all his PE (VGPu 27 Dec 76)
WILLS, John and Draughton, dec'd, e.a.w. their admr., Miles WILLS (VGPu 29 May 78)
WILLS, Mrs. Lucy, consort of Dr. John WILLS, d. on the 16th inst. in Fluvanna Co. (Ex 24 Dec 98)
WILLS, William, appr., 20, ran away from Thomas BREWER, Yorktown, last May and may be headed for N. Carolina (VG 3 Jul 46)
WILLS, Dr. William, surgeon, late of Richmond, dec'd, e.a.w. his ex., Thos.

PROSSER and Turner SOUTHALL (VG and VGR 15 Feb 70)
WILLS, William, who mar. Martha ALEXANDER, has £40 left him in the will of Sarah ALEXANDER dec'd, late of Gloucester Co. (VGR 20 Jun 71)
WILLS, Capt. William, of Warwick Co., dec'd, e.a.w. his ex., Wm. WILLS and Thos. HAYNES (VG 24 Mar 74)
WILLSON, Anthony, appr., 14-15, ran away from John THOMPSON, Pr. Edw. Co. (VGP 17 Nov 74)
WILLSON, William, dec'd, Peter LIGHT advises Nancy WILLSON extx. and Andrew BOGGS and James BRISON ex. of Wm. WILLSON that he will take depositions of Wm. ASKEW, John LIGHT Jr., and Alex. BUCHANAN as witnesses for himself in a suit in the Circuit Ct. of the U.S., District of Va., wherein they are pltfs. and he is def. (BI 2 Oct 99)
WILLSON, Hannah, svt., 30, b. in Denmark, speaks Low Dutch and Eng., [ran away from] Henry BRINKER, Winchester, and is supposed gone away with some sailors who were in the battle on the Monongahela and were going to their ship at Hampton (VG 5 Sep 55)
WILMORE, William, Eng. conv. svt., weaver, ran away from John MARR, Pittsylvania Co. (VGP 15 Jun 75)
WILSON, Aaron, Negro, b. in Brunswick Co., c. 22, says he is free and served Benj. MACKLIN for 21 yrs. in Brunswick Co., N. Carolina, jailed in Wmsbrg. (VGWeA 29 Oct 89); committed to jail in New Kent Co. (VGGA 12 Jan 91)
WILSON, Alexander, merch., mar. Miss CUNNINGHAM, both of Norfolk (NH 19 Oct 99)
WILSON, Andrew, aka John WILLIAMS, aka John GORDON, who enl. three different times and des. as often, was shot in the barracks near this city [Wmsbrg.] on Sat. last agreeable to his sentence (VG 20 Nov 79)
WILSON, Mrs. Anne, wife of Solomon WILSON, formerly a merch. of this town [Norfolk], d. on Thurs. last near Smithfield leaving a husband and three chil. (NH 23 Jan 96)
WILSON, Cornelius, Negro lad, c. 17, bound to Thomas SIKES, tanner, 10 miles from Burlington in East Jersey, sent to Philadelphia with leather in the ship *Ritson* bound to Norfolk from which he ran away (AGNPPA 23 Oct 95)
WILSON, Cumberland, late of Dumfries, dec'd, his admr., Wm. WILSON, James WILSON, and Campbell WILSON, have empowered James LORIMER merch. in Dumfries to collect the outstanding debts (CMAG 10 Jan 99)
WILSON, David, adv. that he came to this country 25 or 26 yrs. ago and does not have a family in Ireland (VGWA 28 Dec 87)
WILSON, Edward, clear mulatto, appr., carpenter and joiner, c. 18, ran away from Philip MALLORY (VG 5 Sep 71)
WILSON, Mrs. Frances, spouse of Col. Josiah WILSON of Norfolk Co., died (VGNI 16 Feb 75)
WILSON, George, of York Co., desires to return to Eng. (VG 1 Jan 67)
WILSON, Goodrich, vendue master at Portsmouth, died (VJAA 22 Dec 85)
WILSON, James, late of Wmsbrg., dec'd, his ex., Ebenezer EWING, will settle his est. (VGWeA 24 Feb 92)
WILSON, James, appr., c. 15, ran away from James WILSON [sic], Mill Cr., Berkeley Co. (BVCG 8 Sep 94 sup)
WILSON, James, appr. joiner, ran away from Hugh CUNNINGHAM Jr. who supposes he has made for Ky. as his brother went there very lately (PGBA 28 Dec 95)
WILSON, the Hon. James Esq., one of the Associate Judges of the U.S. Supreme Ct., d. at Edenton, N. Carolina on the 21st ult. (NH 6 Sep 98, VH 7 Sep 98)
WILSON, James, a member of the Society of Friends and late resident in Yorkshire, Eng., d. in Manchester on the 22nd inst. (VGGA 25 Sep 98, DOB 27 Sep 98)

WILSON, John, aka John WILLIAMS, svt., from Yorkshire, ran away from Zachariah HICKS, Pr. Geo. Co., (VG 20 Apr 39)

WILSON, John, b. in Galway, Ireland, 56, des. from Capt. Robert HODGSON's Independent Co. now raising for the service and defense of S. Carolina (VG 3 Jul 46)

WILSON, John, says his master lives in Va. not far beyond Patowmack, but low down, appears to be about 25, jailed in Baltimore as a runaway in Oct. last (MG 22 Apr 62)

WILSON, John, mulatto, 34, carpenter, ran away from Wm. BLACK on James River (VG 13 Dec 70)

WILSON, John, shoemaker, of Norfolk, died (VG 17 Oct 71); his admrs., Archibald CAMPBELL and Geo. WILSON Jr., will sell his PE; Geo. Wilson Jr. and Co. are carrying on the shoemaker's business (VG 7 Nov 71)

WILSON, Col. John, of Augusta Co., where he had long served as a burgess, d. in his 72nd year (VG and VGR 4 Feb 73)

WILSON, John Esq., of Norfolk Co., died (VG 2 Oct 79)

WILSON, Col. John, dec'd, his admr., Willis WILSON, intends to petition the next assembly for a payment to be made to the est. of Col. WILSON for the destruction of his property in the Northwest (NPJ 10 Sep 88)

WILSON, John, appr., 19, ran away from John LAY[P]OLD, Rockett's; his mother lives near the Merry Oaks in Hanover Co. (VGRMA 13 Mar 94)

WILSON, John, watchmaker from London, d. on Wed. 11 Mar. in Richmond; he was bur. in the churchyard agreeable to the Masonic Order (VGGA 18 Mar 95)

WILSON, John, of Portsmouth, dec'd, a tract of land bel. to his est. near the Northwest Landing and presently occupied by Wm. WILSON Sr. (nfi) to be sold by Willis WILSON of Portsmouth, his admr. w.w.a. (AGGA 6 Sep 96)

WILSON, John Custis, of Somerset Co., Md., intends to petition the next GA to remove some of his slaves to his lands in Accomack and Northampton Cos. (VCGA 7 Jul 94)

WILSON, John, seaman, 25, ran away from the ship *Amelia* lying at Bermuda Hundred (VG 1 Jun 69)

WILSON, Joseph, dec'd, his admr., Wm. WORTHINGTON, will sell nine of his Negroes (PGBA 16 Nov 95)

WILSON, Col. Josiah, of St. Bride's Par., Norfolk Co., d. last Tues. in the 87th year of his age (HNPA 16 May 95)

WILSON, Malachi, of St. Bride's Par., d. on Mon. last (AGNPPA 21 May 94)

WILSON, Peter, ind. svt., c. 24, native of Scotland, butcher, ran away from John SYME, Newcastle (VGPu 28 Jul 75, VGNI 2 Aug 75)

WILSON, Robert, of Frederick Co., dec'd, e.a.w. his admr., Thos. BABB and John WILSON (BVCG 14 Jan 93)

WILSON, Samuel, eld. son of Goodrich WILSON, dec'd, late of Norfolk Co., d. of smallpox sometime in the month of Feb. last on his passage from Glasgow to Portsmouth [epitaph signed "Amicus"] (NPC 9 Apr 91)

WILSON, Sarah, ind. svt., c. 20, ran away from John IRWIN, Westmoreland Co., Pa., near Ft. Pitt, along with John S[O]UDER (VGWA 27 Aug 91)

WILSON, Solomon, dec'd, e.a.w. John EASON in Smithfield or his ex., John GOODRICH, Isle of Wight Co. (NH 15 Jun 99)

WILSON, Thomas, printer, d. in the Federal City last Mon. week (CMAG 1 Mar 96); his admx., Alice WILSON of Washington, will sell his printing office consisting of a good press and upwards of 800 weight of well assorted types (CMAG 30 Apr 96)

WILSON, Thomas, of Buckingham Co., adv. that his wife, Polly WILSON, has for some time past left his bed and board (LWG 2 Mar 99)

WILSON, Thomas, mar. Miss Lucinda POPE on Sat. eve. (VGGA 6 Dec 99)

WILSON, William, aka Wm. RAWSON, of Fauquier Co., executed on Fri. last for horse stealing (VGWeA 6 Dec 87)

WILSON, William [Jr.], of Cedar Point, dec'd, e.a.w. his admr., James KEARNEY, and admx., Jane WILSON (PGBA 13 Feb 95, 5 Sep 95)

WILSON, William, 24-25, b. in Ireland, enl. at Fredsbrg. on 22 Oct. 1794, des. from Ft. Nelson (HNPA 4 Mar 95)

WILSON, Col. Willis, of Gosport, d. suddenly on Tues. at the Great Bridge; he was bur. with military honors (NH 13 Sep 98)

WILTROY, John, Virginia born, soldier in the Corps of Artillerists and Engineers, des. from Ft. Norfolk (NHPA 23 Sep 97)

WIMBISH, Benjamin, dec'd, e.a.w. his extx., Elizabeth WIMBISH, and ex., John WIMBISH (VGWeA 10 Dec 85)

WINCH, William, merch., of New Kent Co., mar. Miss Fanny Parke CUSTIS only dau. to the Hon. John CUSTIS Esq. one of H.M's Council of this colony, on 27 Jun. (VG 29 Jun 39)

WINDER, Edmund, merch., mar. Mrs. Jane WARD relict of the late Capt. James WARD (VHFA 18 Feb 90)

WINEY, Thomas, conv. svt., professes farming, was imp. lately in the *Litchfield*, Capt. JOHNSON, and came from Maidstone Gaol in the county of Kent, Eng., ran away from Wm. FITZHUGH, Westmoreland Co., he reportedly intends for Pa. and from thence to New England (MG 23 Aug 49)

WINFREY, Isaac, dec'd, e.a.w. his ex., Robert DRURY, Kg. Wm. Co. (VGPu 4 Apr 77)

WINFREY, Mrs. Sarah, spouse of Isaac WINFREY, d. lately in Kg. Wm. Co. (VGR 17 Feb 74)

WINGALL, Francis, Eng. svt., 25, shoemaker, ran away from Robert ADAM and Peter WISE, Alexandria (VG 6 Jun 66)

WINN, Richard, dec'd, e.a.w. his admr., Peter WINN of Hanover Co. (VGPA 18 Jun 91)

WINSLOW, Benjamin, ensign in the 5th Regt. and eld. son of Beverly WINSLOW, d. of a malignant fever in his 18th year (VGPu 27 Sep 76 sup)

WINSLOW, Col. Beverly Esq., of Spotsylvania Co., d. on Fri. the 12th inst. in his 60th year (VHFA 18 Jul 93); his ex., Thomas and Wm. WINSLOW, will sell his PE at his late dwelling house [in Spotsylvania Co.] (VHFA 17 Oct 93)

WINSLOW, Miss Polly, dau. of Benj. WINSLOW of Orange Co., d. of smallpox in Fredsbrg. in the bloom of [life] (VHFFA 26 May 97)

WINSLOW, William, of Spotsylvania Co., intends to remove to Ky. early in Oct. (VH 14 Sep 98)

WINSTON, Mrs. Anne, spouse of Col. John WINSTON of Hanover Co., d. on Fri. the 6th inst. in her 32nd year (VIC 11 Nov 89, 18 Nov 89)

WINSTON, Anthony, dec'd, 25 of his slaves to be sold at Amherst Ct. H. on 3 Nov. and 2600 ac. of his land in Buckingham Co. to be sold by his ex., Edmund WINSTON (VGAA 20 Sep 83); Edmund WINSTON of Campbell Co. will sell about 2000 ac. of his land in Buckingham Co. on the road from New London (RMA 18 Oct 96, Arg 3 Jan 97)

WINSTON, Geddes Esq., of Richmond, d. on Tues. morn. last in his 63rd year (VGGA 11 Jun 94, VGRMA 12 Jun 94)

WINSTON, George D., of Chestnut Hill, mar. Miss Dorothea Spotswood HENRY fourth dau. of the Hon. Patrick HENRY Esq. of Long Island, on Thurs. the 18th ult. (RMA 9 Jul 95)

WINSTON, Maj. Isaac, late of Henrico Co., dec'd, e.a.w. his ex., Peter and Isaac WINSTON, and Thomas PROSSER (VG 1 Jan 67)

WINSTON, James, late of Hanover Co., dec'd, e.a.w. his ex., John WINSTON Jr. (VG 28 Jan 73)

WINSTON, Col. John, d. at his seat in Hanover Co. on Sat. the 11th inst. (VGGA 22 Nov 97, VH 29 Nov 97)

WINTERSMITH, Hugh G., son of Dr. Charles WINTERSMITH of Martinsburg, aged 16, d. of dysentery on Sun. last (WG 28 Aug 99)

WINTERTON, Nicholas, dec'd, e.a.w. his admr., Geo. ABYVON of Norfolk (VGR 18 Feb 68)

WINTHROP, Thomas, Eng. svt., b. in Carlisle, c. 25, ran away from Geo. KELLOR, Frederick Co. (VGR 20 Jul 69)

WIROW, John, soldier on duty at Ft. Cumberland, [Tennessee], killed by

Indians on 6 Apr. (VSPW 4 Jun 95)

WISE, Thomas, svt., 25, from Yorkshire, ran away from James MAGINESS, Orange Co. (VGR 24 Mar 68)

WISEACRE, Christopher, young man from Dunmore Co., jailed for murder, escaped from jail in York Co. (VGR 4 Aug 74) [name also given as WISECARVER]

WISEMAN, Catharine, has removed herself from the bed and board of her husband, Adolph WISEMAN (SVG 1 Mar 97)

WISHART Family, HCC, 5 Mar. 1796: James Garnett TALIAFERRO and Wilhelmina his wife (pltf.) and Wm. WISHART and Sydney WISHART, Michael WALLACE and Lettice his wife late the widow of John WISHART, Achilles HORD ex. of Thomas HORD who was the ex. of John WISHART, and Rich. TAYLOR surviving ex. of Wm. ROWLEY (defs.); it appears that TAYLOR is not an inhabitant of this country (VGGA 6 Jul 96)

WISHART, the Rev. James, Rector of Brunswick Par., Kg. Geo. Co., d. on the 10th inst. (VGR 25 Aug 74)

WISHART, Mary, dec'd, her ex. (nfi) of Pr. Anne Co., will sell all her PE in that co. (HNPA 7 Jan 95, AGNPPA 23 Jan 95)

WISHART, Rachel, has eloped from her husband, Nicholas of Rockingham Co. (BVCG 27 Jan 97)

WISMER, Jacob, native of Germany, d. on Sun. the 4th of Feb. last in Bucks Co., Pa.; in Queen Anne's reign he emigrated to N. Carolina where he lived 10 yrs.; he then settled in Pa. where he mar. his third wife with whom he lived 67 yrs. and had 170 chil., grand chil. and great grand chil.; his widow is about 84 (VGWeA 22 Mar 87)

WITHERS, John, late of Stafford Co., dec'd, e.a.w. his ex., George WITHERS (VHFA 5 Jun 95)

WODDROP, John, brother and heir of Robert WODDROP dec'd of Great Britain (VG 28 Nov 71)

WODDROP, John, dec'd, his extx., Anne WODDROP, will sell 15 of his slaves (VGPu 28 Nov 77)

WODDROP, John Jr. and Sr., e.a.w. their ex., Samuel HARWOOD of Charles City Co. (VGPu 3 Jan. 77)

WODDROP, Robert, merch., of Northumberland Co., d. there about the middle of last month (VG 11 Jun 67)

WODROW, Alexander, d. of an apoplectic fit at Falmouth in his 45th year (VGPu 5 Sep 77); his admr., Andrew WODROW, will sell his 212 ac. tract on the Rappahannock River about two miles above Falmouth on which is a merch. mill (VGPu 7 Nov 77); his admr. will sell valuable lots in the town of Falmouth, other items of HHF and a large collection of books (VGPu 19 Sep 77); Andrew WODROW, admr. w.w.a. of Alexander WODROW and John NELSON dec'd, will petition the next assembly for permission to sell certain lands in Frederick, Hampshire, and Stafford Cos. bel. to their est. for the benefit of their heirs and creditors (VHFA 24 Jan 93)

WODROW, Col. Andrew, of Hampshire, mar. Miss Betsey HARRISON of Frederick Co., on Thurs. the 15th inst. (BVCG 23 Sep 96, VHFFA 4 Oct 96); [corrected to] mar. Miss Polly HARRISON on the 8th (BVCG 7 Oct 96)

WOLF, [Ollander], of this town [Fredsbrg.], mar. Miss Fenton KITCHEN of Stafford Co., there on Sun. the 19th inst. (RCFPC 29 Mar 97)

WOLFE, Benjamin, merch., mar. Miss Sophia SAMUEL, both of Richmond, on Wed. eve. last (RMA 30 Jul 95, RC 1 Aug 95)

WOLGAMOTT, Mrs. Catherine, wife of Joseph WOLGAMOTT, long since dead, d. in Martinsburg on Thurs. last aged 80, she was bur. in the German Burying Ground (PGBA 28 Dec 95)

WOLLEY, William, Eng. svt., carpenter, c. 27, imp. this fall in the *Lord Camden* from London, ran away from Rich. Hen. LEE, Westmoreland Co. (VGR 29 Nov 70)

WOLLMAN, Ester, will not go to live where her husband, Elias WOLLMAN of Augusta Co., desires (SS 19 Oct 93)

WOMBLE, Matthew, of Isle of Wight Co. [or Nansemond Co., acc. to VGAA of 29 Jan 85] murdered his pregnant wife and four of his six children last week (VGAA 26 Jun 84, VJAA 1 Jul 84); executed yesterday for murder (VGAA 29 Jan 85)

WOOD, Basil, mar. Miss Peggy RICHARDSON, both of Richmond, on Sat. eve. last (VGGA 19 Jan 91)

WOOD, Edward, Eng. svt., c. 30, ran away from Absolom FOX, Leesburg, Loudoun Co. (VGR 9 Nov 69)

WOOD, Isaac, adv. that Abby WOOD and himself have agreed by mutual consent to separate (VGWeA 24 Jun 91)

WOOD, James, dec'd, his admr., Joseph FORGUSON of Wmsbrg., will sell all his PE (VGGA 10 Apr 98)

WOOD, John, Eng. conv. svt., bricklayer, c. 22, ran away from John HOWLET, Urbanna, Middlesex Co. (VG and VGR 4 Mar 73)

WOOD, John, from Fairfax Co., executed on 12 May for burglary (VGPu 12 May 75 sup)

WOOD, John, aka Peter, black, 37-38, had been in the West Indies, ran away from Francis SMITH, Chesterfield Co. with a black girl 18-19, named Amia; they were with the British at Portsmouth and York; [they] may be in Gloucester Co. (VGAA 2, 9 Feb 82)

WOOD, Joseph, d. at Orange Ct. H., aged about 36 (VHFA 6 Jan 91)

WOOD, Leighton, mar. Miss Polly YOUNGHUSBAND in Richmond on Sat. (VGRMA 19 May 94, VGGA 21 May 94)

WOOD, Mrs. Mary, mother of His Ex. James WOOD Esq., Gov. of the Commonwealth, d. on the night of Mon. the 18th inst. in her 80th year at the seat of Robert WOOD near Winchester; she was bur. on Wed. in the family burying ground (VGGA 10 Jan 98)

WOOD, Richard, Virginian, 20, des. from Capt. Carter HARRISON's Co. (VG 5 Dec 55)

WOOD, Robert, weaver, c. 18, ran away from Thomas ROBINS, Gloucester Co.; he is thought to be in Pr. Geo. Co. (VG 23 Sep 73)

WOOD, Thomas, his wife intends to leave Norfolk to go to her husband (VCGA 11 Apr 94)

WOOD, Valentine Jr., late of Goochland Co., dec'd, his admr. (nfi) asks that [debtors] and creditors come forth (RMA 10 Jan 96)

WOODLIEF, John, of Pr. Geo. Co., died; his death notice was termed "premature" in the 10 Jan. issue (VG 3 Jan, 10 Jan 77)

WOODROW, Isaac, of Winchester, mar. Miss Elizabeth BLAKEMORE of Frederick Co. on Thurs. last (WG 21 Aug 99)

WOODS, James, c. 16, apprehended for housebreaking, but escaped (VGGA 25 Jan 92)

WOOD[S], Capt. John, d. on board the ship *Stanley* now in Alexandria from Liverpool (VJAA 21 Apr 85); e.a.w. his admr., Jesse TAYLOR, Alexandria (VJAA 23 Jun 85)

WOODSIDE, Mrs. Jane, spouse of John WOODSIDE of Norfolk, d. yesterday in an advanced age (VCNPGA 24 Aug 93)

WOODSIDE, John, of Norfolk, tailor, has declined business in favor of his son James (VCNPGA 4 May 93)

WOODSIDE, Joseph, of Norfolk Borough, d. yesterday (NHPA 27 Jan 98)

WOODSON, Charles, d. at his seat in Powhatan Co., on the 10th inst. in his 85th year (RMA and VGGA 17 Feb 96)

WOODSON, Charles Jr., dec'd, e.a.w. his extx., Ann WOODSON of Powhatan Co. (VGGA 22 Aug 92)

WOODSON, David, HCC, 11 Nov. 1786: James DALTON son and heir of Timothy DALTON (pltf.) against David WOODSON son and heir of Obadiah WOODSON and others (nfi) (defs.); it appears that David WOODSON is not an inhabitant of this country; he may have been of Russel Par. Bedford Co. (VIC 10 Sep 88)

WOODSON, Elizabeth, d. on 30 Jan. at her house in Goochland (Arg 14 Feb 97)

WOODSON, John, of Cumberland Co., dec'd, e.a.w. his ex., John WOODSON, Cartersville (VGGA 18 Nov 95, RC 21 Nov 95)

WOODSON, Matthew, of Goochland Co., dec'd, e.a.w. his admx., Elizabeth WOODSON; Thomas WOODSON and Samuel WOODSON (nfi) will sell lands in lower Goochland Co. (RMA 13 Aug 95)

WOODSON, Richard, late silversmith in Petersburg, dec'd, his brother is David WOODSON (VG 2 May 66)

WOODSON, Shadrack, Franklin Co., Ct. of Q.S., 7 Aug. 1798, in chanc.: Wm. AKERS (compl.) against Hezekiah FORD and Susannah his wife widow and relict of Shadrack WOODSON dec'd who is admx. of the sd. Shadrack WOODSON dec'd, and Joseph PRICE (defs.); it appears that FORD and his wife are not inhabitants of the country (LWG 13 Oct 98)

WOODSON, Tucker Jr., of Albemarle Co., dec'd, several of his slaves to be sold by his ex., Samuel WOODSON and Nicholas LEWIS (VGAA 31 Jan 84)

WOODFORD, William Gent., dec'd, 1600 ac. of his land on Nusiponix Run. six miles from Fredsbrg. to be sold by his ex. (VG 12 Sep 55)

WOODWARD, Benj., late of the Par. of Bath, Dinwiddie Co., silversmith, c. 30, suspected of counterfeiting paper money; escaped from jail in Dinwiddie Co. (VG 7 Sep 76)

WOODWARD, Henry, dec'd, e.a.w. his ex., John WOODWARD of Pr. Anne Co. (NHPA 3 Nov 96)

WOODWARD, William, of New Kent Co., is wanted by the sheriff for taking two Negroes; he is about 30; was formerly an inhabitant of New Kent Co. until some yrs. ago he went to Isle of Wight Co. where he lived some considerable time and there married; sometime in the last month he moved back to New Kent; it is supposed he will make for Carolina (VGIC 6 Jun 89 sup)

WOOLEY, Rebecca, Irish svt., very big with child, has been in the country upwards of two yrs., ran away from Geo. and Rich. LEE, Westmoreland Co., it is believed she will attempt to pass as the wife of Edmund CRYER who ran away with her (MG 20 Sep 49)

WOOLFOLK, William and Edward, of Redstone, have removed to the westward and have invested Robert WOOLFOLK of Caroline Co. with full powers to transact their business (VHFA 26 May 95)

WOOLLEN, Magor, d. at the Canal Mills on Fri. eve. last; he had been principal superintendent of the mills for three to four yrs.; he was bound as an appr. to some gentlemen in Baltimore at four yrs. of age and has never seen his parents since, they having removed to the back parts of Pa. immediately after he was put appr.; printers in Baltimore and Fredsbrg. are requested to insert the above notice (VGGA 29 Nov 97)

WOOLRIDGE, William, appr. tailor, c. 13, ran away from Lewis [WERCOR], Richmond (Arg 28 Feb 97)

WOOTON, Richard, mentions land in Isle of Wight Co. sold to him and his wife, Lucy, in 1730; also mentions Wm. WOOTON (nfi) (VGR 25 Feb 73)

WOOTTON, George and Herbert, sons of Sam. WOOTTON of Bishops Castle, Shropshire, Eng. and late of Greenock in Scotland; if they be living, on their applying to the printers of this paper, they will hear of something to their advantage left them by legacy; they have lately sailed out of different ports in America but Norfolk and Baltimore in particular (AGNPPA 21 May 94)

WORD, Charles, his ex., Henry FINCH of New Kent Co., requests his legatees to come to receive their proportional parts of the est. (VGPu 20 Jun 77)

WORMELEY, Mrs. Jane, widow of the late Ralph WORMELEY Esq., d. on Mon the 21st Oct. at Rosegill, aged 67 (VHFA 31 Oct 93, VGGA 6 Nov 93)

WORMELEY, John, of Lancaster Co., dec'd, his PE to be sold by his ex., R. Wormeley CARTER and Ralph WORMELEY (VGAA 13 Aug 85)

WORMELEY, Miss Lucy, second dau. of Ralph WORMELEY Esq., died (VG 8 Apr 73)

WORMELEY, Ralph Esq., of Middlesex Co., mar. Miss Salley BERKELEY, Wmsbrg., yesterday was fortnight (VG 19 Nov 36)

WORMELEY, Ralph Esq., d. on Tues. [or Thurs.] the 19th inst. at Rosegill in

his 75th year (VGGA 25 Aug 90, VGWeA 26 Aug 90)
WORMINGTON, Abraham, of Norfolk Co., dec'd, his acting ex., Wm.
WILSON, will sell some of his land in that co. including a 1200 ac. tract six
miles from the Great Bridge (NPC 8 May 90, 7 Aug 90)
WORSHAM, Charles, appr., 17-18, tailor, ran away from Thomas DAVIS,
Amelia Co. (VG 15 Feb 70)
WORSHAM, Capt. John, late of the 2nd Va. Regt., dec'd, e.a.w. his ex., Wm.
ROYAL and Joseph ROYAL of Amelia Co. (VG 25 Dec 79)
WORSHAM, John Sr., of Bermuda Hundred, dec'd, e.a.w. his ex., Wm. GILES
and Thomas WORSHAM; Mrs. WORSHAM will receive any debts due the
est. (VGR 19 Oct 69 sup)
WORSHAM, Richard, ensign, was adv. as a deserter, but states that he
obtained a furlough for 10 days due to ill health then went home to Hanover
Ct. H. but still being in ill health returned home til the men he was to
recruit should march (VGPu 18 Apr 77 sup)
WORT, Aaron, of Hampshire Co., was drowned in the South Branch on Thurs..
eve. last (BVCG 16 Mar 91)
WOTHERSPOON, James, came to America some years ago from Colehill Par.
of Old Munkland near Glasgow, his father has since d. and left him an est.
(VG 22 Sep 38)
WRAY, Mrs., spouse to Jacob WRAY of Hampton, died (VG and VGR 16 Dec
73)
WRAY, Mrs. Frances "Fanny", wife of James WRAY of Wmsbrg., d. last Mon.
in her 20th year (VG and VGR 11 Aug 74)
WRAY, William, d. on Thurs. last in Manchester (VGRMA 3 Apr 94)
WREN, Mrs. Eleanor, age 28, consort of Daniel WREN of Alexandria, d. on
Sun. night last leaving two chil. and her husband; one of the chil. is only a
few days old (TAA 3 Apr 98)
WREN, Mrs. Mary, widow of Wm. WREN formerly of Kg. Geo. Co., d. on 6 Dec.
1796, Benj. WEST will make a motion to the court of that co. to act. as admr.
for her est. (RCFPC 11 Jan 97)
WRENN, Joseph, dec'd, e.a.w. his admr., John FLOYD of Isle of Wight Co.
(VG 2 Oct 79)
WRIGHT, Ambrose, dec'd, James BOOKER of Essex Co. will settle any
demands against his est. or against BOOKER's wife (VG 15 Aug 77)
WRIGHT, Mrs. Ann, of Norfolk, d. on Tues. last in an advanced age (NH 16
Jun 96, AGNPPA 17 Jun 96, AGGA 17 Jun 96); e.a.w. her ex., Stephen
WRIGHT (NH 28 Jul 96, 29 Mar 98)
WRIGHT, Daniel, Virginian, 22, des. from Capt. Thomas WAGGENER's Co. of
Va. forces (VG 22 Aug 55)
WRIGHT, George, lately a merch. in Amelia Co., d. at Nassau, New
Providence on Tues. 7 Aug. (VGWeA 11 Oct 87)
WRIGHT, James, and his wife Anne, of Henrico Co., acquitted of Felony by the
Grand Jury at Wmsbrg. (VG 20 Oct 52)
WRIGHT, James, appr., ran away from Wm. DUNN, tailor, Norfolk (NHPA 23
Oct 97)
WRIGHT, James, pvt. in the 2nd Regt. of Artillerists and Engineers, native of
Gloucester Co. West Jersey, has not returned from leave and is suspected of
being a deserter (VGGA 13 Nov 98)
WRIGHT, John, svt., glazier, 24, ran away from the ship *Walpole* lying at the
Hundred in James River (VG 13 Oct 38)
WRIGHT, John, svt., from Scotland, c. 24, ran away from John G. FRAZER,
Kg. Wm. Co. (VG 7 Dec 69)
WRIGHT, John, Tobacco Inspector at Fredsbrg., d. suddenly on 11 May, aged
56 (VHFA 19 May 91); of Spotsylvania Co., his extx., Rosomond WRIGHT,
and exors., John STEWARD and Anthony FRAZER, will sell part of his
stock at his plant. known as Catharpin (VHFA 25 Oct 92)
WRIGHT, John, late of Norfolk, d. in Portsmouth last Thurs. (HNPA 11 Apr 95)
WRIGHT, Joshua, appr., c. 17, ran away from John HAMILTON, tailor,

Norfolk (NH 16 Jun 96)
WRIGHT, Mary, aka BRUCE, wife of John BRUCE, Norfolk, who will no longer pay her debts (NH 5 May 96)
WRIGHT, Mary, of Hanover Co., dec'd, the sheriff of sd. co. will administer the est. (VGGA 2 Nov 96)
WRIGHT, Capt. Patrick, of St. Bride's Par., Norfolk Co., dec'd, his land there to be sold by his ex., Geo. KELLY and Rich. E. LEE; his est. items to be sold at the house of Mrs. Lucy WRIGHT (NPJ 18 Jul 87, 21 Nov 87)
WRIGHT, Samuel, mulatto, b. near Hampton, c. 30, ran away from Rich. FRY living in Gloucester Township near Great Egg Harbor [New Jersey] (PC 1 Aug 68)
WRIGHT, Stephen, dec'd, e.a.w. Matthew PHRIPP of Norfolk (VG 24 Jul 79)
WRIGHT, Stephen, dec'd, his ex., Anne WRIGHT, will sell about 200 ac. of his land on the Western Branch near Norfolk (VGWeA 28 Feb 84)
WRIGHT, Maj. Stephen, of Craney Island, mar. Miss Abba CONNOR dau. of Col. Charles CONNOR of the same place on Thurs. eve. (HNPA 20 Jun 95)
WRIGHT, Mrs. Susannah, consort of John WRIGHT on Mine Run, Orange Co., d. suddenly on Wed. the 31st inst. (RCFPC 7 Sep 96)
WRIGHT, Thomas, late of Norfolk, e.a.w. Thomas CROSSLEY, Norfolk (NH 1 Sep 98)
WRIGHT, William, conv. svt., a ditcher by trade, ran away from Abraham SMITH, Dinwiddie Co. (VGPu 27 Mar 78)
WRIGHT, William, of Hanover Co., adv. that his wife, Mary, has for some time past absented herself and neglected to give her assistance towards the support of her children (VG 4 Sep 79)
WRIGHT, William, d. on Mon. last, aged 89 (VHFA 15 Oct 89)
WYAT, Elizabeth, has eloped from her husband, Nathan, Nansemond Co. (VG 5 Nov 67)
WYATT, C., of Gloucester Co., died (VGAA 20 Jul 82)
WYATT, Capt. Cary, d. on Mon. the 13th inst. at Hanover Town (VGGA 22 Feb 92); his ex. (nfi) will sell his HH and KF (VGGA 2 May 92)
WYATT, Hubard, of Pr. Geo. Co., mar. Miss Catherine COCKE of the same co. (VGPu 28 Apr 75)
WYATT, John, of Caroline Co., dec'd (VG 30 Jan 52)
WYATT, Richard Esq., of Caroline Co., mar. Miss Nancy WARE fourth dau. of John WARE Esq. of Goochland Co., on Thurs. the 8th inst. (Arg 16 Dec 96)
WYCHE, Benjamin, of Sussex Co., dec'd, all his PE to be sold by his admx. (nfi) (VG 9 Mar 69)
WYCHE, Capt. Nathaniel, of Sussex Co., dec'd, his ex., Hen. TAZEWELL and Daniel MABRY, will hire out 12 of his Negroes (VG 13 Dec 76); his ex. will sell 12-15 of his Negroes at Hick's Ford in Brunswick Co. (VGPu 13 Jun 77); his ex., Daniel MABRY, intends to leave the state shortly (VG 23 Oct 79)
WYLIE, John, Irish svt., 20, ran away from James CRAIG, Lunenburg Co. (VG 1 Jun 69)
WYNN, Mrs. Mary, of Greensville Co., d. in or about Oct. 1789; the sd. Mary gave to her two sons by will, John and Robert POWELL, a parcel of Negroes; Capt. MANSON of York Co., claims some of the Negroes and Michael MALONE of Sussex Co. also claims them acc. to an advertisement by James POWELL ex. of John POWELL who was ex. of Mary WYNN dec'd and Matthew DAVIS ex. of Robert POWELL (VGPI 28 Apr 97)
WYNNE, The Rev. John, Pastor of the Methodist Episcopal Church in Winchester, age about 27, d. on 27 Apr.; he was bur. in the German Presbyterian Burying Ground (BVCG 5 May 94)
WYTHE, Mrs. Elizabeth, spouse of the Hon. George WYTHE Esq. of Wmsbrg., d. on Sat. the 18th inst. in her 48th year [long obit. in VIC] (VGWeA 23 Aug 87, VIC 29 Aug 87, VGPI 30 Aug 87)

YACTON, Mary, formerly Mary SPINNER, wife of Emanuel YACTON, left home on Wed. last (VCGA 30 Jun 94)

YAGER, Nicholas, dec'd, e.a.w. his ex., Elisha BERRY and A. YAGER of Madison Co. (VHFFA 28 Feb 97)

YANCEY, Archilaus, dec'd, his admr. w.w.a., Charles YANCEY, will sell a tract of his land on Little River in Louisa Co. containing 300-400 ac. and a tract of land in the same co. whereon Mrs. Elizabeth YANCEY now lives agreeable to the will of Henry YANCEY dec'd; Charles YANCEY is apparently Henry's ex. (VGGA 27 Nov 98)

YANCEY, the Rev. Robert, Rector of Trinity Par., Louisa Co., died (VG 5 May 74)

YANCEY, Stephen, of Louisa Co., executed near Richmond on 3 Dec. for the murder of his brother (VGAA 4 Dec. 84); his est. to be sold by Waddy THOMPSON, Garret MINOR, and Charles YANCEY (VGAA 5 Mar 85)

YANCY, Achiles, dec'd, his ex., Wm. PIERCE of Elizabeth City Co., adv. that he wishes to settle his administration of the est. immediately (VGGA 26 Oct 96)

YARBROUGH, Charles, a young man late of Philadelphia, d. on Thurs. the 22nd inst. in Kg. Wm. Co. (Arg 27 Nov 98)

YARBROUGH, William, dec'd, all persons having any demands against his est. are desired to make them known to James Smith YARBROUGH, Pr. Edw. Co. or to Rich. YARBROUGH in Blandford (VG 2 May 71)

YARMOUTH, Jack, Negro, 40, formerly bel. to Gov. GOOCH, ran away from Peter WAGENER, Fairfax Co., suspected of having gone to Hanover Co. (VGR 12 May 68)

YATES, the Rev. Benjamin, dec'd, e.a.w. his admr., Barth. YATES (VGR 13 Jul 69)

YATES, Lt. Bartholomew, of Col. READ's Va. Regt., d. on Fri. last at Princeton, [N. J.]; Edw. R. YATES (nfi) adv. that all persons having demands against his est. are to make them known to Wm. YATES Esq. (nfi) (VG 31 Jan, 21 Mar 77)

YATES, Col. Edward Randolph, of Mecklenburg Co., dec'd, e.a.w. his ex., Lewis BURWELL and Wm. HEPBURN, who will also sell his personal property (VGPI 26 Jul 92, VGGA 4 Oct 92)

YATES, Mrs. Elizabeth, of Mecklenburg Co., died (VGGA 14 Sep 91)

YATES, Dr. Michael, of Caroline Co., dec'd, his livestock to be sold by his admrs., Daniel COLEMAN and Wm. YATES (VHFA 17 Feb 91)

YATES, Robert, Irish, des. from the 4th Co. of the 2nd Bn. for the State of Georgia, enl. in Henry Co. (VGPu 9 May 77 sup)

YATES, the Rev. William, President of William and Mary, Chaplain of the Worshipful House of Burgesses, and Rector of Bruton Par., d. on Sat. (VG-Randolph 21 Sep 64)

YATES, Col. William, dec'd, his admr., Francis MUIR of Pr. Geo. Co. will sell his est. in Dinwiddie Co. and settle his est. (VICGA 17 Mar 90, VGPI 18 Mar 90, VGGA 25 Aug 90)

YEAL, William, left Eng. about eight yrs. ago, a single man, c. 40, if he will apply to Joseph PLEASANTS near Richmond in Henrico Co., he will hear something to his advantage (VGAA 4 May 82)

YEISER, Frederick, dec'd, e.a.w. his admr., Susannah YEISER and Geo. LIGHTER who will attend at the house Nathan GRIFFITH in Baltimore on the first Mon. in May next (TAA 17 Apr 98)

YERBY Family, HCC, 13 May 1790, George YERBY and the sd. Geo. YERBY ex. of John YERBY dec'd and Thomas YERBY eld. son and heir at law of the sd. John YERBY dec'd (pltfs.) [see the TAFF Family] (VGGA 25 Aug 90)

YOAKUM, Matthias, appr., saddler, 16-17, ran away from Henry FRIDLEY (VGWA 23 Sep 90)

YORKE, John, Eng. svt., 22, ran away from Robert GILKISON and David HOGSHEAD near Jennings's Gap (VGR 27 Oct 68)

YOUL, Thomas, b. in Culpeper Co., des. from Ft. Washington (KG 22 Aug 95)

YOUNG, Alexander, late of Henrico Co., dec'd, e.a.w. his ex., Richard YOUNG of Richmond (Arg 12 Feb 99)

YOUNG, Andrew, svt., weaver, 30, ran away from Patrick COUTTS, Richmond (VG 16 May 66)

YOUNG, Charles, merch., mar. Miss Polly DABNEY, both of [Alexandria], at Georgetown, last Thurs. (CMAG 10 Sep 96)

YOUNG, Daniel, svt., ran away from Daniel HORNBY, Richmond Co. (VG 11 May 39)

YOUNG, David, of Alexandria, dec'd, his admr. is David YOUNG (VJAA 13 Jan 85)

YOUNG, David, adv. that his wife, Nancy YOUNG, has left his bed and board (CMAG 9 Nov 97)

YOUNG, Edward, native of Scotland, c. 20, committed suicide on Sun. last; he was an assistant in the store of H. McAUSLAND (VHFA 6 Sep 92)

YOUNG, Edwin, dec'd, his tract of land in Frederick Co. will be sold by his ex., Wm. C. WILLIAMS (BVCG 21 Apr 94)

YOUNG, James, native of Scotland, joiner, came to America many yrs. ago and last resided in Alexandria; Bolling STARK of Petersburg will inform him of something greatly to his advantage (VGR 9 Jun 74); James DAVENPORT, Westmoreland Co., adv. that YOUNG d. in Westmoreland Co. at the house of Edw. SANFORD in Feb. 1765; he d. unmarried (VGR 30 Jun 74)

YOUNG, James, late of Fauquier Co., dec'd, e.a.w. his ex., James NEALE (VH 19 Mar 99)

YOUNG, John, Eng. svt., ran away from Jacob BRAKE, Hampshire Co. (VG 25 Mar 75)

YOUNG, John, executed near Winchester on Fri. 19 Oct. in his 47th year for horse stealing; he was b. in Baltimore [a full biography is given] (BVCG 22 Oct 92, VGRDA 27 Oct 92)

YOUNG, the Rev. John, Minister of the Gospel in Va., mar. this week in Green Castle, Miss Polly CLARKE dau. of Geo. CLARKE of Green Castle ([Hagerstown, Md.] Washington Spy 1 Oct 94)

YOUNG, John, of Richmond, d. on the 7th inst. leaving parents and brothers (RMA 9 Apr 96)

YOUNG, John, 35-36, of Dinwiddie Co., jailed in Petersburg for suspicion of horse stealing, has escaped (VGGA 10 Aug 96)

YOUNG, John, executed yesterday at the gallows near this city [Richmond] for horse stealing (VGWeA 29 Oct 96)

YOUNG, John, late of Richmond, dec'd, e.a.w. Richard YOUNG his admr. (Arg 12 Feb 99)

YOUNG, Nicholas, a venerable old man killed during a robbery near Shepherdstown on the 24 th inst.; Wm. CRUMPTON was found guilty of his murder and sentenced to death on 18 Nov. (PGBA 28 Apr 96, BVCG 21 Oct 96)

YOUNG, Capt. Thomas, of Norfolk Co., d. on 19th ult. in Accomack Co. (AGGA 7 Nov 97)

YOUNG, William, d. on Sat. eve. aged 76 (TAA 1 Oct 98)

YOUNG, William Jr., dec'd, e.a.w. his ex., Wm. DUNN of Essex (VGAA 4 Feb 86)

YOUNG, William Sr., dec'd, his ex., Leroy DANGERFIELD, will sell his 571 ac. tract in Essex Co. near Hobb's Hole (VHFA 13 Sep 92)

YOUNGHUSBAND, Miss Elizabeth C., [an unsigned poem on her death] (VGRDA 25 Oct 92)

YOUNGHUSBAND, Lt. Isaac, d. lately in the service of his country in Gen. WAYNE's Army (VGRMA 12 Jan 95)

YOUNGHUSBAND, Capt. Isaac, d. on Mon. morn. last at his seat near Richmond in a very advanced age (VGGA 29 Apr 95, RMA 30 Apr 95)

YOUNGHUSBAND, Isaac Jr., ex. of his uncle, Thomas YOUNGHUSBAND dec'd; mentions Isaac YOUNGHUSBAND SR. who had brought sundry claims against the est. (VGGA 29 Aug 92)

YOUNGHUSBAND, Mrs. Mary, wife of Pleasant YOUNGHUSBAND of

Richmond, d. at Studley the seat of the Hon. Peter LYONS Esq. in Hanover (VGRMA 15 Apr 93)

YOUNGHUSBAND, Master Peter, only son of Pleasant YOUNGHUSBAND of Richmond, d. on Fri. last at Studley in Hanover Co. (VGRMA 28 Oct 93)

YOUNGHUSBAND, Pleasant, merch., mar. Miss Polly LYONS dau. of the Hon. Peter LYONS Esq. in Hanover Co. on Sun. last (VGAA 5 Jul 86)

Y[O]WELL, David, charged with the murder of Nancy CLARK, was found guilty in Fredsbrg. District Ct. yesterday (VHFA 2 May 93)

YOWELL, William, appr., 20, ran away from Robert BROOKING, Culpeper (VHFA 24 Jun 90)

YRARGAIN, Anner, of Chesterfield Co., dec'd, her ex. will sell the crop of corn and fodder, HH and KF and three Negroes (VGPI 21 Nov 97)

ZANE, Brig. Gen. Isaac, for many yrs. a rep. of Shenandoah Co., d. at Marlbro' Iron Works last night (Winchester disp. of 17 Aug.) (VHFA 25 Aug 95); late of the Marlbro' Iron Works, Frederick Co.; Col. Jacob RINKER, Shenandoah Co., Dr. Robert MACKY, Winchester, Alexander WHITE, Washington, and Miss Sarah ZANE, Philadelphia, will sell his iron works with 9000 adjoining acres plus many other tracts of land (BVCG 22 Jan 96)

ZEAN, Simeon, dec'd, e.a.w. John M'LENACHAN, his admr., of Alexandria (VGAxA 5 Nov 89)

ZOLL, [?], d. of Hemophilia near North Mountain, Frederick Co., aged 19, he had five brothers who also bled to death; they were all children of their father's first wife (VGWA 16 Feb 91, VHFA 3 Mar 91)

Index of Names

Abbernatha, David 247
Abbett, [?] 243
Abbot, Josiah 1
Abbot, Mourning 330
Abbot, Sarah 304
Abbott, Elizabeth 1
Abbott, James 212
Abbott, Jane 1
Abbott, John 1
Abbott, Margaret 1
Abbott, Richard 1
Abbott, Robert 1
Abbott, Sarah 1
Able, Ezekiel 116
Able, Thomas 296
Ablewhite, Thomas 295
Abney, W. 216
Abrams, Capt. Mordecai (see: Abraham, Capt. Mordecai) 1
Abyvon, Geo. 293, 373
Acrill, Wm. 70, 84
Adam 19
Adam, Elizabeth 1
Adam, Robert 45, 73, 100, 160, 176, 197, 204, 295, 306, 343, 354, 373
Adam, Thomas 231
Adams, Alex. 2
Adams, Miss Alice 227
Adams, Benj. 358
Adams, Col. Rich. 2
Adams, E. 69
Adams, Miss Eliz. 282
Adams, Francis 2, 305
Adams, George 2
Adams, Henry 2, 189
Adams, James 2
Adams, Jn. 95, 339
Adams, Rich. 43, 63, 347
Adams, Rich. Jr. 2
Addison, Col. Jn. 225

Aderton, James 169
Aderton, Rebecca 169
Adkins, Robert 2
Adkins, Thomas Sr. 2
Adkisson, Isaiah 2
Aduddell, Elias 5
Agen, Thomas 2
Aiken, Hugh (see: Aitken, Hugh) 3
Ainsworth, Wm. 162
Aitchison, Miss Nancy 177
Aitchison, Wm. 177
Aitken, Wm. 3
Akers, Wm. 376
Akers, Wm. Jr. 259
Alcock, Miss Betsy 287
Alcorn, James 337
Alderson, Jeremiah 1, 239
Aldridge, Dorothy 282
Aldridge, Richard 3
Alexander, Capt. 94
Alexander, Gerrard 51
Alexander, Jn. 99
Alexander, Joseph 194
Alexander, Lucy 3
Alexander, M. 222
Alexander, Martha 371
Alexander, Miss Peggy 139
Alexander, Robert 3, 79, 122, 147, 311
Alexander, Sarah 371
Alexander, Wm. 3, 132, 154, 169, 187, 249, 295
Alfriend, Benj. 3
Alick 297
Allan, Jacob 18, 293
Allan, James 3, 363
Allan, Miss Sally 363
Allegre, Giles 4
Allegre, Miss Jane 260
Allen 4
Allen, Ann 4
Allen, Anne 4

Allen, Aphia 206
Allen, Charles 4, 61
Allen, David 4, 206, 251
Allen, Edward 106
Allen, Elizabeth 4
Allen, Frances 4
Allen, George 4
Allen, Lt. H. 194
Allen, Henry 4
Allen, Hugh 296
Allen, Isham 277
Allen, James 24, 67, 142, 313
Allen, Jn. 99, 156
Allen, Col. John 4
Allen, Julius 4
Allen, Julius Jr. 4
Allen, Julius Sr. 359
Allen, Lucy 4
Allen, Martha 5
Allen, Mary 4
Allen, Nancy 4
Allen, Nathan 327
Allen, Phebe 4
Allen, Rich. 39, 334
Allen, Richmond 5, 334
Allen, Robert P. 4
Allen, Miss Sally 24
Allen, Thos. 4, 5, 201, 254, 277
Allen, Wm. 208, 244, 366
Allen, Col. Wm. 153, 334
Alley, David 93
Allgood, Jn. 369
Allgood, Sarah 369
Allinford, Philip 159
Allison, the Rev. Dr. 148
Allison, Miss Nancy 54
Allison, Nancy Walker 328
Allison, Robert 115, 211, 223
Allison, Sam. 5
Allmand, Lewis 276
Allmond, Wm. Sr. 5
Allmorn, Lewis 150
Almand, Jn. 270
Almand, Lewis 286

Alsop, Maj. Benj. 5
Alvas, Nancy 183
Ambler, Miss Betsey 38
Ambler, Edw. 6
Ambler, Jacquelin 5, 285
Ambler, Jaquelin 38
Ambler, John 5
Ambler, Mary 5
Ambler, Miss Polly 227
Amia 375
Amory, Thomas C. 270
Amy 44
Anderson, Adjutant 195
Anderson, Mrs. 329
Anderson, Ambrose 7, 210
Anderson, Arch. 6
Anderson, Bart. 361
Anderson, Bartelot 6
Anderson, Bartlet 289
Anderson, Bartlett 94
Anderson, Bartt. 7, 370
Anderson, Catharine 29
Anderson, Cicely 6, 8, 185
Anderson, Colbert 91
Anderson, Daniel 7
Anderson, David 6, 7
Anderson, David Jr. 155, 318
Anderson, Edmund 6
Anderson, Edward 254
Anderson, Eliz. 6, 7
Anderson, Fanny 8
Anderson, Mrs. Frances 161
Anderson, Francis 6, 8, 172
Anderson, Geo. 6
Anderson, Handsford 7
Anderson, Ignatius 99
Anderson, Isaac 194
Anderson, James 7

Anderson, Jasper 6
Anderson, Jesse 187
Anderson, Jn. 6, 7, 185, 186, 228
Anderson, Col. Jn. 329
Anderson, Jos. 7
Anderson, Lucy 6, 7
Anderson, Miss Lucy 303
Anderson, M. 179
Anderson, Matthew 128
Anderson, Matthew 207
Anderson, Matthew 6, 7, 92, 128, 207
Anderson, Michael 7
Anderson, Miss Molly 369
Anderson, Nancy 6
Anderson, Nath. 6
Anderson, Nathan 122
Anderson, Nathaniel 6, 56, 185
Anderson, Nelson Jr. 294
Anderson, Nicholas 6
Anderson, Miss Polly 242
Anderson, Rich. 6, 138
Anderson, Ro. 273
Anderson, Robert 6, 127
Anderson, Samuel 6
Anderson, Sarah 6
Anderson, Thos. 6, 7
Anderson, Turner 144
Anderson, Wm. 6, 7, 8, 29, 96, 124, 185, 186, 191, 282, 314, 315
Anderson, Capt. Wm. 235
Andre, Peter Francis 129
Andres, Martin 8
Andrew, Garnet 8
Andrews, Rev. Mr. 8
Andrews, James 39
Andrews, Molly 39

Andrews, Nancy 8
Andrews, Robert 23, 285
Andrews, Wm. 8
Ange, Eleanor 8
Ange, John 8
Angel, Miss 136
Anner, Robert 235
Anson, Thomas J. 370
Anthony 139
Anthony, Jn. 96
Apperson, Jn. 8, 317
Apperson, Samuel 27
Applethwaite, Thomas 343
Applewhaite, John 8
Apthorp, Charles Ward 369
Apthorp, Miss Maria 369
Archdeacon, Parnel 8
Archer, Abraham 9, 37
Archer, Edw. 9
Archer, James 93
Archer, Jn. 12, 33
Archer, Jn. Jr. 36
Archer, Mary 9
Archer, Thos. 8
Archibald, Catherine 9
Arell, Mrs. Phoebe 239
Arell, Rich. 251
Argenbright, George 158
Arlington, James 227
Armentrout, Henry 193
Armistead, [?] 119
Armistead, Miss Betsey 304
Armistead, Miss Betsy 203
Armistead, Miss Betsy Stith 10
Armistead, Dorothy 280
Armistead, Edw. 10
Armistead, Miss Euphan 134
Armistead, Miss Fanny 141

18th-Century Virginia Newspapers 385

Armistead, J. 316
Armistead, James Bray 10
Armistead. Jn. 22, 61, 228, 320
Armistead, Julia 9
Armistead, Katharine 10
Armistead, Lucy 9
Armistead, Maria 10
Armistead, Mary 10
Armistead, Mary 9
Armistead, Miss Molly 50
Armistead, Moss 82
Armistead, Miss Polly 229, 346
Armistead, R. 10
Armistead, Robert 10, 304
Armistead, Miss Sukey 59
Armistead, Thos. 10
Armistead, Wm. 9, 10, 85, 109
Armistead, Wm. Sr. 10
Armston, Freer 120
Armstrong, Alex. 10
Armstrong, Andrew 10
Armstrong, Archibald 10
Armstrong, Elinor 10
Armstrong, Isabella 10
Armstrong, James 218, 228
Armstrong, Jn. 98
Armstrong, Robt. 10
Armstrong, Thos. 10
Armstrong, Wm. 10
Arnatt, Susana 140
Arnatt, Wm. 140
Arnaud (see: Arno) 61
Arno, Jn. Baptist 61
Arnold, Joshua 184
Arnold, Priscilla 184
Arnold, Reuben 332
Arnold, Wm. 11, 306
Arthur, Charles R. 11

Arundell, Jn. 301
Ash, Francis 237
Ashbrook, Aaron 11
Ashbrook, Absolom 11
Ashbrook, Amelia 11
Ashbrook, Eli 11
Ashbrook, Eliz. 11
Ashbrook, John 11
Ashbrook, Levi 11
Ashbrook, Mary 11
Ashbrook, Rhody 11
Ashbrook, Thos. 11
Ashbrook, Wm. 11
Ashburn, Geo. 11
Ashby, Edward 35
Ashby, John 12
Ashby, Margaret 35
Ashby, Robert 12
Ashenhurst, Wm. 12
Ashley, Ann 63
Ashlock, Rich. 97
Ashton, Burdit 356
Askew, Wm. 371
Askin, Vincent 172
Askren, Thomas 156, 341
Astin, Daniel 279
Atcheson, Wm. (see: Aitcheson, Wm.) 3
Ather, Jn. Jr. 113
Atherton, Caleb 76
Atherton, James 12
Atkerson, Jn. 12
Atkerson, Thomas 12
Atkins, Mary 245
Atkins, Philip 96, 97
Atkins, Wyatt 99
Atkinson, Hen. 12
Atkinson, James 12
Atkinson, Jn. 106
Atkinson, Jn. 44, 69, 82
Atkinson, Joseph 63
Atkinson, Miss Nelly 261
Atkinson, Philip 93
Atkinson, Roger 54, 280
Atkinson, Thomas 200
Attkisson, Isaiah 12
Attkisson, Joseph 12

Attwell, Thomas 107, 274
Aubery, Arcutt 12
Austin, Capt. John Jr. 13
Austin, Moses 320
Austin, Susannah 13
Austin, Thomas 12
Austin, Wm. 285
Avery, Miss Polly 14
Avery, Wm. 92
Aydle, James 98
Aylett, Anne 13
Aylett, Jn. 151, 156
Aylett, Mary 13
Aylett, Miss Mary 119
Aylett, P. 13, 287
Aylett, Philip 13
Aylett, Rebecca 13
Aylett, Wm. 13, 59, 124, 129, 220, 223, 225, 274, 297
Aylett, Col. Wm. 119
Ayscough, Anne 13

Babb, Thos. 372
Backhurst, J. 14
Bacon, Nathaniel 14
Bacon, Samuel D. 14
Badger, Joseph 225
Badget, Thomas 125
Badgett, Mary 14
Badgett, Milly 14
Bagley, Dicie 103
Bagley, James 103
Bagners, A. 200
Bagners, Lacoste 200
Bagnois, Mrs. Nancy 354
Bailey, Miss 112
Bailey, Anne 15, 310
Bailey, Charles 99
Bailey, Chester 14
Bailey, Daniel 14
Bailey, David 184
Bailey, Eliz. 14
Bailey, Gabriel 14
Bailey, Hen. 14
Bailey, Jane 14
Bailey, Jeane 184
Bailey, Jn. 15
Bailey, Jn. E. 20
Bailey, Jonathan 14
Bailey, Jos. 14
Bailey, Lemuel 347

Bailey, Parke 14, 309
Bailey, Rich. 305
Bailey, Sarah 14
Bailey, Thomas 358
Bailey, Wm. 14
Bailey, Yancey 15
Bailinge, Larkin 99
Baily, Rich. 349
Bain, Robert 65, 305
Baintone, Josias 72
Baird, James 157
Baird, John 15, 251, 311, 350
Baker, Dr. 15
Baker, Caleb 16
Baker, Edward 283
Baker, Eliz. 107
Baker, Hilary 309
Baker, John 15, 116, 123
Baker, Dr. Jn. 15
Baker, Leonard 111
Baker, Martin 59, 107
Baker, Mary 15
Baker, Rich. 2, 15, 158, 290
Baker, Samuel 108
Baker, Thos. 22
Baker, Wm. 15, 100
Bakewell, T. 16
Balch, Ensign 195
Balentine, Eliz. 7
Baley, Winifred 13
Balfour, Mr. 156
Balfour, James 359
Ball, Miss Betsey 211
Ball, Burges 17
Ball, Burgess 313
Ball, Col. Burges 211
Ball, Henry 24
Ball, James 105
Ball, James Jr. 215
Ball, Jn. 35, 284
Ball, Mary 16
Ball, Spencer 150, 293
Ball, Wm. 193, 194
Ball, Dr. Wm. 16
Ballard, Miss Betsy 8
Ballard, Rich. 17
Ballard, S. 47
Ballard, Thomas 336
Ballard, Wm. 152
Ballard, Wm. 205

Ballendine, Mrs. Anne 344
Ballendine, Thos. W. 17
Ballentyne, Jn. 44
Balmain, the Rev. Alex. 17, 52, 252
Balsh, Ensign 195
Bangham, Humphrey 17
Banister, Miss Fanny 34
Banister, Jn. 17, 18, 244
Banister, Jn. Monroe 17, 18
Banister, Col. Jn. 18, 244
Banister, Theo. Blair 17, 18
Bankes, Judith 18
Bankhead, Miss Jane 109
Bankhead, Miss Nelly 287
Banks, Adam 150, 197
Banks, Eliz. 6, 185
Banks, Miss Nancy 150
Banks, Rich. 6, 185, 325
Banks, Thomas 294
Bannerman, Benj. 18
Bannister, Jn. 292
Baptist, Wm. G. 90
Barber, Col. 348
Barber, Elizabeth 18
Barber, James 295
Barber, Sarah 18
Barbour, Thomas 335
Barclay, George 70
Barclift, Err 227
Bardine, Rich. 226
Barham, Peter 95
Barker, Joseph 335
Barkesdale, Wm. 275
Barkley, Wm. 1
Barksdale, Daniel 19
Barksdale, Jos. 19
Barksdale, Samuel 19
Barlow, Wm, 86
Barnaby, Elias 149, 241
Barnard, Jn. 67

Barnes, A. 170
Barnes, Col. 139
Barnes, Gabriel 19
Barnes, Henry 19
Barnes, Jacob 91
Barnes, Mary 295
Barnes, Rich. 276, 279
Barnet, Ambrose 160
Barnet, James 19
Barnet, Margaret 160
Barnett, Ambrose 220
Barnett, David 94
Barnett, Gerrard 309
Barnett, James 92
Barnett, Jn. 20
Barns, Osborn 92
Barns, Rich. 20
Barr, Miss Sukey 325
Barradall, Edward 87
Barraud, Daniel 16, 320, 332
Barraud, Miss Kitty 75
Barraud, Miss Sally 332
Barret, Jn. 20
Barrett, Rich. 20
Barrett, Tabitha 20
Barrett, Thos. 20, 249
Barrier, Jacob 217
Barrom, Fielding 20
Barron, Capt. 28
Barron, Rebecca 20
Barron, Capt. Robert 20
Barrott, Miles 333
Barry, George 295
Barry, Jn. 75, 93
Barry, Thos. 20
Bartholemus, Jn. 76
Bartlet, Capt. 118
Bartlett, Alex. 97
Bartlett, Edmund 19
Bartlett, James 93
Bartlett, Sarah 19
Bartlett, Wm. 97
Barton, Lt. Col. 29
Barton, Charles 238
Barton, Underhill 228
Barton, Wm. 219
Basco 21
Baskerville, Jn. 21, 220

18th-Century Virginia Newspapers 387

Baskerville, Jn. Sr. 21
Baskerville, Rich. 238
Bass, Drury 93
Bass, Edw. 21
Bass, Francis 21
Bass, Hartwell 356
Bass, James 356
Bass, Jn. 96, 348
Bass, Col. Joseph 301
Bass, Nancy 348
Basset, Col 357
Bassett, Burwell 21
Bassett, Col. Burwell 21
Bassett, Miss Judith 214
Bate, Jn. 295
Bates, Benj. 21
Bates, Eliz. 21
Bates, Fleming 21, 178
Bates, James 21
Bates, Jn. 295
Bates, Thomas F. 166, 260
Bates, William 93
Bathgate, Wm. 21
Batle, Alex. Watson 21
Batle, Eliz. Parham 22
Batle, Francis Beverly 22
Batle, Mary 22
Batle, Wm. 21
Battaile, Hay 22
Batte, Henry 272
Batte, Jn. 27
Batte, Rich. 22
Batte, Wm. 43
Batten, Wm. 92
Battersby, W. 52
Batterton, Eliz. 22
Baughan, Miss Hannah 177
Baylis, Jn. 22
Baylor, Col. 353
Baylor, Gregory 22
Baylor, Col. Jn. 22
Baylor, Mrs. Lucy 50
Bayly, Samuel 308
Bayne, Easworth 22
Bayne, Rich. 155
Baynham, Jn. 22
Bayns, Jn. 127
Bazel, Andrew 193

Bazel, Eliz. 193
Beacham, Isaac 323
Beacham, Prudence 323
Beacham, Sarah 22
Beachy, Felix 117
Beadel, Jn. 241
Beal, Taverner 223, 362
Beale, Anne 343
Beale, Miss Fanny 127
Beale, Jn. 38
Beale, Mary 22
Beale, Miss Mildred 118
Beale, Rich. E. 351
Beale, Thomas 127
Beale, Wm. C. 74
Beale, Wm. Curry 343
Beall, Mr. 193
Beall, Harriet 23
Beall, Matilda 23
Beall, Norbert 23
Beall, Sam. 23, 293
Beally, Ensign 195
Bearcroft, Wm. 93
Beard, George 174
Beasley, Ambrose 23
Beasley, Wm. 23
Beatly, Wm. 93
Beatty, Capt. 78
Beatty, Ensign 195
Beauche, Jn. Baptist 129
Beavans, Wm. 213
Beavars, Wm. 281
Beazely, Sarah 23
Becham, Ann 15
Beckley, Jn. 39, 88, 231
Beckwith, Jonathan 242
Beckwith, Roger 14
Becquith, [?] 24
Becquith, Mary 24
Bedinger, Henry 73, 118, 325, 327
Beeler, Becky 24
Beeler, Benj. 23, 24
Beeler, Benj. Jr. 24
Beeler, Catharine 23
Beeler, Charles 24
Beeler, Christopher 23, 24

Beeler, Eliz. 24
Beeler, Frederick 23, 24
Beeler, Geo. 24, 269
Beeler, Joseph 23, 24
Beeler, Mary 24
Beeler, Michael 24
Beeler, Samuel 24
Beeler, Samuel Jr. 24
Beeler, Wm. 24
Beeson Family 59
Beeson, Jesse 24
Beezley, Edmund 113
Begg, John 24
Belfield, Jn. 330
Bell, Capt. 121, 156 163, 206, 345
Bell, Mr. 38
Bell, Ann 198
Bell, Benj. 195
Bell, Betty 24
Bell, Capt. David 39, 42, 82, 92, 105, 148, 236, 262, 275
Bell, David 24
Bell, Edward 24
Bell, Eliz. 250
Bell, Henry 24, 25
Bell, James 46
Bell, John 24, 322
Bell, Joseph 24
Bell, Miss Lucy 198
Bell, Nathan 182, 198
[Bell], Nell 24
Bell, Perry 250
Bell, Samuel A. 24
Bell, Thos. 25, 96
Bell, Wm. 91
Bellamy, the Rev. Josiah 254
Belsches, James 2, 154
Ben 83, 182, 346
Benger, Dorothea 122
Bennett, Charles 217
Bennett, Henry Astley 217
Bennett, Nat. 99
Bennett, Rich. 296
Bennitt, Joseph 357
Benson, Andrew 98
Benson, Jn. 25, 193
Benson, Miss Margaret 193
Benson, Robert 278

Bentford, Robert 122
Bentley, James 210
Bentley, Samuel 117
Bentley, Wm. 17, 291
Bentley, Col. Wm. 25
Benton, Jn. 195
Beriford, James 57
Berkeley, Edmund 26, 193
Berkeley, Jn. 332
Berkeley, Nelson 26
Berkeley, Miss Salley 376
Berkeley, Wm. 26
Berrier (see: Jn. Barrier) 217
Berrow, Jn. 26
Berry, Elisha 379
Berry, James 96
Berry, Jn. 93
Berry, L. 13
Berry, Mary 248
Berry, Nathaniel 95
Berry, Samuel 130
Berryman, Benj. 54
Berryman, Isaac 26
Berryman, James 186
Best, James 247
Best, Susanna 247
Betaly, Spencer Morgan 93
Bethell, Wm. Jr. 242
Betin, Charles 296
Bettesworth, Wm. 96
Bettis, Christopher 26
Betty 325
Beuford, Warren 133
Beufort, Abraham 238
Beufort, Mary 238
Bever, Eliz. 194
Beverage, Eliz. 201
Beverage, Jn. 201
Beveridge, Wm. 343
Beverley, Miss 74
Beverley, Miss Eveline Byrd 202
Beverley, Robert 40, 202
Beverly, Robert 346
Bickers, Lewis 99
Bickerton, Mrs. Ann (see: Mrs. Ann Dickenson) 100

Bickerton, Mrs. Martha 27
Bickerton, Wm. Francis 242
Biddle, Eliz. 27
Bigbey, Susanna 27
Bigby, Elijah 95
Bigelow, Roderick 27
Biggs, Randolph 93
Bignall, Mrs. 362
Bile, Jacob 91
Bile, Jn. 91
Billey 359
Billups, Mrs. 27
Billups, Miss Betsey 201
Billups, Geo. 224, 239, 355
Billups, Jn. 49, 89
Billups, Miss Mary 109
Billy 19, 266, 267, 316
Binford, Aquila 62
Binford, Eliz. 62
Binford, James 62
Binford, Jn. M. 62
Binford, Mary 62
Binford, Thomas 305
Bingham, Roscoe 27
Bird, Col. 265
Bird, Catherine 55
Bird, Jn. 297
Bird, Richard 28
Bird, Robert Jr. 27
Bird, Robin 167
Bird, Wm. 55
Birmingham, Edward Arthur 296
Bishop, Luman 300, 349
Bissett, Margaret 28
Bissey, Jn. 295
Bissit, Alex. 177
Black, Miss 132
Black, Mrs. 64
Black, Anne 28
Black, James 28
[Black], Judy 28
Black, Miss Nancy 151
Black, Peggy 28
Black, Rudolph 170
Black, Wm. 151
Black, Wm. 372
Black, Wm. 44, 52, 66, 83, 98, 151, 372
Blackburn, Col. 28

Blackburn, Christopher 285
Blackburn, Col. Rich. 28
Blackburn, Edward 237
Blackburn, Maj. R. 335
Blackburn, T. 17, 301
Blackburn, Thomas 129
Blacknall, Mary 29
Blackwell, James 29
Blackwell, Jn. 58, 116, 127
Blackwell, Miss Nancy 38, 43
Blackwell, Thomas 257
Blagrove, the Rev. Mr. 29
Blair, Mrs. 167
Blair, Miss Betsey 337
Blair, Catharine 29
Blair, Mrs. Catherine 83
Blair, Miss Eliz. 143
Blair, Jacob 29
Blair, James 30, 109, 236, 317
Blair, Dr. James 30
Blair, Jn. 8, 18, 29, 30, 59, 74, 278, 279, 330, 337
Blair, Jn. Jr. 5, 29
Blair, Joseph Mitchell 93
Blair, Mary 29
Blair, Miss Molly 8
Blair, Miss Nancy 11, 18
Blair, Miss Sally 59
Blair, Miss Susan 287
Blair, Wm. 29
Blake, James 37
Blake, Philip 296
Blake, Rich. 208
Blakemore, Miss Eliz. 375
Blakey, Smith 173, 257
Blakey, Stith 323
Blakey, Thos. 30
Blamer, Miss Polly 190

18th-Century Virginia Newspapers

Blamire, J. 175, 176, 214
Blancett, Rodman 346
Blanch, Michael 209
Blanchard, Jn. 63
Blanchard, Miss Sarah 63
Blanchlet, Wm. 296
Bland, Maj. 178
Bland, John 1
Bland, Peter Randolph 141
Bland, Rich. 30
Bland, Col. Rich. 30, 137
Bland, Miss Sally 137
Bland, the Rev. Wm. 5, 30
Bland, Theodoric 30, 244
Bland, Thos. 30
Bland, Wm. 30
Blaney, D. 287
Blaney, Helen 30
Blaws, Miss Ann 28
Bledsoe, Col. Isaac 195
Blews, Mary 31
Blick, Benj. 330
Blick, James 94
Blincoe, Thomas 89, 247
Blunt, Benj. 112
Blunt, Rich. 177
Blunt, Washer 282
Blunt, Wm. 112
Blyth, Wm. 15, 155
Boa, Margaret 31
Boa, Mrs. Margaret 290
Boarman, Leonard 51
Boaten, Lewis 210
Boatman, Rich. 221
Bob 141, 251, 330
Bockius, John 31
Bodeley, Matthias 228
Bogan, Jn. 298, 316
Boggess, Ann 31, 356
Boggess, Bennett 31, 171, 356
Boggess, Jn. 31
Boggess, Mary 31
Boggess, Robert 19, 31, 309, 356
Boggs, Andrew 371

Bogue, Jn. 217, 238
Bohannan, Wm. 296
Boisseau, Jn. 301
Boland, Jn. 92
Bolling, Miss 245
Bolling, Alex. 32
Bolling, Mrs. Anne 31
Bolling, Archibald 31, 32
Bolling, Eliz. 31
Bolling, Jn. 31
Bolling, Miss Lucy 278
Bolling, Miss Nancy 206, 217
Bolling, Powhatan 32
Bolling, Robert 31, 32, 176
Bolling, Col. Robert 278
Bond, Jane 32
Bond, Mrs. Jane 369
Bonfield, Charles 188
Bonnaund 32
Bonner, Samuel 100
Bonner, Wm. 100
Bonny, Alex. 127
Bontz, Adam 116
Booker, Edmund 171
Booker, Edw. 32, 330
Booker, Efford 33
Booker, Frances 32
Booker, Geo. 350
Booker, James 32, 277
Booker, James 377
Booker, Jn. 32
Booker, Jn. Jr. 33
Booker, Marshall 33
Booker, Parham 32
Booker, Polly 33
Booker, Rich 32, 33, 172, 331
Booker, Rich. Edward 32
Booker, Rich. Marriott 32
Booker, Rich. Merriot 331
Booker, Richeson 33
Booker, Samuel 244
Booker, Wm. Marshal 32
Boon, Wm. Jr. 33
Boone, Daniel 297

Booth, Miss Betsy 85, 350
Booth, Dr. Geo. 33
Booth, George 307
Booth, Mordecai 33
Booth, Miss Nancy 23
Booth, Robert 33
Booth, Thos. 33
Booth, Wm. 33
Boothman, Jonathan 296
Bordland, Mary 104
Borland, Robert 16, 29, 247
Borland, Robert 29, 247
Borum, Miss 315
Borum, Jn. 315
Bostuck, Parthina 357
Boswell, Miss Betsey 9
Botkin, Jn. 194
Bott, Ann 34
Bott, Col. Jn. 64
Bottom, Jn. 34
Botts, Benj. 154
Boucher, the Rev. Mr. 58
Boucher, Jonathan 203, 319
Boulware, Delphia 85
Boulware, Obadiah 85
Bountin, Wm. 286
Bourniche, Eliz. Swan 48
Bouse, Arthur 64
Boush, Miss Betsey 341
Boush, Charles S. 34
Boush, Elizabeth 34
Boush, Miss Eliz. 314
Boush, Frances M. 34
Boush, Mrs. Frances M. 365
Boush, Goodrich 34
Boush, James 34
Boush, Jn. 34, 365
Boush, Mrs. Margaret 276
Boush, Mary 34
Boush, Miss Nancy 224

Boush, Robert 34
Boush, Samuel 34, 342
Boush, Wilson 34
Boush, Wm. 351
Boushell, James 34, 205
Bowcock, Edw. 18
Bowdoin, Courtney 343
Bowdoin, Frances 18
Bowdoin, Frances Banister 17
Bowdoin, Jn. 34, 343
Bowdoin, John 18
Bowdoin, Peter 18
Bowdoin, Preeson 227, 265, 343, 344
Bowdoin, Preston Jr. 34
Bowdoin, Wm. 242
Bowen, Christopher 35
Bowen, Horatia Skillern 34
Bowen, Jn. 34, 99
Bowen, Jn. Jr. 35
Bowen, Wm. 34, 35
Bowers, Peter 253
Bowes, Rich. 260
Bowler, Rich. 152
Bowles, Benj. 35
Bowles, Sally 35
Bowls, Elisha 93
Bowman, Catharine 91
Bowman, Isaac 133
Bowman, Nicholas 91
Bowman, Thomas 98
Bowness, Eliz. 35
Bowness, Fanny 35
Bowness, Margaret 35
Bowness, Mary 35
Bowness, Thos. 35
Bowness, Wm. 35
Bowyer, Henry 246
Bowyer, Capt. Henry 201
Bowyer, Jugle 161
Bowyer, Mrs. Margaret 246
Bowyer, Col. Wm. 129

Boxley, Benj. 357
Boyce, Daniel 308
Boyce, James 15, 22
Boyce, Wm. 2
Boyd, Lt. 195
Boyd, Mrs. 235
Boyd, Betty 89
Boyd, David 10, 190, 237, 315
Boyd, James 19, 35, 89, 96
Boyd, Robert 89
Boyd, Spencer 89
Boyd, Walter 235
Boyd, Wm. 89
Boyer, Adam 201
Boyer, Christina 201
Bozley, Jn. 73
Bracken, Ensign 194
Bracken, Jn. 49, 53, 58
Bracken, the Rev. Jn. 350
Bracken, the Rev. Mr. 45,
Bracken, the Rev. Mr. J. 87
Brackenridge, Geo. 6, 185
Bradby, Catharine Allen 36
Braddick (see: Mrs. Mary Bradock) 353
Braddock, Gen. 168, 181, 320, 349
Bradford, Capt. 195
Bradford, Maj. 349
Bradford, Mr. 71
Bradford, David 88
Bradford, Mrs. Jane 349
Bradford, Peggy 157
Bradford, Rich. Henry 157
Bradish, Jn. 99
Bradley, Absalom 36
Bradley, James 236
Bradley, Lt. James W, 100
Bradley, Jn. 36
Bradley, Lavinia 36
Bradley, Wm. 36, 76
Bradock, Mrs. Mary 353

Bradshaw, Jeremiah 94
Brady, Jn. 352
Bragg, James 66
Bragg, Mrs. Ann 66
Braikenridge, George 90
Brake, Jacob 380
Bramble, Jn. 36
Bramham, Nimrod 310
Branan, J. 27
Branch, Anderson 36
Branch, Benj. 19, 366
Branch, Hen. 36
Branch, James 316
Branch, Samuel 226
Branch, Thomas 114
Branch, Wm. 36
Brand, Joseph 363
Brander, Jn. 288
Brandt, Rich. 83
Braney, Patrick 37
Branham, Ben. 299
Branham, Stephen 322
Branin, Francis 5
Brannon, Jn. 194
Branson, Thomas 310, 347
Brasel, James 152
Brasfield, George 224
Bratton, Adam 121
Bratton, Eliz. 121
Braxton, Mrs. 50
Braxton, Carter 64, 75, 102, 278
Braxton, Col. Carter 256
Braxton, Geo. 37
Braxton, Col. George 211
Braxton, Miss Molly 256
Bray, Rich. 37
Brazel, James 152
Brazel, Robert 152
Breeding, Rich. 80
Breedwell, Sandford 237
Breillat, Thos. 37
Brenan, Stephen 322
Brend, Thos. 37
Brenon, James 253
Brent, Clare 38

Brent, Daniel Carroll 38
Brent, Eleanor 38
Brent, Mrs. Eliz. 56
Brent, Geo. 38, 105
Brent, Vincent 326
Brent, Wm. 33, 230
Bressie, Capt. 97
Bressie, Henry 344
Bressie, Capt. Thomas 96, 203, 341
Brett, Francis 76
Brett, George 173
Brevoort, Miss 161
Brewer, Thomas 370
Briant, Hawkins 97
Brickey, Christian 38
Brickey, Jared 38
Brickey, Jn. 38
Brickey, [M.] 38
Brickey, Milly 38
Brickey, Nancy 38
Brickey, Patsey 38
Brickey, Peter 38
Brickey, Polly 38
Brickey, Temperance 38
Brickey, Winney 38
Brickhouse, Smith 75
Bride, Jn. 98
Briden, Grizald 38
Briden, Jn. 38
Briden, Robert 38
Briden, Wm. 38
Bridger, Col. Joseph 257
Bridger, Esther 38
Bridger, Jos. 38
Bridger, Mrs. Mary 257
Bridges, Ensign 195
Bridgforth, Benj. 119
Brigendine, Wm. 39
Briggs, David 352
Briggs, Miss Dolly Pleasants 250
Briggs, Gray 16, 250
Briggs, James 39
Briggs, Wm. 78
Brightwell, Eliz. 39
Brightwell, Jn. 39
Brightwell, Thomas 183
Brill, Harman 39

Brillinger, Peter 92
Brinker, Henry 371
Brinkley, Peter 92
Briscoe, Jn. 41
Briscow, Col. 39
Brison, James 371
Bristor, M. 39
Brittan, Jn. 55
Britton, George 31
Britton, Jesse 39
Britton, Miss Rebecca 153
Broaddus, America 39
Broaddus, Capt. Jn. 39
Broaddus, Robert Loury 39
Broaddus, Warner Harwood 39
Broaddus, Wm. 39
Broaderic, Miss Ann 115
Broadnax, Miss 58
Brock, Capt. 98
Brock, Jos. 37, 40, 58, 207, 309
Brock, Capt. Jos. 2, 19, 98
Brock, Wm. 39
Brockenbrough, Arthur 114
Brockenbrough, Miss Eliz. 114
Brockenbrough, Jn. 112
Brockenbrough, Jn. 40, 112
Brockenbrough, Newman 40
Brockman, Samuel 337
Brokenbrough, Miss 202
Bromley, James 40
Bronaugh, Geo. 19
Bronaugh, Patty 19
Bronaugh, Wm. 244
Brook, Joseph 207
Brooke, Clement 58
Brooke, Col. Geo. 40
Brooke, Dudley 41
Brooke, Edmund 40
Brooke, Francis Taliaferro 40
Brooke, Geo. 22, 344

Brooke, Humphrey 40, 152
Brooke, Jn. 77, 221
Brooke, Jn. T. 233
Brooke, Jn. Taliaferro 40
Brooke, Lawrence 40
Brooke, Dr. Lawrence 40
Brooke, Robert 40
Brooke, Miss Susanna 348
Brooke, Thomas 328
Brooke, Wm. 40
Brookes, Jn. 200
Brooking, Col. 118
Brooking, Robert 15, 40, 381
Brooking, Vivian 41
Brooking, Vivion 244
Brooking, Wm. 40
Brooks, Charles 97
Brooks, Ensign 195
Brooks, George 64
Brooks, Len 239
Brooks, Wm. 137
Brooks, Zachariah 202
Brothers, Francis 92
Brough, Robert 30, 306
Brough, Wm. 10
Brounley, Archibald 236
Browder, Rich. 301
Brown Family 132
Brown, Capt. 314
Brown, Capt. 76
Brown, Mrs. 254, 365
Brown, Aaron 94
Brown, Ann 43
Brown, Benj. 167
Brown, Miss Bethina 261
Brown, Beverly 21, 43
Brown, Catherine 43
Brown, Charles 125
Brown, Charlotte 43
Brown, Clement 166
Brown, Edmund 48
Brown, Miss Eliz. 166
Brown, Frances 42
Brown, Francis 66, 254
Brown, George 95

Brown, Hugh 41, 121
Brown, Isaac 176
Brown, James 41, 42, 210, 236, 260
Brown, Jeremiah 96
Brown, Jesse 245, 267
Brown, Jn. 21, 22, 41, 42, 43, 92, 135, 145, 271, 296, 306, 307, 328
Brown, Capt. John 41
Brown, Miss Judith 306
Brown, Miss Judith Walker 207
Brown, Lake 95
Brown, Maj. 195
Brown, Margaret 41
Brown, Mary Bell 48
Brown, Miss Nancy 307
Brown, Miss Peggy 251
Brown, Miss Phoebe 101
Brown, Raleigh 41
Brown, Rebecca 41
Brown, Sally 41
Brown, Samuel 43, 299
Brown, Sarah 41, 121
Brown, Mrs. Sarah 188
Brown, T. 188
Brown, Thos. 41, 96, 174, 347
Brown, Mr. W. 43
Brown, Wm. 143
Brown, Wm. 21, 41, 143, 235, 240, 249
Brown, Wm. Burnet 207
Brown, Wm. C. 262
Browne, Andrew Cochran 43
Browne, Basil 43, 44
Browne, Bennett 18, 43
Browne, Miss Betsy 142
Browne, Charles 43, 44
Browne, Hen. 112
Browne, James 44
Browne, Judith 44
Browne, Mary 43, 44
Browne, Mary Hill 43
Browne, Miss Polly 64
Browne, Priscilla Brooke 43, 44
Browne, Robert 44
Browne, Samuel 44
Browne, Sarah 44
Browne, Wm. 338
Browne, Wm. 44
Browning, Eliz. 162
Browning, Francis 206
Browning, James 184
Brownlow, Jn. 189, 356
Bruce, the Rev. Mr. 162
Bruce, Charles 318
Bruce, Jacob 13, 215, 265
Bruce, James 185
Bruce, Jn. 378
Bruce, Lydia 185
Bruce, Mary 378
Bruce, Rachel 44
Bruce, Robert C. 44
Bruin, Bryan 227, 246
Bruin, Peter Bryan 111
Brunet, Mrs. 44
Brunet, Henry 45
Brunsen, Erastus 100
Bryan, Benj. 102, 163
Bryan, Frederick 9, 273
Bryan, Frederick Jr. 45
Bryan, Mrs. Jane 45
Bryan, Thomas 190
Bryan, Wm. 102
Bryant, Allen 45
Bryant, Isaac 263
Bryant, Joseph 96
Bryant, Mary 45, 53
Bryant, Peter 45
Bryant, Rawleigh 366
Bryant, Rebecca 45
Bryant, Sarah 45
Bryant, Thos. 45, 337
Bryant, Wm. 45
Bryce, Nicholas 45
Bryce, Robert 45, 84
Buchanan, the Rev. Mr. 204
Buchanan, Alex. 371
Buchanan, Miss. Elisabeth 23
Buchanan, Andrew 23, 46, 347
Buchanan, James 103, 146, 302
Buchanan, Neil 18, 292
Buchanan, Neill 139
Buchanan, Sarah 345
Bucher, Jacob 151
Bucher, Miss Susannah 43
Buck, Robert Jr. 46
Buckland, Wm. 15, 22, 118
Buckles, Wm. 46
Buckles, Wm. Jr. 281
Buckley, Wm. 331
Buckner, Frances 187
Buckner, Miss Judy Roy 27
Buckner, Miss Lucy 60
Buckner, Philip 13, 46
Buckner, Wm. 60, 62
Bucktrout, Benj. 87, 228
Budd, Henry 46
Bueil, Count de 342
Buford, Henry 28
Buford, James 104
Buford, Miss Prudence 28
Bulgar, Eliz. 46
Bullard, Cary 184
Bullett, Alex. Scott 47
Bullett, Cuthbert 47
Bullett, Helen 47
Bullett, Thos. 47
Bullifant, James 336
Bullington, Wm. 14
Bullitt, Cuthbert 172, 264, 301

18th-Century Virginia Newspapers 393

Bullitt, Miss Helen E. G. 172
Bullitt, Thos. J. 47
Bullock, Rhoda 47
Bully, Edward 265
Bully, George 194
Bulman, Jn. 95
Bumpass, Jn. 195
Bunbury, Capt. 47
Bundie, the widow 122
Bunns, Jn. 97
Burbridge, Julius King 11, 313
Burch, Mr. 293
Burcher, Jn. 47, 284
Burd, Andrew 186
Burden, Polly 149
Burdett, Christiana 47
Bure, Peter 47
Burgess, Adjutant 195
Burgess, the Rev. Mr. 47
Burgess, Thomas 6, 48
Burghes, the Rev. Mr. 367
Burke, Dr. 48
Burk, Mary 48
Burk, Patrick 48
Burk, Thos. 48, 142
Burke, James 128
Burke, Michael 118
Burke, Mrs. 118
Burke, Patrick 365
Burland, Rich. 140
Burley, Garnet 354
Burley, Jeremiah 95
Burley, Robert 80
Burn, Patrick 295
Burnell, [?] 255
Burner, Jn. Sr. 48
Burner, Michael 122, 215
Burnet, Miss Betsey 6
Burnet, Thomas 92
Burnett, Casson 133
Burnett, Caston 48
Burnett, Jeremiah 133
Burnett, Joseph 133
Burnett, Rich. 133
Burnley, Col. 199

Burnley, Hardin 6, 48, 108, 185, 302
Burnley, Jn. 48, 108
Burnley, Mary Bell 48
Burnley, Rich. 48
Burnley, Zachariah 48, 108
Burnly, Hardin 48
Burns, George 99
Burns, Isabella 48
Burns, Jn. 218
Burns, Patrick 219
Burns, Mrs. Peggy 131
Burns, Wm. 309
Burny, Barnaby 49
Burrough, Rich. 49
Burrow, Jn. Jr. 49
Burrows, Jn. 100
Burrows, Polly 32
Burrows, Wm. Ward 32
Burrus, Charles 49
Burrus, Eliz. 184
Burrus, Jennings 184
Burrus, Samuel 49
Burt, George 130
Burton, Alex. 49
Burton, Charles 10, 49
Burton, Miss Lucy 272, 369
Burton, Martin 49
Burton, Mary 49
Burton, May Jr. 79, 103, 196, 261, 303
Burton, Robert 153
Burton, Thomas 49
Burton, Wm. 255
Burwell, Col 69
Burwell, Miss Alice 126, 369
Burwell, Anne 50
Burwell, Miss Betsey 256
Burwell, Carter 36, 37
Burwell, Col. Carter 50, 345
Burwell, Miss Eliz. 248
Burwell, James 49
Burwell, Lewis 11, 23, 49, 75, 148, 208, 243, 256, 302, 379

Burwell, Col. Lewis 49, 50, 228
Burwell, Nancy 208
Burwell, Nathaniel 22, 23, 49, 171
Burwell, Capt. Nathaniel 50, 191, 253
Burwell, Robert 50
Burwell, Miss Sally 36
Bush, Henry 197
Bush, James 92
Bush, Joseph 51
Bush, Miss Kitty 252
Bush, Matthias 51
Bushop, Wm. 92
Bushrod, Jn. 220
Bushrode, Jn. 124, 129, 223, 225, 348
Buston, James 90
Butler, Gen. 195
Butler, Maj. 257
Butler, Anne 312
Butler, Beckwith 290
Butler, Emma 11
Butler, Gamaliel 3
Butler, Jn. 71, 76, 240
Butler, Jn. Jr. 51
Butler, Laurence 17
Butler, Reuben 312
Butler, Theodore 11
Butler, Thos. 51
Butler, Tristram 151
Butler, Will 121
Butt, Miss Fanny 341
Butt, Francis 252
Butt, Hillary 30, 31, 227, 241
Butt, Rich. 51, 305
Butts, Joshua 318
Butts, Peter 309
Buxton, James 51
Byers, Miss Polly 189
Byrd, Adam 109
Byrd, Miss Betsy 119
Byrd, Jn. 99
Byrd, Miss Maria 256
Byrd, Mary 52
Byrd, Wm. 31, 52, 57, 93, 119, 132, 210, 241, 259
Byrd, Col. Wm. 256
Byrn, Charles 52
Byrn, James 52
Byrn, Peyton 52
Byrne, Andrew 306

Byrne, James 52, 174
Cabell, Miss Eliza 151
Cabell, Joseph 266, 359
Cabell, Nicholas 151
Cabell, Peggy 181
Cabell, Capt. Samuel Jordan 94
Cabell, Wm. 181, 188
Cabell, Wm. Jr. 292
Caddeen, Rich. 294, 302
Caesar 154
Cahoon, George 52
Cain, James 265
Cain, Jn. Lovel 98
Calder, James 322
Caldwell, Geo. 346
Caldwell, Robert 52
Caldwell, Wm. 61
Call, Daniel 121
Call, Jn. 66
Call, Rich. 215, 362
Call, Wm. 238, 301
Callaghan, Rachel 361
Calland, Joseph 23
Calland, Samuel 169
Callender, Capt. Jn. 53, 86, 175
Callender, Jn. Jr. 53
Callender, Miss Nancy 86
Callender, Miss Sukey 175
Callis, George 299, 325
Callis, W. O. 14
Calloway, James 41
Calmes, Betty 53
Calmes, George 53
Calmes, Marquis 53
Calmes, Wm. 53
Calvert, Capt. 132
Calvert, Cornelius 215
Calvert, Cornelius Jr. 216
Calvert, Cornelius Sr. 193, 351
Calvert, Miss Eleanor 83
Calvert, Miss Eliza 332

Calvert, Jn. 253, 332
Calvert, Jn. Savage 53, 76
Calvert, John S. 53
Calvert, Jonathan 53, 76
Calvert, Dr. Jonathan 53
Calvert, Maximilian 53
Calvert, Newton 53
Calvert, Miss Polly 253
Calvert, Rebecca 53
Camabell, Charles 105
Cameron, Jane 217
Camm, Jn. 183, 354
Camm, Rev. and Hon. Jn. 53
Camm, Miss Nancy 353
Cammock, Mary 53
Cammock, Wm. Sr. 53
Camp, Capt. Jn. 348, 356
Camp, Eliz. 142
Camp, Henry 142
Campbell, Mrs. 222, 272
Campbell, Alex. 54
Campbell, Maj. Andrew 170
Campbell, Archibald 54, 84, 135, 372
Campbell, Miss Cecilia 346
Campbell, Charles 238
Campbell, Daniel 91
Campbell, Donald 75
Campbell, Emily 54
Campbell, George 98
Campbell, Gilbert 338
Campbell, Henry 99
Campbell, Isaac 5
Campbell, James 16, 116, 218, 301
Campbell, Jn. 53, 54, 65
Campbell, Joshua 97
Campbell, Miss Molly 297
Campbell, Neil 147

Campbell, Phoebe 238
Campbell, Robert 44
Campbell, Capt. Robert 195
Campbell, Miss Sally B. 271
Campbell, Wm. 46
Campbell, Capt. Wm. 79, 264
Campbell, Gen. Wm. 271
Canaday, Jn. 194
Canby, Benj. H. 332
Canby, Samuel 178
Canby, Samuel 178, 199
Cane, Cornelius 54
Cane, Daniel 54
Cane, David 55
Cane, Edmund 55
Cane, James 54
Cane, Jesse 55
Cane, Jn. 54
Cann, James 349
Cann, Sarah 55
Cannon, Miss Betsy 153
Cannon, Miss Judith 50
Cannon, Luke 74
Cannon, Mary 55
Cannon, Col. Wm. 153
Canterbury, Joseph 94
Caperton, Hugh 116
Capper, Jn. 362
Capron, George 287
Carbery, Philip 44, 61, 302
Cardwell, Obedience 55
Carfs, James 131
Carleton, Wm. 99
Carlile, David 63
Carlisle, Rachel 121
Carlton, Isaac 97
Carlyle, Col. Jn. 55
Carlyle, Jn. 49, 180, 307
Carmichael, Roderick 96
Carncroft, Joseph 90
Carneal, Thomas 144
Carney, Jn. 98
Carney, Patrick 296

Carnyham, Adam 56
Carpenter, Eliz. 56
Carper, Nicholas 305
Carr, Archibald 193
Carr, Miss Betsy 333
Carr, Garland 56
Carr, Jn. 92
Carr, Jn. Fendall 56
Carr, Wm. 56, 105, 165, 185, 333
Carrington, Anne 56
Carrington, Geo. 21
Carrington, Joseph 56, 232, 366
Carrington, Mayo 56
Carrington, Paul 52, 232
Carroll, Dr. Chas. 29, 234
Carroll, Jn. 34
Carson, Beaty 176
Carson, George 166
Carson, Joseph 198
Carter, Col. 37
Carter, Mr. 227
Carter, A. W. 58
Carter, Miss Anne 202, 214
Carter, Benj. 57
Carter, Charles 57, 92, 129, 202, 299
Carter, Charles Jr. 57
Carter, Col. Charles 58
Carter, Counsellor 29
Carter, Dale 276
Carter, Edward 60
Carter, Eliz. 57
Carter, Miss Eliz. 256, 318
Carter, Miss Fanny 230
Carter, Hebe 142
Carter, Jacob 57
Carter, James 58, 183, 220, 222
Carter, Jn. 45, 58, 90, 207, 264, 265, 320
Carter, Jn. Jr. 58
Carter, Joseph 58
Carter, Landon 57, 58, 145, 241, 277

Carter, Col. Landon 57
Carter, Louisa 57
Carter, Miss Louisa 250
Carter, Philadelphia 58
Carter, Polly 320
Carter, Rawleigh 79
Carter, Robert 56, 142, 230, 367
Carter, Robert Jr. 58
Carter, Capt. Samuel 57
Carter, Talitha P. 57
Carter, Theodoric 57
Carter, Thomas 179, 307, 361
Carter, Thos. Jr. 57
Carter, Wm. 58, 59, 179
Carter, Wm. Jr. 59
Carter, Dr. Wm. 58
Carter, Wormeley 58, 376
Cartmell, Mr. 63
Cartmell, Miss Eliz. 213
Cartmell, Martin 59
Cartmell, Thomas 59, 213
Cartwright, Thomas 109
Carty, Letty 335
Carty, Mary 335
Carty, Violet 335
Caruthers, James 29
Carvan, Thomas 298
Cary, Col. 156
Cary, Amey 285
Cary, Archibald 196, 278, 279
Cary, Miss Betsey 157, 196
Cary, Miss Eliz. B. 119
Cary, Joseph 24
Cary, Capt. Miles 70
Cary, Patrick 97
Cary, Robert 285
Cary, Miss Sally 248
Cary, Sylvester 95
Cary, Thomas Jr. 264
Cary, Wilson Miles 5, 59, 118, 119, 248,

Cary, Col. Wilson Miles 59
Case, Archibald 95
Casey, Miss Eliz. 264
Cash, Archibald 59
Cassady, James 44
Cassanave, Anne 60
Cassay, Philip 106
Casteel, Aaron 57
Catlett, Ann 60
Catlett, Charles 133
Catlett, Jn. 14, 87, 156, 332
Catlett, Jn. G. 60
Caton, James 115, 146, 188
Catton, Benj. 59
Catton, Mrs. Mary 60
Catton, Wm. 94
Causin, Gerard B. 83, 89
Cavan, Patrick 76
Cave, Belfield 275
Cavenagh, Tobias 296
Caverly, Miss Phoebe 9
Cawfield, Owen 94
Cawley, Asa 95
Cawn, Fanny 115
Cawn, Jack 115
Cawood, Jn. 30, 173
Cawsey, Capt. Jn. 273
Chafe, Ensign 195
Chaffin, Joshua 33, 113
Challis, Jn. 60
Chamber, Jn. 271
Chamberlain, Edward 160
Chamberlayne, Byrd 349
Chamberlayne, Mary 61
Chamberlayne, Miss Betsy 123
Chamberlayne, Mrs. Eliz. 142
Chamberlayne, Rebecca 61
Chamberlayne, Capt. Rich. 61
Chamberlayne, Wm. 142

Chamberlin, Elijah 221
Chamberlin, James 221
Chambers, Adam 98
Chambers, Jn. 96
Chambers, Joseph 93
Chambers, Samuel 76
Chamier, Daniel 319
Champaigne, Stephen 61
Champe, Jn. 298
Champe, John 24
Champe, Mary 61
Champe, Wm. 61
Chandlee, Miss Polly 337
Chandler, George 147
Chandler, Happy 147
Chandler, Mary 61
Chandler, Susanna 147
Chandler, Thomas 95
Chandoin, Francis 92
Chapin, Miss Betsy 12
Chaple, Jn. 95
Chapman, Allen 138
Chapman, Allen 138, 150
Chapman, Ben. 61
Chapman, Benj. 61
Chapman, Cornelius 92
Chapman, Maj. Henry Henley 61
Chapman, Isaac 177
Chapman, Jn. 177
Chapman, Joseph 46
Chapman, Joseph 46, 92
Chapman, Miss Judith 164
Chapman, Nathan 357
Chapman, Reuben 285
Chapman, Rich. 66, 109, 128, 188
Chapman, Thos. 56, 105
Chapman, Will. 61

Chapman, Capt. Wm. 164
Chappell, Agnes 62
Chappell, Benj. 61, 62
Chappell, Jn. 62
Chappell, Thos. 13, 62
Chappell, Wm. 308
Charberlayne, Mrs. 85
Charlton, Francis 62
Charlton, Miss Jane 367
Charlton, M. 62
Charlton, Mary 62
Charlton, Sarah 62
Chase, Ensign 195
Chastain, the Rev. Mr. 236
Chasteen, Rainy 349
Chenoweth, John 11
Cherry, Jn. 116
Chesley, Jn. 341
Chesley, Miss Rebecca 341
Chesley, Robert 223
Chester, Wm. 195
Chevis, Jn. 62
Chew, Miss Betsy 361
Chew, Jn. 228
Chew, Capt. Nathaniel 186
Chew, Rich. 325
Chew, Robert B. 185
Chew, Roger 62, 74
Chewning, Bartholomew 140
Chewning, Jn. 62
Chichester, Sarah 62
Childers, Jn. 99
Childres, Matthew 93
Childress, Abraham 96
Childs, Wm. 296
Chiles, Henry 119, 219
Chilton, Felicia 343
Chilton, Orrick 343
Chilton, Thos. 74, 314
Chink 62

Chinn, Miss Agatha 196
Chipley, Miss Hanna 46
Chipley, Miss Polley 150
Chipley, Capt. Wm. 46, 150
Chisman, Diana 63
Chisman, Jn. 63
Chisman, Miss Nancy 170
Chiswell, Col. 289
Chiswell, Col. Jn. 293
Chiswell, Jn. 67
Chiswell, Miss Lucy 248
Chiswell, Miss Sukey 289
Choice, Cyrus 63
Choice, Jn. 63
Choice, Tully 63
Choice, Wm. 63
Choisy, Gen. 247
Chowning, Wm. 29
Chrenshaw, Jn. 139, 179
Christian, Col. 63
Christian, Miss Eliz. 87
Christian, Francis 361
Christian, Israel 54
Christian, Jn. 153
Christie, James 63
Christie, Jeremiah 96
Christie, Robert 40
Christie, Thomas 236
Christman, Peter 87
Christopher, Eliz. 359
Christopher, Morton 359
Christopher, Will. 63
Churchbill, A. 172
Churchill, Armistead 64, 183
Churchill, Benj. 64
Churchill, Jn. 63
Churchill, Miss Lucy H. 86
Churchill, Sarah 64
Churchill, Thos. E. 64
Churchill, Will 240

18th-Century Virginia Newspapers 397

Churchill, Col. Wm. 86
Churchwell (see: Ann Churchill) 63
Cirvill, Peter 156
Clack, James 64
Claiborne, Col. 123
Claiborne, Col. Augustine 68
Claiborne, Bathurst 64
Claiborne, Daniel 231
Claiborne, Herbert 294
Claiborne, Jn. 103
Claiborne, Jn. H. 64
Claiborne, Matt. M. 154
Claiborne, Miss Nancy 68
Claiborne, Miss Philadelphia 58
Claiborne, Philip W. 61
Claiborne, Philip Whitehead 55, 157
Claiborne, Miss Polly 64
Claiborne, Thomas 257
Claiborne, Wm. 64, 210
Claiborne, Wm. D. 13
Claiborne, Wm. Sr. 204
Claibourne, Buller 64
Claibourne, Miss Lucy 137
Clamen, Jn. 299
Clapham, Josias 299
Clark, Lt. 195
Clark, Maj. 195
Clark, Christopher 104
Clark, Gilly 65
Clark, James 36, 99
Clark, Jn. 194, 241
Clark, Josiah 95
Clark, Mary 65, 245
Clark, Nancy 381
Clark, Quentin 141, 144
Clark, Rich. 238
Clark, Wm. 295
Clark, Wm. 65, 95, 295
Clarke, Gen. 171
Clarke, Elisha 150
Clarke, Francis 65
Clarke, Geo. 380
Clarke, Isaac 65
Clarke, James 330
Clarke, Jn. 150
Clarke, Joseph 96
Clarke, Lucy 66
Clarke, Mary 65
Clarke, Miss Polly 380
Clarke, Thomas 98, 341
Clarke, Wm. 65, 247
Clarke, Dr. Wm. 265
Clarke, Zachariah 66
Claughton, Thomas 81
Clauzel Family 31
Clay, Charles 66
Clay, Eleazer 66
Clay, Green 66
Clay, Jn. Moore 97
Clay, Martha 66
Clay, Matthew 66
Clay, Priscilla 66
Clay, Samuel 187
Clay, Thomas 66, 188
Clay, Wm. 66
Clayborne, Frances 66
Clayton, Elvy 297
Clayton, Jasper 66
Clayton, Samuel 66
Clayton, Thomas 302
Clayton, Wm. 10, 61, 66, 169, 243, 334, 358
Cleland, Dr. W. C. 66
Clement, Mr. 244
Clements, David 238
Clements, Pitman 67
Clendenning, Andrew 67
Clerico, Joseph 194
Clifford, Jn. 37
Clifton, Eliz. 311
Clifton, Rich. 263
Clifton, Wm. 311
Clopton, George 67, 81
Clopton, George Jr. 275
Clopton, Waller 67
Clough, Mary 67
Clough, Miss Sally 367
Clowes, Mrs. Anne 196
Cloyd, Eliz. 67
Cloyd, Gordon 335
Clubb, Alex. 295
Coagar, Michael 72
Cobbett, Anne 67
Cobbs, Ensign 195
Cobbs, Jn. 301
Cobbs, Jn. L. 67
Cobbs, Sarah 67
Cochran, James 67, 280
Cochran, Lucy 67
Cochran, Wm, 67
Cock, Abraham 185
Cock, Frederick 93
Cock, Jn. 97
Cockarnin, David 18
Cockburn, Jn. 316
Cockburn, Jn. 322
Cocke, Capt. 350
Cocke, Benj. 183
Cocke, Bowler 71, 85
Cocke, Miss Catherine 378
Cocke, Charles 37, 294
Cocke, Chastaine 247
Cocke, Miss Eliza F. 71
Cocke, Eliz. 68
Cocke, Henry 168
Cocke, James 68, 277, 278, 294, 330
Cocke, Jn. 68, 294
Cocke, Jn. H. 295
Cocke, Jn. Hartwell 68
Cocke, Joseph 294, 170
Cocke, Lemuel 68, 159
Cocke, Miss Martha 277
Cocke, Mary 294

Cocke, Pleasant 68
Cocke, Rebecca H. 68
Cocke, Rebecca Hubbard 68
Cocke, Miss Rebekah 183
Cocke, Rich. 68, 159, 183, 294
Cocke, Rich. Jr. 68
Cocke, Robert 68
Cocke, Stephen 355
Cocke, Miss Theodosia 360
Cocke, Wm. 80
Cocke, Wm. Archer 294
Cocke, Dr. Wm. 222
Cockrell, Christopher 69
Cockrell, Joseph 69
Cockrell, Simon 109
Cockrell, Susannah 69
Cody, Redmond 69
Coeur de Roy, Prittraud 97
Coffee, Betty 69
Coffee, Isaac 152
Coffee, Jn. 166, 286
Coffin, Christopher 217
Cohoon, Jn. C. 69
Cohoon, Samuel 326
Coke, Judith 69
Coke, Samuel 69
Coke, Sarah 69
Colbert, Joseph 155
Colden, Alex. 166
Coldin (see: Miss Goldin) 193
Coldwell, Thomas 69
Cole, Mrs. 345
Cole, Col. 97
Cole, David 247
Cole, Miss Dolley 171
Cole, Francis 209
Cole, Jn. 171, 247, 295
Cole, Rich. 169
Cole, Thomas 95
Cole, William 69
Cole, Wm. 70, 196
Coleman, [?] 273
Coleman, Abby 104
Coleman, Betty 70

Coleman, Cornelius 296
Coleman, Daniel 379
Coleman, Francis 19, 267
Coleman, Henry 177
Coleman, Jn. 280
Coleman, Jos. 11
Coleman, Mary 70
Coleman, Miss Nancy 250
Coleman, Rich. 70
Coleman, Robert 70
Coleman, Robert S. 70, 211
Coleman, Samuel 227
Coleman, Thos. 70
Coles, Wm. 71
Colquhoun, Walter 129
Colin, Didier 52, 187
Colley, Charles 181
Colley, James 209
Collick, Cornelius 10
Collier, Ann 200
Collier, Benj. 71
Collier, Catherine 71
Collier, Charles 71
Collier, Francis 71
Collier, Frederick 200
Collier, James 97
Collier, Jn. 71
Collier, Joseph 71
Collins, Miss 203
Collins, Benj. 93
Collins, Frances 227
Collins, Geo. 37
Collins, Henry 71
Collins, James 42, 71, 245, 296
Collins, Josiah 315
Collins, Stephen 203
Colly, Edw. (see: Colley, Edw.) 71
Colquhoun, James 141
Colquhoun, Robert 129
Colquhoun, Walter 44, 317
Colson, Thomas 229
Colson, Thomas 84

Colston, Rawleigh 360
Colston, Wm. 144
Colvard, Benj. 51, 288
Colville, Catherine 72
Colville, Frances 72
Colville, Thos. 72
Combs, Rich. 72
Commodore, Jn. 168
Compton, Catharine 72
Compton, E. 338
Comrie, Dr. Wm. 72
Conley, Wm. 92
Conn, Thomas 40
Connally, Jn. W. 72
Conner, Frances 72
Conner, Lewis 72
Conneran, Thomas 96
Connor, Miss Abba 378
Connor, Col. Charles 378
Conoway, Jn. 185
Conrad, Eliz. 73
Conrad, Mrs. Eliz. 87
Conrad, Frederick 73, 259
Conrad, Jn. 73
Conrad, Miss Kitty 146
Consolvo, Wm. 230
Constantine, Edw. 92
Constantine, P[?] 92
Conway, C. 123
Conway, Catlett 329
Conway, Cornelius 73
Conway, Col. Edwin 118
Conway, Miss Eliz. 123
Conway, Miss Susannah Fitzhugh 329
Cook, Benj. 63
Cook, Capt. Jn. 73
Cook, Eliz. 304
Cook, Fanny 304
Cook, Jn. 304
Cook, Wm. 73

18th-Century Virginia Newspapers

Cooke, Miss Betsy 84
Cooke, Robert N. 255
Cooke, Stephen 299
Cooke, Wm. 140
Cookus, Catherine 73
Cookus, Henry 73
Cookus, Jacob 73
Cooley, Jn. 296
Cooley, Peter 73
Coons, David 73
Cooper, Capt. 127
Cooper, Charles 74
Cooper, E. 178
Cooper, Eliz. 227
Cooper, Francis 74
Cooper, Hamilton 363
Cooper, James 92
Cooper, Jonathan 53
Cooper, Moses 92
Cooper, Wm. Jr. 74
Coots, James 304
Copeland, Charles 109
Copeland, David 46
Copeland, Joseph 92
Copeland (see: David Coupland) 76
Copland, Charles 74
Copland, Peter 74
Coppedge, Charles 360
Copper, Eliz. 74
Coppidge, Jn. 105
Corban, Jn. 92
Corbin, Col. Gawin 74, 344
Corbin, Francis 75, 134, 139, 343
Corbin, Gawin 58, 71
Corbin, Miss Hannah 344
Corbin, Jane 343
Corbin, Jean 74
Corbin, Jn. 66
Corbin, Jn. Tayloe 127
Corbin, Col. Jn. 74
Corbin, Mrs. Lettice 74
Corbin, Rich. 289, 290
Corbin, Rich. H. 360
Corbin, Rich. Henry 343
Corcoran, Thomas 20, 84
Corcory, James 75
Cordell, Jn. 76
Cordill, Dorothy 75
Cornee, Conner 275
Cornelius, Wm. 77
Cornick, Amy 75
Cornick, Jn. 75, 320
Cornick, Miss Nancy 320
Corran, Henry 75
Corries, Jn. 151
Coryell, George 145, 316
Cosby, Charles 140
Cosby, Eliz. 140
Cosby, James 75
Cosby, Overton 113, 193, 293, 360
Cosby, Thomas 360
Cosby, Wm. 215
Coste, Joseph 75
Cottrell, Rich. 111
Couch, Samuel 318
Couchman, Phoebe 78
Couchman, Miss Polly 336
Couper, Miss Peggy 219
Coupland, David 76
Courtney, [?] 69
Courtney, Philip 34
Courtney, Miss Rachel 37
Courtney, Wm. 156
Courts, Betsey 76
Courts, Mary 76
Courts, Wm. 76
Cousins, Geo. 333
Cousins, Henry 105, 165
Coutts, the Rev. Mr. 359
Coutts, Patrick 142, 146, 380
Coutts, Reuben 294
Coutts, Wm. 76
Couture, Patrick 237
Couzens, Fanny 76
Cowan, Alex. 53, 76
Cowan, Eliz. 296
Cowan, Jn. 47
Cowden, Jn. 98
Cowen, Henry 19
Cowles, Thomas 79
Cowley, Abraham 103
Cowling, Josiah 106
Cowling, Slaughter 116
Cowper, Edward 77
Cowper, Jn. 77, 300
Cowper, Josiah 77
Cowper, Robert 77
Cowper, Capt. Robert 117
Cowper, Roe 77
Cowper, Wills 285
Cowper, Wm. 77
Cox, Edward 77, 218
Cox, Mrs. Eliz. 130
Cox, Frederick 116
Cox, George 77
Cox, Jacob 77
Cox, Jn. 77
Cox, Reuben 94, 95
Cox, Rich. 94
Cox, Samuel 146
Cox, Volentine 77
Cozens, Mrs. 78
Craddock, Jn. 147
Craghead, George 75
Craghead, Wm. 91
Craig, Lt. 195
Craig, Alex. 131, 302
Craig, George 76
Craig, Miss Gracie 148
Craig, J. 176
Craig, James 13, 129, 378
Craig, Jn. 78
Craig, Miss Judith 131
Craig, Miss Kitty 129
Craig, Robert 65
Craigen, Jn. 78
Craighead, Capt. Wm. 4
Craighead, Robert 92
Craik, Mrs. S. 111
Craine, Jn. 169, 190
Cralle, Jn. Jr. 78

Cralle, Rodham
 Kenner 94
Cramphin, R. 328
Crampton, Miss Jane
 105
Crandell, Thomas
 179, 220
Crane, James 279
Crane, Jn. 52, 348
Crank, Betsey 140
Crank, Frankey 140
Crank, George 140
Crank, Jn. 140
Crank, Lipscomb 140
Crank, Nancy 140
Crank, Sally 140
Crank, Stephen 140
Crap, James Jr. 48, 78
Crap, John 78
Crap, Rich. 295
Crawford, Mr. 41
Crawford, Andrew 70, 77
Crawford, Anne 79
Crawford, the Rev. Chas. 16
Crawford, David Sr. 79
Crawford, the Rev. Edward 305
Crawford, James 15, 139, 202
Crawford, Margarett 79
Crawford, Nelly 79
Crawford, Wm. A. 9
Crawley, [?] 103
Crawley, Eliz. 79
Crawley, Jn. 79
Crawley, Miss Eliz. 77
Crawley, Robt. 5
Creager, Peter 100
Creagh, Patrick 72, 91, 234, 261, 332
Crebs, Conrad 211
Creighton, Robert 179
Creighton, Wm. Jr. 79
Crenshaw, David 153
Crestmast, Miss Nancy 330
Crews, Benj. 99
Crews, Jn. 281
Crews, Sarah 281

Cri[s]t, Miss Rebecca 59
Cribbs, Capt. 195
Cringan, Dr. 267
Cringan, Dr. Jn. 80
Crissop, Michael 80
Critcher, Easther 80
Critcher, Thomas 80
Critchit, George 53
Critchit, Jn. 53
Critchit, Rich. 53
Critchit, Sarah 53
Critendon, Hannah 6
Crittenden, Thomas 202
Crum, Anthony 246
Croane, Miss Mary 356
Crohon, Matthew 11
Crompton, Capt. 80
Cronean, Daniel 215, 245
Crop, Rich. 97
Cropper, Col. 182
Cropper, Jn. Jr. 271
Cross, James 184
Cross, Jn. 80
Cross, Joseph 80, 131, 230
Cross, Thomas 222
Crossley, Ann 285
Crossley, Thomas 378
Crouch, Miss Eliz. 316
Crouch, Miss Polly 242
Crouly, James 138
Crow, David 133
Crow, James 20
Crowdson, Jn. 222
Cruer, Mr. 18
Crug, Charles 81
Crumley, Sarah 81
Crump, Capt. 315
Crump, Capt. Abner 360
Crump, B. 42
Crump, Benedict 81
Crump, Goodrich 210
Crump, Miss Polly 156
Crump, Richard 19
Crumpton, Wm. 380
Crutcher, Coleman 81
Crutcher, Henry 81

Crutcher, Hugh 81
Crutcher, Robert 81
Crutcher, Sarah 81
Crutcher, Seabert 81
Crutcher, Thomas 81
Crutcher, Wm. 81
Crutchfield, [?] 167
Cryer, Edmund 376
Cubbin, Andrew 188
Cubbin, Andrew 252
Cubbins, Dorothy 81
Cubbs, Capt. 195
Cumbridge, Joseph 195
Cundiff, Ensign 194
Cuningham, Peter 76
Cuninghame, Alex. 223
Cunningham, Miss 321, 371
Cunningham, Ann 81
Cunningham, Edward 216
Cunningham, Eliz. 82
Cunningham, Hugh Jr. 371
Cunningham, Jn. 82, 216
Cunningham, Paul 195
Cunningham, Rox 265
Cunningham, Samuel 82
Cunningham, Wm. 44, 324
Curd, Jesse 82, 114
Curd, Mary 358
Curd, Sarah 82
Curd, Wm. 358
Curdiff, Christopher 150
Cureton, James 82
Cureton, Jeremiah 82
Curle, Col. 362
Curle, Mrs. Mary 362
Curle, Col. Wm. Roscow Wilson 82
Curlet, Thomas 67
Curlett, Nicholas 23
Currie, David 198

18th-Century Virginia Newspapers

Currie, the Rev. Mr.
   David   5
Currie, Miss Frances
   Hill   5
Currie, Miss J.   138
Currie, James   257
Currie, Dr. James
   82
Currie, Peter   92
Currin, Robert   82
Curry, James   37
Curry, Wm.   296
Curson, Rich.   149
Curte (see: Curle, Col.
   Wm. Roscow Wilson)
   82
Curtin, Chloe   83
Curtin, Daniel   165
Curtis, Christopher
   44
Curtis, Will   121
Curtis, Wm.   289
Cushman, Silas   100
Custis, Mrs.   325
Custis, Daniel Parke
   83, 107
Custis, Miss Fanny
   Parke   373
Custis, Jn.   373
Custis, Jn. Parke   325
Cuthbert, Wm.   45
Cuttings, [?]   273

Dabney, Jn.   177
Dabney, Miss Polly
   380
Dabney, Rich.   83
Dabney, Robert   107
Dade, Miss Betsy   206
Dade, Mrs.   123
Dade, Sarah   83
Dade, Townshend   83
Daffin, Miss   236
Daingerfield, Mary
   84
Daingerfield, W.   84
Daingerfield, Wm.
   84, 88
Dalby, Philip   84
Dalgleish, Alex.   328
Dalgleish, Dr. Alex.
   84
Dalgleish, Jn.   84
Dalgleish, Robert   328
Dalsell, James   305
Dalton, Miss   149
Dalton, James   375

Dalton, Jn.   45, 73
Dalton, Timothy   84, 375
Damar, Will   274
Dameron, Aaron   93
Dameron, James   12, 20, 46
Dameron, Martha
   84
Dameron, Miss Nancy
   129
Dames, Jn.   84
Dana, Phinehas   280
Danby, Jn.   186
Dance, Matthew   84
Dancy, Edward   84
Dandridge,
   Bartholomew   109, 313
Dandridge, Miss Betsey
   13
Dandridge, Francis
   85
Dandridge, J.   10
Dandridge, Jane   85
Dandridge, Mrs. Jane
   347
Dandridge, Jn.   85, 109
Dandridge, L.   83
Dandridge, Miss Mary
   319
Dandridge, N. W.   118
Dandridge, Nathaniel
   West   85
Dandridge, Wm.   257, 319, 340
Dandridge, Col. Wm.
   85
Danger, Wm.   255
Dangerfield, Leroy
   380
Dangerfield, Miss
   Betsey   315
Daniel   88, 288
Daniel, Beverley   85
Daniel, Chestley   85
Daniel, Eliz.   369
Daniel, George   85, 240
Daniel, Henry   85
Daniel, James   85
Daniel, Jn.   85
Daniel, Dr. Jn.   85
Daniel, Overton   85
Daniel, Robert   85, 87, 240

Daniel, Royall   117
Daniel, Samuel   163, 294
Daniel, Sarah   85
Daniel, Thomas   85, 369
Daniell, Andrew   305
Daniell, Miss Amey
   158
Daniell, Thomas   85, 158
Dansie, Capt.   341
Dansie, Thomas   13, 127, 172, 319
Dantignac, Anne   86
Dantignac, Jn.   86
Darby, Adam   215
Dark, Wm.   73
Darke, Mrs.   167
Darlington, Jn.   218
Darracott, Jn.   172
Darracott, Capt. Jn.
   86
Darricoatt, Wm.   71
Darringer, Miss Kitty
   80
Darrous, Jn.   208
Davenport, Alixus
   Madder   86
Davenport, Bedford
   86
Davenport, Benj.   86
Davenport, Miss Betsey
   175
Davenport, Birkett
   146
Davenport, Catharine
   86
Davenport, George
   86
Davenport, James
   179, 380
Davenport, Jn.   339
Davenport, the Rev.
   Joseph   87, 175
Davenport, Miss
   Peachy   273
Davenport, Thomas
   Pasteur   86
Davenport, Wm. [?]
   86
Davenport, Wm.   86
Davenport, Wm. Tersyl
   86
Daves, Armistead   255
Davey, George   290
David   70, 252

David, James 18
Davidson, James 352
Davidson, Jn. 352
Davie, Peter 126
Davies, Henry 87
Davies, Jn. 295
Davis, Miss 176
Davis, [Mrs.] 2
Davis, the Rev. Mr. 165, 239
Davis, Augustine 87
Davis, Miss Clarissa 164
Davis, Miss Eliza 20
Davis, Eliz. 167, 168
Davis, Hobble 243
Davis, Isaac Jr. 197
Davis, Jn. 88, 93, 100, 167, 234, 312
Davis, Jn. W. 128
Davis, Mary 12, 88
Davis, Miss Mary 101
Davis, Matthew 378
Davis, Miss Nancy 281
Davis, Robert 291
Davis, Samuel 87, 168
Davis, Thomas 88, 94, 167, 377
Davis, the Rev. Mr. Thomas 64, 176
Davis, Wm. 38, 89, 93, 253
Davison, Ann 88
Davison, Eliz. 88
Davison, Hezekiah 88
Davison, Ithmar 88
Davison, Lucinda 88
Davison, Margaret 88
Davisson, Ithamar 88
Davy 305
Dawley, Col. 184, 348
Dawley, Dennis 91, 117
Dawlin, Jn. 319
Dawson, Capt. 204
Dawson, Commissary 88, 89
Dawney, Alex. 25, 93, 239
Dawson, Benj. 56

Dawson, Jn. 88, 92
Dawson, Thomas 77, 88, 362, 365
Dawson, the Rev. and Hon. Wm. 88
Day, Benjamin 211
Day, Maj. Benj. 338
Day, Jn. 89, 218, 334
Day, Samuel 334
Daylies, Hannah 89
De Bartz, [?] 296
De Clery, Noel 129
De Clovay, Capt. 349
de Gamble, Mons. 343
De Graffenreidt, Tscharner 89
De Klauman, C. C. 48
De La Hoyde, Anne 220
De Rieux, P. 89
De Sigengue, Lewis 90
Deaderick, Miss Polly 131
Deadman, Miss Susanna 288
Deakins, Wm. Jr. 300
Dean, Abel 90
Dean, Benj. 94
Dean, Jonathan 194
Dean, S. 90
Deane, Benj. 95
Deane, Eliz. 90
Deane, Elkanah 90, 174, 274
Deane, Mildred 328
Deane, Wm. 90, 134
Debaptist, Frances 89
Debny, Lewis 250
Debutts, Samuel 90
Degraa, Charles 90
Degraffenreid, Baker 89
Degraffenreid, Sarah 89
Degraffenreid, Vincent 89
Degraffenried, [?] 171
Dejarnatt, Munford 90
Delafield, Wm. 116

Delahaye, Joseph 26, 155
Delap, Felix 135
DeLaporte, Capt. 97
Delasie, Marshall 97
Delbridge, Robert 91
Delk, David 91
Dell, Philip 115
Delony, Henry 91
Delyon, Mr. 189
Demar, Nicholas 8
Demby, Malachi 227
Demissy, [?] 33
Demoss, Charles 91
Demoss, Katherine 91
Demoss, Lewis 91
Demoss, Sarah 91
Demoss, Thomas 91
Demoss, Throckmorton 91
Demoss, Wm. 91
Demsey, Mark 99
Denby, Miss Susan 201
Deneale, G. 342, 350
Denham, Rich. 91
Denniston, Hannah 91
Denny, Rich. 194
Denny, Wm. 96
Dent, Rich. 69
Depreist, Jn. Jr. 179
Depriest, Wm. 93
Derrick, Barbara 91
Derrick, Eve 91
Derrick, Jn. 91
Derrick, Jonathan 91
Derrick, Michael 91
Derrick, Rosanna 91
Derrough, Amos 160
Devine, Eliz. 120
Devine, James 93
Dew, Dolphin 38
Dewbree, John 10
Dewbree, Rebecca 10
Dewbree, Samuel 10
Dick 35, 150, 181
Dick, Alex. 286
Dick, Archibald 269
Dick, Charles 100, 217, 223
Dick, Edward 295
Dick, Elisha C. 9
Dick, Wm. 33, 55, 100, 139

18th-Century Virginia Newspapers 403

Dickenson, Capt. 264
Dickenson, Hannah 100
Dickenson, James 109
Dickerson, Archelaus 100
Dickerson, George 98
Dickerson, Wm. 100
Dickeson, Jn. 301
Dickey, Jn. 100
Dickie, Anne 100
Dickins, Miss Masey 241
Dickinson, Ann 101
Dickinson, S. 300
Dickson (see: Dixon) 102
Diddep, Archibald 106
Didlake, Jn. 89
Diggens, Daniel 109
Digges, Cole 101, 153
Digges, Dudley 50, 101
Digges, Dudley Jr. 101
Digges, Edward 101
Digges, Lt. Edw. 91
Digges, Miss [Patsy] 50
Digges, Miss Polly 101
Digges, Miss Susanna 153
Digges, Thomas 101
Digges, Wm. 101
Digges, Wm. Jr. 101
Digges, Wm. Sr. 101
Diggs, Miss Lucy 324
Dighton, Wm. 276
Dignan, Philip 76
Dildey, Catharine 363
Dildey, Gutlieb 363
Dildey, Maria 363
Dildey, Peter 363
Dillard, James 101
Dillard, Jn 232
Dilley, Aaron 95
Dillon, Edward 216
Dillon, Jn. 111
Dison, Mrs. Sarah 165
Dittond, Anthony Francis 117

Divers, George 51, 288
Dix, Rebecca Marriott 32
Dix, Wm. 32
Dixon, Anne 102
Dixon, Haldenby 87
Dixon, Harry 102
Dixon, Holenby 283
Dixon, James 284
Dixon, Jn. 29, 102, 166
Dixon, Col. Jn. 102, 283
Dixon, Lucy 102
Dixon, Miss Polly 283
Dixon, Peter 344
Dixon, Rachel 107
Dixon, Roger 102, 159
Dixon, Sarah 10, 45, 102
Dixon, Thomas 102
Dixon, Capt. Thomas 45
Dixon, Turner 102
Dixon, Wm. 98
Dobbie, Capt. George 277
Dobbins, Miss Aggy 300
Dobbins, George 300
Dobson, Frances 7
Dobson, Rich. 7
Dobson, Robert 165
Dodd, Griffin 103
Dodson, Daniel 319
Dodson, Jn. 223
Doeber, Christian 103
Doff (see: Henry Orendorff) 290
Dogers (see: Samuel Dogens) 103
Dogge, Miss Virginia Averilla 101
Doggett, George 334
Doggett, Joel 334
Doggins (see: Samuel Dogens) 103
Donald, Mr. 173
Donald, Alex. 103
Donald, Andrew 103
Donald, Ann 104
Donald, George 345
Donald, M. 194
Donald, Robert 49, 51, 103, 255, 259
Donald, Thomas 103

Donald, Wm. 104
Donaldson, Alex. 104
Donaldson, Jn. 104
Donaldson, Joseph 347
Donaldson, Wm. 103
Donaphin, Gerard 85
Donaphin, Mary 85
Donaphin, Nancy 85
Doniphan, Wm. 104
Donnaby, Abby 104
Donoghoe, Daniel 99
Donovan, Jn. 163
Doody, Ann 104
Doogan, James 99
Doolan, Lawrence 76
Dooley, Mr. 152
Dooly, Capt. Jn. 96
Dorell, Sampson 264
Doren, Michael 296
Dorish, Martha 104
Dorlon, Jn. 15
Dorman, James 100
Dorrell, Miss Eliz. 260
Dorsey, Charles 55
Dorsey, Leven 152, 354
Dortel, Noah 328
Dorton, Wm. 94
Dorton, Wm. 95
Doss, Joel 95
Douding, Lucy 105
Dougal, Barbara 105
Dougherty, James 23
Douglas, Archibald 105
Douglas, Catherine 105
Douglas, Dutchess of 105
Douglas, Hugh 105
Douglas, James 105, 296
Douglas, Margaret 105
Douglass, Achilles 310
Douthat, Mrs. Ann 129
Dove, Jn. 98
Dove, Julia Lee 105
Dove, Mrs. Julia Lee 167

Dowdall, J. G. 72
Dowdall, James G. 216, 297
Dowdey, [?] 195
Dowdy, Edmund 350
Dowlin, Dennis 92
Downer, Wm. 105
Downman, Mrs. Anne 86
Downman, Rawleigh 210
Downman, Rawleigh P. 134
Downman, Robert 159, 190
Downman, Wm. 105
Downrichards, Thos. 16
Dowsing, Everard 289
Doxay, Miss Susannah 267
Doyle, Eliz. 106
Doyle, Jn. 39
Doyle, Thomas 92
Drake, Jn. 297
Drake, Mary 281
Draper, Jn. 183
Drew, Benj. 318
Drew, Dolphin 106
Drew, James 276
Drew, Jn. 106
Drew, Wm. 106
Dribon, Lewis 227
Dring, Jonathan 106
Driscol, Catherine 106
Driscoll, Cornelius 106
Driver, Capt. 128
Driver, Anne 106
Driver, Jn. 106
Drummond, Mrs. 33
Drummond, Jn. 170
Drummond, Miss Sally 324
Drummond, Wm. 204, 215
Drury, Mathias 107
Drury, Robert 373
Drynane, Miss Polly 214
Dryskill, Francis 96
Dudley, Miss 53
Dudley, Capt. Robert 223
Dudley, Edward 64

Dudley, Miss Frances 298
Dudley, James 274
Dudley, Lt. Jn. 28
Dudley, Robert 360
Dudley, Robert B. 107
Dudley, Thomas 107
Dudley, Wm. 107
Duerson, Eliz. 184
Duerson, Wm. 184
Duff, Wm. 222
Duffield, Jn. 361
Duffield, Mary 107
Duffy 312
Duffy, Patrick 94
Dugan, Cumberland 149
Dugan, Margaret 149
Duke, [?] 108
Duke, Betty 108
Duke, Burnley 107, 108
Duke, Cleaverse 107, 108
Duke, Eliz. 107, 108
Duke, Henry 108
Duke, James 107
Duke, Mrs. Jane 2
Duke, Jn. 107
Duke, Martha 107
Duke, Mary 107, 108
Duke, Patsy 108
Dukeland, Alexander 98
Dulany, Benj. 64
Dulany, Miss Julia 64
Dulin, Edward 105
Dun, Peter 341
Dunbar, Col. 29, 214
Dunbar, Mrs. Eliz. Hill 311
Dunbar, Jn. 119
Dunbar, John 18
Duncan, Charles 21, 196
Duncan, Howsen 108
Duncan, Jn. 109, 194
Duncan, Joseph 108
Duncan, Moses 108
Duncan, Rawleigh 109
Duncan, Seth 109

Duncan, Thomas 108, 109
Duncan, Townshend 109
Duncanson, James 33, 208, 268
Duncanson, Col. James 109
Duncanson, Miss Polly 268
Duncastle, Thomas 109
Duncle, Jacob 24
Duncle, Mary 24
Dunivan, Daniel 89
Dunlap, Ben. F. 109
Dunlap, the Rev. Wm. 109
Dunleavy, Daniel 296
Dunlop, Archibald 240
Dunlop, James 91, 224, 238
Dunlop, Susanna 109
Dunn, Miss 152
Dunn, Agrippa 109
Dunn, Henrietta 109
Dunn, James 25
Dunn, Joshua 95
Dunn, Michael 76
Dunn, Wm. 109, 141, 377, 380
Dunnabow, Jn. 92
Dunory, Jemima 110
Dunory, Karenhappuch 110
Dunory, Kezia 110
Dunstan, Jane 110
Durant, Miss Ann Jane 309
Durant, Mr. L. E. 110
Durell, Miss Rebecca 149
Durfey, Francis 165
Durham, Thomas 100
Durrant, Joseph 295
Durrett, Wm. 110
Duval, Claiborne 110
Duval, Miss Eliz. 144
Duval, Henry 110
Duval, Jn. 110
Duval, Miss Lucy 272
Duval, Philip 110
Duval, Robert 110
Duval, Samuel 101, 143, 177

Duval, Wm. 11, 110, 144, 227
Duval, Maj. Wm. 110
Duvall, Benj. 220
Duvall, Wm. 74, 166
Dwyer, Jn. 98
Dwyer, Patrick 129
Dyer, Edward 197, 328
Dyer, Samuel 87
Dyke, Isham 97
Dykes, James 141
Dykes, Mungo 110
Dyson, Miss Betsey 251
Dyson, James 110, 251
Dyson, Robert 110

Eachus, Robert 337
Earl, Daniel 188
Earl of Dumfries 44
Earle, Samuel 80
Early, James 19, 296
Early, Jn. 111
Earvin, Miss Polly 31
Easly, Warren 111
Eason, Jn. 372
Eastin, Wm. 111
Easton, David 32
Easton, Sarah 32
Eastwood, Corns. 111
Eaton, Col. 148
Eaton, Alice 111
Eaton, Jn. 296
Eaton, Mrs. Rebekah 111
Eaton, Thomas 16
Eaton, Wm. 111, 158, 272
Echalds, Abraham 111
Echalds, David 111
Echalds, Drucilla 111
Echalds, Jeremiah 111
Echalds, Jn. 111
Echalds, Joel 111
Echalds, Joseph 111
Echalds, Mary 111
Echalds, Moses 111
Echalds, Obadiah 111
Echalds, Rebecca 111
Echalds, Rhoda 111

Echalds, Sarah 111
Echalds, Tabitha 111
Echols, Benj. 111
Echols, Betsey 111
Echols, Elijah 111
Echols, James 111
Echols, Jn. 257
Echols, Nancy 111
Echols, Obadiah 111
Echols, Philip I. 111
Echols, Polly C. 111
Echols, Samuel B. 111
Eckstine, Leonard 111
Eddin, Samuel 314
Eddins, Capt. Samuel 27, 28
Edelen, the widow 137
Edloe, Jn. 68
Edmonds, Jn. 94, 112
Edmondson, James 130, 326, 366
Edmondson, Mrs. Mary 105
Edmondson, Philip 70
Edmonstone, Jn. 112
Edmunds, James Jr. 232
Edmunds, Jn. 44, 177
Edmunds, Sterling 112
Edmunds, Sterling 229
Edmunds, Miss Susan 112
Edmundson, Jn. 98
Edwards, Arthur 156, 341
Edwards, Benj. 112
Edwards, Charles 92
Edwards, Francis 292
Edwards, Ignatius 92
Edwards, Jn. 163
Edwards, Mark 112
Edwards, Miss. Mary Ann 5
Edwards, Miss Nancy 354
Edwards, Mrs. Sukey 320

Edwards, Nathaniel Jr. 112
Edwards, Philemon 93
Edwards, Robert 98
Edwards, Thomas 92
Edwards, Usly 119
Edwards, Wm. 39, 112
Edwerds, Edith 112
Edwerds, Humphrey 112
Egborn, Adelia 112
Ege, Miss Eliza 361
Ege, Eliz. 113
Ege, Jacob 131, 205
Ege, Miss Sally 199
Eggleston, Miss Hannah 177
Eggleston, Joseph 107, 108, 113, 355
Eggleston, Mary 108
Eggleston, Rich. 113, 243
Egglestone, Rich. 355
Egleston, Wm. 113
Egmon, James 97
Egmon, Laurence 20
Egmond, Lawrence 243
Eilbeck, Ann 229
Eilbeck, Jonathan 123
Eilbeck, Wm. 229
Eisdale, Jn. 32
Elam, Rich. 287
Elder, Donald 295
Elder, Thomas 279
Elder, Wm. 295
Elk, Benj. 202
Ellar, George 295
Elle, Jane 62
Ellen, David 93
Elliot, Robert 113
Elliott, Mr. 113
Elliott, Andrew 16
Elliott, Miss Besty 220
Elliott, Chivers 114
Elliott, Jn. 12, 114, 169, 370
Elliott, Peter 2, 20, 187
Elliott, Rich. 113
Elliott, Robert 114
Elliott, Thomas 114
Ellis, Jn. 102, 368
Ellis, Mary 65

Ellis, Mrs. Mildred 364
Ellis, Miss Sukey 220
Ellis, Susanna 114
Ellis, Wm. 114
Ellison (see: Tempest Ellis) 114
Ellyson, Gerard 58, 267
Ellyson, Mrs. Sarah 58
Ellzey, W. 114
Elmore, George 100
Elton, Isabella 115
Elton, Mrs. Isabel 326
Elwood, Absolom 98
Embley, Jn. 115
Embley, Thomas 115
Emerson, the Rev. Mr. 101
Emmerson, the Rev. Mr. 18, 130
Emons (see: Amons) 6
Emrey, Catherine 115
Engleton, Anthony 133
English, Wm. 194
Ennever, Joseph 173
Ennis, Enoch 76
Ennis, Lawrence 112
Epes, Col. Peter 115
Epes, Francis 115, 339, 369
Eppes, Eliz. 115
Eppes, Francis 73, 115, 176
Eppes, George 115
Eppes, Richard 122
Eppes, Temple 115
Eppes, Wm. 344
Epps, Col. Francis 16
Epps, Miss M. B. 16
Estes, Elisha 116
Estes, Richard 116
Estes, Robert 116
Estill, Boyd 116
Estill, Wallace 116
Estill, Zachariah Foster 116
Estis, Robert Sr. 116
Etheredge, Wm. 227
Etheridge, Capt. P. 116
Eustace, Miss Kitty 29

Eustis, Jn. 205
Evans, Mr. 102, 117
Evans, Miss A. 350
Evan, Miss Mary Amena 188
Evans, Ann 279
Evans, Charles 116
Evans, David 117
Evans, Edward 262
Evans, Ephraim 117
Evans, George 117
Evans, Henry 117
Evans, Jn. 193, 316
Evans, Jn. Sr. 117
Evans, Joseph Jr. 117
Evans, Lucy 117
Evans, Nathaniel 118
Evans, Peter 117
Evans, Polly 323
Evans, Miss Sally 252
Evans, Sarah 117
Evans, Thomas 117
Evans, Wilmouth 323
Evans, Wm. 15
Everard, Thomas 175
Ewell, Capt. Thos. 59
Ewell, James 17, 148, 264
Ewell, Maj. James 118
Ewell, Jesse 17, 148
Ewell, Thomas W. 95
Ewing, Ebenezer 371
Ewing, Jn. 118, 220
Eyre, Jn. 323
Ezell, Eliz. 118
Ezell, Isham 118
Ezell, Timothy 118

Fackler, Miss Eleanor 260
Fage, Citizen 240
Fain, Capt. Joseph 194
Fair, Edmund 95
Fair, Sarah 118
Fairfax, Bryan 65, 118
Fairfax, Denny 119, 190
Fairfax, Eliz. 118
Fairfax, Ferdinando 118

Fairfax, George Wm. 118
Fairfax, Sarah 118
Fairfax, Thomas, Lord 190
Fairfax, Wm. 55, 60
Falkenquist, Erland 327
Falkner, Usly 119
Falkner, Wm. 119
Fallen, Miss 91
Fallin, Eliz. 91
Famer, Jn. 285
Famer, Liddy 285
Fanny 132
Fant, Fielding 141
Fantleroy, Miss Nancy 56
Faris, Wm. 323
Farish, Hazlewood 119
Farish, Robert 119, 321
Farish, Thomas 257, 268
Farley, Clay 335
Farley, Eliz. 335
Farley, Francis 119
Farley, James Parke 344
Farley, Jn. 95
Farley, Letty 335
Farley, Miss Rebecca Parks 74
Farley, Wm. 335
Farmer, Wm. 119
Farnan, Matthias 116
Farquharson, Jn. 119
Farquharson, Margaret 119
Farrar, Jn. 226
Farrar, Rebecca H. 226
Farrar, Samuel 14
Farrel, Wm. Jr. 175
Farrell, Mary 120
Farrier, Jn. 214
Farrington, Reuben 96
Farrow, Miss Betsy 297
Faulcon, Edward 120
Faulcon, Jacob 304
Faulcon, Nicholas 120, 304

Faulcon, Nicholas Jr. 112, 338
Faulder, Thomas 120
Faulkner, David 80, 91
Faulkner, Eliz. 343
Faulkner, James 171
Fauntleroy, Jn. 345
Fauntleroy, Samuel Griffin 120
Fausset, Wm. 98
Faver, Thomas 335
Fawcett, Thomas 147
Fear, Henry 96
Fearson, Dorothy 120
Fearson, Wm. 128
Femster, Eliz. 121
Femster, Jn. 121
Femster, Rachel 121
Femster, Sarah 121
Femster, Susannah 121
Femster, Thomas 121
Femster, Wm. 121
Fenaughty, Daniel 200
Fendall, Benj. 159
Fendall, Philip R. 164
Fenny, Thos. 10
Fentress, Hezekiah 92
Fentriss, Nehemiah 94
Ferguson, Maj. 195
Ferguson, James 92
Ferguson, Obadiah 97
Ferguson, Peter 93
Ferguson, Robert 142
Ferguson, Walter 188
Fergusson, Benj. 98
Fergusson, Jn. 47, 79
Fergusson, Joseph 118
Ferr, Jn. 94
Ferrell, Dolly 14
Ferrell, Wm. 14
Feskin, Peter 121
Feury, Patrick 121
Fewqua, Joseph 93
Ficklin, Benj. 81
Ficklin, Susana 81
Ficklin, Wm. 194, 247
Field, Daniel 287
Field, Henry 121
Field, James 121
Field, Jn. 297
Field, Col. Jn. 194
Field, Jn. Shaw 121
Field, Margaret 121
Field, Mary 121
Field, Theophilus 121
Figures, Rebekah 358
Figures, Rich. 358
Finch, Comfort 122
Finch, Edward 63, 274
Finch, Henry 335, 376
Finch, Wm. 122
Findly, James 255
Finlay, Amelia 122
Finlay, Robert Jr. 44
Finn, Derby 91
Finnie, Mrs. Joanna 122
Finnie, Miss Mary 122
Finnie, Col. Wm. 122
Fish, Sarah 260
Fisher, Mr. 129
Fisher, Bolling 123
Fisher, Daniel 41, 123, 320
Fisher, George 123
Fisher, Jn. 97, 123
Fitzgerald, Ann 347
Fitzgerald, Anne 224
Fitzgerald, Francis 76, 185, 186
Fitzgerald, Jn. 48, 125, 298
Fitzgerald, Wm. 240, 367
Fitzgerrald, Capt. Wm. 249
Fitzhugh, Miss Barbara 222
Fitzhugh, Col. Henry 123, 325
Fitzhugh, Dennis 123
Fitzhugh, Mrs. Eliz. 123
Fitzhugh, Jn. 123, 142
Fitzhugh, Maj. Jn. 222
Fitzhugh, Miss Molly 325
Fitzhugh, Theodorick 272
Fitzhugh, Thomas 292
Fitzhugh, Wm. 82, 123, 150, 363, 373
Fitzhugh, Wm. Beverly 308
Fitzjarrel, Morris 190
Fitzpatrick, George 98
Fitzpatrick, Jn. 93
Fitzpatrick, Mary 124
Fitzpatrick, Wm. 355
Flahavan, Miss Biddy 55
Flahavan, Roger 55
Fleet, Frances 124
Fleet, Sarah 43
Fleet, Wm. 1, 43
Fleming, Judge 319
Fleming, Lt. 149
Fleming, Betty 125
Fleming, Charles 93
Fleming, Capt. Charles 94
Fleming, Gardner 218
Fleming, Miss Molly 207
Fleming, Miss Sukey 206
Fleming, Tarlton 125
Fleming, Thomas 32, 124
Fleming, Thomas M. 124
Fleming, Wm. 90, 124
Fleming, Wm. R. 124
Fleming, Col. Wm. 32
Flemming, Miss Sally 271
Flemming, Wm. 354
Flennikin, Wm. 195
Fletcher, Carter 94, 95
Fletcher, James 130, 154
Flieger, Jn. 254
Flin, Anne 125
Flint, Mrs. Margaret 265
Flipps, Wm. 55
Flood, Miss Alice 188
Flood, Edward 243
Flood, Eliz. 125

Flood, Capt. Henry 211
Flood, Nicholas 143
Flood, Dr. Nicholas 215
Flood, Wm. 19, 73
Flood, Wm. P. 300, 357
Flood, Dr. Wm. 153
Flournoy, Jordan 125
Flournoy, Thos. 365
Flower, George 168
Flower, Matthew 92
Floyd, Jn. 377
Floyrnoy, Samuel 279
Folden, Jn. 337
Foley, Dennis 139
Foley, Eliz. 125
Folger, Obed 125
Fontaine, Eliza 126
Fontaine, the Rev. James Maury 126
Forbes, Alex. 126
Ford, Hezekiah 376
Ford, Samuel 255
Ford, Susannah 376
Forest, Philip 287
Forest, Sarah 287
Forester, Eliz. 157
Forester, Jn. 157
Ferguson, Joseph 375
Formicola, Mr. 59
Formicola, Seraphino 126
Forrester, Wm. 158, 198
Forson, Benj. 158
Forson, Sally 158
Forster, James 292
Forster, Wm. 126
Forsyth, Absolom 375
Fox, Adam 91
Fox, Anne 128
Fox, Elisabeth 128
Fox, Eliz. 91, 200
Fox, Jacob 200
Fox, James 128, 318
Fox, Jn. 16, 127, 128
Fox, Joseph 128, 164
Fox, Capt. Nathaniel 353
Fox, Robert 66
Fox, Thomas 225, 228
Francis, Joseph 225
Francis, Tench 275

Frank, Graham 339
Franklin, James 182, 225
Franklin, Jn. 94
Franklin, Thos. 76
Franks, Henry 76
Fraser, Miss Betsy 279
Fraser, David 128
Fraser, Thomas 128
Frawd, Mary 189
Frayser, Thomas 317
Frazer, Anthony 128, 377
Frazer, Esther 174
Frazer, George 174
Frazer, Hugh 334
Frazer, James 95
Frazer, Jn. 128
Frazer, Jn. G. 289, 377
Frazer, Simon 221
Frazier, Alex. 352
Frazier, Wm. Jr. 257
Freeland, Mace 368
Freeland, Peregrine 285
Freeman, Charles 201
Freeman, Robert 24
Freeman, Wm. 44, 93
French, Miss 108
French, George 117, 269
Fridley, Henry 241, 379
Friend, Edward 211
Friend, Joseph 77, 215, 255
Frister, Miss 310
Frizzle, Luke 339
Frothingham, Lt. 195
Fry, Christ. 65, 192
Fry, David 167
Fry, Mary 91
Fry, Philip 91
Fry, Rich. 378
Fryatt, Batholomew 243
Fugate, Randolph 95
Fulkner, Margater 40
Fullmer, Joseph 134, 243, 244, 283
Fulmer, Joseph 130

Funk, Jacob 130, 192
Funk, John 8
Furney, Barbary 309
Furney, Hans Adam 309
Furr, Ephraim 20
Furry, Benj. 130
Furry, Mary 130

Gaffney, Jane 130
Gagahagen, Jn. 296
Gaillard, Jn. 362
Gailliard, Jn. 129
Gaine, Hugh 226
Gaines, Ben. 76
Gaines, Broddus 130
Gaines, Dorothy 130
Gaines, Edward 130
Gaines, Francis 130
Gaines, Geo. 19
Gaines, Harry 162
Gaines, Joseph 130
Gaines, Katey 19
Gaines, Mary 130
Gaines, Rich. 130
Gaines, Sarah 130
Gaines, Solomon 130
Gaines, Susanna 130
Gaines, Thomas 130
Gaines, Wm. Fleming 256
Gainet, Henry 48, 298
Gaither, Ephraim 320
Gaither, Greenberry 347
Galaspie, Mary 131
Gallagher, Thos. 76
Gallego, Joseph 204
Galley, Wm. 116, 214
Galloway, Jn. 131
Galloway, R. 146
Galloway, Robert 131
Galt, Miss 299
Galt, Mrs. Eliz. 131
Galt, J. M. 273
Galt, James 131, 332
Galt, Jn. M. 62, 73, 78, 342
Galt, Dr. Jn. M. 131
Galt, Samuel 131
Galt, Thomas 212
Galt, Wm. 324

18th-Century Virginia Newspapers

Gambill, Matthew 131
Gamble, Joseph 352
Gambrell, [?] 195
Ganby, Jn. 100
Garber, M. Jr. 100
Gardiner, James 132
Gardiner, Jn. 98
Gardiner, Miss Sally 174
Gardner Family 41
Gardner, Anthony 89
Gardner, Francis 132
Gardner, Hanson 335
Gardner, Henry 20, 132
Gardner, James 32
Gardner, Jn. 359
Gardner, Nancy 335
Gardner, Rebecca 132
Gardner, Samuel 275
Gardner, Thomas 132
Gardner, Wm. 93
Garland, Griffin 132, 266, 276, 347
Garland, Jn. 132
Garland, Thomas 162
Garlick, Miss Eliz. 139
Garlick, Samuel 202
Garner, Charles 153
Garner, James 153
Garner, Jn. 153
Garner, Parish 153
Garner, Miss Sally 332
Garner, Thomas 153
Garner, Vincent 153
Garnett, James 125
Garnett, James M. 233
Garnett, Muscoe 203
Garnett, Miss Nancy 283
Garnett, Reuben 251
Garnett, Thomas 132, 236, 283
Garr, Solomon 295
Garrard, Mary 132
Garrard, Wm. 132
Garret, Hen. 6
Garret, James 93
Garret, Martha 6
Garretson, Job 163, 288

Garrow, Wm. 341
Garthright, Benj. 132
Garthright, Miss Eliz. M. 300
Garthright, Jn. 132
Garthright, Samuel 132
Garthright, Thomas 132
Garthright, Wm. 132
Garton, Jesse 77
Garts, Peter 132
Garwood, Daniel 315
Gary, Jn. 303, 318
Gasford, Samuel 58
Gaskin, Thomas Jr. 94
Gasking, Charles 27
Gaskins, Thomas 160
Gates, Jn. 133
Gates, Maj. Gen. Horatio 133
Gatewood, Fleming 133
Gatewood, Fullington 133
Gatewood, Henry 133
Gatewood, Jn. 133
Gatliff, Charles 133
Gatliff, Leah 133
Gay, Archibald 209
Gay, Daniel 280
Gay, Polly 133
Gayle, George 179
Gayle, Thomas 133
Geddy, Miss Betsey 329
Geddy, James 11, 13, 42, 192
Geddy, Miss Nancy 42
Geddy, Miss Polly 271
Gehce, Wm. M. 306
Gennery, Will 134
Geoghegan, Anthony 299
George 117, 123, 257
George, Elsley 134
George, Wm. 134
Gerard, Timothy 95
Gess, Mrs. Kitty 211
Gibbin, Marcus 134
Gibbin, Mrs. Martha 134
Gibbin, the Rev. Jn. 134

Gibbons, Jn. 143
Gibbony, Alex. 32
Gibbs, Gov. 340
Gibbs, James 64
Gibbs, Miss Massy 128
Gibbs, Wm. 134
Gibson, Capt. 103
Gibson, Alex. 134
Gibson, James 134
Gibson, Jn. 197
Gibson, Joseph 135
Gibson, Rowland 116
Giertberg, Jonas 327
Gilbert, Miss. Eliz. 123
Gilbert, Reyner 123
Gilbert, Sarah 135
Gilbert, Thomas 135
Gilchrist, Alex. 194
Gilchrist, Jn. 135
Gilchrist, Robert 19
Giles, Cannon 135
Giles, Eliz. 294
Giles, Grizell 104
Giles, Judith 135
Giles, Knowles 135
Giles, Mary 295
Giles, Nicholas 135
Giles, Tas 295
Giles, Wm. 243, 377
Giles, Wm. B. 328
Giles, Capt. Wm. 135
Gilkeson, Hugh 181
Gilkison, Jn. 348
Gilkison, Robert 281, 379
Gill, Frances 135
Gillart, Felix 135
Gillet, Simon 125
Gilliam, Miss Jeany 108
Gilliam, Jn. Sr. 267
Gilliam, Joseph 103
Gilliam, Reuben M. 136
Gilliam, Robert 154, 326
Gilliam, Miss Susanna 36
Gilliam, Wm. 154
Gilliat, Anthony 139
Gillies, Wm. 141, 288
Gillum, Jn. 136
Gillum, Wm. 136

Gilmer, George 136, 311
Gilmore, Mr. 152
Gilmore, Miss Betsey 140
Gilmore, Peachy 140
Gilmour, Dr. 29, 151
Ginter, John Conrad 17
Gird, Henry 107
Girty, Simon 54
Gist, Joshua 69, 279
Gist, Mordecai 61
Gist, Samuel 6, 8, 121
Glascock, Gregory 126
Glascock, Thomas 126
Glascock, Wm. 136
Glass, Robert 136
Glass, Sarah 165
Glass, Thomas 136, 296
Glass, Wm. 165
Glassell, Jn. 174, 230, 234
Glassell, Wm. 1
Glendening, David 92
Glendy, the Rev. Mr. 53
Glover, Isabella 335
Glover, Wm. 99, 335
Godard, Wm. 63
Goddard, M. K. 106
Goddin, Isham 129
Godfrey, Isabella 136
Godfrey, Matthew 251, 334
Godfrey, Nathaniel 136
Godwin, Mr. 136
Godwin, Anthony 136, 166
Godwin, Miss Betsey 271
Godwin, James 136
Godwin, Jeremiah 136
Godwin, Miles 137
Goffigan, N. 323
Goggin, Robert 301
Golat, Jn. 250

Gold, James 46
Goldie, Thomas 249
Goldin, Miss 193
Goldwell, Mrs. 137
Gooch, Gov. 379
Gooch, Gideon 219
Gooch, Sir Wm. 137
Goodchild, Wm. 31, 126, 186
Goode, Col. Robert 213, 319
Goode, Francis 125
Goode, Mack 173
Goode, Miss Polly 319
Goode, Rich. 176
Goode, Miss Sally 213
Goodin, Miss Sally 49
Goodloe, Aquilla 184
Goodloe, George 184
Goodloe, Henry 184
Goodloe, Jn. 184
Goodloe, Priscilla 184
Goodloe, Robert 184
Goodrich, Bridger 115
Goodrich, Jn. 38, 372
Goodrich, Wm. 38, 115
Goodwin, Capt. Wm. 137
Goodwin, Clara 133
Goodwin, Daniel 38
Goodwin, Eliz. 138
Goodwin, Jn. 7, 133
Goodwin, Mary 7
Goosely, Capt. George 138
Goosley, W. 5, 185
Gordon, Alex. 139, 150, 251, 259, 260
Gordon, Ann 138
Gordon, Miss Ann 70
Gordon, Charlotte 138
Gordon, James 215, 350, 359
Gordon, James Jr. 15
Gordon, Jn. 86, 158, 288, 371
Gordon, Miss Lucy G. 350
Gordon, Mary 139

Gordon, Nathaniel 84
Gordon, Miss Peggy 198
Gordon, Rich. 124
Gordon, Thomas 138, 179, 352
Gordon, Wm. 138
Gore, Jn. 139
Gore, Miss Susannah 192
Gorlier, Francis 105
Gorman, Jn. 99
Gorsuch, Jn. 163, 288
Gosling, Susannah 139
Goss, James 116
Gould, Mr. 139
Govan, Archibald 146, 351
Govan, James 44, 74, 110, 351
Gow, Anne 365
Gow, Mrs. Anne 45
Gowan, James 44
Grace, Capt. 188
Gracie, Jn. 34, 224
Graff, Andrew 227
Graham, Alex. 10
Graham, Catherine 140
Graham, David 299
Graham, Geo. 10
Graham, George 156
Graham, James 98, 177
Graham, Jn. 32
Graham, Miss Polly 32
Graham, Reginald 251
Graham, Rich. 28, 51, 107, 270
Graham, Stephen C. 324
Graham, Thomas 140
Graham, Wm. 139
Grammer, Jn. 140
Granberry, Mrs. 103
Granberry, Josiah 285
Granger, Francis 296
Grant, Daniel 59, 140
Grant, Margaret 61
Grapes, Miss Hannah 303

Grapes, Jacob 140
Grasty, George 235
Gratenread (see: David
 Graffenread) 139
Grattan, Jn. 183, 199
Graven, Morgan 90
Graves, Ann 282
Graves, Mrs. Anne
 141
Graves, Arthur 197
Graves, Edmund 327
Graves, Henry 206
Graves, Howel 140
Graves, James 140
Graves, Jn. 140
Graves, Jn. Jr. 141
Graves, Joseph 141
Graves, Margaret 235
Graves, Rachel 206
Graves, Rice 95, 141
Graves, Rich. 76
Graves, Rich. C. 348
Graves, Samuel 140
Graves, Thomas 141
Graves, W. 273
Graves, Wm. 79,
 141, 273, 301
Gray, Capt. 313
Gray, Alex. 343
Gray, Daniel 197
Gray, David 301
Gray, Edwin 136,
 141, 309
Gray, Etheldred 87
Gray, Isaac 99
Gray, Miss Isabella
 192
Gray, James 360
Gray, Jn. 322
Gray, Lucy 360
Gray, Mary 141, 343
Gray, Peggy 142
Gray, Robert 96,
 141, 192
Gray, Wm. 296
Grayson, Col. 138, 190
Grayson, Dr. 195
Grayson, the Rev. Mr.
 303
Grayson, Alfred 142
Grayson, Benj. 269
Grayson, George 142
Grayson, Robert 142
Grayson, Spence 269
Grayson, the Rev.
 Spence 142
Grayson, Wm. 142

Grayson, Col. Wm.
 96
Greaves, Capt. Wm.
 142
Green, Gen. 277
Green, Abraham 87
Green, Anderson 95
Green, Ann 142
Green, Mrs. Ann 143
Green, Charles 269
Green, Eliz. 143
Green, Fortunatus
 195
Green, Francis Wyatt
 142
Green, George 61
Green, Grief 237
Green, Jn. 142, 143,
 212
Green, Col. Jn. 143
Green, Moses 142, 143
Green, Robert 222
Green, T. 156
Green, Thos. 16
Green, Wm. 99, 142, 143
Green, Wm. Wills
 26
Green, Col. Wm. 142,
 143
Greenfield, Wm. 143
Greenhill, Miss Sally
 278
Greenhow, Robert
 144
Greenhow, Samuel
 144
Greenway, Capt.
 Joseph 144
Greenwood, James
 228
Greenwood, Jn. 198,
 306
Gregg, Hermon 194
Gregorie, James 193,
 245
Gregory, Capt. Jn.
 94
Gregory, Eliz. 144
Gregory, James 193
Gregory, Jn. 144
Gregory, Margaret
 144
Gregory, Mildred 144
Gregory, Rich. 178
Gregory, Roger 144,
 303
Gregory, Wm. 97, 144

Gregs, Edmund 98
Greig, Admiral 144
Gresham, Wm. 34,
 79, 144
Gretter, Michael 121,
 224
Grider, Jacob 161
Grider, Rebecca 161
Grier, Robert 145
Grievous 81
Griffin, Mr. 351
Griffin, the Rev. Dr.
 362
Griffin, the Rev. Mr.
 290
Griffin, Corbin 249
Griffin, Dr. Corbin
 2
Griffin, Cyrus 145,
 196
Griffin, the Rev. James
 78
Griffin, Jn. 8, 75
Griffin, Leroy 34
Griffin, Mary 8
Griffin, Polly 75
Griffin, Samuel 312
Griffin, Susannah
 304
Griffin, Thomas B.
 313
Griffin, Wm. 145
Griffith, Charles 102,
 137, 188
Griffith, Hannah 145
Griffith, Henry Jr.
 102, 137, 188
Griffith, Nathan 379
Grigg, Jn. 95
Griggs, Thomas 53
Grigsby, James 95
Grigsby, Miss Nancy
 293
Grimes 140
Grimes, Agatha 145
Grimes, Jn. 145
Grimes, Philip 145
Grinnan, Daniel 317
Grinnan, Daniel Jr.
 236
Gross, Michael 193
Grove, Christian 133
Grove, Henry 145
Grymes, Benj. 85,
 131, 146
Grymes, Charles 146

Grymes, Col. Charles 213
Grymes, Miss Fanny 213
Grymes, Henry 355
Grymes, Jn. 49, 146, 268
Grymes, Jn. D. 230
Grymes, Miss Lucy 49
Grymes, Ludwell 19
Grymes, Miss Molly 248
Grymes, Philip 50, 146, 248, 252
Grymes, Philip L. 207
Grymes, Philip Ludwell 146
Grymes, Miss Susannah 50
Guerrant, Miss Jane 142
Guerrant, Jn. 183, 299
Guerrent, Daniel 360
Guin, James 92
Gunn, Mr. 279
Gunnell, H. 69
Gunther, Martha 146
Gurley, the Rev. George 146
Guthrie, Capt. 195
Guthrie, Alex. 38
Guthrie, Kesiah 38
Gutridge, Mr. 137
Guttery, Mary 210
Guy, George 152
Guy, Capt. George 303
Guy, James 74
Gwatkin, James 187

Haas, Frederick 39
Hack, Wm. 336
Hackett, Thomas 234
Hackley, Miss Betsey 55
Hackley, Miss Nelly 22
Hackley, Rich. 55
Hackley, Richard S. 147, 179
Haddon, Allen 147
Haden, Anthony 75
Haden, Jn. 95
Hadfield, Thomas 321
Hagley, Peter 147
Hagner, Martin 59

Hague, Francis 121
Hague, Hannah 147
Hague, Jn. 292
Hague, Joseph 91
Haines, Jacob 273
Haines, Margaret 147
Haines, Miss Mary 220
Haines, Wm. 195
Hains, Eliz. 177
Hains, Samuel 177
Hair, Daniel 368
Hair, Miss Nancy 162
Haire, Miss Katey 322
Hales, Jn. 294
Hall, Miss Amelia P. 176
Hall, B. H. 148
Hall, Charles 362
Hall, Col. Elihu 148
Hall, Dr. Elisha 148
Hall, Henry 30
Hall, James 84, 147
Hall, Jemima 147
Hall, Jn. 312
Hall, Capt. Jn. H. 148
Hall, Lt. Jn. 42
Hall, Lucy 312
Hall, Nathaniel 92
Hall, Philip 73, 230
Hall, Polly Hopkins 148
Hall, Samuel 147
Hall, Susanna 147
Hall, Thomas 147
Hall, Wm. 147
Hallam, Mr. 148
Halley, Mary 148
Halley, Wm. 148
Hallier, Simon 10
Halpin, Jn. 298
Hambleton, Robert 96
Hamblin, Charles Jr. 64
Hamilton, Col. 35
Hamilton, Lt. 349
Hamilton, A. 356
Hamilton, Alex. 148, 149
Hamilton, Andrew 103, 311, 345
Hamilton, Eliz. 149
Hamilton, Francis 149
Hamilton, Gavin 124, 148, 149, 357

Hamilton, George 107
Hamilton, Jacobina 149
Hamilton, James 92, 96, 149
Hamilton, Jeremiah 99
Hamilton, Jesse 239
Hamilton, Jn. 149, 212, 219, 253
Hamilton, Robert 180, 331
Hamilton, Thomas 95, 149, 264
Hamlet, Jesse 239
Hammack, Eliz. 149
Hammack, Jn. 149
Hammon, Eleanor 247
Hammon, James 247
Hammon, Jarvis 309
Hammond, Camilla 149
Hammond, Charles 286
Hammond, Charles Jr. 81
Hammond, Edward 95
Hammond, Harriet 149
Hammond, Miss Jane 236
Hammond, Margaret 149
Hammond, Stephen 149
Hammond, Thomas 92
Hammond, Wm. 149
Hamond, Samuel 97
Hampton, Michael 195
Hanby, Jonathan 225
Hancock, Arthur 149
Hancock, Edw. 337
Hancock, Sarah 337
Hankey 304
Hanness, Wm. 96
Hansborough, Miss Betsey 67
Hansborough, Miss Milly 24
Hansborough, Peter 24, 67
Hansfield, Thomas 179

18th-Century Virginia Newspapers 413

Hansford, Charles 53, 164	Hardyman, Wm. 152, 158	Harris, Francis Eppes 77
Hansford, Eliz. 150	Hare, Moses 151	Harris, Frederick 107, 334
Hansford, Miss Eliz. 53	Hare, Parker 44	
	Hare, Wm. B. 14, 151	Harris, Hamblin 54
Hansford, Lewis 150, 369	Harford, Jn. 97	Harris, Hamlin 153
	Hargrave, Jesse 151	Harris, Hugh 94
Hansford, Miss Molly 306	Harl, Jn. Sr. 151	Harris, James 152, 279
	Harl, Leander 151	
Hanson, Col. Samuel 150	Harlan, George 268	Harris, Jane 153
	Harlan, Jehu 151	Harris, Jn. 76, 152, 153, 168, 181
Hanson, Rich. 35, 317	Harlan, Jesse 151	
Hanson, Samuel 24, 235	Harlett, Jane 295	Harris, Jn. Jr. 125
	Harman, Miss 143	Harris, Nathaniel 170
Happer, Mary 150	Harman, Jn. 195	
Happer, Thomas 150	Harmanson, Miss Eliz. 300	Harris, Peyton 152
Harbert, Judith 26		Harris, Rich. 6
Hardage, Wm. 253	Harmanson, Miss Isabella 127	Harris, Robert 152
Hardaman, Susannah 226		Harris, Miss Sally 216
	Harmar, Gen. 126	
Hardaway, Daniel 355	Harmar, Brig. Gen. 195	Harris, Samuel 173
		Harris, Mrs. Sarah 152
Hardaway, Hartwell 150	Harp, Jn. 92	
	Harp, Micajah 151	Harris, Sarah 153
Hardaway, Jn. 70	Harp, Wiley 151	Harris, Sherod 226
Hardaway, Mary 150	Harper, Andrew 282	Harris, Thomas 88
Hardaway, Rebecca 150	Harper, Ann 152	Harris, Wm. 152, 153, 220
	Harper, Ferrel 356	
Hardaway, Thomas 252	Harper, J. W. 303	Harris, Wm. Jr. 28
	Harper, James 349	Harrison, Col. 20, 97, 244
Harden, Cleaverse Duke 107	Harper, Jesse 94	
	Harper, Jn. 86	Harrison, Miss Anne 101
Harden, James 107	Harper, Joseph 126	
Harden, Joseph 250	Harper, Joseph Wells 152	Harrison, Barbara 154
Harden, Nathan 250		
Harden, Rebecca 250	Harper, Margaret 1	Harrison, Ben. Jr. 278
Harden, Rich. 76		
Hardesty, George 150	Harper, Ritter 356	Harrison, Benj. 18, 41, 76, 124, 153, 256, 277, 279
Hardiman, Mary 357	Harper, Samuel 126	
Hardin, Mr. 152	Harper, Thos. 73	
Hardin, Anne 357	Harper, Wm. 152	Harrison, Col. Benj. 278, 284
Harding, Miss Anne 196	Harper, Wyatt 152	
	Harpiron, Mr. 157	Harrison, Benj. Jr. 153
Harding, Joseph 113, 174	Harres, Andrew 92	
	Harrifield, James 97	Harrison, Miss Betsey 374
Harding, Wm. 93	Harringham, James 151	
Hardy, Andrew 94		Harrison, Mrs. Betsy 284
Hardy, Curtis 94, 95	Harrington, Henry 104	
Hardy, Hannah 151		Harrison, Burr 153
Hardy, Miss Nelly 172	Harris, Col. 354	Harrison, Capt. Carter 57, 92, 161, 287, 336, 375
	Harris, Benj. 153, 279	
Hardy, Wm. 94	Harris, Miss Betsey 355	
Hardyman, Mr. 80		Harrison, Col. Carter 286
Hardyman, Mrs. 158	Harris, David 93	
Hardyman, Jn. 173	Harris, Eldridge 53, 104	Harrison, Carter B. 153, 370
Hardyman, Stith 352		
	Harris, Fanny 339	Harrison, Cary 200

Harrison, Catherine 153
Harrison, Charles 153
Harrison, Col. Charles 213
Harrison, Cuthbert 153
Harrison, Edmund 15, 16, 154
Harrison, Edward 201
Harrison, F. S. 353
Harrison, Henry 154
Harrison, Jane 153
Harrison, Miss Jane 255
Harrison, Jn. 179
Harrison, Miss Lucy 278
Harrison, Miss Ludwell 138
Harrison, Mary-Ann 153
Harrison, Miss Mary Anne 351
Harrison, Matthew 153, 351
Harrison, Miss Nancy 76
Harrison, Nathaniel 101, 153, 154
Harrison, Col. Nathaniel 353
Harrison, Peyton 154
Harrison, Miss Polly 374
Harrison, Rich. 202
Harrison, Robert 154
Harrison, Robert C. 154
Harrison, Miss Sally 220
Harrison, Samuel 135
Harrison, Sarah 200
Harrison, Seth 154
Harrison, Miss Susan 352
Harrison, Thos. 47, 99, 153, 154, 313
Harrison, Walter H. 154
Harrison, Willie 154
Harrison, Wm. 153
Harrison, the Rev. Wm. 137, 182

Harriss, Mr. Hamlin 154
Harriss, Wm. 168
Harrow, Gilbert 154
Harry 34
Harry, Evan 71
Harry, James 306
Harston, Eliz. 357
Harston, Geo. 357
Hart, Maj. 195
Hart, Mr. 197
Hart, Adam 215
Hart, Joseph 155
Hart, Josiah 155
Hart, Malcolm 79
Hart, Oliver 155
Hart, Robert 227
Hart, Silas 155
Hartley, Letecia 155
Hartshorn, Capt. 195
Harvell, Peyton 17
Harvey, Frances 343
Harvey, Mungo 290
Harvey, Wm. 155, 343
Harvie, Jn. 11
Harvin, Anthony 296
Harvin, Jn. 296
Harwell, Peyton 21
Harwell, Sterling 263
Harwood, Edward 162
Harwood, Elisha 156
Harwood, Frances 155
Harwood, Humphrey 137, 155, 165, 189, 363
Harwood, James 156
Harwood, Samuel 374
Harwood, Wm. 168
Harwood, Wm. Jr. 155
Haskins, Christopher 160
Haskins, Creed 156
Haskins, Edward 156
Haskins, Joseph 93
Haskins, Miss Mary P. 242
Haskins, Owen 237
Haskins, Robert 211, 341
Haskins, Thomas 156
Hatcher, Miss Eliz. 202
Hatcher, Thomas 299
Hatter 156

Hatterslay, Samuel 156
Hatton, James 92
Hatton, Samuel 156, 231, 246
Hauk, Peter 163
Haw, Capt. Samuel Jr. 62
Hawk, Stephen 97, 98
Hawke, Elijah 328
Hawkins, Arculus 305
Hawkins, James 297
Hawkins, Jn. 107, 310
Hawkins, Mary 108, 157
Hawkins, Reuben 157
Hawkins, Susanna T. 157
Hawkins, Wm. 89
Hawthorne, [James] 29
Hawthorne, Susannah 29
Haxall, Wm. 60
Hay, Anthony 157
Hay, Charles 157
Hay, David 157
Hay, George 157
Hay, Grissel 157
Hay, Helen 157
Hay, James 10
Hay, Jn. 47, 157
Hay, Lydia 157
Hay, Mary 157
Hay, Peter 157
Hay, Robert 157
Hay, Wm. 157
Haycock, Wm. 126
Haydon, Jesse 158
Hayes, Eliz. 158, 258, 295
Hayes, Miss Hetty 178
Hayes, Jn. 31
Hayes, Robert 258
Hayes, Wm. 116
Hayly, Jn. 96
Haymaker, Adam 158
Haynes, A. 158
Haynes, Mrs. Ann 280
Haynes, Catherine 12, 158
Haynes, Curtes 229

18th-Century Virginia Newspapers   415

Haynes, Eaton 158
Haynes, James 158
Haynes, Miss Peggy 88
Haynes, Miss Sally 184, 185
Haynes, Thomas 370
Haynes, Thos. 371
Hays, Anthony 86
Hayth, Wm. 191
Hayward, Araminta 158
Haywood, Jn. 158
Haywood, Willis 158
Haywood, Wm. 158
Hazlegrove, James 51
Hazlegrove, Jn. 277
Hazlehurst, Jn. 274
Hazlett, Wm. 42
Head, Benj. 92
Head, Betsy 158
Head, Eliz. 158
Head, Eliz. Jannatt 270
Head, Eliz. Jannett 158
Head, James 159, 270
Head, Lucy 158
Head, Simon Benj. 158
Heane, Thomas 159
Heard, Jesse 367
Heary, Matthew 159
Heath, Alex. 159
Heath, Jesse 159
Heath, Jn. 159
Heath, Susannah 159
Heathcote, Lydia 296
Heavenridge, Jn. 165
Heavin, Howard 159
Heavin, James 159
Heavin, Jn. 159
Heavin, Rich. 159
Heavin, Wm. 159
Heckie, Peter 200
Hedges, Thomas 159
Heerman, Frederick 81, 121
Heermann, Fre. 297
Hefferson, Jn. 232
Heiges, George 147
Heiskell, Miss Amelia 308
Heiskell, Frederick 308

Helm, Achiles 160
Helm, Barbary 160
Helm, Jn. 82
Helm, Joseph 160
Helm, Leonard 160
Helm, Margaret 160
Helm, Meredith 160
Helm, Thomas 160
Helm, Zachariah 160
Helphinstone, Peter 160
Heman, Jos. 160
Henay, Barbary 201
Henay, Peter 201
Hench, Charles Frederick 160
Hencke, Unich 304
Henderson, Alex. 105, 162, 169, 309
Henderson, James 253, 367
Henderson, Jn. 160
Henderson, Judith 160
Henderson, Rich. 370
Henderson, Wm. 49
Hendrick, Jn. 160
Hendrick, Zachariah 215
Hendricks, James 197, 214
Hendrock, Drucella 117
Hendrock, Moses 117
Hendry, Wm. 160
Hening, David 160
Hening, Samuel 160
Hennessy, Daniel 296
Henninger, Jn. Frederick 160
Henninger, Mary Magdalena 160
Henry, Miss Anne 287
Henry, Miss Betsy 13
Henry, Miss Dorothea Spotswood 373
Henry, Eleanor 161
Henry, James 161
Henry, Jane 161
Henry, Jn. 274
Henry, Capt. N. 100
Henry, Patrick 63, 161, 177, 287, 373
Henry, Sam. 6
Henshaw, Anne 161

Henshaw, W. 81
Hensler, W. 90
Hensley, Joseph 93
Hensley, Thomas 92
Henson, Sam 218
Henton, Peter 161
Henton, Rebecca 161
Henton, Thomas 161
Henton, Wm. 161
Hepburn, Eliz. 161
Hepburn, Miss Nancy 109
Hepburn, Wm. 379
Herbert, Buttler 162
Herbert, Judith 162
Herbert, Martha 162
Herbert, Maximilian 5, 251
Herbert, Miss Tabitha 205
Herbert, Rich. 162
Herbert, Wm. 1, 55
Herderson, Alex. 293
Herdman, James 162
Herges, George 147
Herman, Jn. 226
Hermann, Frederick 297
Herndon, Edward 162
Herndon, Jn. 162
Herndon, Joseph 162
Herndon, Mrs. Mary 162
Herndon, Wm. 40
Herring, Arthur 323
Herring, Mary 323
Herring, Wm. 37, 323
Herringham, Francis 162
Herringham, Mary 162
Herringham, Wm. 162
Herriter, Casper 197
Herron, James 331
Hert, Mr. 41
Hesley, Jn. 47
Heslop, Miss Frances 84
Hessler, George 218
Heston, Robert 194
Heth, Wm. 35, 162
Hewes, Aaron 108
Hewes, Mrs. Eliz. 264
Hewet, Jn. 322

Hewett, Thomas 213
Hewitt, Miss Martha 213
Hewitt, Wm. 162
Heyden, Lewis 162
Hiatt, Isaac 163
Hiatt, James 163
Hiatt, Simeon 163
Hickey, Edward 163
Hicklen, Hugh 281
Hicklin, Thomas 116
Hickman, Jn. 350
Hickman, Peggy 335
Hickman, Samuel 335
Hickman, Thomas 163
Hickman, Wm. 208
Hicks, Capt. 223
Hicks, Mrs. 189
Hicks, Charity 358
Hicks, Edward 354
Hicks, Miss Eliz. 319
Hicks, George 123
Hicks, Isaac 95
Hicks, Jn. 163
Hicks, Nathaniel 358
Hicks, Robert 354
Hicks, Zachariah 123, 372
Hicks, Zachariah 372
Hide, Daniel (see: Daniel Hyde) 176
Hidges, Jn. 97
Hieskell, Christopher 174
Higgens, Ensign 195
Higgens, Jn. 275
Higgins, Jn. 115
Higginson, Miss 152
High, Samuel 187
Higham, Abraham 163
Hildrip, Jn. 45
Hile, Joist 222
Hill, the Rev. Mr. 128
Hill, Baylor 71, 163
Hill, Miss Betsey 109
Hill, Miss Betsy 262
Hill, Edward 88, 163, 223, 240
Hill, Miss Frances 121
Hill, Francis 92
Hill, Geo. 333
Hill, Col. Henry 121

Hill, Humphrey 180, 228
Hill, James 164
Hill, Jn. 118, 163, 164
Hill, Joseph 163
Hill, Judah 227
Hill, Julia 106
Hill, Miss Molly 44
Hill, Nathaniel 263
Hill, Susanna 164
Hill, Thomas 96, 148
Hill, Wm. 93, 163, 164, 358
Hill, Wm. Cortito 323
Hilldrup, Sam. 26
Hilliard Family 159
Hinde, Jn. W. 164
Hinds, Jn. 98
Hinds, Joseph 98
Hinson, Tudor 135
Hipkins, Mrs. 164
Hipkins, Miss A. 26
Hipkins, Miss Eliza 317
Hipkins, Miss Fanny 20
Hipkins, Jn. 20, 84
Hipkins, Leroy 26, 165
Hipkins, Rich. 40
Hipkins, Samuel 165, 266, 347
Hiseler, Mary 165
Hitchcock, Daniel 195
Hitchings, James 295
Hite, Alex. 192
Hite, Col. 264
Hite, Isaac 46, 165, 218, 298
Hite, Isaac Jr. 217
Hite, Miss Kitty 203
Hite, Miss Sally 46, 211
Hite, Mrs. Sarah 363
Hobday 102
Hobday, Jn. 206
Hobson, Ishmas 86
Hobson, Jn. 200
Hobson, Nicholas 80, 264
Hobzenbeeler, Joseph 165
Hockaday, Col. Jn. 165
Hodge, Thomas 162

Hodges, Chainey 165
Hodges, James 97, 165
Hodges, Jesse 165
Hodges, Joseph 165
Hodges, Josiah 4
Hodgson, Jn. 273, 347
Hodgson, Martha 273
Hodgson, Peter 275
Hodgson, Capt. Robert 26, 42, 74, 78, 119, 183, 189, 228, 330, 353, 372
Hodgson, Wm. 35, 324
Hoffman, Philip 192
Hogan, Margaret 166
Hogden, Jos. 38
Hogden, Wm. 38
Hogg, Mr. 117, 126
Hoggard, Mary 166
Hogshead, David 281, 379
Holaman, Jn. 166
Holdcroft, James 199
Holderness, George 104
Holderness, Jas. 15
Holland, Jn. 168
Holland, Jonas 357
Holland, Joseph 95
Holland, Thomas 94
Holland, Wm. 166, 232
Holliday, James 107, 166
Holliday, Jane 167
Holliday, Mrs. Jane 52
Holliday, Jn. 129
Holliday, Thomas 270
Hollidge, Miss Ann 47
Hollingsworth, Jesse 24, 35
Hollingsworth, Stephen 24
Hollis, Bathsheba 145
Holloway, David 309
Holloway, George 94
Holloway, James 286
Holloway, John 26
Holloway, Sarah 167
Hollyday, James 167
Holmes, B. 23
Holmes, David 168
Holmes, Miss Eliz. 219

18th-Century Virginia Newspapers 417

Holmes, Hugh 168
Holmes, Jn. 200
Holmes, Col. Joseph 204
Holmes, Dr. Joseph 73
Holmes, Miss Peggy 204
Holmes, Rebecca 168
Holmes, Miss Rebecca 73
Holmstrom, Swen 327
Holshoo, Michael 167
Holstead, Latimer 110
Holt, Betsey 168
Holt, Miss Betsy 70
Holt, Betty 168
Holt, James 345
Holt, Jn. 39, 168
Holt, Nancy 168
Holt, Rich. 103, 168
Holt, Rich. Jr. 236
Holt, Thomas 144, 263
Holt, Wm. 168
Holtzclaw, Jn. 168
Home, Patrick 174
Honey, Lucy 168
Hood, Jn. 33, 178, 198, 285, 356
Hood, Judith 168
Hood, Wm. 95
Hooe, Bernard 83, 169
Hooe, Miss Catherine 253
Hooe, Jn. 264
Hooe, Col. Jn. 253
Hooe, Robert T. 235
Hooe, Robert Townshend 217
Hooe, Seymour 3
Hooe, Wm. 120
Hook, Jn. 126, 145
Hooker, Miss Love 331
Hoomes, Jn. 19, 113, 135
Hooper, Edmund 169
Hooper, Unity 21, 169
Hoops, Adam 328
Hoops, Miss Sally 328
Hope, George 60, 274
Hopewell, George 169
Hopkins, the Rev. Dr. 246

Hopkins, James 95, 169
Hopkins, Jn. 360
Hopkins, Josiah 106
Hopkins, Keziah 169
Hopkins, Mary Cary 106
Hopkins, Matthias 169
Hopkins, Samuel 180, 268
Hopkins, Capt. Samuel 69, 225
Hopkins, Stephen 205
Hopkins, Wm. 169
Hopper, Lt. 195
Hopwood, Anne 369
Hopwood, Wm. 369
Hord, Achilles 374
Hord, Thomas 169, 374
Horn, Mary 127
Hornby, Daniel 104, 380
Horne, Pooling 162, 169
Hornsby, Joseph 45, 170, 319
Hornsby, Thomas 170
Hornsby, Wm. 170
Horrocks, the Rev. Mr. James 170
Hosca, Samuel 94
Hoskins, Wm. 182
Hotzenbeller, Jacob 170
Hough, Mr. 118
Hough, Edith 155
Hough, Mahlon 170, 319
Hough, Samuel 170, 319
Hough, Wm. 170, 336
Houlton, Daniel 296
House, Colley 170
House, Henry 170
House, Jn. 170, 265
House, Kesiah 170
House, Lawrence 170
House, Mary 170
House, Nancy 170
House, Patsy 170
House, Samuel 170
Houston, Fanny 170
Houston, Hugh 170
Houston, Wm. 125

Hovemaster, Godlove 201
Hovemaster, Sarah 201
How, Rich. 51
Howard, Benj. 170, 295
Howard, Dr. Ephraim 172, 198
Howard, Henry 161
Howard, Jos. 25
Howard, Judah 297
Howard, Miss Sally 8
Howard, Sarah 170, 198
Howard, the widow 264
Howard, Wm. 170
Howdeshell, Henry 195
Howell, Samuel 171
Howell, Simon 171
Howell, Wm. 100
Howerton, Ambrose 171
Howerton, Charles 171
Howerton, Heritage 70
Howerton, Wm. 92
Howle, Absolom 171
Howle, Epaphroditus 171
Howlet, Jn. 375
Howlitt, Thos. 328
Hoy, Jn. 171
Hoye, Daniel 322
Hubard, James 314
Hubbard Family 153
Hubbard, the Rev. Mr. 101
Hubbard, Benj. 42
Hubbard, James T. 103
Hubbard, Mary Blaikley 327
Hubbard, Thomas 327
Huber, George 122
Huber, Jn. 317
Huck, Jn. 24
Huck, Mary 24
Hudale, Henry 189
Hudgens, Mr. 152
Hudnall, James 172
Hudson, Miss Betsey 80

Hudson, Charles 172, 206
Hudson, Christopher 6
Hudson, Francis 172
Hudson, Jn. 172
Hudson, Sarah 6
Hudson, Vincent 95
Huff, Miss Eliza 206
Huff, Jn. 99
Huff, Lawrence 206
Huffman, Samuel 195
Hughes, Emery 187
Hughes, Miss Esther 72, 81
Hughes, George 187
Hughes, James 177
Hughes, Jn. 172
Hughes, Joseph 369
Hughes, Miss Martha 137
Hughes, the Rev. Mr. Thomas 295
Hughes, Wm. 113, 164
Hughes, Wm. Jr. 172
Hughs, Thomas 98
Huie, James 172
Hulett, Jn. James 254, 353
Hull, Rich. 150, 293
Humphrey, Thomas Jr. 121
Humphreys, Mrs. 324
Hundley, George 173
Hundley, Jn. 173
Hunnicut, Jn. Jr. 173
Hunnicutt, [?] 30
Hunnicutt, Glaister 286
Hunt, David 173
Hunt, Gilbert 173
Hunt, Jane 173
Hunt, Wm. 173
Hunter, Adam 174
Hunter, Anne 175
Hunter, Caleb 97
Hunter, David 119, 175, 320
Hunter, Miss Eliz. 23
Hunter, Geo. 125, 360
Hunter, Capt. George 148

Hunter, James 48, 101, 192, 205, 257, 258
Hunter, Jn. 174
Hunter, Mary-Anna 314
Hunter, Miles 173, 175
Hunter, Moses 119, 301, 320
Hunter, Peter 301
Hunter, S. 174
Hunter, Wm. 83, 168, 174
Hunter, Wm. Jr. 1, 197, 213, 283
Hunton, Eliz. 175
Huntsberger, Jacob 175
Hurley, Jn. 198, 310
Hurt, R. S. 299
Hurt, the Rev. Jn. 177
Husslar, Nazy 175
Hussler, George 178
Hutcheson, Miss Eliz. 71
Hutchings, Daniel 251
Hutchings, Eliz. 175
Hutchings, Jn. 175, 276, 343, 367
Hutchings, Joseph 191
Hutchings, Col. Joseph 176
Hutchings, Miss Mary 367
Hutchings, Robert 20, 253
Hutchins, Benj. 219
Hutchinson, Alex. 176
Hutchinson, James 176
Hutchinson, Jane 176
Hutchinson, Jn. 176
Hutchinson, Nancy 176
Hutchinson, Thomas 176
Hutt, Mr. 352
Hutton, Linda 69
Hyde, Henry 356
Hyde, Rebecca 356
Hyland, Francis 244
Hylton, Mrs. 80
Hylton, Daniel L. 17

Hylton, Miss Hetty 54, 83
Hylton, Jn. 176, 359
Hylton, Ralph 80
Hylton, Wm. 54, 192
Hyndman, Jn. 367
Hynes, Joseph 76
Iferlow, Jane 209
Inadell, James 315
Ingalls, Thomas 106, 333
Ingles, Mrs. 82
Inglis, Samuel 65
Ingot, Henry 97
Ingraham, Nathaniel 177
Ingram, Joseph 97
Ingram, Samuel 361
Ingram, Wm. G. 177
Innes, Alex. 195
Innes, Eliz. 177
Innes, Harry 338
Innes, Hugh 177
Innes, James 6, 229
Innes, Col. James 338
Innes, Robert 126
Innes, Miss Sally 338
Innis, Harry 177, 337
Innis, James 177, 337
Innis, Miss Salley 326
Innis, Robert 177
Inskeep, Abraham 177
Inskeep, Hannah 177
Inskeep, James 177
Inskeep, Priscilla 177
Inskeep, Samuel 177
Inskeep, Sobilla 177
Insko, Mary 285
Insko, Thomas 285
Irby, Charles 94
Irby, Francis 144
Irby, Littlebury 151
Ireland, the Rev. Jn. 331
Irey, Jn. 79
Irion, Philip Jacob 40
Irvin, Francis 67
Irvine, Samuel 177
Irwin, Francis 67

Irwin, Jn. 178, 317, 372
Irwin, Mrs. Martha 27
Irwin, Thomas Wm. 341
Isbell, Mary 85
Isbell, Wm. 178
Isham Family 278
Isler, Mary 178
Isler, Mrs. Mazey 86
Isles, Absolom 328
Isles, Betsey 328

Jack 37, 75, 141, 292, 367
Jack, Jn. 247
Jack, Thomas 44
Jackson, Anthony 33
Jackson, Bathsheba 145
Jackson, David 178
Jackson, Hugh 116
Jackson, Jack 266
Jackson, Jn. 87, 178, 195
Jackson, Joseph 58
Jackson, Josiah 179
Jackson, Lowe 178, 295
Jackson, Martha 356
Jackson, Mary 284
Jackson, Matthew 178
Jackson, Miss Mildred 241
Jackson, Mingo 178
Jackson, Polly 358
Jackson, Robert 179, 327, 366
Jackson, Sarah 25
Jackson, Wilson 97
Jackson, Wm. 156, 179, 241
Jacob, Benj. 189
Jacome (see: Jacomi) 179
Jacomi, Emanuel 179
Jaggard, Hope 177
Jaggard, Samuel 177
Jameison, George 165
Jameison, Mrs. Molly 165
James 145, 229
James, Becky 24
James, Edmund 307
James, Edward 97, 266
James, Elias 179
James, Henry 61
James, Jn. 4, 179
James, Joshua 179
James, Micajah 60
James, Rich. 324, 370
James, Miss Sally 51, 227
James, Susanna 266
James, Thomas 97
James, Thruston 307
Jameson, Capt. 262
Jameson, David 138, 180
Jameson, Jn. 180, 206
Jameson, Thomas 180
Jamieson, Alex. 170
Jamieson, Andrew 212, 312
Jamieson, Neil 343
Jamison, Jn. 273
Janes, Ann 180
Janny, Abel 180
Jaquelin, Edward 314
Jaquelin, Miss Molly 314
Jaques, Wm. 178
Jarrett, Abraham 270, 367
Jarvis, [?] 190
Jarvis, Jn. 180
Javen, Daniel 180
Jefferson, Alex. 180
Jefferson, Archer 181
Jefferson, Eliz. 180
Jefferson, Field 180
Jefferson, Frances 180
Jefferson, Jn. 180
Jefferson, Judith 180
Jefferson, Miss Maria 115
Jefferson, Miss Patsey 279
Jefferson, Patsy 180
Jefferson, Peter F. 180
Jefferson, Samuel 180
Jefferson, Thomas 25, 115, 181, 279
Jefferson, Wm. 180
Jeffery, Thomas 96
Jefferys, Samuel 265
Jeffries, Jn. 181
Jeggitt, Garden 10
Jegitts, Joseph 181
Jemm, Peter 69
Jenkins, Anne 181
Jenkins, Charles 359
Jenkins, Eliz. 127
Jenkins, Geo. 9, 201
Jenkins, Margaret 181
Jenkins, Peter 301
Jenkins, Sarah 181
Jenkins, Thomas 181
Jenkins, Wm. 95, 179, 181
Jennings, Edmund 171
Jenny 297
Jerdone, Charles 181
Jerdone, Matthew 181
Jerdone, Reuben 181
Jerdone, Wm. 181
Jerro, Peter 205
Jervis, Jn. 195
Jesse 75
Jesse, Rich. 98
Jeter, Henry 181, 324
Jeter, Thomas 181
Jett, Bersheba 182
Jim 62
Joe 299, 301
John 27, 132, 209, 217, 218, 317, 349
John, Gregory 182
John, Samuel 122
John, Wm. 200
Johnny 11, 41, 152, 345
Johnson, Capt. 314
Johnson, Capt. 373
Johnson, B. 182
Johnson, Ben 25
Johnson, Ben. E. 191, 290
Johnson, Benj. 181, 253
Johnson, Billy 182
Johnson, Charles 363
Johnson, Christopher 182
Johnson, Daniel 35
Johnson, David 182

Johnson, Miss Fanny 60
Johnson, Frederick 183
Johnson, George 96, 206
Johnson, Grace 183
Johnson, Harry 182
Johnson, Henry 182, 295
Johnson, James 61, 92, 134, 182, 316
Johnson, Capt. James 38, 169
Johnson, James B. 68, 183
Johnson, Jeremiah 184
Johnson, Jn. 71, 93, 97, 170, 182, 183
Johnson, Jn. W. 180
Johnson, Joel 94
Johnson, Katy 182
Johnson, Keziah 182
Johnson, Lewis 212
Johnson, Matthew 93
Johnson, Michael 98, 181
Johnson, Rebecca 68
Johnson, Rich. 262
Johnson, Samuel 347
Johnson, Stephen 184
Johnson, Susanna 206
Johnson, Thos. 34, 68, 97, 182
Johnson, Waddel 262
Johnson, Wm. 5, 25, 95, 183, 195, 215
Johnson, Col. Wm. 264
Johnson, Y. 13
Johnston, Aquilla 184
Johnston, Archibald 184
Johnston, Benj. 117, 124, 185
Johnston, Caleb 184
Johnston, Miss Catherine 101
Johnston, Clary 184
Johnston, Daniel 184
Johnston, Capt. Gideon 98
Johnston, James 97, 184
Johnston, Jebediah 184
Johnston, Jn. 47, 98, 184, 205, 270, 308
Johnston, Judkins 99
Johnston, Luthor 194
Johnston, Mary 184
Johnston, Molly 184
Johnston, Nancy 184
Johnston, Patsey 184
Johnston, Peter 330
Johnston, Rich. 1, 70, 184
Johnston, Col. Rich. 101
Johnston, Robert 158, 185
Johnston, Miss Sally 319
Johnston, Samuel 184
Johnston, Sarah 184
Johnston, Stephen 252
Johnston, Wm. 96, 184
Johnston, Wm. E. 158
Johnstone, James 198
Joiner, John 11
Joiner, Molly 189
Joiner, Rebecca 11
Jolliffe, Amos 185
Jolliffe, Eliz. 185
Jolliffe, Jn. 106
Jolliffe, Mary 185
Jones, Maj. 156
Jones, Mr. 180
Jones, Mrs. 46
Jones, Alan 112
Jones, Alex. 79
Jones, Allen 187, 300, 321
Jones, Ambrose 167
Jones, Ann 48
Jones, Anne 121
Jones, Archer 233
Jones, Augustine 186
Jones, Bathurst 7
Jones, Benj. 95, 96, 353
Jones, Miss Betsey 74
Jones, Cadwallader 239
Jones, Maj. Cadwallador 187
Jones, Caleb 194
Jones, Catesby 161
Jones, Charles 279
Jones, Constance 186
Jones, David 99, 296, 359
Jones, the Rev. Mr. David 216
Jones, Elijah 86
Jones, Eliz. 6, 185, 186, 216, 368
Jones, Miss Elizabeth 65
Jones, Eliza 198
Jones, Emmanuel 132
Jones, Francis 186, 187
Jones, Frederick 185
Jones, Gabriel 119, 187, 190
Jones, George 130
Jones, Hambleton 186
Jones, Hamilton 167
Jones, Hannah 359
Jones, Harrison 86
Jones, Henry 96
Jones, Ignatius 92
Jones, James 96
Jones, Jane 186
Jones, Jn. 6, 86, 93, 123, 185, 259
Jones, Jonathan 205
Jones, Joseph 187
Jones, Josiah 94
Jones, Laney 6, 185
Jones, Letitia 279
Jones, Lewellen 187
Jones, Lewis 99
Jones, Lucy 86
Jones, Lunsford 186
Jones, M. 187
Jones, Martin 190
Jones, Miss Mary 216
Jones, Mrs. Mary 185
Jones, Nathan 82
Jones, Peter 185
Jones, Phebe 186
Jones, R. 361
Jones, Reuben 86
Jones, Rich. 187, 261, 366
Jones, Robert 94, 167, 186, 344

Jones, Robert Jr. 292
Jones, Samuel 187
Jones, Strother 46
Jones, Tabitha 186
Jones, Thomas 186, 188, 216, 241, 329, 363
Jones, Col. Thomas 74
Jones, Vinkler 186
Jones, Walter 49, 300
Jones, Willie 187
Jones, Wm. 53, 95, 97, 108, 243, 277, 306
Jones, Wood 181, 188
Jonesten, Wm. 97
Jopling, James 188
Jopling, Josiah 188
Jordan, Miss 157
Jordan, James 63, 96
Jordan, Jn. M. 188
Jordan, Miss Peggy 266
Joshua 198
Judah 359
Jude, Geo. 10
Jude, John 11
Julian, Dr. 109
Julian, Charles 189
Julian, Margaret 189
Julian, Miss Lucy 109
Jurden, James 97

K[?]o, Thomas 149
Kackley, Elias 254
Kavanagh, Patrick 189
Kay, Mrs. 184
Kay, Alex. 189
Kean, Jn. 311
Kean, Miss Eliz. 311
Kearfoot, Samuel 189
Kearnes, Margaret 189
Kearney, James 372
Kearsley, Jn. 285
Kearsley, Miss Sally 285
Keeling, Adam 190
Keeling, Miss Betsy 101
Keeling, Miss Sally 265

Keene, Newton 329
Keene, Wm. 307
Keenor, Jn. G. 55, 131
Keesee, Rachel 125
Keesee, Sally 125
Keggan, James 296
Keith, Bargey 340
Keith, Jn. 65
Kellam, Zerubabel 94
Keller, Eliz. 190
Keller, George 190
Keller, Jacob 190
Kelley, Abraham 76
Kello, S. 364
Kello, Samuel 68
Kellor, Geo. 373
Kelly, [?] 114
Kelly, Andrew 123
Kelly, Emanuel 94
Kelly, Geo. 378
Kelly, James 103
Kelly, Jn. 99
Kelly, Katy 191
Kelly, Margaret 191
Kelly, Michael 116
Kelly, Patrick 99
Kelly, Thomas 94
Kelly, Wm. 48, 78, 107, 187
Kelsey, Andrew 116
Kelsey, Jacob 364
Kelsey, Samuel 259
Kelsick, Capt. 191
Kelsick, Samuel 259
Kelsick, Capt. Samuel 191
Kelso, Lt. 195
Kelso, Joseph 32
Kelso, Robert 191
Kelty, Wm. 42, 43
Kemble, E. 94
Kemp, Ann 191
Kemp, Jn. 191
Kemp, Peter 191
Kemp, Thomas 191
Kemper, George 226
Kempton, Samuel 296
Kemton, Mark 318
Kendal, Col. Custis 192
Kendall, Miss 300
Kendrick, Abraham 192
Kendrick, Barbara 192

Kendrick, Benj. 192
Kendrick, Catherine 192
Kendrick, Christian 192
Kendrick, Eliz. 192
Kendrick, Jacob 192
Kennedy, Daniel 321
Kennedy, David 212
Kennedy, James 100
Kennedy, Jn. 71, 192
Kennedy, Michael 365
Kenner, Matthew 258
Kenner, Matthew Jr. 245
Kenner, Rodham 192, 329
Kennerly, James 254
Kennett, Zachariah 95
Kennon, Miss Nancy 271
Kennon, Miss Polly 279
Kennon, Col. Rich. 279
Kennor, Jn. 240
Kenton, Mark 55
Kephart, Christopher 193
Kephart, Eliz. 193
Kephart, Henry 193
Kephart, Nancy 193
Keppell, Henry 193
Ker, David C. 155, 193
Ker, Edward 282, 357
Ker, James 10, 45, 139, 193
Kerby, Thomas 193
Kercheval, Samuel 310
Kercheval, Wm. 193
Kerfoot, Miss Eliza 318
Kerney, Jn. 335
Kerr, Mrs. 155
Kerr, Ann 193
Kerr, Edward 193
Kerr, Miss Eliz. 238
Kerr, George 193
Kerr, James 194, 238
Kerr, Jn. 193, 321

Kerr, Miss Margaret 199
Kerr, Samuel 174, 199
Kerr (see: George Kier) 235
Kersey, Jn. 95, 116
Key, Jn. 54, 126, 194, 354, 359
Key, Joshua 194
Key, Tandy 194, 228
Keys, Francis 149
Keys, Gresham 149
Keys, Jn. 149
Kibble (see: Rich. Kible) 194
Kidd, Alex. 194
Kidd, Andrew 370
Kidd, Isaac 202
Kier, George 235
Kiger, Adam 331
Kiger, Geo. 221, 316, 355
Kiger, Jacob 361
Kiger, Miss Kitty 316
Kiger, Miss Polly 221
Kilty, Jn. 364
Kimbell, Jn. 195
Kimbrough, Rich. 108
Kinchler, Peter 179
Kinder, Joseph 47
King, Mrs. 126
King, Andrew 97
King, Edward 169
King, Elijah 60
King, Miss Eliz. 309
King, Esther 196
King, George 119
King, Henry 362
King, James 196
King, Jn. 60
King, Dr. Jn. 196
King, Mary 136, 196
King, Michael 196
King, Miles 10, 20, 167, 196, 224
King, Rich. 139
King, Robert 59, 60
King, Sackville 61, 196
King, Wm. 96
Kingston, Samuel 296
Kinney, Jacob 158
Kinsman, Jn. 196, 197
Kippen, Jn. 104
Kirbey, Samuel T. 197

Kirby, Abraham 327
Kirby, Thomas 197
Kirk, Mrs. 197
Kirk, Bridget 197
Kirk, James 176, 204, 306, 354
Kirk, Jn. 197
Kirkpatrick, Capt. Alex. 231
Kirkwood, Capt. 195
Kirley, Thomas 309
Kirtley, Francis 197
Kitchen, Miss Fenton 374
Kleinhoff, Jn. 197
Kleinhoff, Jn. Jocelyn 197
Klug, Samuel 212
Knap, Mary 254
Knapp, Frances 49
Knight, Ambrose 348
Knight, Arpasia 348
Knight, Jn. 197
Knight, Peter 295
Knop, Valentine 91
Knox, Alex. 154
Knox, Ambrose 75
Knox, James 42, 198
Knox, Jn. 76
Knox, Robert 198
Knox, Wm. 73, 198
Kuhn, Jacob 155
Kyle, James 96
Kyzer, Benj. 23, 24
Kyzer, Betsy 24
Kyzer, Catharine 24
Kyzer, Eliz. 24
Kyzer, Geo. 23, 24
Kyzer, Jn. 24
Kyzer, Mary 24
Kyzer, Molly 24

La Puillade 97
Lacy, Jn. 137
Ladbrook, Anne 247
Ladd, Amos 198
Ladd, James 12, 198
Ladd, Wm. 302
Laderdale, James 163
Lafayette, [Marquis de] 71
Lafferty, Wm. 133
Lafong, Miss Angelica 205

Lagan (see: Jn. Legan) 275
Laing, Wm. 199
Laird, James 74
Laman, George 199
Laman, Joseph 251
Laman, Rachel 199
Lamb, Arthur 98, 296
Lamb, Walter 199
Lamb, Wm. B. 129
Lambert, Charles 185
Lambert, Chas. 6, 185
Lambert, David 131, 135
Lambert, James 227
Lambert, Nancy 6, 185
Lambert, Thomas 226
Lambuth, Samuel 156
Lamkin, Sharp 358
Lammond, Peggy 199
Lamoine, Jn. 341
Lamon, George 161
Lampert, Davy 100
Lampkin, Polly 358
Lamson, James 100
Lancaster, Amelia 199
Lancaster, Jn. 94
Land, Richard 285
Landen, Daniel 76
Landrum, Hawkins 111
Lane, Aaron 199
Lane, C. W. 339
Lane, Charles 205
Lane, George 199, 297
Lane, H. 199
Lane, Hardadge 318
Lane, Hardage 89, 247
Lane, James 131, 230
Lane, Jn. 116, 360
Lane, Joseph 185
Lane, Larkin 199
Lane, Miss Nancy 365
Lane, Wm. 199
Lane, Capt. Wm. 95
Lane, Capt. Wm. Jr. 128, 129

Lane, Wm. Carr 25, 235
Lang, Wm. 194
Langford, Mr. 151
Langford, Edward 353
Langhorne, Miss Jane S. 113
Langhorne, Wm. 82
Langley, Lemuel 200
Langley, Robert 200
Langstone, Matthew 187
Lanier, Mrs. 297
Lanier, Colin 200
Lanier, Frederick 356
Lanier, Lewis 301
Lanier, Martha 301
Lanier, Mary 200
Lanier, Tempy 356
Lanier, Thomas 200
Lanier, Wm. 200
Lankford, Benj. 32
Lankford, Henrietta 32
Lankford, [Thomas] 200
Lankford, Wm. 200
Laprade, Jn. 261, 360
Laprade, Wm. 182
Lapsley, Wm. 200
Larew, James 41
Larick, Jn. 219
Lark, Joseph B. 112
Lark, Mary 200
Lark, Samuel 200
Larkin, Betty 200
Larsh, Hannah 200
Larsh, Paul 200
Larue, Jabez 200, 229
Larue, Jacob 283
Larue, James 200, 268
Lashley, Eliz. 356
Lathan, Robert 176
Latil, Joseph 201
Latimer, James 201
Latimer, Wm. 201
Lattimer, Mr. 265
Lattimore, Charles 230
Lau[?]k, A. 53
Lauderback, Abraham 201

Lauderback, David 201
Lauderback, Eve 201
Lauderback, John 201
Lauderback, Joseph 201
Lauderback, Matthias 201
Laughlin, James 201, 285
Laughlin, Martha 285
Laurance, Mr. 39
Laverty, James 87, 111
Lavinder, Robert 201
Lawlor, Susannah 201
Lawrason, James 43
Lawrence, Edward 295
Lawrence, James 201
Lawrence, Jn. 98, 195, 197, 242, 306, 337, 351
Lawrence, Wm. 201
Lawson, Agnes 149
Lawson, Alex. 43
Lawson, Miss Chloe 200
Lawson, Eliz. 43
Lawson, Gavin 292
Lawson, James 149
Lawson, Jn. 130
Lawson, Mary 149
Lawson, Miss Polly 61
Lawson, Ralph 296
Lawson, Robert 149, 217
Lawson, Thos. 310, 223
Lawson, Lt. Wm. 132
Layland, Peter 97
Layne, Wm. 255
Laypold, Jn. 372
Lazerat, Jean 98
Le Blanc, Joseph 129
Le Porte, Miss 54
Leadbeater, Jn. 208
Leahy, James 71, 306
Leak, Josiah 202
Lear, Abraham 94
Lear, Tobias 202
Leath, Peter 202

Leavil, ,Burrell 274
Leckie, Miss Alice 329
Lee, Miss 298
Lee, Frances 202
Lee, Francis Lightfoot 203
Lee, G. 203
Lee, Geo. 81, 366, 376
Lee, Hall 320
Lee, Henry 16, 202, 203, 299
Lee, Col. Henry 202, 203
Lee, James 202
Lee, Jn. 94, 96, 223, 271
Lee, Mary 203
Lee, Miss Molly 121, 148
Lee, Miss Nancy 256
Lee, Philip Ludwell 25
Lee, Miss Portia 165
Lee, R. 202
Lee, Col. R. H. 202
Lee, Rich. 70, 81, 92, 107, 190, 203, 250, 274, 275, 353, 366, 376
Lee, Rich. Bland 165, 202, 232
Lee, Rich. E. 75, 378
Lee, Rich. Evers 349
Lee, Rich. Hen. 202, 203, 357, 374
Lee, Richard 16
Lee, Robert 202
Lee, Miss Sally 168
Lee, Samuel 159, 165
Lee, Sarah 345
Lee, Miss Sarah 202
Lee, Thomas 52, 203, 295
Lee, Thos. L. 309
Lee, W. 203
Lee, Wm. 165, 203
Leed, Jedidiah 271
Leeds, Jedediah 204
Lees, Jn. 204
Leetch, Jn. 195
Leftwich, Augustine 324
Leftwich, Delilah 324
Leftwich, Eliz. 324
Leftwich, Jabez 324

Leftwich, Thomas
204
Lefueur, Catherine
204
Lefueur, David 204
Lefueur, James 204
Legan, Jn. 275
Legg, Thomas 92,
204
Leigh, Walter 200
Leigh, Wm. 204
Leiper, Dr. Andrew
239
Leiper, Miss Lucy 239
Leitch, Andrew 33,
79, 115, 123, 261
Leitch, David 205,
260
Leitch, John 3
Leith (see: David
Leitch) 260
Leland, Jn. 91
Lemberd, Samuel 318
Lemen, Joseph 322
Lemman, John 6
Lennard, Mary 205
Lennard, Will 164
Lenno, Eliz. 205
Lenno, Philip 205
Lenox, Walter 229
Lent, George 225
Leonard, Anna 205
Leonard, Vandevan
212
Lesher, Jn. 205
Leslie, George 65
Lester, Thomas 172
Letuz, G. H. 224
Levan, [?] 107
Levi, Lazarus 38
Levi, Sarah 38
Levy, Isaac 227
Lewellin, Eliz. 186
Lewis, Capt. 7
Lewis, Miss 64
Lewis, Abraham 120,
164
Lewis, Miss Alice 188
Lewis, Andrew 46
Lewis, Benj. 76
Lewis, Miss Betsy 319
Lewis, Mrs. Betty 206
Lewis, Charles 23,
92, 119, 207, 208, 217,
348
Lewis, Col. Charles
194

Lewis, Charles L. 206
Lewis, Col. Warner
207
Lewis, Daniel 76
Lewis, David 206
Lewis, Col. Fielding
206, 327
Lewis, Francis 208
Lewis, George 206
Lewis, Mrs. Hannah
238
Lewis, Jacob 92
Lewis, James 81,
162, 206, 208, 238, 249
Lewis, Jn. 98, 206, 207,
234, 236, 295
Lewis, Capt. Jn. 80,
96, 97
Lewis, Jn. Zachary
207
Lewis, Joseph 120,
164
Lewis, Judith A. 208
Lewis, Lawrence 112
Lewis, Miss Mildred
236
Lewis, Miss Nancy
262
Lewis, Nicholas 206,
207, 376
Lewis, Polly 206
Lewis, Priddy 206
Lewis, Rachel 234
Lewis, Rebecca 206
Lewis, Rich. 96
Lewis, Robert 207
Lewis, Col. Robert
207, 272
Lewis, Miss Roxa 83
Lewis, Miss Sally 272
Lewis, Miss Susannah
348
Lewis, Thomas 200,
206, 263, 265, 317
Lewis, Capt. Thos.
4, 99
Lewis, Thos. W. 63
Lewis, Warner Jr.
206
Lewis, Wm. Terrell
206
Lewis, Zachariah 107,
334
Lewney (see: Peter
Luney) 213
Libscomb, Nathaniel C.
208

Lichens, Jn. 94
Lickins, Lt. 195
Lietch, Margaret 208
Light, Jn. Jr. 371
Light, Peter 371
Lighter, Geo. 379
Lightfoot, Miss Betty
277
Lightfoot, Miss Mildred
71
Lightfoot, Philip 50,
208, 277
Lightfoot, Wm. 20,
21, 71, 208, 243, 366
Ligon, Wm. 208
Lilley, Mr. S. J. 117
Lilly, Miss Peggy 132
Lilly, Robert 132,
208
Linch, James 92
Lincoln, Jn. 39
Lindinberger, George
Jr. 237
Lindsay, Miss Ann Fox
331
Lindsay, Daniel 209
Lindsay, Jacob 209
Lindsay, Jn. 209
Lindsay, Reuben 209
Lindsey, Adam 246
Lindsey, Michael 73
Lingard, Charles 322
Linn, George 209
Linney, James 95
Linsey, Edmund 209
Linsey, Eliz. 209
Linton, George 350
Lipscomb, Daniel 25,
270
Lipscomb, Jn. P. 209
Lipscomb, Sarah 209
Lipscombe, Ambrose
209
Lisle, Miss Nancy 223
Lithgow, Hugh 209
Lithgow, Jn. 209
Little, [?] 99
Little, Charles 55,
217, 361
Little, David 305
Little, Miss Polly 219
Littlejohn 73
Littlepage, Edmund
48
Littlepage, Miss Fanny
321

18th-Century Virginia Newspapers 425

Littlepage, James 11, 38
Littlepage, Rich. 23, 164, 358
Littlepage, Thos. 48
Lively, Constant 210
Livingston, George 210
Livingston, Peter V. B. 210
Livingstone, Cornelius 210
Llewellin, Thos. 1, 353
Lloyd, Jn. 164
Locke, Thomas 11
Locker, Thomas 91, 92
Lockett, Edmund 211
Lockett, Francis 210
Lockett, Mary 66
Lockett, Pleasant 94
Lockett, Stephen 66
Lockhart, Patrick 186
Lockhead, Henry 149
Lockley, Jn. 272
Logan, Charles 141, 267
Logan, James 246
Logan, Jane 246
Logan, Mary 210
Logan, Mrs. Mary 267
Loggins, Anne 281
Loggins, James 281
Logwood, Edmund 211
Logwood, Thomas 211
Logwood, Wm. 211
Loman, Samuel 100
Lomax, Jn. 43
Lomax, Rachel 211
Long, Bromfield Jr. 211
Long, Eliz. 211
Long, George 122, 244
Long, Jonathan 359
Long, Nimrod 211
Long, Miss Polly 322
Long, Samuel 135
Longacre, Joseph Jr. 218
Longan, Augustine 42

Longden, Thomas 211
Lorde, Jane 212
Lorimer, Geo. 347
Lorimer, Hannah Thacker 212
Lorimer, James 371
Lorton, Robert 264
Lorton, Thomas 212
Lothian, Jn. 212
Love, Allan 212
Love, Edmund 97
Love, Fanny 212
Love, Robert 333
Love, Samuel 145
Love, Samuel Jr. 104, 164, 338
Love, Thomas 94
Loveday, Joseph 295
Lovell, George 95, 212
Lovell, Wm. 204
Lovett, Daniel 212
Lovett, Rebecca 212
Lowery, Jn. 94
Lowndes, Benj. 212
Lowndes, Francis 212
Lowndes, Miss Sally 266
Lownes, Miss Deborah 267
Lowry, Jn. 321
Lowry, Miss Olivia 245
Lowry, Thomas 84
Lowry, Thos. 84, 340
Lowther, Miss 256
Lowther, Wm. 256
Loyal, Paul 212
Loyall, Miss Fanny 34
Loyall, Paul 34, 110, 344
Lucas, Daniel 213
Lucas, Fielding 213
Lucas, Capt. James 94
Lucas, Passibella 213
Lucas, Miss Sally 116
Lucas, Thomas 213
Lucas, Zach. 116
Luchas, Ambrose 97
Luck, Samuel 213
Luckey, Joseph 4
Lucy 75
Ludwell, Col. 331

Ludwell, Miss Hannah 204
Ludwell, Philip 204, 213
Luellin, David 172
Lugg, Peter 25, 187
Luke, John 3
Luke, Paul Dale 349
Luke, Sally 349
Lukins, Lt. 195
Lumkin, John 1
Lumkin, Sarah 213
Lumsden, George 107, 108, 351
Lunder, Catharine 11
Lunder, Jacob 11
Lupton, David 213, 219
Lupton, Edward 225
Lupton, Jonathan 213
Luster, Wm. 98
Luthie, Peter 98
Lutrell, Wm. 99
Luttrell, Simon 56
Lutwidge, Mr. 38
Lutz, Catherine 213
Lyde, Mr. 213
Lyle, James 43, 146, 291
Lyle, Jane 213
Lyle, Jonathan 88
Lyle, Lamb 180
Lyle, Martha 213
Lyle, Robert 213, 281
Lyle, Wm. 94, 213
Lyles, Henry 72
Lyles, Wm. 93, 178, 214
Lynar, Jn. 214
Lynch, George 214
Lynch, Jn. 103
Lynch, Peter 116, 131
Lynch, Robert 100
Lyne, W. 214
Lynn, Miss Elizabeth 129
Lynn, Katherine 214
Lynn, Miss Kitty 75
Lynn, Wm. 56
Lynn, Dr. Wm. 147
Lyon, Mrs. 82
Lyon, Elinor 357
Lyon, James 323
Lyon, Peter 234, 243
Lyon, Robert 86

Lyon, Stephen 357
Lyon, Walter 82
Lyons, Miss Kitty 62
Lyons, Miss Lucy 169
Lyons, Peter 21,
62, 64, 169, 171, 214,
276, 289, 304, 361, 381
Lyons, Miss Polly 381

M'Aboy, Eliz. 92
M'Aboy, Murthy 148
M'Adoms, Joseph 252
M'Adooe, Anne 214
M'Alester, Emma 214
M'Alister, James 196, 219
M'Alister, Jn. 215, 219
M'Alister, Miss Sarah 196
M'Alister, Sarah Eliz. 219
M'Allester, Miss Betsey 51
M'Anthony, Wm. 127
M'Atee, Samuel 139
M'Aulay, Thomas 216
McAusland, H. 380
M'Bride, Jn. 313
M'Caa, Sarah 215
M'Cabe, Henry 224, 254
M'Cabe, James 185
M'Call, Archibald 17, 142, 346
M'Call, George 51
M'Call, Margaret 17
M'Callaster, Matthew 215
M'Callmont, Jn. 304
M'Callum, Mrs. 346
M'Callum, Daniel 255, 346
M'Camy, Isabella 215
M'Camy, Jn. 215
M'Cann, Dennis 364
M'Carmack, James 287
M'Carty, Charles 159, 190
M'Carty, Cornelius 296
M'Carty, Daniel 216

McCarty, Miss Maria 230
M'Carty, Thaddeus 178
M'Castle, Murdoch 116
M'Caul, Alexander 44
M'Cauley, James 99
M'Clachan, Robert 130
McClanahan, Miss 134
M'Clanahan, Samuel 75
M'Clannahan, Jn. 78
M'Clellan, Jn. 79
M'Clenachan, Jn. 134, 308
M'Clenachan, Miss Patty 245
M'Clenechan, Miss Eliza 1
M'Clenachan, Capt. Robert 194
M'Clenehan, Nathaniel 110
M'Cleod, Alexander 116
M'Cleod, Daniel 116
M'Cloud, Daniel 100
M'Cloud, Jn. 100, 149
McCloud, Nancy 216
M'Clung, Jn. 3
M'Clur, Andrew 290
M'Clurg, James 216
M'Cluse, David 216
M'Cluse, Eliz. 216
M'Cluse, Jn. 216
M'Connico, Christopher 34, 167, 217, 242, 322
M'Coole, Jn. 286
M'Corkle, James 162
M'Cormack, James 296
M'Cormick, Eliz. 283
M'Cormick, James 97
M'Cormick, Wm. 283
McCoull, Ann 217
McCoull, Jn. 121, 217
M'Coy, Anne 227
M'Coy, Robert 222

McCoy, Thomas 257
M'Crammuck, O'Conner 21
M'Craw, James 107
M'Crea, Mrs. Eliz. 86
McCrea, Robert 197
M'Credie, Robert 322
M'Creery, Jn. 121
M'Creery, Martha 121
M'Croskey, the Rev. Samuel Smith 217
M'Culloch, Anthony 217
M'Culloch, James 217
M'Culloch, Margaret 217
McDaniel, Anne 285
M'Daniel, Clement 111
McDaniel, Edmund 285
M'Daniel, Geo. 324
M'Daniel, James 225
M'Donald, Alex. 295
M'Donald, Angus 143, 217, 218
M'Donald, Anna 217
M'Donald, Miss Anne 167
M'Donald, Archibald 217, 218
M'Donald, Charles 52
McDonald, Charles 69
M'Donald, D. 318
M'Donald, Duncan 45
M'Donald, Miss Eleanor 339
M'Donald, George 99
M'Donald, James 85, 104, 225, 283
M'Donald, Jn. 26, 44, 217, 314
M'Donald, Dr. Jn. 218
M'Donald, Kenneth 116
M'Donald, Mary 217
M'Donald, Patrick 217
M'Donald, Philip 96

M'Donald, Samuel 232
M'Donald, Sarah 52
M'Douall, Jn. 71
M'Dougle, Jn. 218
M'Dowell, James 218
M'Dowgal, Jn. 87
M'Elwaine, Anne 224
M'Enery, Jn. 275
M'Evoy, Jn. 335
M'Fadden, Alex. 218
M'Fadden, James 218
M'Farland, James 97
McFarlane, Alex. 355
M'Farlane, Mary 218
M'Farline (see: M'Farlane) 218
M'Fearson, Jn. 297
M'Gehee, James 140
M'Gehee, Jn. 219
M'Gehee, Samuel 219
M'Gehee, Sarah 140
M'Gehee, Wm. 140
M'George, Jn. 157
M'Gill, Col. Charles 219
M'Gill, Jn. 57
M'Glahon, James 204
M'Grath, Chris. C. 219
M'Grath, Wm. 99
M'Graw, James 76
M'Guier, Thomas 146
M'Guire, Anthony 177
M'Guire, Edward 216, 219, 297
M'Guire, Francis 228
McGuire, Francis 226
M'Henry, Ann 219
M'Henry, James 219
M'Huchin, the widow 312
M'Intosh, Jn. 91
M'Intyre, Alex. 224, 254, 313
M'Intyre, James 76
M'Intyre, Jane 219
M'Iver, Paul 305
M'Kann, Thomas 98
M'Kean, Samuel 62

M'Keand, Jn. 43, 76, 219
M'Keaver, Paul 165
McKechnie, Wm. 65
M'Keel, Miss Abbey 162
M'Kendrick, Archibald 258
M'Kenny, Anne 220
M'Kenzie, Joanna 28
M'Kenzie, W. 294
M'Kenzie, Wm. 28, 68
M'Key, George 295
M'Kim, Andrew 261
M'Kim, Robert 261
M'Kim, Wm. 62, 65, 76
M'Kinzie, Alex. 220
M'Kinzie, Sarah 220
M'Kittrick 339
M'Knight, Judith 237
M'Lane, James 295
M'Laughlin, Eliz. 220
M'Lean, Mr. 7
M'Lean, Aeneas 235
M'Lean, Archibald 197
M'Lellan, Wm. 99
M'Lenachan, Jn. 381
M'Mahan, Maj. 195
M'Manes, Patrick 335
M'Manes, Sarah 335
M'Math, Lt. 195
M'Mechan, David 149
M'Mekin (see: M'Miken) 221
M'Min, Robert 284
M'Minn, James 28
M'Mullen, James 76, 253
M'Mutrey, Capt. 195
M'Neale, Daniel 51
McNeal, Mr. 349
M'Neally (see: M'Neely) 221
M'Nickle, Lt. 195
McNiff, Charles 99
M'Pherson, Archibald 221
M'Pherson, D. 318
M'Pherson, Daniel 206
McPherson, Daniel 201, 219

M'Pherson, Hugh 210
M'Pherson, Isaac 166, 354
M'Pherson, Jn. 247
M'Pherson, Wm. 66
McQueen, Margaret 254
M'Rae, Christopher 221
M'Rae, Jn. 221
M'Rea, James 99
M'Redie, Thomas 221
M'Redie, Wm. 221
M'Robert, Alex. 76, 220
M'Robert, Ebenezer M. 88
M'Robert, Theodorick B. 111
M'Ronald, David 286
M'Sherry, Rich. 221
M'William, Wm. 295
M'Williams, Anne 221

Mabry, Daniel 378
Mabry, Robert 209
Macartney, Mrs. Ariana 81
Macauley, Alex. 262
Macauley, Miss Ann 343
Maccaul, Archibald 15
Maccoy, Robert 222
Macdonald, George 295
Mace, Henry 96
Macgehee, Wm. 222
Macgill, Nathan 222
Macharg, Alex. 222
Machenry, Hannah 222
Machett, Thos. 70
Machie, Miss Eliza 326
Machin, Mrs. Mary Ann 36
Machir, James 222
Maciver, Colin 316
Mackenzie 286
Mackenzie, George 114, 134, 159, 267, 356
Mackenzie, Miss Nancy 28
Mackenzie, Wm. 340

Mackie, Jn. 106
Mackilwean, Capt.
 James 14, 71, 83,
 147, 169, 176,
Mackir, Alex. 222
Mackir, Angus 222
Mackir, Jn. 222
Mackir, Peggy 222
Mackir, Sarah 222
Mackir, Scot 222
Mackland, Hannah
 347
Macklin, Benj. 371
Macky, Dr. Robert
 381
Maclean, Miss Sally
 70
Macleod, Mary 223
Maclin, Miss Eleanor
 321
Macon, Col. Wm.
 Hartwell 354
Macon, Fauntleroy
 312
Macon, Mrs. Grace
 129
Macon, Hartwell 223
Macon, Henry 223
Macon, Jn. 129, 312
Macon, Miss Molly
 186
Macon, Sally 223
Macon, Miss Sally
 354
Macon, Wm. 223
Macon, Wm. H. 223
Macrae, Christopher
 152
Macudie, Thomas
 35
Madden, Michael 137,
 223
Maddox, James 96
Maddox, Thomas 134,
 326
Madison, Maj.
 Ambrose 223
Madison, Miss Eliza
 306
Madison, Francis 306
Madison, Henry 223
Madison, James 23
Madison, Jn. 127
Madison, Mary W.
 223
Magee, Christopher
 98

Magee, George 225
Magee, Miss Sally
 62
Maget, Nicholas 87
Magill, Archibald 104,
 185
Magill, Charles 224
Magill, James 56
Maginess, James 374
Magnien, Bernard
 19, 222
Magruder, Daniel
 250, 329
Magruder, Hezekiah
 250
Magruder, Susannah
 250
Magruder, Thomas
 46
Maguire, Bell 298
Maguire, Patrick 224
Mahane, Timothy 99
Mahany, Stephen 149
Mahony, Florence
 10
Mahony, Henry 98
Maitland, David 364
Maitland, Wm. 216,
 224
Major 179
Major, Anne 340
Major, Bernard 224
Major, Christian 224
Major, Francis 224
Major, Jn. 224
Major, Samuel 27
Major, Wm. 224
Malartie 297
Malcolm, the Rev. Mr.
 58
Male, Miss E. 308
Mallory, Miss Betsey
 256
Mallery, Francis 10
Mallery, Mary 10
Mallory, Edward 224
Mallory, Jn. 291
Mallory, Miss Mary
 205
Mallory, Philip 2,
 371
Mallory, Miss Polly
 78
Mallory, Wm. 205
Malone, Drury 225
Malone, Jn. 224
Malone, Mary 281

Malone, Michael 378
Malone, Wm. 225
Malvir, Isaac 236
Man, Agnes 225
Man, Anna 225
Man, Constant Harden
 225
Man, Jn. 225
Man, Peter Nicholas
 225
Man, Sally 225
Man, Washington
 225
Man, Wm. Miller 225
Mankin, Jn. 225
Manly, Jn. 225
Mann, Henry 225,
 235
Mann, Jn. Sr. 225
Mann, Michael 225
Manning, Geo. 7
Manson, Capt. 378
Manson, Peter 112
Marbury, Maj. Jos.
 2
Mareck, R. 361
Marie 75
Mariner, James 226
Marion, Frederick
 76
Markham, Maj. 266
Markham, Bernard
 257
Markham, George
 215, 226, 255
Markham, Jn. 226
Markham, Vincent
 226
Markham, Wm. 226
Marks, Edward 207
Marks, Solomon 253
Marlatt, Abraham Jr.
 226
Marlatt, Rich. 226
Marles, Meekey 358
Marley, Wm. 226
Marmaduke, Wm.
 305
Marr, Agnes 226
Marr, Anna 226
Marr, Constant
 Harden 226
Marr, George Lent
 Washington 226
Marr, Jn. 226
Marr, Jn. 371

Marr, Peter Nicholas 226
Marr, Sally 226
Marr, Susanna 357
Marr, Susannah 226
Marr, Wm. Miller 226
Marrable, Benjamin 226
Marrable, Edward 226
Marrell, Jn. 98
Marriott, Eliz. 227
Marsden, Miss Anne 313
Marsden, James 123, 227, 259
Marsden, Jn. Greenhow 227
Marsden, Mary 227
Marshall, Alexander 227
Marshall, Benj. 227
Marshall, Charles 227
Marshall, Christopher 227
Marshall, J. 126
Marshall, Miss Jane 331
Marshall, Jn. 238
Marshall, Miss Lucy 6
Marshall, Mrs. Mary 227
Marshall, Sally 38
Marshall, Sarah 227
Marshall, Maj. Thos. 38
Marshall, Wm. 145, 227, 280
Marsteller, P. 154
Marsteller, Philip 283
Marsteller, Philip G. 9
Marston, Wm. 76
Martin, Andrew 150, 251
Martin, Miss Ann 135
Martin, Anthony 125
Martin, Denny 118, 119
Martin, Elenor 111
Martin, Eliz. 228
Martin, F. X. 147
Martin, George 228

Martin, Hannah 300
Martin, J. 228
Martin, James 228, 300
Martin, Jn. 57, 77, 228, 318
Martin, Job 95
Martin, Jonathan 111
Martin, Joseph 96, 285
Martin, Joshua 227
Martin, Martha 14
Martin, Milley 285
Martin, Oliver 296
Martin, Samuel 92, 107
Martin, Col. T. B. 55
Martin, Thomas 95, 97
Martin, Thomas Bryan 119
Martin, Warner 14
Martyr, Rebekah 109
Martyr, Tomkins 109
Marye, Eleanor 142
Marye, Peter 142
Marye, the Rev. James 228
Mask, Wm. 229
Mason, A. Barnes 362
Mason, Miss Betsy 284
Mason, Col. David 284
Mason, Col. George 229
Mason, J. 229
Mason, James 353
Mason, Capt. James 125, 304
Mason, Jn. 48, 76, 136
Mason, Thomas 90, 170, 229, 279
Mason, Thomson 215, 229
Mason, W. 229, 257, 303
Mason, Wm. 93, 229, 288
Massay, Eliz. 147
Massay, Polly 147
Massenburg, Dr. Cargill 165
Massenburg, Jn. 346
Massenburg, Robert 337

Massenburg, Wm. 229, 288
Massey, Edmund 95
Massey, Wm. 86
Massie, Capt. Thomas 22, 153, 259
Massie, Thomas 199
Mastin, Elijah 229
Matey, Louis Joseph 296
Mathesons, David 230
Mathews, Archer 293, 310
Mathews, Sampson 316
Mathews, Thomas 281
Mathews, Wm. 229
Mathias, Ann 227
Mathoney, Ernest Frederick 201
Mathoney, Susanna 201
Matteny, Hezekiah 96
Matterson, Robert 92
Matthews, Miss Betty 178
Matthews, George 111, 194, 268, 271, 320
Matthews, the Rev. Jn. 230
Matthews, Joseph 230
Matthews, Patrick 136
Matthews, Sampson 27, 111, 157, 192, 268, 271, 320
Matthews, Sarah 230
Matthews, Thomas 235
Matthias, Joshua 230
Mattingly, Edward 121
Mattox, Mary 230
Maupin, Gabriel 78, 230, 256
Maury, Ann 231
Maury, Betty 40
Maury, Fontaine 40
Maury, James 231
Maury, Leonard Hill 231
Maury, Ludwell 231
Maury, Mary 231

Maury, Miss Mary 157
Maury, Penelope 231
Maury, Wm. Grymes 231
Mauzy, Joseph 108
Maven (see: James Maiben) 224
Maxey, Edward 258
Maxey, Eliz. 231
Maxwell, Mrs. 280
Maxwell, Arthur 300
Maxwell, James 30, 259
Maxwell, Capt. James 280
Maxwell, Miss Nelly 30
May, Anne 231
May, Edward 231
May, Jn. 244
May, Miss Prudence 363
May, Miss Rosetta 263
Mayes, Matthew Jr. 71
Mayes, Wm. 116
Mayle, Mrs. Lydia 231
Maynard, Jn. 295
Maynard, Mary 231
Mayo, Capt. 117
Mayo, George 231, 301
Mayo, Jn. 101, 231, 274
Mayo, Joseph 232
Mayo, Miss Polly 12
Mayo, Wm. 231, 270, 327
Mayo, Col. Wm. 12, 231
Mazzei, Mrs. Petronilla 232
Meachum, Banks 115
Meade, Capt. 362
Meade, Maj. 232
Meade, Andrew 352
Meade, David 271, 302, 352
Meade, E. 127
Meade, George 89
Meade, Rich. Kidder 232
Meanly, Persons 335
Mears, Jn. 24

Mears, Joseph 361
Mease, Robert 232
Meaux, Jn. G. 232
Meaux, N. B. 232
Meaux, Rich. 232
Medlock, Eady 117
Medlock, Jn. 194
Medlock, Zachariah 117
Meed, Capt. Andrew 158
Meeks, Edward 96
Mekin (see: Miss Molly Macon) 186
Melan, James 322
Melone, Jn. 95
Melton, Absolom 226
Melton, Charles 94
Melvin, James 322
Menitree, Paul 65
Mennis, Maj. Gallowhill 13
Menzies, Ninian 259
Mercer, Capt. 150
Mercer, Anne 233
Mercer, Capt. George 67, 369
Mercer, Gen. Hugh 233, 260
Mercer, J. 232
Mercer, James 233
Mercer, Jn. 55, 65, 100, 351
Mercer, Capt. Jn. 58
Mercer, Miss Nancy 260
Merchant, Wm. 189
Meredith, Ann B. 233
Meredith, Wm. 173, 199, 204, 233
Merewether, David Wood 207
Merewether, Jane 207
Merewether, Mary 207
Merewether, Zachary 207
Merideth, Elisha 188
Meriman, Thomas 185
Meriwether, Lt. James 186
Meriwether, Jn. 233
Meriwether, Polly 6
Meriwether, Thomas 6, 359

Meriwether, Capt. Thomas 137, 254
Meriwether, Wm. 113
Meroney, James 233
Merry, Prettyman 134
Merryman, Jn. 365
Merton, Michael 76
Meshie, Benj. 227
Messenger, the Rev. Mr. 65
Messhie, Barbara 233
Messhie, Christopher 233
Messhie, Eliz. 233
Messhie, Jacob 233
Messhie, Jn. 233
Messhie, Mary 233
Messmore, Nicholas 233
Metcalf, Samuel 33
Mettauer, Jemima 234
Meux, Agnes 234
Meux, Thomas 234
Meux, Wm. 234
Meyers, Anna 234
Michael, Jacob 160
Michaels, Philip 41
Michaux, Paul 62
Michell, Cary 224
Michell, Wm. 234
Michum, Thomas 300
Mickell, Susannah 234
Mickle, Mrs. S. 326
Middlemist, Archibald 4
Middleton, Anne 80
Middleton, Benedict 336
Middleton, Capt. Benedict 199
Middleton, Lucinda 234
Midlemist, Archibald 241
Midlimist, Archibald 149
Miles, Charles 239
Miles, George 116
Miles, Mary 234
Miles, Thomas 79
Milhado, Mary 234
Millen, Alex. 275
Miller, Miss 311

Miller, Alex. 235
Miller, Andrew 235
Miller, David 118, 349
Miller, Edwards 308
Miller, Francis 235
Miller, Hannah 234, 235
Miller, Henry 162, 234
Miller, Hugh 54
Miller, James 26, 98, 234, 235
Miller, Jn. 95, 181, 235, 263
Miller, Miss Katy 258
Miller, Capt. Matthias 234
Miller, Nicholas 16, 287
Miller, Patsey 234
Miller, Philip 97
Miller, Rachel 234
Miller, Robert 28
Miller, Samuel 234
Miller, Susanna 235
Miller, Miss Susanna 16
Miller, Thomas 87, 111, 181
Miller, Wm. 234
Milleson, Ward 235
Millison, Polly 307
Millner, Wm. 304
Mills, Hannah 181
Mills, James 113, 323
Mills, Job 140, 346
Mills, Mary 181
Mills, Thomas 181
Mills, Willis 153
Mills, Wm. 108, 181
Milton, Robert 92
Mims, Martin 291
Minge, Christina 236
Minge, Jn. 70
Mingham, Mrs. Sarah 31
Mingo 41
Minitree, Jacob Andrew 103, 152, 211
Minitree, Miss Mary 35
Minns, Jn. 116
Minon, Garret 107
Minor, Ann 6
Minor, Miss Betsy 8
Minor, Dabney 236
Minor, Garret 334, 379
Minor, James 56
Minor, Jn. 341
Minor, Jn. Jr. 26
Minor, Joseph 116
Minor, Mary 236
Minor, Nicholas 236
Minor, Thomas 259
Minser, Rebecca 236
Minson, Henry 159, 169, 236
Minton, Mary 258
Minzies, Ninion 157
Miskell, Wm. 222
Mitchell, Abraham 225
Mitchell, Andrew 48
Mitchell, Ann 237
Mitchell, Eliz. 356
Mitchell, Frances 236
Mitchell, George 101
Mitchell, James 48, 75, 93, 237
Mitchell, Jane 237
Mitchell, Janet 237
Mitchell, Jn. 33, 54, 97, 98, 142, 292, 322
Mitchell, Rich. 330
Mitchell, Stephen 65, 298
Mitchell, Thomas 164
Mitchell, Wm. 195, 208, 237, 315, 356
Mitchelson, Jn. 32
Mitchum, Mr. 1
Mockbee, Joseph 57
Moffett, George 67
Moffett, Hannah 234
Moffett, James 234
Moffett, Miss Magdalene 67
Mohun, Eliz. 237
Mohun, Joel 237
Moir, James 230
Molloy, Saray 237
Moncure, the Rev. Jn. 301
Mongold, Jn. 308
Monroe, Jn. 237
Monroe, Jo. Jo. 226
Monroe, Mrs. Sarah 237
Montague, Duke of 145
Montague, M. 239
Montfort, Henry 238
Montfort, Joseph 235
Montgomerie, Thos. 4
Montgomery, the Rev. Mr. 150
Montgomery, Alex. 42
Montgomery, James 305
Montgomery, Col. Jn. 195
Montgomery, Joseph 305
Montgomery, Robert 305
Montgomery, Sam. 305
Montgomery, Wm. 126, 305
Moody, Miss Clara 265
Moody, Eliz. 238
Moody, Eliz. Beufort 238
Moody, Francis 238
Moody, Henry 238
Moody, Jesse 297
Moody, Miss Kitty 238
Moody, Margaret 238
Moody, Mary 238
Moody, Matthew 238
Moody, Miss Mildred 183
Moody, P. 238
Moody, Thomas 97, 238
Moody, Wm. 45, 108, 238
Moore, Miss 167
Moore, Mrs. 316
Moore, Alex. 116, 119
Moore, Alfred 246
Moore, Miss Anne 347
Moore, Augustine 236
Moore, Augustine Sr. 10
Moore, Col. Bernard 57
Moore, Catherine 239
Moore, Cato 102

Moore, Daniel 239
Moore, Edw. 178, 206, 296, 336
Moore, Eliz. 230
Moore, Filmer 239
Moore, Francis 94
Moore, Geo. 239, 365
Moore, James 12, 166, 182, 286
Moore, Jeremiah 367
Moore, Jn. R. 329
Moore, Mary 239
Moore, Merritt 193, 288
Moore, Molly 239
Moore, Nancy 45
Moore, Miss Nancy 57
Moore, Nicholas R. 149
Moore, Miss Peggy 102
Moore, Miss Rachel 38
Moore, Reuben 239
Moore, Capt. Reuben 167
Moore, Robert 12, 317
Moore, Samuel 80
Moore, Sarah 149, 239
Moore, Thomas 12, 97, 195, 239
Moore, Wm. 10, 230
Moran, Thomas 240
Moras, the widow 240
Moreland, Francis 224
Moreland, Nancy 224
Morgan, Abraham 240
Morgan, Charles 100
Morgan, Diana 240
Morgan, Drusella 140
Morgan, James 32
Morgan, Jean 140
Morgan, Jn. 93
Morgan, Morgan 91
Morgan, Nathaniel 25
Morgan, Rauleigh 240
Morgan, Thomas 93
Morgan, Wm. 240

Morrel, Louis 95
Morris, Austin 266, 307
Morris, Dabney 263
Morris, Euell 240
Morris, Henry Jr. 241
Morris, Jn. 98, 240, 241
Morris, Moses 241
Morris, Philip 241
Morris, Polly 266
Morris, Rich. 137
Morris, Ruth 31, 356
Morris, Wm. 179
Morrison, Andrew 241
Morrison, Nathaniel 241
Morrison, Miss Sally 2
Morrison, Wm. 179
Morriss, Mrs. 194
Morrow, Charles 73
Morrow, Jn. 240
Morson, Alex. 212
Morson, Arthur 336
Morton, Arch. 241
Morton, Barbara 303
Morton, David 168
Morton, George 241, 242
Morton, James 313
Morton, Jn. 242
Morton, Joseph 241, 242, 340
Morton, Robert 71, 241
Morton, Wm. 239
Mosby, Benj. 293
Mosby, Miss Betsey 343
Mosby, Littlebury 242, 343
Mosby, Samuel 248
Moseby, Benj. 77
Moseley, Alex. 242, 265, 334, 351
Moseley, Anthony 242
Moseley, Bassett 242
Moseley, Daniel 242
Moseley, Edward 175, 211
Moseley, Edward Hack 242
Moseley, Miss Esther 63

Moseley, Robert 242
Mosely, Capt. H. 364
Mosely, Miss Nancy 364
Moses 368
Moses, Mrs. 189
Mosley, Edward 242
Moss, Henry 242
Moss, Jn. 62, 138, 341
Moss, Capt. Jn. 306
Moss, Julia 242
Moss, Miss Polly 306
Moss, Wm. 214
Mossley, Miss Nancy 129
Moulder, Joseph 322
Moulson, Wm. 107
Mount, Ezekial 209
Mountgomery, James 65
Mountjoy, Capt. J. 96
Mountjoy, Jn. 367
Moxley, Miss Betsy 288
Moxley, Hester 243
Moxley, Wm. 243
Moxly, Anne 243
Moyers, Casper 45
Moyers, Jn. 73
Muick, Mr. 195
Muir, the Rev. Dr. 3
Muir, the Rev. Mr. 209
Muir, Eliz. 243
Muir, Francis 138, 379
Muir, George 301
Muir, Jn. 46
Muir, Miss Phebe 301
Muir, Robert 243, 345
Muirhead, John 4
Mulholland, [?] 199
Mullaghan, James 213
Mulligan, Hercules 296
Mullin, Thomas 354
Mullineaux, Wm. 99
Mullins, Conoly 243
Mullins, Jn. 243, 258
Mullins, Wm. 258
Mumford, Thomas 244

Munford, Miss Frances Moseley 34
Munford, Robert 244
Munford, Wm, Green 151, 231
Murchie, James 103
Murchie, Jn. 220
Murdaugh, Josiah 306
Murdaugh, Miss Peggy 306
Murdock, Addison 57
Murphey, Andrew 98
Murphey, Demsey 247
Murphey, Edward 98
Murphey, James 244
Murphey, Jn. 222
Murphey, Martin 244
Murphey, Rachel 247
Murphree, James 126
Murphree, Susannah 244
Murphy, Frances 180
Murphy, George 53, 180
Murphy, Henry 136
Murphy, James 194
Murphy, Miss Mary 82
Murphy, Nancy 53
Murphy, Robert 127
Murphy, Wm. 98
Murray, [?] 66
Murray, Mrs. 15
Murray, Betty 66
Murray, George 246
Murray, James 15, 244, 245
Murray, Jn. 124, 244, 245
Murray, Capt. Jn. 194
Murray, the Rev. Jn. 198
Murray, Margaret 245
Murray, Miss Mary 89
Murray, Miss Molly 138
Murray, Patrick 89, 196

Murray, Peggy 138
Murray, Rachel 245
Murray, Wm. 244, 245
Murray, Capt. Wm. 139
Murrell, Sarah 245
Murril, Samuel 228
Murrill, George 284
Murry, Jno. 205
Muse, Elliott 246
Muse, Hudson 245
Muse, James 246
Muse, Lawrence 245
Muse, Rich. 246
Muse, Thomas 246
Muse, Wm. T. 84, 275
Musick, Daniel 96
Myer, Samuel 69
Myers, Capt. Christopher 246
Myers, Citizen 240
Myers, Lewis 40
Myers, M. M. 246
Myers, Matthew 246
Myers, Samson 246
Myers, Samuel 246
Myles, George 246
Myre, Conrad 243
Mytinger, Daniel 25

Nabb, Jn. 70
Nailing, Samuel 144
Nalle, Wm. 246
Napp, Thomas 127
Nash, Francis 246
Nash, Jn. 246
Nash, Martha 117
Nash, Thomas 246
Nash, Wm. 132, 246
Nat 274
Natchez 268
Nattall, Matthias 247
Neal, Francis Moore 26
Neal, Thomas 295
Neale, Anne 247
Neale, James 380
Neale, Jn. 247
Neale, Shapleigh 134
Neave, Rich. 275
Neaves, Wm. 247
Ned 226
Needham, Miss Sally 188
Negro Bill 161

Negro Billy 161
Negro James 86
Negro Tom 74
Neil, [?] 122
Neile, Jane 190
Neill, Lewis 247
Neilson, Miss Agnes 245
Neilson, Charles 330
Neilson, Miss Jenny 317
Nelmes, Archibald 247
Nelmes, David 247
Nelmes, Mary 247
Nelmes, Sarah 247
Nelms, Samuel 129
Nelson, Capt. 87
Nelson, Miss 366
Nelson, Charles 194
Nelson, Charlotte 338
Nelson, Eliz. 256
Nelson, Francis 248
Nelson, George 161
Nelson, Hugh 94, 248, 256
Nelson, J. 248
Nelson, Jn. 96, 248, 374
Nelson, Miss Mary Eliza 287
Nelson, Nathaniel 256
Nelson, Philip 248
Nelson, Rebecca 248
Nelson, Robert 304
Nelson, Susannah 304
Nelson, Thomas 248
Nelson, Thomas Jr. 307
Nelson, Capt. Thomas 350
Nelson, Wm. 10, 207, 208, 245, 248, 256, 289
Nesbit, Mary 248
Nesbit, Samuel 248
Netherland, the widow 133
Netherland, Anne 248
Netherland, B. 248
Netherland, Jn. 248
Netherland, Jn. Jr. 339
Netherland, Littleberry 248

Netherland, Wade 171
Nevett, Thomas 295
Neville, Joseph 41
Nevison, Jn. 316
New, Edith 249
New, Jesse 95
New, Jn. 232
New, Mary 248
Newby, Ozwald 249
Newby, Pritchard 40
Newlands, Alex. 249
Newman, Capt. 195
Newman, Martha 249
Newman, Thomas 223
Newsom, Benj. 249
Newsum, Amos 93
Newsum, Jn. 68, 99
Newsum, Wm. 196
Newton, Col. 267
Newton, Miss Ailcey 149
Newton, Miss Amy 30
Newton, Andrew 249
Newton, Henry 249
Newton, James 69, 106
Newton, Jn. 145
Newton, Martha 343
Newton, Thomas 98, 175, 270, 344
Newton, Thomas Jr. 343
Newton, Col. Thos. 30
Newton, Willoughby 20, 254
Nice, Wm. 35, 209
Nicholas, Abraham 317
Nicholas, Miss Betsy 277, 311
Nicholas, George 118
Nicholas, Capt. Jn. 95
Nicholas, Jos. 10
Nicholas, Ro. C. 5
Nicholas, Robert Carter 250, 252
Nicholas, Miss Sally 253
Nichols, Benj. 250
Nichols, Casandra 250
Nichols, Edward 250
Nichols, Eliz. 250
Nichols, George 181
Nichols, Hester 181
Nichols, Isaiah 250
Nichols, Rebecca 250
Nichols, Susannah 250
Nicholson, Henry 245
Nicholson, James 251
Nicholson, Jn. 98, 250, 292
Nicholson, Michael 152
Nicholson, Thomas 251
Nicholson, Wm. 251, 295
Nickolls, J. B. 366
Nicolson, Miss Peggy 134
Nicolson, Robt. 15, 42, 100, 157, 250, 302, 303
Nicolson, Wm. 251
Nighswonger, Peter 251
Nivison, Jn. 251
Nixon, Jonathan 316, 320
Nixon, Thos. 4
Nixon, Wm. 93
Nobbs, Miss Wills 148
Noble, Geo. 366
Noel, Joseph 92
Noel, Reuben 125
Noel, Taylor 125
Noel, Ursula 125
Noix, James 86
Noland, Mary 251
Noland, Thomas 251
Nolen, Michael 76
Nolle, Francis 251
Nolle, Jn. 251
Nolling, Col. Robert 32
Norfleet, Miss Sarah 185
Norman, Dr. Samuel 251
Norman, Sally 285
Norris, Joseph 251
Norris, Wm. 191, 295
North, Catherine 252
North, Miss Eliz. 130
North, Robert 9
North, Roger 67, 213
North, Wm. 130
Northern, Juduth 117
Northern, Samuel 117
Norton, the widow 267
Norton, Caroline 343
Norton, Mrs. Catherine 6
Norton, Miss Courtney 207
Norton, Daniel 343
Norton, Jn. 361
Norton, Jn. Harley 252
Norton, Sarah 252
Norvell, George 217
Norvell, Martha 252
Norvell, Miss Patsey 355
Norvell, Reuben 252
Norvell, Wm. 20
Notchet, Peter (see: Peter Nouchet) 252
Nouchel, Peter (see: Peter Nouchet) 252
Nourse, James 252, 357
Nourse, Joseph 252
Nourse, Wm. 252
Nox, Edward 252
Nunan, Wm. 296
Nunnellee, Edward 253
Nutall, Thomas 99
Nutall, Wm. 99
Nutt, Catherine 227
Nutt, Wm. 205, 368
Nutty, Mrs. Betty 346

O'Bannon, Wm., 253
O'Brian, Jn. 37
O'Conner, Francis 295
O'Connor Family 253
O'Connor, Jn. 34
O'Daniel, James 71
O'Deer, Jn. 97
O'Grady, Dr. 197
O'Harrow, Thomas 253

18th-Century Virginia Newspapers   435

O'Neil, Jn. 98
O'Neill, Jn. 254
O'Williams, Dr. Edward 255
Oakes, Charles 148
Obannon, Joseph 78
Ofd, Jn. 201
Oferrall, Jn. 309
Oferrall, Polly 309
Ogborne, Hannah 356
Ogborne, Wm. 356
Ogelsby, Miss 80
Ogilby, Miss Polly 160
Oglevie, the Rev. Mr. 253
Oldham, Col. 195
Olford, George 253
Oliphant, Wm. 180
Oliver, Miss 232
Oliver, Mrs. 303
Oliver, Ben. 363
Oliver, Jn. 254
Oliver, Joseph 254
Oliver, Rachel 254
Olivier, David 236
Omohundro, Wm. 99
Oneal, Francis 99
Orandoeff, Christian 73
Orange, Maj. Wm. 293
Orendorff, C. Jr. 254
Orendorff, Henry 290
Orkney, Earl of 107
Orr, Mrs. 320
Orr, Miss Eleanor 261
Orr, Miss Eliza 270
Orr, Capt. Hugh 254
Orr, Jn. 123
Orr, Wm. 8
Orrell, Ann 238
Orton, Reginald 254, 300
Osborn, David 221
Osborne, Edward 192
Osborne, Miss Nancy 103
Otey, Frances 57
Otey, James 307
Otey, Thos. 57
Otty, Thomas 255
Otway, Robert 192
Overacre, Daniel 115
Overall, Jn. 339
Oversteen, Henry 96

Overston, Samuel 137
Overton, James 255
Overton, Jn. 255
Overton, Samuel Jr. 275
Owen, David 255
Owen, James 86
Owen, Jeremiah 56, 318
Owen, Judith 255
Owen, Thomas 97
Owens, Rose 255
Owens, Wm. 94
Owings, Samuel 177
Owings, Samuel Jr. 151
Owins, Aaron 269
Owins, Wm. 269
Owram, Thomas 255

Packe, Sarah 143
Page, Mrs. 248
Page, Carter 279
Page, Eliz. 256
Page, Gwyn 256
Page, Miss Jeanie 248
Page, Jn. 50, 60, 248, 256
Page, Miss Judith 353
Page, Miss Judy 248
Page, Lucy 256
Page, Miss Lucy 22
Page, Mann 22, 119, 256, 261, 324, 357, 367
Page, Mann Jr. 207
Page, Robert 256
Page, Miss Sally 256
Paine, Miss Fanny 302
Paine, Obadiah 89
Paine, Samuel 189
Paine, Wm. 302
Painter, David 117
Palmer, Alice 257, 328
Palmer, Ann 257
Palmer, Isaac 257
Palmer, Jn. 257
Palmer, Joseph 257
Palmer, Rawleigh 257
Palmer, Robert 257, 328

Palmer, Thomas 257, 328
Palmer, Wm. 257
Pankey, Stephen Jr. 257
Pannell, Nancy 358
Pannill, David 284
Pannill, Jn. 257
Pannill, Wm. 177
Parham, Isham 93
Parham, Lewis 21
Parham, Sarah 22
Parham, Stith 344
Parham, Thomas 257
Parish, Jn. 257
Park, Catharine 257
Park, Mrs. Catherine 229
Park, Jane 257
Parke, George 347
Parker, A. 257
Parker, Agnes 45
Parker, Benj. 157, 272
Parker, Dolly 157
Parker, Jn. 258, 360
Parker, Josiah 88
Parker, Judith 258
Parker, Martha 258
Parker, Mary 258
Parker, Patrick 257, 258
Parker, Rich. 257
Parker, Robert 332
Parker, Susanna 258
Parker, Thomas 17
Parker, Wm. 258
Parkins, David 262
Parks, Charlotte 124
Parks, Daniel 363
Parks, James 94
Parratt, Thos. 72
Parratt, Wm. 47
Parris, Mary Maria Milmount 194
Parris, Rich. 361
Parrish, Joel 258
Parrot, Thomas 286
Parsons, James 191
Parsons, Jonathan 78
Parsons, Miss Nancy 192
Parsons, Miss Polly 229
Parsons, Samuel 259

Parsons, Wm. Ap Thomas 259
Partlow, Lewis 259
Partlow, Sarah 259
Passmore, Joseph 221
Pasteur, Blovet 205
Pate, Jeremiah 259
Pate, Samuel 93
Pate, Thomas 4, 93
Paterson, John 7
Patillo, Sarah 224
Patillo, Solomon 224
Paton, Wm. 19
Patterson, Andrew 98
Patterson, Charles 259
Patterson, George 94
Patterson, James 104
Patterson, Jn. 244, 259
Patterson, Judah 259
Patterson, Mary 259
Patterson, Miss Polly 211
Patteson, David 17, 30, 259
Patteson, Eliz. 260
Patteson, Jonathan 89
Patteson, Leonard 260
Patteson, N. 6
Pattie, James 188
Patton, James 15, 122, 311
Patts, Thomas 98
Paul, Ann 260
Paul, Fanny 260
Paul, James 76
[Paul], John 10
Paup, Joseph 229
Payne, Ben. 339
Payne, Charles 194
Payne, Geo. 332
Payne, Jn. 260
Payne, Joseph 94
Payne, Merryman 260
Payne, Wm. 260
Payntar, Susanna 260
Paynter, Jn. 216
Payton, Miss Frances 328

Peachey, Capt. 290, 314
Peachey, Francis G. 260
Peachey, Leroy 125, 260
Peachey, Miss Susanna 250
Peachey, Thomas Griffin 367
Peachey, W. 369
Peachey, Wm. 9, 125, 151
Peachey, Col. Wm. 34, 250, 260
Peachey, Lt. Col. Wm. 331
Peachy, Thos. G. 15
Peak, Wm. 152
Peale, Robert 94
Pearce, Capt. 145
Pearce, Charles 99
Pearce, Jeremiah 261
Pearce, Mary 166
Pearce, Peter 166
Pearce, Thomas 101
Pearl, Rich. 93
Pearson, Colin 345
Pearson, M. 261
Pearson, Mary M. 261
Pearson, Miss Nancy 3
Pearson, Philip 345
Pearson, Wm. 169, 201, 308, 330, 345, 364
Peart, Miss Polly 252
Peate, Capt. 195
Peck, Adam 305
Peck, Eliz. 305
Peck, Jacob 280, 288
Peck, Simeon 261
Peebles, Capt. Lemuel 82
Peebles, Heartwell 261
Peed, Joshua 7
Peed, Nathaniel 180
Peeling, Jn. 261
Peers, Anderson 261
Peers, Elis S. 348
Peers (see: Maj. Valentine Pearce) 261
Peete, Rich. 261
Peggy 229

Peirce, Joseph 153, 334
Peirce (see: Francis Pearce) 261
Peirce, Thomas 89
Pelham, Capt. 315
Pelham, Miss Sally 29
Pelkington, Rich. 150
Pemberton, Jn. 196
Pendleton, Benj. 156
Pendleton, Edmund 19, 177, 289, 304, 329, 331
Pendleton, Edmund Jr. 22, 133, 135
Pendleton, Jn. 262
Pendleton, Jn. Jr. 146
Pendleton, Miss Polly 307
Pendleton, Philip 106, 119, 301, 361
Pendleton, Miss Sally 366
Pendleton, Spice 368
Pendleton, Wm. 366
Peninton, Isaac 225
Peniston, Thomas 262
Penman, Mr. 60
Penn, Abraham 306
Penn, Gabriel 144
Penn, Col. Gabriel 246
Penn, Miss Matilda 246
Penn, Wm. 262
Penne, James 296
Pennington, Jn. 262
Pennington, Marcus 262, 316
Pennington, Mary 150
Pennington, Wm. T. 150
Pennix, Jn. 103
Pennix, Thomas 103
Pennock, Anne 343
Pennock, Wm. 343
Penticost, Catharine 24, 35
Penticost, Dorsey 12, 35
Penticost, Dorsy 24
Penticost, Geo. Washington 35

18th-Century Virginia Newspapers

Penticost, Jos. Dorry 35
Penticost, Lucy 35
Penticost, Miss Peggy 12
Penticost, Rebecca 35
Penticost, Sarah 35
Pepys, Wm. W. 174
Peritt, Jn. 92
Perkin, Jos. 22
Perkins, Baker 187
Perkins, Betty 224
Perkins, Charles 357
Perkins, Christopher 148
Perkins, David 262
Perkins, Hardin 357
Perkins, Isaac 262
Perkins, Jn. 224, 262
Perkins, Mary 358
Perkins, Nathaniel 262
Perkins, Nicholas Tate 357
Perkins, Peter 357
Perkinson, Anne 262
Perkinson, Wm. 88
Perks, Jn. 276
Peronie, Capt. 349
P[errell], Edw. 11
P[errell], Rachel 11
Perrin, Capt. 347
Perrin, Mrs. 365
Perrin, Jn. 166, 365
Perrin, Miss Nancy 282
Perrin, Samuel 10, 350
Perrow, Charles 263
Perrow, Frances 263
Perry, Dr. 263
Perry, Ignatius 185
Perry, James 20, 191, 241, 305
Perry Miss Margery 185
Perry, Miss Peggy 180
Person, Benj. 263
Person, Dorcas 263
Person, Henry 263
Person, Jn. 263
Person, Wm. 263
Pery, James 358
Pescud, Thomas 307

Peter, Thomas 125, 263
Peter, Walter 112
Peters, Abraham 296
Peters, Ann 263
Peters, James 258
Peters, Jn. 40, 189
Peters, Lucy 258
Peters, Polly 263
Peters, Thomas 258
Peterson, David 99
Petit, Jn. 206
Petit, Joseph 296
Petre, Wm. 72
Pettit, Jn. 158
Pettus, Amy 107
Pettus, Jn. 263
Pettus, Samuel 107
Pettus, Wm. 108, 141, 263
Pettway, Wm. 263
Petty, Jn. 326
Peyten, Wm. 92
Peyton, Anne 318
Peyton, Argel 92
Peyton, Edward 164
Peyton, Miss Eliz. 102
Peyton, Henry 264
Peyton, Jn. 73, 102, 264, 365
Peyton, Mary 264
Peyton, Samuel H. 264
Peyton, Sir Jn. 192, 263, 328
Peyton, Thomas 263
Pharr, Samuel 195
Phelan, Capt. 195
Phelps, Elisha 329
Phile, Frederick 324
Phile, Miss Eliza 324
Philips, Joseph 96
Philips, Mary 87
Philips, Nathan 13
Philips, Thomas 264
Phillippie, Sally 264
Phillips, Capt. Rich. 264
Phillips, Jn. 95
Phillips, Moses 235
Phillips, Rich. 94, 172
Phillips, Robert 3, 182, 219, 295, 367
Phillis, Charles 94
Philon, Capt. 195
Philpotts, Jn. 61

Phipps, James 100
Phripp, Matthew 175, 265, 337, 378
Pickett, Capt. 349
Pickett, Jeremiah 370
Pickett, Mary 285
Pickett, Miss Polly 349
Pickett, Ralph 298
Pickett, Wm. 285, 299
Pied, Joshua 265
Pierce, Miss Alice 141
Pierce, Miss Eliz. 180
Pierce, Miss Fanny 216
Pierce, Jn. 20, 23, 43, 140, 141, 180, 231
Pierce, Joseph 86
Pierce, Wm. 379
Piercefield, Van 194
Piercy, Miss Kitty 220
Pinckard, Mr. 217
Pindall, Ann 265
Pinhard, Lucy Coleman 142
Pinhard, Nathaniel 142
Pinkney, Jn. 286
Pinnock, Jn. 330
Pipeman, Benj. 265
Pipeman, Elenor 265
Pipeman, Kitty 265
Pipeman, Rebecca 266
Piper, Jn. 334
Piper, Jonathan 227
Pitcher, Jn. 266
Pitman, Jn. 152
Pitman, Wm. 266
Pitt, George 143
Pitt, Dr. George 266
Pitt, James 276
Pitt, Mary 38
Pitt, Robert 38
Pitt, Wm. 266
Pitts, Eliz. 81
Pitts, Henry 85, 254
Pitts, Lunsford 81
Pitzer, Jn. 91
Plant, James 99
Plant, Williamson 96
Plater, George 331

Plater, Miss Nancy 316
Plater, Miss Rebecca 331
Player, Eliz. 29
Pleasant, Jn. 289
Pleasants, Miss Clementine 49
Pleasants, Eliza 267
Pleasants, Isaac W. 141, 144
Pleasants, James 324
Pleasants, Jn. 185, 266, 267, 338
Pleasants, Col. Jn. 43
Pleasants, Jonathan 266, 267
Pleasants, Joseph 379
Pleasants, Mrs. Maria 43
Pleasants, Mary 210
Pleasants, Miss Nancy 335
Pleasants, Rich. 266
Pleasants, Robert 144, 266, 267, 335, 368
Pleasants, Samuel 190, 267, 291
Pleasants, Thomas 266
Pleasants, Thomas Mifflin 266
Plowman, Miss 17
Plume, Miss 162
Plume, Wm. 162
Poe, Jacob 364
Poe, Miss Anna 330
Poindexter, Ann 142
Poindexter, Babriel 108
Poindexter, Gabriel 107
Poindexter, Jn. 142
Poindexter, Molly 107, 108
Pointdexter, P. 247
Polk, Miss Eliz. 66
Pollard, Ben. 289
Pollard, Benj. 188
Pollard, Isaac 8
Pollard, Jn. 295
Pollard, Jos. 8
Pollard, Mary 8
Pollard, Miss Nelly 206

Pollard, Nancy 8
Pollard, Robert 161, 266, 267
Pollard, Susannah 8
Pollard, Thomas 176
Pollard, Lt. Thomas 132
Pollard, Wm. 267, 312
Polsan, Mr. 92
Polson, Capt. 349
Poney, Leah 133
Poney, Wm. 133
Pontiffe, Louis 296
Pool, Howard 267
Pool, James 206
Pool, Jn. 227
Pool, Rebecca 206
Pool, Robert 267
Pool, Samuel 267
Poole, Miss Polly 272
Poole, Miss Sally 24
Pope, David 99
Pope, Jn. 95, 98
Pope, Capt. Jn. 131
Pope, Miss Lucinda 372
Pope, Dr. Matthew 268
Pope, Miss Nancy 110, 294
Pope, Nathaniel 268
Pope, Capt. Nathaniel 110
Pope, Thomas 209
Porter, Benj. 221
Porter, Capt. Benj. 95
Porter, Camp 268
Porter, James 130
Porter, Thomas 224
Porter, Wm. 87, 111
Porterfield, Eliz. 268
Porterfield, Matthew 268
Porterfield, Gen. Robert 268
Portlock, Jn. 268
Portlock, Rebecca 268
Portlock, Samuel 268
Posey, Jn. 93
Posey, Thomas 337
Potter, Charles 96
Potter, David 99

Potter, Wm. 187
Pottie, George 269
Pottie, Mary 269
Pottinger, James 269
Potts, Eliz. 269
Potts, Jn. 113, 269
Potts, Johannah 269
Potts, Jonas 269
Potts, Rich. 279
Potts, Thomas 269
Poule (see: Howard Pool) 267
Poulton, Capt. Jesse 269
Pound, Jacob 269
Pound, Jn. 269
Pound, Morris 269
Povey (see: Peter Povall) 269
Powall, Leven 184
Powars, Miss Betsy 55
Powel, Jn. 93
Powell, Benj. 50, 106, 231, 269, 270, 293
Powell, Miss Hannah 106
Powell, James 87, 162, 258, 378
Powell, Jane 270
Powell, Jn. 231, 378
Powell, Levan 270
Powell, Leven 52, 160, 190
Powell, Miss Nancy 50, 352
Powell, Robert 270, 378
Powell, Samuel 101
Powell, Seymour 353
Powell, Dr. Thomas 101
Powell, Wm. 325
Power, Maj. Henry 148
Power, Miss Molly 148
Powers, Wm. 270
Poythress, Miss Agnes 12
Poythress, Eliz. 270
Poythress, Jn. 167
Poythress, Joshua 243, 366
Poythress, Joshua Jr. 258

18th-Century Virginia Newspapers 439

Poythress, Miss Lucy 138
Poythress, Mary 270
Poythress, Miss Nancy 278
Poythress, Peter 270
Poythress, Col. Peter 12, 30, 278
Poythress, Susanna 270
Poythress, Miss Susannah 30
Poythress, Wm. 115
Pradel, Joseph 296
Pratt, Capt. 195
Pratt, Wm. 95
Prelinger, Peter 92
Prentis, Miss Betsey 133
Prentis, Jn. 170
Prentis, Joseph 231
Prentis, Wm. 37, 271
Presley, Col. 2, 309
Presley, Peter 288, 308
Presson, Nicholas 271
Preston, Capt. Wm. 191, 357
Preston, Francis 271
Preston, Jn. 116, 271
Preston, Paul 296
Preston, Wm. 46, 116
Pretlow, Samuel 28, 261
Pretlow, Thomas 261
Pretlow, Thos. 28
Price, Capt. 195
Price, the widow 272
Price, Anne 271
Price, Benj. 321
Price, Bourne 274
Price, Charles 171
Price, Elisha 320
Price, Eliz. 29
Price, Miss Eliz. P. 238
Price, James 190, 272
Price, Jane 272
Price, Miss Jane 105
Price, Jn. 175, 198, 265, 271

Price, Jn. W. 272
Price, Joseph 95, 376
Price, Lewis 272
Price, Nathan W. 61
Price, Nathaniel 271
Price, Nathaniel W. 271
Price, Paul 32
Price, Peter 272
Price, Miss Polly 46
Price, Randolph 271, 272
Price, Robert 40
Price, Samuel 4, 260
Price, Susanna 32
Price, Thomas 96, 300, 359
Price, Wm. 32, 96, 271
Pride, James 16, 146
Pride, Jn. 56
Primus 75
Prince, Francis 304
Prince, Joanna 304
Pringle, Jn. 20, 84
Pringle, Rich. 272
Prior, Jn. 272
Prior, Samuel 272
Pritchard, Stephen 272
Pritchard, Wm. 111
Pritchet, Miss Sally 22
Pritlow, Joseph 302
Proatzman, Miss Mary 210
Probey, Paul 349
Proby, Miss Eliz. 299
Proby, P. 21
Proby, Paul 190, 272
Procter, John 12
Prosser, Miss Patsey 154
Prosser, Miss Susannah 31
Prosser, Thomas 237, 259, 371, 373
Prosser, Maj. Thomas 272
Prothero, Thomas 273
Prunty, Jn. 273
Pryor, Christopher 273

Pryor, Jn. 37
Pryor, Samuel 367
Pucket, Jn. 180
Pugh, Joseph 321
Pughe, Eaton P. 158
Pulaski, Gen. 69
Purcell, Henry 273
Purcell, Peter 273
Purcell, Pierce 69
Purcill, Charles 69
Purdie, Capt. 195
Purdie, Ensign 195
Purdie, Alex. 211, 273
Purrington, Clarissa 348
Purrington, Jn. H. 348
Pursell, Anthony 255
Purtle, Jane 273
Purtle, Martha 273
Purtle, Nicholas 274
Purviance, Eliz. 274
Purviance, Henry 274
Purviance, Isabella 274
Purviance, Letitia 274
Purviance, Robert 274
Purviance, Samuel 274
Purviance, Susanna 274
Purvis, Geo. 306, 354
Purvis, George 176, 204
Puryear, Ellis 274
Puryear, Hezekiah 274
Puryear, Samuel 274
Puryear, Wm. 274
Putrel (see: Thomas Putterill) 274
Pyland, Robert 274
Pyron, James 12

Quarles, Miss Ann 333
Quarles, Miss Betsey 77
Quarles, Francis West 315
Quarles, Capt. Henry 97, 288, 333
Quarles, Lt. Henry 332
Quarles, James 356

Quarles, Jn. 274, 354
Quarles, Col. Jn. 274
Quarles, John Jr. 4
Quarles, Lucy Daingerfield 315
Quarles, Nathaniel 82
Quarles, Robert 356
Quarles, Col. Tunstall 61
Quarles, W. Jr. 257
Quarles, Wharton 315
Quarrier, Alex. 139
Quarrier, Maj. Alex. 274
Quash 274
Quenichett, Joseph 49
Quesenburg, Jn. 95
Quin, Francis 99
Quince Family 39
Quince, Rich. 219
Quinn, James 275
Quinn, Jn. 95
Quinn, Rich. 50
Quisenberry, Aaron 275
Quisenberry, Moses 275

Raborg, Michael 226
Rachel 15, 35
Rackett, Ludwell 275
Radford, Jn. 281
Radford, Milner 281
Radford, Miss Polly 271
Radford, Wm. 6, 271
Ragan, Brice 96
Ragan, Philip 96
Ragland, Evan 275
Ragland, Jn. 275
Ragland, Wm. 275
Ragsdale, Drury 213, 274
Ragsdale, Rich. 237
Railey, Miss Eliz. 339
Railey, James 358
Raines, Isaac 92
Raines, Lt. 261
Raines, Nathaniel 275
Rainey, Wm. 111
Rakestraw, Jn. 275

Rakestraw, Mary 275
Rakestraw, Robert 275
Raleigh, Bryan 92
Ralls, Geo. 11, 215
Ralls, Jn. 70
Ralston, David 88
Ramer, Francis 195
Ramsay, Alex. 65
Ramsay, Dennis 223
Ramsay, Eliz. 276
Ramsay, Miss Eliza 269
Ramsay, Miss Hannah 223
Ramsay, James 265, 276
Ramsay, Dr. James 276
Ramsay, Jane 276
Ramsay, Dr. Jn. 276
Ramsay, Col. Nathaniel 66
Ramsay, Patrick 276
Ramsay, Wm. 223, 276
Rand, Jn. 276
Rand, Sophia 276
Rand, Walter 276
Rand, Wm. 122, 276
Randal, Jn. 276
Randall, Christopher 277
Randall, Hannah 277
Randall, Joseph 277
Randolph, Mr. 148
Randolph, Mrs. 310
Randolph, Miss Betsey 26
Randolph, Betty 278
Randolph, Brett 278
Randolph, Col. Rich. 154, 278
Randolph, David M. 279
Randolph, David Meade 278
Randolph, Edmond 152, 278
Randolph, H. 30
Randolph, Harrison 277
Randolph, Harwell 97
Randolph, Jacob 302, 303
Randolph, James 93

Randolph, Miss Jane 31
Randolph, Jn. 277, 333
Randolph, Miss Judith 323
Randolph, Miss Lucy 50
Randolph, Peter 179, 210, 289
Randolph, Peyton 152, 277, 310
Randolph, Rich. 31, 278, 279, 327
Randolph, Rich. Kidder 277
Randolph, Maj. Richard 1, 355
Randolph, Ry. 157
Randolph, Ryland 277, 278
Randolph, Miss Sukey 154
Randolph, Thomas Isham 278
Randolph, Thomas M. 277, 279
Randolph, Wm. 277, 278, 279, 323
Raney, Daniel 225
Rankin, Judith 279
Ransdell, Edward 279
Ransdell, Mrs. Eliz. 86
Ransone, Ambrose 8
Ransone, Miss Harriot 63
Ransone, Rich. 279
Ratchford, Thomas 295
Ratcliff, Davis 96
Ratcliff, George 94
Ratcliffe, R. 111
Ratekin, James 160
Ratliff, Rich. 84
Rauly, Judith 357
Rauly, Matthew 357
Ravel, Anthony 296
Ravel, Mark 296
Rawleigh, Wm. 280
Rawlings, Mrs. 107
Rawlings, Eliz. 184
Rawlings, Joseph 184
Rawlings, Peter 107
Rawlings, Robert 206
Rawlins, James 116

Rawlins, John 19,
Raworth, Jn. 296
Raworth, Miss Nancy
 90
Rawson, Wm. 372
Ray, Anne 280
Ray, James 93
Ray, Jonathan 280
Razer, Miss Christiana
 194
Rea, Wm. 280
Reaburn, Adam 60
Read, Col. 379
Read, Dr. 187, 280
Read, Clement 246
Read, Coleman 230
Read, Dr. J. K. 18
Read, Dr. Jn. K. 280
Read, Miss Keziah
 149
Read, Miss Lucy
 Franklin 187
Read, Mary 246
Read, Miss Patsy K.
 18
Read, Miss Sally 258
Read, Thomas 246,
 280
Read, Col. Thomas
 247
Reade, Clement 90,
 150
Reade, Hawkins 263,
 280
Reade, Jn. 280
Reade, Robert 280
Reade, Samuel 280
Reader, Robert 65
Reagan, Nicholas 281
Reardon, Jn. 98
Reat, Wm. 281
Redd, Wm. 281
Reddick, Lemuel 263,
 267
Redman, Martin 94
Redmon, Benj. 281
Redmon, Mahaney
 281
Redmon, Mildred 281
Redmon, Thomas 281
Redmon, Wm. 281
Redwood, Henry 295
Redwood, W. 281
Reed, Lt. 195
Reed, Geo. 365
Reed, James 246
Reed, Jn. 16, 287

Reed, Thomas 210,
 267
Reefe, Capt. 195
Rees, Jacob 88
Rees, Jn. 335
Rees, Silas 26
Reese, David 94
Reese, Jordan 165
Reese, Olive 209
Reese, Wm. 99
Reeves, Joseph 296
Regan, Miss Delia
 165
Reid, the Rev. Mr.
 Alex. 282
Reid, Fanny 282
Reid, Francis 104
Reid, George 78,
 137, 345
Reid, Jacobina 149
Reid, James 54,
 282
Reid, Jeremiah 305
Reid, Jn. 281
Reid, Margaret 78
Reid, Capt. Nathan
 96
Reilly, Polly 282
Reily, Miss Syvella
 5
Relfe, Jn. 275
Remine, Samuel 99
Renaud, Areanea 282
Renfroe, Stephen 195
Renick, Wm. 156
Renn, Joseph 282
Rennolds, Eliz. 85
Rennolds, Jn. 14
Rennolds, Robert 71
Reubin, Levi 216
Revell, Edward 282
Revis, Timothy 282
Reynold, Jn. 300
Reynolds, Capt. 282
Reynolds, Miss 183
Reynolds, Mrs. 282
Reynolds,
 Quartermaster 195
Reynolds, David 229
Reynolds, Dorothy
 282
Reynolds, Mrs. Dorothy
 3
Reynolds, Jn. 138,
 282
Reynolds, Jn. Jr. 286

Reynolds, Nathaniel
 282
Reynolds, Thomas
 303
Reynolds, Wm. 59,
 138, 340, 360
Rhodes, Ann 265
Rhodes, Jn. 283
Ricaud, Francis 283
Rice, Edmund 283
Rice, Edward 300
Rice, Eliz. 283
Rice, George 283
Rice, Capt. George
 146
Rice, Jacob 15
Rice, James 283
Rice, Jn. 283
Rice, Patsey 348
Rice, Philip 348
Rice, Miss Polly 218
Rice, Stephen 95
Richards, Mrs. 127
Richards, the Rev. Mr.
 127
Richards, Anthony
 145
Richards, Eleanor
 283
Richards, Jn. 99,
 177, 204
Richards, Martha
 283
Richards, Miss Polly
 204
Richards, Thomas
 283
Richards, Wm. 99,
 209, 368
Richardson Family
 72
Richardson, Alex.
 344
Richardson, Charles
 69
Richardson, Dudley
 160, 307
Richardson, George
 284
Richardson, Jn. 54,
 172, 221, 284, 296
Richardson, Miss
 Peggy 375
Richardson, Rebecca
 321
Richardson, Samuel
 256, 284

Richardson, Sarah 284
Richardson, W. 23
Richardson, Wm. 3, 273, 321
Richardson, Wm. 71
Richerson, David 127
Richeson, Elliott 303
Richeson, Holt 284
Richeson, James 284
Richeson, Peter 284
Richey, Robert 175
Richmond, Wm. 44
Richter, Mary 284
Ricketts, Miss Anne 3
Ricketts, J. T. 343
Ricketts, John Thos. 3
Rickits, James 15
Rickman, Eliz. 285
Riddell, George 60, 222
Riddell, James 285
Riddell, Lewis 285
Riddell, Susanna 285
Riddick, Edward 285
Riddick, Esther 285
Riddick, Robert Moore 285
Riddick, Samuel 285
Riddle, Jn. 105, 285
Riddle, Joseph 345
Riddle, Richard 285
Riddle, Sally 159, 270
Riddle, Thomas 285
Riddle, Wm. 79, 285, 352
Riddle (see: Dr. Geo. Riddell) 285
Ridgely, Joshua 285
Ridlehurst, Francis 285
Ridley, James 285
Ridley, Jane 285
Ried, Lt. 195
Riely, Jn. 296
Rigdon, Thomas 291
Riggs, Thomas 166
Riley, Jn. 54
Riley, Martin 326
Rind, James 200
Rind, Sophia 286
Rind, Wm. 286
Rinker, Col. Jacob 381

Ritchie, Archibald 114, 286
Ritchie, Mary 286
Ritchie, Wm. 150, 286
Ritenour, Jn. 286
Ritson, Miss Nancy 332
Ritson, Thomas 158, 370
Ritter, Philip 370
Rivalain, Lewis 26
Rivers, Thomas 286
Rives, George 336
Rives, Jn. 322
Rivington, James 105
Roach, Micajah 283
Roach, Ruth 283
Roach, Thomas 92, 95
Roach, Tynie 295
Roache, James 77
Roan, Wm. 245
Roane, James 287
Roane, Mary Eliz. Mills 245
Roane, Spencer 287
Roane, Thomas 85, 245
Roane, Wm. 54, 237
Rob, James 62
Robb, Miss Betsey 235
Robb, James 19, 60, 135, 141, 235, 297
Robb, Miss Lucy 141
Robb, Miss Nancy 60
Roberdeau, Gen. 328
Roberdeau, Daniel 5, 244, 288
Roberdeau, Miss Nancy 328
Roberts [Family] 200
Roberts, Burwell 284
Roberts, David 287
Roberts, Easther 31
Roberts, Edward 287
Roberts, Eliz. 106
Roberts, Francis 92
Roberts, Miss Hannah 16
Roberts, Jacob 33
Roberts, James 99, 100
Roberts, Jn. 130, 288
Roberts, Lemuel 107

Roberts, Lucy 288
Roberts, Mary 117, 130, 287
Roberts, Mat. 288
Roberts, Morris 93
Roberts, Olive 288
Roberts, Miss Polly 3
Roberts, Samuel 117
Roberts, Sarah 304
Roberts, Thos. 14
Roberts, Wm. 96, 287
Robertson, Alex. 17, 155
Robertson, Archibald 270
Robertson, Daniel 75
Robertson, Eliz. 288, 357
Robertson, Miss Eliz. 208
Robertson, George 105
Robertson, Gilbert 45, 282
Robertson, Hodge 357
Robertson, Holcombe 184
Robertson, James 288
Robertson, Jn. 44, 99
Robertson, Joseph 145
Robertson, Julius 306
Robertson, Mary 324
Robertson, Moses 288
Robertson, Risden 324
Robertson, Ruth 184
Robertson, Sarah 288
Robertson, Thomas 95
Robertson, Wm. 208, 350
Robin 128
Robins, Francis 265
Robins, Jn. 289
Robins, Thomas 175, 375
Robins, Wm. 37
Robinson, Capt. 140
Robinson, Miss 64
Robinson, Mrs. 145
Robinson, Miss Amelia 209

18th-Century Virginia Newspapers 443

Robinson, Anthony 281
Robinson, Benj. 99, 258, 290
Robinson, Charles Carter 289
Robinson, Christopher 290, 352
Robinson, Esther 174
Robinson, Miss Hannah 143
Robinson, Henry 67
Robinson, James 47, 351
Robinson, Jn. 112, 228, 248, 289, 290, 304, 350
Robinson, Miss Judy 146
Robinson, Miss Katy 350
Robinson, Lucretia 289
Robinson, Peter 79
Robinson, Polly 304
Robinson, Thomas 289, 290
Robinson, Tully 272
Robinson, Wm. 92, 98, 289, 290
Roceau, Joachim 296
Rochester, Nathaniel 80
Rock, Capt. Charles 290
Roddy, Charles 290
Rodgers, Adam 290
Roe, Jn. 332
Roger, Capt. 253
Rogers, Lt. 195
Rogers, the Rev. Dr. 106, 216
Rogers, Achilles 291
Rogers, Cornelius 347
Rogers, Eliz. 347
Rogers, Joseph 291
Rogers, Parmenas 291
Rogers, Priscilla 291
Rogers, Thomas 290, 291
Rogers, Wm. 9
Rollins, Miss Mary 294
Romjeu, Jn. 291
Ronald, Andrew 182, 210, 291
Ronald, Anne 17
Ronald, Betsey 291
Ronald, Betsy 17
Ronald, Nancey 291
Ronald, Wm. 17, 182, 291
Rookings, Eliz. 292
Rootes, George 292
Rootes, Maj. Philip 292
Roper, Jesse 292
Rose, Alex. 177
Rose, Duncan 17, 18, 292
Rose, Ezekial 292
Rose, Hugh 181
Rose, Jn. 40
Rose, Matilda 181
Rose, Patrick 292
Rose, Thomas 247
Rose, Wm. 292
Roseberry, Hausimus 54
Rosebrock, Robert 48
Ross, Alex. 299
Ross, D. 328
Ross, David 18, 164, 231, 246, 267, 291
Ross, Capt. David 127
Ross, Isabella 266
Ross, Jn. 101, 292
Ross, Miss Liza 246
Ross, the Rev. Mr. Robert 218
Ross, the Rev. Robert 143
Ross, Thomas 368
Ross, Wm. 292
Rosson, Joseph 293
Rothery, Mrs. Clara 364
Rothery, Mary 293
Rothery, Mrs. Mary 281
Rothrock, George 293
Roulett, Jn. 293
Roulett, Mackness 293
Rourke, James 326
Rousby, Mrs. 123
Rousby, Jn. 123
Roussau (see: Henry Rosseau) 293
Routh, Ann 51
Routh, David 51
Routh, Mrs. Eliz. 51
Routlidge, Robert 63
Routy, Jn. 52
Row, Wm. 83
Rowand, Jn. 293
Rowe, Jasper 293
Rowe, Mrs. Johanna 109
Rowe, Zachariah 293
Rowelen, Patrick 222
Rowland, Zachariah 110
Rowley, Wm. 374
Rowt, Jn. 63
Rowzee, Jn. 319
Rowzee, Rich. 293
Rowzee, Miss Sally 318
Rowzie, Jn. 40
Roy, Anne 293
Roy, Beverly 75
Roy, Thomas 93
Royal, Joseph 377
Royal, Wm. 377
Royall, Eliz. 294
Royall, Miss Eliz. 288
Royall, Jn. 288
Royall, Jn. Jr. 294
Royall, Wm. 115, 269
Royster, Jn. 135, 231
Royster, Littlebury 120
Royster, Wm. 284, 305
Royston, Rich. Wiatt 294
Rozer, Miss Eliza 108
Rubel, Jn. 294
Ruble, George 228
Rubsamen, Balthasar 294
Rubsamen, Daniel 294
Rubsamen, Jacob 294
Rubsamen, Maria Catharine 294
Rucker, Anthony 48
Rud, Avis 294
Rud, Jn. 294
Rud, Thomas 294
Rudd, [?] 265
Rudd, Samuel 294
Rudder, Charles 237
Ruddle, Deborah 45
Ruddle, Jn. 45

Ruff, Thomas 295
Ruff, Wm. 165
Ruffin, Col. 294
Ruffin, Ben. Jr. 309
Ruffin, Francis 249, 294
Ruffin, Jn. Jr. 294
Ruffin, Maj. Jn. 345
Ruffin, Miss Molly 64
Ruffin, Robert 208
Ruffin, Thomas 294
Ruffin, Wm. 286
Ruffner, Mary 295
Rundell, Robert 359
Rush, James 97
Russel, John 10
Russel, Mary 10
Russel, Miss Sarah 139
Russell, Col. 94
Russell, Mr. 127
Russell, Absolom 130
Russell, Amelia 217, 297
Russell, David 112
Russell, Edmund 130
Russell, Eliz. 130, 297
Russell, Enoch 285
Russell, Francis 130, 216, 297
Russell, George 96
Russell, Hinde 307
Russell, James 23, 216, 297
Russell, Jn. 96
Russell, Margaret 217, 297
Russell, Robert 216, 217, 297
Russell, Ruth 285
Russell, Sanders 130
Russell, Sarah 298
Russell, Susannah 297
Russell, Thomas 297
Russell, Wm. 50, 231, 238, 286, 297
Russell, Capt. Wm. 297
Rust, Benj. 89
Rust, Hannah 89
Rust, Peter 89
Rutherford, Gen. 195
Rutherford, Benj. 298

Rutherford, Dudley 306
Rutherford, Reuben 159
Rutherford, Robert 23, 168, 185, 215, 298
Rutherford, Miss Sally 23
Rutherford, Thomas 279
Rutherford, Thomas Jr. 298
Rutledge, Thos. 76
Rutt, Lettice Lee 315
Rutter, James 93
Ryan, Dennis 214
Ryan, Edward 296
Ryan, Patrick 84, 225
Ryburn, Jn. 238
Rylot, Edward 295
Ryly, Wm. 93

Sack, Jn. 298
Sadler, Jn. 298
Sale, Mrs. Anne 125
Sale, Cornelius 25
Sale, Leonard 125
Sale, Wm. B. 125
Salle, Abraham 114
Sallie, Isaac 39
Sallie, Jn. 315
Salusbury, Jn. S. 154
Samater, Anthony 95
Samith, Mary 360
Samith, Samuel 360
Sample, Quartermaster 195
Sampson, Mary 299
Sampson, Stephen 299
Samuel, Gray 39
Samuel, James 299
Samuel, Reuben 299
Samuel, Sally 39
Samuel, Miss Sophia 374
Samuel, Thomas 299
Sancho 23
Sandal, Osmand 96
Sanders, Miss Mildred 229
Sanders, the Rev. Mr. Nathaniel 229
Sanders, Thomas 242
Sanderson, Capt. 300

Sandford, Hannah Philippa 230
Sandford, Robert 230
Sanford, Capt. Wm. 345
Sanford, Edw. 380
Satchell, Matthew 281
Saunders, the Rev. Mr. 236
Saunders, Alex. 32
Saunders, Betsy 184
Saunders, David 204
Saunders, Miss Eliza 254
Saunders, Jesse 300
Saunders, Jn. 81, 90, 96, 115, 158, 184, 300
Saunders, Jn. Hyde 299
Saunders, Julius 161
Saunders, Margaret 81
Saunders, Mary 161
Saunders, Miss Polly 102
Saunders, Robert 58, 299
Saunders, Robert H. 270
Saunders, Samuel 92, 95
Saunders, Samuel Hyde 189
Saunders, Thomas 286
Saunders, Wm. 39, 161, 295
Saunderson, Miss 134
Savage, Col. Littleton 300
Savage, Margaret 269
Savage, Miss Mary Burton 300
Savage, Nathaniel L. 300
Savage, Thomas L. 300
Savage, Wm. 269, 282
Savenas, Mary 129
Savenas, Nicholas 129
Savey, Abraham 279
Savey, Sarah 279

Saws, Thomas 300	Scott, Thomas 115, 301, 303	Semple, Jn. Walker 304
Sayers, Edward 300	Scott, Wm. 302, 307	Semple, Robert Baylor 304
Sayers, Eliz. 300	Scrosby, Miss Dorothy 46	Sennet, Jn. 304
Sayers, Isham 300	Scrosby, James 158, 303	Senseney, Jn. 217
Sayers, Robert 300	Scruggs, Gross 94	Setlington, Mary 121
Sayers, Wm. Hardyman 300	Scruggs, Littleberry 303	Setlington, Robert 121
Scales, Joseph 358	Scrugs, James 268	Seton (see: Capt. Charles Seaton) 303
Scales, Nicholas 358	Scully, Patrick 98	Settle, Mary 304
Scales, Parthina 358	Seaborn, George 303	Settle, Wm. 35, 137
Scales, Peter 358	Seabrook, Mrs. 286, 343	Seward, Joseph 170
Scales, Robert 358	Seabrook, Nicholas B. 59	Seward, Wm. Jr. 57
Scamble, Jn. 15	Seabrook, Nicholas Brown 341	Sexsmith, Simon 48
Scarburgh, Col. Edmund 301	Seabrook, Miss Polly 343	Sexton, Meshach 274, 347
Scarlet, Mrs. 114	Seabrook, Miss Sally 286	Seyle, Jn. 129, 261, 342
Scasbrooke, Col. Henry 301	Seabrooke, Jn. 303	Seymour, Miss Ann 227
Schoolar, Jn. 239	Seagrove, James 114	Seymour, Jn. B. 305
Schultz, George 99	Searlon, Francis 261	Shackleford, Judith 305
Scot, Archibald 296	Sears, Jn. 240	Shackleford, Lettice 305
Scott, Capt. 195	Seaton, Howson 215	Shackleford, Lyne 43
Scott, Col. 144	Seaward, Benj. 95	Shackleton, Nancy 57
Scott, Mrs. 297	Seawell, Miss Eliz. 365	Shackleton, Wm. 57
Scott, the Rev. Mr. 43, 229	Seayres, Frankey 70	Shadburn, Wm. 135
Scott, Anderson 7	Seayres, Robert 14	Shaffer, Rich. 195
Scott, Ann 302	Sebra 299	Shannan, Theophilus 121
Scott, Charles 181, 247	Seegfried, Jn. 116	Sharkey, James 305
Scott, Gen. Charles 301	Segar, Rich. 303	Sharkey, Jn. 305
Scott, Charles R. 303	Seguin, Pierre 339	Sharkey, Nicholas 305
Scott, Eliz. 32, 301	Selden, Cary 237	Sharkey, Patrick 305
Scott, Eliza 302	Selden, Eliz. 304	Sharp, Daniel 60
Scott, Exum 267	Selden, Jn. 304	Sharp, Hales 36, 147, 305
Scott, Francis 301	Selden, Miles 232	Sharp, Henry 93
Scott, Frankie 302	Selden, Miss 14, 216	Sharp, Jn. 324
Scott, Frederick 301	Selden, Myles Jr. 4	Sharp, Rich. 16, 147
Scott, James 301	Selden, Miss Nancy 37	Sharp, Thomas 235, 296
Scott, James Jr. 79	Seldon (see: Miss Ann Selden) 304	Shaw, Alex. 17, 18
Scott, John 7, 158, 172, 187, 303	Self, Francis 127	Shaw, Haily 165
Scott, Jn. B. 368	Self, James 94	Shaw, Patsey 165
Scott, Joseph 32, 302, 303	Self, Wm. 94	Shaw, Rebecca 165
Scott, Joseph Jr. 193	Sell, George 244, 356	Shaw, Robert 165
Scott, Miss Kitty 43	Semple, Eliz. 304	Shaw, Wm. 54
Scott, Mary 302	Semple, James 155	Shearl, Joseph 93
Scott, Mary Slowman 301	Semple, Jn. 149, 304	
Scott, Maryann 242		
Scott, Peggy 303		
Scott, Robert 105, 303		
Scott, Sall 302		

Shearman, Jn. 95
Sheckel, Diederick 354
Shedden, Jn. 306
Shedden, Robert 280
Shedden, Wm. 59
Sheels, James 76
Sheild, Maj. Robert 306
Sheild, Samuel 53
Sheldreake, George 306
Shelly, James 56
Shelton, Abigail 306
Shelton, Aziriah 306
Shelton, Cuthbert 100
Shelton, Eliphaz 306
Shelton, Elop 306
Shelton, Ezakiah 306
Shelton, James 306
Shelton, Jeremiah 306
Shelton, Jn. 258
Shelton, Joseph 153
Shelton, Liberty 306
Shelton, Mary 306
Shelton, Patrick 306
Shelton, Ralph 306
Shelton, Robert 312
Shelton, Roger 306
Shepard, Nathaniel 247
Sheperd, [?] 21
Shepherd, Abrah. 325
Shepherd, Alex. 306
Shepherd, Andrew 25, 29, 86
Shepherd, Anne 34, 306
Shepherd, Miss Catherine 86
Shepherd, George 81
Shepherd, Miss Helen 29
Shepherd, Jane 295
Shepherd, Joseph 241
Shepherd, Smith 306
Shepherd, Solomon 34
Sheppard, Ann 266
Sheppard, Benj. 241, 307
Sheppard, Eliz. 266

Sheppard, Mrs. J. 332
Sheppard, Jn. 22, 205, 266
Sheppard, Jn. M. 307
Sheppard, Joseph 307
Sheppard, Moseby 266
Sheppard, Nathaniel 306
Sheppard, Philip 266, 307
Sherman, Adam Jr. 190
Sherman, Betsy 109
Sherman, Frances 307
Sherman, Henry Duke 109
Sherman, Rich. 100
Shermer, Mrs. Anne 307
Shermer, Jn. 307
Shermer, Rich. 307
Shermidine, Jn. 307
Sherrard, Robert 307
Sherridan, James 296
Shield, Jn. P. 307
Shield, Samuel 307
Shields, Mrs. 177
Shields, James 256
Shields, Maj. James 307
Shields, Maj. Wm. 308
Shifflet, Thomas 93
Shiphard, Jn. 219, 320
Shipman, Isaiah 312
Shippen, Eliz. Carter 18
Shippen, Thos. Lee 18
Shippen, Wm. 18
Shippey, Jn. 281
Shirley, Philamon 308
Shively, Jacob 308
Shope, Wm. 349
Shore, Henry S. 308
Shore, Jn. 308, 314
Shore, Rich. 92
Shore, Samuel 308
Shore, Thomas 314
Short, George 92

Short, Isaac 73, 230
Short, Thomas 92, 93
Short, Tom 308
Short, Wm. 133
Shortwell, Jn. 81
Shortzraitz, Jn. 75
Shough, Jn. 201
Shreve, Benj. 308
Shreve, Samuel 19
Shuck, Jacob 163
Shuffleton, Ann 285
Shuffleton, Jn. 98
Shule, Andrew 86
Shum, Prudence 308
Shuster, Jacob 36
Shuter, Wm. 308
Sibbald, Capt. 309
Siebolt, Jn. Lewis 98
Siford, Michael 309
Sikes, George 220
Sikes, Thomas 371
Silbey, Jn. 360
Siling, Andrew 309
Siling, Catharine 309
Sills, Corporal 216
Simcock, Rich. 189
Simmons, Mr. 309
Simmons, Benj. 46
Simmons, Henry 46
Simmons, Isaac 281
Simmons, Thos. 46
Simmons, Wm. 288, 309
Simms, Miss 57, 152
Simms, Charles 235
Simms, Eliz. 309
Simms, James 14
Simms, Thomas 309
Simons, Abraham 309
Simons, David 188, 309
Simons, Miss Sally 188
Simpson, George 309
Simpson, Gilbert 309
Simpson, James 290
Simpson, the Rev. James 80
Simpson, Jn. 305
Simpson, Joseph 160, 270
Simpson, Mary 305
Simpson, Moses 309

Simpson, Rich. 101, 309, 310
Simpson, Thomas 351, 352
Simpson, Wm. 310
Simrall, A. 194
Simrall, Miss Fanny 236
Sinclair, Charles 96
Singleton, Daniel 186, 273
Singleton, Miss Eliz. 347
Singleton, James 191
Singleton, Mary 310
Singleton, Menoah 186
Singleton, Menoah 273
Singleton, Peter 310
Sip 173
Sisrall, Francis 310
Sisson, George 299
Sistare, Jn. 310
Sittler, Miss Eliz. 221
Sittler, Isaac 221, 310
Skaife, the Rev. Mr. Jn. 311
Skelton, Bathurst 181
Skelton, Mrs. Martha 181
Skerum, Jn. 170
Skidmore, Edward 310
Skinker, Jn. 3
Skinker, Wm. 311
Skinner, Eliz. 311
Skinner, Miss Betsey 14
Skipwith, Gray 311
Skipwith, H. 272
Skipwith, Miss Mary 279
Skipwith, Peyton 74
Skipwith, Sir Peyton 65, 155, 164, 311
Skipwith, Robert 155
Skipwith, Sir Wm. 279
Slack, Josiah 259
Slaney, Wm. 311
Slater, Edward 249, 326
Slater, Mary 311
Slaughter, Capt. 56

Slaughter, A. 349, 354
Slaughter, Anne 72
Slaughter, J. 110
Slaughter, James 142
Slaughter, Jn. 93
Slaughter, Lawrence 122
Slaughter, Robert Jr. 311
Slaughter, Thomas 142, 311
Sleet, Miss Lucy 338
Slinkey, Jn. 38
Slinkey, Polly 38
Sloan, Jn. 99
Slote, Jn. 298
Slusher, Catharine 312
Sly, Jacob 98
Smallwood, Jn. 268
Smallwood, Mary B. 312
Smallwood, Wm. 142
Smarr, Robert 312
Smarr, Sarah 312
Smelt, Anne 312
Smelt, Dennis 312
Smelt, the Rev. Jn. 312
Smelt, Lucy 312
Smelt, Wm. 312
Smith Family 72
Smith, Capt. 195
Smith, Miss 167
Smith, Mr. 1
Smith, Abraham 312, 378
Smith, Agnes 313
Smith, Alex. 287, 310
Smith, Ann 107, 108, 282
Smith, Anne 313
Smith, Capt. Arthur 94
Smith, Augustine 89, 240, 315
Smith, Austin 332
Smith, Babby 140
Smith, Benj. 312
Smith, Bethiah 316
Smith, Chas. 6, 97
Smith, Dabney 140
Smith, Daniel 317
Smith, Daramis 313

Smith, Edward 123, 315
Smith, Edwin Bathurst 315
Smith, Eliz. 108, 192, 313, 358
Smith, Fanny 140
Smith, Frances 313
Smith, Francis 12, 313, 316, 375
Smith, Francis Jr. 11, 291
Smith, Francis Sr. 13, 192
Smith, Frankey 140
Smith, George W. 315
Smith, George Wm. 315
Smith, Granville 313
Smith, Gregory 33, 231
Smith, Hannah 297
Smith, Harry 316
Smith, Henry 312
Smith, Hill 92
Smith, Hugh 315
Smith, James 8, 92, 254, 315
Smith, Jesse 17, 313
Smith, Jn. 13, 36, 66, 75, 96, 127, 137, 155, 159, 170, 192, 225, 235, 237, 250, 313, 315, 316, 318, 368
Smith, Col. Jn. 332
Smith, Jn. Jr. 297
Smith, John W. 5
Smith, Jonathan 315
Smith, Joseph 116, 314
Smith, Joshua 200
Smith, Josiah 308, 315
Smith, Col. Larkin 315
Smith, Levi 250
Smith, Margaret 318
Smith, Mary 363
Smith, Miss Mary 332
Smith, Meredith 315
Smith, Meriwether 67
Smith, Nancy 140
Smith, Miss Nancy 138, 179

Smith, Nathaniel 95
Smith, Patrick 92
Smith, Philip 313, 370
Smith, Polly 140, 250
Smith, Miss Polly 340
Smith, Rebekah 264
Smith, Reuben 108
Smith, Rich. 92
Smith, Robert 8, 240, 313, 315
Smith, Rose 312
Smith, Sally 140
Smith, Samuel 149, 312
Smith, Sarah 75
Smith, Sukey 140
Smith, Miss Sukey 210
Smith, Thomas 12, 147, 313, 315, 365, 369
Smith, Walter 151
Smith, Wm. 72, 75, 81, 92, 99, 107, 108, 117, 128, 138, 140, 201, 228, 231, 295, 304, 312, 314, 315, 316, 340, 353, 358, 368
Smith, Capt. William 94
Smock, Esme 72
Smock, Wm. 269
Smyth, Francis 227
Snail, Miss Nancy 162
Snapp, Adam Jr. 190
Snapp, Barbara 190
Snapp, Eliz. 190
Snapp, Jacob 190
Snapp, Jn. 190
Snapp, Capt. Lawrence 108
Snapp, Madelina 190
Snapp, Mary 190
Snapp, Miss Peggy 108
Snead, [?] 167
Snead, Wm. 317
Sneed, Eliz. 81
Sneed, James 357
Sneed, Mary 81
Sneed, Parthena 357
Sneed, Wm. 317
Snider, Henry 317
Sniggers, Miss Betsy 324

Snodgrass, Wm. 305
Snyder, Jacob 324, 325
Snyder, Jn. 193
Solomon 40
Solomon, Isham 119
Somerville, Geo. 317
Somerville, James Jr. 317
Sorrell, Jn. 96
Sorter, Abraham 57
Souder, Jn. 317, 372
Sourbeer, Anthony 308
Southall, Miss 243
Southall, Mrs. 324
Southall, Miss Cyntha 340
Southall, Miss Eliz. 278
Southall, Miss Frances 85
Southall, Furnea 77
Southall, Furnew 339
Southall, Henry 240
Southall, James 34, 134, 135
Southall, Col. James 85, 243, 278
Southall, James Jr. 107
Southall, Mrs. Jane 246
Southall, Miss Polly 185
Southall, Turner 28, 110, 146, 237, 371
Southerland, David 177
Southerland, Miss 274
Southwick, Chudleigh 16, 145
Sowell, Thomas 207
Sowers, Miss Eliz. 209
Sowers, Jn. 209
Spadden, Ann 161
Spain, Miss Eliz. 244
Spain, Joshua 80
Spangler, David 318
Spark, George 177
Spark, Mary 177
Sparks, Jn. 127
Sparling, Geo. 39
Sparrow, Jn. 318

Speairs (see: Wm. Spears Sr.) 318
Spear, Miss Mary 250
Spears, Robert 318
Spears, Wm. 318
Speer, Lt. 195
Spencer, Benj. 93
Spencer, Charles 58
Spencer, Capt. Joseph 96, 199
Spencer, Nathaniel 92
Spicer, Randolph 163
Spier, Lt. 195
Spiller, B. C. 186
Spinks, Charles 295
Spinner, Mary 378
Splitdorff, Lt. 349
Spooner, Jn. 330
Spore, Jn. 227
Spotswood, Capt. 159
Spotswood, Col. 71
Spotswood, Alex. 189, 319
Spotswood, Col. Alex. 304, 354
Spotswood, Gen. Alex. 329
Spotswood, Miss Anne Washington B. 329
Spotswood, Jn. 318
Spottswood, Col. 295
Spottswood, Alexander 84, 90
Spratt, Edmund 193
Spreker, Charles 193
Spriggs, Miss 233
Spriggs, Rich. 233
Springer, Mrs. 158
Sprinkle, Henry 256
Sprouse, Charles 95
Sprowle, Andrew 78
Spurk, Peter 296
St. Clair, Gen. 99, 195
St. Clair, Alex. 216
St. George, H. U. 312
St. John, Rich. 70
Stabler, Wm. 319
Stacey, Jn. 319
Stackhouse, Stephen 362
Stacy, Joseph 170
Stafford, Dr. Anthony 148
Stafford, Hannah 141
Stagle, Moses 152

Stainback, Francis 319
Stainback, Wm. 150
Stanard, Beverly 319
Stanard, Larkin 26
Stanard, Miss Lucy Carter 54
Stanard, Miss Sarah C. C. 58
Stanard, Wm. 46, 54, 58
Standford, Joseph 47, 270
Stanhope, Wm. 309
Stanley, Jn. 320
Stanton, Col. 301
Stanton, Miss Lucinda 301
Stanton (see: Jn. Staunton) 320
Stanup (see: Price Stanhope) 319
Staples, Nathaniel 320
Staples, Samuel 306
Stark, Belfield 320
Stark, Bolling 380
Stark, Miss Fanny 318
Stark, Sarah 297
Stark, Wm. 32, 320
Starke, Burwell 207
Starke, Miss Betsy 277
Starke, Miss Nancy 196
Starke, Rich. 320
Starkey, [?] 221
Staten, Reuben 98
Steed, Jn. 191
Steel, Mr. 343
Steel, Bazzel 91
Steel, Jn. 320
Steel, Wm. 296
Steele, Wm. 195
Stephen 187
Stephen, Col. 190
Stephen, Andrew 127
Stephen, Robert 320
Stephens, Debbie 320, 321
Stephens, Eliz. 321
Stephens, Hailey 320
Stephens, Henry 285, 305
Stephens, Jn. 95, 320

Stephens, Joseph 320, 321
Stephens, Joshua 320
Stephens, L. 130
Stephens, Lewis 181
Stephens, Miss Nelly 123
Stephens, Robert 119
Stephens, Samuel 321
Stephens, Thomas 321
Stephenson, David 155
Stephenson, Joseph 91
Stephenson, Marcus 108, 245
Stephenson, the Rev. Mr. 188, 193
Sterling, Lord 320
Stern, Charles Smith 168
Sterrett, James 321
Sterrett, James F. 321
Sterrett, Jn. 321
Sterrett, Joseph 321
Sterrett, Sarah 321
Steuart, Charles 41, 299
Steuart, Hugh 244
Steuart, Jn. 137
Steven, Capt. Richard 94
Stevens, James 184
Stevens, Jn. 92
Stevens, Mary Byrd 184
Stevens, Nathaniel 92
Stevens, Samuel 198
Stevens, Wm. 95
Stevenson, Capt. 235
Stevenson, the Rev. Mr. 204
Stevenson, Edward 245, 295, 354, 367
Stevenson, Frances 321
Stevenson, the Rev. James 302
Stevenson, Jn. 247, 321
Stevenson, Robert 190
Steward, Jn. 377
Steward, Robert 127
Steward, Wm. 224
Stewart, Anthony 217

Stewart, Charles 80
Stewart, Eliz. 358
Stewart, Dr. Geo. 314
Stewart, Hugh 322
Stewart, James 103
Stewart, Miss Jane 80
Stewart, Jn. 3, 318, 322
Stewart, Rich. 322
Stewart, Richardton 218
Stewart, Robert 322
Stewart, Roger 72
Stewart, Walter 125, 322
Stieber, Michael 194, 234
Stiff, Jn. 322
Stigall, Moses 152
Stinson, Capt. 368
Stip, Frederick 322
Stip, Jn. 322
Stith, Anderson 323
Stith, Buckner 187, 232
Stith, Col. Drury 123
Stith, Miss Eliz. 123
Stith, Griffin 327
Stith, Jn. 94
Stith, Maj. Jn. 323
Stith, Joanna 322
Stith, Joseph 130
Stith, Mary 322
Stith, Rich. 130
Stith, Col. Robert 338
Stith, Miss Susan 338
Stith, Thomas 322
Stith, Wm. 327
Stobo, Robert 80, 121, 122, 127, 164
Stocksdill, Wm. 92
Stokes, Batte 323
Stokes, Feraby 323
Stokes, Jn. 96, 323
Stokes, Lt. Jn. 62
Stokes, M. 323
Stokes, Martha 323
Stokes, Rich. 323
Stokes, Shadrack 323
Stokes, Wiley 323
Stokes, Wm. 79, 350
Stone, Anderson 323
Stone, Caleb 339
Stone, Eliz. 324
Stone, Jn. 324

Stone, Marble 323
Stone, Prichard 96
Stone, Thomas 212, 323
Stone, Wm. 98, 199, 323
Stoner, Peter 291
Storey, Robert 268
Storrs, Gervas 324
Storrs, Joshua 113
Stot Family 72
Stouton, Joseph 96
Stoval, Geo. 324
Stoval, Mary 324
Stoval, Thos. 324
Stovall, Ann 324
Stovall, Barnes 324
Stovall, Bartholomew 324
Stovall, Eliz. 324
Stovall, Hezekiah 324
Stovall, Jesse 324
Stovall, Jn. 206, 324
Stovall, Littleberry 324
Stovall, Mary 206
Stovall, Ralph 324
Stover, Barbara 192
Stover, Christian 192
Strade, James 118
Strain, Wm. 325
Stran, Wm. 1
Strange, Berry 117
Strange, Frances 117
Strange, James 129, 313
Strange, Wm. 94
Stras, Geo. F. 324
Stratsman, Joseph 98
Street, David 323
Street, Martha 324
Stretch, Jn. 25
Strickland, George 325
Strickler, Isaac 325
Strickler, Joshua 325
Strikler, Joshua 317
Stringer, Daniel 142
Stringer, Jn. 13, 325
Stringer, Milly 142
Strite, the Rev. Mr. 325
Strobia, Jn. 325
Strode, Jn. 349
Strother, [?] 96

Strother, Anthony 121, 325
Strother, Jn. 325
Strother, Jos. 14
Stroud, Wm. 325
Stuard, Francis 325
Stuart, Alex. 134, 200, 326
Stuart, David 83
Stuart, Jn. 218
Stuart, Rich. 36
Stuart, Wm. 297
Stuart, the Rev. Wm. 309
Stuart, Wm. Gibbons 3
Stubblefield, Joanna 326
Stubblefield, Miss Betsy 113
Stump, Mr. 151
Stunks, Charles 273
Sturdivant, Jn. 326
Sturdivant, Joel 326
Sturdley, Phillis 326
Styers, Jacob 326
Suckey 298
Suggs, Geo. 367
Suggs, Capt. George 326
Suitor, Jn. 54
Sukey 182
Sulivan, Timothy 310
Sullenger, Thomas 326
Sullivan, Conor 97
Sullivan, Eliz. 326
Sullivan, Jeremiah 103
Sullivan, Mary 205
Sullivan, Philip 148
Sullivane, Margaret 72
Sully, Miss 313
Summers, Betty 326
Summers, George 326
Summers, Isabel 326
Summers, Susannah 326
Summers, Wm. 310
Sumner, Luke 47
Sumpter, Jn. 290
Suter, Miss Polly 63
Sutherland, Daniel 295
Sutor, James 327

Sutton, Jn. 121, 219, 224, 327
Swangel, G.S. Charles H. 2
Swann, the Rev. Mr. 220
Swann, Jennett Carson 327
Swann, Jn. 113, 291, 327
Swann, Mrs. Judith 327
Swann, Samuel 113, 200
Swann, Thomas Thompson 327
Swann, Thompson 327
Swann, Wm. 90
Swearengen, Capt. 195
Swearingen, Josiah 327
Swearingen, Thomas 240
Swearingham, Samuel 99
Sweet, Ensign 195
Sweeting, Frances 209
Swenly, Miss Betsy 33
Sweny, Edward 225
Swepson, Thomas 106
Swift, Amy 107, 108
Swift, Archibald 108
Swift, Betsy 108
Swift, Charles 108
Swift, Clevearse 107, 108
Swift, Harriet 107, 108
Swift, Jn. 108
Swift, Jonathan 42, 136, 217
Swift, Maria 108
Swift, Mary 108
Swift, Nancy 108
Swift, Peggy 107
Swift, Rebecca 107, 108
Swift, Rich. 328
Swift, Sally 108
Swift, the widow 148
Swift, Thomas 107, 108

18th-Century Virginia Newspapers

Swift, Wm. 108
Swilavan, Florence 123
Swinton, George 328
Swisher, Valentine 170
Sydnor, Fortunatus 328
Sydnor, Robert 328
Sydnor, Will. 215
Syfers, Sarah 273
Syling, Miss Polly 253
Syling (see: Andrew Siling) 309
Syme, Jn. 139, 179, 372
Syme, Col. Jn. 337
Syme, Miss Jane Isabell 337
Syms, Col. 359
Syphax 156
Syphret, Andrew 328

Tabb, Miss Fanny 293
Tabb, Frances 328
Tabb, Jn. 127
Tabb, Mary 328
Tabb, Philip 33
Tabb, Miss Polly 329
Tabb, Thomas 122, 328
Taff Family 379
Taff, Anne 328
Taff, Betty 328
Taff, Ellen 328
Taff, Francis 328
Taff, Peter 328
Taff, Priscilla 328
Taff, Thomas 328
Taff, Travis 328
Taff, Wm. 328
Taff, Woodbridge 328
Taggart, Lucy 328
Taite, Miss Betsey 342
Taite, Miss Sally 223
Taite, Wm. 89, 168, 256
Talbot, Edward 250
Talbot, Mary 329
Talbot, Miss Polly 158
Talbot, Rebecca 16
Talbot, Susannah 250
Talbot, Wm. 250
Talbott, Benj. 71
Talbott, Edward 329
Talbott, Haly 329
Talbott, Tamer 329
Talbut, Ann 329

Talbut, Benj. 329
Talbutt, Sarah 329
Taliafero, Lawrence 83
Taliafero, Rich. 51
Taliafero, Maj. Wm. 29
Taliaferro, Miss 257
Taliaferro, Eliz. 329
Taliaferro, Francis 283
Taliaferro, James Garnett 374
Taliaferro, Jn. 329, 338
Taliaferro, Col. Jn. 257, 329
Taliaferro, Nicholas 339
Taliaferro, Peter 95
Taliaferro, Philip 329
Taliaferro, Rich. 113, 271, 329
Taliaferro, Robt. 329
Taliaferro, Roderick 329
Taliaferro, Wilhelmina 374
Taliaferro, Wm. 206, 329, 352
Taliaferro, Wm. Harris 95
Taliaferro, Zachary 329
Taller, Wm. 95
Talley, Charles 350
Talley, Elkanah 6, 185
Talley, Mary 6, 185
Talley, Nathaniel 330
Tandy, Roger 15
Tankard, Miss Hannah 301
Tankard, Miss Peggy 77
Tanker, Mary 354
Tankersley, Jn. 14, 156
Tankerville, Earl of 217
Tanner, Branch 330
Tansell, Corbin 330
Tapp, Thomas 96
Tarlton 179
Tarry, Peter 330
Tarry[s], Eliz. 79

Tarry[s], Gracey 79
Tarry[s], Samuel 79
Tarry[s], Thomas 79
Tasker, Benj. 58
Tasker, Miss Frances 58
Tate, Adam 330
Tate, Benj. 24
Tate, Francis 330
Tate, Jn. 158, 330
Tate, Joseph 330
Tate, Robert 94, 98
Tate, Wm. 297
Tatham, Thomas 330
Tayler, Jn. 330
Tayler, Wm. 330
Tayloe, Miss Betty 74
Tayloe, Eliz. 210
Tayloe, Miss Jane 26
Tayloe, Jn. 26, 55, 74, 202, 210, 234, 256, 330, 357
Tayloe, Miss Molly 256
Tayloe, Miss Rebecca 202
Tayloe, Miss Sally 357
Taylor, Col. 326
Taylor, Miss 15
Taylor, Mrs. Ann 62
Taylor, Anne 331
Taylor, Benj. 331
Taylor, Miss Betsy 359
Taylor, Bushrod 324
Taylor, Creed 277, 278
Taylor, E. 17
Taylor, Edmund 331, 334
Taylor, Edward 331
Taylor, Miss Eliz. 105
Taylor, Erasmus 25
Taylor, Francis 331
Taylor, Capt. Francis 42, 62
Taylor, Geo. 327, 331
Taylor, Miss Gracy 118
Taylor, Henry 333
Taylor, Hugh 296
Taylor, Humphrey 18
Taylor, James 16, 17, 93, 99, 171, 209,

237, 241, 276, 314, 315, 331, 338, 344, 345
Taylor, James Jr. 105, 343
Taylor, Miss Jenny 276
Taylor, Jesse 219, 238, 375
Taylor, Capt. Jesse 276
Taylor, John 7, 15, 95, 287, 304, 332, 344, 351
Taylor, Capt. Jn. 62
Taylor, Col. Jn. 331
Taylor, Kaylen 108
Taylor, Miss Kitty 222
Taylor, Miss L. 17
Taylor, Miss Lucy 25
Taylor, Margaret 332
Taylor, Mary 108, 349
Taylor, Miles 51, 120, 259
Taylor, Miss Nancy 27
Taylor, Peter 206
Taylor, Phoebe 238
Taylor, Miss Polly 263
Taylor, Rich. 27, 72, 293, 349, 374
Taylor, Rich. K. 108
Taylor, Rich. S. 61
Taylor, Robert 118, 258, 273
Taylor, Sarah 206
Taylor, Miss Susannah 313
Taylor, Thomas Jr. 332
Taylor, Wm. 7, 32, 98, 331
Tazewell, Mr. 30
Tazewell, Henry 333, 378
Tazewell, Jn. 357
Tazewell, Linton 279
Teare, Polly 216
Tease, Mary 333
Tebbs, Foushee 145
Tebbs, Samuel 333
Tebbs, Willoughby 333
Tebbs, Wm. 254
Teek, Jn. 180
Temple, Liston 333
Temple, S. 281

Templeman, Miss Polly 78
Templeman, Rich. 333
Tenant, Elizabeth 175
Tenant, Thomas 340
Tennant, John 26
Tennant (see: Tennent) 333
Tennent, Jn. 233, 333
Terrel, Chiles 105
Terrell, Capt. 280, 323
Terrell, Chiles 63
Terrell, Richmond 107
Terrill, Edmund 90, 150
Terry, Stephen 334
Teuwell, Mary 334
Tewell (see: Matthew Teuwell) 334
Thacker, Mrs. Mary Eliz. 334
Thacker, the Rev. Chichley 334
Thackston, James 334
Tharp, Capt. 195
Tharp, Matthew 253
Theeds, Eliz. 334
Thenabell, Miss Eliz. 284
Theney 75
Theodorick 1
Thiebaud, M. 129
Thilman, Mrs. 364
Thilman, Jn. 152
Thilman, Capt. P. 334
Thomas, Benj. 334
Thomas, Betty 155
Thomas, Daniel 335
Thomas, Daniel 348
Thomas, Edmund 295
Thomas, Eleanor 335
Thomas, Evan 269, 335
Thomas, Francis 174, 220
Thomas, George 142, 276, 334
Thomas, Capt. George 28
Thomas, James 334

Thomas, Jn. 95, 112, 155, 206, 281, 295
Thomas, Jordan 57
Thomas, Joseph 211
Thomas, Mary 142, 348
Thomas, Miss Nancy 269
Thomas, Nelly 155
Thomas, Rich. 334
Thomas, Samuel 240
Thomas, Sarah 335
Thomas, Wm. 195, 335
Thomasson, David Hix 335
Thomasson, Fanny 335
Thomasson, Jn. 335
Thomasson, Lewis 335
Thomasson, Nancy 335
Thomasson, Patsey 335
Thomasson, Polley 335
Thomasson, Temperance Dumas 335
Thomasson, Unity 335
Thomasson, Unity Smith 335
Thomasson, Winney 335
Thomasson, Wright 335
Thompson, Ann 245
Thompson, Catherine 204
Thompson, Charles 297
Thompson, Eliz. 6, 335
Thompson, G. 337
Thompson, Garland 90, 336
Thompson, George 76
Thompson, Hannah 336
Thompson, Henry 335
Thompson, Isabella 335

18th-Century Virginia Newspapers 453

Thompson, Jacob 336
Thompson, James 70, 128, 335, 336
Thompson, Jn. 23, 38, 296, 335, 336, 337, 371
Thompson, Jn. Jr. 252
Thompson, Jonah 336
Thompson, Mary 335
Thompson, Nancy 335
Thompson, Patton 335
Thompson, Peggy 335
Thompson, Miss Polly 308
Thompson, Rich. 336
Thompson, Robert 197, 204
Thompson, Samuel 336, 337
Thompson, Temperance 38
Thompson, Thomas 279
Thompson, W. 336
Thompson, W. S. 336
Thompson, Waddy 6, 379
Thompson, Winney 38
Thompson, Wm. 38, 97, 98, 197, 335, 337
Thompson, Capt. Wm. 68
Thomson, James 92
Thomson, Miss Catharine 70
Thomson, Robert 180
Thomson, Wm. 264
Thomson, Wm. 310
Thorn, Michael 78
Thornberry, Sam. 281
Thornhill, Amstead 337
Thornhill, Barnett 337
Thornhill, Bryant 337
Thornhill, Edna 337
Thornhill, Ezekiel 337
Thornhill, James 337
Thornhill, Jn. 337
Thornhill, Leonard 337

Thornhill, Reuben 337
Thornhill, Sarah 337
Thornhill, Wm. 337
Thornton, A. 83
Thornton, Anthony 338
Thornton, Miss Betsy 108
Thornton, Daniel 337
Thornton, F. 338
Thornton, Francis 337, 338
Thornton, Francis Sr. 108
Thornton, Geo. 338
Thornton, Jesse 130
Thornton, Jn. 334, 338
Thornton, Lucy 66
Thornton, Mary 337
Thornton, Peter Presley 338
Thornton, Presley 234, 329, 338
Thornton, S. 338
Thornton, Miss Sara 61
Thornton, Sarah 338
Thornton, Sterling 338
Thornton, the Rev. Thos. 61
Thornton, Wm. 66, 337
Thoroughgood, Day 72
Thorowgood, Miss Eliz. 251
Thorpe, Joseph 276
Thorpe, Timothy 338
Threlkeld, Ensign 195
Threlkeld, Col. Elijah 128
Threlkeld, Miss Nancy 128
Throckmorton, Albion 360
Throckmorton, Jn. 304
Throckmorton, Mary 360
Throckmorton, Robert 53, 304, 339
Throckmorton, Miss Sally 338

Throckmorton, T. 64
Throgmorton, Miss P. 75
Thruston, Col. C. M. 73, 85
Thruston, Miss Eliz. 85
Thruston, Miss Fanny 73
Thruston, Miss Polly 224
Thurman, Andrew 339
Thurmon, Eliz. 350
Thurston, Miss Lucy 329
Thwaites, Jn. 339
Thweatt, Henry 55
Thweatt, J. 268
Thweatt, J. J. 268
Thweatt, Jn. 28
Thweatt, Capt. Thomas 96
Tibbs (see: Foushee Tebbs) 333
Tidball, Joseph 141, 142
Tigner, Ann 227
Tignor, Thomas 339
Tillett, Giles 339
Tillett, Samuel 339
Tilley, Ann 339
Timberlake, Betsey 339
Timberlake, Henry 339
Timberlake, J. Jr. 35
Timberlake, Jn. 61, 339
Timberlake, Miss Hannah Thacker 212
Timberlake, Rich. 339
Timberlake, Wm. 339
Timple, Capt. 27
Tinsley, Agnes 340
Tinsley, Anne 356
Tinsley, Jn. 356
Tinsley, Mary 340
Tinsley, Wm. 230, 340
Tippins, Charles 340
Tipple, Capt. 51
Tipton, Capt. 195
Tipton, Samuel 284

Tisdale, Thomas 97
Titsworth, Isaac 340
Titsworth, Jn. 340
Titsworth, Peggy 340
Tod, Mr. 78
Todd, Bernard 340
Todd, Geo. 347
Todd, James 273
Todd, Jane 273
Todd, Jn. 140
Todd, Capt. Joseph 291
Todd, Col. Levi 340
Todd, Mallory 38, 291
Todd, Capt. Robert 340
Todd, Wm. 159, 312
Toffler, Peter 34, 109
Toke, Nicholas 201
Toler, Benj. 6, 185, 186, 340
Tolkin, Jn. 297
Tom 77, 83, 299
Tomkies, Francis 209
Tomkins, Christopher 163
Tomlin, Robert 120
Tomlin, Walker 298
Tomlins, Jn. 295
Tomlinson, Eliz. 165
Tomlinson, Jn. 295
Tompkies, Charles 100
Tompkins, Ben. 341
Tompkins, Christopher 1
Tompkins, Francis 274, 341
Tompkins, Jn. 319
Toney, Peter 171
Tongud, Johnzd 318
Tooley, Ennall 96
Toomer, Jn. 63
Toone, James 26
Torray, Cornet 195
Towers, James 127
Towers, Jn. 106
Towles, Miss Betsey 40
Towles, Henry 260
Towles, Col. Henry 341
Towles, Lt. Henry B. 195

Towles, Oliver 62, 84
Towles, Thomas 207
Towles, Col. Thos. 40
Townes, Wm. 341
Towns (see: Rich. Townes) 341
Townsend, Dormand 227
Trabue, Mr. 151
Trap, Thomas 96
Travis, Edw. C. 343
Travis, Edw. Champion 45
Travis, Edward 125
Travis, Edward Jr. 342
Trebell, Wm. 45, 55, 157, 165, 259, 303, 330, 342
Trent, Alex. 325
Trent, Alex. 342
Trent, Miss Fanny 204
Trent, Peterfield 21, 42, 342
Trevillian, Thomas 152
Trice, Frances 202
Trice, James 140, 202
Trice, Mary 224
Trice, Thomas 224
Trice, Wm. 140
Trigg, Stephen 162
Trimble, Jn. 107
Trimper, Laurence 361
Triplet, Thomas 103
Triplet, Wm. 107
Triplett, Daniel 283, 342
Triplett, Sarah 342
Triplett, Wm. Jr. 201
Troman, Elijah 288
Troop, James 93
Tross, Samuel 183
Trotman, Jn. 127
Trout, Daniel 298
Troutwine, Geo. 365
Truehart, Daniel 227
Trueheart, Bartholomew 343
Trueheart, D. 123
Trueheart, Daniel 323

Trueheart, Miss Patsy 323
Trueheart, Miss Sukey 242
Trueheart, Maj. Wm. 343
Trugen, Mrs. 343
Tuck, Thomas 85
Tucker, Benj. Sr. 212
Tucker, Miss Caroline Henrietta 252
Tucker, Eliz. 343
Tucker, George 344
Tucker, Gideon 93
Tucker, Henry 343
Tucker, J. 305
Tucker, James 62, 120
Tucker, Jesse 116
Tucker, Jn. 291, 323, 343, 344
Tucker, Joanna 343
Tucker, Joel 323
[Tucker], Phoebe 11
Tucker, Polly 323
Tucker, Prescilla 323
Tucker, Robert 148, 369
Tucker, St. G. 54
Tucker, St. George 343
Tucker, Thomas 11, 93
Tucker, Wm. 116
Tuells, Enoch 344
Tuff, James 149
Tuley, Joseph 212
Tully, Jn. 152
Tummins, Edward 344
Tummins, Mary 344
Tummins, Samuel 344
Tummins, Winefred 344
Tunstall, Jane 360
Tunstall, Rich. 344
Tunstall, Richard 121
Tunstall, Wm. F. 360
Turberville, Betty Taylor 343
Turberville, George 74, 78, 181, 229, 262
Turberville, Geo. Lee 343
Turberville, Capt. George Lee 204

Turberville, Jn. 11, 54, 66, 72, 74, 78, 344, 358
Turberville, Martha 344
Turnbull, Charles 345
Turnbull, George 244
Turnbull, Jas. 10
Turnbull, Robert 176, 196
Turner, Col. 159
Turner, Benj. 96
Turner, Edward 98
Turner, Ensign 195
Turner, James 92
Turner, Kenchen 94
Turner, Reuben 330, 345
Turner, Miss Sally 198
Turner, Sarah 345
Turner, Simon 345
Turner, Thomas 147, 269, 345
Turner, Washington 345
Turner, Wm. 91, 345
Turner, Wm. Griffin 181
Turpin, Ephraim 93
Turpin, Horatia 346
Turpin, Joseph 71
Turpin, Peterfield 346
Turpin, Dr. Philip 345
Turpin, Thomas 346
Turpin, Wm. 346
Tutt, Mrs. 239
Tutt, James 249
Twigley (see: Robert Quigley) 275
Twyman, Abraham 346
Tye, Wm. 93
Tyler, Francis 346
Tyler, Jn. 107, 143, 155, 183, 222, 346
Tyler, Miss Johanna 222
Tyler, Judge 346
Tyler, Lewis 180
Tyler, Mary 346
Tyler, Peggy 346
Tyree, Jn. 346
Tyree, Wm. 346

Tyrie, Mrs. Mary 68
Uhler, Erasmus 309
Ultz, Daniel 359
Ultz, Mary 359
Underwood, George 82
Underwood, Jn. 107
Underwood, Thomas 347
Updegraff, Nathan 110
Upp, Valentine 91
Upshaw, James Jr. 125
Urquhart, Charles 109
Urquhart, Wm. 124
Ursula 35
Usher, Ann 347
Usher, Eliz. 347
Usher, James 347
Usher, Joseph 347
Usher, Josiah 347
Usher, Robert 347
Usher, Samuel 347
Usher, Sarah 347
Usher, Thomas 347

Vaderchamp, Simon 129
Vaiden, Jacob 347
Vaiden, Joseph 228, 347
Vaiden, Wm. 228
Valentine, Batchelder 347
Valentine, Charles 97
Valentine, Jacob 347
Valentine, Joseph 347
Valentine, Lynde 357
Valentine, Mrs. 123
Van Bram, Jacob 127
Van Meter, Jn. 302
Van Pelt, [?] 330
Vance, James D. 136, 348
Vance, Wm. 348
Vanderen, Bernard 308
Vandewall, Col. Markes 348
Vandine, Eliz. 344
Vandine, Jacob 344
Vanhorne, Jn. 348

Vass, Eliz. 360
Vass, Philip 360
Vass, Vincent 89
Vaughan, Gennett 285
Vaughan, Henry 63, 236
Vaughan, Hudson 348
Vaughan, Jack 348
Vaughan, James 348
Vaughan, Capt. James 161
Vaughan, Miss Jenny 323
Vaughan, Mary 348
Vaughan, Matilda 348
Vaughan, Matthew 348
Vaughan, Peter 348
Vaughan, Rich. 93
Vaughan, Salathiel 173
Vaughan, Stanhope 348
Vaughan, Thomas 294
Vaughan, Washington 348
Vaughan, Wm. 14, 285
Vaughn, Miss Patsy 307
Vaughn, Thomas 169
Vaulx, Robt. 12, 169, 370
Vaulx, Capt. Robert 172
Vauns, Wm. 65
Veal, Jn. 275
Veale, Samuel 349
Veale, Thos. 55, 349
Veale, Wm. C. 349
Veall, Demse 349
Veall, Eliz. 349
Veall, Nancy 349
Veall, Samuel 349
Veall, Wm. 349
Velts, Aaron 93
Venable, Geo. 11
Ventus, Mary 349
Verell, Jn. 239
Vernon, Abner 174
Vest, Jn. 94, 349
Vestall, Jn. 269

Vestall, Wm. 269
Vickery, Capt. Eli 349
Vidler, Edward 118
Vieller, Edward 59, 171
Vincent, Abraham 349
Vincent, Charles 297
Violet, Sampson 98
Violett, Thomas 218
Vose, Col. 363
Voss, Alexander 257
Voss, Edward 150, 163
Voss, Miss Kitty 144
Voss, Nicholas 163
Vowles, Capt. H. 349
Vowles, Henry 174
Vowles, Mary 174
Vowles, Thomas 350

Wackland, Mary 290
Wackland, Wm. Kook 290
Waddell, Jn. 350
Waddey, Francis 94
Waddy, Jn. 264
Wade, Andrew 350
Wade, Anney 350
Wade, Benj. 350
Wade, Daniel 270
Wade, Eliz. 350
Wade, Henry 350
Wade, Joseph 295, 350
Wade, Martha 350
Wade, Wm. 350
Wagener, Peter 172, 379
Wagener, the Rev. Peter 350
Waggener, Andrew 283
Waggener, Capt. Thomas 77, 87, 100, 181, 212, 302, 323, 377
Waggoner, Abraham 350
Waggoner, Maj. Andrew 303
Waggoner, Catharine 350
Waggoner, Christopher 350
Waggoner, Eliz. 350
Waggoner, F[.....] 350
Waggoner, Jacob 350

Waggoner, Jn. 350
Waggoner, Joseph 350
Waggoner, Mary 350
Waggoner, Mary Barbara 350
Waggoner, Miss Polly 303
Waggoner, Stephen 99
Waggoner, Capt. Thomas 34, 131, 314
Wagpels, Joseph 177
Waite, Wm. 112, 152
Wakefield, Wm. 96
Wakeland, Wm. [K.] 35
Walden, Charles 351
Walden, Jn. 351
Walding, Mrs. Eliz. 160
Wales, Andrew 213, 220, 341
Walke, Anthony 173, 242, 351
Walke, the Rev. Anthony 14, 185, 190, 252
Walke, Mary 351
Walke, Thomas 370
Walke, Wm. 351
Walker 352
Walker, Alice 111, 296
Walker, Anne 358
Walker, Miss Anne 310
Walker, Miss Betsy 249
Walker, Edmund 351
Walker, Miss Fanny 196
Walker, Francis 351
Walker, Freeman 76
Walker, Hugh 318, 351
Walker, James 37, 120, 135, 196, 220, 231, 252, 325, 370
Walker, Miss Jane 207
Walker, Miss Jenny 211
Walker, Jn. 173, 295, 309, 351

Walker, Mary 351, 352
Walker, Miss Mary Ann 24
Walker, Miss Mildred 169
Walker, Miss Nancy 184
Walker, Rich. 352
Walker, Robert 10, 24, 255, 296, 323, 351
Walker, Sam. 305
Walker, Susannah 352
Walker, Thomas 104, 184, 207, 352
Walker, Dr. Thomas 169
Walker, Warren 223
Walker, Wm. 113, 194, 349, 352, 355
Walker, Wm. T. 230
Wall, James 159,
Wall, Rich. 93
Wall, Wm. 93, 353
Wallace, Miss Betsey 319
Wallace, Eliz. 353
Wallace, Mrs. Elizabeth 229
Wallace, Col. G. B. 318
Wallace, James 362
Wallace, Jeane Dunstan 353
Wallace, Lettice 374
Wallace, Michael 374
Wallace, Robert 6, 47, 146, 206, 295
Wallace, Wm. Brown 128
Waller, Mrs. 184
Waller, Ann 353
Waller, B. 90
Waller, Ben. 43, 170
Waller, Benj. 34, 37, 74, 112, 175, 259, 314, 332, 333, 354
Waller, Miss Clarissa 342
Waller, Miss Dorothy Eliz. 333
Waller, Eliz. 354
Waller, Henry 354

18th-Century Virginia Newspapers 457

Waller, Mrs. Isabella 142
Waller, Jn. 112, 273
Waller, Miss Molly 74
Waller, Miss Nancy 34
Waller, Miss Patty 332
Waller, Robert H. 354
Waller, Miss Sally 314
Waln, Jesse 48
Waln, Robert 48
Walsh, John 26
Walsh, Matthew 76
Walsh, Nicholas 76
Walsh, Rich. 12
Walters, Miss Pleasant 210
Walters, Rich. C. 354
Walters, Walter 93
Walthal, Mary Patterson 354
Walton, Geo. 357, 354
Wanless, Mrs. 55
Wanton, Philip 257
Warburton, Miss Frances Booker 45
Ward, Quartermaster 195
Ward, Abigail 355
Ward, Benj. 122, 363
Ward, Capt. James 119, 194, 373
Ward, Cicely 355
Ward, George 234
Ward, Jane 355
Ward, Miss Jane 119
Ward, Mrs. Jane 373
Ward, Joanna 234
Ward, Joseph 49
Ward, Miss Lucy 277
Ward, Miss Polly 176
Ward, Samuel 355
Ward, Seth 278
Ward, Timothy 76
Ward, Wm. 74
Warden, Abraham 355
Warden, Jn. 289
Warden, Wm. 198
Wardope, James 296

Wardrop, James 87, 279, 355
Ware, Jn. 378
Ware, Miss Nancy 378
Ware, Robert 355
Wareham, Reader 150
Waring, Alse 45
Waring, Jn. 45
Waring, Marsham 117
Waring, Robert Payne 312
Waring, Wm. 355
Warner, James 99
Warner, Philip 88
Warner, Samuel 95
Warren, Lt. 195
Warren, Benj. 356
Warren, Miss Betsey 316
Warren, Eliz. 356
Warren, Mrs. Eliz. 62
Warren, Hannah 356
Warren, James 319, 356
Warren, Jn. 356
Warren, Marriott 356
Warren, Martha 356
Warren, Polly 356
Warren, Rebecca 356
Warren, Ritter 356
Warren, Robert 337
Warren, Robt. C. 12
Warren, Susannah 356
Warren, Tempy 356
Warren, Thomas 356
Warren, Toulson 356
Warren, Wilson 356
Warren, Wm. 356
Warrick, Wm. 64
Warricker, Wm. 34
Warrington, Jn. 25, 217, 342
Warrington, the Rev. Mr. Thomas 356
Warwick, Miss Eliz. 110
Wash, Jn. 98
Wash, Lipscomb 300
Washington, Col. 28, 181
Washington, Gen. 27, 83, 123, 184, 203

Washington, Judge 356
Washington, Anne Catharine 356
Washington, Augustine 348
Washington, Charles 357
Washington, Corbin 203
Washington, Mrs. Fanny 202
Washington, Frances Maria 356
Washington, George 41, 72, 118, 318, 357, 360
Washington, Gen. George 356
Washington, Hannah 365
Washington, Miss Harriott 258
Washington, Henry 334, 356
Washington, Maj. Jn. 356
Washington, Jn. A. 357
Washington, Jn. Augustine 203
Washington, Laurence 3
Washington, Lawrence 67
Washington, Lawrence Sr. 32
Washington, Lund 83, 305, 332
Washington, Miss Mildred 203
Washington, Miss Nancy 264
Washington, Nathaniel 356
Washington, Miss Sally 32
Washington, Samuel 258, 357, 368
Washington, Col. Samuel 356
Washington, Sarah 357
Washington, Thomas 357
Washington, Col. Warner 365

Washington, Wm. A. 345, 357
Washington, Wm. Augustine 203
Washington, Wm. H. 3
Wasley, Robert 310
Wassill (see: George Wassell) 357
Waters, Bazil 298
Waters, James 98
Waters, Miss Sally 232
Waters, Wm. 164, 295, 360
Watkins, Anne 358
Watkins, Benj. 226, 357
Watkins, Betsey 358
Watkins, Conny 357
Watkins, David 246
Watkins, Edward 54
Watkins, Eliz. Anne 357
Watkins, Elly 357
Watkins, Henry 172
Watkins, Ichabod 357
Watkins, Isaiah 357
Watkins, Jacob 210
Watkins, Jn. 183, 227, 239
Watkins, Joseph 24
Watkins, Ledwell 357
Watkins, Mary 358
Watkins, Nicholas 357
Watkins, Sarah 210
Watkins, Thos. 6, 295
Watkins, Willis 357
Watson, [?] 51
Watson, Capt. 258
Watson, Miss Betsey 212
Watson, Miss Charlotte 367
Watson, Capt. Edward 358
Watson, James 296
Watson, Jn. 340
Watson, Jn. Jr. 61
Watson, Joseph 359
Watson, Josiah 212
Watson, Nicholas 99
Watson, Thos. 38, 163
Watt, James 221

Watts, Ann 359
Watts, Arthur 127
Watts, Charles 232
Watts, Shadrach 359
Watts, Wm. 125
Waugh, Alex. 359
Wayland, Adam 359
Wayland, Hannah 359
Wayland, Jn. 359
Wayland, Joshua 359
Wayland, Lewis 359
Wayles, Jn. 278
Wayles, Jn. 97
Wayles, Miss Tabitha 311
Wayman, Jn. 359
Wayne, Gen. 116, 214, 273, 380
Wayte, Jn. 37
Weaver, Jacob 217
Weaver, James 323
Webb, Bernard 100
Webb, Capt. Jn. 94, 95
Webb, Francis 360
Webb, George 68, 243, 276, 360
Webb, James 360
Webb, Lewis 27, 243
Webb, Miss Lucy 85
Webb, Mary 295, 360
Webb, Miss Molly 68
Webb, Rich. C. 235
Webb, Thomas 360
Webb, Wm. 28, 360
Webber, Wm. Jr. 183
Webster, Henry 95
Webster, Joanna Catharine 77
Webster, Philip 214
Weedon, George 141, 233
Weedon, Gen. George 360
Weekly, Thomas 98
Weems, the Rev. M. L. 118
Weightman, Rich. 198
Weir, James 104
Weisiger, Anna 361
Weisiger, Daniel 114, 361
Weisiger, Joseph 103

Weisiger, Capt. Joseph 278
Welch, Mr. 99
Welch, Michael 73
Welch, Miss Nancy 176
Wellman, Mrs. Anne 361
Wellman, Edward 95
Wellman, Matthew 188
Wells Family 72
Wells, Mrs. 30
Wells, Abner 273
Wells, Alex. 151
Wells, Benj. 100
Wells, Charles 149
Wells, Daniel 340
Wells, Elijah 328, 361
Wells, Geo. 6
Wells, Jn. 145
Wells, Larkin 328
Wells, Robert 107, 127
Welsh, Jn. 361
Welsh, Wm. 103
Wemmer, Eliz. 361
Wemston, Isaac 103
Wentworth, Mary 361
Wercor, Lewis 25, 376
Wesson, Jn. 272
West, Mr. 190
West, Alley 362
West, Benj. 377
West, Eliz. 362
West, Col. Francis 27
West, Geo. 362
West, Hannah 361
West, Harriot 361
West, James 193
West, Jn. 280, 362
West, Jn. Jr. 72
West, Katy 362
West, Lucy 304
West, Margaret 361
West, Mrs. Margaret 36
West, Miss Mary 13
West, Nancy 362
West, Rachel 362
West, Rich. 54
West, Robert 361
West, Roger 1, 362

18th-Century Virginia Newspapers

West, Stephen 250, 361
West, Thos. 72
West, Capt. Thomas 96
West, Walter 362
West, Wm. 304, 329, 362
West, the Rev. Dr. Wm. 362
Westcot, Capt. Wright 193
Westcote, Miss Fanny 282
Westwood, Eliz. 362
Westwood, Miss Patsy 242
Westwood, Warlich 10
Wetherburn, Henry 307
Wethers, Margaret 124
Wharm, Wm. 297
Wharton, Jn. 268
Wharton, Mary 159
Wharton, Samuel 96
Wharton, Thos. Jr. 38
Whatmore, Jn. 296
Wheatley, Mary 363
Wherdon, Nathaniel 363
Whiddon, Mary 363
Whitacre, Robert 211
Whitbust, Jn. 92
White, Alex. 143, 146, 363, 366, 381
White, Bennett 81, 130
White, Miss Eliz. 78
White, Mrs. Eliz. 364
White, Jacob 254
White, Jane 157
White, Jn. 60, 201, 281, 364
White, Joseph 205
White, Mary 52, 365
White, Miss Mary 190
White, Miss Patty 338
White, Rhoda 364
White, Richard 366
White, Robert 36, 363
White, Samuel 313, 364
White, Thomas 172, 356
White, Wm. 190, 242, 334, 364
Whitefield. Wm. 19
Whitehead, Mr. 64, 110
Whitehead, the Rev. Mr. 82, 201
Whitehead, Edward 114
Whitehead, the Rev. James 3, 30, 88, 118, 162, 267, 364, 365, 367
Whitehead, the Rev. Wm. 299
Whitehouse, Miss Eliz. 348
Whitehurst, Joshua 369
Whitehurst, Levi 94
Whitelock, James 31
Whiteman, Henry 364
Whitfield, Eliz. 365
Whiting, Beverley 365
Whiting, Eliz. 365
Whiting, Francis 357
Whiting, Henry 365
Whiting, Humphrey 365
Whiting, Jn. 365
Whiting, Miss Mary 357
Whiting, Miss Molly 29, 171
Whiting, Miss Nancy 273
Whiting, Thomas 66, 170
Whitlock, Miss Betsey 282
Whitlock, Wm. 365
Whitman, Ezekial 368
Whitney, Eliz. 365
Whitney, Susannah 365
Whitstyene, Jn. 76
Whittaker, Abraham 92
Whittaker, Isaac 92
Whitwell, Capt. 365
Whitworth, Sir Charles 249
Whyte, Alex. 365
Whyte, Euphemia 366
Wiatt 71
Wiatt, Miss Sally 26
Wickersham, Amos 194
Wickliff, David 366
Widewilt, Jn. 294
Wiggenton, Margaret 295
Wiggenton, Robert 295
Wil[t]on, Robt. S. B. 18
Wiley, James 45, 195
Wiley, Mary 305
Wiley, Peter 305
Wilkerson, Eliz. 205
Wilkes, George 184
Wilkins, Daniel 93
Wilkins, Robert 94
Wilkins, Willis 366
Wilkins, Wm. 97
Wilkins, Wm. Sr. 3
Wilkinson, Miss 342
Wilkinson, Miss Eliz. 144
Wilkinson, Gabriel 95
Wilkinson, Jane 367
Wilkinson, Jn. 312, 366
Wilkinson, Mary 366
Wilkinson, N. 69
Wilkinson, Miss Nancy 221
Wilkinson, Nathaniel 12, 66
Wilkinson, Col. Nathaniel 144
Wilkinson, Miss Peggy 61
Wilkinson, Thomas 245, 247
Wilkinson, Willis 118, 367
Will 134, 210
Will, Lauchlane 295
Willcock, Wm. 209, 241
Willey, James 367
William 160
Williams, Capt. 367
Williams, Lt. 206
Williams, Ben 305
Williams, Betty Ann 369

Williams, Daniel 227
Williams, Dr.
 Frederick 272
Williams, Edward
 295, 368
Williams, Elisha 128
Williams, Eliz. 276
Williams, Frances
 367
Williams, Fred. 15,
 22, 176
Williams, George 92,
 368
Williams, Henry 368
Williams, Jacob 368
Williams, James 98
Williams, Jesse 358
Williams, Jn. 93,
 94, 122, 150, 371, 372
Williams, Capt. Jn.
 346
Williams, Jn. S. 368
Williams, Jonas 150
Williams, Joseph 368
Williams, Joshua 92
Williams, Lewelling
 150
Williams, Luke 369
Williams, Marston
 334
Williams, Mary 173
Williams, Nicholas
 166
Williams, Peter 92,
 165, 248
Williams, R. 368
Williams, Samuel
 185
Williams, Sarah 368
Williams, Thomas
 18, 95, 146, 173, 369
Williams, Capt.
 Thomas 368
Williams, W. O. 222
Williams, Wm. 297,
 368
Williams, Wm. C.
 380
Williamson, Allen
 88
Williamson, Archibald
 175
Williamson, George
 261, 313
Williamson, Jesse
 263
Williamson, Jn. 96

Williamson, Jn. Jr.
 14
Williamson, Miss Patty
 136
Williamson, Robt. 27,
 369
Williamson, Samuel
 369
Williamson, Stephen
 367
Williamson, Thomas
 257, 367
Willie (see: the Rev.
 Mr. Wilie) 366
Willie, Wm. 168
Willie, the Rev.
 William 369
Willing, Thomas 101
Willis, Abel 94
Willis, Augustine 16,
 370
Willis, Benj. D. 35
Willis, Miss Betsy 176
Willis, Drury 369
Willis, Edward 369
Willis, Francis 67,
 176, 192, 263, 370
Willis, Col. Francis
 50
Willis, Col. Henry 197
Willis, Jn. 136, 246,
 369, 370
Willis, Capt. Jn. 45
Willis, Maj. Jn. 369
Willis, Martha 370
Willis, Mary 369
Willis, [Mrs.] Mary
 50
Willis, Mildred 370
Willis, Moses 125
Willis, Rich. 369
Willis, Sherwood 369
Willis, Sterling 369
Willis, Thomas 196,
 369
Willis, Wm. 333,
 369
Willison, James 124
Willits, Samuel 109
Willman, Matthew
 39
Willmott, Ambrose
 295
Willmott, Sarah 370
Willock, T. 134
Willock, Thomas 164

Willoughby, Miss E.
 133
Willoughby, Eliz. 276
Willoughby, Jn. 332
Willoughby, Col. Jn.
 370
Willoughby, Miss
 Margaret 249
Willoughby, Miss
 Peggy 362
Willoughby, Miss Polly
 71
Willoughby, Wm. 136,
 226
Willoughly, Alexander
 370
Willoughly, Charity
 370
Willoughly, Joshua
 370
Willoughly, Wm. 370
Wills Family 72
Wills, Draughton 370
Wills, Dr. Jn. 370
Wills, Miles 301,
 370
Wills, Robert 126,
 137
Wills, Willis 370
Wills, Wm. 371
Willson, James 43
Willson, Joseph 205
Willson, Nancy 371
Willson, Capt. Samuel
 194
Willstock, Henry 99
Wilson, Capt. 275
Wilson, Miss 150
Wilson, Miss Agnis
 227
Wilson, Alice 372
Wilson, Andrew 97
Wilson, Miss Anna
 327
Wilson, Archibald
 106
Wilson, Benj. 190
Wilson, Campbell 371
Wilson, Cornelius
 99
Wilson, Cumberland
 23
Wilson, Eleanor 218
Wilson, Geo. Jr. 372
Wilson, George 92
Wilson, James 246,
 371

18th-Century Virginia Newspapers

Wilson, Jane 372
Wilson, Jn. 64, 78, 91, 320, 350, 372
Wilson, Joseph 321
Wilson, Joshua 283
Wilson, Col. Josiah 371
Wilson, Mary 283
Wilson, Miss Mary 227
Wilson, Polly 372
Wilson, Robt. Banister 17
Wilson, Sarah 198
Wilson, Solomon 258, 259, 371
Wilson, Susanna 78
Wilson, Thomas 166
Wilson, Willis 357, 372
Wilson, Wm. 1, 45, 99, 327, 350, 371, 372, 377
Wimbish, Eliz. 373
Wimbish, Jn. 358, 373
Wimbish, Samuel 358
Wimbish, Wm. 358
Wimmer, Jn. 306
Winchester, Col. 195
Winder, Edmund 208
Windsor 125
Winfrey, Isaac 373
Wingfield, Jn. 48, 172
Wingmore, Morgan 184
Wingo, Wm. Jr. 286
Winn, Benj. 184
Winn, Peter 373
Winn, Miss Sally 207
Winning, James 241
Winrow, Mr. 287
Winslow, Benj. 373
Winslow, Beverly 373
Winslow, Thomas 373
Winslow, Wm. 373
Winstin, Capt. 317
Winston, Anthony 185
Winston, Miss Barbara O. 334
Winston, Edmund 373
Winston, Geddes 181
Winston, Geddis 210

Winston, Isaac 373
Winston, Jn. 96, 373
Winston, Capt. Jn. 146
Winston, Col. Jn. 373
Winston, Mary 181
Winston, Miss Patsey 308
Winston, Peter 373
Winston, Miss Rebecca 9
Winston, Miss Sally 298
Winston, Samuel 21
Winston, Will. O. 289
Winterbury, Miss Betsey 51
Wintersmith, Dr. Charles 373
Wise, Dr. Tully R. 259
Wise, Geo. D. 322
Wise, J. 259
Wise, Jacob 308
Wise, Jn. 243
Wise, Peter 100, 160, 214, 343, 373
Wise, Miss Polly 135
Wisecarver (see: Christopher Wiseacre) 374
Wiseham, W. 23
Wiseham, Wm. 62, 291
Wiseman, Adolph 374
Wishart, Jn. 374
Wishart, Nicholas 374
Wishart, Sydney 374
Wishart, Thomas 310
Wishart, Wm. 72, 374
Wislon, Goodrich 372
Withers, George 374
Withers, James 212
Withers, Jn. 186
Withers, Jn. Jr. 326
Withers, Miss Eliza 212
Withers, Wm. 45, 110, 251, 352
Witmore, Henry 295
Woddrop, Anne 374
Woddrop, Robert 374
Wodrow, Andrew 374
Wolff, George 132

Wolford, Catharine 235
Wolford, Henry 235
Wolgamott, Joseph 374
Wollman, Elias 374
Womack, David 97
Wonycott, Nicholas 291
Wood, Abby 375
Wood, David 359
Wood, Drury 313
Wood, Hannah 161
Wood, James 174, 275, 291, 375
Wood, Leighton 340
Wood, Peter 375
Wood, Rich. 92
Wood, Robert 296, 375
Wood, Samuel 220, 221
Wood, Wm. 93
Woodcock, Edward 285
Woodcock, Jn. S. 367
Woodend, James 212
Woodend, Jane 212
Wooderfield, Robt. 98
Woodford, Catesby 58
Woodford, Jn. 98
Woodford, Wm. 338
Wooding, Robert 8
Woodrow, Miss Rachel 247
Woodruff, Wm. 97
Woods, Adam 305
Woods, Anne 305
Woodside, Jn. 267, 375
Woodside, Robert 148
Woodson, Ann 375
Woodson, Miss Ann 268
Woodson, Miss Betsy Ann 115
Woodson, David 84, 376
Woodson, Eliz. 376
Woodson, Jn. 376
Woodson, Miller 261, 265
Woodson, Obadiah 375

Woodson, Miss Sally H. 137
Woodson, Samuel 82, 376
Woodson, Shadrack 375
Woodson, Thomas 376
Woodward, James 15
Woodward, Jn. 376
Woodworth, Capt. David 158
Woolams, Jn. 93
Woolfolk, Agatha 125
Woolfolk, Edward 376
Woolfolk, P. 334
Woolfolk, Paul 139
Woolfolk, Robert 376
Wooling, Joseph 164
Woolsey, George 297, 336
Wooton, Wm. 376
Wootten, Jn. 92
Wootten, Wm. 241
Wootton, Mr. 72
Wootton, Herbert 376
Wootton, Sam. 376
Worley, Caleb 296
Wormax, Sarah 337
Wormeley, Jn. 332, 351
Wormeley, Miss Judith 146
Wormeley, Ralph 118, 146, 289, 330, 376
Wormington, Mrs. 9
Wormley, Jn. 310
Wornack, Jn. 214
Worsham, Mrs. 377
Worsham, R. 346
Worsham, Thomas 128
Worsham, Thomas 377
Worthington, Betsy 222
Worthington, Wm. 222, 372
Wray, Jacob 377
Wray, James 377
Wray, Miss Matilda 58
Wray, Molly 227
Wray, Miss Molly 58
Wren, Daniel 377

Wren, Wm. 377
Wright, Lt. 349
Wright, Alex. 174
Wright, Anne 378
Wright, Augustine 200
Wright, Charles 98
Wright, James 15, 86, 174
Wright, Jn. 378
Wright, Jonathan 39
Wright, Mrs. Lucy 378
Wright, Miss M. 25
Wright, Martin 49
Wright, Mary 378
Wright, Patrick 30, 303
Wright, Peter 174
Wright, Rich. O. 96
Wright, Robert 238
Wright, Rosomond 377
Wright, Sarah 200
Wright, Stephen 377
Wright, Thomas 249
Wright, Wm. 34, 122
Wrinn, Rich. 44
Wyat, Nathan 378
Wyatt, Jemima 181
Wyatt, Jn. 181
Wyatt, Wm. 80, 100, 222, 336
Wyllys, Maj. 195
Wynn, Mary 378
Wynne, Mrs. Polly Harriet 119
Wythe, G. 279
Wythe, George 378

Yacton, Emanuel 378
Yager, A. 379
Yager, Godfrey 359
Yancey, Charles 379
Yancey, Mrs. Eliz. 379
Yancey, Henry 379
Yancey, Nathan 31
Yap, Samuel 276
Yarbrough, James Smith 379
Yarbrough, Rich. 358, 379
Yates, Barth. 379
Yates, the Rev. Mr. Bartholomew 280

Yates, Miss Catherine 338
Yates, Charles 265, 266, 336
Yates, Edward R. 75, 379
Yates, Miss Frances 280
Yates, Robert 73, 171
Yates, the Rev. Robert 338
Yates, Wm. 30, 138, 245, 379
Yeargan, Samuel 67
Yeiser, Susannah 379
Yerby, Geo. 328, 379
Yerby, Jn. 328, 379
Yerby, Thomas 328, 379
Young, Mrs. 370
Young, Adam 246
Young, Charles 249
Young, Daniel 96, 203
Young, David 380
Young, Miss Eliz. 313
Young, Ezekiel 182
Young, Henry 344
Young, James 167, 257
Young, Nancy 380
Young, Nicholas 60, 81
Young, R. 343
Young, Rich. 379, 380
Young, Robert 164
Young, T. 370
Young, Wm. 100, 203
Younger, Joseph 96
Younghusband, Isaac Sr. 380
Younghusband, Pleasant 380, 381
Younghusband, Miss Polly 375
Younghusband, Thomas 380
Younglove, Wm. 98
Yowell, David 65
Yuille, Thomas 180, 330

Zane, Col. Isaac 187

Zane, Isaac 204, 237, 363
Zane, Miss Sarah 381

The following names were accidentally lost from page 408 of the index:

Forsyth, Robert 4
Forsyth, W. 361
Foushee, Charles 81
Foushee, Jn. 81
Foushee, Lucy 81
Foushee, Sarah 81
Foster, Mr. 21
Foster, Betsey 335
Foster, Capt. James 95
Foster, Francis 15, 54
Foster, James 295
Foster, Jn. 126
Foster, Nelson 335
Foster, Peter 66
Foster, Samuel 75
Foster, Wm. 242, 254
Fought, Wm. 99
Foulcon, Jacob 227
Foulder, Miss Hannah 282
Fountain, Maj. 195
Foushee, W. 247
Foushee, Wm. 133, 220, 245
Foushee, Dr. Wm. 127
Foutlaie, Joseph 296
Fowler, Mrs. 302
Fowler, Jn. 116, 127
Fowler, Joseph 13
Fox, Absolom 375

Index of Places, Ships, Military Units, etc.

Aberdeenshire 282
Africa 32
Algiers 6
Alsace [France] 226
Annapolis 59, 72, 80, 88, 91, 118, 120, 148, 163, 171, 196, 225, 233, 234, 253, 261, 266, 284, 294, 314, 325, 332, 340, 360, 362
Antigua 119, 164, 357
Ayreshire 35

Baltimore 11, 12, 16, 17, 18, 19, 31, 32, 34, 35, 38, 39, 40, 46, 52, 59, 60, 61, 62, 66, 72, 89, 96, 98, 103, 106-108, 115, 116, 131, 132, 136, 139, 140, 143, 148, 156, 158, 159, 161, 163, 165-167, 172-175, 179, 192, 197, 205, 207, 209, 217, 225, 237, 240, 243, 244, 247, 249, 250, 252, 257, 255, 275, 276, 281, 284, 285, 287, 288, 289, 299, 306, 308, 312, 314, 317, 319, 325, 327, 331, 340, 348, 355, 359, 362, 364, 367, 368, 372, 376, 379, 380
Barbados 339, 343
Belfast 139
Berlin 197
Bermuda 212, 248, 291, 316, 317
Birmingham [England] 31, 126
Bordeaux 31
Boston 40, 71, 117, 164, 198, 219, 232, 236, 252, 313, 355
Brandenburg 363
Bremen 297
Bristol 27, 44, 48, 87, 90, 151, 159, 213, 228, 270, 273, 276, 303, 318, 319, 365
Brunswick [Germany]155
Buckinghamshire 49

Cambridge 107

Cambridgeshire 204
Canada 52
Carolina 31, 41, 57, 89, 95, 96, 97, 107, 116, 122, 194, 241, 351, 376
Cheshire 62, 279
Companies:
  Allen & Hart 155
  Allmand & Powell 5
  Amos & James Ladd 198
  Anderson & Jamieson 159, 355
  Balfour & Barraud 351
  Blight, Brothers & Co. 273
  Blodget & Eustis 117
  Bogle, Somerville & Co. 334
  Brymer & Belcher 209
  Buchanan & Simmons 46
  Burke & Brunet 48
  Callender & Henderson 53
  Clark & Bixby 64
  Clarke & Bixby 65
  Clarke & Nebaker 247
  Clemison & Johnson 67, 183
  Daniel & Isaac M'Pherson 221
  Daniel Call & Co. 121
  David Ross & Co. 18
  Dekar Thompson & Co. 336
  Duncan & Turnbell 196
  Elliott & Purviance 114
  Eskrigge & Smith 116
  Farell & Jones 277
  Fisher, Bragg & Co. 124
  Gardener & Green 142

  Geo. Wilson Jr. & Co. 372
  George Hite & Co. 73
  Gibson & Robertson 288
  Gilbert Robinson & Munro 244
  Gilliat & Taylor 332
  Glassford & Henderson 309
  Goddard & Langworthy 143
  Gordon & Ramsey 276
  Gregorie & Barksdale 144
  Henry Gird & Co. 41
  Hunt & Adams 335
  James & Adam Hunter 174
  James and Robert Donald & Co. 103
  James Campbell & Co. 156
  James McClatchy & Co. 216
  James Miller & Co. 111
  James Rose & Co. 244
  James Smith & Co. 63
  John & Frederick Conrad 73
  John Hay & Co. 157
  Johnson & M'Dowell 218
  Jones and Broadbent 39
  Joseph Anthony & Co. 261
  Joseph Royle & Co. 294
  Lenox, Scott & Co. 142
  Little & Thompson 209
  Louis Vignon & Co. 349
  M'Call & Shedden 120, 287

Marsden Maxwell &
  Co.   259
Montgomery & Allen
  106
Newton & Kelly 191
Phripp & Bowdoin
  227, 265
Pomery & Isabel
  156
Prentis & Co.   279
Purdie & Dixon 55
Randall & Atkinson
  187
Robert & Walter
  Colquhoun   129
Robertson & Gibson
  288
Robinson, Sanderson
  & Rumney   213
Sloan & Pagan 312
Smith & Hannay
  150
Solomon Wilson &
  Co.   258
Southall and Hay
  317
Strachan & Hall
  70
Stump, Ricketts &
  Co.   276
Taylor & Rogers
  159
Thomas & Van
  Rutherford 298
Thomas W. Cocke &
  Co.   68
Thos. Williamson &
  Co.   369
Wallace & Muir
  62
Webb & Colston 360
William and J.
  Abbott 1
William and James
  Donald & Co. 104
William Forsyth &
  Co.   44, 351
Yundt & Brown 209
Connecticut   63,
  90, 100, 104, 176, 258,
  270, 314, 353, 364, 366
Cork [Ireland]   71,
  72, 306
Cumberland
  [England]180

Delaware   51, 117, 182,
  276, 314, 359
Demerara 153
Denmark 371
Derbyshire 43, 54
Devonshire 56
Dorsetshire 150
Dublin   37, 42, 45,
  78, 90, 93, 106, 116,
  131, 134, 178, 183, 219,
  224, 249, 253, 349, 355,
  365
duel 22, 46, 51, 56, 164,
  180, 198, 263
Durham [Eng.]   28,
  261

East Indies 183, 209
East Jersey 371
Edinburgh 78, , 249,
  283, 290
England   23, 24, 26,
  28, 29, 31, 33, 38, 39,
  41, 42, 49, 52, 64, 79,
  81, 84, 92, 94, 95, 96,
  100, 102, 115, 119, 139,
  142, 148, 150, 151, 154,
  156, 162, 167, 170, 172,
  176, 178, 180, 190, 192,
  196, 199, 201, 205, 210,
  221, 234, 242, 243, 250,
  251, 254, 255, 258, 261,
  267, 268, 269, 270, 273,
  277, 279, 280, 284, 291,
  294, 299, 307, 311, 316,
  327, 328, 333, 342, 345,
  347, 349, 350, 354, 360,
  364, 365, 366, 369, 371,
  373, 376, 379
Essex [England]   134,
  149, 350

Flanders   198
France   22, 31, 52,
  55, 89, 90, 97, 107, 144,
  174, 205, 240, 339, 341,
  342, 343, 361

Gambia   358
Georgia   11, 21, 35,
  80, 83, 89, 96, 111, 121,
  122, 130, 138, 148, 159,
  163, 222, 231, 233, 234,
  246, 257, 270, 272, 276,
  298, 309, 318

Germany   130, 161,
  164, 200, 205, 213, 259,
  296, 303, 306, 324, 374
Glamorgan [South
  Wales] 146
Glasgow   44, 80, 180,
  213, 218, 220, 237, 249,
  283, 320, 342, 372, 377
Gloucester 16
Gloucester
  [England]134
Granada 162
Great Britain   48,
  75, 93, 248
Grenada   131, 292
Groningen 35
Guernsey 254

Hampton-Sydney
  Academy 147
Herefordshire   38,
  122
Hertfordshire   106,
  264
Holland   35, 90, 164,
  201
Huntingdonshire 225

Ireland   3, 15, 19,
  31, 36, 38, 42, 45, 55,
  59, 82, 92, 95, 97, 99,
  100, 106, 107, 116, 120,
  124, 127, 134, 149, 169,
  171, 181, 190, 191, 197,
  212, 213, 214, 224, 228,
  237, 241, 244, 251, 260,
  275, 283, 284, 287, 293,
  300, 305, 316, 328, 337,
  347, 352, 358, 371, 372,
  373,
Isle of Man 92
Italy 3

Jamaica   11, 12, 16,
  27, 49, 54, 169, 192,
  204, 259
Jerseys   105, 204

Kent [England]   162,
  201, 373
Kentucky   13, 17, 25,
  28, 37, 46, 47, 52, 65,
  66, 68, 71, 73, 75. 76,
  85, 105, 108, 109, 110,
  120, 121, 126, 132, 137,
  151, 157, 160, 161, 166,
  169, 170, 172, 177, 188,

189, 192, 195, 197, 199, 200, 203, 211, 220, 221, 229, 232, 233, 239, 240, 242, 248, 250, 255, 266, 269, 274, 279, 282, 288, 299, 301, 311, 312, 321, 325, 326, 331, 334, 337, 340, 342, 348, 358, 371, 373

Lancashire 25, 26, 87, 100, 203, 327
Lancaster [England]293, 328
Leicester [England]159,
Leicestershire 347
Leyden 90
Lincolnshire 274, 280, 359
Lisbon 232
Liverpool 4, 11, 18, 33, 37, 38, 39, 64, 69, 136, 137, 171, 186, 196, 208, 231, 234, 269, 331, 332, 375
London 8, 9, 12, 14, 20, 21, 26, 29, 31, 49, 55, 56, 65, 72, 78, 80, 85, 87, 90, 93, 104, 111, 113, 115-118, 121, 125, 127, 129, 131, 135, 142, 136, 163, 171, 174, 176, 183, 190, 194, 197, 199, 201, 204, 205, 218, 220, 225, 235, 236, 247, 249, 254, 256, 261, 273, 281, 291, 296, 297, 303, 308, 311, 314, 329, 330, 335, 343, 351, 352, 353, 356, 358, 361, 374

Madeira 304, 337, 341
Madrid [Spain] 55
Manchester [England] 120
Martinico 37, 110, 204
Martinique 240
Martinique 89
Maryland 3, 8, 10, 11, 14, 15, 16, 19, 20, 22, 24, 25, 26, 29, 30, 32, 33, 36, 38, 41, 43, 44, 47, 48, 51, 55, 57, 58, 61, 65, 69, 70, 71, 73, 75, 76, 77, 79, 81-84, 88-95, 98, 99, 100, 101,

104-106, 108, 109, 116, 117, 121, 126, 127, 130, 134, 136-139, 142, 148, 150, 151, 152, 154, 155, 157, 159, 161, 163, 165, 166, 167, 171, 172, 173, 177, 178, 179, 183, 186, 188, 190, 191, 196, 197, 198, 201, 202, 210, 212, 213, 219, 220, 223, 224, 228, 229, 230, 234, 235, 239, 240, 241, 244, 245, 250, 257, 259, 261, 262, 265, 266, 269, 270, 271, 272, 273, 277, 279, 281, 284, 285, 286, 287, 290, 293, 294, 295, 296, 298, 299, 300, 302, 303, 304, 308, 310, 312, 314, 320, 323, 325, 326, 329, 330, 331, 332, 333, 335, 340, 341, 346, 347, 348, 350, 354, 356, 359, 360, 362, 364, 367, 369, 372
Massachusetts 63, 65, 83, 100, 177, 290, 355
Military Units:
1st Regt. 115, 127
1st Regt. of Artillery 314
1st U.S. Regt. 98, 353
1st Va. Regt. 35, 58, 81, 183, 186, 248, 260, 264, 315, 350, 362
2nd Georgia Regt. 97
2nd. Regt. 36, 80, 94, 97, 115
2nd Regt. of Art. & Eng. 55
2nd Va. Regt. 42, 62, 96, 283, 345, 362, 377
3rd Regt. of Lt. Dragoons 22
3rd Sub-Legion 17, 42, 99, 101, 103, 126, 150, 163, 243, 314
3rd U.S. [Regt.] 2, 19, 45, 98, 99, 103, 104, 198, 355
4th Sub-Legion 98, 99, 191, 195, 357

4th Troop of Horse 94
4th U.S. Regt. 103, 180, 217, 266, 322, 327
4th Va. Regt. 94
5th Regt. 280
5th Va. Regt. 95, 120, 191, 214, 258, 323, 373
6th Regt. 109
6th Regt. of Continental Regulars 80, 264
6th Va. Continental Regt. 21
6th Va. Regt. 22, 46, 62, 69, 94, 95, 144, 153, 169, 225, 259, 268, 348, 353
7th North Carolina Regt. 161
7th Regt. 96, 120
7th U.S. Regt. 79, 143, 180, 199, 227, 264, 284, 360
7th Va. Regt. 93, 94, 95, 294
8th Brigade 99
8th Regt. 56
8th U.S. Regt. 5, 100, 136, 216, 253, 332
8th [Va.] Regt. 227, 235, 368
9th Regt. 104
9th Va. Regt. 89
10th Va. Regt. 95, 96
11th Regt. of Foot 266
12th Regt. 196
14th British Regt. 126
14th Regt. 146, 272
14th Va. Regt. 96
15th Bn. of Continental Troops 94
15th Va. Regt. 60, 94, 95, 126, 204, 213
16th Regt. of Guards 217
17th British Regt. 254
21st Regt. of Lt. Dragoons 311

43rd [British] 220
54th Regt. 276
French Legion 247
H.M's 56th Regt. 362
Maryland Line 305
New York Regt. 327
Royal American Regt. 320
South Carolina Regt. 363
Stafford Light Infantry 264
Tarlton's Legion 116
Virginia Line 19, 242
Virginia Regt. 7
Monmouthshire 367

Nevis 22, 63, 162
New England 36, 74, 91, 94, 117, 226, 268, 296, 373
New Jersey 96, 99, 126, 143, 156, 180, 258, 268, 350, 358, 378, 379,
New Orleans 52, 343
New Providence 53, 377
New York 7, 11, 17, 19, 20, 23, 24, 29, 30, 35, 40, 41, 42, 47, 52, 63, 70, 71, 78, 82, 83, 90, 93, 99, 105, 106, 131, 151, 156, 159, 161, 163, 166, 168, 182, 196, 208, 209, 210, 220, 225, 226, 235, 237, 247, 249, 256, 295, 296, 299, 300, 304, 321, 327, 336, 341, 369
Norfolk [England] 65
North Britain 139, 143, 155, 199, 212, 220, 282
North Carolina 7, 11, 13, 15, 19, 22, 23, 30, 32, 38, 39, 42, 47, 48, 55, 60, 65, 67, 74, 75, 78, 80, 91, 92, 94, 95, 96, 97, 100, 105, 106, 111, 112, 114, 116, 118, 119, 122, 123, 126, 132, 138, 142, 148, 149, 151, 153, 154, 156, 169, 171, 175, 177, 181, 184, 186-189, 190, 191, 201, 103, 209, 214, 219, 222, 228, 235, 237, 238, 239, 241, 243, 251, 254, 260, 262, 263, 265, 275, 277, 280, 281, 282, 284, 285, 287, 288, 290, 291, 297, 299, 300, 301, 307, 312, 315, 316, 317, 320, 322, 323, 327, 328, 329, 330, 353, 363, 364, 369, 371, 374
Northamptonshire 247, 278
Norwich [England] 33, 167
Nova Scotia 97, 189, 209

Ohio 63, 80, 110, 129, 190, 26, 228, 310
Oxford 129, 354
Oxfordshire 159, 351

Paris 198, 205, 256, 349
Pennsylvania 1, 3, 5, 12, 23, 28, 29, 35, 36, 42, 43, 45, 59, 65, 71, 73, 76, 85, 86, 87, 95, 99, 105, 107, 126, 127, 130, 143, 147, 169, 183, 185, 197, 199, 204, 206, 211, 215, 216, 218, 229, 235, 244, 260, 262, 281, 287, 296, 302, 312, 317, 322, 325, 355, 372, 374, 376
Perthshire 25
Philadelphia 10, 11, 25, 28, 34, 38, 48, 51, 55, 61, 71, 83, 88, 89, 90, 93, 99, 101, 105, 106, 111, 116, 123, 131, 134, 137, 139, 140, 145, 146, 147, 148, 151, 158, 160, 164, 168, 177, 181, 182, 189, 194, 198, 199, 201, 203, 204, 206, 207, 208, 209, 213, 214, 223, 225, 232, 233, 237, 238, 240, 242, 253, 255, 257, 258, 262, 263, 265, 268, 269, 274, 276, 278, 280, 286, 287, 294, 295, 296, 309, 312, 318, 322, 324, 327, 328, 333, 336, 338, 341, 362, 366, 369, 371, 379, 381
Port Glasgow 121
Port-au-Prince 41, 157, 244, 268

Rhode Island 21, 45, 56, 136, 143, 176, 179, 209, 241, 310, 361
Rutlandshire 363

Scotland 25, 35, 38, 44, 48, 67, 83, 92, 103, 108, 109, 135, 138, 141, 145, 149, 164, 168, 172, 185, 192, 208, 216, 217, 218, 220, 222, 235, 237, 250, 276, 285, 287, 290, 292, 296, 320, 322, 345, 352, 355, 357, 360, 372, 376, 377, 380
Sheffield 39, 52
Ships:
Africa 52
Agness 106
Alexandria 14
Allerton 5, 219, 310
Alliance 280
Amazon 341
Amelia 59, 145, 223, 241, 335, 372
America 261
American Congress 93
Ann 342
Anne 113, 347
Ardent 312
Assistance 243
Baltimore 51
Becky 75, 320
Berry 42, 218, 323
Betsey 127, 300
Betsey and Polly 94
Betsy Richmond 120
Betsy 164, 344
Billy 56
Boston 139
Boyne 182
Brenchley 27, 157, 218, 297
Brickdale 254
Brilliant 3, 84, 327
Brothers 273
Brunswick 320
Burwell 106

18th-Century Virginia Newspapers

Caesar 221
Carlisle 106, 122, 222, 367
Cary 158
Catherine 192
Chance 296
Charlotte 240
Charming Peggy 100, 133
Commodore Hood 297
Constellation 16, 126
Constitution 100, 280
Delight 73, 170, 341
Devonshire 53
Donald 295
Dorsetshire 26
Dove 75
Dragon 78
Draper 78
Duke of Argyle 119
Duke of Cumberland 12, 88, 132, 198
Duly-Ann 322
Eliza 69, 204, 341
Elizabeth 258, 297
Encouragement 7, 183, 199, 236, 308
Endeavor 99
Europe 77, 88, 345
Fair Phebe 133
Fairfield 237, 363
Fanny 131, 137, 241
Fewey 106, 216, 363
Flamsborough 128
Flora 11
Fly 11
Fortune 295
Forward Galley 113, 194
Four Friends 48
Frances 352
Franklin 336
Fraw Tabitha 306
Friendship 290
George and Patty Washington 237
Greenvale 104, 262
Greenwood 158
Greyhound 95, 306
Hanbury 116

Hannah 27, 186
Hannibal 45, 81, 145, 148, 368
Hanover 98
Harriet 162
Hector 314
Henry 26, 67
Hero 42, 82, 129, 172, 228, 235
Hodgson 56
Hope 269
Hudibras 200
Idle Times 265
Industrious Bee 47, 207, 226, 228
Industy 310
Innermay 183
Iris 169
Jane 95, 348
Janet 282
Jenny 325
Jerushia 198
John 37, 82, 120, 132, 133, 171, 215, 219, 224, 231, 239, 243, 244, 307, 313
Juno 119
Justitia 1, 4, 22, 67, 72, 107, 115, 143, 159, 183, 212, 249, 261, 266, 268, 271, 296, 361
L'Eclatant 240
Lark 292
Lewis 96
Liberty 93, 274
Litchfield 235, 366, 373
Lord Camden 65, 78, 185, 374
Lord Clive 65
Lydia 69
Lyon 127
Madeira Packet 366
Mally 2, 117, 126
Manly 8, 97
Marlborough 84
Martha 228
Mary Ann 193, 218
Mary 19, 45, 275
Maryland Merchant 26
Mercury 53, 151
Molly 60, 138, 209
Montague 114

Morris 296
Muskito 104, 233, 355
Nancy 204, 332
Nassau 33, 208
Nautilus 288
Neptune 21, 56, 261, 355
Norfolk Revenge 193
Norfolk's Revenge 59
Northampton 96, 205
Page 336
Pamunkey Snow 147, 343
Peggy 3, 140
Planter 195
Polly 56, 117
Prince William 52
Priscilla 295
Queensborough 6
Rachel 142, 205
Randolph 98
Rappahannock 266
Rattler 4
Revenge 56, 368
Rippon 337
Ritson 371
Roba and Betsy 214
Roebuck 169
Romulous 226, 342
Ruby 47
Sally 13, 22, 258, 357
Saratoga 262
Saucy Fox 243
Scarsdale 353
Scorpion 53, 94, 208
Seahorse 80
Speirs 213
Spencer 295
St. Alban's 28
St. Bees 205
Stanley 130, 375
Success's Increase 17, 114
Susannah 129, 188
Swaile 293
Swift 111
Sybille 60, 226, 285
Tartar 96, 270

Tayloe 162, 169
Taylor 296
Thetis 327
Thomas 303, 321
Thornton 58, 295
Triton 147, 281, 343
Tryall 55
Venus 217
Vernon 44
Virginia Packet 171
Virginia 87, 88, 100, 145, 147, 173, 187, 316
Vulture 26
Walpole 377
Washington 72, 345
Waters 311
Westmoreland 27
Wilcox 179
William and Anne 118
York 9, 234, 295
Shropshire 190, 269, 283, 311, 376
Somerset 305
Somersetshire 129, 180, 202, 332
South Carolina 19, 27, 41, 55, 59, 63, 67, 76, 96, 104, 125, 127, 148, 155, 159, 164, 198, 201, 202, 206, 220, 249, 255, 259, 275, 276, 283, 287, 313, 314, 326, 330, 334, 353, 362, 366
South Wales 146
Southampton [Eng.] 81
Spain 89, 312
St. Bartholomew's 280
St. Croix 358
St. Eustatia 358
St. Kitts 243
St. Lucia 228
St. Martin's 171
St. Thomas 358
St. Vincent's 106
Suffolk [England] 159
Surry [England] 49, 108, 296
Sussex [England] 124, 361
Sweden 212, 249
Sweedland 158

Switzerland 107, 269

Tennessee 64, 151, 158, 195, 225, 238, 263, 317, 318, 346, 352, 373

University of Edinburgh 135
University of Paris 121
University of Pennsylvania 103
Wales 181, 187, 281, 299, 319
Warwick 294
Warwickshire 8, 19, 55
Washington, D. C. 197, 202, 372, 381
West Florida 103
West Indies 63, 78, 121, 162, 171, 172, 243, 315, 344, 375
West Jersey 377
Westmoreland [Eng.] 45
Whitehaven 3, 11, 22, 38, 124, 148, 170, 198, 222, 311
William and Mary 53, 88, 129, 159, 170, 183, 223, 227, 250, 278, 298, 323, 354, 379
Wiltshire [England] 137, 143
Windward Islands 11

Yorkshire 15, 45, 48, 51, 60, 67, 81, 146, 176, 178, 198, 221, 225, 230, 249, 255, 287, 310, 330, 354, 355, 359, 371, 372, 374